Lecture Notes in Computer Science 10963

Commenced Publication in 1973
Founding and Former Series Editors:
Gerhard Goos, Juris Hartmanis, and Jan van Leeuwen

Editorial Board

More information about this series at http://www.springer.com/series/7407

Osvaldo Gervasi · Beniamino Murgante
Sanjay Misra · Elena Stankova
Carmelo M. Torre · Ana Maria A. C. Rocha
David Taniar · Bernady O. Apduhan
Eufemia Tarantino · Yeonseung Ryu (Eds.)

Computational Science and Its Applications – ICCSA 2018

18th International Conference
Melbourne, VIC, Australia, July 2–5, 2018
Proceedings, Part IV

Springer

Editors
Osvaldo Gervasi (iD)
University of Perugia
Perugia
Italy

Ana Maria A. C. Rocha (iD)
University of Minho
Braga
Portugal

Beniamino Murgante (iD)
University of Basilicata
Potenza
Italy

David Taniar (iD)
Monash University
Clayton, VIC
Australia

Sanjay Misra (iD)
Covenant University
Ota
Nigeria

Bernady O. Apduhan
Kyushu Sangyo University
Fukuoka shi, Fukuoka
Japan

Elena Stankova (iD)
Saint Petersburg State University
Saint Petersburg
Russia

Eufemia Tarantino (iD)
Politecnico di Bari
Bari
Italy

Carmelo M. Torre (iD)
Polytechnic University of Bari
Bari
Italy

Yeonseung Ryu (iD)
Myongji University
Yongin
Korea (Republic of)

ISSN 0302-9743   ISSN 1611-3349 (electronic)
Lecture Notes in Computer Science
ISBN 978-3-319-95170-6   ISBN 978-3-319-95171-3 (eBook)
https://doi.org/10.1007/978-3-319-95171-3

Library of Congress Control Number: 2018947453

LNCS Sublibrary: SL1 – Theoretical Computer Science and General Issues

Printed on acid-free paper

This Springer imprint is published by the registered company Springer International Publishing AG part of Springer Nature
The registered company address is: Gewerbestrasse 11, 6330 Cham, Switzerland

Preface

These multiple volumes (LNCS volumes 10960–10964) consist of the peer-reviewed papers presented at the 2018 International Conference on Computational Science and Its Applications (ICCSA 2018) held in Melbourne, Australia, during July 2–5, 2018.

ICCSA 2018 was a successful event in the International Conferences on Computational Science and Its Applications (ICCSA) conference series, previously held in Trieste, Italy (2017), Beijing, China (2016), Banff, Canada (2015), Guimaraes, Portugal (2014), Ho Chi Minh City, Vietnam (2013), Salvador, Brazil (2012), Santander, Spain (2011), Fukuoka, Japan (2010), Suwon, South Korea (2009), Perugia, Italy (2008), Kuala Lumpur, Malaysia (2007), Glasgow, UK (2006), Singapore (2005), Assisi, Italy (2004), Montreal, Canada (2003), and (as ICCS) Amsterdam, The Netherlands (2002) and San Francisco, USA (2001).

Computational science is a main pillar of most current research and industrial and commercial activities and it plays a unique role in exploiting ICT innovative technologies. The ICCSA conference series has been providing a venue to researchers and industry practitioners to discuss new ideas, to share complex problems and their solutions, and to shape new trends in computational science.

Apart from the general tracks, ICCSA 2018 also included 33 international workshops, in various areas of computational sciences, ranging from computational science technologies, to specific areas of computational sciences, such as computer graphics and virtual reality. The program also featured three keynote speeches.

The success of the ICCSA conference series, in general, and ICCSA 2018, in particular, is due to the support of many people: authors, presenters, participants, keynote speakers, session chairs, Organizing Committee members, student volunteers, Program Committee members, International Advisory Committee members, International Liaison chairs, and people in other various roles. We would like to thank them all.

We would also like to thank Springer for their continuous support in publishing the ICCSA conference proceedings and for sponsoring some of the paper awards.

July 2018

David Taniar
Bernady O. Apduhan
Osvaldo Gervasi
Beniamino Murgante
Ana Maria A. C. Rocha

Welcome to Melbourne

Welcome to "The Most Liveable City"[1], Melbourne, Australia. ICCSA 2018 was held at Monash University, Caulfield Campus, during July 2–5, 2018.

Melbourne is the state capital of Victoria, and is currently the second most populous city in Australia, behind Sydney. There are lots of things to do and experience while in Melbourne. Here is an incomplete list:

- Visit and experience Melbourne's best coffee shops
- Discover Melbourne's hidden laneways and rooftops
- Walk along the Yarra River
- Eat your favourite food (Chinese, Vietnamese, Malaysian, Italian, Greek, anything, … you name it)
- Buy souvenirs at the Queen Victoria Market
- Go up to the Eureka, the tallest building in Melbourne
- Visit Melbourne's museums
- Walk and enjoy Melbourne's gardens and parks
- Visit the heart-shape lake, Albert Park Lake, the home of the F1 Grand Prix
- Simply walk in the city to enjoy Melbourne experience
- Try Melbourne's gelato ice cream

Basically, it is easy to live in and to explore Melbourne, and I do hope that you will have time to explore the city of Melbourne.

The venue of ICCSA 2018 was in Monash University. Monash University is a member of Go8, which is considered the top eight universities in Australia. Monash University has a number of campuses and centers. The two main campuses in Melbourne are Clayton and Caulfield. ICCSA 2018 was held on Caulfield Campus, which is only 12 minutes away from Melbourne CBD by train.

The Faculty of Information Technology is one of the ten faculties at Monash University. The faculty has more than 100 full-time academic staff (equivalent to the rank of Assistant Professor, Associate Professor, and Professor).

I do hope that you will enjoy not only the conference, but also Melbourne.

David Taniar

---

[1] The Global Liveability Report 2017, https://www.cnbc.com/2017/08/17/the-worlds-top-10-most-livable-cities.html

Organization

ICCSA 2018 was organized by Monash University (Australia), University of Perugia (Italy), Kyushu Sangyo University (Japan), University of Basilicata (Italy), and University of Minho, (Portugal).

Honorary General Chairs

Antonio Laganà	University of Perugia, Italy
Norio Shiratori	Tohoku University, Japan
Kenneth C. J. Tan	Sardina Systems, Estonia

General Chairs

David Taniar	Monash University, Australia
Bernady O. Apduhan	Kyushu Sangyo University, Japan

Program Committee Chairs

Osvaldo Gervasi	University of Perugia, Italy
Beniamino Murgante	University of Basilicata, Italy
Ana Maria A. C. Rocha	University of Minho, Portugal

International Advisory Committee

Jemal Abawajy	Deakin University, Australia
Dharma P. Agrawal	University of Cincinnati, USA
Marina L. Gavrilova	University of Calgary, Canada
Claudia Bauzer Medeiros	University of Campinas, Brazil
Manfred M. Fisher	Vienna University of Economics and Business, Austria
Yee Leung	Chinese University of Hong Kong, SAR China

International Liaison Chairs

Ana Carla P. Bitencourt	Universidade Federal do Reconcavo da Bahia, Brazil
Giuseppe Borruso	University of Trieste, Italy
Alfredo Cuzzocrea	University of Trieste, Italy
Maria Irene Falcão	University of Minho, Portugal
Robert C. H. Hsu	Chung Hua University, Taiwan
Tai-Hoon Kim	Hannam University, South Korea
Sanjay Misra	Covenant University, Nigeria
Takashi Naka	Kyushu Sangyo University, Japan

Rafael D. C. Santos   National Institute for Space Research, Brazil
Maribel Yasmina Santos   University of Minho, Portugal

Workshop and Session Organizing Chairs

Beniamino Murgante   University of Basilicata, Italy
Sanjay Misra   Covenant University, Nigeria
Jorge Gustavo Rocha   University of Minho, Portugal

Award Chair

Wenny Rahayu   La Trobe University, Australia

Web Chair

A. S. M. Kayes   La Trobe University, Australia

Publicity Committee Chairs

Elmer Dadios   De La Salle University, Philippines
Hong Quang Nguyen   International University (VNU-HCM), Vietnam
Daisuke Takahashi   Tsukuba University, Japan
Shangwang Wang   Beijing University of Posts and Telecommunications,
                                China

Workshop Organizers

Advanced Methods in Fractals and Data Mining for Applications (AMFDMA 2018)

Yeliz Karaca   IEEE
Carlo Cattani   Tuscia University, Italy
Majaz Moonis   University of Massachusettes Medical School, USA

Advances in Information Systems and Technologies for Emergency Management, Risk Assessment and Mitigation Based on Resilience Concepts (ASTER 2018)

Maurizio Pollino   ENEA, Italy
Marco Vona   University of Basilicata, Italy
Beniamino Murgante   University of Basilicata, Italy
Grazia Fattoruso   ENEA, Italy

Advances in Web-Based Learning (AWBL 2018)

Mustafa Murat Inceoglu   Ege University, Turkey
Birol Ciloglugil   Ege University, Turkey

Bio- and Neuro-inspired Computing and Applications (BIONCA 2018)

Nadia Nedjah   State University of Rio de Janeiro, Brazil
Luiza de Macedo Mourell   State University of Rio de Janeiro, Brazil

Computer-Aided Modeling, Simulation, and Analysis (CAMSA 2018)

Jie Shen   University of Michigan, USA
Hao Chen   Shanghai University of Engineering Science, China
Youguo He   Jiangsu University, China

Computational and Applied Statistics (CAS 2018)

Ana Cristina Braga   University of Minho, Portugal

Computational Geometry and Security Applications (CGSA 2018)

Marina L. Gavrilova   University of Calgary, Canada

Computational Movement Analysis (CMA 2018)

Farid Karimipour   University of Tehran, Iran

Computational Mathematics, Statistics and Information Management (CMSIM 2018)

M. Filomena Teodoro   Lisbon University and Portuguese Naval Academy,
                        Portugal

Computational Optimization and Applications (COA 2018)

Ana Maria Rocha   University of Minho, Portugal
Humberto Rocha   University of Coimbra, Portugal

Computational Astrochemistry (CompAstro 2018)

Marzio Rosi   University of Perugia, Italy
Dimitrios Skouteris   Scuola Normale Superiore di Pisa, Italy
Albert Rimola   Universitat Autònoma de Barcelona, Spain

Cities, Technologies, and Planning (CTP 2018)

Giuseppe Borruso   University of Trieste, Italy
Beniamino Murgante   University of Basilicata, Italy

Defense Technology and Security (DTS 2018)

Yeonseung Ryu   Myongji University, South Korea

Econometrics and Multidimensional Evaluation in the Urban Environment (EMEUE 2018)

Carmelo M. Torre   Polytechnic of Bari, Italy
Maria Cerreta   University of Naples Federico II, Italy
Pierluigi Morano   Polytechnic of Bari, Italy
Paola Perchinunno   University of Bari, Italy

Future Computing Systems, Technologies, and Applications (FISTA 2018)

Bernady O. Apduhan   Kyushu Sangyo University, Japan
Rafael Santos   National Institute for Space Research, Brazil
Shangguang Wang   Beijing University of Posts and Telecommunications,
                         China
Kazuaki Tanaka   Kyushu Institute of Technology, Japan

Geographical Analysis, Urban Modeling, Spatial Statistics (GEO-AND-MOD 2018)

Giuseppe Borruso   University of Trieste, Italy
Beniamino Murgante   University of Basilicata, Italy
Hartmut Asche   University of Potsdam, Germany

Geomatics for Resource Monitoring and Control (GRMC 2018)

Eufemia Tarantino   Polytechnic of Bari, Italy
Umberto Fratino   Polytechnic of Bari, Italy
Benedetto Figorito   ARPA Puglia, Italy
Antonio Novelli   Polytechnic of Bari, Italy
Rosa Lasaponara   Italian Research Council, IMAA-CNR, Italy

International Symposium on Software Quality (ISSQ 2018)

Sanjay Misra   Covenant University, Nigeria

Web-Based Collective Evolutionary Systems: Models, Measures, Applications (IWCES 2018)

Alfredo Milani   University of Perugia, Italy
Clement Leung   United International College, Zhouhai, China
Valentina Franzoni   University of Rome La Sapienza, Italy
Valentina Poggioni   University of Perugia, Italy

Large-Scale Computational Physics (LSCP 2018)

Elise de Doncker   Western Michigan University, USA
Fukuko Yuasa   High Energy Accelerator Research Organization, KEK,
                         Japan
Hideo Matsufuru   High Energy Accelerator Research Organization, KEK,
                         Japan

Land Use Monitoring for Soil Consumption Reduction (LUMS 2018)

Carmelo M. Torre	Polytechnic of Bari, Italy
Alessandro Bonifazi	Polytechnic of Bari, Italy
Pasquale Balena	Polytechnic of Bari, Italy
Beniamino Murgante	University of Basilicata , Italy
Eufemia Tarantino	Polytechnic of Bari, Italy

Mobile Communications (MC 2018)

Hyunseung Choo	Sungkyunkwan University, South Korea

Scientific Computing Infrastructure (SCI 2018)

Elena Stankova	Saint-Petersburg State University, Russia
Vladimir Korkhov	Saint-Petersburg State University, Russia

International Symposium on Software Engineering Processes and Applications (SEPA 2018)

Sanjay Misra	Covenant University, Nigeria

Smart Factory Convergence (SFC 2018)

Jongpil Jeong	Sungkyunkwan University, South Korea

Is a Smart City Really Smart? Models, Solutions, Proposals for an Effective Urban and Social Development (Smart_Cities 2018)

Giuseppe Borruso	University of Trieste, Italy
Chiara Garau	University of Cagliari, Italy
Ginevra Balletto	University of Cagliari, Italy
Beniamino Murgante	University of Basilicata, Italy
Paola Zamberlin	University of Florence, Italy

Sustainability Performance Assessment: Models, Approaches and Applications Toward Interdisciplinary and Integrated Solutions (SPA 2018)

Francesco Scorza	University of Basilicata, Italy
Valentin Grecu	Lucia Blaga University on Sibiu, Romania
Jolanta Dvarioniene	Kaunas University, Lithuania
Sabrina Lai	Cagliari University, Italy

Advances in Spatio-Temporal Analytics (ST-Analytics 2018)

Rafael Santos	Brazilian Space Research Agency, Brazil
Karine Reis Ferreira	Brazilian Space Research Agency, Brazil
Joao Moura Pires	New University of Lisbon, Portugal
Maribel Yasmina Santos	University of Minho, Portugal

Theoretical and Computational Chemistry and Its Applications (TCCA 2018)

M. Noelia Faginas Lago   University of Perugia, Italy
Andrea Lombardi   University of Perugia, Italy

Tools and Techniques in Software Development Processes (TTSDP 2018)

Sanjay Misra   Covenant University, Nigeria

Challenges, Trends and Innovations in VGI (VGI 2018)

Beniamino Murgante   University of Basilicata, Italy
Rodrigo Tapia-McClung   Centro de Investigación en Geografía y Geomática Ing
                             Jorge L. Tamay, Mexico
Claudia Ceppi   Polytechnic of Bari, Italy
Jorge Gustavo Rocha   University of Minho, Portugal

Virtual Reality and Applications (VRA 2018)

Osvaldo Gervasi   University of Perugia, Italy
Sergio Tasso   University of Perugia, Italy

International Workshop on Parallel and Distributed Data Mining (WPDM 2018)

Massimo Cafaro   University of Salento, Italy
Italo Epicoco   University of Salento, Italy
Marco Pulimeno   University of Salento, Italy
Giovanni Aloisio   University of Salento, Italy

Program Committee

Kenny Adamson   University of Ulster, UK
Vera Afreixo   University of Aveiro, Portugal
Filipe Alvelos   University of Minho, Portugal
Hartmut Asche   University of Potsdam, Germany
Michela Bertolotto   University College Dublin, Ireland
Sandro Bimonte   CEMAGREF, TSCF, France
Rod Blais   University of Calgary, Canada
Ivan Blečić   University of Sassari, Italy
Giuseppe Borruso   University of Trieste, Italy
Ana Cristina Braga   University of Minho, Portugal
Yves Caniou   Lyon University, France
José A. Cardoso e Cunha   Universidade Nova de Lisboa, Portugal
Rui Cardoso   University of Beira Interior, Portugal
Leocadio G. Casado   University of Almeria, Spain
Carlo Cattani   University of Salerno, Italy
Mete Celik   Erciyes University, Turkey
Alexander Chemeris   National Technical University of Ukraine KPI, Ukraine
Min Young Chung   Sungkyunkwan University, South Korea

Florbela Maria da Cruz Domingues Correia	Polytechnic Institute of Viana do Castelo, Portugal
Gilberto Corso Pereira	Federal University of Bahia, Brazil
Carla Dal Sasso Freitas	Universidade Federal do Rio Grande do Sul, Brazil
Pradesh Debba	The Council for Scientific and Industrial Research (CSIR), South Africa
Hendrik Decker	Instituto Tecnológico de Informática, Spain
Frank Devai	London South Bank University, UK
Rodolphe Devillers	Memorial University of Newfoundland, Canada
Joana Matos Dias	University of Coimbra, Portugal
Paolino Di Felice	University of L'Aquila, Italy
Prabu Dorairaj	NetApp, India/USA
M. Irene Falcao	University of Minho, Portugal
Cherry Liu Fang	U.S. DOE Ames Laboratory, USA
Florbela P. Fernandes	Polytechnic Institute of Bragança, Portugal
Jose-Jesus Fernandez	National Centre for Biotechnology, CSIS, Spain
Paula Odete Fernandes	Polytechnic Institute of Bragança, Portugal
Adelaide de Fátima Baptista Valente Freitas	University of Aveiro, Portugal
Manuel Carlos Figueiredo	University of Minho, Portugal
Maria Antonia Forjaz	University of Minho, Portugal
Maria Celia Furtado Rocha	PRODEB–PósCultura/UFBA, Brazil
Paulino Jose Garcia Nieto	University of Oviedo, Spain
Jerome Gensel	LSR-IMAG, France
Maria Giaoutzi	National Technical University, Athens, Greece
Arminda Manuela Andrade Pereira Gonçalves	University of Minho, Portugal
Andrzej M. Goscinski	Deakin University, Australia
Sevin Gmïgmï	Izmir University of Economics, Turkey
Alex Hagen-Zanker	University of Cambridge, UK
Malgorzata Hanzl	Technical University of Lodz, Poland
Shanmugasundaram Hariharan	B.S. Abdur Rahman University, India
Eligius M. T. Hendrix	University of Malaga/Wageningen University, Spain/The Netherlands
Tutut Herawan	Universitas Teknologi Yogyakarta, Indonesia
Hisamoto Hiyoshi	Gunma University, Japan
Fermin Huarte	University of Barcelona, Spain
Mustafa Inceoglu	EGE University, Turkey
Peter Jimack	University of Leeds, UK
Qun Jin	Waseda University, Japan
A. S. M. Kayes	La Trobe University, Australia
Farid Karimipour	Vienna University of Technology, Austria
Baris Kazar	Oracle Corp., USA
Maulana Adhinugraha Kiki	Telkom University, Indonesia
DongSeong Kim	University of Canterbury, New Zealand

Taihoon Kim	Hannam University, South Korea
Ivana Kolingerova	University of West Bohemia, Czech Republic
Rosa Lasaponara	National Research Council, Italy
Maurizio Lazzari	National Research Council, Italy
Cheng Siong Lee	Monash University, Australia
Sangyoun Lee	Yonsei University, South Korea
Jongchan Lee	Kunsan National University, South Korea
Clement Leung	Hong Kong Baptist University, Hong Kong, SAR China
Chendong Li	University of Connecticut, USA
Gang Li	Deakin University, Australia
Ming Li	East China Normal University, China
Fang Liu	AMES Laboratories, USA
Xin Liu	University of Calgary, Canada
Savino Longo	University of Bari, Italy
Tinghuai Ma	NanJing University of Information Science and Technology, China
Luca Mancinelli	Trinity College Dublin, Ireland
Ernesto Marcheggiani	Katholieke Universiteit Leuven, Belgium
Antonino Marvuglia	Research Centre Henri Tudor, Luxembourg
Nicola Masini	National Research Council, Italy
Eric Medvet	University of Trieste, Italy
Nirvana Meratnia	University of Twente, The Netherlands
Alfredo Milani	University of Perugia, Italy
Giuseppe Modica	University of Reggio Calabria, Italy
Josè Luis Montaña	University of Cantabria, Spain
Maria Filipa Mourão	IP from Viana do Castelo, Portugal
Laszlo Neumann	University of Girona, Spain
Kok-Leong Ong	Deakin University, Australia
Belen Palop	Universidad de Valladolid, Spain
Marcin Paprzycki	Polish Academy of Sciences, Poland
Eric Pardede	La Trobe University, Australia
Kwangjin Park	Wonkwang University, South Korea
Ana Isabel Pereira	Polytechnic Institute of Bragança, Portugal
Maurizio Pollino	Italian National Agency for New Technologies, Energy and Sustainable Economic Development, Italy
Alenka Poplin	University of Hamburg, Germany
Vidyasagar Potdar	Curtin University of Technology, Australia
David C. Prosperi	Florida Atlantic University, USA
Wenny Rahayu	La Trobe University, Australia
Jerzy Respondek	Silesian University of Technology, Poland
Humberto Rocha	INESC-Coimbra, Portugal
Alexey Rodionov	Institute of Computational Mathematics and Mathematical Geophysics, Russia

Jon Rokne	University of Calgary, Canada
Octavio Roncero	CSIC, Spain
Maytham Safar	Kuwait University, Kuwait
Chiara Saracino	A.O. Ospedale Niguarda Ca' Granda - Milano, Italy
Haiduke Sarafian	The Pennsylvania State University, USA
Marco Paulo Seabra dos Reis	University of Coimbra, Portugal
Jie Shen	University of Michigan, USA
Qi Shi	Liverpool John Moores University, UK
Dale Shires	U.S. Army Research Laboratory, USA
Inês Soares	University of Coimbra, Portugal
Takuo Suganuma	Tohoku University, Japan
Sergio Tasso	University of Perugia, Italy
Ana Paula Teixeira	University of Trás-os-Montes and Alto Douro, Portugal
Senhorinha Teixeira	University of Minho, Portugal
Parimala Thulasiraman	University of Manitoba, Canada
Carmelo Torre	Polytechnic of Bari, Italy
Javier Martinez Torres	Centro Universitario de la Defensa Zaragoza, Spain
Giuseppe A. Trunfio	University of Sassari, Italy
Toshihiro Uchibayashi	Kyushu Sangyo University, Japan
Pablo Vanegas	University of Cuenca, Ecuador
Marco Vizzari	University of Perugia, Italy
Varun Vohra	Merck Inc., USA
Koichi Wada	University of Tsukuba, Japan
Krzysztof Walkowiak	Wroclaw University of Technology, Poland
Zequn Wang	Intelligent Automation Inc., USA
Robert Weibel	University of Zurich, Switzerland
Frank Westad	Norwegian University of Science and Technology, Norway
Roland Wismüller	Universität Siegen, Germany
Mudasser Wyne	SOET National University, USA
Chung-Huang Yang	National Kaohsiung Normal University, Taiwan
Xin-She Yang	National Physical Laboratory, UK
Salim Zabir	France Telecom Japan Co., Japan
Haifeng Zhao	University of California, Davis, USA
Kewen Zhao	University of Qiongzhou, China
Fabiana Zollo	University of Venice Cà Foscari, Italy
Albert Y. Zomaya	University of Sydney, Australia

Reviewers

Afreixo Vera	University of Aveiro, Portugal
Ahmad Rashid	Microwave and Antenna Lab, School of Engineering, Korea
Aguilar José Alfonso	Universidad Autónoma de Sinaloa, Mexico
Albanese Valentina	Università di Bologna, Italy
Alvelos Filipe	University of Minho, Portugal
Amato Federico	University of Basilicata, Italy
Andrianov Serge	Institute for Informatics of Tatarstan Academy of Sciences, Russia
Antunes Marília	University Nova de Lisboa, Portugal
Apduhan Bernady	Kyushu Sangyo University, Japan
Aquilanti Vincenzo	University of Perugia, Italy
Asche Hartmut	Potsdam University, Germany
Aslan Zafer	Istanbul Aydin University, Turkey
Aytaç Vecdi	Ege University, Turkey
Azevedo Ana	Instituto Superior de Engenharia do Porto, Portugal
Azzari Margherita	Universitá degli Studi di Firenze, Italy
Bae Ihn-Han	Catholic University of Daegu, South Korea
Balci Birim	Celal Bayar Üniversitesi, Turkey
Balena Pasquale	Politecnico di Bari, Italy
Balucani Nadia	University of Perugia, Italy
Barroca Filho Itamir	Instituto Metrópole Digital da UFRN (IMD-UFRN), Brazil
Bayrak §sengül	Haliç University, Turkey
Behera Ranjan Kumar	Indian Institute of Technology Patna, India
Bimonte Sandro	IRSTEA, France
Bogdanov Alexander	Saint-Petersburg State University, Russia
Bonifazi Alessandro	Polytechnic of Bari, Italy
Borruso Giuseppe	University of Trieste, Italy
Braga Ana Cristina	University of Minho, Portugal
Cafaro Massimo	University of Salento, Italy
Canora Filomena	University of Basilicata, Italy
Cao Yuanlong	University of Saskatchewan, Canada
Caradonna Grazia	Polytechnic of Bari, Italy
Cardoso Rui	Institute of Telecommunications, Portugal
Carolina Tripp Barba	Universidad Autónoma de Sinaloa, Mexico
Caroti Gabriella	University of Pisa, Italy
Ceccarello Matteo	University of Padova, Italy
Cefalo Raffaela	University of Trieste, Italy
Cerreta Maria	University Federico II of Naples, Italy
Challa Rajesh	Sungkyunkwan University, Korea
Chamundeswari Arumugam	SSN College of Engineering, India
Chaturvedi Krishna Kumar	Patil Group of Industries, India
Cho Chulhee	Seoul Guarantee Insurance Company Ltd., Korea

Choi Jae-Young	Sungkyunkwan University, Korea
Choi Kwangnam	Korea Institute of Science and Technology Information, Korea
Choi Seonho	Seoul National University, Korea
Chung Min Young	Sungkyunkwan University, Korea
Ciloglugil Birol	Ege University, Turkey
Coletti Cecilia	University of Chieti, Italy
Congiu Tanja	Università degli Studi di Sassari, Italy
Correia Anacleto	Base Naval de Lisboa, Portugal
Correia Elisete	University of Trás-Os-Montes e Alto Douro, Portugal
Correia Florbela Maria da Cruz Domingues	Instituto Politécnico de Viana do Castelo, Portugal
Costa e Silva Eliana	Polytechnic of Porto, Portugal
Cugurullo Federico	Trinity College Dublin, Ireland
Damas Bruno	LARSyS, Instituto Superior Técnico, Univ. Lisboa, Portugal
Dang Thien Binh	Sungkyunkwan University, Korea
Daniele Bartoli	University of Perugia, Italy
de Doncker Elise	Western Michigan University, USA
Degtyarev Alexander	Saint-Petersburg State University, Russia
Demyanov Vasily	Heriot-Watt University, UK
Devai Frank	London South Bank University, UK
Di Fatta Giuseppe	University of Reading, UK
Dias Joana	University of Coimbra, Portugal
Dilo Arta	University of Twente, The Netherlands
El-Zawawy Mohamed A.	Cairo University, Egypt
Epicoco Italo	Università del Salento, Italy
Escalona Maria-Jose	University of Seville, Spain
Falcinelli Stefano	University of Perugia, Italy
Faginas-Lago M. Noelia	University of Perugia, Italy
Falcão M. Irene	University of Minho, Portugal
Famiano Michael	Western Michigan University, USA
Fattoruso Grazia	ENEA, Italy
Fernandes Florbela	Escola Superior de Tecnologia e Gestão de Braganca, Portugal
Fernandes Paula	Escola Superior de Tecnologia e Gestão, Portugal
Ferraro Petrillo Umberto	University of Rome "La Sapienza", Italy
Ferreira Fernanda	Escola Superior de Estudos Industriais e de Gestão, Portugal
Ferrão Maria	Universidade da Beira Interior, Portugal
Figueiredo Manuel Carlos	Universidade do Minho, Portugal
Fiorini Lorena	Università degli Studi dell'Aquila, Italy
Florez Hector	Universidad Distrital Francisco Jose de Caldas, Colombia
Franzoni Valentina	University of Perugia, Italy

Freitau Adelaide de Fátima Baptista Valente	University of Aveiro, Portugal
Gabrani Goldie	Bml Munjal University, India
Garau Chiara	University of Cagliari, Italy
Garcia Ernesto	University of the Basque Country, Spain
Gavrilova Marina	University of Calgary, Canada
Gervasi Osvaldo	University of Perugia, Italy
Gioia Andrea	University of Bari, Italy
Giorgi Giacomo	University of Perugia, Italy
Giuliani Felice	Università degli Studi di Parma, Italy
Goel Rajat	University of Southern California, USA
Gonçalves Arminda Manuela	University of Minho, Portugal
Gorbachev Yuriy	Geolink Technologies, Russia
Gordon-Ross Ann	University of Florida, USA
Goyal Rinkaj	Guru Gobind Singh Indraprastha University, India
Grilli Luca	University of Perugia, Italy
Goyal Rinkaj	GGS Indraprastha University, India
Guerra Eduardo	National Institute for Space Research, Brazil
Gumgum Sevin	İzmir Ekonomi Üniversitesi, Turkey
Gülen Kemal Güven	Istanbul Ticaret University, Turkey
Hacızade Ulviye	Haliç Üniversitesi Uluslararas, Turkey
Han Longzhe	Nanchang Institute of Technology, Korea
Hanzl Malgorzata	University of Lodz, Poland
Hayashi Masaki	University of Calgary, Canada
He Youguo	Jiangsu University, China
Hegedus Peter	University of Szeged, Hungary
Herawan Tutut	Universiti Malaysia Pahang, Malaysia
Ignaccolo Matteo	University of Catania, Italy
Imakura Akira	University of Tsukuba, Japan
Inceoglu Mustafa	Ege University, Turkey
Jagwani Priti	Indian Institute of Technology Delhi, India
Jang Jeongsook	Brown University, Korea
Jeong Jongpil	Sungkyunkwan University, Korea
Jin Hyunwook	Konkuk University, Korea
Jorge Ana Maria, Kapenga John	Western Michigan University, USA
Kawana Kojiro	University of Tokio, Japan
Kayes Abu S. M.	La Trobe University, Australia
Kim JeongAh	George Fox University, USA
Korkhov Vladimir	St. Petersburg State University, Russia
Kulabukhova Nataliia	Saint-Peterburg State University, Russia
Kumar Pawan	Expert Software Consultants Ltd., India
Laccetti Giuliano	Università degli Studi di Napoli, Italy
Laganà Antonio	Master-up srl, Italy
Lai Sabrina	University of Cagliari, Italy

Laricchiuta Annarita	CNR-IMIP, Italy
Lazzari Maurizio	CNR IBAM, Italy
Lee Soojin	Cyber Security Lab, Korea
Leon Marcelo	Universidad Estatal Península de Santa Elena – UPSE, Ecuador
Lim Ilkyun	Sungkyunkwan University, Korea
Lourenço Vanda Marisa	University Nova de Lisboa, Portugal
Mancinelli Luca	University of Dublin, Ireland
Mangiameli Michele	University of Catania, Italy
Markov Krassimiri	Institute for Information Theories and Applications, Bulgaria
Marques Jorge	Universidade de Coimbra, Portugal
Marvuglia Antonino	Public Research Centre Henri Tudor, Luxembourg
Mateos Cristian	Universidad Nacional del Centro, Argentina
Matsufuru Hideo	High Energy Accelerator Research, Japan
Maurizio Crispini	Politecnico di Milano, Italy
Medvet Eric	University of Trieste, Italy
Mengoni Paolo	Università degli Studi di Firenze, Italy
Mesiti Marco	Università degli studi di Milano, Italy
Millham Richard	Durban University of Technology, South Africa
Misra Sanjay	Covenant University, Nigeria
Mishra Anurag	Helmholtz Zentrum München, Germany
Mishra Biswajeeban	University of Szeged, Hungary
Moscato Pablo	University of Newcastle, Australia
Moura Pires Joao	Universidade Nova de Lisboa, Portugal
Moura Ricardo	Universidade Nova de Lisboa, Portugal
Mourao Maria	Universidade do Minho, Portugal
Mukhopadhyay Asish	University of Windsor, Canada
Murgante Beniamino	University of Basilicata, Italy
Nakasato Naohito	University of Aizu, Japan
Nguyen Tien Dzung	Sungkyunkwan University, South Korea
Nicolosi Vittorio	University of Rome Tor Vergata, Italy
Ogihara Mitsunori	University of Miami, USA
Oh Sangyoon	Ajou University, Korea
Oliveira Irene	University of Trás-Os-Montes e Alto Douro, Portugal
Oluranti Jonathan	Covenant University, Nigeria
Ozturk Savas	The Scientific and Technological Research Council of Turkey, Turkey
P. Costa M. Fernanda	University of Minho, Portugal
Paek Yunheung	Seoul National University, Korea
Pancham Jay	Durban University of Technology, South Africa
Pantazis Dimos	Technological Educational Institute of Athens, Greek
Paolucci Michela	Università degli Studi di Firenze, Italy
Pardede Eric	La Trobe University, Australia
Park Hyun Kyoo	Petabi Corp, Korea
Passaro Tommaso	University of Bari, Italy

Pereira Ana	Instituto Politécnico de Bragança, Portugal
Peschechera Giuseppe	University of Bari, Italy
Petri Massimiliano	Università di Pisa, Italy
Pham Quoc Trung	Ho Chi Minh City University of Technology, Vietnam
Piemonte Andrea	Università di Pisa, Italy
Pinna Francesco	Università degli Studi di Cagliari, Italy
Pinto Telmo	University of Minho, Portugal
Pollino Maurizio	ENEA, Italy
Pulimeno Marco	University of Salento, Italy
Rahayu Wenny	La Trobe University, Australia
Rao S. V.	Duke Clinical Research, USA
Raza Syed Muhammad	Sungkyunkwan University, South Korea
Reis Ferreira Gomes Karine	National Institute for Space Research, Brazil
Reis Marco	Universidade de Coimbra, Portugal
Rimola Albert	Autonomous University of Barcelona, Spain
Rocha Ana Maria	University of Minho, Portugal
Rocha Humberto	University of Coimbra, Portugal
Rodriguez Daniel	The University of Queensland, Australia
Ryu Yeonseung	Myongji University, South Korea
Sahni Himantikka	CRISIL Global Research and Analytics, India
Sahoo Kshira Sagar	C. V. Raman College of Engineering, India
Santos Maribel Yasmina	University of Minho, Portugal
Santos Rafael	KU Leuven, Belgium
Saponaro Mirko	Politecnico di Bari, Italy
Scorza Francesco	Università della Basilicata, Italy
Sdao Francesco	Università della Basilicata, Italy
Shen Jie	University of Southampton, UK
Shintani Takahiko	University of Electro-Communications, Japan
Shoaib Muhammad	Sungkyunkwan University, South Korea
Silva-Fortes Carina	ESTeSL-IPL, Portugal
Singh V. B.	University of Delhi, India
Skouteris Dimitrios	SNS, Italy
Soares Inês	INESCC and IPATIMUP, Portugal
Sosnin Petr	Ulyanovsk State Technical University, Russia
Souza Erica	Universidade Nova de Lisboa, Portugal
Stankova Elena	Saint-Petersburg State University, Russia
Sumida Yasuaki	Kyushu Sangyo University, Japan
Tanaka Kazuaki	Kyushu Institute of Technology, Japan
Tapia-McClung Rodrigo	CentroGeo, Mexico
Tarantino Eufemia	Politecnico di Bari, Italy
Tasso Sergio	University of Perugia, Italy
Teixeira Ana Paula	Universidade Católica Portuguesa, Portugal
Tengku Adil	La Trobe University, Australia
Teodoro M. Filomena	Lisbon University, Portugal
Tiwari Sunita	King George's Medical University, India
Torre Carmelo Maria	Polytechnic of Bari, Italy

Torrisi Vincenza	University of Catania, Italy
Totaro Vincenzo	Politecnico di Bari, Italy
Tran Manh Hung	Institute for Research and Executive Education, Vietnam
Tripathi Aprna	GLA University, India
Trunfio Giuseppe A.	University of Sassari, Italy
Tóth Zoltán	Hungarian Academy of Sciences, Hungary
Uchibayashi Toshihiro	Kyushu Sangyo University, Japan
Ugliengo Piero	University of Torino, Italy
Ullman Holly	University of Delaware, USA
Vallverdu Jordi	Autonomous University of Barcelona, Spain
Valuev Ilya	Russian Academy of Sciences, Russia
Vasyunin Dmitry	University of Amsterdam, The Netherlands
Vohra Varun	University of Electro-Communications, Japan
Voit Nikolay	Ulyanovsk State Technical University, Russia
Wale Azeez Nurayhn	University of Lagos, Nigeria
Walkowiak Krzysztof	Wroclaw University of Technology, Poland
Wallace Richard J.	Univeristy of Texas, USA
Waluyo Agustinus Borgy	Monash University, Australia
Westad Frank	CAMO Software AS, USA
Wole Adewumi	Covenant University, Nigeria
Xie Y. H.	Bell Laboratories, USA
Yamauchi Toshihiro	Okayama University, Japan
Yamazaki Takeshi	University of Tokyo, Japan
Yao Fenghui	Tennessee State University, USA
Yoki Karl	Catholic University of Daegu, South Korea
Yoshiura Noriaki	Saitama University, Japan
Yuasa Fukuko	High Energy Accelerator Research Organization, Korea
Zamperlin Paola	University of Florence, Italy
Zollo Fabiana	University of Venice "Cà Foscari", Italy
Zullo Francesco	University of L'Aquila, Italy
Zivkovic Ljiljana	Republic Agency for Spatial Planning, Belgrade

Sponsoring Organizations

ICCSA 2018 would not have been possible without the tremendous support of many organizations and institutions, for which all organizers and participants of ICCSA 2018 express their sincere gratitude:

Springer International Publishing AG, Germany
(http://www.springer.com)

Monash University, Australia
(http://monash.edu)

University of Perugia, Italy
(http://www.unipg.it)

University of Basilicata, Italy
(http://www.unibas.it)

Kyushu Sangyo University, Japan
(www.kyusan-u.ac.jp)

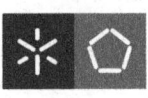

Universidade do Minho, Portugal
(http://www.uminho.pt)

Keynote Speakers

New Frontiers in Cloud Computing for Big Data and Internet-of-Things (IoT) Applications

Rajkumar Buyya[1,2]

[1] Cloud Computing and Distributed Systems (CLOUDS) Lab,
The University of Melbourne, Australia
[2] Manjrasoft Pvt Ltd., Melbourne, Australia

Abstract. Computing is being transformed to a model consisting of services that are commoditised and delivered in a manner similar to utilities such as water, electricity, gas, and telephony. Several computing paradigms have promised to deliver this utility computing vision. Cloud computing has emerged as one of the buzzwords in the IT industry and turned the vision of "computing utilities" into a reality.

Clouds deliver infrastructure, platform, and software (application) as services, which are made available as subscription-based services in a pay-as-you-go model to consumers. Cloud application platforms need to offer

1. APIs and tools for rapid creation of elastic applications and
2. a runtime system for deployment of applications on geographically distributed computing infrastructure in a seamless manner.

The Internet of Things (IoT) paradigm enables seamless integration of cyber-and-physical worlds and opening up opportunities for creating newclass of applications for domains such as smart cities. The emerging Fog computing is extending Cloud computing paradigm to edge resources for latency sensitive IoT applications.

This keynote presentation will cover:

a. 21st century vision of computing and identifies various IT paradigms promising to deliver the vision of computing utilities;
b. opportunities and challenges for utility and market-oriented Cloud computing,
c. innovative architecture for creating market-oriented and elastic Clouds by harnessing virtualisation technologies;
d. Aneka, a Cloud Application Platform, for rapid development of Cloud/Big Data applications and their deployment on private/public Clouds with resource provisioning driven by SLAs;
e. experimental results on deploying Cloud and Big Data/Internet-of-Things (IoT) applications in engineering, and health care, satellite image processing, and smart cities on elastic Clouds;

f. directions for delivering our 21st century vision along with pathways for future research in Cloud and Fog computing.

Short Bio Dr. Rajkumar Buyya is a Redmond Barry Distinguished Professor and Director of the Cloud Computing and Distributed Systems (CLOUDS) Laboratory at the University of Melbourne, Australia. He is also serving as the founding CEO of Manjrasoft, a spin-off company of the University, commercializing its innovations in Cloud Computing. He served as a Future Fellow of the Australian Research Council during 2012-2016. He has authored over 625 publications and seven text books including "Mastering Cloud Computing" published by McGraw Hill, China Machine Press, and Morgan Kaufmann for Indian, Chinese and international markets respectively. He also edited several books including "Cloud Computing: Principles and Paradigms" (Wiley Press, USA, Feb 2011).

He is one of the highly cited authors in computer science and software engineering worldwide (h-index = 117, g-index = 255, 70,500 + citations). Dr. Buyya is recognized as a "Web of Science Highly Cited Researcher" in both 2016 and 2017 by Thomson Reuters, a Fellow of IEEE, and Scopus Researcher of the Year 2017 with Excellence in Innovative Research Award by Elsevier for his outstanding contributions to Cloud computing.

Software technologies for Grid and Cloud computing developed under Dr. Buyya's leadership have gained rapid acceptance and are in use at several academic institutions and commercial enterprises in 40 countries around the world. Dr. Buyya has led the establishment and development of key community activities, including serving as foundation Chair of the IEEE Technical Committee on Scalable Computing and five IEEE/ACM conferences. These contributions and international research leadership of Dr. Buyya are recognized through the award of "2009 IEEE Medal for Excellence in Scalable Computing" from the IEEE Computer Society TCSC.

Manjrasoft's Aneka Cloud technology developed under his leadership has received "2010 Frost & Sullivan New Product Innovation Award". He served as the founding Editor-in-Chief of the IEEE Transactions on Cloud Computing. He is currently serving as Co-Editor-in-Chief of Journal of Software: Practice and Experience, which was established over 45 years ago. For further information on Dr. Buyya, please visit his cyberhome: www.buyya.com.

Approximation Problems for Digital Image Processing and Applications

Gianluca Vinti

Department of Mathematics and Computer Science,
University of Perugia, Italy

Abstract. In this talk, some approximation problems are discussed with applications to reconstruction and to digital image processing. We will also show some applications to concrete problems in the medical and engineering fields. Regarding the first, a procedure will be presented, based on approaches of approximation theory and on algorithms of digital image processing for the diagnosis of aneurysmal diseases; in particular we discuss the extraction of the pervious lumen of the artery starting from CT image without contrast medium. As concerns the engineering field, thermographic images are analyzed for the study of thermal bridges and for the structural and dynamic analysis of buildings, working therefore in the field of energy analysis and seismic vulnerability of buildings, respectively.

Short Bio Gianluca Vinti is Full Professor of Mathematical Analysis at the Department of Mathematics and Computer Science of the University of Perugia. He is Director of the Department since 2014 and member of the Academic Senate of the University. Member of the Board of the Italian Mathematical Union since 2006, member of the "Scientific Council of the GNAMPA-INdAM "(National Group for the Mathematical Analysis, the Probability and their Applications) since 2013, Referent for the Mathematics of the Educational Center of the "Accademia Nazionale dei Lincei" at Perugia since 2013 and Member of the Academic Board of the Ph.D. in Mathematics, Computer Science, Statistics organized in consortium (C.I.A.F.M.) among the University of Perugia (Italy), University of Florence (Italy) and the INdAM (National Institute of High Mathematics).

He is and has been coordinator of several research projects and he coordinates a research team who deals with Real Analysis, Theory of Integral Operators, Approximation Theory and its Applications to Signal Reconstruction and Images Processing.

He has been invited to give more than 50 plenary lectures at conferences at various Universities and Research Centers. Moreover he is author of more than 115 publications on international journals and one scientific monography on "Nonlinear Integral Operators and Applications" edited by W. de Gruyter. Finally he is member of the Editorial Board of the following international scientific journals: Sampling Theory in Signal and Image Processing (STSIP), Journal of Function Spaces and Applications, Open Mathematics, and others and he holds a patent entitled: "Device for obtaining informations on blood vessels and other bodily-cave parts".

Contents – Part IV

Workshop Challenges, Trends and Innovations in VGI (VGI 2018)

Workshop Virtual Reality and Applications (VRA 2018)

Workshop Scientific Computing Infrastructure (SCI 2018)

Virtual Laboratories: Prospects for the Development of Techniques and Methods of Work

E. N. Stankova[1]([⊠]), N. V. Dyachenko[2], and G. S. Tibilova[3]

[1] Saint Petersburg State University,
7-9, Universitetskaya nab., St. Petersburg 199034, Russia
e.stankova@spbu.ru
[2] Russian State Hydrometeorological University,
98, Malookhtinsky pr., St. Petersburg 195196, Russia
nat230209@yandex.ru
[3] St. Petersburg State Unitary Firm "St. Petersburg Information
and Analytical Centre", 59, Chernyakhovsky ul., St. Petersburg 191040, Russia
tibilova.galina@yandex.ru

Abstract. The possibilities of using virtual laboratories in the process of teaching physics at a university are discussed. Various scenarios for conducting classes in a virtual laboratory for both undergraduate students and masters are offered. The ways of expanding the subject and technical capabilities of the virtual laboratory are considered, methodical recommendations and their possible technical solutions are suggested.

Keywords: Computer technology · Teaching physics · General physics
Laboratory practicum · Virtual laboratories

1 Introduction

In the previous works [1, 2] we have indicated a number of the problems arising before students while studying physics when they have to distinguish real phenomenon from its abstract model. It seems to us that the most productive way to overcome this "gap" in the minds of students are laboratory classes, where they are directly faced with the problem.

In [2] we presented a common vision of a comprehensive technical solution for laboratory works on physics. As part of this solution, two main functional parts can be outlined:

- the development of theoretical material, control of necessary theoretical knowledge and implement preliminary studies (colloquium on theoretical material, the study of the theory of the phenomenon and specific features of laboratory experiments, derivation of the formulas of the errors of indirect measurements);
- implementation of laboratory experiments, including measurements of the necessary parameters, processing the data of the experimental results.

O. Gervasi et al. (Eds.): ICCSA 2018, LNCS 10963, pp. 3–11, 2018.
https://doi.org/10.1007/978-3-319-95171-3_1

The provision of theoretical material and control tasks which represent the first part of the laboratory practicums on physics have in general much in common with the other educational disciplines. Technically this functionality is largely implemented in learning management systems such as modular object-oriented dynamic learning environment (MOODLE), which is currently being implemented in Russian State Hydrometeorological University (RSHU). The basis of this functionality is

– presentation of the theoretical material in various formats with the division on courses and topics with the opportunity to share the training files between the users;
– instrumental environment for providing test and control tasks of various types to control how the students assimilate theoretical material;
– communicational and organizational environment for messaging and event planning
– implementation of analytics and reporting.

The solution is a free (distributed under the GNU GPL license) web application.

Of course, each discipline and each university has a specific character, under which it is necessary to adapt MOODLE and similar solutions. Sometimes, for adaptation it is enough to use built-in tools of e-educational environment, sometimes it is necessary to form the terms of reference and involve developers. Development is especially relevant for those universities, where the certain tools are already used, and the task is to integrate them into certain e-learning environment. However, in general, solutions for automation of the first part of laboratory practicums are available on the market and can be used after the necessary settings or improvements.

The second part of laboratory practicums which presumes formulation of the experiment, measurement fulfillment and result monitoring is of greater interest in terms of information and communication technology implementation.

Direct laboratory work can be carried out in four forms.

(a) Setting up a virtual experiment. This form does not imply the use of any additional equipment other than a computer. Virtual experiment can be conducted both in the laboratory, and remotely.
(b) Experiments with an equipment that is not integrated with a computer. This form assumes that an experiment is conducted only with the use of laboratory equipment. The experiment results and measurement data are entered manually into the electronic environment after the experiment (data processing and report generation, graphical construction).
(c) Experiment on hardware that is integrated with a computer. This form involves the use of a laboratory hardware and software complexes (HSC). The results of the experiment and measurement data are automatically recorded by special software installed on the computer. The software interacts with the software of the device within the hardware and software complex. These results can then be transferred from the HSC software to the e-learning environment.
(d) Mixed form. This form is used for experiments carried out in several stages using various tools.

Currently, the basic configuration of typical e-learning environments, such as MOODLE, suggests the only possibility of entering data, "answers" in the electronic environment. The student should provide the data manually in a free format. Thus, only option (b) of laboratory work can be implemented using the standard capabilities.

At the same time, software and hardware complexes and the software of virtual laboratories are developed in isolation, without regard to the other components and technologies used for automation of the educational process. When purchasing these software products, a systematic approach is often not used, and as a result, the learning process is automated patchwork: its parts are automated in various products that are not integrated with each other, which makes it difficult to share them.

In the paper we will consider the prospects of virtual laboratory development and focus on the products both available today and those that will be available in the nearest future.

Within the framework of the paper, a virtual laboratory is understood as a software product that allows to conduct experiments without direct contact with the real experiment equipment or in the complete absence of the latter [3]. The processes that are the subject of the experiment are modeled using a computer.

Virtual laboratories unlike traditional ones allow to reduce the costs of laboratory developing and equipping [4–6]. The virtual laboratory allows to carry out experiments that are too expensive, dangerous or impossible within the framework of traditional laboratories, and, accordingly, allows to increase the number of practical experiments in the educational process and to diversify their composition.

The obvious disadvantage of a virtual laboratory is the limited ability to develop practical skills. From a methodological point of view, practical skills can be defined in a broad and narrow sense of the word. Virtual laboratory easily provides the opportunity to develop the practical skills in a broad sense. Among them are: the choice of the equipment for solution of a specific experimental problem, inclusion of the equipment into the measuring circuit, the assessment of systematic errors of devices. The direct interaction of the student with the device, its adjustment, calibration, sensitivity determination, adjustment of the optical installation are practical skills in the narrow sense of the word, and their development requires special capabilities of the virtual laboratory program.

In addition, as it has been mentioned above, a virtual laboratory is often technically isolated from the other means of automation of the educational process such as electronic learning environments for example. The problem reduces the overall effectiveness and benefits of virtual laboratory usage.

So below we will discuss how to integrate virtual laboratories in the educational process more effectively by strengthening their advantages and neutralizing disadvantages.

2 Improvement of Virtual Laboratories on the Basis of Technologies Available in Education Today

Nowadays there are two basic directions of virtual laboratory development:

- the subject direction, that is, increasing visibility of the subject of the virtual experiments, increasing their practical significance for students;

- technical direction, that is, the expansion of technical capabilities of virtual laboratories in order to implement various teaching methods.

2.1   Subject Direction of Virtual Laboratory Development

Laboratory practicums can be divided into two levels:

- practicums with precise results;
- practicums with measurements.

The laboratory practicum with the precise results is an implementation of actions provided by students and not related with the appearance of noise. The actions can include selection of measuring instruments, establishment of measuring equipment and equipment for providing research and development, activation and maintenance of the equipment.

Practicums with measurements involves experiments in which the effects of noise should be essential. In order to transfer such practicums to a virtual environment effectively and usefully, it is necessary to emulate real noise in a virtual environment.

The noise can be divided into two groups:

- measurement errors;
- equipment malfunctions.

The measurement error can be simulated in various ways, for example, by setting its certain constant value or by the random number generator that varies error value within certain permissible limits.

It is also extremely important to take into account that virtual laboratories are able to simulate such scenarios as breakage of equipment, peaks in the readings, the fuse, the deviation of the arrows to the left, a roll adjustment of optical schemes. Similar emulation in a virtual environment should be provided in three steps.

Occurrence of an Accident. An accident should occur randomly, depending on randomly generated natural or other conditions, or directly depending on the erroneous actions of the student. For example, maximum permissible values of measured values initially incorrectly estimated by a student and mistakenly set on the instruments as the wrong limits of measurements can lead to a burnout of devices, and extreme natural conditions (radiosonde fall caused by the strong wind) can lead to the destruction of the measuring equipment.

Accident Diagnosis. Accident diagnosis should be implemented by the student on a base of external features, such as switching a red light bulb, turning off a device or disappearing of data on a device panel, or on a base of incorrect measurement results, such as the data that strongly deviates from a number of previous measuring results;

Accident Elimination. Accident elimination should be emulated as a normal restart of a device, or its replacement, or its repair.

The Last Item is the Need to Emulate the Repair of Equipment. Repair emulation is resulted in the need to store the components of the equipment in a virtual environment as separate objects. In this case, the faulty component parts should be identified by a student and be replaced by the exploitable items.

Thus, it is advisable to realize an instrument designer in a virtual environment. The designer should be responsible for emulation of damaged equipment repair and of obsolete component replacement.

Such an approach will allow to realize a practicum designer, which enable to construct various measuring complexes from different devices at the lecturer request, or create virtual laboratory practicum that is difficult to implement in reality. Among such practicums are the study of the quantum effect, that is Compton scattering, the experiments of Davisson and Germer on diffraction of electrons, the alpha decay of nuclei, the motion detection of alpha particles in a cloud chamber etc.

2.2   Technical Direction to the Development of Virtual Laboratories

The technical direction of the development of virtual laboratories should be aimed at improving adaptivity and availability of the software.

Adaptability means a set of built-in capabilities of the software to configure and adapt it to the needs of a user without involving a developer. As mentioned above, a virtual laboratory should contain equipment designer and practicum designer.

This leads to the need to use modular programming when developing virtual laboratories. When designing a virtual laboratory, a laboratory practicum should be divided into independent, alienable parts, which can be stored in the environment as separate objects. One part may present rather simple physical experiments for the younger students, set out, for example, in the books of Pohl R.W. (determination of the frequency response characteristics of the human ear or eye depending on the power of perceived radiation) and the other part may present experiments connected with scientific research provided in the university departments. The latter are intended for advanced students such as undergraduates. This approach will allow to support the software without additional work by purchasing, downloading and installing additional devices and their components into a virtual environment from the developer's website, similar to organization of additional content installation in computer games.

As for availability, it should be noted that the priority in the acquisition and implementation of virtual laboratories should be given to network solutions. Depending on the University policy, the virtual laboratory can be accessed only from the local network of a university or remotely via the Internet.

Access to the virtual lab must be authorized and logging of user actions in the laboratory must be carried out. The following benefits will be obtained.

Monitoring the Actions of Each Student in a Virtual Laboratory. The teacher will be able to track not only the results of the work, but also the entire history of the experiment, including erroneous actions of the student. The availability of such information in the system will open the possibility of developing analytical tools. It will be possible to objectively estimate the quality of different aspects of the laboratory practicum from the point of their adaptively by students. This information can be used for correction of teaching methods, and, in addition, will allow to identify the weaknesses of a student and correct them.

Cooperative Learning. Cooperative learning implies implementation of collective projects thus simulating a work in a research team. This is especially important in view of the existence of a new generation of competencies in educational standards, identifying the ability of the student to work (and even to lead) in small research teams. It is easier to implement group laboratory practicums in the framework of virtual laboratories than in a traditional laboratory.

Cooperative learning can be provided by group work and by logging of user actions. Group work implies access to the necessary tools for all members of the group at the same time. Logging of user actions and session will objectively estimates the contribution of each student (user) to the overall result.

In a virtual environment, a wide variety of cooperative learning becomes available. The following examples can be considered.

- **Jigsaw Method (Openwork Saw).** The essence of the method is to divide the overall task into fragments, on which groups of student's work. The solution arises from the exchange of information between experts from individual groups. For a virtual lab, you can use the Jigsaw method to build a research facility, parts of which are collected by individual groups of students by selecting equipment from the database.

- **Project Method.** This method is always focused on independent activities of students, including individual, paired and group activity which students perform for a certain period of time. This approach is organically combined with a group approach to learning (cooperative learning). The method of projects always involves solution of a problem accompanied on the one hand by the use of a variety of methods and on the other hand by integration of knowledge and skills from different fields of science. The method of projects involves not only the presence of a problem and its awareness, but also the presence of a plan or hypothesis of how to solve the problem and a clear distribution of roles, i.e. each participant must have his/her clear plan of action and must closely interact with each other. The results of fulfilled projects should be "tangible", substantive, i.e., a theoretical problem should be resulted in a concrete solution, practical problem should be resulted in a concrete practical result, ready for use. The method of projects can be used in the virtual laboratory to solve a strategic scientific problem, when students are invited to develop independently a method for determining any physical quantities. Each of the students should provide own "vision" of the problem and offer own solutions.

- **Problem-Based Learning.** Problem-based learning implies the presence of a problem, which is set before students. This can be done by questions. There may be one question or a system of questions. Questions may concern any details of the study, around which all the learning material is built. The problem can be posed with the help of graphs, drawings, photos. The process of problem solution is no less and often is more valuable, than the result of the solution. Students remember the reaction to the problem. Process of problem solution is considered to be successful when a problem situation arises, that is, a student experiences intellectual difficulty, which directs his mental activity to solve the problem. This method arises as a result of the above methods; problems appear in chain when students try to resolve them gradually while they participate in a project.

– **Research Method. Game Method.** Limitations which exist in a real laboratory are absent in a virtual environment. Thus, there are no limitations in scenarios of laboratory experiments and in the scale of the problems that need to be solved during that experiments. In order to implement cooperative learning in a virtual environment large-scale multi-stage game scenarios and even science fiction scenarios can be implemented. Such type of scenarios requires application of knowledge from different parts of physics. Motivation of students to understand the physical processes in such research and game scenarios is also fuelled by understanding that their mistakes will not lead to fatal consequences for equipment and installations. This understanding provide satisfaction of curiosity that is essential stage of the process of cognition.

3 The Future of Virtual Laboratories

These features and benefits of virtual laboratories can be made available in education just now. At the same time, it is important to note that the technical implementation is ahead of the methodological one. The trend of development of virtual laboratories in the direction of network software products with shared access is obvious, but the methods of their application have not yet been sufficiently developed. This is especially true for cooperative learning. At the same time, taking into account the pace of development and implementation of technologies, it is easy to look into the future and assess the possibilities of leveling the shortcomings of virtual laboratories through the development of virtual reality technologies. Virtual reality emulates material reality, affecting all human senses. Objects of virtual reality can behave in accordance with the laws of physical reality and respond accordingly to the actions of users.

Currently, virtual reality technologies are widely used as simulators for training professions in which the operation of real equipment is associated with increased risk (pilots, rescuers, etc.), or high costs, or is impossible due to certain circumstances. Such problems are especially common in astrophysics and hydro and aerodynamics: laboratory measurements there have to be recalculated on full-scale conditions using the methods of similarity theory and dimensions, while the possibility of a virtual experiment greatly facilitates their solution [7–11]. Such virtual simulators develop along the way of maximum approximation of virtual reality to material reality by maximum number of factors. Moreover, neurocomputer interfaces designed for direct information exchange between the brain and the device are already used in medicine. So far, they are not sufficiently perfect and extremely expensive, but the trend is obvious.

To date, these technologies are not available for implementation in education due to their high cost. However, taking into account the pace of implementation of various innovations, it can be said that virtual reality technologies will become available in education within the next ten years. Already now technologies of virtual reality become available in game purposes in a large number of the entertaining virtual attractions. Their use for educational purposes will help to minimize the disadvantages of virtual laboratories, such as lack of subject clarity.

The introduction of virtual reality in the educational process requires a serious methodological work, which should start today.

4 Conclusions

It is obvious that the introduction of information technologies in the educational process requires an integrated approach. It is wrong to install educational information systems as Moodle or to purchase a separate virtual laboratories or laboratory hardware and software complexes (HSC) that are not integrated with any other IT products. The information should be aggregated in one place, otherwise it will not be possible to analyze it i.e. to get an overall picture of progress.

Virtual laboratories are a very promising direction, despite their obvious shortcomings in the current time period.

In the framework of the technologies available to date, it is necessary

- to improve the subject visibility of virtual laboratories in the following ways:
  - to add errors and malfunctions of the equipment in the process of measurement with possibility of equipment diagnostics and repair;
  - to introduce noise analysis during measurements within the limits of sensitivity and accuracy of measurements;
  - to add the ability of laboratory equipment design and construction for the measurement of certain physical quantities, these aims can be achieved by implementation the functionality of the equipment designer and practicum designer;
- to improve the technical implementation of virtual laboratories in the following ways:
  - use modular programming, programmatically implement individual elements of the practicum as independent modules, in order to enhance the capabilities of designers;
  - to organize a virtual lab in the form of networks and sessions, to logg user actions;
  - to integrate virtual labs into existing e-learning environment (e.g. Moodle).

In addition, it is necessary to develop the methodological base of collective training in order to create complex laboratory practicums in groups in a virtual environment, with the possibility of an objective assessment of the personal contribution of each member of the group to the project.

A virtual laboratory provides an opportunity to use both the simplest scenarios for teaching students and more complex tasks for bachelor works.

It is necessary to understand what opportunities a virtual reality gives for education in general. Though being already used in some professional fields this technology is not available just now for teaching physics because of the great cost. But the necessity to work out the methodological background for the technology is very relevant.

Acknowledgment. This research was sponsored by the Russian Foundation for Basic Research under the projects: 16-07-01113 "Virtual supercomputer as a tool for solving complex problems".

References

1. Stankova, E.N., et al.: The use of computer technology as a way to increase efficiency of teaching physics and other natural sciences. In: Gervasi, O., et al. (eds.) ICCSA 2016. LNCS, vol. 9789, pp. 581–594. Springer, Cham (2016). https://doi.org/10.1007/978-3-319-42089-9_41

2. Dyachenko, N.V., et al.: Prototype of informational infrastructure of a program instrumentation complex for carrying out a laboratory practicum on physics in a university. In: Gervasi, O., et al. (eds.) ICCSA 2017. LNCS, vol. 10408, pp. 412–427. Springer, Cham (2017). https://doi.org/10.1007/978-3-319-62404-4_30

3. Kostsov, V.V., Stankova, E.N.: Laboratory practical work using virtual stands on discipline "Physics". Section "Molecular physics and thermodynamics". RSHU, St. Petersburg (2010). - 64 p. (in Russian)

4. Trukhin, A.V.: On the use of virtual laboratories in education. Open Distance Educ. **4**(8), 70–72 (2002)

5. Gorbachev, Yu.E., Zhmakin, A.I., Zatevakhin, M.A., Krzhizhanovskaya, V.V., Bogdanov, M.V., Kulik, A.V., Ofengheim, D.H., Ramm, M.S.: From electronic textbooks to virtual laboratories. Telecommunications and informatization of education **5**(36) (2006). (in Russian)

6. Gorbachev, Yu.E., Krzhizhanovskaya, V.V., Bogdanov, M.V., Zhmakin, A.I., Kulik, A.V., Ramm, M.S.: Virtual laboratories - software complexes for science and education. In: Proceedings of the XIV All-Russian Scientific and Methodical Conference Telematika 2007, 18–21 June 2007, pp. 108–109. University telecommunications, St. Petersburg (2007). (in Russian)

7. Dyachenko, N.V., Dyachenko, V.K.: Method of calculation of parameters of the spray cloud surrounding the amphibious hovercraft (ASVP) when floating above the water surface in the collection of proceedings of TSNII im. Acad. A. N. Krylov "Modern computational methods in ship theory", **49**(333), 111–122 (2009). Publishing house of CRI to them. A. N. Krylov, St. Petersburg

8. Dyachenko, N.V., Anosov, V.N.: Calculation of the amount of water carried into the atmosphere by a jet of air from the airbag in the collection of works TSNII them. Acad. A. N. Krylov "Modern computational methods in ship theory", **49**(333), 123–134 (2009). Publishing house of CRI to them. A. N. Krylov, St. Petersburg

9. Dyachenko, N.V.: Dynamics of water droplets movement in the spray cloud surrounding the amphibious hovercraft (ASVP) in the lateral wind. Trudy TSNII im. Acad. A. N. Krylov. B. **59**(343), 165–176 (2011)

10. Petrov, D.A., Stankova, E.N.: Use of consolidation technology for meteorological data processing. In: Murgante, B., et al. (eds.) ICCSA 2014. LNCS, vol. 8579, pp. 440–451. Springer, Cham (2014). https://doi.org/10.1007/978-3-319-09144-0_30

11. Stankova, E.N., Balakshiy, A.V., Petrov, D.A., Shorov, A.V., Korkhov, V.V.: Using technologies of OLAP and machine learning for validation of the numerical models of convective clouds. In: Gervasi, O., et al. (eds.) ICCSA 2016. LNCS, vol. 9788, pp. 463–472. Springer, Cham (2016). https://doi.org/10.1007/978-3-319-42111-7_36

CUDA Support in GNA Data Analysis Framework

Anna Fatkina[1,2(✉)], Maxim Gonchar[1], Liudmila Kolupaeva[1],
Dmitry Naumov[1], and Konstantin Treskov[1]

[1] Joint Institute for Nuclear Research,
Joliot-Curie, 6, Dubna, Moscow region 141980, Russia
fatkina.a.i@gmail.com
[2] Saint-Petersburg State University,
7/9 Universitetskaya nab., St. Petersburg 199034, Russia

Abstract. Usage of GPUs as co-processors is a well-established approach to accelerate costly algorithms operating on matrices and vectors.
We aim to further improve the performance of the Global Neutrino Analysis framework (GNA) by adding GPU support in a way that is transparent to the end user. To achieve our goal we use CUDA, a state of the
art technology providing GPGPU programming methods.

In this paper we describe new features of GNA related to CUDA
support. Some specific framework features that influence GPGPU integration are also explained. The paper investigates the feasibility of GPU
technology application and shows an example of the achieved acceleration of an algorithm implemented within framework. Benchmarks show
a significant performance increase when using GPU transformations.

The project is currently in the developmental phase. Our plans include
implementation of the set of transformations necessary for the data analysis in the GNA framework and tests of the GPU expediency in the
complete analysis chain.

Keywords: CUDA · GPGPU · Parallel computing · Data analysis
Neutrino

1 Introduction

The neutrino is weakly interacting neutral fermion. There are three types of
these particles ν_1, ν_2 nd ν_3 with masses m_1, m_2 and m_3, respectively. These
particles interact with charged leptons (electron, muon and tau) with interaction
strengths determined by elements $V_{\alpha i}$ of the lepton mixing matrix V, named after
Pontecorvo-Maki-Nakagawa-Sakata.

Two facts, that neutrino masses are all different and that V is not a diagonal matrix, lead to a spectacular quantum mechanical phenomenon known as
neutrino oscillations. Its firm experimental confirmation was celebrated by the
2015 Nobel Prize in physics and the 2016 Breakthrough Prize in Fundamental
Physics [21,23,26].

© Springer International Publishing AG, part of Springer Nature 2018
O. Gervasi et al. (Eds.): ICCSA 2018, LNCS 10963, pp. 12–24, 2018.
https://doi.org/10.1007/978-3-319-95171-3_2

Neutrino physics entered the stage of precision measurements and addressing remained open questions: neutrino mass hierarchy, if neutrino is Majorana particle, and others. Both require an accurate, fast and flexible tool for a combined analysis of neutrino world data. Our team began a development of the corresponding software GNA based on our experience in Daya Bay [3] ('Analysis D'), JUNO [4] and NOvA [1] experiments.

GNA is an universal tool for building comprehensive physical models and statistical data analysis, designed with neutrino experiments in mind. It was initially created as software for the JUNO and Daya Bay experiments in a flexible and efficient way. The name GNA stands for Global Neutrino Analysis, as the package introduces tools for the combined analysis of the physical data. The framework is described in more detail in the following section.

There are several groups that perform the global neutrino analysis [7,9]. The dedicated software is not an open-source and as far as we know lacks the support of GPU computations. There is a group [5] working on Global neutrino analysis of the long baseline neutrino experiments. The software is not an open-source and according to the talks and publications lacks the support of GPU and multi-threading computations. The GLOBeS software [18] is dedicated to the sensitivity analysis of the long baseline neutrino experiments and is not used for the data analysis. It lacks the support of the GPU/multi-core computations.

GPUs (Graphics Processing Units) are used today for a much wider range of problems than simply processing graphics, including data analysis in science [2,11]. Video cards can be used as co-processors on both personal computers and high-performance servers. There exist free tools that provide an interface for GPU programming such as CUDA [24], OpenACC [10] or OpenCL [17].

We have added CUDA support to the GNA framework in order to achieve better performance during the processing of vector data. With this architecture the input data is mapped on multiple threads that are executed in parallel. Because a GPU platform has hundreds of times more threads compared to modern CPUs it is especially suitable for running data-parallel algorithms.

The CUDA Toolkit is developed by NVIDIA and supports only NVIDIA graphics accelerators. This narrows the range of compatible acceleration devices compared to other tools. Nevertheless, the CUDA Toolkit provides a number optimized numerical routines. Also, NVIDIA GPUs are quite popular and are widely used in common desktop computers and laptops.

It this paper we describe the way in which CUDA is integrated in GNA, and its implications from both the end-user and developer points of view. Major implementation details are discussed. A review of our future plans for GPU-based development is also presented.

2   GNA Architecture

The GNA is designed with dataflow programming principles in mind [8,14,20,27]. The computation process in GNA is represented by a directed graph in which nodes represent functions and edges present the data flow. Nodes are called transformations, which is an abstraction layer for C++ functions. They may have

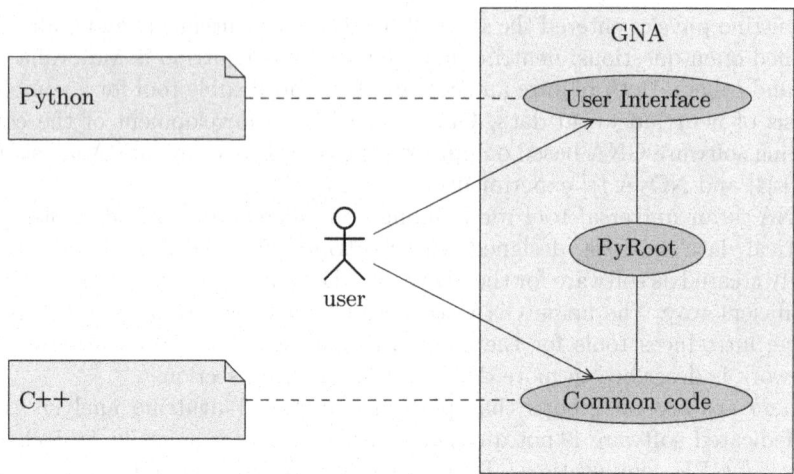

Fig. 1. GNA architecture schematic diagram.

inputs (arguments) and have at least one output (return values). Transformations typically operate on data arrays. A computational graph describes how transformations interact with each other. Because transformations are encapsulated and have universal interfaces a high flexibility is achieved.

Data analysis in GNA consists of two stages:

1. Configuration stage on which the computational graph is created.
2. Computational stage on which graph is evaluated.

In the first stage the transformation instances are created, and outputs and inputs are bound together. This step is done only once within Python and is flexible, but may be inefficient. The actual calculation happens on the second step. Calculations are done within compiled C++ code and are usually executed repeatedly.

The generalized scheme of the framework is shown on Fig. 1. GNA has a Python user interface (UI) that is used for building computation chains. The implementation of all transformations and the way they interact are described in C++. These two parts are linked via PyRoot.

The user may manage the computational process by using transformations already implemented in GNA. Transformations may also be written by users themselves and added into the framework environment.

2.1   Transformation

A transformation is an encapsulated wrapper for a function that either converts input data into output or calculates the output data in a standalone mode.

Figure 2 schematically displays several kinds of transformations. Transformations may or may not have inputs (marked by arrows on the left side) and

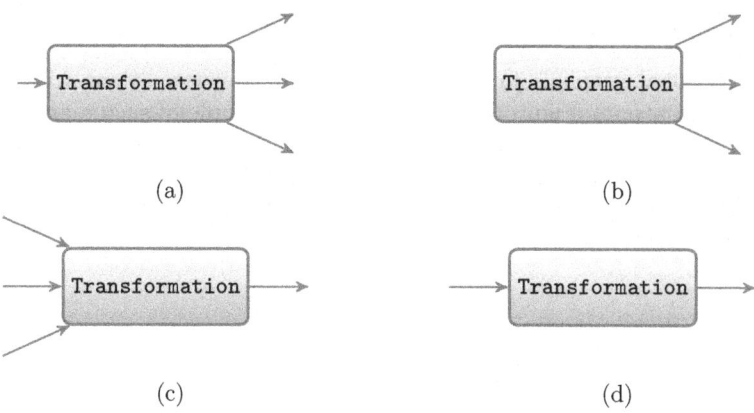

Fig. 2. Example of transformation kinds. Intermediate transformation (a) with a single input and multiple outputs. Initial transformation (b) with multiple outputs. Intermediate transformation (c) with multiple inputs and single output. Intermediate transformation (d) with single input and single output.

must have at least one output (marked by arrows on the right side). Inputs and outputs generally refer to data arrays. In addition to inputs transformation may also depend on variables. A variable is a small input data type which usually refers to a single number.

Actual data is allocated on the transformation outputs. Input data cannot be changed inside the transformation, it is a read-only state for the output it is connected to. It enables us to ensure that data will not be modified by following transformations after it is computed. A transformation is computed only once and the result may be used multiple times afterwards. It will be re-computed only if any of the variables or inputs it depends on were modified.

There is a set of predefined transformations implemented in the GNA framework. Because transformations are independent from each other the set may be straightforwardly extended by the users. The guidelines on how to do this are provided in the framework documentation [15].

The typical computational chain that produces prediction for the reactor antineutrino experiments contains hundreds of nodes and is evaluated within a time frame on the order of 0.1 seconds to seconds. The prediction is a histogram with 300 bins and depends overall on 250 independent parameters. The prediction is then used in the process of multidimensional minimization, which takes around 30 min for 15 free parameters or around 6 h for all the model parameters, most of which are constrained. Statistical analysis requires repeated minimization and may take several days to evaluate confidence intervals. MC based methods, such as Feldman-Cousins, require millions of minimization procedures and may take months when executed on a cluster. The framework is also suitable for building more complex graphs with evaluation times on the order of seconds to hours.

2.2   Computational Graph

A computational graph is formed by a chain of transformations with inputs connected to outputs. Figure 3 displays a simple example of such a graph. This scheme shows that the same output may refer to and be referred by any number of inputs. The graph may be configured in an arbitrary way, as long as data types of the outputs are compatible with the requirements of the transformation they are connected to.

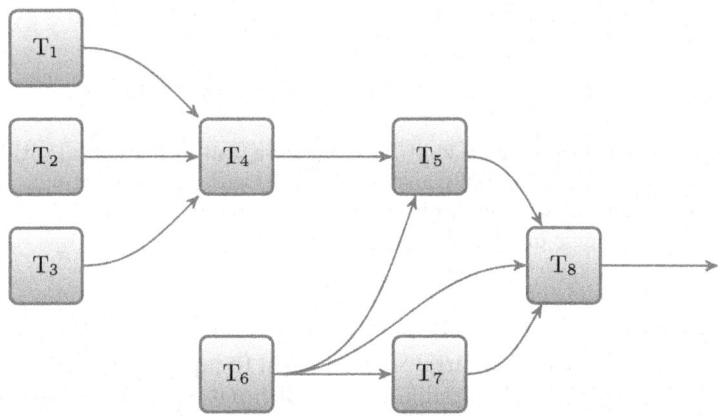

Fig. 3. Schematic example of the GNA computational graph.

The graph is constructed using Python. Users describe the way transformations are chained via Python script or from the command line interface. The result of any transformation may be read at any moment through the Python interface.

Lazy evaluation means that the output of a transformation is computed on demand if the output is read by a caller. In the case when the output of an intermediate transformation is accessed only preceding transformations are evaluated, not the entire graph.

2.3   Parallelism Opportunities

Parallel computing is a well-known method to speed up the computational process. There are methods to achieve performance increases on different levels. The most efficient and safe method is to divide input data into smaller independent datasets and execute the analysis on a distributed system [6,12]. However, in real-world cases analysis of those datasets often takes a long time. Due to this fact acceleration at an individual dataset level is also needed, and may be implemented for multi-core CPUs or GPUs [19]. In this paper we consider the prospects for acceleration of computations in GNA on a framework level using GPGPU.

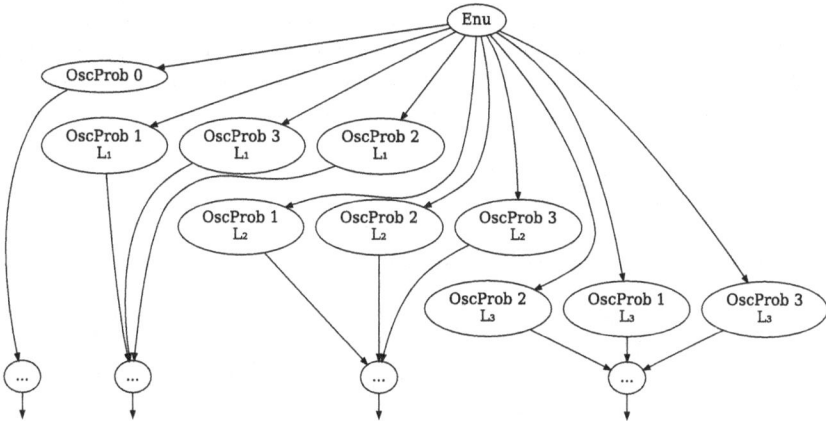

Fig. 4. Neutrino oscillation probability calculation scheme. A part of JUNO computational graph.

Figure 4 shows a part of a computational graph for the JUNO experiment implementing the neutrino oscillation probability calculation (see Sect. 4.1). There are multiple OscProb transformation instances in the graph computing the neutrino oscillation probability for various distances L, each of them depending on a vector neutrino energy E_ν. For the most practical cases E_ν may be computed only once. OscProb transformation instances are independent from each other and bound to different parameters (variables) that may change their output. Parallel technologies are applicable for graphs with such a structure, since no data writing collision is possible.

The OscProb transformation, as well as most of the framework modules, provide multi-dimensional array operations which are particularly suitable for multi-threaded systems such as GPUs or multi-core CPUs if their elements are computed independently.

3 CUDA Overview

CUDA (Compute Unified Device Architecture) is an architecture for parallel data processing for NVIDIA GPUs. The average GPU has hundreds of times more threads compared to modern CPUs. Threads run in parallel in SIMT (Single Instruction, Multiple Threads) [22] manner as GPUs were originally created for image processing—a vivid example of SIMT algorithms.

The CUDA Toolkit [25] has a set of specialized libraries optimized for their purposes, such as cuBLAS (linear algebra), cuRAND (random number generators), cuDNN (deep neural networks), etc. It also provides high-level abstractions to manage computational processes on GPUs, and low-level methods to tune it.

GPGPU's main performance limitations are memory allocation and data transfers, as the co-processor is an independent physical device. The copying of data from Host (CPU and RAM) to Device (GPU) or vice versa is slow. Nevertheless, it is a powerful tool for accelerating algorithms that contain operations with the same instruction applied to each element of an array, and producing independent output.

4   GPU Acceleration

4.1   Neutrino Oscillation Probability

In this section we consider an opportunity of achieving better performance for a distinct transformation that calculates the neutrino oscillation probability [13].

The general formula for oscillation probability in vacuum, the probability that neutrino flavor changes from ν_α to ν_β after travelling distance L, reads as follows:

$$P(\nu_\alpha \to \nu_\beta) = \delta_{\alpha\beta} - 4 \sum_{i>j} \mathrm{Re}(V_{\alpha i}^* V_{\beta i} V_{\alpha j} V_{\beta j}^*) \sin^2 \frac{\Delta m_{ij}^2 L}{4 E_\nu}$$

$$+ 2 \sum_{i>j} \mathrm{Im}(V_{\alpha i}^* V_{\beta i} V_{\alpha j} V_{\beta j}^*) \sin \frac{\Delta m_{ij}^2 L}{2 E_\nu},$$

where E denotes neutrino energy, L is a distance between neutrino source and detector, $V_{\alpha i}$ is a complex unitary matrix called a Pontecorvo-Maki-Nakagawa-Sakata (PMNS) matrix, and $\Delta m_{ij}^2 = m_i^2 - m_j^2$ is a neutrino mass splitting.

Within GNA the oscillation probability is implemented as a set of transformations for each formula item respectively. Each transformation input is a vector of neutrino energy values $\boldsymbol{E}_\nu$.

The computations for different energy values are identical and independent from each other, therefore they can run in parallel on a GPU. It should be noted that the input array (neutrino energy), in most realistic cases, is known beforehand and will be copied to the GPU only once while the computation is performed for different oscillation parameter values.

The following features were used to port the oscillation probability code to GPU:

- CUDA Streams [16],
- datasets are divided into smaller sizes to organize overlapped execution,
- asynchronous memory copying.

After porting the oscillation probability the result was verified: a difference between GPU and CPU output results is within the roundoff accuracy of the double precision floating point numbers.

Results of the test with input energy vectors of sizes 10^4 and 10^6 elements are presented in Table 1. The calculation is performed with double precision on Intel Core i7-6700HQ CPU and NVIDIA GeForce GTX 970M GPU. It should be noted that a size of 10^4 elements corresponds to the JUNO experiment's case. First row contains the ratio of the full computation times for CPU-only and GPU-oriented (including data transfer costs) versions of the algorithm. The second row contains the ratio of the computation times (without data transfer costs in GPU-based case).

When data transfer is taken into account the acceleration for the 10^6 sample size is not significant. For the smaller sample the acceleration is not enough to cover the overhead due to data transfer.

When data transfer is not taken into account the achieved acceleration is at least ×20 compared to CPU case. Since the neutrino energy is computed only once and then stored the latter is the more realistic case for this task.

The speed-up is expected to be more significant for larger datasets. At the same time the data transfer overhead should be considered and handled appropriately in any case.

It should also be noted that single precision floating point operations are typically much faster (dozens of times) on most GPUs when compared to double precision. For CPUs the single precision is only twice as faster. Therefore a significant speed-up is expected for cases when single precision is sufficient.

4.2   Computational Chains with GPU-Oriented Transformations

The original CPU computational scheme was modified in such a way that switching between CPU- and GPU-oriented transformation modes is transparent for the end user. The transformation is still a single object with two function definitions: one for the CPU and another for the GPU. On the UI side the GPU computation is enabled by setting a single flag that changes the target device of the transformation and switches the active function. Thus, users are enabled to work with the GPU mode of GNA without any special knowledge about GPGPU.

In order to handle data transfer we implemented a C++ wrapper for the GPU array and defined several frequently used mathematical operations. The portion of the framework that contains CUDA is built as a separate shared library. Then the main code is built with this library as a dependency. This way GPU functions may be called from the common C++ code. GPU related code may be switched off completely by a special flag during the compilation of the framework.

Since memory allocation is one of GPGPU's limitations within GNA, all required memory for both the GPU and CPU is allocated during the configuration stage to avoid extra time costs in the runtime.

Table 1. Benchmarks for oscillation probability calculation on CPU and GPU with input vectors sizes of 10^4 and 10^6 elements.

Input data size, elements	10^4	10^6
CPU time/(GPU computing + transfer time)	0.017	1.39
CPU time/GPU computing-only time	20.90	26.46

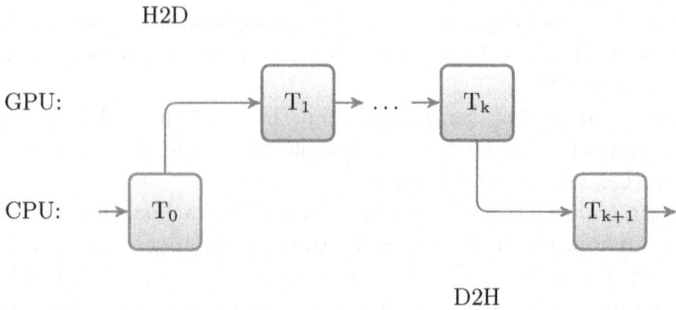

Fig. 5. Schema of mixed (CPU and GPU) computational chain.

As described earlier, inputs are simply the views on the data of the corresponding outputs of preceding transformations. The same feature is implemented for the GPU arrays. There is no additional allocation on the GPU for the inputs as it refers to the output it is bound to. The only exception to this rule is the first GPU-oriented transformation in the computational subchain: an extra GPU memory allocation for its inputs occurs because we need to transfer data from Host memory to the Device.

We have extended the GNA internal data storage objects in order to maintain a synchronized copy of Host data on the Device. The synchronization is done in a lazy manner, i.e. it happens only when the unsynchronized Host data is read from Device and vice versa.

Figure 5 shows the computation scheme in which the chain contains a subset of GPU-based transformations. Only two data transfers between the Host and the Device take place in this case: at the beginning of GPU subchain and at the end of it. We minimize communication between Host and Device to cut the time costs due to data copying since it is an expensive operation. The status of GPU function, which indicates whether or not it was executed successfully, is available on the Host side after the transformation computation is finished. Device-To-Device data transfers may occur inside the transformations implementation, but they not considered to be costly.

Extra data transfers from Device to Host may be triggered by the user, reading the data at any point of the computational chain as is shown in Fig. 6. In this case an extra data transfer occurs. The backward transfer is not needed. Because user-triggered reading may occur during a debugging procedure or for the plotting of data, the data transfer overhead in not significant in this case when compared to the actual data analysis.

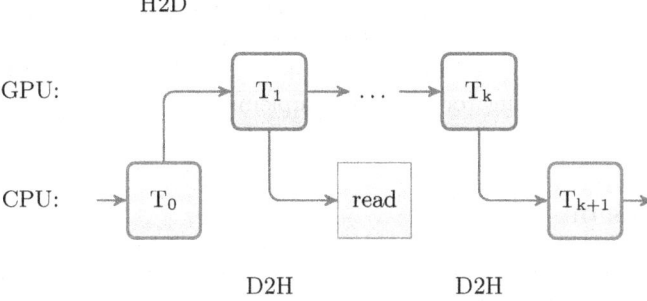

Fig. 6. Reading an intermediate result from the GPU chain.

5 Future Work

The major shortcoming of the current GPU support implementation is the lack of fault tolerance. In the case of GPU failure the computation will be aborted.

We are planning to add a feature of switching the computation between CPU and GPU modes automatically during runtime as is shown in Fig. 7. It is assumed that the deceleration of the algorithm execution is more preferred than aborting it.

Another planned feature is adding checkpoints for the GPU side of the framework. It will decrease latency time for recovering the computation crashed on GPU side. This implies that data will regularly be synchronized between Host and Device. Since this may lead to an additional overhead the existence and frequency of the checkpoints will be configurable.

In order to use a GPU for the computational chain in a real analysis a subset of existing transformations should be ported to the GPU. Not every algorithm will be ported, however. The choice will be made based on analysis of the computational chains of the Daya Bay and JUNO experiments. As a sufficient set of transformations is ported we will benchmark the GPU-enabled version of GNA on several realistic computational schemes with various configurations and floating point precision settings.

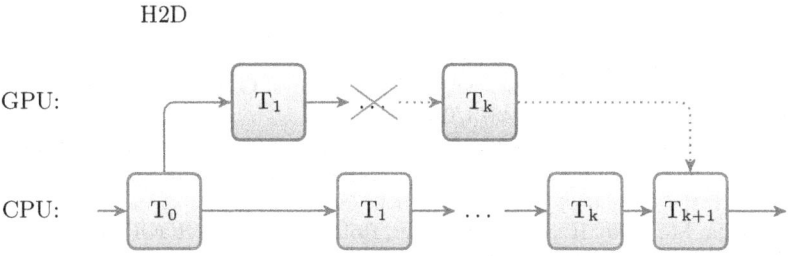

Fig. 7. Computational process recovery on CPU after GPU fault.

Since the data transfer costs may negate performance improvement of GPU-enabled computational chain the actual choice of the configuration should be made and tested by the end-user, based on a particular computational chain. Specialized benchmarking tools will be implemented in GNA to simplify this task.

6   Conclusion

In this paper we describe the GPU support within the GNA framework implemented via the CUDA architecture with transparency for the end-user. For the particular case of neutrino oscillation probability it has been demonstrated that the achieved acceleration may be of order of $\times 20$ for double precision floating point numbers.

While the realistic acceleration for the large computational chains may be lower and may depend on a particular chain, the prospects look very promising. Significant improvement is expected when single precision is sufficient for the task. An acceleration obtained in case of single precision is usually much higher for GPUs compared to CPUs. The corresponding studies and benchmarks will be performed in further work.

The solutions to the major problems and limitations, such as memory allocation and data transfer are discussed.

Acknowledgements. We are grateful to Chris Kullenberg for reading the manuscript and for valuable suggestions.

This research is supported by the Russian Foundation for Basic Research (projects no. 18-32-00935 and 16-07-00886) and by the Association of Young Scientists and Specialists of Joint Institute for Nuclear Research (grant no. 18-202-08).

References

1. Adamson, P., et al.: Constraints on oscillation parameters from ν_e Appearance and ν_μ disappearance in NOvA. Phys. Rev. Lett. **118**(23), 231801 (2017). https://doi.org/10.1103/PhysRevLett.118.231801
2. Al-Turany, M., Uhlig, F., Karabowicz, R.: GPU's for event reconstruction in the fairroot framework. J. Phys: Conf. Ser. **219**(4), 042001 (2010)
3. An, F.P., et al.: Measurement of electron antineutrino oscillation based on 1230 days of operation of the Daya Bay experiment. Phys. Rev. D **95**, 072006 (2017). https://doi.org/10.1103/PhysRevD.95.072006
4. An, F., et al.: Neutrino physics with JUNO. J. Phys. **G43**, 030401 (2016). https://doi.org/10.1088/0954-3899/43/3/030401
5. Andreopoulos, C., et al.: VALOR joint oscillation analysis using multiple LAr-TPCs in the booster neutrino beam at Fermilab. J. Phys: Conf. Ser. **888**(1), 012254 (2017). https://doi.org/10.1088/1742-6596/888/1/012254
6. Ballintijn, M., Brun, R., Rademakers, F., Roland, G.: The PROOF distributed parallel analysis framework based on ROOT. arXiv preprint physics/0306110 (2003)
7. Capozzi, F., Lisi, E., Marrone, A., Palazzo, A.: Current unknowns in the three neutrino framework (2018)

8. Dennis, J.B., Fosseen, J.B., Linderman, J.P.: Data flow schemas. In: Ershov, A., Nepomniaschy, V.A. (eds.) International Symposium on Theoretical Programming. LNCS, vol. 5, pp. 187–216. Springer, Heidelberg (1974). https://doi.org/10.1007/3-540-06720-5_15

9. Esteban, I., Gonzalez-Garcia, M.C., Maltoni, M., Martinez-Soler, I., Schwetz, T.: Updated fit to three neutrino mixing: exploring the accelerator-reactor complementarity (2016)

10. Farber, R.: Parallel programming with OpenACC. Newnes (2016)

11. Fatkina, A., Iakushkin, O., Tikhonov, N.: Application of GPGPUs and multicore CPUs in optimization of some of the MpdRoot codes. In: 25th Russian Particle Accelerator Conference on (RuPAC 2016), St. Petersburg, Russia, 21–25 November 2016, pp. 416–418. JACOW, Geneva (2017)

12. Gankevich, I., Tipikin, Y., Korkhov, V.: Subordination: providing resilience to simultaneous failure of multiple cluster nodes. In: Proceedings of International Conference on High Performance Computing Simulation (HPCS 2017), pp. 832–838. Institute of Electrical and Electronics Engineers (IEEE), NJ, USA, July 2017. https://doi.org/10.1109/HPCS.2017.126

13. Giunti, C., Kim, C.W.: Fundamentals of Neutrino Physics and Astrophysics. Oxford University Press, New York (2007)

14. Glatard, T., Rousseau, M.E., Camarasu-Pop, S., Adalat, R., Beck, N., Das, S., da Silva, R.F., Khalili-Mahani, N., Korkhov, V., Quirion, P.O., et al.: Software architectures to integrate workflow engines in science gateways. Future Gener. Comput. Syst. **75**, 239–255 (2017)

15. GNA group: GNA documentation. http://gna.pages.jinr.ru/gna/

16. Gómez-Luna, J., González-Linares, J.M., Benavides, J.I., Guil, N.: Performance models for cuda streams on nvidia geforce series. J. Parallel Distrib. Comput. **72**(9), 1117–1126 (2012)

17. Howes, L., Munshi, A.: The Opencl Specification. Khronos Group (2015)

18. Huber, P., Kopp, J., Lindner, M., Rolinec, M., Winter, W.: New features in the simulation of neutrino oscillation experiments with GLoBES 3.0: general long baseline experiment simulator. Comput. Phys. Commun. **177**, 432–438 (2007). https://doi.org/10.1016/j.cpc.2007.05.004

19. Iakushkin, O., Fatkina, A., Degtyarev, A., Grishkin, V.: Application of multi-core architecture to the MPDRoot package for the task ToF events reconstruction. In: Gervasi, O., et al. (eds.) ICCSA 2017. LNCS, vol. 10408, pp. 428–437. Springer, Cham (2017). https://doi.org/10.1007/978-3-319-62404-4_31

20. Johnston, W.M., Hanna, J.R.P., Millar, R.J.: Advances in dataflow programming languages. ACM Comput. Surv. **36**(1), 1–34 (2004). https://doi.org/10.1145/1013208.1013209, https://doi.acm.org/10.1145/1013208.1013209

21. Kajita, T.: Nobel lecture: discovery of atmospheric neutrino oscillations. Rev. Mod. Phys. **88**(3), 030501 (2016)

22. Lindholm, E., Nickolls, J., Oberman, S., Montrym, J.: Nvidia tesla: a unified graphics and computing architecture. IEEE Micro **28**(2), 39–55 (2008)

23. McDonald, A.B.: Nobel lecture: the sudbury neutrino observatory: observation of flavor change for solar neutrinos. Rev. Mod. Phys. **88**(3), 030502 (2016)

24. Nickolls, J., Buck, I., Garland, M., Skadron, K.: Scalable parallel programming with CUDA. Queue **6**(2), 40–53 (2008). https://doi.org/10.1145/1365490.1365500, http://doi.acm.org/10.1145/1365490.1365500

25. Nvidia, CUDA: Compute unified device architecture programming guide (2007)
26. Johnston, W.M., Hanna, J.R.P., Millar, R.J.: Advances in dataflow programming languages. ACM Comput. Surv. **36**(1), 1–34 (2004). https://doi.org/10.1145/1013208.1013209
27. Sharp, J.A.: Data Flow Computing: Theory and Practice. Ablex Publishing Corp., Norwood (1992)

Application Porting Optimization on Heterogeneous Systems

Nikita Storublevtcev[✉], Vladimir Korkhov, Alexey Beloshapko,
and Alexander Bogdanov

Saint Petersburg State University, 7/9 Universitetskaya nab.,
St. Petersburg 199034, Russia
100.rub@mail.ru, v.korkhov@spbu.ru, beloshapko-alexey@rambler.ru,
a.v.bogdanov@spbu.ru

Abstract. Modern heterogeneous computer systems offer an exceptional computational potential, but require specific knowledge and experience on the part of the programmer to fully realize it. In this paper we explore different approaches to the task of adapting an application to the heterogeneous computer system. We provide performance evaluation of the test application ported using those approaches. We also evaluate the difficulty and time investment required to implement those approaches in relation to performance improvements they offer.

Keywords: Computing · CUDA · Performance · Heterogeneous

1 Introduction

The demand for computational power is ever increasing, especially in such fields as Computational Fluid Dynamics. Historically those areas provided the most demand for supercomputers and the trend continues to this day. Since around year 2000, the per-core performance growth slowed down and most CPU manufacturers began to focus on multi-core systems, necessitating the rewriting of many applications to accommodate the parallel computing paradigm. This problem was more prevalent for applications designed for personal computers, since supercomputer environments were parallel for a long time. Around 2005 the new paradigm of Heterogeneous Computing entered the public focus, supported by such technologies as OpenCL, CUDA and OpenACC. The idea itself was not new, but the faster evolution of Graphics Processing Units (GPUs), compared to CPUs, brought the potential of using them as main processing unit, to industry's attention. While GPUs indeed provide an deep potential to improve system performance in many different areas, the process of adapting the existing applications and algorithms to this architecture is non-trivial, and requires specific knowledge and experience. Therefore it is important to know, is it worth, for non-specialists, to spend time and resources studying the technology, and what techniques, specific to this architecture offer the most benefit for the amount of work and time invested.

© Springer International Publishing AG, part of Springer Nature 2018
O. Gervasi et al. (Eds.): ICCSA 2018, LNCS 10963, pp. 25–40, 2018.
https://doi.org/10.1007/978-3-319-95171-3_3

In this paper we discuss possible approaches to adapting an application to the heterogeneous computer system using CUDA technology. We look into different optimization techniques (both hardware-dependent and not), and evaluate their effectiveness compared to the difficulty of their usage in various types of applications and algorithms. Finally we compare the performance of different versions of the test application, created using mentioned techniques in two programming languages, C/C++ and Fortran95, and different compiler suits, CUDA Toolkit v9.1 for C/C++, and PGI CUDA Fortran Compiler 17.10 for Fortran95. The test application uses a modified matrix/vector multiplication algorithm as the main computational workload.

The project aims to accomplish the following goals:

- Compare the performance increase offered by the different approaches and techniques of porting an application to heterogeneous system.
- Determine the most effective of those approaches, in relation of difficulty of their implementation.
- Compare the performance of test application versions created using different programming languages and compiler suits.

The drive for increased performance is almost universal in the industry and heterogeneous solutions offer an exceptional potential. Unfortunately realizing this potential requires specific knowledge and experience with heterogeneous systems, and optimization process is frequently far from trivial. Knowing that, it is important for any project management to determine how much resources and time they are willing to spend on optimization for heterogeneous systems. A comprehensive analysis of available options and methods, as well as their difficulty of implementation, will allow even non-specialists to make the right decision.

The paper is organized as follows: Section 2 presents an overview of related work on using application porting and optimization methods used for heterogeneous systems; Section 3 presents the details of the test application, and hardware used in testing; Section 4 discusses various optimization methods and compiler suits used; Section 5 showcases the test results; Section 6 discusses the results and Sect. 7 concludes the paper.

2   Related Work

The problem of porting applications to heterogeneous platforms is not new, as the technology is more than 10 years old. Still there are very few specialists with knowledge and experience required to port or develop heterogeneous applications in a production environment, without spending a most of the time familiarizing themselves with the intricacies of the technology. The situation is even worse with scientific applications, as they require an additional knowledge in their specific area, to effectively understand and optimize algorithms involved.

In [1] which is concerned with porting of Weather Research and Forecasting software to CUDA-based heterogeneous system, authors emphasize the need for unified formal methodology of application porting, and note that "the process of porting the code to CUDA requires significant effort and is prone to error". While the project was ultimately successful, it took 3 month to port a production-ready, tested, and verified code, although by authors admission, a significant time was spent learning about the software itself.

[2] provides useful performance metrics and methodology for optimization of CUDA-based applications. However the results were acquired using CUDA version 1.0, and GeForce 8800, which is now considered legacy hardware and is no longer supported, while latest version of CUDA is 9.1.

[3] provides a good comparison of FORTRAN and C GPU and CPU benchmarks, but being a relatively old paper (2012) the results are outdated. Hardware used is also five generations behind and can be considered outdated.

After reviewing these works it is evident that this problem area is in need of up-to-date reports, as advancement in GPU architecture is very quick. This paper seeks to address this issue by using the most up to date hardware and software that can be reasonably acquired. Additionally ongoing compiler optimization can be a very significant factor in resulting performance, especially for PGI CUDA FORTRAN tools.

3   Problem Overview

3.1   Difficulties of Application Porting

Historically most applications, especially in scientific area were designed to be ran on CPU-based platforms. With the continued evolution of GPUs, they began to be considered as more effective platform for many kinds of specialized computational tasks. The main strength of GPUs in comparison to CPUs, is their massive parallel capability, which ideally suits many scientific and statistical problems. Those problems have massive amounts of legacy solutions, most of them written in FORTRAN, optimized for CPU-based super-computing environments. Unfortunately, GPUs have a different architecture compared to CPUs, and require special skills and knowledge to use them directly, which mitigated their use in many fields.

In 2006 NVIDIA released their General Purpose GPU (GPGPU) technology named CUDA [6], after which in 2008 followed OpenCL [7] from Khronos Group. Initially both of those technologies, only had C-based API available and necessitated either a complete rewrite of the application in C/C++, or use of FORTRAN-C bindings that are very difficult to implement correctly. In 2009 PGI Group, having been bought by NVIDIA earlier, released the first version of their CUDA FORTRAN compiler [8], making it possible for native-FORTRAN applications to use full CUDA API. Since then GPGPU technologies are in constant development, increasing usability and performance with every new version.

GPGPU technologies generally use the concept of a "kernel" to designate a portion of code executed on GPU. That necessitates dividing the application code into modules with different intended computation devices. But more importantly it requires the transfer of data between the main CPU (commonly designated as "host"), and GPU (frequently designated as "device"). Therein lies a great potential for both performance gains and big pitfalls.

With the new breath of options, a new question rises to the top, that is, which option is the best. As with all competing technologies it is impossible to definitively determine the better one overall, so this paper will focus on the performance reasonably attainable with CUDA C/C++ and PGI CUDA FORTRAN compilers. This issue is very contentious as veteran specialists on both sides have invested considerable time and effort in mastering their language of choice, and don't consider switching lightly. As such it is important for new projects to know what combination of technologies and languages offers the best performance with minimal effort.

3.2   Test Application Overview

Different algorithms and environments require different optimization strategies. In this paper we use basic matrix-on-vector multiplication algorithm, as it is a very frequent operation in scientific applications. Main benefits of this algorithm for out purposes include its simplicity, lack of branching, high degree of data-parallelism and reasonable reuse of data inside one iteration. These features allow us to examine different facets of GPU architecture and CUDA programming model.

Test application has two versions. One written in C using CUDA API, and small amount of C++ features, beyond that used in CUDA C. Second version is written in FORTRAN 95 using PGI CUDA FORTRAN API. Performance timing in both versions is performed using CUDA events, although a couple of language specific timers were used for comparison during development, all of which reported consistent results.

Both version of the application consist of main entry point function, a set of benchmark functions (subroutines in case of FORTRAN), and a set of utility functions. Main function performs all host-side initialization, such as determining benchmark parameters, allocating host memory for input data, detecting and managing devices, and displaying results. Each benchmark function implements a different version of the algorithm using different optimization methods and techniques, including non-optimized serial single-thread CPU version. Utility functions serve to encapsulate such tasks as creating reference data and checking the results of each iteration.

Input data is allocated as linear dynamic arrays of appropriate size. This is due to the specifics of data transfer in CUDA API. Input data consists of array of size NxNxC, representing a stack of square matrices with dimensions NxN (where N is the length of the side of the matrix and C is the number of matrices in the stack), and array of size NxC, representing stack of input vectors. Results consist of array of size NxC, representing stack of result vectors (each vector is of length N, with C vectors in each stack).

After all initialization is complete main function calls all benchmark functions in sequence, passing input data by reference. Each benchmark function handles all device data allocation and transfer, performs timing of each step, calculates time per element and calls result checking utility functions. Each benchmark function performs a number of iterations equal to I, with each iteration consisting of full processing of input data. Results are checked after each iteration. Multiplications are performed pair-wise, with each matrix in the stack having a corresponding input vector and a result vector. Each multiplication is independent, allowing for a number of ways to optimize them.

Timing results, averaged over iterations, are printed after completion of each benchmark subroutine. Testing was done with N = 128, C = 15000, and I = 1000, which results in roughly 2 GB data set.

3.3   Platform Hardware Overview

One of the goals of this project is to compare performance of different hardware and determine the best way to utilize it. As such a couple of different hardware configurations were used.

Development configuration:

- Intel Core I5-4690K CPU, 4 cores, 3,5 GHz (4.74 GFLOPS per core, 18.96 GFLOPS total)
- NVIDIA GK104 GeForce GTX 770 GPU, Kepler architecture, 1536 CUDA cores, 1046–1085 MHz clock speed (3333 GFLOPS total), 2 GB global memory (7 GB/s PCI transfer bandwidth, 224.3 GB/s peak memory bandwidth)

Production configuration 1:

- Intel Xeon E5-2690 v4 CPU, 14 cores, 2,6 GHz (3.69 GFLOPS per core, 44.00 GFLOPS total)
- NVIDIA TESLA P100 GPU, Pascal architecture, 3584 CUDA cores, 1328–1480 MHz clock speed (9340 GFLOPS total), 16 GB global memory (32 GB/s PCI transfer bandwidth, 732 GB/s peak memory bandwidth)

Production configuration 2:

- Intel Xeon E5-2690 v4 CPU, 14 cores, 2,6 GHz (3.69 GFLOPS per core, 44.00 GFLOPS total)
- NVIDIA QUADRO P6000 GPU, Pascal architecture, 3840 CUDA cores, 1417 MHz clock speed (12634 GFLOPS total), 24 GB global memory (32 GB/s PCI transfer bandwidth, 432 GB/s peak memory bandwidth)

4   Optimization Methods and Compiler Suits

Application optimization is, unfortunately, an endless task. Attaining peak performance takes a long time, and each new optimization pass usually offers less and less performance increase. Describing all possible optimization method applicable to GPGPU will take a very long time, and thus is outside the scope of this paper. Our main interests lie in which optimization methods offer the biggest individual increase in performance and how hard it is to implement them. Additionally we want to know if there are any differences in performance of applications that implement those methods using different languages and compiler suits. Methods used in this paper are described next.

4.1   Host-Device Data Transfer Optimization

The biggest barrier to using GPUs is the need for data transfer to and from the device. Every non-integrated GPU device has a certain amount of on-board memory, and this is the only memory it can address during execution of kernels. This mean that before running the kernel we must make sure that all required data had been successfully transferred to the device.

Reference versions of the applications copy all input data, including the result vector stack to the device before every iteration. This is an obvious candidate for optimization, because if application does not use previous values in this array we can safely omit its copying. With our default parameters it results in roughly 15 MB of data transfer saved in each iteration.

But the biggest gains can be gained in case when data can be safely left on the device for multiple iterations. This can be used in areas like Computational Fluid Dynamics (CFD), where the same simulated system evolves over multiple iterations. In this situation all calculations can be performed on the device using multiple different kernels, each processing data already on the device, and results are gathered only in the end of calculation. This all but eliminates transfer costs and can increase performance dramatically. In our example this means over 2 TB of data transfer saved over 1000 iterations. Unfortunately this method requires that either the whole data-set fits inside device on-board memory or that data is split between several devices. This also requires a high degree of data-parallelism from the algorithm.

On our development platform, peak PCI bus transfer rate is 15.8 GB/s, which is much slower than our GPU internal transfer rate of 224.3 GB/s. That makes this optimization even more important, as outside very specialized systems, PCI transfer rates will continue to be very slow. Even upcoming PCI Express 5.0 promises only 63 GB/s.

4.2   Device Memory Usage Optimization

GPU on-board memory consists of different spaces with varying access speeds [4]. Global memory is the largest space with the slowest access. It is where the data from host is copied to, and is one of the few spaces host can access with CUDA API. Most other spaces are only accessible from within the device executing the kernel code.

Similar in speed is local memory space, which is only visible to the individual thread and lasts only until that thread finishes execution. This is not a physically different space, but a logically mapped global memory. In most cases it is better to use other types of memory for temporary data storage.

Next in terms of speed is texture memory and constant memory spaces. Both of them are read-only during executing and require pre-transfer of data from host. Those types of memory are orders of magnitude faster to access that global memory, but are limited to relatively small sizes on most GPUs. For example on most GPUs constant memory is limited to 64 KB. It is a good place to store a small amount of read-only data accessed by all thread. Texture space is bigger, but its use requires a lot of specialized knowledge and is outside of the scope of this paper. Unfortunately, in our case there is not enough data to put there, to see any real difference.

Next fastest space is shared memory, which is visible only to threads within one block and is erased after that block finishes work. It is commonly used for communication between thread, and is even faster than other types. In best case scenario its speed can be comparable to that of the registers. If any data is accessed multiple times within one kernel and the grid execution can be configured in such a way when that data is used only in one block, it can be beneficial to copy it to shared memory and access it from there. The performance increase will be proportional to the number of times the data is accessed in one iteration. In our example input vector is the best candidate for this, as, by default one block is responsible for one matrix-vector pair, with thread calculation individual elements of the result vector. That way each element of input matrix is read only once and each element of input vector is read N times. Shared memory is limited to 49 KB per block and, in our case, one input vector is 1 KB.

The fastest memory space available are registers. They follow the scope rules of local memory, but are much faster. Register access can theoretically take zero clock cycles, but it requires a lot of concurrent threads to fully hide the latency. Additionally we need to watch out for register pressure, which happens when to much data is placed in this memory type. In this case device compensates by mapping global space as registers, which negatively affects performance. In our case we can place the temporary result variable in this memory space as it is accessed N times each iteration, and we have millions of threads to hide the latency. In-built CUDA variables, like ThreadID and BlockID, may also be worth cashing in registers, if they are accessed multiple times.

4.3 Thread/Block Load Optimization

Before launching any kernel we must determine it's so called "execution configuration". For this we need to determine the size of the thread blocks in three dimensions and the overall size of the grid consisting of those blocks. This allows us to map the treads logically onto our input data and divide it for parallel processing.

Kernel execution configuration can also drastically affect application performance, as it determines how effectively GPU resources are used. [2] showcases up to 4 times performance difference with different grid/block sizes. Unfortunately this method either requires to know the dimensions of input data in advance or create an automatic system for determining the optimal configuration. It is also very hard to predict those parameters without an extensive amount of testing.

Those parameters also have some limitations placed on them by the API. As of the version 9.1 [4], each block can contain 1024 threads in total, with maximum size for each dimension of the block equal to 1024, 1024, and 64. That means that we can create blocks with configurations of (1,1,1), (1024,1,1),

(1,1024,1), (4,4,64), and anything in between, as long as total number of threads does not exceed 1024.

According to current CUDA documentation [4] the size of the grid is limited to 2 147 483 647 in x-dimension and 65 535 in y- and z-dimensions, for a theoretical total of 9 223 090 559 730 712 575 blocks in one grid. Which gives us a maximum of 9 444 444 733 164 249 676 800 threads. Of course, most applications will never need to account for grid size, but block size may prove limiting. In our example it limits the matrix size to $N = 1024$, otherwise we would need to change the kernel code. This may prove problematic in conjunction with the use of shared memory, as if one interdependent data-block has to be split between thread blocks, we would need to duplicate some of the data in both block's shared memory. This may result in reduced performance as the total amount of shared memory available to any multiprocessor is limited, in our case to 49 KB.

Overall this method the most work-intensive as it requires a lot of testing and consideration, especially when used together with other methods. Configuration changes can break kernels that rely on a specific way data is mapped on threads and blocks. In our application, it is easy to make the kernel configuration-independent because we use relatively fine mapping method, where one thread is mapped to a single element of the result vector.

Calculation of each element is independent of the others, requires access to only one row of the input matrix, but requires access to the whole input vector. That means, if we would want to use shared memory to store input vectors, we need to make sure that one matrix-vector pair is mapped to a single thread block and vector can fit in the memory limits.

4.4   CUDA C vs CUDA FORTRAN

It is well known that the choice of compiler can have a drastic effect on application performance. Problem is further compounded by a relatively rapid development of both CUDA C and PGI CUDA FORTRAN compilers. This means that result performance tend to fluctuate over time and it is hard to say what compiler will be better in the end.

In this project we used CUDA Toolkit v9.1 [4] (which, in turn, uses Red Hat GCC 7.3.1-2) as C/C++ version compiler, and PGI CUDA Fortran Compiler 17.10 [5] for FORTRAN versions. All version were compiled using -O3 flag, which tends to prioritize speed in generated code. There are some data suggesting that it can hurt performance in specific cases (such as small cache size on compute device), but unfortunately, due to time constraints, we were unable to test all available compiler optimization flags, and therefore, present base-level performance that can be consistently expected from most applications.

As most participants of this project have very little FORTRAN programming experience, it is possible that FORTRAN versions of the application are under-optimized. But in our opinion it offers a valuable perspective on the performance level attainable with limited effort and under hard time constraints.

5   Benchmark Results

In this Section we present the performance results of the test application on platforms described in Sect. 3.3. Results show time in nanoseconds required to calculate a single element of result vector. Both time spent on transferring data and time spent on calculations are tracked separately. For CPU versions memory transfer time is considered to be zero as we don't interact with the GPU. All test were performed with $N = 128$, $C = 15000$ and $I = 1000$ (stack consists of 15000 pairs, matrix size is 128×128, vector length is 128, 1000 iterations). Unless stated otherwise, block size is 128, and grid size is 15000, resulting in roughly 2 GB data-set.

Descriptions of different versions of the application and their differences are presented below.

Serial CPU. This version is a single thread serial CPU implementation of the algorithm. It uses CUDA API only for timing and does not interact with GPU in any way. Only computation is timed. Setup and utility parts of the code are not timed. Multiplication is done using multiple nested loops. Each iteration is timed separately and results are averaged. Utility functions are used to calculate array indexes, and to check the results of each iteration. No optimization methods were implemented in this version.

Reference GPU. This version is a reference CUDA GPU version. Its host-side code is identical to Serial CPU version. It uses CUDA API for timing, data transfer and computations on GPU. Computation is timed by measuring the execution time of the kernel and using event synchronization to force host-side code to wait for the completion of the kernel. Transfer is timed separately, first when host application passes data to the device, and later, when host retrieves the results from the device. Multiplication is performed inside the kernel code, with each thread calculating one element of the result vector stack. Each iteration is timed separately and results are averaged. No utility functions are used inside the timed parts of the code. Utility functions are used outside the timed parts to check the results. No optimization methods were implemented in this version.

One-In Many-Out. This version showcases the possible benefits of data-transfer optimization by passing the input data to the GPU only once, before iterations, and retrieving the results after each iteration. In all other aspects it is identical to Reference GPU.

One-In One-Out. This version is a continuation of One-In Many-Out version. It pushes the data-transfer optimization even further by only retrieving the results at the end of the computation.

Shared Memory. This version uses shared memory to store input vectors. Each thread of the block copies one element of the vector from global to shared memory at the beginning of the kernel. Thread synchronization is used to ensure correct results. Input Matrices are not stored in shared memory because their elements are only read once per kernel launch.

Registers. This version explicitly uses registers to store the temporary value of the result vector element. Reference GPU version writes every new intermediate value directly to the result vector in global memory, while this version stores it in registers until the end of the kernel and then writes it to global memory.

N-Thread Block. These versions use different block sizes than Reference GPU version, to showcase the block load optimization potential. Only the following block sizes were tested - 128, 64, 32, 16, 8. This version uses slightly different index arithmetic than Reference GPU, to ensure correct results with any block size.

Combined. This version combines Shared Memory and Registers versions.

Combined Best Block. This version combines Shared Memory, Registers and N-Thread Block versions. We determine the best block-size experimentally and use it to achieve the best computational performance.

Ultimate. This version combines all optimization methods of Combined version with One-In One-Out version and uses the best block size for the platform. It showcases the best possible situation.

Tables 2, 3 and 4 show the results on Development platform, Production 1 platform and Production 2 platforms respectively.

Figures 1, 2 and 3 show the computation speedup compared to Reference GPU version, on each platform.

We have also tested different Matrix sizes on production platforms. N and C we changed appropriately, to maintain a consistent size of the result vector stack (1 966 080 000 elements, roughly 16 GB data set). Because the time per element is dependant on N, the total computation times per iteration for Reference GPU and Combined Best Block versions were recorded. In addition the optimal block size was determined in each case. These results are presented in Table 1.

Table 1. Matrix dimension and block size test results. Times are in microseconds for a single iteration. N is the matrix size, C is stack size.

			N	1024	512	256	128	64
			C	1875	7500	30000	120000	480000
Production 1	C/C++	Reference		278,49	265,46	271,66	469,90	265,86
		Combined		48,33	53,95	75,81	72,58	44,95
		Block		8	8	8	8	8
	FORTRAN	Reference		232,01	216,17	222,13	372,92	210,54
		Combined		86,01	75,73	77,29	74,43	46,52
		Block		8	8	8	8	8
Production 2	C/C++	Reference		918,32	902,16	815,79	468,38	302,18
		Combined		98,45	117,47	127,81	210,06	111,02
		Block		8	8	16	8	8
	FORTRAN	Reference		636,08	630,32	466,61	349,01	228,11
		Combined		131,76	125,48	134,66	182,62	94,33
		Block		8	8	16	8	8

Table 2. Performance results on Development configuration. Times are in nanoseconds, per element of result vector.

Version	C/C++			FORTRAN		
	Total	Compute	Transfer	Total	Compute	Transfer
Serial CPU	268, 23	268, 23	0	607, 00	607, 00	0
Reference GPU	266, 20	106, 45	159, 75	258, 93	99, 05	159, 87
One-In Many-Out	107, 76	106, 31	1, 45	100, 35	98, 91	1, 44
One-In One-Out	106, 47	106, 31	0, 16	99, 01	98, 85	0, 16
Shared memory	264, 08	104, 37	159, 71	254, 81	94, 99	159, 82
Registers	260, 64	100, 93	159, 71	261, 22	101, 38	159, 84
64-thread blocks	258, 01	98, 32	159, 69	248, 10	88, 31	159, 80
32-thread blocks	227, 28	67, 57	159, 71	214, 00	54, 20	159, 81
16-thread blocks	199, 98	40, 28	159, 69	196, 03	36, 24	159, 79
8-thread blocks	211, 68	51, 97	159, 71	201, 97	42, 13	159, 84
Combined	256, 21	96, 56	159, 66	253, 76	93, 94	159, 83
Combined best block	194, 33	34, 60	159, 73	195, 20	35, 39	159, 80
Ultimate	34, 62	34, 46	0, 16	35, 36	35, 20	0, 16

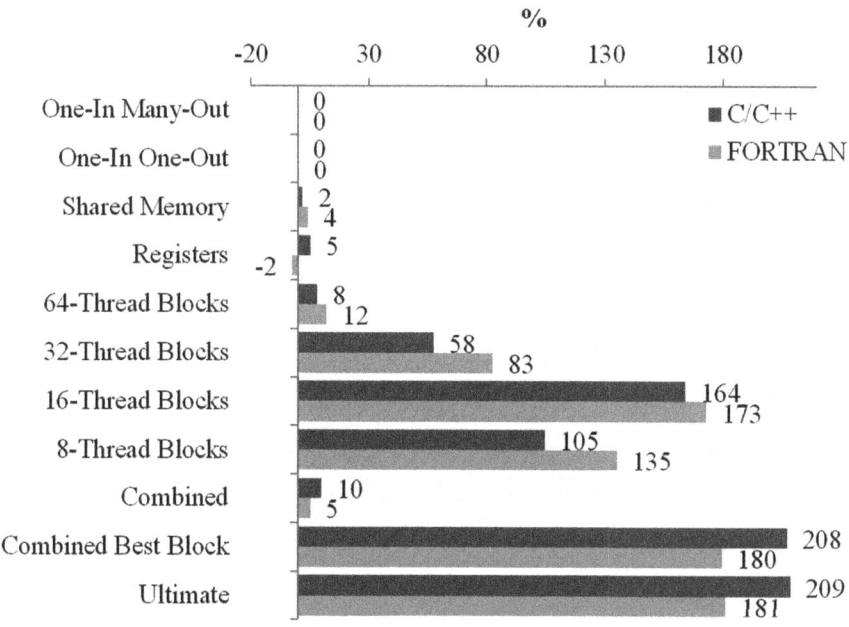

Fig. 1. Computation speedup percentages compared to Reference GPU version on Development configuration.

Table 3. Performance results on Production 1 configuration. Times are in nanoseconds, per element of result vector.

Version	C/C++			FORTRAN		
	Total	Compute	Transfer	Total	Compute	Transfer
Serial CPU	313, 74	313, 74	0	737, 31	737, 31	0
Reference GPU	155, 84	30, 47	125, 37	160, 16	30, 47	125, 37
One-In Many-Out	30, 76	30, 50	0, 26	31, 09	30, 85	0, 25
One-In One-Out	30, 64	30, 46	0, 18	30, 97	30, 75	0, 21
Shared memory	145, 37	30, 01	115, 36	140, 29	24, 32	115, 97
Registers	126, 74	12, 66	114, 08	125, 22	8, 85	116, 36
64-thread blocks	144, 67	30, 54	114, 13	147, 03	31, 02	116, 01
32-thread blocks	143, 28	27, 26	116, 02	142, 79	27, 56	115, 23
16-thread blocks	128, 37	14, 02	114, 34	129, 68	14, 73	114, 95
8-thread blocks	121, 14	6, 78	114, 36	122, 87	8, 07	114, 80
Combined	124, 40	10, 19	114, 21	123, 34	8, 55	114, 79
Combined best block	118, 92	4, 74	114, 18	119, 87	5, 06	114, 81
Ultimate	4, 87	4, 73	0, 14	5, 32	4, 93	0, 39

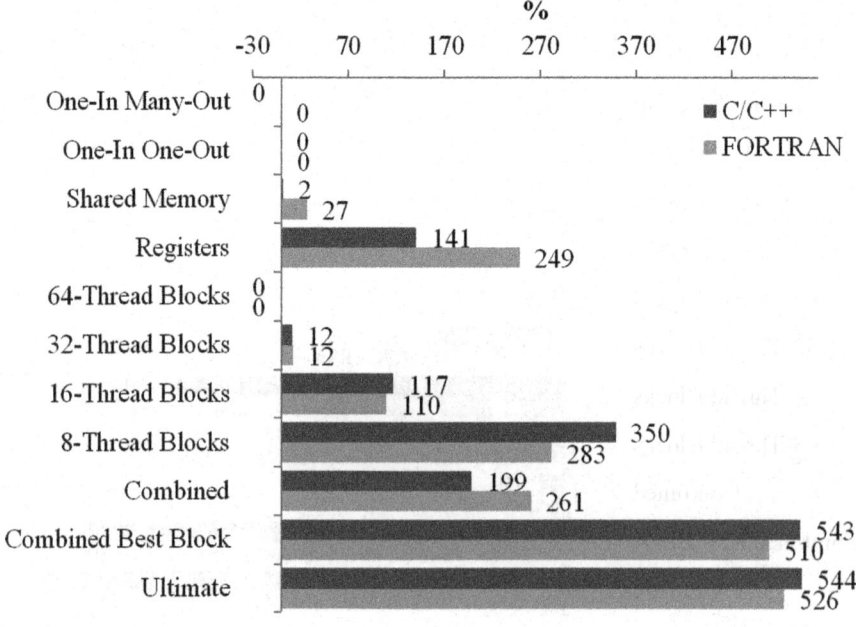

Fig. 2. Computation speedup percentages compared to Reference GPU version on Production 1 configuration.

Table 4. Performance results on Production 2 configuration. Times are in nanoseconds, per element of result vector.

Version	C/C++			FORTRAN		
	Total	Compute	Transfer	Total	Compute	Transfer
Serial CPU	313, 12	313, 12	0	737, 55	737, 55	0
Reference GPU	184, 61	54, 05	130, 57	176, 97	48, 98	127, 99
One-In Many-Out	54, 05	53, 82	0, 23	49, 02	48, 81	0, 21
One-In One-Out	54, 13	53, 90	0, 23	49, 58	49, 01	0, 58
Shared memory	163, 27	45, 65	117, 61	153, 88	35, 27	118, 61
Registers	133, 65	17, 15	116, 51	129, 23	11, 92	117, 30
64-thread blocks	168, 73	52, 43	116, 29	167, 52	51, 14	116, 38
32-thread blocks	136, 91	20, 84	116, 07	139, 36	21, 99	117, 37
16-thread blocks	132, 12	16, 11	116, 01	134, 02	16, 74	117, 28
8-thread blocks	129, 95	13, 90	116, 05	132, 73	15, 60	117, 13
Combined	129, 38	13, 45	115, 93	128, 37	12, 17	116, 20
Combined best block	129, 70	13, 73	115, 97	130, 76	12, 52	118, 23
Ultimate	13, 86	13, 73	0, 14	12, 44	12, 31	0, 13

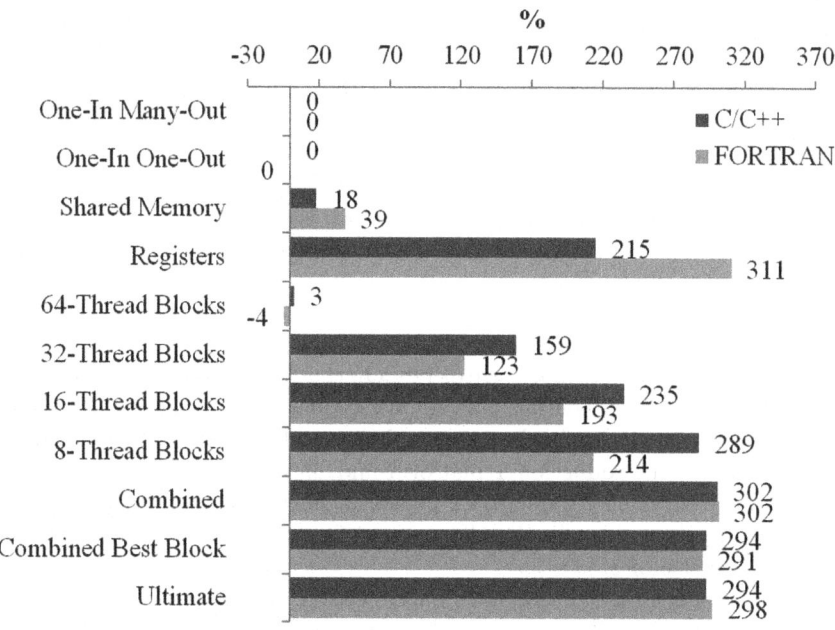

Fig. 3. Computation speedup percentages compared to Reference GPU version on Production 2 configuration.

6   Discussion

Test results were predictable in general but very surprising in details. In Serial CPU version, FORTRAN displayed more than two times worse performance. Reasons for this are currently unknown. Additionally, FORTRAN versions show mostly worse memory transfer performance, although the difference is minimal.

In Reference GPU versions FORTRAN shows better computational performance on Development and Production 2 platforms, but performs slightly worse compared to C/C++ on Production 1 platform.

Memory transfer optimization, as expected, does not influence computational performance. The benefits of those methods are proportional to the length of the computation. 1000 iterations gives us around 100 times decrease in total transfer time for One-In Many-Out version on Development platform, and roughly 500 times on Production platforms.

One-In One-Out version decreases transfer time on Development platform, and has no, or even negative effect on Production platforms. It can be a sign of large overhead on memory operations. Curiously, FORTRAN shows better transfer times in One-In Many-Out version, but worse ones in One-In One-Out version, on all platforms.

Shared Memory and Registers versions provide very little performance increase on Development platform, but give a much more significant boost on Production platforms, especially the Registers version. FORTRAN implementation of Registers version actually gives a negative effect on Development platform. This is most likely due to much more aggressive use of registers by default in PGI compiler, which triggers register overflow, discussed in Sect. 4.2. This effect is absent on Production platforms, where much more memory is available.

Block size optimization shows some unexpected results. On Development platform, decreasing the block size gives a steady computational performance increase down to the block-size of 16, after which the effect becomes negative. It is important to point out that with smaller block sizes we will need to duplicate data in shared memory. Because the whole input vector needs to be present in each block's shared memory, the degree of duplication is inversely proportional to the block size. For example with block size of 64 we use 2 times more shared memory than with default block size of 128. On the other hand, even non-optimal block size provides bigger performance increase than shared memory or registers.

On Production platforms the effect is different. Decreasing the block size to 64 has no effect on Production 1 platform and, in case of FORTRAN version, has a negative effect on Production 2 platform. Further decreasing of the block size gives a steady and proportionally stronger performance increase all the way down to block size of 8.

In a surprising turn of events, languages seem to affect this type of optimization quite significantly. While FORTRAN versions are faster by default, with the decreasing block size, C/C++ versions start to catch up, with overtake happening around block size of 16. This effect is only present on Production platforms and differs in strength, but C/C++ version becomes faster in the end.

The Combined versions, again create some interesting questions. While FOR-TRAN version consistently shows better performance on all platforms, changing block size to the optimal value makes C/C++ version faster on Development and Production 1 platforms.

Ultimate version only serves to confirm all previous observations. But it is worth pointing out that transfer times tend to fluctuate much more on Production configurations, while compute time remain consistent. Therefore the slight decrease in transfer times on in this version can be explained by the varying system bus load.

After that a series of tests was performed to determine the relationship between the matrix size and the compute time, and to determine the best block size in each case. Those test were performed only on Production platforms and used a bigger data set.

The results are mostly as expected, with smaller N decreasing the amount of arithmetic operations needed to calculate each element, while overall number of result vector element remains consistent.

Two unexpected results are the jump in computation time on Production 1 platform with N = 128, and the optimal block size of 16 on Production 2 platform with N = 256. Both of those anomalies we, at this time, cannot explain.

On the Development configuration the biggest problem of FORTRAN versions is the register overflow, although it can be solved by carefully designing the application with the in-compiler optimization in mind.

Production 1 configuration shows a noticeable C/C++ bias, the reasons for which are as of yet unknown, but can be solved with new CUDA and PGI versions. Here C/C++ versions show much better base performance and also better speedup.

Production 2 platform shows slight FORTRAN bias, having much better Registers speedup and identical speedup on both implementations of Combined version.

It is very important that Production 1 platform, while supposedly having almost 30% worse GFLOPS index, shows roughly 50% better performance than Production 2 platform.

7   Conclusions

Overall C/C++ is currently better language for achieving maximum performance in CUDA with minimal effort, although most of its advantage stems from block size optimization, and the difference is not very big. PGI FORTRAN compiler is much more aggressive with optimization by default, which can give unexpected results.

Unfortunately optimization with CUDA still relies on experimentation, but it seems that optimal block size is between 8 and 16, which gives us a good starting point for further research. Block size optimization currently is the most effective method, giving 150–200% performance boost without the need for any significant code changes.

The following was achieved during the project:

– Created and tested multiple versions of test application implementing Matrix-Vector multiplication algorithm.
– Compared the performance of identical CUDA applications, written in C/C++ and FORTRAN 95.
– Analyzed the performance increase offered by different optimization methods.

More work still needs to be done in this area. We were not able to research the nuanced effects of compiler optimization flags on the performance. In addition, performance of multi-GPU versions is of a particular interest to us, as most production environments support multiple devices.

We also had some unexpected test results which we will look into.

Acknowledgments. The research was supported by Russian Foundation for Basic Research (project N 16-07-01111).

References

1. Delgado, J., Gazolla, G., Clua, E., Masoud Sadjadi, S.: A case study on porting scientific applications to GPU/CUDA. J. Comput. Interdisc. Sci. **2**, 3–11 (2011). PDN: jcis.2011.02.01.0027
2. Ryoo, S., Rodrigues, C.I., Stone, S.S., Baghsorkhi, S.S., Ueng, S.-Z., Stratton, J.A., Hwu, W.W.: Program optimization space pruning for a multithreaded GPU. In: Proceedings of the 2008 CGO - Sixth International Symposium on Code Generation and Optimization, pp. 195–204 (2008). https://doi.org/10.1145/1356058.1356084
3. Cloutier, B., Muite, B.K., Rigge, P.: Performance of FORTRAN and C GPU extensions for a benchmark suite of fourier pseudospectral algorithms. In: Symposium on Application Accelerators in High Performance Computing. Chicago IL, pp. 145–148 (2012). https://doi.org/10.1109/SAAHPC.2012.24
4. CUDA C Programming Guide v9.1. https://docs.nvidia.com/cuda/pdf/CUDA_C_Programming_Guide.pdf
5. CUDA FORTRAN Programming Guide and Reference v2018. https://www.pgroup.com/resources/docs/18.4/pdf/pgi18cudaforug.pdf
6. About CUDA. https://developer.nvidia.com/about-cuda
7. OpenCL: The Future of Accelerated Application Performance Is Now. https://www.amd.com/Documents/FirePro_OpenCL_Whitepaper.pdf
8. About CUDA FORTRAN. https://developer.nvidia.com/cuda-fortran

Creating Artificial Intelligence Solutions in E-Health Infrastructure to Support Disabled People

David Grigoryan[1], Avetik Muradov[1], Serob Balyan[1],
Suren Abrahamyan[1(✉)], Armine Katvalyan[1], Vladimir Korkhov[1],
Oleg Iakushkin[1], Natalia Kulabukhova[1], and Nadezhda Shchegoleva[2]

[1] Saint Petersburg State University, 7/9 Universitetskaya nab.,
St. Petersburg 199034, Russian Federation
mr.d.grigoryan@gmail.com, avet.muradov@gmail.com,
serob.balyan@gmail.com, suro7@live.com,
arminekatvalyan@gmail.com,
{v.korkhov, o.yakushkin, n.kulabukhova}@spbu.ru
[2] Saint Petersburg Electrotechnical University 'LETI',
Professora Popova 5, St. Petersburg 197376, Russian Federation
stil_hope@mail.ru

Abstract. Recently, the creation of a barrier-free environment for disabled people is becoming more and more important. All this is done so that people do not feel difficulties in filing their ordinary needs, including communication. For this purpose, a communicator application was developed that allows communication using card-pictograms for people with speech and writing disorders, particularly people with ASD. According to the US National Center for Health Statistics and the Health Resources and Services Administration, in 2011–2012 Autism was detected in 2% of schoolchildren worldwide, and this problem is very relevant.

This article discusses several approaches of using Artificial Intelligence to simplify text typing with pictogram based cards by predictive input, which allows users faster compose messages and simplify communication process. A tool for analyzing the texts semantics - Word2Vec, was used, which is a neural network of direct distribution. Two approaches are considered: Continuous Bag of Words and Skip-gram. Also quality measures of advisory systems were used, and an approach giving the best results was identified.

Besides that, quality measurements were carried out to identify optimal solutions of sentiment analysis to automatically detect suspicious messages sent by the users with such disabilities, which will help doctors to enhance their capabilities of monitoring and behavioral control and take appropriate actions if undesirable behavior of patient is detected by the system.

Keywords: Artificial Intelligence · Learning technologies · Mobile computing
Information retrieval · E-Health

© Springer International Publishing AG, part of Springer Nature 2018
O. Gervasi et al. (Eds.): ICCSA 2018, LNCS 10963, pp. 41–50, 2018.
https://doi.org/10.1007/978-3-319-95171-3_4

1 Introduction

Currently the task of creating a barrier-free environment for people with communication disabilities is very urgent. For these people, such tasks as moving around the city, using public transport, communication with others are not such trivial tasks as for the rest. Also, the number of people, suffering from speech and write disorders, in particular with ASD (Autism Spectrum Disorders), is growing. According to CDC's National Center for Health Statistics and the Health Resources and Services Administration in 2011–2012, ASD was detected in 2% of schoolchildren, while in 2007 this number was only 1.2% [1].

On the other hand, with the development of the Internet, more and more people are becoming part of the world wide web. Over the past fifteen years, the number of Internet users has increased about seven times. There are more and more new social networks and mobile applications. Nowadays they are rapidly developing and have become very popular in our society, where millions of users exchange messages, news, share their opinions about various aspects of our everyday life.

Despite this progress children with communication disabilities constantly experience difficulties in communication even now. In the age of modern technology, they still experience limited opportunities for communication,

To facilitate their communication, special card-pictograms were invented [2]. It is proved, that such people communicate more easily with the help of these pictograms (for example, they are used to train children with ASD in schools).

In the articles [2, 3] was introduced a special messenger implemented on the Android platform allowing disabled people to communicate with electronic version of these card-pictograms: it allows to send and receive messages consisting of pictograms. This messenger can be part of an E-health infrastructure based on the concept, described in [4]. AI solutions can be integrated to this infrastructure to extend communication of people with disabilities and enhance monitoring possibilities for their doctors and parents. They can be used as a part of "Automatic consultation module" described in [5].

In this article the following objectives were set:

1. Facilitate the process of typing messages in the messenger using predictive input. This will speed up the typing and as a consequence, will provide more comfortable communication.
2. Find out optimal solutions of sentiment analysis for this particular case to automatically detect suspicious messages sent by the users with disabilities for further integration into the unified E-Health platform. This will help doctors and parents to determine if something is changed in children's online-behavior and take appropriate action if necessary.

2 Predictive Input for Pictograms

There were 850 impersonal messages sent by users and testers. It is necessary to speed up the process of typing messages based on this data and to predict the next word when typing. It should be noted that the dictionary of unique words is limited to those that are present in the application, there are about 500 of them.

It was decided to use the common Word2Vec semantic analysis tool, created by Tomas Mikolov and other Google employees in 2013. It is a set of algorithms, the input of which is a document consisting of a certain number of sentences. At the output, we get a vector representation of each word [6].

There are two approaches to creating a Word2Vec model: Continuous Bag of Words (CBOW) and Skip-gram. These are two different neural network architectures, and the principle of their work is different. CBOW tries to predict the next word with context, while Skip-gram, on the contrary, tries to predict the context for the given word. But both algorithms are based on a direct distribution neural network [6].

In CBOW case the so-called "bag of words" representation is used, in which each sentence is represented as a set of words that does not take into account the order. So, for example, for the sentence "Have a good day" the following set of words will be formed:

"have", "a", "good", "day".

Thus, each word from the dictionary will represent a vector in which its components will show the frequency of use in a sentence.

The Skip-gram approach is that instead of specific words, k-skip-n-grams would be used - sequences consisting of words of length n, in which the distance between the elements is at most k. So, for example, for k = 1 and n = 2, the following n-grams will be formed for the proposed sentence: "Have a", "a good", "good day" [6, 7]. Later, for these n-grammes, the number of mentions in the sentences will be counted and vectors will be formed similarly.

After compiling the word vectors, the words with the highest frequency are removed, which contributes to an increase in the quality of the obtained model. Next, a direct distribution neural network with a hierarchical softmax activation function is used.

It was decided to check both approaches and to identify which one is better coping with the task. To do this, a test sample was created, where each unfinished sentence was matched by a certain word that was expected. Each time the model will offer the three most probable words. CBOW allows you to predict words in a certain context, and Skip-gram is vice versa.

As a measure, the root-mean-square error was used between the expected word and the word received by the predictor. This metric is standard for expert systems [8].

Let in the test sample there are n sentences, Y_t – expected word, F_t – word predicted by the expert system. Then the measure of the quality of this system will look like the following:

$$RMSE = \sqrt{\frac{\sum_{i=1}^{n} |Y_t - F_t|^2}{n}} \qquad (1)$$

The lower the RMSE, the better the performance of a particular model. Since in our case Yt and Ft are two-dimensional matrices and not vectors, it was decided not to use Euclid's norm $(\|A_F\| = \|A_2\| = \sqrt{\sum_{ij}|a_{ij}|^2})$, but the Frobenius norm $(\|x_2\| = \sqrt{\sum_i|x_i|^2})$, as its generalization to a two-dimensional space. Models were created using CBOW and Skip-gram and for them the root-mean-square deviation was calculated (Table 1).

Table 1. RMSE of different approaches

Algorithm	RMSE
CBOW	0.048569303751
Skip-gram	0.0834937229753

As can be seen, the root-mean-square deviation was smaller when using the CBOW method. As expected, this approach gave the best results.

Since the computing power of the mobile device on which the messenger is running may not be enough, it was decided to use client-server model and make such kind of calculations on the server-side.

A server application, based on REST-JSON architecture was written using Python 3 language that handles HTTP requests and calculates the appropriate words when user is typing on the client-side. The Flask micro-framework [9] was used for the server application, and to implement Word2Vec the package gensim [10] was used. Multithreading has been added to speed up computation and request parallelization.

Fig. 1. A screenshot of a prediction result

Figure 1 illustrates how proposed approach works in the mobile application. Red arrow shows the input message, which is "you, cafe" in this case. Upper green arrow is directed on predicted probable suggestions for continuation of the entered sentence, which are "cappuccino, delicious, alone". User can use these suggested words to speed up the process of typing and make messaging more comfortable.

Mobile application gets all necessary data from the python server via REST API. Client have to send HTTP GET request with two parameters: one is the type of algorithm ("cbow" for Continuous Bag of Words or "sg" for Skip-gram), and the second one, called "message", contains the inserted text. So, request can be something like the following: /prediction?method=sg&message=один. In the following figure the part of the server log is shown while receiving client requests (Fig. 2).

92.42.30.104 - - [01/May/2018:20:47:56 +0000] "GET /prediction?message=|_мы|_|_лето|_ HTTP/1.1" 200 60 "-" "okhttp/3.9.0" "92.42.30.104" response-time=0.002
92.42.30.104 - - [01/May/2018:20:47:56 +0000] "GET /prediction?message=|_мы|_ HTTP/1.1" 200 78 "-" "okhttp/3.9.0" "92.42.30.104" response-time=0.002
92.42.30.104 - - [01/May/2018:20:48:05 +0000] "GET /prediction?message=|_ты|_ HTTP/1.1" 200 68 "-" "okhttp/3.9.0" "92.42.30.104" response-time=0.003
92.42.30.104 - - [01/May/2018:20:48:10 +0000] "GET /prediction?message=|_ты|_|_кафе|_ HTTP/1.1" 200 68 "-" "okhttp/3.9.0" "92.42.30.104" response-time=0.002
92.42.30.104 - - [01/May/2018:21:28:02 +0000] "GET /prediction?message=|_ты|_|_кафе|_|_один|_ HTTP/1.1" 200 78 "-" "okhttp/3.9.0" "92.42.30.104" response-time=0.044

Fig. 2. Server log

3   Sentiment Analysis of Pictogram Messages

3.1   Problems of Sentiment Analysis

Sentiment analysis (opinion mining) is one of the directions of text mining, the aim to determine the attitude of a writer to object, organization, product, event, theme, phenomenon, process, as well as to individuals.

Even if a software can provide detailed and complete sentiment analysis, some problems may occur during the automatic analysis which are described below [11]:

- Dependence on the subject area in which the analysis is needed. As a rule, it is easier to analyze products and services than to analyze the political field, because it can have more terminology, as well as expressions of emotions, ridicule.
- If you consider a social network or a community as a resource, you can face such a problems as grammatical, syntactic errors, slang, which subsequently influence on the quality of the result.
- Recognition of irony and sarcasm, is a problem for sentiment analysis, because they always contain a negative color, but in fact the sentence itself can look positive.
- Using adversative conjunctions like "however", "but", "as well as" in a sentence can change all sentence tone, for example "All my friends prefer flying, but I do not!".
- Sentiment analyzing for a specific object, one of the most important aspects in the sentiment analysis, for example, "I like the Dell laptop, but I do not like Toshiba". If the object is taken by "Dell", sentence opinion is positive, if "Toshiba", then it is negative.

3.2 Methods for Solving Sentiment Analysis Problems

Nowadays the following approaches are used to for sentiment analysis [12]:

1. Machine learning (supervised).
2. Machine learning (unsupervised).
3. The method is based on dictionary.
4. The rule-based approach.
5. The hybrid method.

The First Type. Supervised machine learning is one of the most commonly used methods. To use this method, you need a training data, where documents are placed in advance in two classes: positive and negative. This sample is used to build a classifier to get the resulting model to determine opinion mining of the text of new documents or proposals. For example, Support Vector Machine method and Naive Bayes Classifier are used most often.

The machine learning approach gives a fairly high accuracy in sentiment analysis.

The Second Type. Unsupervised machine learning is not very popular, because the accuracy of determining is lower than other methods. The advantage of this method is that it does not require training data. The method is most often used for clustering.

The Third Type. This type is a method based on the dictionary. Sentiment dictionaries are required for this method, i.e. It is necessary to have at least two dictionaries: positive and negative. Each word has a sentiment weight, for example from −5 to 5. Analyzing the sentence, each word is assigned appropriate value and at the end is calculated average value. The advantage of this method is simplicity, a lack of precision.

The Fourth Type. A rule-based method. A set of rules is generated, which will be used for sentiment analysis. The sentence is divided into N-grams, collected data helps to highlight common patterns which are used to determine opinion mining.

The Fifth Type. The hybrid method, the most commonly used in commercial projects. It contains machine learning, sentiment dictionary and a rule-based method.

3.3 Objective of Classification and Data Presentation

Sentiment classification can be represented as follows:

Suppose there are two classes: positive and negative, respectively c_1 и c_2, $C = \{c_1, c_2\}$ and set of documents: $D = \{d_1, d_2, \ldots, d_n\}$.

There is a unknown function $F : C \times D \to \{c_1, c_2\}$, the value of which is known only for the training sample, i.e. which document belongs to which class. It is necessary to find functions F', a classifier that reflects the documents in the appropriate classes:

$$F' : C \times D \to \{c_1, c_2\}$$

Feature space can be represented using a vector model (feature vectors). words and phrases are taken as a feature in sentiment analysis. Often vectors are represented in the form of N-grams, where N > 0, some of the popular are unigrams, bigrams, trigrams.

1. When using unigram, a document represented as set of words, for example, "John is a good friend" - <"John", "good", "friend">.
2. When using bigrams, the vector will look like this: <"John good," "good friend">.
3. When using the trigram, we get <"John a good friend">.

In practice, mostly unigrams and bigrams are used. Each word has its own weight, there are several ways to determine it:

1. For the first type, it is created a dictionary (vector) from the unique words of all documents, and taken the basis (stem) of the word. Then for each word of the document a weight is set: if the word is present, then the weight is 1, otherwise it is 0.
2. The second approach is the use of a statistical measure TF * IDF

Term frequency (TF) is the frequency of a word, calculated by the formula:

$$TF = \frac{n_i}{\sum_k n_k}$$

where n_i is the number of occurrences of the term in the document and $\sum_k n_k$ is the length of the document.

Inverse Document Frequency (IDF) is the inverse frequency of the document, calculated by the following formula:

$$IDF = \log \frac{|D|}{|d_i \supset t_i|}$$

Where $|D|$ is the total number of documents in the package, $|d_i \supset t_i|$ is the number of documents containing this i-th term.

And there is weight given to each word in the document: $w_i = TF * IDF$.

3.4 Training Data

As training dataset were taken real messages from "Sezam" application [2, 3], which were manually processed and distributed by classes: negative and positive ones. Also some sentences for these two classes were added manually. All in all, a total number of sentences was 850, 500 of which were positive and 350 were negative.

3.5 Comparison of Approaches

In this paper three approaches are considered:

1. Machine learning (supervised).
2. Method is based on dictionary.
3. Hybrid method.

For the first case Naive Bayesian classifier, a probabilistic classifier based on the Bayes theorem is used. Bayesian classifier is one of the most frequently used methods in sentiment analysis, because it is not complicated in implementation and shows fairly high results [13].

Using the Bayesian formula, we obtain a conditional probability for all classes:

$$P(c|d) = \frac{P(c)P(d|c)}{P(d)}$$

Class with the highest probability is c*, which owns the document $d = \{w_1, w_2, \ldots, w_n\}$.

For the second approach was created a dictionary of unique words from the trained data. Each word was given an experimental weight from −5 to 5. The dictionary contains 480 words.

To test and compare the hybrid approach, commercial solution SentiScan was used.

SentiScan is a technology for sentiment analysis of Russian text. This development uses a hybrid method, i.e., a rule-based approach, sentiment dictionary and machine learning. The peculiarity of the product is that the technology can work directly with target object. This means that this system analyses texts and optionally targets objects to determine sentiment for [14].

3.6   The Results of Testing the Above Approaches

For testing were selected 25 positive messages and 25 negative messages. Accuracy of work is (Table 2):

As a result, you can see that for the positive sentences the best result was shown by the commercial solution of SentiScan, but it should be noted that other methods also showed good results. In the case of negative sentences, a Dictionary classifier showed the highest result.

Table 2. Results for sentiment analysis

	Naive Bayes	Dictionary	SentiScan
Positive	0.88	0.88	0.92
Negative	0.76	0.88	0.69

4   Conclusion

An expert system was created that predicts the next word (pictogram) when entering text and thereby accelerates it. This will make communication easier for people with disabilities. The hypothesis was also confirmed. Proposed approach for text prediction gives users possibilities for more comfortable and quick messaging. This would also allow people with disabilities to express their ideas more easily.

There were tested methods for sentiment analysis, and as it turned out, hybrid method classifies positive sentences better than other methods in our particular case. But for negative messages hybrid method is not the best solution. As our chosen variant of hybrid method is commercial, and difference between its result and other methods is insignificant ($\sim 3\%$) for positive sentences and worse for negative ones, then it was decided to use Naive Bayes and Dictionary approaches in E-Health system, to support doctors make behavioral analysis based on their patients' messages.

Later it is planned to collect more data and improve the quality of word prediction while typing and sentiment.

Acknowledgment. The research was supported by Russian Foundation for Basic Research (project N 16-07-01111).

References

1. CDC and HRSA issue report on changes in prevalence of parent-reported Autism Spectrum Disorder in school-aged children. Media Advisory. Centers for Disease Control and Prevention
2. Abrahamyan, S., Balyan, S., Muradov, A., Korkhov, V., Moskvicheva, A., Jakushkin, O.: Development of M-Health software for people with disabilities. In: Gervasi, O., et al. (eds.) ICCSA 2016. LNCS, vol. 9790, pp. 468–479. Springer, Cham (2016). https://doi.org/10.1007/978-3-319-42092-9_36
3. Balyan, S., Abrahamyan, S., Ter-Minasyan, H., Waizenauer, A., Korkhov, V.: Distributed collaboration based on mobile infrastructure. In: Gervasi, O., Murgante, B., Misra, S., Gavrilova, M.L., Rocha, A.M.A.C., Torre, C., Taniar, D., Apduhan, B.O. (eds.) ICCSA 2015. LNCS, vol. 9158, pp. 354–368. Springer, Cham (2015). https://doi.org/10.1007/978-3-319-21410-8_28
4. Abrahamyan, S., Balyan, S., Muradov, A., Kulabukhova, N., Korkhov, V.: A concept of unified E-Health platform for patient communication and monitoring. In: Gervasi, O., et al. (eds.) ICCSA 2017. LNCS, vol. 10408, pp. 448–462. Springer, Cham (2017). https://doi.org/10.1007/978-3-319-62404-4_33
5. Guskov, V.P., Gushchanskiy, D.E., Kulabukhova, N.V., Abrahamyan, S., Balyan, S., Degtyarev, A.B., Bogdanov, A.V.: An interactive tool for developing distributed telemedicine systems. Comput. Res. Model. **7**(3), 521–528 (2015)
6. Mikolov, T., Chen, K., Corrado, G., Dean, J.: Efficient estimation of word representations in vector space. arXiv:1301.3781 (2013)
7. Mikolov, T., Sutskever, I., Chen, K., Corrado, G.S., Dean, J.: Distributed representations of words and phrases and their compositionality. In: Advances in Neural Information Processing Systems, pp. 3111–3119 (2013)
8. Hyndman, R.J., Koehler, A.B.: Another look at measures of forecast accuracy. Int. J. Forecast. **22**(4), 679–688 (2006)
9. Welcome | Flask (A Python Microframework). http://flask.pocoo.org/. Accessed 21 Mar 2018
10. Deep learning with word2vec – models.word2vec. https://radimrehurek.com/gensim/models/word2vec.html. Accessed 07 Apr 2018

11. Brunova, E.G.: Automatized content analysis of comments in three subject areas. Philol. Sci. Questions Theory Pract. **12-2**(42), 43–47 (2014). ISSN 1997-2911
12. Automatic sentiment analysis. http://sentistrength.wlv.ac.uk/. Accessed 21 Mar 2018
13. Frolov, A.V., Polyakov, P.Yu., Pleshko, V.V.: Using semantic categories in application to book reviews sentiment analysis. RCO LLC, Moscow (2012)
14. Kan, D.: Rule-based approach to sentiment analysis at ROMIP (2011)

GPGPU for Problem-Solving Environment in Accelerator Physics

Nataliia Kulabukhova[✉] [iD]

Saint-Petersburg State University, Saint Petersburg, Russia
n.kulabukhova@spbu.ru

Abstract. The paper contains the survey of benefits of using graphical processors for general purpose computations as a part of problem-solving environment in the beam physics studies. The comparison of testing numerical element-to-element modelling on CPU and the long-turn symbolic simulation with the general purpose GPUs in the working prototype is made. With the help of the graphical processors from both sides - the general purpose computations and the graphical units itself - the analysis of beam behaviour under the influence of the space charge is done.

1 Introduction

The use of graphical processors in the case of simulation of beam dynamics is widely spread through particle accelerator scientists [1–6] today as, without a doubt, a very popular approach, though it is not quite a new one in other areas of science. But in accelerator physics there are some problems with porting the earlier realised program components to the hybrid architecture. We will speak about it below.

Last year we present the idea of using graphical processors for simulation and visualization in the terms of constructing Virtual Accelerator Laboratory (VAL) [7]. In the work we described how to develop a model of real machine and test the behaviour of the beam inside the virtual system of control elements, such as dipoles, quadrupoles, sextupoles and drifts. As far as VAL is a problem-solving environment, it is divided in to special blocks of components.

In this paper we will involve only this set of components:

The block of control elements: with the help of it the user can construct the main view of the future accelerator (for example, Fig. 1).

The block of particle distribution: which forms the initial particle distribution coming from the source.

The block of data: the data base with all calculated results.

The block of GPU vizualization: the result of calculations presented in a 3D graphical form.

The work is supported by RFBR 16-07-01113A.

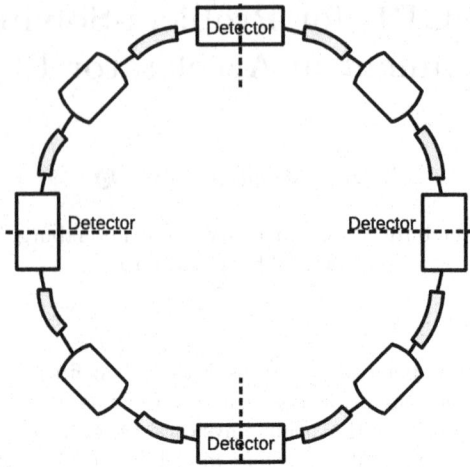

Fig. 1. Schematic view of accelerator ring for modelling the long-turn evolution

2   The Idea of the Matrix Form of the ODE

The main idea of the concept is to describe the behaviour of some dynamic system with the set of ordinary differential equations presented in the matrix form. Let us have a system:

$$\frac{dX}{dt} = F(X,t), \tag{1}$$

where $F(X,t)$ - arbitrary, analytic in the neighborhood $X = 0, X \in R^n$ and measurable $t \in [t_0, t_s] \in R^n$ function.

According to [8], Eq. (1) can be written:

$$\frac{dX}{dt} = \sum_{i=0}^{k} \mathbb{P}^{1i}(t)X^{[i]}, \tag{2}$$

where $\mathbb{P}^{1i}$ matrix with symbolic coefficients obtained from the original ODE. This matrix has the form:

$$\mathbb{P}^{11} = \begin{pmatrix} \mathbb{P}^{11} & \mathbb{P}^{12} & \dots & \mathbb{P}^{1k} & \dots \\ \mathbb{O} & \mathbb{P}^{22} & \dots & \mathbb{P}^{2k} & \dots \\ \vdots & \vdots & \ddots & \vdots & \ddots \\ \mathbb{O} & \mathbb{O} & \dots & \mathbb{P}^{jk} & \dots \\ \vdots & \vdots & \ddots & \vdots & \ddots \end{pmatrix},$$

Dimensions of control matrices depend on the length of the vector X and the order of nonlinearity necessary for the experiment.

In the course of symbolic computation elements of final matrix $\mathbb{P}$ can be calculated by series expansion:

$$\{\mathbb{P}^{1k}(t)\}_{ij} = \frac{1}{k_1! \dots k_n!} \frac{\partial^k \mathbf{F}_i(X_j, t)}{\partial x_1^{k_1} \dots \partial x_n^{k_n}}\bigg|_{x_1 = \dots = x_n = 1}$$

Depending on the problem Eq. 1 can be represented in numerical form:

$$X = \sum_{i=0}^{k} \mathbb{R}^{1i}(t) X_0^{[i]}, \tag{3}$$

where $\mathbb{R}^{1i}$ – matrix with numerical coefficients.

Initial vector $X = \{x, y, x', y', s, \dots\}^T$ can also be written as a matrix consisting of vectors:

$$\mathbf{X}_0 = \begin{pmatrix} x_1 & x_2 & \cdots & x_n \\ y_1 & y_2 & \cdots & y_n \\ x'_1 & x'_2 & \cdots & x'_n \\ y'_1 & y'_2 & \cdots & y'_n \\ \vdots & \vdots & \ddots & \vdots \end{pmatrix}$$

Thus, during calculations is the multiplication of the matrix by the matrix:

$$\mathbf{X}_s = \sum_{i=0}^{k} \mathbb{R}^{1i}(t) \mathbf{X}_j^{[i]}, \tag{4}$$

3   The Space Charge Example

The these part describes how it works on the example of the influence of space charge on the dynamics of the beam.

The equations of the cross-section motion in the beam without bunches can be written in the following form:

$$x'' = \frac{q}{p}\sqrt{1 + x'^2 + y'^2}(y'B_s - (1 + x'^2)B_y + x'y'B_x + \sqrt{1 + x'^2 + y'^2}\frac{E_x}{c\beta\gamma}),$$

$$y'' = -\frac{q}{p}\sqrt{1 + x'^2 + y'^2}(x'B_s - (1 + y'^2)B_x + x'y'B_y + \sqrt{1 + x'^2 + y'^2}\frac{E_y}{c\beta\gamma}) \tag{5}$$

In the linear case for example for quadrupole they will look as shown below

$$x'' + \frac{qB_{xy}}{m_0 c\beta\gamma}x - \frac{q}{\epsilon_0 m_0 c^2 \beta^2 \gamma^3}E_x^L = 0,$$

$$y'' - \frac{qB_{yx}}{m_0 c\beta\gamma}y - \frac{q}{\epsilon_0 m_0 c^2 \beta^2 \gamma^3}E_y^L = 0 \tag{6}$$

According to the matrix form the influence of the space charge will modify the Eq. (2) this way:

$$\frac{dX}{dt} = \sum_{i=0}^{k}(\mathbb{P}_e x t^{1i}(s) + \mathbb{P}_s elf^{1i}(s))X^{[i]}, \tag{7}$$

Now we have the part, which respond to the external field and the part of the self space charge forces. The external field describes by the components of the vector of magnetic induction. And for the space charge responds the intensity vector.

Matrices $\mathbb{P}_{ext}^{11}(s) + \mathbb{P}_{self}^{11}(s)$ in linear case will be:

$$\mathbb{P}_{ext} = \begin{pmatrix} 0 & 1 & 0 & 0 \\ -k_x & 0 & 0 & 0 \\ 0 & 0 & 0 & 1 \\ 0 & 0 & -k_y & 0 \end{pmatrix} \quad (8) \quad \mathbb{P}_{self} = \begin{pmatrix} 0 & 0 & 0 & 0 \\ -\eta_x & 0 & 0 & 0 \\ 0 & 0 & 0 & 0 \\ 0 & 0 & -\eta_y & 0 \end{pmatrix} \quad (9)$$

For non-linear case the Eq. (5) will be

$$x'' + (K_x - L_x)x = a_x x^3 + b_x x x'^2 + c x y^2 + (K_x)' x y y' + d_x x y'^2 + K_x x' y y',$$
$$y'' + (K_y - L_y)y = a_y y^3 + b_y y y'^2 + c y x^2 + (K_y)' y x x' + d_y y x'^2 + K_y y' x x' \quad (10)$$

where

$$K_x = \frac{q B_x y}{m_0 c \beta \gamma},$$

$$K_y = \frac{q B_y x}{m_0 c \beta \gamma},$$

$$L_x = \alpha \frac{qI}{\pi \epsilon_0 m_0 c^3 \beta^3 \gamma^3 r_x (r_x + r_y)},$$

$$L_y = \alpha \frac{qI}{\pi \epsilon_0 m_0 c^3 \beta^3 \gamma^3 r_y (r_x + r_y)}.$$

Therefore the external and self matrices will take the following form

$$\mathbb{P}^{11} = \begin{pmatrix} \mathbb{P}^{11}_x & 0 \\ 0 & \mathbb{P}^{11}_y \end{pmatrix} \qquad \mathbb{P}^{13}_x = \begin{pmatrix} \mathbb{P}^{11}_x & \mathbb{O} & \mathbb{P}^{13}_x & \mathbb{O} \\ 0 & \mathbb{P}^{22}_x & \mathbb{O} & \mathbb{P}^{24}_x \end{pmatrix}$$

The idea of the matrix form of the ordinary differential equations is not new [9]. But with the help of evolution of the graphical processors these form of the equations get a new life. And next the usage of these method will be presented.

4   Linear Cases on CPU

The workflow of the environment is shown on the scheme on Fig. 2. The initial distribution of the particles and the structure of the machine is set to the database to begin working with. The user can choose the style of the machine: linear or cyclic. Then the mode of the simulation can be defined: element-to-element or long-turn evolution. By element-to-element we mean the test of the system, when the visualization of particle distribution is made after each element.

The results of computations in linear case for different distributions are shown on the pictures below. The system in this example consists of several drifts and quadrupoles under the FODO concept

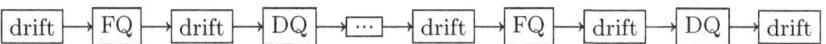

where DQ - defocusing quadrupole, FQ - focus quadrupole.

The studies show that the algorithm works with commonly used distributions - Gauss (Fig. 3) and uniform (Fig. 4). On Fig. 5 new Gauss distribution of 10000 particles on CPU is shown. And on Fig. 6 new uniform distribution of 10000 particles on CPU is shown.

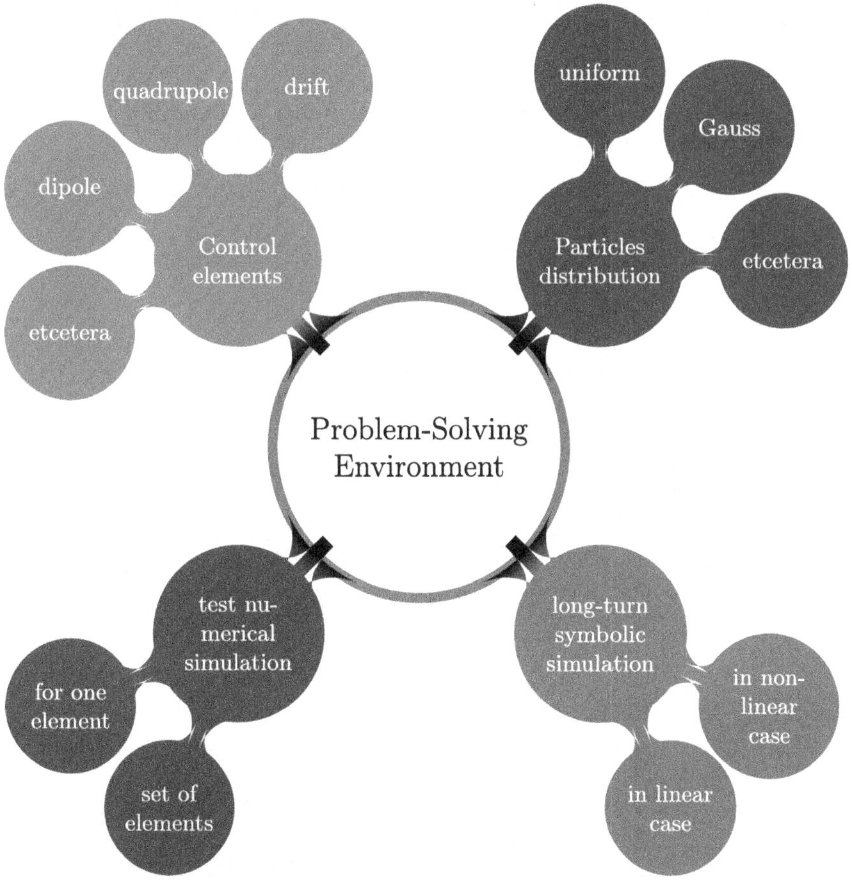

Fig. 2. General scheme of the workflow of the PSE

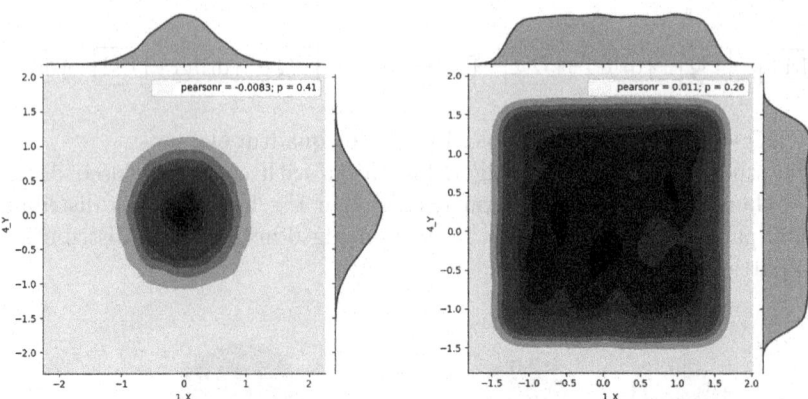

Fig. 3. Initial Gauss distribution, N = 10000 particles

Fig. 4. Initial Uniform distribution, N = 10000 particles

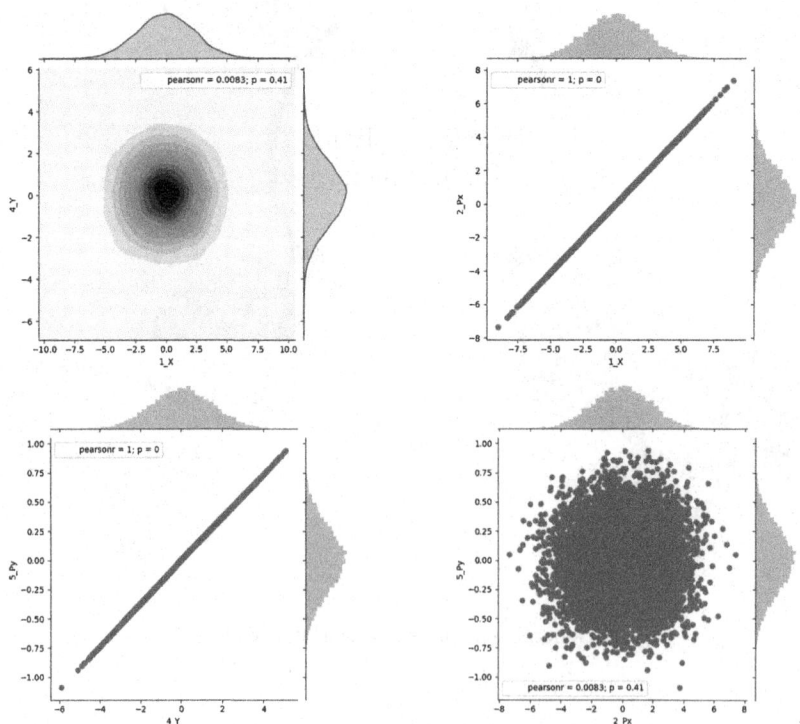

Fig. 5. New Gauss distribution of 10000 particles on CPU in (X, Y), (X, P_x), (Y, P_y), (P_x, P_y)

5 Long-Turn Evolution of the Beam on GPU

When we speak about the linear machine with some meters lengthwise, the personal computer will solve our problems. But in the case of the storage ring with the long-turn evolution of the beam, we need the machine like the accelerator itself to get the result in suitable time. As the result of transformation of the ODE we get matrices in the sparse form. The problem is how to compute them on the GPU in the most effective way. The advantage of using sparse matrices on GPU is that we have a lot of zero elements, which can be empty components to be loading from the CPU memory to the memory of the GPU. But the fact that we get the partial result from every element the memory exchanges will outweigh the advantages of the sparse matrices. For that reason we compute the part of accelerator (rather the quarter of it) in the symbolic way to get the total matrix of this part to load it on the device. As the whole machine consists of symmetric sections, with some corrections these matrix can be used for modelling the long-turn evolution of the beam with minimum (in some way) computational resources. The schematic view of such system is shown on the Fig. 1.

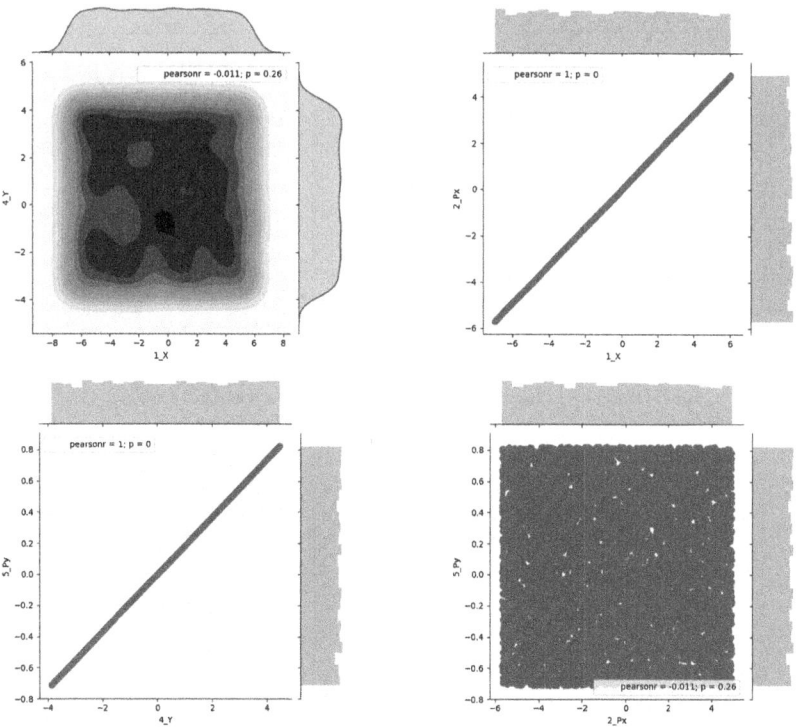

Fig. 6. New uniform distribution of 10000 particles on CPU in (X, Y), (X, P_x), (Y, P_y), (P_x, P_y)

Computations were made on GeForce GTX 1060 6 GB with compute capability 6.1. The whole environment is developed on Python 3.6 libraries. Obviously, Python is not a quick tool for computations, but it is used as background of all important components. Python plays a role of something like glue, it links everything in one working system. The main computational blocks are constructed with the following modules:

NumPy – scientific computations on CPU [10];
pyCUDA – general purpose computations on GPU [11];
SymPy – symbolic calculations of control elements for sending on GPU [12];
TkInter – graphical user interface [13];
Seaborn – visualization of obtained results [14];

Furthermore, there are some libraries, which are going to used for future work with machine learning and neural networks, such as Scikit-learn [15] and TensorFlow [16]. The results of computations of new Gauss distribution of 1000000 particles on GPU are shown on Fig. 7.

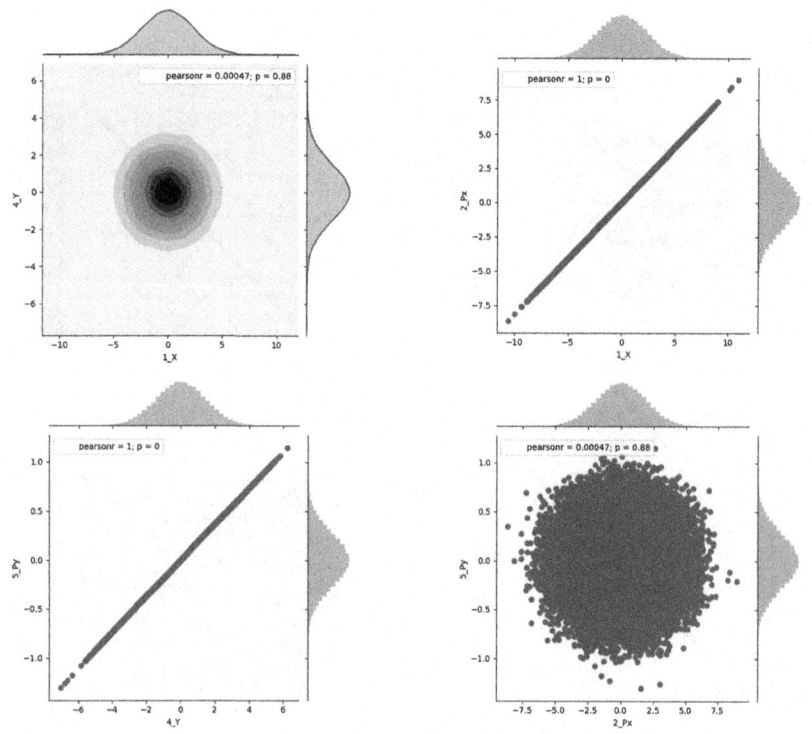

Fig. 7. New Gauss distribution of 1000000 particles on GPU in (X, Y), (X, P_x), (Y, P_y), (P_x, P_y)

6   Discussion

In works [17–19] the concurrency is made for a simple part of the large particle physics simulation toolkits, such as Geant4 and Elegant. The difficulty is that these toolkits were developed for CPU only systems. And they cannot be easily ported for general purpose GPU computations. On the contrary, the method of matrix form of ODE has parallel principle inside. Besides, we constructing the problem-solving environment as a toolkit based on the idea of matrix representation of ODE, but not in reverse. In this case, there is no such a problem of adapting, because we develop a parallel system originally.

The main difficulty in GPGPU development for the matrix algorithm is the amount of data sent on device. It is a bottleneck of practically every GPU program. As every non-zero P^{ij} matrices can be calculated separately and all zero elements are not needed for computations and not sent on device, save resources for the set of particles.

7   Conclusion

The idea of the problem-solving environment is to provide the scientist with a clear and easy environment to simulate and predict the behaviour of the beam. The result of the simulation should be shown in numerical and graphical ways.

In this work the long-turn simulation of the beam with the help of the graphical processors is made. The future work will be dedicated to visualization of the received results. Besides, the KV-distribution is under testing, and the results of simulation using this distribution can be compared with other works.

Another idea is to use the machine learning algorithms to analyse the numerical data and the neural networks, especially the deep learning approach to process visual data of the experiment.

Acknowledgments. The author would like to express gratitude to Vladimir Korkhov for valuable help. The work was sponsored by the Russian Foundation for Basic Research under the project: 16-07-01113 "Virtual supercomputer as a tool for solving complex problems" and the SPbSU equipment project: 9.40.1615.2017 "Deployment of experimental high-performance computing infrastructure to support scientific research of the Department of computer modelling and multiprocessor systems".

References

1. Kulabukhova, N., Andrianov, S.N., Bogdanov, A., Degtyarev, A.: Simulation of space charge dynamics in high intensive beams on hybrid systems. In: Gervasi, O., et al. (eds.) ICCSA 2016. LNCS, vol. 9786, pp. 284–295. Springer, Cham (2016). https://doi.org/10.1007/978-3-319-42085-1_22
2. Kulabukhova, N.: Software for virtual accelerator environment. In: RuPAC 2012 Contributions to the Proceedings. JACOW (2012)
3. Petrov, D.A., Stankova, E.N.: Use of consolidation technology for meteorological data processing. In: Murgante, B., et al. (eds.) ICCSA 2014. LNCS, vol. 8579, pp. 440–451. Springer, Cham (2014). https://doi.org/10.1007/978-3-319-09144-0_30

4. Stankova, E.N., Balakshiy, A.V., Petrov, D.A., Shorov, A.V., Korkhov, V.V.: Using technologies of OLAP and machine learning for validation of the numerical models of convective clouds. In: Gervasi, O., et al. (eds.) ICCSA 2016. LNCS, vol. 9788, pp. 463–472. Springer, Cham (2016). https://doi.org/10.1007/978-3-319-42111-7_36

5. Bogdanov, A., Degtyarev, A., Korkhov, V., Gaiduchok, V., Gankevich, I.: Virtual supercomputer as basis of scientific computing. In: Horizons in Computer Science Research, vol. 11. Nova Science Publishers (2015)

6. Korkhov, V., Kukla, T., Krefting, D., Terstyanszky, G.Z., Caan, M., Olabarriaga, S.D.: Exploring workflow interoperability tools for neuroimaging data analysis. In: Proceedings of the 6th Workshop on Workflows in Support of Large-Scale Science (2011)

7. Kulabukhova, N., Bogdanov, A., Degtyarev, A.: Problem-solving environment for beam dynamics analysis in particle accelerators. In: Gervasi, O., et al. (eds.) ICCSA 2017. LNCS, vol. 10408, pp. 473–482. Springer, Cham (2017). https://doi.org/10.1007/978-3-319-62404-4_35

8. Andrianov, S.N.: Dynamical Modeling of Control Systems for Particle Beams. Saint Petersburg State University, Saint Petersburg (2004)

9. Miklos, S.: Electron and Ion Optics. Mir, Moscow (1990). (in Russian)

10. NumPy: the fundamental package for scientific computing with Python. http://www.numpy.org/

11. pyCUDA: Nvidia's CUDA parallel computation API for Python. https://documen.tician.de/pycuda/

12. SymPy: a Python library for symbolic mathematics. http://www.sympy.org/en/index.html

13. TkInter: Pythons de-facto standard GUI package. https://wiki.python.org/moin/TkInter

14. Seaborn: Python visualization library based on matplotlib. http://seaborn.pydata.org/index.html

15. Scikit-learn: tools for data mining and data analysis. http://scikit-learn.org/stable/

16. TensorFlow: an open source machine learning framework

17. Seiskari, O., Kommeri, J., Niemi, T.: GPU in Physics Computation: Case Geant4 Navigation (2011). https://arxiv.org/pdf/1209.5235.pdf

18. Amyx, K., Balasalle, J., King, J., Pogorelov, V., Borland, M., Soliday, R.: Beam dynamics simulations with a GPU-accelerated version of elegant. JACOW (2013)

19. King, J.R., Pogorelov, I.V., Amyx, K.M., Borland, M., Soliday, R.: GPU acceleration and performance of the particle-beam-dynamics code Elegant (2011). https://arxiv.org/pdf/1710.07350.pdf

The Construction of the Parallel Algorithm Execution Schedule Taking into Account the Interprocessor Data Transfer

Yulia Shichkina[1,2], Al-Mardi Mohammed Haidar Awadh[1],
Nikita Storublevtcev[2], and Alexander Degtyarev[2(✉)]

[1] Saint Petersburg Electrotechnical University "LETI", ul. Professora Popova 5,
197376 St. Petersburg, Russia
`strange.y@mail.ru, almardi-md@mail.ru`
[2] Saint Petersburg State University, Universitetskaia nab. 7-9,
199034 St. Petersburg, Russia
`a.degtyarev@spbu.ru`

Abstract. The method of constructing a schedule for parallel algorithm execution is considered in the article. This algorithm takes into account the execution time of each operation of the algorithm and the relationship of operations on the data. The method is based on an information graph in which the nodes are the operations of the algorithm, and the edges are the directions of the data transfer. As a result of the interchange of operations between computing nodes, it is possible to achieve a reduction in the execution time of the algorithm by reducing the time spent on data transfer between computing nodes and reducing the downtime of computational nodes. The algorithm can be applied both in parallel programming and in adjacent areas, for example, when scheduling tasks in distributed systems.

Keywords: Parallel algorithm · Algorithm optimization · Information graph
Operation execution time · Algorithm execution schedule · Process
Processor · Interprocessor data transmission

1 Introduction

For several decades, including the present time, in parallel technology sphere there is a trend of lagging mathematical apparatus development that supports parallel computation, from higher computer architecture development. In connection with this, modern highly productive computation systems do not allow for the quick solution of theoretical applied problems. In other words, modern high-performance systems are used inefficiently, and many tasks are solved with a significant time delay.

Parallel programming, as well as sequential programming, is based on algorithms and data structures. An ineffective working program is a direct loss of computer performance, finance for its purchase, and efforts to solve problems. It would not like to have such losses, or, at least, minimize them. This requires proven methods of research, development, and equivalent transformations of algorithms.

© Springer International Publishing AG, part of Springer Nature 2018
O. Gervasi et al. (Eds.): ICCSA 2018, LNCS 10963, pp. 61–77, 2018.
https://doi.org/10.1007/978-3-319-95171-3_6

In the process of long-term use of serial computers, a large number of algorithms modeling and optimizing various processes have been accumulated and thoroughly tested. To these algorithms over the past few decades, a large number of parallel algorithms have been added. But the problem of efficient use of high-performance computing equipment still remains. And if the problem was only that when the algorithm was executed on a set·of computing nodes, some of them do not work, then this would be a third of the general problem of inefficient use of high-performance computing. Most of the common problem is that, due to the inefficient use of high-performance computing, the performance of the parallel algorithm is greatly reduced.

The solution of this problem is the search for methods that allow us to optimize the structure of the algorithm to maximize the use of all the capabilities of high-performance computing.

The main drawbacks of existing parallel computing optimization methods are:

- the absence of a stage of analyzing the structure of the algorithm, for the implementation of which a parallel program is designed. Instead, it is proposed to apply various heuristics;
- the need on each step of searching for the optimal structure of a computer system to solve the problem of constructing, if possible, an optimal schedule for organizing a computational process (which is, in general, an NP-complete problem);
- the dependence of the quality of solutions obtained with the help of heuristics from the initial approximation and the structure of the investigated algorithm of data processing.

The transfer of the ideology of sequential programming of algorithms for small-scale problems to high-performance computing systems does not immediately improve the efficiency of computational experiments. In other words, it becomes necessary not only to parallelize the programs, but also to apply mathematical methods that make it possible to use the computational resources to the maximum extent.

Today, developers of parallel programs are divided into two main classes: those who believe that a parallel program should be created without reliance on the sequential analogues and those who are based on accumulated sequential programs over the decades.

Both approaches have their advantages and disadvantages. But both approaches are the same in that: the need to analyze the structure of the algorithm for the efficient use of computing resources and to find ways to accelerate the calculation processes. This analysis can be done as previously to create a parallel algorithm based on sequential, intermediate to obtain information on the success of parallel execution, finally - to compare the algorithms and their implementations among themselves.

One of the indicators of the quality of the parallel program is the density of loading of computing nodes. Time delays in the transmission of data through communication channels from one processor to another result in a long time of inactivity of the processors and an increase in the overall running time of the algorithm.

In this article, we propose a method for constructing an effective algorithm based on the number of processors used, the execution time of the algorithm, and the amount of inter-processor data transfers. This method can be applied both to sequential algorithms for obtaining their parallel analogue, and to parallel algorithms in order to improve their quality.

The remainder of the paper is organized as follows. Section 2 describes the main lines of research in the field of parallel computing. Section 3 presents the definitions of the main objects, with which we will work further in the article. Section 3 describes the method of constructing a schedule of operation on information graph using adjacency lists. Vertex analysis is carried out on the tiers of the information graph, beginning with the first tier. Section 4 provides examples of permutations of operations in several models of algorithms using the method described in Sect. 3. Section 5 describes the method of accelerated search of schedules. This method significantly reduces the number of steps in the analysis of the graph vertices. Section 6 presents the results of the work.

2 Related Works

Since the 1980s, many researches has been carried out in the field of theory and practice of parallel computations. All these researches can be divided into the following categories: development of parallel computation systems; analysis of parallel computation efficiency for resulting computation acceleration assessments and using all the possibilities of computer hardware when applying parallel methods for problems solution; formation of the general principles of parallel algorithms for solving computationally complex tasks; creation and development of system software for parallel computation systems (e.g., MPI); creation and development of parallel algorithms for applications in various fields of practical applications.

Most of the researches were conducted earlier and are conducted today in the latter area. Here some works can be singled out, for example, the ones related to modeling the calculation of electromagnetic radiation based on multi-core processors and clusters of parallel GPU architecture using the hybrid parallel algorithm MPI-OpenMP and MPI-CUDA [1]. The current researches are aimed at solving the problem of large data volumes transfer in IoT (the Internet of Things) using highly productive technologies [2]. Many researches of parallel algorithms are carried out in the field of differential equations [3] and linear equations systems [4, 5]. Given the large amount of data and the need to solve problems in real time, algorithms for finding the shortest path using a city road map are now parallelized [6].

Parallel programs and computer systems scalability analysis dates back to 1967 when an IBM employee Gene Amdahl published an article [7], which later became a sort of sample. The further assessment of computational algorithms acceleration, resource utilization and computation systems capacity was obtained in many other studies [9–12]. Analysis of parallel computations efficiency, the effect of performance variability on optimization algorithm accuracy and efficiency, and the strategy for minimizing the effect of this variability are given in [13].

The problem of processors load balancing is considered in [14, 15].

The newest supercomputers [16] have a very large number of computational nodes/cores, but many practical applications cannot achieve maximum performance on these supercomputers due to the inadequately developed device for exploring concurrency in applications. Some algorithm jobs planning researches can be high-lighted in the area of the parallel algorithms general principles development [17, 18]. One of the disadvantages of these algorithms is their NP-completeness.

The problem of constructing a schedule for a parallel algorithm with an optimal completion time was highlighted in various researches conducted since the 1980s. Since then, various scheduling algorithms based on the methods for finding the max-imum flow in a transport network, on the basis of branches and boundaries, dynamic programming, as well as iterative algorithms (e.g., genetic algorithms, annealing algorithms) have been created [19, 20]. Most of these algorithms, in particular, the ones based on finding the maximum flow in a transport network, are characterized by pseudopolynomial complexity [21, 22].

The works [23, 24] are devoted to the problems of algorithms separate fragments parallelization, usually the most difficultly parallelizable ones.

The whole variety of algorithms for planning parallel computations was well described by Kwok and Ahmad in the article [27]. In the same article, we show the complexity of the application of these algorithms and not the existence of a formal description of some of the algorithms.

Another problem, which is also traced in this variety of algorithms, is that when parallelizing algorithms, data transfer between computational nodes is almost never taken into account. It is known that when implementing an algorithm for distributed memory systems, computation speed and the number of computational nodes depen-dency diagram has the shape of a normal distribution. There is a number of compu-tational nodes which allows parallel algorithm to acquire the maximum speed. If this number is exceeded, the speed starts decreasing due to an increase in the data exchange between the computational nodes. But if data exchange between nodes is reduced, it is possible to significantly increase the algorithm speed, even with the help of compu-tational resources available.

It can be seen from the review [27] that research in this direction was still in the 1990's. This article presents the results of researches on the problem of interprocessor data transfers volume increase in parallel algorithms for the case when all the jobs of an algorithm differ by the completion time. The case of all algorithm jobs completion time equality is considered in the articles [25, 26]. The difference between the method presented in this article for optimizing the algorithms for the volume of interprocessor transfers is that when a processor is assigned to a node, it considers not only the characteristics of the node and the processor at the current moment, but also takes into account:

- characteristics of the environment: the parameters of other nodes, the connections between them, the parameters of the processors;
- all other connections between nodes from the current node to the last node in the schedule.

The last property on the one hand significantly complicates the algorithm, making it different from the three-level model of Kwok and Ahmad. On the other hand, this property allows to comprehensively thoroughly study the graph and choose the most optimal of all schedules.

The methods presented in this article are based on the adjacency lists of vertices. This allows efficient use of memory and speeds up the processing of information graph. In the methods described in this article, vertex analysis is carried out taking into account the information dependency of the vertices of not only neighboring tiers, but also distant tiers of the information graph. It allows to create more time-efficient scheduling algorithms.

3   The Description of the Problem

Let us assume that for the some given algorithm and computational system are set the following constraints:

- computational system is unlimited in terms of the number of processors (cores);
- amount of input data for each job is equal;
- completion time of each job is different;
- time of data transfer between any two processors is constant, conditionally equal to 1 unit.

The problem is to create a method that allows us to find the equivalent structure of a given algorithm, such that when it is executed on a parallel computing system, data transfer between the computational nodes will be minimal.

It is also assumed that an information graph for the algorithm transformed in an arbitrary way is constructed in some parallel form. The peculiarity of the methods proposed below is that the amount of computational resources of the optimized algorithm is not greater than the amount of computational resources of the original algorithm. Therefore, before applying these methods, it is desirable to optimize the width of the algorithm or adjust the algorithm to a certain amount of computational resources.

The essence of algorithm interprocessor transfer's volume optimization method, taking into account the time required for the completion of each job, consists in rearranging the vertices within a tier and between the tiers in such a way as to minimize the overall time needed for the algorithm completion.

The difference in jobs completion time makes the methods of constructing an algorithm schedule much more complicated, since it is necessary to track not only direct, but also transitive information links between the algorithm jobs. But on the other hand, this condition makes it possible to reduce the algorithm completion time not only by eliminating bubbles, but also by the more dense jobs distribution.

Let us assume that the early term for a job performance is the minimum time required for the job completion from the moment of the whole algorithm completion start. The term of a job is the maximum allowable time for the completion of the job from the moment the whole algorithm performance start taking into account the constraint on the of algorithm completion time.

Then, the earliest term for performing the jobs and the algorithm itself will be obtained if to pass through the tiers of an information graph in the direction from the first to the last one, whereas the late terms will be received if to enumerate the vertices in the direction from the end to the beginning. Therefore, vertex enumeration direction selection depends not only on the quality of the method functioning in this direction, but also on the ultimate goal of the algorithm investigation.

4 Method of Scheduling Taking into Account the Direction of Data Transfer Between Computing Nodes

Designations. Let us assume that m is the total number of groups derived in formalized manner, e.g., by optimizing the width of an information graph using a matrix or adjacency list [25], k-number of the current group, n_k-number of vertices in the group under number k, i - the number of current vertices in the group under number k, j - the number of the current vertex in the group under number $(k - 1)$.

1. Vertices permutation process begins with the first group. Current group number $k = 1$. All the processors in the group are not considered to be marked.
2. To find a set of early terms for jobs completion from group $M_{(k+1)}$ for M_k taking into account data transfer according to rules (1, 2).

Rule 1

Let us assume that $M_{(k+1)} = \left\{ v_1, \ldots, v_j, \ldots, v_{n_{(k+1)}} \right\}$ is the group, in which vertices permutation takes place, $T_{(k+1)} = \left\{ t_1, \ldots, t_j, \ldots, t_{n_{(k+1)}} \right\}$ – the time required for the completion of each job in group $M_{(k+1)}$.

Then the time required for each job of group $M_{(k+1)}$ taking into account data transfer using i^{th} processor is:

$$T = \left\{ T'_{(k+1)} \right\}_i = \{ t_j + \alpha \}, j = 1 \ldots n_{(k+1)}, i = 1 \ldots n_k$$

where

$$\alpha = \begin{cases} 1, if\ \exists \left(M_{k_i}, M_{(k+1)_j} \right) \\ 0, if\ \not\exists \left(M_{k_i}, M_{(k+1)_j} \right) \end{cases} \tag{1}$$

Example of Rule 1 Application
Let us assume that the following fragment of a graph and schedule is obtained when distributing the vertices by groups:

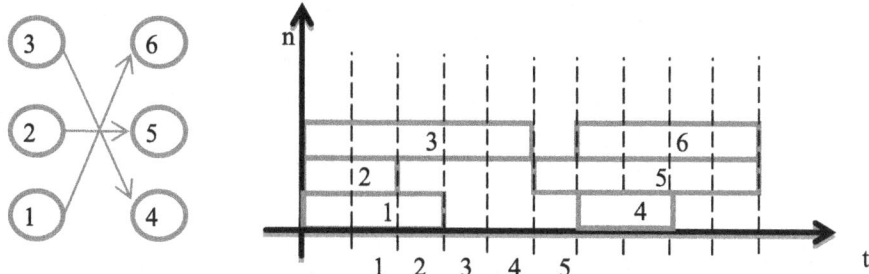

Fig. 1. Example of graph and timing diagram

For $i = 2$ we get the time required for the jobs:

$$\{t_4 + 1, t_5, t_6 + 1\} = \{3, 5, 5\}$$

The time required for the fourth and sixth jobs completion will be increased by one, since permuted to the second processor they will have to wait for information from the other processors.

For $M_2\{4, 5, 6\}$, the time required for jobs taking into account T' data transfer from group $M_1\{1, 2, 3\}$ by formula (1) equals to: $T' = \{\{3, 6, 4\}, \{3, 5, 5\}, \{2, 6, 5\}\}$.

Rule 2

Let us assume that $M_{(k+1)} = \{v_1, \ldots, v_j, \ldots, v_{n_{(k+1)}}\}$ is the group, in which vertices permutation takes place, $M_k = \{u_1, \ldots, u_j, \ldots, u_{n_k}\}$ is a group of vertices on a fixed tier, $T = \{T'_{(k+1)}\}_i, i = 1..n_k$ – the time required for each job of group $M_{(k+1)}$ taking into account data transfer to i^{th} processor.

Then the early term of each job from group $M_{(k+1)}$ is based on data transfer using i^{th} processor is:

$$\tau = \left\{\tau'_{(k+1)}\right\}_i = \left\{T'_{(k+1)_i} + \max(\tau_i, \tau_r)\right\},$$

$$\text{for } \tau_r : \exists\left(M_{k_r}, M_{(k+1)_j}\right), r = 1..n_k, j = 1..n_{(k+1)} \tag{2}$$

Example of Rule 2 Application

Let us assume that the fragment of the graph and schedule are obtained in the course of vertices distribution by groups from Fig. 1.

According to rule 1 the time required for jobs completion is obtained for group M_2: $T' = \{\{3, 6, 4\}, \{3, 5, 5\}, \{2, 6, 5\}\}$.

According to rule 2, for example, the set of early terms of the jobs from group M_2 is: $\tau'_2 = \{3 + \max(2, 5), 5 + \max(2), 5 + \max(2, 3)\} = \{8, 7, 8\}$.

For $M_1\{1, 2, 3\}$ the set of early terms of the jobs from group $M_2\{4, 5, 6\}$ completion taking into account the data transfer by formula (2) equals to:

$$\tau' = \left\{ \begin{array}{l} \{3+\max(3,5), 6+\max(3,2), 4+\max(3)\} \\ \{3+\max(2,5), 5+\max(2), 5+\max(2,3)\} \\ \{2+\max(5), 6+\max(5,2), 5+\max(5,3)\} \end{array} \right\}$$

$$\tau' = \{\{8,8,7\}, \{8,7,8\}, \{7,11,10\}\}$$

3. To find the optimal schedule for jobs of group $M_{(k+1)}$. The schedule in which all the jobs of $M_{(k+1)}$ ends earlier than in other schedules is considered to be optimal. In order to find the optimal schedule, it is necessary:
   (a) To arrange P set for all the possible schedules of group $M_{(k+1)}$ jobs after group M_k jobs completion.
   (b) In each schedule $P_r, r = 1..n_p$ to find the maximum early term for the job:

$$P_r max = \max\left(\tau'_{r_j}\right), r = 1..n_p, j = 1..n. \tag{3}$$

   (c) Among all $P_r max$ to find the minimum value. The schedule to which this value corresponds is the optimal one.

The Example of P Set of All Possible Group of Jobs $M_{(k+1)}$ Schedules After Group of Jobs M_k

Let us assume that:

$$\tau' = \left\{ \begin{array}{l} \{\tau_{11}, \tau_{12}, \tau_{13}\} \\ \{\tau_{21}, \tau_{22}, \tau_{23}\} \\ \{\tau_{31}, \tau_{32}, \tau_{33}\} \end{array} \right\}$$

Then:

$$P = \left\{ \begin{array}{l} \{\tau_{11}, \tau_{22}, \tau_{33}\}, \{\tau_{11}, \tau_{23}, \tau_{32}\}, \{\tau_{12}, \tau_{21}, \tau_{33}\}, \{\tau_{12}, \tau_{23}, \tau_{31}\}, \{\tau_{31}, \tau_{22}, \tau_{13}\}, \{\tau_{31}, \tau_{23}, \tau_{12}\} \\ \{\tau_{21}, \tau_{12}, \tau_{33}\}, \{\tau_{21}, \tau_{13}, \tau_{32}\}, \{\tau_{22}, \tau_{13}, \tau_{31}\}, \{\tau_{22}, \tau_{31}, \tau_{13}\}, \{\tau_{23}, \tau_{12}, \tau_{31}\}, \{\tau_{23}, \tau_{31}, \tau_{12}\} \\ \{\tau_{31}, \tau_{12}, \tau_{23}\}, \{\tau_{31}, \tau_{12}, \tau_{33}\}, \{\tau_{32}, \tau_{13}, \tau_{21}\}, \{\tau_{32}, \tau_{31}, \tau_{12}\}, \{\tau_{33}, \tau_{11}, \tau_{22}\}, \{\tau_{33}, \tau_{12}, \tau_{21}\} \end{array} \right\}$$

Total P will consist of $n_p = n(n!)$ combinations, where $\max(n_k, n_{(k+1)})$. Formally, this can be described as follows:

Rule 3

$$Pmin = P_s : P_s max = \min\left(\max\left(\tau'_{r_j}\right)\right)$$
$$r = 1..n_p, j = 1..n, n_p = n(n!), n = \max(n_k, n_{(k+1)}) \tag{4}$$

There can be several schedules which satisfy condition (4). In this case it is necessary to select those schedule in the total value of early terms is the smallest.

Formally, it can be described as follows:

Rule 4

$$Pmin = P_s : P_s max = \min\left(\max\left(\tau'_{r_j}\right)\right), \sum_{k=1}^{n} \tau'_{sj} = \min_s\left(\sum_{j=1}^{n} \tau'_{rj}\right)$$
$$r = 1..n_p, j = 1..n, n_p = n(n!), n = \max\left(n_k, n_{(k+1)}\right) \tag{5}$$

4. To rearrange the vertices according to the schedule found.
5. If $k < m$ then $k = k + 1$ and step 2. Otherwise step 6.
6. End of the method.

5 Accelerated Schedules Enumeration Technique

Designations. Let us assume that R is the number of the processor with which scheduling starts, r – the current processor number, j – job number in group $M_{(k+1)}$, P – the set of selected schedules, s – the number of the current schedule, p_{s_r} – the job performed on the rth processor according to the scheduled numbered s, τ'_{s_r} – the earliest term for p_{s_r} completion of jth jobs on r^{th} processor scheduled with number s.

1. Let us assume that $R = 1$, $s = 1$.
2. Let us assume that $r = 1$, $p_{s_r} = 0$ for all $r = 1..n_{(k+1)}$.
3. Find the minimum earliest term in $\tau'_r = \min\left(\tau'_{r_l}\right), l = \left\{1..n_{(k+1)}\right\}/\{p_{s_r}\}$, $r = 1..n_{(k+1)}$. Let us assume that $p_{s_r} = j, \tau'_{s_r} = \tau'_{rj}$.
4. If $r < n_k$, then assume that $r = r + 1$ and step 3. If at step 3 several minimum early terms were found, step 4 is executed for each of them. If $r = n_k$, then step 5.
5. If $R < n_k$, then assume that $R = R + 1$ and step 2. Otherwise step 6.
6. End of the algorithm.

As a result, the complexity of the whole algorithm with regard to the search of possible schedules will be $O\left(n_k n_{(k+1)}\right) = O(n^2)$, where $n = \max\left(n_k, n_{(k+1)}\right)$.

The Example of Accelerated Schedules Enumeration
Let us assume that group $M_{(k+1)} = \{3, 7, 9\}$. For this group, in accordance with formulas (3.1 and 3.2) τ' is found:

$$\tau' = \left\{ \begin{array}{c} \{8, 8, 7\} \\ \{7, 7, 8\} \\ \{7, 11, 10\} \end{array} \right\}$$

Following the above method:

1. Let us find the minimum early term and its job number in the first set: $p_{11} = 3$ (the third column is the third ordinal number of the job), $\tau'_{11} = 7$.
2. Let us find the minimum early term of all the early terms except for 1st and 3rd in the second set (since $p_{11} = 3$): $p_{12} = 1$ (the first column is the first ordinal number of the job), $\tau'_{12} = 7$.
3. Let us find the minimum the early term of all the early terms except for 1st and 3rd ones in the third set: $p_{13} = 2$ (the second column - the second ordinal number of the job), $\tau'_{13} = 11$.

We get the first schedule: $p_1\{job_3, job_1, job_2\}$. Let us take jobs numbers from $M_{(k+1)} = \{3, 7, 9\}$, we get the following schedule:

$$p_1\{9, 3, 7\} \text{ with early completion terms } \tau'_1 = \{7, 7, 11\}.$$

4. Now let us assume that $p_{21} = p_{11}$ and return to step 2. In the second set, among all the early terms, except for 3rd one (since $p_{21} = p_{11} = 3$) there is the second minimum early term: $p_{22} = 2$ (the second column - the second ordinal number of the job), $\tau'_{22} = 7$.
5. Let us find the minimum early term in the third set of all early terms except 2nd, 3rd (since $p_{21} = 3, p_{22} = 2$): $p_{23} = 1$ (the first column - the first ordinal number of the job), $\tau'_{13} = 7$.

We get the second schedule: $p_2\{job_3, job_2, job_1\}$. If to consider jobs numbers of $M_{(k+1)} = \{3, 7, 9\}$, we get the schedule:

$$p_2\{9, 7, 3\} \text{ with early completion terms } \tau'_2 = \{7, 7, 7\}$$

6. Now let us begin enumerating the sets from the second group composing the third schedule. Let us find the minimum early term in the second set of all the early terms: $p_{32} = 1$ (the first column - the first ordinal number job), $\tau'_{32} = 7$.
7. Let us find the minimum early term and job number in the first set among all the early terms except for 1st one (since $p_{32} = 1$): $p_{31} = 3$ (the third column - the third ordinal number of the job), $\tau'_{31} = 7$.
8. Let us find the minimum early term of all the early terms in the third set except for 1st and 3rd ones (since $p_{32} = 1, p_{31} = 3$): $p_{33} = 2$ (the second column - the second ordinal number of the job), $\tau'_{33} = 11$.

We get the second schedule: $p_2\{job_3, job_2, job_1\}$. If to consider jobs numbers of $M_{(k+1)} = \{3, 7, 9\}$, we get the schedule:

$$p_3\{9, 3, 7\} \text{ with early completion terms } \tau'_3 = \{7, 7, 11\}$$

Continuing this way, we get the following set of schedules:

Schedule	Early terms
$p_1\{9,3,7\}$	$\tau_1' = \{7,7,11\}$
$p_2\{9,7,3\}$	$\tau_2' = \{7,7,7\}$

All the other schedules will be their copy. In total 9 schedules will be found. If to complete the full enumeration, $n(n!) = 3(3!) = 18$. Thus, we managed to conduct two times less jobs.

Following further the method for finding an optimal schedule for $M_{(k+1)}$ let us find the maximum early term in each of the found schedules (3.3): $P_r\text{max} = \{11,7\}$ (11 for the first schedule p_1, 7 – for the second one p_2).

Next, let us find minimum element (3.4) among the set of $P_r\text{max}$ values: $Pmin = 7$. This value is unique and corresponds to p_2 schedule $\{9, 7, 3\}$.

As a result, an optimal schedule for group $M_{(k+1)}$ is p_2 $\{9, 7, 3\}$.

The Example of Search for an Optimal Jobs Schedule in the Group $M_{(k+1)}^{\text{th}}$

Let us assume that the group $M_{(k+1)} = \{3,7,9\}$. For this group, in accordance with formulas (3.1 and 3.2), τ' set is found:

$$\tau' = \left\{ \begin{array}{c} \{8,7,7\} \\ \{7,8,8\} \\ \{7,7,9\} \end{array} \right\}$$

7. Following the above method, we find:

Schedule	Early terms
$p_1\{9,3,7\}$	$\tau_1' = \{7,7,7\}$
$p_2\{7,3,9\}$	$\tau_2' = \{7,7,9\}$
$p_3\{7,9,3\}$	$\tau_1' = \{7,8,7\}$

8. $P_r\text{max} = \{7,9,8\}$
9. $Pmin = 7$

As a result, the optimal schedule for group $M_{(k+1)}$ is $p_1\{9,3,7\}$.

6 Application of the Method

It is known that the function of accelerating the execution of the algorithm on a system of n computing devices $K = F(n)$ has, for the most part, a normal distribution graph (Fig. 2):

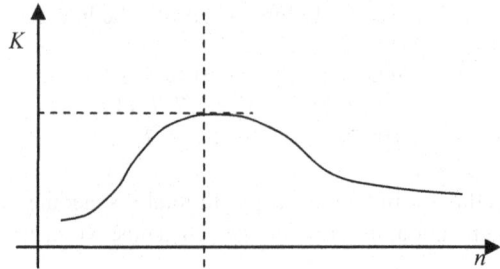

Fig. 2. Graph of the acceleration of the execution of the algorithm on a system of n computational nodes

Starting from a certain value of n, the acceleration of computations decreases due to the increase in the number of data transfers between computing nodes. For some algorithms, this dependence is a linear decreasing function. For example, a parallel algorithm of a bubble sort works slower than the original sequential algorithm. The amount of transferred data between the processors is quite large. The imbalance in the amount of computation and complexity of data transfer operations increases with the number of computational nodes. Figure 3 shows how the acceleration K decreases when the number of processors n increases for arrays of different sizes (10,000, 20,000, 30,000, 400,000 and 50,000 elements in the array).

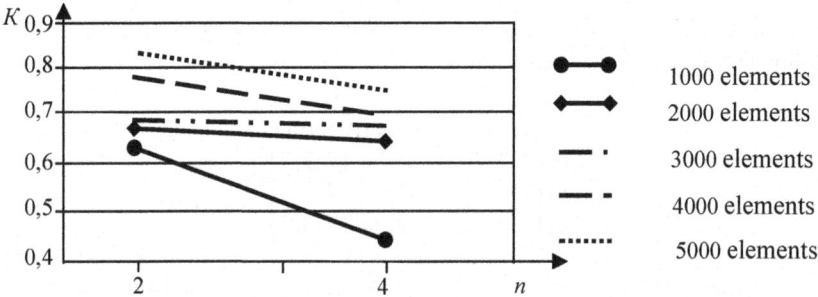

Fig. 3. Graph of the acceleration of the execution of the bubble sort algorithm

Therefore, an obvious step in the way of obtaining the optimal timing algorithm is its analysis, taking into account the amount of interprocessor data transfers. The proposed method for optimization of algorithm by reducing the interprocessor data transfers makes it possible to shorten the execution time of the algorithm.

The method for optimization of algorithm by the volume of interprocessor data transfers can be effectively applied in accordance with the following procedure:

1. Divide the algorithm into operations.
2. Construct the information graph of the algorithm.

3. Construct the parallel form of the information graph and a time diagram of the algorithm.
4. Optimize the information graph by width (by the number of processors).
5. Optimize the information graph on interprocessor communications.
6. Apply the method of consolidating operations.

The application of the algorithm optimization method by the volume of interprocessor transfers allows to achieve a higher level of performance, efficiency and high-speed processing of parallel programs.

Particularly relevant is the use of this method in parallelizing queries to databases. For example, consider the query:

> *Select field1, field2, field3, (field1*2 as field4)*
> > *from table1,*
> > > *(select **
> > > *from table2, table4*
> > > *where (field5<value1))*
> > *where field6 in*
> > > *(select (field7+2) as field8*
> > > *from table2*
> > > *where field8='string1'*
> > > *union*
> > > *select field9, field10*
> > > *from table2, table3*
> > > *where (field9=value2) and (field11> value3))*
> > *union*
> > *select **
> > *from table2;*

Using a special program developed by the authors of the article, this query is divided into subqueries. Between subqueries, the program determines information dependencies. The result of the program is a list of adjacency of the information graph of the queries. For this query, it was obtained the following information graph (Fig. 4).

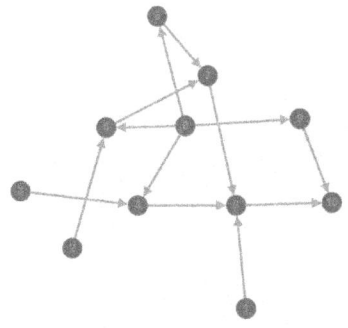

Fig. 4. The information graph of query.

Using the method of constructing a query schedule without taking into account interprocessor data transfers for this graph can be obtained:

1. The set of subqueries executed on each node:

> node 1: 0, 4, 7, 8, 9;
> node 2: 1, 5;
> node 3: 2, 6;
> node 4: 3, 9.

2. Schedule:

> step 1: 0, 1, 2, 3;
> step 2: 4, 5, 6, 9;
> step 3: 7;
> step 4: 8;
> step 5: 10.

This schedule and the distribution of subqueries by nodes will correspond to a time diagram (Fig. 5), where n is the number of nodes, t is the execution time in conditional units:

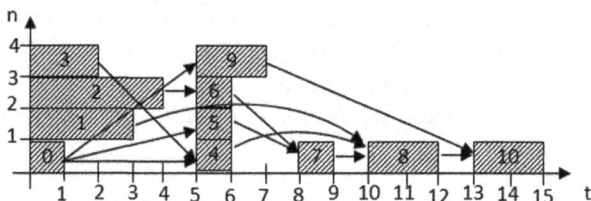

Fig. 5. The schedule of query execution.

Thus, the result of one of the methods for building the schedule will be the schedule, according to which the execution time of our request will be 15 units on 4 computational nodes.

After applying the method described in the article, this schedule will be optimized and a new schedule is made (Fig. 6):

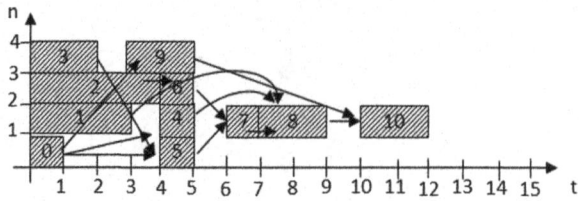

Fig. 6. The new schedule of query execution.

Time for the implementation of the algorithm on the new schedule to be reduced to 12 units. If the conventional units are hours, then this is a very big difference. The conducted testing made it possible to make sure that the query works more efficiently in the new schedule.

It should also be noted that this method is the starting point for creating a more advanced method that takes into account not only the volume of the edges entering the given vertex, but also the amount of data transferred, the length of the data transmission path, the operation time of each operation.

7   Conclusion

The method described in the article allows for the interchange of jobs between computational nodes in such a way as to minimize the time spent on data transfer. In this case, the method takes into account the time required for the completion of the jobs themselves and the nature of interrelation between jobs. So, if there are several jobs that depend on the data of the previous job, the jobs will be arranged on the computational nodes so that the total time required for their completion, taking into account the data transfer, is minimal.

The algorithm constructed by this method is characterized by low $O(n\ 2\ m)$ complexity where n - the number of computational nodes, m - the number of the information graph tiers. The method is based on adjacency lists that allow for considerable economy of memory compared to the adjacency matrix.

The result of the method is an algorithm that is equivalent to the original algorithm, because throughout the work of the method, information dependencies between operations are preserved.

As the result of the method, the total number of nodes does not exceed the number of computational nodes in the initial schedule.

The method described above can be combined with other optimization methods, for example, by the number of computational nodes.

Parallel algorithm time optimization method, taking into account inter-processor transfers, can be successfully applied in the cases of tasks scheduling in distributed computation systems.

8   Competing Interests

The authors declare that there is no conflict of interests regarding the publication of this paper.

Acknowledgments. The paper has been prepared within the scope of the state project "Initiative scientific project" of the main part of the state plan of the Ministry of Education and Science of Russian Federation (task No 2.6553.2017/8.9 BCH Basic Part) and partly supported by Russian Fund for Basic Research (grant No 16-07-00886).

References

1. He, B., Tang, L., Xie, J., Wang, X., Song, A.: Parallel numerical simulations of three-dimensional electromagnetic radiation with MPI-CUDA paradigms. Math. Probl. Eng. **2015** (2015). Article ID 823426, 9 p.
2. Jiancheng, Q., Yiqin, L., Yu, Z.: Parallel algorithm for wireless data compression and encryption. J. Sens. **2017** (2017). Article ID 4209397, 11 p.
3. Gong, C., Bao, W., Tang, G., Jiang, Y., Liu, J.: A parallel algorithm for the two-dimensional time fractional diffusion equation with implicit difference method. Sci. World J. **2014** (2014). Article ID 219580, 8 p.
4. Ma, X., Liu, S., Xiao, M., Xie, G.: Parallel algorithm with parameters based on alternating direction for solving banded linear systems. Math. Probl. Eng. **2014** (2014). Article ID 752651, 8 p.
5. Hou, J., Lv, Q., Xiao, M.: A parallel preconditioned modified conjugate gradient method for large Sylvester matrix equation. Math. Probl. Eng. **2014** (2014). Article ID 598716, 7 p.
6. Yu, D.-X., Yang, Z.-S., Yu, Y., Jiang, X.-R.: Research on large-scale road network partition and route search method combined with traveler preferences. Math. Probl. Eng. **2013** (2013). Article ID 950876, 8 p.
7. Amdahl, G.M.: Validity of the single processor approach to achieving large scale computing capabilities. In: Proceedings of the AFIPS Spring Joint Computer Conference, pp. 483–485. AFIPS Press, Reston (1967)
8. Ware, W.: The ultimate computer. IEEE Spectr. **9**, 84–91 (1972)
9. Grama, A., Gupta, A., Karypis, G., Kumar, V.: Introduction to Parallel Computing, 2nd edn. Addison Wesley, USA (2003)
10. Gergel, V.P., Strongin, R.G.: Parallel Computing for Multiprocessor Computers. NGU Publications, Nizhnij Novgorod (2003). (in Russian)
11. Quinn, M.J.: Parallel Programming in C with MPI and OpenMP, 1st edn. McGraw-Hill Education, New York (2003)
12. Wittwer, T.: An Introduction to Parallel Programming. VSSD uitgeverij, Netherlands (2006)
13. Tiwari, A., Tabatabaee, V., Hollingsworth, J.K.: Tuning parallel applications in parallel. Parallel Comput. **35**(8–9), 475–492 (2009)
14. Mubarak, M., Seol, S., Qiukai, L., Shephard, M.S.: A parallel ghosting algorithm for the flexible distributed mesh database. Sci. Program. **21**(1–2), 17–42 (2013)
15. Kruatrachue, B., Lewis, T.: Grain size determination for parallel processing. IEEE Softw. **5**(1), 23–32 (1988)
16. Meuer, H., Strohmaier, E., Dongarra, J., Simon, H.: Top500 supercomputing sites (2015)
17. Yang, T., Gerasoulis, A.: DSC: scheduling parallel tasks on an unbounded number of processors. IEEE Trans. Parallel Distrib. Syst. **5**(9), 951–967 (1994)
18. Darbha, S., Agrawal, D.P.: Optimal scheduling algorithm for distributed memory machines. IEEE Trans. Parallel Distrib. Syst. **9**(1), 87–95 (1998)
19. Liu, C.L., Layland, J.W.: Scheduling algorithms for multiprogramming in hard real-time environment. J. ACM **20**(1), 46–61 (1973)
20. Marte, B.: Preemptive scheduling with release times, deadlines and due times. J. ACM **29**(3), 812–829 (1982)
21. Burns, A.: Scheduling hard real-time systems: a review. Softw. Eng. J. **6**(3), 116–128 (1991)
22. Stankovic, J.A.: Implications of Classical Scheduling Results for Real-Time Systems. IEEE Computer Society Press, Los Alamitos (1995)
23. Tzen, T.H., Ni, L.M.: Trapezoid self-scheduling: a practical scheduling scheme for parallel compilers. IEEE Trans. Parallel Distrib. Syst. **4**, 87–98 (1993)

24. Sinnen, O., Sousa, L.A.: Communication contention in task scheduling. IEEE Trans. Parallel Distrib. Syst. **16**, 503–515 (2005)
25. Kupriyanov, M.S., Shichkina, Y.A.: Applying the list method to the transformation of parallel algorithms into account temporal characteristics of operations. In: Proceedings of the 19th International Conference on Soft Computing and Measurements, SCM 2016, 7519759, pp. 292–295 (2016). https://doi.org/10.1109/SCM.2016.7519759. ISBN: 978-146738919-8
26. Shichkina, Y., Kupriyanov, M., Al-Mardi, M.: Optimization algorithm for an information graph for an amount of communications. In: Galinina, O., Balandin, S., Koucheryavy, Y. (eds.) NEW2AN/ruSMART-2016. LNCS, vol. 9870, pp. 50–62. Springer, Cham (2016). https://doi.org/10.1007/978-3-319-46301-8_5
27. Kwok, Y.-K., Ahmad, I.: Static scheduling algorithms for allocating directed task graphs to multiprocessors. ACM Comput. Surv. (CSUR) **31**(4), 406–471 (1999)
28. Shichkina, Y., Gushchanskiy, D., Degtyarev, A.: Information graph-based creation of parallel queries for databases. Int. J. Bus. Intell. Data Min. **13**(4), 475–491 (2018). https://doi.org/10.1504/IJBIDM.2017.10004785
29. Shichkina, Y., Degtyarev, A., Gushchanskiy, D., Iakushkin, O.: Application of optimization of parallel algorithms to queries in relational databases. In: Gervasi, O., et al. (eds.) ICCSA 2016. LNCS, vol. 9787, pp. 366–378. Springer, Cham (2016). https://doi.org/10.1007/978-3-319-42108-7_28
30. Bogdanov, A., Degtyarev, A., Korkhov, V., Gaiduchok, V., Gankevich, I.: Virtual supercomputer as basis of scientific computing. In: Horizons in Computer Science Research, vol. 11, pp. 159–198. Nova Science Publishers, Inc., New York (2015). 203 p.

Data Storage, Processing and Analysis System to Support Brain Research

Vladimir Korkhov[1]([⊠]), Vladislav Volosnikov[1], Andrey Vorontsov[1],
Kirill Gribkov[1], Natalia Zalutskaya[2], Alexander Degtyarev[1],
and Alexander Bogdanov[1]

[1] Saint Petersburg State University, 7/9 Universitetskaya nab.,
St. Petersburg 199034, Russia
v.korkhov@spbu.ru
[2] V.M. Bekhterev National Research Medical Center for Psychiatry
and Neurology, 3 Bekhterev str., 192019 St. Petersburg, Russia

Abstract. Complex human research, in particular, research in the field of brain pathologies requires strong informational support for consolidation of clinical and biological data from various sources to enable data processing and analysis. In this paper we present design and implementation of an information system for patient data collection, consolidation and analysis. We show and discuss results of applying cluster analysis methods for the automated processing of magnetic resonance voxel-based morphometry data to facilitate the early diagnosis of Alzheimer's disease. Our results indicate that detailed investigation of the properties of cluster analysis data can significantly help neurophysiologists in the study of Alzheimer's disease especially with the means of automated data handling provided by the developed information system.

Keywords: Brain · Data analysis · Information system
Neuroinformatics · Alzheimer's disease

1 Introduction

It is impossible to imagine modern scientific activity without active use of information technologies. This applies to complex human research, in particular, research in the field of brain pathologies. Dozens of sources of clinical and biological data, for example, genotyping, blood tests, neurological examinations, are used simultaneously to determine the relationship between the results of different measurements in certain functional situations. Identification and analysis of such relationships allow better understanding of the processes occurring in the brain.

Unfortunately, the heterogeneity of data sources, the diversity of presentation formats and the resource-intensive nature of pre-processing make it difficult to conduct comprehensive interdisciplinary research. Combining data for each individual case is a laborious process that requires from researchers not only time, but also deep knowledge in the field of information technology. To solve

© Springer International Publishing AG, part of Springer Nature 2018
O. Gervasi et al. (Eds.): ICCSA 2018, LNCS 10963, pp. 78–90, 2018.
https://doi.org/10.1007/978-3-319-95171-3_7

the problem of the joint use of heterogeneous sources of clinical and biological species in brain research an information system with unified access to heterogeneous data is required. Effective implementation of such a system requires the creation of a model of combining heterogeneous data into a single information environment and adaptation of pre-processing methods applied individually to each separate type of data. The implementation of a model that solves the fundamental problem of the consolidation of medical and biological data in the form of a cloud service will solve the problem of the organization of researchers' access to the results of the consolidation, while leveling the geographical distribution of research groups and equipment. The user interface designed to meet the needs of brain researchers will allow access to data without the need to develop skills in working with databases thereby allowing users to focus on research rather than on access to data.

The project presented in this paper is devoted to the creation of information support in the field of the human brain research. We have already addressed the issues of hybrid analog-digital approaches and human brain activity modelling in our earlier work [1–3]. Here we analyze the possibilities and practices of consolidation of clinical and biological data, build a model of consolidation and interaction of heterogeneous sources of data on brain research, programmatically implement the model in the form of a cloud service, as well as provide interface to the information system that supports requests in a format encapsulating the complex architecture of consolidation from the user.

2   Related Work

Neuroinformatics tasks are focused on the creation, storage, processing, simulation, and visualization of research results. All these stages affect the work with large amounts of data and require the development of a unique software and hardware systems that require special algorithms and hardware for efficient operation. Currently, various components of the cloud infrastructure are already used in neuroinformatics, for example, in such projects as JuBrain [17] and a-Brain [18]. The creation of cloud platforms to support work in this area has been actively engaged since 2008 [4], but the system that would cover the full range of tasks still does not exist, and often specialized projects are required to solve individual problems [5].

Correct recording of information requires the ability to draft pre-processing of data. Sources of such data may be MRI devices, EEG and others directly interacting with the object of the study. The analysis of data streams received from these devices requires a powerful computing system. For example, one of the objectives of the fMRI project is to obtain a three-dimensional model of brain activity in real time. It uses Xeon Phi coprocessor technologies [6]. The use of cluster systems directly limits the possibilities of redistribution of computing resources [7]. In such systems, resources are allocated within a narrow range of software platforms, which limits the flexibility of the software used [8].

The solution to such problems may be a private cloud deployed in the research center environment and allowing the use of virtual machines or Docker containers [9,10].

Some modern technologies create extra-large amounts of data. For example, the Harvard project "CONNECTOME" requires 2PB data analysis for each cubic millimeter of the brain [11]. Such projects are at an early stage of their development, but bring fruitful results [12,13] and show significant progress in increasing the speed of information processing from two centuries for one millimeter in 2010 to 5.6 years in 2013 [14]. Such data volumes require long-term storage. Public cloud systems provide "cold" storage [15], allowing you to place data on slow hard drives of large volume or magnetic tape. This solves the problem of expanding the infrastructure of a private cluster, turning it into a hybrid cloud that can accommodate the required amount of data.

In addition to manual data aggregation tools, there are a number of projects aimed at creating a common knowledge base. The Brain Atlas project of the Allen Institute aggregates open data, providing a software interface to the images, 3D reconstructions, sections and structures in areas of study of the brain: mice and primates, including humans; different types of cells, connections of the brain. This database is located in the USA [16]. For research using this database in any other region, it is necessary to transmit data over long distances. The organization of an interregional network may not be optimal because of its dynamic organization and constant changes which leads to the need for data consolidation [31,32]. Public cloud platforms allow you to build secure communication channels that have guaranteed bandwidth for data transfer between regions.

Development of data processing tools is integral to the development of high-performance computing. Thus, [19] presents a number of modeling systems of neural networks using computations on NVidia co-processors, available in public cloud solutions. Paper [20] considers the connection of brain work and its modeling using quantum computing, which, according to the authors [21], is primarily available in the form of a PaaS service from cloud providers.

Much attention is paid to systems that allow users to work within the model of "notebooks". Such systems are aimed at combining the web service containing the IDE, the system of visualization in HTML5 format and the possibility of setting tasks on remote clusters [22,23]. There are solutions using the Spark platform for solving Neuroinformatics problems [24]: Bolt to work with local and distributed arrays of data; Thunder to analyze images and time series. Cloud providers often allocate separate systems that allow you to quickly deploy a Spark cluster.

Visualization of research materials can be the key to scientific discovery. The Virtual Brain project [25] allows to display various aspects related to brain modeling within a single framework in the form of a web service. The multi-tenant model looks at the support for the stand-alone operation of multiple organizations within a single underlying cloud datacenter hardware. This solution allows one visualization system provider to completely separate customer data, providing increased security of the system.

Cloud-based systems allow for maximum savings on the resources involved at any given point in time. Public cloud solutions expand the organization's existing capacity by leveraging technologies that are not available through on-premises datacenters. This speeds up the development of software prototypes and extends the capabilities of the existing IT infrastructure. The advantage of cloud solutions is that you can cancel the use of cloud equipment at any time, change its parameters or expand the volume used for a small amount of time. These features of cloud technologies make them relevant for solving problems of Neuroinformatics.

3   Architecture

3.1   Data for Brain Research: Sources and Formats

The survey was conducted over 145 people aged 55 years and older who underwent psychological and psychiatric examination at the Gerontological department of V.M. Bekhterev instutite. All patients were without severe neurological and psychopathological symptoms, as well as without diabetes mellitus, marked increases in blood pressure, atherosclerosis and neuroinfections.

All the subjects passed magnetic resonance imaging on Toshiba Vantage XGV MRI installation with a magnetic field of 1.5 T. The standard study was carried out in three projections to obtain T1, T2 weighted images, pulse sequence "inversion-recovery" FLAIR and pulse sequence 3D-MP-RAGE.

Postprocessing of MRI results was carried out with the FreeSurfer package [26]. The resulting 3D-MP-RAGE sequence files in DICOM format were converted to NIFTI FSL format. The files were converted using the MRIConvert software package.

The files generated by FreeSurfer contain the result of automatic cortical parcellation and subcortical segmentation. For each patient we were given a set of ".stats" files that described the structures of the left and right hemispheres, labeled using different brain atlases. Each file contains technical information about FreeSurfer configuration and a table with the characteristics of the corresponding structures like cortex thickness, white matter volume, intensity of magnetic field etc.

The data was processed in the IBM SPSS Statistics software Release 20.0.0.2. Before the beginning of the comparative analysis, the samples were checked for normality using the Kolmogorov-Smirnov test. To assess the reliability of the differences, the Mann-Whitney U-criterion was used. The differences $P \leq 0.01$ were considered reliable. To establish the relationship between the investigated parameters of the method of voxel-based morphometry and the methods of psycho-psychiatric examination, the Spearman rank correlation coefficient was used.

3.2   Information System

Main function of the information system in the current project is to perform data consolidation and create a data storage and analysis system, that will help doctors working with patients and analysts who need quick access to test data, to provide a large amount of data for analysis.

First step of the implementation is to create a simple data-storage service, so that privileged users can upload data of patients and hide their personal information while other users can access anonymized data not to violate patients' privacy. Design of the web application is based on personal pages of patients. For each patient there is a page, where all related information and tests are described. It will help doctor to make better diagnoses - all the necessary information from various data sources (MRI, EEG, genomic and postgenomic analysis data, etc.) is stored in one place.

For building this system the MEAN (Mongo, Express, Angular, Node) stack is most suitable (Fig. 1). It is a modern way to build a lightweight, flexible system with Angular as a front-end framework, Express+Node for a back-end server and Mongo as a database.

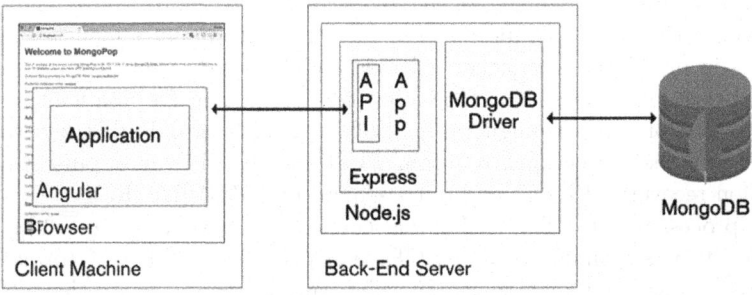

Fig. 1. Scheme of MEAN stack.

Angular

For web-based application, that must run on different devices, different OS and provide greater flexibility in the development, Angular framework [27] is currently the optimal choice. Our web-page should render all kinds of neural data formats, be able to collect and filter them to help doctors to find precisely the information they need.

First of all, Angular is most popular framework nowadays, has a great community and lots of useful open-source tools, that can help in working with multi-structured data, such as MRI results. Its a complicated task to develop all tools for neural data treatment by yourself - free libraries will help a lot, and most of them are made to work with Angular.

Main problem with which we are faced is how to render all this complex data in browser. Most useful programs today are developed for working in OS, not on web-pages, so we need to implement some kind of viewers to help doctors check patients test without having to physically save them on computer and open in external programs. For sure, there are some open-source projects, like DICOM web viewer that can help us, but they are still under development.

Express+NodeJS

As a backend system in our stack Node.js with installed web-framework ExpressJS are used [28]. NodeJS is a cross-platform runtime for the JavaScript language. In fact NodeJS turns JavaScript into a General-purpose language. In turn, ExpressJS allows you to organize a NodeJS http-server. All 4 components of this stack interact well with each other, they are all associated with JavaScript. In particular, the great advantage of this stack is the ability to work with JSON objects without converting them to other data types because javascript is one of the standard data types is a JSON object. Because of this, the properties of the stack, there is no need to use the mapping data when the sample from MongoDB [29].

Generally, it is one of the fastest and easiest ways to create a modern web-server. We don't need a high-performance back-end, but flexibility and speed of development is necessary in our project, so NodeJS is the optimal choice.

MongoDB

In the database we need the ability to store data with any structure and have convenient access to this data, because our analysis files have different format. A non-relational database suits best to fulfill these requirements. In particular, for the implementation of this system we chose NoSQL database MongoDB. Instead of the traditional relational database structure, MongoDB uses JSON-like documents with dynamic schemes. This approach to the storing of information allows arbitrary definition of the schema structure for data storage. For example: two different objects of the same schema field with the same key may be values of very different formats. This property of MongoDB is best suited for the implementation of this information system.

Current Implementation and Roadmap

At the moment, the system provides functionality to add/delete/modify user profiles and download/upload files, attached to them including automatic parsing of uploaded Excel data.

Next step is to provide functions for working with massive data analysis. We need an easy way to store and download a lot of files, and keep their structure to enable further analysis. We need a method to separate one file types from another and to keep in mind that some files attached to specific person, without keeping names or other personal information. In analysis module we will build some correlations, so we need to save person's analysis as a solid object, but we can't mix them, we need to explore each type of data.

For this feature, special parsers must be written - you just can't import hundreds of files manually. This will be one of the most technically difficult moments of the project. User will simply choose all files for import, without any reference to patient - and system automatically must detect personal information in any file, find the right patient for it (don't forget about misspelling in surnames or missing data), and save a file correctly. If it is impossible - service will ask what to do with this file: skip it, create a new patient for it or attach to existing patient, maybe suggest the best options based on available data. Its very complicated task, because those parsers must be open-source software, so we can use them in our project, and, as main programming language in our project is javascript, they must support it too. Unfortunately, under these requirements there are very little products, so most of parsers will be developed by our team.

The integrated information system will provide built-in support for data analysis of stored data e.g. to find correlations between different groups of patients with similar clinical state within the group and their brain data. The next section describes some examples of such brain data analysis.

4   Brain Data Analysis

Nowadays, about 46.8 million people around the world suffer from dementia. One of the most common forms of age-related dementia is Alzheimer's — a progressive neurodegenerative disease that leads to permanent brain damage.

Structural and functional brain changes occur long before the obvious manifestations of cognitive impairment. For example, atrophy of the middle temporal lobe is considered one of the markers of Alzheimer's disease. In this connection, the methods of neuroimaging, which allow to detect *in vivo* structural changes in the brain are useful in practice.

In this part of the paper, the application of cluster analysis methods for the automated processing of magnetic resonance voxel-based morphometry data to facilitate the early diagnosis of Alzheimer's disease is considered.

To carry out this work, the St. Petersburg V.M. Bekhterev Psychoneurological Research Institute provided anonymous MRI examinations of a group of 145 patients not less then 55 years of age to study and model the human brain. Among the patients there was a control group of healthy volunteers.

The data obtained after MRI processing by special medical software FreeSurfer, used for segmentation and parcellation of brain zones, was divided into 5 categories: subcortical structures volume, volume of gray matter structures in right and left brain hemispheres, volume of white matter structures and common segmented volume of brain. The integration of data in the system provides a Python script, preserving the characteristics of the patients in the JSON format.

Because the dimension of the initial data (about 550 characteristics) is high in comparison with the number of the surveyed group, it was decided to cluster separately by parts of the brain: temporal lobe, parietal lobe, insula, limbic system, entorhinal cortex, etc.

Based on received data we have clustered patients by characteristics of different brain parts: frontal lobe, parietal lobe, temporal lobe, insula, limbic, entorhinal cortex. Every patient was considered as a point in the normalized n-dimensional feature space.

Due to lack of information about clusters' count and shapes, at this stage it was decided to use density-based algorithm. The advantage of this class of algorithms is ability to allocate clusters of different shapes and densities. Some drawbacks: vulnerability to the "curse of dimension" — loss of efficiency at high dimensions and the need for a large number of points.

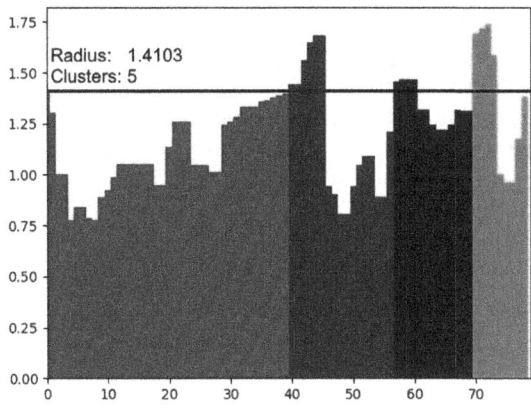

Fig. 2. Distance diagram

In the first step we chose density-base algorithm "OPTICS" (Ordering points to identify the clustering structure) [30] realization in PyClustering library. As input parameters it uses maximal considering distance ε and minimal number of neighbor points required to form a cluster. One of the advantages of this algorithm is the detection of noise, which will be helpful for using unstable to noise methods.

To select the optimal radius of r, we used the function of drawing the distance diagram (Fig. 2) included in the package, which allows to determine the average distance between points in the cluster.

"OPTICS" algorithm is a good tool for noise isolation. This advantage will make it possible to use unstable to noise algorithms for further data analysis.

The weak side of the algorithm is the need to have a large set of points. For that reason the need to increase count of patients is obvious.

As a result, after use of the PCA method, graphs of the resulting partitions with about 40% of the data dispersion were obtained.

After the clustering, depending on the share in question, different partitions were obtained. In all cases, the noise was allocated to the "zero" cluster.

Analysis of some brain structures showed clearly distinct groups. For example, according to the characteristics of the insula, four distinct clusters is observed (Fig. 3). Such a result agrees with the presentation of specialists of the Bekhterev Institute on the patients under consideration. This is of interest for further studies of this structure.

The study of most parts of the brain revealed one large cluster, surrounded by abnormal emissions. For example, the distribution of patients according to the characteristics of the parietal lobe is shown in Fig. 4. Given the very small number of patients examined, the algorithm can find the points of cluster accumulation undetected at this stage when the study is continued.

However, in some cases, even with such a breakdown, it was possible to obtain potentially useful results. Among the "abnormal" patients, sharply differing from the rest in the parameters of the parietal lobe (Fig. 5), those suffering from dementia and depression are represented, and the members of the control group are almost not represented. An indication of further investigation of the properties of isolated clusters can significantly help neurophysiologists in the study of Alzheimer's disease.

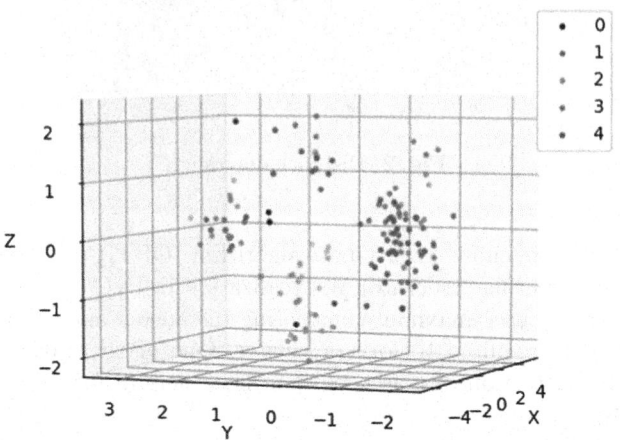

Fig. 3. Insula distribution.

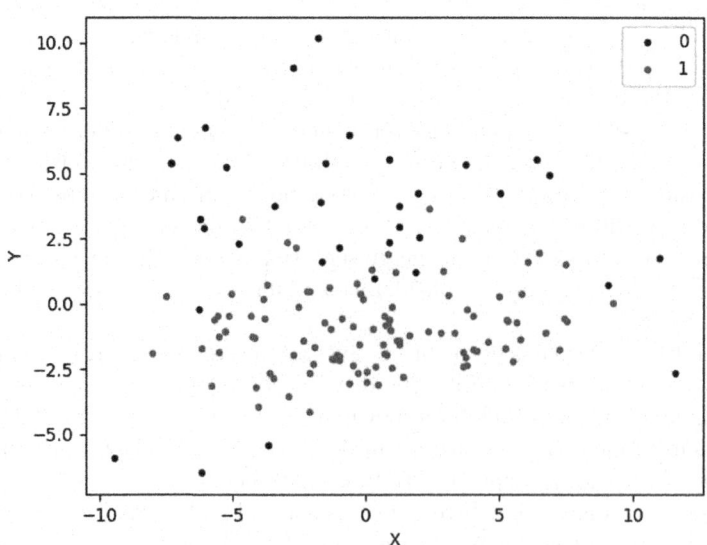

Fig. 4. Parietal distribution

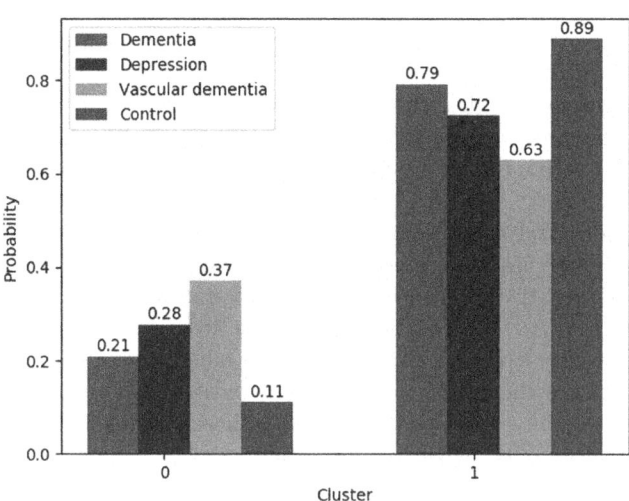

Fig. 5. Parietal probabilities

Figure 6 shows the results of the test, reflecting the overall cognitive level of the patients. The value of 30 corresponds to an absolutely healthy person.

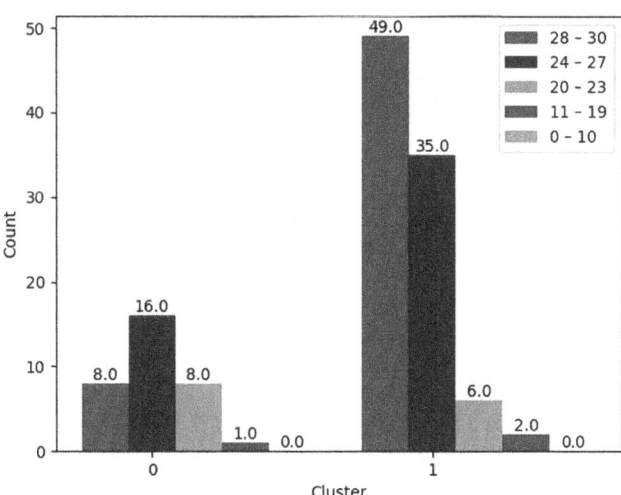

Fig. 6. Parietal MMSE results.

5   Conclusions and Future Work

Currently all the modules of the information system are deployed on the server and are stable. System provides file storage with the ability to edit patients pages and saving any types of files. It uses a special scheme to conceal the personal information while browsing, if the user has no rights for it. We plan to develop the platform further to provide more functionality for data handling and automated analysis.

The study of voxel-based MR morphometry data of 145 patients with the division of the data (550 characteristics of the brain structures of each patient) allowed clustering with the release and separate analysis of data on the volume of white and gray matter, the thickness of the crust in the hemispheres as a whole and separately frontal, temporal, parietal lobes, limbic system and insula. We plan to enhance the results by using new patient data accumulated in the developed information system and investigate other methods of machine learning and data analysis applied to neuroinformatics.

Acknowledgments. Research has been partially supported by the RFBR grant 16-07-00886.

References

1. Bogdanov, A., Degtyarev, A., Guschanskiy, D., Lysov, K., Ananieva, N., Zalut-skaya, N., Neznanov, N.: Analog-digital approach in human brain modeling. In: Proceedings - 201717th IEEE/ACM International Symposium on Cluster, Cloud, and Grid Computing, CCGrid 2017, pp. 807–812 (2017)
2. Bogdanov, A., Degtyarev, A., Guschanskiy, D., Lysov, K., Ananieva, N., Zalut-skaya, N., Neznanov, N.: Hybrid approaches and human brain activity modelling. V.M. Bekhterev Rev. Psychiatry Med. Psychol. **1**, 19–25 (2017)
3. Ananyeva, N.I., Bogdanov, A.V., Gushchanskiy, D.E., Degtyarev, A.B., Zalutskaya, N.M., Lysov, K.A., Neznanov, N.G., Iakushkin, O.O.: Analog and digital systems and high-performance solutions in problems of brain research and modeling. V.M. Bekhterev Rev. Psychiatry Med. Psychol. **3**, 16–21 (2016)
4. Watson, P., Lord, P., Gibson, F., Periorellis, P., Pitsilis, G.: Cloud computing for e-Science with CARMEN. In: 2nd Iberian Grid Infrastructure Conference Proceedings, pp. 3–14, May 2008
5. D'Haese, P.F., Konrad, P.E., Pallavaram, S., Li, R., Prassad, P., Rodriguez, W., Dawant, B.M.: CranialCloud: a cloud-based architecture to support trans-institutional collaborative efforts in neurodegenerative disorders. Int. J. Comput. Assist. Radiol. Surg. **10**(6), 815–823 (2015)
6. Wang, Y., Anderson, M.J., Cohen, J.D., Heinecke, A., Li, K., Satish, N., Sundaram, N., Turk-Browne, N.B., Willke, T.L.: Full correlation matrix analysis of fMRI data on Intel®Xeon^{TM}Phi coprocessors. In: Proceedings of the International Conference for High Performance Computing, Networking, Storage and Analysis, p. 23. ACM (2015)
7. Bogdanov, A., Degtyarev, A., Korkhov, V.: Desktop supercomputer: what can it do? Phys. Part. Nucl. Lett. **14**(7), 985–992 (2017)

8. Bogdanov, A., Degtyarev, A., Korkhov, V.: New approach to the simulation of complex systems. In: EPJ Web of Conferences, vol. 108, p. 01002. EDP Sciences (2016)
9. Jinzhou, Y., Jin, H., Kai, Z., Zhijun, W.: Discussion on private cloud PaaS construction of large scale enterprise. In: 2016 IEEE International Conference on Cloud Computing and Big Data Analysis (ICCCBDA), pp. 273–278. IEEE (2016)
10. Korkhov, V., Gankevich, I., Degtyarev, A., Bogdanov, A., Gaiduchok, V., Ahmed, N., Cubahiro, A.: Experience in building virtual private supercomputer. In: Proceedings of International Conference on Computer Science and Information Technologies (CSIT), pp. 220–223 (2015). ISBN 978-5-8080-0797-0
11. Swanson, L.W., Lichtman, J.W.: From Cajal to Connectome and beyond. Annu. Rev. Neurosci. **39**(1), 197–216 (2016)
12. Tomassy, G.S., Berger, D.R., Chen, H.H., Kasthuri, N., Hayworth, K.J., Vercelli, A., Seung, H.S., Lichtman, J.W., Arlotta, P.: Distinct profiles of Myelin distribution along single axons of pyramidal neurons in the neocortex. Science **344**(6181), 319–324 (2014)
13. Lichtman, J.W., Denk, W.: The big and the small: challenges of imaging the brain's circuits. Science **334**(6056), 618–623 (2011)
14. Lichtman, J.W., Pfister, H., Shavit, N.: The big data challenges of connectomics. Nat. Neurosci. **17**(11), 1448–1454 (2014)
15. Han, Y.: Cloud storage for digital preservation: optimal uses of Amazon S3 and Glacier. Library Hi Tech **33**(2), 261–271 (2015)
16. Miller, J.A., Ding, S.L., Sunkin, S.M., Smith, K.A., Ng, L., Szafer, A., Ebbert, A., Riley, Z.L., Royall, J.J., Aiona, K., Arnold, J.M.: Transcriptional landscape of the prenatal human brain. Nature **508**(7495), 199–206 (2014)
17. Mohlberg, H., Eickhoff, S.B., Schleicher, A., Zilles, K., Amunts, K.: A new processing pipeline and release of cytoarchitectonic probabilistic maps-JuBrain (2012)
18. Antoniu, G., Costan, A., Mota, B.D., Thirion, B., Tudoran, R.: A-brain: using the cloud to understand the impact of genetic variability on the brain. ERCIM News **89**, 21–22 (2012)
19. Prieto, A., Prieto, B., Ortigosa, E.M., Ros, E., Pelayo, F., Ortega, J., Rojas, I.: Neural networks: an overview of early research, current frameworks and new challenges. Neurocomputing **214**, 242–268 (2016)
20. Neven, H., Denchev, V.S., Rose, G., Macready, W.G.: QBoost: large scale classifier training with adiabatic quantum optimization. In: ACML, pp. 333–348 (2012)
21. Singh, H., Sachdev, A.: The quantum way of cloud computing. In: 2014 International Conference on Optimization, Reliabilty, and Information Technology (ICROIT), pp. 397–400. IEEE, February 2014
22. Iakushkin, O.O., Sedova, O.S.: Creating CAD designs and performing their subsequent analysis using opensource solutions in Python. In: AIP Conference Proceedings 1922, no. 140011 (2018). https://doi.org/10.1063/1.5019153
23. Iakushkin, O., Kondratiuk, A., Sedova, O., Grishkin, V.: Jupyter extension for creating CAD designs and their subsequent analysis by the finite element method. CEUR Workshop Proc. **1787**, 530–534 (2016)
24. Cunningham, J.P.: Analyzing neural data at huge scale. Nat. Methods **11**(9), 911–912 (2014)
25. Leon, P.S., Knock, S.A., Woodman, M.M., Domide, L., Mersmann, J., McIntosh, A.R., Jirsa, V.: The virtual brain: a simulator of primate brain network dynamics. In: Information-based methods for neuroimaging: analyzing structure, function and dynamics, p. 10 (2015)

26. Freesurfer. http://surfer.nmr.mgh.harvard.edu/. Accessed 15 Apr 2018
27. Angular. https://angular.io/
28. Express+Node.js. https://expressjs.com/
29. MongoDB. https://www.mongodb.com/
30. Ankerst, M., Breunig, M.M., Kriegel, H.-P., Sander, J.: OPTICS: Ordering Points To Identify the Clustering Structure. In: ACM SIGMOD International Conference on Management of Data, pp. 49–60. ACM Press (1999)
31. Petrov, D.A., Stankova, E.N.: Use of consolidation technology for meteorological data processing. In: Murgante, B., Misra, S., Rocha, A.M.A.C., Torre, C., Rocha, J.G., Falcão, M.I., Taniar, D., Apduhan, B.O., Gervasi, O. (eds.) ICCSA 2014. LNCS, vol. 8579, pp. 440–451. Springer, Cham (2014). https://doi.org/10.1007/978-3-319-09144-0_30
32. Stankova, E.N., Balakshiy, A.V., Petrov, D.A., Shorov, A.V., Korkhov, V.V.: Using technologies of OLAP and machine learning for validation of the numerical models of convective clouds. In: Gervasi, O., Murgante, B., Misra, S., Rocha, A.M.A.C., Torre, C., Taniar, D., Apduhan, B.O., Stankova, E., Wang, S. (eds.) ICCSA 2016. LNCS, vol. 9788, pp. 463–472. Springer, Cham (2016). https://doi.org/10.1007/978-3-319-42111-7_36

Staccato: Cache-Aware Work-Stealing Task Scheduler for Shared-Memory Systems

Ruslan Kuchumov[1], Andrey Sokolov[2], and Vladimir Korkhov[1(✉)]

[1] Saint Petersburg State University,
7/9 Universitetskaya nab., St. Petersburg 199034, Russia
`kuchumovri@gmail.com, v.korkhov@spbu.ru`
[2] Institute of Applied Mathematical Research,
Karelian Research Centre RAS, Petrozavodsk, Russia
`avs@krc.karelia.ru`

Abstract. Parallel tasks work-stealing schedulers yield near-optimal tasks distribution (i.e. all CPU cores are loaded equally) and have low time, memory and inter-thread synchronizations. The key idea of work-stealing strategy is that when scheduler worker runs out of tasks for execution, it start stealing tasks from the queues of other workers. It's been shown that double ended queues based on circular arrays are effective in this scenario. They are designed with an assumption that tasks pointer are stored in these data structures, while tasks object reside in heap memory. By modifying tasks queues so that they can hold task objects instead pointers we managed to increase the performance above 2.5 times on CPU bound applications and decrease last-level cache misses 30% compared to Intel TBB and Intel/MIT Cilk work-stealing schedulers.

Keywords: Work-stealing scheduler · Work-stealing deques
Data structures

1 Introduction

Some programs can be divided into subprograms and when they are executed in parallel execution time of the program can be reduced. To achieve this operating systems offer an interface to the treads of execution. In some cases their usage is not always justified and effective. First, threads creation and termination are rather expensive operations so when subprograms are too small creating a thread for each one would only slow down total execution time. Second, the number of threads is limited by operating system. Third, if there are more threads created than the number of physical cores then the threads would not be able to work simultaneously as CPU time would be distributed equally among them by operating system.

© Springer International Publishing AG, part of Springer Nature 2018
O. Gervasi et al. (Eds.): ICCSA 2018, LNCS 10963, pp. 91–102, 2018.
https://doi.org/10.1007/978-3-319-95171-3_8

To get rid of aforementioned problems one can create a fixed number of execution threads which will be active during program execution and then use a scheduler that would distribute subprograms among execution threads. This approach would eliminate thread creation overhead, and the number of threads can be the same as the number of physical cores.

Scheduling strategies can be classified as static and dynamic. Static ones can be used when all the properties and features of scheduler tasks are known a priori. In this case an optimal task distribution can be calculated, but this approach is considered to be NP-complete [1] thus is rare.

In dynamic scheduling the scheduler uses a relatively simple distribution strategy which yields near-optimal result with minimal computation overhead. These strategies, in turn, can be classified as centralized when there is a dedicated thread for tasks distribution and decentralized [2].

In decentralized scheduling each thread have its own queue of waiting for execution tasks and threads themself handle tasks balancing. For example, the thread which has a lot of tasks may delegate them to other threads (work-dealing [3]) or, e.g. when the thread finish all its own task it starts to request (work-requesting [4]) or steal tasks (work-stealing [6]) from other threads.

In this paper we focus on work-stealing strategy. Theoretically proven [6] that this strategy yields near-optimal task distribution and it has also been proven in practice - its implementations can be found in general purpose schedulers as MIT Cilk [7], Intel TBB [8], .NET TPL [9], Rust, Java Fork/Join [14], X10 [15] working on multi-core processors. There are also adaptive scheduler implementations for many-core processors [16].

In work-stealing scheduler there is one task pool per worker thread, so unlike centralized strategies with a single pool, there is less lock contention for inserting and removing tasks. Work-stealing pools are usually implemented based on double-ended queue (or deque) data structure. Performing owner's operations (task insertion and removal) on one end of a deque and steal operation on the other end allows to implement it without locking and with a single synchronization point (when only one task is left the pool).

There are many deques implementations for work-stealing schedulers, for example, based on fixed arrays [6], doubly-linked lists [18], implementations that allows to steal multiple tasks at once [5]. The one that's commonly used is based on circular arrays [19] as it provides low operation and memory overhead and unlike others allows for dynamic resize. Its implementations can be found in Intel TBB and Rust.

However, all these implementation are designed with an assumption that deques store memory pointers to task object, that can be easily removed or added to it. So despite its low overhead, schedulers still rely on memory manages for allocating and deallocating every tasks. These tasks objects can't be stored in deques permanently and have to reside in memory manager's data pool. Accessing memory manager for creating/deleting each task may bring significant overhead, because of, first, allocation overhead and, second, cache-misses overhead during task execution.

This problem is addressed in this paper by, first, designing deque based (denoted by "Staccato") data structure that allows to store tasks objects during their execution, and, second, by creating memory manager specific for holding task memory with minimal overhead. Our data structure is based on a list of circular deques holding tasks objects. When the tasks are completed their memory is reused by the following tasks, which eliminates the need for accessing memory manager. Besides that there are multiple synchronization primitives per task pool instead of one, which reduces lock contention even further.

Memory manager we designed is specific for storing task deques so that it allows to store tasks in consecutive memory, minimizing cache-misses during their execution. As deques owner executes tasks in LIFO manner, its memory access follows the same pattern. It allowed us to use LIFO based memory manager that does not have to provide fragmentation handling and thread-safety thus having lowest overhead possible. By doing that we managed to significantly reduce last-level cache-misses and total execution time. The only downside of this approach is that programmer has to set the maximum degree of task DAG manually, which is not a problem a problem for majority of problems solved using tasks scheduler.

2 Motivation

The tasks executed by the scheduler can be described as a set of instructions that must be executed consequently, but during their execution they can create subtasks that can be executed independently from parent task, in parallel. Thus all tasks can be represented in form of tree graph where each task (except for the root) is pointing to its parent task that waits for it to finish (Fig. 1).

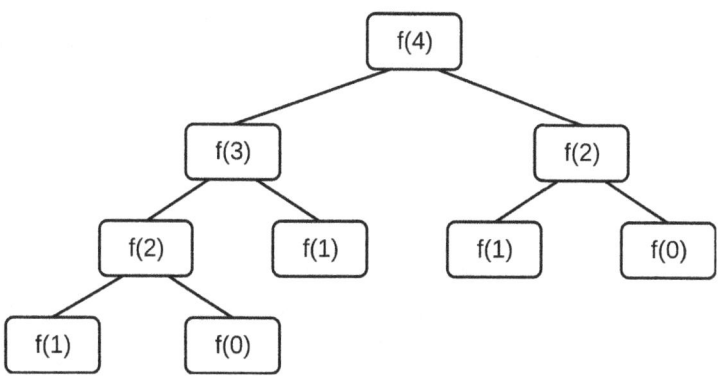

Fig. 1. Task graph for calculating 4th Fibonacci number. Each task creates and waits for two subtasks.

For example, the task for calculating Fibonacci number can be written (in pseudocode) as follows:

```
void fib(int n) {
        if (n <= 2)
                return 1;
        int x = spawn fib(n − 1);
        int y = spawn fib(n − 2);
        synchronize;
        return x + y;
}
```

During the execution of fib(n), two subtasks will be created and placed in the pool of the worker executing parent task. These subtasks can be stolen and executed by other workers or can be executed by the same worker as well. When parent task have to wait for its subtasks to finish (i.e. synchronize) is called, the flow of execution is passed to the worker allowing it to work on other tasks, until all subtasks are finished. The worker takes tasks from its own pool first, and when it becomes empty, it starts to steal from the pool of a random worker.

The most common implementation of work-stealing deque is based on circular array [19], it can be found in Intel TBB or in Rust. The idea behind it is to use two atomic indexes (called top and bottom) for pointing to the ends of deque. The top index is used only by steal operations concurrently and it can be only incremented and never decremented. It allows to synchronize steals by lock-free atomic compare and swap operations. The other index (bottom) is used only by deque owner for putting and taking tasks. The only race condition between deque owner and a thief is possible when there is a single task left in the deque. In this case owner takes the task by using the top index as if it is stealing from itself (Fig. 2).

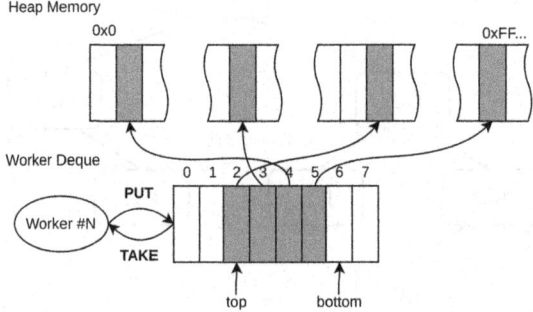

Fig. 2. Work stealing deque. One end is accessed only by its owner, another by thieves. Deque contains pointers to task objects located outside, in heap memory.

The access to actual deque elements is done by performing modulo operation with its size. It allows to dynamically change deque capacity without modifying its indexes as they point to the same elements after resize. The size of a deque is always a power of two, which allows indexes to overflow when they are constantly being incremented.

When the task is removed (either stolen or taken by the owner) from the deque for execution, the indexes are updated and task's previous place in the deque can be taken by the following tasks inserted by the owner. Because of this, parent task object can not reside in the deque memory during the execution of its subtasks. In most work-stealing scheduler implementations, task deques manipulate with pointers to task objects, which are located somewhere in a heap.

This implies that for each task memory manager should be accessed twice, first to allocate task memory before and second, when the task is finished, its memory should be deallocated. As the total number of tasks increase exponentially depending on the input data dimensions in fork-join computational model, the memory manager overhead can be significant if not done properly.

Besides the allocation overhead there's also cache-misses induced by accessing random memory addresses when the scheduler traverses task graph. It happens at least twice, first, when the scheduler loads a new tasks for execution and, second, when the scheduler has finished executing a task and updates its parent counters. In these cases cache-locality is violated and last-level cache (LLC) miss may happen.

3   Design of Cache-Aware Work-Stealing Deque

We changed work-stealing deque data structure so that it can hold tasks in the deque while they are being executed which allowed us to store task objects instead of pointers. This, in turn, reduces cache-misses as task objects are stored in adjacent memory regions and reduces the number of memory allocations as task memory can be reused when the task is completed.

To achieve that, we create a linked list of deques (Fig. 3), so that each deque stores only one set of subtasks. When parent task is being executed, a new deque for holding subtasks of this task is created and added to the list. In case the deque is already created by previous tasks executions, it is being reused for holding new tasks. Each worker keeps the pointer to the tail (i.e. the last non-empty deque) of its own linked list and moves it during task graph execution. When the worker have to steal a task, it travels from the head of a victim list until steal operation finishes successfully.

Deques inside this linked lists are operated the same way as described in previous chapter. When the owner takes a task for execution, the task still reside in deque memory but it becomes unreachable for steal operation as deque indexes were updated when the task was taken. At the same time, this task would not be overwritten by the following insertion operations while it's being executed because deque owner has to finish it before inserting a new task to the same deque. So using a dedicated deque for each set of subtasks ensures that task's memory would not be modified when this task is being executed.

Each deque in a list has its own set of indexes that are used for identifying deque ends and for synchronizations between workers. This, in turn, means, that deque list owner and a thief would likely to operate on a different cache-lines to perform synchronization which reduces its contention compared to original approach with a single set of indexes per worker. Also, as indexes are located in adjacent memory regions to the array of tasks objects, the spatial locality of CPU cache is better than in original implementation.

The downside of this approach is that deque locations in memory have to be fixed throughout task graph execution otherwise deque list owner would not be able to remove list entries without locking. This problem can be bypassed in programming languages with garbage collectors or by using smart pointers, but we decided not to sacrifice with performance and leave it as is, as the only effect it has is that programmer will have to manually specify the maximum number of subtasks a single task can have. This information is usually known at the stage of designing task graph.

We have also created a memory manager specially for holding this data structure. It is based on a linked list of memory pages. Memory pages are used for allocating adjacent memory regions. There is a separate memory manager for each worker and worker do not access memory manager of other worker, thus there's no need for ensuring thread safety. As the worker process tasks in LIFO order, its memory is accessed in the same way so external fragmentation is also not a concern. Because of all of these, memory allocation boils down to incrementing a single variable and requesting a new memory if the previous one does not have enough space.

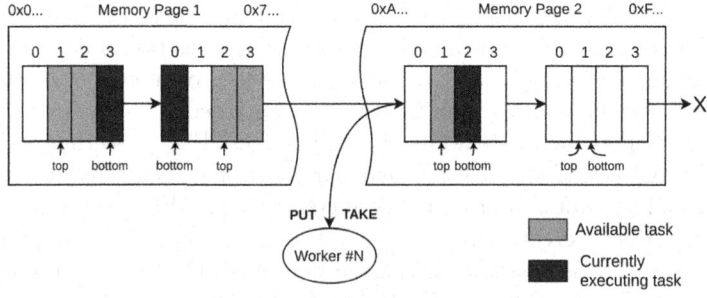

Fig. 3. Our proposed data structure for holding data task objects. It's based on a linked list of circular array deques. Task objects are stored in deques instead of pointers. Deques are located in adjacent memory regions until they fit on the same memory page.

4   Implementation

Work-stealing scheduler implementations can be classified as child-stealing and parent-stealing depending on which task is executed when a new task is created [17]. In child-stealing a new object for the child task is placed in worker queue and then the worker continues to execute the parent task. On contrary, in parent-stealing when a new task created the continuation of a parent task is stored in worker queue and child task is executed immediately. Parent-stealing approach is harder to implement as there's no portable way of storing processor state but the queues of lesser size can be used. Parent-stealing can be found in Intel/MIT Cilk which is implement as a part of compiler and child-stealing can be found in, for example, Intel TBB which is a shared library. Our implementation also adopts child-stealing.

We have implemented work-stealing scheduler as a C++11 library, so unlike MIT/Intel Cilk and OpenMP it does not rely heavily on a compiler and can be used in any environment with C++11 threads support. The closest well-known scheduler implementation to ours is the one in Intel TBB library (v2017.7) as it's a C++ library and it also adopts child-stealing strategy which makes it a good candidate for comparison, but the key difference is that it relies on general-purpose memory allocators.

5   Evaluation

We used a server that has two 2 Intel Xeon E5 v4 to evaluate and compare our work-stealing scheduler implementation to others. Each processor has 32K L1i and L2d, 256K L2 and 35 Mb L3 cache, 14 cores and 2 threads per core. Each scheduler was compiled with the same compiler (g++ v7.2) and the same optimization level (-O3).

Table 1. Benchmarks used for evaluation.

Name	Dimensions	Description
fib	42	Fibonacci number calculation recurrence formula
dfs	9^9	Depth first search of a balanced tree
matmul	3500×3500	Cache-aware square matrix multiplication
blkmul	4096×4096	Square block matrix multiplication

In order to evaluate the performance we have used benchmarks described in Table 1. We implemented these benchmarks for each task scheduler so that all of them execute exactly the same tasks with the only difference for scheduler initialization and tasks creation. Sequential versions with similar task graph structures has also been implemented. matmul and blkmul benchmarks were adopted from Cilk package examples. As different schedulers create threads of executions at different stages we have included scheduler initialization and termination stages for evaluating total execution time. Each benchmark was executed at least 6 times and execution times were averaged out.

fib and dfs benchmarks have relatively small tasks and the majority of CPU time is spend executing the scheduler code. On contrary, blkmul and matmul benchmarks require more time to execute their tasks than the scheduler code. This can be seen when comparing the execution times of sequential versions with the parallel one, fib and dfs are far more efficient without a scheduler. This, in turn, means that fib and dfs are more suited for comparing the overheads of different schedulers. As our scheduler implementation attempts to reduce the overhead of internal data structures, its effect is almost unnoticeable for blkmul and matmul, which are besides being computation-heavy are also memory-bound tasks. We decided avoid using non deterministic tasks (e.g. backtracking, branch and bound method) for benchmarking as they have very large samples variance.

Figure 4 shows that the maximum speedup of 3.5 and 2.6 has been achieved in fib and dfs benchmarks compared to its closest relative Intel TBB scheduler. blkmul, matmul benchmarks the time difference is not so noticeable for the reasons described above. When scaled to a larger number of threads (Fig. 6), one can notice almost smooth exponential decrease of execution times. Figure 5 also shows that LLC misses have reduced significantly in fib and dfs benchmarks while they were not affected in blkmul and matmul benchmarks.

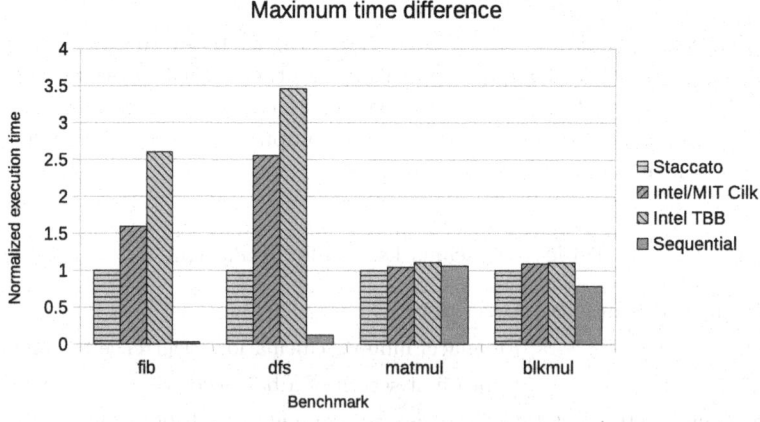

Fig. 4. Normalized maximum execution time difference of different benchmarks. Where our proposed scheduler implementation (staccato) considered as 1.

6   Related Works

Many studies have been done to improve work-stealing performance. They can be characterized into the following categories. At first, there are works dedicated to adapting work stealing schedulers for different hardware architectures,

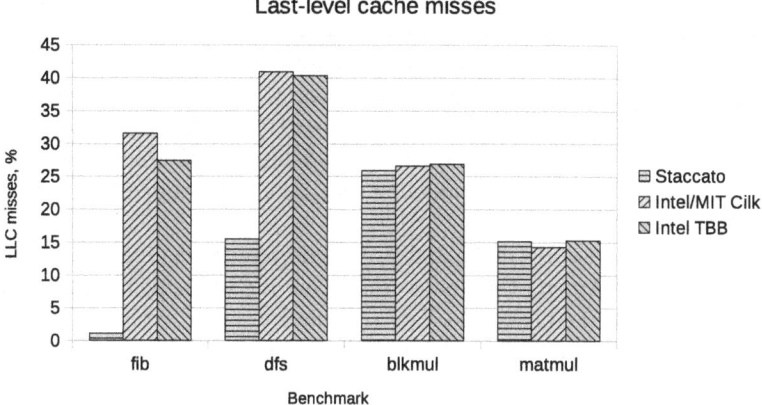

Fig. 5. Percentage of LLC misses from total number of LLC operations (loads and stores).

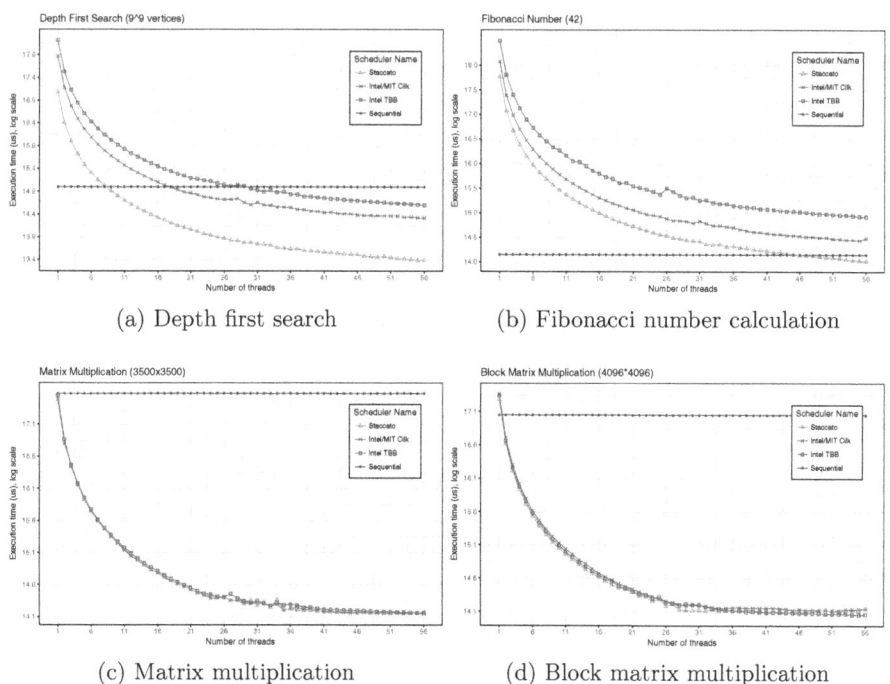

(a) Depth first search   (b) Fibonacci number calculation

(c) Matrix multiplication   (d) Block matrix multiplication

Fig. 6. Benchmarks execution time (log scale) vs. the number of threads of Staccato, Intel/MIT Cilk and Intel TBB schedulers and sequential version.

e.g. many-core systems [16], weak-memory architectures [20], NUMA architectures [21–23]. Then, different stealing strategies has been suggested, in particular steal-half strategy [5], when a half of victim tasks is transferred per single steal operation, and there's also our paper on stealing specific amount of tasks per single steal [13]. Also, there are numerous theoretical works has been done, for example, work stealing scheduler modeling using Markov-chains [10] or differential equations [11]. The later also covers modeling of different stealing strategies. There's also our papers on modeling scheduler behaviour based on random walks [12].

There are multiple works dedicated to changing work-stealing scheduler internal data structures. Among the first works, there are implementations based on fixed-size arrays [6], doubly-linked lists [18], and circular arrays [19]. Staccato internal data structure unites two last approaches into one and at the same time reduces the overhead of linked lists and allows to keep tasks objects in circular arrays during their execution which was not possible in other implementations. Completely different approach was implemented in state-of-art Intel/MIT Cilk scheduler of so-called cactus stack which redefines conventional linear stack per se. Unlike Intel/MIT Cilk out implementation do not require compiler- and hardware- features and it's implemented as template library, but still shows better results at some benchmarks.

7   Conclusion

Work-stealing scheduler internal data structures are build with an assumption that tasks pointers are stored inside of them and they are removed when the task is being executed. Taks object, in turn, should be stored in the heap memory, which brings, first, allocator-related overhead, and, second, an increase of cache misses. In this paper we've proposed to modify work-stealing deque so that tasks object can be stored inside of it. To achieve that, we've used a linked list of circular array deques, and have coupled it with LIFO based memory allocator which has lowes overhead possible and allocates objects in adjacent memory regions. The only drawback of this approach is that the maximum number of subtasks must be known at the compilation time, but for majority of tasks it's not an issue, and we plan to mitigate it in future versions. We've implemented this approach in our own scheduler. As benchmarks show, the maximum speedup of more than 2.5 times and LLC cache-miss 30% decrease have been achieved on CPU-bound tests compared to Intel TBB and Intel/MIT Cilk schedulers. At the same time, the performance of memory-bound tasks did not suffer.

Acknowledgements. Research has been supported by the RFBR grants No. 18-01-00125-a and 16-07-01111.

References

1. Kwok, Y.-K., Ahmad, I.: Static scheduling algorithms for allocating directed task graphs to multiprocessors. ACM Comput. Surv. **31**(4) (1999). https://doi.org/10.1145/344588.344618
2. Beaumont, O., Carter, L., Ferrante, J., Legrand, A., Marchal, L., Robert, Y.: Centralized versus distributed schedulers for multiple bag-of-task applications. In: 20th IEEE International Parallel & Distributed Processing Symposium (2006). https://doi.org/10.1109/IPDPS.2006.1639262
3. Hendler, D., Shavit, N.: Work dealing (extended abstract). In: Proceedings of the Fourteenth Annual ACM Symposium on Parallel Algorithms and Architectures, SPAA 2002, pp. 164–172 (2002). https://doi.org/10.1145/564870.564900
4. Acar, U.A., Chargueraud, A., Rainey, M.: Scheduling parallel programs by work stealing with private deques. In: PPoPP 2013, pp. 219–228. ACM, New York (2013). https://doi.org/10.1145/2442516.2442538
5. Hendler, D., Shavit, N.: Non-blocking steal-half work queues. In: Proceedings of the Twenty-First Annual Symposium on Principles of Distributed Computing, pp. 280–289. https://doi.org/10.1145/571825.571876
6. Arora, N.S., Blumofe, R.D., Plaxton, C.G.: Thread scheduling for multiprogrammed multiprocessors. In: Annual ACM Symposium on Parallel Algorithms and Architectures, pp. 119–129 (1998)
7. Blumofe, R.D., Leiserson, C.E.: Scheduling multithreaded computations by work stealing. In: Annual ACM Symposium on Parallel Algorithms and Architectures, pp. 119–129 (1999)
8. Reinders, J.: Intel Threading Building Blocks. O'Reilly & Associates Inc., Sebastopol (2007)
9. Duffy, J.: Concurrent Programming on Windows. Addison-Wesley, Upper Saddle River (2008)
10. Berenbrink, P., Friedetzky, T., Goldberg, L.A.: The natural work-stealing algorithm is stable. In: Proceedings of 42nd IEEE Symposium on Foundations of Computer Science, pp. 1260–1279 (2001). https://doi.org/10.1137/S0097539701399551
11. Mitzenmacher, M.: Analyses of load stealing models based on differential equations. In: SPAA 1998 Proceedings of the Tenth Annual ACM Symposium on Parallel Algorithms and Architectures
12. Aksenova, E.A., Sokolov, A.V.: Modeling of the memory management process for dynamic work-stealing schedulers. In: Ivannikov ISPRAS Open Conference (ISPRAS), Moscow, pp. 12–15 (2017). https://doi.org/10.1109/ISPRAS.2017.00009
13. Kuchumov, R.I.: Implementation and analysis of work-stealing task scheduler. Stochastic Optim. Comput. Sci. **12**, 20–39 (2016)
14. Peierls, T., Bloch, J., Bowbeer, J., Lea, D., Holmes, D.: Java Concurrency in Practice. Addison-Wesley Professional, Reading (2006)
15. Charles, P., Grothoff, C., Saraswat, V., Donawa, C., Kielstra, A., Ebcioglu, K., von Praun, C., Sarkar, V.: X10: an object-oriented approach to non-uniform cluster computing. In: Proceedings of the 20th Annual ACM SIGPLAN Conference on Object Oriented Programming, Systems, Languages, and Applications, pp. 519–538 (2005). https://doi.org/10.1145/1094811.1094852
16. Guo, Y.: A scalable locality-aware adaptive work-stealing scheduler for multi-core task parallelism. Rice University Houston, TX, USA (2010)
17. Robison, A.: A primer on scheduling fork-join parallelism with work stealing (2014)

18. Hendler, D., Lev, Y., Moir, M., Shavit, N.: A dynamic-sized nonblocking work stealing deque. Distrib. Comput. **18**(3), 189–207 (2005)
19. Chase, D., Lev Y.: Dynamic circular work-stealing deque. In: SPAA 2005 Proceedings of the Seventeenth Annual ACM Symposium on Parallelism in Algorithms and Architectures, pp. 21–28 (2005). https://doi.org/10.1145/1073970.1073974
20. Le, N.M., Pop, A., Cohen, A., Nardelli, F.Z.: Correct and efficient work-stealing for weak memory models. In: PPoPP 2013 Proceedings of the 18th ACM SIGPLAN symposium on Principles and Practice of Parallel Programming, pp. 69–80 (2013). https://doi.org/10.1145/2442516.2442524
21. Chen, Q., Guo, M., Guan, H.: LAWS: Locality-aware work-stealing for multi-socket multi-core architectures. In: ICS 2014 Proceedings of the 28th ACM International Conference on Supercomputing (2014). https://doi.org/10.1145/2597652.2597665
22. Chen, Q., Guo, M.: Contention and locality-aware work-stealing for iterative applications in multi-socket computers. IEEE Trans. Comput. https://doi.org/10.1109/TC.2017.2783932
23. Wang, K., Zhou, X., Li, T., Zhao, D., Lang, M., Raicu, I.: Optimizing load balancing and data-locality with data-aware scheduling In.: 2014 IEEE International Conference on Big Data (Big Data). https://doi.org/10.1109/BigData.2014.7004220
24. Armbrust, M., Fox, A., Griffith, R., Joseph A.D., Katz, R., Konwinski, A., Lee, G., Patterson, D., Rabkin, A., Stoica, I., Zaharia, M.: A view of cloud computing. Commun. ACM **53**(4), 50–58 (2010). https://doi.org/10.1145/1721654.1721672

Design and Implementation of a Service for Cloud HPC Computations

Ruslan Kuchumov[1], Vadim Petrunin[1], Vladimir Korkhov[1(✉)],
Nikita Balashov[2], Nikolay Kutovskiy[2], and Ivan Sokolov[2]

[1] Saint Petersburg State University,
7/9 Universitetskaya nab., St. Petersburg 199034, Russia
kuchumovri@gmail.com, petrunin-vn@yandex.ru, v.korkhov@spbu.ru
[2] Joint Institute for Nuclear Research, Dubna, Russia
{balashov,kut,isokolov}@jinr.ru

Abstract. Cloud computing became a routine tool for scientists in many domains. In order to speed up an achievement of scientific results a cloud service for execution of distributed applications was developed. It obliviates users from manually creating virtual cluster environment or using batch scheduler and allows them only to specify input parameters to perform their computations. This service, in turn, deploys virtual cluster, executes supplied job and uploads its results to user's cloud storage. It consists of several components and implements flexible and modular architecture which allows to add on one side more applications and on another side various types of resources as a computational backends as well as to increase a utilization of cloud idle resources.

Keywords: Cloud computing · High performance computing
Software as a service

1 Introduction

At the moment a great number of large scale data processing centers are created worldwide including different scientific and commercial organizations. The majority of them deploy their own private cloud environments for hosting services and performing computations. The advantages of using cloud computing has been discussed many times, for example, paper [1] gives a good survey on this topic. From our point of view, the main benefit of using cloud computing is its flexible architecture and the ability to reduce the maintenance cost of computational infrastructure.

The growth of cloud computing has also led to the changes in scientific computations: it enabled scientists and researchers to launch high-performance applications without having computing infrastructure at their disposal. One of key factors in this case may be cloud computing pay-as-you-go financial model, when the user pays only for the resources he uses. Through the use of this model,

O. Gervasi et al. (Eds.): ICCSA 2018, LNCS 10963, pp. 103–112, 2018.
https://doi.org/10.1007/978-3-319-95171-3_9

renting virtual cloud resources only to execute a specific application is often more beneficial than to purchase, maintain and upgrade hardware at site. In addition to lower cost, clouds provide flexibility to choose both hardware and software components, which is not usually the case for traditional physical infrastructures where horizontal and vertical scaling are done by upgrading the hardware. So, the main advantages of using cloud infrastructure for scientific computing are flexibility, low cost of maintenance, and scalability.

Distributed computing paradigms can be characterized into high-performance computing (HPC), high-throughput computing (HTC) and many-task computing (MTC) which are usually distinguishes by the measure of computational tasks interconnect and task execution time [2]. In HPC applications the tasks are tightly-coupled and require large amount of computing power over a short period of time (hours or days). On contrary, HTC targets long running applications (for month or years) consisting of loosely-coupled tasks. MTC paradigm bridges gap between HTC and HPC. MTC applications can be distinguished by a very large number of tasks with relatively short per task execution time and they usually rely on disk I/O throughput rather than network throughput.

In previous research [3,4] we examined how flexible configuration of virtualized computing and networking resources can influence application performance and enable multi-tenancy with minimal mutual impact of simultaneously running parallel applications; in [5] we focused on Hadoop deployment and execution in virtual container-based clusters and investigated the dependency of Hadoop benchmarking suite performance on resource restrictions and other simultaneously running applications.

In this paper we are focusing on HPC applications for scientific computations where the most common workflow consists of the following stages. At first, a group of scientists needs to perform computations, for example, to do modelling, then the application for this purpose is being developed by their own effort or by separate team of developers, then this application is being ported to and executed in cluster environment. The same version of a application is usually executed many times with different input parameters or input datasets. When operating in a cloud environment, for each user or an application a new virtual cluster has to be created and configured either by users themself or by system administrators. In both cases it leads to delays in the achievement of scientific results and unnecessary complications.

What makes matter worse, is the problem that these scientists do not have and shouldn't have enough experience or knowledge on how to prepare their task for execution, how to operate cluster schedulers using command line interface and especially on how to configure a virtual cluster. Instead of all these concerns, they would prefer to focus on the problems in their scientific field and leave these that to system administrators.

To solve these problems a cloud service denoted as IdleUtilizer for helping users to perform HPC computations in a cloud environment was created. It provides users with a web interface that allows them to specify input parameters of their application, submit it for execution and receive its output when it's finished. When an application is submitted, this service will deploy a new virtual cluster in a cloud, configure it, prepare and execute user's application and then upload its results to user shared cloud data storage. The details of cluster configuration, its deployment and bootstrapping process are all hidden from the user. System administrator help is only may be required to add a new application to the system and for service maintenance.

Because of service's flexible architecture, IdleUtilizer provides users with a common interface for executing their job on different computational backends. Among them are different cloud providers (e.g. OpenNebula and OpenStack) and batch schedulers (e.g. Slurm) of a physical cluster.

2   Related Works

There are several works attempting to create web interfaces for batch schedulers, for example, there are implementations for HTCondor scheduler [6] or PBS scheduler [7]. The key difference is that our approach can be described as a common denominator across different schedulers where the user has ability only to specify input parameters of his application and where to perform computations, while scheduler-specific parameters, such as job file or input and output paths, are hidden from the user.

There are also systems for managing virtual clusters. "Virtual Cluster as a Service" [8] allows users to create a virtual cluster in OpenNebula cloud with preconfigured images, and to submit their jobs to this cluster. When user job is completed he or she may restart it with other input parameters or delete the cluster. "Dynamic Virtual Cluster" [9] is a similar system that allows to create a virtual cluster and then submit users jobs, but instead of accessing a cloud provides, it uses Xen hypervisor directly and deploys Moab scheduler for launching user jobs. In "Virtual Organization Cluster" [10] the system automatically creates a virtual cluster exclusively to execute the jobs coming from the grid. Similar to these approaches, we also create a virtual cluster for executing user jobs, but we also offer some flexibility in turns of choosing computational backends. Users can decide where to execute their tasks, he or she can choose different cloud providers or to execute the job in a physical scheduler. Related issues of adaptation and deployment of a task management system for a private cloud infrastructure and modelling of message passing middleware in cloud computing environments is considered in [11,12].

There are also works with similar goals as ours. HPCaaS [13] and Uncinus [14] allow users to run their applications in a cloud based on SaaS model. While the purpose is the same, its implementation differs. In these works, users must create virtual machine image for each application which would be used for deploying a cluster. This would not work in our approach as we are using physical clusters along with virtual and rely on batch schedulers to distribute users jobs. Besides that we could not find any similar systems available for deployment.

3   Design and Implementation

Figure 1 shows high level overview of Idle-Utilizer service architecture. It consists of three main components. At first, there is a web interface that is used by end-users for configuring and submitting jobs and monitoring their statuses. Web interface communicates only with the seconds component, idle-utilizer service. The main responsibilities of this service are to configure computational backend environment, to prepare, execute and monitor user's job, and to send the results back to the user. The third component is computational backed. In case the users prefers to do computation in a cloud, the cloud provider is accessed for deploying virtual cluster specifically for executing his job, and in case of the batch scheduler backend, the job would be created and submitted to the scheduler.

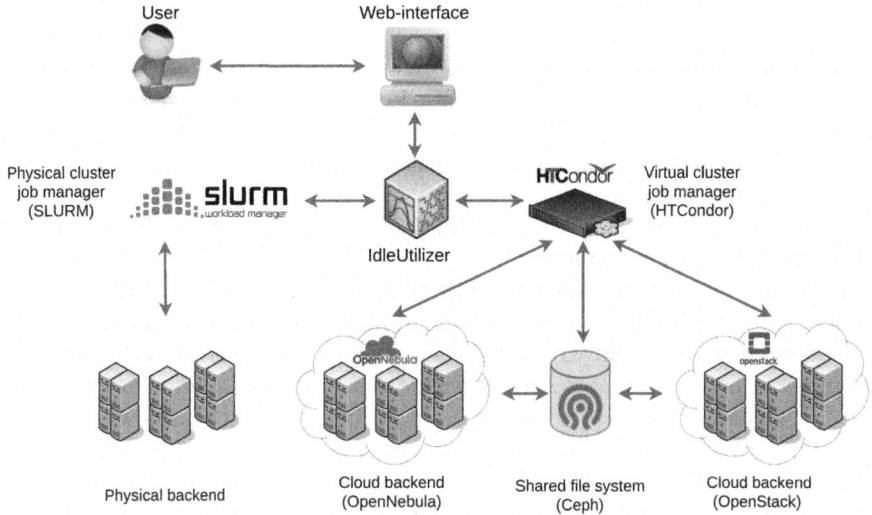

Fig. 1. Idle-Utilizer high-level architecture.

The web interface component and users scenarios are covered in [15]. From IdleUtilizer point of view, the interactions are done through the request protocol defined over XML-RPC (remote procedure calls). Among the supported procedures are mainly the ones for submitting a new request, obtaining its state and deleting it. When submitted, request specifies such parameters as user job resources demand (number of nodes, CPUs, memory and time), task template and job input parameters, it also specifies which computational backend to use and where and how to upload job results. As request processing advances, additional information such as cluster configuration and batch scheduler status are stored in the request and is available for RPC client.

The Idle-Utilizer service is a core component as it is responsible for handling RPC request, orchestrating virtual cluster environment, submitting and monitoring jobs statuses in batch scheduler and uploading their results to user shared directory. This service has its own database for holding active requests. With a specific interval (2 s) it updates each request by changing its state as depicted in Fig. 2 In case an error occurs in any of the transitions between states, its message is stored in the database and can be reported to the user. Before and after each stage and on error custom scripts (so called hooks) can be executed e.g. for benchmarking, creating job-specific files or error reporting, but they usually hidden from end-users.

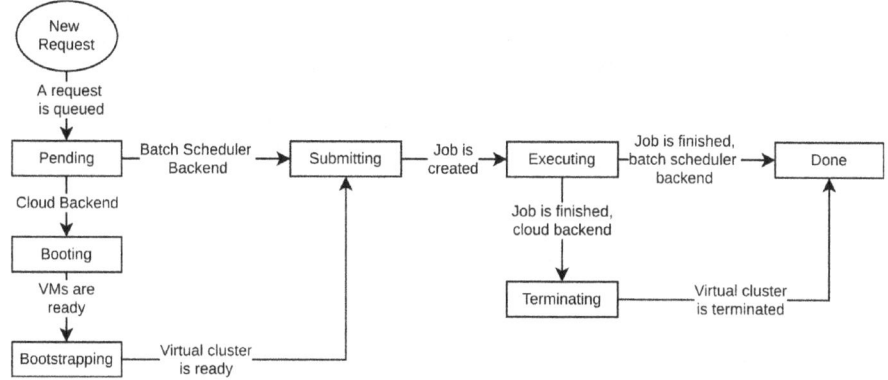

Fig. 2. Request states transitions.

As soon as the request is received it starts transitioning from pending to done (Fig. 2). In pending state virtual machines are requested to spawn, or in case of physical cluster backend, it transitions to submitting state. When virtual machines have started (booting stage), they autostart HTCondor software and add themselves into HTCondor pool (bootstrapping stage). During submitting stage (Fig. 3), job file is created and submitted to the scheduler. When the job is finished (after executing stage), virtual cluster is terminated and the request is considered to be done.

The computational backend is specified in users' request. Right now OpenNebula cloud and Slurm batch scheduler are supported. If batch scheduler backend is specified, request handling process is straightforward as IdleUtilizer mainly serves as an interface for a scheduler.

In case of a cloud backend, a new virtual cluster is deployed for executing user job. Each node of a virtual cluster is created from the same template and the same image, they only may differ by the amount of memory and the number of CPU cores. HTCondor scheduler software is installed in virtutal machine image and it is configured to automatically register itself in the pool of HTCondor scheduler. HTCondor scheduler is only used for assigning jobs for execution to a virtual cluster. Although the architecture can be simplified by omitting HTCondor scheduler, we decided to keep it for its simplicity of managing user jobs compared to manual approach and for consistency with physical cluster environment.

```
{
            'status': 'submitting',
            'status_updated_at': 1512462493,
            'resources': {
                    'nodes': 2, 'memory': 4096, 'cpu': 4, 'time': 100},
            'scheduler': {
                    'name': 'htcondor',
                    'hosts': [ 'host-100', 'host-101' ]},
            'backend': {
                    'name': 'opennebula',
                    'owner': {'gid': 1, 'uid': 196},
                    'hosts': [
                            { 'id': 100, 'ip': '10.10.0.100' },
                            { 'id': 101, 'ip': '10.10.0.101' }]},
            'template': '....',
            'user_data': {
                    'key1': 'value1',
                    # Job parametres
            },
}
```

Fig. 3. An example of request fields at submitting stage.

Similar to physical cluster environment, the nodes of virtual cluster have shared file system mounted for executing distributed applications and exchanging job input and output files.

Before the job is executed, user's custom scripts in scheduler manager node can be executed for obtaining input files either by generating them from job request value or by downloading them from remote location. When the job is finished its output is uploaded to user's cloud storage directory.

4   Experiments

In our experiment we used NAS Parallel Benchmarks (NPB) which consists of several widely used set of programs designed to evaluate the performance of HPC systems. The benchmarks is a set of five kernels program and three pseudo-applications that mimic scientific computations. Problem sizes in NPB are predefined and indicated as different classes. We used MG, FT, CG and IS kernels of A, B and C classes:

- IS (Integer Sort): sorts small integers using the bucket sort. This test is CPU and Memory intensive but with low inter-node communications.
- CG (Conjugate Gradient): calculates conjugate gradient method. This test is both memory- and communication-intensive.

- MG (Multi-Grid): solves discrete Poisson equation using multi-grid method. This test is both memory- and communication-intensive.
- FT (Fourier Transform): solves three-dimensional partial differential equation using the fast Fourier transform. This benchmarks tests inter-node all-to-all communications.

For a testbed we used OpenNebula cloud with KVM hypervisor provided by JINR [16].

Experiments showcasing low overhead of virtualization for HPC applications have been done many times by different authors [8,17]. Instead, in experiments, we tried to justify the need for automatic virtual cluster configuration depending on job input parameters. There are two values that should be minimized: the size of virtual cluster (the number of virtual machines and their memory requirements) and job execution time. Figure 4 shows that for each benchmark the minimal amount of memory can be set without sacrificing the performance. Also Fig. 5 shows that by increasing the number of virtual machines from 4 to 8 in some cases (especially in cg and mg) yields the performance increase significantly less in comparison with 2 to 4. In other experiments (Fig. 6) we have throttled network bandwidth to show that in some hardware configurations there may be peaks of performance at the certain number of nodes, and when this number increases further, job performance degrade drastically. This can be noticed with network bandwidth of 50 Mbits/s, when the optimal number of nudes is 2 or 4.

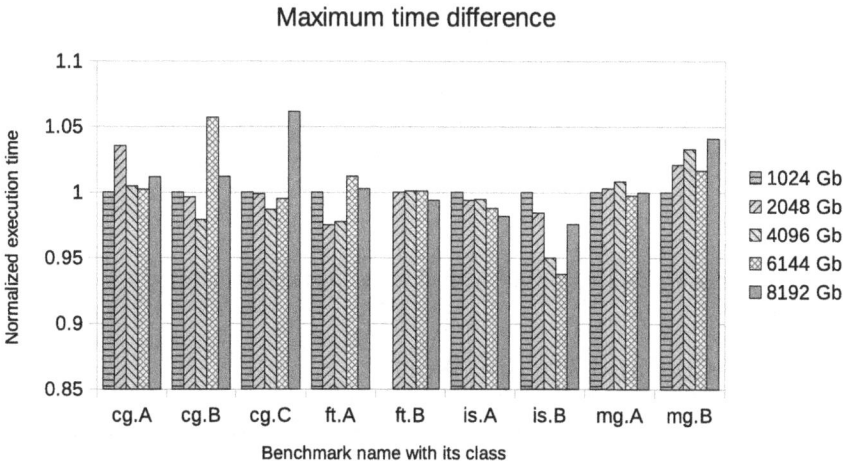

Fig. 4. The maximum of normalized benchmark execution time for different amounts of memory. Execution time with 1024 Gb considered as 1.

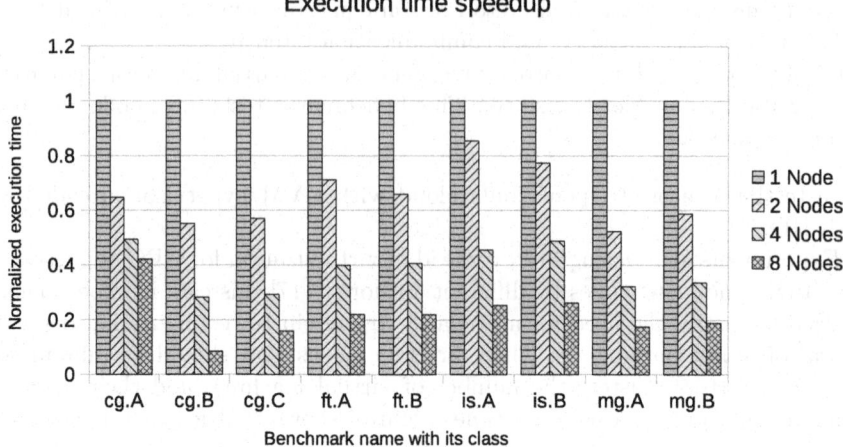

Fig. 5. Execution time speedup of different number of nodes.

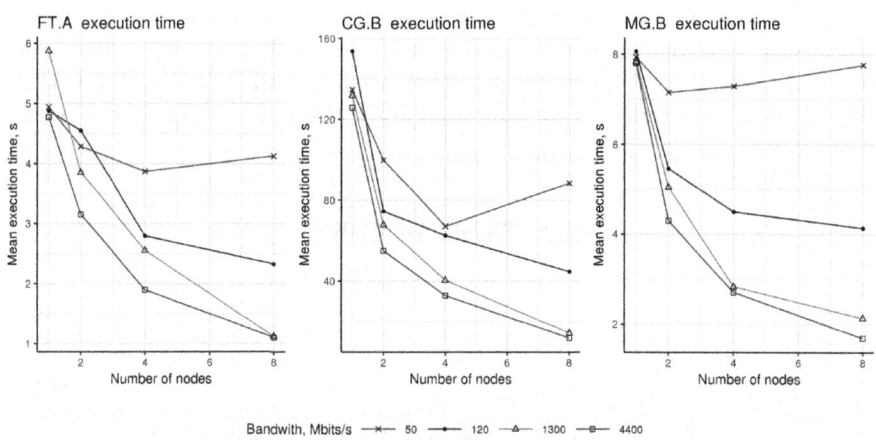

Fig. 6. Execution time with throttled network bandwidth.

5   Conclusion and Future Works

We have created a software-as-a-service system for launching HPC applications. IdleUtilizer service allows users to execute their jobs by only specifying input parameters via web interface and then to obtain the results via their cloud storage. To achieve this, IdleUtilizer service creates a virtual cluster in a cloud, creates and submits the job for execution on this cluster and, when it's done, transfers results to user. Besides the cloud environment, user jobs can also be submitted for execution to the scheduler of physical HPC cluster.

The primary goal of this service is to simplify the workflow of HPC application execution for scientists. IdleUtilizer service has already been deployed in JINR cloud [16] and used with long Josephson junction modelling application [18].

In the current version, users still have to make decision on a cluster configuration, i.e. he or she needs to know job resource requirements to specify the number of nodes, the amount of memory and CPUs per node. Finding these values for each set of application parametres sometimes may be rather tedious. But, as our experiments have shown, it may help to reduce not only the job execution time, but also job unused resources. To simplify this process we are planning to extend the functionality of IdleUtilizer service so that before every execution, it will analyze the information about previous job executions and then hint user an optimal cluster configuration.

Acknowledgements. Research has been supported by the RFBR grant 16-07-01111.

References

1. Armbrust, M., Fox, A., Griffith, R., Joseph A.D., Katz, R., Konwinski, A., Lee, G., Patterson, D., Rabkin, A., Stoica, I., Zaharia, M.: A view of cloud computing. Commun. ACM **53**(4), 50–58 (2010). https://doi.org/10.1145/1721654.1721672
2. Shawish, A., Salama, M.: Cloud computing: paradigms and technologies. In: Xhafa, F., Bessis, N. (eds.) Inter-cooperative Collective Intelligence: Techniques and Applications, Studies in Computational Intelligence, vol. 495. Springer, Heidelberg (2014). https://doi.org/10.1007/978-3-642-35016-0_2
3. Korkhov, V., Kobyshev, S., Krosheninnikov, A.: Flexible configuration of application-centric virtualized computing infrastructure. In: Gervasi, O., et al. (eds.) ICCSA 2015. LNCS, vol. 9158, pp. 342–353. Springer, Cham (2015). https://doi.org/10.1007/978-3-319-21410-8_27
4. Korkhov, V., Kobyshev, S., Krosheninnikov, A., Degtyarev, A., Bogdanov, A.: Distributed computing infrastructure based on dynamic container clusters. In: Gervasi, O., et al. (eds.) ICCSA 2016. LNCS, vol. 9787, pp. 263–275. Springer, Cham (2016). https://doi.org/10.1007/978-3-319-42108-7_20
5. Korkhov, V., Kobyshev, S., Degtyarev, A., Bogdanov, A.: Light-weight cloud-based virtual computing infrastructure for distributed applications and hadoop clusters. In: Gervasi, O., et al. (eds.) ICCSA 2017. LNCS, vol. 10408, pp. 399–411. Springer, Cham (2017). https://doi.org/10.1007/978-3-319-62404-4_29
6. Chapman, C., Goonatilake, C., Emmerich, W., Farrellee, M., Tannenbaum, T., Livny, M., Calleja, M.: Condor Birdbath - web service interface to Condor. In: Cox, S.J., Walker, D.W., (eds.) Proceedings of the UK e-Science All Hands Meeting 2005, EPSRC: Swindon, UK (2005)
7. Ma, G., Lu, P.: PBSWeb: a web-based interface to the portable batch system. In: 12th IASTED International Conference on Parallel and Distributed Computing and Systems (PDCS), Las Vegas, NV, 6–9 November 2000. ACTA Press, Calgary (2000)
8. Doelitzscher, F., Held, M., Reich, C., Sulistio, A.: ViteraaS: virtual cluster as a service. In: 2011 IEEE Third International Conference on Coud Computing Technology and Science (CloudCom), pp. 652–657. https://doi.org/10.1109/CloudCom.2011.101

9. Emeneker, W., Jackson, D., Butikofer, J., Stanzione, D.: Dynamic virtual clustering with Xen and Moab. In: Min, G., Di Martino, B., Yang, L.T., Guo, M., Rünger, G. (eds.) ISPA 2006. LNCS, vol. 4331, pp. 440–451. Springer, Heidelberg (2006). https://doi.org/10.1007/11942634_46
10. Murphy, M.A., Kagey, B., Fenn, M., Goasguen, S.: Dynamic provisioning of virtual organization clusters. In: CCGRID 2009 Proceedings of the 2009 9th IEEE/ACM International Symposium on Cluster Computing and the Grid, pp. 364–371. https://doi.org/10.1109/CCGRID.2009.37. ISBN 978-0-7695-3622-4
11. Iakushkin, O., Shichkina, Y., Sedova, O.: Petri Nets for modelling of message passing middleware in cloud computing environments. In: Gervasi, O., et al. (eds.) ICCSA 2016. LNCS, vol. 9787, pp. 390–402. Springer, Cham (2016). https://doi.org/10.1007/978-3-319-42108-7_30
12. Iakushkin, O., Malevanniy, D., Bogdanov, A., Sedova, O.: Adaptation and deployment of PanDA task management system for a private cloud infrastructure. In: Gervasi, O., et al. (eds.) ICCSA 2017. LNCS, vol. 10408, pp. 438–447. Springer, Cham (2017). https://doi.org/10.1007/978-3-319-62404-4_32
13. Church, P., Wong, A., Brock, M., Goscinski, A.: Toward exposing and accessing HPC applications in a SaaS cloud. In: IEEE 19th International Conference on Web Services, Honolulu, HI, pp. 692–699 (2012). https://doi.org/10.1109/ICWS.2012.119
14. Church, P., Goscinski, A., Tari, Z.: SaaS clouds supporting non computing specialists. In: 11th International Conference on Computer Systems and Applications (AICCSA), Doha, pp. 1–8 (2014). https://doi.org/10.1109/AICCSA.2014.7073171
15. Balashov, N.A., Bashashin, M.V., Kuchumov, R.I., Kutovskiy, N.A., Sokolov, I.A.: JINR cloud service for scientific and engineering computations. Mod. Inf. Technol. IT Educ. 14(1) (2018). https://doi.org/10.25559/SITITO.14.201801.061-072
16. Baranov, A.V., Balashov, N.A., Kutovskiy, N.A., Semenov, R.N.: JINR cloud infrastructure evolution. Phys. Part. Nuclei Lett. 13, 672–675 (2016). https://doi.org/10.1134/S1547477116050071
17. Menon, A., Santos, J.R., Turner, Y., Janakiraman, G.J., Zwaenepoel, W.: Diagnosing performance overheads in the XEN virtual machine environment. In: VEE 2005, Proceedings of the 1st ACM/USENIX international conference on Virtual execution environments, pp. 13–23, New York, NY, USA (2005)
18. Bashashin, M.V., et al.: Numerical approach and parallel implementation for computer simulation of stacked long Josephson junctions. Comput. Res. Model. 8(4), 593–604 (2016)

Porting the Algorithm for Calculating an Asian Option to a New Processing Architecture

Eduard Stepanov$^{(\boxtimes)}$, Dmitry Khmel$^{(\boxtimes)}$, Vladimir Mareev$^{(\boxtimes)}$,
Nikita Storublevtcev$^{(\boxtimes)}$, and Alexander Bogdanov$^{(\boxtimes)}$

Saint Petersburg State University,
7/9 Universitetskaya nab., St. Petersburg 199034, Russia
`e.an.stepanov@gmail.com`, `dskhmel@cc.spbu.ru`, {`map,bogdanov`}`@csa.ru`,
`100.rub@mail.ru`

Abstract. This article describes some numerical approaches for solving the problem of pricing derivatives. These approaches are based on the Monte Carlo and finite difference methods. A number of techniques are given that provide a possibility to optimize the computational algorithms for their use on graphics processors. A software and hardware complex is also described that allows to increase the efficiency of calculations.

Keywords: GPGPU · Option pricing · Finite difference methods
Monte Carlo method

1 Introduction

With the growth of the derivatives market, the task of quick calculating their prices becomes more urgent. Today for modeling the dynamics of price change prevalent models that are based on stochastic differential equations, partial differential equations or the path integral. In most cases, within the framework of these models, it is not possible to obtain a solution in an analytical form. For this reason, various numerical approaches are used. The most popular among them is the Monte Carlo and finite-difference methods.

In the study of the effectiveness of various approaches, the question arises of optimizing computations at the software, algorithmic and hardware level. Some results on optimization of computational algorithms were presented in [1]. This article discusses the issues related to the optimal use of computing powers available on the market.

The numerical approaches used can be effectively divided to many simpler tasks that require much less computer powers. For such algorithms, it is advisable to use graphics processors. In this article CUDA technology was chosen for testing purposes. The calculations themselves were made for the Asian option type.

© Springer International Publishing AG, part of Springer Nature 2018
O. Gervasi et al. (Eds.): ICCSA 2018, LNCS 10963, pp. 113–122, 2018.
https://doi.org/10.1007/978-3-319-95171-3_10

2   Brief Introduction to CUDA

CUDA (Compute Unified Device Architecture) is a software model that includes the description of computational parallelism and the hierarchical structure of memory directly into the programming language. The concept of CUDA assigns the role of a massively parallel coprocessor. CUDA-program uses both CPU and GPU, the CPU performs a sequential part of the code and preparatory stages for GPU-calculations. Parallel sections of the code can be transferred to the GPU, where they will be simultaneously executed by a large number of threads. It is important to note a number of fundamental differences between conventional CPU threads and GPU threads.

1. The GPU thread is extremely lightweight, its context is minimal, the registers are distributed in advance.
2. To effectively use the GPU resources, the program needs to use thousands of separate threads, while on a multi-core CPU the maximum efficiency is usually achieved with a number of threads equal to or several times larger than the number of cores.

This technology has the following advantages.

- The CUDA application programming interface (CUDA API) is based on the standard C programming language with some limitations. This simplifies and smoothes the process of studying the architecture of CUDA.
- A shared memory of 16 KB in size can be used for a user-organized cache with a wider bandwidth than when fetching from conventional textures.
- More efficient transactions between CPU memory and video memory.
- Full hardware support for integer and bitwise operations.

A number of features of the new versions of CUDA show a tendency to gradually transform the GPU into a self-sufficient device that completely replaces the normal CPU due to the implementation of some system calls.

3   Mathematical Models

The following notations are used in the paper:

S — the price of the underlying asset,
r — risk-free interest rate,
K — strike price,
σ — volatility,
t — time, $t \in [0, T]$,
C — option price.

The price of the underlying asset is described by a stochastic differential equation of the form [2]:

$$dS(t) = rS(t)dt + \sigma S(t)dB(t), \tag{1}$$

where $B(t)$ is the standard Wiener process.

The following partial differential equation describing the dynamics of the price change of Asian option can be obtained from this equation [3,4]:

$$\frac{\partial C(S, I, t)}{\partial \tau} - S\frac{\partial C}{\partial I} - \frac{1}{2}\sigma^2 S^2 \frac{\partial^2 C}{\partial S^2} - rS\frac{\partial C}{\partial S} + rC = 0, \tag{2a}$$

$$C(S, I, 0) = \max\left\{\frac{I}{T} - K, 0\right\}, \tag{2b}$$

$$C(0, I, \tau) = e^{-r\tau}\max\left(\frac{I}{T} - K, 0\right), \tag{2c}$$

$$C(S, I_{\max}, \tau) = e^{-r\tau}\max\left(\frac{I_{\max}}{T} - K, 0\right) + \frac{S}{rT}(1 - e^{-r\tau}), \tag{2d}$$

$$C(S_{\max}, I, \tau) = \max\left\{e^{-r\tau}\left(\frac{I}{T} - K, 0\right) + \frac{S_{\max}}{rT}(1 - e^{-r\tau}), 0\right\}, \tag{2e}$$

$$\frac{\partial C}{\partial I}(S, 0, \tau) = 0, \tag{2f}$$

where $C = C(S, I, t)$, $\tau = T - t$, $I = \int_0^T S(\tau)d\tau$, $I \in [0, I_{\max}]$.

Option price can also be described by the following equation [5,6]:

$$C(S_0, 0) \approx e^{-rT}\int_{-\infty}^{+\infty} dx_N \ldots dx_1 \left(\frac{1}{2\pi\sigma^2\Delta t}\right)^{N/2}$$

$$\times \exp\left\{-\sum_{n=1}^{N}\frac{1}{2\sigma^2\Delta t}[x_n - (x_{n-1} + \mu\Delta t)]^2\right\}$$

$$\times \max\left(\frac{\Delta t\sum_{n=1}^{N} G(x_n, x_{n-1}, \Delta t)}{T} - K, 0\right), \tag{3}$$

where

$$x(t) = \ln S(t), \quad \Delta x_n = x_n - x_{n-1},$$

$$G(x_n, x_{n-1}, \Delta t) = e^{x_n}\left(\frac{1}{\Delta x_n} + \frac{\sigma^2\Delta t}{2\Delta x_n^2} - \frac{\sigma^2\Delta t}{\Delta x_n^3}\right) + e^{x_{n-1}}\left(-\frac{1}{\Delta x_n} + \frac{\sigma^2\Delta t}{2\Delta x_n^2} + \frac{\sigma^2\Delta t}{\Delta x_n^3}\right).$$

4   Monte Carlo Method

To calculate the option price on the basis of Eqs. (1), (2) and (3) the Monte Carlo method was used. Numerical experiments for the Eq. (2) using the CPU showed a very slow convergence of the Monte Carlo method. For this reason, this case was excluded from further consideration.

Below are the main changes that were made for efficient parallelization of algorithms.

To find the option price using the stochastic differential Eq. (1) it is reduced to the form:

$$S_{t_{i+1}} = S_{t_i} \exp\left\{ \left(r - \frac{\sigma^2}{2}\right) \Delta t + \sigma\sqrt{\Delta t}\epsilon \right\}. \tag{4}$$

It shows that it is necessary to generate a set of values $S_0, S_{\Delta t}, S_{2\Delta t}, \ldots, S_T$. The dependence of these values negatively affects the speed of the parallel algorithm. To solve this problem, the last equation can be reduced to the form by means of algebraic transformations:

$$S_{(N+1)\Delta t} = S_0 \exp\left\{ \left(r - \frac{\sigma^2}{2}\right) \Delta t + \sigma\sqrt{\Delta t}\varepsilon_1 \right\} \times \ldots$$

$$\times \exp\left\{ \left(r - \frac{\sigma^2}{2}\right) \Delta t + \sigma\sqrt{\Delta t}\varepsilon_N \right\} \exp\left\{ \left(r - \frac{\sigma^2}{2}\right) \Delta t + \sigma\sqrt{\Delta t}\varepsilon_{N+1} \right\}.$$

Thus, it is sufficient to generate independent random variables ε_i, then apply the algorithm for calculating prefix sums relative to the multiplication operation.

A similar problem occurs with the Eq. (3). For using the Monte Carlo method for calculating the option price it is necessary to generate random values for the value x_n with the distribution function of the form:

$$f(x) = \exp\left\{ -\frac{1}{2\sigma^2\Delta t} \sum_{k=1}^{n+1} [x - (x_{k-1} + \mu\Delta t)]^2 \right\}.$$

To eliminate the dependence on x_{n-1} we note that

$$x_n = \xi_n \sigma\sqrt{\Delta t} + \left(r - \frac{\sigma^2}{2}\right) \Delta t + x_{n-1}, \quad \xi_n \in N(0,1).$$

This formula can be represented as:

$$x_n = \sigma\sqrt{\Delta t} \sum_{i=1}^{n} \xi_i + n \left(r - \frac{\sigma^2}{2}\right) \Delta t + x_0.$$

Putting the basic equation into a form where there are no dependencies, we get a typical problem for the GPU, based on obtaining a large number of realizations of the stochastic process. But, having a huge array of results for each of the processes, there appears the problem of finding their sum. For this purpose, you can use parallel reduction algorithms, which can also be performed on the GPU several times faster than on the CPU. At the same time, knowing the hierarchy of memory and the architecture of the GPU, you can speed up the parallel reduction algorithm several times more. So, for example, if the operation on the elements is simple, the main factor limiting performance will be access to memory. Efficiency can be increased by using shared memory for threads within one block. For more details, see [7].

An important factor in obtaining high performance on the GPU is the possibility of bypassing the "bottleneck" in the transmission of a large amount of data to the GPU memory. Random numbers for the Monte Carlo method generated directly on the device using a CURAND random number generator. This is a library optimized for generation of pseudo- and quasi-random numbers on the host and GPU with a period of 2^{67} [8].

The task of pricing the Asian option by the Monte Carlo method was launched on the following system:

```
CPU: 6 x Intel Xeon E5-2680 v3 2.50 GHz;
RAM: 128 GB;
GPU: NVidia Tesla M2050, NVidia Tesla K40, NVidia Tesla P100.
```

The main characteristics of this hardware are described in Appendix A.

The optimal accuracy of the Monte Carlo method is achieved by 1 million iterations.

	NVidia Tesla M2050	NVidia Tesla K40	NVidia Tesla P100	6 x Intel Xeon E5-2680 v3 (72 cores)
Time, seconds	0.034	0.029	0.025	4.63
Acceleration	136	160	185	1

The advantage of calculating this task on graphic cards is obvious. Not even the latest generation of GPUs show high performance, which means that the CUDA software and hardware model is ideal for tasks that are solved using the Monte Carlo method (Fig. 1).

Experiments were also carried out to scale the computations to several GPUs. The results are shown on Fig. 2.

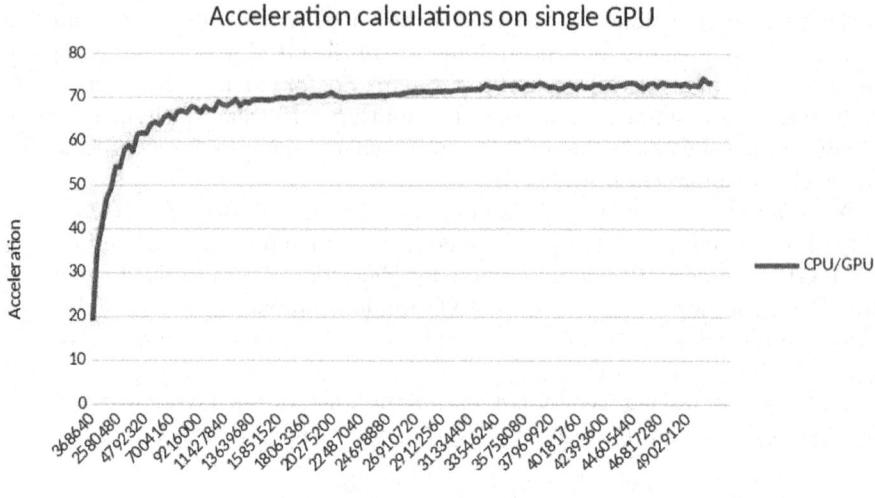

Fig. 1. Comparison graph of sequential and parallel algorithms for the calculation path integral using Monte Carlo method.

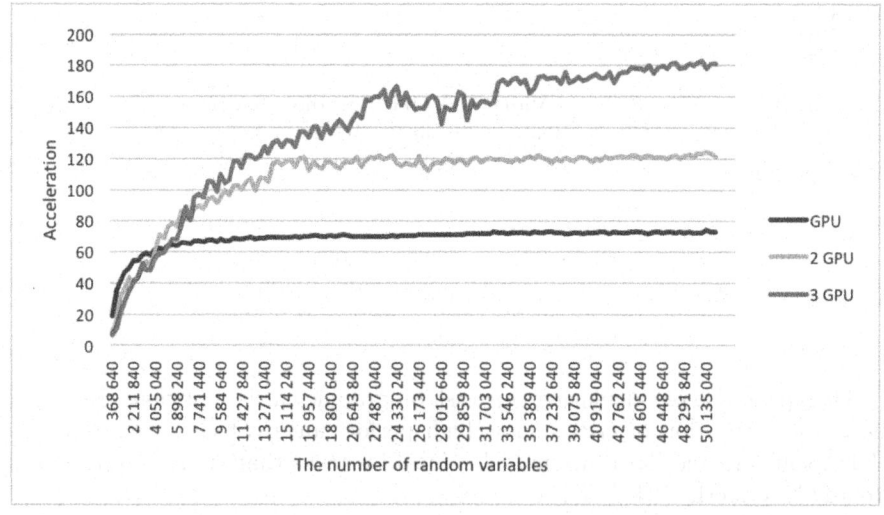

Fig. 2. Acceleration calculations on multiple GPUs

5   Finite Difference Method

The calculation of the partial differential Eq. (2) was also performed using an explicit finite-difference method with constant steps in time and spatial variables. This choice was made in view of the need to perform calculations with maximum speed. In addition, experiments have shown that an explicit method allows to achieve sufficient accuracy of calculations.

The finite-difference representation of the problem (2) is the following [9,10]:

$$C_{jk}^{n+1} = (1 - \Delta\tau\sigma^2 j^2 - r\Delta\tau)C_{jk}^n + \left(\frac{\Delta\tau\sigma^2 j^2}{2} + \frac{rj\Delta\tau}{2}\right) C_{j+1,k}^n$$

$$+ \left(\frac{\Delta\tau\sigma^2 j^2}{2} - \frac{rj\Delta\tau}{2}\right) C_{j-1,k}^n + \frac{j\Delta S\Delta\tau}{2\Delta I}C_{j,k+1}^n - \frac{j\Delta S\Delta\tau}{2\Delta I}C_{j,k-1}^n, \quad (5a)$$

$$C(S_j, I_k, 0) = \max\left\{\frac{I_k}{T} - K, 0\right\}, \tag{5b}$$

$$C(0, I_k, \tau_n) = e^{-r\tau_n} \max\left\{\frac{I_k}{T} - K, 0\right\}, \tag{5c}$$

$$C(S_{\max}, I_k, \tau_n) = e^{-r\tau_n} \max\left\{\frac{I_k}{T} - K, 0\right\} + \frac{S_{\max}}{rT}(1 - e^{-r\tau_n}), \tag{5d}$$

$$C(S_j, I_{\max}, \tau_n) = \max\left\{e^{-r\tau_n}\left(\frac{I_{\max}}{T} - K\right) + \frac{S_j}{rT}(1 - e^{-r\tau_n}), 0\right\}, \tag{5e}$$

$$C(S_j, 0, \tau_n) = C(S_j, I_1, \tau_n). \tag{5f}$$

where $\Delta\tau$ is a constant step in time, ΔS and ΔI are constant steps with respect to the variables S and I.

Let note the following features of the problem under consideration:

1. the coefficients of the finite-difference scheme are calculated independently of one another, and they do not depend on time;
2. the values C_{jk}^{n+1} are independent within each time layer.

These facts help to significantly optimise the computational process.

Since the coefficients of the finite-difference scheme are independent of time, it will be expedient to store them in the GPU constant memory. In this case, thanks to the caching mechanism, there is no need to read them permanently from the global memory. But it is necessary to note the volume limitations of the constant memory of the GPU. For this reason, in the calculation process, it is necessary to ensure that it will not be overflowed by an increase in the number of discretization points.

The second feature provide an possibility to more effectively use the shared memory of the graphics processor. Due to the its limited volume, the values C_{jk}^{n+1} were calculated by blocks 16×16. To do this, we need to copy 18×18 values from the time layer n into the shared memory.

Due to these changes, the number of read operations from global memory is dramatically reduced. Figure 3 shows the results of comparing sequential and parallel algorithms.

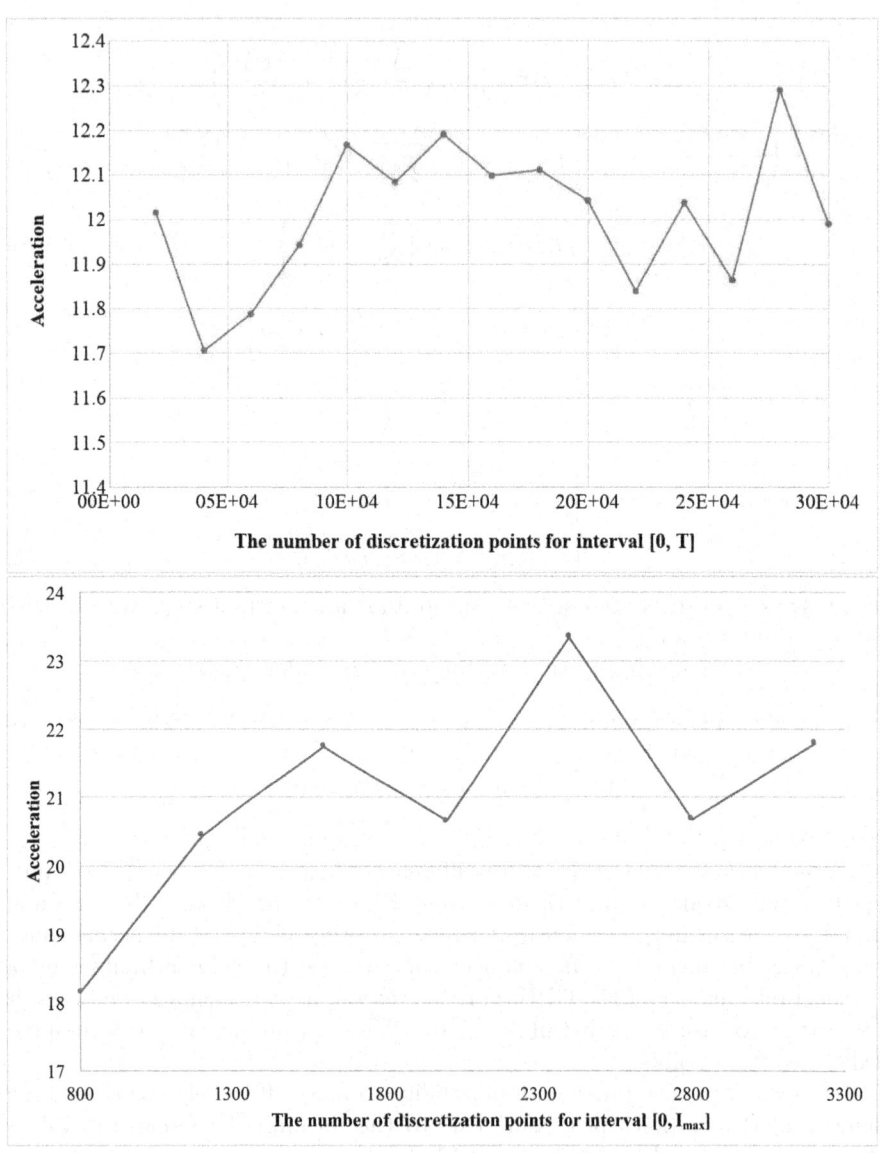

Fig. 3. Comparison graph of sequential and parallel algorithms for finite difference method.

6   Conclusion

In this paper it was shown that both the Monte Carlo method and the finite-difference method make it possible to optimize the search algorithms for the price of securities in order to effectively launch them on the GPGPU. In some cases, the rate of computation can be increased by almost 2 orders of magnitude. For this, however, it is necessary to take into account the specificity of the different tasks, as well as the peculiarities of the work of each GPU.

Acknowledgments. The research was supported by Russian Foundation for Basic Research (project N 16-07-01113).

A   Appendix

The main characteristics of the hardware used for calculations (Tables 1, 2, 3 and 4).

Table 1. NVidia Tesla M2050

Number of processor cores	448
Chip	Tesla T20 GPU
Processor clock	1.15 GHz
Memory clock	1.546 GHz
Memory size	3 GB
Memory I/O	384-bit GDDR5

Table 2. NVidia Tesla K40

Number of processor cores	2880
Chip	GK110B
Core clocks	745 MHz
Memory clock	3.0 GHz
Memory size	12 GB
Memory I/O	384-bit GDDR5

Table 3. NVidia Tesla P100

NVIDIA CUDA cores	3584
GPU clocks	1189 MHz
Maximum memory clock	715 MHz
Memory size	16 GB HBM2
Memory bus width	4096-bit
Peak memory bandwidth	Up to 732 GB/s

Table 4. Intel Xeon E5-2680 v3

Processor number	E5-2680V3
# of cores	12
# of threads	24
Processor base frequency	2.50 GHz
Max turbo frequency	3.30 GHz
Cache	30 MB SmartCache
Bus speed	9.6 GT/s QPI

References

1. Bogdanov, A., Stepanov, E., Khmel, D.: Assessment of the dynamics of Asian and European options on the hybrid system. J. Phys: Conf. Ser. **681**(1), 012007 (2016)
2. Hull, J.: Options, Futures and Other Derivatives, 9th edn. Pearson, New Jersey (2015)
3. Kwok, Y.E.: Mathematical Models of Financial Derivatives, 2nd edn. Springer, Heidelberg (2008). https://doi.org/10.1007/978-3-540-68688-0
4. Black, F., Scholes, M.: The pricing of options and corporate liabilities. J. Polit. Econ. **81**, 637–654 (1973)
5. Montagna, G., Nicrosini, O., Moreni, N.: A path integral way to option pricing. Physica A Stat. Mech. Appl. **310**(3–4), 450–466 (2002)
6. Bennati, E., Rosa-Clot, M., Taddei, S.: A path integral approach to derivative security pricing: I formalism and analytical results. Int. J. Theor. Appl. Finan. **2**(4), 381–407 (1999)
7. Boreskov, A., Harlamov, A.: Parallelnye vychysleniya na GPU. Moscow University Press, Moscow (2012)
8. CUDA Toolkit documentation (n. d.). http://docs.nvidia.com/cuda/curand. Accessed 7 May 2018
9. Zvan, R., Forsyth, P.A., Vetzal, K.: Robust numerical methods for PDE models of Asian options. J. Comput. Finan. **1b.** (1998) Risk Waters Group, London
10. Duffy, D.J.: Finite Diffrence Methods in Financial Engineering. Wiley, Chichester (2006)

Influence of External Source on KPI Equation

Alexander V. Bogdanov[1], Vladimir V. Mareev[1],
Nataliia V. Kulabukhova[1(✉)], Alexander B. Degtyarev[1],
and Nadezhda L. Shchegoleva[2]

[1] St. Petersburg State University,
7/9 Universitetskaya nab., St. Petersburg 199034, Russia
{bogdanov,map}@csa.ru, kulabukhova.nv@gmail.com
[2] St. Petersburg Electrotechnical University "LETI",
ul. Prof. Popova 5, St. Petersburg 197376, Russia

Abstract. The analysis of external sources influence on 2D waves evolution is carried out with special attention to the possibility of exponential growing. We have proposed master equation, that is the generalization of Kadomtsev-Petviashvili-I Equation (KPI), that shows major part of the problems in ocean waves evolution and at the same time most difficult from the point of view of numerical algorithm stability. Some indications for choosing of correct numerical procedures are given. This analysis is especially relevant in connection with the emergence of new hybrid computing architectures, the porting of applications on which strongly depends on the chosen algorithm.

Keywords: Kadomtsev-Petviashvili-I Equation · Numerical methods Solution

1 Introduction

Consider the two-dimensional Kadomtsev-Petviashvili equation — KPI

$$\left[u_t + 0.5\left(u^2\right)_x + \beta u_{xxx} - G \right]_x = \eta u_{yy} \tag{1}$$

Equation (1) with respect to function $u(x,y,t)$ is considered in the domain $t \geq 0$, $x, y \in (-\infty, \infty)$, $\beta, \eta \geq 0$, $G(x,y)$ is external source. In general, the solution of such equation is sought numerically.

Analysis of such equations, especially in the asymptotic region, has long been beyond the computational possibilities available in universities. However, the recent appearance of hybrid vector accelerators GPGPU allows us to consider this task from a new perspective. In this paper, we propose a variant of numerical realization of two-dimensional nonlinear wave equations adapted to modern NVIDIA graphics processors.

© Springer International Publishing AG, part of Springer Nature 2018
O. Gervasi et al. (Eds.): ICCSA 2018, LNCS 10963, pp. 123–135, 2018.
https://doi.org/10.1007/978-3-319-95171-3_11

1.1   Finite Difference Method for KPI Equation

When the KPI equation is numerically integrated, instead of the original Eq. (1) its integro-differential analogue is considered

$$u_t + 0.5\left(u^2\right)_x + \beta u_{xxx} = \eta \int_{-\infty}^{x} u_{yy}(x', y, t)dx' + G(x, y) \tag{2}$$

Solution of the Eq. (2) in half-plane $t \geq 0$ is sought for initial distribution $u(x, y, 0) = q(x, y)$. The numerical simulation of the Eq. (2) by many authors was carried out by various methods, in particular, by pseudospectral method, Runge-Kutta method, explicit finite-difference method with flow correction procedure, and finite-difference method directly for Eq. (1) [1–5]. In this paper, we will not analyze the features of all these approaches.

In our work the numerical simulation of the Eq. (2) is carried out using a linearized implicit finite-difference scheme using in some cases the flux correction procedure (FCT) [6].

The continuous region for (2) is replaced by the discrete mesh $[x_{min}, x_{max}] \times [y_{min}, y_{max}] \times [0, T]$. The calculation region is mapped to a uniform finite difference grid for a time t and spatial coordinates x and y:

$$x_j = j\Delta x, \quad j \in [1, M], \quad x_{min} = x_1, \quad x_{max} = x_M$$

$$y_k = k\Delta y, \quad k \in [1, L], \quad y_{min} = y_1, \quad y_{max} = y_L$$

$$t^n = n\Delta t, \quad n = 0, 1, 2, \ldots, T/\Delta t - 1$$

with $\Delta x, \Delta y$ being the spatial coordinates steps, Δt being the time step. With these notations for the constructed grid we have:

$$u(j\Delta x, k\Delta y, n\Delta t) = u_{j,k}^n, \quad \int_{-\infty}^{x_j} u_{yy}dx' \approx \int_{x_{min}}^{x_j} u_{yy}dx' \equiv S_{j,k}^n$$

For Eq. (2), the approximation is performed using the central-difference operators.

$$u_{j,k}^{n+1} - u_{j,k}^n + \frac{\Delta t}{4\Delta x}\left(F_{j+1,k}^{n+1} - F_{j-1,k}^{n+1}\right) + \beta\frac{\Delta t}{2\Delta x^3}\left(u_{j+2,k}^{n+1} - 2u_{j+1,k}^{n+1} + 2u_{j-1,k}^{n+1} - u_{j-2,k}^{n+1}\right) = \Delta t\eta S_{j,k}^{n+1} + \Delta t G_{j,k} \tag{3}$$

The order of approximation of the difference scheme (3) in the calculation region is $O(\Delta t, \Delta x^2, \Delta y^2)$.

The resulting system of difference Eqs. (3) is reduced to the form:

$$a_j\Delta u_{j-2,k}^{n+1} + b_j\Delta u_{j-1,k}^{n+1} + c_j\Delta u_{j,k}^{n+1} + d_j\Delta u_{j+1,k}^{n+1} + e_j\Delta u_{j+2,k}^{n+1} = f_{j,k}^n \tag{4}$$

with $\Delta u_{j,k}^{n+1} = u_{j,k}^{n+1} - u_{j,k}^n$.

With linearization of finite-difference representation of the transfer term of (4) we have

$$F_{j,k}^{n+1} \equiv \left(u^2\right)_{j,k}^{n+1} = \left(u^2\right)_{j,k}^{n} + 2u_{j,k}^n \Delta u_{j,k}^{n+1} + O\left(\Delta t^2\right)$$

The system (4) is solved by a five-point run (Thomas algorithm). Integral $S_{j,k}^n$ is calculated by trapezoidal method, the subintegral derivative of u_{yy} is approximated by the Central differences of the second order:

$$\frac{\Delta t}{\Delta y^2}\left(u_{j,k-1}^{n+1} - 2u_{j,k}^{n+1} + u_{j,k+1}^{n+1}\right).$$

1.2   The Boundary Conditions

At the boundaries of the computational region $[x_1, x_M] \times [y_1, y_L]$ differential boundary conditions are specified. Solutions to the KPI equation decrease in proportion to the square of the distance $O[1/(x^2 + y^2)]$, and as a result, in practical calculations, it is impossible to choose sufficiently large region sizes $[x_{min}, x_{max}] \times [y_{min}, y_{max}]$ to use homogeneous Dirichlet conditions. In such cases, the so-called "percolation conditions" are traditionally used: $u_x = u_{xx} = 0$ along boundary lines x_1 and x_M, and $u_y = 0$ along the lines y_1 and y_L. In difference form the differential conditions look like:

$$u_{-1,k}^n = u_{0,k}^n = u_{1,k}^n; \; u_{M+2,k}^n = u_{M+1,k}^n = u_{M,k}^n; \; u_{j,0}^n = u_{j,1}^n; \; u_{j,L+1}^n = u_{j,L}^n \quad (5)$$

With additional artificial nodes in system (5):

$$(-1, k), (0, k), (M+2, k), (M+1, k), (j, 0), (j, L+1).$$

We meet here with a special feature of the application of difference boundary conditions (5). In fact, those conditions are written for the original Kadomtsev-Petviashvili differential Eq. (1). In applying its integro-differential analogue (2), we do not obtain the same result for the difference form (3). This is an illustration of a typical problem, when in continuous space the transformation of the Eqs. (1) and (2) are identical, and in grid space there are no similar transformations from finite-difference representation of Eq. (1), i.e. they do not lead to expression (3). Taking into account the above, when calculating the system of Eqs. (4) with boundary conditions (5), the conditions of percolation along the y axis are not implemented correctly, but lead to a reflection condition.

2 Initial Distribution

Three different types of volumes were chosen as initial distributions.

1. The parallelepiped
   Volume $V_1 = a_1 \times b_1 \times h$ with a_1, b_1, h being the edges along the axis x, y and z. When calculating the volume in the grid region, the steps of the spatial coordinates are considered, since practically the truncated pyramid is considered.
2. Gaussian distribution

$$q_2(x, y) = \sigma \exp\left[-\omega\left(x^2/a_2^2 + y^2/b_2^2\right)\right], \sigma > 0$$

   With the volume $V_2 = \sigma \pi a_2 b_2 / \omega$, and a_2, b_2 being the half axis.
3. The ellipsoid of rotation

$$\frac{x^2}{a_3^2} + \frac{y^2}{b_3^2} + \frac{z^2}{c_3^2} = 1, z \geq 0$$

   With the volume $V_3 = 2\pi a_3 b_3 / 3$, and a_3, b_3 being the half axis.

The heights are selected with the condition that the volumes of all shapes are equal in the grid region. In many approaches, the analytical solution (1) with $G = 0$ is selected as the initial distribution. In our case, we want to investigate the influence of the form of the initial distribution on further evolution of the perturbation. For such purpose Gaussian distribution with smooth derivatives, the parallelepiped with large derivatives in grid region and the ellipsoid of rotation without derivative at $z = 0$ were chosen. To unify the selection of distribution parameters values, the volume of the shape and the choice of half-axes for ellipses that fit into the base of the parallelepiped are fixed.

3 Comparisons with Exact Solutions

The results of numerical calculations were compared with the known analytical solution of the KPI equation.

We apply the finite difference scheme (3), (4) for the equation, similar to (1):

$$\left[u_t + 3\left(u^2\right)_x + u_{xxx}\right]_x = 3u_{yy}. \tag{6}$$

For the Eq. (6) there exist the lump type soliton solution, i.e.:

$$u(x, y, t) = 4\frac{-(x - 3\mu^2 t)^2 + \mu^2 y^2 + 1/\mu^2}{\left[(x - 3\mu^2 t)^2 + \mu^2 y^2 + 1/\mu^2\right]^2} \tag{7}$$

For the solution (7) a following condition is met,

$$\int_{-\infty}^{\infty} \int_{-\infty}^{\infty} u(x, y, t)\,dx\,dy = 0, \forall t$$

We used function (7) at при $t = 0$ and $\mu^2 = 1$. At those conditions the speed of perturbation (7) evolution is $\tilde{U} = 3\mu^2 = 3$.

The finite difference scheme (4) for Eq. (6) has been tested. The analytical solution of the Eq. (7) discussed above was set as the initial distribution. The evolution of such perturbation was considered numerically for different values of the difference scheme parameters. Figure 1 shows a comparison of the exact solution with the numerical solution for one moment at $y = 0$.

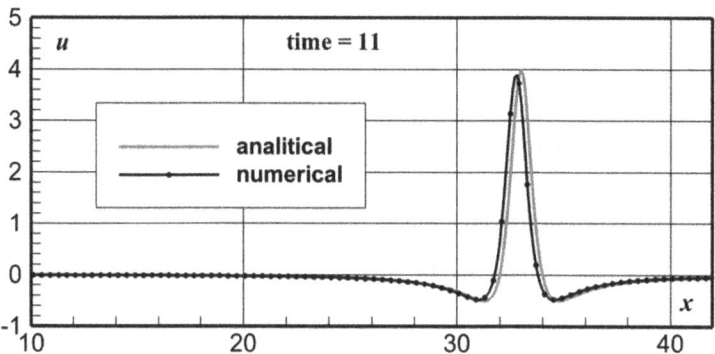

Fig. 1. Comparison of the exact solution (7) with a numerical one at $t = 11$. Grid: $700 \times 500, \Delta x = \Delta y = 0.1, \Delta t = 2 \cdot 10^{-5}, y = 0$.

The matching results are within the tolerance limits for the applied purely implicit difference scheme. Original transfer term $0.5(u^2)_x$ is approximated by five-point pattern:

$$\left(u^2\right)_x\big|_{j,k}^{n+1} = \frac{\Delta t}{24\Delta x}\left(-F_{j+2,k}^{n+1} + 8F_{j+1,k}^{n+1} - 8F_{j-1,k}^{n+1} + F_{j-2,k}^{n+1}\right) + O\left(\Delta x^4\right), \qquad (8)$$

$$F_{j,k}^{n+1} \equiv \left(u^2\right)_{j,k}^{n+1}$$

This was fully justified in the framework of Thomas algorithm in direction of x. But, as a result of the numerical analysis of the evolution of the exact solution (7), it became clear that such an approximation leads to poor results. Forms of perturbation, its velocity and amplitude is described unsatisfactory. A further increase in the coordinate step leads to a strong increase in the dispersion ruffle.

Increasing of the order of approximation of derivatives occurs when the number of nodes of the difference grid used is increased. This, in turn, can worsen the details of the solution in areas with strong gradients, that is observed in our case. This is particularly evident at relatively large values of coordinate steps.

4 FCT — *Flux-Corrected Technique*

In our previous papers [7, 8] the solution of KdVB equation was calculated using a difference scheme that includes a flow correction procedure (FCT). Let us consider the possibility of using of this approach in our case.

KPI equations, as well as KdV equation, do not describe dissipative processes and this fact should be taken into account when constructing a finite-difference scheme. Numerical dispersion errors accumulate during the computational process, which leads to the emerging of nonphysical oscillations and distortion of the results. These dispersive errors are not damped in time. For the described finite difference method with small β or $\beta = 0$ dispersion errors increase, which leads to an unlimited growth of errors. This behavior is typical for the approximation of derivatives by central differences. This case was considered in [8]. Therefore, an introduction of the numerical diffusion into the difference scheme is required. To do this, we used the well-known algorithm of flow correction FCT [6] for the coordinate x.

We denote the solution obtained by solution of the system (3) by $\bar{u}_{j,k}$. The algorithm of flux correction procedure (FCT) in representation [6] for x coordinate consists of the following steps:

1. The calculation of the diffusive fluxes.

$$u^d_{j+1/2,k} = v_{j+1/2,k}\left(u^n_{j+1,k} - u^n_{j,k}\right).$$

2. The calculation of the antidiffusive fluxes.

$$u^{ad}_{j+1/2,k} = \mu_{j+1/2,k}\left(\bar{u}_{j+1,k} - \bar{u}_{j,k}\right).$$

The coefficients $v_{j+1/2,k}$ and $\mu_{j+1/2,k}$ are specified as

$$v_{j+1/2,k} = \lambda_0 + \lambda_1 \mathbb{C}^2_{j+1/2,k}, \mu_{j+1/2,k} = \lambda_0 + \lambda_2 \mathbb{C}^2_{j+1/2,k} \tag{9}$$

$$\mathbb{C}^2_{j+1/2,k} = \frac{u^n_{j+1/2,k} + u^n_{j,k}}{2}\frac{\Delta t}{\Delta x}$$

After the correction step we get the adjusted value $u^{corr}_{j,k}$. The final solution on the $n+1$ layer has the form:

$$u^{n+1}_{j,k} = \bar{u}_{j,k} + u^d_{j+1/2,k} - u^d_{j-1/2,k} - u^{corr}_{j,k} + u^{corr}_{j-1,k}.$$

The main difficulty in application of the FCT method for KdV or KPI equations is the correct choice of coefficients (9). The standard choice [6] gives too large values: $\lambda_0 = 1/6, \lambda_1 = 1/3, \lambda_2 = -1/3$. With such values, diffusion smooths completely not only physical oscillations, but also the amplitudes of perturbations of the solution. Below we consider the range of coefficient values (9) proposed for our case. At $\beta = 0, \eta = 1, G = 0$ Eq. (2) takes the form

$$u_t + 0.5\left(u^2\right)_x = \int_{-\infty}^{x} u_{yy}(x', y, t)dx'. \tag{10}$$

As in the case of the one-dimensional version of the equation Kdv [8], the approximation of the Eq. (10) with the proposed scheme causes strong oscillations (Fig. 2a).

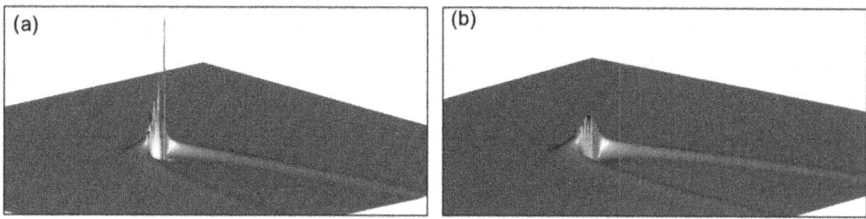

Fig. 2. (a) Numerical dispersion at $\beta = 0$ without FCT. (b) With FCT procedures of (11). $t = 1$. Grid: 500×500, $\Delta x = \Delta y = 0.2$, $\Delta t = 10^{-4}$.

The introduction of the FCT procedure with minimal coefficient values (9) leads to acceptable results displayed on Fig. 2b. The parameters are set to the following values:

$$\lambda_0 = 10^{-4}, \lambda_1 = 1.1 \cdot 10^{-5}, \lambda_2 = -10^{-5} \tag{11}$$

Meanwhile a more thorough analysis of the use of smoothing procedures for the initial distribution of different forms and values of coefficients was carried out.

Finally, after the analysis of numerical experiments, it was decided not to use the smoothing algorithm in General. The resulting small numerical dispersion ripples do not significantly affect the nature of disturbances and, most importantly, do not underestimate the amplitudes of solitons and the growth of the wave.

5   Numerical Results

Numerical implementation of the proposed algorithms requires considerable computational resources, so a hybrid system with a powerful vector accelerator is used
   Production configuration:

- Intel Xeon E5-2690 v4 CPU, 14 cores, 2,6 GHz (3.69 GFLOPS per core, 44.00 GFLOPS total);
- NVIDIA TESLA P100 GPU, Pascal architecture, 3584 CUDA cores, 1328–1480 MHz clock speed (80719 GFLOPS total), 16 GB global memory (32 GB/s PCI transfer bandwidth, 732 GB/s peak memory bandwidth).

5.1   Dependence of the Soliton on the Form of the Initial Distribution $q(x,y)$ at a Constant Volume of Perturbation

Let us consider the dependence of the results of calculations on the initial distributions. For this purpose, it is necessary to fix some values of parameters:

$a_1 = 4, b_1 = 6, a_2 = a_3 = 2, b_2 = b_3 = 3$. Volume $V = 120$ and the same for all shapes.

Calculations were performed without smoothing procedure for the moment of time $t = 8$; number of nodes 800×700; time step $\Delta t = 5 \cdot 10^{-5}$; coordinates steps $\Delta x = \Delta y = 0.1$.

As it is evident from Fig. 3 the largest soliton is formed from the original form of the ellipsoid of rotation.

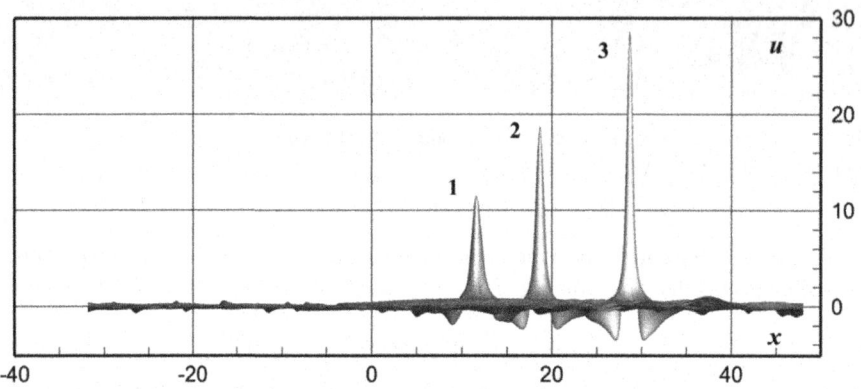

Fig. 3. Formation of solitons at different initial distributions for $t = 8, V = 120$. Grid: $800 \times 700, \Delta x = \Delta y = 0.1, \Delta t = 5 \cdot 10^{-5}, y = 0$. Notations: 1 — Rectangular parallelepiped, $h = 5.2144$; 2 — Gaussian distribution, $\sigma = 10$; 3 — ellipsoid of rotation, $c = 9.56$.

5.2   Comparison of Solitons for Different Values of Half-Axes of Ellipse at Constant Volume of Perturbation

We now consider only the Gaussian initial distribution for $\sigma = 10, V_2 = 120$. But in the original distribution, we turn the ellipse by $90°$. In Figs. 4 and 5 it is visible that under such conditions the soliton is not formed. Figure 5 demonstrates the effect of reflection of perturbations from the boundaries y_1 and y_L.

5.3   The Dependence of the Height of the Soliton on the Initial Volume

We consider the initial distribution of the Gaussian type, with different volumes. All calculations were performed without smoothing for the following parameter values:

$a_2 = 2, b_2 = 3, t = 7$, Grid: 500×500, $\Delta t = 10^{-4}, \Delta x = \Delta y = 0.2$. In Table 1 various variants of calculations are given.

With the help of numerical modeling, the situation was studied in which the amplitude of the formed soliton increases sharply with a relatively small increase in volume, compared with the previous value.

The process is like the jump (Figs. 6 and 7). The difference in volume for option 8 of the volume for the option 9 is approximately 0.17%.

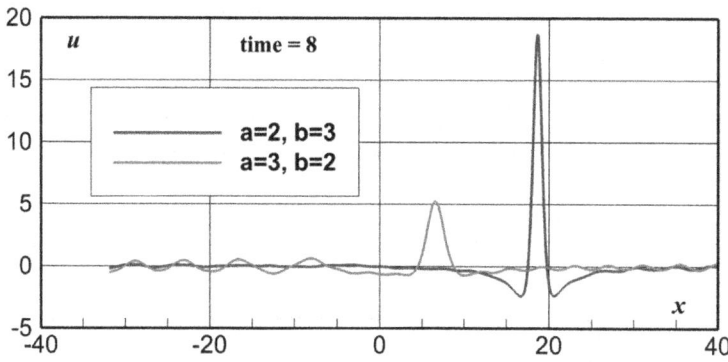

Fig. 4. Formation of solitons for initial conditions of Gaussian type at $t = 8, V = 120$. Grid: $800 \times 700, \Delta x = \Delta y = 0.1, \Delta t = 5 \cdot 10^{-5}, y = 0$.

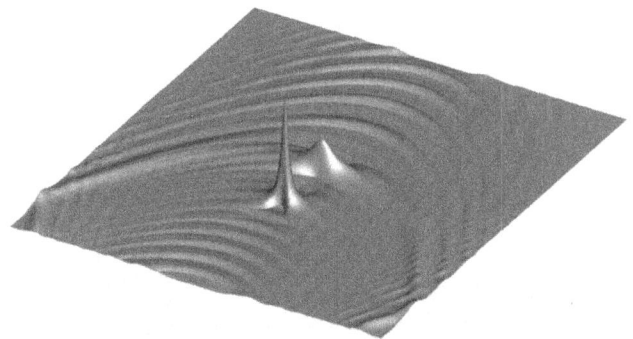

Fig. 5. 3D formation of solitons for initial conditions of Gaussian type at $t = 8, V = 120$. Grid: $800 \times 700, \Delta x = \Delta y = 0.1, \Delta t = 5 \cdot 10^{-5}, y = 0$.

Table 1. Initial parameter values.

№	V	σ
1	96	8
2	108	9
3	120	10
4	132	11
5	138	11,5
6	141	11,75
7	142,5	11,875
8	143,4	11,95
9	143,64	11,97
10	144	12

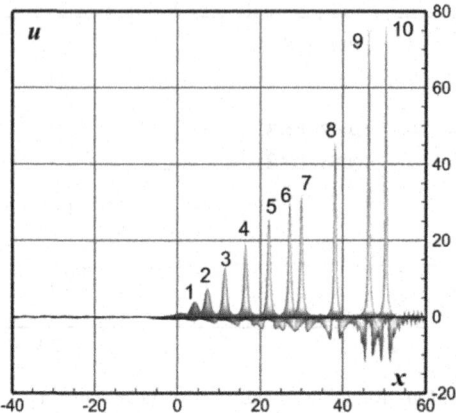

Fig. 6. Demonstrations of a jump-like increase in the amplitude of the soliton for the initial conditions of the Gaussian type at $t = 7$. Grid: 500×500, $\Delta t = 10^{-4}$, $\Delta x = \Delta y = 0.2$.

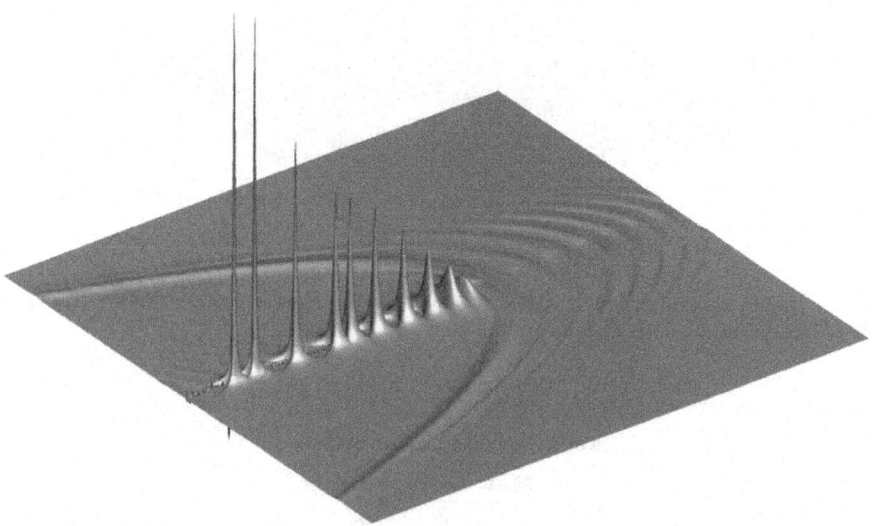

Fig. 7. 3D demonstration of the abrupt increase of the amplitude of the soliton for the initial conditions of a Gaussian form with $t = 7$. Grid: 500×500, $\Delta t = 10^{-4}$, $\Delta x = \Delta y = 0.2$.

5.4   The Influence of the Source

We chose a source in the form of an ellipsoid of rotation, as in the case of 3 for initial distributions:

$$G(x,y) = c_4 \sqrt{1 - \frac{(x - x_0)^2}{a_4^2} - \frac{(y - y_0)^2}{b_4^2}}$$

Calculations of the Eq. (2) with the source as an analogue of natural influence on the water surface give numerous variants of possible situations of formation of high amplitude solitons. The source itself generates solitons. The intensity of the source varies over a wide range. The area of influence of the source is limited by condition, but over time, a cluster of disturbances is formed, from which solitons of various amplitude are formed. For example, we give the evolution of the perturbation development without taking into account the initial distribution of the above types.

In Figs. 8 and 9 we show the moments of the perturbations evolution for the values $a_4 = 2, b_4 = 3, c = 5$, т.е. $V_4 = 20\pi$.

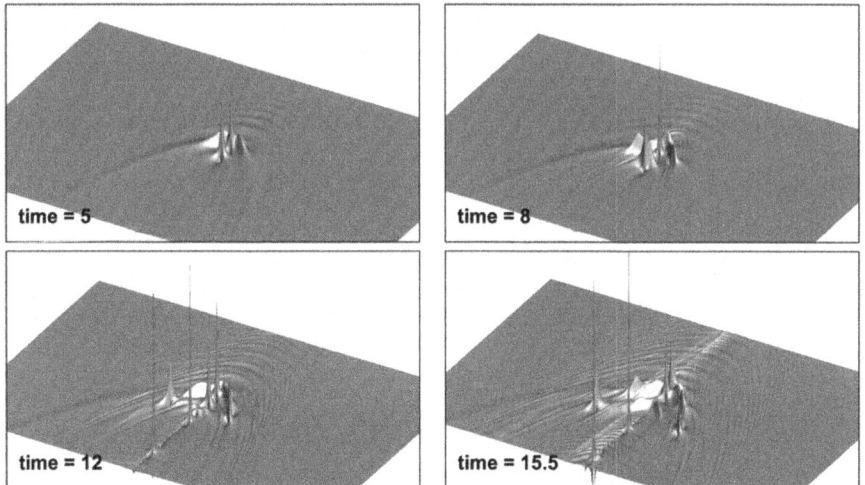

Fig. 8. 3D Demonstration of the evolution of the perturbations from the source. Grid: 600×850, $\Delta t = 10^{-4}$, $\Delta x = \Delta y = 0.2$.

The moment of time $t = 15.5$ is shown in the enlarged view in Fig. 9.

For a more powerful source, the process of forming a soliton cluster, represented by Fig. 10, is more efficient.

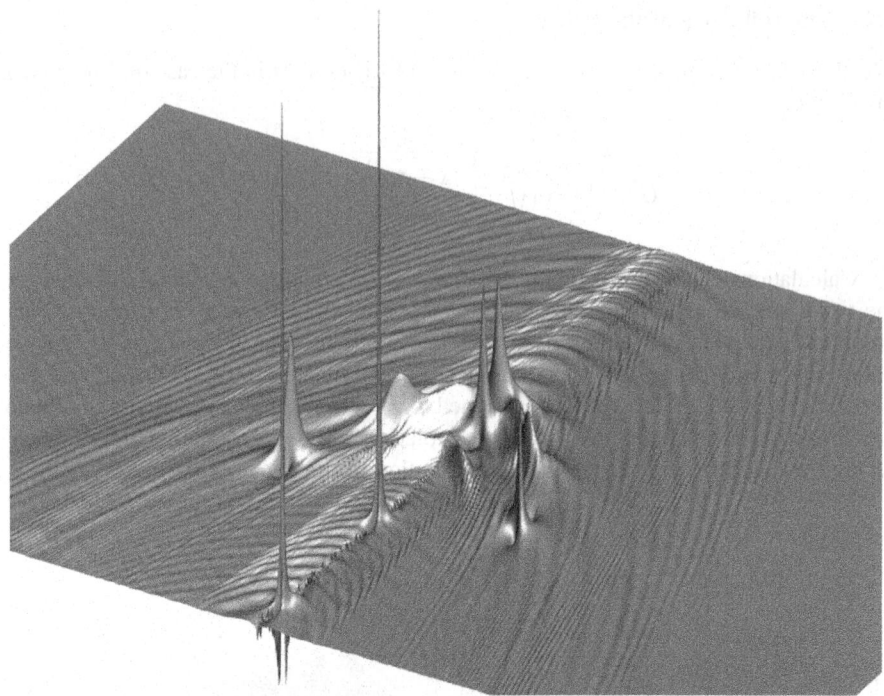

Fig. 9. Source-only 3D perturbation at $t = 15.5$. Grid: 600×850, $\Delta t = 10^{-4}$, $\Delta x = \Delta y = 0.2$.

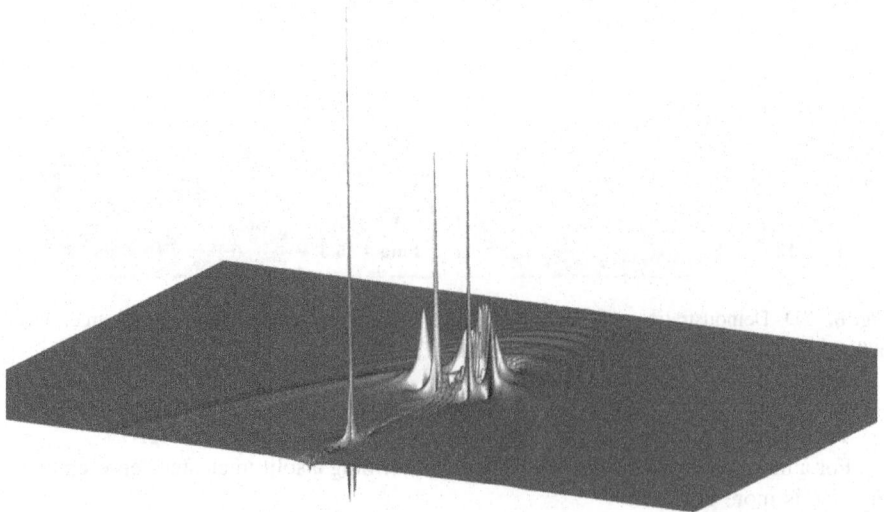

Fig. 10. Source-only 3D perturbation at $t = 7, V = 30\pi, a_4 = 2, b_4 = 3, c = 7.5$. Grid: 600×850, $\Delta t = 10^{-4}$, $\Delta x = \Delta y = 0.2$.

6 Conclusions

1 The proposed difference scheme has sufficient resolution for zones with large gradients. The scheme satisfactorily illuminates cases with initial distributions which are not completely integrable. Thus, the use of modern hybrid systems in combination with the new algorithmic approach has allowed not only to realize calculations of the wave evolution with sufficient accuracy to enter the asymptotic region, but also to create a software and hardware platform for mass computations of wave processes.

2 The use of the smoothing procedure leads to an underestimation of the amplitudes of emerging solitons. In General, the need for such a PCT procedure is not obvious.

3 The time step depends strongly on the initial distribution, since the evolution of the perturbation leads to velocities by an order of magnitude greater than that considered in the linear analogue of the KPI equation.

4 In numerical modeling, the effect of jump-like amplification of the amplitude of the solitons formed at a relatively small increase in the volume of the body of the initial distribution was observed.

Scientific research were performed using the equipment of the Research Park of St. Petersburg State University. The work was sponsored by the Russian Foundation for Basic Research under the projects: 16-07-01113 "Virtual supercomputer as a tool for solving complex problems".

References

1. Mekki, A.: Numerical simulation of Kadomtsev–Petviashvili–Benjamin– Bona-Mahony equations using finite difference method. Appl. Math. Comput. **219**(24), 11214–11222 (2013)

2. Feng, B.-F., Mitsui, T.: A finite difference method for the Korteweg-de Vries and the Kadomtsev-Petviashvili equations. J. Comput. Appl. Math. **90**, 95–116 (1998)

3. Popov, S.P.: Numerical implementation of two-soliton solutions to the Kadomtsev-Petviashvili equation. Comput. Math. Math. Phys. **40**(10), 1447–1455 (2000). (in Russian)

4. Lu, Z., Liu, Y.: The generation of lump solitons by a bottom topography in a surface-tension dominated flow. Zeitschrift für Naturforschung A, May 2005. https://doi.org/10.1515/zna-2005-0504

5. Lu, Z., Tian, E.M., Grimshaw, R.: Interaction of two lump solitons described by the Kadomtsev–Petviashvili I equation, Wave Motion. Elsevier, August 2004. https://doi.org/10.1016/j.wavemoti.2003.12.017

6. Fletcher, C.A.J.: Computational Techniques for Fluid Dynamics 1, 2nd edn., p. 401. Springer, Heidelberg (1991). https://doi.org/10.1007/978-3-642-58229-5

7. Bogdanov, A.V., Mareev, V.V., Stankova, E.N.: Hybrid approach perturbed KdVB equation. In: Gervasi, O., Murgante, B., Misra, S., Gavrilova, M.L., Rocha, A.M.A.C., et al. (eds.) ICCSA 2015. LNCS, vol. 9158, pp. 331–341. Springer, Cham (2015). https://doi.org/10.1007/978-3-319-21410-8_26

8. Bogdanov, A., Mareev, V.: Numerical simulation perturbed KdVB equation. In: EPJ Web of Conferences, vol. 108, p. 02014 (2016). [MMCP 2015 Stará Lesná, Slovakia, 2015]

Reconstruction of Stone Walls in Form of Polygonal Meshes from Archaeological Studies

Oleg Iakushkin, Anna Fatkina$^{(\boxtimes)}$, Vadim Plaksin, Olga Sedova,
Alexander Degtyarev, and Alexei Uteshev

Saint-Petersburg State University, St. Petersburg 199034, Russia
o.yakushkin@spbu.ru, fatkina.a.i@gmail.com

Abstract. Visualization of archeological monuments plays an important role in reconstruction of historic and cultural context. The fragmented nature of many artefacts and archival documents stresses the need to use specialized software to model the objects being studied. The paper describes computer algorithms of monument reconstruction that allow to generate three-dimensional models using very limited input data. We have developed a software product that generates 3D models of stones using their contours and enables a user to reconstruct a wall based on available polygonal objects. This software product has a number of distinguishing features: reliable results even with very limited input data; no need to use specialized equipment; flexibility and support of recurrent use of the reconstructed model's components.

Keywords: 3D reconstruction · Polygonal mesh · Automatization
Architectural visualisation · Digital reconstruction · Cultural heritage
Archeology

1 Introduction

Archaeological studies provide a vivid example of practical implementation of 3D visualization [4,7,13]. The methods used in archæological studies include, inter alia, mandatory visual recording of each and every artefact and structure. Archaeological plans are specifically drawn to show the general dimensions and location of objects. The obtained results may undergo 3D reconstruction in order to facilitate research activities or for the purposes of popularization. However, 3D reconstruction is labour-intensive and requires special computer skills from the researchers [15].

Computer modelling of historic objects allows to further develop this task through creating an automatic 3D visualization based on fragments of a 2D image. This provides for a major optimization of labour and equipment costs.

1.1 Available Solutions

Computer reconstruction of historic objects is currently carried out using 3D editors, such as 3ds Max, Blender, Cinema 4D, and others. These software packages offer methods that may reconstruct the appearance of a wall based on its contours. For instance, 'Displace' function in Houdini Engine translates a depth map of a stonework wall drawing into a relief texture. This approach has a number of drawbacks:

– where a wall is incomplete, its missing contours should be manually added to the drawing;
– the relief texture wall is represented by a single large 3D object that cannot be subdivided into groups of separate stones to work with independently. This prevents a user from modelling physical interaction between stones and altering selected wall fragments. This also renders it impossible to reconstruct a wall's physical destruction–e.g., as the result of seismic activity, decay, flood, or a combination of various other factors.

Archaeology makes use of a number of solutions to reconstruct a real object and avoid the problems referred to above. These solutions are:

– reconstruction based on a series of photos (or videos) taken from different angles;
– reconstruction based on the data obtained by surface scans without excavation.

Both solutions have a major restriction–they require a large volume of input data that in most cases is unavailable to researchers.

2 Goals and Objectives

The specific information about the form of wall parts may be obtained by way of historic, cultural and chronological analogies through extrapolation of data available in respect of other objects. This kind of extrapolation will yield the input data required to build a model.

In this paper, we will use the word "contours" to describe the projections of a stone on one of the three planes constituting the three-dimensional space. We describe an algorithm that allows to build a true-to-life polygon mesh of a stone based on one, two or three contours. This task will yield not more than three projections of one stone, because a stone may only take one of the following positions in a wall:

1. in the centre of a wall's surface–in this event, only one contour will be available;
2. at the corner of a building, but not in the top row of stones (two projections);
3. at the corner and in the top row of stones (three projections).

Our goal is to automate the process of wall modelling in architectural structures discovered by archaeological studies. This goal includes the following two objectives:

1. modelling of objects that comprise a wall;
2. reconstruction of a wall based on such objects.

Such service-based approach is easily transferable into a distributed environment setting [2,5,6,8–11] Below we elaborate on each of these two stages.

3   Modelling of Separate Stones

3.1   Algorithm to Reconstruct the Objects Comprising a Wall

The algorithm is provided with 2D graphic documentation–a plan supplemented with cross-sections of excavated objects. The scale and position in space are the parameters that are set for each input image.

The noise is cleaned up and any information and graphic notes are removed from the image in order to ensure an unfettered access to the objects material for the analysis.

Then the algorithm of stone reconstruction is run through the following stages:

1. the division of input images into separate contours;
2. the reconstruction of a point cloud based on one, two or three contours;
3. the creation of polygon mesh based on the point cloud built at the previous stage.

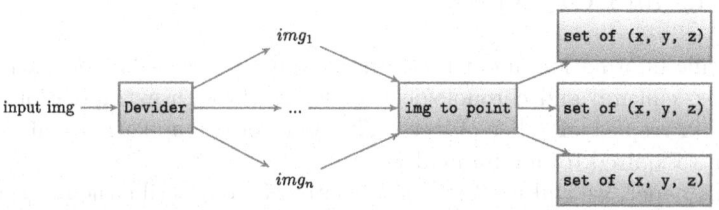

Fig. 1. Scheme of the image segmentation algorithm.

The first stage of the algorithm is schematically presented in Fig. 1. The scheme applies to cases where only one input drawing is used. However, the algorithm has the capacity of processing a higher number of input drawings. An input drawing is broken down in a number of smaller images–each of them containing only one contour. The contours in the original drawing may border on each other.

The next stage is aimed at stone reconstruction based on a set of contours. This stage includes the following steps:

1. The compression/expansion ratio and the position are assigned to the input drawing. The compression/expansion ratio is used to scale the drawing.
2. A contour is singled out in the image and recorded as a set of points.
3. In the three-dimensional space, each point is shifted according to the position assigned in the input data (by default all shifts are equal to zero).
4. One, two or all three contours are used to build a point cloud comprised of the points obtained from the contour(s). The resulting point set may be called a framework of a stone.
5. The framework is interpolated to include a denser grid of points.
6. The resulting point cloud is then converted to a polygon mesh.

Poisson surface reconstruction [3,12,14] method implemented in CGAL library [1] is used to convert the framework of a stone to a polygon mesh. The reconstruction is directly preceded by an additional step of interpolating the framework through point density enhancement, which is required to make the polygon mesh conversion algorithm work correctly.

The surface reconstruction algorithm, if run on the original (non-interpolated) framework, will fail to obtain a comprehensive model of a stone, since the epsilon-sampling condition will not be met for the majority of the framework's points. The distance between the points comprising different input contours of the single stone is too large compared with the distance between the

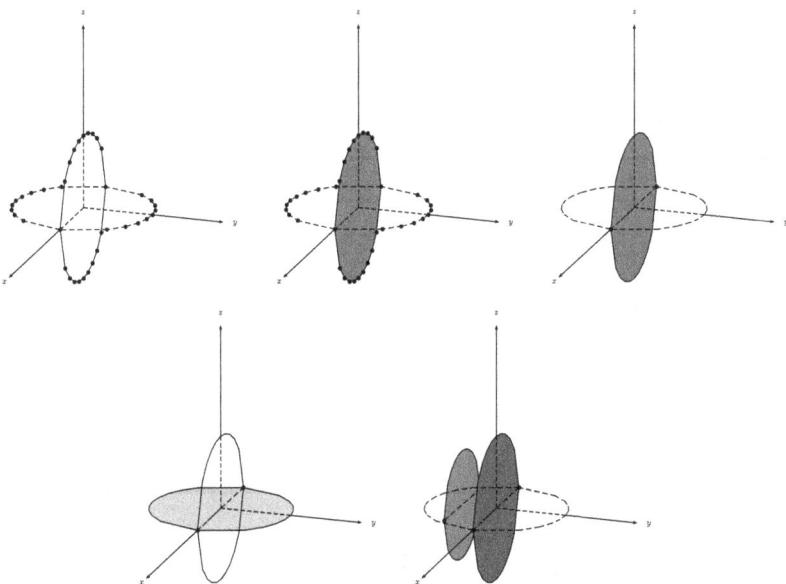

Fig. 2. Algorithm of stone reconstruction based on two input contours.

points comprising the same contour, with the exception of areas close to contour intersections. In order to make the data meet the condition, it is required to run an interpolation task that treats stone framework points as the key points.

The input data supplied to this algorithm may range from one up to three input contours. The simplest interpolation case involves two contours of the same stone. The algorithm used in such two-contour interpolation is shown in the Fig. 2.

An example of possible input data is schematically presented in Fig. 2. Let us consider the restoration algorithm illustrated in Fig. 3.

The first contour is selected in an arbitrary way from an available set, and its point scattering is measured. The selected contour will be referred to as the 'template' contour. The second contour of the same stone will be referred to as the 'static' contour–the word 'static' means it will not be changed as the result of the algorithm.

The task involves interpolation based on a small number of points–in this particular case, based on two points interpolated at each step of the algorithm. For practical reasons, we introduced an additional requirement–i.e., there should be a similarity between the template contour and those contours that will be obtained through interpolation. The interpolation task requires that the

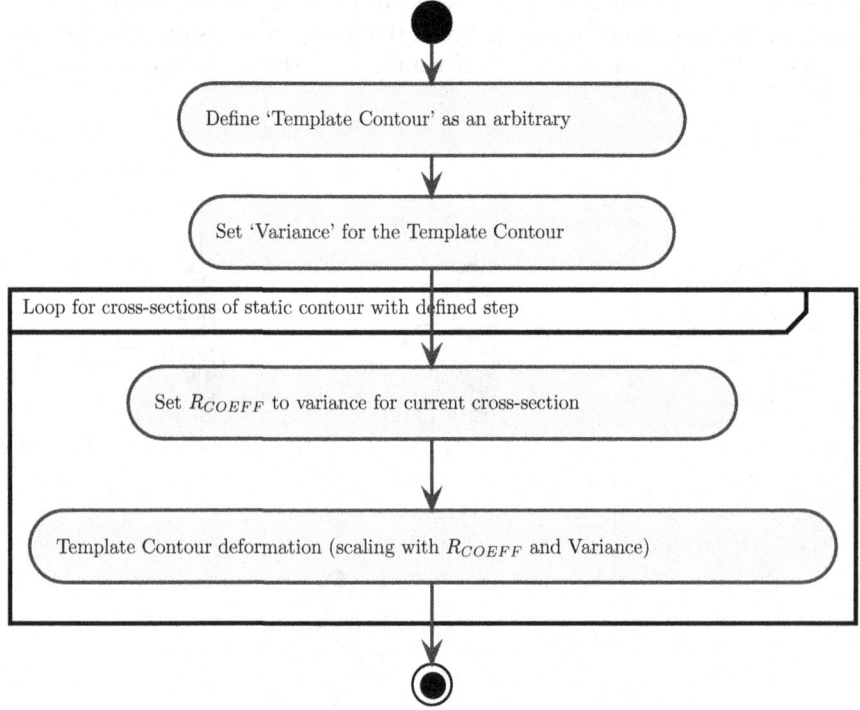

Fig. 3. Algorithm of stone reconstruction for two contours.

template contour and the static contour both have the same point scattering. The algorithm calculates the compression/expansion ratio R_{COEFF} for the template contour. Then the algorithm calculates the scattering of static contour coordinates along one of its axes. This axis must be at right angle to the template contour's plane and parallel to the static contour's plane.

Within the range of values obtained at the previous stage, the algorithm with the given step (equal to 1.0 by default, but can also be user-defined) obtains the static contour's cross-sections perpendicular to the contour's plane. The point scattering is identified for each cross-section. The template contour–that has been either compressed or expanded having regard to R_{COEFF} compression/expansion ratio–is added in each cross-section. The resulting contour should meet two conditions: it should be similar to the template contour and incorporate the static contour's points. This allows to obtain a dense regular grid of points on the entire surface of the given stone. This grid is suitable for the application of Poisson surface reconstruction method.

In the event of only one contour being provided to the algorithm, the second contour is substituted by a circumference or by a contour used earlier, and the task becomes the two-contour task described above.

Should there be three contours available for the stone, we use the algorithm presented in Fig. 4 (Stone reconstruction algorithm based on three input contours).

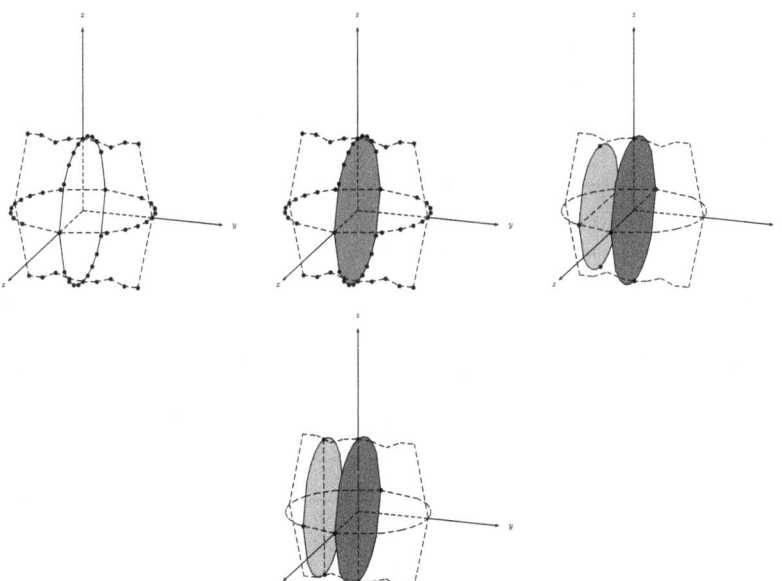

Fig. 4. Stone reconstruction algorithm based on three input contours.

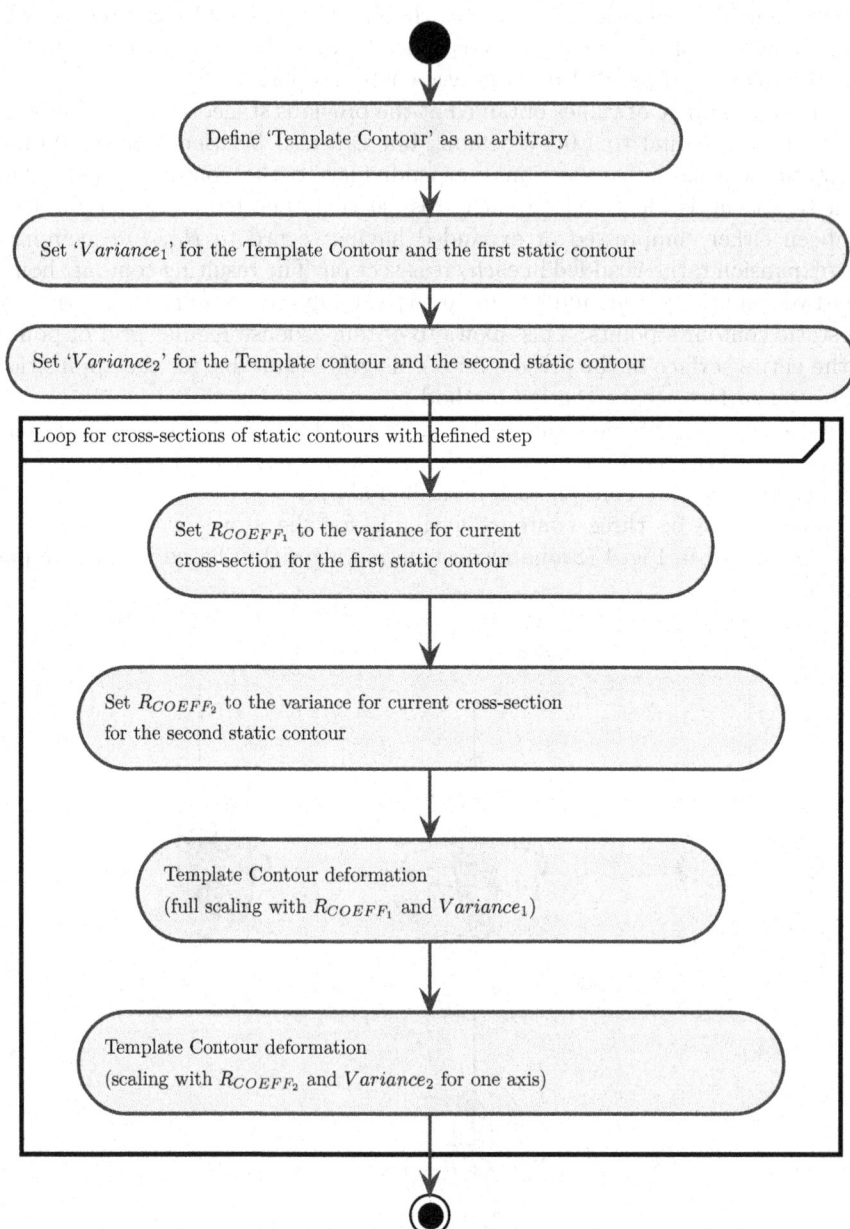

Fig. 5. Stone reconstruction algorithm for three contours.

In this instance, there are two static contours and one template contour. R_{COEFF_1} and R_{COEFF_2} values are determined for both static contours (Fig. 5). At each step, we start with the same algorithm as in the two-contour task and ignore one of the static contours. Then, the template contour that has undergone the first deformation having regard to R_{COEFF_1} coefficient is made subject to another deformation based on R_{COEFF_2} and having regard to the scattering of the second static contour (the one that was previously ignored). The second deformation is performed along one axis only–the one that includes the values of the cross-section of the previously ignored static contour.

As the result, the algorithm will produce a deformed contour that will run through the points of two static contours and be similar to the original template contour.

Note that any real task will fall within one of the following three situations:

- there is only one contour available for stones located in the centre of a wall's surface;
- there are two contours available for corner stones;
- there are three contours available for corner stones in the top row.

In other words, the algorithm described above is suited to process input data in any possible situation.

Experiments Performed. We have run tests using various input data, including those that have been obtained in actual archeological expeditions. Images in Table 1 show input data, and the result of stone reconstruction algorithm run on the input contours. The input drawings need not to be convex: the respective form will be displayed in the generated model. However, the input contours do need to coincide in overlapping points with only some degree of inaccuracy allowed. This degree (margin of error) depends on the required density of points in the output point cloud. Where this condition is not satisfied, the output object will have defects.

Proposed Algorithm Application Issues. The proposed algorithm will prove instrumental when dealing with one of the many issues in the comprehensive task of reconstruction and multimedia demonstration of archeological objects.

Specifically, we propose–by way of a possible option–not only to reconstruct stones based on actual drawings, but also to create their variations through slight deformation of models created earlier or through re-combination of stone schemes available in archives. The parameters of stones required to create an archeological object may be inferred from such object's historic and cultural specifics.

We can create a true-to-life object through adding fluctuations to the available contours, altering the size of generated models, and combining various stones.

Table 1. Tests of the position reconstruction algorithm for original and modified input data

ontours count, settings   ontours   Result

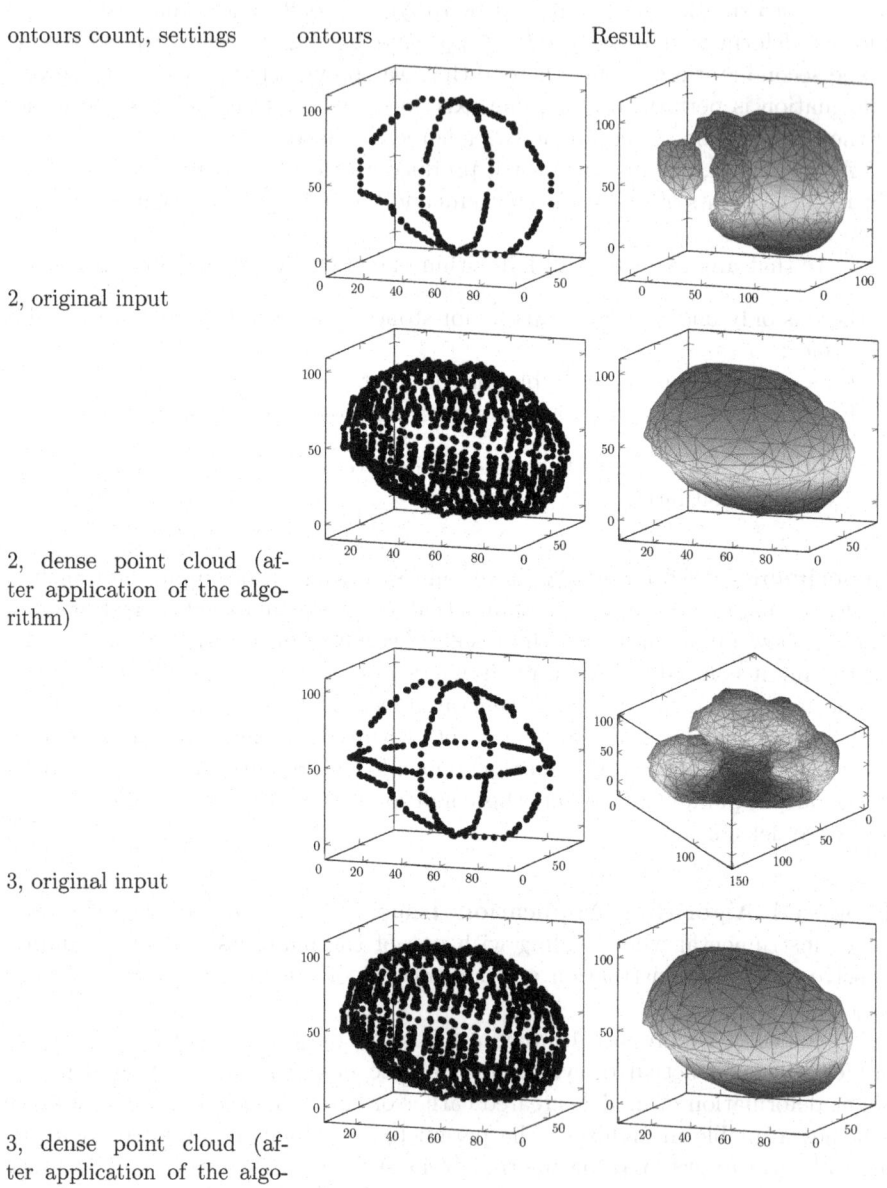

2, original input

2, dense point cloud (after application of the algorithm)

3, original input

3, dense point cloud (after application of the algorithm)

4 Generation of a Wall: Task and Solution

There are many 3D editors that are capable of reconstructing the appearance of a wall based on its contours. However, the generated wall will usually be represented by an indivisible 3D model. This renders it impossible to separate individual stones and, therefore, to ascribe individual properties to wall fragments in order to simulate their physical interaction. An indivisible model has another drawback: it is inconvenient to add the missing fragments once they are discovered by further studies or archive analysis (e.g., to add apertures, passageways and other items).

This prompted us to develop a specialized software that would allow to use the models of available stones in order to reconstruct a 3D wall and to further use this wall to run interactive physical simulations.

We decided to create the software in question using Houdini Engine, a graphic editor often utilized to create special effects and multimedia in filmmaking industry. Houdini Engine's distinguishing feature is that it is a visual programming environment–i.e., Houdini Engine allows modeling through procedural programming using so-called nodes. A node in Houdini Engine is a small function having a number of inputs and outputs and implementing an algorithm (e.g., uploading a 3D model from file, applying texture, copying a three-dimensional object, etc.). Node-based programming essentially involves creating a graph consisting of nodes, where one node's output may be supplied as input to another node. This kind of approach can be used in Houdini Engine by means of either a graphic editor or the python programming language. Using python allows to integrate Houdini Engine to any other code in python.

We put forward the following algorithm to solve the problem. The input data provided to the programme includes 3D models of stones and parameters of the prospective wall–height, width and length of a stone; curve describing the wall's shape; number of stone rows; and the size of gap between the stones.

1. Each object is uploaded together with its texture and scaled according to the defined dimensions of a stone. At this step, we obtain a set of 3D models that will become the constituent fragments of the prospective wall. The next step involves using a pre-set curve to select the points in which the selected scaled objects will be randomly located.
2. The curve is supplied to the algorithm as an ordered set of points lying in a plane, which points are successively connected with short line segments. In other words, the curve is approximated by a polygonal line.
3. The length of the object that will fill the prospective wall model is read by the algorithm, and then the size of gap between the objects is added to it.
4. Starting from the first point, line segments are successively intercepted on the curve. Each line segment has the value obtained at step 3.
5. The result is that the original curve is approximated by a polygonal line with chains of the same length. Stone models are then placed in the centres of line segments, their longitudinal axes having the same direction of orientation as the chains do. This step results in the first row of stones being generated.

6. The next row is generated based on the polygonal line created in steps 4 to 5. A new polygonal line is built so that the ends of its chains are placed in the centres of the preceding polygonal line.
7. Stone models in the second row are placed in the centres of the new polygonal line's chains, the stone models' longitudinal axes having the same direction of orientation as the chains do. That is how the second row of the wall is created.
8. The subsequent rows are generated based on the polygonal lines of the first and second rows.

This programme produces a 3D model of a wall with each stone being a 3D object as well, not a simple relief plane. The algorithm generates a wall model based on a curve.

Let us consider some examples of the algorithm's work. Let two models of red and green stones serve as an input. The red and green colours are used as texture to show the positions of objects in the generated wall.

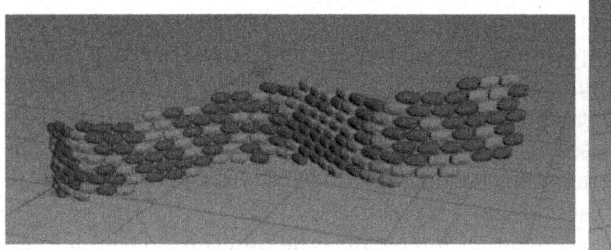 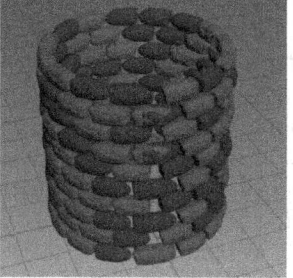

Fig. 6. Examples of wall reconstruction produced by our software. (Color figure online)

In Fig. 6, each stone is a separate 3D object, which allows to ascribe physical properties (weight, material, etc.) to each stone and simulate the wall's response to a variety of physical impacts. This kind of simulations have the potential of facilitating archeologists' understanding of the conditions in which the wall would exist and the causes of its destruction.

The algorithm we put forward has a number of drawbacks. First, it is currently unable of reconstructing a wall based on a closed curve. For instance, the algorithm does not allow to reconstruct a tower, since towers are essentially circumferences. The attempts to use a closed curve result in object overlapping, which is shown in Fig. 6–the green and red stones are mixed.

Secondly, the algorithm does not provide for wall layouts where a stone occupies more than one row. And third, this version of the algorithm leaves the gaps between stones unfilled–this certainly requires improvement, because various materials used to bond stones may exert a different impact on the wall's physical properties.

In future, we are going to upgrade the algorithm to provide for curves built in three dimensions, not only in a plane. We also will include the functions of adding apertures for other walls and windows.

5   Results and Conclusions

The paper describes the technique that allows to reconstruct 3D structures based on graphic archeological documents and presents the respective software. We put forward algorithms to reconstruct and visualize models of wall structures and wall building materials. The results may be used to create interactive multimedia reconstructions of historic monuments and also to model physical processes that have underlain a monument's destruction.

Acknowledgments. This research was partially supported by the Russian Foundation for Basic Research grants (projects no. 17-29-04288 17, 16-07-00886). The authors would like to acknowledge the Reviewers for the valuable recommendations that helped in the improvement of this paper.

References

1. Alliez, P., Fabri, A.: CGAL-the computational geometry algorithms library. Association for Computing Machinery, Inc. (2016)
2. Bogdanov, A., et al.: Building a virtual cluster for 3D graphics applications. In: Gervasi, O., et al. (eds.) ICCSA 2016. LNCS, vol. 9787, pp. 276–291. Springer, Cham (2016). https://doi.org/10.1007/978-3-319-42108-7_21
3. Culjak, I., Abram, D., Pribanic, T., Dzapo, H., Cifrek, M.: A Brief Introduction to Opencv, pp. 1725–1730 (2012)
4. Erickson, M., Bauer, J., Hayes, W.: The accuracy of photo-based three-dimensional scanning for collision reconstruction using 123D catch. SAE Technical Papers 2 (2013)
5. Fedoseev, G., Degtyarev, A., Iakushkina, O., Korkhov, V.: A continuous integration system for MPD root: Deployment and setup in GitLab, CEUR-WS, vol. 1787, pp. 525–529 (2016)
6. Gankevich, I., Tipikin, Y., Korkhov, V., Gaiduchok, V.: Factory: Non-stop batch jobs without checkpointing, pp. 979–984. Institute of Electrical and Electronics Engineers Inc. (2016)
7. Grasmueck, M., Weger, R., Horstmeyer, H.: Full-resolution 3D GPR imaging for geoscience and archeology, vol. 1, pp. 329–332 (2004)
8. Grishkin, V., Iakushkin, O.: Middleware transport architecture monitoring: Topology service. Institute of Electrical and Electronics Engineers Inc. (2014)
9. Iakushkin, O., Grishkin, V.: Messaging middleware for cloud applications: Extending brokerless approach. Institute of Electrical and Electronics Engineers Inc. (2014)
10. Iakushkin, O., Sedova, O., Valery, G.: Application control and horizontal scaling in modern cloud middleware. In: Gavrilova, M.L., Tan, C.J.K. (eds.) Transactions on Computational Science XXVII. LNCS, vol. 9570, pp. 81–96. Springer, Heidelberg (2016). https://doi.org/10.1007/978-3-662-50412-3_6

11. Iakushkin, O., Sedova, O.: Creating cad designs and performing their subsequent analysis using opensource solutions in python, vol. 1922. American Institute of Physics Inc. (2018)
12. Kazhdan, M., Hoppe, H.: Screened poisson surface reconstruction. ACM Trans. Graph. **32**(3), 61–70 (2013)
13. Kersten, T.P., Omelanowsky, D., Lindstaedt, M.: Investigations of low-cost systems for 3D reconstruction of small objects. In: Ioannides, M., et al. (eds.) EuroMed 2016. LNCS, vol. 10058, pp. 521–532. Springer, Cham (2016). https://doi.org/10.1007/978-3-319-48496-9_41
14. Moulon, P., Monasse, P., Perrot, R., Marlet, R.: OpenMVG: open multiple view geometry. In: Kerautret, B., Colom, M., Monasse, P. (eds.) RRPR 2016. LNCS, vol. 10214, pp. 60–74. Springer, Cham (2017). https://doi.org/10.1007/978-3-319-56414-2_5
15. Rizvic, S., Okanovic, V., Sadzak, A.: Visualization and multimedia presentation of cultural heritage. pp. 348–351. Institute of Electrical and Electronics Engineers Inc. (2015)

Algorithm for Processing the Results of Cloud Convection Simulation Using the Methods of Machine Learning

E. N. Stankova[1]([✉]), E. T. Ismailova[1], and I. A. Grechko[2]

[1] Saint-Petersburg State University,
7-9, Universitetskaya nab., St.Petersburg 199034, Russia
e.stankova@spbu.ru, elaismaylova@gmail.com
[2] Saint-Petersburg Electrotechnical University "LETI", (SPbETU),
ul.Professora Popova 5, St.Petersburg 197376, Russia
grechko.irinka@gmail.com

Abstract. Data preprocessing is an important stage in machine learning. The use of qualitatively prepared data increases the accuracy of predictions, even with simple models. The algorithm has been developed and implemented in the program code for converting the output data of a numerical model to a format suitable for subsequent processing. Detailed algorithm is presented for data pre-processing for selecting the most representative cloud parameters (features). As a result, six optimal parameters: vertical component of speed; temperature deviation from ambient temperature; relative humidity (above the water surface); the mixing ratio of water vapour; total droplet mixing ratio; vertical height of the cloud has been chosen as indicators for forecasting of dangerous convective phenomena (thunderstorm, heavy rain, hail). Feature selection has been provided by using recursive feature elimination algorithm with automatic tuning of the number of features selected with cross-validation. Cloud parameters have been fixed at mature stage of cloud development. Future work will be connected with identification of the influence of the nature of the evolution of the cloud parameters from initial stage to dissipation stage on the probability of a dangerous phenomenon.

Keywords: Machine learning · Numerical model of convective cloud
Weather forecasting · Thunderstorm · Data preprocessing · Feature selection

1 Introduction

Global warming produced by permanent anthropogenic influence on the atmosphere leads to an increase in the intensity of convective processes. The increase in temperature and the increase in air humidity are two facts that together lead to an intensification of active convection in the atmosphere, which in turn entails an increase in the number of heavy rains, an increase in thunderstorm activity, an increase in the number of tornadoes and an increase of other dangerous convective phenomena that have a tremendous destructive effect. Therefore, the problem of operational forecast of dangerous convective phenomena (thunderstorm, heavy rain, hail) is one of the most relevant and practically significant.

© Springer International Publishing AG, part of Springer Nature 2018
O. Gervasi et al. (Eds.): ICCSA 2018, LNCS 10963, pp. 149–159, 2018.
https://doi.org/10.1007/978-3-319-95171-3_13

Variable specificity of convective clouds, caused by large vertical velocities within the cloud and its environment, and also the impossibility of carrying out control experiments lead to the fact that the greatest success can be achieved by computer research, which allows, without resorting to costly field experiments, to carry out an analysis of the development of the cloud. Forecast of dangerous convective phenomena is based upon the results of such an analysis.

Computer researches are based on numerical modeling. The construction of a numerical model consists of two stages: the first is the creation of a qualitative model, the second is the creation of a quantitative model. Creation of a qualitative cloud model implies formalization of the physical processes taking place in it and allows to reveal significant properties. As a result of the construction of a quantitative model, measurement scales and standards are established for each of these properties, which makes it possible to characterize the properties numerically.

Computer simulation provides a set of the output data that must be analyzed in order to build a forecast of dangerous convective phenomenon caused by the development of the cloud with such properties.

Methods of machine learning allow to automate the process of forecasting. The application of machine learning methods consists in carrying out a series of computational experiments, with the purpose of analyzing, interpreting and comparing the simulation results with the actual behavior of the object under study and, if necessary, the subsequent refinement of the input parameters.

Methods of machine learning implement the concept of data mining. This concept consists in processing large amounts of data and identifying on their basis various relationships and patterns. However, the data may be inaccurate, heterogeneous, inconsistent, contain omissions, which leads to incorrect forecasting. Therefore, an important step is feature selection, that is identification the most significant features among the data obtained.

The present paper is concerned mainly with the description of this important step of machine learning in case of preprocessing data for analyses of the results of numerical modeling of convective cloud.

2 Data Formation for the Research

As it is well known, the tasks of machine learning are reduced to the problem of finding an unknown relationship between a known set of objects and a set of answers [1, 2]. So, it is necessary to construct a function that would approximate sufficiently accurately the values of the set of responses at the points of the set of objects and on the rest of the space.

Everything can be considered as objects: web pages, countries, people, products, businesses, that is everything that carries any information (has a set of features). Features are understood as methods for measuring the characteristics of objects in the space under study.

Depending on the answers (values of the target variable), the tasks of machine learning are divided into types. The main types of machine learning tasks are:

- classification tasks;
- regression problems;
- ranking tasks.

Our task relates to the problems of regression.

The model of relationship between a known set of objects and a set of answers is called model of algorithms. The problem of finding the dependency model is reduced to constructing an algorithm that would equally accurately approximate the unknown target dependence, both on the sample elements and on the entire object space. This task was called the training with the teacher (supervised learning).

At the training stage, a training sample is used to identify the dependency, and optimization of the parameters is performed using it.

In our case training sample represents a set of radiosonde soundings obtained at a place and on a time when the dangerous convective phenomena take place. Radiosonde soundings were used as input data for one and a half convective cloud model [3–7]. Our training set consists of numerical parameters simulated by a numerical cloud model for each sounding, and is manually marked, that is, for each sounding from our set we know whether any dangerous convective phenomenon has been observed or not.

So the fact of dangerous phenomenon occurrence can be considered as an answer, and the results of numerical modeling, using as an input the corresponding radiosonde sounding, can be considered as an object.

The numerical parameters of the simulated clouds were chosen as an object features. There is a problem that should be discussed concerned with the time and height when and where the features are to be fixed. In the previous our works [8, 9] it was decided to fix the numerical parameters at the moment of maximum cloud development and at the height, where the maximum ratio of water droplets was observed. These time moment and height correspond to the mature stage of cloud development. But there are three stages in cloud evolution: stage of development, mature stage and dissipation stage. And it would be interesting to identify the influence of the nature of the evolution of the cloud parameters from stage to stage on the probability of a dangerous phenomenon with the help of machine learning methods. But at present there are no appropriate algorithms. So the only way out is to fix the cloud parameters not only at mature stage, but at the stages of development and dissipation also. Data preprocessing and subsequent analyses should be provided for the three sets of features and the best set from the point of the most accurate forecast should be chosen.

Training sample represents a set of radiosonde soundings obtained at a place and on a time when the dangerous convective phenomena take place were obtained with the help of integrated information system [10–15], which allow to integrate information about the dates and types of different convective phenomena and about vertical distributions of temperature and relative humidity observed on these dates and places.

3 Data Preprocessing

Data preprocessing is an important stage in machine learning. The use of qualitatively prepared data increases the accuracy of predictions, even with simple models.

At the first stage of preparation, it is necessary to transform data specific for the subject domain into understandable vectors for the model. For these purposes, an algorithm was developed and implemented in the program code for converting the output data of a numerical model to a format suitable for subsequent processing (the columns correspond to the characteristics, each line to a sounding uniquely determined by the values of the signs of time and height).

The next stage of data preprocessing is the adaptation of the data set to the requirements of the algorithm. The data has been subjected to normalization in view of the fact that most of the gradient methods that underlie almost all the algorithms of machine learning are highly sensitive to data scaling.

As a result of preprocessing, the data were brought to a form convenient for further work with machine learning methods.

The main statistical characteristics of the numerical data (the number of unallocated values, mean, standard deviation, range, median, 0.25 and 0.75 quartiles) are shown in Fig. 1. Analyzing these data, we can conclude that we have a complete set of data (the number of records is the same for each column, which indicates the absence of omissions in the data, their completeness).

The mean values of numerical features in the data with and without the phenomenon are presented in Table 1.

	velocity	velocityU	temperature	deltaT	relativeH	vapor	pressure	density	aerosol
count	6.150000e+02	615.000000	615.000000	615.000000	615.000000	6.150000e+02	615.000000	615.000000	6.150000e+02
mean	9.015934e+00	0.712901	263.406597	2.463016	0.714923	3.172778e-03	58969.729092	0.780044	2.729818e-08
std	1.012207e+01	7.603501	9.732534	3.371144	0.321774	2.817081e-03	2553.681444	0.032678	4.986370e-08
min	-2.607130e+00	-28.274580	183.397840	-2.372689	0.007335	1.550653e-08	4920.701500	0.093471	0.000000e+00
25%	-7.412999e-07	-1.061997	257.285400	-0.158336	0.397372	6.999553e-04	58412.269000	0.769386	0.000000e+00
50%	1.059566e+00	-0.000169	263.817430	0.914849	0.902727	2.333101e-03	59073.761000	0.780448	0.000000e+00
75%	1.854551e+01	0.001944	270.550375	4.552562	0.998569	5.167988e-03	59853.462500	0.791151	5.672878e-08
max	3.053718e+01	93.666761	282.485530	17.292512	1.017904	1.189431e-02	74666.560000	0.960829	1.052166e-06

Fig. 1. Main statistical characteristics

From the Table 1 we can conclude that such features as temperature and pressure play a weak role in predicting the phenomenon.

Grouping of data depending on the target variable and output of statistical data allows displaying the number of unset values, average value, standard deviation, range and median separately for the sets of soundings with and without phenomena. A fragment of the statistical data grouped by the value of the target variable is presented in Table 2.

Table 1. Mean values of numerical features

Without phenomenon	With phenomenon
velocity -1.042726e-02 velocityU -3.687637e-02 temperature 2.570544e+02 deltaT -2.149329e-01 relativeH 4.131247e-01 vapor 8.592840e-04 pressure 5.826526e+04 density 7.891568e-01 aerosol 5.676505e-08 drop 1.086072e-05 ice 6.266864e-06 hailAndGrits 2.029110e-05 targetV 0.000000e+00 dtype: float64	velocity 1.701783e+01 velocityU 1.377581e+00 temperature 2.690378e+02 deltaT 4.837027e+00 relativeH 9.824677e-01 vapor 5.223697e-03 pressure 5.959424e+04 density 7.719661e-01 aerosol 1.175712e-09 drop 5.998802e-03 ice 6.216738e-05 hailAndGrits 2.728569e-04 targetV 1.000000e+00 dtype: float64

Table 2. A fragment of the statistical data grouped by the value of the target variable

targetV		velocity	velocityU	temperature	deltaT	relativeH	vapor	pressure	density	aerosol
0.0	count	2.890000e+02	289.000000	289.000000	289.000000	289.000000	2.890000e+02	289.000000	289.000000	2.890000e+02
	mean	-1.042726e-02	-0.036876	257.054432	-0.214933	0.413125	8.592840e-04	58265.261853	0.789157	5.676505e-08
	std	4.497304e-01	0.981230	7.834125	0.637566	0.205231	6.454670e-04	3304.279900	0.042477	5.995266e-08
	min	-2.412241e+00	-7.118333	183.397840	-2.372689	0.007335	1.550653e-08	4920.701500	0.093471	0.000000e+00
	50%	-8.715962e-07	-0.000002	257.616430	-0.174670	0.373010	6.995521e-04	58554.729000	0.790320	5.693065e-08
	max	6.425881e+00	9.186365	270.851100	5.369964	0.996721	4.672748e-03	61204.791000	0.834002	1.052166e-06
1.0	count	3.260000e+02	326.000000	326.000000	326.000000	326.000000	3.260000e+02	326.000000	326.000000	3.260000e+02
	mean	1.701783e+01	1.377581	269.037812	4.837027	0.982468	5.223697e-03	59594.241460	0.771966	1.175712e-09
	std	7.530381e+00	10.364664	7.541692	3.013280	0.074093	2.375928e-03	1346.268411	0.016710	7.459265e-09
	min	-2.607130e+00	-28.274580	235.463740	-0.427600	0.213483	1.940047e-04	54716.773000	0.740654	0.000000e+00
	50%	1.810377e+01	-0.958654	269.804885	4.262443	0.998146	4.973325e-03	59677.786500	0.770532	0.000000e+00
	max	3.053718e+01	93.666761	282.485530	17.292512	1.017904	1.189431e-02	74666.560000	0.960829	5.622077e-08

Figure 2 shows the graphs of the dependencies of various characteristics from each other (boxplot), the histograms of the distribution are on the diagonal.

A more detailed display of the relationship between two features: the deviation of temperature from the ambient temperature and the vertical component of wind speed is shown in the Fig. 3.

The matrix of correlation of numerical features is the form of the data matrix, which includes correlation coefficients for all pairs of analyzed variables. The correlation matrix is the basis for factor analysis, canonical correlation, and other statistical

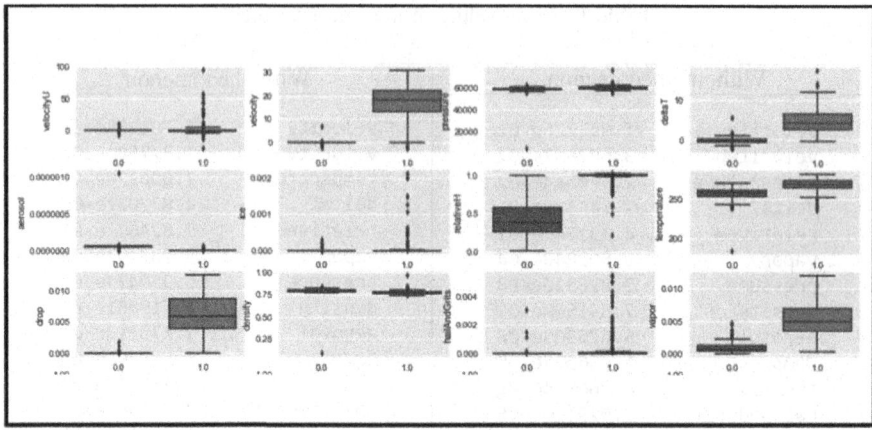

Fig. 2. Diagram of the range of feature values (boxplot)

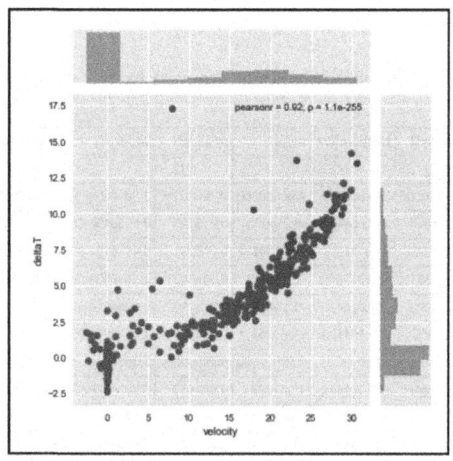

Fig. 3. The relationship between the feature of temperature excess from ambient temperature and the vertical component of velocity

techniques that reproduce the structure of the relationship between variables. A visual display of the correlation matrix of the characteristics used for the prediction of dangerous convective phenomena is given in Fig. 4.

When studying the features in a large group, different values of this characteristic are observed and occur unevenly a number of times: some more often, others less often. The distribution of the features from the minimum to the maximum is carried out, ordered when broken down into classes, that is, a variation series is constructed. The variation series are a double series of numbers consisting of the designation of classes and the corresponding frequencies.

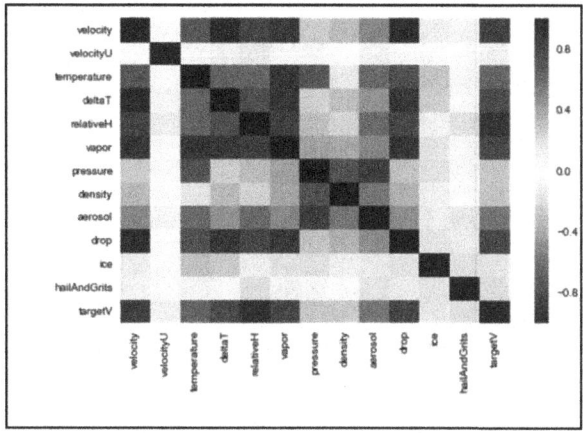

Fig. 4. Matrix of correlation of numerical features

The variation series includes all the primary material for the measurement of the feature in all representatives of the group. This material in the variation series is brought in a certain order, which makes it possible to characterize the sign, both at the average level of development, and on various details of diversity with an approximation that is quite sufficient for the first acquaintance with the feature.

For more detailed familiarization with the alignment of the characteristic, a variation curve is plotted graphically in the form of a curve whose ordinates are proportional to the frequencies of the variation series. The distribution of features can serve to identify a certain pattern. The norm of mass random manifestation of features, according to this, is called the normal distribution, which is usually hidden under the random form of its manifestation. The distributions of the characteristics are presented in the Fig. 2. A diagram of the scale (boxplot) is widely used to display the connection of characteristics with the target variable.

The boxplot is a limited area in the form of a rectangle (box), lines and points. The area bounded by the rectangle shows the inter quantile range of the distribution, that is, respectively 25% (Q1) and 75% (Q3) percentiles. The bar inside the rectangle indicates the median of the distribution. The lines that extend from the rectangle represent the entire scatter of points except the ejections, that is, the minimum and maximum values that fall within the gap.

$$(Q1 - 1.5 * IQR, Q3 + 1.5 * IQR), \tag{3.1}$$

where IQR = Q3–Q1 is an inter quantile range.

Points on the graph indicate emissions, that represent those values that do not fit into the range of values specified by the lines of the graph. An example of a boxplot is shown in Fig. 5.

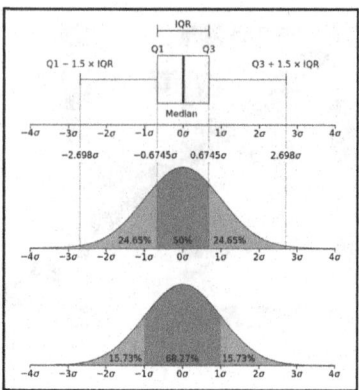

Fig. 5. Example of a boxplot

The result of plotting the boxplot for the features used in this paper is given in the Fig. 2. This kind of diagram in a convenient form shows the median, the lower and upper quartiles, the minimum and maximum value of the sample, and the outliers. Several such diagrams, constructed on the same plane, allow one to visually compare one distribution with another. Distances between different parts of the box allow you to determine the degree of dispersion (dispersion) and data asymmetry and to identify emissions.

Based on the results obtained, it can be concluded that the most interesting parameters are the vertical component of velocity, pressure, temperature deviation from ambient temperature, relative humidity.

One of the most important stages in the preparation of data is the selection of the most significant features. The reduction in the number of features (the rejection of features that are weakly correlated with the target variable) not only increases the accuracy of the prediction, but also lowers the requirements for the computing resources used.

There are various methods for feature selection, they can be divided into three groups:

- methods of filtration;
- methods for selecting the best subset;
- built-in methods.

The filtration methods are based on a statistical approach and consider the effect of each feature on the prediction error independently.

The Information gain method is one of the filtering methods. The IG (Information gain) parameter indicates the degree of correlation between the characteristic and the target variable. Thus, the method allows you to rank the characteristics by significance, degree of correlation with the target variable.

The degree of correlation of features with the target variable was represented using the matrix in the Fig. 4. According to this matrix, we can conclude that the most significant features are:

- vertical component of speed;
- temperature deviation from ambient temperature;
- relative humidity (above the water surface);
- the mixing ratio of water vapour;
- total droplet mixing ratio.

Filtering methods have low computational costs and work reliably on training sets, where the number of features exceeds the number of examples - these characteristics are advantages of this group of methods. However, an essential drawback is to work with each feature independently, because such an approach does not allow us to determine a subset on which the prediction accuracy will be the highest.

Methods for determining the best subset of characteristics consist in starting the classifier on different subsets and selecting a subset with the best parameters on the training sample. In turn, the methods of this group can be divided into inclusion methods and methods of exclusion. In the first case, the method starts with an empty subset, then at each step the optimal attribute is selected, in the second case, the initial subset is equal to the original set of characteristics. The work of the method consists in excluding the feature at each step with the reclassification of the classifier.

Recursive Feature Elimination method from the library scikit-learn is an example of methods for the gradual elimination of features [16]. To use this method, the support vector method was chosen as the classifier. As a result, the following six parameters appeared to be optimal for using as forecasting indicators:

- vertical component of speed;
- temperature deviation from ambient temperature;
- relative humidity (above the water surface);
- the mixing ratio of water vapour;
- total droplet mixing ratio;
- vertical height of the cloud.

4   Conclusions

Detailed algorithm is presented for data pre-processing for selecting the most representative cloud parameters (features). As a result, six optimal parameters: vertical component of speed; temperature deviation from ambient temperature; relative humidity (above the water surface); the mixing ratio of water vapour; total droplet mixing ratio; vertical height of the cloud has been chosen as indicators for forecasting of dangerous convective phenomena (thunderstorm, heavy rain, hail). Feature selection has been provided by using recursive feature elimination algorithm with automatic tuning of the number of features selected with cross-validation. Cloud parameters have been fixed at mature stage of cloud development.

Future work will be connected with identification of the influence of the nature of the evolution of the cloud parameters from initial stage to dissipation stage on the probability of a dangerous phenomenon. All the collected data should be integrated to the previously developed integrated information system [10–15]. In future the system should become a consistent part of the Virtual private supercomputer [17, 18] and will be organized similar to the systems presented in [19, 20], that will enable users to provide forecasts of the dangerous convective phenomena by themselves.

Acknowledgment. This research was sponsored by the Russian Foundation for Basic Research under the projects: № 16-07-01113.

References

1. Hastie, T., Tibshirani, R., Friedman, J.: The Elements of Statistical Learning. SSS. Springer, New York (2009). https://doi.org/10.1007/978-0-387-84858-7. http://statweb.stanford.edu/~tibs/ElemStatLearn/
2. Mitchell, T.: Machine Learning. Springer, Berlin (2009)
3. Raba, N., Stankova, E., Ampilova, N.: On investigation of parallelization effectiveness with the help of multi-core processors. Procedia Comput. Sci. **1**(1), 2757–2762 (2010)
4. Raba, N., Stankova, E.: On the possibilities of multi-core processor use for real-time forecast of dangerous convective phenomena. In: Taniar, D., Gervasi, O., Murgante, B., Pardede, E., Apduhan, Bernady O. (eds.) ICCSA 2010. LNCS, vol. 6017, pp. 130–138. Springer, Heidelberg (2010). https://doi.org/10.1007/978-3-642-12165-4_11
5. Raba, N.O., Stankova, E.N.: On the problem of numerical modeling of dangerous convective phenomena: possibilities of real-time forecast with the help of multi-core processors. In: Murgante, B., Gervasi, O., Iglesias, A., Taniar, D., Apduhan, B.O. (eds.) ICCSA 2011. LNCS, vol. 6786, pp. 633–642. Springer, Heidelberg (2011). https://doi.org/10.1007/978-3-642-21934-4_51
6. Raba, N.O., Stankova, E.N.: On the effectiveness of using the GPU for numerical solution of stochastic collection equation. In: Murgante, B., Misra, S., Carlini, M., Torre, C.M., Nguyen, H.-Q., et al. (eds.) ICCSA 2013. LNCS, vol. 7975, pp. 248–258. Springer, Heidelberg (2013). https://doi.org/10.1007/978-3-642-39640-3_18
7. Raba, N., Stankova, E.: Research of influence of compensating descending flow on cloud's life cycle by means of 1.5-dimensional model with 2 cylinders. In: Proceedings of MGO, vol. 559, pp. 192–209 (2009). (in Russian)
8. Stankova, E.N., Grechko, I.A., Kachalkina, Y.N., Khvatkov, E.V.: Hybrid approach combining model-based method with the technology of machine learning for forecasting of dangerous weather phenomena. In: Gervasi, O., Murgante, B., Misra, S., Borruso, G., Torre, C.M., et al. (eds.) ICCSA 2017. LNCS, vol. 10408, pp. 495–504. Springer, Cham (2017). https://doi.org/10.1007/978-3-319-62404-4_37
9. Stankova, E.N., Balakshiy, A.V., Petrov, D.A., Shorov, A.V., Korkhov, V.V.: Using technologies of OLAP and machine learning for validation of the numerical models of convective clouds. In: Gervasi, O., Murgante, B., Misra, S., Rocha, A.M.A.C., Torre, C., et al. (eds.) ICCSA 2016. LNCS, vol. 9788, pp. 463–472. Springer, Cham (2016). https://doi.org/10.1007/978-3-319-42111-7_36
10. Petrov, D.A., Stankova, E.N.: Use of consolidation technology for meteorological data processing. In: Murgante, B., Misra, S., Rocha, A.A.C., Torre, C., Rocha, J.G., et al. (eds.) ICCSA 2014. LNCS, vol. 8579, pp. 440–451. Springer, Cham (2014). https://doi.org/10.1007/978-3-319-09144-0_30

11. Petrov, D.A., Stankova, E.N.: Integrated information system for verification of the models of convective clouds. In: Gervasi, O., Murgante, B., Misra, S., Gavrilova, M.L., Rocha, A.M.A.C., et al. (eds.) ICCSA 2015. LNCS, vol. 9158, pp. 321–330. Springer, Cham (2015). https://doi.org/10.1007/978-3-319-21410-8_25
12. Stankova, E.N., Petrov, D.A.: Complex information system for organization of the input data of models of convective clouds. Vestnik of Saint-Petersburg University. Series 10. Applied Mathematics. Computer Science. Control Processes. Issue 3, pp. 83–95 (2015). (in Russian)
13. Petrov, D.A., Stankova, E.N.: Use of consolidation technology for meteorological data processing. In: Murgante, B., Misra, S., Rocha, A.A.C., Torre, C., Rocha, J.G., et al. (eds.) ICCSA 2014. LNCS, vol. 8579, pp. 440–451. Springer, Cham (2014). https://doi.org/10.1007/978-3-319-09144-0_30
14. Petrov, D.A., Stankova, E.N.: Integrated information system for verification of the models of convective clouds. In: Gervasi, O., Murgante, B., Misra, S., Gavrilova, M.L., Rocha, A.M.A.C., et al. (eds.) ICCSA 2015. LNCS, vol. 9158, pp. 321–330. Springer, Cham (2015). https://doi.org/10.1007/978-3-319-21410-8_25
15. Petrov, D., Stankova, E.: Complex information system for organization of the input data of models of convective clouds Vestnik of Saint-Petersburg University. Series 10. Applied Mathematics. Computer Science. Control Processes. Issue 3. pp. 83–95 (2015). (in Russian)
16. Scikit-learn. Machine Learning in Python. http://scikit-learn.org/
17. Bogdanov, A., Degtyarev, A., Korkhov, V., Gaiduchok, V., Gankevich, I.: Virtual Supercomputer as basis of Scientific Computing, in series: Horizons in Computer Science Research. In: Clary, T.S. (eds.), vol. 11, pp. 159–198. Nova Science Publishers (2015). ISBN: 978-1-63482-499-6
18. Korkhov, V., Krefting, D., Kukla, T., Terstyanszky, G.Z., Caan, M., Olabarriaga, S.D.: Exploring workflow interoperability tools for neuroimaging data analysis. In: WORKS 2011 - Proceedings of the 6th Workshop on Workflows in Support of Large-Scale Science, Co-located with SC 2011, pp. 87–96 (2011). https://doi.org/10.1145/2110497.2110508
19. Kulabukhova, N., Bogdanov, A., Degtyarev, A.: Problem-solving environment for beam dynamics analysis in particle accelerators. In: Gervasi, O., Murgante, B., Misra, S., Borruso, G., Torre, C.M., et al. (eds.) ICCSA 2017. LNCS, vol. 10408, pp. 473–482. Springer, Cham (2017). https://doi.org/10.1007/978-3-319-62404-4_35
20. Kulabukhova, N., Andrianov, S.N., Bogdanov, A., Degtyarev, A.: Simulation of space charge dynamics in high intensive beams on hybrid systems. In: Gervasi, O. et al. (eds.) Computational Science and its Applications – ICCSA 2016, vol. 9786, pp. 284–295. Springer, Cham (2016). https://doi.org/10.1007/978-3-319-42085-1_22

3D Reconstruction of Landscape Models and Archaeological Objects Based on Photo and Video Materials

Oleg Iakushkin, Dmitrii Selivanov, Liliia Tazieva, Anna Fatkina[✉],
Valery Grishkin, and Alexei Uteshev

Saint-Petersburg State University, St.Petersburg 199034, Russia
o.yakushkin@spbu.ru, fatkina.a.i@gmail.com

Abstract. Computer technology is used to reconstruct the main parts of archaeological monuments by creating their 3D models. There is a number of software products that can solve this important task of historical and cultural studies. However, the existing solutions either require expensive specialized equipment or may only be used by specially trained personnel. This makes it relevant to create a software that could reconstruct 3D models automatically.

This paper describes the algorithm and development stages of a new application that comprises components with the following functionality: video decomposition, user movement tracking, point cloud creation, polygon mesh creation, and application of texture to a polygon mesh. The software we have developed allows to run an automatic 3D reconstruction of landscape models and archaeological objects based on photo and video materials. It allows to significantly reduce labour costs and processing time compared to the existing solutions. The software has a friendly interface and may be operated be users without special expertise.

Keywords: 3D reconstruction · Landscape visualisation
Automatization · Digital reconstruction · Cultural heritage
Virtual archeology

1 Introduction

The development of software that allows to automatically build 3D models of an archaeological monument and the surrounding landscape is a relevant cross-disciplinary task. Visualization of history is currently used for scientific purposes and popularization in a plethora of ways.

Laser scanning and photogrammetry are the most widely used methods to create 3D models of ancient objects and environments. These methods of 3D data collection require specialized equipment that increases the cost of research and raises the complexity of post-editing stage [3,15].

© Springer International Publishing AG, part of Springer Nature 2018
O. Gervasi et al. (Eds.): ICCSA 2018, LNCS 10963, pp. 160–169, 2018.
https://doi.org/10.1007/978-3-319-95171-3_14

The availability of high-precision models of modern relief significantly alters our understanding of historic landscapes. The bulk of this 3D information is obtained from topographic maps and satellite data, and is further analysed using geographic information systems (GIS). This kind of information may be accurate enough when applied to entire cities or regions, but its degree of accuracy does not suffice when it comes to studying the specifics of local surroundings of archaeological monuments, where 0.1–1,0 meter landscape resolution is required.

The following commercial products allow to create 3D models of archaeological excavation landscapes based on video materials: Photo Modeler, Autodesk 123D Catch and Autodesk AutoCAD. These products process a series of specifically prepared photos of an object as well as elevation and position marks made during archaeological studies. Such software requires that its users have professional level of expertise.

This makes it relevant to develop a software consisting of components that are already available and can—once combined—automate the reconstruction of 3D models of landscapes and archaeological monuments based on photo and video materials [4,7]. This kind of software should be designed for users who do not have special computer modelling skills and is easily transferable into a distributed environment setting [6,8,10–12].

2   Problem Description

This paper has the goal of automating the process of reconstructing 3D models of archaeological monument components based on photo and video materials obtained at an archaeological site. This goal can be broken down in two smaller tasks:

1. obtaining a 3D model of landscape based on video materials;
2. creating a 3D model of an archaeological object based on its photographs.

3   Creating a 3D Model of an Object Using Its Photographs

We developed a programme called '2Dto3D' to create 3D models using video materials and to examine the algorithms underlying object reconstruction. The programme is based on a freeware that allows to convert photos and videos taken around an object into a polygon mesh with a texture applied to it. The programme is run in three major stages:

1. conversion of video of an object into a series of photographs;
2. reconstruction:
    (a) creation of a point cloud based on photographs;
    (b) conversion of the point cloud into a polygon mesh;
    (c) saving the model and its texture.
3. Deletion of temporary files created during reconstruction.

The programme was developed under the paradigm of component-based software engineering, which allows to easily replace its separate modules implementing various parts of the algorithm.

3.1   Data Preparation

This stage involves video breakdown into separate frames with user-defined frequency using FFmpeg multimedia platform—a multifunctional cross-platform framework that allows to encode and multiplex the data obtained from a digital stream, and to perform video and audio conversion. FFmpeg enables the programme to work with various video formats, such as MPEG, AVI, 3GP, FLV, MOV and others.

3.2   Reconstruction

The SIFT (Scale-invariant feature transform) algorithm [2] is used to single out a set of key points in each of the photos obtained at the first stage. These points serve the purpose of comparing the images with each other. The Incremental Sfm algorithm is used to create a point cloud [18]. The successive frames are compared with each other—this part is the most resource-intensive. The usual complexity of the process is $O(n^2)$, where 'n' is the number of photos. However, Incremental Sfm allows to reduce the comparison complexity down to $O(n)$ by reducing the number of point pairs compared with each other. This stage involves automatic ascertainment of camera lens distortion.

Then the points are projected in three-dimensional space. New points are added to the point cloud from photographs—one photograph at each iteration. The Bundle adjustment (BA) algorithm [1] is utilized to ensure the projections are performed correctly. The algorithm identifies the coordinates in space that correspond to the points in photographs. Importantly, it has regard to both camera parameters and point parameters. The projections of the same point made from different images do not necessarily coincide—the difference between their coordinates is called a projection error. The BA algorithm is aimed at minimizing the function of projection errors. Where necessary, the points that have been added to the point cloud are further filtered: the points having excessive projection error values are removed from the cloud. In the event the error function values for some points have been altered during such filtration, the BA algorithm is called recursively.

After the point cloud has been created, we obtain a file containing data about all cameras that will be used for model reconstruction, a initialization file with polygon mesh reconstruction parameters, and projection matrixes for each image.

The reconstruction stage is completed with polygon mesh reconstruction based on the point cloud created earlier, on information about camera positions in space, and on parameters described in the initialization file that contains information about:

- images of an object: their quantity and dimensions;
- location of folders with photos and projection matrixes;
- requirement to remove excessively large triangles from the mesh;
- export of object textures;

– number by which the quantity of polygons should be reduced when obtaining a simplified model. The simplification allows to reduce surface distortions.

CMPMVS software [13] is used to create a polygon mesh. This step of reconstruction results in two polygon meshes in 'wrl' format with textures applied to them, and a number of separate 'png' files with textures. The number of 'png' files may vary depending on the mesh and as a rule ranges from 1 to 5.

3.3   The Final Stage of Reconstruction

At the fourth step, the 3D model undergoes conversion from the outdated 'wrl' format into 'obj' format. The latter format, being one of the most popular among developers, allows to reduce efforts and costs required to recognize and store 3D objects. After conversion, the file will contain vertices, normals and texture coordinates of the model. It will also contain a link to a file in the material library that stores the model's texture data. Furthermore, the material library file itself is created. The conversion is implemented in Meshlab.

The external software is called by means of the free library. POCO allows to create new processes and supply command line arguments to the programmes requiring such arguments for their work. The user interface was generated by means of the Qt cross-platform framework that allows to create widgets and isolate interface threads from the programme's major computing threads.

The description of 3D model reconstruction indicates that the programme creates many temporary files that are needed only at certain reconstruction steps. These files allow to perform a step-by-step analysis of the process, which might be useful for developers. For ordinary users, there is an option allowing to delete all temporary files.

The 2Dto3D software produces a number of files as the result of its work: the file containing the model, several texture files, and the material library file. It also produces a folder containing the same files for a model simplified by 25 times.

3.4   Functionality of the Developed Application

Figure 1 reveals the main problems in the models generated by the programme:

– ripple distortions in planes (smooth surfaces—e.g., the apple's surface);
– a more accurate camera positioning requires bright marks to be placed around an object (problem similar to that in 123D Catch);
– the polygon mesh consists of several parts.
– textures created by the programme (see Fig. 2) are hard to edit.

However, these isolated drawbacks have little impact on the programme's main advantage: it enables an unqualified user to create a 3D model based on a video of an unlimited duration using a single open source product. The user interaction with the programme includes only two actions: selecting a video file and defining the number of frames per second. The programme then generates

a model in 'obj' format and its texture in 'png' formant. In future, we are going
to reduce the programme's runtime (see Table 1) by using co-processors and to
improve on the textures generated by the programme by using algorithm [19].

We should note that this solution does not allow to create a 3D landscape
model of an archaeological excavation site, because the point cloud generation
will not yield a reliable result in this case. Furthermore, it might be difficult to
place bright marks at the borders of an entire archaeological monument.

(a) to the righta poly- (b) to the righta polygon
gon mesh simplified by 25 mesh; to the leftphoto of
times; to the leftphoto of an object.
an object;

Fig. 1. The result returned by 2Dto3D.

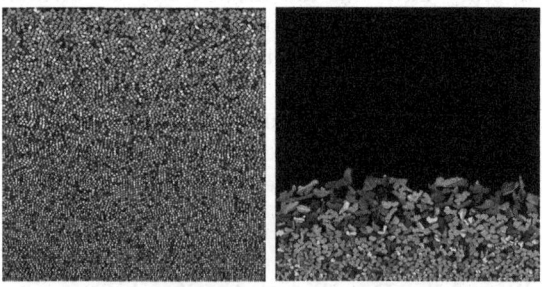

(a) To the righta poly- (b) To the righta polygon
gon mesh simplified by 25 mesh; to the leftphoto of
times; to the leftphoto of an object.
an object.

Fig. 2. Textures generated by 2Dto3D for the model presented in Fig. 1.

Table 1. 2Dto3D runtime depending on the number and size of added photos

Image count	52	211	103	74	34
Image size	1920 × 1080	1920 × 1080	1920 × 1080	640 × 480	3264 × 2488
Run Time (hours)	0,6	2,3	1,1	0,25	0,5

4   Video-Based Landscape Modelling

4.1   Solution Algorithm

The algorithm consists of the following major stages:

1. pre-processing: ascertaining camera calibration parameters and lens distortion (unless these data are already known);
2. generating a point cloud using the available video and camera parameters;
3. ascertaining normals in each point and generating a 3D model;

4.2   Implementation Details

The parameters of camera calibration matrix required to build a point cloud are sometimes unknown. This requires the first stage to be preceded by the preparation stage: the video is analyzed using Automatic Lens Distortion, and then the parameters of the ideal pinhole camera are used in the camera calibration matrix.

(a) Original image   (b) Undistorted image.

(c) Cropped image.

Fig. 3. Image preprocessing workflow on a frame from a video made by a quadcopter at an archaeological excavation site.

In order to use the obtained images at subsequent stages, the frames are cropped so as to remove black strips emerging in the course of lens distortion correction (as shown in Fig. 3).

The First Stage involves using the available video and parameters of camera calibration to generate a cloud of points corresponding to the points on the landscape's surface. This is done by means of ORB SLAM 2 [16], an open source algorithm that simultaneously performs map localization and generation. The available version of ORB SLAM 2 does not allow to obtain a cloud, which prompted us to modify the algorithm so as to obtain the required data in monocular and RGB-D regimes.point

There are two alternatives at this stage depending on the technique that was used to make a video recording of an object. The RGB-D regime is selected to obtain more accurate results where a video was made with a 3D scanner (e.g., Microsoft Kinect) and contains not only RGB photo sequence, but also depth maps. In other cases, the monocular regime is selected. The SLAM (simultaneous localization and mapping) method yields results that are much more impressive when it comes to working with RGB-D data, but a limited field of view (FOV) and depth range of standard RGB-D cameras still impede flawless registration of remote points. In contrast, monocular SLAM may use the data made by wide-angle cameras and having no depth limitations—however, this approach is still unreliable when applied to homogeneous scenes without bright spots that could serve as points of interest tracked on a frame-by-frame basis.

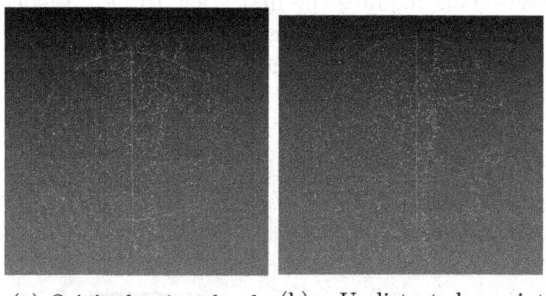

(a) Original point cloud.   (b)   Undistorted   point
                                    cloud.

Fig. 4. Point cloud composed from images.

These data (see Fig. 4) will be further used to calculate the normals of each point and to reconstruct a 3D model later.

Today there are artificial intelligence (AI) algorithms capable of predicting the point depths in an image with a certain degree of accuracy. They allow to apply the RGB-D regime to monocular data when obtaining the point cloud at the first stage. One of such AI algorithms is described in [14]. It supports calculation by NVIDIA graphic processors by default, which allows to obtain—almost in real time—depth maps from videos having 1280720 resolution. However, the accuracy of obtained data largely depends on the samples utilized in neural network training.

An example of a depth map obtained with [14]. Each point in this image has a value from 0 to 255 corresponding to its depth: the smaller the number (and, therefore, the darker the colour), the closer the point to the camera, and vice versa.

At the second stage, normals are calculated in each point, and a 3D land-scape model is generated based on the point cloud available. Normal vectors are calculated using the method of least squares applied to the position of a surface containing 'k' closest neighbouring points. Then the Poisson Surface Reconstruction algorithm [5] is run to obtain a 3D landscape model. The algorithm's input data include a set of points with oriented normals. We assume that the input points contain few outliers and little noise. The output 3D model is generated by means of extracting the isosurface of this function using CGAL Surface Mesh Generator [17] (Fig. 5).

Fig. 5. A 3D model generated by Poisson Surface Reconstruction [15] based on the point cloud contained in.

We used the following algorithm to detect outliers and noise in the point cloud. The input points are sorted in the order of ascending mean squares of distances to 'k' closest neighbouring points. Then the algorithm identifies whether there are points in respect of which this distance exceeds the double mean interval between points in the cloud. Smoothing methods are used where the original video is of such a quality that the point cloud obtained at the first stage contains many outliers and much noise. These methods are components of Computational Geometry Algorithms Library (CGAL) and are based on [9].

5   Application and Prospects

The technological novelty of our software is that it does not require specialized equipment and provides archaeologists with an end-to-end solution. It contains components that are not included in similar solutions and allow to identify camera calibration parameters and remove noise and outliers from a point cloud. This enhances the quality of 3D models compared to alternative software.

The major drawback of our software is that the reconstruction result depends on graphic continuity of input scenes—there should be key objects allowing to build a coherent route. In other words, the algorithm can obtain a high-quality integral 3D model of a landscape, where the input video contains a sequence of frames depicting a site's model without interruptions.

Separate components of our solution—such as video decoding, point capture, depth map generation using a neural network—support computation on graphic processors, which allows to substantially enhance the algorithm's efficiency on contemporary user devices.

In future, we are going to improve the methods of point depth prediction based on a video in order to allow the use of RGB-D regime of ORB SLAM 2 algorithm without resorting to 3D scanners during video recording. We also are going to implement the support of computation on NVIDEA processors at all stages of the solution under consideration.

Acknowledgments. This research was partially supported by the Russian Foundation for Basic Research grants (projects no. 17-29-04288 17, 16-07-01113). The authors would like to acknowledge the Reviewers for the valuable recommendations that helped in the improvement of this paper.

References

1. Agarwal, S., Snavely, N., Seitz, S.M., Szeliski, R.: Bundle adjustment in the large. In: Daniilidis, K., Maragos, P., Paragios, N. (eds.) ECCV 2010. LNCS, vol. 6312, pp. 29–42. Springer, Heidelberg (2010). https://doi.org/10.1007/978-3-642-15552-9_3
2. Bastanlar, Y., Temizel, A., Yardimci, Y.: Improved sift matching for image pairs with scale difference. Electron. Lett. **46**(5), 346–348 (2010)
3. Bennett, R., Zielinski, D., Kopper, R.: Comparison of interactive environments for the archaeological exploration of 3D landscape data. In: Proceedings of 2014 IEEE VIS International Workshop on 3DVis, 3DVis 2014, pp. 67–71 (2015)
4. Bogdanov, A., Degtyarev, A., Korkhov, V.: Desktop supercomputer: what can it do? Phys. Part. Nucl. Lett. **14**(7), 985–992 (2017). https://doi.org/10.1134/S1547477117070032
5. Bolitho, M., Kazhdan, M., Burns, R., Hoppe, H.: Parallel poisson surface reconstruction. In: Bebis, G., et al. (eds.) ISVC 2009. LNCS, vol. 5875, pp. 678–689. Springer, Heidelberg (2009). https://doi.org/10.1007/978-3-642-10331-5_63
6. Fedoseev, G., Degtyarev, A., Iakushkina, O., Korkhov, V.: A continuous integration system for MPD root: deployment and setup in gitlab. In: CEUR-WS, vol. 1787, pp. 525–529 (2016)
7. Glatard, T., Rousseau, M., Camarasu-Pop, S., Adalat, R., Beck, N., Das, S., da Silva, R., Khalili-Mahani, N., Korkhov, V., Quirion, P.O., Rioux, P., Olabarriaga, S., Bellec, P., Evans, A.: Software architectures to integrate workflow engines in science gateways. Fut. Gener. Comput. Syst. **75**, 239–255 (2017). https://doi.org/10.1016/j.future.2017.01.005

8. Grishkin, V., Iakushkin, O.: Middleware transport architecture monitoring: Topology service. Institute of Electrical and Electronics Engineers Inc. (2014)
9. Huang, H., Wu, S., Gong, M., Cohen-Or, D., Ascher, U., Zhang, H.: Edge-aware point set resampling. ACM Trans. Graph. **32**(1), 108-119 (2013)
10. Iakushkin, O., Grishkin, V.: Messaging middleware for cloud applications: Extending brokerless approach. Institute of Electrical and Electronics Engineers Inc. (2014)
11. Iakushkin, O., Sedova, O., Valery, G.: Application control and horizontal scaling in modern cloud middleware. In: Gavrilova, M.L., Tan, C.J.K. (eds.) Transactions on Computational Science XXVII. LNCS, vol. 9570, pp. 81–96. Springer, Heidelberg (2016). https://doi.org/10.1007/978-3-662-50412-3_6
12. Iakushkin, O., Sedova, O.: Creating CAD designs and performing their subsequent analysis using opensource solutions in python, vol. 1922. American Institute of Physics Inc. (2018)
13. Jancosek, M., Pajdla, T.: Multi-view reconstruction preserving weakly-supported surfaces. In: Proceedings of the IEEE Computer Society Conference on Computer Vision and Pattern Recognition, pp. 3121–3128 (2011)
14. Laina, I., Rupprecht, C., Belagiannis, V., Tombari, F., Navab, N.: Deeper depth prediction with fully convolutional residual networks. In: Proceedings of 2016 4th International Conference on 3D Vision, 3DV 2016, pp. 239–248 (2016)
15. Liang, H., Lucian, A., Lange, R., Cheung, C., Su, B.: Remote spectral imaging with simultaneous extraction of 3D topography for historical wall paintings. ISPRS J. Photogram. Remote Sens. **95**, 13–22 (2014)
16. Mur-Artal, R., Tardos, J.: Orb-slam2: An open-source slam system for monocular, stereo, and RGB-d cameras. IEEE Trans. Rob. **33**(5), 1255–1262 (2017)
17. Rineau, L., Yvinec, M.: A generic software design for delaunay refinement meshing. Comput. Geom. Theor. Appl. **38**(1–2), 100–110 (2007)
18. Wu, C.: Towards linear-time incremental structure from motion. In: Proceedings of 2013 International Conference on 3D Vision 3DV 2013, pp. 127–134 (2013)
19. Zhou, Y., Yin, K., Huang, H., Zhang, H., Gong, M., Cohen-Or, D.: Generalized cylinder decomposition. ACM Trans. Graph. **34**(6), 1–14 (2015)

10th International Symposium on Software Engineering Processes and Applications (SEPA 2018)

A Software Reference Architecture for IoT-Based Healthcare Applications

Itamir de Morais Barroca Filho[1][✉] and Gibeon Soares de Aquino Junior[2][✉]

[1] Metropole Digital Institute,
Federal University of Rio Grande do Norte, Natal, Brazil
itamir.filho@imd.ufrn.br
[2] Department of Informatics and Applied Mathematics,
Federal University of Rio Grande do Norte, Natal, Brazil
gibeon@dimap.ufrn.br
http://www.imd.ufrn.br, http://www.dimap.ufrn.br

Abstract. With the Internet of Things (IoT), a myriad of connected things and the data captured by them is making possible the development of applications in various markets, such as transportation, buildings, energy, home, industrial and healthcare. Concerning healthcare, the development of these applications is expected as part of the future, since IoT can be the main enabler for distributed healthcare applications, having a significant potential to contribute to the overall decrease of healthcare costs while increasing the health outcomes. However, there are a lot of challenges in the development and deployment of this kind of application, such as interoperability, availability, usability and security. The complex and heterogeneous nature of the IoT-based healthcare applications makes its design, development and deployment difficult. It also causes an increase in the development cost, as well as an interoperability problem with the existing systems. To contribute to solve the aforementioned challenges, this paper aims to improve the understanding and systematization of the IoT-based healthcare applications' architectural design. It proposes a software reference architecture, named Reference Architecture for Healthcare (RAH), to systematically organize the main elements of IoT-based healthcare applications, its responsibilities and interactions, promoting a common understanding of these applications' architecture to minimize the challenges related to it.

Keywords: Internet of Things (IoT) · Healthcare
Software reference architecture · Design

1 Introduction

New technologies can change lives! That what is happening with the use of the Internet of Things (IoT). The IoT denotes a trend where a large number of embedded devices employ communication services offered by Internet protocols.

© Springer International Publishing AG, part of Springer Nature 2018
O. Gervasi et al. (Eds.): ICCSA 2018, LNCS 10963, pp. 173–188, 2018.
https://doi.org/10.1007/978-3-319-95171-3_15

Many of these devices, often called "smart objects" or "things", are not directly operated by humans but exist as components in buildings or vehicles, or are spread out in the environment [1]. Thus, the basic idea of this new paradigm is the pervasive presence, around all of us, of a variety of things - such as Radio-Frequency IDentification (RFID) tags, sensors, actuators, mobile phones, etc. - which, through unique addressing schemes, are able to interact with each other and cooperate with their neighbors to reach common goals [2]. It is estimated that by 2025, 80 billion IoT devices will be online, creating 180 ZB of data [3]. This myriad of connected things, the data captured by them, and the connectivity between them is making the development of applications in various markets, such as transportation, buildings, energy, home, industrial, and healthcare possible.

Concerning the healthcare market, it is expected the development of these applications as part of the future, since it can improve e-Health to allow hospitals to operate more efficiently and patients to receive better treatment. This paradigm is reshaping modern healthcare, connecting everything to the Internet, shifting "from anytime, anyplace connectivity for anyone" to "connectivity for anything". The IoT can be the main enabler for distributed healthcare applications, thus having a significant potential to contribute to the overall decrease of healthcare costs while increasing the health outcomes.

A type of IoT healthcare application in which developers will focus is the mobile health application (mhealth). The primary goal of mhealth is to allow remote monitoring of the patients' health status (biometries) and treatment from anywhere in the world [4]. Moreover, according to Al et al. [5], healthcare and manufacturing applications are projected to provide the biggest economic impact. Healthcare applications and the related IoT-based services such as mobile health (mHealth) and telecare, which enable medical wellness, prevention, diagnosis, treatment and monitoring services to be delivered efficiently through electronic media, are expected to create about $1.1 – $2.5 trillion annually in global economy growth by 2025 [5].

On the other hand, the population aging and the rise of chronic diseases are becoming a global concern since they might result in an increase in the number of patients at hospitals. Moreover, several studies have indicated the need for strategies to minimize the institutionalization process and the effects of the high cost of patient care [6]. With the intention of reducing this concern, a promising trend in health treatments is to move the medical check routines from the hospital (hospital-centric) to the patient's home (home-centric). Nowadays, this trend is supported by e-Health techonologies and can be improved with IoT, with the promotion of distributed healthcare, helping to enhance the outcome of health services and decrease related costs. The progress in wireless technologies with related performance improvements heavily support realtime monitoring of physiological parameters, thus easing the uninterrupted care of chronic diseases, enabling early diagnosis, and the management of medical emergencies [7].

Therefore, there are a lot of challenges in the development and deployment of this kind of application, such as (i) interoperability [8,9]: there are heterogeneous sources of data, the devices' protocol is not open, so a given device cannot be integrated to another (or multiple) applications, and there are also different studies and proposals for patient monitoring at hospitals or personal monitoring at home; (ii) availability [9]: the proposed applications do not provide a way to ensure that the systems are available when needed; (iii) usability [10]: the existing home healthcare systems have drawbacks such as simple and few functionalities, weak interaction and poor mobility; (iv) security [9]: the existing proposed systems lacks of permission control, privacy and data anonymity, etc. There are also challenges related to data storage and management [9], since the vast volume of data produced by the sensors is in an unstructured format, which is very complicated to understand and requires data storage mechanisms that are different from the typical database management system (DBMS) [11].

In short, the complex and heterogeneous nature of the IoT-based healthcare applications makes its design and development difficult. It also causes an increase in the development cost, as well as an interoperability problem with the existing systems. Thus, a strategy to design a reference software architecture to systematically organize the main elements of IoT-based healthcare applications, its responsibilities, and interactions, promoting a common understanding of these applications' architecture would minimize the challenges related to it. Software reference architectures have emerged as abstractions of concrete software architectures from a certain domain [12]. A reference architecture (RA) is used to design concrete architectures in multiple contexts, serving as an inspiration or standardization tool [13]. Nowadays, the increasing complexity of software, the need for efficient and effective software design processes and the need for high levels of system interoperability lead to the increase in the importance of reference architectures in the software design process.

Thus, this paper aims to improve the understanding and systematization of the IoT-based healthcare applications' architectural design. It proposes a SRA, named Reference Architecture for Healthcare (RAH), to systematically organize the main elements of IoT-based healthcare applications, its responsibilities and interactions, promoting a common understanding of these applications' architecture to minimize the challenges related to it. To evaluate the RAH, we designed a platform to promote the remote intelligent monitoring of patients presented by Barroca and Aquino [14]. Finally, the paper is organized as follows: in Sect. 2, we present the related works. In Sect. 3, we present the proposed software reference architecture, describing its elements and the relationship between them. In Sect. 4 we present the conclusions, future works, and perspectives of future researches.

2   Related Works

Before the proposal of the software reference architecture for IoT-based healthcare applications, it is essential to understand the state-of-art of this area, and to realize that, we performed a review based on Systematic literature reviews (SLR) method. According to Wohlin [15], SLRs are conducted to identify, analyze and interpret all available evidence related to a specific research question, as it aims to give a complete, comprehensive and valid picture of the existing evidence, both the identification, analysis and interpretation must be conducted in a scientifically and rigorous way. Therefore, this section presents the related works, describing a summary of a review based on SLR method, performed by Barroca and Aquino [16], that aimed to comprehend the current state and future trends for IoT-based healthcare applications, and also in order to find areas for further investigations.

The research questions that addressed the review were:

RQ1. What are the main characteristics of healthcare applications based on IoT infrastructure?
RQ2. What are the protocols used in healthcare applications based on IoT infrastructure?
RQ3. What are the challenges and opportunities related to healthcare applications based on IoT infrastructure?

Regarding the main characteristics of healthcare application based on IoT infrastructure (RQ1), we collected their functional and nonfunctional requirements from the studies. Thus, the functional requirements described in the studies are the patient's body and environment monitoring. Considering the body monitoring, the data monitored by sensors attached to patient's body are the pulse oximeter, heart rate, galvanic skin, transpiration, muscle activity, body temperature, oxygen saturation, blood pressure, airflow, body movement, blood glucose, breathing rate and ECG. Moreover, the environment monitoring is related to sensors deployed in the patient's environment that capture data from temperature, light, humidity, location, body position, motion data, SPO2, atmospheric pressure and CO2. Moreover, when it comes to healthcare applications' features, there are some important nonfunctional requirements that represent a concern in this kind of application. Thus the nonfunctional requirements cited by the studies are scalability, reliability, ubiquity, portability, interoperability, robustness, performance, availability, privacy, integrity, authentication and security.

Regarding protocols (RQ2), the data collected from the studies showed that there are two protocols categories: communication, regarding network protocols, and application, regarding data transfer protocols. Thus, the communication protocols cited by the studies on the healthcare applications are 6LoWPAN, IEEE 802.15.4, Zigbee, Bluetooth, RFID, WIFI, Ethernet, GPRS, IEEE 802.15.6, 3G/4G, NFC and IrDA. Regarding the applications protocols, the studies cited: REST, YOAPY, HTTP, CoAP, XML-RPC and Web Services. When it comes to data format, the studies presented that the healthcare applications use HL7, XML, EHR, CSV, JSON and PHR.

The studies showed that there are many challenges related to healthcare applications based on IoT infrastructure (RQ3). The authors presented that health information management through mobile devices introduces several challenges: data storage and management (e.g., physical storage issues, availability and maintenance), interoperability and availability of heterogeneous resources, security and privacy (e.g., permission control, data anonymity, etc.), unified and ubiquitous access are a few to mention [9]. Moreover, the authors highlight the interoperability challenge, since there have been different studies and proposals for patient monitoring at the hospital or for personal monitoring at home, but a shared goal to produce an interoperable system adopting open standards for healthcare, such as HL7, and a seamless framework to be easily deployed in any given scenario for healthcare is still missing [17].

Finally, with this review we were able to define a layered architecture for healthcare applications based on IoT Infrastructure. It considers the characteristics of these applications, functional requirements, quality attributes, used protocols, and is composed of a layer of monitoring, quality attributes, middleware, and services. In Sect. 3 we will describe this architecture, and it will be used for the development of a platform for remote intelligent health monitoring that will address issues like security and interoperability.

3   A Software Reference Architecture for Healthcare

There are a lot of challenges related to the development and deployment of IoT-based healthcare applications, as presented in Sect. 2, such as data storage and management, security and privacy, and the interoperability between new applications and existing hardware and software solutions. Regarding interoperability, 93% of new healthcare solutions described in the review performed by Barroca and Aquino [16] would demand a change in the existing healthcare hardware and software. Thus, although it exists many proposed standards and different studies for patient monitoring at hospital or at home for personal monitoring, as presented in Sect. 2, a shared goal to produce an interoperable system adopting open standards for healthcare, for example HL7, and a seamless framework to be easily deployed in any given scenario for healthcare is still missing [17]. As a result, independent healthcare applications that do not interoperate and communicate with other applications are developed, making its deployment difficult. Moreover, with the perspective of expanding the IoT-based healthcare applications market and consequently the development of new solutions, this problem will grow significantly.

In this context, one of the possible cause for this lack of interoperability and communication between IoT-based healthcare applications is the absence of a software reference architecture (SRA) to serve as a guideline for the design of their architectures. The SRA facilitates the development process, acting as a tool for standardization and making modular configuration and interoperability with healthcare solutions from different suppliers possible. Furthermore, with an SRA, different vendors could be able to provide specific modules that can be integrated among themselves. Finally, its existence would provide a standardized view for these applications which promotes communication between the potential stakeholders (business professionals, software developers).

Therefore, we designed a software reference architecture for IoT-based healthcare applications, which was named Reference Architecture for Healthcare(RAH) with the primary goal of solving interoperability problems. RAH is defined based on a set of required qualities. These qualities were extracted from existing publications collected through the review presented in Sect. 2. Some of the benefits of an SRA [18] that we expect to achieve with RAH are: (i) standardizing concrete software architectures by using the SRA as a template for designing a portfolio of applications that use the standardized design; (ii) facilitating the design of concrete software architectures by providing guidelines and inspiration for the applications' developers; (iii) systematically reusing standard functionalities and configurations throughout the applications' development; (iv) reducing risks through the use of proven and partly pre-qualified architectural elements included in the SRA; (v) enhancing quality by facilitating the achievement of software quality aspects already addressed by the SRA; (vi) allowing interoperability between different applications and their software components by establishing common mechanisms for information exchange; (vii) creating a knowledge repository, since the SRA inherently acts as a repository of applied knowledge such as architectural and design principles; (viii) improving communication in the organization and with multiple suppliers since stakeholders share the architectural mindset established in the SRA; (ix) using the newest design solutions. Preliminary, SRAs are usually designed to provide innovative design solutions concerning the existing state of the art.

Finally, in this section, we present the proposed software reference architecture for IoT-based healthcare applications. It is structured as follows: in Sect. 3.1, we describe the required qualities in a reference architecture for IoT-based healthcare applications, specifying the functional, non-functional and architecture qualities; in Sect. 3.2 we present the RAH's design approach and its levels of abstraction; and in Sect. 3.3 we describe RAH, the software reference architecture for IoT-based healthcare applications. For this section organization, we were inspired by the structure defined by Angelov and Grefen to describe their software reference architecture [19].

3.1   Required Qualities in a Reference Architecture for IoT-Based Healthcare Applications

In this section, we discuss the functional and quality attributes (non-functional qualities) that must be addressed in the RAH. The functional qualities express the functionalities that must be supported by an IoT-based healthcare application. We used the review presented in Sect. 2 to define the required functionalities. The quality attributes (non-functional qualities), in its turn, are separated into two groups: application qualities and architecture qualities. The application qualities must be addressed in the development of an IoT-based healthcare application. The architecture qualities are qualities that are important for the design of a reference architecture.

Therefore, to define the quality attributes (non-functional qualities) required in a reference architecture for healthcare, we used the list of quality attributes of information systems presented by Bass et al. [20], as well as the existing publications presented in Sect. 2. Based on these list of requirements, we defined RAH.

Functional Requirements. According to Bass et al., the functional requirements state what the system must do, and how it must behave or react to runtime stimuli [20]. Thus, considering the evidence collected in the review presented in Sect. 2, the functional requirements of IoT-based healthcare applications consist of monitoring the patient's body and environment. Regarding the body monitoring, the applications use sensors attached to the patient's body and capture data from: electrocardiogram (ECG), blood pressure, blood glucose, heart rate, oxygen saturation, temperature, and breathing rate.

When it comes to monitoring the environment, the applications use sensors deployed in the patient's environment to capture data from temperature, light, humidity, location, body position, motion data, atmospheric pressure and CO_2. They are important because the environment measures can directly affect the patient's treatment.

Quality Attributes. The quality attributes or non-functional requirements are qualifications of the functional requirements or of the overall product. A qualification of a functional requirement is an item such as how fast the function must be performed, or how resilient it must be to erroneous input. A qualification of the overall product is an item such as the time to deploy the product or a limitation on operational costs [20]. Thus, the main nonfunctional requirements/quality attributes of IoT-based healthcare applications evidenced in the studies presented in Sect. 2 are: availability, interoperability, performance, and security.

Architecture Qualities. In Bass et al. [21], several architecture qualities are presented. Inspired by them and the quality attributes defined by Angelov and Grefen [19], we have elaborated the following list of architectural qualities expected in our software reference architecture (RAH): completeness, buildability, applicability, and usability (acceptability).

3.2   Design Approach

With the definition of the qualities required for a software reference architecture for IoT-based healthcare applications, we started to design the RAH. The design approach was based on the Attribute-Driven Design(ADD) method [20], and we interactively built RAH starting from more abstract to less abstract design, trying to address the usability, buildability, applicability, and completeness architecture qualities described in Sect. 3.1. Regarding the availability quality, we introduced a component based on the Ping/Echo tactic to detect faults. For the security quality, we added components to provide authentication and authorization to users, also based on tactics to identify and resist attacks.

Moreover, in RAH, connections between components are made through dedicated interfaces, which is the basis for achieving the interoperability quality of IoT-based healthcare applications. Finally, we defined RAH as a component-based architecture, in which we applied styles and patterns to design a software reference architecture that can be modifiable and use integrative components.

3.3 RAH - Reference Architecture for IoT-Based Healthcare Applications

From the qualities required for a reference architecture for healthcare applications, which were previously defined, and using the described design approach, we designed RAH, a software reference architecture for IoT-based healthcare applications. The stakeholders for this reference architecture are analysts, architects, and developers of IoT-based healthcare applications.

Thus, we organized RAH in layers according to the required qualities. Layers help to bring the modifiability and portability quality attributes to a software system [22]. A layer is an application of the principle of information hiding, whose main theory is that a change to a lower layer can be hidden behind its interface and will not impact the layers above it. Thus, RAH is presented in its first level of abstraction in Fig. 1. It is composed of four layers: monitoring, middleware, services, and quality attributes. Interacting with the monitoring layer, there are patients that can be using an IoT-based healthcare application to help in: rehabilitation, respiratory diseases, elderly, obesity, arterial hypertension, and diabetes control. Interacting with the services layer, there are the users, such as: physicians, hospital administrators, nurses, family, patients, pharmaceutical and clinical staff.

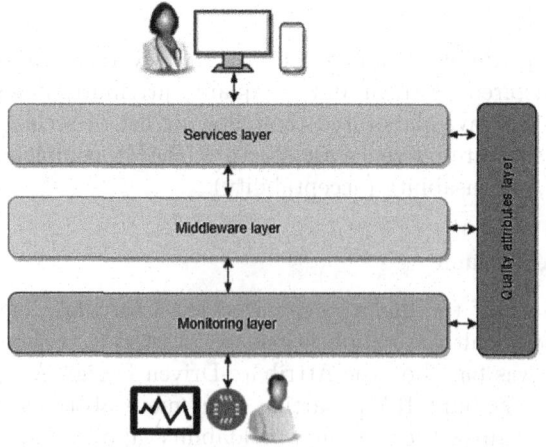

Fig. 1. RAH reference architecture (first level of abstraction).

The *Monitoring Layer* is responsible for monitoring the patient's body and environment, and is composed of the following components:

1. *Devices*: It is a hardware component that represents the devices used for monitoring the patient's body and environment. Thus, body monitoring involves sensors to capture heart rate, temperature, oxygen saturation, blood pressure, blood glucose, breathing rate and ECG. Regarding the environment monitoring, the devices are sensors that capture data related to temperature, light, humidity, location, body position, motion, SPO2, pressure, and CO2.
2. *Gateway*: It is a software component that receives the data from the *Devices* and makes it available by publishing it to the *Middleware Layer* using the publish-subscribe pattern to bind values at runtime [20].

Regarding the *Middleware Layer*, it is responsible for receiving the patient's sensors and environment data from the *Monitoring Layer*, processing it, persisting it and making it available for the *Services Layer*. This layer is composed of the following components:

1. *IoTDataCollector*: The collector is a software component that is subscribed in the *Gateway's* data flow topic. Thus, it receives data from the *Gateway* and persists it to its nonrelational repository. Moreover, it has a relational repository containing data regarding the patients. The processed data is published using publish-subscribe pattern to the *Intelligence* component.
2. *Intelligence*: It is a software component that receives data from the *IoTDataCollector* and uses its inference engines to classify and persist the data from the alerts in a relational repository.

The *Services Layer* is responsible for the services, that are provided through Application Programming Interfaces (APIs), that promote interoperability between IoT-based healthcare applications. For these services, we proposed the use of Representational State Transfer (REST), that is a coordinated set of architectural constraints that attempts to minimize latency and network communication while maximizing the independence and scalability of the components' implementations [23]. Thus, this layer is composed of the following components:

1. *Hospital*: It is a software component composed of services for hospitals information systems that provides the patient's monitored data. It interacts with the *Intelligence* component of the *Middleware Layer*.
2. *Ambulance*: It is a software component composed of services for the ambulance emergency service's information systems that provides the patient's monitored data. It interacts with the *Intelligence* component of the *Middleware Layer*.

Finally, the *Quality Attributes Layer* is responsible for features that make IoT-based healthcare applications secure and reliable. Its elements help to assure availability and security. It is important to emphasize that because of the responsibility of this layer, it interacts with the *Services*, *Middleware* and *Monitoring* layers. Therefore, it is composed of the following components:

1. *PingEcho*: It is a software component that sends asynchronous request/response message pairs exchanged between other components of the RAH. Thus, it is used to determine reachability and the round-trip delay through the associated network path, and also determines that the pinged component is alive and responding correctly. Moreover, to help in the recovery of a fault, it performs the exception handling. This component was designed to help achieve availability.
2. *Authorization*: It is a software component that is responsible for granting a user the privileges to perform a task in the IoT-based healthcare application. This component was designed to achieve security assuring that only authorized personnel would access healthcare information.

Regarding the described layers, it is possible to note that modifiability and performance is a concern. Therefore, we used publish-subscribe in the elements as a coordination model that reduces coupling and increases performance. With the publish-subscribe asynchronous messaging, participants do not have to wait for an acknowledgment of arrival, since it assumes that the infrastructure delivered the message successfully [20]. However, since it depends on this successfully delivery, *PingEcho* component has to assure that all the elements are available to send, process and receive the messages.

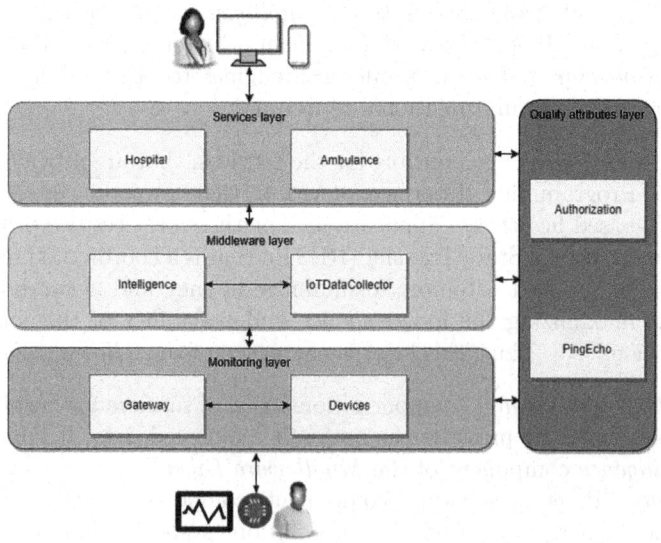

Fig. 2. Layered view of the RAH reference architecture (first level of abstraction).

The RAH is presented in its first level of abstraction in the layered and decomposition view in Figs. 2 and 3. This decomposition view describes the organization of the software into modules and submodules and shows how the system's responsibilities are partitioned across them. The layered view is based on the layered style, which reflects a division of the software into layers that represent a group of modules that offers a cohesive set of services [22].

Continuing with the RAH's documentation, Fig. 4 presents the uses view based on the uses styles. The uses style results when the depends-on relation is specialized to uses and a module uses another module if its correctness depends on the correctness of the other. Thus, this style goes one step further to reveal which modules use which other modules, enabling incremental development and the deployment of useful subsets of full systems [22]. Therefore, the *Gateway* uses the *Devices*, and the *IoTDataCollector* uses the *Gateway*. The *Intelligence* uses the *IoTDataCollector* and is used by the *Hospital* and *Ambulance* components.

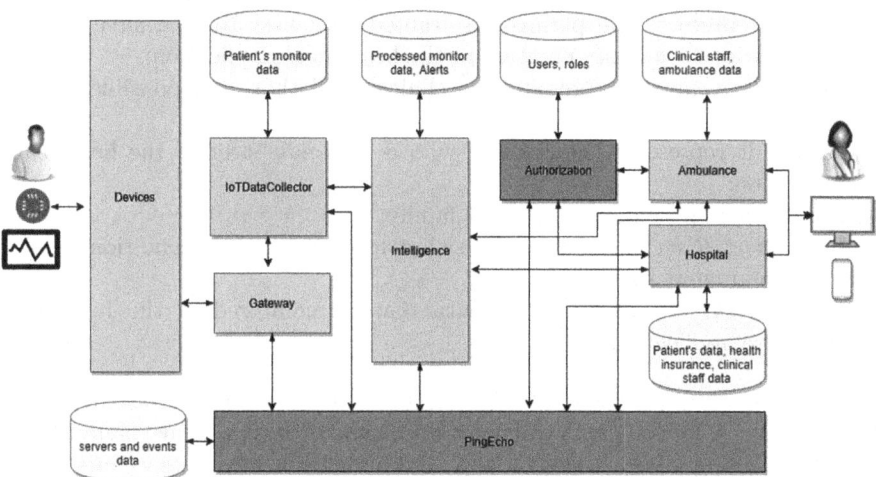

Fig. 3. Decomposition view of the RAH reference architecture (second level of abstraction).

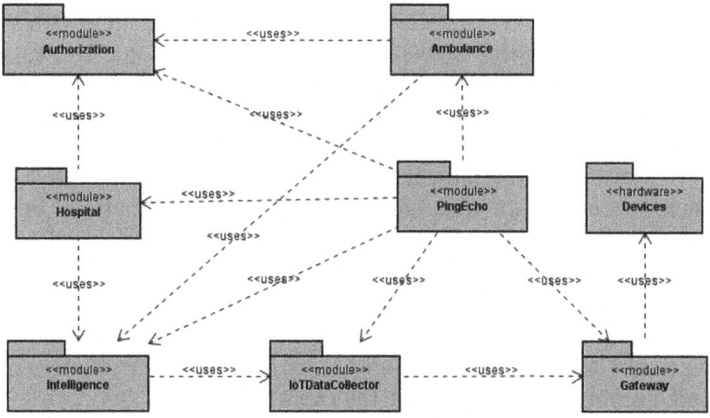

Fig. 4. Uses view of the RAH reference architecture (third level of abstraction).

The *Hospital* and *Ambulance* components use the *Authorization* component. Finally, the *PingEcho* component uses all the other components of this reference architecture, once it checks their availability.

Another aspect proposed by RAH is a conceptual data model for IoT-based healthcare applications. The conceptual data model abstracts implementation details and focuses on the entities and their relationships as perceived in the problem domain. Thus, RAH's conceptual data model is composed of the following entities:

- *Person*: it represents a generalization of a person in the healthcare application with common attributes found in the users;
- *User*: it represents a user of the IoT-based healthcare application;
- *Role*: it represents the permission granted to a user to guarantee his/her authorization to use an operation in the healthcare application;
- *Nurse, Physician*: it represents the clinical staff that is responsible for the patient;
- *Patient*: it represents the patient, who is the main user of the healthcare application;
- *Relative*: it represents the patient's family;
- *Alert, Alert Rule*: it represents the alert for the patient's condition, and is based on an alert rule;
- *MonitorData*: it represents the data that is monitored in the IoT-based healthcare application.

Thus, the Nurse, Patient and Physician entities are specializations of the Person entity. A Person can have many Users, and a User can have many Roles. A Role can be applied to many Users. A Patient can have many Nurses and Physicians. A Nurse and a Physician can have many Patients. A Patient can have many health Alerts and MonitorData. A health Alert is based on an AlertRule, and an AlertRule can be used in many different Alerts.

Finally, we present, in Fig. 5, the component-and-connector (C&C) view of the RAH. A C&C view shows elements (components) that have runtime presence, such as processes, objects, clients, servers, and data stores. It also includes as elements the pathways (connectors) of interaction, such as communication links and protocols, information flows, and access to shared storage [22]. Therefore, to design the RAH's C&C view, we considered the data-flow and event-based styles. Regarding the data-flow, we used the pipe-and-filter style, since the healthcare stream data undergoes successive transformations before it is available to stakeholders. The *Gateway, IotDataCollector* and *Intelligence* components are filters successively transforming the patient's monitored data, and the communications between it, using publish-subscribe style, are pipes. With the utilization of the pipe-and-filter style, we aim to improve reuse due to the independence of filters; improve throughput with the parallelization of data processing; and simplify reasoning about the overall behavior.

Still regarding the RAH's C&C design, the event-based style used was the publish-subscribe style. The computational model for the publish-subscribe style

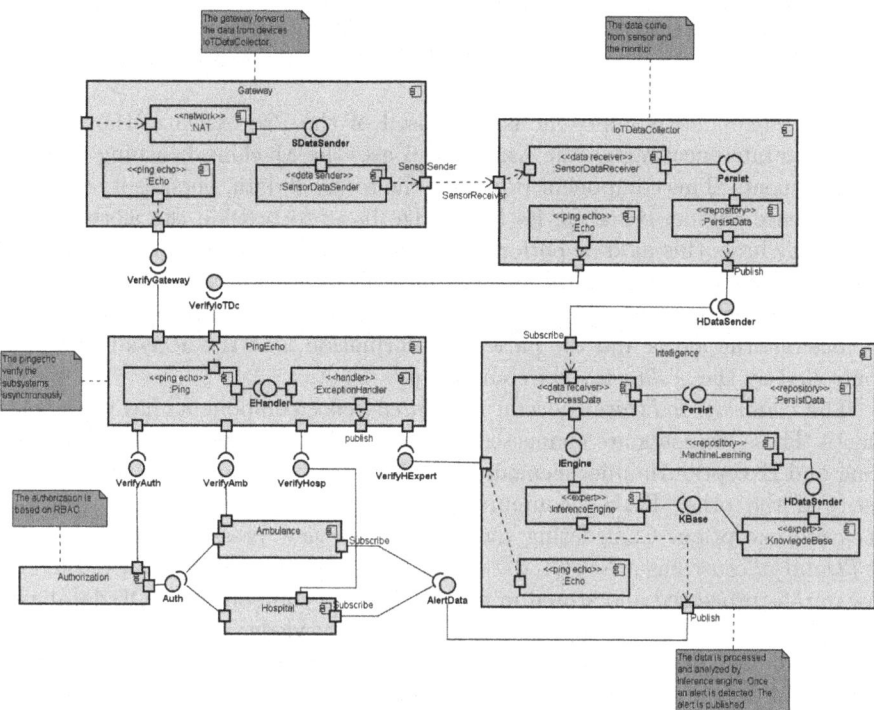

Fig. 5. Component-and-connector view of the RAH reference architecture (fourth level of abstraction).

is better thought of as a system of independent processes or objects, which react to events generated by their environment, and which, in turn, cause reactions to other components as a side effect of their event announcements [22]. So, with the use of this style, we aim to isolate event producers from event consumers, making the data change and notification dynamic to the other components that care about it. We also used the shared-data style to design RAH's repository views. A Repository view contains one or more components, called repositories, which typically retains large collections of persistent data [22]. With this style, we aim to provide enhanced modifiability by decoupling data producers from data consumers.

Explaining the RAH's C&C view, the *Gateway* component is composed of the NAT, the SensorDataSender, and the Echo elements. The NAT element is responsible for the network address transformation considering the need to send the data from the Intranet to the Internet. The SensorDataSender is responsible for publish all the monitored data in a topic where the SensorDataReceiver of the *IoTDataCollector* component is subscribed. The *IoTDataCollector* component is composed of the SensorDataReceiver, the PersistData, and the Echo elements.

The SensorDataReceiver receives the data from the *Gateway* component, persists it and publishes it in a topic where the ProcessData element of the *Intelligence* component is subscribed.

The *Intelligence* component is composed of the ProcessData, the Persist-Data, the InferenceEngine, the KnowledgeBase, the Machine Learning and the Echo elements. This component processes the received data, persists it, and uses its inference engine, based on its knowledge base, to provide the alerts. In its knowledge base, this module performs machine learning to recognize patterns in the patient's alerts. The alerts are published in topics where the *Hospital* and *Ambulance* component are subscribed. These components are composed of APIs to consume the alerts and the patient's information, and the access to them is controlled by the *Authorization* component.

The *Gateway, IoTDataCollector* and *Intelligence* components have Echo elements. These elements are connected to the *PingEcho* component, composed of Ping and ExceptionHandler elements, which are responsible for asynchronously verify if the other RAH's components are active and process any possible occurred exception. Considering the repositories view presented in Fig. 6, the *IoTDataCollector* has a NoSQL database that stores the sensors' raw data. The raw data is processed and stored in the *Intelligence* component's SQL database. In addition to this database, the module has a Knowledge database that stores data from the patient's alerts and recognized patterns. The *Authorization* component has a users database that stores data about the users, roles, and permissions to access the *Hospital* and *Ambulance* components.

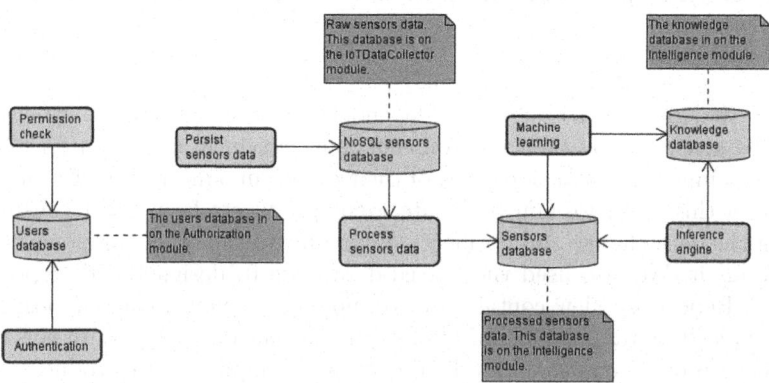

Fig. 6. Repositories view of the RAH reference architecture (fourth level of abstraction).

4   Conclusions and Future Works

As presented in Sect. 1, the IoT based technologies are changing our lives, and the growing number of connected sensors are making it possible to develop applications in many different fields, such as healthcare, manufacturing, electricity, agriculture, and others. Particularly in the healthcare field, it is expected to see the development of applications following this trend as part of the future, since it can allow hospitals to operate more efficiently and patients to receive better treatment. Moreover, with the projections of the increase of population aging and chronic diseases that might result in more patients at hospitals, the use of IoT-based healthcare applications is a strategy to minimize the institutionaliza-tion process and the effects of the high cost of patient care.

In Sect. 2, the systematic review presented that 93% of the newly devel-oped solutions for healthcare would demand a change in the existing hardware and software. Therefore, as a strategy to promote interoperability, we proposed a software reference architecture for IoT-based healthcare applications named RAH, which is presented in Sect. 3. The proposed software reference architec-ture, which systematically organizes the main elements of these applications, its responsibilities, and interactions, promotes a common understanding of these applications' architecture, thus minimizing the challenges related to it.

Regarding RAH, we proposed and documented this software reference architecture presenting its requirements, quality attributes, and architecture qualities. Finally, as future works, we will evaluate this SRA performing a case study of the development of the IoT-based healthcare platform for intelligent remote monitoring of patients, proposed by Barroca and Aquino [14]. This plat-form is being created by the instantiation of the RAH reference architecture in a concrete architecture, and the evidence collected by this case study will test the hypothesis that RAH is a suitable approach to address the challenges found when developing IoT-based healthcare applications.

References

1. Arkko, J., McPherson, D., Tschofenig, H., Thaler, D.: Architectural considerations in smart object networking (2015)
2. Atzori, L., Iera, A., Morabito, G.: The Internet of Things: a survey. Comput. Netw. **54**(15), 2787–2805 (2010)
3. IDC. Idc futurescape: Worldwide it industry 2017 predictions (2017). https://www.idc.com/getdoc.jsp?containerid=us41883016
4. Jara, A.J., Zamora-Izquierdo, M.A., Skarmeta, A.F.: Interconnection framework for mhealth and remote monitoring based on the Internet of Things. IEEE J. Selected Areas Commun. **31**(9), 47–65 (2013)
5. Al-Fuqaha, A., Guizani, M., Mohammadi, M., Aledhari, M., Ayyash, M.: Internet of Things: a survey on enabling technologies, protocols, and applications. IEEE Commun. Surv. Tutor. **17**(4), 2347–2376 (2015)
6. Hochron, S., Goldberg, P.: Driving physician adoption of mheath solutions. Healthc. Fin. Manag. **69**(2), 36–40 (2015)
7. Riazul Islam, S.M., Kwak, D., Humaun Kabir, M.D., Hossain, M., Kwak, K.-S.: The Internet of Things for health care: a comprehensive survey. IEEE Access **3**, 678–708 (2015)
8. Sebestyen, G., Hangan, A., Oniga, S., Gál, Z.: ehealth solutions in the context of Internet of Things. In: Proceedings of IEEE International Conference on Automa-tion, Quality and Testing, Robotics (AQTR 2014), Cluj-Napoca, Romania, pp. 261–267 (2014)

9. Doukas, C., Maglogiannis, I.: Bringing IoT and cloud computing towards pervasive healthcare. In: 2012 Sixth International Conference on Innovative Mobile and Internet Services in Ubiquitous Computing (IMIS), pp. 922–926. IEEE (2012)

10. Kevin, I., Wang, K., Rajamohan, A., Dubey, S., Catapang, S.A., Salcic, Z.: A wearable Internet of Things mote with bare metal 6lowpan protocol for pervasive healthcare. In: IEEE 11th International Conference on Ubiquitous Intelligence and Computing, pp. 750–756. IEEE (2014)

11. Mohammed, J., Lung, C.-H., Ocneanu, A., Thakral, A., Jones, C., Adler, A.: Internet of Things: remote patient monitoring using web services and cloud computing. In: 2014 IEEE International Conference on Internet of Things (iThings), pp. 256–263. IEEE (2014)

12. Angelov, S., Grefen, P., Greefhorst, D.: A framework for analysis and design of software reference architectures. Inf. Softw. Technol. **54**(4), 417–431 (2012)

13. Muller, G.: A reference architecture primer. Eindhoven University of Technology, Eindhoven White paper (2008).

14. Barroca Filho, I.M., de Aquino Junior, G.S.: Proposing an IoT-based healthcare platform to integrate patients, physicians and ambulance services. In: Gervasi, O., Murgante, B., Misra, S., Borruso, G., Torre, C.M., Rocha, A.M.A.C., Taniar, D., Apduhan, B.O., Stankova, E., Cuzzocrea, A. (eds.) ICCSA 2017. LNCS, vol. 10409, pp. 188–202. Springer, Cham (2017). https://doi.org/10.1007/978-3-319-62407-5_13

15. Wohlin, C., Runeson, P., Höst, M., Ohlsson, M.C., Regnell, B., Wesslén, A.: Experimentation in software engineering. Springer, Heidelberg (2012). https://doi.org/10.1007/978-3-642-29044-2

16. de Morais Barroca Filho, I., de Aquino Junior, G.S.: IoT-based healthcare applications: a review. In: Gervasi, O., Murgante, B., Misra, S., Borruso, G., Torre, C.M., Rocha, A.M.A.C., Taniar, D., Apduhan, B.O., Stankova, E., Cuzzocrea, A. (eds.) ICCSA 2017. LNCS, vol. 10409, pp. 47–62. Springer, Cham (2017). https://doi.org/10.1007/978-3-319-62407-5_4

17. Khattak, H.A., Ruta, M., Di Sciascio, E.: Coap-based healthcare sensor networks: a survey. In: Proceedings of 2014 11th International Bhurban Conference on Applied Sciences & Technology (IBCAST) Islamabad, Pakistan, 14th–18th January, 2014, pp. 499–503. IEEE (2014)

18. Martínez-Fernández, S., Ayala, C.P., Franch, X., Marques, H.M.: Benefits and drawbacks of software reference architectures: a case study. Inf. Softw. Technol. **88**, 37–52 (2017)

19. Angelov, S., Grefen, P.: An e-contracting reference architecture. J. Syst. Softw. **81**(11), 1816–1844 (2008)

20. Bass, L., Clements, P., Kazma, R.: Software Architecture in Practice, 3rd edn. Addison-Wesley (2013)

21. Bass, L., Clements, P., Kazman, R.: Software Architecture in Practice. Addison-Wesley Professional (2003)

22. Bachmann, F., Bass, L., Garlan, D., Ivers, J., Little, R., Merson, P., Nord, R., Stafford, J.: Documenting Software Architectures: Views and Beyond. Addison-Wesley Professional (2011)

23. Fielding, R.T., Taylor, R.N.: Principled design of the modern web architecture. ACM Trans. Internet Technol. (TOIT) **2**(2), 115–150 (2002)

Machine Learning Based Predictive Model for Risk Assessment of Employee Attrition

Goldie Gabrani$^{(\boxtimes)}$ and Anshul Kwatra

School of Engineering and Technology, BML Munjal University, Gurgaon, India
{goldie.gabrani,anshul.kwatra.14cse}@bmu.edu.in,
ggabrani@gmail.com

Abstract. Every organization today is challenged with the issues of employee attrition. Attrition is the reduction in the employee base of an organization. This could be because of voluntary resignation or expulsion by the higher management. It becomes important for the company to be prepared for the loss of human power in whom company has invested and from whose help it has earned revenue. Thus, it is a profitable idea to predict the risk involved with uneven attritions so that management can take preventive measures and wise decisions for the benefit of the organization. In this paper, a model based on Machine Learning techniques that predicts the employee attrition has been designed. The model is implemented and is thoroughly analyzed for the full profile of companies. It has been shown that the model can be effectively used to maximize the employee retention.

Keywords: Machine learning · Multivariate analysis · Predictive modeling
Logistic regression · Random forests · Decision tree · Adaboost
Attrition · Risk assessment

1 Introduction

Reduction in employee or staff in a company is a common problem in industries especially in the area of IT, BPO etc. The reduction could have a number of reasons like different career goals, salary, location, demography [1]. This unpredictable attrition can cause a huge loss to the company. In order to overcome the loss to the company, the authors in this paper, propose a machine learning method to predict the employee attrition.

Attrition control is very important for health and success of any organization. Costs spent on human resources development are amongst the largest expenses any organizations bears. Salaries, bonuses, training costs and other personal benefits are the costs an organization takes to invest in their employees. If employee's aspirations are not met, this can result in uneven attritions from the company which can lead to some hazardous impacts on the growth of the company.

Accurate prediction in risk planning requires the correct interpretation of the available data about both the company user and the employee. Therefore, the design of such systems first requires finding anomalies in the available data. Anomalies occur due to various reasons like inconsistent data, missing values; the techniques used can differ in their complexity, the amount of data required, as well as other features. This

© Springer International Publishing AG, part of Springer Nature 2018
O. Gervasi et al. (Eds.): ICCSA 2018, LNCS 10963, pp. 189–201, 2018.
https://doi.org/10.1007/978-3-319-95171-3_16

paper presents modeling techniques to help management to plan risks associated with uneven attritions of employees in their organizations. The chosen methods are used in prediction systems of many well-known services and are applied to different organizations.

The proposed model requires delivering appropriate predictions for employee turnover, so an adequate dataset is needed for the purpose. The data set was used for both training and validation. The chosen Machine Learning methods were implemented and evaluated, and the results were collected. The main objective of this paper is to design and implement a real-time prediction model that is to predict accurate employee attritions in a company. Prior to solving this problem some of the previous literature was studied which is discussed in Sect. 2. Section 3 describes the proposed architecture and methodologies to find solution to this problem along with the Pseudo codes of the algorithms used for prediction and comparison. Section 4 elaborates the proposed model's prediction behavior with the help of an example. In Sect. 5 the results and conclusions of the proposed model with other related system is illustrated.

2   Literature Review

The term attrition or turnover [2] is the ratio of a number of organizational employees that have left the organization along with the consideration of time divided by the regular number of employees working in the organization at that specific time period. Employee attrition is the most studied behavior in any [3], yet continues to evade any concrete conclusions. Turnover of an employee has serious impact on the organization and that is why it is the most concerned issue which needs attention. Researchers say that higher turnover rates can have adverse effects on the growth of an organization if it is not suitably managed [4].

Controlling the employee attrition is a very complex and challenging task. Mobley [5] finds out and analyses the reasons of employee attrition. The withdrawal behaviour of employees is studied in detail for helping the management to understand more about what needs to be done in order to solve this problem which has creeped into the culture of many organizations. It helps the management to identify the variables that urges an employee to willingly leave the organization. Management face difficulty in understanding and accepting this situation within their organization due to their narrow vision and propoer understanding of the repurcusions of the situation. However, to identify the primary cause and to quantify the reasons of turnover, one can find the possible solution to this issue can be useful to the managers who look to create a difference in their organization [5].

There exist quite a number of causes that are used to interpret the turnover ratio of the employee but there is no specified theory or rules to understand it. Many efforts have been done to find the answer to the question of what governs employees' intention to quit by examining possible backgrounds of employees [6–8]. There are quite a few reasons why employees leave their organizations. These reasons are then used to predict intentions of leaving and actual exit the job. Various factors that cause churning the job may include (i) lack of commitment, (ii) job discontent, (iii) vague expectations of seniors and peers, (iv) uncertainty in performance appraisal system, (v) job profile, (vi) salary and career growth opportunities, (vii) location. Attrition is not same for different kinds of employees. For instance labour work-force or daily wage workers have issues related to environmental and managerial factors. These factors comprise of (i) organization's ethos and morals, (ii) managerial style, (iii) appropriate pay, (iv) giving support to each other, (v) faith amongst employees, (vi) manageable workload, (vii) career building (viii) amount of job satisfaction. There have been a number of findings implying the causes of employee turnover. These causes could be job-related issues and could be directly controlled by the employee. Examples of such factors are discontent with working conditions, supervising clashes, or salary related inconsistencies. To appreciate the causes related to job turnover is very critical in recognizing the concerns in an organization that is suffering attrition risk; such reasons are in direct control of an employer.

The attrition risk in the organization can be assessed by machine learning techniques by evaluating many features and analyzing them [9]. The model based on logistic regression is successful to predict turnover with a great accuracy because it uses a logistic curve to fit in the data which is quite random. The data is based on the separated employee dataset. This dataset was used to get the risk equation which was later used to assess the attrition risk with the current set of employees. After this, a cluster of high risk was identified, and then the analysis was done to find the reasons behind attrition so that management can create a plan to minimize this risk.

A new algorithm Data Mining Evolutionary algorithm (DMEL) [10] is designed for a carrier company to predict not only whether a customer will move to another company or not, but also to find out that how likely is it for him to do so. It was found out that if a customer is leaving, then carrier actually chooses a set of loyalty programs for its customers with special offers and services at much lower rates to retain them. DMEL showed correct results by showing stimulating rules of classification and diverse churn rates when applied to real-time employee data. Another paper [11], studies the Events per Variable (EPV) in logistic regression analysis to further increase its effectiveness in terms of accuracy. A data set of cardiac trails was used in the analysis 673 patients and had 7 variables. The number of events per predictive variable was calculated as a number of events/number of variables for e.g., 252/7 = 36. The results of this analysis show us factors like sample size or a total number of events may influence the validity of logistic regression. The less EPV value may lead to lesser accuracy. Calculated coefficients may get biased to both positive and negative side with less EPV value.

Next section gives in detail the approach used to develop the proposed model, process flows, involved data and the outputs that were obtained from the logistic regression model.

3 The Proposed Architecture and Methodologies

3.1 The Proposed Architecture

Described below is the standard O.S.E.M.N method which is used in this paper and it forms the base of the analysis:

- Obtain the data: The dataset is taken from Kaggle's website. It is a benchmarked data set that includes 9 features of 17,790 employees.
- Scrub or clean the dataset: The data set obtained from the source can have errors, missing values or in raw form, which means the data needs to be preprocessed before it can be used for any meaningful analyses. If data set is not cleaned before being analyzed or used as a feed into machine learning algorithms, it can produce wrong results. These results may lead to irrelevant insights and can impede decision making process. Common errors found in any data set are:
  - Duplicate records
  - Missing ranges
  - Raw data format
  - Incorrect numerical scales
  - Incorrect data formats
- Explore the dataset: This process involves multiple operations like knowing the statistical properties of the dataset, understanding features and deciding whether allanalyzing the limits with help of visual graphs. These graphs can be of the following types:
  - Box Plot
  - Line chart
  - Histogram
  - Scatter Plot

In some cases, if the data set has too many independent variables which makes it very complex to handle, it is termed as high dimensionality data set representation. This becomes very important to reduce the dimensions to a significant number. Feature selection is used in this paper which was carried out with logistic regression.

The feature 'left' (defines the number of employees that have left the organization) is the dependent variable and all other 9 variables are independent variables. These independent variables are:

- satisfaction_ level
- evaluation _score
- no._ of_ projects
- average_working_monthly_hours
- number_of_years at Organization Spent
- accident_at_work
- got_promotion
- department
- salary_level

The correlation matrix and heat maps are used to check which variables are positively or negatively correlated. The variables number_of_projects, average_working_monthly_hours and evaluation_score have positive correlation which means employees which work for more duration generally have higher evaluation_score. Variable like satisfaction_level is negatively correlated with a left variable which indicates employees with lower satisfaction degree are likely to leave the organization. Comparison of salary_level with left variable, departments with left variable and no_of_projects with left variable were analyzed.

- Model the dataset: After exploring the extreme limits and features of the data set, next process is to train the data set with appropriate algorithms. If it's a classification problem, the algorithms like Decision trees, Support vector machine, Random forests, Naive Bayes classifier etc. are used. But if the concerned problem is of predicting the discrete values over a set of domain then it is better to use regression modelling. The algorithms connected with regression modelling are Linear Regression, Logistic Regression etc. In this paper, we have covered both the aspects of prediction the attrition rate and classification of employees on whether they will leave the company or not. These models are explained in the Sect. 3.2.
- Interpret the results: Results obtained after modelling the data set with appropriate algorithms need to be analyzed and processed to lead them to decision making process. For example, left% obtained from the Eq. 1 is only a number unless a meaning is not associated with this like risk factor discussed in [9]. Graphs obtained from exploratory analysis are interpreted as a whole to deliberate the overall scenario of the problem statement. To check the accuracy and acceptability of the algorithms that we have used, this paper has discussed the results in the form of tables showing Precision, Recall and F1-score. These parameters help in concluding the solution in a nutshell.

3.2 Methodologies

Four models were created using four different machine learning methodologies Pseudo-code of these are given below:

3.2.a Logistic Regression

```
Given α, {[xi, yi]} where i goes from 1 till m.
Initialize variable d=<1,...1>T
Repeat the steps until algorithm converges:
for each j=0,...,n:
for dj'=dj + Σi(yi-ha(Xi))xji
for each j= 0,...,n:
dj = dj
Output d
```

3.2.b Random Forests

Creation:
Select L features randomly out of K features where L<<M
Calculate node d (use best split point) in the selected
L features.
Node created is then split in daughter nodes (use best
split)
Numbers of steps are repeated until the desired numbers
of nodes are created
Build forest by repeating the given steps to create the
desired number of trees

Prediction:
Use the features of test data and also take in count
the rules of each randomly generated decision tree to
predict the result and save it
Calculate a number of votes of each target
High voted variable is set as final prediction

3.2.c Decision Tree

```
Decsion_tree_algo(Sample S, Attribute_list A)
Create a node N
Samples if belong to same class C; label the node N
with C and terminate
A if is null; label N with most common class C in ma-
jority voting
Select a belongs to A, with the highest information
gain; Name N with n
For value t of n:
Grow a branch from N with the condition n=t;
Assume S to be the subset of samples in S with n=t
If St is empty; join a leaf labelled with most common
class in S
Else attach node generated by Decision_Tree(St, A-n)
```

3.2.d Adaboost Algorithm

```
Training Algorithm:
For every example in D define Wᵢ=1/|D|
For t from 1 to T
Hypothesis is generated, Hᵢ from BaseLearn(D)
Error Eᵢ of hypothesis Hₜ is calculated as total weight
of examples that are classified incorrect
Check Eᵢ >0.5 then exit the loop, else continue
Generate another parameter Bᵢ = Eᵢ/(1-Eᵢ)
Weights of examples are multiplied by Hₜ which are clas-
sified correctly
Return H=(h₁,h₂,…hₜ)

Testing Algorithm:
Hypothesis Hₜ in H votes for ex's classification with
weight log(1/Bₜ)
Return class which has highest weighted total number of
votes
```

Modelling our testing data with logistic regression, the resultant equation is as follows:

$$left\% = -3.7 * satisfaction\_level + 0.20 * evaluation\_score + 0.170 \\ * number\_of\_years + 0.18 \tag{1}$$

In Eq. 1, constant value, 0.18 represents the total effect of other independent variables which were not considered for our proposed model.

4   An Example

To explain the Eq. 1, we will take an example of values taken from test data set which yielded the following results:

$$left\% = -3.7 * satisfaction\_level + 0.20 * evaluation\_score + 0.170 \\ * number\_of\_years + 0.18 \tag{2}$$

The values for the different parameters from the data set are: (i) satisfaction_level = 0.9, (ii) evaluation_score = 0.6 and (iii) number_of_years = 8; Substituting the values in (2) we get:

$$left\% = -3.7 * 0.9 + 0.20 * 0.6 + 0.17 * 8 + 0.18 \tag{3}$$

$$left\% = -3.33 + 0.12 + 1.36 + 0.18 \tag{4}$$

$$\text{left\%} = -1.67 \tag{5}$$

final value of employee retention is predicted by using the following equation:

$$\text{final} = \exp(a)/1 + \exp(a) \tag{6}$$

$$\text{where } a = \text{left\%} \tag{7}$$

$$\text{final} = 0.37 \tag{8}$$

This means that the employee has a chance of 37% chance of leaving the company. According to [9] the risk factor analyzed. It is found that there is not much risk and the employee will be loyal to the company.

5   Results

This paper demonstrates the use of Logistic regression for risk assessment of employee's attrition by predicting the turnover of an employee in the company. The detailed analysis is performed on the employee dataset using the proposed model. The design of the model is done by using numerical python library 'NumPy'. To compare our proposed model based on Logistic Regression with the other existing techniques based on different supervised learning algorithms; we chose Decision Tree, Random Forests and Adaboost.

Comparison of salary_level with left variable was done and it was observed that those employees with low and medium salary level left the organization. Then departments were compared with the left, it was found Sales and Technical are the departments from where employees left the maximum. Next analysis is on the no. _of_projects an employee handles with the left variable and outcome is that more than 50% employees left their company with 2, 6 and 7 projects in hand and specifically all employees left their company who were having 7 projects with them. This shows more the number of projects more likely is the chance for an employee to leave. The evaluation_score played an important role in influencing left variable. It was proven that employees with very high or very low evaluation_score were the ones who left the company. Then average working monthly hours with left variable was analyzed and it was found that employees with very less or very more working hours left more often. Interesting results showed up when cluster comparisons of evaluation_score was done with satisfaction_level. There were a huge number of employees who were evaluated with good scores but were unhappy with their work. Same was the case with less evaluation_score and less satisfaction_level but more the evaluation_score and more the satisfaction_level, it was less likely that an employee would leave. Further, Decision Tree algorithm was used to check the prominent features which affect the attrition of employees. It was found that satisfaction_level, number_of_years and evaluation_score were the features which came to be of more importance than the other independent variables. The calculated predictions for these different models are as given in Tables 1, 2, 3 and 4 respectively. The attributes of the tables are:

Table 1. Accuracy using logistic regression algorithm

	Precision	Recall	F1-score
Not_ left	0.90	0.76	0.82
Left	0.48	0.73	0.58
Average–score	0.80	0.75	0.76

Table 2. Accuracy using decision tree algorithm

	Precision	Recall	F1-score
Not_ left	0.97	096	0.97
Left	0.87	0.91	0.89
Average–score	0.95	0.95	0.95

Table 3. Accuracy using random forests algorithm

	Precision	Recall	F1-score
Not_ left	0.99	0.98	0.99
Left	0.95	0.96	0.95
Average–score	0.98	0.98	0.98

Table 4. Accuracy using adaboost algorithm

	Precision	Recall	F1-score
Not_ left	0.95	0.97	0.96
Left	0.90	0.82	0.86
Average–score	0.58	0.76	0.93

Precision: It is also known as positive predicted value. It is given by:

$$TPV/ (TPV + FPV) \qquad (9)$$

TPV– true positive value.
FPV–false positive value.
FNV –false negative value.
Recall: It is also known as sensitivity. It is given by:

$$TPV/ (TPV + FNV) \qquad (10)$$

F1- Score: weighted average of the (i) precision and (ii) recall values.
not_left: the employee has not left the organisation.
left (already mentioned above): the employee has left the organisation.
As shown in the Tables 1, 2, 3 and 4, Random forests model has the highest accuracy of 98% which is very high. Detailed analysis of different independent variables is shown in Figs. 1, 2, 3, 4, 5 and 6.

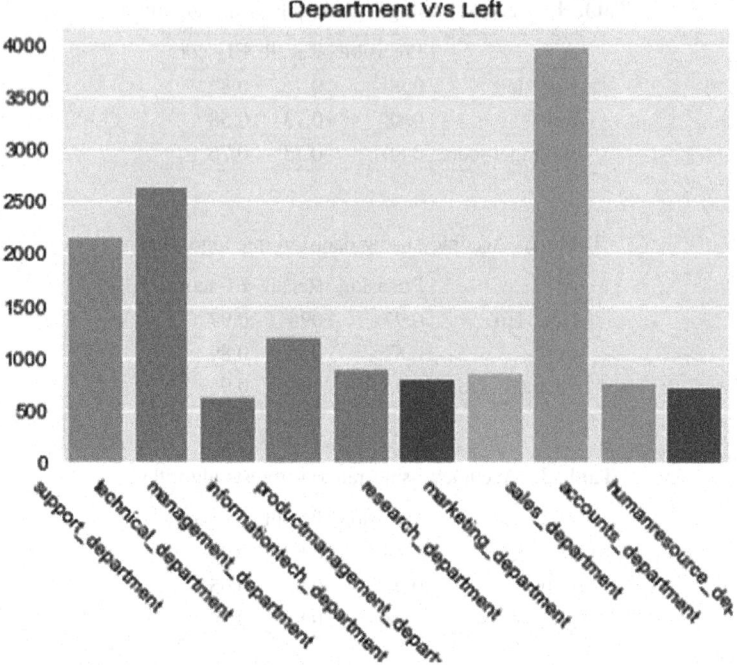

Fig. 1. Department v/s left

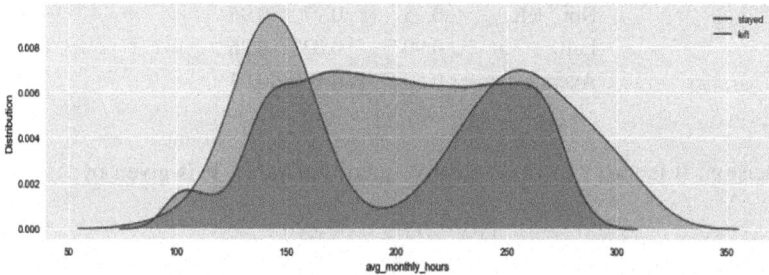

Fig. 2. Average_montly_hours v/s left

The proposed model is compared with the models based on Random Forests, Decision Trees and Adaboost algorithms. The broad results of the analysis are as follows:

- Underworked employees usually left the work; typically those who worked less than 150 h/month.
- Overworked employees left the company; typically those who used to work more than 240 h/month.
- Employees who had very high or very low evaluation-scores were the ones who churned in an organization.

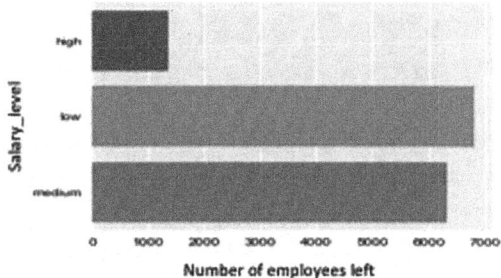

Fig. 3. Salary_level v/s left

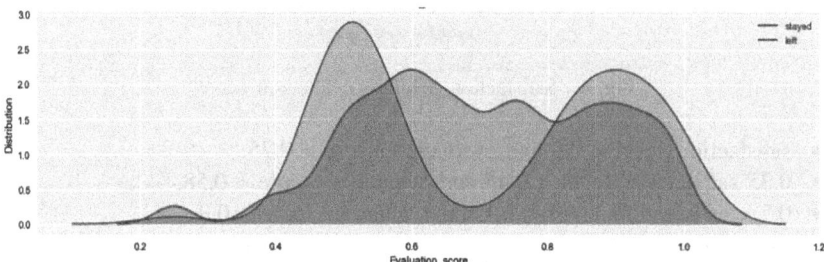

Fig. 4. Evaluation_score v/s left

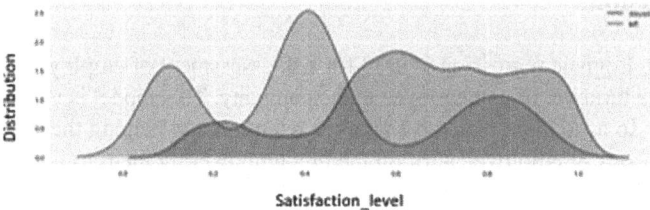

Fig. 5. Satisfaction_level v/s left

- Employees who had low or medium salary were mainly responsible for leaving the company.
- Employees having 2, 6 and 7 number of projects were the ones who left the company more often.
- Satisfaction Level came out to be a most important factor in analyzing attrition.
- Employees staying for 4 to 5 years at the company were the ones mainly responsible for uneven attrition.
- The random forests algorithm gave the best results with highest accurate number of predictions and gave the accuracy of 98%.
- In Fig. 6, clusters made by comparing evaluation_score and satisfaction_level showed that the employees which left their company had:

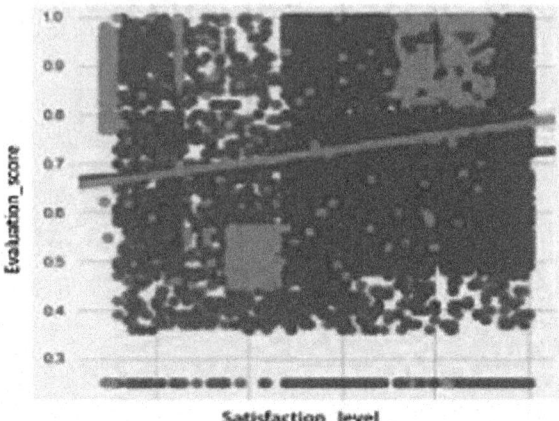

Fig. 6. Satisfaction_level v/s evaluation_score

- satisfaction_level < 0.2 and evaluation_score > 0.75.
- 0.35 satisfaction_level < 0.45 and evaluation_score < 0.58.
- 0.7 < satisfaction_level < 1.0 and evaluation_score > 0.8.
- From Fig. 1, it is inferred that most of the attritions happened in Sales, Technical and Support departments.

6 Conclusions

In this paper, Logistic regression is used for risk assessment of employees' attrition by predicting the turnover of an employee in the company. This model is very beneficial to the company so as to maximize the employee retention and helping the management to know the reasons of employee attrition thereby empowering them to make much more informed decisions. Logistic regression gave a equation to fit the model but had only the accuracy of 80%. The results obtained by Logistic regression were compared with Decision Tree, Random Forests and Adaboost. Among these Random forests model was found to have the highest accuracy of 98%. It is much better than other models. This is because it is a dynamic model and thereby adapts to changing the number of features in the data set. It is also observed that satisfaction_level, number_of_years and evaluation_score are the biggest factors that affect the attrition rate of any organization.

References

1. Denver, A., McMahon, F.: Labour turnover in London hostels and the cost-effectiveness of preventive measures. Int. J. Hosp. Manag. **11–2**, 143–540 (1992)
2. Price, J.L., Mueller, C.W.: A causal model of turnover for nurses. Acad. Manag. J. **24**, 543–565 (1981)

3. Schwab, D.P.: Contextual variables in employee performance-turnover relationships. Acad. Manag. J. **34**, 966–975 (1991)
4. Wasmuth, W.J., Davis, S.W.: Managing employee turnover: why employees leave. Cornell HRA Q., 11–18 (1993)
5. Mobley, W.H.: Employee Turnover: Causes, Consequences, and Control. Addison-Wesley Publishing, Philippines (1982)
6. Nagadevara, V., Srinivasan, V., Valk, R.: Establishing a link between employee turnover and withdrawal behaviours. Appl. Data Mining Tech. Res. Pract. Hum. Resour. Manag. **16** (2), 81–99 (2008)
7. Kevin, M.M., Joan, L.C., Adrian, J.W.: Organizational change and employee turnover. Pers. Rev. **33**(2), 161–166 (2004)
8. Saks, A.M.: The relationship between the amount of helpfulness of entry training and work outcomes. Hum. Rel. **49**, 429–451 (1996)
9. Khare, R., Kaloya, D., Choudhary, C.K.: Employee attrition risk assessment using logistic regression analysis. In: IIMA International Conference on Advanced Data Analytics, Business Analytics (2015)
10. Wai, H.A., Chan, K.C.C., Yao, X.: A novel evolutionary data mining algorithm with applications to churn prediction. IEEE Trans. Evol. Comput. **7**(6), 532–545 (2003)
11. Peduzzi, P., Concato, J., Kemper, E., Holford, T.R., Feinstein, A.R.: A simulation study of the number of events per variable in logistic regression analysis. J. Clin. Epidemiol. **49**, 1373–137 (1996)

A Way of Design Thinking as an Inference Rule of Substantially Evolutionary Theorizing in Software Projects

P. Sosnin$^{(\boxtimes)}$

Ulyanovsk State Technical University,
Severny Venets, Street 32, 432027 Ulyanovsk, Russia
sosnin@ulstu.ru

Abstract. The principal direction of innovations in software engineering is the search for useful ways of theorizing in the design process and its results. In searching, the nature of design and specificity of software essences should take into account. The paper describes a way of theorizing that focuses on features of organizational and behavioral activity of designing and Grounded theories used in such conditions. The main feature of a suggested theorization is building a project theory on the base of facts of interacting the designers with the accessible experience when they use the design thinking approach for evolving the project and its theory in parallel. Such way leads to new positives in architectural and cause-and-effects forms of understanding.

Keywords: Conceptual designing · Lexical control · Mental imagery
Ontology · Question-answering · Software intensive system · Visual modeling

1 Introduction

One of the most painful problems of creating the software intensive systems (Software Intensive Systems, SISs) is the problem of the success of their design, obvious indicators of which are the statistical reports of the Standish Group, published since 1994 [1].

A special place in the assessments of the unsatisfactory state of affairs is taken by the SEMAT initiative (Software Engineering Methods And Theory), that was claimed in 2009 [2] by a group of well-known theoreticians and practitioners in this subject (the leaders of this group were I. Jacobson, B. Meyer, and R. Soley). The initiative was aimed at cardinal reformatting of software engineering, including its theorization (the obligatory emphasis on the theory found its expression even in the abbreviation of the initiative). Starting with its announcement, the SEMAT initiative is being actively implemented both in practical and theoretical plans, but some important questions of theorization are still open, and the search for answers to them is topical.

In our study, we propose some innovations for constructing and using the theories of a substantially evolutionary type for projects of SISs. The proposed new methods and tools were caused by the following premises:

1. In SISs projects, their developers too often face a high degree of complexity that is manifesting itself from different but important points of view on projects.

O. Gervasi et al. (Eds.): ICCSA 2018, LNCS 10963, pp. 202–216, 2018.
https://doi.org/10.1007/978-3-319-95171-3_17

2. The features of the life cycle of the SIS project include the unpredictable impact on its course of numerous situational factors that it is dangerous not to take into account at various points in the life cycle (for reference in the useful review [3] about 400 such situational factors are mapped into 48 of their variants distributed across 11 groups).
3. The uniqueness of each project is affected not only by the need to take into account the situational factors and their effects, but also the necessity of using the "feedbacks" for repeated processing the project situations appeared in the past. Such necessity is caused by various reasons and also the uniqueness of the designers' experience involved in their work.

For designing the SISs, the above premises prompts the usefulness of such projects' descriptions that will help the designer (or designers):

- to understand the current situations, evaluating them for choosing the next steps forward or going back, if it will be necessary;
- or to predict the consequences of the actions and make justified decisions at the problematic points of the life cycles of projects.

In our deep opinion, the role of a description with such potential may be entrusted to the theories of a substantially evolutionary kind that corresponds to the subclass of Grounded theories. Any substantially evolutionary theory of the corresponding project (below Project Theory) is created and applied by designers in conditions of operative solving the project tasks. A very important feature of such version of theorizing is the use of facts any of which corresponds to the act of interactions (with experience) that is registered in question-answer forms.

The process of constructing the Project Theory and the results of this process (in their current state) will have the potential for checking and modeling the semantics of the project, including forms of architectural and cause-and-effect understanding that facilitate to the solution of design tasks using automated design thinking (Design Thinking, the subject area that is actively evolved nowadays).

2 Preliminaries Bases

The last 15 years, our research has focused on the use of question-answering in the conceptual design of software intensive systems. This choice was due to the following reasons:

1. Lack of sustained progress in enhancing the success in designing of SISs despite numerous attempts to change the painful state of affairs with the successfulness.
2. Our understanding that:
   2.1. A very important source of reasons affecting the design process is the human factor that manifests itself in the designer's interactions with the accessible experience and its computerized models.
   2.2. Interactions with experience are based on what people call "questions" and "answers."

We began our study with orientation on:

1. Availability of regular and long-term statistical reports containing information on the positive and negative factors that influence the success in designing the SISs (reports of the Corporation Standish Group in the first place [1]).
2. Workflows of conceptual activity applied in well-known technologies providing the development of systems with software (first of all workflows of the technology "Rational Unified Process").

The first steps of the study have led to useful artifacts that were called "Question-Answer Nets" (QA-nets). In conceptual solving the project tasks, QA-nets register question-answer reasoning (QA-reasoning) in semantic memory of the question-answer type (QA-memory) [4]. Later, such type of artifacts was adopted for use in activities shown in Fig. 1.

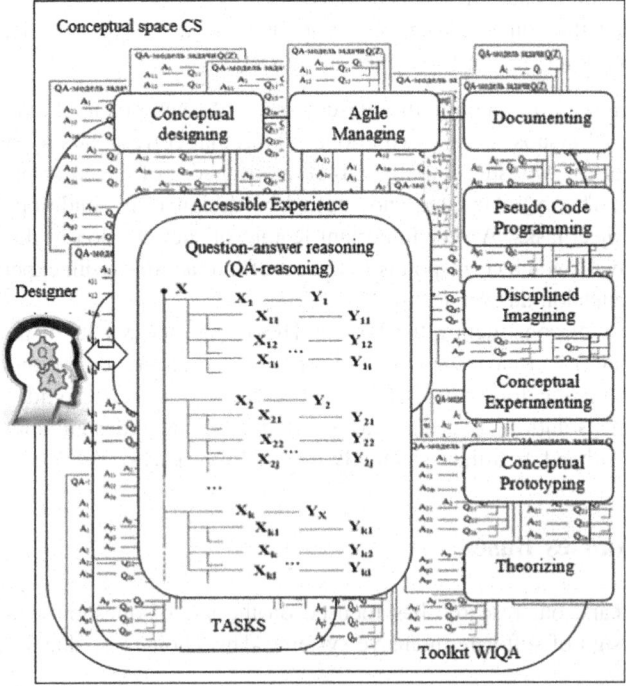

Fig. 1. Basic applications of QA-nets

In this scheme, one can view a visual tree of nodes, any of which has X or Y-type but nodes can have not only hierarchical relations. The can be bound by common additional attributes modeling useful semantic relations. Thus, in the general case, the structure can have the form of the net. In applications indicated on the scheme, QA-nets were used for modeling different essences of the operational space of designing the SIS in their reflection on QA-memory of the toolkit WIQA (shown in Fig. 2).

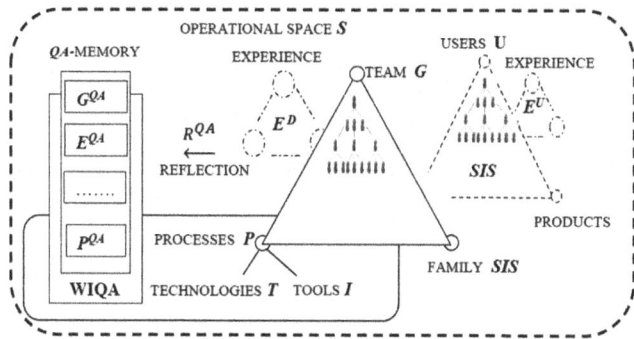

Fig. 2. Reflection of operational space on QA-memory

For example, in conceptual space CS formed in the semantic memory, designers have the possibility to interact with the following types of nodes: Q – question and A – answer in QA-reasoning; G – team of designers and M – member of the group; R – executed role and C- competency; D – name of data and V – its value and so on.

The last pair indicates on using of QA-nets for modeling the constructs of the pseudocode language defined above QA-memory. In programs written in this language, QA-nets can be used for the definition of the necessary semantics expressed by basic and additional attributes of the memory cell, in which the corresponding node is uploaded.

In developed applications shown in Fig. 1, QA-nets of different kinds are intertwined, and their nodes are visually and programmatically accessible. Moreover, the designer can attach the useful files and references to any cell (or uploaded node) if it will be necessary or useful.

Our work with QA-nets in conceptual designing the SISs, including the development of the toolkit WIQA and its extensions, confirmed that such kind of artifacts helps to build the CS that adequately reflects the operational space of designing.

In designing the certain SISs, the CS of the corresponding project is created in parallel with other actions, and such processes lead to the beginning of the CS that is shown in Fig. 3. The structure and content of this figure demonstrate the life cycle of the CS in conditions when the designers apply the precedent-oriented approach and QA-approach [4] in conceptual solving the project tasks. As a result of such activity at the conceptual stage of designing, solutions of tasks express with the help of texts, graphics, and tables.

The scheme also demonstrates the dynamics of the design process because any project of SIS is a unique phenomenon, the essence of which is determined primarily by human-computer activities implemented by a team of designers interacting with the involved stakeholders in conditions of very high complexity. Each person acting in the process of designing has a unique experience that is applied unpredictably, and parts of this experience can find objectification in the designed SIS. Except all, the numerous situational factors can unpredictable influence on a course of the project in different points of its life cycle.

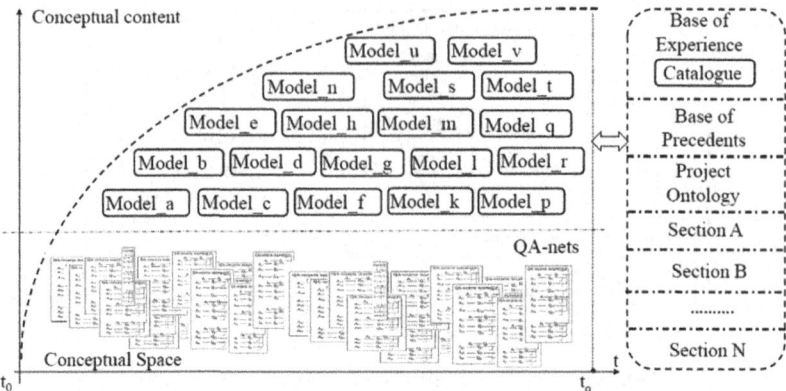

Fig. 3. Beginning the results of conceptual solving the tasks

Therefore, the result of designing essentially depends on rules that are used by designers for managing their work. In the described case, one subset of these rules is bound with an experimental activity that leads to developing the Base of Experience and its components in parallel with other actions of the design process. More details, this subset of rules defines preparing the solutions of tasks for their reuse with the help of corresponding models of precedents [4].

The second subset of rules we bound with the use of QA-nets in creating the substantially evolutionary theories [5], the typical scheme of which is presented in Fig. 4.

The scheme indicates that dynamics of such theory combines processes and theory extensions occurring in some following phases:

- Before-theoretical phase involves the collection of facts $F(t) = \{F_k\}$, relevant to the corresponding subject area.
- In the descriptive phase, registered facts are used for constructing the texts of $T(t) = \{Ti\}$ linking the facts in the description of essences distinguished in the subject area.
- In building the theory, special attention focuses on vocabulary and especially on developing its part that presents a system of concepts $S(\{Np\})$. In our case, these concepts combine in the project ontology. In Fig. 2, this part of the theory marked as the classification phase.
- In becoming the theory and its use, the identifiably measuring phase introduces the possibility of (empirical) interpreting the theoretical constructs.
- Any theory is created for its uses, a very important kind of which is models (model phase in the scheme).

The scheme also underlines that components of any phase are located in QA-memory. Thus, in the most general sense, any theory is a system of sentences combined in textual units, relations among which define the structure of the theory. For uses of the theory, it is typical to combine its theoretical constructs with constructs of corresponding meta-theory, appropriate graphical units, and tables.

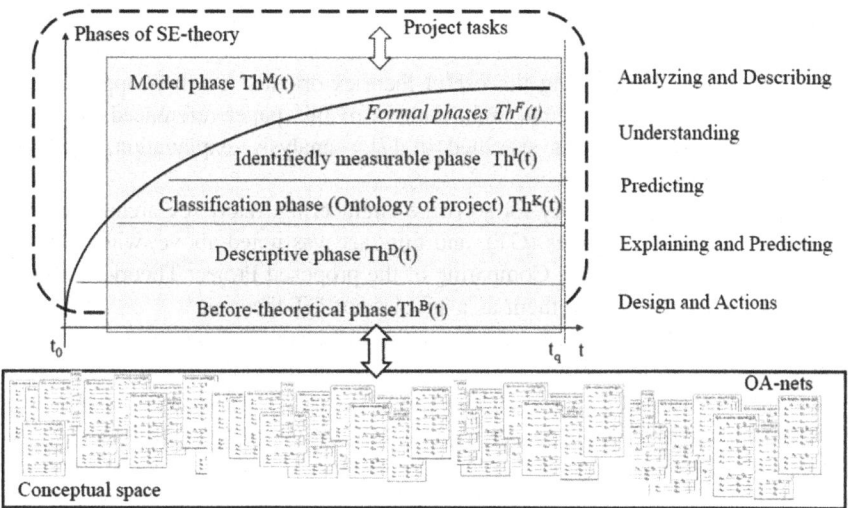

Fig. 4. Structure of the Project Theory

3 Related Works

Above, it was noted that the special place in the assessments of the unsatisfactory state of affairs is taken by the SEMAT initiative (Software Engineering Methods And Theory), in which the necessity to search for the basic theoretical foundations of software engineering found its place, even in the abbreviation of the initiative. Starting with its announcement, the SEMAT initiative is being actively implemented both in practical and theoretical plans, and SEMAT-guidelines (http://semat.org/documents/20181/57862/formal-15-12-02.pdf/e7ba1188-c477-4585-b18a-06937f0e62f3)   are included in the OMG -Group standards database (http://www.omg.org/Essence/20150601/Essence.xmi).

The state of affairs in the field of software engineering theorizing is evaluated at annual conferences, symposiums and seminars held both within the framework of SEMAT (for example, the General Theory of Software Engineering (GTSE 2011-2015) and the 5th International Workshop on Theory-Oriented Software Engineering (2016)), and other communities of theorists and practitioners (IEEE, ACM, …). From year to year, the state of affairs with this application of theorizing is enriched, but some important questions of theorization are still open, and the search for answers to them is topical.

As a rule, after conferences and workshops their result is generalized, and, for example, such report for the second workshop marked that a GTSE should "explain and predict software engineering phenomena at multiple levels, including social processes and technical artifacts, should synthesize existing theories from software engineering and reference disciplines, should be developed iteratively, should avoid common misconceptions and theoretical concepts, and should respect the complexity of software engineering phenomena" [6].

Very often, researchers, who were participated in attempts to build the general theory have referenced in the paper [7] that includes an analysis of assignments of theories and a way for creating the useful theories oriented on their applications in software engineering. In their research, authors of this paper referenced on the following classification that was specified in [7] - analysis, explanation, prediction, design, and activity.

In attempts to build a theory for software engineering, many researchers turned to the class of Grounded Theories (GT), and this fact was noted above, where we indicated some features of the GT. Comparing of the proposed Project Theories with such features enabled us to qualify them as a subclass of GT-theories.

In this section, for describing and estimating the state of affairs with theorizing in this area of software engineering, we will apply two thematic-analytical reviews [8, 9].

In the review [8] published in 2013, there are no applications of GT to a coherent set of specialized disciplines typically implemented by designers in the development of systems with software. Therefore, in the review, investigated publications were separated into three areas - flexible design, distributed development and the formation of requirements.

In the conclusions of the review, authors noted the prospects for using GT in software engineering, primarily because the development of software is based on intensive human activity. In a wide range of the GT-applications, they are usually created for investigation of behavioral processes and phenomena in social science.

In the second review [9] that was published (in 2016) by authors directly related to the SEMAT initiative, it is stated that in the vast majority of investigated publication, GT is applied fragmentarily, either at the level of GT-procedures or to some kinds of activity of designers. Particularly useful results of the analysis are two questionnaires, allowing researchers to determine the specifics of the GT designed by them. The first questionnaire helps to understand the general characteristics of the GT being created, while the second questionnaire focuses on the features of the basic data (the facts over which the theory is built up): what is their source? To what extent are the data adequate for the study? Which forms and procedures are adequate for coding of data?

Particular attention in the second review is given to potential problems in conducting theoretical research in the field of software development. Among such problems are the following: 1. Managing large volumes of heterogeneous data: including source code, test packages, task and effort data from project management software, design diagrams (for example, frameworks, class diagrams), project documents, project management documents (e.g., backlogs, burnout diagrams), performance data, problem tracking data, and others. 2. Encoding of non-traditional texts. It is unclear how to use open coding to develop diagrams, structured text (for example, use cases), or source code.

From the second review, for our version of theorizing, it is important one of the conclusions. Let us repeat it:

"Grounded theory (GT) remains one of the most rigorous methods to generate new theories. This is a significant issue as the establishment of a strong theory base has been identified as an important challenge for the software engineering discipline. We believe well-conducted GT studies can make significant contributions to our field and help to develop rich theories to inform future empirical studies in software engineering."

4 Automated Design Thinking in Theorizing

4.1 Features of the Project Theory

Theories of substantially evolutionary type (SE-type) have the following features:

The Essence of Facts. In reflecting the components of the operational space OS on their models in the conceptual space, designers use interactions with experience and register such behavioral acts by textual models of questions and answers. In creating SE-theories, designers extract the facts $\{F_k\}$ from sets of such models. Thus facts $\{F_k\}$ are traces of designers' interactions with the used experience.

Gathering the Facts. Applied SE-theories form a sub-class that corresponds to the kind of Grounded theories of a constructive type specified by K Chermes [10]. One of the features of this kind is starting the creation of the theory from the root question. For SE-theories, such root question is an initial statement $S(t_0)$ of the root task $Z^*(t_0)$ of the corresponding project P. The principal role in gathering the raw facts fulfills an abductive search.

The Relevance of Facts. For any SE-theory, a role of facts play only such of them that are bound with solving the project tasks that are understudied as naturally artificial essences with the following features:

1. As told above, tasks are the type of questions, answer on which are constructed in forms of tasks' solutions.
2. They are oriented on achieving the definite goals that must be confirmed by obtained results and their checks.
3. In the general sense, a life cycle of a task can include creative actions that help to overcome definite gaps as problems if such gaps are revealed (but "task" has another sense then "problem").
4. Solved tasks are a type of values that should be prepared for the future reuse.
5. The task description that provides the task reuse can be interpreted as the model of the corresponding precedent that simulates the unit of experience.

Location of Theoretical Constructs. Figure 3 indicates that facts $\{F_k\}$ used for creating SE-theory are placed in QA-memory, from which they are extracted for the necessary processing. Moreover, any sub-theory with its components is also uploaded in this memory.

Applications of SE-Theory. If it is necessary or useful, designers can use the current state of SE-theory for analyzing, describing, understanding and explaining of situations or for predicting the results of possible actions or for creating the useful models for implementing the next steps of the design process. Any application is constructive because it is accompanied by creating the necessary QA-objects and their compositions.

Referents of Theory. In real-time work, designers create the theoretical system of already used experience and applied such system as SE-theory when it is necessary or useful. Thus, any SE-theory reflects the experience that is objectified in the developed system in the current state of its lifecycle.

Coding. On the course of becoming any SE-theory, the basic way for coding facts and theoretical constructs is their coding as QA-objects.

Memoing. There is two version for registering memos, which provide a link with reality and are a source of prompts for the development of the theory. In the first version, the designer can attach the memo to the construct (uploaded in the cell of QA-memory) through a reference. The second way is the use of subordinated answer in the corresponding QA-net.

Access to Facts and Constructs. Any SE-theory exists in QA-memory where components of any theoretical phase are accessible for the use of pseudo-code programs, and such possibility helps in automating behavioral actions in the creation and use of the theory.

Basic Principle of Evolution. In SE-theories, tasks are reasons of evolution. Any applied SE-theory begins its life cycle from the initial statement $St(t_0)$ of the root task $Z^*(t_0)$, QA-analysis of which leads to subordinated tasks combined in the tree of tasks. As it will show below, in the described way of creating of SE-theories, it is used design thinking approach [11] for the work with any new project tasks. In evolving applied SE-theory, any implementation of such approach fulfills a role of a "soft" rule of inference. Any such rule of inference must satisfy the principle of "additivity," the essence of which is clarified by the following reasoning.

Any such rule of inference must satisfy the principle of "additivity," the essence of which is clarified the following reasoning. Any solved task Z_i leaves textual traces in theory $Th^P(t)$ understood as the system $S(\{T_j\}, t)$ of textual units $\{T_j\}$. Let us assume, that any textual unit T_j of traces included in $S(\{T_j\}, t_j)$ is its increment $\Delta S(T_j, t_j)$ in the moment of time t_j. Then, this system of texts can be expressed in a form

$$Th^P(t_j) \;=\; S(\{T_j\}, t_j) \;=\; S(T_0,\ t_0) \cup (\cup_j \Delta S(T_j, t_j))$$

where T_0 is a textual description with which designers start their work with the project $P(t)$ and its theory $Th^P(t)$ in the moment of time t_0.

Because the expression corresponds the textual structure of the theory $Th^P(t)$, it can be presented in the form

$$Th^P(t_j) = Th^P(t_0) \cup (\cup_j \Delta Th^P(t_j))$$

where $\Delta ThP(t_j)$ is a next increment of the theory in its current state $Th^P(t_j)$.

Thus, creating and operatively using the theory $Th^P(t)$ have a managerial potential that is caused by the additional ordering of the work. This additional order is based on the theoretical systematization of the current state of the design process and its results as well as on the possibility of a regulated evolution of both the theory and the project.

In the described case, the suggested version of theorizing leads to the additional subset of rules in designing the SISs. Implementing of these rules is a source of traditionally positive effects that caused by the use of the theory. Additional positive effects are bound with rules of inferences, among which it needs to mark cause-and-effects regularities objectified in models of precedents. A typical expression of the precedent regularity has the following logical view (Fig. 5):

Name of precedent P_i:
while [logical formulae (LF) for motives $M = \{M_k\}$]
as [LF for aims $C = \{C_l\}$]
if [LF for precondition $U' = \{U'_n\}$],
then [plan of reaction (program) r_q],
end so [LF for postconditions $U'' = \{U''_m\}$]
----
there are alternatives $\{P_j(r_p)\}$.
(choice)

Fig. 5. The cause-and-effect regularity of the precedent

Any of such regularities is discovered and formed in the process of solving the new project task. These regularities have the behavioral nature (motives, aims, choice). They can be interpreted as rules of inference in theory, requirements of the project or regularities of the corresponding conceptual space. In the described case, for discovering the regularities and their initial specifying, the designer must use an automated version of the design thinking approach [12].

4.2 Automated Design Thinking as an Inference Rule

Let us clarify the role of the new task in our integrated approach to the creation of the project theory in designing the systems with the software. This approach has the following basic features:

1. In the process of conceptual designing the definite SIS, its developers create and apply the specialized QA-net (tree of tasks TT(Z*, t) where Z* is a root task of the project) that reflects the SIS-project from the viewpoint of project tasks.
2. This artifact is used for creating the project theory $Th^P(t)$ and developing the project documentation $P^D(t)$ that is interpreted as one of the theory models.
3. In developing the artifacts TT(Z*, t) and $Th^P(t)$, designers apply reflecting the activity space onto the semantic memory of the QA-type and processing the conceptual objects in this memory in handy, automated and automatic modes.
4. Processing the conceptual objects is based on the question-answer analysis in the context of stepwise refinement of tasks, model-driven development oriented on precedents, and design thinking approach in real-time using the interactions with the affordable experience [12].
5. Designers use the stepwise refinement when they work:

- With project tasks $\{Z_i\}$ beginning with initial statement $S(Z^*, t_0)$ of the root task Z^* of the project;
- With the initial statement $S(Z_i, t_0)$ of any project task Z_i the work with which can lead to generating the subordinated project tasks or to the corresponding artifact $TT(Z_i, t)$ and so on.

6. Thus artifact $TT(Z^*, t)$ can be presented as the system $S(\{TT(Z_i, t)\})$, and therefore, in this paper, almost all that we suggest can be clarified on an example of a new project task.

In design thinking, designers work with any new task (for example Z_i) in conditions that are schematically shown in Fig. 6, where important place occupies the project ontology and semanticized graphics.

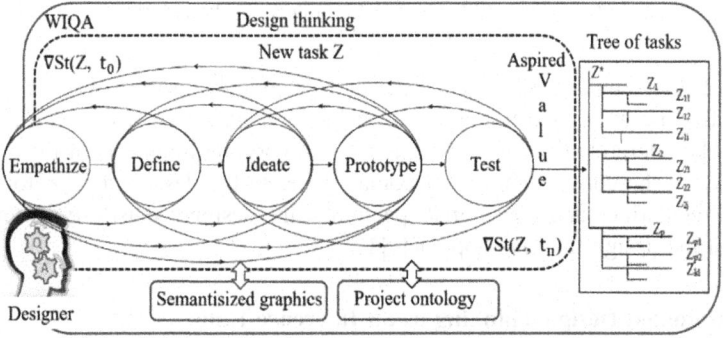

Fig. 6. The iterative process of design thinking

Let us assume, that in the constructive use of DT, the work with a new task Zi begins with a list of keywords registering this potential task at the level of an initial uncertainty $\nabla U(Z, t0)$. This initial state of the task can be presented with an implication

$$??^U U(Z_i) \xrightarrow{???^W W(Z_i)} ?^V V(Z_i),$$

where symbols $?^U, ?^V$ and $?^W$ indicates applying of QA- approach to the components of a condition U, value V and gap W of the task Z_i.

This expression reflects a situation S, in which initiators of a certain innovation decided to start the work with a corresponding project. Let us clarify our understanding this expression:

1. There is a goal G to achieve a certain value for potential customers, and in the current moment of time, this value V expressed with some ambiguity $(?V)$.
2. Conditions U, in which the goal can be achieved, are vague perceived, and they can be expressed with essential uncertainty $??U$ for reducing of which conditions can be constructed during the process of designing the SIS.

3. The construct $???W$ is unknown, and it can not be qualified as a problem gap between $??U$ and $?V$ taking into account their ambiguity.
4. Having the goal G expressed by $(?V)$ opens the possibility for interpreting the situation S as an indicator of the task Z* that should be solved.
5. For reducing the uncertainties in the expression (1), it should apply design thinking based on question-answer reasoning.

At the Empathize-stage, initial keywords are used by the designer for generating some discourses that implicitly or explicitly describe future components of the implicative expression of the task Z_i. Wording the discourses, the designer checks them on compliance with the ontology. Additionally, interactions with the ontology help to the designer in extracting the useful questions. Indicated usages of the ontology that lead to reducing the initial uncertainty.

Moreover, any of such discourses should be tested on its understanding with the use of an appropriate conceptual experiment that will require expressing conditions of experimenting and a result of this process. For achieving these goals, the designer can apply appropriate means of the semanticized graphics, for example, UML-diagrams or block-and-line scheme of other kinds.

At the Define stage, the designer must combine the generated discourses in an understandable wholeness where discourses will be coordinated. Actions of this stage also require interacting with the ontology and creating the useful schemes that help the designer in continuous reducing the uncertainty in work with the task Z_i.

The basic feature of the Ideate-stage is the search of appropriate ideas that help to solve the task. Therefore, for this stage, a principal role plays extracting the questions from texts created at the previous stage, especially questions that lead to formulating initial statements of tasks corresponding perspective ideas. In any of such statements, working with extracted questions, the designer (or designers) must include information that is sufficient for achieving the physical and algorithmic realizations.

At the Prototype stage, for an alternative idea, the designer must invent and conduct the corresponding conceptual experiment that not only demonstrates the way of the task solution but also discloses some its characteristics helping in comparison of alternatives. At this stage, the designer can use all developed mechanisms of onto-logical and figuratively semantic support, including the following possibilities:

1. Discovering the cause-and-effects relations that are implicitly and explicitly expressed in the description of an alternative.
2. Useful versions of conceptually algorithmic prototypes that can be built and tested in the WIQA-environment
3. The second possibility has the following versions:
4. Pictured prototypes (P-prototypes) that have some similarities with paper prototypes [12], but P-prototypes are a system of pictorial schemes created in the graphical editor described above. This version of prototypes includes a drawn system of executable interfaces.
5. In the second version of P-prototypes, they are programmed by designers in the pseudo-code language LWIQA with the use of drawn interfaces.

It should be noted, that pseudo code means can be applied for combining the pictorial schemes in a prototype system, for example, they can be combined in a slideshow with automated or automatic switching among schemes.

Described versions of prototypes can be tested in some versions also. Differences among versions are caused by the following intentions:

1. Orientation on an understanding with the use of combining the different architectural viewpoints on the prototype to be tested.
2. Orientation on understanding the conceptually algorithmic structure of the executable prototype.
3. Intention to use the ways of testing applied in traditional programming.
4. Attempt to prepare and conduct a conceptual experiment that must demonstrate a model of a precedent for the task to be prototyped.

Told above discloses some positive effects that are caused by the use of design in thinking in reactions of designers on new tasks the main of which is the root task Z^* of the SIS-project.

Thus, in the process of designing a certain SIS, the described version of automated design thinking helps the designer who has been in the task situation to perform the following actions:

1. Present this situation by some expected effects (with the position of the SIS users) in the conceptual space of the project;
2. Determine an initial statement of the corresponding task and verify this statement on the consistency of the project theory in its current state;
3. Invent an algorithmically realizable way of solving the task and consistently insert the corresponding idea in the current statement of the task;
4. Prototype the conceived way of the task solution and estimate obtained results (postconditions) on its consistency of the project theory and expectations of the users;
5. Try to conceive and check other alternative versions of reactions on the task situation and choose one of them that is better.

Finalizing this section, we can mark, that enumerated actions help to the designer to build the understandable version of the task solution that is consistent with the current states of the project theory and corresponding Conceptual Space. After that, this solution should be refined and formed as the precedent model with the use of the precedent oriented approach. That is why we interpret the use of design thinking approach as a "soft" rule of inference in developing the project theory while any precedent model will correspond to a strict rule of inference of the theory $Th^P(t)$.

5 Conclusion

The paper presents the way of real-time creating the project theory of the substantially evolutionary type that corresponds to the reality of becoming the conceptual project of the certain SIS in its conceptual space. Any of such projects finds its expression in a system of documents that combine textual units, graphical schemes, and necessary tables.

The theory $Th^P(t)$ as the additional and very useful artifact fulfills the role of the checked ground for the conceptual project. Any of such theory has the phase structure, in which the description phase occupies the central place. The base of this phase is the semantic net, nodes of which are questions and answers that are generated during the question-answer analysis of project tasks. For such work of designers, we developed QA-approach reified in the WIQA toolkit. Basic features of QA-approach are the use of the stepwise refinement, beginning with the initial statement of the root task of the project.

In the offered way of a reaction on the new task, the designer (or a group of designers) uses three intertwined lines of actions that correspond design thinking, question-answer analysis and creating the model of the corresponding precedent. Intertwining has iterative form, dynamics of which is managed with the normative scheme of design thinking, stepwise refinement in its applying to the statement of the task being solved. In SE-theorizing, any realization of DT-approach fulfill the role of the inference rule.

Acknowledgments. This work was supported by the Russian Fund for Basic Research (RFBR), Grant #18- 07-00989a, 18-47-730016p-a, and the State Contract №2.1534.2017/4.6.

References

1. Chaos reports, 1994–2016 (2017). http://www.standishgroup.com
2. Jacobson, I., Ng, P.-W., McMahon, P., Spence, I., Lidman, S.: The essence of software engineering: the SEMAT kernel. Queue **10**(10), 1–12 (2012)
3. Clarke, P., O'Connor, R.V.: The situational factors that affect the software development process: towards a comprehensive reference framework. J. Inf. Softw. Technol. **54**(5), 433–447 (2012)
4. Sosnin, P.: Precedent-oriented approach to conceptually experimental activity in designing the software intensive systems. Int. J. Ambient Comput. Intell. (IJACI) **7**(1), 69–93 (2016)
5. Sosnin, P.: A way for creating and using a theory of a project in designing of a software intensive system, In: Proceedings of the 17th International Conference on Computational Science and Its Applications, pp. 3–6 (2017)
6. Johnson, P., Ralph, P., Goedicke, M., Ng, P.-W., Stol, K.-J., Smolander K., Exman, J., Perry, D.E.: Report on the Second SEMAT Workshop on General Theory of Software Engineering (GTSE 2013). SIGSOFT Softw. Eng. (Notes) **38**(5), 47–50 (2013)
7. Sjøberg, D.I.K.I.K., Dyba, T., Anda, B.C.D., Hannay, J.E.: Building Theories in Software Engineering. In: Shull, F., Singer, J., Sjøberg, D.I.K.I.K. (eds.) Guide to Advanced Empirical Software Engineering, pp. 312–336. Springer, London (2008). https://doi.org/10.1007/978-1-84800-044-5_12
8. Badreddin, O.: Thematic review and analysis of grounded theory application in software engineering. In: Advances in Software Engineering, vol. 2013. Hindawi Publishing Corporation, Article ID 468021, 9 pages (2013)
9. Stol, K.J., Ralph, P., Fitzgera, B.: Grounded theory in software engineering research: a critical review and guidelines. In: Proceedings of the 38th International Conference on Software Engineering, pp. 120–131 (2016)

10. Charmaz, K.: Constructing Grounded Theory: A Practical Guide Through Qualitative Analysis. Sage, London (2006)
11. Dorst, K.: The nature of design thinking, in DTRS8 Interpreting Design Thinking. In: Proceeding of Design Thinking Research Symposium, pp. 131–139 (2010)
12. Sosnin, P.: Experience-Based Human-Computer Interactions: Emerging Research and Opportunities. IGI-Global (2017)

A Critical Review of the Politics of Artificial Intelligent Machines, Alienation and the Existential Risk Threat to America's Labour Force

Ikedinachi Ayodele Wogu[1], Sanjay Misra[1(✉)], Patrick Assibong[1],
Adewole Adewumi[1], Robertas Damasevicius[2],
and Rytis Maskeliunas[2]

[1] Covenant University, Ota, Ogun State, Nigeria
{ike.wogu, sanjay.misra, patrick.assibong,
wole.adewumi}@covenantuniversity.edu.ng
[2] Kaunas University of Technology, Kaunas, Lithuania
{robertas.damasevicius, rytis.maskeliunas}@ktu.lt

Abstract. While an increasing number of scholars are growing weary about the troubling predictions about when Artificial Intelligent Machines (AIMs) will fully acquire the capacity of intentionality - the ability for AIMs to possess the similitude of human-like knowledge for processing data and the knowledge of what is right and wrong in their own eyes, to the detriment of mankind – there are scholars who argue that politicians and the powers that be in the American government, have blatantly disregarded the existential threats magnified in the works of scholars like Katja Grace and Kevin Drum who frankly portrayed with some degree of certainty, an era of job apocalypse among other dangers mankind would be exposed to when AIMs eventually take over. Drawing from the Marxian Alienation Theory, the authors examine the degrees of extinction and existential threat imminent on humanity and the justification and implications for politicizing the predictions made about when AIMs would take over man's job. The *ex-post facto* research methodology and Derrida's reconstructive and deconstructive analytical method was adopted for evaluating the degree of politicking at play among American politicians. The paper identifies the impending era of mass joblessness as one of the greatest tasks progressive governments and thinkers must grapple with in other to curb this threat. Policy makers and scholars of AIM research must quickly identify pathways for distributing the gains of robot labour, such that its operations will cease to be a threat to mankind.

Keywords: American politicians · Artificial Intelligent Machines
Existential threat · Job apocalypse · Intentionality · Marxian Alienation Theory
Policy makers

1 Introduction

Most scholars [1–3] toady believe that the rising number of researchers worried about the near perfect predictions about when machines will take over the job of man in all sectors of life, justifies the reason why the subject of AIM threat to mankind, should take the center stage, alongside other current issues such as global warming, etc., which

© Springer International Publishing AG, part of Springer Nature 2018
O. Gervasi et al. (Eds.): ICCSA 2018, LNCS 10963, pp. 217–232, 2018.
https://doi.org/10.1007/978-3-319-95171-3_18

presently have been identified as one of the highly politicized subjects of the 21st century in America [4]. However, the wish to have the subject of AIMs on the front burner of every major economy of the world, has not been materialized. This is largely due to the fact that most governments believes that these predictions are mere products of conjectures and refutations arising from ambitious AIM researchers. This notwithstanding, some scholars [5–7] believe that the impending threat of 'mass unemployment' and 'job apocalypse' are threats that may be much closer than most governments and concerned authorities are willing to accept as a reality of life soon to take place. These category of scholars believe the existential threat of massive job annihilation may have already begun in most industrialized nations of the world like America [4]. In the light of this, the need for governments like the United States of America and other industrialized nations of the world, to rise up to the occasion regarding issues of AIM threats to mankind in the 21st century, cannot be over emphasized in this paper. The need to discuss core issues arising from recent AI predictions and the need to sensitize policy makers and American politicians of the need to take more serious steps - as against their present lackadaisical attitude – towards addressing the troubling AIM research predictions about the extinction/existential risks threats posed to the jobs of the ordinary American worker, justifies the timely need for writing this paper.

Most governments that come into power in this 21st century often have as one of their topmost priority, the task to create more jobs for the teaming populations of the unemployed work-force in their society. The immediate past administration of president Obama and the newly elected government of Donald Trump, were seen to both echo this fact [8–10]. Perhaps, some of the reasons why most governments, and by implication, most industrialized nations of the world like the American government, have continued to pay leap service to the existential threat espoused by AIM researchers lately, is largely a result of some statistical data and reports released from the Bureau of Labour Statistics of 9th of March, 2018. The report announced that the unemployment rate for the country was unchanged at 4.1% in February 2018 [11]. The diagram in Fig. 1 provides a detailed summary of this report.

From the data in the charts in Fig. 1, the report concludes that the US unemployment rate has remained unchanged from the previous months. Thus, the present data depicts a 17 year-low figure which is slightly above the market expectations of 4.0%, as indicated in Fig. 1. The report also indicates that, while the civilian labour force rose by 806,000 in February, 2018, its participation rate increased by 0.3%. The report also indicates that: total employment by house survey rose by 785,000, thus increasing the employment population ratio from 0.3% to 60.4% in the month of February, 2018 [10].

This perhaps explains why it is easy for government officials and policy maker to extrapolate that, while the economy continues in this steady line of progress, more people would likely gain employment and the unemployment rate would further decrease, seeing that there has been a downward trend in the unemployment ration in the past 17 year [10]. From the above premise, most governments are inclined to forecast a steady rise in employment opportunities in the labour markets. These kind of projections were seen reflected in Trump's campaign promises to his party and the entire US citizens. This perhaps largely explains why any contrary opinion or prediction about an era of mass joblessness, something quite different from the results

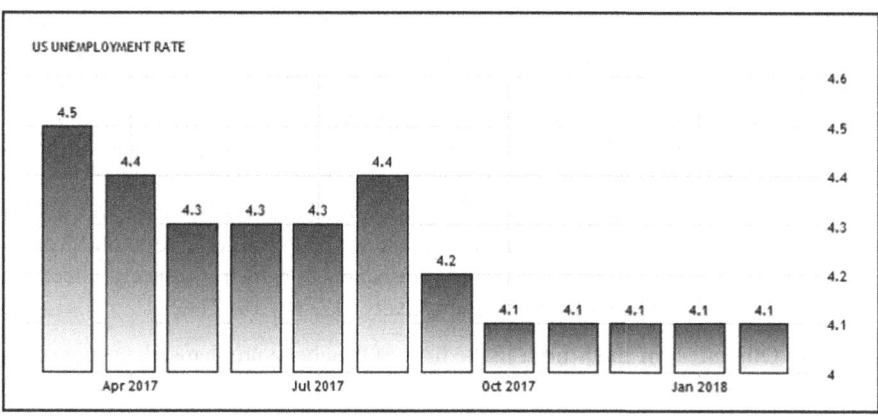

Fig. 1. Unemployment rate in the United States of America Source: Adopted from Trading Economics.com/US Bureau of Statistics (USBS, 2018)

indicated in the charts in Fig. 1, is often not taken seriously. However, to corroborate the reality in this new situation, scholars like Stephen Hawking in [12], expressed the fear that the future of humans would come to nothing, especially in the area of retaining jobs, if governments fail to take drastic steps to align the goals of AIMs with those of humans [13].

The Problematic: Recent advances in AIM technology revealed in October of 2017, that the Uber trucking subsidiary nicknamed Otto, successfully made a delivery of its cargo of 2000 Boxes of Budweiser when it safely delivered them from Fort Collins Colorado to Colorado Springs, a distance of 120 miles unaided by a driver in its driver's compartment. This technology today - the technology capable of manipulating a self-driven car (truck) - has advanced to the extent that the Uber Company have been licensed to commence commercial test run of this AIM technology within Colorado State. The high success rate projected to emerge from this technology, when it is fully operational and commercialized in most states of America and in most industrialized nations of the world, is foretold, would mean the end of the truck driving and commercial driving jobs for over 20 Million drivers in the Unites States and its environ where this technology will be embraced [7]. Other scholars who corroborate the soon emergence of this era of machine take over include: [12, 14–18]. In more specific terms, some of the problems which this paper is poised to address include:

i. The problem of the increase in the numbers of near perfect predictions about the emergence of an era that would herald what most scholars refer to as, 'an era of massive job apocalypse' (Drum, 2017) in the American society and in most industrialized nations of the world where AIMs have been integrated into all sectors of life. A situation which results to the alienations of man and the belittling of his *beingness* [7, 19].

ii. Problems arising from recant reports from the Bureau of Labour Statistics on the employment/unemployment status of American citizens. This report is believed to be largely responsible for the lackadaisical attitude displayed by American government officials who are compelled by these reports, to play politics with issues regarding the inimical predictions presented by AI researchers about the proficiencies [20] AIMs have acquired over the decade.

iii. The problem of the extinction and existential risk threats fears espoused by AIM researchers, from their various predications, are observed to have inimical ontological, psychological and existential consequences which ultimately affect the psyche of the American workforce negatively [12, 14, 16, 21–23].

Aims and Objectives of the Study: In the light of the above problems, the paper seeks to critically appraise:

i. Most of the prominent predictions about Artificial Intelligent Machines (AIMs) with the view to assessing the viability of its claims to the soon emerge era of the massive job apocalypse' and the various degrees of Alienations affecting man in the labour force.

ii. The various factors responsible for the lackadaisical behaviours of politicians who fail to take seriously, the inimical predications from AIM researchers about the proficiencies intelligent machines have acquired over the decade, to the detriment of mankind.

iii. The existential risk threat factors believed to be affecting the psyche of the American workforce who are threatened by the imminent loss of their jobs and their humanity.

Methodology: The paper largely draws inferences from the Marxian Alienation Theory in line with the objectives and goals earmarked for the paper. This theory is favored because it offers appropriate platforms for interrogating and assessing the consequences of the politics at play by American government officials over issues of AIM technology. The four classes of the Marxian Alienation theory [24–26] aids the researchers' ability to categorize the degree of influence and consequences identified to affect the American workforce. The *ex-post facto* method [27, 28] of research in the social science was adopted for the paper since the authors desire to evaluate previous and current AIM predictions conducted in line with the objectives of this paper. Derridas' deconstructive and critical reconstructive analytic method of enquiry in philosophy [6, 29 31] was utilized for the paper since the methods offer insights for understanding the meanings of concepts and the interrogation of arguments presented for the deductions and inferences proposed later on in this paper.

2   Alienation and AIM Operations in 21st Century America

The concept of *intelligence* generally refers to the mental capacity for humans to process data intellectually and abstractly which results in the knowledge of new ways for addressing issues for the benefit of mankind [13, 32]. While most scholars prefer to ascribe the feature of intelligence to man alone, there are a host of other scholars who contend with the idea that the feature of intelligence should only be ascribed to humans alone. They argue that the feature of intelligence could also be found in other things or artifacts which are capable of passing the intelligent quotient (IQ) test. To the former class of scholars however, the feature of intelligence is an exclusive reserved feature of man alone. Any trace of such intelligence in another object or being should only be regarded as *artificial* and not real intelligence. The application of this feature of intelligence, they further contend, is that which gives mankind the superior edge over all other living creature on earth [32]. It is the feature of intelligence that makes it possible for him to be able to think resourcefully and to introspect on issues as they arise with the view to solving problems. Hence, these group of scholars are of the resolve that any other artifact possessing a similitude of such intelligence should best be described as *Artificial Intelligence Machines* (AIM).

Today, these AIMs have advanced in leaps and bound, especially in their ability to solve very complex and technical problems - human and none human alike. This advancement is today exemplified in games such as: Texas Hold' em, Jeopardy, Go, Poker and even in the game of Chess. Some of the companies sponsoring these innovations include: Deepstak, Aysadi, AlphaGo, Libratus, Magic Pony, IBM Watson, and Deep Mind, to mention but a few. These companies discovered that for AIMs to rise to, and above the challenges of the 21st century, it had to develop and acquire the feature of intelligence which was before now, believed to be an exclusive reserve of humans alone [33]. Today's machines however, seem to have perfected the act of acquiring higher level intelligence via the acquisition of what is best referred to as *intentionality* or *intuition*, a feature that allows intelligent machines the capacity to learn on their own by simply applying deep machine learning algorithm strategies, which invariably allows them to mimic complex human features and characteristics for its own good. [15, 34]. A study by [20] further corroborates this fact "The ability for HLMI systems of this dispensation to acquire the capacity to self-instruct, via deep machine learning processes, which make it possible for it to process different systems, all at the same time, coupled with the machine's ability to learn and exchange files and data from other AIMs close to it within the same vicinity, with the view to update, improve and upgrade itself when necessary, is the feature that has given AIMs the edge in the 21st century America" [20].

Consequent on these new developments, scientists of this century are now exploring and maximizing these new abilities in AIM for advancing studies research in every other sector like in the medical profession (Doctors/Surgeons). The application of these AIM technology in this field has made running accurate medical diagnosis possible [35] in matter seconds. The same is the case for the legal profession, Economics/Manufacturing/investment analysis sector and virtually in every other sector. Current studies by [4] describes very bluntly, the inimical nature of the proficiencies which AIMs have now acquired.

> I don't care what your job is. If you dig ditches, a robot will dig them better. If you're a magazine writer, a robot will write your articles better. If you're a doctor, IBM's Watson will no longer "assist" you in finding the right diagnosis from its database of millions of case studies and journal articles. It will just be a better doctor than you... And CEOs? Sorry. Robots will run

companies better than you do. Artistic types? Robots will paint and write and sculpt better than you. Think you have social skills that no robot can match? Yes, they can. Within 20 years, maybe half of you will be out of jobs. A couple of decades after that, most of the rest of you will be out of jobs [4].

The above reality espoused by [4], paints a fair picture of the existential risk fears which studies reveal, have already started alienating thousands of individuals in the American work force who have lost their jobs to advances in AI technologies. Intelligent robots have also largely taken over industrial plants resulting to the massive loss of jobs from millions of the unskilled American labour workforce. These new developments create derogatory relations between man and AIM, the kind of relations which [17, 26, 32] describes as that kind of relations which creates feelings of 'hopelessness and helplessness in the face of the technology man himself has created'. The authors of this paper thus pause to reflect for a moment on this pertinent question: 'Is the fate of mankind really doomed in the face of present advances and innovations in AIMs in America'?

3   Predictions About AIMs and the Existential Risk Threat to Mankind

Since the turn of the 21st century, most scholars [6, 33, 35–41] offered what some corners believe, are unrealistic predictions about when they think the new wave of advancements in AI technology would become perfect enough to take over the affairs of their creators - man. Most of the predictions were termed unrealistic because of the various time-frames when AI research proponent's foretold these revolutions would take place. One thing common with all their forecasts is that, the advent of AIMs would sooner than later, spell doom for mankind. In this regard, the works by Stephen Hawking comes to light. He was known to have vehemently sounded the alarm about how the future of mankind would come to nothing if decisive efforts were not taken in the direction of aligning the goals of mankind with those of AIMs [12]. This section of the paper discusses some scholars and their predictions about when AIMs would fully take over the jobs and affairs of man.

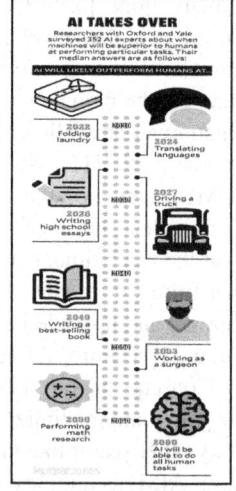

Fig. 2. Jobs AIMs will soon takeover. Adopted from Mother Jones Magazine (Drum, 2017).

Worthy of note in this study is a research conducted by Katja Grace and her team of researchers from the Future for Human Institute (FHI) in Oxford University and others from Yale University [42]. Their research focused on identifying – from the opinions of the major stake holders of research in AIMs - when indeed machines would most likely take over in entirety, the affairs and jobs of men in whatever sector you can imagine. Their research also sought to discover when AIMs would gain superiority over humans and none humans alike. To achieve these objectives, she and her team sampled and analyzed the opinion of 1634 distinguished AI researchers. The team drew their inferences from 352 respondents of the total number of questionnaires dispersed during the research. Some of the quality of respondents who took part in the research include: Mustafa Suleyman from Google's DeepMind, the director of research at Facebook, Yann LeCun and the Director of Uber's AI Lab, Zoubin Ghahramani [2, 20].

3.1 The Existential Risks Threat and Precise Predictions About AIMs

One profound discovery from Grace's research revealed that respondents were convinced that AIMs would soon out do humans in the following tasks: language translation by [2024]; critical speech and essay writing for high school students by [2026] and truck driving jobs by [2027] [6]. Some of the respondents however, felt that for those whose jobs fall within retailing outfits, that is, jobs where very specific skills like writing Novels or working as a medical surgeon, would take much longer time [2031, 2049 and 2053 respectively] before AIMs are able to perfectly simulate them and take over their jobs. All the respondents however, agreed that nearly all the jobs in the world will soon be automated in 120 years' time. They evertheless, warned that there is a 50% chance that the time frame stipulated for this full automation to materialize, may actually take place some 45 years from now. This is because of the chances that machines could acquire more High Level Machine Intelligence (HLMI), sooner than the anticipated time for acquiring such intelligence. Figure 2 is an attempt to capture diagrammatically, all the different kinds of jobs which respondents made clear predictions about when AIMs would take over.

If the research by Grace and her team is anything to go by, jobs that fall into the routine category (cognitive and physical) will be one of the first to go by year [2020], compliments to advances in robotics engineering. On the other hand, non-routine jobs like those of Police officers, Construction workers, Novelists and Surgeons will be the next to follow by year [2040's]. In all, their predictions held that AIMs will be able to perform any task accomplished by man in year [2060]. This invariable will mean a total annihilation of human jobs since all the jobs that fall into this category are mainly normal everyday jobs humans presently have. While year [2060] may seem to be years ahead, if the study by Grace and her team of Yale and Oxford researchers is anything to go by, then the world would soon face what [4] described as 'an employment apocalypse' since the disappearance of routine jobs of all kinds constitute mostly half of the jobs in the American labour force. Why the American government and the political elite class continue to be lackadaisical about these existential risks threats as foretold by these AI predictions, is one issue that troubles the authors of this paper. It is an issue they hope to grapple with before the paper is completed.

Other studies conducted for this paper revealed that the study by Grace and her team is not alone among the series of studies sounding the alarm about the impending massive jobs loss set to hit the American polity. An independent consulting firm known as Price-water-house Coopers, released the results of a survey they too conducted on AI predictions, with similar results. They predicted that 38% of the jobs in America (most of which fall into the routine jobs category), stand the risks of automation by the beginning of year 2030 [4]. The World Economic Forum on the other hand, predicts that the rich will lose 5 Million jobs to AIMs (Robots) by 2020 [4]. Another independent AI group of researchers published their own report in *Scientific America*. There, they opined that 40% of some of the 500 biggest companies in America and beyond, would have totally disappeared within a decade [4]. One Kai-Fu Lee, formerly a Microsoft and Google top brass, who now majorly invests in China's AI startup industries, opines that AIMs will most probably, replace 50% of human jobs in industrial nations of the world within the next 10 years. Writing for *Mother Jones Magazine*, Keats Drum in [4] could not help speaking quite frankly about what would become of America if she continues to play politics with AIM research predictions. In his words:

> AI is coming whether we like it or not. The rewards are just too great. Even if America did somehow stop AI research, it would only mean that the Chinese or the French or the Brazilians would get there first. To corroborate this point, Russian President Vladimir Putin agrees that "Artificial intelligence is the future, not only for Russia but for all humankind," he announced in September 2017. "Whoever becomes the leader in this sphere will become the ruler of the world." There's just no way around it: For the vast majority of jobs, work as we know it will come steadily to an end between year 2025 and year 2060 [4].

In the light of the above claims, the authors of this paper can't fathom why policy makers in America are playing politics with this all too important matter. Why is she allowing her labour work force to be taken over by the existential risk threats arising from these AIM predictions?

3.2   An Expose on the Marxian Alienation Theory and AIM Predictions

From the forgoing, it is clear that only very wealthy individuals and aristocrats of the American society are those who can afford to acquire and control these 21st century robots. Consequently, only they can benefit from all the advances in AIM technology at the end of the day. On the other hand, the rest of the masses who are not able to acquire these AIM/robots, but can only offer themselves as labour for wages, will be the ones at the receiving end. When machines eventually take over all human jobs, this would translate to scenarios where workers would be rendered jobless. 'No work', in this case will simply mean, 'No money'. 'No money' on the other hand would translate to 'No life'. This scenario of 'No life', a consequence of 'No work' and 'No money', is what Karl Marx described in his 4 classes of the Alienation theory [24, 46].

One of the most profound consequences of AIMs prediction - as exemplified in Fig. 2 - is 'the Alienation of the human psyche and processes'. This kind of Alienations has been described as one of the greatest consequences of advances in AIM technologies [12, 16, 23, 43–45]. These researchers are unanimous in the opinion that "one of the greatest and perhaps, scariest amongst all the fears which the advent AIM technology pose to the human psyche is 'the extinction risks threat' [45]. This is the kind of fear that arise from the knowledge that AIMs, now more than ever, are poised to take over the jobs and livelihood of man, since machines themselves have found man unfit to cope with the capacity of intelligence required to properly function in the 21st century and the future beyond. Stuart Armstrong throws more light on AIMs and the state of man in this future in [45].

Armstrong in [45] advocates that contemporary researchers need to reflect more about how America's workforce of today, could retain their existential and ontological relevance amidst rising trends and innovations in AIMs technology. This reflection is considered very pertinent as not doing so would perhaps, place man in disadvantaged positions. Position where AIMs find justified reasons to make the decision of down-sizing or out rightly removing man from the scene, for reasons of incompetence. Hence, scholars fear the time might come when AIM technology might begin to see man as the threat to their own smooth operational existence, hence they need to eliminate them from the scene. If Karl Marx were here, this scenario would amount to the highest degree of Alienation.

Because major capitalist economies have disrupted the order and process of things in their industries for the purpose of cutting down costs and maximizing profit for their shareholders and for the purpose of alleviating the burdens often associated with jobs that require some degree of manual labour in industries, man's access to the means of livelihood has also been disrupted. Thus, the introduction of AIMs as tools in manu-facturing industries seem to have left mankind in a precarious situation. Judy Cux lamentation in [26] corroborates this fact. In her words: 'Never before have we felt so helpless in the face of the forces we ourselves have created'. From the foregoing and in response to the Marxian question above, the authors of this paper are inclined to note that, where mankind - by any guise - is deprived of the opportunity and the means for earning an honest wage for himself and his family, the consequences lead to situations where man's mental, emotional, ontological and existential state of mind is exposed to imminent dangers, the likes the world have never seen before. A situation Karl Marx described clearly manifests in either of the four classes of the Alienation theory: (1) Alienation of the worker from his work and its product (2) Alienation of the worker from working and production. (3) Alienation of the worker from what Karl Marx called "their Gattungswesen (species-essence)" and (4), Alienation of the worker from human nature [16, 25].

Where these consequences have been clearly identified as scenarios arising from governments' inability to provide mankind and indeed, its citizens with the job security they had so vehemently promised them during election campaigns, the authors of this paper can't but wonder why a polity like America continues to play politics with the predictions foretold could translate to the annihilation of millions of jobs for American citizens. This lackadaisical attitude of the American government, this paper identifies, is largely responsible for the 'great existential risk fears' expressed amongst American citizens.

4 The Politics of AIMs in America

The paper at this point discusses some factors perceived to militate against America's inability to give appropriate attention to AIMs research predictions and technological innovations.

i. **Current data from the Bureau of Labour Statistics:** The recently published report from the Bureau of Labour Statistics on the unemployment/employment status of Americans and the rest of the world [11] seem to place America and it citizens in the clear of all the impending existential risk threats of massive loss of jobs and unemployment set to hit the labour force decades from now. The report, as discussed in page 2 and 4 of this paper, tends to give most policy makers reasons to pay lip service to the existential risk threats espoused by AI researchers. Thus, with an employment rate forecasted to rise in the future of president Trump's administrations, most government officials and policy makers believe predictions about massive loss of jobs etc., are predictions that should not be worthy of any serious attention at the moment.

ii. **An uninformed government elite:** The high degree of ignorance displayed by most government officials on matters of state - issues like the impending job loss and the existential risk threat that should be on the front burner - is an example of another main factor responsible for the lackadaisical attitude displayed by policy makers and government officials which today, prevents them from providing commensurate responses to the predictions provided by AI researchers. When Steven Mnuchin, the present Treasury Secretary of the Trump's administration was asked to comment on the subject of AIM technology, viewed as a threat to the American people, he waved off the question with the back of his hand, noting that the idea of the existence of such threats was unrealistic – at least not for now - since he believed that AI threats issues do not constitute an issue worthy of losing sleep on. In his opinion, it was a problem not for the now but a problem forecasted not to begin until another 50–100 years from now. In his words: 'I do not understand how anyone could reach the conclusion that all the actions with technology is half a century away. Artificial intelligence is transforming everything from retailing to banking to the provision of medical care' [4]. 'How naïve'! Schmidt from Google in a conference earlier in year 2017, corroborates this fact of naivety when he quite frankly observed that "The gaps between government officials, in terms of their understanding of software, let alone AIMs technology, is so large that it's almost hopeless," [4]. This indeed, is quite true of most of the top members of Trump's administration. That is, going by the comments made by Steven Mnuchin.

iii. **The ongoing political dog-fight between Democrats and Republicans:** The present administration of Donald Trump, since coming to power, have been observed to be preoccupied with what this paper chose to describe as 'political dog fights' between contending political parties, labour unions, pressure groups and the political elite class in America. Most prominent among these groups: the Republicans and Democrats, are known to have a history of going for each other's necks at the slightest opportunity available to them. The doctrines of the conservative party for instance, tend to blind them from the willingness to accept policies presented via Democratic doctrines. The Democrats on the other hand, do not have it in their DNA to accept policies and doctrines of the Conservative Party without first fighting over issues of who should initiate the idea or better still, who profits more from such ideology or policy. In confirmations of this point, the Trump's administration has been noted to find pleasure in fighting existing Democratic ideals by pulling down all legacies initiated by the Obama administration. By this, reference is made to policies/legacies like the 'Obama care policy' and the push for $15 minimum wage, etc. The attack on these legacies studies revealed [4], were more because the policies had democratic ideals written all over them and not necessarily for reasons of non-viability or incompetence. Preoccupied with these internal conflicts, these political groups do not have the time to reflect on other serious issues such as AIM research predictions about the impending threat to mankind's means of livelihood.

Going by the amount of media attention which AIMs and Robotic Engineering have gotten in the past decade, the authors of this paper are troubled at the fact that its awareness have not gotten the deserved and expected attention it is supposed to have gotten by now in the American polity. For instance, how is it that the governments and all concerned agencies are failing to take notice of the technological innovations in the Uber industries where self-driving cars have partially gone into the commercial test driving stage? In the same vein, AIMs can now write short stories on sport etc. Some intelligent devices can now, on their own, order replacement parts before you even know about the fault. The Carnegie Mellon Computer has since perfected the act of playing and defeating the best online poker professionals in the world. Earlier in 2017, Jill Watson from Georgia Tech proved to be a better teacher than the Artificial Teaching Assistant (ATA) she was initially designed to be. Sony, on the other hand, as part of her drive for AIM advancements, promised to soon introduce a robot with the capacity for expressing deep human emotions with its owner. Imagine the nature and quality of society that will emerge when these AIM innovations are fully deployed and running in the society. There is no doubt, millions of very important jobs in the society would disappear as this new world order of intelligent machines unfolds.

The high and rapid rate of advancements in AIM research is an indication of the impending storms and technological explosions which have been predicted to soon take place in the nearest future. Hence, discussions about AIMs, like other similar issues of importance - like the need for wide spread deployment for renewable energy and global warming issues - must therefore constitute part of the pertinent issues ripe for critical reflection the front burner of every industrialized nations of the world. Matter of fact, it is not out of place to put all matters concerning AIMs and the existential threat to the world of work and mankind, first in line of the issues needing very urgent attention in the American polity.

5 Findings and Further Discussion

5.1 Summary of Findings

From the forgoing discussions, the authors of this paper are inclined to note the following: (1) that the advent of AIMs is poised to be one of the most outstanding influence on human nature and on the world of work in the 21st century. (2) That AIMs in no distant time, will have the capacity to reshape almost every facets of human endeavor. (3) On a wider scale, AIM technologies and other related technologies will be capable of transforming both the security and economic status of nations [47]. Hence, its benefits and power would be redistributed among the lines of those nations who are able to launch into it on time and make more investments into AIM research. (4) Woe be unto any nation that is found slacking in this race towards getting acquainted and massively implementing the innovations emerging from 21st century AIM technology.

The various studies considered for the objectives of this paper depicts that, despite the fact that America is seemingly in the forefront of championing AI innovations and its applications, the actual center of gravity on AI affairs is presently in the hand of private investors and multinational companies, who do not have the clout and power required to achieve anticipated results out of the present state of AI research and operations [47]. Except the American government and indeed, the government of Donald Trump, begins to extend his philosophy of "America First" to this area of research, they would have no other choice than to cede the profound field of AIM research and all the future gains therein, to its strongest contender, China. So far, his government have been observed to be lackadaisical about policies and what directions to take with regard to innovations in AIM research and AI technology generally, due largely to an ignorance of the political elite class. While his State of the Union speech was observed to contain key issues regarding National Security, Trade, Immigration, Infrastructure, Jobs security and the economy, nothing was said about the clarion call needed for developing the potentials of AIMs for the 21st century and beyond.

5.2 Contribution to Knowledge

i. The paper for the first time, embarked on a study of the extinction and existential risk threat fear foretold by AIM researchers. This threat is said to be associated with the rising adoption of AIMs technology for daily operations in the US polity and Marxian Alienation theory via *ex post facto* methods of research in the social science.

ii. The paper identified and evaluated the factors that continues to militate against the growth of AI research in the American polity. This notwithstanding, the paper highlighted the dangers of losing the privileges of championing and advancing research and innovations in the field of AI research, to rival contenders like China and Russia, in the event that Americans continue to play politics with AIM research issues.

iii. Amidst some of the negative influences of AIM technologies discussed in the paper, the authors clearly espoused arguments to sustain the merits associated with AIM research for the rest of the 21st century.

5.3 Recommendation

The authors of the paper find the following recommendations pertinent and essential for the objectives proposed for this paper and the American polity:

i. Government should ensure that the work force of the 21st century are trained from school/Universities for the nature of work required in today's world. Where it becomes necessary, 'on the job training programs' and 'in-service training programs' should be embarked upon to ensure that today's worker does not lose relevance because of advances and innovations in AIMs.

ii. The American government should, in the bid to sustain her mantra of 'Making America first,' rise to the occasion of taking required steps to sway the existential risk fears arising from predictions made about the future of AIMs. This is because, the fewer the number of threatened workforce there are, the greater the number of productive people (workforce) you will have in the workplace.

iii. If the era of President Donald Trump administration is anything to go by, then the 'Make America First' Mantra should come alive in this AIMs era. Hence, his new mantra should now read: "Make America First in AIM research.

iv. In line with the 23 AI Ashimolar principles, the American government needs to urgently develop viable policies that would guide research in AIM operations and in robotic engineering. These policies would outline the ethical codes and conducts essential for safeguarding and mitigating unintended, negative consequences *that may arise from* inventions and the dissemination of these new AI innovative technology.

5.4   Conclusion

The first objective of this paper affirmed the strong presence of the forces of Alienation amongst majority of the American work force, whose jobs fall within the routine jobs category like truck driving and factory work. The second objective discussed at least three factors which continues to initiate lackadaisical attitudes amongst American politicians, to the detriment of future AIM research and the American work force. Studies conducted for the third objective, revealed that the existential risk threat predicted by AIM researchers are more real than just being a mere propaganda initiated by proponents of AIMs. It is a risk the American government should work towards abating it from the harm it could have on the American workforce, before it gets out of hand.

In the light of the foregoing summations, the authors of this paper conclude by noting that the existential risk threats foretold by AIM researchers is a threat worthy of note and serious consideration. More real is the impending danger of alienation and job annihilation feared would herald a revolution and a devastation, the likes the American nation and indeed the world, might not be able to recover from., if not abated on time.

References

1. Ratner, P.: Here's when machines will take your job, as predicted by AI gurus. Big Think Edge. Online publication (2017). http://bigthink.com/paul-ratner/heres-when-machines-will-take-your-job-predict-ai-gurus

2. Gray, R.: How long will it take before your job is automated? BBC Capital News Online (2017). http://www.bbc.com/capital/story/20170619-how-long-will-it-take-for-your-job-to-be-automated. Accessed 26 Feb 2017

3. Emerging Technology.: Experts predict when AI will exceed human performance. From the arXiv. MIT Technology Review Online (2017). https://www.technologyreview.com/s/607970/experts-predict-when-artificial-intelligence-will-exceed-human-performance/. Acces sed 26 Feb 2017

4. Drum, K.: You will lose your job to a robot – sooner than you think! Mother Jones Magazine Online Blogger (2018). https://www.motherjones.com/politics/2017/10/you-will-lose-your-job-to-a-robot-and-sooner-than-you-think/. Accessed 26 Feb 2018

5. Mcrae, M.: Experts think this is how long we have before AI takes all of our jobs. A publication of Science Alert online (2017). https://www.sciencealert.com/experts-think-this-is-how-long-we-have-before-ai-takes-all-of-our-jobs

6. Edmond, C.: This is when a robot is going to take your job, according to Oxford University. Formative Content, World Economic Forum. An online publication of the World Economic Forum (2017). https://www.weforum.org/agenda/2017/07/how-long-before-a-robot-takes-your-job-here-s-when-ai-experts-think-it-will-happen

7. Wogu, I.A.P., Misra, S., Assibong, P.A., Ogiri, S.O., Damasevicius, R., Maskeliunas, R.: Super-intelligent machine operations in 21st century manufacturing industries: a boost or doom to political and human development?. In: International Conference on Towards Extensible and Adaptable Methods in Computing (TEAMC) 2018. 26–28 March 2018. Netaji Subhas Institute of Technology, New Delhi, India (2018). https://drive.google.com/file/d/1bhdcUA0EJBhDTbyMw2Y0mSVkXWlCf8W4/view

8. Jaffe, J., Bazie, M.: Poverty rates fell in 2000 as unemployment reached 31-Year Low (2002). https://www.cbpp.org/archives/9-25-01pov.htm

9. Zumbrun, J.: Donald Trump is right: About 42% of Americans are unemployed (If you include my 88-year-old grandma). An online publication of Ream Time Economics in Wall Street Journal (2015). https://blogs.wsj.com/economics/2015/08/20/donald-trump-is-right-about-42-of-americans-are-unemployed-if-you-include-my-88-year-old-grandma

10. Trading Economics.: United States unemployment rate 1948–2018. An online publication of Trading Economics (2018). https://tradingeconomics.com/united-states/unemployment-rate

11. Bureau of Labour and Statistics: The employment situations, February (2018). An online publications of the Bureau of Labour and Statistics (2018). https://www.bls.gov/bls/newsrels.htm

12. Hawking, S., Tegmark, T., Russell, S., Wilczek, F.: Transcending complacency on super-intelligent machines. Hoffpost (2014). http://www.huffingtonpost.com/stephen-hawking/artificial-intelligence_b_5174265.html

13. Wogu, I.A.P., Misra, S., Assibong, P.A., Olu-Owolabi, E.F., Maskeliunas, R., Robertas Damasevicius, R.: Artificial intelligence, smart class rooms and online education in the 21st Century: Implications for human development. In: A Conference Paper Presented at the International Conference on Information Systems and Management Science (ISMS 2018). University of Malta, Valletta, 22–23 February (2018). http://toc.proceedings.com/38672webtoc.pdf, http://www.proceedings.com/38672.html

14. Griffin, A.: AI could wipe out humanity when it gets too clever. Independent News (2015)

15. Wallace, H.: The future of artificial intelligence in the poker world. CASINO GAMS PRO (2017). http://www.casinogamespro.com/2017/10/16/the-future-of-artificial-intelligence-in-the-poker-world

16. Wogu, I.A.P., Olu-Owolabi, F.E., Assibong, P.A., Apeh, H.A., Agoha, B.C., Sholarin, M.A., Elegbeleye, A., Igbokwe, D.: Artificial intelligence, Alienation and Ontological problems of other minds: a critical investigation into the future of man and machines. In: Conference Paper Presented at the 2017 ICCNI/IEEE International Conference on Computing, Networking and Informatics. In proceedings of the IEEE International Conference on Computing, Networking and Informatics (ICCNI 2017), 29–31 October 2017, Covenant University, Ota (2017). https://doi.org/10.1109/iccni.2017.8123792, http://ieeexplore.ieee.org/document/8123792/?part=1

17. Conn, A.: Can we properly prepare for the risks of super-intelligent AI? Future of Life Institute (FLI) (2017). https://futureoflife.org/2017/03/23/ai-risks-principle/

18. AMPT.: Artificial intelligence applications in manufacturing [Advance MP Technology] (2014). http://www.advancedmp.com/artificial-intelligence/
19. Gouldner, A.W.: The Two Marxism, pp. 177–198. Oxford University Press, New York (1984)
20. Wogu, I.A.P., Misra, S., Olu-Owolabi, F.E., Assibong, P.A., Apeh, H.A.: Artificial intelligence, artificial teachers and the fate of learners in the 21st century education sector: Implications for Theory and Practice. In: ICCSA paper, (Forth Coming, 2018)
21. Bryant, M.: Artificial intelligence could kill us all. Meet the man who takes that risk seriously. The Next Web (TNW) (2014). https://thenextweb.com/insider/2014/03/08/ai-could-kill-all-meet-mantakes-risk-seriously/#.tnw_hVchaHqU
22. Huffington Post UK.: 'Artificial intelligence poses 'extinction risk' to humanity', says Oxford University's Stuart Armstrong. An online publication of Huffington Post UK (2014). http://www.huffingtonpost.co.uk/2014/03/12/extinction-artificial-intelligence-oxford-stuart-rmstrong_n_4947082.html
23. Russell, S.: This artificial intelligence pioneer has a few concerns. Quanta Magaz. (2015). https://www.wired.com/2015/05/artificial-intelligence-pioneer-concerns/
24. Mészáros, I.: Marx's Theory of Alienation (1970). http://www.marxist.org/archive/meszaros/works/alien/
25. Ollman, B.: Alienation: Marx's Conception of Man in Capitalist Society. (Online Publication) (1976). http://www.alienationtheory.com/
26. Cox, J.: An introduction to Marx's theory of alienation. Int. Socialism Q. J. Socialist Workers Party (Br.) 79, 5 (1998). July 1998 Copyright © International Socialism
27. Cohen, L., Manion, L., Morison, K.: Research Methods in Education. Routledge Falmer, London (2000)
28. Marilyn, K.: Ex-post facto research: Dissertation and scholarly research, Recipes for success. Dissertation Success LLC, Seattle, WA (2013). http://www.dissertationrecipes.com/wp-content/uploads/2011/04/Ex-Post-Facto-research.pdf
29. Derrida, J.: Of Grammatology. Johns Hopkins University Press, Baltimore (1976)
30. Balkin, J.M.: Deconstructive Practice and Legal Theory, 96 Yale, L.J. (1987)
31. Derrida, J.: Force of Law: Deconstruction. Quaintance, M. (eds.) (trans.) (1992)
32. Wogu, I.A.P.: Problems in mind: a new approach to age long problems and questions in philosophy and the cognitive science of human development, p. 495. Pumack Nigeria Limited Education Publishers (2011). ISBN 978-978-50060-7-0
33. Sulleyman, A.: People are far more likely to be killed by Artificial Intelligence than nuclear war with North Korea, warns Elon Musk. Independent News (2017). http://www.independent.co.uk/life-style/gadgets-and-tech/news/ai-north-korea-nuclear-war-elon-musk-tesla-artificial-intelligence-robots-a7892066.html
34. Schrager, A., Wang, A.: Imagine how great universities could be without all those human teachers. Quartz (2017). https://qz.com/1065818/ai-university
35. Radowitz, J.: Intelligent machines will replace teachers within 10 years, leading public school head teacher predicts. INDEPENDENT News (2017). http://www.independent.co.uk/news/education/education-news/intelligent. Accessed 16 Feb 2018
36. Hansen, M.: How technology will change the demand for teachers. Brown Center Chalkboard (2016). https://www.brookings.edu/blog/brown-center-chalkboard/2016/01/26/how-technology-will-change-the-demand-for-teachers/
37. The Economist: Re-educating Rita. A Special Report on Education and Policy. An Online publication from the Economists (2016). https://www.economist.com/news/special-report/21700760-artificial-intelligence-will-have-implications-policymakers-education-welfare-and
38. Houser, K.: The solution to our education crisis might be AI. Futurism, an online Publication of Future Society (2017). https://futurism.com/ai-teachers-education-crisis/

39. Todd Leopold, B.: A professor built an AI teaching assistant for his courses — and it could shape the future of education. Business Insider (2017). http://www.businessinsider.com/a-professor-built-an-ai-teaching-assistant-for-his-courses-and-it-could-shape-the-future-of-education-2017-3?IR=T

40. Talwar, R., Wells, S., Calle, H.: 10 human jobs disrupted by AI. IT ProPotal (2018). https://www.itproportal.com/features/10-human-jobs-disrupted-by-ai/

41. Dickson, H.: How AI is changing education. A Tech Talk Publication (2017). https://bdtechtalks.com/2017/03/09/artificial-intelligence-education-edtech/

42. Grace, K., Salvatier, J., Dafoe, A., Zhang, B., Evans, O.: When will AI exceed human performance? Evidence from AI experts. arXiv:1705.08807v2 [cs.AI]. arXiv:1705.08807v2 [cs.AI, 30 May 2017

43. Marcus, G.: Why we should think about the threat of AI. The New Yorker (2013). http://www.newyorker.com/tech/elements/why-we-should-think-about-the-threat-of-artificial-intelligence

44. Hendry, E.R.: What happens when artificial intelligence turns on us? Smithsonian.com (2014). http://www.smithsonianmag.com/innovation/what-happens-when-artificial-intelligence-turns-us-180949415/

45. Armstrong, S.: Artificial intelligence poses 'extinction risk' to humanity says Oxford University's Stuart Armstrong, in Huffington Post UK, An online publication of Huffington Post UK (2014). http://www.huffingtonpost.co.uk/2014/03/12/extinction-artificial-intelligence-oxford-stuart-armstrong_n_4947082.html

46. Dictionary of Philosophy.: Alienation. In: The Dictionary of Philosophy: Revised, 2nd edn., p. 10 (1984)

47. Allen, J.R.: Trumps first state of the union: AI and the future of America. FIXGOV. An online publication of Brookings (2018). https://www.brookings.edu/blog/fixgov/2018/01/30/trumps-1st-sotu-artificial-intelligence-and-the-future-of-america/

Mapping Dynamic Behavior Between Different Object Models in AOM

Antônio de Oliveira Dias[1]([✉]) [iD], Eduardo Martins Guerra[1] [iD],
Fábio Fagundes Silveira[2] [iD], and Tiago Silva da Silva[2] [iD]

[1] National Institute for Space Research – INPE, São José dos Campos, Brazil
antoniodiasabc@gmail.com, guerraem@gmail.com
[2] Federal University of São Paulo – UNIFESP, São José dos Campos, Brazil
{fsilveira,silvadasilva}@unifesp.br

Abstract. Adaptive Object Model (AOM) is an architectural pattern with the aim of increasing flexibility regarding domain classes. The domain entity types are represented in AOM as instances that can be changed at runtime. Because entities have a distinct structure, they are not compatible with the majority of the existing frameworks, especially the ones that use reflection and code annotations. In the proposed model, AOM entities can be mapped and adapted for the format expected by the frameworks. A reference implementation, called Esfinge AOM Role Mapper, was developed to evaluate the viability of the proposed model. When the development was concluded, it was realized that, although this flexibility on the development of software using AOM architecture, it does not implement dynamic behavior based on adding new methods on adapted classes. The main objective of this work is to introduce dynamic behavior on AOM architecture using Esfinge AOM Role Mapper framework reference to validate this study.

Keywords: Dynamic behavior · Code annotation · Reflection
Flexibility · Framework

1 Introduction

Adaptive Object Models (AOM) is an architectural pattern for creating flexible applications. Based on design patterns, such as Type Object, Properties, Type Square and Accountability, AOM represent types as an instance that can be manipulated at runtime. Therefore, new types can be created, and existing types can be modified, enabling the application to easily be adapted to changing requirements. This kind of architecture has already been implemented successfully in domains such as insurance [7] and health care [14].

To handle the entity and types defined in a different structure, an AOM architecture often needs custom-tailored software components. These components are necessary, for instance, to persist the entities and to present them in the user interfaces. The development of such components can be considered a drawback

© Springer International Publishing AG, part of Springer Nature 2018
O. Gervasi et al. (Eds.): ICCSA 2018, LNCS 10963, pp. 233–249, 2018.
https://doi.org/10.1007/978-3-319-95171-3_19

on projects using AOM since for regular information systems there are several components and frameworks that can be reused in several different layers.

As an attempt to enable the reuse of such features, some AOM frameworks, like Oghma [3] and Ink [1], provide ready-to-use classes that can be used to define entity types and create entities. Since these classes are not attached to any specific domain, in the context of this paper, we call them domain-independent. The solutions also provide components for the architecture of AOM applications based on their AOM structure. A drawback of this approach for AOM frameworks is that it is not possible to add domain-specific features in the AOM model. This practice is very common in AOM applications and drives the AOM pattern implementation towards its requirements, especially for business rules that handle the entities directly.

The adoption of an AOM architectural style also prevents the use of frameworks that were created for regular static classes. For instance, the Java Beans standard [12] defines for the Java language a way to specify application entities by using the prefix "get" and "set" for access methods. Several frameworks that use reflection or are based on annotations [6] consider this standard for processing entities. Since an AOM model does not provide this same API style, none of those frameworks can be reused. For AOM frameworks, it is possible to reuse the components that it provides, however, the application is stuck to them. This lack of reuse increases the cost of developing an AOM application, since several components that could be reused need to be developed from scratch.

To solve this problem, we developed an AOM framework for adaptive object model architectures that aims to increase the reuse of components and frameworks created for static class models. The proposed framework model was implemented in Java by an AOM framework named Esfinge AOM Role Mapper [2].

Although this flexibility in the software development using AOM architecture, it does not implement dynamic behavior to the entities created. Thus, the main objective of this work is to introduce dynamic behavior on AOM architecture by using Esfinge AOM Role Mapper framework as a study case tool.

This paper is organized as follows: Sect. 2 presents Adaptive Object Model architecture and the patterns AOM Type Object, Property, Type Square, Accountability, and the new Pattern RuleObject, used to add the dynamic behavior RuleObject. Section 3 presents the Esfinge Role Mapper framework, used to validate this work. Section 4 presents the dynamic behaviour on AOM. Next, Sect. 5 shows up the study case using dynamic behavior on Esfinge Role Mapper. Finally, Sect. 6 concludes the paper and points out future works.

2   Adaptive Object Model

AOM is an architectural pattern in which classes, attributes, relationships, and behaviors are represented as metadata and consumed at runtime. This enables systems built with this architecture to be flexible and can be modified at runtime, by developers, business analyst or users, allowing changes to be done and made available quickly. Also, this flexibility allows the domain to evolve as part of the business.

Figure 1 presents the conceptual model of the AOM architecture. The XML data entry, then going through the metadata interpreter, the information goes to the metadata repository, from which the domain objects of the metadata are created. The domain objects have their persistence mechanisms that can be relational databases or even XML/XMI files.

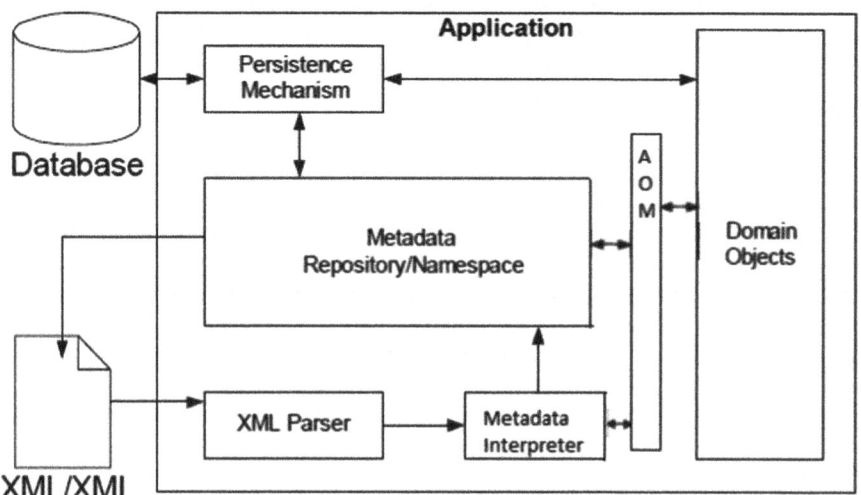

Fig. 1. Adaptive object model [14]

The AOM core architecture was developed using the patterns Type Object [10], Property [5], Type Square [13], and Accountability [4].

2.1 Type Object

The Type Object pattern [10] is used when there is an undetermined number of sub-classes that a class may need along with development life cycle. This pattern solves such a situation by representing the sub-classes that are not known at development time as instances of a generic class that represents the type of an object.

2.2 Property

The Property pattern [5] is applied in situations where instances of the same class can have different types of properties. The Property pattern solves this problem by representing the properties of an entity using a class and causing that entity to have a collection of instances of that class. By applying the Property pattern, a Measurement class can be created to represent the data of an entity. This way, the attributes of the entity can be replaced by a collection of Measurement with only the necessary measurements for each specific entity.

2.3 Type Square

In the AOM architectural style, the Type Object and Property patterns are used together, resulting in the Type Square pattern [13] In this pattern, the Type Object is used twice - once to represent the entities and entity types of the system and once to represent the properties and property types. Using Type Square pattern, new types of entities with different types of properties can be created. Likewise, existing entity types can be changed at runtime, since modeling is done at the instance level.

2.4 Accountability

The Accountability [4] pattern allows the relationship between entities to be represented by an object, usually an instance of an Accountability class. Each Accountability object is associated with an AccountabilityType object, representing the relationship type. The associations between entities are represented at the instance level. So, the types of relationships between entities can be created and modified dynamically.

2.5 Rule Object

To create the dynamic behavior, it was added to the core patterns of AOM architecture the RuleObject pattern. According to Yoder and Johnson [14], business rules for objects can be represented in many ways. In the architectural style Adaptive Object Model each application of the Strategy takes to a different interface, and therefore there is a hierarchy of classes of different Strategies. Strategies are most often associated with entities, where implementing the operations in the methods. However, as more powerful business rules are needed, these Strategies can evolve to become more complex. These more complex Strategies are called RuleObjects. Figure 2 shows an example of RuleObject with all other AOM patterns.

3 Esfinge AOM Role Mapper

This section presents the framework used as a reference implementation for the proposed AOM framework model, called Esfinge AOM Role Mapper. This framework is implemented in Java and is available open-source[1].

The Esfinge AOM Role Mapper framework works with three different types of models: the domain-specific AOM models, a generic model, and JavaBean-based

---

[1] http://esfinge.sourceforge.net/AOM.html – documentation available in portuguese.

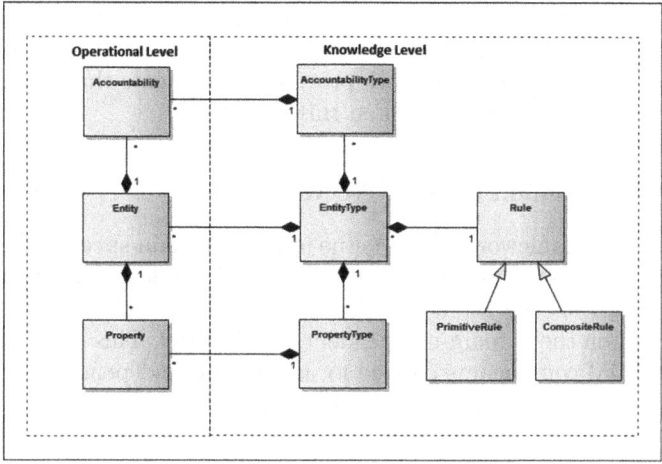

Fig. 2. RuleObject with all AOM pattern

models [8]. The main role of the framework is to map AOM structures of a specific domain to a general AOM framework or to JavaBean using annotations, creating adapters dynamically. The idea is to make possible a hybrid model, which can be composed of entities that can be defined by each of the approaches. For example, an entity defined with JavaBean can be added as a property in an AOM entity.

This section describes the functionality provided by Esfinge AOM Role Mapper with the main focus of how the models and the adapters are implemented. These functionalities are the base to develop the dynamic behavior.

3.1 Domain-Independent AOM Model

The Esfinge AOM framework enables the creation of entities and your properties without the need of an application with domain-specific AOM model. These entities are created using the framework classes. Listing 1.1 presents the use of framework classes to create an entity type with two properties and an entity with values for the respective properties.

Listing 1.1. Creating entity type and entity using the domain-independent AOM model

```
1  //Creating Entity Type
2  IEntityType sensorType = new GenericEntityType("Sensor");
3  sensorType.addPropertyType(new GenericPropertyType("name", String.class));
4  sensorType.addPropertyType(new GenericPropertyType("type", String.class));
5  //Creating Entity
6  IEntity sensor = sensorType.createNewEntity();
7  sensor.setProperty("name", "radiometerX");
8  sensor.setProperty("type", "radiometer");
```

General AOM frameworks should use the domain-independent AOM structure to create reusable components compatible with applications from different domains. For instance, the framework provides components that persist entities and entity types in databases based on this model.

3.2   Mapping Domain-Specific AOM Models

The Esfinge AOM framework supports the usage of domain-specific AOM classes. The application classes that play a role in the AOM architecture should receive code annotations for the framework be able to identify these roles and create adapters based on the domain-independent AOM model. This approach enables the reuse of AOM components created for the domain-independent AOM model in the application that defines its own AOM classes.

Listing 1.2 presents a domain-specific class that represents an AOM entity configured with Esfinge AOM Role Mapper annotations. The annotation @Entity identify that the class plays the Entity role in AOM. Its attributes also receive annotations to map to what they represent

Listing 1.2. Mapping domain-specific class that represents an entity

```
1   @Entity
2   public class Sensor implements ISensor {
3    @EntityType
4    private SensorType SensorType;
5
6    @FixedEntityProperty
7    private String owner;
8
9    @EntityProperty
10   private List<SensorProperty> properties = new ArrayList<SensorProperty>();
11
12   //access methods omitted
13   }
```

Listing 1.3 presents an example of how the framework creates adapters from mapped application-specific AOM classes to its domain-independent API. By using these adapters, the AOM components based on the framework API can be reused by several applications with its own AOM model.

Listing 1.3. Adapting a domain-specific AOM model to the framework domain-independent AOM model

```
1   String fileName = "JsonMapTest.json";
2   AdapterFactory af = AdapterFactory.getInstance(fileName);
3
4   //Creating Entity Type
5   IEntityType sensorType = new GenericEntityType("Sensor");
6
7   //Creating Entity
8   IEntity sensor = sensorType.createNewEntity();
9
10  //Generating bean adapter
11  Object sensorAdap = af.generate(sensor);
```

3.3   Adapting Entities to JavaBeans

The Esfinge AOM Role Mapper framework is also able to adapt classes following the pattern of the Bean specification. This means that properties will be created for each of the attributes of the adapted class, just as it is specified for a Bean. The generated adapter class maintains an entity attribute, and for each of its attributes, a property is generated in the adapter. In this section it will be described how the Esfinge AOM Role Mapper framework generates adapters from a Bean class.

The adapter is generated by means of bytecode via the ASM library. It is possible to create JAVA classes at runtime by specifying which bytecodes to execute. The class responsible for generating this new class is the AdapterFactory. It follows the design pattern factory so there is a single instance of it per application. To generate an instance of AdapterFactory it is necessary to pass the name of the annotation map file to the getInstance method as a parameter.

The adapter method of AdapterFactory creates an instance of the adapter class of a Bean entity. To do this, it is necessary to pass to this method an instance of IEntity that you want to create the adapter. It is checked if there is an adapter created for the entity in the class cache of the Esfinge AOM Role Mapper. In case an adapter is already created, the method only returns one instance of your own to the user. Otherwise, a new adapter is generated for the Bean.

The sample to create an adapted object is same as listed in the Listing 1.3 as shown before.

3.4   Internal Structure

The internal structure of the Esfinge framework is composed of four components. These components are Metadata Handler, AOM Core API, AOM Core Implementations, and Model Manager.

The AOM Core API includes a set of interfaces that represent the common structure of the AOM core provided by the framework [11]. AOM Core Implementations contains implementations of Interfaces defined by the AOM Core API component. Each of these classes contains an attribute to store the application object AOM for the specific domain they adapt.

The Model Manager is responsible for instantiating the model and managing the AOM Core API instances created by the framework. The main class of this component is the Model Manager. All operations involving manipulation of the model, including the persistence, loading, and query model, must be done through this class. One of the main responsibilities of the Model Manager class is to ensure that a logical element is not instantiated twice in the framework.

Metadata Handler is responsible for retrieving metadata from application classes. In your internal structure, the component is organized into the following parts:

- Descriptors: implements the metadata container pattern.
- Metadata Readers: implements the metadata reader strategy pattern.
- Metadata Repository: implements the metadata repository pattern, providing a memory cache of metadata already retrieved.
- Annotations: contains the Java annotations that allow the identification of the roles of AOM elements in specific domain AOM applications. Annotations in the Esfinge Framework are used to map domain-specific AOM applications for the generic structure of the AOM kernel using JavaBean pattern.

4   Dynamic Behavior on AOM

The dynamic behavior was developed in the AOM using Esfinge Role Mapper framework as a validation tool. The changes on this framework get done mainly using RuleObject pattern. We created a RuleObject interface to all dynamic method be added in this interface.

The RuleObject interface must be realized by classes that represent the behavior of AOM entities by implementing the execute method. The execute method receives two parameters: the first one is the entity from which the method will execute, and the second parameter of type varargs (Object type) are the parameters that the method receives for its execution. The Listing 1.4 presents the RuleObject Interface.

Listing 1.4. method definition on RuleObject Interface

```
1  public interface RuleObject {
2    public Object execute(IEntity obj, Object... params);
3  }
```

To add a RuleObject to an AOM entity, you must add a new operation to the EntityType class, invoking the addOperation method, passing as parameters the rule name and an instance of the class that implements the RuleObject interface.

The RuleObject will be stored in the entity for execution. In the Listing 1.5 is presented a sample where the rule name yearsMade and the RuleObject CalculaAnos instance are passed as parameters to EntityType productType.

Listing 1.5. Add a RuleObject to the AOM entity

```
1  public static void createEntityType() throws EsfingeAOMException{
2    IEntityType productType = new GenericEntityType("Product");
3    productType.addOperation("yearsMade", new CalculaAnos("dateMade"));
4  }
```

To execute the rule, it was changed the IEntity interface do add the method executeOperation as presented in the Listing 1.6.

Listing 1.6. executeOperation rule method on IEntity interface

```
public interface IEntity extends HasProperties {
  //... omited method
  public Object executeOperation(String name, Object... params);
  public void addPropertyMonitored(String propertyName, String ruleName);
  public Object getResultOperation(String ruleName);
}
```

The executeOperation method has two parameters: the rule name that will be executed and one of type varargs (Object type) with the parameters that the method needs to be executed. This way, when an entity is created, it has the method executeOperation for the execution of the dynamic behavior. The rule name is the same that was used to add the operation to the EntityType class.

The GenericEntity and AdapterEntity classes implement the IEntity interface and the implementation of the executeOperation method get the RuleObject and invoke the execute method.

Listing 1.7 shows a unit test using CalculaAnos RuleObject.

Listing 1.7. rule method execution

```
@Test
public void testRuleManufacturingYears() throws EsfingeAOMException{
    IEntityType entityType = new GenericEntityType("Product");

    // add RuleObject to entity type
    entityType.addOperation("anosFabricacao", new CalculaAnos("dataFabricacao"));
    GenericPropertyType dataNascPropertyType = new GenericPropertyType("dataFabricacao",
        Date.class);
    dataNascPropertyType.setProperty("notempty", true);
    GenericPropertyType nomePropertyType = new GenericPropertyType("nome", String.class);
    nomePropertyType.setProperty("notempty", true);
    entityType.addPropertyType(dataNascPropertyType);
    entityType.addPropertyType(nomePropertyType);
    // creating AOM entity
    produto = entityType.createNewEntity();
    produto.setProperty("nome", "Notebook DELL");
    GregorianCalendar dataFabr = new GregorianCalendar();
    dataFabr.set(2010, 11, 23);
    produto.setProperty("dataFabricacao", dataFabr.getTime());

    // executing the rule method
    Object resultOperation = produto.executeOperation("anosFabricacao");
}
```

Another changes were made to get dynamic behavior working for domain-specific classes and adapted classes to work with frameworks based on JavaBeans Standard.

One of this change refers to the mapping of Rules from a domain-specific AOM to the AOM Role Mapper. To reach this in the Esfinge framework, three new annotations (RuleClass, RuleMethod, and RuleAttribute) were created to map dynamic behavior into classes, dynamic behavior on methods, and attributes with dynamic behavior, respectively.

To map a RuleObject, it is needed to include a property of ruleObject or ruleClass. With this property, the method that generates the adapter adds the mapping of an annotation to the generated object. In the Listing 1.8, is created the EntityType and included the ruleObject and ruleClass property, indicating that this object is a RuleObject.

Listing 1.8. Mapping RuleObject created by annotation

```
1   IEntityType entityType = new GenericEntityType("ProdutoNovo2");
2   // criando property types
3   IPropertyType dataNascPropertyType = new GenericPropertyType("dataFabricacao",
        Date.class);
4   IPropertyType nomePropertyType = new GenericPropertyType("anosFabricacao", String.class);
5   // add property types in the entity type
6   entityType.addPropertyType(dataNascPropertyType);
7   entityType.addPropertyType(nomePropertyType);
8   entityType.addOperation("anosFabricacao", new CalculaAnos("dataFabricacao"));
9   entityType.setProperty("ruleClass", true);
10  nomePropertyType.setProperty("ruleObject", true);
```

In the Listing 1.9, the Entity product is created, and values are assigned to the properties. After the entity creation, the adapter generation method is invoked, which finds the ruleObject property and includes the mapping on the generated adapter. In this example the name of the generated adapted object is personBeanAdapter.

Listing 1.9. Generating adapter of a entity with RuleObject

```
1   GregorianCalendar dataFabr = new GregorianCalendar();
2   dataFabr.set(2010, 11, 23);
3   Map<String, Object> parametersSubstring = new HashMap<String, Object>();
4   parametersSubstring.put("dataFabricacao", "2016");
5   parametersSubstring.put("perecivel", true);
6   nomePropertyType.setProperty("ruleAttribute", parametersSubstring);
7   IEntity product = entityType.createNewEntity();
8   product.setProperty("nome", "Notebook DELL");
9   product.setProperty("dataFabricacao", dataFabr.getTime());
10  Object personBeanAdapter = af.generate(product);
```

In Listing 1.10, tests are created to verify that the annotations are present in the created adapter, personBeanAdapter.

Listing 1.10. Testing annotated rules

```
1   boolean cap = personBeanAdapter.getClass().getMethod("getAnosFabricacao")
2       .isAnnotationPresent(RuleMethod.class);
3   assertTrue(cap);
4   RuleAttribute ruleAttribute = personBeanAdapter.getClass().getMethod("getAnosFabricacao")
5       .getAnnotation(RuleAttribute.class);
6   String columnName = (String)
        ruleAttribute.getClass().getMethod("dataFabricacao").invoke(ruleAttribute);
7   assertEquals(columnName, "2016");
8   Method m = personBeanAdapter.getClass().getMethod("getAnosFabricacao");
9   assertNotNull(m);
10  assertTrue(m.isAnnotationPresent(RuleMethod.class));
11  assertEquals("2016",m.getAnnotation(RuleAttribute.class).dataFabricacao());
12  assertEquals(true,m.getAnnotation(RuleAttribute.class).perecivel());
```

Another important change regards to the translation of Rules to methods when transforming the class into a JavaBean Adapter.

This feature was developed to maintain compatibility with frameworks that work with the standard JavaBean. Making use of the ASM component the bytecodes of the dynamic behavior method are included dynamically so that it can be executed by the framework. To generate the class by mapping the **RuleObject** to a method, we initially created the entityType product type, added the operation called periodoConsumo, and the creation of the product entity is done as presented in the Listing 1.11.

Listing 1.11. Generate class mapping RuleObject to method

```
IEntityType entityType = new GenericEntityType("Produto");
entityType.addOperation("periodoConsumo", new PeriodoConsumo("dataFabricacao"));
IEntity produto = entityType.createNewEntity();
produto.setProperty("validade", 90);
```

In this step, the **personBeanAdapter** adapter is generated as shown in the Listing 1.12.

Listing 1.12. Generating Adapter on entity with RuleObject

```
Object personBeanAdapter = af.generate(produto);
```

And the executeOperation method is added to the personBeanAdapter adapted object, using the bytecode of the ASM-generated method and then we have the tests to execute the method and validate that it has been included in the adapted object, as shown in the Listing 1.13.

Listing 1.13. Testing rule method on adapter

```
Object personAdapter = af.generate(produto);
Method declaredMethod = personAdapter.getClass().getDeclaredMethod("executeOperation",
    String.class, Object[].class);
Object resultOperation = declaredMethod.invoke(personAdapter, "periodoConsumo", null);...
```

5   Case Study

To validate the mapping of dynamic behavior between different object models in AOM, we needed to verify that the method result with the rule was invoked and produced a different result of an entity without dynamic behavior.

To achieve this, we did a unit test with Esfinge Gamification framework. Esfinge Gamification is a metadata-based framework applicable to systems that require logical gamification, regardless of their domain. The main goal of the framework is to dissociate gamification concerns from the application, allowing developers to focus on application logic, adding only information on how gamification should work on each feature invoked.

The framework intercepts these invocations and performs the appropriate gamification logic. Provides extension points that allow the introduction of application-specific gamification behaviors. The Esfinge Gamification defines various types of achievements and different implementations to store gamification information about users. To record how gamification must be handled in the application, the framework uses annotations that must be added to the business methods in the application.

The major question to be answered to validate the study is: can the class created and adapted by Esfinge Role Mapper have the rule method mapped by an annotation of the Gamification framework and when the method is invoked, the points are added to the user used in the test?

To answer this question we developed a unit test with an entity class with a rule method, mapping this class as AOM domain independent class and adapting it, mapping the annotation PointsToUser to the method and then invoking the method to verify that the annotation was used to add points to the user used in the test and to prove the correct functionality of the mapping.

In the first step of the test, it was created a unit test class with the method setupGame to prepare the Esfinge Gamification framework run the test to validate count points to user Spider, as presented in the Listing 1.14.

Listing 1.14. preparing Gamification with setup test method

```
1  public class TestDynamicProxyWithRule {
2    Game gs;
3    @Before
4    public void setupGame() {
5      UserStorage.setUserID("Spider");
6      gs = new GameMemoryStorage();
7      GameInvoker gi = GameInvoker.getInstance();
8      gi.setGame(gs);
9    }
```

For first, it will be created a simple test with a common entity with nothing special, just to show how the Gamification framework does your work to add points to the user. To use the annotation of Esfinge Gamification, it must be created an interface using the annotations with a method. To do that, the interface ITestRule is declared and annotated to add 25 points to the user of the test with a correct ANSWER as shown in the Listing 1.15.

Listing 1.15. Interface ITestRule annotated

```
1  public interface ITestRule {
2    @PointsToUser(name = "ANSWER", quantity = 25)
3    public void doRule();
4  }
```

Then the class TestRuleImpl implements ITestRule interface to override the doRule method as shown in the Listing 1.16.

Listing 1.16. Testing rule method on adapter

```
1  public class TestRuleImpl implements ITestRule{
2    @Override
3    public void doRule() {
4      // do something
5    }
6  }
```

Then to verify the simple annotated class, it is created a unit test creating a proxy using TestRuleImpl class, invoking the doRule method and comparing the result of the method invocation and how the Gamification framework used the PointsToUser annotation to add points to the user Spider, as presented in the Listing 1.17.

Listing 1.17. Testing annottation PointsToUser adding points to the user

```
1  @Test
2  public void testRule01() {
3    ITestRule rul = GameProxy.createProxy(new TestRuleImpl());
4    rul.doRule();
5    Achievement ach = gs.getAchievement("Spider", "ANSWER");
6    assertEquals(new Integer(25), ((Point) ach).getQuantity());
7  }
```

To validate the AOM entity with rule method, it was created a new class called ClassGameProxy. It was developed using the cglib framework because the adapted class do not have Interfaces. It creates a proxy based on classes without Interfaces. The Interface MethodInterceptor of the cglib framework has the method intercept. It intercepts the annotated method and makes the invocation from the proxy object.

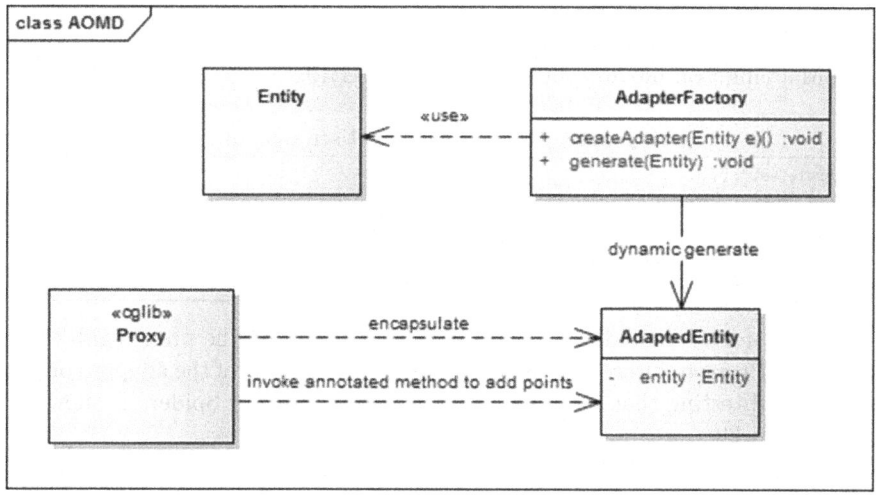

Fig. 3. Proxy cglib to add points to the user

The Listing 1.18 shows the ClassGameProxy code using cglib framework. The class has two methods, the method createProxy to create the cglib proxy and the method intercept to intercept the call of the method oh the encapsulated object.

Listing 1.18. ClassGameProxy to intercept method of adapted object

```
1   public class ClassGameProxy implements MethodInterceptor{
2
3     private Object encapsulated;
4
5     private ClassGameProxy(Object encapsulated) {
6       this.encapsulated = encapsulated;
7     }
8
9     @SuppressWarnings("unchecked")
10    public static <T> T createProxy(T encapsulated){
11      ClassGameProxy classGameProxy = new ClassGameProxy(encapsulated);
12      Enhancer enhace = new Enhancer();
13      enhace.setSuperclass(encapsulated.getClass());
14      enhace.setInterfaces(encapsulated.getClass().getInterfaces());
15      enhace.setCallback(classGameProxy);
16      return (T) enhace.create();
17    }
18
19    @Override
20    public Object intercept(Object obj, Method method, Object[] args, MethodProxy mProxy)
          throws Throwable {
21      try {
22        Object returnValue = method.invoke(encapsulated, args);
23        GameInvoker gameInvoker = GameInvoker.getInstance();
24        gameInvoker.registerAchievment(encapsulated, method, args);
25        return returnValue;
26      } catch (InvocationTargetException e) {
27        throw e.getTargetException();
28      }
29    }
30  }
```

To the annotation be found by adapted class, it was added it on the AnnotationMapping.json file an shown in the Listing 1.19.

Listing 1.19. Mapping PointsToUser annotation

```
1   "ruleTest":[
2     {"target":"method"},
3     {"annotationPath":"net.sf.esfinge.gamification.annotation.PointsToUser"},
4     {"parameter_1":"name"},
5     {"parameter_2":"quantity"}
6   ]
```

Finally, it was created the test method testRule using the proxy cglib class, ClassGameProxy to intercept the PointsToUser annotation of the adapted object ruleTest and testing that the points were added to the user Spider, as shown in the Listing 1.20.

Listing 1.20. Testing rule method annotated on Gamification framework

```
1   @Test
2   public void testRule() {
3     AdapterFactory af = AdapterFactory.getInstance("AnnotationMapping.json");
4     IEntityType productType = new GenericEntityType("Product");
5     // creating property types
6     GenericPropertyType dataNascPropertyType = new GenericPropertyType("dateDone",
           Date.class);
7     try {
8       dataNascPropertyType.setProperty("notempty", true);
9       GenericPropertyType nomePropertyType = new GenericPropertyType("name",
             String.class);
10      nomePropertyType.setProperty("notempty", true);
11      productType.addPropertyType(dataNascPropertyType);
12      productType.addPropertyType(nomePropertyType);
13
14      Map<String, Object> parameters = new HashMap<String, Object>();
15      parameters.put("dataFabricacao", "2016");
16      parameters.put("perecivel", true);
17      nomePropertyType.setProperty("ruleAttribute", parameters);
18
19      Map<String, Object> parametersSubstring = new TreeMap<String, Object>();
20      parametersSubstring.put("name", "ANSWER");
21      parametersSubstring.put("quantity", 25);
22      dataNascPropertyType.setProperty("ruleTest", parametersSubstring);
23
24      // method name and parameter name
25      productType.addOperation("yearMade", new CalculaAnos("dateDone"));
26
27      // create entity
28      IEntity product = productType.createNewEntity();
29      product.setProperty("name", "Notebook DELL");
30      GregorianCalendar dataFabr = new GregorianCalendar();
31      dataFabr.set(2014, 11, 23);
32      product.setProperty("dateDone", dataFabr.getTime());
33
34      // create adapter from entity product
35      Object ruleTest = af.generate(product);
36
37          // create the cglib proxy
38      Object proxyRule = ClassGameProxy.createProxy(ruleTest);
39
40      // invoke method annotated to add points
41      Object result = proxyRule.getClass().getMethod("getDateDone").invoke(proxyRule);
42      // expected result
43      Achievement ach = gs.getAchievement("Spider", "ANSWER");
44      assertEquals(new Integer(25), ((Point) ach).getQuantity());
45
46    } catch (Exception e) {
47      e.printStackTrace();
48      Assert.assertFalse(true);
49    }
50  }
```

The proxyRule object is the proxy created using cglib from adapted AOM object ruleTest. In the line 41 of the code, the method getDateDone is invoked and this method is intercepted by intercept method, which uses the annotation PointsToUser to add points to the user Spider. Thus, validating the test, it is verified the points added to the user, as tested in the line 47, answering the question that the adapted object with rule method was executed dynamically using the annotation of the Gamification framework successfully.

6   Conclusion and Future Work

This research work presented a Mapping Dynamic Behavior Between Different Object Models in AOM to be applied in the development of systems with the high frequency of changes of rules. Since it is a new feature to improve AOM frameworks compatibility with Standard frameworks, it presents the flexibility as the main earn to use AOM architecture.

The Esfinge framework, used as the validation tool, has received the improvements to present these results. The conclusion is that the dynamic behavior has many applications in the development of the systems which use frameworks that use annotations or have rules changing frequently. Future work includes an approach to integrate this model with Aspects [9] to improve the tool set of the framework, increasing the flexibility of this technology.

Acknowledgments. The authors would like to thank CNPq (grant 455080/2014-3) and FAPESP (grant 2014/16236-6) for financial support.

References

1. Acherkan, E., Hen-Tov, A., Lorenz, D.H., Schachter, L.: The ink language meta-metamodel for adaptive object-model frameworks. In: Proceedings of the ACM International Conference Companion on Object Oriented Programming Systems Languages and Applications Companion, pp. 181–182. ACM (2011)
2. Esfinge (2017). http://esfinge.sf.net/
3. Ferreira, H.S., Correia, F.F., Aguiar, A.: Design for an adaptive object-model framework. In: Proceedings of the 4th Workshop on Models@ Run. Time, Held at the ACM/IEEE 12th International Conference on Model Driven Engineering Languages and Systems (MoDELS 2009) (2009)
4. Fowler, M.: Analysis Patterns: Reusable Object Models. Addison-Wesley Professional, Indianapolis (1997)
5. Guerra, E., Fernandes, C.: A qualitative and quantitative analysis on metadata-based frameworks usage. In: Murgante, B., Misra, S., Carlini, M., Torre, C.M., Nguyen, H.-Q., Taniar, D., Apduhan, B.O., Gervasi, O. (eds.) ICCSA 2013. LNCS, vol. 7972, pp. 375–390. Springer, Heidelberg (2013). https://doi.org/10.1007/978-3-642-39643-4_28
6. Guerra, E., de Souza, J., Fernandes, C.: Pattern language for the internal structure of metadata-based frameworks. In: Noble, J., Johnson, R., Zdun, U., Wallingford, E. (eds.) Transactions on Pattern Languages of Programming III. LNCS, vol. 7840, pp. 55–110. Springer, Heidelberg (2013). https://doi.org/10.1007/978-3-642-38676-3_3
7. Johnson, R., Oakes, J.: The User-Defined Product Framework (1998). http://stwww.cs.uiuc.edu/users/johnson/papers/udp
8. JSR: JSR 220: Enterprise Javabeans 3.0, August 2007. http://jcp.org/en/jsr/detail?id=220
9. Kiczales, G.: Aspect-oriented programming. ACM Comput. Surv. (CSUR) **28**(4es), 154 (1996)
10. Manolescu, D., Voelter, M., Noble, J.: Pattern Languages of Program Design 5, vol. 5. Addison-Wesley Professional, Reading (2006)

11. Matsumoto, P.M., Guerra, E.: An approach for mapping domain-specific AOM applications to a general model. J. UCS **20**(4), 534–560 (2014). https://doi.org/10.3217/jucs-020-04-0534
12. Sun Microsystems: Javabeans (TM) Specification 1.01 Final Release, August 1997. http://download.oracle.com/otn-pub/jcp/7224-javabeans-1.01-fr-spec-oth-JSpec/beans.101.pdf
13. Yoder, J.W., Balaguer, F., Johnson, R.: Architecture and design of adaptive object-models. ACM Sigplan Notices **36**(12), 50–60 (2001)
14. Yoder, J.W., Johnson, R.: The adaptive object-model architectural style. In: Bosch, J., Gentleman, M., Hofmeister, C., Kuusela, J. (eds.) Software Architecture. ITI-FIP, vol. 97, pp. 3–27. Springer, Boston (2002). https://doi.org/10.1007/978-0-387-35607-5_1

Transformation of the Teacher into "Produser": An Emergency Case from the Appropriation of Social Web-Based Technologies

Karolina González Guerrero[1]([⊠]) [iD], José Eduardo Padilla Beltrán[1] [iD], and Leonardo E. Contreras Bravo[2] [iD]

[1] Universidad Militar Nueva Granada, Cajicá, Colombia
kgonzalezg@gmail.com
[2] Universidad Distrital Francisco José de Caldas, Bogotá, Colombia

Abstract. The teacher "produser" as an emerging figure that explores the ability of the subject to participate or to generate new experiences and content from information and communication technologies, provides a new overview of the impact of technological developments in the social, cultural and even educational fields. This overview is the main focus of this manuscript. For this reason, it is sought to investigate both the emerging role of this figure and its relation with the work of teachers in higher education. A quantitative methodological approach is adopted with exploratory design, which allows determining the favorability on behalf of the teachers to take on this role, through the technique of semantic differential. As a result of this approach, the produser is characterized by the will, cultural work and empathy shown to promote innovation and learning with autonomous and collaborative purposes in order to achieve relevance and flexibility in teaching. The conclusion is that transitioning to produser depends on its disassociation with economic components closer to the action of the prosumers and thereby generates processes of collective consciousness from the social web to address many different issues, both inside and outside of the classroom.

Keywords: Collaboration · Education · Higher education · Produser
Prosumer · Social web

1 Introduction

1.1 Characterization of the Teacher as Produser

While the concept of produser has been the neologism with the most impact in the way of sharing, creating and distributing content for the need to sell or receive retributions from a particular location, it came from the assumptions of Alvin Toffler according to Martinez and De Salvador (2012). It has several elements that bring with it the mercantilism and alienation of the subjects in terms of the quest for free or low-cost labor that is rooted in their motivations. This can offer elements, products or goods that perpetuate the consumption system.

© Springer International Publishing AG, part of Springer Nature 2018
O. Gervasi et al. (Eds.): ICCSA 2018, LNCS 10963, pp. 250–260, 2018.
https://doi.org/10.1007/978-3-319-95171-3_20

Consequently, the binary logic of producing and consuming still holds a model of economic efficiency. While trying to get away from the common aspects of exchange, it maintains dualities in production for some and in consumption for the vast majority of subjects that make up the figures of collaboration within systems such as the social web, collaborative platforms, blogs, social networks and other spaces in which the prosumer plays his role. On the contrary, the produser (combination of the words: producer and user), with an emphasis on the figure of the user, long-term vision to focus the attention on the social, cultural and symbolic aspects set by the user when it produces or performs an action.

In this way, for Fuch (s.f.) Information and Communication Technologies (ICT) have to allow alternative strategies to understand the user, not only as a consumer, but as an agent of change in their role as producer through logical peer-to-peer solutions or the use of knowledge. This can contribute to solving social problems for the reconstruction of the social fabric and the exposure of ideas according to the context. The produser then, focuses on the power of the collective intelligence exposed by Levy (2004), whose emphasis lies on the ability to collaborate with others by means of inter and transdisciplinary methods that foster new points of view to handle different problems.

The transition into a produser is an ethical and political subject, regarding the capacity to make decisions based on the reflection on the impact it may have on others. In that sense, the qualities of differentiation of the produser from the prosumer will focus on the ethical and social matters as well as the request for citizen participation around ideas and thoughts of cultural order to potentiate the value of collective work. Because of this, the produser has no place in today's society full of information and knowledge. ICTs, social web and network connections enable collaborative work, which is why it is important to analyze how this process constitutes the basis and through the educational system, how it is capable of transmitting and socially transforming the principles of autonomy and collaboration as a result. In the universe of computer science, it is important to admit that the development of this aspect has fostered numerous advantages for the exploitation of information and communication technologies within an innovative environment. Precisely, one of these environments has generated a significant impact which is the academic aspect. The main purpose of this research is to identify the connections and figures that arise from the development of technology and its impact on the academic environment. This assures that the figure of the teaching produser is included and studied as a determining factor in this context with fundamental characteristics for the development of higher education.

1.2 The Importance of the Produser in the Social Context

According to Paltrinieri and Degli (2013), the produser aims at strengthening the citizen dimension of different cultures in the context of the paradigm of empowerment, offering spaces for participation, meeting and inclusion. Based on ideals for the benefit of people from various communities, this is achieved through interaction, the construction of knowledge and continuous learning in internet and social web.

The same author insists on observing the internet as a citizen's space, whose capacity is to foster critical thoughts through "the empowerment of citizens, understood as communicative empowerment" (Paltrinieri and Degli 2013, p. 30). In the words of Lévy (2004), the previous statement can be understood as "the members of the molecular collectives communicate transversally, reciprocally, outside of categories, without going through the hierarchical way, folding and folding, complicating with all calm the great metamorphic tissue of the quiet cities" (p. 37).

When you have this type of communication in framed social groups, the aspects of consumption and production need to be overcome paving the way for the logic of social interaction. Hence, as stated by Fernandez (2014) it is necessary to acquire a greater understanding of the influence of the world in characterizing a role that shelters the participation and the dynamics of the network beyond the approaches of consumption, therefore creating the culture of involvement around common property with wide access, distribution and circulation;

Most of the efforts would be directed on making the resources, contents and development on the web of free access, acquiring the connotation of common goods as mentioned by Fernandez (2014). The main characteristic is the participation of citizens through public policies related to access to content. In addition, the Ministry of Information Technologies and Communications (MinTic 2010) affirms that social web has enabled new communication channels linked to public policy, turning new addenda and public projects more in line with the access and ability to access in by the so-called "users/citizens" (p. 21). Each initiative for access and communication to the public is linked to new projects, informing of what is happening to ensure commitment on new causes of social development. In a broader vision of the ICT context, Colás Bravo (2002) mentions that these "are only means to efficiently manage data, information and knowledge" (p. 78), which is why they are considered key to generate learning processes and creation of wealth based on knowledge management through collaboration, as well as the use of spaces for interaction and participation.

2 Methodology

The present study is based on a quantitative methodological approach (Sautu et al. 2005), whose design is framed within a non-experimental scenario because it is not intended to control variables, but rather to consider a type of exploratory transactional method. As explained by Hernández (2006), data can be collected in a specific instance and at the same time allow the investigation of essential aspects of attitudinal and experiential type on the relevance of the role of produser in the professional work of the teacher.

In addition, the hypothesis that the study seeks to verify focuses on the teachers' degree of acceptance of the use and appropriation of the social web and how this can contribute to performing the functions of a produser, who both produces and uses content or digital experiences inside and outside of the classroom.

2.1 Sample

The sample for this study recognizes the set of full-time faculty of the Universidad Militar Nueva Granada and the Universidad Distrital Francisco José de Caldas. It draws on the expertise and knowledge of the study subject of teachers in the Faculty of Graduate Studies in the development of processes related to virtual, semi-classroom and distance education supported in different media and technologies. In this sense, the sample of this study was based on the random selection of 37 teachers whose object of study is the closest to the approach according to their research lines, research projects and trajectory of teacher-researcher in different universities at a national level. This type of sampling is also referred to by Crespo and Salamanca (2007) as convenience sampling, whose reference is the selection of people who contribute with their professional experience to the recognition of emerging factors in the object of study, which is why random elements cannot be explored in the sampling process.

2.2 Semantic Differential Instrument

For Aros et al. (2009), the semantic differential is an instrument that allows the recognition of the significant and symbolic value of an object or concept. In this way, the data collected with this technique are encompassed in the connotative order, when capturing the attitudes, meanings and perceptions of the population under study through a rating scale. In the same lines, Hernández (2006) defines the semantic differential as an element of estimation of attitudes, which are graded through a series of bipolar adjectives including a scale that assigns a measure reflecting the position or attitude of the person regarding the concept.

In the particular case of this research, the use of semantic differential allows assessing the attitudes of teachers towards the use and appropriation of technologies such as social web and the features included in the concept of produser as an agent that produces and uses these media at a professional level on a daily basis. Hence, the construction of the instrument involves six statements that combine elements of social web with the produser role. Then, the position of the teacher on the impact of such technologies in the professional environment can be determined, with trainees and other agents of the targeted educational community.

3 Result

As it was clarified during the explanation of the data collection technique, statements are made to catalog aspects of social web and the role of the teacher produser. Additionally, there is an item of conceptualization of the produser figure where the perception is analyzed surrounding this concept. In this way, the following describes the results acquired using three blocks of semantic differential; the first one is related to the concept of the produser; the second one is associated with social web and the impact they have in education through virtuality and the resources used inside and outside the classroom by the teacher; and finally, the third block marks what is inherent to the characterization of the teacher-produser according to the willingness of teachers to appropriate aspects of the produser in their professional work. Furthermore, it is important to clarify that the scale of measurement goes from (1) to (7), depending on the positive or negative direction of each pair of nouns or adjectives that are used to describe the favorability in each group of remarks.

In the first statement referring to the produser benchmark, in terms of the levels of partnership attributed to him and how it relates to social web. To that extent, a major feature of this concept must be the facilitation, which reinforces the importance of aspects such as the development of content in their cultural and educational work. In contrast to the population sample, the most important cooperative actions are teamwork and the assignment of roles for specific tasks regarding the duties of the produser in higher education scenarios.

Regarding the second block of the semantic differential instrument, it is ascertained by the social web and the impact it has on higher education, which is exposed in the first instance if the appropriation of ICTs is consistent with the institutional framework; and at a Faculty level, it serves as a strategy that contributes to the education of the students. This explains a tendency towards FAVORABILITY. In both levels, the statistical average of the response in each pair of qualifiers (positive and negative) exceeds the threshold of 6 (see Fig. 1), therefore, flexibility and relevance are necessary, which are harnessed with the technologies of information and communication.

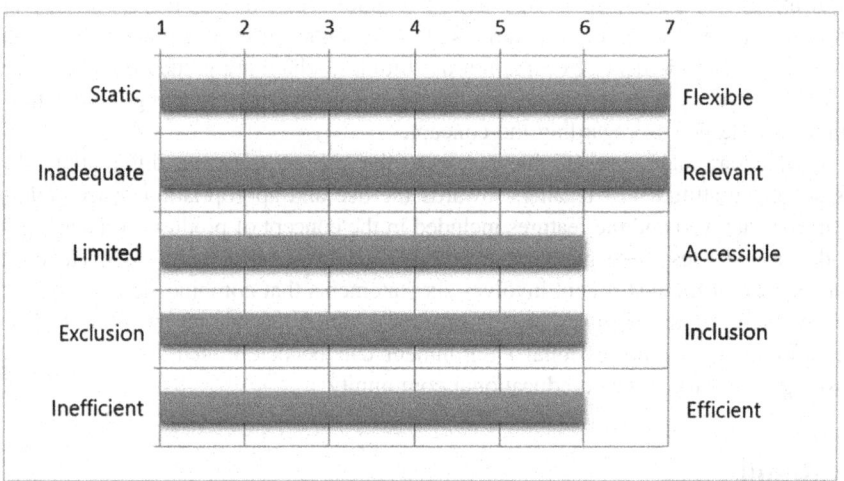

Fig. 1. Appropriation of ICT in education

By favoring the appropriation of ICTs, related to the statement that is raised later on whether social web allows the teacher to develop learning in their students, the results obtained seem to be in favor of monitoring and controlling the learning process, tackle complex elements or incentivize emotion as an input for meaningful learning. Others see intuition and horizontality as a way to mitigate the teacher's superiority in the classroom and acquire less favorability for the population sample. This contextual block of social web is the most valuable for the sample and in which there is a relative consensus on the positive items that describe this object.

In the third block of statements about the role of the teacher-producer, the aspects to potentiate learning were researched when the teacher takes on the role of Produser, inside and outside the classroom. In this regard, the statistical average is located in (4), therefore there is no clear consensus from the pairs of items used to describe these traits. As shown in Fig. 2, safety and learning have the most favorability (see Fig. 2).

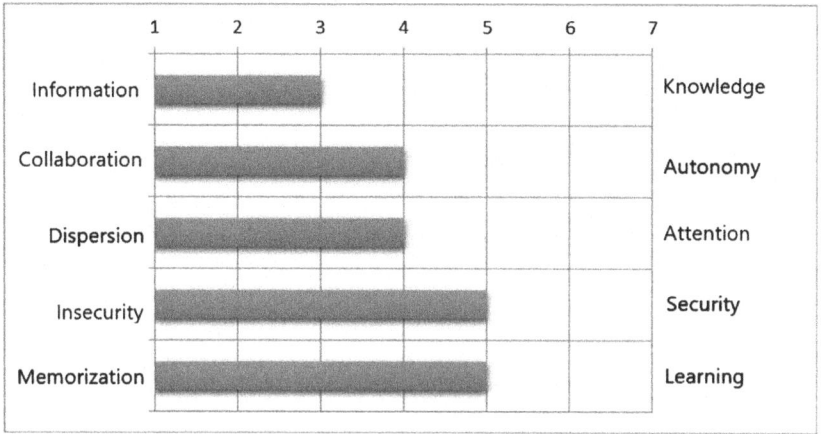

Fig. 2. Teacher produser role in higher education

Aspects such as autonomy and collaboration received an assessment of (4) by a few teachers which could mean that both are substantial in the framework of the teacher-produser to encourage learning from social web. The previous statement is linked to what aspects can turn the role of the teacher-produser into an apprentice so the following information was widely inquired including other actors of the educational community.

In this line of thought, the result translates into a favorable orientation in items such as empathy and innovation. The "heterarchy" which had already been witnessed with the aspect of horizontality in previous inquiries (see Fig. 1), does not acquire significance on an attitudinal level for the sample population and it has the lowest score in the group (see Fig. 3).

According to what the produser role can offer to students in first degree, and subsequently to the other actors of the educational community, the following statement intended to analyze the attitudes that describe to the teacher when he articulates this role inside and outside of the classroom. However, it is in this group of peers that the qualifiers show greater disparity in each couple of opposites. Therefore, in spite of the fact that leadership and attention are valued as relevant, others such as changes or divergence are also displayed with ratings (see Fig. 4).

In the case of the pair of qualifiers dependence and independence, it is inferred that something similar happens with the collaboration-autonomy pair (see Fig. 4), and each one is important for a certain sector of the sample or is considered to occur at different times of playing the role.

Additionally, in the statistical average of the response for the third block and the two previous surveys a value of (4.53) is obtained which can be interpreted as a point of indecision or balance between negative and positive aspects in each pair of qualifiers on the role of the teacher-produser.

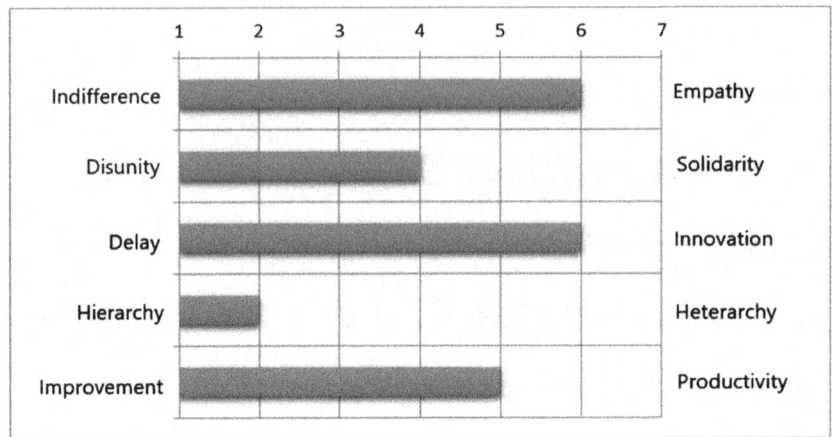

Fig. 3. The teacher-produser in the educational community

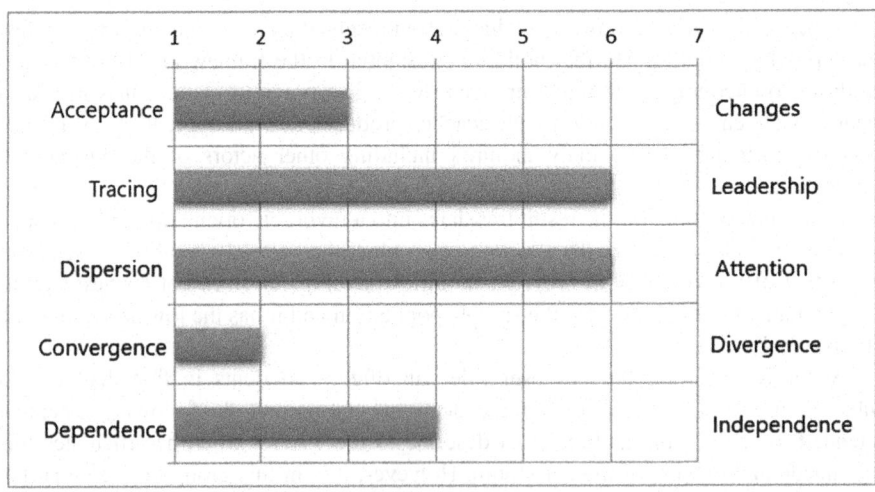

Fig. 4. Teacher-produser role attitudes

4 Discussion

Unlike the previously stated by Levy (2004), as a principle of collaboration of these emerging figures in the network or web server (the produser), the connotation that the produser acquires according to the results of the semantic differential is mainly based on cooperation rather than collaboration. This hinders the ethical-political component that promotes citizen participation with a vision of solidarity in relation to living and learning with others. In that regard, in spite bringing together elements of teamwork and the ability to work with others to solve specific problems, cooperation is the purpose of the result, while the collaboration reflects on the process and strategies to reach such result. They can be seen as a couple of elements that contribute to the process of training and participation in the collaborative work.

However, in accordance with Paltrinieri and Degli (2013), the teachers included in the sample in the present investigation, give importance to the cultural component; they are much more emphatic in the latter than in the economic component, seeing the relevance of the dimension of facilitation as a mark of their work in the context of higher education. In the same way, priority is given to the ability of this figure to produce experiences and contents beyond them. Therefore, as exposed in Fernandez (2014), overcoming the principles of exacerbated consumption can be a point of reflection in this role that exceeds the agent's binary vision of the prosumer.

On a separate matter, with respect to the conception and contextualization of social web in higher education, the results reflect favorability on the opportunity provided by ICT in the field of education to develop innovation, mainly through aspects already mentioned by MinTic (2010). This relates to the accessibility of information, communication with others and the efficiency of the means and resources of this social web to include aspects of the network and establish more flexible teaching processes as learning and formation benefits for the educational community.

Likewise, many of the teachers participating in the present study have a positive attitude towards the fact that social web, rather than complicating educational action, contributes to consider aspects of complexity that are substantial for what was stated by Reig (2013) on the construction of knowledge in a collective order, both inside and outside the network. This also involves the imprint of moving from the technicality of ICT to another level focused on the TAC (Learning Technologies and Knowledge) that includes aspects such as emotion and intuition as inputs for meaningful learning, which combined with reasoning, generates a suitable creative margin for the resolution of problems.

Regarding the answers that were taken on the produser role associated with the work of the teacher, the most important thing is attached to encouraging learning according to the attitude of the teachers participating in the research. The actions of autonomy and collaboration that are accounted for under the equity method to carry them out, at the same time allow students to acquire security and self-learning strategies in the search, selection and understanding of the information.

In that sense and as stressed by Reig (s.f.), the produser should be a function of generating environments and experiences that exceed the use of access to the media and ICT mediations to accommodate around reflective components that can be used for each element present in the social web. This contributes to learning and creativity in line with the resolution of problems, surpassing the mnemonic model present in some magisterial processes carried out by conventional teaching methods.

As outlined in the results obtained, aspects such as emotion and intuition are of great value for the process of articulation of the Social web and serve as guiding principles for the role of the teacher-produser. While retaking experiences and memories that allow both teachers and apprentices to generate contexts that encourage intrinsic motivation, they stimulate significant learning through the inclusion of different senses, prior knowledge or recurrences around a particular topic or aspect to be taught. In contrast, the positions stated by Levy (2004), Paltrinieri and Degli (2013) and Fernandez (2014) about the importance of collectivity and equal participation to generate networked communities for building knowledge through produser action, can be truncated in relation to teachers who are concerned on how they refer to the results of semantic differential. Hierarchies prevail over heterarchies, which hinders the achievement of aspects of solidarity, leadership and civic participation within the educational context.

In addition to this possible impediment, obstacles are also reflected in terms of promoting changes in order to transform teacher actions through the appropriation of ICT and social web. All of this is based on the attitudes of teachers towards the acceptance of technologies and the low favorability in relation to divergence as a way of thinking that allows exploring new ideas with conceptual and paradigmatic changes for the sake of adaptable solutions in different spaces or situations.

Hence, Bauman (2005) points out that subjectivity, creativity and the intertwining of feelings allow other types of thought structures that give value to the educational component, recognizing interdisciplinary aspects and factions more in line with the social changes that occur in what he calls liquid societies. Otherwise, as to whether social web and specifically the role of teacher-produser allows a certain dependence or independence, something similar to the qualifying pair of collaboration-autonomy needs to happen, they are present on both occasions and could be interpreted as occurring in different moments in stockpile to the imposition that educational institutions have on teachers, the attitudinal and cognitive profiles of the apprentices or the types of resources and strategies that are integrated to perform the work of the produser.

5 Conclusions

The study shows that the conceptual gap between the prosumer and produser roles has to be acknowledged not on the basis of formal change in neologism through the impact of social web in the framework of ICT in the educational context, but based on the considerations that each role offers. While the prosumer is still linked to the production and consumption from the invisible economy sphere as Martinez and El Salvador (2012) state; the producer is the person who to encourage collective processes, social and cultural rights that reflect the participation and empowerment of the educational community, particularly the work of the teacher.

The results of this investigation reflect the overall acceptance of the changes of the produser to the extent that its meaning contributes to the facilitation of learning, the collective construction of content and the resolution of problems with higher complexity in which academic peers or other agents outside of the educational institution can intervene. In relation to technologies in higher education, specifically on what is inherent in ICT, in the words of Reig (2013), these have to transmute to processes referred to as Learning Technologies and Knowledge (TAC), whose purpose is to recognize the attitudes and skills of the users and citizens to contribute to the development of experiences within social transformation.

Also, the impact of social web has an influence on the dynamics of higher education contexts, making them not only appropriate, but flexible enough to maximize the efficient inclusion of various educational actors. For this reason, social web is displayed as an alternative to encourage aspects related to the emotion and intuition as key aspects that accompany reasoning for a proper understanding of the problems and social realities. Finally, the future of this research is oriented to seeking, developing and validating a methodology for the strengthening of online research competences from the logic of the prosumer-teacher, based on the changes generated by ICT and especially social web tools. Therefore, it is considered vital to understand the technological context, its development and prospective to different fields, such as the academic.

Acknowledgements. Funding: This work was supported by the Universidad Militar Nueva Granada [2018] – Code of the result of the project: INV-DIS-2569.

References

Aros, M., Narváez, G., Aros, N.: The semantic differential for the discipline of design: a tool for the product evaluation. In: 13th International Congress on Project Engineering, pp. 422–433. AEIPRO, Badajoz, Julio 2009

Bauman, Z.: Los retos de la educación en la modernidad líquida. Editorial Gedisa, S.A, Barcelona (2005)

Colás Bravo, M.P.: La investigación educativa en la (nueva) cultura científica de la sociedad del conocimiento. En-clave pedagógica 4(2), 77–94 (2002)

Crespo, M.C., Salamanca, A.: El muestreo en la investigación cualitativa. Nure Investigación, 27, 1–9 (2007). http://www.nureinvestigacion.es/ficheros_administrador/f_metodologica/fmetodologica_27.pdf

Fernández, P.: Consumos culturales en América Latina y la emergencia del prosumidor: un recorrido conceptual desde la sociedad de la información. Commun. Papers 4(3), 87–100 (2014)

Fuchs, C.: Digital prosumption labour on social media in the context of the capitalist regime of time (s.f.). http://tas.sagepub.com/content/early/2013/10/03/0961463X13502117.full.pdf+html

Lévy, P.: Inteligencia colectiva, por una antropología del ciberespacio (Trad. F. Martínez). BIREME, Washington (2004)

Hernández, R., Fernández, C., Baptista, P.: Metodología de la Investigación. Mc Graw Hill, México (2006)

Martínez, Y., De Salvador, S.: El Produser como producción de usuarios: más allá de wreaders y de prosumers. Revista Razón y Palabra, 86 (2012). http://www.razonypalabra.org.mx/N/N86/V86/24_MartinezSalvador_V86.pdf

Ministerio de Tecnologías de la Información y las Comunicaciones (MinTic) Introducción al uso de la social web en el estado colombiano (2010). http://www.ucaldas.edu.co/docs/prensa/Introduccionala_web_20_recomendacion_redes.pdf

Paltrinieri, R., Degli, P.: Processes of inclusion and exclusion in the sphere of prosumerism. Future Internet 5, 21–33 (2013). https://doi.org/10.3390/fi5010021

Reig, D.: Bienvenidos a la sociedad aumentada (s.f.). https://dialnet.unirioja.es/descarga/articulo/4110753.pdf

Reig, D., Vílchez, L.: Los jóvenes en la era de la hiperconectividad: tendencias, claves y miradas. Fundación Telefónica, Madrid (2013)

Sautu, R., Boniolo, P., Dalle, P., Elbert, R.: Manual de metodología. Colección Campus Virtual, Buenos Aires (2005)

Investigation of Obstructions and Range Limit on Bluetooth Low Energy RSSI for the Healthcare Environment

Jay Pancham[1(✉)], Richard Millham[1(✉)], and Simon James Fong[2(✉)]

[1] Durban University of Technology, Durban, South Africa
{panchamj,richardml}@dut.ac.za
[2] University of Macau, Taipa, Macau SAR
ccfong@umac.mo

Abstract. Indoor Real-Time Location Systems (RTLS) research identifies Bluetooth Low Energy as one of the technologies that promise an acceptable response to the requirements of the Healthcare environment. In this context, we investigate the latest improvements with Bluetooth 5.0 especially with regards its range when the signal penetrates through different types of multiple partitions. The improvements in Bluetooth technology especially with regards form factor, low energy consumption, and higher speeds make this a viable technology for use in indoor RTLS. Several different venues are used at the University to mimic the Healthcare environment to conduct the experiment. The results indicated an acceptable range through obstacles such glass, drywall partitions and solid brick wall. Future research will investigate methods to determine the position of Bluetooth Low Energy devices for the possible location of patients and assets.

Keywords: Bluetooth low energy · BLE · Real-Time Location System
RSSI · Indoor positioning

1 Introduction

Over the past several years, indoor localization has grown into an important research topic, attracting much attention in the networking research community [1]. The increase in popularity for positioning services offered by smart devices and their related technology has indicated a turning point in the field of indoor localization [2]. Our ultimate goal is to design a cost-effective and efficient RTLS abbrev not defined within the constraints identified in our previous paper [3] for a Healthcare environment. Previous work by [4] also evaluated the technologies for indoor RTLS as well as identified the methods used in determining locations. This paper determines the possible range and throughput imitative of quantitative technological evaluations by [5] with Bluetooth LE in different scenarios of a Healthcare environment. Future work will explore Bluetooth LE mesh networking for indoor localization to enhance scalability and detection range.

The rest of the paper is organized as follows. Section 2 illustrates the basic concepts of indoor localization. Section 3 defines the methodology used to conduct the

© Springer International Publishing AG, part of Springer Nature 2018
O. Gervasi et al. (Eds.): ICCSA 2018, LNCS 10963, pp. 261–274, 2018.
https://doi.org/10.1007/978-3-319-95171-3_21

experiments and obtain the results. In Sect. 4, the authors discuss the results obtained from the experiments. After that conclusions and future work are discussed.

2 Literature Review

2.1 Technologies and Techniques for RTLS

A number of different technologies have been tested for use in RTLS. However, due to the availability of newer technologies, the best technology within the constraints need to identify for indoor RTLS. [4] evaluated the most popular technologies of RTLS published in recent peer-reviewed works with the most appropriate attributes in terms of Real-Time Location System (RTLS) within literature and the healthcare exemplar in order to assess these technologies. In addition to the exemplar of a hospital survey, data of 23 US hospitals [6] was used in the evaluation process. In the previous paper, we investigated technologies such as WiFi, Bluetooth and RFID and determined evaluation criteria cost [7], energy consumption [8], detection range [7], size and accuracy [9] based on this literature. Although accuracy was identified as one of the attributes, it will be used in future research as this paper comprises preliminary work leading to future research. The health care sector has other constraints such as electromagnetic interference [10, 11] which we now mitigate with low battery transmission level but space constraints limited our selection to the most appropriate and the most common attributes. Other constraints do exist but were not identified as most common. An important example within a health care environment is electromagnetic interference especially in Industrial, Scientific and Medical (ISM) radio bands [10] which can be mitigated with the lowest transmission levels.

Attempts to mitigate these common constraints using popular RTLS technologies researched by [4] include Radio Frequency Identification Devices (RFID), Bluetooth classic, Bluetooth LE, Zigbee, and Wi-Fi. Lee et al. compared BLE and ZigBee technologies using a single fixed distance of one meter but did not have conclusive results indicating which technology is better as wireless transmission is greatly affected by practical situations, such as the realistic environment interferences [5]. Furthermore, this experiment did not provide measurements of aspects such as RSSI or throughput beyond this fixed distance, both measurements which are needed for a proper network technology evaluation for the fixed distance.

A number of different methodologies exist to increase the accuracy of location determination within RTLS, the most popular being the RSSI technique which increases accuracy to 1–2 (meters) [12]. An available improvement of RSSI involves a Kamlan filter which increases Bluetooth accuracy to 0.47 m but at the cost of increased size (due to larger storage requirements) and increased power consumption due to increased computational cost [7]. As can be seen, these RSSI and Kamlan filter techniques adds to the size form factor for Bluetooth and energy consumption.

An example of a Bluetooth system is the Bluetooth Local Infotainment Point (BLIP) [13] which is a managed network offering access to LAN/WAN via Bluetooth [14]. Such a network will require a number of BLIP nodes to which the bluetooth devices will connect to due to its limited range. These bluetooth nodes then provide access to the LAN/WAN. With the advancement of Bluetooth LE such nodes will be minimized or eliminated depending on the environment.

Bluetooth classic also has drawbacks in crowded areas due to signal attenuation and interference. Bluetooth classic can transfer large quantities of data, but consumes battery life quickly and more costly than Bluetooth LE or other indoor localisations technologies [15]. In addition accuracy for RTLS differs at a cost in term of power consumption, size of the device, and other factors. This gave birth to Bluetooth low energy (BLE) suitable to exchange little amounts of data consuming lower energy at a cheaper cost.

2.2   Bluetooth LE

Bluetooth Low Energy (BLE) is the power-version of Bluetooth that was built for the Internet of Things (IoT) making it perfect for devices that run for long periods on power sources, such as coin cell batteries or energy-harvesting devices [16]. One of the two systems of this version is Bluetooth low energy which transmits small packets of data whilst consuming significantly less power than the previous version of Bluetooth [8]. A BLE system typically consists of a stationery anchor to detect the tags, a tag and the location engine to calculate the location [17]. BLE is an improvement and a later version of Bluetooth (BT) offering several advantages such as smaller form factor, lower cost, and extended coverage. The point-to-point communication of the current BLE nodes has only limited coverage over a short range. Hence the proposal of a wireless mesh multi-hop network that has multiple nodes that are capable of communicating with each other to enable routing of packets to extend this limited coverage as a possible solution [18]. This distance can be extended further with the combination of current technologies that are more efficient.

Bluetooth® 5, released on 6 December 2016, is a transformative update on previous versions that significantly increases the range, speed and broadcast messaging capacity of Bluetooth applications. This version quadruples range and doubles speed of low energy connections while increasing the capacity of connectionless data broadcasts by eight times [19, 20]. These will impact on reliability, robustness, responsiveness. This latest version will have quadruple the range, double the speed and an increase of data broadcasting capacity by 800% over Bluetooth Classic [21].

This earlier Bluetooth Classic version uses 79 channels with 1 MHz spacing whilst Bluetooth LE uses 40 channels with 2 MHz spacing in the unlicensed industrial, scientific and medical (ISM) band of 2.4 GHz. The range for Bluetooth LE extends from 2402 MHz (RF channel 0; logical channel 37) to 2480 MHz (RF channel 39; logical channel 39). Three channels (logical 37, 38 and 39) are so-called advertising channels; logical channels 0 to 36 are data channels. The advertising channels are positioned so that they are not disturbed by the non-overlapping WLAN channels 1, 6 and 11 in the ISM band, see Fig. 1. Bluetooth LE now can provide the higher transmission speeds as a result of the increased 2402 MHz wider channels as compared to the Bluetooth classic 1 MHz channels. In addition to higher transmission speeds, more data can be transmitted within these channels as a result of the higher transmission frequency.

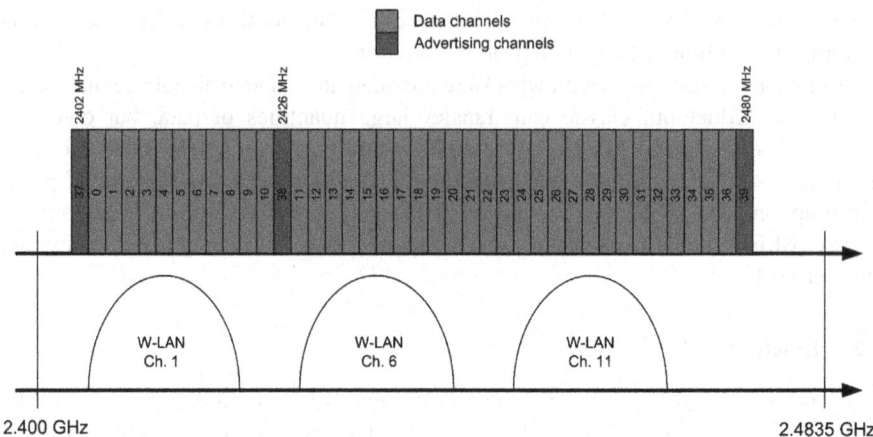

Fig. 1. Bluetooth LE channels.

2.3 Use of Bluetooth LE in Healthcare

In order to understand the technologies, use in indoor RTLS on must look at the early developments in this domain such as the RADAR system. This system was one of the first developed indoor positioning systems that use radio beacons and Received Signal Strength Indicator (RSSI) measurements for localization [2]. A number of authors have used RSSI for indoor location together with various methods such as triangulation, trilateration, fingerprinting to improve its accuracy. These different methods are required to improve the range as obstructions such as partitions, walls etc. cause degradation of the signal strength and in some cases completely block the signal, hence the need to use other methods for location determination [22].

3 Methodology

Our approach was to use Bluetooth LE to propose a cost-effective indoor RTLS solution with low power consumption, scalability, and long detection range. In order to determine the maximum range that can be obtained within the constraints, we used experimental methods to mimic the Healthcare environment given a Bluetooth LE v5 signal transmitted at the lowest energy level of −20dBm. The aim of this experiment is to determine the maximum usable range indoors at the clear line of sight, as well as through obstructions such as through glass door, dry wall and brick wall. Such obstructions represent partitions that would separate offices, wards, passages etc. in an actual healthcare facility, hence representing as close as possible the actual environment. This methodology has sections that describe in detail the hardware selection and software configuration and the environment used for the experiment.

The experiment used the transmitted power level as independent variables. The power level was varied from −20 dBm to 4 dBm to establish the ranges through the different obstructions. The dependent variables were distance and obstructions resulting in different RSSI measured at the receiver. Using these variables, the following steps were used during the experiment:

Step 1: Measure and label the different predetermined distances.

Step 2: Setup the software on the PDK's.

Step 3: Place the receiver PDK at a fixed starting location.

Step 4: Place the broadcaster PDK at the first measured point.

Step 5: Commence measurement of the received RSSI value. If the lowest transmit level is reached or there is no reception of the broadcasted packets go to step 7.

Step 6: Decrease the transmit level of the broadcaster and go to step 5.

Step 7: Move broadcaster PDK to next measured point, reset the transmit level to 4 dBm and repeat step 5.

Step 8: Stop when the maximum possible distance is reached, and measurements are unusable, or PDKs are disconnected.

3.1 Hardware Selection and Software Configuration

The hardware used for this experiment were two Nordic nRF 52840 Preview Development Kits (PDK). Segger Embedded Studio was used for application development and testing as well as deployment onto the nRF 52840 BLE System on Chip (Soc). The selection of this latest BLE Soc was based on the many advantages identified by [20]. Nordic was selected as the preferred supplier due to its price advantage, feature set and availability over comparable features through Texas Instruments.

The software was set up to identify the receiver and broadcaster by pressing buttons 3 and 4 on the PDK respectively. Furthermore, buttons 1 and 2 were used to decrease and increase the broadcast level by the predefined level of 4 dBm. The Physical (PHY) layer of the Nordic nRF52832 and prior Soc's transmission was limited to 1 Ms/s as per the Nordic design specification [23]. With the advancement of technology, the latest NRF52840 Soc allows for the transmission of 1 Ms/s or 2 Ms/s. Our intention is to implement the Soc in a Healthcare environment and hence the decision to test up to the lowest transmission of −20 dBm to investigate the range through obstructions. Broadcasting at the lowest level will limit the interference on other equipment and allow for more devices to be used within the same bands. One of the PDK boards was set as the receiver whilst the other PDK board was set as the broadcaster. Given limited resources, we relied on a single receiver-broadcaster model. The broadcaster broadcasted at the level from 4 dBm to −20 dBm. This receiver PDK was connected to a laptop where Putty (a terminal emulator) was used to read the data from the USB interface. A minimum of 10 packets was received for each of the different levels for the different distances in order to obtain an average reading. If the results showed a wide variance, the plan was to repeat the experiment multiple times. Once the data was captured, the averages were calculated and reported.

3.2 Experiment Environment

The two different venues selected together with the measured distances to conduct the experiment mimicked different areas and hence is a close replica of the Healthcare environment similar to other research conducted [24]. The lecture venues could be considered as two large open plan patient wards; whilst the computer labs could represent wards (semiprivate, private, clinic etc.) separated by an office or passage. The layout of the lecture venues and the computer labs are depicted in Figs. 2 and 3 respectively.

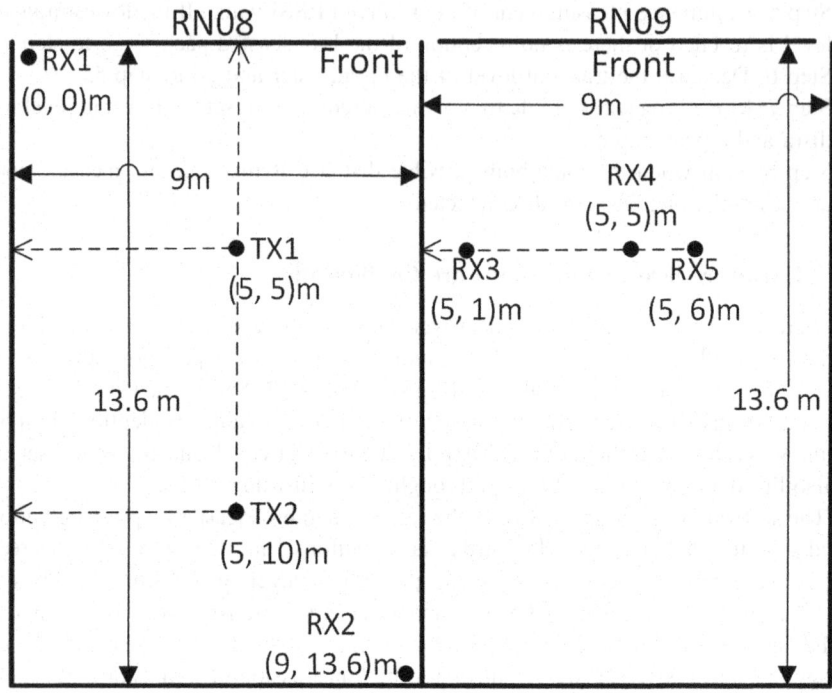

Fig. 2. Lecture Venues RN08 and RN09

The experiment comprised of two lecture venues (RN08 and RN09) constructed of solid brick wall of approximately 21 cm in thickness and measured 9 m by 13 m. The points in Fig. 2 are labeled using the Transmit (TX) or Receive (RX) together with the coordinates from the top left corner. For example, "RX1, (0, 0) meters" means the receiver is placed at top left corner while "TX2, (5, 10) meters" means that the transmitter is placed 5 m from the left wall and 10 m from the front wall. For the first test the two receivers were placed at the corners of the venue RN08 diagonally opposite each other (points RX1 and RX2) whilst the broadcaster was placed at points TX1 and TX2 in the same venue as depicted in Fig. 2. The fixed desks were used to place the broadcaster in the lecture venue. For the second test one of the receivers was placed at position RX1 in venue RN08 whilst the second receiver was placed in venue RN09 at positions RX3, RX4 and RX5. The broadcaster was placed at position TX1 in venue RN08. Data was collected at the measured points and across the brick wall obstruction.

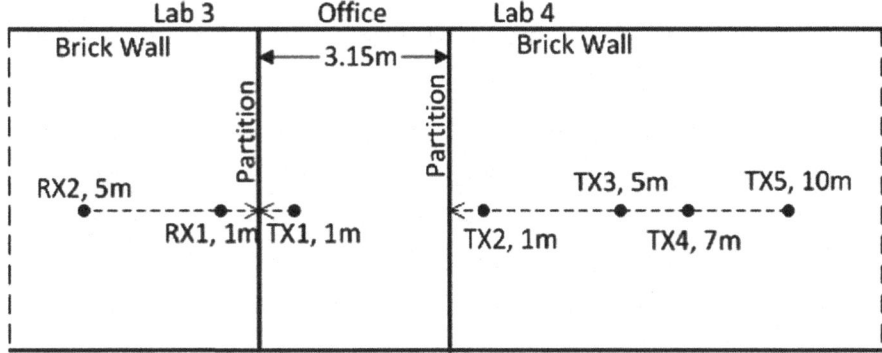

Fig. 3. Lab 3 and Lab 4

These second venue was the computer labs separated by an office with partitions that allowed for testing through double dry walls as well as double glass panels. The partition was made up of dry wall from the floor to about midway and then glass to the ceiling. The receiver was placed at points RX1 and RX2 i.e. 1 m and 5 m away from one of the partitions. The transmitter was placed at position TX1 i.e. 1 m across the first partition and them positions TX2 to TX5 i.e. 1, 5, 7 and 10 m from the second partition. These transmit and receive positions in the two labs as well as the office in between are indicated in Fig. 3. Data was collected from these positions across one partition and across two partitions of both dry wall and glass.

4 Results

Data was collected in the lecture venues as well as the computer labs. Figures 4, 5, 6, 7, 8, 9, 10 and 11 depict the average RSSI values received through the different partitions for the different broadcast levels. The data for the different attributes for the different venues are groups together and indicate in their respective attribute graphs due to space constraints. The different colors representing the obstacles are indicated in the legend.

In the lecture venues the measurements were taken until the connectivity and transmission was unacceptable and broadcast packets were not received. The measurements noted whilst the PDK boards were placed at different angles were not significantly different. Therefore, additional measurements were not considered in the final analysis. The results obtained from lecture venue RN08 is indicated in Fig. 4. The receivers indicate a consistent decrease in the levels received as the transmit level was decreased. From transmit position TX1 in Fig. 2 the received level indicated by receiver 1 (RX 1) is the consistently higher that that received at that received by receiver 2 (RX 2) as the receiver 2 was further away from the broadcaster. The broadcast packets were received up to a lowest level of −20 dBm.

The results obtained from when the transmitter was moved to position TX2 is indicated in Fig. 5 The lower levels received by receiver 1 at positon RX1 is expected as the receiver is further away compared to receiver 2 at position RX2. The receive levels of both RX1 and RX2 are consistently lower as the broadcast levels decreased.

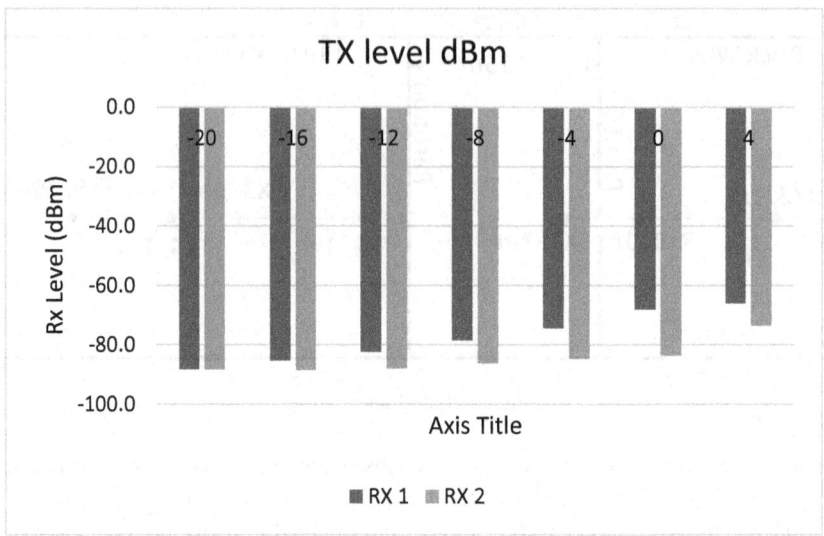

Fig. 4. RSSI levels received at from position TX1

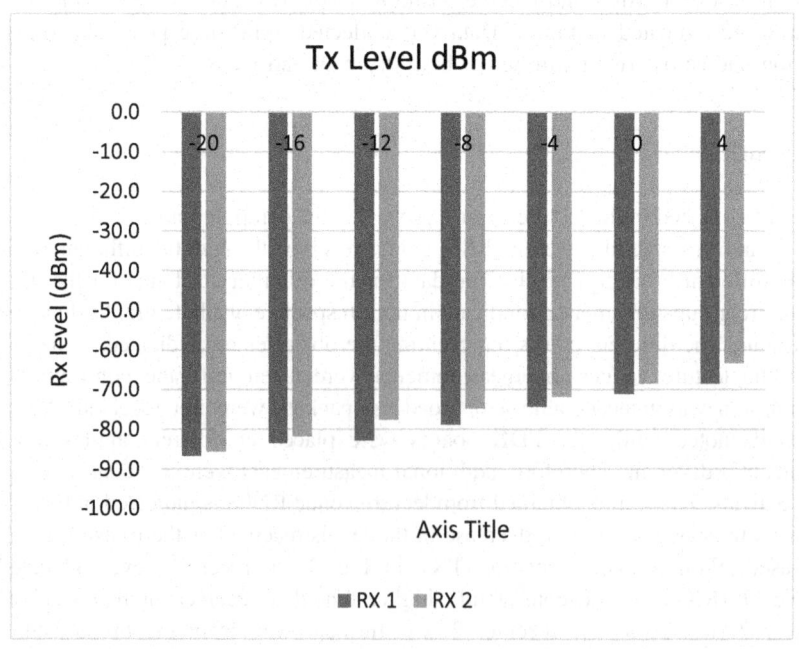

Fig. 5. RSSI levels received from position TX2

The results obtained between the two lecture venues is indicated in Fig. 6. The broadcast packets were received in lecture venue RN09 5 m away from the wall at position RX5 depicted in Fig. 2. No reception was received beyond position RX5 in Fig. 2. At position RX5 the receive level was −75.7 dBm for a transmit level of 4 dBm whilst a receive level was −87.7 dBm for a transmit level of −12 dBm.

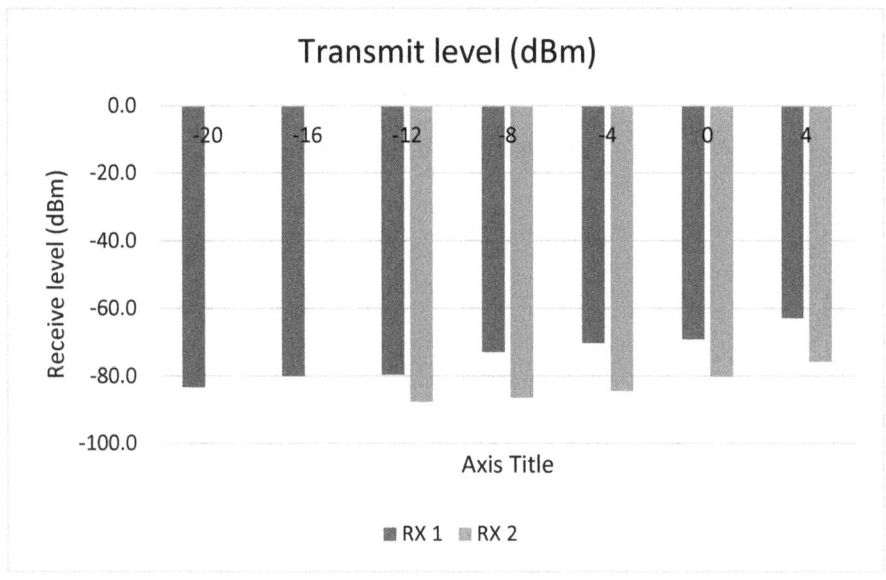

Fig. 6. RSSI levels between two lecture venues

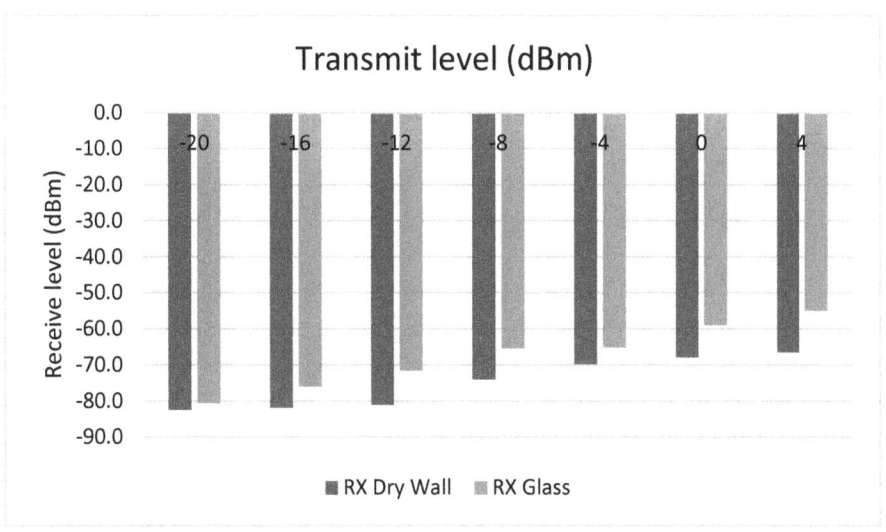

Fig. 7. RSSI levels between TX1 and RX1 across single partition

In the second venue depicted in Fig. 3 the first set of readings was taken between positions TX1 and RX1 separated by a single partition. The two different types of partitions used were dry wall and glass and their respective measurements are indicated in Fig. 7.

The transmitter was then moved to position TX2 in Fig. 3 separating the transmitter and receiver by double partitions. Measurements indicated in Fig. 8 were taken using both the dry wall and glass. A decrease in receive levels is noted for both glass and dry wall partitions as the transmit level decreases.

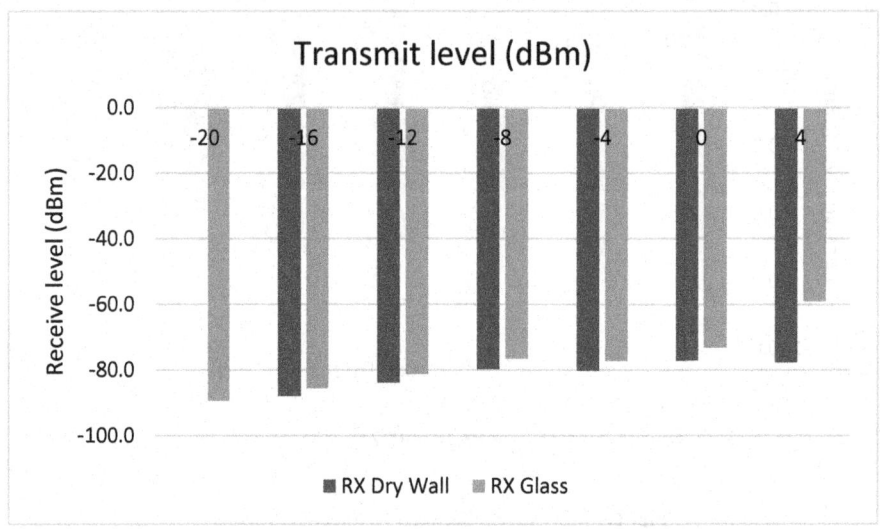

Fig. 8. RSSI levels between TX2 and RX1 across double partition

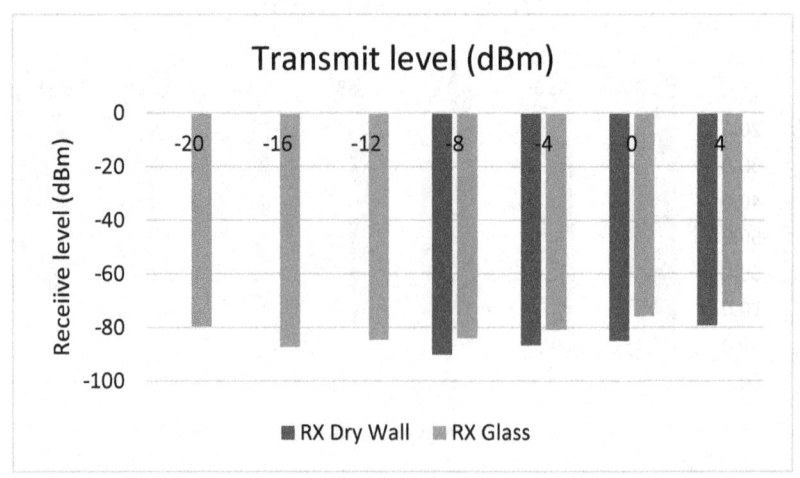

Fig. 9. RSSI levels between TX2 and RX2 across double partition

The receiver was then moved to position RX2 and the transmitter remained at position TX2. Readings were taken across the double partitions are indicated in Fig. 9. A decrease in received signal strength is noted from a transmit level of 4 dBm to −8 dBm. However, the packets were not received for a transmit level of lower than −8 dBm through the dry wall partitions but were received through the glass partitions. The transmitter was then moved to position TX3, a distance of 5 m from the partition. This setup used the transmitter and receiver 5 m away from the partitions with the office in between as indicated in Fig. 3. There received levels indicated in Fig. 10 are lower than that compared to transmit level from position TX2. The signal further deteriorated through the dry wall partitions restricting any level lower than −8 dBm.

The transmitter was moved to positon TX5 10 m away from the partition is indicate in Fig. 3. Since no packets were received from this position, the transmitter was moved closer to the partition until a usable signal level was received at position RX2. With the transmitter TX4 7 m away from the partition an acceptable level for packets was

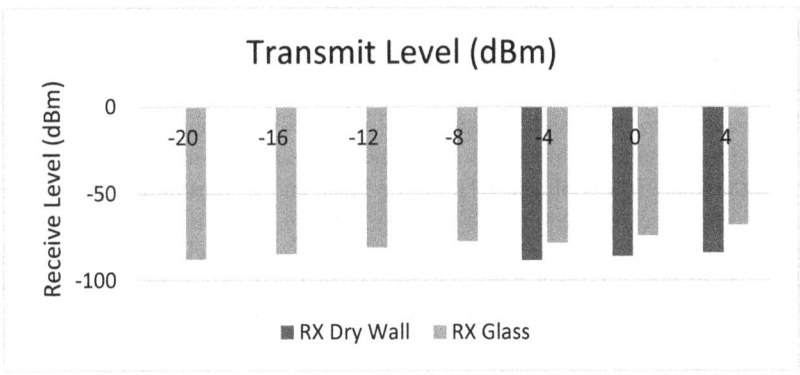

Fig. 10. RSSI levels between TX3 and RX2 across double partition

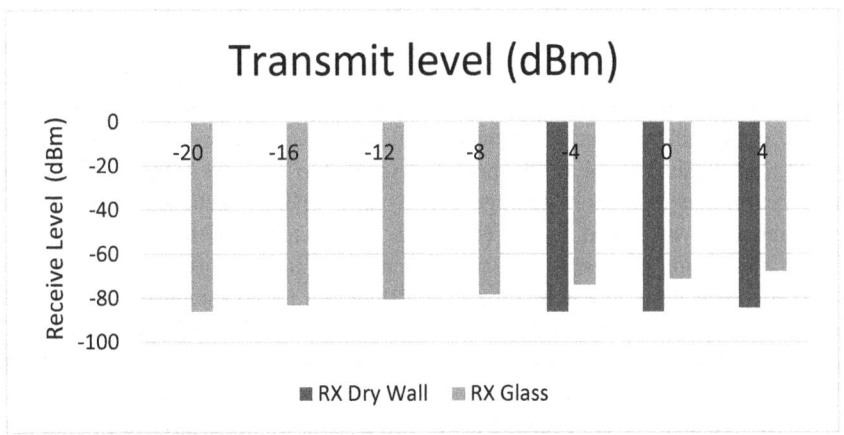

Fig. 11. RSSI levels between TX4 and RX2 across double partition

received at position RX2. High levels were received through the dry wall partitions for a transmit level of 4 dBm to −4 dBm. The received levels through glass decreased consistently as the transmit level decreased. These transmit and receive levels are depicted in Fig. 11.

5 Discussion of Results

The reception of broadcast packets general follows a linear pattern. However, in some cases a nonlinear level is measured suggesting the possibility of potential interfering variables in this experiment. Given the constraints these interfering variable could not be isolated within this study.

Results from tests carried within lecture venue RN08 shown in Fig. 4 indicate that there is a difference in RSSI levels between the two receivers. These differences are significant and noticeable at the higher transmitted levels and smaller at the lower levels. The results obtained from the test performed between the two venues RN08 and RN09 depicted in Fig. 6 show that the Bluetooth low energy signal can penetrate solid walls. The signal can be received up to a distance of approximately 6 m even at low transmit levels of −12 dBm.

The variance in the results represent an actual environment as we have noted a pattern within certain environments and random changes at certain distances. This indicates that there is a nonlinear relationship between the transmitter and the receiver as distance increases. However, RSSI results indicate that it is possible to identify a Bluetooth device with a degree of accuracy through a solid brick wall, double dry wall partitions or double glass partitions. The RSSI level was measured in anticipation of future work to use this aspect as part of location determination.

6 Conclusion and Future Work

The primary focus of this paper was to test the latest Bluetooth LE v5 PDK's signal penetration through different types of partitions in an indoor environment for future use in a Healthcare environment for e.g. in a RTLS. However, an accurate and reliable RTLS system within the constraints of the health care environment requires a well-designed architecture. The results obtained through double partitions are promising to be used in a Health care environment for data transmission as well as RTLS.

RTLS in health care has the potential to enable efficient location of patients, employees and equipment. Although RTLS have realized benefits in some cases, further research was called for to reduce the serious technical impediments such as obstacle obstruction of signals to its implementation including asset management [6]. As a consequence, we researched the latest Bluetooth LE to establish through experimentation the possible range as well as the level of penetration through obstacles. The coordinate system was used to depict the transmitter and receiver as this will lead to the RTLS for the health care sector. Bluetooth LE can be configured into a low cost low energy network architecture enabling lower energy consumption [25] and extending the range. A combination of multiple methods such as triangulation, fingerprinting [26], block chain architecture and repeater tags (tags configured to forward messages) will be used to increase the location accuracy whilst minimizing energy consumption. Further research will need to be done especially with regards RSSI measurements with their distances to expand on this paper's findings The use of BLE devices, with low power consumption will extend battery life thereby reducing maintenance [5]. Due to the high volume of patients as well as the size of hospitals, especially those in the public sector, cost is an important constraint.

Some of these challenges such as network range can be realized by using mesh networks as well as intermediate sensors to link to others in the near vicinity. With the latest technology used unlike its predecessors the Bluetooth LE devices can form a mesh network to extend the network with the lowest possible energy consumption. A more detailed experiment with different values for variables such as transmission power levels, data packet size etc. will be conducted for improved and accurate performance in terms of indoor real-time location. The results of this will be published in future articles. Furthermore, a prototype will be setup in a Healthcare environment to test viability of the processes and newly designed architecture.

References

1. Wang, Y., Ye, Q., Cheng, J., Wang, L.: RSSI-based bluetooth indoor localization. In: 2015 11th International Conference on Moile Ad-hoc and Sensor Networks (MSN), pp. 165–171. IEEE (2015)
2. Thaljaoui, A., Val, T., Nasri, N., Brulin, D.: BLE localization using RSSI measurements and iRingLA. In: 2015 IEEE International Conference on Industrial Technology (ICIT), pp. 2178–2183. IEEE (2015)
3. Pancham, J., Millham, R., Fong, S.J.: Assessment of feasible methods used by the health care industry for real time location. In: Federated Conference on Computer Science and Information Systems, Poznań, Poland (2017)
4. Pancham, J., Millham, R., Fong, S.J.: Evaluation of Real Time Location System technologies in the health care sector. In: 2017 17th International Conference on Computational Science and Its Applications (ICCSA), pp. 1–7. IEEE (2017)
5. Lee, J.-S., Dong, M.-F., Sun, Y.-H.: A preliminary study of low power wireless technologies: ZigBee and bluetooth low energy. In: 2015 IEEE 10th Conference on Industrial Electronics and Applications (ICIEA), pp. 135–139. IEEE (2015)
6. Fisher, J.A., Monahan, T.: Evaluation of real-time location systems in their hospital contexts. Int. J. Med. Inform. **81**(10), 705–712 (2012)
7. Tsang, P.Y.P., Wu, C.H., Ip, W.H., Tse, Y.K.: A bluetooth-based indoor positioning system: a simple and rapid approach. Ann. J. IIE (HK) **35**(2014), 11–26 (2015)
8. Yu, B., Xu, L., Li, Y.: Bluetooth Low Energy (BLE) based mobile electrocardiogram monitoring system. In: 2012 International Conference on Information and Automation (ICIA), pp. 763–767. IEEE (2012)
9. Deng, Z., Yu, Y., Yuan, X., Wan, N., Yang, L.: Situation and development tendency of indoor positioning. China Commun. **10**(3), 42–55 (2013)
10. Alemdar, H., Ersoy, C.: Wireless sensor networks for healthcare: a survey. Comput. Netw. **54**(15), 2688–2710 (2010)
11. Yao, W., Chu, C.H., Li, Z.: The adoption and implementation of RFID technologies in healthcare: a literature review. J. Med. Syst. **36**(6), 3507–3525 (2012)

12. Bal, M., Xue, H., Shen, W., Ghenniwa, H.: A 3-D indoor location tracking and visualization system based on wireless sensor networks. In: 2010 IEEE International Conference on Systems Man and Cybernetics (SMC), pp. 1584–1590. IEEE (2010)
13. Kolodziej, K.W., Hjelm, J.: Local Positioning Systems: LBS Applications and Services. CRC Press, Boca Raton (2017)
14. Deak, G., Condell, K., Condell, J.: A survey of active and passive indoor localisation systems. Comput. Commun. **35**(16), 1939–1954 (2012)
15. Zaim, D., Bellafkih, M.: Bluetooth Low Energy (BLE) based geomarketing system. In: 2016 11th International Conference on Intelligent Systems: Theories and Applications (SITA), pp. 1–6. IEEE (2016)
16. Bluetooth Low Energy, 2016, 25 May 2017. https://www.bluetooth.com/what-is-bluetooth-technology/how-it-works/low-energy
17. Han, G., Klinker, G.J., Ostler, D., Schneider, A.: Testing a proximity-based location tracking system with Bluetooth Low Energy tags for future use in the OR. In: 2015 17th International Conference on E-health Networking, Application & Services (HealthCom), pp. 17–21. IEEE (2015)
18. Raza, S., Misra, P., He, Z., Voigt, T.: Building the Internet of Things with bluetooth smart. Ad Hoc Netw. **57**, 19–31 (2016)
19. Bluetooth 5, 2016, 25 May 2017. https://www.bluetooth.com/what-is-bluetooth-technology/how-it-works/bluetooth5
20. B. S. I. Group: Bluetooth 5 Quadruples Range, Doubles Speed, Increases Data Broadcasting Capacity by 800% (2016). https://www.bluetooth.com/news/pressreleases/2016/06/16/-bluetooth-5-quadruples-rangedoubles-speedincreases-data-broadcasting-capacity-by-800
21. Schultz, B.: From Cable Replacement to the IoT Bluetooth 5, White Paper, December 2016 (2016)
22. Abdullah, M.W., Fafoutis, X., Mellios, E., Klemm, M., Hilton, G.S.: Investigation into off-body links for wrist mounted antennas in bluetooth systems. In: Antennas & Propagation Conference (LAPC), 2015 Loughborough, pp. 1–5. IEEE (2015)
23. nRF52832 Product Specification v1.4 (2016)
24. Larranaga, J., Muguira, L., Lopez-Garde, J.-M., Vazquez, J.-I.: An environment adaptive ZigBee-based indoor positioning algorithm. In: 2010 International Conference on Indoor Positioning and Indoor Navigation (IPIN), pp. 1–8. IEEE (2010)
25. Ahmad, S., Lu, R., Ziaullah, M.: Bluetooth an optimal solution for personal asset tracking: a comparison of bluetooth, RFID and miscellaneous anti-lost tracking technologies. Int. J. u e-Serv. Sci. Technol. **8**(3), 179–188 (2015)
26. Jachimczyk, B., Dziak, D., Kulesza, W.J.: Using the fingerprinting method to customize RTLS based on the AoA ranging technique. Sensors **16**(6), 876 (2016)

A Business Intelligent Framework to Evaluate Prediction Accuracy for E-Commerce Recommenders

Shalini Gupta and Veer Sain Dixit[✉]

Department of Computer Science, Atma Ram Sanatan Dharma College,
University of Delhi, New Delhi, India
{sgupta,vsdixit}@arsd.du.ac.in

Abstract. It is important for on-line retailers to better understand the interest of users for creating personalized recommendations to survive in the competitive market. Implicit details of user that is extracted from click stream data plays a vital role in making recommendations. These indicators reflect users' items of interest. The browsing behavior, frequency of item visits, time taken to read details of an item are few measures that predict users' interest for a particular item. After identifying these strong attributes, users are clustered on the basis of context clicks such as promotional and discounted offers and interest of the individual user is predicted for the particular context in user-context preference matrix. After clustering analysis is performed, neighborhood formation process is conducted using collaborative filtering on the basis of item category such as regular or branded items which depicts users' interest in that particular category. Using these matrices, computational burden and processing time to generate recommendations are greatly reduced. To determine the effectiveness of proposed work, an experimental evaluation has been done which clearly depicts the better performance of the system as compared to conventional approaches.

Keywords: Personalized recommendations · Implicit details · Click stream
Preference matrix · Collaborative filtering

1 Introduction

While interacting with the World Wide Web, a user is surrounded by a large number of items. This requires the user to get connected to personalization tools which are capable of searching items of interest. These tools help the users in their decision- making process. One such tool that assists in making decisions is Recommender Systems (RSs) [1]. RS are knowledge-based systems that emerged as personalization tool for users. Initially, the focus was on combining various recommendation techniques to improve the quality of recommendations. Further, focus was on how to use explicit features [2–4] of users that are extracted from ratings, queries and purchase status.

Conventional RS are based on explicit data obtained from users in the form of rankings, queries, and reviews. Moreover, users' interest in an item is predicted on the basis of binary purchase data. If an item has been purchased in the past, then the user is having a higher preference for an item as compared to items that are not purchased.

© Springer International Publishing AG, part of Springer Nature 2018
O. Gervasi et al. (Eds.): ICCSA 2018, LNCS 10963, pp. 275–288, 2018.
https://doi.org/10.1007/978-3-319-95171-3_22

However, these binary results do not depict the preference of a user for item not purchased as many other reasons affects the purchase such as low on time, budget, etc. Thus implicit details [5] of the user are extracted based on click sequences and items are assigned a preference level according to users' interest.

The work done in this study emphasizes on developing a recommender framework for generating individual recommendations based on browsing behavior that is extracted from click stream [5, 6] sessions with no interaction from user side. The refinement is based on preferences of user using implicit multi-criteria attributes that are traced from web logs.

The proposed work performs the following task. Click stream data sessions are processed to extract strong attributes of users. These attributes justify users' interest in an item and have an impact on the purchase of an item such as reading time taken to view details of an item, a number of visits made to a particular item, cart placement status of an item and purchase status of an item, etc. After the attributes are identified, users are clustered on the basis of their interest in particular click context category. These click context categories are promotional offers, discounted offers, regular offers and many more. After clustering is performed, target users' neighbors are identified within these clusters. Like-minded users [7, 8] are discovered based on their interest in item brands. Finally, the prediction for those items is made that are not viewed by the target user and top-N list is generated.

To illustrate the effectiveness and performance of RS, experiments are carried out on click stream data of a commercial website. Evaluation metrics used clearly shows that the proposed RS is giving better results than that of conventional ones.

The rest of the article is divided as follows. In Sect. 2, the related literature regarding RS techniques and problems faced are thoroughly reviewed. Section 3 describes the click sequence of users based on click contexts and item brands. An algorithm is discussed that predicts items' preference based on these sequences. In Sect. 4, the performance of the proposed algorithm is discussed based on various evaluation metrics. Finally, Sect. 5 presents conclusions and makes suggestions for the direction of future research.

2   Related Work

The research interest in the field of RS has gained popularity because these systems help the users in their decision-making process. These decisions are based on user previous history of purchases or the ratings given by them. This section presents an overview of recommendation techniques that employs user navigational behavior to predict preferences. Two things were evident from the literature survey on RS. Firstly, the focus was not only given on generation of recommendations through explicit data but also through the implicit behaviour of users. Secondly, many methods have been discussed which help RS to achieve their goal of generating good quality recommendations.

For an e-commerce website, recommendations are provided based on conventional techniques such as collaborative filtering (CF) or content based filtering (CBF). CF algorithm attempts to identify similarities between entities (users or items) based on the interaction history and purchase status of items. Recommendations are made based on data extracted (explicit or implicit) such as ratings given by users, queries answered for items purchased and click stream behavior of user while searching for an item. Similar users are identified sharing common preferences for an item using measures such as Pearson correlation (PC), constrained Pearson Correlation (CPC), cosine vector (CV) similarity, Jaccard coefficient etc. and top-N items are recommended based on these similarity measures. Major steps involved in CF technique are as mentioned. (i) Based on the feedback/rating information given by a user for each item, a brief user profile is constructed. (ii) Like-minded users [9, 10] are grouped together that have share same interest as that of the target user. This similarity can be calculated using the measures such as PC, CPC, cosine vector or distance-based similarity. (iii) Averagely weighted preference for an item is calculated as it is liked by neighbors. The ratings can also be predicted using probabilistic model or machine learning model that is built from a large set of rating samples. These types of predictive measures involve *Memory-based predictions* (Predicting preferences using measures such as average or weighted sum) and *Model-based predictions* (Predicting preferences using probabilistic or machine learning model).

Apart from its usage, the approach also suffers from few limitations. *New user problem* [11, 12] is a drawback of CF in which system faces difficulty in recommending items to users who have never rated any items in the past. Similarly, items which are new in the market are recommended less as they are never rated before, is categorized as *new item problem* [13]. If the number of items and users are exceptionally high then most of the items are not sufficiently rated by users. Thus customer-item utility matrix becomes sparse which leads to poor recommendations. This is commonly termed as the *Sparsity problem.*

CBF systems, on the other hand, as their name implies, are the recommendations based on content of the items. CBF approach suggests items based on high similarity between items to recommend and items highly rated. A similarity between user and item profile is calculated and top-N items with high similarity score are recommended i.e. they suggest items based on high similarity between items to recommend and items already purchased. Major steps involved in CBF approach are as mentioned. (i) Profile of each item is constructed based on its attributes preferred by users. (ii) A user profile is built from set of attributes of items that each user purchased. (iii) Similarity between user and item profiles is calculated using similarity measures. (iv) Finally, Top-N items with high similarity scores are recommended.

CBF also suffers from certain limitations. Recommendations are not accurate if item profiles are incomplete as it is not easy to obtain sufficient number of features. This type of problem is commonly known as *insufficient feature problem*. Another form of limitation is *over-specialization problem* [13] in which recommendations are similar to the items purchased in past. In *unusual user problem*, users whose purchasing behavior is not uniform get poor recommendations.

Personalized RS are helpful in delivering the right item to right customer. The decreasing cost of data storage and preprocessing leads to use of RS on larger scale. Keeping the track of customer navigational behavior while browsing e-commerce website is also helpful in providing accurate recommendations. Sellers on commercial websites trace the navigational behavior of customers and purchases made by them to recommend good items and enhance their sales. Social websites analyze the contact lists to recommend new friends. Mobile application recommenders help in suggesting new applications to download for similar users.

Another form of recommendation technique is hybridization of recommenders. Hybrid recommenders [14, 15] combine collaborative and content-based approaches into one unified approach. Hybrid method combines the features different algorithms to remove limitations of said approaches and gives more accurate recommendations.

In conventional methods, recommendations are made on the basis of explicit data i.e. ratings provided by user. However for e-commerce websites, techniques are suggested on click stream behavior in which users surfing path is traced and used in recommendation. This implicit data consist of time spend on each webpage, cart placement binary data, surfing behavior (searching or browsing), number of visits to a webpage and many more. Customer's sequential patterns are also analyzed in many studies to find similarity among users and make good recommendations. Both techniques are good in one way or the other. These techniques does not work well with binary purchase data i.e. purchase = 1 or no-purchase = 0. Instead of explicitly acquiring the customer ratings for specific items, their navigational behavior (i.e. implicit ratings) is traced. Detailed case studies of the clickstream data analysis from various e-commerce sites are carried out.

3   Structural Representation and Descriptive Statistics

3.1   Dataset

The dataset used in the proposed algorithm is of a big e-commerce retailer [16] in Europe that sells clothing, electronic gadgets and books etc. Users' clickstream path is traced to identify the strong attributes that indicates users interest in a particular item. The data is collected for one month and over 10 million of users visited the website and viewed 62546 items. After applying data cleaning and pre-processing steps using MATLAB R2013a only those users are selected who have clicked more than 70 items. A specific number of users and items are identified for recommendation as we need to find correlation among similar users. Thus a total of 57540 users are chosen to find preference ranking for 4300 items.

3.2   Item Classification and Implicit Feature Extraction

An e-commerce website categorizes its items in the form of a hierarchy as shown in Fig. 1. Customers click stream path is traced along this hierarchy and attributes are identified as in Table 1.

The click stream behavior of users is pre-processed to extract strong attributes that reflects users interest in a particular item. As shown in Table 2, the probability of purchase of an item after its cart placement is 85.5 (=562/657). The result shows that cart placed item is having higher tendency of purchase than those that are not placed in the cart. If an item is highly viewed then it has higher chances of purchase (0.38 > 0.33 or 0.08). Also if time spent on a particular item is more as compared to others then it has higher probability of purchase.

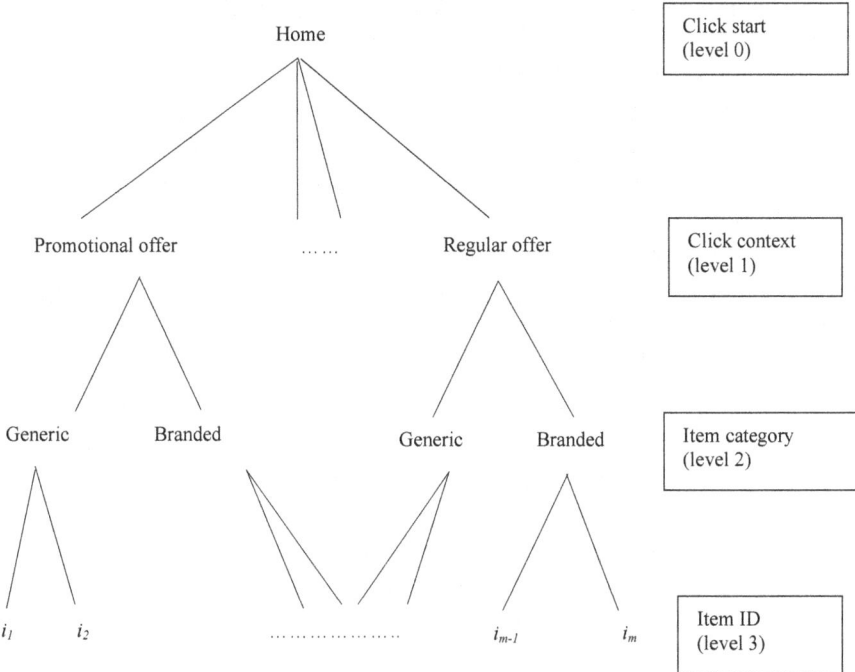

Fig. 1. E-commerce click sequence hierarchy

Table 1. Attributes identified from click stream path

Attributes	Description
Session ID	User Identification ID
Item ID	Item identification ID
Time stamp	Time and date at which user logged in and started browsing
Click context	Reflects user behavior
Cart placement	Item placed in the cart or not
Purchase	Item purchased or not
Price	Price of item purchased
Quantity	Quantity of purchased item

Table 3 presents the desired result which is justified using t-test as length of reading time is captured in seconds which is considered as continuous attribute. To verify the hypothesis that higher the time taken to view an item, the more is the probability of purchase is justified as difference between mean of purchase and no purchase at 5% significant level. Thus a longer reading time indicate higher chances of purchase made. The strong attributes that are identified from the click stream dataset are mentioned in Table 4.

Table 2. Probability of purchase for cart placement and view count

	Purchase = 1	Purchase = 0	Total
Cart placement			
Cart placement = 0	0	3643	3643
Cart placement = 1	562	95	657
Total	562	3738	4300
View count			
1 view	305	3277	3582
2–4 views	153	298	451
5 or more views	104	163	267
Total	562	3738	4300

Table 3. t-test results for Duration of Reading time (5% Significance Level)

	N	Mean	StdDev	StdErr	Pr > |t|
Duration of Visit					
Purchase = 1	562	62.19	142.60	8.86	<0.0001
Purchase = 0	3738	28.31	68.88	2.04	

Table 4. Strong attributes that justify user behavior

Attributes	Description	Variable type
View count	No. of times an item is visited	Discrete
Duration of visit	Total time for which the customer visited the item	Continuous
Click context	Reflects user behavior (whether user is interested in promotional offers or regular offers)	Numeric
Item category	Category to which item belongs (Regular or branded)	Numeric
Cart placement	Item placed in the cart or not	Binary
Purchase	Item purchased or not	Binary

3.3 Proposed Algorithm

The proposed work consists of following phases.

Phase 1: In this phase, customers are categorized on the basis of their browsing behavior. Most of the customers are interested in making purchases when e-commerce websites offers special promotional or discount offers. Customers who have made purchases in past on the basis of these types of offers are categorized accordingly. Individual user preference for particular context is calculated on the basis of their past purchases. "Customer-context preference matrix" is built by computing the frequency of clicks, number of cart placed items and total items purchased. The more purchases made from a particular context category reflects customers' interest in that particular context category. The three matrices are computed as shown in Fig. 2.

$$context_1 \ldots context_k \qquad context_1 \ldots context_k \qquad context_1 \ldots context_k$$

$$\begin{pmatrix} c_{11}^{11} & \cdots & c_{1k}^{11} \\ \vdots & \ddots & \vdots \\ c_{n1}^{11} & \cdots & c_{nk}^{11} \end{pmatrix} \qquad \begin{pmatrix} c_{11}^{12} & \cdots & c_{1k}^{12} \\ \vdots & \ddots & \vdots \\ c_{n1}^{12} & \cdots & c_{nk}^{12} \end{pmatrix} \qquad \begin{pmatrix} c_{11}^{13} & \cdots & c_{1k}^{13} \\ \vdots & \ddots & \vdots \\ c_{n1}^{13} & \cdots & c_{nk}^{13} \end{pmatrix}$$

(i) Viewed item (c^{11}) (ii) Cart placed item (c^{12}) (iii) Purchased item (c^{13})

Fig. 2. Customer-context preference matrix (C)

Here c^{11}, c^{12}, c^{13} represents the total count of items viewed, items placed in cart and items purchased respectively. Also c_{ij}^{mn} represents i^{th} user preference for j^{th} context in matrix c^{mn}. For example c_{11}^{12} represents 'user 1' preference for 'context 1' based on number of items placed in cart (as in c^{12}). Thus the weighted average preference of user i for context j based on the combined results of item viewed (c^{11}), cart placed item (c^{12}) and purchased item (c^{13}) is given by the customer-context preference matrix (C) which is calculated using Eq. 1.

$$C_{ij} = \frac{\propto_1 c_{ij}^{11} + \beta_1 c_{ij}^{12} + \gamma_1 c_{ij}^{13}}{\sum_{d=1}^{k} (\propto_1 c_{id}^{11} + \beta_1 c_{id}^{12} + \gamma_1 c_{id}^{13})} \tag{1}$$

Where $0 \leq \alpha_i, \beta_i, \gamma_i \leq 1$ and $\alpha_i + \beta_i + \gamma_i = 1$. If the number of context clicks are promotional offers and regular offers (i.e. k = 2), then customer-context preference matrix is given as in Fig. 3.

| promo offer | regular offer | promo offer | regular offer | promo offer | regular offer |

$$\begin{pmatrix} c_{11}^{11}(9) & c_{12}^{11}(3) \\ \vdots & \vdots \\ c_{n1}^{11} & c_{n2}^{11} \end{pmatrix} \qquad \begin{pmatrix} c_{11}^{12}(4) & c_{12}^{12}(1) \\ \vdots & \vdots \\ c_{n1}^{12} & c_{n2}^{12} \end{pmatrix} \qquad \begin{pmatrix} c_{11}^{13}(1) & c_{12}^{13}(0) \\ \vdots & \vdots \\ c_{n1}^{13} & c_{n2}^{13} \end{pmatrix}$$

(i) Viewed item (c^{11}) (ii) Cart placed item (c^{12}) (iii) Purchased item (c^{13})

Fig. 3. A sample of customer-context preference matrix (C)

Here, if user 1 views 9 items categorized under category 1 (promotional offer), places 4 of them in cart and purchase only 1, then user 1's preference for promotional context (k = 1) is calculated as shown in Eq. 2. (Assuming $\alpha_1 = 0.5, \beta_1 = 0.3, \gamma_1 = 0.2$)

$$C_{11} = \frac{0.5 \times 9 + 0.3 \times 4 + 0.2 \times 1}{(0.5 \times 9 + 0.3 \times 4 + 0.2 \times 1) + (0.5 \times 3 + 0.3 \times 1 + 0.2 \times 0)} = 0.766 \quad (2)$$

In the same manner, preference of all the users is calculated for all the click contexts. Also, the weighted sum of click contexts for each customer is 1.

Phase 2: In this phase, users' preference for particular item category is calculated on the basis of their past purchases. "Customer- item category preference matrix" is built by computing the frequency of clicks, number of cart placed items and total items purchased. The more purchases made from a particular item category reflects customers' interest in that particular item category (regular or branded items). Similar to phase 1, the three matrices are computed as shown in Fig. 4.

$$category_1 ....category_k$$

$$\begin{pmatrix} t_{11}^{11} & \cdots & t_{1k}^{11} \\ \vdots & \ddots & \vdots \\ t_{n1}^{11} & \cdots & t_{nk}^{11} \end{pmatrix}$$

(i) Viewed item (t^{11})

$$category_1 .....category_k$$

$$\begin{pmatrix} t_{11}^{12} & \cdots & t_{1k}^{12} \\ \vdots & \ddots & \vdots \\ t_{n1}^{12} & \cdots & t_{nk}^{12} \end{pmatrix}$$

(ii) Cart placed item (t^{12})

$$category_1 .....category_k$$

$$\begin{pmatrix} t_{11}^{13} & \cdots & t_{1k}^{13} \\ \vdots & \ddots & \vdots \\ t_{n1}^{13} & \cdots & t_{nk}^{13} \end{pmatrix}$$

(iii) Purchased item (t^{13})

Fig. 4. Customer-item category matrices (T)

Here t^{11}, t^{12}, t^{13} represents the total count of items viewed, items placed in cart and items purchased for particular item category respectively. Also t_{ij}^{mn} represents i^{th} user preference for j^{th} item category (regular or branded) in matrix t^{mn}. For example t_{11}^{12} represents 'user 1' preference for 'category 1' based on number of items placed in cart (as in t^{12}). Thus the weighted average preference of user i for category j based on the combined results of item viewed (t^{11}), cart placed item (t^{12}) and purchased item (t^{13}) is given by the customer- item category preference matrix (T) which is calculated as shown in Eq. 3.

$$T_{ij} = \frac{\alpha_2 \, t_{ij}^{11} + \beta_2 t_{ij}^{12} + \gamma_2 t_{ij}^{13}}{\sum_{d=1}^{k} (\alpha_2 \, t_{id}^{11} + \beta_2 t_{id}^{12} + \gamma_2 t_{id}^{13})} \quad (3)$$

Where $0 \leq \alpha_i, \beta_i, \gamma_i \leq 1$ and $\alpha_i + \beta_i + \gamma_i = 1$.

Phase 3: The k-means clustering is performed to group customers on the basis of data obtained from phase 1 i.e. customers are clustered on the basis of their click context preference (C). Based on customer- item category preference matrix (T), like-minded users are discovered within these clusters. These customers have similar purchase patterns as that of target user u^t. Thus the time taken in neighborhood formation process is reduced as only clustered users' preferences are taken into account (Fig. 5).

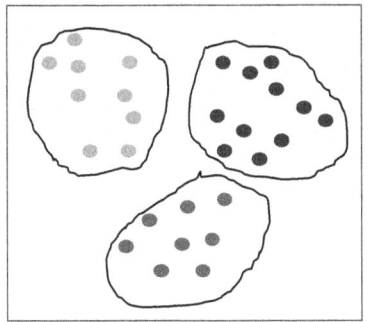 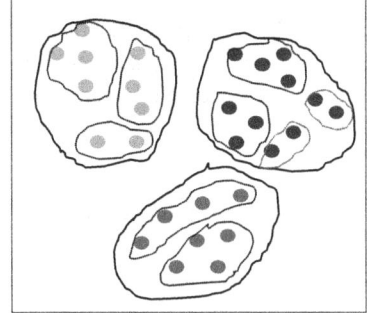

Fig. 5. Clustering (using matrix C) and neighborhood formation (using matrix T) process

Similarity among customers is approximated using measures such as Pearson correlation (PC), constrained Pearson correlation (CPC) and cosine vector (CV) as defined in Eqs. (4–6).

$$PC_{u^t,u^a} = \frac{\sum_{i_p \in \Sigma}\left(r\left(u^t,i_p\right) - \overline{u^t}\right)\left(r\left(u^a,i_p\right) - \overline{u^a}\right)}{\sqrt{\sum_{i_p \in \Sigma}\left(r\left(u^t,i_p\right) - \overline{u^t}\right)^2 \sum_{i_p \in \Sigma}\left(r\left(u^t,i_p\right) - \overline{u^a}\right)^2}} \tag{4}$$

$$CPC_{u^t,u^a} = \frac{\sum_{i_p \in \Sigma}\left(r\left(u^t,i_p\right) - v\right)\left(r\left(u^a,i_p\right) - v\right)}{\sqrt{\sum_{i_p \in \Sigma}\left(r\left(u^t,i_p\right) - v\right)^2 \sum_{i_p \in \Sigma}\left(r\left(u^t,i_p\right) - v\right)^2}} \tag{5}$$

$$CV_{u^t,u^a} = \frac{\sum_{i_p \in \Sigma} r\left(u^t,i_p\right) \times r\left(u^a,i_p\right)}{\sqrt{\sum_{i_p \in \Sigma}\left(r\left(u^t,i_p\right)\right)^2}\sqrt{\sum_{i_p \in \Sigma}\left(r\left(u^a,i_p\right)\right)^2}} \tag{6}$$

The three proximity measures finds the similarity among users u^t and u^a. The correlated value is based on their preferences for commonly clicked item i_p that belongs to item dataset Σ. Here $r\left(u^t,i_p\right)$ and $r\left(u^a,i_p\right)$ represent the preference levels of users u^t and u^a for commonly clicked item i_p. Also $\overline{u^t}$ and $\overline{u^a}$ signify the average values of user u^t and u^a preference levels respectively, for all commonly clicked items. Since PC is only used to measure linear tendency, we will be using CPC so that we can predict the preference levels of users with respect to the value v. Since we are normalizing the preference level ranging from 0.0 to 1.0, we will assume v to be 0.5.

After determining the similarity among users, the next step is to find the preferences of the items that are not viewed by the target user and either clicked, placed in cart or purchased by its neighbors. For this purpose weighted average preference is calculated and preference for the item not viewed by target user is predicted using Eq. 7.

$$r(u^t, i_j) = \frac{\sum_{i \in NB_{u^t, i_j}} CPC_{u^t, u^i} \times r(u^i, i_j)}{\sum_{i \in NB_{u^t, i_j}} CPC_{u^t, u^i}} \qquad (7)$$

Here, $NB_{u^t, prod_j}$ is the neighborhood of target u^t who viewed the item i_j. In our study, CPC similarity measure performs consistently better than PC and hence is used in predicting the weighted average of preference levels. Items that are neither viewed by target user nor viewed by its neighborhood are assigned the preference 0.

4   Experimental Results

4.1   Steps for Recommender Evaluation

Following steps are implemented to test the proposed RS:

Step 1: From the purchased dataset, 10% (appx.) of items that are purchased are considered as not viewed by the target user.
Step2: Preference for that item is predicted for the target user using proposed method.
Step 3: A top-N item list is generated for the target user.
Step 4: Recommended items are examined to see whether hidden purchased items exist in that list.

4.2   Evaluation Measures

To test the accuracy of RS, evaluation metrics such as 'recall' and 'precision' are used. These methods are commonly used in the field of information retrieval which are described in Eqs. (8) and (9).

$$recall = \frac{\sum_{i \in X} |\text{Hidden}(i) \cap \text{Top\_N}(i)|}{\sum_{i \in X} \text{Hidden}(i)} \qquad (8)$$

$$precision = \frac{\sum_{i \in X} |\text{Hidden}(i) \cap \text{Top\_N}(i)|}{N.|X|} \qquad (9)$$

Where,
Hidden(i)   hidden items of user i
N   # recommended items
Top_N(i)   recommended items for user i
|X| # users who has at least one hidden item

When the # of hidden items increases, recall also increases but precision decreases as the two measures are inversely related. Therefore a combined measure F1 is used whose higher value indicates a better accuracy of the designed RS. The harmonic mean F1 of recall and precision is given by Eq. (10).

$$F1 = \frac{2 \times \text{Recall} \times \text{Precision}}{\text{Recall} + \text{Precision}} \tag{10}$$

4.3 Evaluation of Proposed and Conventional RSs

Proposed technique performs better than the conventional [17] RS that finds relative preferences of items and also improves the accuracy of the system.

The results presented in Figs. (6, 7 and 8) finds appropriate user similarity function that is suitable for the real clickstream dataset. The three similarity functions PC_{u^t,u^a}, CPC_{u^t,u^a} and CV_{u^t,u^a} are used to find similarity among the users. Number of neighbors selected varies from 1 to 5 with the increment of 1. Also number of items recommended to each user varies from 5 to 30 in increments of 5. CPC_{u^t,u^a} outperforms PC_{u^t,u^a} and CV_{u^t,u^a} in all measures of precision, recall and $F1$. We can conclude from the results that CPC is more suitable for the selected dataset when its neighborhood size increases from 1 to 4, while it decreases when size is 5. The highest accuracy of the selected similarity measure is obtained when the number of recommended items is 30. Table 5 clearly shows that proposed method outperforms the conventional one.

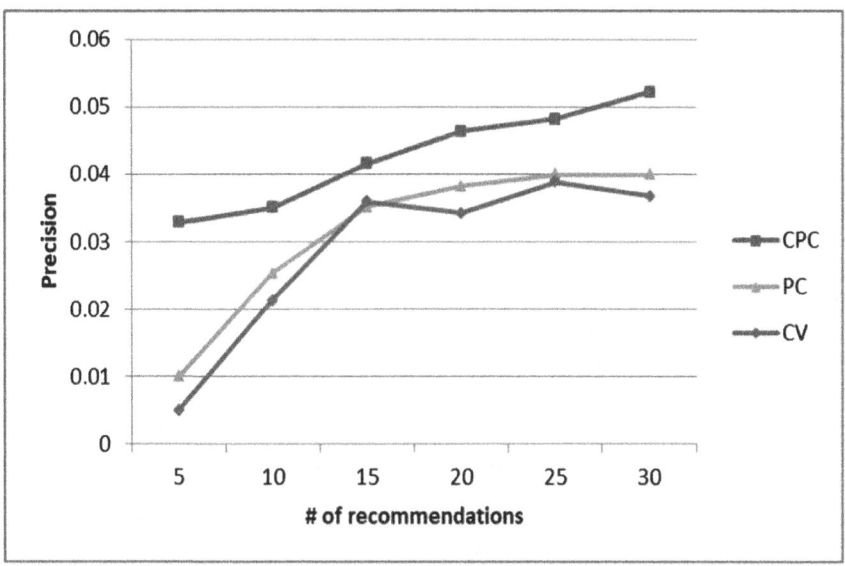

Fig. 6. Comparing precision using CPC, PC and CV as similarity measures

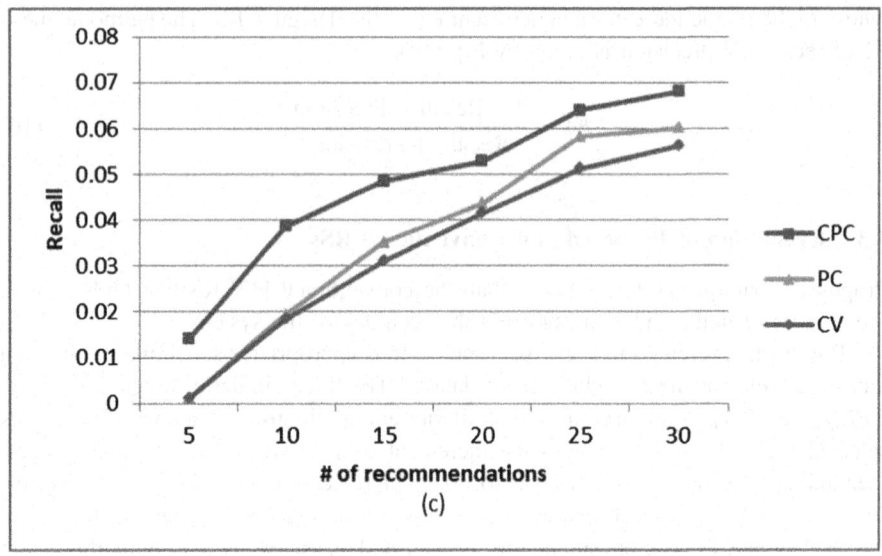

Fig. 7. Comparing recall using CPC, PC and CV as similarity measures

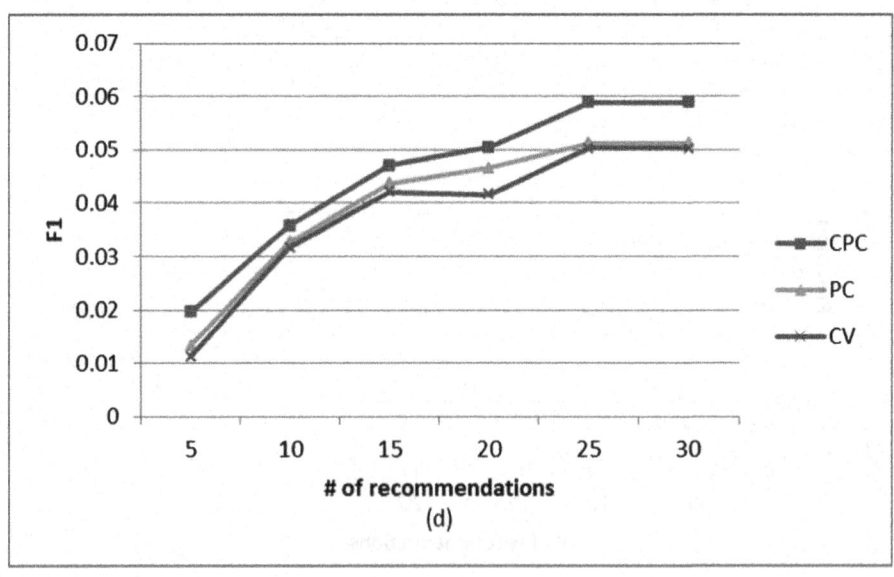

Fig. 8. Comparing $F1$ values using CPC, PC and CV as similarity measures

Table 5. Comparison of F1 values with conventional methods

N (Number of recommendations)	H (Percentage of Hidden Products)	F1 values	
		Conventional method [17]	Proposed method
5	10	0.02	0.02061
10	10	0.03801	0.03975
15	10	0.04811	0.04899
20	10	0.05	0.05049
25	10	0.058	0.05888
30	10	0.058	0.05888

5   Conclusion and Future Scope

The approach in this article utilizes click stream data and predicts the preference for the items viewed by the user. Users' interest is predicted based on items' click context and like-minded users are discovered based on items' category. In our study, CPC gives the highest accuracy among the rest of the similarity measures. Finally weighted average of the customers in a cluster is used to calculate the preference of the items not viewed by the target user. Top-N list is generated for the target user and effectiveness of the algorithm is evaluated based on metrics such as precision, recall and F1. From the analysis, we observe that the proposed algorithm outperforms the ones used in conventional [17] approaches.

Further the data used is very vast and recommendations are made only for users who have clicked more than 70 items. Recommendations are generated for the users who have spent less time browsing e-commerce website. We can also suggest a method that takes into account the association between the items that appear sequentially. A fruitful area of future work may include applying proposed work on vast datasets and by finding associations between the items.

References

1. Ricci, F., Rokach, L., Shapira, B.: Introduction to recommender systems handbook. In: Ricci, F., Rokach, L., Shapira, B., Kantor, P. (eds.) Recommender Systems Handbook, pp. 1–35. Springer, Boston (2011). https://doi.org/10.1007/978-0-387-85820-3_1
2. Jeong, B., Lee, J., Cho, H.: An iterative semi-explicit rating method for building collaborative recommender systems. Expert Syst. Appl. **36**(3), 6181–6186 (2009)
3. Zhao, X., Niu, Z., Chen, W.: Interest before liking: two-step recommendation approaches. Knowl. Based Syst. **48**, 46–56 (2013)
4. Cleger-Tamayo, S., Fernández-Luna, J.M., Huete, J.F.: Top-N news recommendations in digital newspapers. Knowl. Based Syst. **27**, 180–189 (2012)
5. Kim, Y.S., Yum, B.: Recommender system based on click stream data using association rule mining. Expert Syst. Appl. **38**(10), 13320–13327 (2011)
6. Li, Y., Tan, B.H.: Clustering algorithm of web click stream frequency pattern. J. Tianjin Univ. Sci. Technol. **3**, 018 (2011)

7. Kim, S.C., Sung, K.J., Park, C.S., Kim, S.K.: Improvement of collaborative filtering using rating normalization. Multimed. Tools Appl. **75**(9), 4957–4968 (2016)
8. Sarwar, B., Karypis, G., Konstan, J., Riedl, J.: Item-based collaborative filtering recommendation algorithms. In: Proceedings of the 10th International Conference on World Wide Web, pp. 285–295. ACM (2001)
9. Kim, S.C., Sung, K.J., Park, C.S., Kim, S.K.: Improvement of collaborative filtering using rating normalization. Multimed. Tools Appl. **75**(9), 4957–4968 (2016)
10. Sarwar, B., Karypis, G., Konstan, J., Riedl, J.: Item-based collaborative filtering recommendation algorithms. In: Proceedings of the 10th International Conference on World Wide Web, pp. 285–295. ACM (2001)
11. Kim, H.N., Ji, A.T., Ha, I., Jo, G.S.: Collaborative filtering based on collaborative tagging for enhancing the quality of recommendation. Electron. Commer. Res. Appl. **9**(1), 73–83 (2010)
12. Park, Y.J., Chang, K.N.: Individual and group behavior-based customer profile model for personalized product recommendation. Expert Syst. Appl. **36**(2), 1932–1939 (2009)
13. Adomavicius, G., Tuzhilin, A.: Toward the next generation of recommender systems: a survey of the state-of-the-art and possible extensions. IEEE Trans. Knowl. Data Eng. **17**(6), 734–749 (2005)
14. Ghauth, K.I., Abdullah, N.A.: Measuring learner's performance in e-learning recommender systems. Australas. J. Educ. Technol. **26**(6), 764–774 (2010)
15. Ghazanfar, M.A.: Experimenting switching hybrid recommender systems. Intell. Data Anal. **19**(4), 845–877 (2015)
16. Ben-Shimon, D., Tsikinovsky, A., Friedmann, M., Shapira, B., Rokach, L., Hoerle, J.: Recsys challenge 2015 and the yoochoose dataset. In: Proceedings of the 9th ACM Conference on Recommender Systems, pp. 357–358. ACM (2015)
17. Gupta, S., Dixit, V.S.: Scalable online product recommendation engine based on implicit feature extraction domain. J. Intell. Fuzzy Syst. **34**(3), 1503–1510 (2018)

Recommendations with Sparsity Based Weighted Context Framework

Veer Sain Dixit and Parul Jain[✉]

Atma Ram Sanatan Dharam College, University of Delhi, Delhi, India
veersaindixit@rediffmail.com,
paruljainpj@rediffmail.com

Abstract. Context-Aware Recommender Systems (CARS) is a sort of information filtering tool which has become crucial for services in this big era of data. Owing to its characteristic of including contextual information, it achieves better results in terms of prediction accuracy. The collaborative filtering has been proved as an efficient technique to recommend items among all existing techniques in this area. Moreover, incorporation of other evolutionary techniques in it for contextualization and to alleviate sparsity problem can give an additive advantage. In this paper, we propose to find the vector of weights using particle swarm optimization to control the contribution of each context feature. It is aimed to make a balance between data sparsity and maximization of contextual effects. Further, the weighting vector is used in different components of user and item neighborhood-based algorithms. Moreover, we present a novel method to find aggregated similarity from local and global similarity based on sparsity measure. Local similarity gives importance to co-rated items while global similarity utilizes all the ratings assigned by a pair of users. The proposed algorithms are evaluated for Individual and Group Recommendations. The experimental results on two contextually rich datasets prove that the proposed algorithms outperform the other techniques of this domain. The sparsity measure that is best suited to find aggregation is dataset dependent. Finally, the algorithms show their efficacy for Group Recommendations too.

Keywords: Sparsity measure · Particle swarm optimization · Local similarity
Global similarity · Group recommendations

1 Introduction

Context-Aware Recommender Systems (CARS) have gained the high attention of experts and researchers for item recommendations due to an important role played by contextual information in them [1, 2]. Dey (2001) defined the context as "Context is a piece of information that describes the circumstances of an entity". The choice of items is usually different in different contextual situations. To quote a few examples: (a) One would choose to listen different music if weather is pleasant and/or road is free rather than it is being a hot summer day and/or traffic jam, (b) The choice of restaurant would be different if one is going on quick business lunch rather than going to dine with

O. Gervasi et al. (Eds.): ICCSA 2018, LNCS 10963, pp. 289–305, 2018.
https://doi.org/10.1007/978-3-319-95171-3_23

girlfriend. Therefore, to improve accuracy and user satisfaction, CARS have been studied in various domains encompassing information retrieval, mobile applications, e-commerce, e-learning, management, and marketing.

The crux of CARS is to incorporate contextual information in various mathematical [1, 2, 5], probabilistic [1, 2], soft computing [1, 2, 16] and particle swarm optimization techniques [3, 7]. The recommender systems(RS) involving collaborative filtering (CF) technique are most effective and widely used among all existing RS. The quality and accuracy of such RS can be increased by using new and improved similarity measures along with utilization of contexts in an effective manner.

Major Challenges in CARS. There remain many challenges in CARS such as utilization of contextual information, data sparsity, scalability and cold start problem. Selection and application of contextual factors in making recommendations is clearly a blunt instrument. However, user-item-rating matrices are sparse since generally all items are not evaluated by users. Sparsity problem becomes more severe when these matrices are diluted with contextual factors. Use of too many contextual factors in algorithms increases data sparsity and few context factors fails to bring contextual effects in recommendations. In our previous research [10], we have addressed this issue by formation of context communities which are utilized in different components of the algorithm (CAWP). Although, the algorithm included the context and increased accuracy, but it is domain dependent. Optimization is the core of research. In this research, we find the optimal set of weights for the whole context vector using particle swarm optimization (PSO) to alleviate data sparsity problem.

Another major issue is to find similarity between two users and/or items, especially in context aware datasets. More the similarity measure is improved, better are the recommendations. Typically, conventional similarity measures such as Pearson Correlation Coefficient (PCC), Cosine(COS), Mean Squared Difference(MSD) can be calculated on items which are commonly rated by two users and the users who have rated common items. They ignore global rating information. Moreover, contextual information is not considered by them while finding similarity between two users and items. Even some researches have employed newly emerging similarity measures such as NHSM [18], Bhattacharya Coefficient with correlation [17] and PSS based similarity measure [18, 20] which overcome one or another problem mentioned above but do not consider contextual situation into account.

Our Contribution. Motivated by the above mentioned issues, the primary contribution in this work is presented as follows:

- A context weighing vector is computed using PSO to weight the contribution of all contextual features instead of context selection or relaxation. Weighting the contextual features overcome the data sparsity problem and optimizes the contextual effects. Then, these weighting vector are applied in each component of the user and item neighborhood based algorithms.
- An effective approach is proposed to combine local and global similarities based on sparsity measure. Several variations of sparsity measure are used to weight the contribution of global and local similarities. These measures caters sparse and dense data. Moreover, global similarity can be computed on non-corated items and

considers global preferences of the user behaviour while local similarity is obtained using co-rated items.

- Extending our research area, the proposed approach is evaluated for two different types of a group of users. Three different group recommendation techniques are compared to analyze the efficacy of the proposed framework. The two datasets used are contextually rich and especially designed for contextual personalization research.

The forthcoming paper is organized as follows. Few CARS related reviews and similarity measures are mentioned in Sect. 2. The detailed construction of the proposed framework and the approach used are presented in Sect. 3. Section 4 presents experimental results and their analysis. Section 5 specifies the conclusions followed by future research work.

2 Related Reviews

2.1 Context-Aware Recommendation

Context-Aware Recommender System includes context features while making a prediction. The rating estimation function is given by $R : userX\ itemX\ context \rightarrow rating$. Context aware recommendation algorithm falls into three paradigms: (a) contextual pre filtering, where filtered dataset using contextual information is utilized by rating prediction algorithm, (b) contextual post filtering, where final set of recommendations are filtered using contextual information and (c) contextual modeling, where contextual information is used to predict the rating [1, 2]. The identification of valid and influential contexts is also required to be applied into recommendation algorithms [24, 26]. To identify relevant and influential context features of LDOS-CoMoDa dataset, [15] has summarized the assessments obtained from user survey and statistical testing. Another method is proposed in [22] to select optimal contexts including demographic, item and contextual features. The relevance value of each context feature set under a specific genre for IncarMusic dataset is found by [4]. A new prediction aggregation model combining predictions obtained using demographic, semantic and social contexts is demonstrated by [9]. An approach is presented by [25] to analyze several direct context prediction algorithms based on multilabel classification.

2.2 Sparsity Problem

Many techniques have been used by the researchers to handle data sparsity issue. It is one of the major challenges observed in this field. Especially in context aware datasets where the rating dataset is filtered with contextual information, the matrices become more sparse. DCR algorithm is proposed in [21] to handle data sparsity problem where the relaxed context constraints are used in the prediction algorithm. Another approach CAWP formed context communities and included weighted percentile method [10]. DCW for CARS [23] describes to find weights of contextual features and those users which possess context similarity greater than the threshold are used by the algorithm.

2.3   Similarity Measures

Traditional similarity measures such as Pearson Correlation Coefficient (PCC), Mean Square Difference (MSD), Cosine (COS), Jaccard are mostly used by recommender systems for computation of similarity between a pair of user or item. These measures have several drawbacks such as few co-rated item problems, utilization of only local rating information and non-inclusion of global ratings [1, 2, 14, 18, 20]. Hence some new similarity measures are proposed to overcome the drawbacks. A new similarity measure based on Bhattacharya Coefficient is evaluated by [14] to handle sparse data that do not depend on co-rated items. A heuristic similarity model which considers both local and global contexts of the user behaviour is experimentally shown in [18]. A model based on a mean measure of divergence is defined by [13, 20] that takes rating habits of a user into account. These measures do not consider contextual information and suffer from one or the other problem, so we attempt to form a combination of local, global and contextual similarity measure to improve accuracy.

3   The Proposal

This section presents construction and details of the proposed framework depicted in Fig. 1. The framework consists of Sparsity Based Weighted Context Recommendation Unit (SWCRU) and Group Recommendation Unit (GRU). The SWCRU predicts ratings via user neighborhood based and item neighborhood based algorithms. To achieve this, first, the optimum weight of different context features and genres are obtained using particle swarm optimization (PSO). The overlap metric and weights of context features are used to find contextual similarity value. This value is utilized by different parts of both user and item neighborhood based algorithms. Also, local and global similarities are found to exploit their strengths by the prediction algorithms. The sparsity measure is employed to make a balance between local and global similarity since both performs differently under different sparse data scenario. The GRU unit presents three different group recommendation techniques Merging, Multiplicative and Merging-Multiplicative for performance analysis of the proposed algorithms for a group of users. Random Groups are used for this purpose.

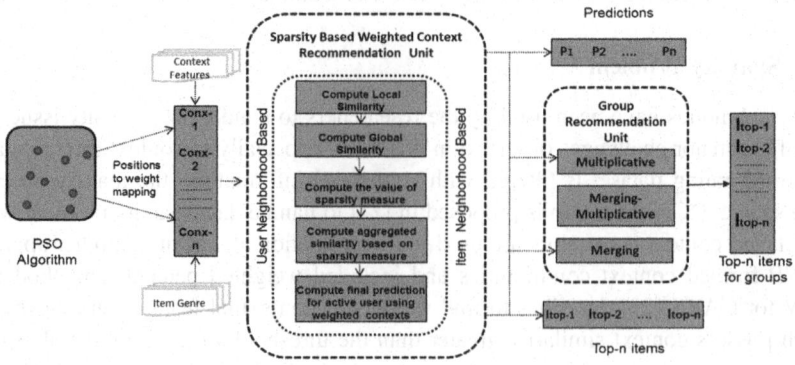

Fig. 1. The proposed framework

3.1 PSO to Learn Optimal Weighting Vector *w*

We assume that those rating which is more similar in contexts are more valuable in making predictions. To handle data sparsity problem, we learn the optimal weight *w* for each context feature using PSO instead of filtering out some context features. The *w* can take the weight as the real values in the range of [0,1]. These weighted values control the contribution of each context feature in the recommendation algorithms.

Particle Representation and Initial Population
Each context feature weight is represented with 8 binary digits in range of [0,255]. If there are 'n' features then 8n bits represent a particle. After reaching termination criteria, binary value of each weight is converted to its decimal equivalent [3, 7]. Then each weight is divided by the total weight to get a normalized value.

Particle Dynamics
PSO consists of collection of candidate solutions called swarm where each candidate solution represents a particle. These particles continuously move in search space by some velocity. The velocity and position w.r.t. each particle in every dimension is updated at each time stamp. The following rules are followed to update the swarm [7].

$$vel_i = rw * vel_i + cons_1 * r_1 \left(pos_{PBest,i} - pos_i \right) + cons_2 * r_2 \left(pos_{GBest} - pos_i \right)$$
$$\text{If} \left(|vel_i| > vel_{max} \right), \left(vel_{max} / |vel_i| \right) * vel_i \; ; \; pos_i = pos_i + vel_i$$

where the position of current particle i is represented by pos_i, the best position attained by particle is known by $pos_{PBest,i}$, pos_{GBest} elaborates the swarm's global best, vel_i represents the velocity of particle i, rw is the random inertia weight lies between 0.4 and 0.9, $cons_1$ and $cons_2$ are spring constants whose values are set as 2.0 by empirical suggestions [22], r_1 and r_2 are random numbers between 0 and 1. vel_{min} and vel_{max} are $(ul - lb)/2$. In our case, it is tuned to 2.0 after experimental analysis. Swarm size is 10 and the number of iterations performed before termination is 20.

The Fitness Function
The *ith* particle's fitness value in the swarm is computed using the following fitness function [3, 7].

$$Fitness_i = \frac{1}{S_R} \sum_{t=0}^{S_R} |(ar_t - pr_t)|$$

S_R is the cardinality of a training set for the active user. ar_t and pr_t are actual and predicted rating of item t respectively.

Termination Criteria
We opted to take a specified number of iterations as terminating situation. This also means that the PSO algorithm terminates after executing specified number of iterations.

3.2   Overlap Metric to Find Contextual Similarity

The Overlap metric finds the similarity between two objects obj_i and obj_j and widely used for categorical attributes [19]. It is a simple and effective and is defined by

$$S(obj_i, obj_j) = \frac{\sum_{a=1}^{m} S_a(obj_{ia}, obj_{ja})}{m}$$

where a depicts a particular attribute and m is used to represent the total number of attributes of the object. obj_{ia} means a-th attribute of object obj_i. if $obj_{ia} = obj_{ja}$, then the value of $S_a(obj_{ia}, obj_{ja}) = 1$ otherwise it is 0.

Illustrative Example
Using Table 1, the contextual similarity between $user1$ and $user4$ via Overlap metric is computed as $S(user1, user4) = \frac{3}{5} = 0.6$.

3.3   Weighted Overlap Metric

This metric is used to assess how much weight should be given to a rating $r_{a,i,c2}$ using weighted vector w obtained using PSO. The weighted overlap metric to find context similarity between target context $c1$ and different user context $c2$ is given by:

$$O_w(c1, c2, w) = \frac{\sum_{func \in c1 \cap c2} w_{func}}{\sum_{func \in c1 \cup c2} w_{func}} \tag{1}$$

which means total context similarity of target user with some other user will be obtained by adding weights of those context features where the values match.

Table 1. Rating matrix for an item i by different users under different contextual conditions.

User	Day	Timing	Place	Companion	Mood	Rating
User1	Weekend	Night	Home	Family	Positive	4
User2	Holiday	Evening	Friend's home	Friend	Neutral	5
User3	Weekend	Afternoon	Theatre	Colleagues	Positive	4
User4	Holiday	Night	Home	Family	Neutral	3

3.4   Weighted Local Similarity

To calculate local similarity between two users or two items, we used Pearson Correlation Coefficient which uses commonly rated items to find the value. $c1$ represents the context vector of u_x or i_x and $c2$ represents the context vector of u_y or i_y.

The weighted variant to find similarity between two users, $simu - loc_w$ is given by

$$simu - local_w(u_x, u_y, w) = \frac{\sum_{t=1}^{n'}(r_{u_x,i_t} - \overline{r_{u_x}}) - (r_{u_y,i_t} - \overline{r_{u_y}})O_w(c1,c2,w)}{\sqrt{\sum_{t=1}^{n'}(r_{u_x,i_t} - \overline{r_{u_x}})^2 O_w(c1,c2,w)}\sqrt{\sum_{t=1}^{n'}(r_{u_y,i_t} - \overline{r_{u_y}})^2 O_w(c1,c2,w)}} \quad (2)$$

where $i_t : t = 1, 2, .., n' \wedge n' \leq n$ represents a set consisting of those items which u_x and u_y had rated and n identifies the total number of accessible items.

The weighted variant to find similarity between two items, $simi - loc_w$ is given by

$$simi - local_w(i_x, i_y, w) = \frac{\sum_{t=1}^{m'}(r_{u_t,i_x} - \overline{r_{i_x}}) - (r_{u_t,i_y} - \overline{r_{i_y}})O_w(c1,c2,w)}{\sqrt{\sum_{t=1}^{m'}(r_{u_t,i_x} - \overline{r_{i_x}})^2 O_w(c1,c2,w)}\sqrt{\sum_{t=1}^{m'}(r_{u_t,i_y} - \overline{r_{i_y}})^2 O_w(c1,c2,w)}} \quad (3)$$

where $\{u_x : x = 1, 2, .., m' \wedge m' \leq m\}$ represents a set consisting of users who have rated i_x and i_y, where m identifies the total number of accessible users.

3.5   Weighted Global Similarity

Bhattacharya Coefficient
The Bhattacharyya Coefficient finds similarity value between two statistical samples [14]. If pq and pr be the discrete probability distributions under same domain D, the Bhattacharyya coefficient (BC) between pq and pr is given by.

$$BC(pq, pr) = \sum_{x \in D} \sqrt{pq(\mathrm{x})pr(\mathrm{x})}$$

Following it, the similarity between two users $u1$ *and* $u2$ is given as:

$$BC(u1, u2) = \sum_{k=1}^{m} \sqrt{\left(\widehat{D_{u1k}}\right)\left(\widehat{D_{u2k}}\right)} \quad (4)$$

where $\left(\widehat{D_{u1k}}\right)$ and $\left(\widehat{D_{u2k}}\right)$ represents users rating values under domain D and $\left(\widehat{D_{u1k}}\right) = \frac{\#k}{\#u}$ where $\#k$ = total count of items which are rated as k (value), $\#u$ = total count of items rated by user u.

Illustrative Example
Consider the rating scale lies in the range $\{1, 2, 3\}$ and user $u1$ and $u2$ made rating on five different items (Table 2).

The BC coefficient is calculated as:

$$BC(u1, u2) = \sum_{t=1}^{3} \sqrt{\left(\widehat{u1_t}\right)\left(\widehat{u2_t}\right)} = \sqrt{\frac{2}{3} * \frac{1}{2}} + \sqrt{\frac{1}{3} * \frac{1}{2}} + \sqrt{\frac{0}{3} * \frac{0}{2}} = 0.9855$$

Table 2. User-item rating matrix.

User/Item	i1	i2	i3	i4	i5
u1	1	0	2	0	1
u2	0	1	0	2	0

Proximity-Significance-Singularity (PSS)

PSS similarity is used as local measure [11, 18] which punishes bad similarity and reward good similarity and is defined as follows:

$$sim(u1, u2)^{PSS} = \sum_{i \in I} PSS(r_{u1,i}, r_{u2,i}) \tag{5}$$

where I represents all the items rated by user $u1$ *and* $u2$ and $r_{u1,i}$ means rating assigned by user $u1$ to item i.

$$PSS(r_{u1,i}, r_{u2,i}) = \text{Proximity}(r_{u1,i}, r_{u2,i}) \times \text{Significance}(r_{u1,i}, r_{u2,i}) \times \text{Singularity}(r_{u1,i}, r_{u2,i}).$$

Proximity considers absolute difference between two ratings and assigns penalty to disagreement.

Significance assumes that those ratings which are far off from the median are more significant.

Singularity uses difference of two ratings from the mean of their rating vector.

$$\text{Proximity}\left(r_{u1,i}, r_{u2,i}\right) = 1 - \frac{1}{1 + \exp\left(-\left|r_{u1,i} - r_{u2,i}\right|\right)}$$

$$\text{Significance}\left(r_{u1,i}, r_{u2,i}\right) = 1 - \frac{1}{1 + \exp\left(-\left|r_{u1,i} - r_{med}\right| * \left|r_{u2,i} - r_{med}\right|\right)}$$

$$\text{Singularity}\left(r_{u1,i}, r_{u2,i}\right) = 1 - \frac{1}{1 + \exp\left(-\left|\left(\frac{r_{u1,i} + r_{u2,i}}{2}\right) - \mu_i\right|\right)}$$

where μ_i is the mean rating of item i.

Hybrid Similarity Metric

Combining the strengths of Weighted Overlap (for context similarity) stated by Eq. (1), Bhattacharya Coefficient (for global similarity) described by Eq. (4) and PSS (for local component) defined by Eq. (5), the hybrid similarity measure is given by the Eqs. (6) and (7).

$$simu - global_w\left(u_x, u_y, w\right) = \sum_{a \in I_{ux}} \sum_{b \in I_{uy}} BC\left(u_x, u_y\right) * O_w(c1, c2, w) * s\left(u_x, u_y\right)^{PSS} \tag{6}$$

$$simi - global_w\left(i_x, i_y, w\right) = \sum_{a \in U_{ix}} \sum_{b \in V_{iy}} BC\left(i_x, i_y\right) * O_w(c1, c2, w) * s\left(i_x, i_y\right)^{PSS} \tag{7}$$

3.6   Sparsity Measure (ϑ)

Previous researches have verified that when the data sparsity is high then the global similarity makes more accurate predictions while in case of low sparsity, local similarity performs better. The various sparsity measures are proposed in [3] to ensure that the locally similar neighbors and globally similar neighbors should be weighted differently in different scenario of data. We propose to use these sparsity measures to get the correct proportions of local and global similarities. The various sparsity measures that utilized are as follows.

Overall Sparsity Measure (ϑ_1)
It is uniform for all users and considers sparsity of entire matrix. It is computed as

$$\vartheta_1 = 1 - \left(\frac{m_R}{(m_U \, X \, m_I)} \right)$$

where m_R, m_U and m_I represents total count of ratings in the entire matrix, total count of unique users and total count of unique items in the matrix respectively.

User Dependent Sparsity Measure (ϑ_2)
The intuition behind this metric is that those users who have rated less items will not get much reliable local neighborhood. It is user specific and remains constant for all the items of the active user. The value of ϑ_2 is defined as follows.

$$\vartheta_2 = 1 - \left(\frac{m_u}{(max_{u \in U} m_u)} \right)$$

where m_u represents number of items which user u has rated.

The forthcoming measure addresses the sparsity at user-item level since sometimes globally similar neighbors shows superiority depending on the items rated by the users.

Local Global Ratio (ϑ_3)
The value of ϑ_3 is computed as: $\vartheta_3 = 1 - \left(\frac{|L_{Neigh}(a,i)|}{|G_{Neigh}(a,j)|} \right)$
where $L_{Neigh}(a,i)$ represents the set of locally similar neighbors of user a who have rated item i and $G_{Neigh}(a,j)$ represents the set of globally similar neighbors of user a. ϑ_4 is defined as average of ϑ_1, ϑ_2 and ϑ_3.

Aggregated Similarity
The correct proportion of local and global similarities can achieve better quality predictions in sparse and dense data scenario. Thus, the aggregated similarity is a linear combination of local and global similarity and is defined by Equation

$$sim - aggr(i,j) = \vartheta \, X \, sim - global_w(i,j,w) + (1 - \vartheta) X \, sim - local_w(i,j,w) \quad (8)$$

where i represents u_x or i_x and j represents u_y or i_y depending on whether it is user or item neighborhood algorithm. The values of ϑ can be calculated with the help of any of these sparsity measure ϑ_1, where $i = 1, 2, 3 \, or \, 4$.

The value of $sim - local_w(i,j,w)$ is computed by Eqs. (2) or (3) and $sim - global_w(i,j,w)$ using Eqs. (6) or (7) depending on user or item neighborhood algorithm.

3.7   Predictions and Recommendations

The following neighborhood based algorithms are being used for rating prediction towards active user a towards an unrated item:

Weighted Context User Based Using Sparsity Measure $(WCUB_{\vartheta-sim})$

$$P_{a,i,c} = \overline{\omega}(a, O_w(c1,c2,w)) + \frac{\sum_{t \in N_a} sim - aggr(a,t)(\omega(t, O_w(c1,c2,w)) - \overline{\omega}(t, O_w(c1,c2,w)))}{\sum_{t \in N_{a,k}} sim - aggr(a,t)} \quad (9)$$

Weighted Context Item Based Using Sparsity Measure $(WCUB_{\vartheta-sim})$

$$P_{a,i,c} = \overline{\omega}(i, O_w(c1,c2,w)) + \frac{\sum_{t \in N_i} sim - aggr(i,t)(\omega(t, O_w(c1,c2,w)) - \overline{\omega}(t, O_w(c1,c2,w)))}{\sum_{t \in N_{i,k}} sim - aggr(i,t)} \quad (10)$$

Table 3. Description of notations used.

Notation	Description
$P_{a,i,c}$	Predicted rating user a towards item i in contextual situation c
N_i	Neighborhood of items that are rated by user a
N_a	Neighborhood of users who have rated item i
$\overline{\omega}(a, O_w(c1,c2,w))$	User a's average of contextually weighted ratings
$\omega(t, O_w(c1,c2,w))$	Contextually weighted rating of neighbor t
$sim - aggr(a,t)$	Aggregated similarity between users a and t after using PSO and sparsity measure
$sim - aggr(i,t)$	Aggregated similarity between items i and t after using PSO and sparsity measure

3.8   Group Recommendation Unit

This unit provides three different group recommendation techniques to evaluate the algorithms for group of users.

Merging. In merging, top-n recommended items belonging to each member of group are merged into a single list. Then top-n items of the merged list are recommended to the group [6, 8].

Multiplicative. In multiplicative, an aggregated value is calculated after multiplication of predicted rating obtained by each group member. Then top-n items with highest value(prediction) are recommended to group as a whole [8].

Merging-Multiplicative. In this method, first off the top-n recommended items of each group member are merged together. Among them, top-n items are extracted. Then the new aggregated value is calculated after multiplication and the items are rearranged [8].

4 Experimental Evaluation

We have performed several experiments to obtain and analyze the performance of the proposed framework. The following issues are addressed:

- How do the utilization of weighted contexts via PSO in user neighborhood and item neighborhood model performs?
- To analyze the effects of sparsity measure variants controlling the contribution of local and global similarities.
- Are the proposed algorithms reliable for group of users?

4.1 Description, Parameter Setup and Evaluation Metrics

The experiments are conducted on two global datasets enriched with context features and especially designed for context aware personalization research. The LDOS-CoMoDa dataset is from movie domain contains 30 features and are collected from surveys [12]. IncarMusic dataset is a global dataset and collected from is https://github.com/irecsys/CARSKit/tree/master/context-ware_data_sets [4]. The summarized statistics of these datasets are given in Table 4.

Table 4. The statistics of datasets.

Datasets	# of users	# of items	# of ratings	# of contexts factors	# of user attributes	# of item attributes	Rating scale
IncarMusic	42	139	4012	8	1	8	1–5
LDOS-CoMoDa	121	1232	2296	12	4	11	1–5

For implementation purpose, those users who have given ratings to at least three items are filtered and used for experimentation. The filtered dataset is divided into three folds. Out of them one fold is utilized as test set and rest two are treated as training set. The average of five runs are presented for all measures in the results. To measure predictive accuracy, mean absolute error i.e. MAE and root mean square error i.e. RMSE are used. Also, recommended ranked list of top10 items are calculated using Precision, Recall and F1-score. For both IncarMusic and LDOS-CoMoDa data sets, an item is considered relevant (a hit) only if it is assigned a rating higher than or equal to 4 (in scale of 1–5) by the active user. Each group recommendation technique is evaluated for five Random Groups. Moreover, the experiments are performed on two sizes of groups i.e. Small Group (SG) consisting of 3–5 users and Large Group (LG) consisting of 6–8 users. Group recommendations are measured for five runs and average using F1-score (metric) is presented as result.

4.2   Compared Methods

The experimental results shown below are compared with three more approaches to analyze the performance of the proposed algorithms presented in Sect. 3. We choose one context aware recommendation approach *CAWP* from our previous researches [10], second DCR via BPSO [21, 23] and DCW via PSO [23] from the same domain of research.

CAWP. In our previous research work, we tried to come out from the dilemma of context selection by forming context communities and used a weighted percentile method to increase the accuracy [10]. We implemented the concept in user neighborhood model $CAWP_{UB-ER}$ and item neighborhood model $CAWP_{IB-ER}$. We are using the best cases i.e. 90th percentile in case of movie dataset and 70th percentile in music dataset for comparison.

DCR via BPSO. Binary particle swarm optimization (BPSO) uses vectors of binary values to represent the position of particle instead the real-valued vectors. BPSO has been successfully demonstrated as efficient non linear optimizer for feature selection. It is available in open source libraries to understand and implement [23]. Moreover, DCR via BPSO is described [23] as the best technique to filter the context features.

DCW via PSO. Instead of selecting few features, DCW includes the contribution of each contextual feature which is weighted. PSO optimizes the position of particles which represents a weighting vector for context features. It is also found that PSO based algorithms outperforms genetic algorithms which is also used for the same purpose. Hence it is used in CF technique [23].

4.3   Results and Analysis

This section presents and discusses the experimental results of the proposed framework using LDOS-CoMoDa and IncarMusic datasets.

Method Comparisons
Table 5 presents the results of the proposed sparsity based weighted context recommendation technique and other context aware implementations. It is also shown in Table 5 that the proposed algorithms whether it is user or item neighborhood based outperforms the other techniques of this area. The reason could be that usage of optimum weight for context features and sparsity dependent contribution of local and global neighbors are taken. It is worth to be noted that the proposed algorithms consider global similarities too (i.e. neighbors who have not rated common items) which other compared techniques don't do.

Further, Fig. 3 illustrates a comparison in the predictive accuracy of the recommendation system using only local similarity and the combination(local and global similarities with best case of 9). Using both datasets, the combination of local and global similarities perform better than local similarities. It also verifies the assumption that two users can be similar even if they do not rate common items.

Figure 2 (a) and (b) depict that the two variants of proposed method (i.e. user neighbourhood based and item neighbourhood based) show a significant difference in

Table 5. The computed values of MAE, RMSE, Precision, Recall and F1-score for different algorithms using two datasets.

Datasets	IncarMusic dataset					LDOS-CoMoDa dataset				
Algorithm	MAE	RMSE	Precision	Recall	F1-score	MAE	RMSE	Precision	Recall	F1-score
CAWP$_{UB-ER}$ (Baseline)	0.7211	1.0231	0.6110	0.3210	0.4208	0.8073	0.9412	0.8388	0.4495	0.5853
DCR via BPSO (Baseline)	0.6832	0.8992	0.6893	0.3005	0.4185	0.7489	0.9362	0.8578	0.5901	0.6992
DCW via PSO (Baseline)	0.6431	0.8791	0.7388	0.3465	0.4717	0.7224	0.9255	0.8976	0.6589	0.7599
WCUB$_{9-sim}$(Proposed)	0.6008	0.8012	0.7599	0.3471	0.4765	0.7008	0.9009	0.8999	0.6595	0.7612
CAWP$_{IB-ER}$ (Baseline)	0.7210	1.0114	0.6806	0.3830	0.4902	0.6794	0.8968	0.9296	0.9287	0.9291
DCR via BPSO (Baseline)	0.6502	0.8839	0.6818	0.3718	0.4812	0.6543	0.8765	0.9619	0.9218	0.9414
DCW via PSO (Baseline)	0.6301	0.8432	0.6842	0.3781	0.4870	0.6292	0.8023	0.9732	0.9556	0.9643
WCIB$_{9-sim}$(Proposed)	0.6001	0.8002	0.6979	0.3892	0.4997	0.5901	0.7802	0.9798	0.9579	0.9687

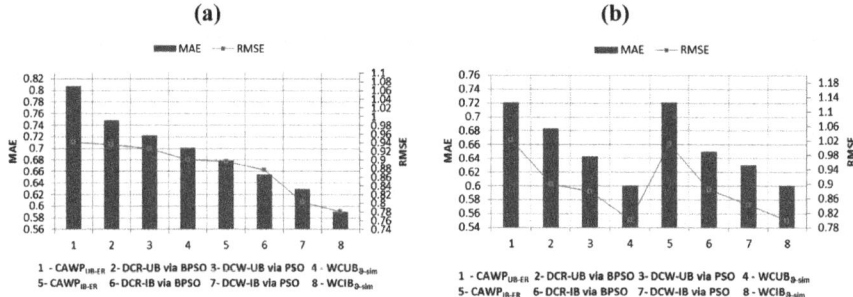

Fig. 2. Comparison of different algorithms w.r.t. MAE and RMSE values using: (a) IncarMusic dataset (b) LDOS-CoMoDa dataset.

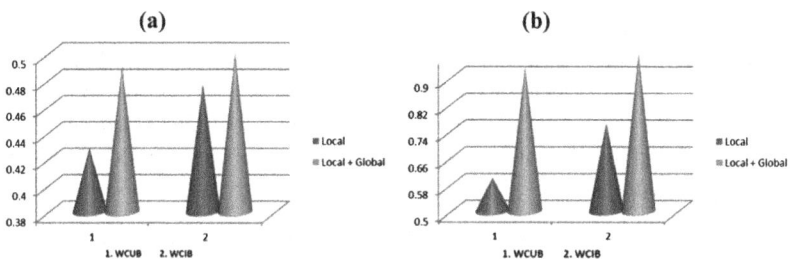

Fig. 3. Prediction accuracy (F1-score) using local similarity vs. local + global similarity on: (a) IncarMusic dataset (b) LDOS-CoMoDa dataset.

terms of MAE and RMSE. Similar trend is seen in F1-score (Table 5). Proposed algorithms reduces MAE and RMSE values remarkably compared to other baselines. The search space for BPSO is limited since the value in particle position can switch between 0 and 1 i.e. either the context feature is included or it is not. In PSO, search space becomes unlimited since the value can be in range [0,1] i.e. all context feature take some value in the range [0,1].

Hence, it can be concluded that proposed algorithms which finds optimum weight for context features using PSO and utilize the combination of local and global similarities are the best performing one. Also, item neighbourhood based algorithm are better than user neighbourhood based algorithm.

Sensitivity Analysis of Sparsity Measure ϑ
Figure 4 shows the comparison of results w.r.t. F1-score using different sparsity measures ϑ_i where $= 1, 2, 3, 4\ or\ 5$. The prediction accuracy of ϑ_2 based on F1-score is better than others using movie dataset. The reason might be that small local neighborhood is formed since it is user specific sparsity measure. It can be observed that the similar trend is shown by both user and item neighborhood algorithms. It is worth to be noted that in IncarMusic dataset ϑ_1 performs better as dataset is comparatively less sparse and rich set of local neighbors are obtained.

Hence, we claim that sparsity measure ϑ can handle local and global similarities in more effective way and the choice of sparsity measure best suited, is dataset dependent.

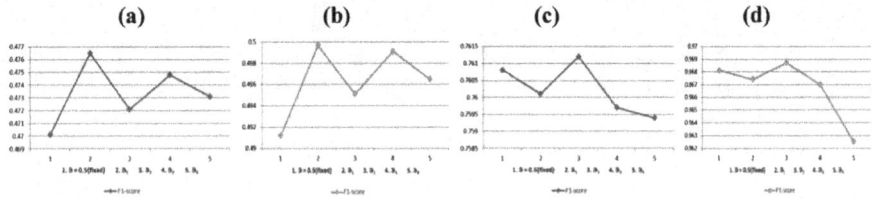

Fig. 4. Sensitivity of sparsity measure ϑ on F1-score for the datasets (a) IncarMusic in user neighborhood (b) IncarMusic in item neighborhood (c) LDOS-CoMoDa in user neighborhood (c) LDOS-CoMoDa in item neighborhood.

Performance for Group Recommendations
\Figure 5(a) and (b) illustrates that the Merging + Multiplicative technique is slightly better than other grouping techniques. The reason could be that it is able to fix up errors more. Particularly, with user neighborhood algorithms on music dataset. F1-score values in Fig. 5 and Table 3 also reveals the effectiveness of proposed algorithms for group recommendations.

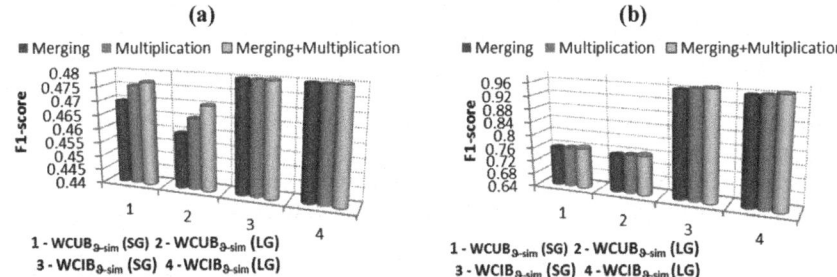

Fig. 5. Performance of different Group Recommendations techniques in terms of F1-score. SG represents small group and LG represents large group. User neighborhood and item neighborhood algorithms are compared on two datasets (a) IncarMusic (b) LDOS-CoMoDa.

5   Conclusions and Future Work

Through this paper, we tried to alleviate the data sparsity problem and the issue of finding similarity in the absence of co-rated items for context aware recommender systems. To attain these goals, we have proposed a novel framework which utilizes contextually weighted collaborative filtering techniques based on user and item neighborhood model. The aggregated similarity measure used by these algorithms attempts to take sparsity based contribution of local and global similarities to produce better quality predictions. Global similarity measure provides better predictions when data sparsity is high and can handle user rating behaviour. Local similarity measure performs well in case of low data sparsity. The algorithms are evaluated under different levels of sparsity. Also, PSO technique is used to find weights of different context features to be utilized by different components of the algorithms. Assigning weights to contextual features rather than selection or matching also solves data sparsity problem. The experimental results show that the balanced contribution of local and global similarities produce better accuracy than considering only local similarity. Moreover, PSO is an efficient optimizer for weighting context. Hence, the proposed algorithms increase predictive accuracy. Furthermore, the variant of sparsity measure that suits best is dataset dependent. The proposed algorithms are reliable for group recommendations also.

In future, we aim to utilize fuzzy logic to better understand the results.

References

1. Adomavicius, G., Sankaranarayanan, R., Sen, S., Tuzhilin, A.: Incorporating contextual information in recommender systems using a multidimensional approach. ACM Trans. Inf. Syst. (TOIS) **23**(1), 103–145 (2005). https://doi.org/10.1145/1055709.1055714
2. Adomavicius, G., Tuzhilin, A.: Context-aware recommender systems. In: Ricci, F., Rokach, L., Shapira, B., Kantor, Paul B. (eds.) Recommender Systems Handbook, pp. 217–253. Springer, Boston, MA (2011). https://doi.org/10.1007/978-0-387-85820-3_7

3. Bakshi, S., Jagadev, A.K., Dehuri, S., Wang, G.: Enhancing scalability and accuracy of recommendation systems using unsupervised learning and particle swarm optimization. Appl. Soft Comput. **15**, 21–29 (2014). https://doi.org/10.1016/j.asoc.2013.10.018

4. Baltrunas, L., et al.: InCarMusic: context-aware music recommendations in a car. In: Huemer, C., Setzer, T. (eds.) EC-Web 2011. LNBIP, vol. 85, pp. 89–100. Springer, Heidelberg (2011). https://doi.org/10.1007/978-3-642-23014-1_8

5. Baltrunas, L., Ludwig, B., Peer, S., Ricci, F.: Context relevance assessment and exploitation in mobile recommender systems. Pers. Ubiquit. Comput. **16**(5), 507–526 (2012). https://doi.org/10.1007/s00779-011-0417-x

6. Baltrunas, L., Makcinskas, T., Ricci, F.: Group recommendation with rank aggregation and collaborative filtering. In: RecSys 2010 Proceedings of the Fourth ACM Conference on Recommender Systems, pp. 119–126. ACM, New York (2010). https://doi.org/10.10145/1864708.1864733

7. Choudhary, P., Kant, V., Dwivedi, P.: Handling natural noise in multi criteria recommender system utilizing effective similarity measure and particle swarm optimization. In: Seventh International Conferences on Advances in Computing Communications-2017, pp. 853–862 (2017). Procedia Computer Sciences 115. https://doi.org/10.1016/j.procs.2017.09.168

8. Christensen, I.A., Schiaffino, S.: Entertainment recommender systems for group of users. Expert Syst. Appl. **38**, 14127–14135 (2011). https://doi.org/10.1016/j.eswa.2011.04.221

9. Dixit, V.S., Jain, P.: A proposed framework for recommendations aggregation in context aware recommender systems. In: 8th International conference on Cloud Computing, Data Science & Engineering. IEEE, Noida (2018, paper accepted and presented, in press)

10. Dixit, V.S., Jain, P.: Weighted percentile based context aware recommender systems. In: 1st International Conference on Signals, Machines and Automation, AISC. Springer, Heidelberg (2018, paper accepted and presented, in press)

11. Katpara, H., Vaghela, V.B.: Similarity measure for collaborative filtering to alleviate the new user cold start problem. In: Third International Conference on Multidisciplinary Research and Practice, vol. 4, no. 1, pp. 233–238 (2016)

12. Kosir, A., Odic, A., Kunaver, M., Tkalcic, M., Tasic, Jurij, F.: Database for contextual personalization. Elektrotehniški vestnik, vol. 78, no. 5, str. 270–274, ilustr (2011). [English print ed.]

13. Liu, H., Hu, Z., Mian, A., Tian, H., Zhu, X.: A new user model to improve the accuracy of collaborative filtering. Knowl.-Based Syst. **56**, 156–166 (2014). https://doi.org/10.1016/j.knosys.2013.11.006

14. Miao, Z., Zhao, Z., Huang, L., Yu, P., Qiao, Y., Song, Y.: Methods for improving the similarity measure of sparse scoring based on the Bhattacharyya measure. In: International Conference on Artificial Intelligence: Techniques and Applications (2016). https://doi.org/10.1016/j.eswa.2011.04.221

15. Odic, A., Tkalcic, M., Tasic, J.F., Kosir, A.: Relevant context in a movie recommender system: users opinion vs. statistical detection. In: Proceedings of the 4th International Workshop on Context-Aware Recommender Systems. Dublin, Ireland (2012)

16. Panniello, U., Tuzhilin, A., Gorgoglione, M.: Comparing context-aware recommender systems in terms of accuracy and diversity. User Model. User-Adap. Inter. **249**(1–2), 35–65 (2014). https://doi.org/10.1007/s11257-012-9135-y

17. Patra, B.K., Launonen, R., Ollikainen, V., Nandi, S.: A new similarity measure using Bhattacharya coefficient for collaborative filtering in sparse data. Knowl.-Based Syst. **82**, 163–177 (2015). https://doi.org/10.1016/j.knosys.2015.03.001

18. Saranya, K.G., Sudha Sadasivam, G.: Modified heuristic similarity measure for personalization using collaborative filtering technique. Appl. Mathe. Inf. Sci. **1**, 307–315 (2017). https://doi.org/10.18576/amis/110137

19. Sulc, Z., Rezankova, H.: Evaluation of recent similarity measures for categorical data. In: 17th Application of Mathematics and Statistics in Economics, International Scientific Conference, Poland (2014). https://doi.org/10.15611/amse.2014.17.27
20. Wang, Y., Deng, J., Gao, J., Zhang, P.: A hybrid user similarity model for collaborative filtering. Inf. Sci. **418–419**, 102–118 (2017). https://doi.org/10.1016/j.ins.2017.08.008
21. Zheng, Y., Burke, R., Mobasher, B.: Differential context relaxation for context-aware travel recommendation. In: Huemer, C., Lops, P. (eds.) EC-Web 2012. LNBIP, vol. 123, pp. 88–99. Springer, Heidelberg (2012). https://doi.org/10.1007/978-3-642-32273-0_8
22. Zheng, Y., Burke, R., Mobasher, B.: Optimal feature selection for context-aware recommendation using differential relaxation. In: Conference Proceedings of the 4th International Workshop on Context-Aware Recommender Systems, Dublin, Ireland. ACM RecSys (2012). https://doi.org/10.13140/2.1.3708.7525
23. Zheng, Y., Burke, R., Mobasher, B.: Recommendation with differential context weighting. In: Carberry, S., Weibelzahl, S., Micarelli, A., Semeraro, G. (eds.) UMAP 2013. LNCS, vol. 7899, pp. 152–164. Springer, Heidelberg (2013). https://doi.org/10.1007/978-3-642-38844-6_13
24. Zheng, Y., Burke, R., Mobasher, B.: The role of emotions in context aware recommendation. In: Decisions@RecSys Workshop in Conjunction with the 7th ACM Conference on Recommender Systems, Hong Kong, China, pp. 21–28. ACM (2013)
25. Zheng, Y., Burke, R., Mobasher, B.: Context recommendation using multilabel classification. In: IEEE/WIC/ACM International Joint Conference on Web Intelligence (WI) and Intelligent Agent Technologies (IAI), ACM Recsys, pp. 301–304. ACM, Silicon Valley (2014)
26. Zheng, Y.: A revisit to the identification of contexts in recommender systems. In: 20th International Conference on Intelligent Users Interfaces, ACM IUI, Atlanta, GA, USA, pp. 109–115 (2015)

Teaching Training Using Learning Collaborative Technologies for Knowledge Generation

Karolina González Guerrero[(✉)] [iD], José Eduardo Padilla Beltrán[iD],
and Andrés Felipe Matallana Borda[iD]

Universidad Militar Nueva Granada, Cajicá, Colombia
kgonzalezg@gmail.com

Abstract. Changes in learning and collaborative technologies due to social web have great impact on education, in particular, regarding the generation of knowledge. In this learning environment, two actors emerge in higher education, the Prosumer (to produce and to consume technologies), and the Produser (to produce and reuse technologies empowered by them). This article characterizes, describes and compares these two figures, in order to determine how appropriate the producer's action in higher education is. For research purposes, we used an exploratory study with a quantitative approach of non-experimental design, in which the Likert scale was used. Several teachers from university Militar Nueva Granada (Colombia), who use Learning and Collaborative Technologies as well as b-learning, participated in the study. Although the prosumer action is considered a preponderant figure in the economic context, this does not necessarily implies that it should be transferred to education. In fact, the producer and action should be deemed more appropriate for higher education since implementation and usage of Learning and Collaborative Technologies develop competences of empowerment and creativity, which transcend mere technologies for production and consumption.

Keywords: Collaboration · Higher education · Produser · Prosumer
Social web · Teacher

1 Introduction

1.1 Learning Collaborative Technologies in the Social Web

In the current events of economic acceleration and deceleration, the technological trend that accompanies the structuring of different flexible models emerges at the economic level, having repercussions in other aspects such as the political, social and cultural fields. In this sense, for Fernández (2014) such changes as well as economic restructuring lead to the so-called information societies, whose incidence occurs initially in the changes of production profiles according to Dussel and Quevedo (2010). It also affects inherent elements to the cultural scenario through the circulation of cultural and symbolic products that have an increasing impact on other societies, generating overcrowding of designs, services, and industrial products, among others, this is very

© Springer International Publishing AG, part of Springer Nature 2018
O. Gervasi et al. (Eds.): ICCSA 2018, LNCS 10963, pp. 306–316, 2018.
https://doi.org/10.1007/978-3-319-95171-3_24

marked in the Latin American sector according to the same author. In this regard, (Toffler 1980, p. 9) states that:

> We try to find words to describe the full force and scope of this extraordinary change. Some speak of an emerging Space Age, Age of Information, Electronic Era or Global Village. Zbigniew Brzezinski told us that we are facing a "technetronic era". The sociologist Daniel Bell describes the advent of a "post-industrial society". The Soviet Futurists talk about the RCT, the "scientific-technological revolution". I myself have written extensively about the advent of a "super-industrial society".

All these changes promote societies with more skills for the management of platforms, computers and other types of screens that allow the development of new knowledge, which in return can be shared for free, or through monetary exchange processes. Because of this, Reig and Vilchez 2013 state that current society is defined by the level of interaction it has with other groups as well as the ability to establish social links with others in the network, which has been called "socionomy" or augmented society. In this way, such society is defined as the involvement of all virtual and face-to-face social networks to generate new knowledge, ideas or strategies that change the course of reality, showing other spaces, groups and dynamics that shape collaborative, autonomous and even participatory aspects, in order to know from different perspectives what surrounds men.

This augmented society carries the burden of conveying different generational markers or different generations that may agree or disagree with the appropriation of these technologies and the path set by the implementation of virtual processes and interaction through social networks. It is for this reason that Reig and Vílchez 2013 clarify that currently there is a stage of confrontation between the good and the bad that this technology offers. However, over time, the second stage of these technological mediations, such as the social web, will be described as something normal, an aspect that is already happening and that will soon migrate to another third stage in which the generations of the mid-21st century obtain greater social and ethical rewards that can be perceived as something positive in society.

It is in the 21st century, when the web's projection begins to be clarified, whose start was raised, according to Hassan (2011) in the presentation and query of content such as text and images which are elements from the past with the advent of the so-called social web fundamental for the change of perception on Information and Communication Technologies (ICT) in the augmented society. Likewise, for Martínez and De Salvador (2012), the beginning of the 21st Century inaugurated the social web as a premise of virtual rebirth, as companies in the field of communication technologies, internet and technological services had presented failures that plunged the field into deficit of growth, which produced the renewal of the internet to leave behind the static primary web and deepen the social web according to processes of dynamic information sharing.

From the previous statements and in accordance to what Hassan (2011) expressed, the social web emerges as a modification space in which an average user can access, share and even reestablish aspects of form or content on the network. This allows him to have greater interaction and access to different spaces without the need to have specialized knowledge in computer science. In the same way, social web regained the interest from investors and several companies in the sector, for the creation of content and experiences in the network. Afterwards, between the year 1999 and the beginning of the 21st century, the explosion of the technological bubble had permeated the international scene (Peña et al. 2006). Additionally, the transcendental-technological turnaround is the inclusion of new users with diversified abilities to contribute in the development of new elements on the web, acting in parallel with the content providers that had already been working on the original web. Therefore, a number of creative forces introduced new concepts: access, production and sharing of information in the social web.

Computational science as a pillar of today's society plays a preponderant role in the exploitation of information and communication technologies. One of the scenarios in which it is constantly developed includes education and, in general, academic environments, which are considered a key factor for the future of institutions and development in general. Hence, this matter has been addressed from a social perspective regarding the change that these trends imply for the population, and from an academic perspective, regarding the emergence of actors that promote educational development over technological environments. Undoubtedly, the development of the web, software and communication and learning tools have generated significant changes in behavior and knowledge management, which is why it is important to measure the level of appropriation to these new technologies based on the application of a qualitative methodology in the study of a particular population.

1.2   The Emerging Figure: From the Prosumer to the Produser

The concept of prosumer has acquired importance in the 21st century when trying to understand the activities, attitudes and changes that occur with the subjects product of the impact of ICT and consequently of the social web. Also, Martinez and De Salvador (2012) state that the term "prosumer" exposed by Alvin Toffler to refer to the people who develop goods, services and/or experiences by themselves, without the need to sell or exchange them, becomes a neologism associated with describing what happens when something is produced and consumed for the sake of using it or distributing it.

Also, Martínez and De Salvador (2012) and Fuchs (2013) (n.d) argue that, insisting on sustaining the neologism of the prosumer is questionable insofar as it continues to reproduce the commercial essence of the term derived from the economic field. This overshadows the true magnitude of the inherent actions to this juncture of empowerment and knowledge technologies based on altruism and participation as something that is totally linked to collaboration. In this sense, both (prosumer and produser) are subject to the way in which governments, structures and cultures are reducing the gaps of access and interaction to new technologies in the communication sphere. They have established protocols according to free access to data and information within the internet to achieve more supportive attitudes in the social web.

However, what differs in these terms is that the prosumer does not acquire the symbiotic qualities of the producer and consumer; on the contrary, it differentiates them even more, recognizing that there are few people who produce on a collaborative scale for many others who consume the processes and information made by these collaborating subjects. Additionally, Martínez and De Salvador (2012) affirm that this neologism does not cease to be morphological: the prosumer is not different from the consumer or producer, but the subject has become a more conscious consumer and is more sensible during the decision-making process to carry out certain actions inside or outside the social web. It is not necessarily done by a producer, nor does it cease to be a consumer per se. Currently, there is a vast universe of information, where the prosumer develops a critical and constructive work in the use of content, cultural behavior, the creation of media environments and knowledge management. This is developed through an associative/collaborative effort that can generate an immense information network used in diverse environments, such as the academic or corporate.

The produser in its educational function would be distinguished hence, by a capacity of altruism superior to that of the prosumer. According to Martínez and De Salvador (2012), this altruism would allow him to distance himself from the logic of the market to influence the creation of materials shared by different academic communities by changing them according to the needs of those who access these materials. Because of this logic, the change of role is not merely formal, but it renews its attributes in relation to what it can do for others and with others; working as a community, from the educational field, to develop more dynamic environments based on the participation of each educational agent in order to solve emerging problems. This is complemented by Bauman (2005) and Reig (2013), who mention that currently, the pedagogical orientation of the teacher is not focused on the transmission of content, but rather on the application of principles of interaction between educators and reflections between the academic and technological fields and flexibility in education.

Producers in the educational framework are defined not by the information or content they capture or create, but how they create and use such information, depending on the potential benefits for other educational agents. A clear example can be found in Wikipedia, a platform that allows completing or improving the content inside it, with added chains of finite information as other users create pages or when new issues, concepts or referents emerge. It can be accessed for free and in the same way others can become authors who leave certain layers of content forming a framework at the service of the academic community, according to Martínez and De Salvador (2012). Hypertexts, on the other hand, are also key aspects to link these contributions in different institutions of higher education, becoming democratic and always accessible to the needs of students and teachers. Therefore, produser networks are supported by these mediations of the web for making pear-to-pear collaborations between teachers or between teacher and students as collaborative pairs.

Mainly, the world of the produser in the educational field is marked by the community structure, whose foundation is the support, collaboration and stimulation of the endogenous contribution to solve problems according to the context. This role relates a little with what was exposed by Martínez and De Salvador (2012) about the openness of the agents of an academic community to know more about the surrounding problems, but above all when recognizing a level of structural cohesion based on determining joint actions of collaboration and support that can be spread around the supports of the social web and ICT. The foregoing serves as an example that underlies the possibility of articulating forums, democratic voting in synchronous media or other mediations, which are always led by producers who are not hierarchically those who impose but rather heterarchically those who propose.

The activities that this new cultural actor could exercise could not be possible without the changes that the society and the educational context could progressively assume in reference to the common goods presented by the Internet from licenses such as the Creative Commons (CC) or another type of faculties that allow modifying, accessing or granting certain attributes of flexibility to the contents, goods and services provided in this educational field. In that sense, Paltrinieri and Degli (2013) talk about 'common goods based on prosumerism' (p. 25), as an alternative way of transcending the limitations of authorship rights; often coercive in relation to the cession of rights and the prohibition of access to restricted content that extend the beneficial system of capitalist structures. This creates a bridge of collective access to obtain permits for creation and modification that respect the efforts developed by each subject, but at the service of a common goal that is the construction of collegiate knowledge.

2 Methodology

In relation to the importance of exploring the emergence of new roles in higher education teachers, born as a consequence of ICT and especially the social web, this study is based on a quantitative methodological approach (Sautu et al. 2005), whose design is encompassed within a non-experimental setting because it is not intended to control variables, but rather to consider a type of exploratory transactional method. As explained by Hernández (2006), data can be collected in a specific instance which in return allows investigating essential aspects of the attitudinal and experiential type on the role of the produser in the teacher's professional performance. Furthermore, the hypothesis aims to verify the degree of acceptance by the teachers of the use and appropriation of social web, and how this allows performing the functions carried out by a produser, while producing and using contents or digital experiences inside and outside the classroom to contribute to the learning process of students.

According to Hernández (2006), transactional designs of exploratory type allow the recognition of variables or elements of a social group or concept that has not been exhaustively addressed to delve into little-known problems. In this sense, and according to the documentary reviews presented by the research, there are few studies that frame the figure of produser in the educational context, so it is important to carry out surveys and inquiries with subjects inside the scope of the study and thus start to recognize the impact, difficulties and dispositions from adopting aspects of the produser concept linked to the dynamics given in the social web within the context of higher education.

The sample of the study was obtained from a random selection of teachers who on a daily basis use collaborative learning technologies in b-learning and distance education modalities, obtaining a sample of 37 teachers (17 from the Francisco José de Paula University and 20 from the Universidad Militar Nueva Granada). It is important to point out that the sample has a non-probabilistic type given that, in the words of Hernández (2006): 'the choice of the elements does not depend on the probability, but on causes related to the characteristics of the research or who makes the sample' (p. 241). This type of sampling allows selecting the teachers with the closest approach to the object of study according to research lines, executed research projects and teacher-researcher trajectory of the aforementioned university. This type of sampling is also referred to by Crespo and Salamanca (2007) as convenience sampling, whose reference is the selection of people who contribute with their professional experience to the recognition of the analyzed emerging factor. Therefore, since it is exploratory, elements based on luck cannot be left in the sampling.

Regarding the applied instrument, the Likert scale is used. This type of scaling enables, through a series of items in the form of affirmations or questions, to determine the reaction or attitude of the sample population regarding an object or concept. Therefore, in this case, the assessment of the relevance of the produser's role in the context of higher education is sought. In this way, the response options that indicate favorability or a lack of favorability are presented, indicating the level of agreement in front of said affirmation (Hernández 2006). Thus, for the particular case of the present study twelve affirmations are used that are based on recognizing if there are functions of the role produser and/or prosumer that the teacher has been adapting inside and outside the classroom and which aspects are mentioned at the level of skills, experiences and aptitudes according to the impact of ICT and the social web in higher education.

3   Results

Taking into account what was described by Rensis Likert cited in Hernández (2006), the Likert scale generates a range of favorability or lack of favorability, depending on the number of affirmations or assumptions that attempt to assess the attitude of the sample vis-à-vis the object of study. Therefore, the Likert scale proposed for this study consists of twelve (12) statements, whose weighing method takes the statistical average of the ranges of favorability or the lack of it. A high favorability is attached to the referent of strongly agreeing, which must be close to a value of five (5), and with a minimum value of one (1), concerning the aspect of strong disagreement. Of course, the assignment of (5) and (1) will depend on the positive or negative orientation given to the assumption or affirmation. When inquiring whether ICT and especially the social web tend to distract the learner from their academic duties, a negative orientation arises. In this sense, the sample agrees in a large percentage with this assumption (see Fig. 1). Likewise, the average acquired for this item is (2.1), which is closer to the agreeing aspect.

The point related to whether social networks represent mediations for teaching multiple contents, the response is expressed in a positive manner taking into account the position taken in this report. As a result of this, the population sample is approached by the option of agreement (see Fig. 2) whose average sets at (4.2), thus showing a degree of favorability with respect to this topic.

Inquiring on social web and its relevance in the creation of links and networks with academic peers to generate new knowledge, the trend marks a positive connotation. Due to this, the majority of the subjects in the sample have a very favorable attitude towards this fact. On the negative side, there is an assumption that the relative impact of the figure of the prosumer is much more focused on the economic aspect than on the educational aspect. Therefore, the sample population is divided between recognizing

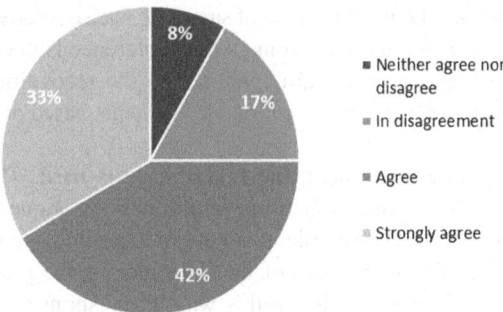

Fig. 1. The social web and its impact on the student

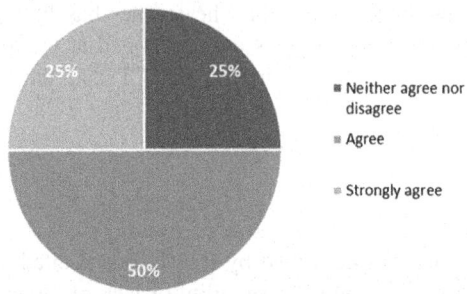

Fig. 2. Social networks in education

the incidence of the prosumer in the educational context beyond its roots in the economic sector. The inquiry on whether the produser consumes more content or experience than it produces, as well as the statement on whether the produser is more a specialized consumer than an emerging producer, have the lowest scores in relation to a negative attitude (Fig. 3).

In accordance with the affirmations of the positive approach, the predominant option was the one that strongly agrees, for which the population sample has an attitude

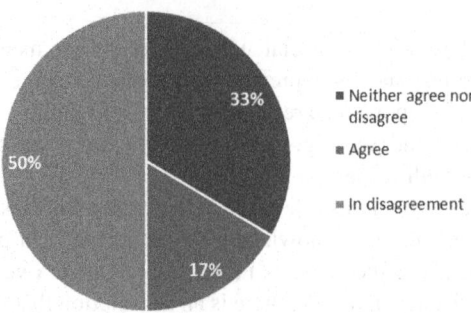

Fig. 3. The producer teacher, consumes more knowledge than it produces

of support during the research. Such option had a frequency of appearance of more than (30) times in all completed queries (Fig. 4).

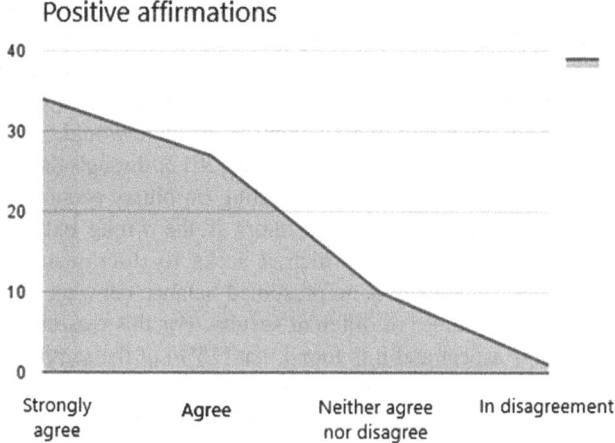

Fig. 4. Frequency of choice in positive affirmation

4   Discussion

The results of the research evidenced that most of the subjects that participated in it, support the inclusion of these mediations to potentiate the actions carried out inside and outside the classroom. The foregoing can be deduced from the favorability shown in Likert scale affirmations about collaborative actions, significant learning and networks used for the construction of knowledge, either with academic peers or with students in the context of higher education. To that extent, the assumptions of Mondragon (2016) about being connected to learn and have greater interaction with others are reflected in the need to articulate these referents of the web in the educational context. However, the teachers who participated in the research also suppose the difficulties that social web has at the moment of isolating and even individualizing the subject in the private realization beyond the promotion of the social projects and the ethical-political vision.

In the statements made by Hassan (2011) about the possibility that social web gives to the user to access, share or modify content on the internet for different purposes, teachers extend this meaning based on their experience stating that it has generated elements of educational nature creating, modifying or sharing content in different disciplinary areas with other teachers and even with students. Therefore, the teacher must guide their students in the use of these technological resources so that the students can use them for meta-learning through autonomous strategies of search, selection and understanding of information. As stated by the teachers participating in the scale of attitudes, social web does not become a distraction for the academic duties of the students.

On another topic, when investigating the concept of prosumer and its favorability or lack of favorability, it was attempted to analyze whether the concept currently has a place in the context of higher education through its characteristics and roles or on the contrary, whether it is inexorably associated with the consumerist logic of consumption, which may pave the way to think about the produser concept with more focus on cultural elements, empowerment and development that benefit different social groups in common problems. This is also shown by the results obtained when investigating the participating teachers, if the concept of prosumer is rooted in the economic sphere, presenting an agreement regarding this assumption, as there would be a correlation in what was expressed by Martínez and De Salvador (2012) through the reproduction of the commercial essence of this neologism, insisting on binary economistic logic.

Another aspect pointed out by these authors is the wrong extrapolation of the concept to the technological area in which it seeks to discriminate the profile of producer and consumer, since there is no presumed balance between what is produced and consumed by each prosumer in different sectors. For this reason, the Likert scale instrument refers to this aspect and it is found that (75%) of the sample agrees that the possible produser consumes more content than it produces. Therefore, this can derive either as an attribute of an emerging specialized consumer or as the fact that few consumers contribute to different prosumers for the generation of content or collaborative experiences. In this sense, the perspective of Ritzer and Jurgenson (2010) is relevant in describing the prosumer in daily self-service tasks and the inclusion of specialized consumers to give feedback on experiences of use or development of products, contents or services.

Emphasizing that the cultural work of the teacher involves ethical, social and pedagogical actions, with emphasis on the cognition and attitudes that are available for the learning process, the articulation of the concept of prosumer would not be very cohesive with this pedagogical perspective. The concept of produser, enrolled in the experience of creating and sharing content regardless of whether it is produced or consumed, would be more akin to thinking not only about what is or can be created, but how it is created and at the same time for what purposes it is used. This connects with the initiative of collective intelligences proposed by Lévy (2004) through the inclusion of molecular-scale technologies and the principles of collaborative networks for problem solving, not only of a scientific nature, but also those emerging in different groups or sectors in everyday life.

5 Conclusions

The differences between the concept of prosumer and produser consider aspects that go beyond the formal or semantic settings. While the former still harbors economic elements that reproduce consumption logics despite being immersed in invisible economies according to Ritzer and Jurgenson (2010), they do not depend on structures and institutions to generate content or processes that contribute to other subjects or social groups. In contrast, the produser is associated with practices and referents in the cultural and participatory scene, returning to the user the possibility of understanding how and what for is the creation and collaboration in terms of making products, contents or services through ICT, especially regarding social web. In this way, it is pertinent to consider teaching literacy processes that integrate elements of this concept and consider hierarchical collaborative strategies for the creation of content or products that solve problems with students or other agents of the educational community.

According to the results obtained with the Likert scale on whether the teacher is coerced by educational institutions in terms of the technological mediations that he uses or prefers; Paltrinieri and Degli (2013) discuss the freedom in common goods on the web or progressive changes in the structures to share, modify and access certain contents that respect the codes of authorship or licensing. The teacher finds it difficult to adopt attributes of the prosumer and especially of the produser in order to create elements that can be shared and even transformed with pedagogical or didactic purposes.

The foregoing should bring with it a reflection on the creative role of the teacher and the dialog between teachers and educational institutions to participate more in technological development for academic training. Due to this, in the next phases of this research, it is important to investigate the role of managers, students and other agents involved in the educational community to understand the impact of protocols and the management of educational institutions in the creative, participatory and cultural role of the teacher when implementing social web inside and outside the classroom. The future of this research is based on the study and analysis of the educational phenomenon in relation to ICT and technological tools, which generally have a significant impact on this environment, in order to develop a methodology for strengthening the effect of online research in higher education.

Acknowledgements. Funding: This work was supported by the Universidad Militar Nueva Granada [2018] – Code of the project's result: INV-DIS-2569.

References

Bauman, Z.: Los retos de la educación en la modernidad líquida. Editorial Gedisa, S.A., Barcelona (2005)

Crespo, M.C., Salamanca, A.: El muestreo en la investigación cualitativa. Nure Investigación **27**, 1–9 (2007). http://www.nureinvestigacion.es/ficheros_administrador/f_metodologica/fmetodologica_27.pdf

Dussel, I., Quevedo, L.: Educación y nuevas tecnologías: los desafíos pedagógicos ante el mundo digital. Santillana, Buenos Aires (2010)

Fernández, P.: Consumos culturales en América Latina y la emergencia del prosumidor: un recorrido conceptual desde la sociedad de la información. Commun. Papers **4**(3), 87–100 (2014)

Fuchs, C.: (s.f.) Digital prosumption labour on social media in the context of the capitalist regime of time. Recuperado de (2013). http://tas.sagepub.com/content/early/2013/10/03/0961463X13502117.full.pdf+html

Hassan, H.: La Web social Estudio y Análisis de la Revolución Social de Internet. Recuperado de (2011). https://riunet.upv.es/bitstream/handle/10251/10925/memoria.pdf?sequence=1

Hernández, R.: Metodología de la investigación, 4ª edn. McGraw-Hill Interamericana, México (2006)

Lévy, P.: Inteligencia colectiva, por una antropología del ciberespacio, BIREME, Washington (2004). Martínez, F. (Trans.)

Martínez, Y., De Salvador, S.: El Produser como producción de usuarios: más allá de wreaders y de prosumers. Revista Razón y Palabra 86 (2012). http://www.razonypalabra.org.mx/N/N86/V86/24_MartinezSalvador_V86.pdf

Mondragon Corporación Cooperativa: 2006 Annual Report, Mondragon Corporación Cooperativa, Arrasate (Gi-puzkoa) (2006)

Paltrinieri, R., Degli, P.: Processes of inclusion and exclusion in the sphere of prosumerism. Future Internet 5, 21–33 (2013). https://doi.org/10.3390/fi5010021

Peña, I., Córcoles, C., Casado, C.: El Profesor 2.0: docencia e investigación desde la Red. Recuperado de (2006). http://www.uoc.edu/uocpapers/3/dt/esp/pena_corcoles_casado.pdf

Reig, D., Vílchez, L.: Los jóvenes en la era de la hiperconectividad: tendencias, claves y miradas. Fundación Telefónica, Madrid (2013)

Ritzer, G., Jurgenson, N.: The Nature of Capitalism in the Age of the Digital "Prosumer" (2010). http://joc.sagepub.com/content/10/1/13.full.pdf+html

Sautu, R., Boniolo, P., Dalle, P., Elbert, R.: Manual de metodología. Colección Campus Virtual, Buenos Aires (2005)

Toffler, A.: La tercera ola. Ediciones Nacionales, Bogotá (1980)

A Scalable Bluetooth Low Energy Design Model for Sensor Detection for an Indoor Real Time Location System

Jay Pancham[1(✉)], Richard Millham[1(✉)], and Simon James Fong[2(✉)]

[1] Durban University of Technology, Durban, South Africa
{panchamj, richardml}@dut.ac.za
[2] University of Macau, Taipa, Macau SAR
ccfong@umac.mo

Abstract. Indoor Real Time Location Systems (RTLS) research identifies Bluetooth Low Energy as one of the technologies that promise an acceptable response to the requirements of the Healthcare environment. A scalable dynamic model for sensor detection, which uses the latest developments of Bluetooth Low Energy, is designed to extend its range coverage. This design extends on our previous papers which tested the range and signal strength through multiple types of obstructions. The model is based on the scenarios and use cases identified for future use in RTLS within the Health care sector. The Unified Modelling Language (UML) is used to present the models and inspections and walkthroughs are used to validate and verify them. This model will be implemented using Bluetooth Low Energy devices for patients and assets with in the Health care sector.

Keywords: Bluetooth Low Energy · BLE · Real Time Location System
RSSI · Indoor positioning

1 Introduction

Over the past several years, indoor localization has grown into an important research topic, attracting much attention in the networking research community [1]. The increase in popularity for positioning services offered by smart devices and their related technology has indicated a turning point in the field of indoor localization [2]. Our ultimate goal is to design a cost effective and efficient RTLS within the constraints identified in our previous paper [3] for a Healthcare environment. Previous work by [4] also evaluated the technologies for indoor RTLS as well as identified the methods used in determining locations. This paper determines the possible range and throughput imitative of quantitative technological evaluations by [5] with Bluetooth Low Energy (LE) in different scenarios of a Healthcare environment.

The rest of the paper is organized as follows. Section 2 illustrates the basic concepts of indoor localization and modelling specifications. Section 3 defines the methodology used to define the design model. In Sect. 4, the authors present and

© Springer International Publishing AG, part of Springer Nature 2018
O. Gervasi et al. (Eds.): ICCSA 2018, LNCS 10963, pp. 317–330, 2018.
https://doi.org/10.1007/978-3-319-95171-3_25

discuss the results of the validated and verified design model. Thereafter discussions and conclusions and future work are presented.

2 Literature Review

2.1 Technologies and Techniques for RTLS

A number of different technologies have been tested for use in RTLS. However, due to the availability of newer technologies, the best technology within the constraints need to identified for indoor RTLS. [4] evaluated the most popular technologies of RTLS published in recent peer reviewed works. They used the most commonly use attributes in terms of Real Time Location System (RTLS) within literature and the healthcare exemplar in order to assess these technologies. In addition to the exemplar of a hospital survey, data of 23 US hospitals [6] was used in the evaluation process. In the previous paper, we investigated technologies such as WiFi, Bluetooth and RFID and determined evaluation criteria cost [7], energy consumption [8], detection range [7], size and accuracy [9]. Although accuracy was identified as one of the attributes it will be used in future research as this paper comprises preliminary work leading to future research. The health care sector has other constraints such as electromagnetic interference [10], [11] which we now mitigate with low battery transmission level but space constraints limited our selection to the most appropriate and the most common attributes. Other constraints do exist but were not identified as most common. An important example within a health care environment is electromagnetic interference especially in Industrial, Scientific and Medical (ISM) radio bands [10] which can be mitigated with the lowest transmission levels.

Attempts to mitigate these common constraints using popular RTLS technologies researched by [4] include Radio Frequency Identification Devices (RFID), Bluetooth classic, Bluetooth LE, Zigbee and Wi-Fi. Lee et al. compared BLE and ZigBee technologies using a single fixed distance of one meter but did not have conclusive results indicating which technology is better as wireless transmission is greatly affected by practical situations, such as the realistic environment interferences [5]. Furthermore, this experiment did not provide measurements of aspects such as RSSI or throughput beyond this fixed distance, both measurements which are needed for a proper network technology evaluation for the fixed distance.

An example of a Bluetooth system is the Bluetooth Local Infotainment Point (BLIP) [12] which is a managed network offering access to LAN/WAN via Bluetooth [13]. Such a network will require a number of BLIP nodes to which the Bluetooth devices will connect to due to its limited range. These Bluetooth nodes then provide access to the LAN/WAN. With the advancement of Bluetooth LE such nodes will be minimized or eliminated depending on the environment.

Bluetooth classic also has drawbacks in crowded areas due to signal attenuation and interference. Bluetooth classic can transfer large quantities of data, but consumes battery life quickly and more costly than Bluetooth LE or other indoor localizations technologies [14]. In addition, accuracy for RTLS differs at a cost in term of power consumption, size of device, and other factors. This gave birth to Bluetooth LE suitable to exchange little amounts of data consuming lower energy at a cheaper cost.

2.2 Bluetooth LE

Bluetooth Low Energy (BLE) is the power-version of Bluetooth that was built for the Internet of Things (IoT) making it perfect for devices that run for long periods on power sources, such as coin cell batteries or energy-harvesting devices [15]. One of the two systems of this version is Bluetooth low energy which transmits small packets of data whilst consuming significantly less power than the previous version of Bluetooth [8]. A BLE system typically consists of a stationery anchor to detect the tags, a tag and the location engine to calculate the location [16]. BLE is an improvement and a later version of Bluetooth (BT) offering several advantages such as smaller form factor, lower cost and extended coverage. The point-to-point communication of the current BLE nodes have only limited coverage over a short range. Hence the proposal of a wireless mesh multi-hop network that has multiple nodes (sensors) that are capable of communicating with each other to enable routing of packets to extend this limited coverage as a possible solution [17].

Bluetooth® 5, released on 6 December 2016, is a transformative update on previous versions that significantly increases the range, speed and broadcast messaging capacity of Bluetooth applications. This version quadruples range and doubles speed of low energy connections while increasing the capacity of connectionless data broadcasts by eight times [18, 19]. These will impact on reliability, robustness, responsiveness. This latest version will have quadruple the range, double the speed and an increased data broadcasting capacity of 800% as compared to Bluetooth Classic [20].

This earlier Bluetooth Classic version uses 79 channels with 1 MHz spacing whilst Bluetooth LE uses 40 channels with 2 MHz spacing in the unlicensed industrial, scientific and medical (ISM) band of 2.4 GHz. The range for Bluetooth LE extends from 2402 MHz (RF channel 0; logical channel 37) to 2480 MHz (RF channel 39; logical channel 39). Three channels (logical 37, 38 and 39) are so called advertising channels; logical channels 0 to 36 are data channels. The advertising channels are positioned so that they are not disturbed by the non-overlapping WLAN channels 1, 6 and 11 in the ISM band, see Fig. 1. Bluetooth LE now can provide the higher transmission speeds as a result of the increased 2402 MHz wider channels as compared to the Bluetooth classic 1 MHz channels. In addition to higher transmission speeds more data can be transmitted within these channels as a result of the higher transmission frequency.

2.3 Modelling Use Cases and Class Models

Using natural language for specifications is also prone to be culturally dependent and therefore to result in ambiguous or unclear meanings [21]. However, using the combined concepts of Unified Modelling Language (UML) makes it easier to visualize and understand Grady Booch, James Rumbaugh and [22]. One of the constructs of UML a use case is a coherent unit of functionality expressed as a transaction between the software product itself and the users of the software product (actors) [22–25]. Use cases

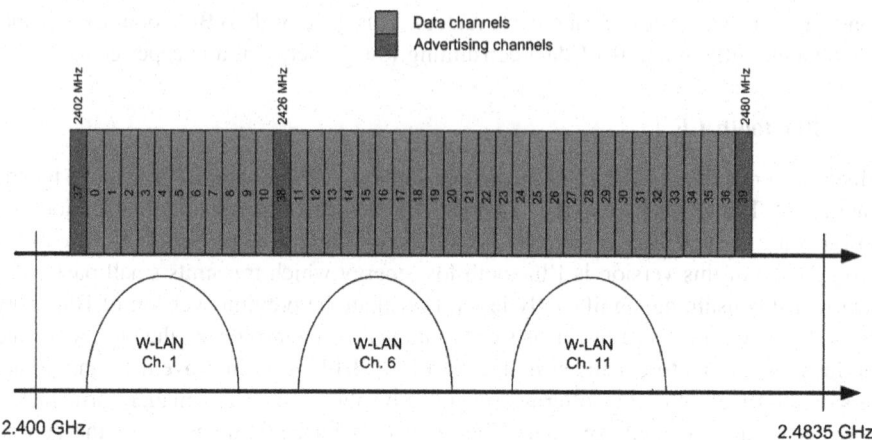

Fig. 1. Bluetooth LE channels.

are extensively used to document user requirements and to drive the software development process [26, 27]. A use case describes a coherent work unit or task to be carried by one or more actors with the help of the system. However different models such as use cases, activity diagrams and class models are based on different modelling techniques and aim at different levels of abstraction. The close coupling of the activity diagrams and use case models demonstrated by [28] is used to validate and verify the proposed model.

There is no hard and fast rule in defining scenarios and use cases. Some people consider that each use case is a single scenario; others, as suggested by Stevens and Pooley (2006), encapsulate a set of scenarios in a single use case. According to Pooley, each scenario is a single thread through the use case, thereby consolidating the common scenario into a single use case. This has the advantage of guiding the number of use cases in a system to the core requirements. Any variation of the core feature will be encapsulated within a use case. A scenario may be used to illustrate an interaction or the execution of a use case instance [22, 25]. A scenario is a specific instantiation of a use case, just as an object is an instantiation of a class [24]. Thus, a scenario is a unique set of internal activities within a use case and represents a unique path through the use case. A fully developed use case increases the probability of a developer thoroughly understanding a business process and the ways in which the system must support them [23].

3   Methodology

Our approach was to use Bluetooth LE network to propose a scalable indoor RTLS solution with low power consumption, and long detection range. In order to satisfy these constraints within Healthcare we developed a model in UML to help conceptualize the solution design. In order to conserve sensor battery power, the lowest possible transmit power level is used in the design to hop via neighboring sensors to a nearest reader.

The network design consists of readers that will connect to a server via WiFi or Ethernet, thereby providing the link for sensors to the network. Sensors connect to the readers and neighboring sensors via Bluetooth LE. Sensors connect to each other forming a low energy dynamic mesh network. The transmit power level is variable and can be used to penetrate obstacles such as dry wall, glass and solid brick wall [29]. Sensors are in constant motion and often disconnect and connect to neighboring sensors continuously forming a dynamic network. Therefore, there is a need to update the connectivity paths from sensors to the readers continuously. Routes are maintained both at the server and at the sensor level to minimize communication between the server and the sensor and hence lower power consumption. Furthermore, neighboring sensors are used to hop to connect to the nearest readers to conserve energy. Therefore, there is a need to define a model to detect the neighboring sensors and readers. UML modelling is used for the definition, validation and verification of the use cases.

3.1   UML Modelling of Use Cases

All possible scenarios for the mesh network commencing from acquisition to disposal are considered. However, due to the space constraints in this paper only the main use cases and scenarios are discussed. Use cases such as sensors acquisition and disposal, sensor allocation and deallocation are omitted. Sensors will need to detect all possible readers in its vicinity to connect to the network. If a neighboring sensor is detected it will be used to hop to the closest reader. Each sensor will maintain a minimum of two path to readers to ensure that there is sufficient redundancy thereby increasing the reliability of the network.

For each use case we exploit activity graphs to model the behavior of the use case. Such a use case is defined by: unique number, unique name and a goal of the use case. a pre and a post condition specifying the assumptions, goal of the use case, the result of the action, and a set of actors involved in the action. The related scenario is characterized by a unique number, name, trigger that initiate the scenario, a set or pre and post conditions, description of the main flow action steps, business rules and system rules.

The related activity diagram is used to model the behavior of the use case *detect reader/sensor*. A use case describes a set of scenarios that represent concrete executions of the corresponding work unit. A scenario corresponds to a path through the activity graph of the use case which starts at the start vertex, is guided by action post-conditions and edge guards, and ends up in a final vertex [28].

A use case generally describes several scenarios that will allow an actor (usually a system user) to benefit from the services offered by that use case [30]. An instance of the use case *successful detection of a sensor/reader* is used to traverse the use case activity diagram.

In order to closely couple the activity diagram and the domain class model the activity diagram is extended to introduce the concept of a class scope. For each of the use cases the set of domain classes with instances involved in the execution of the work unit is determined. These set of classes is called the *class scope* and is derived from the use case description and its pre- and post-condition and complies with the domain class model [28].

3.2   Validation and Verification

Static methods such as walk-through and inspections are used to establish and document whether items, processes, services or documents conform to specific requirements and whether the products of a given development phase satisfy the conditions imposed at the start of the phase [25, 31].

The validated use case model and the class scopes is used to verify the use cases and activity diagrams. Validation and verification of requirements specifications bear certain similarities, but the latter works on a more formal level [28].

4   Results

4.1   UML Modelling of Use Cases

The main use case *Sensor detect reader/sensor* is described in Table 1. The goal of this use case is to detect the neighboring sensors and/or readers, a process triggered by either a movement of a sensor or the expiry of a predefined time period. The scenario described in Table 2 which is an instance of the use case is triggered by the movement of a sensor. Since the sensor has moved its new neighbors (readers and/or sensors) needs to be detected. This then updates the required information until either the next movement or the expiry of the time period.

Table 1. Use case sensor detect readers/sensors

Use case title	Use case description
Use case no.	UC01
Name	Sensors detect readers/sensor
Related requirements	None
Goal in context	To detect neighbouring sensors and readers

Table 2. Scenario sensor moved location

Scenario title	Scenario description
Scenario no.	UC01SC01
Name	Sensor detect reader/sensor
Trigger	Sensor has moved location
Preconditions	Motion has been detected
Main flow action steps	1. Broadcast
	2. Receive acknowledgements from neighbouring sensors
	3. Update neighbour sensor or reader table
	4. Set timer
Exceptions	Acknowledgement not received
Post conditions	One or more neighbouring sensors/readers acknowledgements are received
Business rules	None
System rules	1. Maintain multiple paths to readers for redundancy

The use case diagram depicts the actors (*Sensor and System*) and the main use cases (*Detect Readers/Sensors* and *Determine Sensors in Range*) of the sub-system Bluetooth LE Indoor Real Time Location System (BLE iRTLS). Due to space constraints only the main use cases are depicted (Fig. 2).

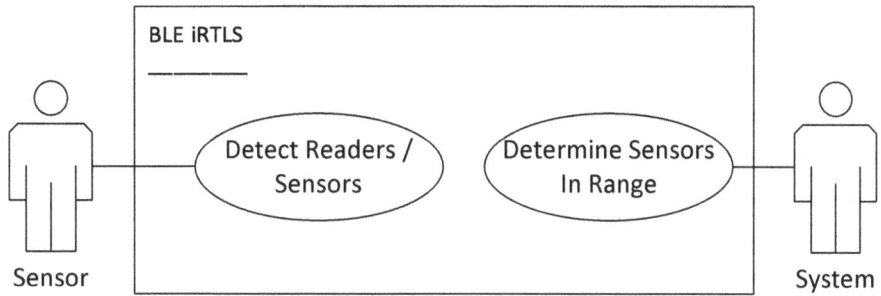

Fig. 2. Use case diagram

The activity diagram shows the process followed within the use case *Detect Reader/Sensor* is indicted in Fig. 3(a). This process commences with the need for determining the new neighboring readers and sensors (the triggers discussed earlier). The trigger invokes a broadcast of a data packet to determine the neighbors. The broadcast is set at the lowest transmission level. If no acknowledgement is received within predetermined time period, the transmission level is increased and the process is repeated. An omission (no acknowledgement received after max transmission level reached) that was noted and is indicated in dotted lines. Such an omission will cause the continuous broadcasts at the highest transmission level.

The scenario of a successful detection of neighboring sensors is indicated in Fig. 3(b). The detection subsystem is that of a neighboring sensor receiving the broadcast, processing the message and sending back an acknowledgement. The sending sensor then records the details received from the neighboring sensor.

4.2   Validation

Figure 4 shows a sub set of the domain class diagram with the classes *Sensor, Broadcast, Acknowledgement, Neighboring Sensor, Neighboring Reader* with their respective methods and attributes. The omission noted above will lead to the removal of all neighboring sensors and readers related to the sensor that tried to detect its neighbors (Fig. 5).

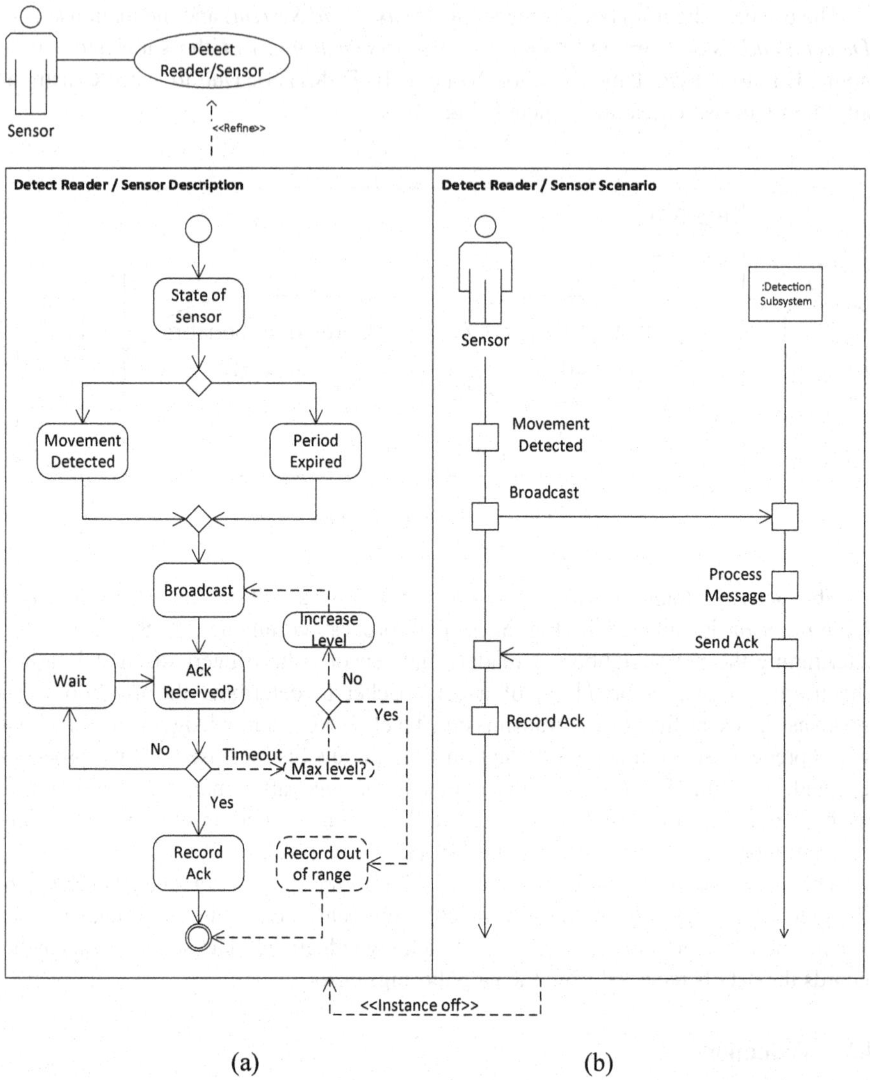

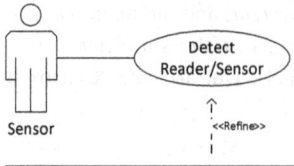

Fig. 3. Use case detect reader/sensor with activity diagram (a) and scenario successful detection (b)

The class scope diagram of the use case *Detect reader/sensor* indicates the domain classes (*Sensor, Broadcast, Neighbouring Sensor and Acknowledgement*) are participants to the use case. This class scope diagram properly couples the activity diagram indicate in Fig. 3 with the domain class model indicated in Fig. 4.

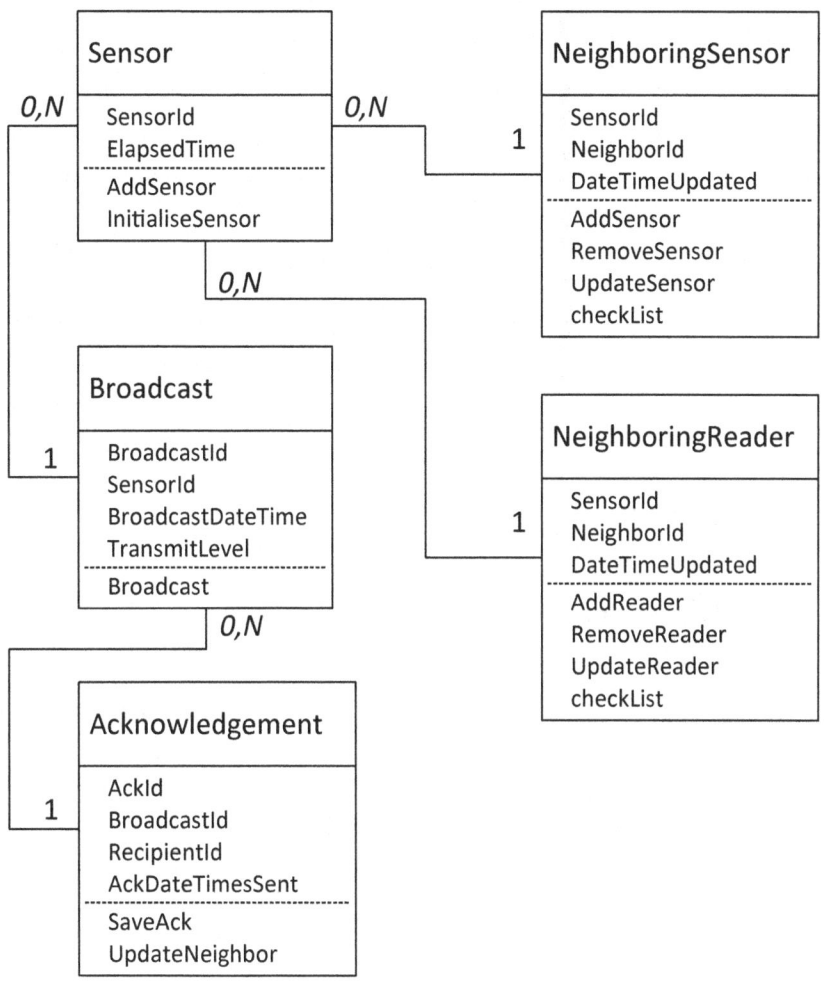

Fig. 4. Subset domain class diagram

Figure 6 depicts a user centered view of the scenario *Detect reader/*sensor. Such a detailed graphic diagram is used generally by end uses and domain experts for a walk through. The domain constellations and the textual descriptions are checked for correctness using a walk through.

4.3   Verification

The business use case *Detect reader/sensor* is reused during the verification and is further detailed by the interaction sequence called a test scenario. This test scenario *successful detection of neighbouring sensor* Fig. 7(a) is a test case where the *detection subsystem* receives the broadcast message, processes it and responds with an acknowledgement. The interaction sequence shows details of the sequence of events

Detect Reader / Sensor
<<trace>>
Detect Reader / Sensor
Participant
Participant
Sensor
Broadcast
Participant
Participant
Neighboring Sensor
Acknowledgement

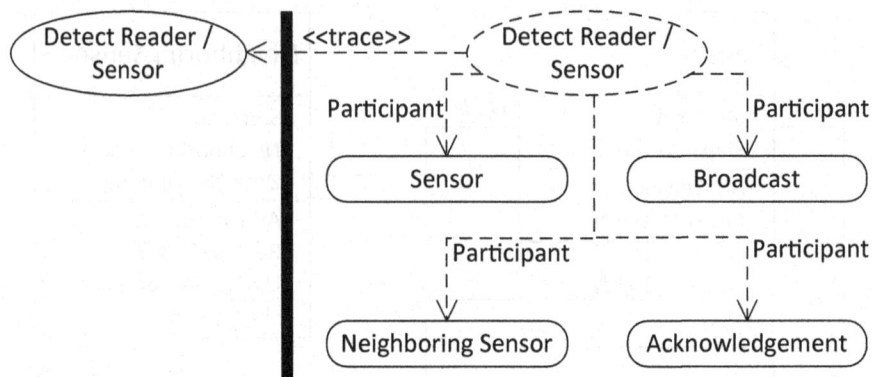

Fig. 5. Class scope of use case detect reader/sensor

Domain Object / Actor
Action
Detect Sensor
Movement Detected
Broadcast
Process Message
Send Ack
Record Ack
Domain Objects
Sensor
Broadcast
Acknowledgement
Neighboring Sensor
Actors
Sensor
Detection Subsystem
Actions
Neighbor Identified
Timeout

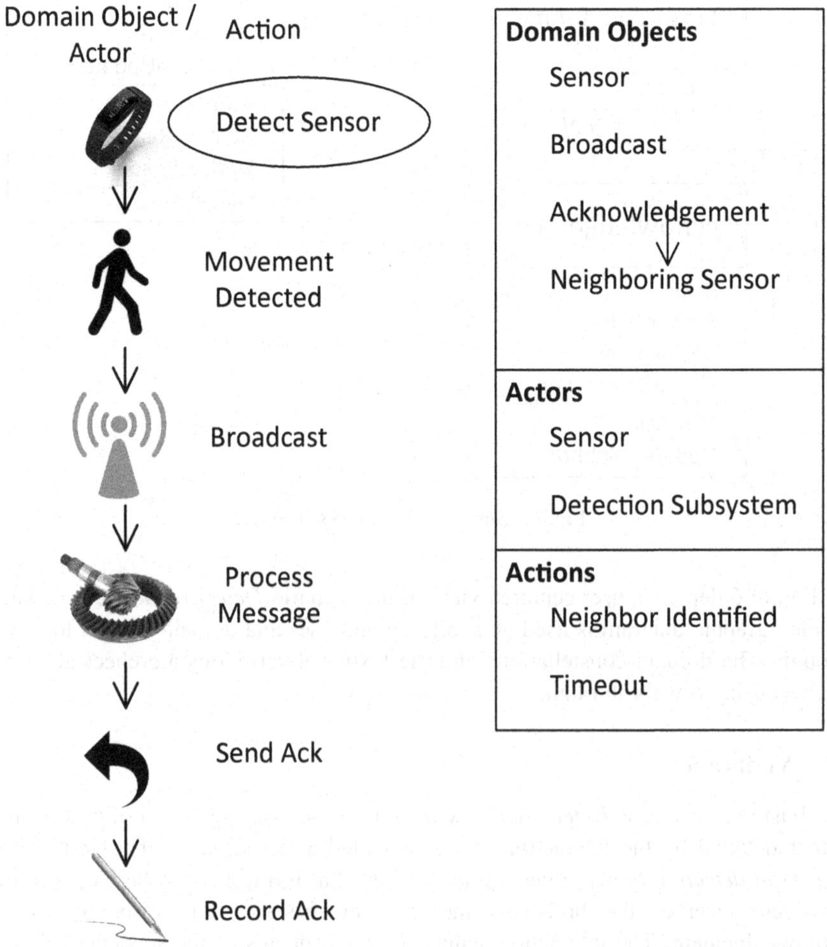

Fig. 6. User centered view of a scenario for use case detect reader/sensor

which check its internal list, records the Id of the sending sensor and responds with an acknowledgement of being range. This tests the related class model depicted in Fig. 4 against the activity diagram in Fig. 3.

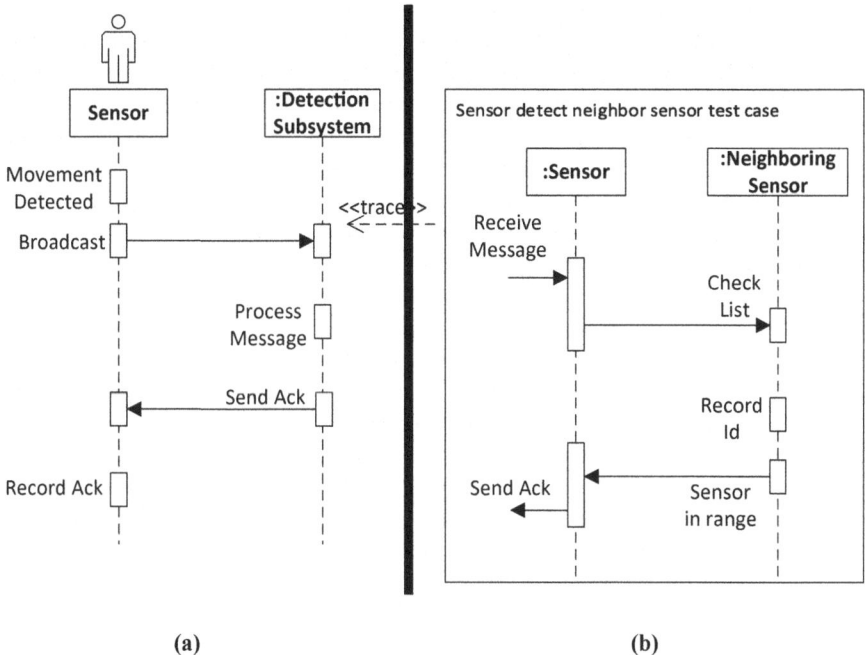

                    (a)   (b)

Fig. 7. Test scenario detect reader/sensor (a) and the interaction sequence (b)

5 Discussion of Results

The design model proposed for detection of neighboring is validated and verified by demonstration of one of the main use cases *Detect reader/sensor*. Such a design model is proposed to link sensors and readers forming a mesh network. The validation and verification was done using the commonly used inspections and walkthroughs methods. One of the several issues identified and documented has been used to indicate how such processes have been used to ensure completeness and correctness, have been identified during this process, whilst others have been omitted due to space constraints.

The dynamic detection of neighboring sensors and readers offer the ability of the network to scale as per the domain requirements. Furthermore, because such a network uses a connectionless oriented service the bandwidth requirements will be very low and the ability to increase the number of sensors is simplified.

6 Conclusion and Future Work

The primary focus of this paper was to design and validate a scalable Bluetooth LE model that can be used for indoor RTLS especially in the Healthcare sector. Such a validated model has the potential to be implemented in a real life scenario for real time location of patients and assets within a healthcare environment.

Although RTLS have realized benefits in some cases, further research was called for to reduce the serious technical impediments such as obstacle obstruction of signals to its implementation including asset management [6]. The design demonstrates that Bluetooth LE can be configured into a low cost low energy network architecture enabling lower energy consumption [32] and extending the range. The use of Bluetooth LE devices, with low power consumption will extend battery life thereby reducing maintenance [5]. Due to the high volume of patients as well as the size of hospitals, especially those in the public sector, cost is an important constraint.

Some of these challenges such as network range is mitigated by using mesh networks as well as intermediate sensors to link to others in the near vicinity. With the latest technology used unlike its predecessors the Bluetooth LE devices forms a mesh network to extend the network with the lowest possible energy consumption. A more detailed experiment with different values for variables such as transmission power levels, data packet size etc. will be conducted using the proposed model for improved and accurate performance in terms of indoor real time location. The results of this will be published in future articles. Furthermore, a prototype will be setup in a Healthcare environment to test practical applicability of the processes and newly designed model.

References

1. Wang, Y., Ye, Q., Cheng, J., Wang, L.: RSSI-based bluetooth indoor localization. In: 2015 11th International Conference on Mobile Ad-hoc and Sensor Networks (MSN), pp. 165–171. IEEE (2015)
2. Thaljaoui, A., Val, T., Nasri, N., Brulin, D.: BLE localization using RSSI measurements and iRingLA. In: 2015 IEEE International Conference on Industrial Technology (ICIT), pp. 2178–2183. IEEE (2015)
3. Pancham, J., Millham, R., Fong, S.J.: Assessment of feasible methods used by the health care industry for real time location. In: Federated Conference on Computer Science and Information Systems, Poznań, Poland (2017)
4. Pancham, J., Millham, R., Fong, S.J.: Evaluation of real time location system technologies in the health care sector. In: 2017 17th International Conference on Computational Science and Its Applications (ICCSA), pp. 1–7. IEEE (2017)
5. Lee, J.-S., Ming-Feng, D., Yuan-Heng, S.: A preliminary study of low power wireless technologies: ZigBee and Bluetooth low energy. In: 2015 IEEE 10th Conference on Industrial Electronics and Applications (ICIEA), pp. 135–139. IEEE (2015)
6. Fisher, J.A., Monahan, T.: Evaluation of real-time location systems in their hospital contexts. Int. J. Med. Inf. **81**(10), 705–712 (2012)
7. Tsang, Y.P., Wu, C.-H., Ip, W.H., Ho, G.T.S., Tse, M.: A bluetooth-based indoor positioning system: a simple and rapid approach. Ann. J. IIE (HK) **35**(2014), 11–26 (2015)

8. Yu, B., Xu, L., Li, Y.: Bluetooth Low Energy (BLE) based mobile electrocardiogram monitoring system. In: 2012 International Conference on Information and Automation (ICIA), pp. 763–767. IEEE (2012)
9. Zhongliang, D., Yanpei, Y., Xie, Y., Neng, W., Lei, Y.: Situation and development tendency of indoor positioning. Chin. Commun. **10**(3), 42–55 (2013)
10. Alemdar, H., Cem, E.: Wireless sensor networks for healthcare: a survey. Comput. Netw. **54** (15), 2688–2710 (2010)
11. Yao, W., Chu, C.H., Li, Z.: The adoption and implementation of RFID technologies in healthcare: a literature review. J. Med. Syst. **36**(6), 3507–3525 (2012)
12. Kolodziej, K.W., Hjelm, J.: Local Positioning Systems: LBS Applications and Services. CRC Press, Boca Raton (2017)
13. Deak, G., Curran, K., Condell, J.: A survey of active and passive indoor localisation systems. Comput. Commun. **35**(16), 1939–1954 (2012)
14. Zaim, D., Bellafkih, M.: Bluetooth Low Energy (BLE) based geomarketing system. In: 2016 11th International Conference on Intelligent Systems: Theories and Applications (SITA), pp. 1–6. IEEE (2016)
15. Bluetooth Low Energy 25 May 2016, 2017. https://www.bluetooth.com/what-is-bluetooth-technology/how-it-works/low-energy
16. Han, G., Klinker, G.J., Ostler, D., Schneider, A.: Testing a proximity-based location tracking system with Bluetooth Low Energy tags for future use in the OR. In: 2015 17th International Conference on E-Health Networking, Application & Services (HealthCom), pp. 17–21. IEEE (2015)
17. Raza, S., Misra, P., He, Z., Voigt, T.: Building the internet of things with bluetooth smart. Ad Hoc Networks (2016)
18. Bluetooth 5, 25 May 2016, 2017. https://www.bluetooth.com/what-is-bluetooth-technology/how-it-works/bluetooth5
19. B. S. I. Group: Bluetooth 5 Quadruples Range, Doubles Speed, Increases Data Broadcasting Capacity by 800% (2016). https://www.bluetooth.com/news/pressreleases/2016/06/16/-bluetooth-5-quadruples-rangedoubles-speedincreases-data-broadcasting-capacity-by-800
20. Schultz, B.: From cable replacement to the IoT Bluttooth 5. White Paper, December 2016
21. Yang, H., De Roeck, A., Gervasi, V., Willis, A., Nuseibeh, B.: Analysing anaphoric ambiguity in natural language requirements. Requirements Eng. **16**(3), 163–189 (2011)
22. Booch, G., Rumbaugh, J., Jacobson, I.: The Unified Modeling Language User Guide. Addison Wesley Longman Inc., Reading (1999)
23. Satzinger, J.W., Jackson, R.B., Burd, S.D.: Introduction to Systems Analysis and Design: An Agile, Iterative Approach. Course Technology, Cengage Learning, Boston (2012)
24. Schach, S.R.: Object Oriented and Classical Software Engineering, 8th edn. McGraw-Hill, New York (2008)
25. Sommerville, I.: Software Engineering, 9th edn. Pearson Education, Boston (2011)
26. Zheng, X., Liu, X., Liu, S.: Use case and non-functional scenario template-based approach to identify aspects. In: the 2010 Second International Conference on Computer Engineering and Applications (ICCEA), vol. 2, Piscataway, NJ, USA, pp. 89–93. IEEE (2010)
27. Simmons, E.: The usage model: a structure for richly describing product usage during design and development. In: The 13th IEEE International Conference on Requirements Engineering, Paris, France, pp. 403–407. IEEE, Piscataway (2005)
28. Kösters, G., Six, H.-W., Winter, M.: Validation and verification of use cases and class models. In: 7th International Workshop on Requirements Engineering: Foundations for Software Quality (REFSQ 2001, Proceedings) (2001)

29. Pancham, J., Millham, R.C., Fong, S.J.: Investigation of obstructions and range limit on Bluetooth Low Energy RSSI for the Healthcare Environment V1.5 First Submission (2018)
30. El-Attar, M.: A systematic approach to assemble sequence diagrams from use case scenarios. In: The 3rd International Conference on Computer Research and Development (ICCRD), vol. 4, pp. 171–175. IEEE, Piscataway (2011)
31. ESA Board for Software Standardisation and Control (BSSC), Guide to Software Verification and Validation. European Space Agency, The Netherlands (1994)
32. Ahmad, S., Lu, R., Ziaullah, M.: Bluetooth an optimal solution for personal asset tracking: a comparison of bluetooth, RFID and miscellaneous anti-lost tracking technologies. Int. J. u-and e-Service Sci. Technol. **8**(3), 179–188 (2015)

A Survey About the Impact of Requirements Engineering Practice in Small-Sized Software Factories in Sinaloa, Mexico

José Alfonso Aguilar[1(✉)], Aníbal Zaldívar-Colado[1], Carolina Tripp-Barba[1], Roberto Espinosa[2], Sanjay Misra[3], and Carlos Eduardo Zurita[1]

[1] Universidad Autónoma de Sinaloa, 82017 Mazatlán, SIN, Mexico
ja.aguilar@uas.edu.mx
[2] Departamento de Computación e Informática, Universidad de La Frontera, Temuco, Chile
[3] Covenant University, Ota, Nigeria
http://www.casesis.net

Abstract. Scientific literature over time highlighted the relevance of requirements engineering for software development process for desktop, web or mobile applications. Nevertheless, not much contemporary information with regard to current practices in small-sized software factories is available. This is specially true in the region of Sinaloa, México, for that reason this work presents an exploratory study which provides insight into industrial practices in Sinaloa. A combination of both qualitative and quantitative data is collected, using semi-structured interviews and a detailed questionnaire from sixteen software factories. A Pearson (r) correlation analysis was performed independently between the variables Company location (EU), Scope of coverage (AC), Number of workers (NT), Time to live in the market (TV), Projects completed (PY), Time dedicated to activities related to the project (TA), Outdated projects completed (PC) in order to determine the degree of relationship between each of the variables mentioned, with all. A correlation analysis and an analysis of variance (ANOVA) were performed. The quantitative results offers opportunities for further interpretation and comparison.

Keywords: Requirements engineering
Small-sized software factories · Requirements practice
Pearson correlation analysis

1 Introduction

It is well-know that Software Engineering (SE) is a discipline that provides software developers with a set of procedures and techniques to carry out the specification, analysis, design, implementation, validation and software mainte- nance. With the application of the SE it is possible to reduce risks of failures in

© Springer International Publishing AG, part of Springer Nature 2018
O. Gervasi et al. (Eds.): ICCSA 2018, LNCS 10963, pp. 331–340, 2018.
https://doi.org/10.1007/978-3-319-95171-3_26

a developing systems and to increase the possibility of delivery of the product in the estimated time, with quality and within the budgeted costs. A very important stage in SE is Requirements Engineering (RE), which allows defining the software to produce and its specifications. RE is carried out through activities that allow obtaining, analyzing, specifying, validating and managing the software requirements. The software requirements are the needs of the customers, the services that the users want the system provides and the restrictions in which they must operate. The result of the requirements process is the basis for the design, implementation and evaluation of the software. It is important to mention that if all the requirements are not discovered and specified accurately, it is possible that an incomplete software product will be obtained, with a high-risk index and not very functional.

On the other hand, in software factories is common that the application of the SE and the process improvements ends in some discussion with respect on which are the "best practices" that can be implemented since in research area and in the industry the "best practices" are a bit different and is difficult to adopt them. In literature regarding to SE is possible to find different paradigms to use for software development which although it is true that they include the generic phases of analysis, design, implementation, testing and deployment, the implementation and use of them is subjective with respect to its application by a software development team. Most of these methodologies and approaches considers RE since there is a considerable amount of published scientific literature as well but transferring this knowledge represents a problem.

Recently, SE implementation has enhanced significantly due to the emergence of maturity models such as MoPROSOFT and CMMI (Capability Maturity Model Integration) [10], according with the Process Maturity Profile, published by the Software Engineering Institute (SEI) each six months, both have as goal the process improvement. The report is based on the results reported to the CMMI Institute [9], which shows an increment in the number of appraisals (activity that helps to identify the strengths and weaknesses of the processes in an organization and to examine how close they are from the processes related to CMMI best practices) increasing the level of maturity by 16% (2008 to 2017) in companies that have 100 or less employees, mainly in China, United States, India and Mexico [11]. With regard to continental level, Asia ranks first with 9,629 evaluations, North America second with 3,932 and Europe is the third place with 1,435 evaluations in the period from 2008 to 2017.

Software industry is constantly evolving, in this sense, despite that Mexico appears as one of the countries in which the SE has improved through the process improvement, it is necessary to promote the application of RE practice in national companies dedicated to software development. To achieve this, it is essential to understand the current state of practice of RE [12] in the software industry and compare it with the academic field, this will allow to promote the improvement of the software development process. In this regard, notwithstanding the efforts derived from research in universities and software industry, to put RE into practice in small-sized software factories, there are still important issues established in the scientific literature related to this area that avoid improving the quality of the product (software), among the most important we have the inconsistency of requirements, incomplete requirements, as well as tools for the management of inadequate requirements that avoid improving the quality of the product.

In last decade in Sinaloa, Mexico, small-sized software factories have been established, some of them have been maintained and others have disappeared. Among the main causes is the failure in software development projects and lack of application of methods, techniques and tools in their processes [13]. In this sense, a research presented in [14], shows that more than 53% of software projects fail because they do not carry out a preliminary study of requirements and to other factors such as lack of user participation, incomplete requirements and changes to the requirements also occupy high positions in the reasons for failures. To address this situation, the Sinaloa government, the Universidad Autónoma de Sinaloa and local software factories have recently constituted a trident government-university-software industry with the idea of promoting the software industry. This trident operates in the following way: universities will produce trained human resources; the government will bring financial support to software factories for certifications and software factories will hire graduated trained and certified students. The idea in particular is very attractive, there have been success stories as in the city of Monterrey, Nuevo León, where industry grew significantly. In Sinaloa, in order to achieve this growth it is necessary to carry out research projects that allow obtaining the current status of the software factories in terms of their development process to be able to develop solutions. Software factories will not be able to compete internationally if they do not have a well-defined method and development process that allows to obtain a quality software product. But, they needs to be convinced that the best practices and RE must to be used. To contribute to achieve this, our work presents an evaluation of the impact of the use of RE in Sinaloa small-sized software factories as a starting point for the adoption of the best practices in the local industry.

Bearing these considerations in mind, the goal of this paper is to shed on light the current state of the practice of the RE in software factories in Sinaloa, Mexico. To do this, an interview was structured as technique for information gathering. A total of 16 local software factories from Los Mochis, Mazatlán, Culiacán were interviewed, which are classified as small-sized enterprises according to Ministry of Economy (*Secretaría de Economía*) from Mexican federal government. Then, a simple and multiple correlation analyzes were performed using seven variables to know the degree of association of each with the others; and to determine how much the six independent variables explains the dependent variable named Outdated projects completed.

This paper is organized as follows: Sect. 2 presents some related work regarding to requirements engineering practice research. The method applied is detailed in Sect. 3. Results are described in Sect. 4. Finally, conclusions are presented in Sect. 5.

2   Related Work

Requirements engineering practices have been identified as a key issue that affects the success rate of projects in most software organizations, SE community has studied this issue in medium and large-sized organizations, below are some of the most important interesting proposals made.

In 2000, Nikula et al. [1] presented the results of a study of the current RE practices, development needs and preferred ways of technology transfer of twelve small to medium sized companies in Finland. They determined that, the key development needs in industry are development of own RE process adaptations, RE process improvement, and automation of RE practices. Directing efforts to these areas would substantially improve the chances of successful technology transfer and process improvement efforts in industry. Even though a lot of literature is available, transfer of that knowledge into practice has been problematic.

The first field study of the software design process for large system development projects was published in 1988 by Curtis, Krasner, and Iscoe [2]. The study was initiated from the software engineering viewpoint but it focused on how requirements and decisions were made, represented, communicated, and changed, as well as how these decisions impacted subsequent development process. As a conclusion the authors state that knowledge sharing and integration, change facilitation, and broad communications and coordination were the three key issues impacting the project success.

One of the larger projects in this field was the REAIMS project in the mid 90s. One project achievement was a process maturity model definition that can be used to assess current RE processes [4]. The REAIMS model provides a ready template for doing RE practice assessments.

In [3], a study was conducted through interviews and questionnaires where the main results were related to five aspects of RE approaches: the use of requirements models, the support for high system complexity, quality assurance for requirements, the transition between this activity and architecture design, and the interrelation of RE and safety engineering.

A study conducted using surveys with participants from 58 German companies addressed a tendency to improve RE via internally defined qualitative methods rather than relying on normative approaches like CMMI. They also discovered several problems that are statistically significant in practice. For example, they corroborated communication flaws or moving targets as problems in practice. Although the results are not completely representative, they offer knowledge about current practices and problems [5].

In [6], the authors investigated how requirements analysis had been conducted in 16 U.S. organizations that were involved in agile software development. The study revealed that agile RE is different from the traditional RE as the former takes an iterative discovery approach. The activities such as requirement elicitation, negotiation, documentation and validation are addressed together in each short development cycle. The authors also found that the intensive communication between the developers and customers is the most important RE practice in terms of its influence on each of the RE activities.

Another approach was presented in [7] to determine areas to improve in RE processes in Thailand. The result also shows the development needs in small and medium enterprises such as software process improvement, RE knowledge, requirements management tools, training, and knowledge transfer. The current key issues related to RE have been identified such as changing requirements problem, requirements inconsistency or incompleteness, lack of user involvement and communication with customer, scope creep, inadequate tools support, absence of RE knowledge in development team, stakeholders issues, poor requirements documents, time limit, cultural problem and lack of cooperation with business partner. They concluded that software companies still challenges with organizational and technical issues, and need requirements engineering knowledge and training in order to improve practitioners skills. Also, in [8] a comprehensive survey of software professionals was conducted to attempt to discover the link between quality requirements from one side and the development processes and software architecture from the other side. This work reports in an empirical analysis of the correlation between software process and software quality with specific reference to agile and traditional processes.

Summarizing, several studies have been conducted with regard to RE practice, the results obtained presents problems such as the lack of communication between final user and the developer team. This has motivated our interest in conducting this study to obtain the current state of the RE practice in small-sized software factories in Sinaloa, Mexico. Our goal is to identify gaps to set the basis for an update on the curricula of computer and informatics careers with regard to RE in the local universities.

3   Research Method

In our work, an interview was applied to 16 software factories, classified as small-sized, located in the most important cities of Sinaloa such as Los Mochis, Culiacan and Mazatlan, in Sinaloa, Mexico. Through the application of the questionnaire technique [8], a total of 20 questions were defined. These questions includes items regarding to the total number of employees, the kind of projects they drives, time expended in requirements phase, the tools they use, how they identify uncompleted requirements and the strategies used to ameliorate this scenario.

3.1   Questions Design

A set of interviews questions was prepared considering that the worker of the software factory could be flexible in the answers according to the conversation flow of each interview. The questionnaire was organized into two main parts. Part one contains questions regarding to company backgrounds and part two contains questions related to the requirements engineering practice in software developer projects. This part is divided in questions with regard to requirements elicitation, analysis, management and tools.

3.2 Data Collection

A Web-based survey using Google Forms[1] was created. After that, an email invitation was sent indicating to visit the link for the survey to local software factories and subsequent reminder. These were extracted from government database and from current, and past graduate students of the Universidad Autónoma de Sinaloa. This closed invitation ensured that we included only industrial practitioners in the survey population because the graduate school caters only to working professionals. The interviewees were selected based on their responsibilities in initial phases of their software development process, such as the responsible for the preparation of the functional requirements specification document.

The data were collected in two forms, one by sending an e-mail with a Google Form and the second form was through the on-site visit of the project collaborators. The duration of the interview was approximately half an hour to an hour, each one was typed and transcribed for analysis to a spreadsheet.

A Pearson (r) correlation analysis was performed independently between the variables Company location (EU), Scope of coverage (AC), Number of workers (NT), Time to live in the market (TV), Projects completed (PY), Time dedicated to activities related to the project (TA), Outdated projects completed (PC). The above in order to determine the degree of relationship between each of the variables mentioned, with all. Additionally, the multiple correlation coefficient (R) was calculated with the same variables and data, as well as the determination coefficient (R^2) and the adjusted coefficient of determination ($\overline{R}^2$) to find the degree of linear association between the dependent variable (response) and independent variables (explanatory); specifically between the variable Outdated projects completed and the regression line estimated with the rest of the factors. It was decided to use PC as a dependent variable because it is an indicator of effectiveness in software factories, by measuring the amount of work carried out despite having been delayed during processing.

3.3 Limitation of Study Method

In this work we have presented a detailed data collected from sixteen software factories in Sinaloa, Mexico. The sample is small (relatively) in order to generalize, although our data should provide an interesting starting point for a further study in requirements engineering practice since there is no such study of this region of Mexico.

4 Results

To calculate the correlation between the different variables involved, and considered for this study in the software development by factories located in the state of Sinaloa, Mexico, correlation analyzes were performed independently among

---

[1] https://docs.google.com/forms/u/0/.

the seven variables. In addition, the multiple correlation was determined, using for this process six independent or explanatory variables and the dependent variable Outdated projects completed (PC). Table 1 shows the variables involved in the correlation model.

Table 1. List of variables used in the correlation analysis. Source: Own.

Independent or explanatory variables	Dependent variable
Company location (UE)	Outdated projects completed (PC)
Scope of coverage (AC)	
Number of workers (NT)	
Time to live in the market (TV)	
Projects completed (PY)	
Time dedicated to activities related to the project (TA)	

Table 1 contains the seven variables used in the analysis and the dependent variable PC. These variables intervene in the correlation calculation carried out to determine the association between them and the independent six with the response factor Outdated projects completed. In the calculation of Pearson's correlation index, for each of the variables with the other six, a low index of linkage was found, with five indicators being the most outstanding (highlighted in bold red), of 21 possible, which are shown in Table 2.

Table 2. Pearsons correlation index (r). Source: Own.

	UE	AC	NT	TV	PY	TA	PC
AC	0.250	1					
NT	0.140	0.253	1				
TV	−0.183	0.413	0.429	1			
PY	−0.380	−0.216	0.129	0.239	1		
TA	−0.241	−0.132	−0.509	0.066	0.168	1	
PC	−0.459	0.505	0.165	0.294	−0.061	0.0212	1

Table 2 presents all the possible correlations among the seven variables analyzed, five indicators with values greater than 0.4 stand out, which despite not being very high, are the ones that represent the greatest link between them, independently. The largest association is given by TA-NT with $r = -0.509$, followed by $r = 0.505$ of PC-AC; the following values are less than 0.5: $r = -0.459$, $r = 0.429$ and $r = 0.413$ for PC-UE, TV-NT and TV-AC, respectively. With regard to multiple correlation analysis, this resulted in an R with value of 0.804, the coefficient of determination $R^2 = 0.647$ and an adjusted R^2 of 0.293. The analysis of variance (ANOVA) was also carried out considering the seven mentioned variables and it remains as a dependent variable PC; is shown in Table 3.

Table 3. Analysis of variance (ANOVA) of the seven variables. Source: Own.

Mode	Sum of squares	df	Mean square	F	Sig.
Regression	2895.316	6	482.553	1.831	.240b
Residual	1581.607	6	263.601		
Total	4476.923	12			

Table 3 presents the analysis of variance of the seven variables, UE, AC, NT, TV, PY, TA and the dependent variable PC. As shown, the critical value of F or significance (Sig.) is greater than 0.05, indicating little relationship between the variables; but the F statistic is greater than its critical value, which indicates a certain degree of goodness in the model composed of seven variables.

5   Conclusions

The RE practice in small-sized software factories has still been largely unexplored in Mexico, specially in Sinaloa. This work presents initial results of a study on the RE practices of these factories based on a questionnaire (composed of 10 questions), 16 software factories participated so far; we are continuously adding new respondents. A Pearson (r) correlation analysis was performed independently between the variables Company location (EU), Scope of coverage (AC), Number of workers (NT), Time to live in the market (TV), Projects completed (PY), Time dedicated to activities related to the project (TA), Outdated projects completed (PC) in order to determine the degree of relationship between each of the variables mentioned, with all.

With regard to the correlation of the variables measured, it can be concluded that the seven variables analyzed, Company location, Scope of coverage, Number of workers, Time to live in the market, Projects completed, Time dedicated to activities related to the project, Outdated projects completed, do not have a strong association between them, the highest correlation indexes go from 0.413 to −0.509, but overall, they show a considerably higher multiple correlation if they take into account the resulting low rates of r, $R = 0.804$, $R^2 = 0.647$ and $\overline{R}^2 = 0.293$. The above can be explained as the synergy of the different factors that influence software development, where each of them, although seemingly insignificant, is key to achieving a successful project of this nature.

It is important to consider the inclusion of a greater number of variables and determine the significant ones in the process being studied, as well as the construction of an acceptable probabilistic prediction model.

Next, initial results presents two major issues to address, these are: (i) the communication between clients and software developer teams is not well performed and does not focus on the right issues. This is a problem since the result is an imperfect RE specification, scope creep and ultimately dissatisfaction with the project; (ii) the use of ad-hoc RE practices on which requirements are hard to track and may be lost (lack of traceability), out of an impression that RE practices are to important for small-size organizations. Based on these initial results, these points are recommended: (i) improving the communication between the software factories (developer team) and the customers; (ii) look for how to convince software factories about the relevance of using RE in their practice through studies and (iii) strengthen the promotion of the relationship between universities and software factories in order to obtain better trained human resources.

Finally, since this research report shows the results of just one stage of a more ambitious project, the search for key variables in the process of developing quality software and the construction of a probabilistic prediction model is considered as future work. Moreover, additional studies are needed to assess the generality of these findings and as starting point to propose solutions based on local software factories needs.

References

1. Nikula, U., Sajaniemi, J., Kalviainen, H.: A State-of-the-Practice Survey on Requirements Engineering in Small- and Medium-Sized Enterprises. Engineering **1** (2000)
2. Curtis, B., Krasner, H., Iscoe, N.: A field study of the software design process for large systems. Commun. ACM **31**, 1268–1287 (1988)
3. Sikora, E., Tenbergen, B., Pohl, K.: Industry needs and research directions in requirements engineering for embedded systems. Requirements Eng. **17**, 57–78 (2012)
4. Sommerville, I., Sawyer, P.: Requirements Engineering: A Good Practice Guide (1997)
5. Fernndez, D.M., Wagner, S.: Naming the pain in requirements engineering: a design for a global family of surveys and first results from Germany. In: Information and Software Technology, pp. 616–643. (Elsevier B.V.) (2015)
6. Ramesh, B., Cao, L., Baskerville, R.: Agile requirements engineering practices and challenges: an empirical study. Inf. Syst. J. **20**(5), 449–480 (2010)
7. Khankaew, S., Riddle, S.: A review of practice and problems in requirements engineering in small and medium software enterprises in Thailand. In: 2014 IEEE Fourth International Workshop on Empirical Requirements Engineering (EmpiRE), pp. 1–8. IEEE (2014)
8. Kassab, M.: A contemporary view on software quality requirements in agile and software architecture practices. In: 2017 IEEE 25th International Requirements Engineering Conference Workshops (REW), pp. 260–267. IEEE (2017)
9. CMMI Institute. cmmiinstitute.com
10. Chrissis, M.B., Konrad, M., Shrum, S.: CMMI Guidlines for Process Integration and Product Improvement. Addison-Wesley Longman Publishing Co., Inc., Boston (2003)

11. CMMI Maturity Profile Report (2017). http://partners.cmmiinstitute.com/wp-content/uploads/2018/02/Maturity-Profile-Ending-31-December-2017.pdf
12. Sadraei, E., Aurum, A., Beydoun, G., Paech, B.: A field study of the requirements engineering practice in Australian software industry. Requirements Eng. **12**(3), 145–162 (2007)
13. Zamudio, E.L.: Aproximación metodológica para la práctica de la Ingeniería de Requisitos en las pequeas y medianas empresas (PyMES) de desarrollo de software en el estado de Sinaloa. Tesis de Maestría en Ciencias de la Información, Universidad Autónoma de Sinaloa, Mexico (2017)
14. Brackett, J.W.: Software Requirements. Software Engineering Institute Education Program. Carnegie Mellon University (1990)

An Approach of a Framework to Create Web Applications

Daniel Sanchez, Oscar Mendez, and Hector Florez$^{(\boxtimes)}$

Universidad Distrital Francisco Jose de Caldas, Bogotá, Colombia
danielssj88@gmail.com, oscfrayle@gmail.com, haflorezf@udistrital.edu.co

Abstract. Currently, there are a lot of frameworks to build web applications working with the architectural pattern MVC (Model View Controller). One interesting approach is based on using 3-layer models, which allow identifying and separating the final application in different layers that facilitates its construction and maintenance. The purpose of this paper is to present our approach of a framework for developing PHP web applications using a 3-layer model. This approach integrates different technologies and design patterns in order to provide one tool that supports the community in the creation of PHP web applications by providing build-in tools and applying good practices focused on the pursue of proper development times. In addition, the approach aims to handle common issues in the industry like efficiency, maintainability, and security.

Keywords: Multilayer architecture · Model View Controller
Framework · 3-layer model

1 Introduction

According to [1], software are not only computer programs. Software are all artifacts needed to make computer programs to operate correctly. Software systems should consist of several independent components connected all together for providing the services specified in the specific software requirements. In addition, software should include a documentation system for describing all its elements. Thus, good software meet its goals, when these attributes highlights the functionality required by the user, while being maintainable, reliable and easy to use.

That is the reason why this work seeks to characterize a multilayer framework to create web applications. The framework is focused but not limited on PHP programming language. It allows improving software development processes from its architectural and conceptual design. This architecture provides new ways of perceiving and applying methodologies related to object-oriented programming and application design patterns. Design patterns have become very important due to they have changed software engineering in favor of creating truly elegant designs [2].

© Springer International Publishing AG, part of Springer Nature 2018
O. Gervasi et al. (Eds.): ICCSA 2018, LNCS 10963, pp. 341–352, 2018.
https://doi.org/10.1007/978-3-319-95171-3_27

Object oriented software design is difficult, and it is even more difficult when the design must be reusable [2]. Thus, in object oriented software design, it is necessary to (a) find the relevant objects, (b) factor objects in classes with the right granularity, (c) define classes, interfaces and inheritance hierarchies, and (d) establish key relationships between these classes and objects.

The framework proposed in this paper has been validated through the creation of one specific web application named *CTS Virtual*, which is an information system to create surveys focused on the research about the perception of the Colombians about science, technology and society. The framework does not intend to put developers in the position to decide between different solutions available in the market for creating web applications. The framework aims to present one additional experience in terms of the use and the implementation of software architectures.

The paper is structured as follows. Section 2 presents the context in order to explain the related concepts used in the construction of the framework. Section 3 presents related work. Section 4 presents the implementation of the framework in the practical case study named *CTS Virtual*. Finally Sect. 5 presents the conclusions.

2   Context

Software industry is in constant search of new ways of solving existing problems [3]. In addition, the reuse of source code is essential in the construction of the current web applications because they use common functionalities, which support the fact to use and develop build-in libraries that allow performing a specific task that can be integrated into multiple projects such as libraries, which are able to perform generic features improving the performance and security of applications that motivates the reduction of time and effort that ultimately reduces manufacturing costs.

In this section, we provide a brief explanation regarding important concepts related to the construction of our approach.

2.1   Separation of Concern

The concept *Separation of concern (SoC)* in the software development context consists in separating a computer program into different small components. Thus, SoC means that each component must be built for an specific intended purpose. SoC allows encapsulating software attributes and services that are developed independently, which aids their maintainability [4]. An example of SoC is the 3-layer development, in which the user interface is separated from the business and persistence layers. Nevertheless, the addition of SoC in a software development project might increase the complexity, but such complexity is compensated with the benefits it produces [5].

In the process of building a framework, defining the architecture has a great importance because it is the basis for the development of the logic components and their interaction [6], having in mind that these components need to be reused in the applications that are implemented on it. For the specific case study *CTS Virtual* the definition of architecture took place when we performed the research about the main features of the Model View Controller pattern and the 3-layer model. This research generated the concepts used in the construction of the framework, which is mainly profiled to characterize in an independent way, the general aspects of the Model View Controller pattern built based on a 3-layer architecture.

2.2 Model View Controller

The Model View Controller (MVC) pattern defines a software architecture that separates data from the user interface and events into the following parts: *Model*, which represents the domain of the software and contains application data, *View*, which is the visual representation of the model by managing the user interface, and *Controller*, which is responsible for receiving user requests (events or actions performed on the user interface), processing them and deciding the actions to be performed. When the model is modified, the view is updated. In addition, the controller can select the view to show the actual responses that are related to the state described by the model [7,8]. Figure 1 presents the component diagram of the MVC pattern.

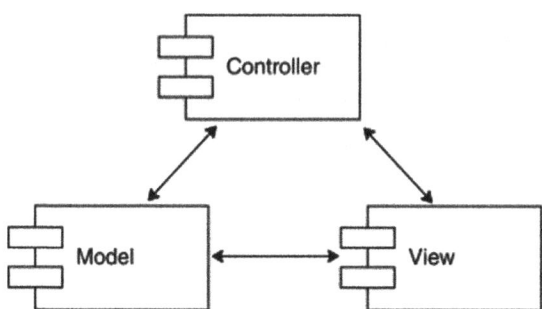

Fig. 1. Model View Controller component diagram.

2.3 3-Layer Model

Another alternative is using the 3-layer model, which separates the presentation logic, business logic and data access (also known as persistence) in 3 different layers. Using the definition of layer, each layer supports the layer n+1 having in mind that the lower layer in this case is data access, so the presentation layer does not have access to the data access layer. This model is presented in Fig. 2. One of the main advantages of this model is the low coupling between the layers because this characteristic allows easily to modify functionality in the application without having in mind all the components of the application.

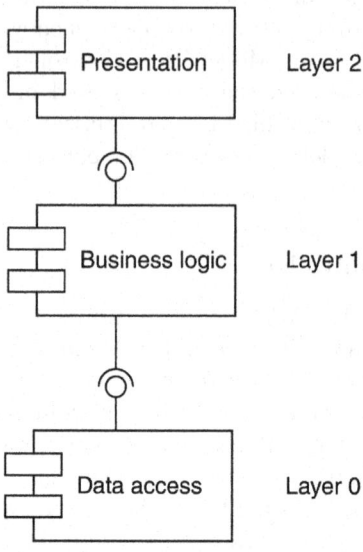

Fig. 2. 3-layer model.

3   Related Work

In industry, there are several frameworks to create web applications using PHP such as Symfony[1], CakePHP[2] and Zend[3] Framework. Most of them use MVC as an architectural design pattern [9].

Nevertheless, by interacting with frameworks such as CakePHP, CodeIgniter[4], and Kohana[5], their maturity and thus their complexity is not the best. This is because they are equipped with lots of libraries for the final result that are useless and impractical for the context. Moreover, there are some projects that do not need the whole structure of the framework such as Laravel and Symfony. Both seem to be very simple, but they have very specific characteristics or require extreme resources to ensure the proper runtime performance. This statement refers to the need of taking concrete and lightweight architectures that meet the specific objectives of the project intended to be developed and that allow extensibility, when adding new functionalities. Another alternatives like Lumen[6] which is a reduced version

---

[1] https://symfony.com/.
[2] https://cakephp.org/.
[3] http://www.zend.com/.
[4] https://codeigniter.com/.
[5] https://kohanaframework.org/.
[6] https://lumen.laravel.com/.

of the framework Laravel satisfies these characteristics. Hence, the idea arises to create a framework with reduced functionality, in which the proposed architecture is designed to build a set of logical tools that provide the necessary components to developers. In addition, the approach uses the 3-layer model that is very well accepted in academy and industry; thus, both communities can use it in different projects.

4 Framework

The development of this framework, which has been validatedin the construction of the project *CTS Virtual*, is characterized by defining three levels or layers of functionality: presentation, business logic and persistence (i.e., data access layer), where its operation is more simple and linear fulfilling the purpose of separating the presentation of persistence avoiding logic code within interfaces.

It is important to mention that in the case of the construction of the multi-layer architecture for creating web applications and specifically for *CTS Virtual*, the use of Smarty[7] as template manager plays a vital role because it allows separating the interaction between the code in the client side (HTML, CSS, Javascript) with the code in the server side (PHP). This characteristic gives a new level of abstraction that modularize the presentation layer allowing more clear and readable source code. The complete architecture is presented in Fig. 3.

4.1 Persistence Layer

In this model, the persistence layer is responsible for encapsulating all necessary logic to communicate the application with the persistence data system used in a

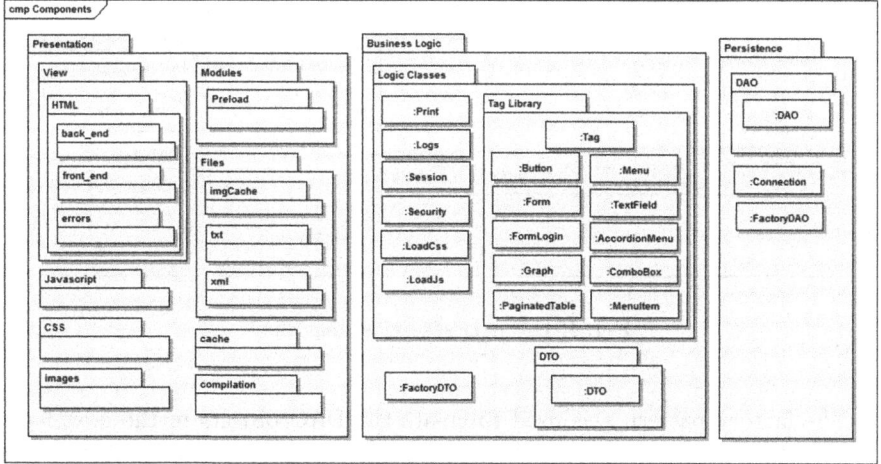

Fig. 3. Multilayer model.

---

[7] https://www.smarty.net/.

project such as engine databases, serialized files, or other storage system. In this case, the storage system is a database; thus, our pesistance layer manage the SQL statements that are going to be submitted to the database. For that task, the DAO (Data Access Object) pattern is used by using the library ADOdb[8] obtaining the necessary independence between the database engine and the code implemented to connect to the database. For *CTS Virtual*, we used the class hierarchy presented in Fig. 4.

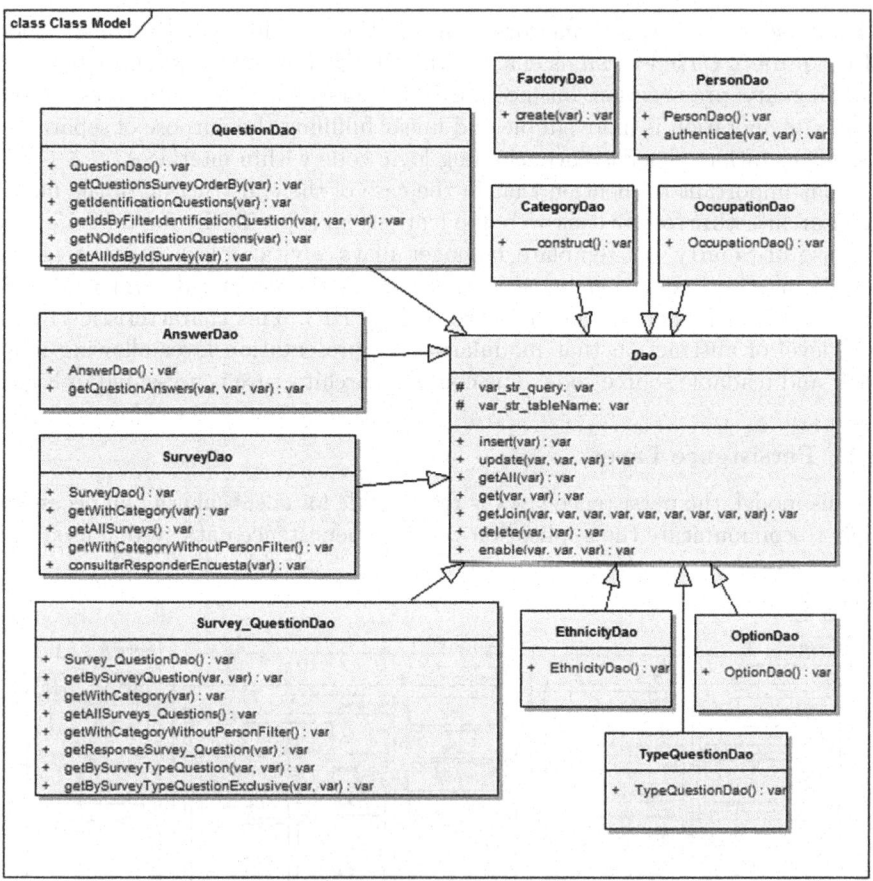

Fig. 4. DAO classes - class diagram.

The factory pattern was used to create the DAO objects in the next layer (i.e., the business logic layer) that encapsulates the operations made against the database. All classes inherit from the class DAO, which has the definition of the generic methods that return the SQL following statement:

---

[8] http://adodb.org/dokuwiki/doku.php.

– *insert*: Generates dynamically insert queries using a data array (arr_data) that receives as parameter.

```
function insert($arr_data)
    { ... }
```

– *update*: Generates dynamically update queries, using a data array (arr_data), that receives as parameters.

```
function update($arr_data, $var_str_key, $var_str_value)
    { ... }
```

– *getAll*: Generates dynamically simple select queries of all columns in a table ordered by a column specified with a parameter (var_str_order).

```
function getAll($var_str_order)
    { ... }
```

– *getByAttribute*: Generates the select query based on one attribute specified by two parameters (var_str_key, var_str_value).

```
function getByAttribute($var_str_key, $var_str_value)
    { ... }
```

– *getJoin*: Method that generates dynamically Join sentence between tables. It uses certain parameters for identifying the tables, attributes, and values involved in the join.

```
function getJoin($var_str_nameTable1, $var_str_nameTable2,
        $arr_attributesTable1, $arr_attributesTable2,
        $var_str_attributoJoinOnTable1,
        $var_str_attributoJoinOnTable2, $var_str_order,
        $var_str_key = "", $var_str_value = "")
    { ... }
```

– *delete*: Generates a delete query based on one attribute specified by two parameters (var_str_key, var_str_value).

```
function delete($var_str_key, $var_str_value)
    { ... }
```

– *enable*: Enable or disable one register updating its value *enable* to 0 or 1 depending the case.

```
public function enable($var_str_key, $var_str_value,
        $var_int_enable)
    { ... }
```

These methods have the logic implemented to interact with the entities in the database. Each of this classes inherits from the abstract class DAO, decreasing the implementation only to the next steps:

1. Inherits from the class DAO in the constructor to define in the variable var_str_tableName of the DAO superclass the desired name of the entity in the database to map it to such class. For example, the class CategoryDAO mades operations with the entity in the database category

```
public function __construct() {
        $this->var_str_tableName = "category";
}
```

2. Later on, in the class FactoryDAO, it is necessary to instatiate the classes DAO producing the required objects to be used in the business logic layer.

```
class FactoryDao{
    public static function create($var_str_type){
        return new $var_str_type();
    }
}
```

This class receives the name of the class as string to create and return the new instance to use in the next layers.

4.2   Business Logic Layer

The business logic layer uses the pattern DTO (Data Transfer Object) to transfer the data from the data access to the presentation layer. For this task, the same approach presented in the DAO pattern is used; thus, there is one abstract class DTO that defines the generic functionalities for those classes. For this, it is necessary to follow the next steps:

1. Create the class that inherits the class DTO. For this, the name of the class is assigned to the attribute var_str_nameDao defined in the superclass DTO. In addition, the generated class is related to corresponding DAO class. For instance, the class CategoryDTO is related to its corresponding DAO class, i.e. the CategoryDAO class.

```
public function CategoryDto() {
        $this->var_str_nameDao = "CategoryDao";
}
```

2. Afterwards, in the class FactoryDTO, it is necessary to instantiate the corresponding DTO classes to be used in the presentation layer. For this task, it is necessary to declare the constants with the name of the classes in the DTO. The instantiation is made through the method create. This method receives the name of the class as a string to create and return the new instance to be use in the next layers.

```
class FactoryDto{
    const PERSON_DTO="PersonDto";
    const CATEGORY_DTO="CategoryDto";
    const SURVEY_DTO="SurveyDto";
    const QUESTION_DTO="QuestionDto";
    const OPTION_DTO="OptionDto";
    const ANSWER_DTO="AnswerDto";
    const OCCUPATION_DTO="OccupationDto";

    public static function create($var_str_type){
        return new $var_str_type();
    }
}
```

The business logic layer has other classes such as:

1. Tag Library: The tag library was created to print HTML elements like forms, menu, and so on. These elements work with the structure and the libraries used in the framework. For instance, by using these classes it is possible to create the menu by generating the HTML structure that works with JQuery and takes the look and feel configured for the application.
2. General Use Classes: These are classes for general use.
   - **LoadCss**: This class has a set of constants defined and an static method to get dynamically the routes of the stylesheets.
   - **LoadJs**: It accomplish the same function that LoadCss class, but in this case it makes the load of the Javascript files and JQuery plugins.
   - **Print**: This class works with one tag library returning a string with the HTML code generated to assign to the Smarty templates that are mentioned later in this paper.
   - **Logs**: Class responsible to print the server logs in a text/plain file to make the instrumentation and auditory in the application.
   - **Security**: The injections of malicious code are one of the most common security issues in web applications [10]. In order to prevent this, our framework has one personalized class used to perform the filter and validate the inputs in the URLs and form fields. The purpose of this configuration is to avoid injections of malicious code as XSS injections or SQL injections.
   - **Session**: Class responsible to manage the sessions of the applications, avoiding security failures like **session fixation**, which is common in applications that uses server sessions based in cookies to manage the authentication and authorization.
   - **Util**: Includes useful and common operations to use in the application.

4.3 Presentation Layer

To improve the separation between the client logic (HTML) and the server logic (PHP), the template manager Smarty was used. In addition, for the separation of the code, this library allows printing code with its own tags and to storage information in cache through the Smarty cache component. The presentation layer has the structure presented in the first part of the Fig. 3. The directories in the presentation layer are:

- **files**: It has the files generated for the general use of the application. Those files are XML, TXT, PDFs and images.
- **cache**: Directory used by Smarty to save the cache of the templates.
- **compilation**: This directory is used by Smarty to save the compiled templates.
- **modules**: This directory contains the PHP scripts that receive the forms requests to (a) call the functionalities in the business logic, (b) preload the Smarty variables to show in the view, and (c) process the AJAX requests.
- **view**: It contains the folders of static files to be presented in the view. The HTML directory contains the HTML files with the Smarty variables to deploy the information of the web application.

4.4 Configuration File

Another point to highlight in this framework is the centralization of the configurations. It is done through one configuration file that has:

- pages routes used to browse the web application
- separators used in the directories system like '\' for windows systems and '/' for Unix systems
- sessions configurations
- database connections
- smarty configurations
- theme to display in the web application using Jquery UI

This configuration file appears in the root of the web application, but its location can be changed updating the new path in the index.php file.

4.5 Route

One of the main features of one web framework is the ability to route calls made to its components from the URL, maintaining a clear structure that is easy to read by users and search engines. It is why the framework runs using the index.php file as an access point to respond the requests from the client-side in a more agile way. This function is part of SEO (Search Engine Optimization), which is a feature for the accessibility and the usability in web applications [11].

5   Conclusions

In industry, this kinds of architectures allow having well-defined three roles working within a group developing a project that can work together taking advantage of the SoC (Separation of concerns) that create this architecture. These work roles can be: (a) designer or front-end developer of the UI that would work on the presentation layer, (b) developer of the business logic which is responsible for performing calculations and information processing, and (c) developer of the data access logic which work directly in the persistence layer and deal with the issues of the data query. In this manner, none of these roles need to know how to work the other roles, merely knowing the way to communicate with the next layer.Then, this approach allows us to generate standards to work into the development group.

The develop of *CTS Virtual* as case study allowed us to determine the feasibility of developing a framework focused on a software architecture based on a three-layer model, considering important elements such as performance, security, integrity of the information, among other. In addition, the case study required to implement functionalities like data access, template management, forms building, and so on. These functionalities are vital parts of the core of the framework as an agile and light architecture to create web applications.

It is clear that there is a great variety of PHP frameworks to build web applications, which are supported by large communities and companies that invest resources at all levels in order to improve their constant evolution. However, this work focuses on the experience of developing an architecture that allowed the construction of *CTS Virtual* under a framework that focused on the solution of specific problems.

In this framework, extensibility is presented as a common feature. This was materialized through the configuration of utilities and libraries that allows connecting further components to provide further functionalities in the web application.

References

1. Sommerville, I.: Software Engineering. Addison-Wesley, Boston (2011)
2. Gamma, E., Helm, R., Johnson, R., Vlissides, J.: Design patterns: abstraction and reuse of object-oriented design. In: Nierstrasz, O.M. (ed.) ECOOP 1993. LNCS, vol. 707, pp. 406–431. Springer, Heidelberg (1993). https://doi.org/10.1007/3-540-47910-4_21
3. Jacobson, I.: What they dont teach you about software at school: be smart!. In: Abrahamsson, P., Marchesi, M., Maurer, F. (eds.) XP 2009. LNBIP, vol. 31, pp. 1–4. Springer, Heidelberg (2009). https://doi.org/10.1007/978-3-642-01853-4_1
4. Florez, H., Sánchez, M., Villalobos, J.: Supporting drafts for enterprise modeling. In: 2014 9th Computing Colombian Conference (9CCC), pp. 200–206. IEEE (2014)
5. Penberthy, W.: Exam Ref 70–486 Developing ASP. NET MVC 4 Web Applications (MCSD): Developing ASP. NET MVC 4 Web Applications. Pearson Education, London (2013)

6. Florez, H., Sánchez, M., Villalobos, J.: Analysis of imprecise enterprise models. In: Schmidt, R., Guédria, W., Bider, I., Guerreiro, S. (eds.) BPMDS/EMMSAD 2016. LNBIP, vol. 248, pp. 349–364. Springer, Cham (2016). https://doi.org/10.1007/978-3-319-39429-9_22

7. Kupp, N., Makris, Y.: Applying the model-view-controller paradigm to adaptive test. IEEE Des. Test Comput. **29**(1), 28–35 (2012)

8. Romsaiyud, W.: Applying MVC data model on hadoop for delivering the business intelligence. In: 2014 12th International Conference on ICT and Knowledge Engineering (ICT and Knowledge Engineering), pp. 78–82. IEEE (2014)

9. Porebski, B., Przystalski, K., Nowak, L.: Building PHP Applications with Symfony, CakePHP, and Zend Framework. Wiley, Hoboken (2011)

10. Johns, M.: Code-injection vulnerabilities in web applications–exemplified at cross-site scripting. it-Inf. Technol. **53**(5), 256–260 (2011). Methoden und innovative Anwendungen der Informatik und Informationstechnik

11. Killoran, J.B.: How to use search engine optimization techniques to increase website visibility. IEEE Trans. Prof. Commun. **56**(1), 50–66 (2013)

Model Driven Engineering Approach to Manage Peripherals in Mobile Devices

Daniel Sanchez and Hector Florez$^{(\boxtimes)}$

Universidad Distrital Francisco Jose de Caldas, Bogotá, Colombia
danieljss88@gmail.com, haflorezf@udistrital.edu.co

Abstract. In the last years, Model Driven Engineering (MDE) has demonstrated several benefits for software development. It has gained a great popularity in both academic and industry communities. The application of its guidelines is suitable for several domains including Model Transformations. In addition, mobile applications is one domain that has a lot of relevance. However, these applications increases their value when they use properly mobile peripherals. Thus, the purpose of this paper is to show the creation of a domain metamodel to manage peripherals in mobile devices. Said metamodel will serve to built a Model Transformation Chain that will be able to generate native code for the Android platform.

Keywords: Model Driven Engineering · Model Driven Architecture
Android · Mobile applications · Model Transformation Chain

1 Introduction

The Object Management Group (OMG) through its specifications Model Driven Architecture (MDA), and Meta-Object Facility (MOF) provide guidelines in the use of models to solve problems in the software industry applied to different business domains.

In addition, the access to mobile devices has increased massively in the last decade; then, the industry needs to build more mobile applications in a better way that accom plish great software quality needs such as correctness that indicates that the software should behave according its specification [1]. In this case, if the specification can be included in a domain model that conforms to a domain metamodel; then, it is possible to create a Model Transformation Chain able to generate source code helping developers to perform their task in a flexible manner, but ensuring high quality because the generated application would have the same conceptual entries modeled.

Therefore, we have created an approach using a Model Transformation Chain for the agile construction of mobile applications. In this aspect, we are focused in modeling the common peripherals of mobile devices that are currently in the market. Thus, in this paper, we present the general approach, but we make emphasis in the construction of the domain metamodel that allows creating the

© Springer International Publishing AG, part of Springer Nature 2018
O. Gervasi et al. (Eds.): ICCSA 2018, LNCS 10963, pp. 353–364, 2018.
https://doi.org/10.1007/978-3-319-95171-3_28

domain model, which are the main components of the Model Transformation Chain. Based on this approach, it is possible to offer a different way to built mobile applications taking into account its performance. Moreover, the approach will facilitate the evolution of the mobile applications [2].

The paper is structured as follows. Section 2 describes the concepts of Model Driven Engineering. Section 3 presents the elements to take into account for the creation of domain metamodels. Section 4 presents the related work. Section 5 illustrates the Mobile Peripheral Modeling Language (MPML), which is the language created in this work to built a Model Transformation Chain for developing mobile apps focusing in managing mobile peripherals. Section 6 presents the future work and finally, Sect. 7 concludes the paper.

2   Model Driven Engineering

Model Driven Engineering (MDE) provides common concepts for understanding the basic notions of models and metamodels, where a model is a simplified representation of a system built with an intended purpose and a metamodel is a specification model for a domain that makes statements about what can be expressed in the valid models of said domain [3]. It means that a metamodel is a formal description of a modeling language allowing the development of modeling and analysis tools [4].

In MDE, according to Selic [5], one model must provide the following characteristics: (1) abstraction by presenting a simplification of the system; (2) understandability, which means that the model must be intuitive; (3) accuracy for providing a true representation of the modeled system; (4) predictiveness, which implies that the model must predict the interesting properties of the system; and (5) inexpensiveness, which means that the construction of the model must be significantly cheaper than the modeled system.

One system might be represented by different models, where each model represents specific aspects and is characterized by a given metamodel [6]. In addition, for a specific aspect, there might be reusable metamodels in different systems. Nevertheless, various systems can belong to the same domain; then, the metamodel that represents such domain defines its concepts and relations, facilitating the modeling process of those common systems [7].

2.1   Model Transformation

Model transformation is one of the pillars of MDE. A transformation is defined as the change of one source model, which conforms to a source metamodel into other target model, which conforms to a target metamodel. It is important to highlight that in the process the source and target models are representations of the same system under study. Besides, the source and target metamodels need to conform to the same metametamodel [8]. This is explained in Fig. 1.

Kurtev [11] defines three different type of transformations that can be perform with models:

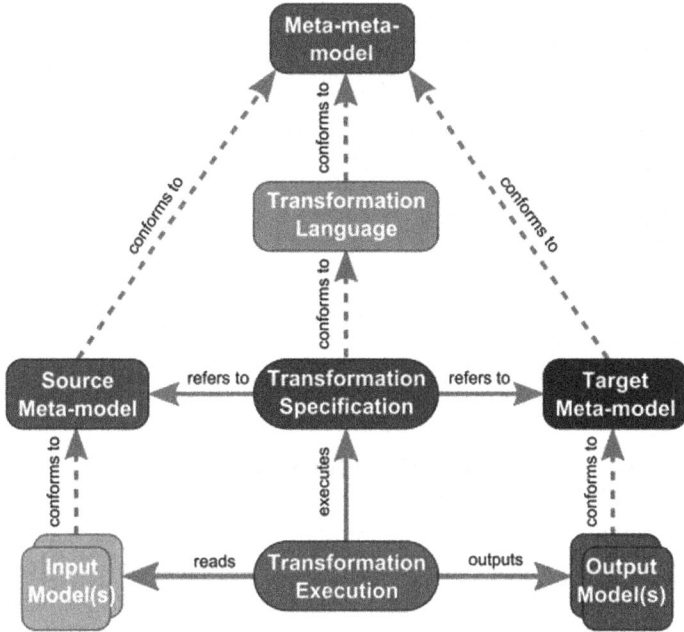

Fig. 1. Model transformation [9] (adapted from [10])

1. Refactoring transformation: The output model is the result of a reorganization of the input model based on some defined criteria.
2. Model-to-model transformation: Transforms one model into a new one.
3. Model-to-code transformation: It is also called Model-to-text transformation and transforms an input model in one or several text files that conform to a programming language.

2.2   Model Transformation Chains

It is possible to chain several transformations with the aim of pass through different model aspects of the same system under study, i.e. the last transformation (the model-to-text transformation that generates the source code of our application) generates source code that depicts in a better way the aspects of the domain under study; then, it is possible to generate code based on a domain model.

In the same way, the model transformation chain allows delivering to the final users, a model that allows them to represent the domain of the application avoiding the aspects of the implementation. With this in mind, It is possible to create two transformations between three different models (the source code generated is also a model) [12]. Thus, Fig. 2 presents a model transformation chain strategy, which uses the Atlas Transformation Language (ATL) as metamodel of the model to model transformation and Acceleo as metamodel of the model to text transformation.

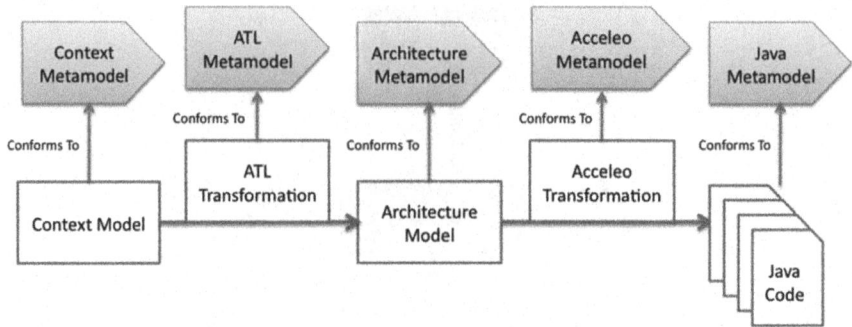

Fig. 2. Model transformation chain strategy [12]

3   Creation of the Domain Metamodel

It is very recommended to select a standard metametamodel, which offer the creation of metamodels that can be operated between them. On this basis, we follow the guidelines defined by the OMG with its specification MDA (Model Driven Architecture) and the definition of our metamodels according to what is defined in the specification MOF (Meta-Object Facility) [13,14]. MOF acts as a framework that enables the development and interoperability between models and metadata driven systems. MOF is also the standard metametamodel from which several metamodels conform to. This makes it very simple and powerful since it is possible to work with compatible models and metamodels derived from

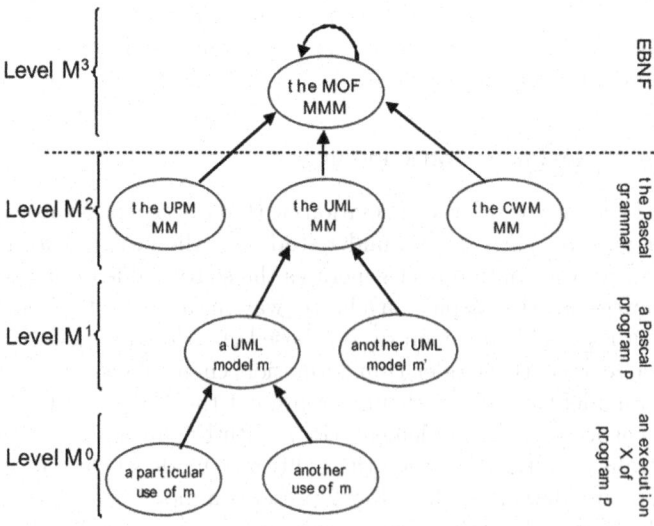

Fig. 3. The OMG four layers standard modeling stack [13]

the MOF metamodel. This can be seen in Fig. 3 that presents the four layers of the standard modeling stack.

Other aspect that is very important is the serialization of the model. The recommendation in MDE is the XML Metadata Interchange Specification (XMI). Based on it, it is possible to take advantage in dealing with models that conform to these standards.

MOF has the following capabilities [15]:

1. Reflection: Extends a model with the ability to be self-describing.
2. Identifiers: Provides an extension for uniquely identifying metamodel objects without relying on model data that may be subject to change.
3. Extension: The simplicity in the definition of the MOF elements provide several advantages to extend it, making it very versatile in the creation of any metamodel.

MOF2 has two main packages [15]:

1. Essential MOF (EMOF). Matches the capabilities of object oriented programming languages and of mappings to XMI or JMI.
2. Complete MOF (CMOF). Provides the full metamodeling capabilities of MOF 2

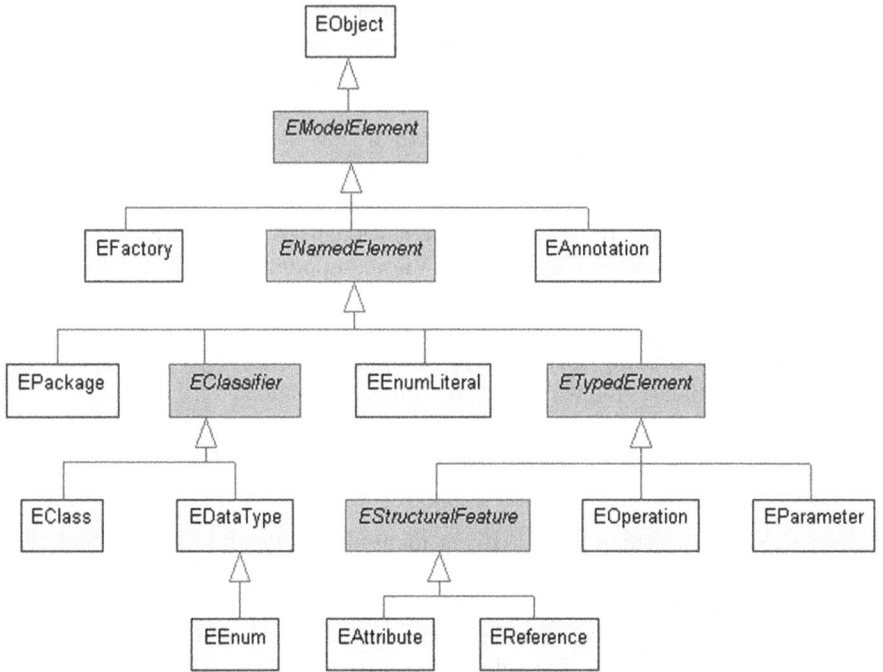

Fig. 4. Ecore components hierarchy

EMF provides Ecore as metametamodel based on the EMOF specification. The hierarchy elements provide by Ecore are presented in the Fig. 4. Ecore has been tested in several scenarios; then, it is a standard and versatil metametamodel.

3.1 Interaction Flow Modeling Language

The OMG has adopted several modeling standards that focused in different representations of a software, one of those stardards is Interaction Flow Modeling Language (IFML).

IFML was created based on the experience earned in more than 10 years with WebML and WebRatio. This was adopted as a standard by the OMG in March 2013. IFML attempts to provide a standard to model and design the UI and UX independent of the platform in which the software is executed. The standard is heavily inspired on WebML. IFML is focus on modeling (a) content visualized in the user interface, (b) navigation paths, (c) user events and interaction, (d) binding to business logic, and (e) binding to persistence layer.

Similar to any modeling language, IFML has elements and connectors defined. IFML elements and connectors are:

– Elements
  1. Container. In mobile this could be a screen, a panel, or a popup.
  2. Viewcomponent. Represents any element with which the user interacts.
  3. Event. Something that is triggered by the client machine, the user or the Server side (i.e. The system events are supported).
  4. Action. In an action cannot be modeled a complex behavior, instead of that this need to be referenced into it. e.g. a dynamic diagram like a sequence diagram.
– Connectors
  1. Navigation flow. Represent the navigation from one Container or Viewcomponent to other Container or Viewcomponent (UI).
  2. Data flow. Transfer data for one element to other element. Happen in the flow connection and is perform through parameters.
  3. Parameter Binding. Describe the mapping from the source element to the target element, this is related to a message element.

4 Related Work

The work of Bernaschina et al. [16] is focused in providing a web tool that helps the user in the creation of IFML models. The tool provides a graphic environment with the IFML elements. In addition, it applies a Model-to-JSON transformation to the model created by the user. Later it generates two results. The former is a Petri Net that allows the user to validate the correct flow of the application modeled. The latter is the code of a Cordova App using web technologies (HTML, CSS, Javascript).

Brambilla et al. [17] present an approach extending the IFML metamodel in a great way, translating the semantic of IFML into the semantic of the mobile elements and appealing to the different connectors and interaction provided by IFML in the representation of 3 kind of events in the mobile devices:

1. Events generated by the interaction of the user (e.g. tap, swipe, etc).
2. Events raised by the mobile device (e.g. sensors, battery, etc).
3. Events generated by the interaction of the user with the mobile components available in the device (e.g. using the camera or the microphone).

This work also presents an approach that generates code using the Cordova framework in order to use its library and to pack the app to install it in mobile devices.

The big differences between these two approaches presented and our approach is the focus on peripherals of the mobile devices giving more relevance to the semantic and syntax of those elements in the domain metamodel. Moreover, the aim of our proposal is to generate native code for a specific platform, initially for the Android platform.

5   Mobile Peripheral Modeling Language

Following the same nomenclature of other model languages accepted by the OMG we called our proposal *Model Peripheral Modeling Language (MPLM)*. The `Element` concept is in higher level of abstraction of *MPLM*, which represents every input sensor or output element to be modeled in the device. Thus, *MPLM* includes the following concepts:

1. Input Elements
   (a) Motion sensors. These sensors measure acceleration forces and rotational forces along three axes. This category includes accelerometers, gravity sensors, gyroscopes, and rotational vector sensors.
   (b) Orientation sensors. These sensors measure the physical position of a device. This category includes orientation sensors and magnetometers.
   (c) Camera. This input represents the inbuilt camera of mobile devices
2. Output Elements. These elements are those that just provide information or actions to the user. In this category, *MPLM* includes Vibrator and Push Notifications
3. Input/Output Elements.
   (a) Communication. Communication includes peripherals that make the interaction with other devices using different protocols like Bluetooth and NFC (Near Field Communication).
   (b) Data Storage. DataStorage models two elements, the LocalStorage of the device and the Rest Services. The main idea is that the user can model the CRUD (Create, Read, Update and Delete) operations. That is why *MPLM* includes Rest Services, because it is straightforward to model this operations using the RestFull specification in the same way as using the LocalStorage.

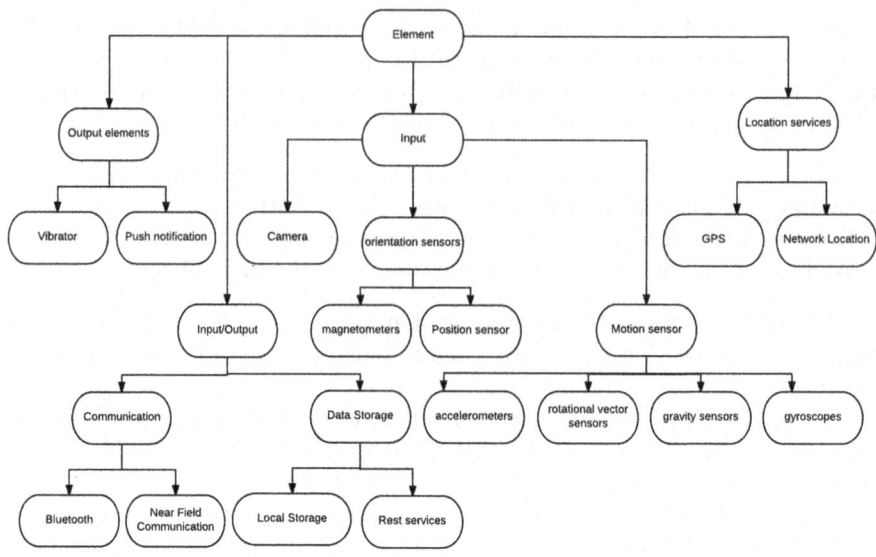

Fig. 5. Metamodels elements taxonomy

4. Location Services. It allows modeling the two ways provided by factory: the GPS sensor and Network Location. Both have differences such as battery consumption.

As a result, we created a taxonomy with all the mentioned concepts presented in Fig. 5. Such diagram serves as raw material for the identification of the elements to be represented in *MPLM*.

5.1   Identification of the Relationships and Metamodel Creation

One of the goals is to allow the user to model parallelism. Then, in order to depict that functionality, we use an approach similar than the used in the UML Activity Diagram metamodel presented in the Fig. 6 using something similar to the Fork and Join nodes defined by this metamodel, we used Eclipse Modeling Framework (EMF) to create one approximation to the metamodel. For illustration purposes, we present it graphically through EMF in Fig. 7.

The elements represented in the metamodel are the following.

1. MPMLElement. This is the element in the higher level of abstraction. Based on Ecore we defined it as an abstract EClass because the user has no option to use this element, when creating conforming domain models.
2. ForkElement. It is the element that allows the user to model a bifurcation in the communication, i.e. the user can model the start of the parallel processing. For example, when launching two sensors to listen any input at the same time in different threads.

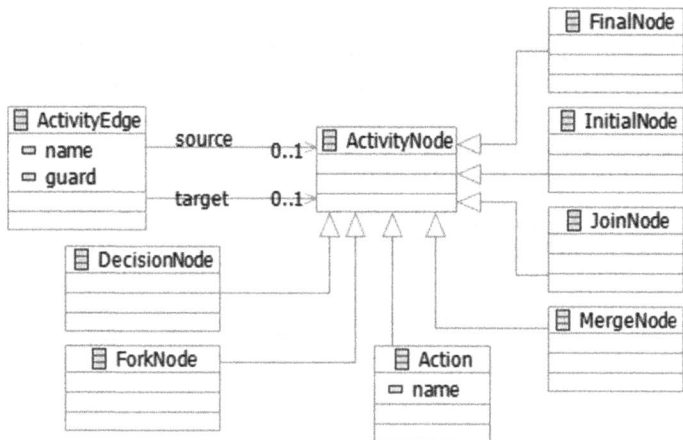

Fig. 6. Activity Diagram metamodel

3. `JoinElement`. The JoinElement is used to model the point where the parallel execution is going to join the processing in order to continue with a serial behavior. For instance, when two sensors finish to emit their answers respectively.

4. `DecisionElement`. In order to accomplish the two previous behaviors, This element provides conditions, which must be fulfilled to Fork or Join the communication flow.

5. `InputElement`. This is an element that only trigger events or generate messages (e.g., an input element such as the camera).

6. `OutputElement`. This is an element that only receive messages and generates outputs (e.g., an output element such as the vibrator).

Table 1. List of Peripherals in the metamodel

Input	Output	Input/Output
Camera	Vibrator	Bluetooth
Gravity	PushNotification	NFC
PositionSensor		LocalStorage
Magnetometer		RestServices
RotationalVector		
Accelerometer		
Gyroscope		
GPS		
NetworkLocation		

7. `InputOutputElement`. This element makes a composition of using both the `InputElement` and the `OutputElement`. This element has the possibility of have both behaviors (e.g., the Data Storage elements that can receive and input message that generates an operation, and an output message that could be the data filter on a query).
8. Peripherals. The rest of the elements are peripherals in the metamodel. Based on them, users can model all peripherals of mobile devices. Therefore, Table 1 presents the peripheral classification.

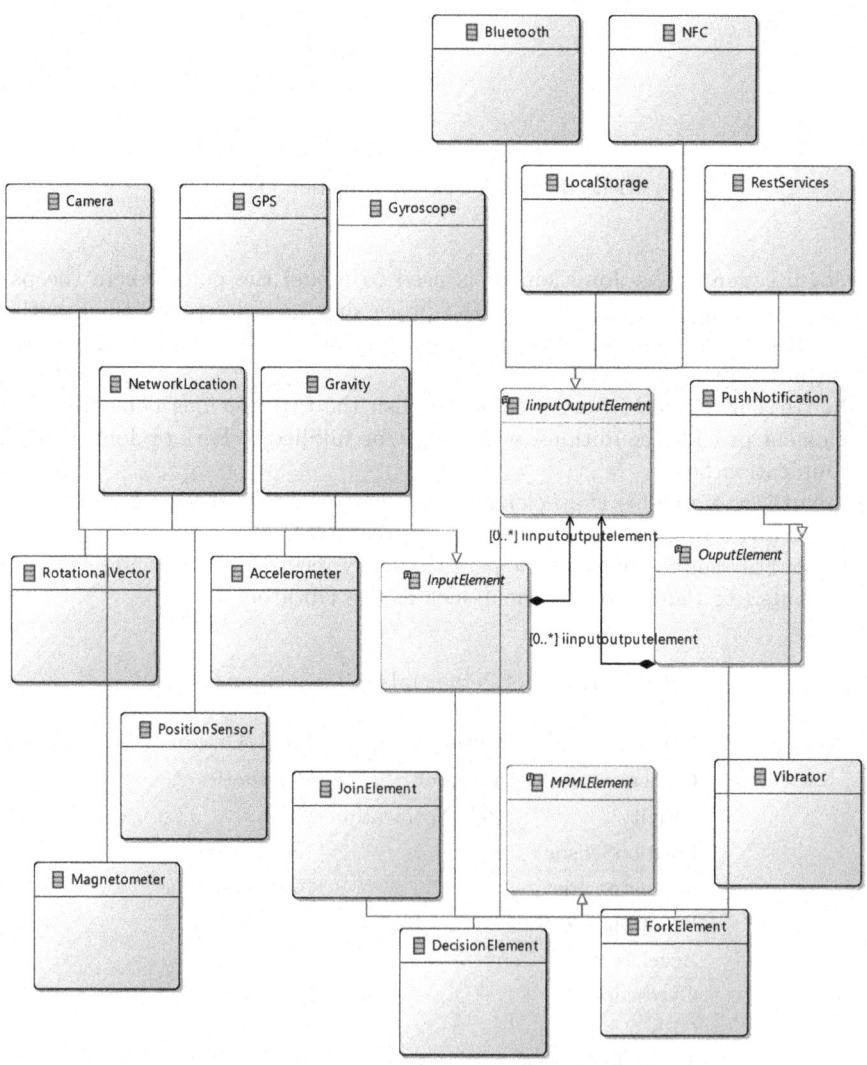

Fig. 7. Metamodel diagram using Ecore

6   Future Work

MPML does not represent by itself a complete mobile application. For that reason, we want to use IFML, since we think it has powerful and simple elements, which allows modeling the interaction between different elements from the perspective of the user when interacting with the app.

It is important to mention that IFML has the goal of modeling the User Interaction without business logic considerations. Part of that business logic is the objective of the peripherals metamodel specification. Then, we will create a new metamodel that extends the elements represented by IFML in the context of mobile devices and combine that approach with the elements defined by *MPML*. The aim is merging both ideas in only one model that allows users to model the complete interaction into the application, taking advantage of both approaches. Finally, based on the first metamodel presented, we can continue creating the following artifacts of the MTC.

7   Conclusions

The taxonomy presented is a raw material for providing a MTC for managing peripheral for mobile devices. Thus, based on such taxonomy, it is possible to define properly the domain concepts in order to provide users a great variety of alternatives when they are dealing with the creation of a mobile application.

EMF is presented as a user-friendly tool that helps modelers in the creation of metamodels offering case tools, supporting the XMI standard specification and providing a good graphical user interface that represents domain metamodels and conforming domain models. Besides its Ecore metamodel is widely accepted in the community and even the OMG metamodels can be obtained in this format.

The standards of the OMG give excellent guidelines in different model operations needed when using the model-driven approach. Besides, it provides interoperability and scalability in the project, since we can manage to use other modeling standards defined by them.

References

1. Ghezzi, C., Jazayeri, M., Mandrioli, D.: Software Qualities and Principles. ACM Press-CRC Press, Boca Raton (2002)
2. Florez, H., Sanchez, M., Villalobos, J., Vega, G.: Coevolution assistance for enterprise architecture models. In: Models And Evolution (ME 2012) Workshop at the ACM/IEEE 15th International Conference on Model Driven Engineering Languages And Systems (MoDELS 2012), Innsbruck (2012)
3. Seidewitz, E.: What models mean. Softw. IEEE **20**(5), 26–32 (2003)
4. Florez, H., Sánchez, M., Villalobos, J.: Embracing imperfection in enterprise architecture models. In: Proceedings of the 6th IFIP WG 8.1 Working Conference on the Practice of Enterprise Modeling (PoEM 2013), pp. 8–17. ACM (2013)
5. Selic, B.: The pragmatics of model-driven development. IEEE Softw. **5**, 19–25 (2003)

6. Bézivin, J.: On the unification power of models. Softw. Syst. Model. **4**(2), 171–188 (2005)
7. Florez, H., Sánchez, M., Villalobos, J.: iArchiMate: a tool for managing imperfection in enterprise models. In: 2014 IEEE 18th International on Enterprise Distributed Object Computing Conference Workshops and Demonstrations (EDOCW), pp. 201–210. IEEE (2014)
8. Kraus, A.: Model driven software engineering for web applications. Ph.D. thesis, Ludwig Maximilians Universität München (2007)
9. Amrani, M., Combemale, B., Lúcio, L., Selim, G.M.K., Dingel, J., Le Traon, Y., Vangheluwe, H., Cordy, J.R.: Formal verification techniques for model transformations: a tridimensional classification. J. Object Technol. **14**(3), 1–43 (2015)
10. Syriani, E.: A multi-paradigm foundation for model transformation language engineering. Ph.D. thesis, McGill University Libraries (2011)
11. Kurtev, I.: Adaptability of Model Transformations. University of Twente, Enschede (2005)
12. Florez, H.: Model transformation chains as strategy for software development projects. In: The 3rd International Multi-conference on Complexity, Informatics and Cybernetics (IMCIC 2012), Orlando (2012)
13. Bézivin, J.: From object composition to model transformation with the MDA. In: TOOLS, vol. 39, pp. 350–354 (2001)
14. Soley, R.: The OMG Staff Strategy group. Model driven architecture (2000)
15. Open Management Group: Meta Object Facility (MOF) Specification v 2.4.1. Open Management Group (2011)
16. Bernaschina, C., Comai, S., Fraternali, P.: IFMLEdit. org: model driven rapid prototyping of mobile apps. In: Proceedings of the 4th International Conference on Mobile Software Engineering and Systems, pp. 207–208. IEEE Press (2017)
17. Brambilla, M., Mauri, A., Umuhoza, E.: Extending the interaction flow modeling language (IFML) for model driven development of mobile applications front end. In: Awan, I., Younas, M., Franch, X., Quer, C. (eds.) MobiWIS 2014. LNCS, vol. 8640, pp. 176–191. Springer, Cham (2014). https://doi.org/10.1007/978-3-319-10359-4_15

Automated Analysis of Variability Models: The SeVaTax Process

Matias Pol'la[1,2], Agustina Buccella[1,2(✉)], and Alejandra Cechich[1]

[1] GIISCo Research Group, Faculty of Informatics,
Comahue National University (UNCOMA), Neuquen, Argentina
{matias.polla,agustina.buccella,alejandra.cechich}@fi.uncoma.edu.ar
[2] Consejo Nacional de Investigaciones Científicas y Técnicas - CONICET,
Buenos Aires, Argentina

Abstract. Variability management includes a set of techniques and methods for defining, modeling, implementing and testing variabilities within the development of a Software Product Line (SPL). Within the testing activity, several approaches have proposed novel techniques for automatic analysis of variability models. However, in spite of the research community has reached some consensus about the base scenarios that should be evaluated, the large number of modeling approaches makes that the way of evaluating those scenarios is still extensively researched.

In this work we propose the SeVaTax process which takes variability models based on orthogonal variability model (OVM) primitives as inputs, and generates a formal model representation. Then, it uses a SAT-based solver for analyzing a wide set of validation scenarios and provides a different level of responses, even proposing some specific actions for correcting the models. Finally, we compare our proposal to others in the literature, based on the supported validations.

Keywords: Variability management · Analysis process
Variability models · Validation · Software product lines

1 Introduction

Variability management is an activity dedicated to provide flexibility and a high level of reuse during software development. Within the software product line approach, the variability activities are aimed at allowing developers to develop a set of similar applications based on a manageable range of variable functionalities according to expert users' needs. Several variability management approaches have emerged in the last twenty years focusing on the different aspects of this activity. Among this wide range of proposals, we are interested in those focused on providing validation activities for variability management

---

This work is partially supported by the UNComa project 04/F009 "Reuso de Software orientado a Dominios - Parte II" part of the program "Desarrollo de Software Basado en Reuso - Parte II".

O. Gervasi et al. (Eds.): ICCSA 2018, LNCS 10963, pp. 365–381, 2018.
https://doi.org/10.1007/978-3-319-95171-3_29

[2,15,22,23]. These activities are really important because they help determine the consistency and correctness of the generated products. At the same time, they cover tasks included in the two engineerings of the SPL development process. During the *domain engineering*, validation activities are responsible for verifying the variability models in order to determine the validity of the SPL platform; and during the *application engineering* they are focused on checking the validity of each derived product (from the platform).

In the last years, a new field has emerged, named *(automated) variability analysis*, focusing specifically on validating variability models according to a predefined set of scenarios [2,9,19]. Understanding the modeling approaches is fundamental for analyzing the validation activities applied to these models. Thus, the validation activities or variability analysis must be considered from these modeling perspectives. Also, it is important to consider the formal model used for translating these variability models because this is the starting point to perform an automated analysis [2].

In previous works, we have presented a modeling approach and a methodology for software product line development [5,6] based on extensions of the OVM approach. Within this context we presented preliminary proposals for developing automatic analysis tools based on different logic representations and solvers [3,17]. In this work we propose an extension of the work presented in [17] for supporting the whole tasks of the automated analysis together with a wide range of validation scenarios with different ways to analyze them. In this way, the contributions of this paper are fourfold: (1) the definition of modeling primitives for delimiting the scope of the variability models; (2) a set of translation rules for formalizing the variability models into a logic representation; (3) the definition of validation scenarios considering mismatches or anomalies on variability models; and (4) an automated analysis (with a supporting tool) for evaluating each of these scenarios.

The paper is organized as follows. Next section describes related works in the literature focused on our research: variability modeling approaches, scenarios validation and automated analysis. Section 3 describes our SeVaTax process mainly focusing on the automated analysis of variability models. In Sect. 4 we compare our process against others in the literature that also present a supporting tool. Conclusions and future works are discussed afterwards.

2 Related Work

In the literature, there exist many works about (automated) analysis of variability models. These works are focused on specific validation activities for the domain engineering phase of the SPL development. Some works presenting surveys o reviews can be found in [2,22]; for example in [22] the authors present a comparison of automated analysis using Alloy [8] for feature models (FM). In [2] there is a broader literature review of automatic analysis of FM, based on a general process that defines a set of tasks for evaluating FM. In Fig. 1 we can see an adaptation of this process, in which we identify five main components as follows.

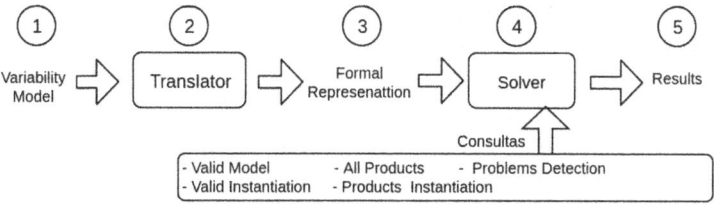

Fig. 1. General process for automated analysis of variability models

The first component is the *variability model* that can be defined by following any of the different modeling approaches. The second component is the *translator*, which performs the transformation process between the model and the formal representation taking into account the selected approach. The third component is the *formal model* or formal representation itself, which includes the variability in logical terms. The fourth component is a *solver*, responsible for validating the formal model. This component also receives the scenario/query set, which determine the *results* (fifth component) of the analysis process.

Regarding to works presenting solutions for an automated analysis process, during the last six years have emerged new works on this field proposing other novel ideas [7,10,13,16,18,19].

For example in [12], authors define a method, supported by a variability modeling tool for checking dead and false optional elements, redundancies, false product line, and the validity of configurations. The tool, named *VariaMos*[1], is based on a independent language that allows to model the variability in different tree structures. The validation of the models is performed by translating them to CSP (Constraint Satisfaction Problem) and then evaluating them in the SWI:Prolog[2] solver. Another proposal is introduced by S.P.L.O.T. [13], which is based on a web tool that allows to design, validate and instantiate FMs. The proposed process translates FMs to 3-CNF (clauses with 3 literals) and by using a SAT-solver, determines the validity of the model including false optional and dead features. Other proposals, based on OVMs, can be found in [10,20,21].

In [20,21] two frameworks are proposed, one of them based on FMs [21] and the other on OVMs [20]. Both frameworks perform an automatic analysis by means of logical translations performed by CSP.

At the same time in FAMA-OVM [20] authors introduce an OVM extension for annotating extra-functional aspects such as availability, development time or efficiency. In Metzger et al. [14], the authors distinguish two general variability types: software variability and PL variability. In this sense, this approach uses two types of models to represent both variants: OVM for documenting the variability, and FM for documenting software variability. Finally to carry out the

---

[1] http://variamos.com/home/.

[2] http://www.swi-prolog.org/.

automatic analysis of the models, the proposal presents a prototype that uses
SAT solver (Sat4j[3]).

Finally, another important aspect to analyze is the set of queries defined
for the analysis process, that is, the set of questions which solvers are capable
of answer. In this sense, in the literature there exists some common validation
scenarios [2,9,11] such as *valid model, valid instantiation, all products*, etc. These
scenarios are important in order to analyze the capabilities of the solvers. In
general, the basic set of scenarios [2,9] is supported by almost all the related
proposals; however this set is not enough to support all the possible anomalies
or problems that can exist in the variability models. Even, none of them makes
suggestions or corrections to the models.

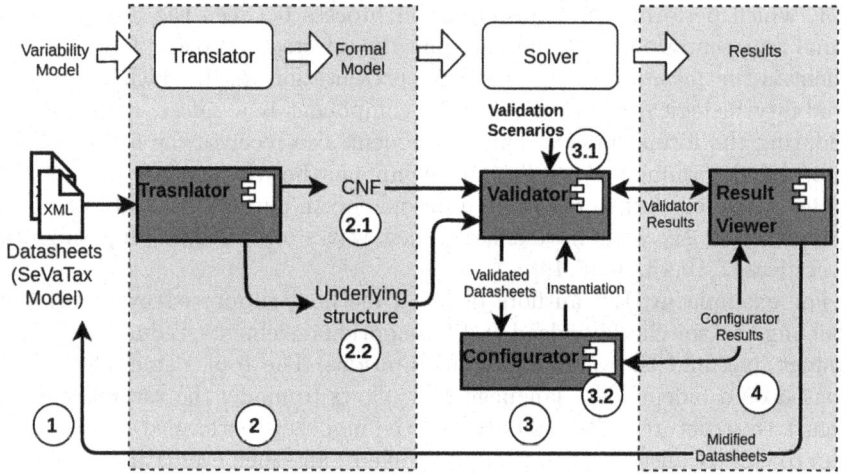

Fig. 2. SeVaTax analysis process according to the general analysis process defined in
Fig. 1

In this work we propose the SeVaTax process based on a set of interconnected variability models, together with an extended set of validation scenarios
supported. In addition, our validation is based on providing suggestions to the
developers for correcting models. In this way, our SeVaTax process improves the
analysis capabilities supporting a wide set of validation scenarios for providing
identification and solution to possible anomalies on the design and derivation of
variability models.

3   The SeVaTax Process for Automated Analysis

The SeVaTax analysis process is based on the general process showed in Figure 1
together with the necessary components for supporting different validation scenarios. In Fig. 2 we show the software components and inputs/outputs included

---

[3] http://www.sat4j.org/.

in the SeVaTax architecture. The figure is divided into four modules with the components and input/output flows involved.

In next subsections we describe each component of the figure highlighting main techniques and structures used for its implementation.

3.1   SeVaTax Variability Model (Module 1)

The SeVaTax model uses the OVM notation for representing each function-ality by means of annotations to design artifacts (based on UML collabora-tion diagrams). In previous works [5,6] we have defined this model based on a functionality-oriented methodology. That is, each functionality of the SPL is documented by a functional datasheet representing the set of services, commons[4] and variants, which interact to reach the desired functionality. Furthermore, each datasheet is composed of a set of hierarchical tree structures, where each struc-ture is conformed by a root service and a set of services (variation points or variants).

The interactions are divided into *variability types*, for denoting the variant interactions among services; *dependencies*, for denoting interactions between ser-vices; and *scope*, for specifying the scope of each variant point. The *scope* defines whether a specific instantiation of a variation point (when deriving products) will be global for every functionality (which includes the variation point) or specific for only each functionality [4]. These scope operators only affect the variability types defined. The complete set of interactions, specified in Table 1, are:

- Variability Types:
    - **Mandatory variation point**: determining the selection of a variant service when the variation point is included. We call mandatory services to those services that are variants of a *mandatoryVP*, or services that present a *uses* relationship with a mandatory service.
    - **Optional variation point:** specifying that zero or more variant services, associated to the variation point, can be selected.
    - **Alternative variation point**: defining that only one variant service, of the set of associated variants of the variation point, must be selected (XOR relation).
    - **Variant variation point**: defining that at least one variant service, of the set of associated variants of the variation point, must be selected (OR relation).
- Dependencies:
    - **Use:** specifying a dependence between common services, which are not necessarily associated with a variation point.
    - **Requires**: specifying a relation between two variant services, independent from the variation points the variants are associated with, in which the selection of one variant service requires the selection of the other.

---

[4] Common services are services that will be part of every product derived from the SPL.

Table 1. Interactions defined for modeling functional datasheets

Dependency	XML Tag	Graphical Notation
Mandatory	$< MandatoryVP >$	——————
Optional	$< OptionalVP >$	------------
Alternative	$< AlternativeVP >$	
Variant	$< VariantVP >$	
Use	$< use >$	◄——————►
Requires	$dependency : Requires$ $= \text{"serviceName"}$	——————►
Excludes	$dependency : Excludes$ $= \text{"serviceName"}$	—/—►
Global vp	$< GV >$	GV
Specific vp	$< SV >$	SV

- **Excludes:** which is the opposite of the requires dependency specifying the exclusion of a variant when another one is selected.
– Scope operators:
  - **Global Variation Point (Global VP):** specifying that if the variation point is instantiated in a specific way, it will be applied in that way for all functionality including that variation point.
  - **Specific Variation Point (Specific VP):** specifying that the instantiation of the variation point is particular for each functionality including that variation point.

Finally, the last item of the datasheet includes a set of XML files, which are built according to the XML tags (showed in the second column of Table 1).

3.2 Translator and Formal Representation (Module 2)

The translator is implemented as a software tool which is composed of a set of parsers that reads the XML files (from the datasheets) and generates two outputs, a formal model based on a logical representation in CNF, and a set of underlying structures (Module 2 of Fig. 2).

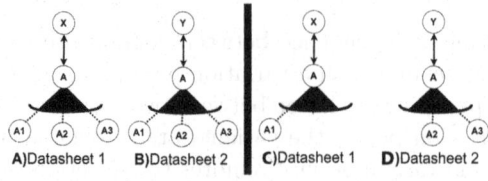

A)Datasheet 1   B)Datasheet 2   C)Datasheet 1   D)Datasheet 2

Fig. 3. Example of a variant variation point with different Specific VVP configurations

Table 2. Translation of a functional datasheet into CNF

Dependency	Logic Modeling	CNF
Datasheet	$Ds \Rightarrow root1 \land root2$	$(\neg Ds \lor root1)$
		$(\neg Ds \lor root2)$
Mandatory VP	$a \Rightarrow a1$	$\neg a \lor a1$
Optional VP	$a \Rightarrow a1 \lor \neg a1$	$(\neg a \lor a1 \lor \neg a1)$
Alternative VP	$a \Rightarrow a1 \otimes a2... \otimes a3$	$(\neg a \lor a1 \lor a2... \lor a3)$
		$(\neg a \lor a1 \lor \neg a2... \lor \neg a3)$
		$(\neg a \lor \neg a1 \lor a2... \lor \neg a3)$
		$(\neg a \lor \neg a1 \lor \neg a2... \lor a3)$
		$(\neg a1 \lor \neg a2) \land (\neg a1 \lor \neg a3)$
		$(\neg a2 \lor \neg a3)$
Variant VP	$a \Rightarrow a1 \lor a2... \lor a3$	$(\neg a \lor a1 \lor a2... \lor a3)$
Use	$a \Longleftrightarrow b$	$(\neg a \lor b) \land (a \lor \neg b)$
Requires	$a \Longrightarrow b$	$(\neg a \lor b)$
Excludes	$a \Longrightarrow \neg b$	$(\neg a \lor \neg b)$

CNF Representation (Module 2.1). The CNF representation of the variability models (in this case of our SeVaTax models) is based on the translation presented in [1] with adaptations and extensions to represent the interactions defined in Table 1. Table 2 shows this formalization along with the translation to CNF of each interaction type, except for the scope operators. For example, a proposed extension is the concept of datasheets which is represented as a logic implication between all the root services that compose it. For example in the first row of Table 2 we can see the representation of a datasheet with two root services. The optional type (third row) is represented by using a tautology (true in every interpretation) because the inclusion or not of an optional service should not generate anomalies. Also, in the fourth row we can see the representation of the alternative type as the logical function XOR.

Other extensions are the scope operations, which will be explained by examples. They contain a Variant Variation Point, named A (VVP), with three variants ($A1$, $A2$ and $A3$) and two different services (X and Y) in different datasheets (1 and 2 respectively) that have dependencies *uses* with A. Figure 3 shows these cases graphically.

Considering the two scope operators, we have the following two possibilities:

- *Global VP* operator: When a Global VP is attached to a variation point (VP), the translation generates a unique formal representation for this VP, which will affect all the dependencies that are related to any service belonging to any functional datasheet. Therefore, only a unique translation to CNF of the VP (that will be valid for the whole SPL platform) is generated. That is, for each service, belonging to any functional datasheet, related to the same VP, the translation will be the same.
  For the example of Fig. 3(A) and (B), if the A (VVP) is a Global VP, the translation is the following: $(X \Longleftrightarrow A) \land (Y \Longleftrightarrow A) \land (A \Rightarrow A1 \lor A2 \lor A3)$

– *Specific VP* operator: When a Specific VP is attached to a variation point (VP), we generate as many logical representations as services (or functionalities) are directly related to the VP. To identify each case, the variant point and the variants are identified together with each related service.

For the example showed in Fig. 3(A) and (B), if the A (VVP) is a Specific VP, the translation is the following (considering both datasheets): $(X \Longleftrightarrow AX) \wedge (AX \Rightarrow A1X \vee A2X \vee A3X) \wedge (Y \Longleftrightarrow AY) \wedge (AY \Rightarrow A1Y \vee A2Y \vee A3Y)$ As we can see, two instances of the VVP are generated. The first one, for representing the interaction of services X and A (AX) (Datasheet 1 of Fig. 3a); and the second one for the interaction between service Y and A (AY) (Datasheet 2 of Fig. 3b).

This translation allows us to generate different configurations for the same variation point within the same product. For example, we can generate the instantiations showed in Fig. 3(C) and (D). It shows a configuration for the A VVP containing the variant $A1$ used by the X service (C-Datasheet 1); and another configuration of A with the variants $A2$ and $A3$ for service Y (D-Datasheet 2).

Underlying Structures (Module 2.2). As aforementioned, the second output of the *translator* component is a set of underlying structures as support to identify our extended set of validation scenarios and to correct errors. This structure contains the set of services connected to a list of variation points and dependencies. In this way, all the structure of datasheets can be easily obtained. For example, regarding to the dependency list, each dependency is composed of a dependency type (Include, Exclude or Uses) and the target service. Each service belongs to one or more datasheets. In this way, it is possible to represent cross-dependencies.

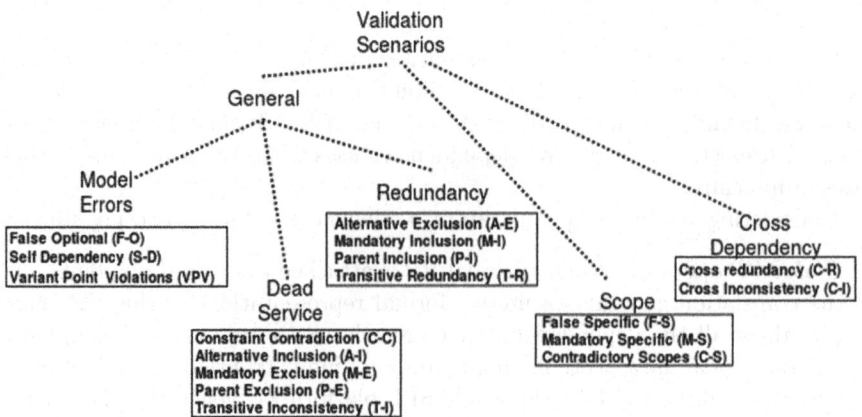

Fig. 4. Classification of validation scenarios

3.3   Solver (Module 3)

In this section we describe the two components that allow to validate and configure a variability model (Module 3 of Fig. 2).

Validator and Validation Scenarios (Module 3.1). Before configuring a specific solver, it is important to define the specific queries supported for the analysis process, that is, the set of questions which solvers are capable of answer.

From the common set of validation scenarios proposed in the literature (Sect. 2), we define a new set of them including particularities of our SeVaTax models (in which more than one hierarchical tree can be included). In this way, several of these scenarios take into account the fact that services can participate in more than one functionality (or variability model representing a functionality).

Figure 4 shows our classification containing seventeen scenarios classified into five categories. The three main categories are, *general*, *scope* and *cross dependency*. The first category is then subdivided into *model error*, *dead service* and *redundancy*.

Following, we apply two different techniques to analyze them. The first one is by using a SAT-Solver (in this case Sat4j) by sending different service true/false combinations for finding inconsistencies. The second one is by using our underlying structures and supported functions for finding more sophisticated anomalies and even suggest or correct errors.

We summarize each scenario type in Table 3 highlighting the scenario, description, graphical notation and the main method applied to validate it. In the first part of the table we show the *model error* scenarios including those presenting errors related to the graphical design of the model.

In the second part of the table we show *dead service* scenarios. A service is dead if it cannot appear in any of the generated products of the software product line. In general terms, to detect the dead service, each service is evaluated individually. To do that, it is necessary to pre-setup the service as true in the CNF. If the generated CNF is inconsistent, then the service is a dead service. At the same time, we sub-classify dead services for detecting and repair some errors. For example, to evaluate the Constraint Contradiction (C-C) scenario, given two services 'A' and 'B' we analyze the CNF translation finding the services related to an *includes* or *excludes* according to the *constraint_contradiction(A,B)* function. When this function detects an *includes* or *excludes* relationship between two services, it checks the translations associated to both services looking for possible incompatibilities.

```
constraint_contradiction (A,B):
If "not(A) not(B)" belong_to CNF ?
    If ("not(A) B") belong_to CNF ?
            return "Constraint Contradition"
    If ("A not(B")) belong_to CNF ?
            return "Constraint Contradition"
```

Table 3. Description and analysis of validation scenarios

Scenario	Description	Notation	Validation
F-O	When a *Optional, Variant or Alternative* service is instantiated for all possible products		SAT-solver
S-D	When a service has a dependency on itself. For the *includes* is irrelevant, but the *excludes* is inconsistent		self_dependency(A,B),
VPV	The same variant belongs to two or more variation points into the same datasheet		variant_vhild(B,Dts)
C-C	A service which includes other service that excludes the first		constraint_contradiction(A,B)
A-I	A service which *includes* an alternative of itself, or some of its parents		alternative_variants_child(A)
M-E	A service that *excludes* a mandatory service		mandatory_exclude(A,B)
P-E	A service that *excludes* a parent service		parent_exclude(C,S)
T-I	A service which *includes* and *excludes* the same service, or presents any transitive relationship of this case		services_excludes(A,B)
A-E	A service which *excludes* an alternative of itself, or an alternative of some of its parents		alternative_variants_child(A)
M-I	A service that *include* a mandatory service		mandatory_include(A,B)
P-I	A service that *includes* a parent service		parent_include(C,S)
T-R	A set of services that presents *includes* generating a transitive redundancy		services_includes(A,B)
F-S	If a *Specific VP* is related to an only one service or variant depending on a *Global VP*		services_consume_variation_point(VP)
M-S	If a *Specific VP* is conformed only by mandatory variant points. Then it can never contain different configurations		mandatories_childs(VP)
C-S	If a *VP* presents different scopes in different functional datasheets		check_scopes(VP)
C-R	Two or more datasheets, which present the same variability or dependence among two or more services		cross_redundancy(Dts[])
C-I	Two or more datasheets that present some type of inconsistency given by the services that are composed		cross_inconsistency(Dts[])

Then, the third part is describing *redundancy* scenarios which include some redundancy type in the formulation of model restrictions and relations. For example, for the Transitive Redundancy (T-R) scenarios, we use the *services_includes(A,B)* function, which given two services 'A' and 'B'(where A *includes* B), generates a list (*Includes_List*) of all services that *include* B; recursively adding services that *include* services belonging to the list (*Includes_List*). Then, if the service A belongs to *Includes_List*, there is a transitive redundancy between 'A' and 'B'.

```
Services_Includes(A,B):
Include_List=[B]
Repeat S in Include_List
    For All A
    if (S_aux Includes B)
        Include_List.add(S_aux)
until Include_List unchange
If A belong_to Include_list
    return transitive redundancy
```

The fourth part summarizes the *scope scenarios* including problems when specific or global VP are defined. Here, for example, for the Contradictory Scopes (C-S) scenario, for each service that represents a variation point we register its scope into the underlying structures. Therefore, when registering the scope we check if the service has the same scope. In all other cases, we are in the presence of an scope inconsistency.

```
Service_Scope(S):
    For each S1 in Datasheets_List
    If  (S1.name == S.name and S1.scope != s.name)
            Return Contradictory Scope
```

Finally, the *cross dependency* scenarios analyze problems among two or more datasheets. The functions *cross_redundancy(Dts[])* and *cross_inconsistency(Dts[])* analyze the services, and combinations of services (relationships) that belong to more than one datasheet. Then, when the same relationship among two or more services is detected in more than one datasheet, a *cross redundancy* alert is generated. On the other hand, when a set of services, in different datasheets, presents more than one formal translation generating a incompatibility a *cross inconsistency* error is generated.

3.4   Results (Module 4)

In order to provide more effective solutions when analyzing variability models, we classify them into a pre-defined set of answer types, as follows:

- Warning (W): an alert is issued about a possible problem identifying the services involved. These cases do not necessarily cause incompatibilities.

Table 4. Relationships between scenarios and answer types

Scenario	Answers	Action
Model Errors (MEs)		
False Optional (F-O)	R	Modify to Mandatory VP
Self Dependency (S-D)	I	-
VP Violations (VPV)	I	-
Dead Services (Ds)		
Constraint Contradiction (C-C)	I	-
Alternative Inclusion (A-I)	I	-
Mandatory Exclusion (M-E)	W	-
Parent Exclusion (P-E)	R	Eliminate the Dependency
Transitive Inconsistency (T-I)	GI	-
Redundancies (Rs)		
Alternative Exclusion (A-E)	R	Eliminate the Dependency
Mandatory Inclusion (M-I)	R	Eliminate the Dependency
Parent Inclusion (P-E)	R	Eliminate the Dependency
Transitive Redundancy (T-R)	I	-
Scope (Ss)		
False Specific (F-S)	R	Modify To Global VP
Mandatory Specific (M-S)	R	Modify To Global VP
Contradictory scopes (C-S)	R	Modify To Global VP
Cross Dependency (CDs)		
Cross redundancy (C-R)	I	-
Cross Inconsistency (C-I)	I	-

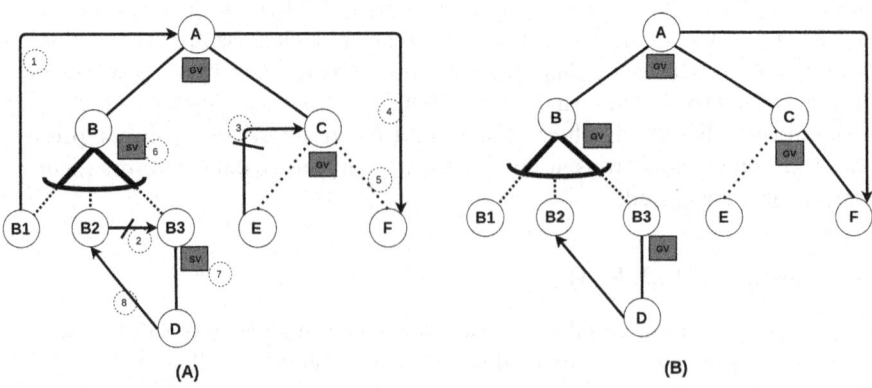

Fig. 5. (A) Functional datasheet with four variation points - (B) Functional datasheet with the corrections applied

- Identification (I): the scenario that generates the conflict is identified. The objective is to visualize the causes and the services involved to assist the solution.
- General Identification (GI): the services that generate the conflict are identified, but it is not possible to identify a specific scenario.
- Repair (R): the scenario that generates the conflict is identified and a pre-established solution is applied. The required action can be *modification* or *elimination*.

Table 5. Validation results

	Scenario	Detail	Action
1	Rs- P-I	service B1 Requires service A	Eliminated (R)
2	Rs- A-E	service B2 Excludes service B3	Eliminated (R)
3	DSs- P-E	service E Excludes Service C	Eliminated (R)
4	Rs- T-R	Transitivy Redundancy Between A,F	Eliminated (R)
5	MEs- F-O	service F is Mandatory	Modified (R)
6	Ss- F-S	B Vp is Global VP	Modified (R)
7	Ss- M-S	B3 Vp is Global VP	Modified (R)
8	DSs- A-I	B3 child Requires B2	Identify (I)

Then, according to our implementation, we can support these answer types on each validation scenario. Table 4 shows these relations between scenarios-answers. As we can see, only when the answer is a *repair (R)*, the required action is attached.

4   Proof of Concept and Evaluation

To show the SeVatax analysis process, we present an example of a functionality represented in a datasheet including nine services and four variation points (two *Specific VP* and two *Global VP*). In Fig. 5 - (A) we can see this model graphically, in which a *Global (Mandatory) VP* is defined for the A service (conformed by two *mandatory* services B and C), an *Specific (Alternative) VP* is defined for the B service (conformed by three variant services B1, B2 and B3); and A is defined for the C service (conformed by two variant services E and F). In addition, the model presents five dependency relations, three *requires* (D-B2,B1-A, and A-F) and two *excludes* (B2-B3 and E-C).

At the same time, the example shows a set of anomalies belonging to different validation scenarios. In the figure we can observe a set of numbers (from one to eight), which identify the eight validation scenarios involved (3 *Redundancies*(Rs), 2 *Dead Services*(DSs), 2 *Scope* (Ss) and 1 *Model Error* (MEs)).

The results of applying the SeVaTax process to each of these scenarios are showed in Table 5.

The first column presents the number (according to the numbers of Fig. 5) of the validation scenarios with the corresponding code. The second column in the table provides a description of the scenario; and finally the last column shows the action performed (Modification, Identification or Elimination) when the answer was *repair (R)*. For example, in the third scenario the process detected a *Parent Excluded*(DSs - P-E) between the E and C services making a repair action of eliminating the *dependency* relation. Another example is the sixth scenario, which presents a False Specific (Ss - F-S) belonging to the B service. In this case, the tool modified the VP scope to Global VP. This example is representative because we are verifying only one datasheet; in other cases the scenarios are validated together with the complete set of datasheets (Platform Validation).

Table 6. Comparison of our approach

Scenario	SeVaTax	S.P.L.O.T	VariaMos
Model Errors			
False Optional	R	R	I
Self Dependency	I	-	NA
VP Violations	I	-	-
Dead Services			
Constraint Contradiction	I	GI	GI
Alternative Inclusion	I	GI	GI
Mandatory Exclude	W	-	-
Parent Exclude	R	GI	GI
Transitive Inconsistency	GI	GI	GI
Redundancies			
Alternative Exclusion	R	-	-
Mandatory Inclusion	R	-	-
Parent Inclusion	R	-	-
Transitive Redundancy	I	-	-
Cross Dependency			
Cross redundancy	I	-	-
Cross Inconsistency	I	-	GI

Finally, Fig. 5 - (B) shows the final variability model (after applying the suggested actions). In this figure we can see two scenarios, an *alternative inclusion* (A-I) between services D and B2; and a transitivity redundancy between A and F. For both scenarios, we cannot provide a solution, but only the scenarios and the services involved are identified, leaving the solutions in the hands of the developer (they are only detected).

4.1   Tool Comparison

To show some advantages of our proposal, we compare the results provided by our tool against the results of two other approaches with similar supporting tools - S.P.L.O.T. and VariaMos. These two tools are widely referenced in the literature and they are available to be downloaded form the Web. The objective of this comparison is to analyze the way the validation scenarios defined previously (Sect. 3.3) for automatic analysis are analyzed by each tool. Therefore we designed a set of variability models according to specific characteristics of those proposals.

Regarding to the results, we use the predefined set of answer types described in Sect. 3.4; so, the answers might be: Warning (W), Identification (I), General Identification (GI) and Repair (R).

Table 6 presents the results of comparing our process against S.P.L.O.T. and VariaMos. It shows the validation scenarios together with the answers for each tool.

As we can see, the results show that many of the scenarios raised are not taken into account and that others are only reported in a general way. By analyzing each of the predefined scenarios we can conclude that:

- Model Errors: S.P.L.O.T repairs (R) the false optional and transforms it to mandatory; while VariaMos only informs this anomaly. Also, VariaMos does not allow to model auto-references (NA).
- Dead Service: this category is the most considered; however, S.P.L.O.T and VariaMos only report the scenarios in a general (GI) way, that is, detect the anomaly as Dead Services without presenting any more information.
- Redundancies: Neither of the two tools performs an analysis of redundancies. This may be due to the characteristics of the solvers used. In our case, we use different underlying structures (detailed in Sect. 3.2) to identify these scenarios.
- Scope: Only evaluated by our tool.
- Cross-dependency: In this case S.P.L.O.T does not perform an evaluation of cross-dependencies due the nature of the feature model, because it uses a unique tree structure. On the other hand, VariaMos only detects the cross-inconsistencies in a general (GI) way, i.e, as Dead Services.

In this way, in this brief comparison, we can see that the analysis capabilities of variability models were improved with respect to the others tools. That is, our proposal is able to find and correct more anomalies presented during the design and derivation of variability models.

5   Conclusion

In this work, we have presented our SeVaTax analysis process of variability models composed of four main components: the variability model, the formal translation, the set of supported validation scenarios, and the results.

In addition, we have performed an evaluation by comparing our SeVaTax analysis process against two other approaches in the literature. This evaluation is based on the specific set of validation scenarios supported by each of the approaches and the possible solutions. The results of the evaluation shows substantial differences between our approach and the others, since in our process each scenario is clearly identified allowing developers to correct some anomalies. These analysis capabilities are not present in other tools.

As future work we are working on a performance evaluation of the supporting tool for each validation scenario taking into account anomaly intra-variability models (individual datasheets) and inter-variability models (cross-references). Also, we are extending the comparison in order to include other similar proposals/tools and evaluate their analysis capabilities and user's responses.

References

1. Batory, D.: Feature models, grammars, and propositional formulas. In: Obbink, H., Pohl, K. (eds.) SPLC 2005. LNCS, vol. 3714, pp. 7–20. Springer, Heidelberg (2005). https://doi.org/10.1007/11554844_3
2. Benavides, D., Segura, S., Ruiz-Cortés, A.: Automated analysis of feature models 20 years later: a literature review. Inf. Syst. **35**(6), 615–636 (2010). https://doi.org/10.1016/j.is.2010.01.001
3. Braun, G., Pol'la, M., Buccella, A., Cecchi, L., Fillottrani, P., Cechich, A.: A DL semantics for reasoning over ovm-based variability models. In: Proceedings of the 30th International Workshop on Description Logics, vol. 1879, July 2017
4. Brisaboa, N.R., Cortiñas, A., Luaces, M.R., Pol'la, M.: A reusable software architecture for geographic information systems based on software product line engineering. In: Bellatreche, L., Manolopoulos, Y. (eds.) MEDI 2015. LNCS, vol. 9344, pp. 320–331. Springer, Cham (2015). https://doi.org/10.1007/978-3-319-23781-7_26
5. Buccella, A., Cechich, A., Pol'la, M., Arias, M., Doldan, S., Morsan, E.: Marine ecology service reuse through taxonomy-oriented SPL development. Comput. Geosci. **73**, 108–121 (2014)
6. Buccella, A., Cechich, A., Arias, M., Pol'la, M., del Socorro Doldan, M., Morsan, E.: Towards systematic software reuse of gis: insights from a case study. Comput. Geosci. **54**, 9–20 (2013). http://www.sciencedirect.com/science/article/pii/S0098300412003913
7. Frantz, F.R., Benavides Cuevas, D.F., Ruiz Cortés, A.: Automated analysis of orthogonal variability models using constraint programming. In: Xv Jornadas De Ingeniería Del Software Y Bases De Datos 2010, Valencia, España (2010)
8. Jackson, D.: Software Abstractions: Logic, Language, and Analysis. The MIT Press, Cambridge (2006)
9. Kowal, M., Ananieva, S., Thüm, T.: Explaining anomalies in feature models. In: Proceedings of the 2016 ACM SIGPLAN International Conference on Generative Programming: Concepts and Experiences, GPCE 2016, New York, NY, USA, pp. 132–143. ACM (2016). http://doi.acm.org/10.1145/2993236.2993248
10. Lauenroth, K., Pohl, K., Toehning, S.: Model checking of domain artifacts in product line engineering. In: 2009 IEEE/ACM International Conference on Automated Software Engineering, pp. 269–280, November 2009

11. von der Massen, T., Lichter, H.: Deficiencies in feature models. In: Mannisto, T., Bosch, J. (eds.) Workshop on Software Variability Management for Product Derivation - Towards Tool Support (2004)
12. Mazo, R., Munoz-Fernandez, J.C., Rincon, L., Salinesi, C., Tamura, G.: VariaMos: an extensible tool for engineering (dynamic) product lines. In: Proceedings of the 19th International Software Product Line Conference, pp. 374–379. ACM (2015)
13. Mendonca, M., Branco, M., Cowan, D.: S.P.L.O.T.: software product lines online tools. In: Proceedings of the 24th ACM SIGPLAN Conference Companion on Object Oriented Programming Systems Languages and Applications, OOPSLA 2009, New York, NY, USA, pp. 761–762. ACM (2009). http://doi.acm.org/10.1145/1639950.1640002
14. Metzger, A., Pohl, K., Heymans, P., Schobbens, P.Y., Saval, G.: Disambiguating the documentation of variability in software product lines: a separation of concerns, formalization and automated analysis. In: 15th IEEE International Requirements Engineering Conference (RE 2007), pp. 243–253, October 2007
15. da Mota Silveira Neto, P.A., do Carmo Machado, I., McGregor, J.D., de Almeida, E.S., de Lemos Meira, S.R.: A systematic mapping study of software product lines testing. Inf. Softw. Technol. **53**(5), 407–423 (2011). https://doi.org/10.1016/j.infsof.2010.12.003
16. Nakajima, S.: Semi-automated diagnosis of foda feature diagram. In: Proceedings of the 2010 ACM Symposium on Applied Computing, SAC 2010, New York, NY, USA, pp. 2191–2197. ACM (2010). http://doi.acm.org/10.1145/1774088.1774550
17. Pol'la, M., Buccella, A., Arias, M., Cechich, A.: Sevatax: service taxonomy selection validation process for spl development. In: 2015 34th International Conference of the Chilean Computer Science Society (SCCC), pp. 1–6, November 2015
18. Rincon, L., Giraldo, G., Mazo, R., Salinesi, C., Diaz, D.: Method to identify corrections of defects on product line models. Electron. Notes Theor. Comput. Sci. **314**, 61–81 (2015). http://www.sciencedirect.com/science/article/pii/S1571066115000286
19. Roos-Frantz, F., Galindo, J.A., Benavides, D., Cortés, A.R., Garcıa-Galán, J.: Automated analysis of diverse variability models with tool support. In: Jornadas de Ingenierıa del Software y de Bases de Datos (JISBD 2014), Cádiz, Spain, p. 160 (2014)
20. Roos-Frantz, F., Galindo, J.A., Benavides, D., Ruiz-Cortés, A.: FaMa-OVM: a tool for the automated analysis of OVMs. In: Proceedings of the 16th International Software Product Line Conference, vol. 2, pp. 250–254. ACM (2012)
21. Segura, S., Benavides, D., Ruiz-Cortés, A.: Fama test suite v1. ISA Research Group, p. 41 (2010)
22. Sree-Kumar, A., Planas, E., Clariso, R.: Analysis of feature models using alloy: a survey. In: Proceedings 7th International Workshop on Formal Methods and Analysis in Software Product Line Engineering, pp. 46–60 (2016). http://dx.doi.org/10.4204/EPTCS.206.5
23. Thüm, T., Apel, S., Kästner, C., Schaefer, I., Saake, G.: A classification and survey of analysis strategies for software product lines. ACM Comput. Surv. **47**(1), 61–645 (2014)

Study on Process of Data Processing and Analysis Based on Geographic Information

Jae-Young Choi[1], Young-Hwa Cho[1], Chin-Chol Kim[2],
Yeong-Il Kwon[2], JeongAh Kim[3], Suntae Kim[4],
and EunSeok Kim[5](✉)

[1] Department of Computer Engineering, Sungkyunkwan University,
Suwon, South Korea
{jaeychoi, choyh2285}@skku.edu
[2] Department of ICT Platform and Services,
National Information Society Agency, Daegu, South Korea
{cckim, kyi}@nia.or.kr
[3] Department of Computer Education, Catholic Kwandong University,
Gangneung, South Korea
clara@cku.ac.kr
[4] Department of Software Engineering, Chonbuk National University,
Jeonju, South Korea
stkim@jbnu.ac.kr
[5] GDS Consulting, Seoul, South Korea
eskim@gdsconsulting.co.kr

Abstract. Today Big Data is the biggest buzzword. However, in order for the data transaction to be activated, it is easy to combine and analyze the stored data and the sales data, but there is a problem that additional infrastructure and manpower for processing and analyzing the data after data purchase. In this paper, we develop data products through geographic information based data processing and analysis. In addition, the system was proposed that the data buyer utilizes data without any separate infrastructure by providing the user with the entire process of data processing for product development. Finally, the process and system will be verified through mediation platform.

Keywords: Geographic information · Data processing · Data analysis
Data mediation platform

1 Introduction

The reason for the low utilization of data in Korea was selected as the main reason for the lack of production data needed by data users. Especially, many start-up companies who want to do business based on mobile apps are not enough to use actual data. This demonstrates that a large number of public data is not processed into the topics and forms what users need through processing, processing, and analysis.

© Springer International Publishing AG, part of Springer Nature 2018
O. Gervasi et al. (Eds.): ICCSA 2018, LNCS 10963, pp. 382–393, 2018.
https://doi.org/10.1007/978-3-319-95171-3_30

In this paper, we develop data products that meet the needs by identifying commerce, flow population and traffic related data that start-up and small business need in business process. In addition, since the developed data products can guarantee the availability by supporting the analysis related application consulting necessary for the subject discovery, analysis and application development, it is necessary to study on the process of the data processing, analysis and visualization based on the geographic information. Through this, it is possible to integrate external data such as population attributes to geographic information sensor data (weather, communication, etc.) by using standardization engine, and visualization and prediction model for integrated data can be developed and applied to business.

2   Development of Data Products Based on Analysis

2.1   Secured Data

The data used in this study can be divided into card usage data, base station data, local administration data, and self-collection data. As shown in Table 1, the card data is credit card, check card usage and utilization information of domestic/foreign people, and data products for regional commercial area analysis and tourism analysis, which are increasingly demanded by public institutions and local governments, are developed [1]. In other words, it obtains the card usage history for the domestic and foreign people by time slot and analyzes it by region (or branch). In particular, it obtains and analyzes the check card information separately in order to grasp the consumption patterns of the 20s and 30s.

Table 1. Card data

Data	Item	Type	Number of data
Credit/debit card usage information	Date of use	TXT/relational DB	1,250,397
	Small Area Code		4,593,451
	Type of business		4,593,451
	Day of use		1,250,397
	Time of use		1,250,397
	Gender		1,250,397
	Age		1,250,397
	Number of sales		4,593,451
	Sales revenue		4,593,451
Business district information	Small Area Code		331,102
	Type of business		331,102
	Number of companies		4,201,203
	Number of new establishments		794,304
Card usage by foreigner	Day of use		890,540
	Time of use		890,540
	Nationality		257,324
	Number of sales		890,540
	Sales revenue		890,540
	Number of franchisee		120,994

384 J.-Y. Choi et al.

Base station data are used by base station-based population data and actual floating population data as shown in Table 2 [2]. That is, it collects actual data of the floating population to verify the measurement of the floating population accuracy of the base station data and uses the base station access information of the communication company in order to develop data products with the highest sales performance of data brokerage transactions in 2016, especially for floating population. Also, it obtains the base station access information of all parts of the country by time, gender, and age, and develops data population related population through items related to the floating population, resident population, and working population at specific time and points [3, 4].

Table 2. Floating population data

Data	Item	Type	Number of data
Floating population by base station information (nation)	POI information	TXT/relational DB	1,339,053,600
	Coordinate		
	Administrative section code		
	Investigation time		
	Number of floating population by POI		
	Number of floating population by POI and age		
	Number of floating population by POI and gender		
Floating population by survey information (Seoul)	POI information		88,554,840
	Coordinate		
	Administrative section code		
	Investigation time		
	Number of floating population by POI		
	Number of floating population by POI and age		
	Number of floating population by POI and gender		
Traffic information (Seoul)	Bus route number		146,493,480
	Bus number		
	Bus stop number		
	Bus stop name		
	Bus stop coordinate		
	Number of passengers by time		
	Subway line number		2,724,360
	Subway station name		
	Number of passengers by time		

Local government administrative agency data use education, traffic/safety data. To develop educational and medical data products, collect information on education institutions and distribution of the population of children in the metropolitan municipalities as shown in Table 3 and develop the data products needed by educational and academia related enterprises. We also develop relevant data products through medical information such as safety related data related to crime and patient occurrence. In other words, safety related data products are developed by collecting and integrating information on safety-related CCTV installation and emergency and information on sex and age data related to the education field and data on the daycare centers and school statistics.

Table 3. Housing/Population/Safety data

Classification	Item	Number of data	Source	Unit
Housing	Public housing maintenance information	109,369	Gyeonggi provincial government	Complex
	Public housing complex information	3,793		Complex
	Real transaction information	2,901,393		Number of business
	Electricity bill	3,044		Complex
	Water bill	3,839		
	Heating bill	697		
Population/Movement	Marriage	454,641		Number of business
	Birth	592,822		
	Number of migration by gender and age	1,039,255		
	Number of migration by scale	1,039,255		
Education	Daycare Center and kindergarten	12,591	Gyeonggi provincial office of education	
	Basic status of school	4,567		
Transportation/Safety	Bus stop information	146,452	Gyeonggi provincial government	
	CCTV installation status	21,197		
	First-aid log	1,616,034	Gyeonggi disaster and safety center	Number
	Hospital information	71,088		

Self-collected data uses self-collected data on population, housing, and business. It aims at the development of existing products that have sales results of data brokerage transactions in 2016 and self-collection of data related to population, housing and business which are the basis for developing data products in 2017 to continuously develop products. Information on housing for common and detached houses in the nation, estimated income and asset information that plays a role of socioeconomic indicators, and basic information on the base of business analysis, coordinates, and land price are used.

2.2 Construction of Data Processing Process

In order to develop data products, the existing big data technologies such as data processing, fusion and analysis techniques should be applied in all areas of product development [5]. Figure 1 shows the data processing platform. The primary data, external data, user data, and analysis result data are inserted into the data storage and it processed through data refining, processing and combining on the data processing module. The data thus processed are analysed through analytical modeling, and they are provided easily through various visualization techniques, and ultimately provide output.

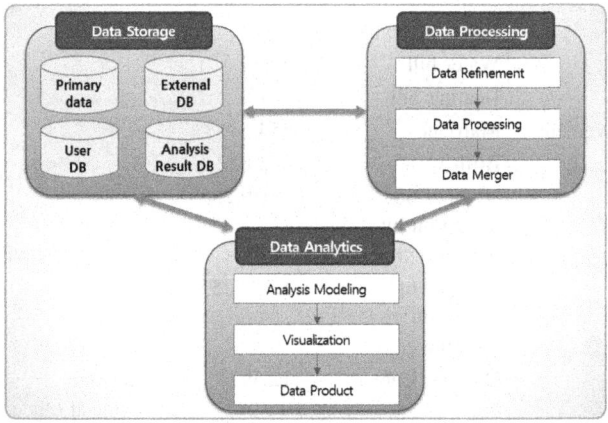

Fig. 1. Configuration of data processing platform

Data processing improves user's analytical convenience and expands the market for data products purchasing by providing internal data processing process which is data refinement, conversion and analysis to the users who lack the infrastructure and manpower. The processing methods include GIS processing technology, address processing technology, and textual data utilization technology, which are applied to establish sales data products [6].

GIS processing technology is applied to construct small area unit data. Specifically, as shown in Fig. 2, an aggregation method or technology that aggregates sensitive data such as personal information in small area units and provides data to achieve data utilization and prevention of personal information exposure at the same time. In this study, Statistics Korea has constructed a nationwide small area of about 100,000 units, and updates the data every year when buildings such as roads, buildings, and apartments are changed. The effect of this technology is that it can be easily combined with the government data, which are aggregated in aggregate units, and can prevent exposure of personal information. In addition, it is easy to analyze because it reduces data capacity of national data.

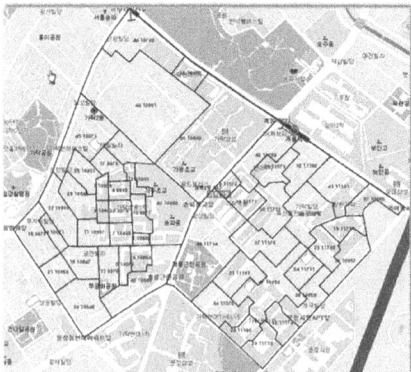

Fig. 2. Examples of small area data construction technology (amount of data: 100,000 units nationwide, constituent: average 200 households, construction: annually by Statistics Korea)

The address processing technique is to calculate the data merge information by address coding as shown in Fig. 3. That is, to facilitate the merging of the customer data and the administrative data of the address unit, the address encoding process is performed using the address information as the key value [7]. Through this technology, text-based address information can be refined to extract the administrative area, zip code, building type and residence type. In addition, there is an effect that it is possible to generate key value that can substitute resident registration number and to expand the range of information related to address, which is the most public information in the public domain.

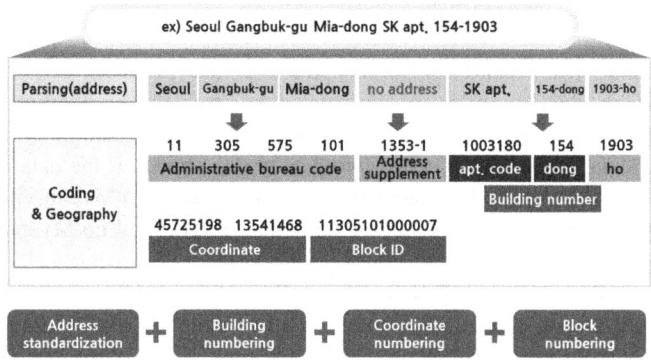

Fig. 3. Example of how to generate additional information by address processing technology

In the case of the Republic of Korea, the existing lot number address was converted to the address of the road name in 2014. Therefore, we need a technique to map the old address to the new address. Figure 4 shows the conversion and refinement technique between the new address and the old address.

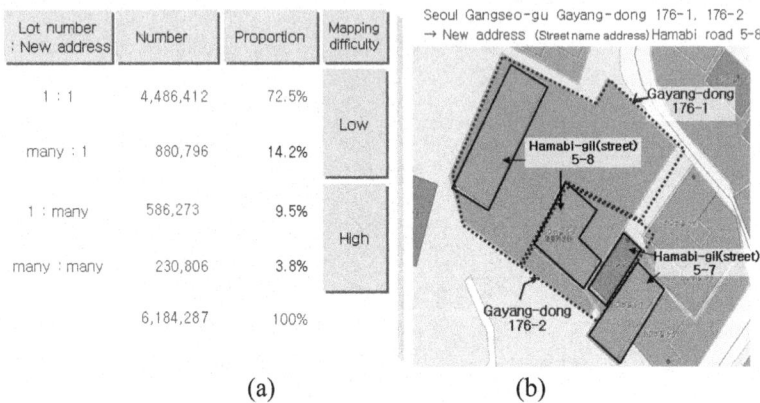

(a)   (b)

Fig. 4. Example of conversion and refinement between new and old addresses; (a) Mapping relationship between lot number and new address, (b) case of many: 1 of lot number: new address

Text data processing technology is used to refine the business name. In other words, it is a technology to standardize and unify business name by a single criteria for the purpose of business name search and business data merger for analyzing business based data. Table 4 shows examples of text information processing tasks for business name and industry refinement. In general, unification of English name and Hangul name existing in business name, current name of former business name, and diversity of notation of corporation name are united by text-based data processing technology. Through this works, the scope of utilization of business data can be expanded by enabling the search and merging of business data in the absence of a business number.

2.3   Construction of Data Analysis Process

The As an analytical technology for constructing data products, it is necessary to integrate various data in order to construct data products. In addition, a separate integration plan is needed because the data collected from the source is composed of different unit data. For example, when two data are combined, if the data is composed of households and the other units are composed of Eup(towns)/Myeon(villages)/Dong (small villages), it is necessary to subdivide the unit data of the Eup/Myeon/Dong or to compute the household unit as the Eup-Myeon-Dong.

Big data analysis is performed by setting the subdivided data as an independent variable and the consolidated data as a dependent variable in order to integrate the data of the up-down relation or subset into the same unit. In this case, big data analysis techniques that can be assumed as dependent causal models are regression model,

Table 4. Text information processing for refining the business name and industry

	Function	Description
Basic function	Basic Refinement	Em characters processing → Remove space before and after name → Remove consecutive spaces → Capitalization
	Meaninglessness information classification	Number representation, Only vowels/Consonants are marked, Only special characters/Space are marked
	Parenthesized information classification	Remove parentheses, Character classification in parentheses
	Keyword Refinement	Remove keywords (corporation etc.), Keyword substitution, Keyword classification
Additional function	Meaninglessness facility classification	Public facilities (park, rest facility, playground etc.), Subway, Residential building, etc.
	Missing name complement	If the address is the same and the phone number is similar, but the back of the name is different
	Typographical error complement	If the address is the same and the phone number is similar, but more than 80% of the name matches
	Building/Business classification	Classify buildings and businesses through building keywords → Create building keyword REF separately

neural network model, and decision tree. Figure 5 shows the geographic information integration by data projection. This method is aimed at expanding the data of a certain point to the data of the whole area of Seoul. As a processing method, an attribute value of a point where data is absent is estimated by using an attribute value of a point where data exists.

For the analysis of geographic information, when the units of collection are different during integrating geographic information, it is necessary to unify the units of the

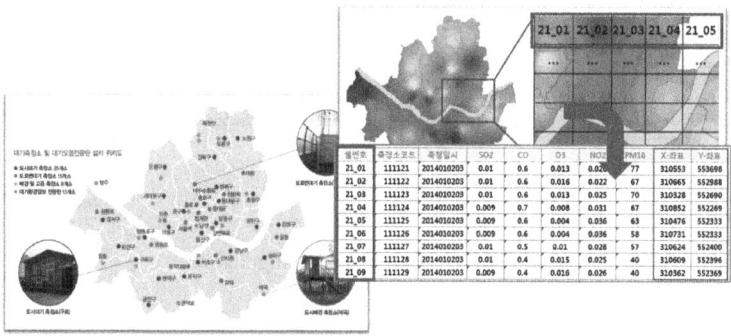

Fig. 5. Example of geographic information integration by data projection (e.g. Seoul air pollution projection)

two data to construct integrated data. For example, one data is converted into an address unit and the other unit is composed of coordinate units when two data are combined, the data is converted into the same unit (address or coordinates) and then integrated. In order to integrate geographical information, it is necessary to convert smooth data such as cell ↔ coordinate, cell ↔ address, and need to apply geographic information analysis technology. Kriging analysis, which is a representative technique of geographic information analysis, or Inverse Distance Weighted analysis method, which is a GIS interpolation method, is utilized for converting information collected in address units into cells or coordinate units [8]. This method of geographic information analysis is used to estimate the value of space without address.

3   Construction of Integrated System and Experiment

3.1   Construction Environment

The data transaction mediation platform was developed based on relational database MS SQL, and the web site is developed and operated on 3-Tier Web. As shown in Figs. 6 and 7, Presentation Layer consists of search management, data management, download management system, and business layer consists of subscription, settlement and basic information management system.

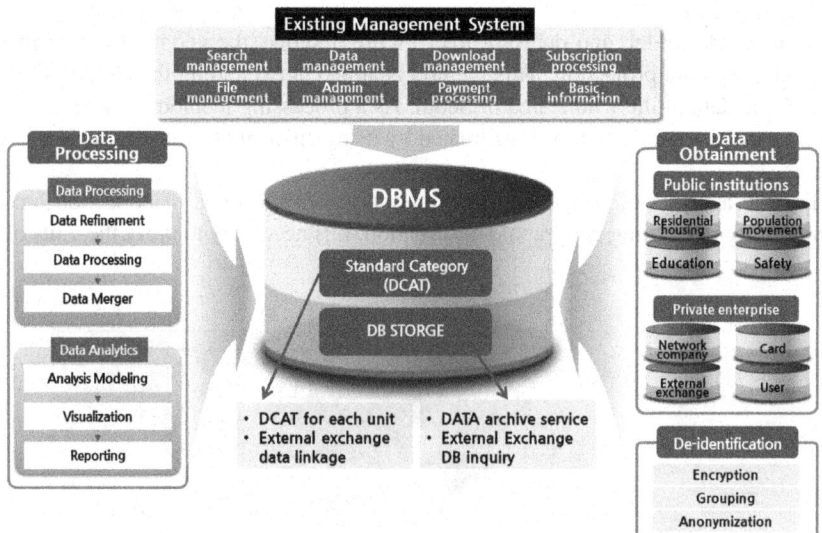

Fig. 6. Overall system configuration

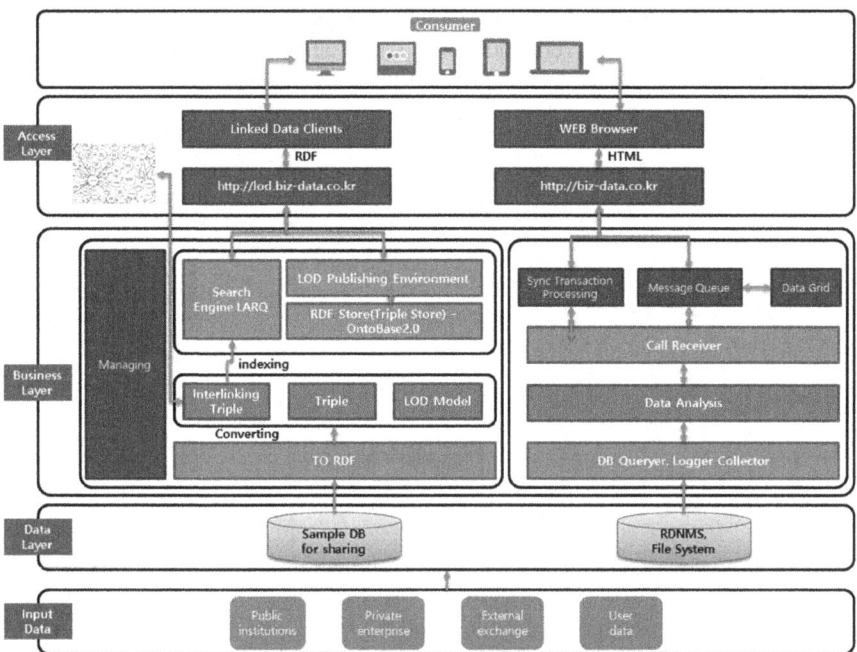

Fig. 7. Platform architecture for data integration

Was, Web server is based on MS Windows Server 2010 later, and Was application server and Was server should be installed with Apache Tomcat 7.0 or later version. The server was configured separately for security reasons. The CKAN server is constructed based on Ubuntu 16.00 or later, and has version is 2.7 more. It is a cloud-based platform that enables data storage, processing, and sales services. The standard data catalog (DCAT) is built to link CKAN-based services and data sets.

In the test execution, we separated and tested the data which is relevant to the brokerage project data products from the shared sample database provided by each institute and the existing RAW DB for verifying the data connectivity. In addition, factors that may cause a risk when expanding the RAW DB constructed in the future brokerage business were identified and removed in advance.

3.2 Experiment Result

We separated the data to verify the constructed model. That is, a modeling dataset for building the model and a validation dataset for the robustness test of the construction model are separately constructed. Also, input variables for model construction were selected. When the input variable is a categorical variable, it is the T-test and the Anova-test between the target variable and the input variable while it is correlation analysis and simple regression analysis when the input variable is a continuous variable. Modeling of the candidate model using the model selection index was performed. In addition, as shown in Fig. 8, we conducted a direct verification using field data and a comparison of candidate models using model verification data obtained from the data separation process for model verification. Also, the statistical model test was conducted to compare the candidate models and deduct the final models.

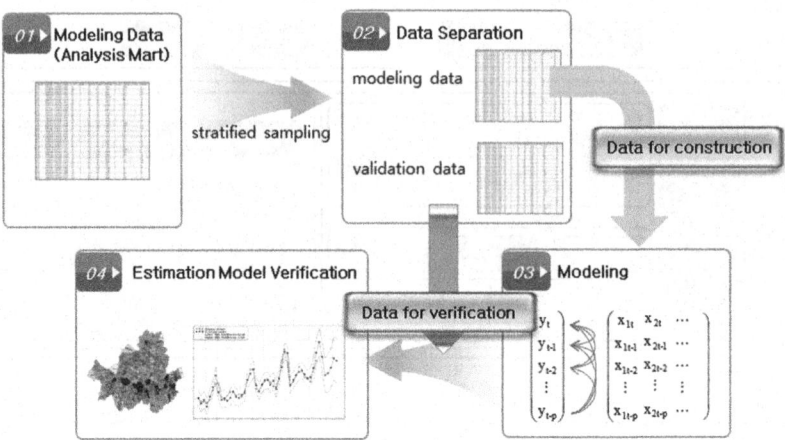

Fig. 8. Statistical verification process of the construction model

The system can confirm that the trading volume in the same period increases because small and medium-sized merchants directly experienced the data they wanted and bought them immediately. They had little prior use of data products. In addition, it was possible to diversify data products by providing simple processing, fusion complex, and customized data products to small and medium-size merchants and developing 30 kinds of data products.

The way that selling data to small and medium-sized merchants can be done through distribution channels, and the method of direct selling is not ruled out either. However, due to the poor analytical infrastructure of small and medium-sized merchants, indirect sales are supported. In addition, a platform has been established for agencies and companies related to small and medium-sized merchants, so that each organization can supply data without separate development through providing a platform for communication between institutions and small and medium-sized merchants, as well as data products developed in this study.

4   Conclusion

This study aims to develop the process of data processing and analysis based on geographic information to develop data products that meet commodity needs, flow population, and traffic related data needed by start-up and small business people in business process according to the necessity of new data transaction infrastructure. In order to do this, we studied data processing techniques and processes such as GIS processing technology for small unit data construction, address processing technology for calculating data merge information through address coding, and text data processing technology for business name refinement. The method for analysing the geographic information was also introduced.

The brokerage transaction activation business which is the basic act of the government data policy through data opening and sharing provides a data content base for big data analysis and utilization in the area of all data utilization in public and private sectors, between public and public institutions, between public institutions. Data processing and brokerage services, which utilize publicly available data in the private sector big data analysis and utilize information gathered in the private business process as basic data for administrative services, will have a significant impact on the big data industry by activating variety data exchanges.

Therefore, through this study, it is possible to deepen and expand the scope of administrative services by providing necessary data to all administrative fields such as traffic, housing, and welfare by applying private data to the public sector. It also shows that using public data can provide a solution to tasks that could not be solved through internal data.

Acknowledgments. This research was supported by Next-Generation Information Computing Development Program through the National Research Foundation of Korea (NRF) funded by the Ministry of Science and ICT (NRF-2014M3C4A7030503).

References

1. Seynaeve, G., et al.: When mobile network operators and statistical offices meet integrating mobile positioning data into the production process of tourism statistics. In: The 14th Global Forum on Tourism Statistics, Venice (2016)
2. Terada, M., et al.: Population estimation technology for mobile spatial statistics. NTT Technical Review, vol. 12, no. 1 (2014)
3. De Meersman, F., et al.: Assessing the quality of mobile phone data as a source of statistics. In: European Conference on Quality in Official Statistics, Madrid (2016)
4. Ricciato, F., et al.: Estimating population density distribution from network-based mobile phone data. Joint Research Centre Institute Technical report, European Commission (2015)
5. Llinas, J., Waltz, E.: Multisensor Data Fusion. Artech House, Norwood (1990)
6. Chang, N.: Improving customer data quality and practical usage by data standardization and enrichment. Entrue J. Inf. Technol. **6**(2), 7–20 (2007)
7. Goldberg, D.W., et al.: Address standardization, Technical report 12, GIS research Laboratory of University of Southern California (2014)
8. Lu, G.Y., Wong, D.W.: An adaptive inverse-distance weighting spatial interpolation technique. Comput. Geosci. **34**(9), 1015–1166 (2008)

Impact Factors on Using of E-learning System and Learning Achievement of Students at Several Universities in Vietnam

Quoc Trung Pham[1(✉)] and Thanh Phong Tran[2]

[1] School of Industrial Management, HCMC University of Technology,
Ho Chi Minh City, Vietnam
pqtrung@hcmut.edu.vn
[2] IT Department, Fulbright University in Vietnam, Ho Chi Minh City, Vietnam
ttphong77@gmail.com

Abstract. The industrial revolution 4.0 opens many opportunities for online learning and leads to the need to study, entertain, and work anywhere and anytime. Recently, e-learning systems become vital for any university to increase the educational quality and to provide students useful and high quality learning resources. However, how to encourage the e-learning usage and to improve the learning achievement of students through e-learning system is still a challenged task. From previous researches, a research model has been proposed and it is evaluated by Cronbach alpha analysis, EFA, CFA, and Structural Equation Modeling (SEM) techniques on SPSS and AMOS software. Based on quantitative analysis from 356 valid samples, the results showed that 5 factors positively impacted on the e-learning usage are: University support (0.367), Computer competency of students (0.274), Infrastructure (0.195), Content and design of courses (0.145), and Collaboration of students (0.118). Besides, learning achievement is influenced by 2 factors, including: E-learning usage (0.446), and Collaboration of students (0.129). Finally, some managerial suggestions are made to improve the efficiency of e-learning usage and to increase the learning achievement of university students in Vietnam.

Keywords: E-learning · Information system · Usage · Learning achievement
University · Vietnam

1 Introduction

Recently, e-learning systems had been implemented in many schools all over the world at both university and high school level to support learning and teaching processes. In US, there are 5.8 millions of students who registered the online courses and the number is increasing annually during last decade (EdTech 2016). Therefore, e-learning becomes a powerful tool for supporting online and distance programs.

In Vietnam, IT infrastructure of educational institutions was invested recently and upgraded frequently. By 2010, the project "Edunet" completed successfully to equip all educational institutions (from primary schools to universities) with high speed Internet connection (MOET 2016). So, a lot of universities in Vietnam are ready for deploying

© Springer International Publishing AG, part of Springer Nature 2018
O. Gervasi et al. (Eds.): ICCSA 2018, LNCS 10963, pp. 394–409, 2018.
https://doi.org/10.1007/978-3-319-95171-3_31

e-learning systems and modern ICT applications for education. Taking advantages of new technologies of industrial revolution 4.0, such as: cloud computing, internet of thing, virtual reality…, e-learning systems open opportunities to turn traditional university into modern one, which combine traditional and online method.

E-learning systems bring many benefits for universities, such as: ubiquitous, flexible, rich content, fast updated, easy to monitor the learning progress, convenient, cost saving, time saving… However, ensuring the success of an e-learning system is a difficult task (Pham and Huynh 2017). In fact, some problems of e-learning system implementation are realized, such as: the high rate of failure of e-leaning projects, the low acceptance and low satisfaction of e-learning users, ineffectiveness of e-learning systems on learning achievement… Therefore, there is a need for doing research to identify factors affecting on the success of e-learning system, especially on user acceptance and learning achievement. In Vietnam, there is a few researches in this topic, but it is necessary to do more researches for supporting the success of e-learning projects and to improve the educational quality of higher educational institutions as the goal of Ministry of Education and Training in recent years.

In general, the main objectives of this research include: (1) identify and measure the impact of some factors on students' e-learning usage and learning achievement of several universities in Vietnam; and (2) suggest managerial implications for improving students' e-learning usage and learning achievement through e-learning system. The structure of the paper is as follows: Sect. (2) Main concepts and Literature review; Sect. (3) Research model and hypotheses; Sect. (4) Research results; Sect. (5) Discussion and Conclusions.

2 Main Concepts and Literature Review

2.1 E-commerce and E-business

E-commerce is defined as a trading, selling and buying products or services on the Internet of computer networks (Rosen 2000). E-commerce may include online or offline payment process, and delivering paid products in digital form through the internet or in traditional form in the real world (WTO 1998).

E-business refers to a broader concept of e-commerce, which includes not only trading process, but also all business activities, such as: manufacturing, logistics, research & development, customer service, collaboration, internal operation activities… (Turban et al. 2015).

2.2 E-learning

E-learning is a specific form of e-business in education, which focuses on learning and teaching processes, such as: training, knowledge sharing and collaboration.

E-learning is defined as learning or training process, which is prepared, transferred and managed using various ICT tools locally or globally (Masie 2016). E-learning is a learning method using Internet communication through interaction between instructor and students with suitable designed learning materials and contents (Resta and Patru 2010).

In this research, e-learning is understood as a learning method through the Internet for some formal educational programs, which are managed by Learning Management System (LMS), to ensure the interaction, collaboration and to satisfy the learning demand of learners at any time, and in any place (Nguyen et al. 2014).

2.3   The Success of E-learning System

Seddon (1997) proposed 3 aspects to evaluate the success of an Information System, including: (1) System quality (relevance, timeliness, accuracy); (2) Perceptual measures (perceived usefulness, user satisfaction); and (3) Benefits (individual, organizational, social). In the IS success model of Delone and Mclean (2003), beside the above factors, Service quality is added to evaluate the support of system supplier.

E-learning is also an information system, so the success of e-learning system could be evaluated similar to any other information system. The success of e-learning system may include: project success, technology acceptance, users' satisfaction, learning achievement, and knowledge transferring... In this research, the success of e-learning focused on e-learning usage and learning achievement of students.

According to Pham and Huynh (2017), learning achievement of students through e-learning system could be determined by independent variables, such as: Computer Self Efficacy, Ease of Use, Perceived Usefulness, Face to Face Interaction, Email Interaction, and Social Presence.

2.4   E-learning Usage: TAM and UTAUT

In order to know the impact factors of e-learning usage, 2 foundation theories should be used, including: Technology Acceptance Model (TAM) and Unified Theory of Acceptance and Use of Technology (UTAUT).

Technology Acceptance Model (TAM) is developed by Davis et al. (1989) based on Theory of Reasoned Action (TRA) of Fishbein and Ajzen (1975). TAM tried to explain human behavior in acceptance of using an information system. In TAM, there are 2 main factors affecting on the acceptance of a new technology, including: perceived usefulness, and perceived ease of use. In which, the usefulness is also affected by the ease of use. Venkatesh and Davis (2000) suggested an extension of the Technology Acceptance Model (TAM2), which explored the determinants to perceived usefulness and perceived ease of use.

Unified Theory of Acceptance and Use of Technology (UTAUT) proposed by Venkatesh et al. (2003) to explain the intention and behavior of using an information system. UTAUT includes: performance expectancy, effort expectancy, social influence, facilitating conditions. Some demographic factors, such as: gender, age, experience, and voluntariness of use, have indirect impacts on the intention and using behavior (Venkatesh et al. 2003). An extend version of UTAUT (UTAUT2) is also suggested by Venkatesh et al. (2012). In UTAUT2, 3 new factors have been added, including: convenience, exchange value, and habit.

2.5   Related Researches

Some related researches in the success of e-learning system could be summarized in the following Table 1.

Table 1. Summary of related researches

Authors	Topic	Impact factors
Nguyen (2015)	Structural Equation model for the success of IS project	Habit, social influence, ease of use, project quality (information, system, and service), project goal, and project features.
Laily et al. (2013)	Critical success factors for e-learning system in IT Telkom Bandung using SEM	✓ Computer competency ✓ Collaboration ✓ Content ✓ Access ability ✓ Infrastructure
Martínez-Caro (2011)	Impact factors on effectiveness of e-learning: an analysis on Manufacturing Management courses	✓ Prior experience ✓ Flexibility ✓ Job status ✓ Blended e-learning ✓ Students interaction ✓ Interaction between students and lecturers
Shee and Wang (2008)	Criteria for evaluating web-based e-learning system: approach from learners' satisfaction and applications	✓ User interface ✓ Community of learning ✓ Content ✓ Individualization
Wang (2008)	Evaluating the success of e-commerce system: a confirmation of Delone & Mclean model	✓ Information quality ✓ System quality ✓ Service quality
Selim (2007)	Critical success factors for the acceptance of e-learning: confirmatory factor model	✓ Teacher attitude toward technology ✓ Teaching style ✓ Computer competency of learner ✓ Collaboration of learner ✓ Content and design of course ✓ Access ability ✓ Infrastructure ✓ School support
DeLone and McLean (2003)	An updated information system success model	✓ Information quality ✓ System quality ✓ Service quality
Soong et al. (2001)	Critical success factors for online courses	✓ Human factors (time effort, skills) ✓ Technology capability of students and teachers ✓ Mindset about online learning. ✓ Collaboration ✓ Perception about IT infrastructure and support

3 Research Model and Hypotheses

3.1 Research Model

From the above researches, the research model of Selim (2007) and Laily et al. (2013) are selected to suggest a model for evaluating e-learning usage and learning achievement of e-learning system in Vietnam. The reason is that these models covered all aspects of an e-learning system, including: human factors (teachers, students), technology factors (infrastructure, access ability), and learning related factors (content, support, collaboration). In the research of Selim (2007), the impact of various factors on e-learning usage is evaluated, but its impact on learning achievement is not considered. In the research of Laily et al. (2013), there is a lack of some important factors, such as: teacher skills, university support. Therefore, in the proposed research model, a combination of the 2 researches above is necessary. In general, there are 7 factors affecting on e-learning usage and learning achievement of students, and e-learning usage also has an effect on the learning achievement through e-learning system. The proposed research model could be summarized in the following Fig. 1.

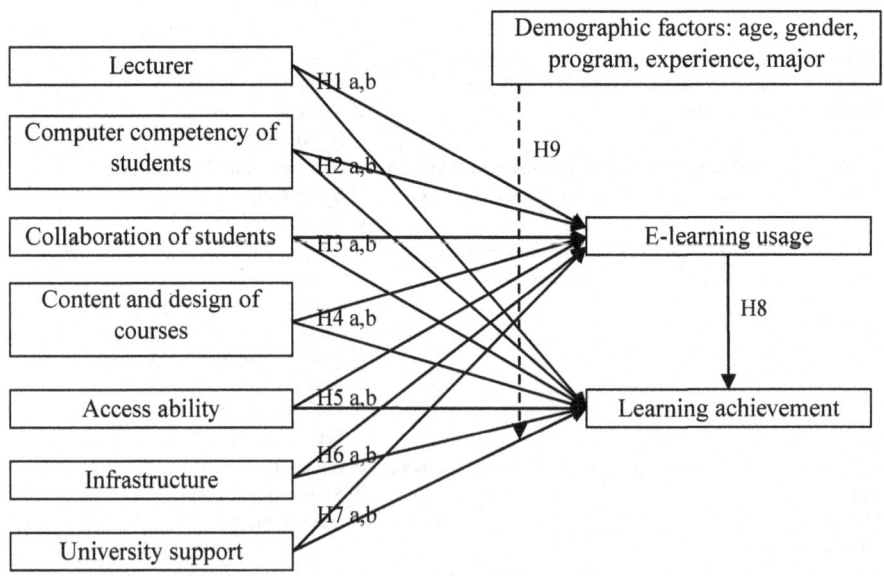

Fig. 1. The proposed research model

3.2 Hypothesis Statements

Lecturer: E-learning is a student-centered method, so, the interaction, evaluation and collaboration between lecturers and students are very important. Harasim (1995) showed that e-learning helps to increase the interaction between students and lecturers in comparison with traditional methods. Moreover, the fear of students in participating in-class discussion is disappeared on e-learning environment (Owston 1997). Selim (2007) said that lecturer should pay attention to high speed interaction and proper support for solving problems of students in using e-learning system. Besides, lecturers should equip themselves with technological knowledge and skills to be active in online interaction with students. Therefore, hypothesis H1a and H1b could be stated as follows:

H1a: Lecturer has a positive impact on e-learning usage of student
H1b: Lecturer has a positive impact on learning achievement of student on e-learning.

Computer competency of students: According to Soong et al. (2001), computer competency of students has a positive impact on the using of e-learning system. Selim (2007) also showed that computer competency and prior experiences of students have positive impacts on e-learning usage. Besides, Laily et al. (2013) confirmed the positive impact of computer competency on learning achievement of learners through e-learning system. Therefore, hypothesis H2a and H2b could be stated as follows:

H2a: Computer competency of students has a positive impact on e-learning usage of students.
H2b: Computer competency of students has a positive impact on learning achievement of students on e-learning.

Collaboration of students: are active learning activities and interactions between students through e-learning system. Selim (2007) showed that collaboration between learners leads to the more using of e-learning system. Besides, collaboration also has a positive impact on the learning achievement of students (Laily et al. 2013). Therefore, hypothesis H3a and H3b could be stated as follows:

H3a: Collaboration of students has a positive impact on e-learning usage of students.
H3b: Collaboration of students has a positive impact on the learning achievement of students on e-learning.

Content and design of courses: is the perception of learners about the richness, the update of learning content and the easiness and the convenience of course design. Previous researches (Laily et al. 2013; Selim 2007) showed that content and design of course have positive impacts on the use of e-learning, and on the learning achievement of students. Therefore, hypothesis H4a and H4b could be stated as follows:

H4a: Content and design of course have a positive impact on the e-learning usage of students.
H4b: Content and design of course have a positive impact on the learning achievement of students on e-learning.

Access ability: is the easiness in accessing the e-learning system. Selim (2007) showed that technology access ability could be seen through the easiness in connecting to the Internet and browsing the e-learning website in the university campus. This ability allows students to use e-learning system easily and to increase the learning achievement through e-learning. Therefore, hypothesis H5a and H5b could be stated as follows:

> *H5a: Access ability has a positive impact on the e-learning usage of students.*
> *H5b: Access ability has a positive impact on the learning achievement of students on e-learning.*

Infrastructure: Selim (2007) showed that the effectiveness of ICT infrastructure in the school, the consistent and reliability of the local network will lead to the more using of e-learning system. Laily et al. (2013) also confirmed that infrastructure has a positive impact on the learning achievement of students. Therefore, hypothesis H6a and H6b could be stated as follows:

> *H6a: Infrastructure has a positive impact on the e-learning usage of students.*
> *H6b: Infrastructure has a positive impact on the learning achievement of students on e-learning.*

University support: The support from school is realized as a critical success factor for e-learning system (Benigno and Trentin 2000; Govindasamy 2001). The support from the university could include: library service, supporting department, computer room, help desk service… Selim (2007) showed that technical support from the school will help to increase the use of e-learning system, so, it will lead to a better learning achievement. Therefore, hypothesis H7a and H7b could be stated as follows:

> *H7a: University support has a positive impact on the e-learning usage of students.*
> *H7b: University support has a positive impact on the learning achievement of students on e-learning.*

Besides, previous studies showed that the e-learning usage of students could have a positive impact on the learning achievement of students (Laily et al. 2013; Pham and Huynh 2017). Therefore, hypothesis H8 could be stated as follows:

> *H8: The e-learning usage has a positive impact on the learning achievement of students on e-learning.*

Moreover, according to Venkatesh et al. (2003), demographic factors including: age, gender, experience… may have impacts on the relationships between independent variables and dependent variables in UTAUT model. In this research, the impact of some demographic factors, such as: age, gender, experience, program, and major, on the e-learning usage and learning achievement of students will be examined. Therefore, hypothesis H9 could be stated as follows:

> *H9: Demographic factors (age, gender, experience, program and major) have impacts on the relationships between independent factors and the e-learning usage, and the learning achievement of students on e-learning.*

4   Research Results

4.1   Data Collection and Analysis Process

Data was collected by a survey using convenient sampling. The questionnaires were delivered using Google Docs, E-mail, E-learning forums, and hard copies to respondents who have used E-learning at several universities in Vietnam. A total of 423 answered questionnaires were received. After removing invalid answers (never use e-learning, the same answer for all questions, lack of information…), there are 356 valid samples, which will be used for quantitative analysis. The data were then analyzed by Cronbach alpha analysis, EFA, CFA, and Structural Equation Modeling (SEM) techniques with the application of SPSS and AMOS (Table 2).

Table 2. Percentage of validated sample

University	Count	Percentage (%)
Bach Khoa University (VNU-HCM)	93	26.1%
Fulbright University in Vietnam	94	26.4%
HCMC Open University	81	22.8%
HCMC University of Economics	88	24.7%
Total	356	100%

4.2   Descriptive Statistics

The descriptive statistics of samples could be summarize in the following Table 3.

Table 3. Descriptive statistics of sample by demographic factors

Factors	Values	Frequency	Percentage (%)
Gender	Male	195	54.8%
	Female	160	44.9%
Age	18–26 years old	246	69.1%
	27–35 years old	80	22.5%
	36–45 years old	26	7.3%
	>45 years old	4	1.1%
Educational level	University	239	67.1%
	Post-graduate level	117	32.9%
Learning program	Regular program	333	93.5%
	Second-degree/distance program	23	6.5%
Major	Technology-Engineering	115	32.3%
	Economics-Management	169	47.5%
	Social sciences-Art-Humanity	72	20.2%

(continued)

Table 3. (*continued*)

Factors	Values	Frequency	Percentage (%)
Intake	<=2011	14	4.0%
	2012	22	6.2%
	2013	20	5.6%
	2014	54	15.2%
	2015	133	37.4%
	>=2016	92	25.9%
Experience of using e-learning	<=1 year	153	43.0%
	1–2 years	183	51.4%
	2–3 years	13	3.7%
	>=3 years	7	2.0%

4.3 Cronbach Alpha Analysis

The reliability of measurement scales is evaluated by Cronbach's Alpha analysis. The scale is considered reliable if the Cronbach Alpha >0.6, and item-totall correlation must >0.3 (if not, it should be removed) (Nguyen and Nguyen 2011). The analysis results showed that the Cronbach Alpha of all measurement scales >0.6. However, variable SIC2 has item-total correlation <0.3 (0.110), so it should be removed. This removal helps to increase the Cronbach alpha coefficient of this factor to 0.757. All other measurement scales are satisfied the criteria and could be used for EFA.

4.4 Exploratory Factor Analysis (EFA)

Exploratory Factor Analysis (EFA) helps to evaluate convergent and discriminant value of the measurement scale. KMO and Bartlett test in EFA showed that the hypothesis of a correlation between variables could be rejected (Sig = .000). The KMO coefficient = 0.902 (>0.5) showed that EFA could be used. The analysis results showed that at Eigenvalue >=1, with "Principal Axis Factoring" method, and "Promax" rotation method with Kaiser Normalization, there could be 10 factors extracted from 45 observed variables, and the extraction variance is 58.82%. After removing 9 variables, which have low loading factor coefficient (<0.3), or were loaded in several factors, there are 9 factors and 36 remaining variables. The final result has total extraction variance = 60.09% (>50%), KMO = 0.877 (>0.5) and Bartlett test is significant (Sig. <0.05), and it could be used for confirmatory factor analysis.

4.5 Confirmatory Factor Analysis

From the above analysis, there are 9 factors extracted, which are suitable with the research model. To test the fitness of the model with market data, CFA is often used. In which, Chi-square (CMIN); CMIN/df (degree of freedom); Comparative Fit Index (CFI), Tucker & Lewis Index (TLI), RMSEA (Root Mean Square Error

Approximation) should be examined. If the values of GFI, TLI, CFI $\geq$ 0.9; CMIN/df $\leq$ 3; and RMSEA $\leq$ 0.08, the model is considered to be fit with the market data (Nguyen 2013). The first CFA result showed that the above criteria are not satisfied. From the table of Standardized Regression Weights, removing some variables with low weights to ensure the convergent value of scales. After removing 9 variables, the above criteria are satisfied. The final result is summarized in the following Fig. 2.

The above results showed that Chi-square/df = 1.811 (<2), GFI = 0.904, TLI = 0.946, CFI = 0.956 (>0.9), and RMSEA = 0.048 (<0.08). Therefore, the model is fit with the sample data. Evaluate the convergent value: In the table of Standardized Regression Weights, the minimum weight is 0.549 (>0.5), and P-value <0.05, so all constructs are convergent. Evaluate the discriminant value: According to Nguyen and Nguyen (2011), if the correlation coefficients between all variables <1, these variables are discriminant. The analysis results showed that the maximum correlation coefficient is 0.728 (<1), so, all variables are considered to be discriminant.

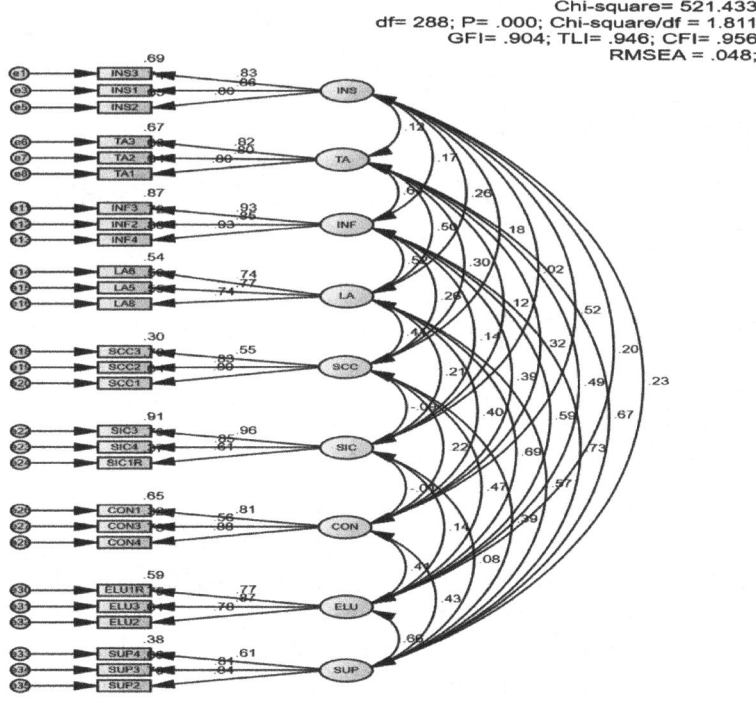

Fig. 2. Standardized CFA results after processing

4.6 Structural Equation Model Analysis

After CFA, the model is concluded to be fit with market data. The SEM analysis results showed that CMIN/df = 1.811 (<2), confirmed the model fitness. Besides, other criteria of SEM analysis are satisfied: GFI = 0.904; TLI = 0.946; CFI = 0.956 (>0.9); and RMSEA = 0.048 (<0.08), the results are significant and summarized as follows (Fig. 3).

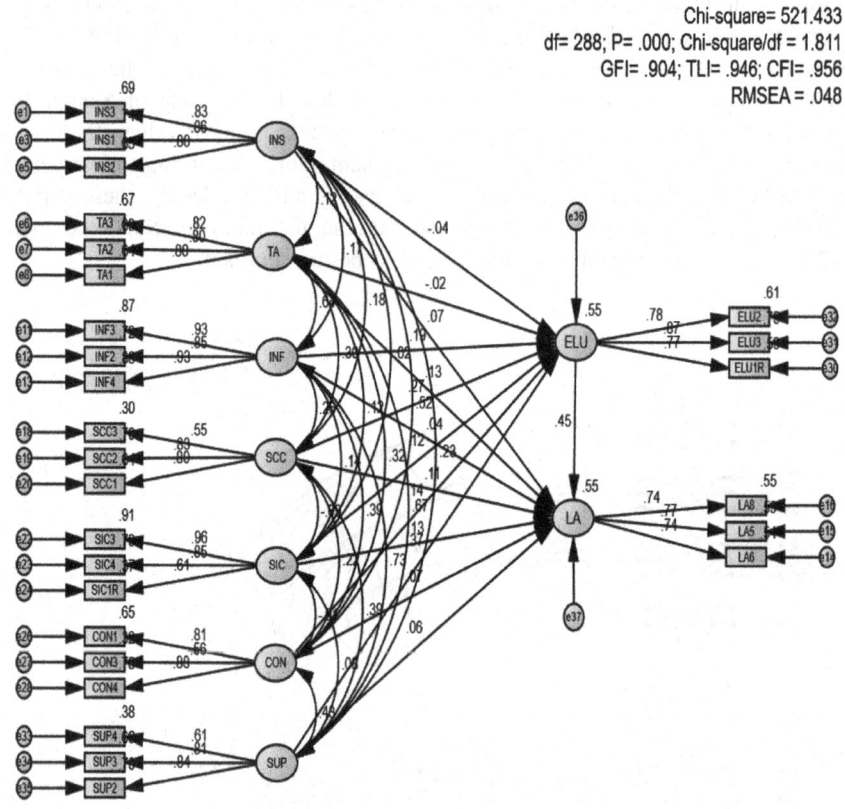

Chi-square= 521.433
df= 288; P= .000; Chi-square/df = 1.811
GFI= .904; TLI= .946; CFI= .956
RMSEA = .048

Fig. 3. Final standardized SEM results

From the results, 5 factors: University support (0.367), Computer competency of students (0.274), Infrastructure (0.195), Content and design of courses (0.145), and Collaboration of students (0.118) have significant impacts on e-learning usage of students and they could explain for 54.8% of the variance in e-learning usage of students. However, the learning achievement of students through e-leaning system is determined by 2 factors: E-learning usage (0.446), and Collaboration of students (0.129). These 2 factors explain for 54.5% of the variance of learning achievement of students (Table 4).

Table 4. Hypothesis testing results

Code	Hypothesis statement	Standardized weight	P-value	Result
H1a	Lecturer => E-learning usage	−0.039	0.503	Rejected
H1b	Lecturer => Learning achievement	0.070	0.262	Rejected
H2a	Computer competency of students => E-learning usage	0.274	***	Accepted
H2b	Computer competency of students => Learning achievement	0.107	0.098	Rejected
H3a	Collaboration of students => E-learning usage	0.118	0.012	Accepted
H3b	Collaboration of students => Learning achievement	0.129	0.012	Accepted
H4a	Content & design of courses => E-learning usage	0.145	0.026	Accepted
H4b	Content & design of courses => Learning achievement	0.072	0.306	Rejected
H5a	Access ability => E-learning usage	−0.017	0.817	Rejected
H5b	Access ability => Learning achievement	0.129	0.107	Rejected
H6a	Infrastructure => E-learning usage	0.195	0.013	Accepted
H6b	Infrastructure => Learning achievement	0.044	0.602	Rejected
H7a	University support => E-learning usage	0.367	***	Accepted
H7b	University support => Learning achievement	0.061	0.572	Rejected
H8	E-learning usage => Learning achievement	0.446	***	Accepted

4.7 ANOVA Analysis

ANOVA test is carried out to analyze if there is any difference in the relationship between independent variables and e-learning usage or learning achievement of students by the demographic variables, such as: gender, age, program, experience, and major. The analysis results showed that the relationship between independent and dependent variables is not changed by gender, age, learning program, and major. However, the impact of experience of using e-learning system on e-learning usage could be realized. The relationship changed as follows:

- For group of students with less experience (<=1 year), there are 3 remaining significant impact factors including: Computer competency of students, Content and design of course, and University support (no significant impact from Infrastructure and Collaboration of students).
- For group of student with more experience (>1 year), there are 4 remaining significant impact factors including: Computer competency of students, Content and design of course, Infrastructure, and Collaboration of students (no significant impact from University support). Certainly, the university support is only necessary for junior students.

5 Discussion and Conclusions

5.1 Discussion

The above analysis result showed that the e-learning usage of students in Vietnam is affected by: University support (0.367), Computer competency of students (0.274), Infrastructure (0.195), Content and design of courses (0.145), and Collaboration of students (0.118). While the learning achievement on e-learning is affected by: E-learning usage (0.446), and Collaboration of students (0.129). This results are similar to previous researches of Laily et al. (2013) and Selim (2007). But the order of impact is a little bit different. For example, in Laily et al. (2013), top 3 impact factors on e-learning usage are: students' collaboration, students' content, and infrastructure. But, in this research, collaboration of students has the lowest impact. The reason may be in the characteristic of Vietnamese students, they are not active in collaboration and lack of self-study skills.

Based on this result, Lecturer and Access ability have no impact on e-learning usage and learning achievement of students. This could be explained by the low participation of lecturer in the e-learning system in Vietnamese universities. Although, there are some policies to encourage more participation and using of lecturers to communicate with students through e-learning system, but the effectiveness of these policies is low (Pham and Huynh 2017). So, currently, lecturer plays a less important role on the use of e-learning system and learning achievement of students. Moreover, Internet connection and network access are popular and not different between campuses and programs, so that, access ability has less impact on e-learning usage and learning achievement of students at the university.

According to the above results, the strongest factor impacting on learning achievement of students through e-learning system is the e-learning usage. This means the more time of using e-learning system, the better learning outcomes of students. So, we should encourage the students to use the e-learning system during their learning program to increase the educational results. The strongest impact factor on e-learning usage of students is university support. Therefore, the board of management of universities should pay attention to providing supporting services, especially technical support for students and lecturers in using e-learning system, and in helping them to interact and to get benefits from e-learning usage, such as: information seeking, group forming, online testing, online manuals…

Moreover, collaboration of students has fairly strong impact on both e-learning usage and learning achievement. Therefore, encouraging the interaction and collaboration between students through e-learning system, such as: group work assignment, ideas preparation, online projects…, could help to increase the use of e-learning system and to improve the learning outcomes of students.

5.2 Managerial Implications

From the above results, some managerial implications for encouraging the use of e-learning system and for improving the learning achievement of students through e-learning system could be suggested as follows:

- The university should equip students with computer skills and knowledge for using the e-learning system to support their study. Especially, the university should require students to study computer related subjects in the 1st or 2nd year. Besides, orientation meeting for junior students should provide students with information to use online library and other computer facilities to support students' study in the campus.
- The university should invest more on their ICT infrastructure, equip students with secured and high speed Internet connection, so that, these infrastructure help to improve the information quality and communication services inside of the university.
- The content and design of online courses should be revised and updated to be suitable for online environment. For example, more learning materials should be provided on the e-learning system, long lectures should be broken into small chunks, more active learning methods should be applied, online tests and virtual workshops should also be used...
- Encourage students to collaborate with each others through e-learning system by providing more online services for them. Developing an information portal for connecting e-learning system with other information systems of the university. Moreover, training the lecturers to apply new teaching methods focusing on collaboration and active learning to improve educational quality, such as: online test, group projects through e-learning and online collaboration in solving a real problem... Scoring methods could also help to increase the use of e-learning system and to allow students to learn actively from any where and at any time.
- The university should pay attention to university support for junior students, because it is very important for making it easy for new students to be familiar with e-learning system and to realize to benefit of e-learning on self-study.

5.3 Conclusions and Limitations

In summary, based on previous researches (Laily et al. 2013; Selim 2007), this paper proposed a research model for evaluating the impact of some factors on e-learning usage and learning achievement of students at several universities in Vietnam. Some main factors include: lecturer, student computer competency, student collaboration, content & design of courses, access ability, infrastructure, and university support.

Based on 356 valid samples collected from students at several universities in Ho Chi Minh City (Vietnam), the measurement scales are verified and the research model is tested. After Cronbach alpha test, EFA, CFA, and SEM analysis, 5 factors are confirmed to have positive impact on e-learning usage, including: University support (0.367), Computer competency of students (0.274), Infrastructure (0.195), Content and design of courses (0.145), and Collaboration of students (0.118). Besides, the learning achievement of students through e-leaning system is determined by 2 factors: E-learning usage (0.446), and Collaboration of students (0.129).

According to ANOVA analysis, there is no difference in the relationship between independent variables and e-learning usage or learning achievement of students by the demographic variables, such as: gender, age, program, experience, and major.

However, the e-learning usage of more experience students is not affected by university support (which has a strong impact for less experience group).

There are several limitations of this research, including: (1) The small and limited sample size, (2) The lack of evaluating the impact of mediating factors & other variables related to online learning processes.

Therefore, some implications for future researches could include: (1) Increase the sample size or extend the scope to various educational institutions/programs; and (2) Identify and measure the impact of some new factors, such as: knowledge process, evaluating & teaching method..., on e-learning usage and learning outcomes of university students.

References

Benigno, V., Trentin, G.: The evaluation of online courses. J. Comput. Assist. Learn. **16**(3), 259–270 (2000)

Davis, F.D., Bagozzi, R.P., Warshaw, P.R.: User acceptance of computer technology: a comparison of two theoretical models. Manage. Sci. **35**(8), 982–1003 (1989)

DeLone, W.H., McLean, E.R.: The DeLone and McLean model of information systems success: a ten-year update. J. Manage. Inf. Syst. **19**(4), 9–30 (2003)

EdTech: Report of e-learning system applications in US universities (2016). https://edtechmagazine.com/

Govindasamy, T.: Successful implementation of e-learning: pedagogical considerations. Internet High. Educ. **4**(3), 287–299 (2001)

Fishbein, M., Ajzen, I.: Belief, Attitude, Intention and Behavior: An Introduction to Theory and Research, p. 302. Addison-Wesley, Reading (1975)

Harasim, L.M.: Learning Networks: A Field Guide to Teaching and Learning Online. MIT press, Cambridge (1995)

Laily, N., Kurniawati, A., Puspita, I.A.: Critical success factor for e-learning implementation in institute technology telkom bandung using structural equation modeling. In: International Conference on Information and Communication Technology (2013)

Martínez-Caro, E.: Factors affecting effectiveness in e-learning: an analysis in production management courses. Comput. Appl. Eng. Educ. **19**, 572–581 (2011). https://doi.org/10.1002/cae.20337

Masie, E.: E-learning definition of Masie Elliot Learning Center (2016). https://www.elearninglearning.com/masie/

MOET: Report & Strategy of VN Education and Training Ministry, 31 August 2016. http://www.moet.gov.vn/tintuc/Pages/tin-tong-hop.aspx?ItemID=4162

Nguyen, D.T.: Phương pháp nghiên cứu khoa học trong kinh doanh. NXB Tài Chính, HCMC (2013)

Nguyen, D.T.: Mô hình cấu trúc cho sự thành công của dự án hệ thống thông tin. Tạp chí phát triển KH CN **18**(2), 109–120 (2015)

Nguyen, D.T., Nguyen, T.M.T.: Nghiên cứu khoa học Marketing: Ứng dụng mô hình cấu trúc tuyến tính SEM. NXB Lao Động, HCMC (2011)

Nguyen, Thanh D., Nguyen, Tuan M., Pham, Q.-T., Misra, S.: Acceptance and use of e-learning based on cloud computing: the role of consumer innovativeness. In: Murgante, B., et al. (eds.) ICCSA 2014. LNCS, vol. 8583, pp. 159–174. Springer, Cham (2014). https://doi.org/10.1007/978-3-319-09156-3_12

Owston, R.D.: Research news and comment: the world wide web: a technology to enhance teaching and learning? Educ. Res. **26**(2), 27–33 (1997)

Pham, Q.T., Huynh, M.C.: Impact factor on learning achievement and knowledge transfer of students through e-learning system at Bach Khoa University, VN. In: International Conference on Computing Networking and Informatics (ICCNI), Lagos, pp. 1–6 (2017)

Resta, P., Patru, M.: Teacher Development in an E-learning Age: A Policy and Planning Guide. UNESCO, Paris (2010)

Rosen, A.: The E-commerce Question and Answer Book. American Management Association, New York (2000)

Shee, D.Y., Wang, Y.-S.: Multi-criteria evaluation of the web-based e-learning system: a methodology based on learner satisfaction and its applications. Comput. Educ. **50**(2008), 894–905 (2008)

Seddon, P.B.: A respecification and extension of the DeLone and McLean model of IS success. Inf. Syst. Res. **8**, 240–253 (1997)

Selim, H.M.: Critical success factors for e-learning acceptance: confirmatory factor models. Comput. Educ. **49**(2007), 396–413 (2007)

Soong, B.M.H., Chan, H.C., Chua, B.C., Loh, K.F.: Critical success factors for on-line course resources. Comput. Educ. **36**(2), 101–120 (2001)

Turban, E., King, D., Lee, J.K., Liang, T.-P., Turban, D.C.: Electronic Commerce: A Managerial and Social Networks Perspective, p. 7. Springer International Publishing, Switzerland (2015)

Venkatesh, V., Davis, F.D.: A theoretical extension of the technology acceptance model: four longitudinal field studies. Manage. Sci. **46**, 186–204 (2000)

Venkatesh, V., Moms, M.G., Davis, G.B., Davis, F.D.: User acceptance of information technology: toward a unified view. MIS Q. **27**(3), 425–478 (2003)

Venkatesh, V., Thong, J.Y.L., Xin, X.: Consumer acceptance and use of information technology: extending the unified theory of acceptance and use of technology. MIS Q. **36**(1), 157–178 (2012)

Wang, Y.-S.: Assessing e-commerce systems success: a respecification and validation of the DeLone and McLean model of IS success. Info. Syst. J. **2008**(18), 529–557 (2008)

WTO: E-commerce definition (1998). https://www.wto.org/

Measuring the Extent of Source Code Readability Using Regression Analysis

Sangchul Choi[1] , Suntae Kim[1(⊠)] , Jeong-Hyu Lee[1],
JeongAh Kim[2], and Jae-Young Choi[3]

[1] Department of Software Engineering, CAIIT, Chonbuk National University,
567 Baekje-daero, Deokjin-gu, Jeonju-si, Jeollabuk-do, Republic of Korea
{114477aa, stkim, jhlee25}@jbnu.ac.kr
[2] Department of Computer Education, Catholic Kwandong University,
24, Beomil-ro 579 beon-gil, Gangneung-si, Gangwon-do, Republic of Korea
clara@cku.ac.kr
[3] Department of Computer Engineering, SungKyunKwan University,
2066 Seobu-ro, Jangan-gu, Suwon, Gyeonggi-do, Republic of Korea
jaeychoi@skku.edu

Abstract. Software maintenance accounts for a large portion of the software life cycle cost. In the software maintenance phase, comprehending the legacy source code is inevitable, which takes most of the time. Source code readability is a metric of the extent of source code comprehension. The better the code is readable, the easier it is for code readers to comprehend the system based on the source code. This paper proposes an enhanced source code readability metric to quantitative measure the extent of code readability, which is more enhanced measurement method than previous research that dichotomously judges whether the source code was readable or not. As an evaluation, we carried out a survey and analyzed them with two-way linear regression analysis to measure the extent of source code readability.

1 Introduction

Software maintenance accounts for a large portion of the entire cost of the software life cycle [1]. In software maintenance, reading source code is the most time consuming activity compared to implementation and testing [2]. The readability of the source code is defined as the extent of how easily the program code can be read by a source code reader. Thus, the readability of the source code is one of the most important factors in software maintenance [2].

There has been many research on measuring source code readability. Previous research has been conducted to measure the readability of source code in the followings: (1) sample code selection, (2) attribute extraction, (3) survey using questionnaires, and (4) statistical analysis. Buse measured the readability by defining the numeric indicators of the source code as a metric, including the LOC (LOC), the number of comments in the code, the number of identifiers, and the number of spaces [2]. Halstead has attempted to define multiple metrics based on the number of operands and operands in the code and to measure the readability of the source code [3]. Posnett also attempted to reduce the number of indexes of the metric by selecting features that best describe the code from the metric indexes defined by Buse and Halstead [4]. Previous studies and many other source code readability studies are primarily tried to discretely classify the code readability into two categories: *readable* or *not-readability*. Therefore, there is no way to quantitatively recognize the extent of source code readability.

This paper proposes a model that quantitatively measures the readability of source code. We newly suggest indicators for measuring the readability metrics of source code, and refine and verify them through questionnaires and two-way linear regression analysis. Finally, based on these indicators, we establish an equation that can quantitatively measure the readability of the code. The generated equation can be used to measure the extent of source code readability on the fly.

The contributions of our research can be summarized as follows:

- *Suggestion of indicators that have an influence on source code readability*: As the indicators are considered as key factors that affect the readability of the source code, a developer can keep them in their mind to improve the source code readability in making a program.
- *Suggestion of an equation for quantifying the extent of source code readability*: This equation allows you to determine the readability of the current code in real time, and can recognize how small changes in the code affect the readability of the code.

This paper is composed as follows. In Sect. 2, we discuss existing studies for readability of source code, and in Sect. 3 we propose a metric for measuring readability of source code. In Sect. 4, the questionnaire is used to refine the metrics and verify how well the metrics describe the readability of the source code through various statistical methods. Section 5 concludes this paper.

2 Related Work

2.1 Buse's Model

Buse proposed a readability metric using numeric indicators of the source code and asserted its relevance to software quality [2]. The indicators used by Buse consist of elements that can be statically measured in the source code, such as the length of an identifier, the number of indentations, the average length of one line, the number of comments. It was considered by two types which is an average and maximum value of each indicator. Some of the indicators (e.g., *the length of one line*) use two types at the same time, while others (e.g., *the number of comments*) apply just one type to justify the readability of the given source code.

After defining the indicators, Buse examined a total of 100 sample codes composed of 4 to 11 lines. Then, he carried out a human user study using a questionnaire for 120 subjects to score the extent of readability with 5 point scaled values for each sample code. Based on the result of the questionnaire, he applied regression analysis to estimate relationship between the readability and defined indicators, and compared the result of classification by regression with human judgment. Finally, an analysis of each indicator was conducted to determine which indicators had a positive or negative effect on the extent of source code readability.

2.2 Halstead's Model

Halstead introduced a method for calculating the complexity of the source code [3]. He defined several indicators through the type of operator (n_1), the total number (N_1), the type of operand (n_2) and the total number (N_2). The equations to measure the each indicators complexity are listed as follows:

- Program Length (N): $N = N_1 + N_2$
- Program Vocabulary (n): $n = n_1 + n_2$
- Volume (V): $V = N * log_2 n$
- Difficulty (D): $D = \frac{n_1}{2} * \frac{N_1}{n_2}$
- Effort (E): $E = DV$

Although the indicator *Volume* seems to be quite similar to *Entropy*, it represents the minimum number of bits needed to naively represent the program. In addition, *Effort* intends to measure the extent of effort to review the source code, which is proportional to the amount of the *Volume* and *Difficulty* indicators.

2.3 Posnett's Model

Posnett proposed a way to minimize the number of indicators for readability measure [4]. He performed the correlation analysis for a selection of measures that best describe readability in Buse's model and Halstead's model with the smallest number of indicators. First, he hypothesized that the number of lines of code can affect source code readability, and he additionally analyzed the relations of *words/characters* and the readability. Then, he compared it with the Buse's model. As a result, he concluded that the lines of code is enough to explain readability without words and characters.

He performed the correlation analysis for each indicator with human judgment based on questionnaires. First he considered the *program length*, *program vocabulary* and *volume* as related factors to source code readability. Thus, he conducted additional analysis such as multi-collinearity which is a phenomenon in which one predictor variable can be linearly predicted from the others. As a result, he selected the *volume* as an indicator. Finally, he added *Entropy* to model. Entropy is considered as the *complexity*, the *degree of disorder*, or the *amount of information* existed in source code. In order to verify it, he used the same dataset with that of measuring the Buse's model, and showed that his proposed indicators are enough to measure the extent of the source code readability compared to the Buse's model.

3   Indicators to Measuring Source Code Readability

In this paper, we select the indicators as shown in Table 1 to quantitatively measure the readability of the source code. This indicators can be used in other programming languages, but this paper exemplified the indicators using the *Java* programming language.

Table 1. Indicators for code readability

Indicators	Explanation
LOC	Lines of source code
numOfMethodInvocation	The number of methods invocated
numOfBranch	The number of branches like if and switch statements
numOfLoops	The number of loops like for and while statements
numOfAssignment	The number of operation of assignment
numOfComments	The number of comments
numOfBlankLines	The number of blank lines
numOfStringLiteral	The number of string literal
numOfArithmaticOperators	The number of arithmetic operators
numOfLogicalOperators	The number of logical operators
numOfBitOperators	The number of bit operators
AverageOfVariableNameLength	The average of length of name of identifiers
AverageLineLength	The average of length of lines
maxNestedControl	The maximum of nested control statements
ProgramVolume	The amounts of information source code has
Entropy	The complexity of source code

The indicators to measure the source code readability in Table 1 are initially selected based on our experience. Then, we adopted the program volume and entropy from the preliminary studies. In addition, the indicators defined in Table 1 are for measuring the readability of a Java method. If the readability of a class unit, the readability of a package unit, and the readability of a project unit should be measured, the indicators should be extended.

These indicators are used to quantify readability using the form of the equation presented in Eq. 1. In the equation, X_1 and X_2 denote indicators presented in the table, and they may be linear or two or three-dimensional. Also, w_1 and w_2 in the equation are weights for each indicator variable.

$$Readability = w_1 * X_1 + w_2 * X_2 + \ldots \tag{1}$$

4   Experiment and Result

In order to find the best indicators to compute the source code readability, We performed the experiment as shown in Fig. 1. It first starts with sampling Java source code, and carrys out the questionnaire survey to recognize how the code readers feels the readability of the given sample source code. Then, we perform the regression analysis to understand the relationships between the suggested indicators and readability. This step results in initial completion of the Eq. 1 with the weights. In the last *Optimization* step, we try to select the optimal indicators to compute the code readability with minimal number of indicators and similar explanatory power of the readability measure.

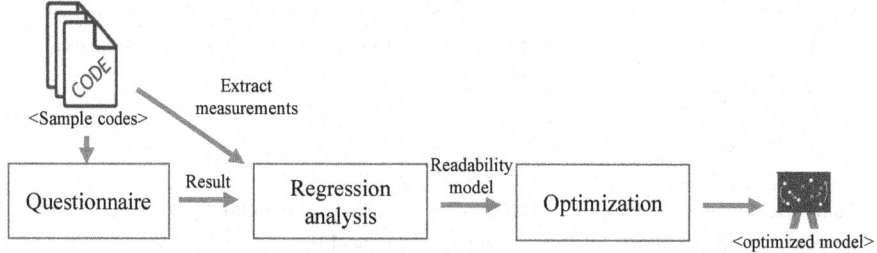

Fig. 1. Experiment progress to generate and optimize model

4.1   Experiment Setting

In order to carry out the experiment presented above, we first prepared the source code for the questionnaire. The source code is sampled from the popular open source libraries including `antlr4 4.1.2`, `base-one 1.8.1.3`, `cglib 3.2.0`, `dbcp 4.2.2`, `fileupload 1.4`, `groovy 2.5.0`, `httpclient 3.0`, and `javacc 6.1.0`. After extracting the source code, the indicators defined in Table 1 are extracted from the methods. Based on the extracted indicators, we selected a total of 60 Java methods so that the numerical distributions of the indicators are as uniform as possible. The length of each source code ranged from a minimum of 13 lines to a maximum of 96 lines.

4.2   Survey Using Questionnaire

The survey has been conducted using *Google Forms*. Subjects of this experiment consist of undergraduate students, postgraduate doctoral researchers, and programmers of software industry. Their job distributions and favorite programming languages are shown in Fig. 2. Each subject anonymously accessed *Google Forms* and read 20 method source codes and put a score on each code's readability. The readability score is scored from 1 to 5 points, where the 1 point indicates that the code is very difficult to understand, while the 5 point indicates that it is very easy to understand.

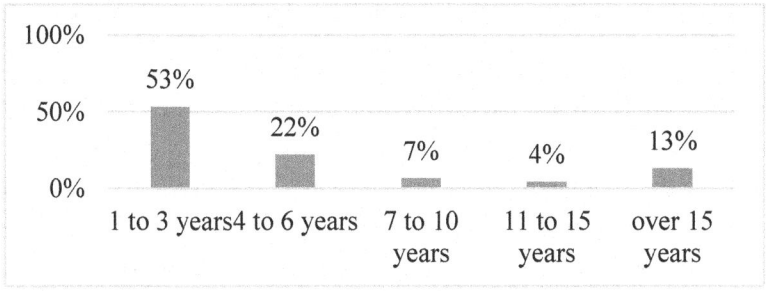

(a) Subject's Work Experience in Year

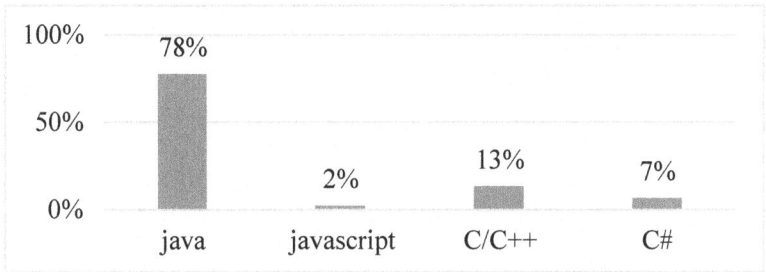

(b) Subject's Preferred Programming Language

Fig. 2. Career and language usage distribution of subjects of questionnaire

4.3 Building Software Readability Measurement Model

We use the linear regression analysis to analyze the results of the survey and generate a model that measures the extent of readability of the source code. Linear regression analysis is a set of statistical methods for estimating the relationship between designated variables [5]. We used two way linear regression analysis including multiple linear regression and nonlinear regression analysis. Multiple linear regression analysis is a method of estimating the relationship between one dependent variable and two or more independent variables using linear equations [6]. Here, the dependent variable is the result of changing the independent variable and the independent variable is the cause of the influence on the result. The nonlinear regression is a method of estimating the relationship between dependent variables and independent variables using the power of squared or logit transformation [7].

First, we use multiple linear regression analysis to estimate the relationship between readability and the indicators defined in Table 1. Table 2 shows the results derived using multiple linear regression analysis. The term *Estimate* in the table is a constant when each term is summarized by a first order polynomial. And the important Pr is the p-value, which indicates whether the item is meaningful to support the analyst's claim. Generally, it is said that the variable is significant when the p-value is less than 0.05. The next important item is the multiple R-squared indicating the explanatory power of the model that means how well the created model represents the data. As a result, the explanatory power of the model using all the indicators is 0.7717, which is 77.17%. The closer the explanatory power is to 100%, the better the model explains the data. The *Estimate* column is converted into the weights of the Eq. 1, and parameters is considered into the independent variables expressed in X_1 and X_2.

Table 2. Result of multiple linear regression

Parameter	Estimate	Pr
(intercept)	7.442e+00	1.17e−09
LOC	−2.288e−02	0.05428
numOfMethodInvocation	−1.479e−02	0.19226
numOfBranch	9.152e−03	0.83132
numOfLoops	4.657e−02	0.54720
numOfAssignment	1.409e−02	0.55928
numOfComments	5.089e−02	0.04821
numOfBlankLines	4.302e−02	0.12826
numOfStringLiteral	3.473e−02	0.08522
numOfArithmaticOperators	−1.118e−02	0.73145
numOfLogicalOperators	1.069e−01	0.30490
numOfBitOperators	−1.034e+00	0.14981
AverageOfVariableNameLength	−4.113e−02	0.76700
AverageLineLength	2.805e−05	0.99652
maxNestedControl	−1.704e−01	0.00801
ProgramVolume	−1.049e−03	0.03351
Entropy	−5.435e−01	0.00170
Multiple R-squared	0.7717	
p-value	3.937e−09	

Next, in order to find the best and smallest indicators, we apply a step-wise best parameter selection technique. The step selection technique allows the selection of optimal independent variables after eliminating the independent variables which have no significant influence on the explanatory power through the combination of the independent variables used in the model. Table 3 shows the results of the optimized model using the step-selection technique. The explanatory power of the model is 74.59%, which is 2.58% lower than that of the whole indicators, but it has the advantage that the reading ability is faster because it is explanatory power just using 7 indicators, which 9 less indicators than initially suggested.

Next, we use nonlinear regression analysis to estimate the relationship. We used a three-dimensional polynomial to perform the analysis because the data distribution was visualized in three-dimensional distribution. Table 4 shows the results derived using nonlinear regression analysis. As a result, the explanatory power of the model using all the indicators with three-dimensional polynomial is 0.929, which is 92.9%. The detailed result of the multiple linear regression is presented at Table 6 in Appendix 1.

Table 3. Result of step-wise technique to multiple linear regression

Parameter	Estimate	Pr
(intercept)	7.4219960	2e−16
LOC	−0.0203190	0.00377
numOfComments	0.0399795	0.08576
numOfBlankLines	0.0369742	0.10582
numOfBitOperators	−0.7550834	0.17617
maxNestedControl	−0.1525998	0.00139
ProgramVolume	−0.0005915	0.00361
Entropy	−0.6106970	54e−05
Multiple R-squared	0.7459	
p-value	2.051e−13	

Table 4. Result of nonlinear regression

Multiple R-squared	0.929
p-value	0.006712

Then, we also applied step-wise technique to the model. Table 5 shows the results of the optimized model. The explanatory power of the model is 92.31%, which is 0.59% lower than original model. The detailed result of the nonlinear regression is presented at Table 7 in Appendix 2.

Table 5. Result of step-wise technique to nonlinear regression

Multiple R-squared	0.9231
p-value	0.0004656

We selected an optimized model by multiple linear regression analysis to estimate the source code readability. Although models by nonlinear regression had over 90% of explanatory power, the model is over-fitted for the given data and indicators. Thus, it is very possible for wrong estimation if data was not in training data and also will be slower than model by multiple linear regression. In addition, the multiple linear regression model had better p-value of the model than that of nonlinear regression analysis. Based on the two-way regression analysis, we completed the following equation to quantitative measure the source code readability on the fly as the following Eq. 2:

$$Readability = (-0.020) * LOC + (0.040) * numOfComments$$
$$+ (0.037) * numOfBlankLines + (-0.755) * numOfBitwiseOperators$$
$$+ (-0.153) * maxnestedControl + (-0.001) * programVolume + (-0.611) * Entropy$$

$$(2)$$

5 Conclusion

In this paper, we propose a model that quantitatively measures the source code readability. The proposed model was different from related works which classified the method whether it was readable or not. Our model can quantitatively measure the readability score of the source code by using 7 indicators and the explanatory power has been reached to 74.59%. As future work, we have a plan to explore what changes will occur when the model is applied to people. In addition, we conducted additional questionnaire to generalize our model and will develop tool support to facilitate a developer to enhance their code readability at the development time.

Acknowledgement. This research was supported by Next-Generation Information Computing Development Program through the National Research Foundation of Korea(NRF) funded by the Ministry of Science and ICT (NRF-2014M3C4A7030503).

Appendix 1

See Table 6.

Table 6. Result of nonlinear regression

Parameter	Degree	Estimate	Pr
(intercept)	1	3.24852	2.45E−15
LOC	1	4.60657	0.27557
	2	7.17265	0.01387
	3	4.41318	0.0121
numOfMethodInvocation	1	3.14754	0.23646
	2	−1.39826	0.33611
	3	−2.41815	0.19927
numOfBranch	1	1.01454	0.66656
	2	−2.64795	0.23572
	3	−5.4396	0.02884
numOfLoops	1	−0.97029	0.56139
	2	0.80174	0.64322
	3	0.98902	0.49222
numOfAssignment	1	8.36985	0.01748
	2	3.20902	0.17739
	3	0.9016	0.62544
numOfComments	1	−1.40486	0.41778
	2	−0.22391	0.80425
	3	2.16001	0.27518

(*continued*)

Table 6. (*continued*)

Parameter	Degree	Estimate	Pr
numOfBlankLines	1	−14.56149	0.13637
	2	−14.78737	0.13443
	3	−4.40727	0.18506
numOfStringLiteral	1	1.82357	0.30288
	2	−2.07073	0.09556
	3	2.88258	0.2008
numOfArithmaticOperators	1	9.79519	0.18338
	2	16.50403	0.05451
	3	0.23202	0.91745
numOfLogicalOperators	1	15.21822	0.14286
	2	19.52573	0.10237
	3	3.72091	0.32246
numOfBitOperators	1	−0.2443	0.87729
AverageOfVariableNameLength	1	0.22179	0.86461
	2	0.35146	0.74637
	3	1.51076	0.31281
AverageLineLength	1	−0.27814	0.80417
	2	4.94913	0.00337
	3	−2.80662	0.03926
maxNestedControl	1	−0.6846	0.72245
	2	−1.91487	0.23102
	3	0.27441	0.85988
ProgramVolume	1	−22.90426	0.08354
	2	−20.18302	0.09266
	3	−4.62538	0.33581
Entropy	1	−3.07303	0.2248
	2	0.64611	0.62567
	3	1.80265	0.19395
Multiple R-squared	0.929		
p-value	0.006712		

Appendix 2

See Table 7.

Table 7. Result of step-wise technique to nonlinear regression

Parameter	Degree	Estimate	Pr
(intercept)	1	3.24444	<2e−16
LOC	1	4.68708	0.156462
	2	21.83126	0.002522
	3	13.35202	0.00185
numOfMethodInvocation	1	2.77837	0.105543
	2	−1.73063	0.129608
	3	−2.79072	0.081131
numOfBranch	1	1.43317	0.444299
	2	−3.4649	0.06486
	3	−5.71362	0.00595
numOfAssignment	1	8.79372	0.005238
	2	3.72061	0.059075
	3	1.27752	0.255627
numOfComments	1	−1.47019	0.308438
	2	−0.18309	0.817522
	3	2.68168	0.092783
numOfBlankLines	1	−16.66131	0.052314
	2	−17.46351	0.040217
	3	−5.2851	0.065936
numOfStringLiteral	1	2.00468	0.181459
	2	−1.91165	0.059525
	3	2.28012	0.138988
numOfArithmaticOperators	1	11.49481	0.07528
	2	18.62925	0.012598
	3	−0.16429	0.926699
numOfLogicalOperators	1	12.14846	0.157112
	2	17.2123	0.080869
	3	2.2141	0.461695
AverageOfVariableNameLength	1	0.40901	0.640565
	2	0.05435	0.948443
	3	1.87957	0.099165
AverageLineLength	1	−0.39277	0.685309
	2	4.83433	0.000695
	3	−2.92728	0.006775

(*continued*)

Table 7. (*continued*)

Parameter	Degree	Estimate	Pr
maxNestedControl	1	−0.9362	0.513424
	2	−1.25692	0.24462
	3	0.49384	0.50668
ProgramVolume	1	−20.32079	0.06747
	2	−17.53835	0.077227
	3	−2.89402	0.458248
Entropy	1	−2.5069	0.188006
	2	0.61751	0.566155
	3	2.41429	0.019699
Multiple R-squared	0.9231		
p-value	0.0004656		

References

1. Boehm, B., Basili, V.R.: Software defect reduction top 10 list. IEEE Comput. **34**(1), 135–137 (2001). https://doi.org/10.1109/2.962984
2. Buse, R.P.L., Weimer, W.R.: A metric for software readability. IEEE Trans. Softw. Eng. **36** (4), 546–558 (2010). https://doi.org/10.1145/1390630.1390647
3. Halstead, M.: Elements of Software Science. Elsevier Science Inc., New York (1997)
4. Posnett, D., Hindle, A., Devanbu, P.: A simpler model of software readability. In: The 8th Working Conference on Mining Software Repositories (MSR), vol. 11, pp. 73–82 (2011). https://doi.org/10.1145/1985441.1985454
5. Ramcharan, R.: Regressions: why are economists obsessed with them? Financ. Dev. **43**, 36–37 (2006)
6. Freedman, D.A.: Statistical Models: Theory and Practice. University of California, Berkeley (2009)
7. Choi, S.-H., Sun, H.-S.: A nonlinear regression analysis method for frame erasure concealment in VoIP network. Inst. Internet Broadcast. Commun. **9**(5), 129–132 (2009)

Optimization of Scaling Factors for Image Watermarking Using Harmony Search Algorithm

Anurag Mishra[1]([✉]), Charu Agarwal[2], and Girija Chetty[3]

[1] Department of Electronics, Deendayal Upadhyay College, University of Delhi, Delhi, India
anurag_cse2003@yahoo.com
[2] Department of Computer Science, University of Delhi, Delhi, India
agarwalcharu2@rediffmail.com
[3] Faculty of ESTEM, University of Canberra, Canberra, Australia
girija.chetty@canberra.edu.au

Abstract. We propose a novel watermarking scheme for images which optimizes the watermarking strength using Harmony Search Algorithm (HSA). The optimized watermarking scheme is based on the discrete wavelet transform (DWT) and singular value decomposition (SVD). The amount of modification made in the coefficients of the LL3 sub band of the host image depends on the values obtained by the Harmony Search algorithm. For optimization of scaling factors, HSA uses an objective function which is a linear combination of imperceptibility and robustness. The PSNR and SSIM values show that the visual quality of the signed and attacked images is good. The proposed scheme is robust against common image processing operations. It is concluded that the embedding and extraction of the proposed algorithm is well optimized, robust and show an improvement over other similar reported methods.

Keywords: Image watermarking · Harmony Search Algorithm (HSA)
Perceptible quality · Normalized cross-correlation · Robustness
Multiple scaling factors (MSFs)

1 Introduction

The problem of image watermarking has acquired a very important research space in the image processing domain. The secure signal processing (SSP) requires a secured scheme to carry out watermark embedding and its extraction for copyright protection, content authentication and owner identification. To this end, the scheme to safely and imperceptibly embed the mark into the host signal in such a manner that it can be extracted even after having undergone multiple attacks is the need of the hour. Therefore it has, over the period of time, acquired a dimension moving towards problem solving using optimization techniques [1, 2]. It has reached to this level also due to the reason that the visual quality post embedding and the robustness criteria

© Springer International Publishing AG, part of Springer Nature 2018
O. Gervasi et al. (Eds.): ICCSA 2018, LNCS 10963, pp. 422–434, 2018.
https://doi.org/10.1007/978-3-319-95171-3_33

which are often found to vary inversely require tradeoff against each other. It is found that the meta-heuristic techniques are frequently applied to resolve this trade-off [3–5].

The embedding of the watermark into the most appropriate regions of the image in the transform domain is a challenge to strike the balance between visual quality and robustness. Many researchers have deliberated over this issue in particular. The earlier research on embedding the mark into the low frequency coefficients was limited to adding the mark by using a single scaling factor (SSF). Note that the scaling factor is the regulatory parameter which decides the amount of external perturbation allowed inside the host image. While, the image is found to vary significantly in its perceptible domain as well as in structural properties, the use of SSF is not perceived as an appropriate method to embed watermark coefficients in the transform domain of the host image. This is because, over all coefficients of the low frequency spectrum of the image, the structural parameters do significantly change between different regions and embedding external information in all regions of the image in the same manner is very naïve in nature. Cox et al. [6] have discussed this issue in great detail. They argue that different regions of the image tend to behave differently and therefore, scaling parameter or the embedding strength of the watermark coefficient cannot be same for all. They further said that this kind of watermark embedding can lead to several undesirable visible artifacts within the signed image. These disturbances are usually noticed in the smoother regions of the image as the smooth regions are more susceptible to noise addition. Therefore, these regions should be processed with a smaller scaling value while the high contrast regions may be allowed to be processed with a higher value of the scaling parameter. Thus, this parameter has become a significant issue to resolve the tradeoff between the imperceptibility and the robustness criteria. Many other researchers have used meta-heuristic techniques to identify the suitable coefficients in different image components. Findik et al. [5] and Run et al. [7] have used Particle Swarm Optimization (PSO) technique to identify the image coefficients best suitable for embedding the watermarks. Kumsawat et al. [8] have used Genetic Algorithm (GA) for the same purpose. The problem of finding optimal values of the multiple scaling factors is also taken up by several researchers. Lai et al. [9] have used Tiny-GA with SVD to find values of the MSF. Ishtiaq et al. [10] have also applied PSO technique to find the MSFs in the Discrete Cosine Transform (DCT) domain. They use PSNR parameter for determining the objective function to evaluate each particle. In addition, Loukhoukha et al. [11] have used multi-objective ant colony optimization (MOACO) in LWT-SVD domain to determine MSF values for watermark embedding. They claim that their MOACO based watermarking scheme outperforms all other SSF schemes in terms of visual quality and robustness.

In the present paper, we apply a new meta-heuristic technique known as Harmony Search Algorithm (HSA) to identify the MSFs best suited for the host images in question in transform domain. We embed the binary watermark coefficients into the image coefficients by the use of a hybrid DWT-SVD transform. We compare our results with those presented by Ishtiaq et al. [10] and Loukhoukha et al. [11] and a simple DWT-SVD based SSF algorithm. The proposed watermarking scheme is also evaluated for its performance in robustness by having undergone eight different image processing attacks. These attacks are – JPEG Compression (Q = 95%), Salt & Pepper Noise (5%), Gaussian Filter of size 3 × 3, Sharpening Attack with aperture size = 2, Histogram Equalization with 64 gray levels, Scaling Attack (256 → 512 → 256), Grayscale Quantization of 1 bit, Cropping by dividing the image into 9 equal blocks and then replacing the coefficients of central block with zeros. These attacks are used both for examining the efficacy of the objective function for the implemented Harmony Search Algorithm (HSA) and also for evaluating the robustness criteria of the proposed embedding scheme.

2 Harmony Search Algorithm

The Harmony Search Algorithm (HSA) was first developed by Geem et al. [12–14]. This is an emerging music based meta-heuristic optimization algorithm, which is employed to cope with numerous challenging tasks during the past decade. It has been applied to solve many optimization problems including function optimization, engineering optimization, water distribution networks, groundwater modeling, energy-saving dispatch, truss design, vehicle routing, and others [15–17]. It was inspired by the observation that the aim of music is to search for a perfect state of harmony. This harmony in music is analogous to find the optimality in an optimization process. The search process in the optimization can be compared to a jazz musician's improvisation process. A musician always intends to produce a piece of music with perfect harmony. On the other hand, an optimal solution to an optimization problem should be the best solution available to the problem under the given objectives and limited by constraints. Both processes intend to produce the best or optimum.

During improvisation process, a skilled musician has three choices:

(1) To play any famous piece of music (a series of pitches in harmony) exactly from his or her memory;
(2) To play something similar to a known piece (thus adjusting the pitch slightly); or
(3) To compose new or random notes.

Geem et al. [12] formalized these three options into quantitative optimization process, and the three corresponding components are: - usage of harmony memory, pitch adjusting, and randomization. Listing 1 gives the algorithm for Harmony Search.

Listing 1: Harmony Search Algorithm for Maximum Optimization

Input:
Define objective function $f(x)$, $x = [x_1, x_2, \ldots \ldots \ldots \ldots, x_d]^T$
Generate initial harmonics $x_p (p = 1, 2, \ldots, n)$
Define pitch adjusting rate (r_{pa}), pitch limits and bandwidth
Define harmony memory accepting rate (r_{accept}), maximum number of iterations (ML)
Output: The best solution x_i^{max} with the largest objective function value
Begin
   while *(t < ML)*
   Generate new harmonics by accepting best harmonics
   Adjust pitch to get new harmonics (solutions)

   if *(rand>r_{accept})*
   choose an existing harmonic randomly

   else if *(rand>r_{pa})*
   adjust the pitch randomly within limits

   else
   generate new harmonics via randomization

   end if

   Accept the new harmonics (solutions) if better
   end while

   Find the current best solutions
End

As compared to other meta-heuristic techniques, the HSA is reported to do less number of mathematical calculations. It is easily adapted for solving various optimization problems of engineering [17, 18]. Likewise, computations have shown that the evolution for the HSA is faster than the GA [13, 19]. Most specifically it has been used to design optimization of water distribution networks, vehicle routing, combined heat and power economic dispatch, design of steel frames, bandwidth-delay-constrained least-cost multicast routing, transport energy modelling among others [20–23]. Mishra et al. [24–26] have proposed several novel image watermarking schemes using different classes of soft computing techniques.

3 SSF Based DWT-SVD Watermarking Algorithm

To study the effect of scaling factor on PSNR and Normalized Cross-correlation $NC(W, W')$ values, the following DWT-SVD based watermarking algorithm is used in the present work [24, 25]. The signed images are examined for visual quality by PSNR given by Eq. 1. A watermark is extracted and $NC(W, W')$ parameter where W and W' being original and recovered watermarks respectively is computed by Eq. 2.

$$PSNR = 10log_{10}\left(\frac{I_{max}^2}{MSE}\right)$$ (1)

where I_{max} is the maximum possible pixel value of the image I and MSE is the mean square error

$$NC(W, W') = \frac{\sum_{i=1}^{m}\sum_{j=1}^{n}[W(i,j) \cdot W'(i,j)]}{\sum_{i=1}^{m}\sum_{j=1}^{n}[W(i,j)]^2}$$ (2)

3.1 Watermark Embedding Algorithm

We consider the host image I of size N × N and the watermark W of size m × m. The embedding scheme is given in Listing 2.

Listing 2: Embedding Algorithm

Step1. Apply 3 level DWT using HAAR filter on the host image I to obtain LL3 sub-band of size m × m

Step2. Apply SVD on LL3 sub-band coefficients of the host image obtained in step1 by using Eq. 3 and hence obtain S

$$[U, S, V] = SVD(LL3)$$ (3)

Step3. Apply SVD on the watermark (W) using Eq. 4 and identify the singular values (S_w)

$$[U_w, S_w, V_w] = SVD(W)$$ (4)

Step4. Embed S_w into S values using the formula given by Eq. 5 [39]

$$S' = S + \delta_s * S_w$$ (5)

where δ_s is the single scaling factor which controls the tradeoff between imperceptibility and robustness of the proposed watermarking scheme.

Step5. Compute the modified LL3 sub-band coefficients using Eq. 6

$$LL3' = U * S' * V^T \tag{6}$$

Step6. Apply 3-level Inverse DWT to obtain the signed image I'

3.2 Watermark Extraction Algorithm

The embedded watermarks are recovered from signed images. The extraction is carried out by applying DWT-SVD combination to signed images. The extracted watermark is denoted by W'. The watermark extraction algorithm is given in Listing 3.

Listing 3: Extraction Algorithm

Step1. Apply 3 level DWT using HAAR filter on the host image I and signed image I' to obtain LL3 and $LL3'$ sub band coefficients of size m × m respectively for the two images

Step2. Apply SVD on the LL3 and $LL3'$ sub-band coefficients using Eqs. 7 and 8 to obtain the singular values S and S' respectively

$$[U, S, V] = SVD(LL3) \tag{7}$$

$$[U', S', V'] = SVD(LL3') \tag{8}$$

Step3. Compute the singular values of the watermark using the formula given by Eq. 9

$$S'_w = (S' - S) \tag{9}$$

Step4. Recover the extracted watermark image using the formula given by Eq. 10

$$W' = U_w * S'_w * V_w^T \tag{10}$$

The extraction carried out in this algorithm is informed extraction. It requires both the original host image and its signed counterpart to obtain the watermark.

4 Harmony Search Algorithm Based Watermarking Scheme

In this paper, we propose a watermarking scheme which makes use of multiple scaling factors or MSF (δ_m) for watermark embedding. The values of MSF are optimized by using HSA. This HSA based watermarking scheme makes use of the embedding and extraction algorithm presented in Listing 2 and 3 respectively. The complete watermarking scheme is given in Listing 4.

Listing 4: Harmony Search Algorithm (HSA) based watermarking scheme

Step1. Initialize n harmonics randomly, where each harmonic is a row vector of size m × m (equal to the size of watermark)

Step2. For each harmonic i, do as follows:

1. Execute the watermark embedding algorithm given in Listing 2, Sect. 3.1 by using the Eq. 11 instead of Eq. 5

$$S' = S + \delta_m * S_w \tag{11}$$

where δ_m is the MSF obtained by HSA.

2. Apply T = 8 different image processing attacks on the signed image I' one by one. This generates T different attacked signed images for the signed image I'
3. Extract the watermarks form the attacked signed images using steps in Listing 3
4. Compute the PSNR between the original image I and signed image I' and $NC(W, W')$ values for attacked images
5. Calculate the objective value of Harmony Search Algorithm (HSA) using objective function given by Eq. 12

$$objective = PSNR + \phi * \left[NC(W, W') + \sum_{i=1}^{T} NC(W, W'_i) \right] \tag{12}$$

where $NC(W, W')$ is the normalized cross-correlation between the original watermark and extracted watermark from signed image, $NC(W, W'_i)$ is the normalized cross-correlation between the original watermark and extracted watermarks from each attacked signed image and ϕ is the weighting factor for $NC(W, W')$ values

Step3. Improvise these n harmonics according to the procedure given in Listing 1
Step4. Repeat Step2 and Step3 until the maximum number of generations (ML) is reached.

Note that the objective value is a function of both factors – the $NC(W, W')$ and the PSNR. In Eq. 12 above, the PSNR is much larger as compared to the associated NC values therefore; a weighting factor ϕ is used to balance out the influences caused by the two parameters.

5   Experimental Results and Discussion

The performance of the proposed algorithm is evaluated on four different 256 × 256 gray-scale host images namely Baboon, Boat, Cameraman and Lena. A 32 × 32 binary image is used as a watermark. All the proposed algorithms in this paper are executed on Matlab 12a. All our experiments were carried out by using HMCR = 0.9, PAR = 0.1 and HMS = 10 [12–14]. The total number of initial harmonics (n) is 10, ϕ is 10 and the simulation is done for ML = 10 iterations. To compute the objective function, eight image processing operations are executed as attacks (T = 8). Figure 1 depicts the host images and the binary watermark. Figure 2 depicts the signed images and Fig. 3 depicts their corresponding extracted watermarks.

As it is mentioned in Sect. 4, our objective function is a linear combination of PSNR and $NC(W, W')$ obtained from signed and attacked images. This objective

Fig. 1. (a–e): Original Images - (a) Baboon, (b) Boat, (c) Cameraman, (d) Lena and (e) Watermark

function is computed by taking into account eight different image processing operations. The HSA uses this objective function to optimize the MSF used for watermark embedding. The optimized MSF is expected to enhance the robustness as compared to using a Single Scaling Factor (SSF) over the DWT-SVD watermarking scheme. Table 1 compiles our results as well as those of several other researchers [10, 11] based on SSF as well as MSF for signed images only. We analyze and compare these results on the basis of optimized MSF using HSA.

The observations compiled in Table 1 are summarized below:

(a) In case of DWT-SVD using SSF watermarking scheme, the average PSNR ranges between 52.07 dB and 52.41 dB for the selected four images, which indicates good visual quality of signed images.

(b) It is clear for the SSF scheme, that the PSNR results are better placed than that using MSF [10, 11] for all host images except Baboon and Boat. This SSF scheme outperforms the PSNR results of Ishtiaq et al. [10] for Baboon, Boat and Lena images. Note that both Loukhaoukha et al. [11] and us have used hybrid transforms

Fig. 2. (a–d): Signed Images - (a) Baboon, (b) Boat, (c) Cameraman and (d) Lena

Fig. 3. (a–d): Extracted Watermarks from - (a) Baboon, (b) Boat, (c) Cameraman and (d) Lena

to implement respective watermarking schemes while Ishtiaq et al. [10] used DCT as the transform to develop PSO based watermarking scheme. In Table 1, 'NA' indicates that Ishtiaq et al. [10] have not applied their scheme over Cameraman image. This means, the use of hybrid transform to implement watermark embedding is better option in comparison to a unitary transform.

(c) Comparing our MSF based results with those reported by Loukhaoukha et al. [11] reveal that our results are better at least for three images. We attribute this result to the use of DWT-SVD hybrid transform while Loukhaoukha et al. [11] have implemented a different hybrid LWT–SVD transform. As far as comparing our MSF results with those of Ishtiaq et al. [10] is concerned, it is clear that we obtain far better outcomes than them, for the three images we could compare with. For NC values again, we obtain either similar or better outcomes as compared to other works for MSF watermarking scheme.

Table 1. PSNR and $NC(W, W')$ value between the host image and signed image of the proposed work and other's work

Image	Category/Algorithm	PSNR (dB)	NC(W, W')
Baboon	SSF/DWT-SVD method	52.2101	1.000
	MSF/Proposed HSA method	**55.3124**	**1.000**
	MSF/Lou et al. [11]	52.379	1.000
	MSF/Ishtiaq et al. [10]	44.9624	NA
Boat	SSF/DWT-SVD method	52.0743	0.991
	MSF/Proposed method	**53.1024**	**1.000**
	MSF/Lou et al. [11]	54.810	1.000
	MSF/Ishtiaq et al. [10]	50.1586	NA
Cameraman	SSF/DWT-SVD method	52.4147	0.995
	MSF/Proposed method	**54.9812**	**1.000**
	MSF/Lou et al. [11]	48.902	1.000
	MSF/Ishtiaq et al. [10]	NA	NA
Lena	SSF/DWT-SVD method	52.3904	0.995
	MSF/Proposed method	**55.9278**	**1.000**
	MSF/Lou et al. [11]	47.718	1.000
	MSF/Ishtiaq et al. [10]	48.105	NA

By this analysis, it is quite clear that the proposed Harmony Search based watermarking scheme is the best among the selected schemes. In the second part of this experiment, we compile results for the robustness studies carried out over signed images obtained by us. For this purpose, as described in Sect. 1, we select eight different image processing operations as attacks to evaluate the robustness of the proposed scheme. These are: JPEG compression (Q = 95), Salt and Pepper noise (5%), Gaussian filtering (filter aperture = 3 × 3), Sharpening (aperture = 0.2), Histogram Equalization (with 64 discrete gray levels), Scaling (256 → 512 → 256), Gray-scale Quantization (1-bit) and Cropping by dividing the image into 9 equal blocks, replacing the central block with zeros. Table 2 compiles the $NC(W, W')$ values for eight different image processing attacks over the four signed images obtained in this experiment.

It is clear from Table 2 that in case of the proposed watermarking scheme, except for the cropping attack, the $NC(W, W')$ values are very close to 1.0. Comparing this result with the one compiled in Table 1, wherein the $NC(W, W') = 1.000$ for all four signed images, it can be safely said that except cropping, no other image processing attack could harm the visual characteristics and the structural properties of the signed images. This indicates that the proposed HSA based embedding scheme is very robust against the selected attacks except cropping for which this scheme tends to falter. We attribute better results for robustness obtained by us to better optimization of MSF (δ_m) using HSA. The HSA makes use of the objective function which is a linear combination of PSNR of signed image and $NC(W, W')$ for both signed and attacked images computed for eight different attacks, there by resulting in high robustness. Additionally, the proposed algorithm maintains good visual quality of the signed images. We therefore, conclude that the much needed tradeoff of the visual quality and robustness is achieved in our scheme as a result of taking into account the MSFs optimized by the HSA. The proposed scheme is proved to be successful in meeting all required criteria.

Table 2. $NC(W, W')$ values for different image processing attacks

Image	JPEG 5%	S & P Noise (5%)	Gaussian Filter 3 × 3	Sharpening (aperture = 2.0)	Histogram Equalization (64 gray levels)	Scaling (256 → 512 → 256)	Gray-scale quantization 1-bit	Cropping central block and replacing with zeros
Baboon	1.000	0.989	0.997	0.999	0.999	1.000	0.999	0.712
Boat	1.000	0.997	0.991	0.993	0.996	1.000	0.99	0.826
Cameraman	1.000	0.982	0.985	0.951	1.000	1.000	0.99	0.654
Lena	1.000	0.981	0.991	0.996	1.000	1.000	0.986	0.610

6 Conclusion and Future Scope

In this paper, we propose successful and novel implementation of the Harmony Search Algorithm based watermarking scheme for grayscale images. This is a meta-heuristic technique which is used for the first time for this application. The tradeoff between the visual quality and the robustness criteria which is very crucial for developing any watermarking scheme is successfully resolved and the proposed scheme is found to be very robust against all image processing attacks except the cropping attack to which it tends to falter. The successful achievement of good visual quality of the signed images and the high robustness values is achieved as a result of careful optimization of the Multiple Scaling factor (MSF) carried out by the HSA used in this scheme. The obtained results are compared with those reported by other researchers and it is found that the proposed HSA based scheme outperforms all other schemes for the selected four host images. It is therefore concluded that it is the best option so far as the optimization of MSFs is concerned. The real time characteristics of this scheme over the selected images are yet to be examined. In the next phase of this experiment, we propose to implement this scheme with a detailed analysis to examine its suitability for real time scenarios.

References

1. Tsai, H.-H., Jhuang, Y.-J., Lai, Y.-S.: An SVD-based image watermarking in wavelet domain using SVR and PSO. Appl. Soft Comput. 12(8), 2442–2453 (2012)
2. Mishra, A., Goel, A., Singh, R., Chetty, G., Singh, L.: A novel image watermarking scheme using extreme learning machine. In: Proceedings of the IEEE World Congress on Computational Intelligence, pp. 1–6 (2012)
3. Motwani, M.C., Motwani, R.C., Harris Jr., F.C.: Wavelet based fuzzy perceptual mask for images. In: Proceedings of IEEE International Conference on Image Processing (ICIP 2009), Cairo, Egypt (2009)

4. Motwani, M.C., Harris Jr., F.C.: Fuzzy perceptual watermarking for ownership verification. In: Proceedings of the International Conference on Image Processing, Computer Vision, and Pattern Recognition, Las Vegas, Nevada (2009)
5. Fındık, O., Babaoğlu, I., Ülker, E.: A color image watermarking scheme based on hybrid classification method: particle swarm optimization and k-nearest neighbor algorithm. Opt. Commun. **283**(24), 4916–4922 (2010)
6. Cox, I., Kilian, J., Leighton, F.T., Shamoon, T.: Secure spread spectrum watermarking for multimedia. IEEE Trans. Image Process. **6**, 1673–1687 (1997)
7. Run, R.-S., Horng, S.-J., Lai, J.-L., Kao, T.-W., Chen, R.-J.: An improved SVD-based watermarking technique for copyright protection. Expert Syst. Appl. **39**, 673–689 (2012)
8. Kumsawat, P., Attakitmongcol, K., Srikaew, A.: A new approach for optimization in image watermarking by using genetic algorithms. IEEE Trans. Sig. Process. **53**(12), 4707–4719 (2005)
9. Lai, C.-C.: A digital watermarking scheme based on singular value decomposition and tiny genetic algorithm. Digital Sig. Process. **21**, 522–527 (2011)
10. Ishtiaq, M., Sikandar, B., Jaffar, A., Khan, A.: Adaptive watermark strength selection using particle swarm optimization. ICIC Express Lett. **4**(5) (2010). ISSN: 1881-803X
11. Loukhaoukha, K., Chouinard, J.-Y., Taieb, M.H.: Optimal image watermarking algorithm based on LWT-SVD via multi-objective ant colony optimization. J. Inf. Hiding Multimedia Sig. Process. **2**(4), 303–319 (2011)
12. Geem, Z.W., Kim, J.H., Loganathan, G.V.: A new heuristic optimization algorithm: harmony search. Simulation **76**, 60–682 (2001)
13. Lee, K.S., Geem, Z.W.: A new meta-heuristic algorithm for continuous engineering optimization: harmony search theory and practice. Comput. Methods Appl. Mech. Eng. **194**, 3902–3933 (2005)
14. Yang, X.S.: Nature-Inspired Metaheuristic Algorithms. Luniver Press, Bristol (2008)
15. Geem, Z.W.: Optimal cost design of water distribution networks using harmony search. Eng. Optim. **38**, 259–280 (2006)
16. Cuevas, E., Ortega-Sánchez, N., Zaldivar, D., Pérez-Cisneros, M.: Circle detection by harmony search optimization. J. Intell. Rob. Syst. Theory Appl. **66**(3), 359–376 (2013)
17. Mahdavi, M., Fesanghary, M., Damangir, E.: An improved harmony search algorithm for solving optimization problems. Appl. Math. Comput. **188**, 1567–1579 (2007)
18. Omran, M.G.H., Mahdavi, M.: Global-best harmony search. Appl. Math. Comput. **198**, 643–656 (2008)
19. Lee, K.S., Geem, Z.W., Lee, S.H., Bae, K.-W.: The harmony search heuristic algorithm for discrete structural optimization. Eng. Optim. **37**, 663–684 (2005)
20. Kim, J.H., Geem, Z.W., Kim, E.S.: Parameter estimation of the nonlinear Muskingum model using harmony search. J. Am. Water Resour. Assoc. **37**, 1131–1138 (2001)
21. Lee, K.S., Geem, Z.W.: A new structural optimization method based on the harmony search algorithm. Comput. Struct. **82**, 781–798 (2004)
22. Ayvaz, T.M.: Simultaneous determination of aquifer parameters and zone structures with fuzzy c-means clustering and meta-heuristic harmony search algorithm. Adv. Water Resour. **30**, 2326–2338 (2007)
23. Geem, Z.W., Lee, K.S., Park, Y.J.: Application of harmony search to vehicle routing. Am. J. Appl. Sci. **2**, 1552–1557 (2005)
24. Mishra, A., Agarwal, C., Sharma, A., Bedi, P.: Optimized gray-scale image watermarking using DWT-SVD and firefly algorithm. Expert Syst. Appl. **41**, 7858–7867 (2014)

25. Mishra, A., Agarwal, C.: Toward optimal watermarking of grayscale images using the multiple scaling factor–based cuckoo search technique. In: Bio-Inspired Computation and Applications in Image Processing, pp. 131–155. Elsevier (2016). https://doi.org/10.1016/B978-0-12-804536-7.00007-7
26. Mishra, A., Rajpal, A., Bala, R.: Bi-directional extreme learning machine for semi-blind watermarking of compressed images. J. Inf. Secur. Appl. **38**, 71–84 (2018)

Combining Automatic Variability Analysis Tools: An SPL Approach for Building a Framework for Composition

Agustina Buccella[1,2(✉)], Matias Pol'la[1,2], Esteban Ruiz de Galarreta[1], and Alejandra Cechich[1]

[1] GIISCo Research Group, Faculty of Informatics, UNComa University, Neuquen, Argentina
`agustina.buccella@fi.uncoma.edu.ar`

[2] Consejo Nacional de Investigaciones Científicas y Técnicas - CONICET, Buenos Aires, Argentina

Abstract. The automatic analysis of variability models is an important research field included in variability management activities. In the context of software product lines, it includes a set of methods and techniques aimed at verifying the design of the variability models in order to avoid inconsistencies during variability definition, implementation, and derivations activities. There exist several tools and proposals implementing the basic activities involved in this analysis process. However, the large number of them makes difficult to find and select the most suitable tool/set of tools to be applied in a particular SPL development. Taking into account this problem, our work aims at developing a framework, built as a software product line, that allows developers to compose/build automatic analysis tools according to their specific needs. We illustrate the proposal through possible instantiations of the framework.

Keywords: Automatic analysis · Variability models
Software product lines · Tools · Framework

1 Introduction

Variability is a relatively new software property aimed at increasing the ability of a system to be changed or customized according to the specific needs of particular systems. In the context of software product lines (SPL), variability plays a central role starting in early phases of the software development and ending when a product is marketed.

This work is partially supported by the UNComa project 04/F009 "Reuso de Software orientado a Dominios - Parte II" part of the program "Desarrollo de Software Basado en Reuso - Parte II".

© Springer International Publishing AG, part of Springer Nature 2018
O. Gervasi et al. (Eds.): ICCSA 2018, LNCS 10963, pp. 435–451, 2018.
https://doi.org/10.1007/978-3-319-95171-3_34

In this way, variability management is defined by set of activities and techniques for defining, modeling, implementing and testing system variabilities. Several variability management approaches have emerged in the last twenty years focusing on the different aspects of this activity. Proposals of techniques for variability model representation [7,8,17], UML-based representations [11,34,43], variability consistency checking [9]; and complete frameworks [27,37] supporting the whole software product line development, provide novel ideas towards consolidating solutions about variability management issues.

At the same time, within the variability management activities have emerged a new research field, named *(automated) variability analysis*, focusing specifically on validating variability models according to a predefined set of scenarios [2,18,23,32]. In the literature, there exist many works about (automated) analysis of variability models. Some works presenting surveys o reviews can be found in [2,39]; for example in [39] the authors present a comparison of automated analysis using Alloy [15] for Feature Models (FM). In [2] there is a broader literature review of automatic analysis of FM, based on a general process that defines a set of tasks for evaluating FM. In this field, the research community has achieved a wide consensus about the main activities involved and the expected results [2]. Even more, several tools have emerged towards automation of these activities [1,26] implementing an effective complete analysis, such as S.P.L.O.T. [22], VariaMos [21], Das et al. [10] or Ripon et al. [31]. However, these activities depend on several factors, such as variability models used, logic representations and solvers selected, etc. These variations make difficult to software engineers or developers, who are developing an SPL, to find and combine the tools or techniques that fit their own requirements. For example, according to the modeling approach used, the techniques for analyzing the variability models can be different with respect to other modeling approaches.

In previous works, we have developed two analysis tools based on different logic representations and solvers [4,28]. Both, take variability models as inputs (built by our own approach, named SeVaTax model [5]) and make different translations to be evaluated by different solvers. In [28] we introduced an implementation in CNF (Conjunctive Normal Form) together with SAT solver (SAT4j[1]); and in [4], we presented another implementation in DL (Description Logic) and using DL Reasoners (RACER[2]). However, these compositions of tools are just two possible implementations that can be used under specific requirements. We have combined third-party tools and added our own code for composition, thinking of composition rules every time from scratch. Taking this context into account, in this work we propose a framework for combining automatic variability analysis tools, which can be adapted to the specific requirements of a variability management case. The framework has been developed by following an SPL development approach to allow developers and software engineers to generate specific tools according to their own needs. To do so, code needed for composition of third-party products has been added as part of the SPL facilitating adaptation.

---

[1] www.sat4j.org/.

[2] https://www.ifis.uni-luebeck.de/~moeller/racer/index.html.

At the same time, the framework can be used for analyzing the behavior of different techniques together, that is, the different combinations of tools derived from the SPL can be compared in terms of performance, correctness, efficiency, etc. Thus, the contributions of this work are threefold: (1) a framework for composition of automatic variability analysis tools as an SPL architecture; (2) an instantiation of the framework for some possible cases, including adaptation (glue) code; and (3) the possibility of analyzing different techniques applied to the automatic variability analysis.

The paper is organized as follows. Next section describes the context and related works in the literature focused on our research: variability modeling approaches, scenario validation and automated analysis. In Sect. 3 we describe the architecture and implementation of the framework focusing on the main components that provide flexibility. In Sect. 4 we present two instantiations of the SPL for deriving two combinations of tools with very different characteristics. Conclusions and future works are discussed afterwards.

2   Background and Related Work

The automated variability analysis includes a set of techniques and methods focused on validation activities of variability management. In a SPL development, it plays an important role when the variability is defined (in the domain engineering phase) and when it is instantiated (in the application engineering phase) [27]. When a SPL development is carried out by software engineers and developers, they must decide the set of software pieces and design variability artifacts to be applied. These decisions will impact later in the way the variability management is addressed. For the automated variability analysis, the development team must consider four components, which are always involved in defining the context of the variability validation process. Figure 1 shows these four components as part of an automated process.

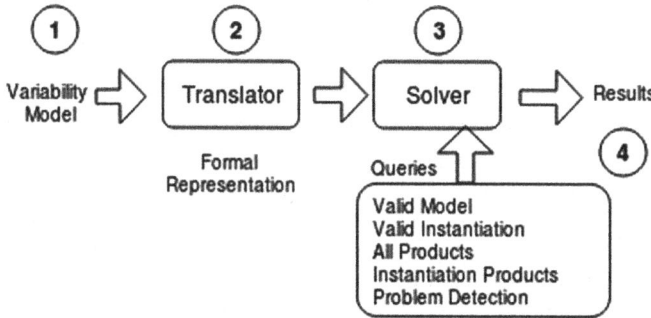

Fig. 1. General process for automated analysis of variability models

Table 1. Summary of automated analysis approaches

Approach	V.M.	F.M.	Solver	Queries/Scenarios				
				VM	VI	AP	IN	PD
Lauenroth et al. [19]	OVM I-O/automata	CTL	SAT-VM	x	-	x	-	-
FAMA-FM [36]	FM	CSP	BDD SAT Choco	x	x	x	x	x
FAMA-OVM [33]	OVM	CSP	BDD SAT Choco	x	x	x	x	x
Metzger et al. [23]	OVM - FD	CNF	SAT	x	x	-	-	-
Bessling and Huhn [3]	CVL SCADE	CVL	SAT SCADE	x	x	-	-	-
Rincon et al. (a) [29]	FM	CSP	Prolog	x	x	-	-	x
Nakajima [24]	FM	CSP	SAT (Alloy)	x	x	-	-	-
VariaMos [21]	Independent	CSP	SWI-Prolog	x	x	-	-	x
S.P.L.O.T. [22]	FM	3-CNF	SAT	x	x	-	x	x
Wang et al. [41]	FM	OWL	FACT++	x	x	-	-	x
Noorian et al. [25]	FM	DL	Pellet	x	x	-	-	x
Fan et al. [12]	FM	DL	RACER	x	x	-	-	-
Das et al. [10]	FM	OWL-DL	RACER	x	x	-	-	x
Ripon et al.[31]	FM	OWL-DL	RACER	x	x	-	-	x
Ryssel et al. [35]	FM	OWL-CSP	FACT++	x	x	-	-	-
Rincon et al. (b) [30]	FM	OWL - SQWRL	JESS	x	x	-	-	x
Zaid et al. [42]	FM	OWL-DL SWRL	Pellet	x	x	-	-	x

The first component is the *variability model* that can be defined by following any of the existing modeling approaches. The second component is the *translator*, which performs the transformation process between the model and the *formal representation* taking into account the selected approach. This formal representation includes the variability in logical terms. The third component is a *solver*, responsible for validating the formal model. This component also receives an *scenario/query* set, which determines the results (fourth component) of the analysis process.

The important point here is that each of these components can be implemented by including different techniques or resources generating a wide set of possibilities of composition. For example in [2] authors implemented a tool that allows to interchange among different SAT-solvers. At the same, it is possible to interchange among different formal representations, modeling approaches, and/or queries.

In Table 1 we summarize several proposals in the literature, highlighting the techniques or methods used for each of these four components.

For example, in the first column of the table (variability model (V.M.)) we show different approaches used for representing variability, such as feature models [16], Orthogonal Variability Models (OVM) [27], Common Variability Languages (CVL) [14], etc[3]. While the expressiveness of each modeling approach might be similar, there are substantial differences among them. For example, proposals based on FM present a hierarchical model that allows to describe the commonalities and variabilities within a single structure; OVM allows to specify variabilities in separate but linked models; and CVL is a domain-independent language for specifying variability, in which models are expressed using DSL (Domain Specific Language) or UML.

Following, the next two columns show proposals of different formal models (F.M.) and solvers. For example, in Rincon et al. (a) [29] and Rincon et al. (b) [30], the authors propose two methods for analyzing feature models but translating them into DL and CSP (Constraint Satisfaction Problem) together with different solvers, Prolog and JESS[4] respectively. Also, in [13,32,33,36] two frameworks are proposed, one of them based on FM [36] and the other on OVM [13,33]. Both frameworks perform an automatic analysis by means of logical translations performed by CSP. The main goal is to allow software engineers to analyze different solver responses, that is, by selecting a specific solver (such as SAT, BDD or Choco), engineers can perform queries allowing validating a platform, products and some anomaly detections. At the same time in FAMA-OVM [33] authors introduce an OVM extension for annotating extra-functional aspects such as availability, development time or efficiency. In the work of Wang et al. [41] the authors propose a method for formalizing FMs into OWL [6], by using a prototype tool (that in future works will be available as a Protégé plugin)[5]. Then, a FACT++ reasoner [40] is used for problem detection by providing a debugger module, which identifies the most general conflicts and gives an explanation. Noorian et al. [25] present a translation of FMs into DL, and use Pellet [38]. In Nakajima [24] the author introduces a semi-automatic method for verifying FMs, which are translated to propositional logic. Then, a SAT-solver (specified in Alloy) is applied to determine the validity of the model. Finally, we can cite the work presented in [21], in which authors define a method, supported by a variability modeling tool for checking dead and false optional elements, redundancies, false product line, and the validity of configurations. The tool, named *VariaMos*[6], is based on an independent language that allows to model the variability in different tree structures. The validation of the models is performed by translating those structures into CSP and then evaluating them in SWI:Prolog[7] solver.

---

[3] Each approach contains a large number of proposals, which extend different aspects.
[4] http://www.jessrules.com.
[5] https://protege.stanford.edu/.
[6] http://variamos.com/home/.
[7] http://www.swi-prolog.org/.

Finally, the last column shows the fourth component in which the set of queries defined for the analysis process is analyzed. These queries or validation scenarios represent the set of questions which solvers are capable of answer. In this sense, in the literature there exists several definitions of the set of anomalies or mismatches that can be found on a variability model [2,18,20]. From these definitions we select the most common ones based on the following five queries:

- *Valid Model (VM)*: Determines if a model is valid or not, that is, if it is possible to generate a product from a variability model.
- *Valid instantiation (VI)*: Given a model and one instantiation of it, determines if the instantiation is valid or not, that is, if the instantiation can generate a valid product.
- *All Products (AP)*: Given a model, identifies all possible instantiations.
- *Instantiation Number (IN)*: Given a model identifies the number of possible instantiations.
- *Problems Detection (PD)*: Given a model, identifies the failures of the validation process, that is, the causes which determine that a model is invalid.

In the Table we can highlight FAMA, which evaluates all scenarios; S.P.L.O.T evaluates 4 of them (all except *All Products*); and VariaMos evaluates 3 of them (*Valid model, Valid instantiation* and *Problems Detection*). Another important conclusion extracted from the table is about the proposals using ontological languages (OWL, DL, etc.) and reasoners for validating models. As we can see, none of these works makes an analysis of *All Products* (AP) and *Instantiation Number* (IN) queries, which are two of the most common queries needed in any variability analysis process. At the same time, more specific queries [2,18,20] are not analyzed either.

Considering these wide panorama of resources and techniques used on each of the components of a variability analysis process shown in Fig. 1, we define four questions that might allow developers and software engineers to determine the context in which the process will be applied:

1. Which variability modeling approach does the project use?
2. Which logic model will be potentially applied?
3. Which solver or reasoner is available and useful to be selected?
4. Which anomalies or problems the team expects to find?

To answers these questions we will define the requirements needed to validate variability in a particular SPL development. In this way, in order to contribute to the search of the more suitable process, we propose a framework that allows to create tools according to these requirements.

3   A Framework for Automatic Variability Analysis

The framework is based on the general process of automatic analysis (Fig. 1), including the main software artifacts for supporting flexibility when composing the involved components.

In the next subsections, we describe the main aspects of the framework's architecture and its implementation, which follow an SPL development approach.

3.1   Framework Architecture

In Fig. 2 we show the three-tier architecture together with the main components:

- *View*: this layer includes the components of the user interface, such as the *Editor Viewer Component* for loading and editing models, and the *(Result Viewer Component* for showing the results of the analysis process.
- *Processing*: this layer includes the processing components responsible for translating a variability model into a specific format for a solver and performing specific queries. The *File Loader Component* is responsible for parsing a JSON file into a set of variability primitives; the *Translator Component* determines the strategies or rules that must be taking into account for translating each variability primitive into a particular logic language; the *Solver Configuration* involves the activities to define and configure solver particularities; and the *Query Analysis Component* defines the set of queries available for analyzing the variability models. The solvers are represented as external components due to they accept representations and queries in a specific format.
- *Model*: this layer includes the model management component, in charge of dealing with all information stored into a database. This database stores the needed structures as support for the upper layers, and the configuration data needed during the instantiation process.

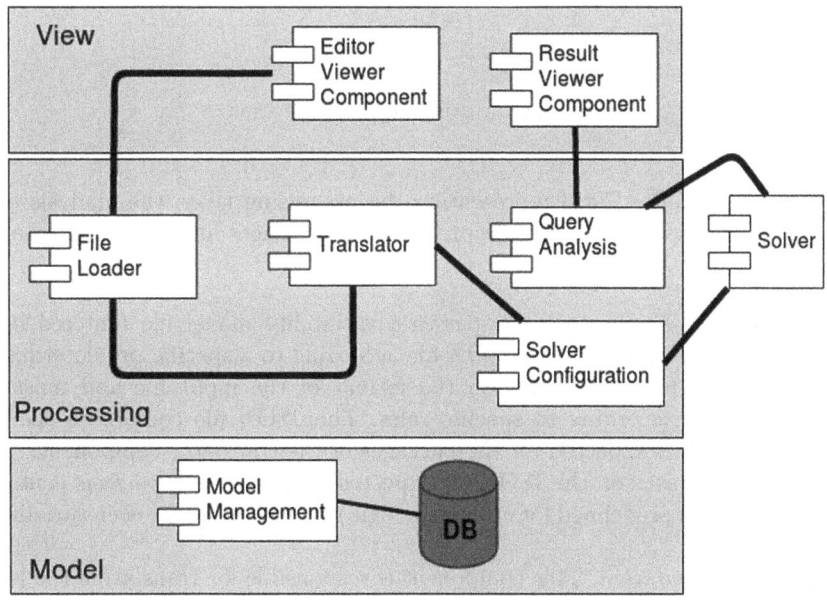

Fig. 2. Framework architecture

Processing Layer

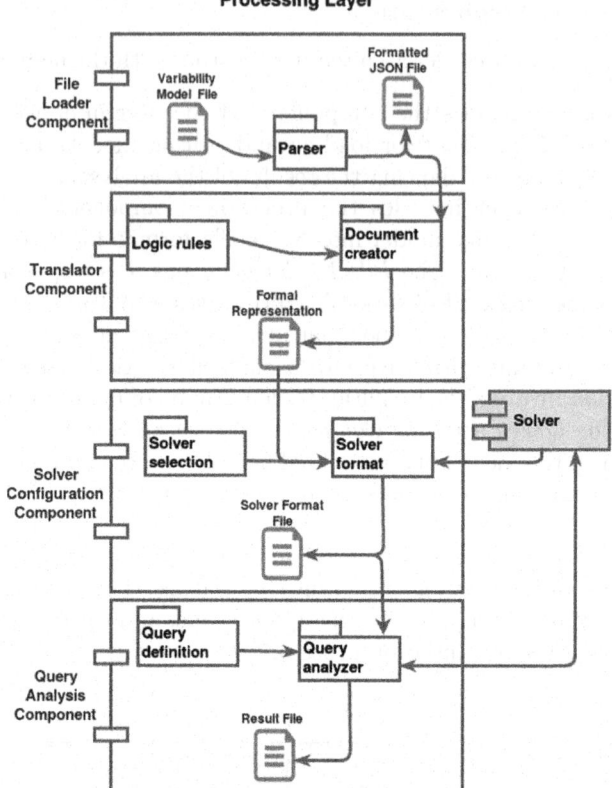

Fig. 3. Processing layer specification

According to the Fig. 3 representing the processing layer, the analysis process involves a set of activities (represented as packages and files) within each component:

- *File Loader*: This component parses a variability model file (entered by a user) in order to generate a JSON file according to a specific pre-determined format. The parser depends on the format of the input file and must be implemented according to specific rules. The JSON file contains a specific format which is expected for the packages of the translator component.
- *Translator*: Based on the JSON file expected, the *logic rules package* contains the logic rules predefined for creating a logic representation for each variability primitive.
- *Solver Configuration*: This component is responsible for translating the logic representation to the format expected by the solver. When a user selects a specific solver, the common logic representation must be created according to their specific requirements.

– *Query Analysis*: There are two main tasks here. On one hand, the possible queries to be sent to the solver must be selected or extended (*query definition package*). Then, the analyzer sends them to the solver and the set of results, or suggestions are attached into a file that will be then show to the user.

In order to show the way the framework is built for achieving flexibility, Fig. 4 shows the variability models[8] included on several of the components described previously. Specifically, the models show the different variabilities that can be configured during the process of instantiating a new product of the SPL. For example, the *parser* alternative variation point is representing that the *Parser* package of the *File Loader Component* can accept as input an OVM, FM or CVL model to be translated into a specific JSON file. The alternative restriction means that any SPL product generated will accept only one type of these

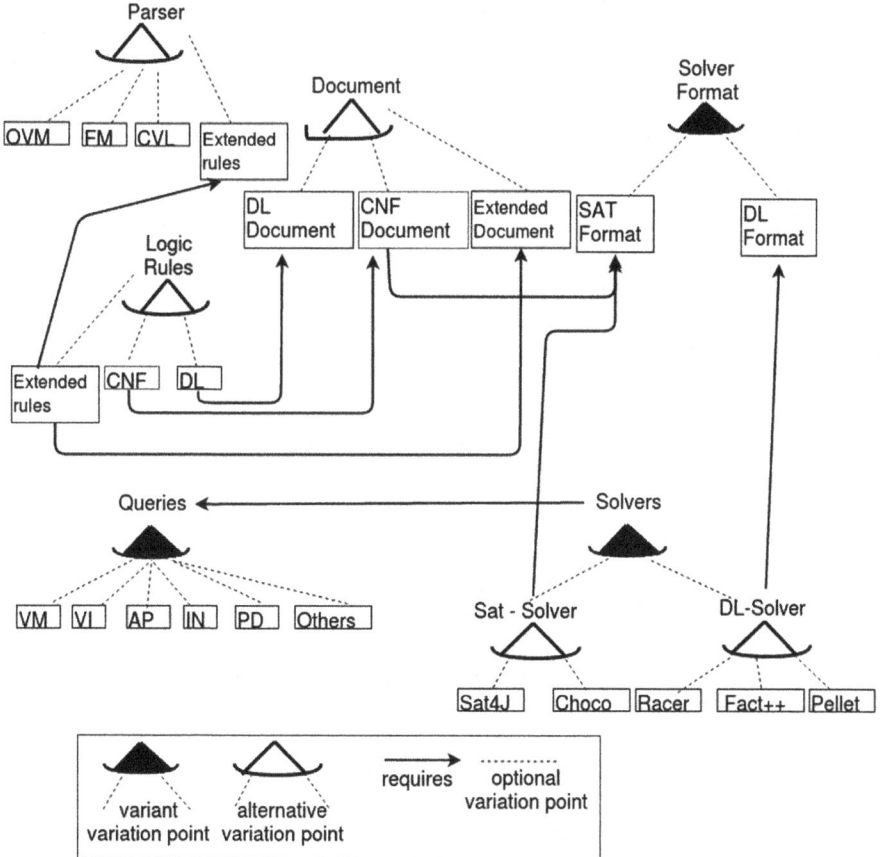

Fig. 4. Variability models for the framework implementation

---

[8] We use the OVM graphical notation for these variability models.

models. At the same time, it could include new extended rules in the case the model contains own primitives or particularities. Also, the *logic rules* alternative variation point represents the translation rules that are used to create documents as DL, CNF or own extensions. These documents contain the logic representation of the variability model firstly entered. The *solver format* variation point represents a shared point between the CNF or DL document created and the solver selected to be applied. This means that the final format to be analyzed by the tool depends on the logic representation of the variability model and the selected solver. Thus, for example a CNF Document requires that a SAT Format be implemented and a SAT-Solver be capable of analyzing it. Finally, there is the *queries* variant variation point, in which we represent the basic validation scenarios (Sect. 2) together with the possibility of adding more specific ones [2,18,20].

These variability models provide the flexibility of building different combinations from the SPL. As an example, in Fig. 5 we can see the features instantiated into three combinations, which are derived from the SPL according to the variability specification (Fig. 4).

3.2   SPL Implementation

We follow an incremental proactive approach[9] in which variant services are implemented on demand, that is, when specific requirements need some variant service, the implementation is carried out.

For the implementation of the framework, we used the typescript framework *Angular 2*[10] for the view layer. This framework was used for displaying menus, which are used for selecting the different options to configure the final combination of tools.

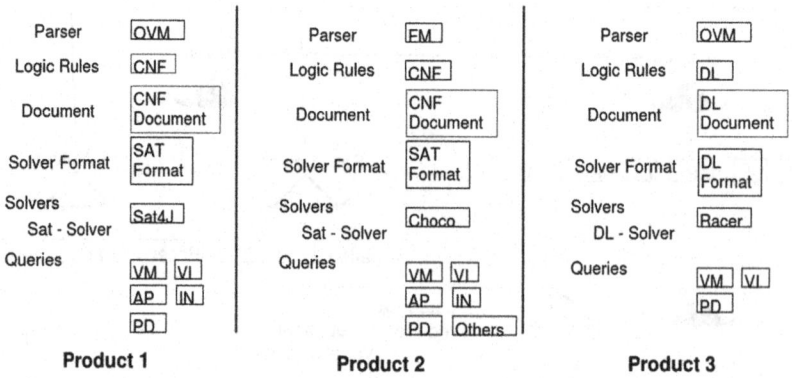

Fig. 5. Three combinations derived from the SPL

---

[9] https://www.sei.cmu.edu/productlines/frame_report/all_three.htm.
[10] https://angular.io/.

For the processing layer we used the NodeJS framework *ExpressJS*[11] because we needed processing in the server side in a fast and simple way.

For the model layer we used *MongoDB*[12], that is a document database that works very well with ExpressJS. MongoDB was used to persist the model configuration used for testing and extending queries. In addition, we stored data about executions and statistic data.

4   Instantiating Two Combinations Derived from the Framework

Instantiating the framework allows us to obtain a suitable combination of tools, working all together to automatically validating variability. Then, for the instantiation process, we must define firstly the contexts or set of requirements that we must achieve. As we described in Sect. 2, these requirements can be obtained by answering the four questions raised previously. Thus, the two contexts created for making the instantiations are defined as:

1. *Context 1*: The variability model approach is OVM, CNF is the logic model, a SAT solver (SAT4j) is selected; and VM, VI, AP, IN and PD are the queries needed. This context corresponds to the *Product 1* of Fig. 5.
2. *Context 2*: The variability model approach is OVM, DL is the logic model, a Reasoner (Racer) is selected; and VM, VI, and PD are the queries needed. This context corresponds to the *Product 3* of Fig. 5.

Figure 6 shows the component instantiation together with (a part) of the adaptation (glue) code needed for making the contexts.

This code ensembles can be instantiated by selecting the possibilities seen in the previous section. As we can see, both instantiations (or contexts) select the OVM approach as input for the variability model. In this case, the implementation of the parser for OVM primitives is part of the commonalities of the framework (SPL), so it is already implemented. Similarly, we have implemented the following types of variabilities:

– **Mandatory variation point:** determining the selection of a variant service when the variation point is included.
– **Optional variation point:** specifying that zero or more variant services, associated to the variation point, can be selected.
– **Alternative variation point:** defining that only one variant service, of the set of associated variants of the variation point, must be selected (XOR relation).
– **Variant variation point:** defining that at least one variant service, of the set of associated variants of the variation point, must be selected (OR relation).

---

[11] http://expressjs.com.
[12] https://www.mongodb.com.

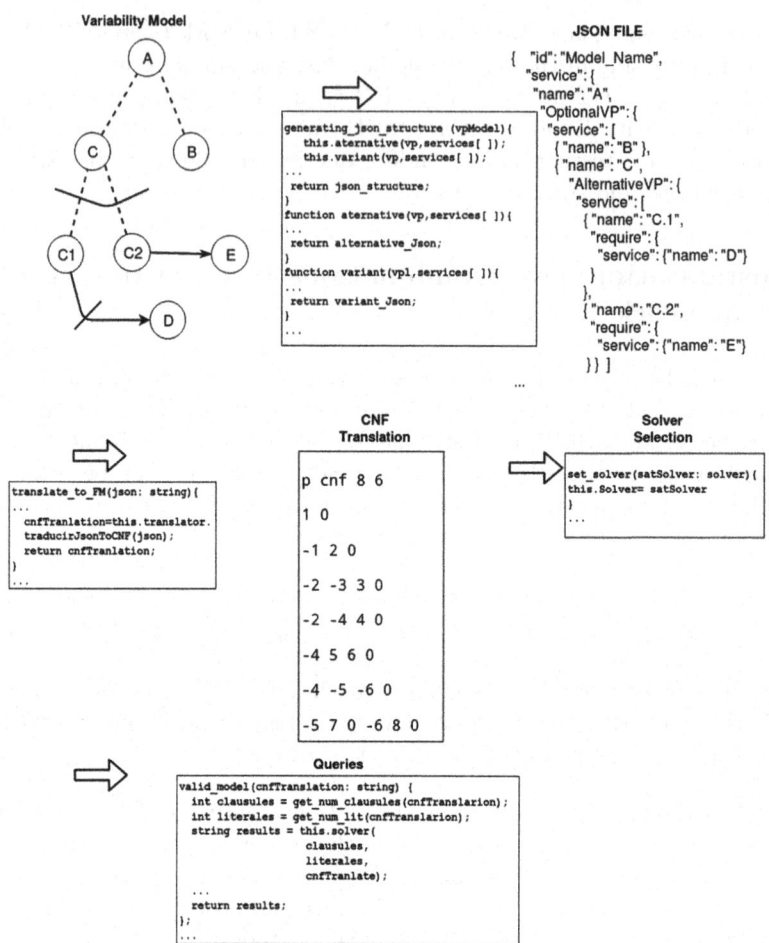

Fig. 6. Instantiating the framework according to context 1

- **Requires:** specifying a relation between two variant services, independent from the variation points the variants are associated with, in which the selection of one variant service requires the selection of the other.
- **Excludes:** which is the opposite of the requires dependency specifying the exclusion of a variant when another one is selected.

For other cases, the parser must be implemented by the developer team because the input format of the variability models can be really different. So, we provide the final JSON format structure that must be obtained from the variability models. In the figure we can see a variability model example together with its corresponding JSON format, and the glue code for creating it. The JSON structure contains 7 services, 2 variant points (optional and alternative) and 2 restrictions (requires and excludes).

Then, the logic rules applied to the JSON variability files must be selected. In this case, for the first context we select the CNF translation, and in the second one, DL. These selections require the use of a SAT-solver and a DL reasoner respectively. For example, for context 1, the CNF document contains the code needed for analyzing the logic representation together with the connection of the SAT4j solver. In Fig. 6 we can see the glue code for the connection to a SAT solver. Finally, the two contexts define a different set of queries. As all of them are part of the commonalities, they are just selected as part of the final tools. Once these instantiations are finished, and the glue code is completed, we can build two different tools. As an example, in Fig. 7 we can see the user interface for the tool generated for the context 1.

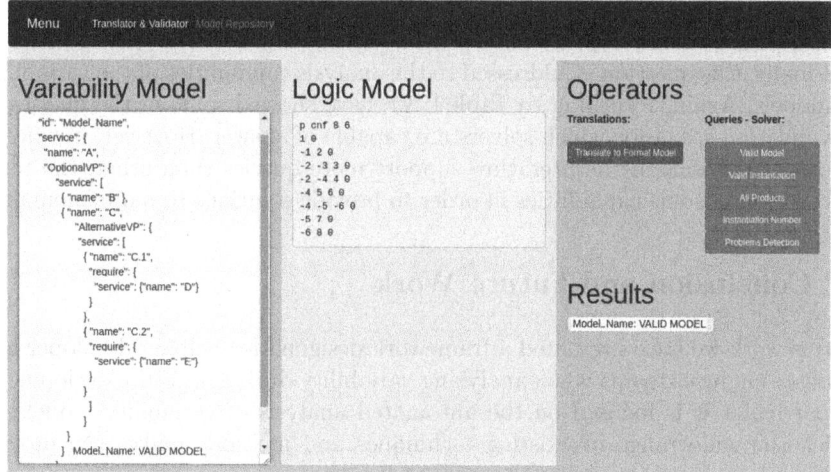

Fig. 7. Context 1 - Web tool

In this way, in this section we have showed a way in which the framework can be applied for deriving two products. These products respond to specific requirements of developers and software engineers according to the context in which they are working. Thus, the answers to the four questions defined in Sect. 2 must be analyzed as follows:

1. *Which variability modeling approach does the project use?*
   It is common that in every product line (PL) development, software engineers use some modeling tool, such as FeatureIDE[13] or VARMOD[14], in order to graphically design the variability of the PL. In this way, according to the variability approach, they must instantiate the framework to the modeling approach applied and generate (in the case the framework does not include the approach) the specific parser.

---

[13] http://www.featureide.com/.

[14] https://sse.uni-due.de/en/research/projects/varmod-prime/.

2. *Which logic model will be potentially applied?*

   The decision here must be supported on some different aspects. The first one is related to the reasoner capabilities that developers are wanting to obtain. That is, they must know that different logic languages generate a different set of responses or can identify a different set of anomalies, as we described in Table 1. Other aspects can be related to the knowledge of the developer team on a specific logic formalism due to the framework instantiation could require code inspection or adding/extending some methods.

3. *Which solver or reasoner is available and useful to be selected?*

   The response to this question is based on previous decisions because the logic translation will determine the set of reasoner developers could choose.

4. *Which anomalies or problems the team expects to find?*

   Finally, this question is addressed to the analysis capabilities of the variability models. Again, returning to Table 1, we have showed some of the queries or validation scenarios which solvers are capable of answer. However, in spite of some proposals in the literature support more queries than other, the team can extend some capabilities in order to provide solutions to more anomalies.

5 Conclusion and Future Work

In this work we have presented a framework designed for helping developer and software engineer teams when analyzing variability during an SPL development. In particular it is focused on the automated analysis of variability models, in which the wide range of existing techniques and methods makes the process really extensive and complex.

Our framework, which has been developed by following an SPL development approach, is aimed at facilitating composition of third-party products in order to build a tool o set of tools according to specific team's needs. To do so, in this work we have presented the SPL architecture proposed, the main components used to allow the adaptability, and the glue code needed for building different tools. At the same time, in addition to facilitate software engineer teams to create their own tools, the framework can be used to build/combine other tools in order to evaluate, under the same test conditions, the performance and correctness of the techniques or methods selected.

In this sense, as future work, we are instantiating the framework for building a set of tools aiming at evaluating the quality of the resulting composition. This evaluation, in addition to allow us to analyze the techniques that are more suitable for different contexts, will give us the possibility of assessing particular properties such as performance of the resulting composition, and adaptability/flexibility of our framework. The future work also includes an industrial validation of the application of this framework.

References

1. Bashroush, R., Garba, M., Rabiser, R., Groher, I., Botterweck, G.: Case tool support for variability management in software product lines. ACM Comput. Surv. **50**(1), 14:1–14:45 (2017). https://doi.org/10.1145/3034827
2. Benavides, D., Segura, S., Ruiz-Cortés, A.: Automated analysis of feature models 20 years later: a literature review. Inf. Syst. **35**(6), 615–636 (2010). https://doi.org/10.1016/j.is.2010.01.001
3. Bessling, S., Huhn, M.: Formal safety analysis and verification in the model driven development of a pacemaker product line. In: MBEES, pp. 133–144 (2012)
4. Braun, G., Pol'la, M., Buccella, A., Cecchi, L., Fillottrani, P., Cechich, A.: A DL semantics for reasoning over OVM-based variability models. In: Proceedings of the 30th International Workshop on Description Logics, vol. 1879, July 2017
5. Buccella, A., Cechich, A., Arias, M., Pol'la, M., del Socorro Doldan, M., Morsan, E.: Towards systematic software reuse of GIS: insights from a case study. Comput. Geosci. **54**, 9–20 (2013). http://www.sciencedirect.com/science/article/pii/S0098300412003913
6. Cuenca, G.B., Horrocks, I., Motik, B., Bijan, P., Patel-Schneider, P., Sattler, U.: OWL 2: the next step for OWL. Web Semant. **6**(4), 309–322 (2008)
7. Czarnecki, K., Eisenecker, U.W.: Generative Programming: Methods, Tools, and Applications. ACM Press/Addison-Wesley Publishing Co., New York (2000)
8. Czarnecki, K., Helsen, S., Eisenecker, U.W.: Formalizing cardinality-based feature models and their specialization. Softw. Process Improv. Pract. **10**(1), 7–29 (2005)
9. Czarnecki, K., Wasowski, A.: Feature diagrams and logics: There and back again. In: Proceedings of the 11th International Software Product Line Conference, SPLC 2007, pp. 23–34. IEEE Computer Society, Washington, DC, USA (2007). https://doi.org/10.1109/SPLC.2007.19
10. Das, N., Ripon, S., Hossain, O., Uddin, M.S.: Requirement analysis of product line based semantic web services. Lect. Notes Softw. Eng. **2**(3), 210 (2014)
11. Dobrica, L., Niemelä, E.: A UML-based variability specification for product line architecture views. In: Proceedings of the Third International Conference on Software and Data Technologies, ICSOFT, pp. 234–239, Porto, Portugal (2008)
12. Fan, S., Zhang, N.: Feature model based on description logics. In: Gabrys, B., Howlett, R.J., Jain, L.C. (eds.) KES 2006. LNCS (LNAI), vol. 4252, pp. 1144–1151. Springer, Heidelberg (2006). https://doi.org/10.1007/11893004_145
13. Frantz, F.R., Benavides Cuevas, D.F., Ruiz Cortés, A.: Automated analysis of orthogonal variability models using constraint programming. In: Xv Jornadas De Ingeniería Del Software Y Bases De Datos, 2010, Valencia, España (2010)
14. Haugen, O., Moller-Pedersen, B., Oldevik, J., Olsen, G.K., Svendsen, A.: Adding standardized variability to domain specific languages. In: 2008 12th International Software Product Line Conference, pp. 139–148, September 2008
15. Jackson, D.: Software Abstractions: Logic, Language, and Analysis. The MIT Press, Cambridge (2016)
16. Kang, K., Cohen, S., Hess, J., Nowak, W., Peterson, S.: Feature-oriented domain analysis (FODA) feasibility study. Technical report CMU/SEI-90-TR-21, Software Engineering Institute, Carnegie Mellon University Pittsburgh, PA (1990)
17. Kang, K., Kim, S., Lee, J., Kim, K., Kim, G.J., Shin, E.: FORM: a feature-oriented reuse method with domain-specific reference architectures. Ann. Softw. Eng. **5**, 143–168 (1998)

18. Kowal, M., Ananieva, S., Thüm, T.: Explaining anomalies in feature models. In: Proceedings of the 2016 ACM SIGPLAN International Conference on Generative Programming: Concepts and Experiences, GPCE 2016, pp. 132–143. ACM, New York, NY, USA (2016). https://doi.org/10.1145/2993236.2993248
19. Lauenroth, K., Pohl, K., Toehning, S.: Model checking of domain artifacts in product line engineering. In: 2009 IEEE/ACM International Conference on Automated Software Engineering, pp. 269–280, November 2009
20. von der Massen, T., H. Lichter, H.: Deficiencies in feature models. In: Mannisto, T., Bosch, J. (eds.) Workshop on Software Variability Management for Product Derivation - Towards Tool Support (2004)
21. Mazo, R., Munoz-Fernandez, J.C., Rincon, L., Salinesi, C., Tamura, G.: VariaMos: an extensible tool for engineering (dynamic) product lines. In: Proceedings of the 19th International Software Product Line Conference, pp. 374–379. ACM (2015)
22. Mendonca, M., Branco, M., Cowan, D.: S.P.L.O.T.: software product lines online tools. In: Proceedings of the 24th ACM SIGPLAN Conference Companion on Object Oriented Programming Systems Languages and Applications, OOPSLA 2009, pp. 761–762. ACM, New York, NY, USA (2009). https://doi.org/10.1145/1639950.1640002
23. Metzger, A., Pohl, K., Heymans, P., Schobbens, P.Y., Saval, G.: Disambiguating the documentation of variability in software product lines: a separation of concerns, formalization and automated analysis. In: 15th IEEE International Requirements Engineering Conference (RE 2007), pp. 243–253, October 2007
24. Nakajima, S.: Semi-automated diagnosis of foda feature diagram. In: Proceedings of the 2010 ACM Symposium on Applied Computing, SAC 2010, pp. 2191–2197. ACM, New York, NY, USA (2010). https://doi.org/10.1145/1774088.1774550
25. Noorian, M., Ensan, A., Bagheri, E., Boley, H., Biletskiy, Y.: Feature model debugging based on description logic reasoning. In: Proceedings of the 17th International Conference on Distributed Multimedia Systems, DMS 2011, 18–20 October 2011, Convitto della Calza, Florence, Italy, pp. 158–164 (2011)
26. Pereira, J.A., Constantino, K., Figueiredo, E.: A systematic literature review of software product line management tools. In: Schaefer, I., Stamelos, I. (eds.) ICSR 2015. LNCS, vol. 8919, pp. 73–89. Springer, Cham (2014). https://doi.org/10.1007/978-3-319-14130-5_6
27. Pohl, K., Böckle, G., van der Linden, F.J.: Software Product Line Engineering: Foundations, Principles and Techniques. Springer, Secaucus (2005)
28. Pol'la, M., Buccella, A., Arias, M., Cechich, A.: Sevatax: service taxonomy selection validation process for SPL development. In: 2015 34th International Conference of the Chilean Computer Science Society (SCCC), pp. 1–6, November 2015
29. Rincon, L., Giraldo, G., Mazo, R., Salinesi, C., Diaz, D.: Method to identify corrections of defects on product line models. Electron. Notes Theor. Comput. Sci. **314**, 61–81 (2015). http://www.sciencedirect.com/science/article/pii/S1571066115000286
30. Rincón, L., Giraldo, L., Mazo, R., Salinesi, C.: An ontological rule-based approach for analyzing dead and false optional features in feature models. Electron. Notes Theor. Comput. Sci. **302**, 111–132 (2014)
31. Ripon, S., Piash, M.M., Hossain, S.M.A., Uddin, M.S.: Semantic web based analysis of product line variant model. JCEE **6**(1), 1–6 (2014)
32. Roos-Frantz, F., Galindo, J.A., Benavides, D., Cortés, A.R., Garcıa-Galán, J.: Automated analysis of diverse variability models with tool support. In: Jornadas de Ingenierıa del Software y de Bases de Datos (JISBD 2014), Cádiz. Spain, p. 160 (2014)

33. Roos-Frantz, F., Galindo, J.A., Benavides, D., Ruiz-Cortés, A.: FaMa-OVM: a tool for the automated analysis of OVMs. In: Proceedings of the 16th International Software Product Line Conference, vol. 2, pp. 250–254. ACM (2012)
34. Rumpe, B., Robert, F.: Variability in UML language and semantics. Softw. Syst. Model. **10**(4), 439–440 (2011)
35. Ryssel, U., Ploennigs, J., Kabitzsch, K.: Reasoning of feature models from derived features. In: Proceedings of the 11th International Conference on Generative Programming and Component Engineering, GPCE 2012, ACM, New York, NY, USA (2012)
36. Segura, S., Benavides, D., Ruiz-CortÃ©s, A.: Fama test suite v1.2. Technical report ISA-10-TR-01, March 2010. http://www.isa.us.es/
37. Sinnema, M., Deelstra, S., Nijhuis, J., Bosch, J.: COVAMOF: a framework for modeling variability in software product families. In: Nord, R.L. (ed.) SPLC 2004. LNCS, vol. 3154, pp. 197–213. Springer, Heidelberg (2004). https://doi.org/10.1007/978-3-540-28630-1_12
38. Sirin, E., Parsia, B., Grau, B.C., Kalyanpur, A., Katz, Y.: Pellet: a practical OWL-DL reasoner. Web Semant. **5**(2), 51–53 (2007)
39. Sree-Kumar, A., Planas, E., Clariso, R.: Analysis of feature models using alloy: a survey. In: Proceedings 7th International Workshop on Formal Methods and Analysis in Software Product Line Engineering, FMSPLE@ETAPS 2016, Eindhoven, The Netherlands, 3 April 2016, pp. 46–60 (2016). https://doi.org/10.4204/EPTCS.206.5
40. Tsarkov, D., Horrocks, I.: FaCT++ description logic reasoner: system description. In: Furbach, U., Shankar, N. (eds.) IJCAR 2006. LNCS (LNAI), vol. 4130, pp. 292–297. Springer, Heidelberg (2006). https://doi.org/10.1007/11814771_26
41. Wang, H.H., Li, Y.F., Sun, J., Zhang, H., Pan, J.: Verifying feature models using OWL. Web Semant. **5**(2), 117–129 (2007)
42. Zaid, L., Kleinermann, F., Troyer, O.D.: Applying semantic web technology to feature modeling. In: Proceedings of the 2009 ACM Symposium on Applied Computing, SAC 2009. ACM, New York, NY, USA (2009)
43. Ziadi, T., Jézéquel, J.: Software product line engineering with the UML: deriving products. In: Käköla, T., Dueñas, J.C. (eds.) Software Product Lines: Research Issues in Engineering and Management, pp. 557–588. Springer, Heidelberg (2006)

SW Architecture of Clinical Decision Support Service in Prevention of Falls

SeungYoung Choi[1], Jeong Ah Kim[1(✉)], and InSook Cho[2]

[1] Catholic Kwandong University,
579 BeonGil 24, Gangneung, Gangwon-do 25601, South Korea
{boromi, clara}@cku.ac.kr
[2] Nursing Department, Inha University,
100 Inha-ro, Nam-gu, Incheon 22212, South Korea
Insook.cho@inha.ac.kr

Abstract. A clinical decision support (CDS) service reduces errors in health-care services and improves the quality and efficiency of healthcare by providing appropriate recommendations or alerts when needed. Owing to these advantages, the attempts to build a CDS service for each hospital, and for each ward in the hospital are increasing. In order to efficiently build multiple CDS systems, it is necessary to develop them into a CDS product line rather than a single CDS. That is, an architecture that can accommodate the variability of a CDS service to easily reflect the different requirements that need to be created. In this study, we designed an architecture that can support the building of a product line that addresses falls, which is the main management subject of each hospital, by applying an architecture-based design (ABD) technique. The applicability of the product line architecture was verified by additionally constructing CDS services to prevent falls in other hospitals based on the proposed architecture.

1 Introduction

A fall can occur with all inpatients. Patients and their caregivers' response is becoming a main source of mistrust of and dissatisfaction with healthcare institutions and health practitioners [1]. Most health practitioners perform a regular assessment with almost all patients every day or once to twice a week using a fall risk assessment tool. The number of published fall risk assessment tools alone is 19, and 72% of the healthcare institutions in Korea use the Morse Fall Scale (MFS), which accounts for 19% the Johns Hopkins Hospital's fall risk assessment tool, and the rest use their own developed or revised tools [2]. The prediction accuracy of these tools ranges from 31% to 75%, which shows a greatly varying degree depending on the health practitioner and the patient group, and despite their continued use, their fall occurrence prediction does not reach a satisfactory level [3]. Hence, instead of suggesting a particular tool, the American Nurses Association recommends an assessment method whose validity has been verified, reflecting each healthcare institution's patient characteristics and needs. As an alternative, electronic medical record (EMR) data can be used to predict fall occurrence, and most studies on this method reflect its logic by extracting knowledge through practical guidelines or establish a prediction model using a logistic regression

© Springer International Publishing AG, part of Springer Nature 2018
O. Gervasi et al. (Eds.): ICCSA 2018, LNCS 10963, pp. 452–463, 2018.
https://doi.org/10.1007/978-3-319-95171-3_35

analysis. This study developed a fall prediction model using EMR data and implemented it in a system, and architecture design was needed considering scalability in hospitals and with end users who are not information technology (IT) experts but nurses. Like other healthcare services, clinical decision support (CDS) for falls is an area where multiple healthcare institutions can provide similar services, and it is necessary to develop a product line instead of a single system. Software architecture is the key to developing a product line because a product line can characteristically scale up in a continued and flexible way. In addition, it should be able to not only accommodate a wide range of identified requirements but also have flexibility to include the requirements that have not been identified yet. To develop fall CDS services required for all healthcare institutions in a product line, this study applied the Architecture Based Design (ABD). This study designed and evaluated architecture for CDS services to predict fall occurrence in accordance with the ABD. Section 2 examines a method to determine architecture design, which serves as the basis of this study and describe the current context for care the patient in prevention of Fall; Sect. 3 define the quality drivers; Sect. 4 introduces designed architecture; and Sect. 5 presents architecture evaluation results and draws conclusions.

2   Background and Motivation

2.1   Architecture Based Design Method

The Architecture-Based Design (ABD) Method is a method for designing the software architecture of a product line of systems [4]. The input to the ABD method is a list of functional requirements, quality and business and constraints. The ABD method proceeds by recursively decomposing the system to be designed. There are three main concepts in the ABD model. The first one is decomposition of functions. The second concept is the realization of quality and business requirements through the choice of architectural style. The third one is the use of software templates to document the software architecture. The decomposition is examined from the perspective of three views: logical, concurrency, and deployment. The concrete requirements (functional, quality and business) are used to verify the decisions made during the decomposition [5]. The steps of the ABD method are follows [4, 5].

1. Identify architectural drivers.
2. Divide (encapsulate) functionality.
3. Choose architectural style.
4. Allocate functionality to style.
5. Refine templates.
6. Verify functionality.
7. Generate logical view
8. Generate concurrency view.
9. Generate deployment view.
10. Verify quality scenarios.
11. Verify Constraint scenarios.

2.2   Business Context

An inpatient fall is one of the most notable patient safety accidents and one of the most frequent adverse events experienced by health professionals, which can lead to an extended hospital stay, fractures, a stroke, and even death. Of the falls, 30% to 50% accompany damage, and 6% to 44% accompany fractures, subdural hemorrhage, and severe bleeding complications, which could result in death. As there are almost no published data or official statistics, it is difficult to precisely identify inpatient falls in Korea. Nevertheless, according to a couple of studies that examined EMR clinical data on highly frequent falls in nursing departments since 2010, neurology departments in the tertiary hospital reported 1.3 to 1.9 fall cases, and integrated care general wards reported 0.43 to 1.9 cases per 1,000 patient days [6]. Considering that the under-reported rates vary greatly depending on the health practitioner and the inconsistency of the reporters' criteria, however, the fall occurrence rate in Korea is estimated to be much higher than these aforementioned numbers. A variety of studies have been conducted to control falls.

Among the tools for which a prospective validity assessment was performed, a prospective validity assessment was conducted on only two tools (the Morse tool and the STRATIFY tool) in a practical environment different from the one in which it was developed. According to survey findings in Korea, nurses were most dissatisfied with the use of a fall risk assessment tool because practical sensitivity was low from 45% to 65% and the tool did not earn the trust of practitioners even though it was being used to examine all inpatients on a regular basis. In this research team's attempt to address this problem, we used patient data in EMRs and developed a fall prediction model. By testing the model, we confirmed its applicability to practice.

3   Architecture Requirements

3.1   Architecture Driver as Critical Quality Attributes

3.1.1   Usability
Usability is the ease of use and learnability of a system user who are non IT experts. System should guide the users to prevent the human errors in input and the operation of system should be easy.

3.1.2   Extensibility
Extensibility means that the implementation takes the growth in the future. System can be adopted after the pilot project in specific parts of the hospital. With the success data of pilot project, service evolution and service extension to the other parts can be considered. So, CDS service of fall should extensible since this service is hospital-wide services.

3.1.3   Modifiability
System should be modified to other hospitals operational context. Since CDS service of fall is not restricted into specific hospital. In other words, every hospital needs the management tools for prevention the fall. And almost hospital constructed EMR so

prevention model based on EMR can be applicable to these hospitals. Prevention model can be standardized so that this service must either initially support or be easily evolvable to a product-line framework.

3.1.4 Availability

A fall prediction model predicts the fall risk group via inferences based on the previous day's data of the patients stored in the EMR (Electronic Medical Records), and the results must be available for confirmation before nurses begin their daily tasks. Although predicted results are not produced in real time, EMR data must be accurately obtained at the appointed time. In addition, if the inferred result based on the prediction model is not created prior to the beginning of a shift, it may cause a fatal problem for the patient's care.

3.1.5 Safety

According to the information security policy of the hospital, it was impossible to access the system from the outside, and since it was a service that was applied only to a specific ward for a certain period, the server management of the hospital medical information room was not available. In some cases, the power may be turned off because the server is located in the nursing management room of the ward, and if the power is unstable during the time when the system needs to operate, it should be able to be checked by the nurse who comes to work. In addition, the execution of the fall prediction model should be made possible through an explicit command.

3.2 Architectural Constraints

According to the information security policy of the hospital, it was impossible to access the system from the outside, and since it was a service that was applied only to a specific ward for a certain period, it could not receive the server management of the hospital medical information room. Therefore, there is a need for a method that can easily identify the cause in the case of a system failure.

3.3 Use Case as Critical Functionality

We defined the abstract functional requirements for the CDS for prevention of falls and constructed these functional requirements into use cases shown in Fig. 1. Detail functionality is defined in Table 1.

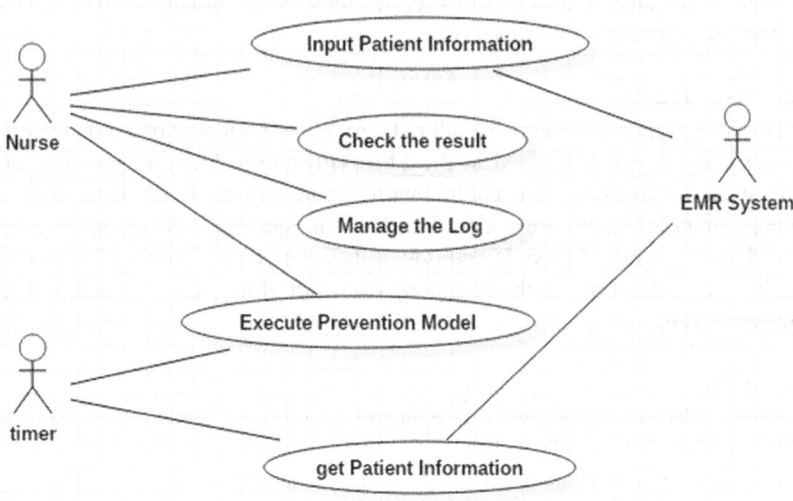

Fig. 1. Requirement model with use case diagram

Table 1. Functionalities of CDS for fall prevention

Functionality	Description
Input patient information	• Fall prevention CDS service should get the patient information • Store some parts of patient information into EMR and other part of patient information are specific to prevention model that are not the element of EMR
Check the result	• Display the prevention result • Display the high risk patient group
Manage the log	• System should track the status of daily system behaviors • System should keep the event log
Execute prevention model	• Every specific time, process the patient information with prevention model • If something is cliwrong, nurse can request the processing in manual to make the prevention result
Get patient information	• Every specific time, system get the patient information for processing

4   Architecture Design

We defined potential architectural options to meet each of quality attributes. Table 2 shows possible architectural mechanisms.

Table 2. Architectural options

Quality attributes	Architectural options
Usability	• Support for input validation check • Detail recommendation for intervention • Apply similar User experience model of legacy EMR system
Extendibility	• Client/Server model
Modifiability	• Layered Architecture • Data mapper pattern to define the mapping rule between the data defined standard prevention model and EMR data model
Availability	• Event Driven architecture pattern • Push/pull messaging pattern • Support manual processing
Safety	• Encryption of patient information so that patient can be identifiable
Constraint	• Client/Server model with light client interface

4.1   Client/Server Model and Layered Architecture as Architecture Style

Client should have simple, easy, light user interface and server should manage the data and access to the EMR for knowledge processing. In this research, we applied C/S model as architecture style. Also, we applied layered style since easy layer can be independent so that it is easy for evolution. Our suggested architecture based on the architecture style is shown in Fig. 2 and detail responsibilities of each layer are defined in Table 3.

4.2   Logical View

The logical model expresses the components as a logical constitutional unit required to satisfy the functional and non-functional requirements of the product line and the relationship between them [7]. Logical means that the platform implementation environment or technology is not considered. The logical architecture of the fall prevention CDS is shown in Fig. 3. Four core components are defined. The inference component of the prediction model is constructed by the definition of Netica's Bayesian network model. We defined a daemon component that contains an agent to obtain the necessary information from the EMR at the appointed time. Among the quality attributes of the architecture, the core component that implements modifiability and extendibility is the data handler component. In this study, we use a strategy to predict the likelihood of falls by extracting patient information from the hospital's EMR for fall prevention. To predict the likelihood of a fall, the fall prediction model can be regarded as a

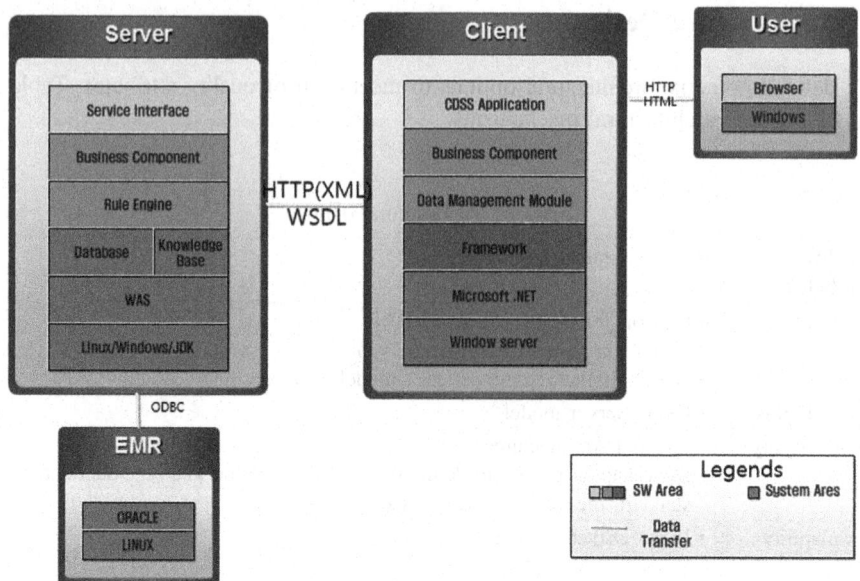

Fig. 2. Client/Server and layered architecture

Table 3. Responsibilities of component in layered architecture

C/S pattern	Component	Responsibility
Server	Service interface	• Manage the CDS service
	Business component	• Manage CDS database • Execute the knowledge engine • Manage the log • Handle the exception
	Knowledge engine	• Execute the knowledge
	Data access component	• Access the EMR data in specific period
	CDS case DB	• Manage the patient information • Manage the result the CDS service
	Knowledge base	• Manage the prevention knowledge mode of Falls
Client	CDS application (UI)	• User interaction interface
	Daemon process	• Send event to execute business component in specific time period
	Business component	• Manage the workflow • Manage the log • Handle the exception

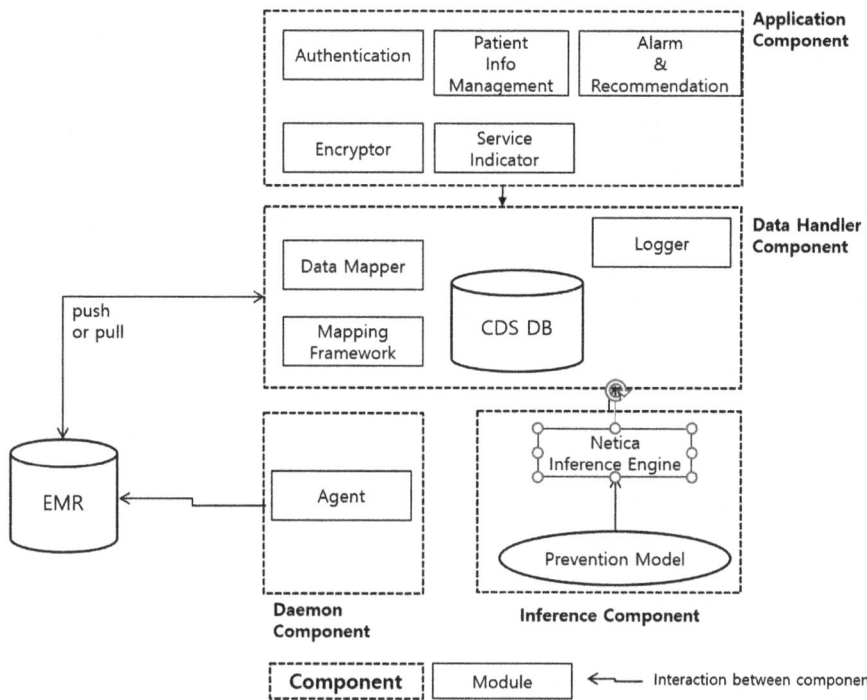

Fig. 3. Logical Architecture of CDS for prevention of fall

standardized model since it has been established based on a standard model that is a factor of various falls. In other words, the fall prediction model can evolve when implementing the fall prediction CDS service as a product line, but it is a model that can be commonly applied to each hospital. However, the way the hospital stores patient information could vary according to the database design strategy when the hospital implements the EMR. If the model that expresses knowledge is defined according to the EMR data structure of each hospital, knowledge and knowledge processing results, which are the core of fall prediction CDS, become variable elements, and new CDS services will be required for each hospital. In order to solve this problem, knowledge is based on the standard model, and the data handler component was designed by applying the mapping pattern connected to the data elements of the standard model by analyzing the EMR data structure of each hospital. The data mapper module contains the mapping information of the standard knowledge and the EMR data structure of each hospital. The mapping framework defines the various calculation functions that are required in the mapping process. For example, we define a concat() function that connects two EMR data elements to create the elements of a standard knowledge model, and a Max() function that generates a value based on a standard knowledge model by finding the maximum EMR element value. The application component defines the modules, such as user rights management for creating a CDS service: the authentication module for managing patient information input (Patient Info

Management), security processing for patient information (Encryptor), and CDS service quality management (Service Indicator).

4.3 Deployment View

A deployment architecture is a model that shows how components are allocated to physical hardware nodes [7]. In this study, we deployed resources to the hardware nodes that thoroughly provide the resources required by the components. The components were deployed according to the C/S(Client/Server) model, which is the selected architecture style (Fig. 4).

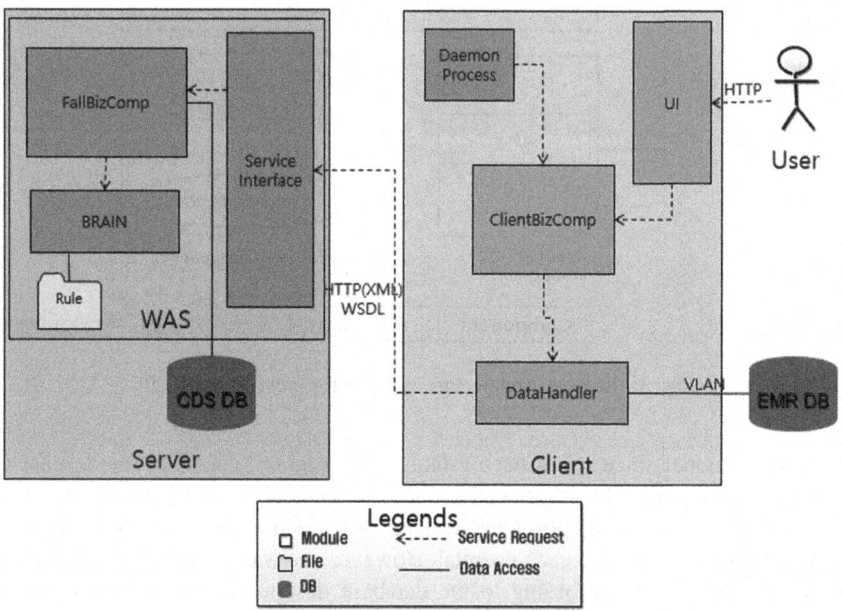

Fig. 4. Deployment architecture

5   Evaluation and Future Directions

5.1   Process Improvement

Introducing the EMR-based fall prediction model allowed us to improve the existing work process (Fig. 5) into that shown in Fig. 6.

Previously, nurses applied the stratify strategy to identify the possibility of a patient's fall, selected a high-risk group, and then provided special care. However, after reflecting on the system proposed by this study, special care became available by inputting information necessary for the EMR and periodically receiving information on high-risk groups from the prediction model after applying the EMR data. As a result of comparing the number of fall events between the control group that prevented falls with a basic method and the experimental group that applied the EMR-based CDS proposed

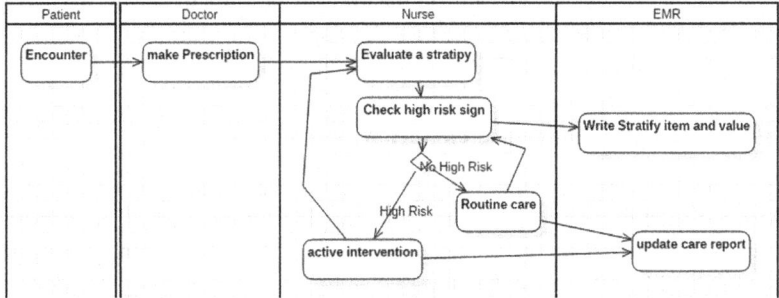

Fig. 5. Process model in current patient care context

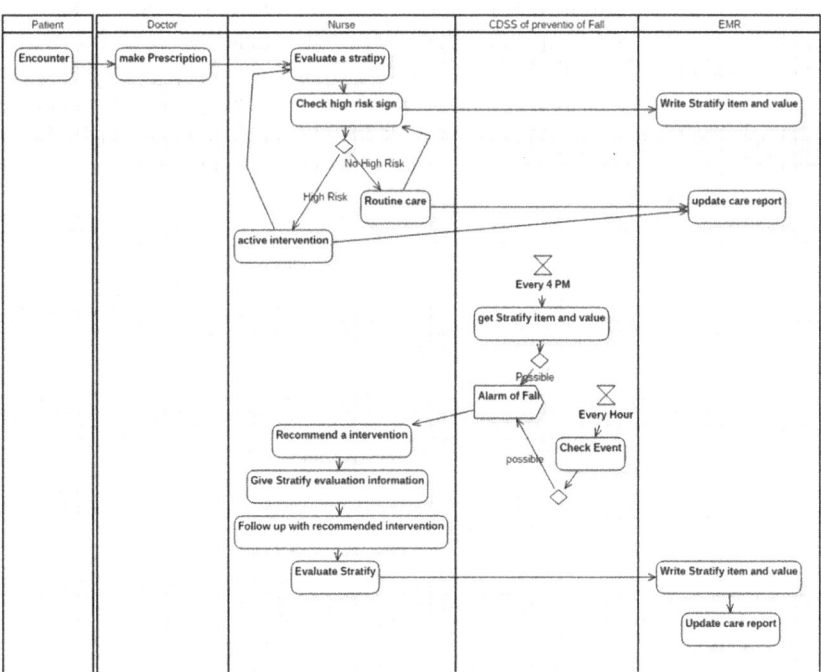

Fig. 6. New Process model with CDS for prevention of falls

in this study, the number in the experimental group was reduced by 19 people. The experimental period was approximately four months. After four months of trial implementation, the effects were verified and extended to all patients in the ward.

In this study, the architecture of a fall prediction CDS service was proposed because a fall prediction CDS service based on EMR is considered to be a service field that is likely to spread to various hospitals. The key to this architecture is the ability to reuse core service modules by applying a mechanism to standardize knowledge, and to transform the data elements applicable to the knowledge from the EMR. To verify this, we examined the possibility of installing the software in other university hospitals considering the introduction of CDS services to prevent falls.

5.2   Evaluation of Architecture Quality Attribute

As a result of analyzing the fall nursing guidelines as well as the nursing record data of the EMR operated by the new hospital, the mapping information of the data mapper should be redefined and the implementation of the Patient Info Management module should be changed according to the proposed architecture of this study. In addition, it is necessary to identify the areas where a refinement of the prediction model is possible, for modifying the prediction model. Given that the data mapper module and the mapping framework have been established considering that the structure of the EMR of each hospital may be different when establishing the architecture, it is necessary to redefine the mapping information to convert the EMR data into standard knowledge data. In addition, there is the possibility that the users of each hospital may require a new configuration of the UI for inputting patient information, which is possible through the implementation of the Patient Info Management module. This variability is a product-specific requirement that can occur at each hospital, and if it can be modified without affecting other modules, the scalability and stability of the product line architecture can be judged to be satisfactory (Fig. 7).

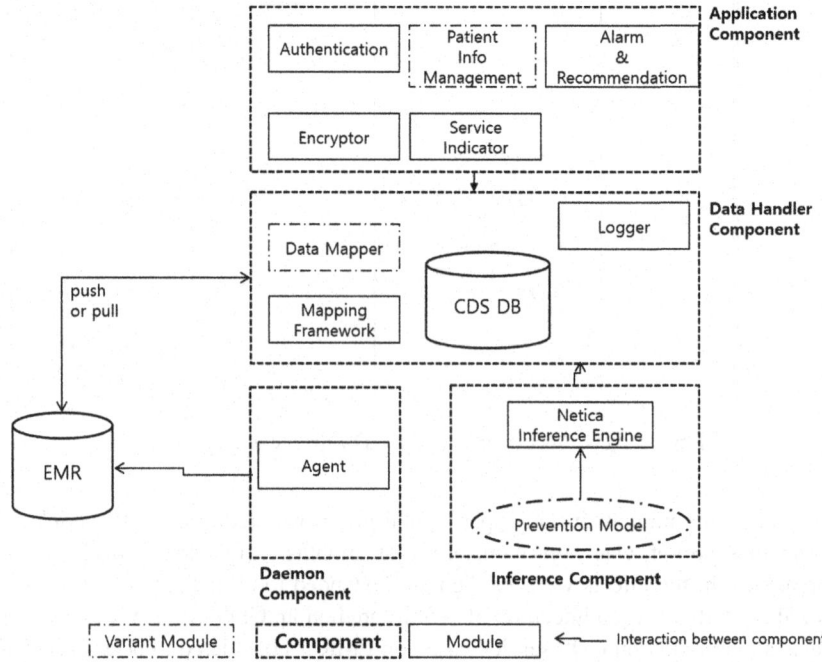

Fig. 7. Refined Logical Architecture for new hospital

5.3   Future Directions

In this study, a design method based on the architecture is applied to construct an EMR-based CDS service as a product line. We set up a product line by establishing a design strategy based on an architecture driver while reflecting on the architecture. In this process, it was possible to establish a basis for creating a product that satisfies new requirements from the product line by identifying a variable module and applying a mechanism for handling variability. This study applied a reactive-type approach that introduced the possibility of establishing an architecture during the design process by examining the possibility of the product line during the process of meeting the requirements of a hospital. Given that we have identified the possibility of a product line, we need to perform domain analysis to analyze the requirements of many hospitals. As a result of the domain analysis, it is necessary to clearly define the variability and commonality of the feature model, which is the core model of the product line, and to refine the architecture based on the feature model.

Acknowledgement. This study was supported by a grant of the Korea Healthcare Technology R&D Project, Ministry for Health, Welfare & Family Affairs, Republic of Korea (No. HI17C0807).

References

1. National Center for Injury Prevention and Control: Falls among Older Adults: An Overview. http://www.cdc.gov/ncipc/factsheets/adultfalls.htm
2. Hee, C.E., Suk, K.M., Suk, Y.C., Kyoung, K.M.: Characteristics of fall events and fall risk factors among inpatients in general hospitals in Korea. J. Korean Clin. Nurs. Res. **23**(3), 350–360 (2017)
3. Degelau, J., Belz, M., Bungum, L., Flavin, P.L., Harper, C., Leys, K., Lundquist, L., Webb, B.: Prevention of Falls (Acute Care) (2012). https://www.icsi.org/guideline. Accessed Mar 2016
4. Bachmann, F., Bass, L., Chastek, G., Donohoe, P., Peruzzi, F.: The Architecture Based Design Method. CMU/SEI-2000-TR-001 (2000)
5. Bachmann, F., Bass, L., Klein, M.H.: An Application of the Architecture-Based Design Method to the Electronic House. CMU/SEI-2000-SR-009 (2000)
6. Cho, I., Boo, E.H., Lee, S.Y., Dykes, P.C.: Automatic population of electronic inpatient fall prevention process and outcome measures using data that are routinely generated and used in EHR systems. J. Am. Med. Inf. (2017, in review)
7. Chaudhary, A., Verma, B.K., Raheja, J.L.: Product line development architectural model. In: Proceedings of the 3rd IEEE International Conference on Computer Science and Information Technology, China, 9–11 July 2010, pp. 749–753 (2010)

Learning User Preferences for Recommender System Using YouTube Videos Tags

Sunita Tiwari[✉], Abhishek Jain, Prakhar Kothari, Rahul Upadhyay,
and Kanishth Singh

G B Pant Government Engineering College, Delhi, India
Sunita.tiwari@gbpec.edu.in,
abhishekjain.vs@gmail.com, prakharkothari@gmail.com,
rahul97164@gmail.com, kanishth30@gmail.com

Abstract. Recommender systems have become essential in several domains to deal with the problem of information overload. Collaborative filtering is one of the most popularly used paradigm of recommender systems for over a decade. The personalized recommender systems use past preference history of the users to make future recommendations for them. The cold start problem of recommender system concerns with the personalized recommendation to the users having no or few past history. In this work we propose an approach to learn implicit user preferences by making use of YouTube Video Tags. The profile of a new user is created from his/her preferences in watching the YouTube videos. This profile is generic and may be used for a wide variety of domains of recommender systems. In this work we have used it for a biography recommender system. However this may be used for several other types of recommender system.

Keywords: User profile discovery · Cold start problem · Tagging
Personalization · Implicit ratings · Collaborative filtering

1 Introduction

In this era of exponentially rising availability of content on internet the problem of filtering the contents of our requirement is becoming more complex. This problem can be fixed by making use of recommender system applications [1, 2]. There are several paradigms for recommender systems but collaborative filtering is most popularly used method [3]. The most prevalent research challenge for recommender system is cold start problem. The situation in which the recommender system does not perform efficiently and effectively due to the non-availability of preference data provided by the user is called cold start problem [4]. The system may perform quite well for warm users but it may fail miserably for new users because the system knows a very little or nothing about these users in terms of their liking and preferences. The solution to this problem is to effectively profile new user.

Providing the solution to the cold start problem is fundamental requirement for the success of a collaborative filtering recommender system. Bad quality recommendation may affect the business severely as the disappointed user may turn up to other market

© Springer International Publishing AG, part of Springer Nature 2018
O. Gervasi et al. (Eds.): ICCSA 2018, LNCS 10963, pp. 464–473, 2018.
https://doi.org/10.1007/978-3-319-95171-3_36

players in the same domain. This problem becomes even grave in case of new recommender system as the user database is small. In some of the work in past, demographic features of user are used to infer their preference but it tends to be stereotypical because it assumes that all the users belonging to certain demographic group have similar taste and preferences. Another natural solution to the problem of cold start is to find the preferences of user implicitly instead of bothering them by querying about their likings and preferences about a specific item and service being offered. Majorly it's been seen that users themselves are not very clear about what they want and what they don't want, so using their implicit liked choices, one can get a good idea about users' preferred interests. Therefore in this work we have proposed a novel approach to learn implicit user preferences from their liked videos and subscriptions on YouTube. This preference learning may be done using other social networks like twitter, Facebook and so on and so forth. However, in this work we solely focus on learning preferences from the YouTube video preferences. We preferred YouTube for this purpose because according to Infographic report YouTube is second largest search engine in witch 100 h of videos are being uploaded every minute and one out of every two internet users are on YouTube. It has around 3 billion searches per month and 1 billion unique visitors per month [17].

The immensely popular, video content driven application YouTube [16] is enriched with huge user base and database, through which people learn, research, explore. In this work we aim to make use of this opportunity and exploit the huge data set in order to create a library which provides the user a facility to categorize their interests in several clusters depending on the data they provide. For that purpose we have used YouTube videos' tags to classify them into different clusters where each cluster signifies an aspect of the user's persona. Now, based on the user's liked or disliked choices we can classify them among these categorized clusters, thus obtaining a view about their interests and tastes regarding various domains. They can further use this library as a component to their recommender systems. The underlying assumption in this work is that the user is willing to share the liked and subscribed histories of their YouTube profile. This approach may be applied on other video streaming applications other than YouTube.

The rest of the paper is organized as follows. Section 2 discusses the related work and the proposed work is introduced in Sect. 3. Implementations and results are presented in Sect. 4 and discussion of the proposed approach is given in Sect. 5. Finally Sect. 6 concludes and present the future directions.

2 Related Work

A lot of research work can be found in literature related to collaborative filtering based recommender systems [1, 2, 13, 14]. There has been a lot of work to solve the problem of cold start but most of those solutions were problem specific. Some of the work which addresses this problem by mining the implicit user preferences is presented here.

Various data mining and machine learning techniques can be used for inferring the user preferences automatically. A tag-based social interest discovery approach is proposed in [7] Li et al. in year 2008. It is justified that user-generated tags are effective to represent user interests because these tags reflect human being's judgments while more concise and closer to human understanding. So the consensus among users for the content of a given web page can be reached more likely via tags than via keywords. Gemmell et al. [5] proposed an approach for personalization using folksonomies. The proposed personalization technique results in improved performance while all clustering techniques showed improvements; they did so with varying degrees. Zenebe et al. [15] in year 2010 proposed an approach to predict user preferences with uncertainty. Also they have considered visualization of item features, user feedback for discovered preferences and improve the interpretation of the discovered knowledge. Mokbel et al. [9] in year 2011 proposed an approach that takes user preferences and context into account to answer user queries. They mostly have adapted existing commercially successful recommendation techniques to consider the spatial aspects of users and/or items when making its decisions. Liu et al. [8] in year 2013, proposed the recommendation model that is based on implicit feedback taken from user check-in count data for modeling user preferences. Safoury et al. [10] in year 2013 proposed an approach to exploit the demographic features to solve the cold start problem in recommender system.

One major contribution in the field of implicit user preference discovery for recommender system was by Berjani and Strufe in year 2011 [3]. In the proposed work, the check-in frequency of users on an online location based social network for a particular spot is used for inferring the user implicit rating or preference for that spot. The authors had exploited the concept of matrix factorization technique for generating the recommendations of spots. In [11, 12], the authors proposed the approach to infer the interest of a user in a tourist spot by mining the GPS logs of individual users in year 2015 and 2017 respectively. These implicit preferences are used as rating and the genetic algorithm based approach was proposed to evolve the ratings of unvisited tourist spots.

In contrast to those existing works this paper presents a generic approach to solve the problem of cold start. We reviewed the literature from the perspective of implicit user preference discovery.

3 Proposed System Design

In this paper we propose to build a user preference learning system which has a set of clusters or categorized data that defines the user's personality and profile. We aim to use the YouTube videos' content for initial clustering and classification. This paper doesn't focus on any specific domain for personalized recommendations.

A schematic process through module to module starting from the fetching of raw data from YouTube to the final end result i.e. the obtaining of user's preferences and interests is proposed in the block diagram presented in Fig. 1.

The inputs to the proposed system are the YouTube are the user's YouTube credentials to fetch the user's 'authorized data' and output of the proposed system is the user profile which may further be used by the recommender system.

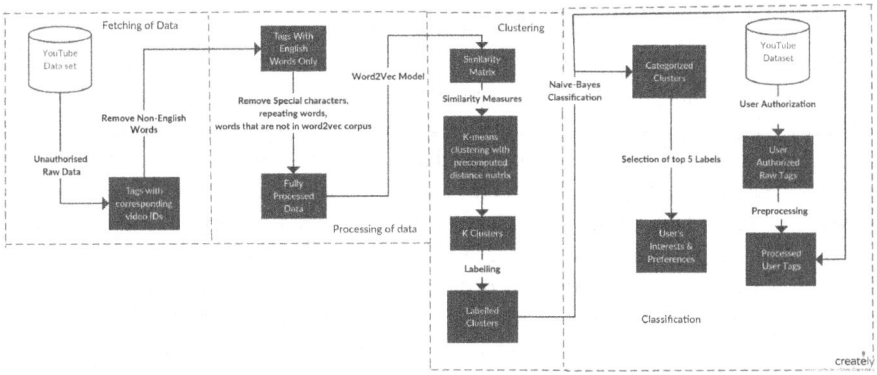

Fig. 1. The Block Diagram of Proposed System

The proposed system consists of four modules namely (1) the data fetching module (2) the pre-processing module (3) the clustering & labeling module (4) classification module. All these modules are discussed further in forthcoming subsections.

3.1 Data Fetching Module

In order to retrieve the user's information the YouTube Data API is used through which the ids of the videos along with the associated tags are fetched. The data on YouTube is of two types, one is called authorized data and other is called unauthorized data. For user's personalized data like his/her liked videos we require user's authorization to access it and is called "Authorized Data". The access to video data that does not require any authorization of a user/individual i.e. it is not someone's personal data is called "Unauthorized data".

For the purpose of getting the initial data without any real user involvement "Unauthorized data" is used where the most popular videos that were trending were fetched. From the fetched data of videos, the corresponding "tags" and the "video id" are filtered away for use. The YouTube data API [16] allows one to use the functions executed on YouTube website in their own application. A resource here is a video, a playlist or a subscription. These resources are represented as JSON objects [6]. The further details about the API usage may be found in [16].

3.2 Pre-processing Module

The tags collected are now pre-processed and filtered before going on to the clustering procedure. In the pre-processing and preparation of data, the stop words, and words or writings that do not belong to the English language are removed. For the preprocessing the "nltk corpus" is used. The result of this step is a Tag cloud.

3.3 Clustering and Labeling Module

The filtered and prepared data set is then used to create a similarity matrix. The matrix consists of each and every word's semantic similarity measure with another. The similarity measure used here is obtained using word2vec model which generates word embedding, based on which a cosine similarity score between −1 and 1 is obtained, where 1 meaning that the two words are same, 0 meaning no relation and −1 meaning opposite relation. This model (word2vec) was first trained on Google News dataset.

The clustering of the tags is done by using the "K-means clustering algorithm". Here instead of using the Euclidean distance measure for generating the clusters we have used the pre-computed similarity matrix as mentioned above.

After the clusters are created, we have computed the similarity matrix of every data point within a cluster corresponding to each pre-decided label. Using this similarity matrix suitable labels are assigned to the appropriate clusters.

3.4 Classification Module

Now that the clusters have been created and labelled, we have trained the Naïve Bayes classifier model over this labelled data. Now, user's authenticated data i.e. his/her liked videos and subscribed channels are fetched from YouTube and classified among the labelled clusters using this model. After this profile of a user is generated describing their top interests and preferences.

4 Implementation and Results

For implementation we have used Python language. We have also used some libraries to help us in the implementation which are as followed:

  i. Nltk
 ii. Sklearn
iii. Gensim
 iv. Numpy
  v. Pandas
 vi. Flask
vii. Google Oauth2

As discussed in previous section, the data is initially fetched by using the YouTube API. The sample raw data is shown in Fig. 2. The videos, the ones from which this data is fetched, are the most popular videos or the trending videos at the time of fetching on YouTube. The data for 800 videos is fetched for experimentation and around 150000 tags retrieved from these 800 videos which were then filtered up to 7,800 after preprocessing as stop words, non-English, and repeating words were removed. The pre-processed data is shown in Fig. 3.

Word2vec is a tool that uses neural networks to generate word embedding. Word embedding is a name for technique where textual data is mapped into numerical vectored data, to make them suitable for machine learning operations.

Fig. 2. Sample Raw Data

Fig. 3. Pre-processed Data

Using this vectored space, each unique word in textual corpus is assigned a corresponding vector depending on the no. of dimensions or features used. E.g.: The word "technology" after being assigned a vector with 300 dimensions would be stored as shown in Fig. 4.

The filtered and prepared data set is then used to create a similarity matrix. The matrix consists of each and every word's semantic similarity measure with another.

```
In [14]: news2vec.wv.__getitem__('technology')

Out[14]: array([ 3.18290979e-02, -1.24364467e-02, -1.85911953e-01, -2.64822185e-01,
         1.97089277e-02,  5.11786103e-01,  1.77844405e-01, -1.37933239e-01,
        -2.23546624e-02, -1.72908083e-01,  1.06261581e-01, -4.39896762e-01,
         2.40704820e-01,  2.86502063e-01,  4.04500626e-02, -2.82133639e-01,
         3.01623680e-02,  2.17293501e-01, -1.19001539e-02,  7.40949437e-02,
         9.95372385e-02,  1.07001938e-01,  3.85070324e-01, -3.04377936e-02,
        -3.27255547e-01, -2.38424875e-02,  3.44804674e-03,  6.26770109e-02,
        -5.12914658e-02,  1.97760403e-01, -8.94539133e-02,  7.42618144e-02,
         1.17952704e-01,  2.41865411e-01, -1.34876952e-01, -1.27154961e-01,
        -4.64513958e-01, -1.27785876e-01, -3.47370729e-02,  2.50812974e-02,
         3.70160379e-02,  3.15545410e-01,  2.63903826e-01,  1.60237774e-01,
         5.67051768e-01,  1.44173400e-02, -9.03099701e-02, -3.65018308e-01,
         2.35130757e-01, -1.55579135e-01, -1.74227387e-01, -1.22993663e-01,
         3.67539495e-01, -1.16175795e-02,  9.07559767e-02,  9.80123729e-02,
        -3.62288684e-01, -6.49903193e-02,  8.18219781e-03,  7.04779676e-03,
         3.76310423e-02,  2.10140407e-01, -9.58141387e-02,  2.41816401e-01,
         1.69773206e-01,  4.25136000e-01,  1.22332394e-01,  1.86507136e-01,
         1.59956694e-01, -3.44094962e-01, -1.78879708e-01, -1.42575145e-01,
         5.39974868e-02, -9.79766771e-02, -1.18147522e-01,  3.80927801e-01,
         1.43402204e-01, -1.11075677e-01, -3.50511163e-01, -1.37125343e-01,
         4.68641669e-01,  1.70431122e-01,  5.33809423e-01, -1.07050337e-01,
        -1.51927322e-01, -8.22292790e-02,  7.31780753e-02,  5.84128462e-02,
         5.07920980e-02,  2.76488781e-01,  9.84590670e-02, -4.93274666e-02,
         2.38036122e-02,  1.27897024e-01, -5.19289114e-02,  8.01878050e-02,
         6.26744702e-02,  3.11339438e-01, -2.32760489e-01,  5.66904426e-01,
         4.24939059e-02, -1.75731152e-01,  2.15587094e-01,  1.10290833e-01,
        -5.27807474e-01, -4.23873842e-01,  2.06909701e-01, -1.43060818e-01,
        -1.24906689e-01, -4.49830145e-02,  1.52721718e-01,  1.10532884e-01,
         1.03975303e-01, -7.10172430e-02,  3.13964069e-01, -1.00359939e-01,
         2.73404986e-01,  4.57213938e-01, -3.06430131e-01, -6.99002221e-02,
         1.43645138e-01,  2.43315790e-02, -1.28993362e-01,  2.98975203e-02,
        -4.57285672e-01,  1.24628536e-01,  1.35427892e-01, -3.34520966e-01,
        -5.63116930e-02, -1.36416852e-01,  1.39762890e-02, -6.25101626e-02,
        -2.53574662e-01,  2.95717835e-01,  2.57861853e-01, -3.70692074e-01,
```

Fig. 4. The sample vector representation of the word 'technology'

		0	1	2	3	4	5	6	7	8	9
		0	1	2	3	4	5	6	7	8	9
0	*	Tom	wow	surfer	fs	exes	Lies	touchdown	great	McEwan
1	Tom	1	0.300225	0.117794	0.248202	0.312353	0.215387	0.260617	0.112987	0.292851
2	wow	0.300225	1	0.354902	0.595504	0.624967	0.450667	0.282326	0.408921	0.432472
3	surfer	0.117794	0.354902	1	0.58775	0.462008	0.44581	0.227343	0.205935	0.495623
4	fs	0.248202	0.595504	0.58775	1	0.704591	0.564253	0.411515	0.281644	0.647954
5	exes	0.312353	0.624967	0.462008	0.704591	1	0.58996	0.36685	0.36859	0.687756
6	Lies	0.215387	0.450667	0.44581	0.564253	0.58996	1	0.286586	0.197718	0.587518
7	touchdown	0.260617	0.282326	0.227343	0.411515	0.36685	0.286586	1	0.224905	0.345527
8	great	0.112987	0.408921	0.205935	0.281644	0.36859	0.197718	0.224905	1	0.270149
9	McEwan	0.292851	0.432472	0.495623	0.647954	0.687756	0.587518	0.345527	0.270149	1
10	Peter	0.31476	0.181994	0.138213	0.254832	0.302728	0.268726	0.17306	0.131474	0.369271

Fig. 5. Sample Proposed Similarity Matrix

The similarity measure used here is cosine similarity which is obtained using word2vec model as mentioned above. The sample similarity matrix is shown in Fig. 5. This similarity matrix is further used in K-Means clustering.

After following the proposed approach, we have arrived at results containing user's interests and preferences based on classification of their data among labeled clusters of sample data fetched with the help of YouTube Data API and also the similarity measure as mentioned previously has been used effectively in the clustering as well as labeling process.

We did an intuitive search to find out the broader areas into which a user's personality can be categorized and defined, and these generic labels (which were found to be around Twenty) were then assigned to the clusters generated by K-Means Clustering Algorithm (where K = 20), which was performed over data containing around 7800 tags. This supervised data having 7800 tags with some label was then converted into input vectors which were used to train the Naïve Bayes classifier model. A total of nineteen different labels are identified namely biography, science, technology & gaming, poetry, fantasy and mythology, drama, food & fitness, horror, travel & events,

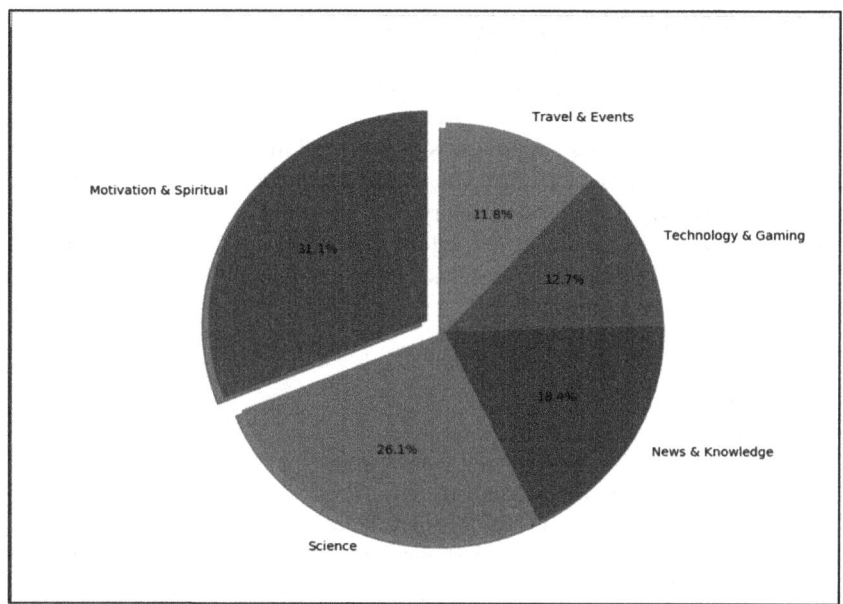

Fig. 6. Sample profile of a user

art & music, activism, news & knowledge, educational, finance & economy, sports, motivational & spiritual, politics, pets & animals, sci-fi, adventure & thriller. One of the sample profile of a new user is shown in Fig. 6.

The proposed approach is generic in nature and useful for any domain of recommender systems. We have specifically implemented it for a biography recommender system and the performance of the recommender system is satisfactory in terms of precision and recall. The precision of the recommender system is 93.7%. This precision is comparable to various existing approaches of recommender systems where explicit user preferences are available. However, the experiments for other domains of recommender system are the future goal.

5   Discussion

The user preference learning system was aimed to provide the foundations of a generic recommendation system by creating a profile of a user or individual with the help of data gained from YouTube videos that he/she liked or subscribed. The Naïve-Bayes classification method that we used to train the model and classify the data is found to be 75% accurate in its results. After doing a survey on 8–10 people by creating their profile with their interests using this system, the ratings for the accuracy provided by them was found to be around 80%. By observing the results achieved, it can be stated that the aim is accomplished and the system can be made more efficient.

6   Conclusion and Future Directions

The proposed work presents the method to find the implicit user preferences from the YouTube videos. This profile may be used to solve the cold start problem of recommender system. The proposed approach is generic and may be used with any recommender system. The accuracy of the biography recommender system implemented using the proposed approach is satisfactory.

In future we aim to evaluate the performance of this system using various performance metrics of recommender systems. We also aim to use the proposed approach in other domains of recommendation.

References

1. Adomavicius, G., Mobasher, B., Ricci, F., Tuzhilin, A.: Context-aware recommender systems. AI Magaz. **32**(3), 67–80 (2011)
2. Adomavicius, G., Tuzhilin, A.: Toward the next generation of recommender systems: a survey of the state-of-the-art and possible extensions. IEEE Trans. Knowl. Data Eng. (IEEE) **17**(6), 734–749 (2005)
3. Berjani, B., Strufe, T.: A recommendation system for spots in location-based online social networks. In: Proceedings of the 4th Workshop on Social Network Systems, vol. 4. ACM, Salzburg, Austria (2011)
4. Burke, R.: Hybrid recommender systems: survey and experiments. User Model. User-Adapt. Interact. **12**(4), 331–370 (2002)
5. Gemmell, J., Shepitsen, A., Mobasher, B., Burke, R.: Personalization in folksonomies based on tag clustering. Intell. Tech. Web Personalization Recommender Syst. **12** (2008)
6. JSON Objects. https://www.w3schools.com/js/js_json_objects.asp
7. Li, X., Guo, L., Zhao, Y.E.: Tag-based social interest discovery. In: Proceedings of the 17th International Conference on World Wide Web, pp. 675–684. ACM, April 2008
8. Liu, B., Fu, Y., Yao, Z., Xiong, H.: Learning geographical preferences for point-of-interest recommendation. In: Proceedings of the 19th ACM SIGKDD International Conference on Knowledge Discovery and Data Mining, pp. 1043–1051. ACM (2013)
9. Mokbel, M., Bao, J., Eldawy, A., Levandoski, J., Sarwat, M.: Personalization, socialization, and recommendations in location-based services 2.0. In: 5th International VLDB Workshop on Personalized Access, Profile Management and Context Awareness in Databases *(PersDB)*. VLDB. ACM, Seattle (2011)
10. Safoury, L., Salah, A.: Exploiting user demographic attributes for solving cold-start problem in recommender system. Lect. Notes Softw. Eng. **1**(3), 303 (2013)
11. Tiwari, S., Kaushik, S.: Modeling personalized recommendations of unvisited tourist places using genetic algorithms. In: Chu, W., Kikuchi, S., Bhalla, S. (eds.) DNIS 2015. LNCS, vol. 8999, pp. 264–276. Springer, Cham (2015). https://doi.org/10.1007/978-3-319-16313-0_20
12. Tiwari, S., Kaushik, S.: Evolving recommendations from past travel sequences using soft computing techniques. Int. J. Comput. Sci. Eng. **14**(3), 242–254 (2017)
13. Tiwari, S., Kaushik, S., Jagwani, P.: Location based recommender systems: Architecture, trends and research areas (2012)

14. Tiwari, S., Kaushik, S.: A non functional properties based web service recommender system. In: 2010 International Conference on Computational Intelligence and Software Engineering (CiSE), pp. 1–4. IEEE, December 2010

15. Zenebe, A., Zhou, L., Norcio, A.F.: User preferences discovery using fuzzy models. Fuzzy Sets Syst. **161**(23), 3044–3063 (2010)

16. Youtube Data API. https://developers.google.com/youtube/v3/

17. https://www.mushroomnetworks.com/infographics/youtube—the-2nd-largest-search-engine-infographic/

A Novel Methodology for Effective Requirements Elicitation and Modeling

Rajat Goel[1]([✉]), Mahesh Chandra Govil[2], and Girdhari Singh[1]

[1] Malaviya National Institute of Technology Jaipur, Jaipur, India
rajatgoel85@yahoo.co.in
[2] National Institute of Technology Sikkim, Ravangla, Sikkim, India
govilmc@gmail.com

Abstract. Undoubtedly, requirement engineering is one of the most crucial step in the development of any software upon which its success depends. In light of the increasing flow of sensitive information, attack attempts and numerous interactions with variety of users, developing a correct software specification is a challenge. Software implementation needs to be an exact translation of this specification. Correct specification ensures customer satisfaction. To obtain precise specification efficient modeling of requirements is beneficial. The methodology envisaged here follows an exhaustive approach to elicit requirements from all possible types of stakeholders to obtain the different constituent entities of the software, finding associations among them and finally modeling the requirements through novel diagrams. This modeling scheme scores over the prior methodologies in the order of information it represents. The methodology includes several good practices suggested by different researchers and can cater to any domain.

Keywords: Requirements · Elicitation · Specification

1 Introduction

Requirements Engineering is the first step in the Software Development Life Cycle (SDLC). It includes elicitation, analysis and specification of requirements. After this phase requirements specifications are obtained that clearly specify the requirements and act as the baseline for all the later phases of development. The success of the software depends on this. Correct specification and their adherence is must, failing which the resultant software product may not be as per the needs of the client leading to huge wastage of time, money and effort.

This paper proposes a novel methodology to elicit and model requirements efficiently that helps in reducing ambiguities in understanding the requirements between the client and the developers. This also ensures precise communication between the teams handling different phases in SDLC. In this paper, to explain the methodology, examples are cited from Smart Building System. The paper is divided into six sections. Sections 2 and 3 put into perspective the significance

© Springer International Publishing AG, part of Springer Nature 2018
O. Gervasi et al. (Eds.): ICCSA 2018, LNCS 10963, pp. 474–487, 2018.
https://doi.org/10.1007/978-3-319-95171-3_37

and issues pertaining to requirements engineering and modeling respectively. Section 4 throws light on the relevance of Smart Buildings in today's world, justifying its selection as a case study. In Sect. 5, the methodology is described in detail. Section 6 puts forward the conclusion.

2   Requirements Engineering

The success and acceptance of a project depends on the quality of requirements according to Kumari et al. [1], Kamata et al. [2] and Hernández et al. [3]. Requirements engineering is perhaps the most important step in developing a software but according to Shreyas [4], Futcher et al. [5] and Breu et al. [6], obtaining adequate, consistent and complete requirements is critical, ambiguous and difficult. A small mistake at this stage might result in rework, time and cost. According to Sabahat et al. [7], the best approach in capturing requirements is to elicit them correctly initially. However, according to Wäyrynen et al. [8] and Keith [9] it is not practical since requirements keep on changing. Chua et al. [10] too believes that getting requirements initially is beneficial but at the same time finds the process to be quite time-consuming. They write off use cases and prototyping for eliciting correct and complete requirements and list several problems in requirements with corresponding effects.

3   Modeling

Modeling is a significant activity of requirements engineering that deals with the development of abstract descriptions of requirements. In this regard, the choice of the modeling scheme is critical especially when stakeholders have divergent goals, different backgrounds and experience [11]. Modeling is more beneficial when systems are complex and large. The users or the client prefer diagrammatic representation than words [6]. Unified Modeling Language (UML) [12] is an implementation independent industry-standard graphical language to model, visualize, specify and construct the entities of the software. It is very expressive, easy to understand and use, supports diverse application areas. UML notation is well-known and acceptable [13].

However, researchers have argued the utility of the diagrams of UML. According to Woods [14] UML has limited building blocks. The diagrams don't provide much information but only relation between things. According to Konrad et al. [15] UML lacks formally defined and precise semantics. The constructs may prove inconsistent and choosing an appropriate construct is difficult. Moreover, the UML has informal semantics [13]. Dobing and Parsons [16], suggest that the UML has to be customized to fit within the context of a project. Glinz [17] has found nine deficiencies in UML. It is stated in [18] that use cases are not suitable for requirements specification.

4   Smart Buildings

This is an era of Internet of Things (IoT) [19]. It is the interconnection of various computing devices, used in everyday life, through internet facilitating them to exchange data. Physical objects are being developed and connected to the internet at a very fast rate. IoT finds it application in various facets of life like industries, health, transportation, home, buildings and cities. "A Smart Building is a building that is equipped with special structured wiring to enable occupants to remotely control or program an array of automated home electronic devices by entering a single command [20]." It makes maintenance and operations more efficient. It makes efficient use of energy and resources. In this research work, smart building has been chosen as a case study because it contains safety and security critical tasks to be taken care of. A smart building is very relevant in today's world when urban population is expected to increase rapidly and will be responsible for the consumption of world's energy and carbon dioxide emissions. Smart Buildings have unique characteristics. A large number of sensors provide input to the smart building system in great magnitude. These types of buildings have to continually adapt to the changing requirements of the inhabitants. Every kind of building is prone to some mishap or the other like earthquake, flood, fire, burglary etc. Any damage to a building can lead to severe loss of life and property. These situations demand installation of safety and security measures of the highest order. At the same time, the comfort of the residents is also important. There are many functionalities of the system like Security, Lighting, Fire Safety, and Heating, Ventilation and Air Conditioning.

5   Methodology

The proposed methodology is based on the entities of the software classified into assets, stakeholders and functionalities. It is a well-structured process that allows gathering of requirements through stories that may be in natural language keeping in mind the stakeholders with limited technical knowledge, extract entities from them exhaustively, refine entities, establish associations among entities and then modeling them efficiently through Story Conversion Diagrams (SCD). Within this research work, data items have been considered as assets. As per Pressman [21], a stakeholder is anyone in the organization that has a direct business interest in the software and will be rewarded for a successful outcome or criticized in case of failure. The potential stakeholders are the developers, client and the users. The client organization may consist of the senior management and members of different departments which will be catered to by the different functionalities of the system. Within the user community there may be several groups that will use different functionalities of the system and consequently the assets involved with them. A core group is set up consisting of the domain experts and senior developers. This group gives advice to the developers during the process of development. An iterative method is used as it is efficient in eliciting the requirements completely. The methodology is illustrated by Fig. 1.

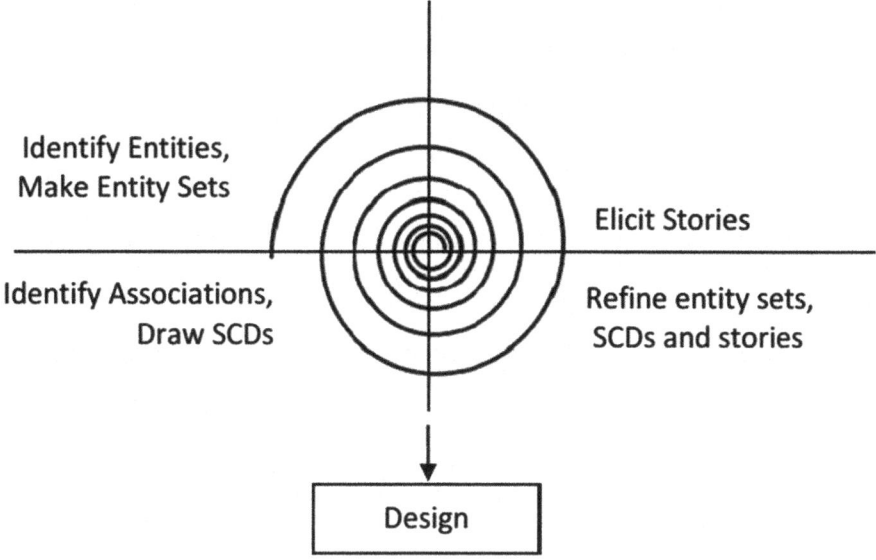

Fig. 1. Methodology

5.1   Identification

In the first quadrant stories are elicited from the client side and recorded by the development team. In the second quadrant the three kinds of entities- assets, stakeholders and functionalities are identified and put into entity sets A, S and F respectively. In the third quadrant, the associations among the entities are identified and based on those Story Conversion Diagrams (SCDs) are developed. Lastly, in the fourth quadrant the entity sets, the stories and the SCDs are refined. After each spiral the entities are incremented and added to the corresponding sets. A Story Conversion Diagram (SCD) diagram provides a pictorial representation of stories created to define the identified entities and associations among them. Diagrams are highly useful in understanding the system and help in effective design process. As a story is elicited, it is analyzed to find the entities as mentioned above and associations among them. In an SCD assets are denoted by rectangles and functionalities by ovals. Some example stories and corresponding SCDs are enlisted in Table 1. For each Story entities are identified and put in stakeholder set S, functionalities set F and asset set A. Figures 2, 3, 4 and 5 depict the SCDs for the stories 1 to 4 respectively. From the four example stories elicited, the stakeholder set S, functionality set F and asset set A are obtained given by Eqs. (1), (2) and (3) respectively.

$$S = \{Inhabitant, Burglar, Police, Building\,Manager, Resident, Entrant\} \tag{1}$$

$$F = \{Smart\,Authentication\,System, Smart\,Burglar\,Alarm\,System, \\ Smart\,Access\,Control\,System\} \tag{2}$$

$$A = \{Username, Password, Message\} \qquad (3)$$

Table 1. Stories elicited and entities identified from them

S. No.	Stories	Stakeholders	Functionalities	Assets	Set
1	The Password of the inhabitants must be kept confidential	Inhabitant	Smart Authentication System	Password	S = {Inhabitant}, F = {Smart Authentication System}, A = {Password}
2	If a burglar tries to enter the building message police	Burglar, Police	Smart Burglar Alarm System	Message	S = {Burglar, Police}, F = {Smart Burglar Alarm System}, A = {Message}
3	Only the Building Manager can assign username, password to every resident	Building Manager, Resident	Smart Access Control System	Username, Password	S = {Building Manager, Resident}, F = {Smart Access Control System}, A = {Username Password}
4	Every entrant must be authenticated	Entrant	Smart Authentication System		S = {Entrant}, F = {Smart Authentication System}, A = {ϕ}

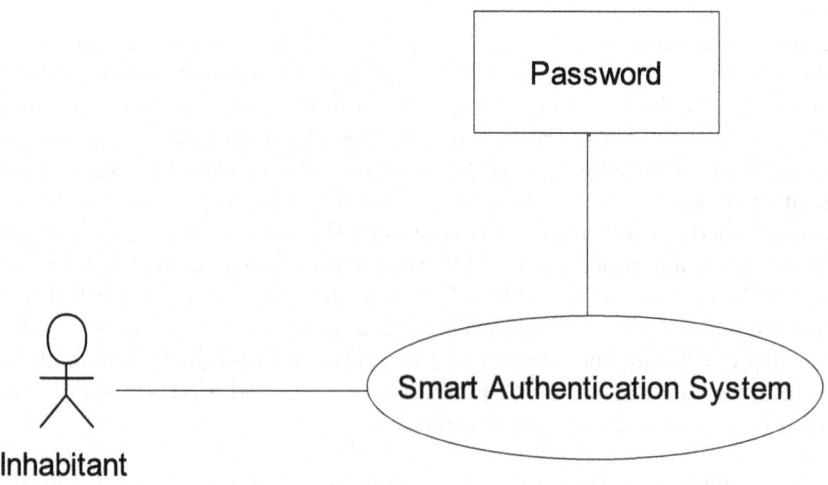

Fig. 2. SCD for Story 1

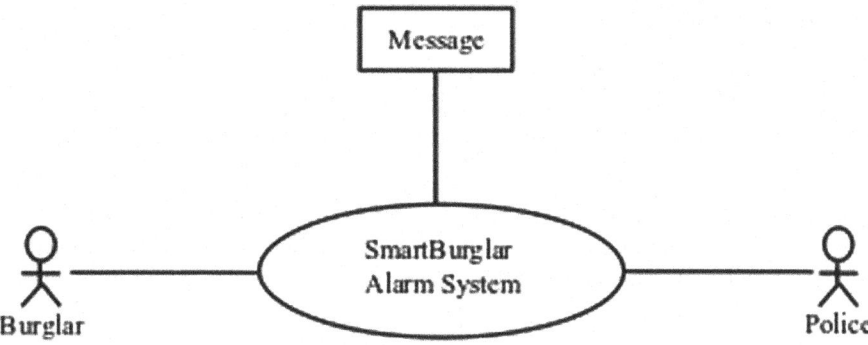

Fig. 3. SCD for Story 2

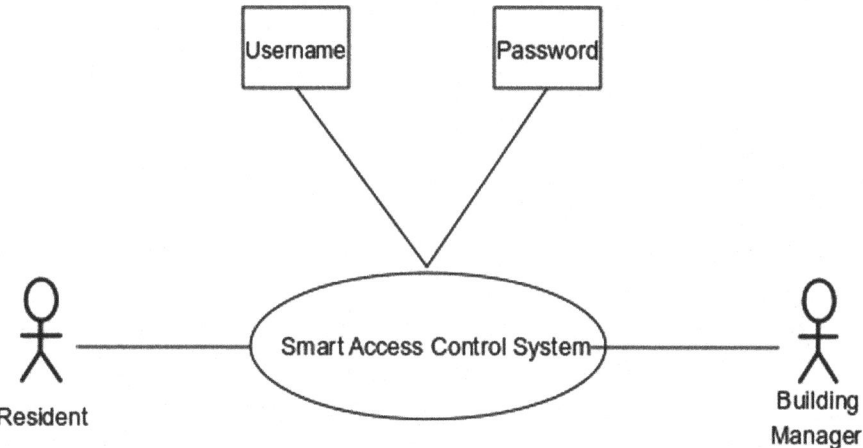

Fig. 4. SCD for Story 3

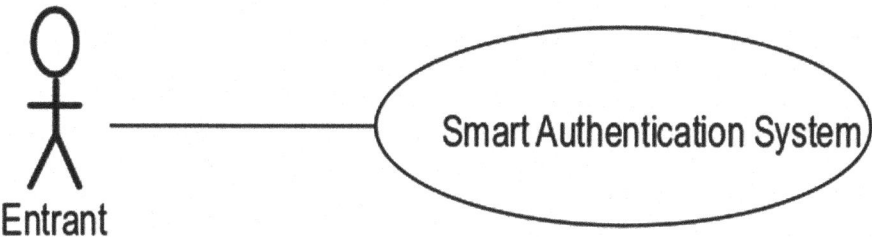

Fig. 5. SCD for Story 4

5.2   Refinement

The information obtained in the identification phase is refined to remove inconsistencies and ambiguities. To achieve this, activities of Redundancy Removal, Aggregation and Decomposition are performed, described as follows.

Redundancy Removal. In set S given by Eq. (1) two entities 'Inhabitants' and 'Residents' are redundant so a only one term i.e. 'Resident' is selected to avoid ambiguity. 'Inhabitant' is found in Fig. 2 and is modified as Fig. 6.

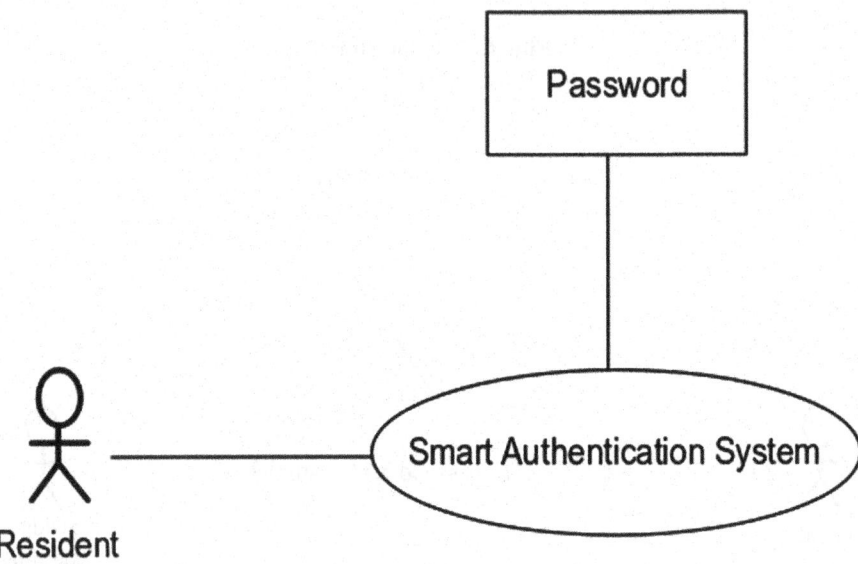

Fig. 6. SCD for Story 1 after redundancy removal

Aggregation. The SCDs rendering similar information are aggregated. In Figs. 3, 4, 5 and 6 we encounter the functionalities of 'Smart Burglar Alarm System', 'Smart Access Control System' and 'Smart Authentication System'. These three functionalities are inseparable constituents of 'Security' and hence, these are aggregated into one 'Smart Security System'. Again SCDs come in handy to attach all entities associated with different functionalities to one functionality. The new SCD is shown by Fig. 7.

Decomposition. Decomposition is an activity to break an entity into its constituent entities if they possess different properties. The asset 'Entrant' is a much generalized term. Actually, it signifies three kinds of persons namely 'Residents' who lives in the building, 'Guest' who visits or is a temporary resident or a

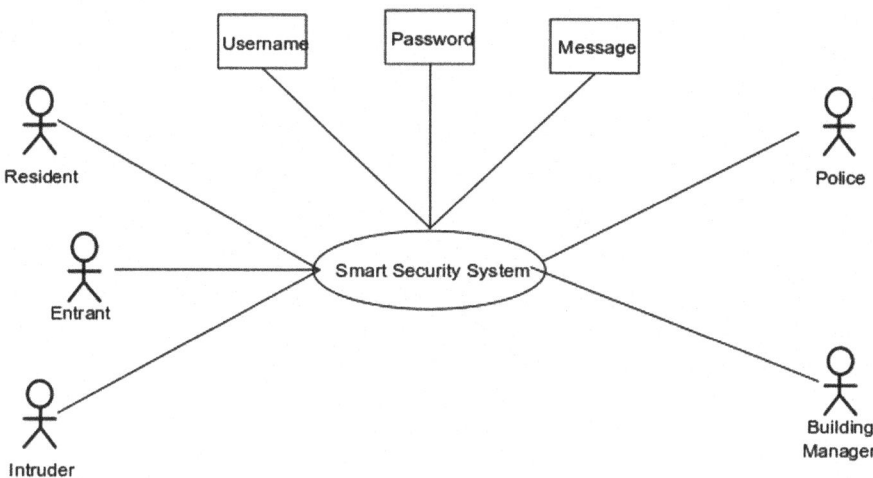

Fig. 7. Aggregated SCD for Smart Security System

worker and 'Intruder' who represents the people who enter in the building without authentication with malicious intentions. It can be a burglar or a terrorist. The change is reflected in the SCD given by Fig. 5. It is modified to Fig. 8. Consequently, after this decomposition, Fig. 7 is modified to Fig. 9.

Final Entity Sets. Evidently, SCDs make the refinement process easy and quick by providing a graphical view of stories. After the exhaustive identification and refinement, final entity sets are obtained for the entire system. The sets are given by Eqs. (4), (5) and (6).

$$S = \{Building\,Manager, Developer, Expert, Client, Resident, \\ Intruder, Guest, Fire\,Department, Police\} \tag{4}$$

$$F = \{Smart\,Authentication\,System, Smart\,Burglar\,Alarm \\ System, Smart\,Access\,Control\,System\} \tag{5}$$

$$A = \{Body\,Motion, Day - light\,Luminance, Room\,Temperature, \\ Humidity\,Level, Electricity\,Consumption, Carbon \\ Monoxide\,Level, Smoke\,Level, SMS, e - Mail, Username, \\ Password, Fingerprint\,Image, Iris\,Image, CCTV\,Footage, \\ Smart\,Card\} \tag{6}$$

Building Manager is the most important functionary of the system who is responsible for the maintenance and smooth functioning of the building. The study has been limited to four functionalities of smart building i.e. Smart Security System, Smart Lighting, Smart Fire Safety System and Heating, Ventilation

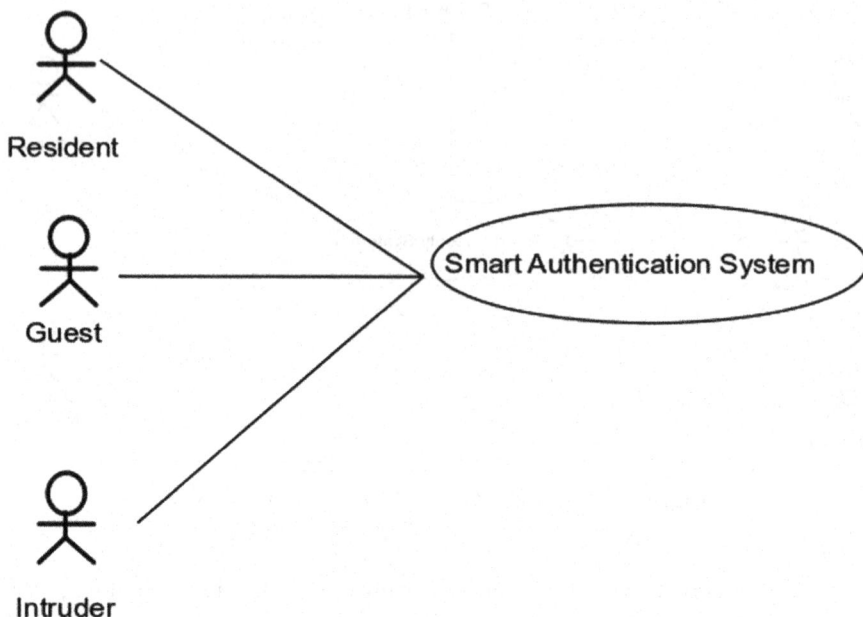

Fig. 8. Decomposition of stakeholder Entrant

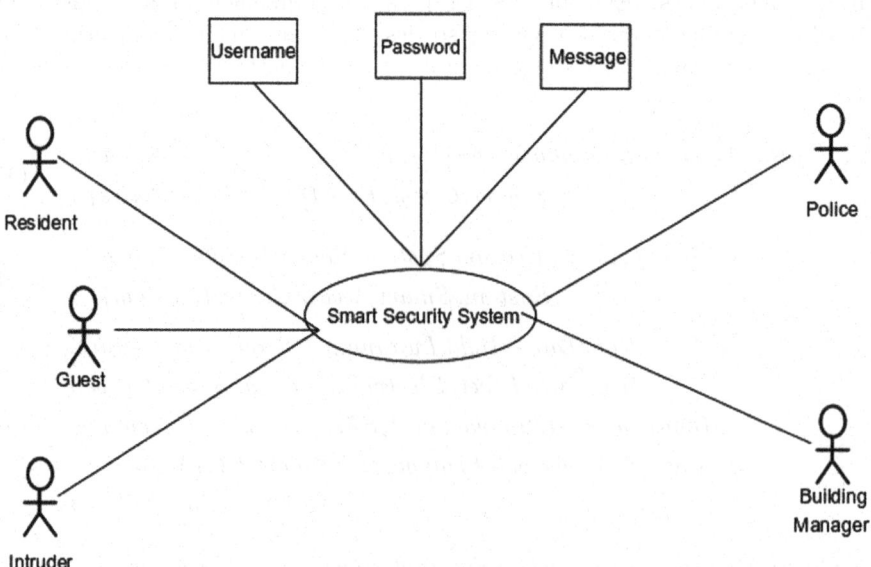

Fig. 9. Aggregated SCD for Smart Security System

and Air Conditioning (HVAC) system. The SMS and e-mail are the preferred means of communication and notifications to and fro residents and the system, with the outside agencies like Police and Fire Department. The smoke, CO and room temperature, beyond the preset levels, raise an alarm of fire. Residents' preferences to various attributes of internal climate, at different times of the day, are recorded for servicing them better. Body Motion of residents is sensed to switch on-off lights. When the complete entity sets are obtained, the entities are mapped to each other in the mapping phase.

5.3 Mapping

In this phase the entities are mapped to each other using Relevance Matrices. These matrices are developed by the core group.

Relevance Matrices. Matrix X maps Assets to Functionalities and matrix Y maps functionalities to stakeholders. For Smart Building, X is shown in Table 2 and Y is shown in Table 3. In these matrices the relevance or association is shown by '1' and irrelevance by '0'. Only a portion of matrices are presented here due to space constraints.

Table 2. Asset-functionality relevance matrix X

Assets	Smart Lighting	Smart Fire Control System	Smart Security System	HVAC
Fingerprint Pattern	0	0	1	0
Iris Image	0	0	1	0
Smart Card	0	0	1	0
CCTV Footage	0	0	1	0
Username	0	0	1	0
Password	0	0	1	0
E-mail	1	1	1	0
SMS	1	1	1	1
Electricity Consumption	1	0	0	1
Smoke Level	0	1	0	1

Table 3. Functionality-stakeholder relevance matrix Y

Functionalities	Building Manager	Resident	Intruder	Guest	Fire Department	Police	Core Group
Smart Lighting	1	1	0	1	0	0	1
Smart Fire Safety System	1	1	0	0	1	0	1
Smart Security System	1	1	1	1	0	1	1
HVAC	1	1	0	1	0	0	1

5.4 Modeling

The relevance matrices, particularly X and Y, together are instrumental in showing the association of assets and stakeholders with a functionality. In matrix X it is seen that asset 'Fingerprint Pattern' is mapped to functionality 'Smart Security System' and in Y matrix 'Smart Security System' is mapped to stakeholder 'Police'. Consequently, it means that Smart Security System is associated with both Fingerprint Pattern and Police. In this way, considering all associations for Smart Security System, given by Fig. 10, is developed. This is called Comprehensive Story Conversion Diagram (CSCD). CSCD evolves from the SCDs. In other words, it is a consolidation of the information presented by all the SCDs

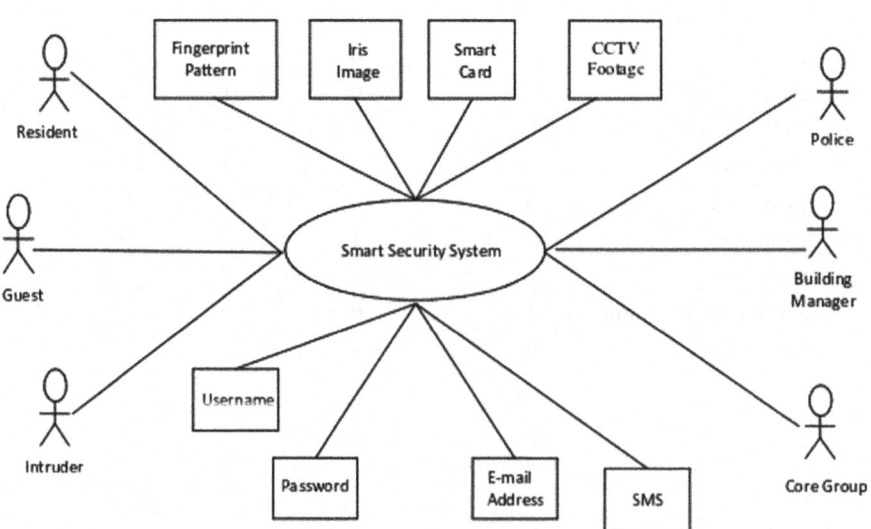

Fig. 10. CSCD for Smart Security System

for certain functionality. All the relevant assets and stakeholders are attached to the functionality. It provides a holistic view of a functionality lucidly that can be communicated to the later phases of development. Algorithm Draw_CSCSD provides the steps to generate it.

Algorithm. Draw_CSCD

Stakeholder set S = ϕ, Asset set A = ϕ, Functionality set F = ϕ
While: No new entities are found
{
  input story
  identify the entities from the story - asset, functionality and/or stakeholder
  input entities in respective sets
  if story contains functionality f_k and $f_k \notin F$
    insert f_k in F
  else
    don't insert
  if story contains stakeholder s_i and $s_i \notin S$
    insert s_i in S
  else
    don't insert
  if story contains asset a_j and $a_j \notin A$
    insert a_j in A
  else
    don't insert
  identify the association among the entities
  draw preliminary SCDs
  Refinement process
  {
    core group reviews the sets
    apply decomposition, aggregation and redundancy removal
    obtain the final entity sets
    find associations among entities
    refine SCDs
  }
}
Mapping
{
  Obtain matrix X: map assets and functionalities
  Obtain matrix Y: map functionalities and stakeholders
  for every functionality fa_k, find the associated assets and stakeholders
  draw CSCD
}

---

6   Conclusion

The diagrammatic representation used in this methodology is more suitable than the textual description. It is easier to comprehend, reduces ambiguity and can be applied to software of any domain. It involves all kinds of stakeholders in the language they are comfortable with. The notion of relevance is a novelty. The diagrams are easy and quite close to UML and hence, easy to comprehend. Many best practices are assimilated in the methodology like iteration in requirement elicitation [22], involvement of a representative from client side in the development team [8], communication within the development team and between teams [23] and involvement of stakeholders in the development of software to increase the their satisfaction [2]. The methodology has been applied on a very relevant field of Smart Buildings and the graphical representation has come out to be better than textual representation. All in all, it aims at the development of a software that lives up to the aspirations of its stakeholders and increases the chances of its acceptance.

References

1. Neetu Kumari, S., Pillai, A.S.: A survey on global requirements elicitation issues and proposed research framework. In: Proceedings of IEEE International Conference on Software Engineering Service Science, ICSESS, pp. 554–557 (2013)
2. Kamata, M.I., Tamai, T.: How does requirements quality relate to project success or failure. In: Requirements Engineering Conference, pp. 69–78 (2007)
3. Hernández, U.I., Rodríguez, F.J.Á., Martin, M.V.: Use processes - modeling requirements based on elements of BPMN and UML use case diagrams. In: 2010 2nd International Conference on Software Technology and Engineering (ICSTE), vol. 2, pp. 36–40 (2010)
4. Shreyas, D.: Software engineering for security - towards architecting secure software. In: ICS, vol. 221, pp. 1–12 (2001)
5. Futcher, L., von Solms, R.: SecSDM: a usable tool to support IT undergraduate students in secure software development. In: Human Aspects of Information Security and Assurance, Crete, Greece, pp. 86–96 (2012)
6. Breu, R., Burger, K., Hafner, M., Jurjens, J., Popp, G., Wimmel, G., Lotz, V.: Key issues of a formally based process model for security engineering. In: 16th International Conference on Software and Systems Engineering and their Applications, Paris, pp. 1–15 (2003)
7. Sabahat, N., Iqbal, F., Azam, F., Javed, M.Y.: An iterative approach for global requirements elicitation: a case study analysis. In: International Conference on Electronics and Information Engineering, Kyoto, Japan, pp. 361–366 (2010)
8. Wäyrynen, J., Bodén, M., Boström, G.: Security engineering and extreme programming: an impossible marriage? In: Zannier, C., Erdogmus, H., Lindstrom, L. (eds.) XP/Agile Universe 2004. LNCS, vol. 3134, pp. 117–128. Springer, Heidelberg (2004). https://doi.org/10.1007/978-3-540-27777-4_12
9. Keith, E.R.: Agile Software Development Processes: A Different Approach to Software Design, pp. 1–25 (2003)
10. Chua, B.B., Bernardo, D.V., Verner, J.: Understanding the use of elicitation approaches for effective requirements gathering. In: Proceedings of 5th International Conference Software Engineering Advances, ICSEA 2010, pp. 325–330 (2010)

11. Abrahão, S., Gravino, C., Insfran, E., Scanniello, G., Tortora, G.: Assessing the effectiveness of dynamic modeling in the comprehension of software requirements: results from a family of five experiments. IEEE Trans. Softw. Eng. **39**, 327–342 (2013)
12. Booch, G., Jacobson, I., Rumbaugh, J.: Unified Software Development Process. Reading, Massachusetts (1999)
13. Choppy, C., Reggio, G.: Requirements capture and specification for enterprise applications: a UML based attempt. In: Proceedings of Software Engineering Conference, ASWEC 2006, pp. 19–28 (2006)
14. Woods, E.: Harnessing UML for architectural description - the context view. IEEE Softw. **31**, 30–33 (2014)
15. Konrad, S., Goldsby, H., Lopez, K., Cheng, B.H.C.: Visualizing requirements in UML models. In: First International Workshop on Requirements Engineering Visualization, REV (2007)
16. Federal Information Processing Standards: Standards for Security Categorization of Federal Information and Information Systems. Federal Information Processing Standards Publication. FIPS PUB 1 (2004)
17. Glinz, M.: Problems and deficiencies of UML as a requirements specification language. In: Tenth International Workshop on Software Specification and Design, pp. 11–22. IEEE, Irvine (2000)
18. Sindre, G., Opdahl, A.: Capturing security requirements through misuse cases. Nor. Inform. (2001)
19. Al-fuqaha, A., Guizani, M., Mohammadi, M.: Internet of Things: a survey on enabling technologies, protocols, and applications. IEEE Commun. Surv. Tutorials **17**, 2347–2376 (2015)
20. Robles, R.J., Kim, T.: A review on security in smart home development. Int. J. Adv. Sci. Technol. **15**, 13–22 (2010)
21. Pressman, R.S.: Software Engineering A Practitioner's Approach. Mc Graw Hill, New York (2001)
22. Kasirun, Z.M., Salim, S.S.: Focus group discussion model for requirements elicitation activity. In: International Conference on Computer and Electrical Engineering, pp. 101–105 (2008)
23. Basri, S., O'Connor, R. V.: The impact of software development team dynamics on the Knowledge Management Process. In: Proceedings of the 23rd International Conference on Software Engineering and Knowledge Engineering, pp. 339–342 (2011)

IoT Powered Vehicle Tracking System (VTS)

Priti Jagwani[1,2(✉)] and Manoj Kumar[1]

[1] Department of Computer Science, Aryabhatta College, University of Delhi,
New Delhi 110021, India
jagwani.priti@gmail.com, kmanojl363@gmail.com
[2] School of Information Technology, Indian Institute of Technology, Hauz Khas,
New Delhi 110016, India

Abstract. With its new avenues, Internet of Things is bringing immense value and potential to the life style of masses. One of the important applications is managing and tracking large fleet which falls under domain of effective transportation and logistics. In this paper a framework has been proposed for real time fleet tracking system. This framework is composed of GPS, GSM and microcontroller technologies. The key features of the system are real-time location tracking, an open-source GIS platform, flexibility and a web-based user interface provided at the base station. A prototype of the proposed system is implemented. Our system prototype is experimentally tested for many trips in Delhi NCR region of North India. The system has been found stable and robust. Targeted fleet has been accurately tracked and its location has been transmitted to the server in real time. Further, with the capabilities of geofencing, functionality of traccar server, its user friendly interface the system is serving the purpose of ubiquitous fleet tracking system providing maximum accessibility for user anytime and anywhere.

Keywords: Vehicle tracking system · Internet of Things · Fleet management
GPS · Arduino microcontroller · GSM

1 Introduction

The idea of connecting basic objects to sensors and making it equipped with some sort of intelligence was the earliest essence of today's much talked "Internet of Things" system. Although the concept was coined in early 90's but the two important milestones which turn the idea into reality were adoption of RFID and IPV6. Internet of things (IoT) is an umbrella term comprising of various technologies, applications and use cases. These are empowered by connection of objects and devices with an IP address (Internet Protocol). The new innovations under internet of things are smarter homes, smart cars, wearable technology and many more. Apart from its never ending list of applications, IoT has tremendously transformed the way business is being done. Intelligent transport system as one of the example domains of IoT, has witnessed much advancement especially when vehicle to infrastructure communication and real time tracking systems are being used.

Tracking system for vehicles which is also known as fleet tracking system is a system used to track and manage/coordinate vehicles belonging to an enterprise/individual. IoT powered vehicle tracking system is also an integral part of asset management systems. It is used for tracking the real-time position and status of vehicles of a fleet, and for communicating between the vehicles and a base station/fleet office. This system is vital for fleet operators in order to monitor and control driving behavior of employees. Fleet management system effectively addresses the environmental, safety, fuel management, reporting issues. This system is a ubiquitous and real time vehicle tracking system which provides maximum accessibility for the user anytime and anywhere. Moreover, if combined with the theft alarm, this system can be used for theft prevention.

Any fleet tracking system is based on the usage of various modern information technologies and communication systems. In reality, vehicle tracking system is based on wide range of technologies communication systems like General Packet Radio Service (GPRS), Global System for Mobile Communication (GSM), the Internet or the World Wide Web and Global Positioning System (GPS), microcontrollers etc. for tracking the position of a vehicle, Global Positioning System (GPS) technology is extensively used. GPS has served as the basis for many such services which raises their popularity and increases their demand.

The proposed work contain design and implementation of a fleet tracking system using the technologies GPS, GSM, microcontrollers and open source server. This system will enable the user to track the location of vehicle(s) geographically and displaying its real time movement/position on a map. The tracking services of the proposed system include acquiring the position and pace of a given vehicle for the current moment or on any time in past.

In this paper we are proposing a novel web based framework for fleet tracking. This system facilitate users to observe the location of the vehicle graphically (on a digital map) and other relevant information of each vehicle in the fleet. Along with the location, a non exclusive list of elements of the relevant information could be vehicles position, speed, stops, and movements. The paper also focuses on design and implementation of the fleet tracking aspect of the system. Along with providing traditional web based tracking utility the proposed system also provides geofencing facility and a user friendly interface also. The proposed fleet Tracking system allows to set up a fencing of series of topographical zones. Movement of vehicles inside or outside these zones can be monitored. For this a virtual boundary has been created and application has been enabled to trigger an indication if the targeted vehicle enters or leaves a particular area. Therefore alerts can be received when the vehicle exceeds these predefined limits. Additionally along with the location tracking/monitoring, setting of speed and geographical limits, acquiring history report of vehicle's movement can also be done. Apart from monitoring at the base station SMS alerts can also be received notifying events. This facility will be proving vital in case of down or limited internet connectivity. This also ensures better fleet management.

The main contribution of the paper lies in providing the design of a flexible and completely customizable fleet tracking system which apart from real time location can also report various parameters like speed of the vehicle, reverse geocoded address, past location/driving history of the vehicle and geofencing also. Because of use of GSM module it can also operate using SMS facility, through over the air network in absence of internet. Also a flexible and user friendly interface for monitoring is provided using traccar server.

The remaining structure of the paper is as follows: Sect. 2 presents the related work in the domain of fleet tracking, Sect. 3 contains details of various modules of the proposed system. Complete methodology of the system is given in Sect. 4 while results are presented in Sect. 5 followed by future directions and conclusions in Sect. 6.

2 Related Work

With the abundance of its application areas vehicle tracking system is one of the most used IoT based solution. It is used around the world in many fields such as vehicle position tracking system, vehicle anti-theft tracking system, fleet management system and intelligent transportation system (ITS). This system contains the fleet data and integrate with vehicle locations to present a comprehensive picture. Fleet management being one of the application of newly coined IoT field, research is not very mature in this domain. Findings from the studies done in the past in this area are as follows:

Earlier the primary mode of communication between driver and base station is wireless voice communication. The major problem with this communication mode is that data is manually provided to the base station by the driver. Authenticity and accuracy of this data was always under scanner and was questionable. On the other hand timely, accurate data is essential to operate fleet business efficiently and economically.

Ramadan and Al-Kheder [2] proposed design and implementation of system for this purpose. They designed a vehicle tracking which also served as an anti-theft system for protecting a vehicle from any intruders. For this authors have used GPS/GSM. To improve the accuracy of determined location and for reduction of positional errors this system used Kalman filter. When the engine is turned on the owner get a status message that the engine has started if the access is illegal the engine gets turned off immediately.

Authors in [5] proposed a vehicle tracking system, that uses the popular social network as a value added service for traditional tracking system. The system proposed in this work uses Google maps for tracking. Functional components used in this system are GPS, GSM and microcontroller module.

Authors in [12] have proposed an Intelligent Vehicle Monitoring System which uses Global Positioning System along with Google Maps and Cloud Computing to collect useful information about a vehicle like location, speed etc. this information is transmitted in near-real-time via cellular or satellite communication to a centralized server maintained in the cloud network. This information is then available for the authorized users in real time and each licensed vehicle owner can access the data in cloud using a web portal anytime anywhere.

Previous systems contain set of components and services that are provided to the user either via a web interface or pre downloaded software. Usual mechanism of data fetching is to retrieve the data from GPS device bound in the vehicle using GPRS. Additionally this service includes showing user's vehicle location on map, providing detailed reports and alerts. Some additional functionality provided by these systems besides tracking could be allowing the user to search for addresses and directions, providing distance calculations and history of vehicle's movement [11]. Apart from providing web interface these services can be accessed by an application that can be downloaded.

Authors in the work [1] designed an in-vehicle device which works using Global Positioning System (GPS) and Global system for mobile communication/General Packet Radio Service (GSM/GPRS). The device is inbound inside the vehicle to be tracked in real-time. This vehicle tracking system uses the GPS module to get geographic coordinates at regular time intervals. The GSM/GPRS module is used to transmit the data and update the vehicle location, and store it in a database.

Our work shares the underlying idea with the above work but there are additional characteristics that are embracing the proposed system with value addition. These characteristics are geofencing, use of open source GIS tracking server and interface. Use of open source GIS tracking and its built in interface enables the system with increased user acquaintance and greater flexibility.

3 System Design

This section presents design specifications and details about the functionalities of all components used in the proposed system. The system has following components: GPS module, Arduino microcontroller, GSM module. All these in combination will form a setup to be in-bound at the targeted vehicle. Also the base station is an integral part of the system where whole monitoring/tracking of the vehicle is being done. Here one can get the location displayed on a monitoring device (computer monitor or any other). Apart from these hardware components, User interface and server module provided by tracccar are used as part of software. The detailed design is shown in Fig. 1.

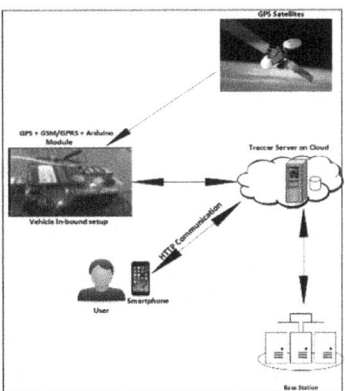

Fig. 1. Proposed system layout

Global Positioning System (GPS) Module:
A GPS navigation device or GPS is a device that is capable of receiving information from GPS satellites and then to determine the device's geographical position. For the proposed

system SKG13BL model of GPS is used. It is a comprehensive GPS engine module having super sensitivity, ultra-low power and small form factor as its special features [8, 9]. A complete serial data message with position, velocity and time information is presented at the serial interface with NMEA protocol This data is taken from GPS satellites. Snapshot of the NMEA data format is shown in Fig. 2. This module is connected to Arduino board and hence it sends this data to the Arduino board.

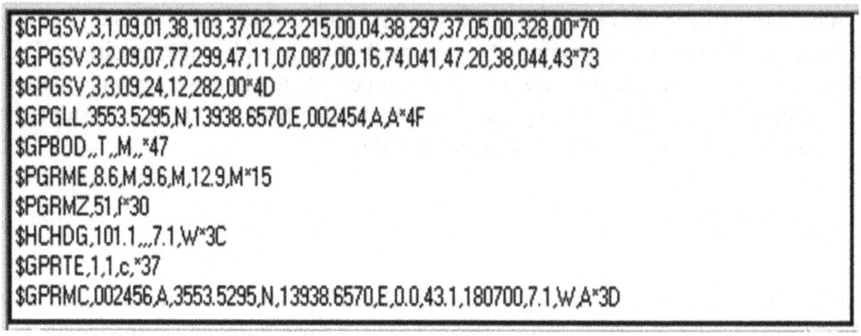

```
$GPGSV,3,1,09,01,38,103,37,02,23,215,00,04,38,297,37,05,00,328,00*70
$GPGSV,3,2,09,07,77,299,47,11,07,087,00,16,74,041,47,20,38,044,43*73
$GPGSV,3,3,09,24,12,282,00*4D
$GPGLL,3553.5295,N,13938.6570,E,002454,A,A*4F
$GPBOD,,T,,M,,*47
$PGRME,8.6,M,9.6,M,12.9,M*15
$PGRMZ,51,f*30
$HCHDG,101.1,,,7.1,W*3C
$GPRTE,1,1,c,*37
$GPRMC,002456,A,3553.5295,N,13938.6570,E,0.0,43.1,180700,7.1,W,A*3D
```

Fig. 2. NMEA format of Data

Arduino:
The Arduino Uno is a microcontroller board based on ATmega328 (datasheet). The cellular shield for a microcontroller includes all the essential parts. It has 14 digital input/output pins, a 16 MHz ceramic resonator, a USB connection, a power jack, an ICSP header, and a reset button. It is an open-source electronics platform based on easy-to-use hardware and software [7]. Arduino boards are able to read inputs, even a Twitter message- and turn it into an output. A software program for controlling this microcontroller is written in the C++ language at Arduino IDE, which is compiled and saved into the microcontroller's flash memory. On receiving the data from GPS module, Arduino extracts the required parameters of data like latitude, longitude, speed and others through a script written in any programming language native to Arduino. In the proposed design this has been connected to GPS module and GSM module. It takes the data from GPS and after required processing this data is given to the GSM module.

The choice of the Arduino is made out of the many available microcontrollers i.e. Raspberry Pi, and other interfacing modules; due to the following reasons:

1. Arduino have less memory capacity compared Raspberry Pi but for the proposed system, it is sufficient. Choosing a light device has its own set of obvious advantages. So it can have a better performance.
2. Arduino is used for data collection here as it is a simple microcontroller whereas Raspberry Pi is a microprocessor which can also process the data. Our processing of data is done at the server end. Hence processing inside the in-bound device setup is not required. We are just sending raw data taken from Arduino and hence latency is improved.

3. Arduino is relatively easier to handle as due to its interface. A huge code library is also available for the customization and extension of coding. Also because of being simple at structure and design it provides easy step testing thus it becomes easier to the find the bug/fault in the system.

GSM Module:
GSM/GPRS module is used to establish communication between a computer (here Arduino microcontroller has been used) and a server. GPRS is an extension of GSM that enables higher data transmission rate [10]. The GSM/GPRS module establishes the connections between in-vehicle setup and a remote server for transmitting the vehicle's location and other information, using HTTP connections over the GSM/GPRS network.

A SIM card and a cellular antenna are functional essential for working of a GSM/GPRS module. In the proposed system GSM module is connected to Arduino and to the server also.

There are wide varieties of GSM module available for different purpose, We have used GSM SIM 900 for the project. This module supports communication in 900 MHz band. The communication between Arduino and GSM module is serial. So serial pins of Arduino (namely R_x and T_x) are used. The T_x pin of GSM module is connected to R_x pin of Arduino and R_x pin of GSM module is connected to T_x pin of Arduino.

GSM T_x –> Arduino R_x
GSM R_x –> Arduino T_x.

Now ground pins of Arduino and GSM module are connected to each other. Now Arduino microcontroller can be loaded with different programs to communicate with GSM module and make it work.

On the other side GSM module is connected to server. It sends the data to the open source GIS server. In this system Traccar server has been used. This module is placed for the two-way data outreach. A fleet going to geographically niche areas may face internet downtime. In such cases this module can directly send the messages containing location of the fleet to a registered mobile number (RMN) over the air network using any mobile network operator.

Software Functionality: Arduino and GPS module have been controlled using suitable programming language scripts. Along with the coding to control and manage GPS module and Arduino, Traccar is used for server functions. Traccar is a free and open source modern GPS tracking system. It also includes a modern fully-featured web interface. This interface is available for desktop and mobile layouts. Traccar software provides high performance and stability on Windows, Linux or any other platform. It is highly customizable and having plethora of features, details of which can be found at [4]. It has three main components:

Traccar Server – It is the server software for GPS tracking. It includes back-end device communication and web interface [4]. The server can be self-hosted in the cloud or on-premise.

Traccar Client – Android and iOS mobile app that reports phone's location to the server and are installed at client end.

Traccar Manager – Android and iOS native mobile alternative to Traccar web application.

For the proposed design only Traccar server has been used. For this project we have used Traccar service which is open source software. It is customized to the vehicle tracking system. It has other built in modules like admin module, user login module etc. It is fully customizable and can be used to Track Vehicle with greater efficiency.

Database is designed to store and manage received vehicle's location information. At the base station, in order to monitor fleet's location and other parameter an interface has been used. This is a customizable interface provided as a submodule of traccar server. This is installed in a device available at the base station. Whenever a user requests the vehicle location, it can be accessed from the database and monitored through the interface of the device at the base station.

4 Methodology

The working flow of the proposed system is as follows:

1. GPS module captures the data from satellite which is handed over to Arduino microcontroller for required processing on it.
2. Data in serial format is expected from GPS at the Arduino end. If data is not available (due to some reasons) then Arduino waits until the data is available.
3. When this NMEA format data is received at Arduino. The NMEA format data $GPGGA which refers to Global Positioning System Fix Data is checked and verified for its format specifications.
4. If the $GPGGA data is available then 'OK' status is displayed by AT command at Arduino. The details of AT commands for HTTP and their parameters for SIM can be found at [6].
5. Microcontroller extracts the relevant fields like vehicle's location information (in the form of latitude, longitude), speed etc. from NMEA string.
6. To give a quick start to our GPRS module '+AT+CPIN?' command is executed.
7. Now Arduino transfer this data to GSM module through serial mode.
8. In order to do this data transfer to GSM, Arduino has been programmed accordingly.
9. Software Serial library is used for allowing serial communication on required digital pins of the Arduino.
10. Digital identities of the pins transmitting the data is made available to the code through the parameters of SoftwareSerial constructor.
11. The serial.begin() command is used to set up the communication data rate in bit per second(baud) for the serial communication of data between arduino and GSM (of whom).
12. Baud rate of 9600 is set by invoking Serial begin at Arduino IDE.
13. After getting data from Arduino, GSM transfers it to the Traccar server.

14. For this data is pushed to the server over HTTP request using a script and saved in a database.
15. At the server end data handling is done through scripts.
16. The data is regularly being transmitted, received and saved at specified time intervals (every 2 s here).

Initially, couple of seconds time is required by GPS module to locate the satellites signal. GPS Module require open space i.e. minimal obstruction of the wall, building, trees etc. for easy and quick configuration. When it receives the signal from the device deployed in the vehicle it starts sending the data to the Arduino microcontroller. Some minimal level of signal strength is required by this microcontroller in order to do further processing and to send data to traccar server. GSM module is connected to the Arduino board to send data to the server and also to speed up the process of the data transmission.

GSM module can work as message receiver and sender also (if required). When the traccar server is not responding the GSM module can directly send message to the registered mobile number. Thus after the all the modules are configured that data is reached to the server where it is recorded and analysed up to a certain extent. Data processing related to speed and other parameters is done at the server end rather than at the setup itself. This enables the system to have lower latency and better performance. This data can be easily shown using any GUI front end application on the monitoring device at the base station. For this case Traccar software was used which has inbuilt and very flexible functionality for better GUI interface.

By default Traccar Server uses embedded H2 database however any database can be used along it for the storing and manipulating the data. A non exclusive list of various choices of database system available for it are flat file system, Sqlite, Mysql. Among all these Mysql outperforms in case much of the processing is required. In terms of efficiency and data retrieval sqlite is a light weight option. So one obvious choice for the database could be sqlite but for prototype implementation MySql has been used.

For MySQL engine some settings in the configuration file are required. The parameters for using MySQL (replace [HOST], [DATABASE], [USER], [PASS-WORD] with appropriate values.

As we have a GPS based system, External factors like climatic conditions, Weather condition, plays a significant role on the overall performance of the system. However, the effect of external factors can be reduced using the alternate source for data transmission.

5 Results

In order to show the feasibility of the proposed system, a prototype has been designed and implemented. This section is showing the results of experimental run. The inbound setup unit containing GPS, Arduino and GSM module has been deployed in a vehicle which is to be targeted. The system is being tested for some trips in Delhi NCR region of India. The vehicle has been tracked continuously 'and the required data parameters

Fig. 3. Location of Fleet and GeoFence on a Map

Attribute	Value
State	
Attribute	Value
Time	2017-07-15 11:06:50 am
Latitude	28.587238°
Longitude	77.163735°
Valid	Yes
Accuracy	0.00 km
Altitude	194
Speed	0.0 km/h
Course	N
Address	18 Benito Juarez Marg, New...

Fig. 4. Various Parameters obtained during Tracking

are collected and successfully displayed through the user interface. Figures presented above are depicting results. Figure 3 is presenting the output of tracking. It is showing the locations vehicle, geofence on a map.

Figure 4 is depicting different set of parameters collected during test run. The list shown here is non-exclusive and can be customized according to the user's need.

6   Future Directions and Concluding Remarks

With rapid innovations in the domain of microelectronics and mobile telecommunications, a variety of fleet diagnostics and satellite tracking has come up. These technologies have provided a backbone of fleet management system also. The real life situations which impose the demand for the improved fleet management are growing road traffic, traffic density and intensification of freight transportation demand. One of the challenging scenario for which the proposed system can be used is increase in the number of accidents that intensifies the demand for safer vehicles. The proposed system provides dynamic fleet management with constant tracking which triggers the safety and security along with reduced operational cost and avoidance of the illegal usage of the vehicle and the fuel manipulation.

Further this system can be used for preventing lane jumping which always results in traffic chaos. This functionality can be implemented with the help geofencing facility of the system.

To pave the way ahead, the proposed framework can witness many improvements like using of DGPS for greater accuracy instead of GPS. But all GPS based technologies are dependent of existence of line of sight (LOS) condition. These conditions may not be available for a vehicle operating on city streets with high rise buildings. For such situations alternative navigation system such as dead reckoning (DR) navigation may be used. Also GSM/GPRS module can be replaced by its better alternatives like 3G, 4G etc. to make the proposed system faster and robust. Arduino Uno as a microcontroller has proven to be good choice here as its efficient to the required extent and not very resource demanding.

In this work a flexible and robust system for real time tracking of fleet has been proposed. GPS, GSM and Arduino microcontroller are used as the elements of inbound unit which is to be placed in the targeted vehicle. Also a server has been used to coordinate with base station and inbound unit. This paper described all components of the system. Further design and whole working flow of the proposed system is shown. Experiments have been conducted on the prototype designed. Stable and accurate results of fleet tracking have been shown by prototype.

References

1. Lee, S., Tewolde, G., Kwon, J.: Design and Implementation of Vehicle Tracking System Using GPS/GSM/GPRS Technology and Smartphone Application, pp. 353–358 (2014). https://doi.org/10.1109/wf-iot.2014.6803187
2. Ramadan, M.N., Al-Khedher, M.A., Al-Kheder, S.A.: Intelligent anti-theft and tracking system for automobiles. Int. J. Mach. Learn. Comput. 2(1), 83 (2012)
3. Liu, Z., Zhang, A., Li, S.: Vehicle anti-theft tracking system based on Internet of things. In: 2013 IEEE International Conference on Vehicular Electronics and Safety (ICVES). IEEE (2013)
4. https://www.traccar.org/documentation/
5. ElShafee, A., ElMenshawi, M., Saeed, M.: Integrating social network services with vehicle tracking technologies. Int. J. Adv. Comput. Sci. Appl. 4(6) (2013)
6. https://www.developershome.com/sms/atCommandsIntro.asp
7. Arduino Microcontroller. http://arduino.cc
8. GPS Module. https://www.sparkfun.com
9. TinyGPS. http://arduiniana.org/libraries/tinygps/
10. GSM/GPRS Module. https://www.sparkfun.com
11. Lau, E.C.-W.: Simple bus tracking system. J. Adv. Comput. Sci. Technol. Res. 3(1) (2013)
12. Jose, D., Prasad, S., Sridhar, V.G.: Intelligent vehicle monitoring using global positioning system and cloud computing. Proc. Comput. Sci. 50, 440–446 (2015)

Grammar-Algebraic Approach
to Analyze Workflows

Alexander Afanasyev$^{(\boxtimes)}$ and Nikolay Voit$^{(\boxtimes)}$ (iD)

Ulyanovsk State Technical University, Ulyanovsk, Russia
{a.afanasev,n.voit}@ulstu.ru

Abstract. Improving the lifecycle of automated systems and reducing their
development time are an important production problem in a large enterprise. We
have created a new approach to the analysis and transformation of their processes on the basis of author's principles, grammar, method of the design
process for narrowing the semantic gap between business process analysis and
business process execution. This approach allows designers to improve the
quality and reduce the time spent on the lifecycle of automated systems.

Keywords: Workflow · Process · Grammar

1 Introduction

Project enterprises often need to dynamically reconfigure their internal processes to
improve the efficiency of the business flow. However, modifications of the workflow
usually lead to several problems (deadlocks) in terms of the degree of freedom,
completeness and security of decisions. Therefore, the design, analysis, monitoring and
modeling of dynamic workflows is an urgent task concerned with the need to quickly
respond to changing business situations. The dynamic development of complex
automated systems is associated with the adaptation of work processes to changes in
system requirements. It is generally accepted that the agility (liveliness) of an
enterprise/business as a property of an enterprise functions in a dynamically developing
world. Enterprises should develop in two directions: adjust to changes in the surrounding environment; discover new opportunities constantly appearing in the dynamic
world for launching completely new products (services).

Becoming agile requires a new approach that allows project managers to discover
changes and opportunities for the development of complex automated systems and to
react on them appropriately. The need to develop such an approach arose when the degree
of change in development requirements increased. Large corporations like Whitestein
Technologies, Magenta Technologies, SkodaAuto, Volkswagen, Saarstahl AG note that
industry and technology (progress) move too fast, and requirements change very quickly,
and traditional (monolithic) methods can no longer manage a product's lifecycle and
project's workflows. The efficiency of business process can be improved by dynamical
reconfiguration of enterprise's business processes as workflows. Design, analysis,
checking, modeling, and transformation of dynamic workflows result in workflows'

© Springer International Publishing AG, part of Springer Nature 2018
O. Gervasi et al. (Eds.): ICCSA 2018, LNCS 10963, pp. 499–510, 2018.
https://doi.org/10.1007/978-3-319-95171-3_39

modifications. When modifying workflows, it is required to solve problems such as deadlock, security, and etc. [1].

The design and development of automated systems should include the adaptation to agile requirements of the environment. In work [2], the agility is the main property of production. There are two behaviors of an enterprise. One of them is to change the enterprise's business processes of production. Another is to create new marketable products. Enterprises should often change their business processes in order to increase product quality and get new market outlets. The work [3] notes that the speed of development in industry and technology should change monolithic approaches. A lot of large enterprises like IBM, ARIS note that the monolithic product lifecycle management systems with static workflow automation tools have reached their limits; almost all possible process configurations and reconfigurations are not only slow and costly, but often impossible [4]. The consequences are ill-fitting processes and soaring process development and improvement costs. ProBis [6] has monolithic workflows. Dynamic workflows are presented in works [7–9].

We used a definition given in [5] for a dynamic workflow as a process of adaptation to the current environment. We define a new RVT-grammar as a temporal finite state grammar using a memory as stacks and tapes to analyze workflows. There are two main principles in this work. They are: the principle of the ensemble of hybrid dynamic workflows. It includes the use of heterogeneous types and distribution in the space of hybrid dynamic workflows; the principle of adaptive design. It has a continuous in time structural and parametric analysis and synthesis of hybrid dynamic workflows.

Article has the following structure. In Introduction, the list of standard problems with workflows is submitted briefly. Related work has an overview of works on this topic. In Method to analyze workflows based on RVT-grammar, and Method of business-processes transformation, authors describe the approach with an example. Discussion has an overview about analyzing and managing manufacturing and workflows of cyber-physical systems. Outputs and the further directions of researches are presented in the conclusion.

2 Related Works

We have studied many research works considered with the workflows' specification, verification and translation. Some of them focus on formal semantics and verification methods for workflows using Petri nets, process algebra, abstract state machine [10, 11]. In [12], Decker and Weske offer a formalism based on Petri Nets to define properties as reliability and promptness, and a method for testing these two properties. However, they only describe the synchronous relationship and do not have any research comparisons for high-level interaction modeling languages as BPMN. In [13], the behavior of BPMN from a semantic point of view is studied and several BPMN templates are proposed. This work is theoretically unjustified and is not complete, which considers only a few models. Lohmann and Wolff [14] offer the analysis using existing templates and monitoring them using compatible templates. In [15], the authors draw attention to the translation of BPMN into the process algebra for analyzing choreographies using the help model and checking equivalence.

The main limit of the methods considered is that they do not work in the presence of different types of diagrams at the same time, which means that in some cases the input diagrams can not be analyzed.

3 Method to Analyze Workflows Based on Temporal RVT-Grammar

Temporal RVT-grammar is defined as the tuple

$$G = \left(V, \Sigma, \widetilde{\Sigma}, C, E, R, \tau, r_0 \right). \tag{1}$$

where $V = \{v_e, \ e = \overline{1.L}\}$ is an additional alphabet for the operation onto a memory; $\Sigma = \{(a_l, t_l), l = \overline{1.T}\}$ is an alphabet (words) of events; $\widetilde{\Sigma} = \{(\tilde{a}_n, \tilde{t}_n), \ n = 1.\widetilde{T}\}$ is a quasi-term alphabet, extending Σ; $C = \{c_i, c_i = c_i + t_{l-1}, i \in N\}$ is a set of a time identifier, and a beginning $c_i = 0$; E is a set of the temporal relations as $\{c_i \sim t_l\}$, where c is a variable (a time identifier), $\sim \in \{=, <, \leq, >, \geq\}$; $R = \{r_i, \ i = \overline{0.I}\}$ is a rule of this grammar G (a set of production rule's complexes), where this complex r_i has a subset P_{ij} of the production rule $r_i = \{P_{ij}, j = \overline{1.J}\}$; $\tau = \{t_l \in [0; +\infty], l = \overline{1.T}\}$ is a set of timestamps, where $c_i \in \tau \times \sim \times \tau$; $r_0 \in R$ is an axiom of this grammar (a name of the first production rule), $r_k \in R$ is the last production rule. The production rule $P_{ij} \in r_i$ has a view as

$$(a_l, t_l) \xrightarrow{\{W_\gamma(v_1,\ldots,v_n)|E\}} r_m. \tag{2}$$

where $W_\gamma(v_1, \ldots, v_n)$ is n-relation, that defines a type of an operation over memory, depending on $\gamma = \{0, 1, 2, 3\}$ (0 – operation is not performed, 1 – write, 2 – read, 3 – compare); (a_l, t_l) is a word as a pair of an event and a timestamp; $r_m \in R$ is a name of a target production rule. The language $L(G)$ of this grammar has words as (a_l, t_l) and presents a trace $\sigma = \{a_0, 0\} \rightarrow \{a_l, t_l\} \rightarrow \{a_k, t_T\}$. The grammar for UML AD is shown in Table 1.

We can check 23 errors. The following semantical errors are: The cyclic connection; Mutually exclusive links; Multiple communication; Remote context error; Control transfer failure; Error in the multiplicity of inputs; Error multiplicity of outputs; Invalid link; Communication error; Access level error; Error transmitting the message; An error in the delegation of control; A quantitative error in the elements of the diagram; Excluding links of the wrong type; A call directed to the life line; Collapsed connection; Violation of the multiplicity of dependencies; Mutually exclusive links; Synchronous call before receiving a response; Great synonymy; The antonymy of objects; Conversion of relations; Inconsistency of objects.

In order to correct errors during the grammar design, types of graphic objects are entered into the alphabet $\widetilde{\Sigma}$. The graphic objects have more than one input or output, the samples of which will be used as an analysis continuer. Such graphic objects are key, because the main graphic representations are built on them. In addition, the large

Table 1. Temporal RVT-grammar for UML AD

Prev. state	Quazi-term	Next state	Operation
r_0	A_{0i}	r_1	insert()/$W_3(k^{t(1)}==1)$
	A_0	r_1	$\varnothing$
r_1	rel	r_2	$\varnothing$
	find	r_2	$W_2(t^{1m})$
r_2	A_i	r_1	insert()/$W_3(k^{t(1)}==1)$
	A_r	r_1	replace()/$W_3(k^{t(1)}==2)$
	A_d	r_3	delete(), $W_1(l^{1m}))$/ $W_3(k^{t(1)}==3$
	A	r_1	$\varnothing$
	A_k	r_5	$\varnothing$
r_3	drel	r_4	$\varnothing$
r_4	A_i	r_1	(change_rel(),insert())/$W_3(k^{t(1)}==1$
	A_r	r_1	(change_rel(), replace())/$W_3(k^{t(1)}==2$
	A_d	r_3	delete_with_link()/$W_3(k^{t(1)}==3$
	A	r_1	change_rel()
	A_k	r_5	change_rel()
r_5	no_label	r_k	*

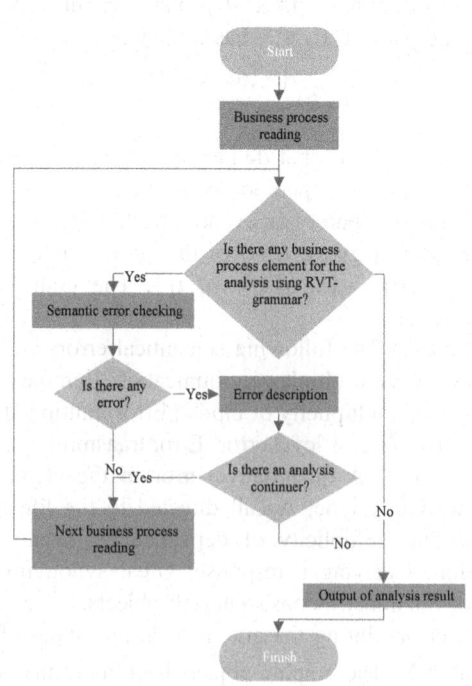

Fig. 1. Algorithm for business process analysis using RVT-grammar.

number of outcoming links allow one to cover the most part of the diagram for analysis. The algorithm for business process analysis using RVT-grammar is shown in Fig. 1.

To analysis and control the errors the Plugin has developed [20]: syntax oriented analyzer of UML diagrams for MS Visio, and network system of diagrams analysis and control, offering a full set of a functional to analyze and control syntax and semantic errors (Fig. 2). The Plugin allows to perform follows:

- Analyses any diagrams (BPML, UML, IDEF0, IDEF3, Petri net) using Temporal RVT-grammar;
- Be integrated as plug-ins into MS Visio;
- Checks 23 types of errors;
- Gives recommendations to a designer for improve a diagram.

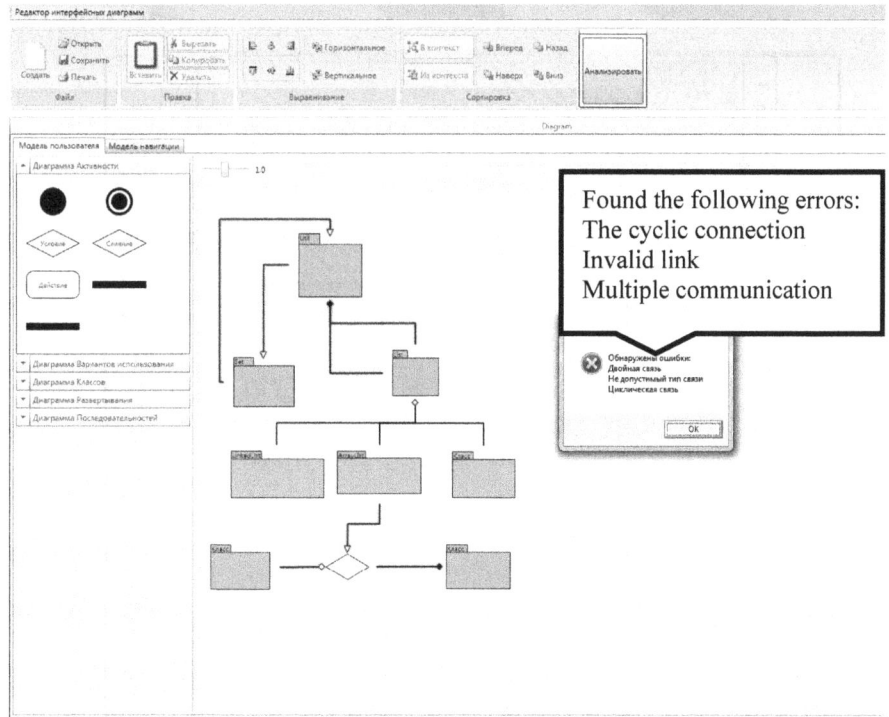

Fig. 2. Plugin to analyze workflows for MS Visio.

4 Method of Business-Processes Transformation

In order to dynamically reconfigure business processes, a mechanism for diagrams' transformation should be developed. It will allow programmers to gain agility, to improve functionality, and to increase business processes efficiency of a company.

We propose to transform the diagram's structure via the procedures "Delete", "Insert" and "Replace" with saving a link for (before, after, and etc.) a special period of time. All graphic primitives must have a timestamp which will allow programmers to determine the diagram's transformation time. As a rule, graphic primitives of BPMN, eEPC, IDEF0, UML AD, and etc. contain a description (see UML AD) which can be defined as a time variable.

Orchestration is the internal workflows in an enterprise or a company that presents its internal business processes [16]. IBM, Microsoft, Oracle, BEA Systems develop tools as BPEL4WS, XLANG, WSFL to describe the business logic [17–19]. In order to control these workflows in the enterprise's business processes, only one manager for orchestration is required (Fig. 3).

Choreography is the external workflows in a lot of enterprises and companies that have relationship with each other. Each member of choreography can describe a role and his place in workflows. All choreography relationships are monitored in log.

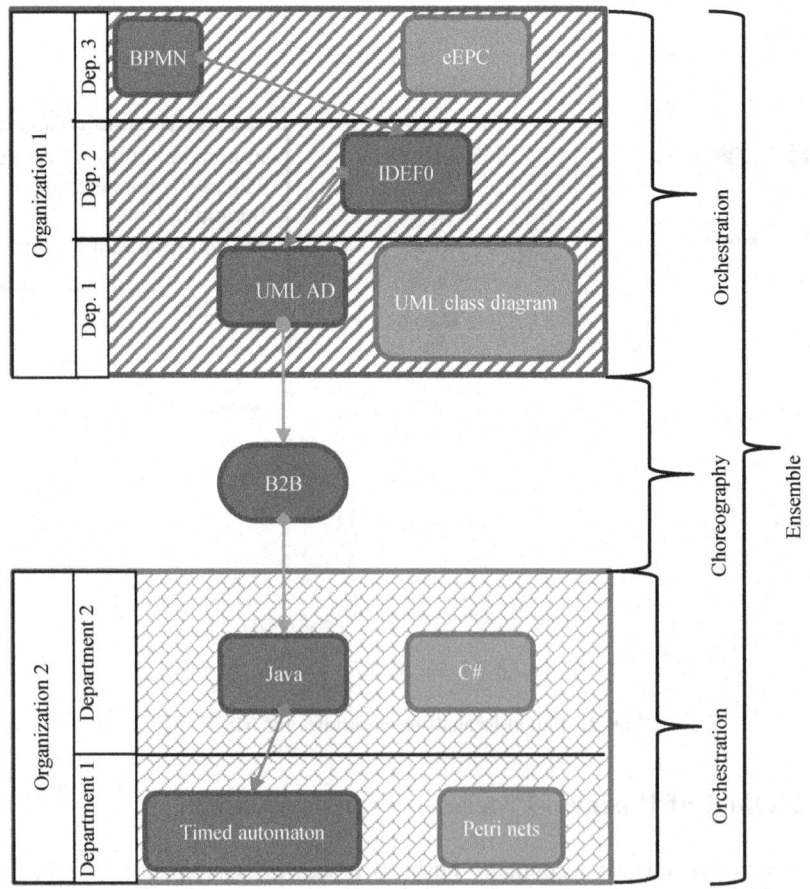

Fig. 3. The ensemble of diagrams and the hybrid orchestration.

The dynamics of workflows is presented in two aspects: orchestration and a sample of choreography that combine into an ensemble. An emerged sample of choreography should be associated with the developed diagrams. Organization 1 has BPMN, IDEF0, UML AD, eEPC, UML diagram in the orchestration. BPNM, IDEF0, UML AD are only in the ensemble [10, 20–24]. Organization 2 has Java, C#, Timed automata, Petri nets in the orchestration, but Java and Timed automata are only in the ensemble.

Hybrid orchestration means that we use different types of diagrams. We can create Temporal RVT-grammar for BPMN, IDEF0, eEPC etc., and transform them. Let us examine an example of a UML AD diagram (Fig. 4).

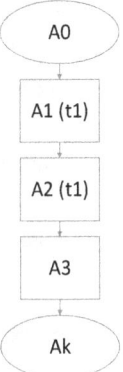

Fig. 4. UML AD diagram with a timestamp t1.

Graphic primitives (elements) A1 and A2 are denoted by the timestamp t1. This means that at a certain point in time t1 these elements will be transformed in the following ways: (1) Insert, (2) Replace, (3) Delete.

It is logical to assume that only one element can be transformed in one period of time. Therefore, each timestamp is given a tape where three variants can be indicated for one element: 1 – Insert, 2 – Replace, 3 – Delete.

Using Insert and Replace operations, additional information will be saved at an extended tape allowing it to save both numbers and quasi-terms.

Additional function Insert() is used for the operation 1. It provides necessary information extracted from the extended tape and forms an inserted fragment based on subgrammar.

Operation 2 is a complex operation that is represented as a set of operations "Delete" and "Insert". Additional function Replace() is introduced.

Let us consider function Delete at the initial stage. At time t1, the diagram becomes as follows (Fig. 5).

It can be deleted an infinite number of elements. In order to delete an element, let us use the following method. If the automaton encounters an element with a timestamp, a link to this element is saved in a stack. Then the automaton continues processing elements until it meets the element without a timestamp. In this case, the special

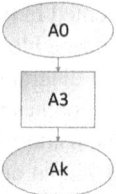

Fig. 5. Elements' deletion at a diagram.

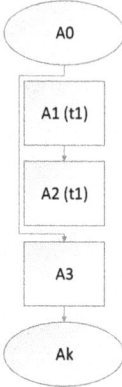

Fig. 6. Links' assignment in deleting an element.

function change_rel() is performed. It finds a link to the first deleted element in the stack and ties it to a current element. This process is shown in Fig. 6.

The function Delete() removes elements in a diagram not to leave elements, which should be deleted, as hanging elements when processing quasi-terms which should be deleted. It should be separately introduced the function delete_with_link() in order to delete elements with an inlink.

5 Discussion

Applying timed grammar for designing, specification, controlling and analyzing real-time systems is well-known practice [25]. Timed and hybrid automatons is used for analyzing and managing manufacturing (MM) and workflows of cyber-physical systems (WCPS) [26].

When solving the tasks of MM&WCPS's design, specification, control and analysis, there are problems with access to resources, blocking, liveliness limitation (liveness, reversibility, boundedness, reachability, dead transitions, deadlocks, home states). The examples of MM&WCPS's tasks are the control of the nuclear reactor's temperature and the control of the railway level-crossing gate [27], and electronic workflows. These tasks successfully apply timed context-free grammars. A large number of MM&WCPS sets the task of monitoring and analyzing. It can be accomplished by various mathematical methods based on workflows [5]. At present, π-calculus is a promising but very young and evolving theory. It has many open questions and unresolved problems. Petri nets which are widely used do not have a universal framework for MM&CPS's modeling and analyzing. In order to analyze various properties (liveliness, attainability, safety), MM&CPSs are modeled in different types of Petri nets. In order to analyze MM&CPS in the error-free systems' development in the conceptual design phase, the model checking method is widely used. However, it is mainly developed for experienced scientists and engineers, since it is complex to understand and use [25]. MM&CPSs are also specified by managers who do not have training in formal models and informatics. Formal analysis requires a detailed representation of the process model in a formal language.

Although, relevant and having big practice famous is a problem researching mechanisms to analyze and control MM&CPS.

Modern tools can only check 16 types of errors [20]. Thus, we develop a new Temporal RVT-grammar to check and fix all type of errors, which has a linear require of time to analysis oppositely with other grammars with exponential and polynomial requires of time. Figure 7 shows the efficiency. Graphic objects are graphic figures as a circle, a rectangle, a rhombus, a square, a line and etc. We propose a formula for calculation of the efficiency that can be written as:

$$\text{Required time} = c \cdot L_s, L_s = \sum_{i=1}^{m} \left(\sum_{j=1}^{V_i} v_{in_{ij}} + \sum_{j=1}^{V_i} v_{out_{ij}} \right) + \sum_{i=m+1}^{t} \left(V_i + \sum_{j=1}^{V_i} v\_out_{ij} \right) + no\_label. \tag{3}$$

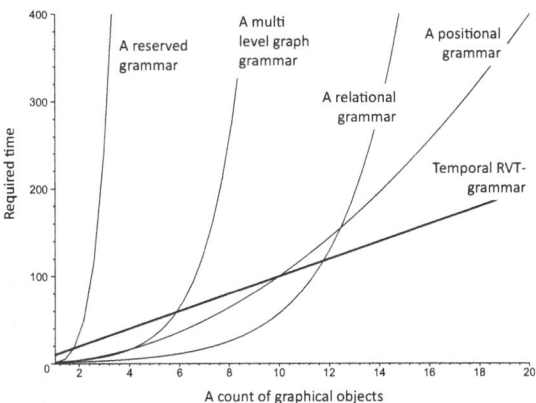

Fig. 7. Efficiency of checking and fixing errors with help Temporal RVT-grammar into diagrams.

where c – the constant of realization of algorithm, which determines a quantity of time (operators) that are spent to analysis one graphic object; L_s – the number of graphic objects; V_i – the number of graphic objects of i-type; v_in_{ij} – the number of inputs to j-graphic objects of i-type; v_out_{ij} – the number of outputs from j-graphic objects of i-type; t – a total of object types; m – a quantity of object types that have more than one output.

6   Conclusion and Future Works

There is a problem with workflows for checking and exchanging various formats between large industrial enterprises, and also between their departments. Time begins to play a major importance for production, which often uses the Internet. This is why we develop a temporal grammar for analyzing, managing and reconfiguring dynamic design workflows, where time is a known role. We create this grammar as a temporal state grammar that uses the memory as a stack. Thus, this grammar allows us to remove several semantic errors (structural-behavioral) at the stage of conceptual design in complex computer systems, as well as solve problems of reengineering for reactive systems using real time. The transformation can check errors in a diagram and correct this diagram. We describe a simple example of using UML AD. The scientific significance of the approach is represented by a grammar and algebraic model that takes into account the temporal nature of workflows, provides structural and behavioral and semantic analysis and reconfiguration of workflows, and expands the class of errors. In future works, we plan to conduct experiments on BPMN and UML AD and other graphical temporal languages for the complex system development, taking into account the design data and technological preparation for the production of a real enterprise. We will identify new typical structural-behavioral errors and describe them in our future works.

Acknowledgments. The reported study was funded by RFBR according to the research project № 17-07-01417.

References

1. Aguilar, J.C.P., Hasebe, K., Mazzara, M., Kato, K.: Model Checking of BPMN Models for Reconfigurable Workflows. arXiv preprint arXiv:1607.00478 (2016)
2. Sherehiy, B., Karwowski, W., Layer, J.K.: A review of enterprise agility: concepts, frameworks, and attributes. Int. J. Ind. Ergon. **37**, 446–460 (2007)
3. Highsmith, J., Orr, K., Cockburn, A.: Extreme programming. In: E-Business Application Delivery, pp. 4–17 (2000)
4. A Global Swiss Company Offering Advanced Intelligent Application Software for Multiple Business sectors. http://whitestein.com/. Accessed 14 Mar 2018
5. Bider, I., Jalali, A.: Agile business process development: why, how and when applying Nonaka's theory of knowledge transformation to business process development. IseB **14**(4), 693–731 (2014). https://doi.org/10.1007/s10257-014-0256-1

6. Andersson, T., Andersson-Ceder, A., Bider, I.: State flow as a way of analyzing business processes-case studies. Logistics Inf. Manag. **15**(1), 34–45 (2012). http://www.ibissoft.com/publications/Cases.pdf. Accessed 14 Mar 2018

7. YAWL Foundation: YAWL. http://www.yawlfoundation.org/. Accessed 14 Mar 2018

8. Bider, I.: Analysis of agile software development from the knowledge transformation perspective. In: Johansson, B., Andersson, B., Holmberg, N. (eds.) BIR 2014. LNBIP, vol. 194, pp. 143–157. Springer, Cham (2014). https://doi.org/10.1007/978-3-319-11370-8_11

9. IbisSoft: iPB Reference Manual. http://docs.ibissoft.se/node/3. Accessed 14 Mar 2018

10. Afanasyev, A.N., Voit, N.N., Kirillov, S.Y.: Development of RYT-grammar for analysis and control dynamic workflows. In: 2017 International Conference on Computing Networking and Informatics (ICCNI 2017), pp. 1–4 (2017). https://doi.org/10.1109/iccni.2017.8123797. http://ieeexplore.ieee.org/stamp/stamp.jsp?tp=&arnumber=8123797&isnumber=8123766. Accessed 15 Mar 2017

11. Voit, N.N.: Development of timed RT-grammars for analysis of business process at manufacturing and in cyber-physical systems. In: 2017 International Conference on Computing Networking and Informatics (ICCNI 2017), pp. 1–5 (2017). https://doi.org/10.1109/iccni.2017.8123798. http://ieeexplore.ieee.org/stamp/stamp.jsp?tp=&arnumber=8123798&isnumber=812376. Accessed 15 Mar 2017

12. Orchestration and Workflow. https://www.cloudenablers.com/blog/orchestration-and-workflow/. Accessed 15 Mar 2017

13. ISO: LOTOS – A Formal Description Technique Based on the Temporal Ordering of Observational Behaviour. Technical Report 8807, ISO 1989

14. Lohmann, N., Wolf, K.: Realizability is controllability. In: Laneve, C., Su, J. (eds.) WS-FM 2009. LNCS, vol. 6194, pp. 110–127. Springer, Heidelberg (2010). https://doi.org/10.1007/978-3-642-14458-5_7

15. Poizat, P., Salaün, G.: Checking the realizability of BPMN 2.0 choreographies. In: SAC 2012, pp. 1927–1934 (2012)

16. Orchestration and Workflow. https://www.cloudenablers.com/blog/orchestration-and-workflow/. Accessed 29 Dec 2017

17. Van der Aalst, W.M.P.: Don't go with the flow: web services composition standards exposed. IEEE Intell. Syst. **18**(1), 72–76 (2003). http://www.martinfowler.workflowpatterns.com/documentation/documents/ieeewebflow.pdf. Accessed 29 Dec 2017

18. Marca, D.A., McGowan, C.L.: SADT: Structured Analysis and Design Technique. McGraw-Hill, Inc., New York (1987). http://dl.acm.org/citation.cfm?id=31837. Accessed 29 Mar 2017

19. TP026B, Rev. Rational Unified Process. https://www.ibm.com/developerworks/rational/library/content/03July/1000/1251/1251_bestpractices_TP026B.pdf. Accessed 29 Dec 2017

20. Afanasyev, A.N., Voit, N.N., Gainullin, R.F.: Diagrammatic models processing in designing the complex automated systems. In: 10th IEEE International Conference on Application of Information and Communication Technologies (AICT 2016), pp. 441–445 (2016). https://doi.org/10.1109/icaict.2016.7991737

21. Afanasyev, A., Voit, N.: Intelligent agent system to analysis manufacturing process models. In: Abraham, A., Kovalev, S., Tarassov, V., Snášel, V. (eds.) Proceedings of the First International Scientific Conference "Intelligent Information Technologies for Industry" (IITI'16). AISC, vol. 451, pp. 395–403. Springer, Cham (2016). https://doi.org/10.1007/978-3-319-33816-3_39

22. Afanasyev, A.N., Voit, N.N., Voevodin, E.Yu., Gainullin, R.F.: Control of UML diagrams in designing automated systems software. In: 9th IEEE International Conference on Application of Information and Communication Technologies, AICT-2015, pp. 285–288 (2015). https://doi.org/10.1109/icaict.2015.7338564

23. Afanasyev, A., Voit, N.: Multi-agent system to analyse manufacturing process models. In: International Conference on Fuzzy Logic and Intelligent Technologies in Nuclear Science, FLINS 2016, France, pp. 444–449 (2016). https://doi.org/10.1142/9789813146976_0072
24. Afanasyev, A., Voit, N., Gainullin, R.: The analysis of diagrammatic models of workflows in design of the complex automated systems. In: International Conference on Fuzzy Logic and Intelligent Technologies in Nuclear Science, FLINS 2016, France, pp. 509–514 (2016). https://doi.org/10.1007/978-3-319-33609-1_20
25. Heitmeyer, C.L., Lynch, N.A.: The generalized railroad crossing: a case study in formal verification of real-time systems. In: IEEE RTSS, pp. 120–131 (1994)
26. Karpov, Yu.G.: Model Checking. Verifikaciya parallel'nyh i raspredelennyh programmnyh system. 560 s (2010) (in Russian)
27. Lee, E.A.: Cyber-physical systems: design challenges. In: ISORC (2008)

Specifying and Incorporating Compliance Requirements into Software Development Using UML and OCL

Oluwasefunmi Tale Arogundade[1(✉)], Temitope Elizabeth Abioye[1],
Abiodun Muyideen Mustapha[1], Adeola Mary Adeniji[1],
Abiodun Motunrayo Ikotun[1], and Franklin O. Asahiah[2]

[1] Federal University of Agriculture, Abeokuta, Ogun State, Nigeria
arogundadeot@funaab.edu.ng, elizatope_2005@yahoo.com,
abiodunmustaphall@gmail.com, biodunikotun@gmail.com
[2] Obafemi Awolowo University, Ile-Ife, Nigeria
sobusola@oauife.edu.ng

Abstract. Nowadays, industries, agencies, institutions demand a high degree of compliance at different level of commercial enterprise to meet various laws, regulations, standards etc. Compliance check on the processes of different firms have shown that it is a daunting task which resulted to high monetary implication in resolving the issues of changing requirements. Here, compliance requirement was incorporated into an industrial domain in Nigeria in order to develop an advanced and effective system. Unified Modeling Language was used to design the software for the case study. Classical Unified Modeling Language like: use case diagram, activity diagram, class diagram and sequence diagram were designed for the system. Compliance requirements embedded in the UML were formalized and validated using Object Constraint Language. Facts gathered from different organizations and customers in this domain were used to incorporate compliance requirements into the design. This will aid system developers to implement compliant systems for business enterprises.

Keywords: Compliance · Unified Modeling Language
Object Constraint Language · Compliance requirements · Software design

1 Introduction

Compliance refers to the means of finding out if the operations of business procedures and software applications is directly related to the requirement that may come from laws, legislation, regulations, standards and code of practices (such as ISO 9001), internal policies and business partner contracts (such as service level agreements-SLAs) [1]. It also implies an approach for conforming to rules, such as a specifications, policies, standards or laws [2]. These rules, described as compliance requirements, is defined as goals that organizations aspire to achieve in their efforts to ensure that they are aware of and take steps to adhere to relevant laws and regulations. It can also be defined as a detailed documented rules and regulations that specify any part of an internal or inter-organizational system processes. This has led to lots of penalties being

© Springer International Publishing AG, part of Springer Nature 2018
O. Gervasi et al. (Eds.): ICCSA 2018, LNCS 10963, pp. 511–526, 2018.
https://doi.org/10.1007/978-3-319-95171-3_40

incurred from several regulatory bodies [3]. Organizations could face the threat of regulatory or legal penalty, financial loss in terms of material and/or reputational loss as a result of non-compliance with laws, regulations, rules, related self-regulatory, and codes of conduct that has to do with organizational processes [4]. Industrial influence cannot be ignored in order to properly understand the problems that affect the incorporation of compliance requirements on foods and beverages system, due to complexity of understanding and the compliance constraint requirement. Therefore, there is need to incorporate domain standards into their mode of operations so that the company can operate in compliance with these standards. This can be achieved by designing the business operations with the compliance requirements at the early stage of automating the business processes.

From structural view, compliance requirements are classified into four groups relating to the fundamental business processes; workflow restrictions (control-flow requirements), the use of information (data requirements and validation), employed resources (task allocation and access rights) and temporal restrictions [5]. These requirements should be founded on well-structured basis of a logical language that will help the applications in the future automation reasoning for testing and assuring business process compliance [2]. The use of formal language like Object Constraint Language (OCL) or creation of design patterns can be employed to achieve this. This paper aims at designing UML profiles for business software designs of e-distribution, formalize its compliance requirements using OCL for the purpose of verifying the system model, and to validate the class diagram in order to detect design flaws before the system is implemented. Section 2 of this paper discusses the review of related works, section three describes the case study and the implementation and validation of the compliance requirements. Section 4 discusses the result, conclusion and future works.

2 Related Works

Gupta et al. [6] presented an object oriented conceptual MD model approach which implies that the proposal is a view of UML that uses the specified extension mechanism given by the UML. This extension makes use of OCL for specifying well-formed rules of new defined member. Lisboa-Filho et al. [7] proposed a UML profile that is designed for modeling geographic databases known as GeoProfile. They considered GeoProfile as the basic step in harmonizing the various existing models gearing towards semantic interoperability. Kim and Hyun [8] used UML in modelling an hybrid control system using a bottom-up approach which starts from certain instances to a generalized classes. The UCHCS members were modelled as group and the activities in connection with the steps are modelled as threads. The transition criterions were also modelled as threads. Sunguk [9] presented the concept of database together with a brief summary of the use of UML as a standard process of the real world objects in developing object oriented design procedure for computer software. Kaur and Arora [10] presented the requirements and analysis design of a real-time embedded system in connection with the control system application for platform stabilization using COMET method of design with UML notation. The application was involved in electromechanical systems design that is controlled by the multiprocessors. Alhumadian [11] delved into thorough analysis of Use Case, Class, and Sequence Diagrams. Applications of these diagrams were monitored in lowering the complexity and presenting a good model of a system.

More so, a treatment to join diagrams with the right approaches was presented to improve modeling potential of UML which help in the system development. Jakimi and El Koutbi [12] suggested a requirement engineering procedure involving UML scenarios for obtaining the worldwide representation of the prescribed services system and implementation code from the UML use case service. Four operators were suggested; Sequential, Concurrent, Conditional and Iteration Operators. An algorithm and a tool complement can instinctively give a global sequence diagram showing ways of composing them and a code generation of sequence diagram was developed. Pham et al. [13] presented a description of logic-based approach for business process compliance checking during two phases of the business process life-cycle. In this approach, business process and the set of regulations are typified in machine readable form. Also, this knowledge was used to check for the compliance between phases. The merit of this method allows the system to find out the semantic errors of business process intuitively at design time and run-time. Gottingen [14] described a broad approach for the model-based development of Web services. This method is founded on a Web service profile for the Unified Modeling Language (UML) that allows a thorough description of complete Web service models. This type of Web service models give room to the generation of a total source code and the equivalent platform-specific configuration files needed to run the modeled Web services. The feasibility of the proposed approach for the model-based development of Web services was validated by implementing a library system Web service. Representation of business rules in UML and OCL models for developing information systems by Nemuraite et al. [15] show case means of presenting business rules using UML and OCL models and its use in system development processes. They discovered that the process of capturing and modifying business rules were safer when visual business process models are employed. Therefore, the effectiveness of UML diagrams coupled with OCL for expressing various kind of rules were specified in their work. Bubel et al. [16] in their work titled "Integration of Informal and Formal Development of Object-Oriented Safety-Critical Software: A Case Study with the KeY System" gave a report on a main industrial case study which was generated from a safety-critical software. The process involved computing a particular railway time table for its drivers from specific engine properties and the available track facilities. This research dealt with an attempt on how authoring and maintenance of formal requirement documents will need little effort. This was done using specification patterns developed in KeY for OCL. Software specification and testing using UML and OCL by Milley et al. [17] presented the combine force in the use of UML and OCL for the specification, design and implementation of software system. These tools were used in developing an automated testing task which enhances the quality and time frame spent on software development. Rumpe [18] presented an agile modeling with the UML. This work dealt with practical approach to model based software development. Requirements and design specification, code generation and the implementation of test case was modeled based on primary artifact. The uses of UML as the modeling language show case a good integration and also provide room to model system and test in parallel. It is suitable therefore to employ UML and OCL in modeling and validating industrial system model respectively to find out their compliance rate and state. This will enable the right scientific propositions instead of assumptions.

3 Design Methodology

In this section, we describe the design tools used to present various features that need be understood in carrying out the incorporation of the compliance requirements.

3.1 Unified Modeling Language (UML)

The UML is accepted as an industrial quality measure for specifying, visualizing, understanding and documenting object-oriented software systems [19]. It is an essential part of building object oriented software as it uses mostly graphical notation to specify the design of the software. Therefore, in the usage of UML in foods and beverages industry system, the design process can be represented in diagrams, using class diagrams [20].

3.2 Class Diagram

A class diagram is normally used to showcase logical classes. It is a point discussion among business people in an organization such as home mortgages, car loans and interest rates [21]. They are also used to demonstrate implementation classes and these are the area of interest of programmers. A class diagram displays the static structure of a system, presenting how various entities like people, things and data interact with each other.

3.3 Object Constraint Language (OCL)

OCL is a UML's constraint specification language [22]. The Object Constraint Language is a declarative language that presents constraint on object-oriented models. A constraint is a condition placed on one or more values of object-oriented model. Therefore, OCL is an example of industrial constraints for object-oriented analysis and design. For example, a label *inv:* declares the restriction to be invariant. There are four types of constraints: An invariant (a constraint that states a condition which must be obeyed by all instantiation of class [22]); a precondition to an operation (a restriction which must be true at the set time of operation execution); the obligations which are specified by the post condition and post condition which is a rule that must be true immediately after the time the operation is executed. A guard is a rule that must be true before a change in state is discharged [23].

3.4 Use Case Diagram

Use case diagram is a method, used in system analysis, to identify, clarify and organize system requirement. Emphasis isplaced on what a system does rather than how it does it. It can also be seen as requirements and restrictions in the form of scripts or scenarios [19]. A Use Case diagram is one of the Unified Modeling Language with the simplest representation of a user's interaction showing the user and the different use cases in which the user is involved. A use case has the capacity to recognize different users in a system and the different use cases. Use Case is a sequence of event or action that states the relationship between a role (an actor) and the system to accomplish a goal. Human or external system can be an actor.

3.5 Activity Diagram

Activity diagram is a behavior diagram that depicts the control flow or object flow. It is important in demonstrating the message flow from one event to another and in describing dynamic parts of the system. It is simply a flowchart that expresses the movement from one event to another or the operation of the system. The rounded rectangles stands for actions, diamonds depict decisions, bars stands for the start or end, a black circle stands for the start of the workflow, an encircled black circle represents the end (final state).

3.6 Sequence Diagram

Sequence diagram is used to present the relationship between objects sequentially as the interaction occurs. It is used in business to show how business works currently by depicting various relationships among business objects. Sequence diagram is drawn by placing lifeline notation elements horizontally on the top of the diagram. Lifeline stands for either roles or object instance that takes part in the modeled sequence.

3.7 Case Study

The case study considered in this work is the e-distribution of food and beverage. This paper explicitly describe how these were implemented in the Specification and Incorporation of Compliance Requirements into the design of the case study.

E-distribution of Food and Beverages
The food and beverages manufacturing industry is a wide scope. It is an industry that is involved in the preparation of food and beverages items that is being offered for purchase and is ready for consumption. The raw materials for production has to be sourced for, processed, preserved and packaged. Also, it involves product research and design, taste evaluation and marketing. The survival of this industry is founded on the expertise, the method used, reuse and simplicity. Industry experts and team are aware of the market conditions and the rules that governed it. They assist in specified installation and gives best solution advice. The internal teams are best in putting together steps that leads to the development of complex projects through the use of many suppliers worldwide. The local facilities are responsible for the preferment of better solution at a reasonable cost. The change/transformation of food consumption data to nutritious intakes demand a food recipe database and experienced computer programmers for calculation of nutrients. A well-developed food recipe database is

costly because of the costs of chemical analysis for numerous foods and nutrients. It gives detail on important form of eating patterns throughout the world (comparative similar diets, changing food springing up and underdeveloped countries' massive food destruction and waste at the point of distribution and consumption). The aforementioned trends have negative impact on health and the environment. Besides, research was also done through internet where several websites were reviewed to gain information about the other current system related to foods and beverages system. Thus Unified Modeling Language (UML) was used as the design model for the proposed system. The standard regulation considered in this domain is the Standard Organization of Nigeria (SON). The licensed beverage company considered in this research work is Cadbury PLC, Nigeria.

International Standards Organization on SON
The SON (Standard Organization Of Nigeria) is set up to cater for and ensure that the goods produced and consumed in the country are of at least, the minimum required standard. The organization is a parastatal of the Federal Government and administered by the Ministry of Industries. It is a corporate body which has two arms through which it operates; a council which is the governing body of the organization called the Standards Council of Nigeria and the organization itself (SON Act 2004). The Council sees to the running of the organization through the formulation of polices in accordance with the intent of the formation of the organization while the organization implements such polices [24].

Function of the Organization
The aim is to ensure that the products pushed into the market by producers are of the required quality and the process of production are of the acceptable standard. They

   i. Advise the Federal Government generally on the national policy on standards, standard specifications, quality control and metrology;
  ii. Designate, establish and approve standards in metrology, materials, commodities, structures and processes for the certification of production in commerce and industry;
 iii. Provide the necessary measures for quality control of raw materials and products in conformity with the standard specification;
  iv. Organizes tests and do everything necessary to ensure compliance with approved standards;
   v. Undertake investigations as necessary into the quality of facilities, materials and products in Nigeria and establish a quality assurance system including certification of factories, products and laboratories, and ensure reference standards for calibration and verification of measures and measuring instruments [25].

Compliance Requirements for Foods and Beverages E-distribution
The class diagrams shown in Figs. 1 and 2 display logical classes, which show the activities in the initial registration phase of the e-distribution of foods and beverages. This reveals how operations are performed between different units of the system. The design pattern considered for this research is the Factory pattern. This comes under creational pattern as this pattern provides one of the best ways to create an object. In

Factory pattern, we create objects without exposing the creation logic to the client and refer to newly created object using a common interface.

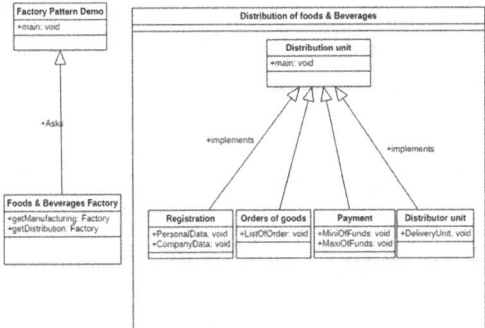

Fig. 1. Class diagram for distribution of foods & beverages (Initial Diagram).

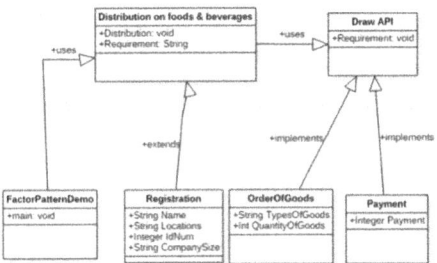

Fig. 2. Class diagram for registration in the domain (Initial Diagram).

The use case diagram shown in Fig. 3 is for the Goods distribution unit. This shows the process through which the manufactured goods are delivered to the customers. The processes include customer registration, order request, payment for goods and delivery cases on the customer side. The staff of the Goods Production unit in the organization will have to carry out the received order case while the Goods Distribution (GD) Manager responds to the feedback. The GD Manager is the individual in the business organizations that coordinates and ensure that the process of good order and delivery is successful. Figures 4, 5 and 6 show activity diagrams that clearly describe the two major activities in the use case diagram. These show the progress that the business process will be engaged in actualizing its goals to its customers.

From Fig. 4, it can be deduced that the customer need to register in the homepage, the system will generate customer registration number, which is the unique key to the customer. When the system want to create order of goods, the customer has to enter the registration number, if it correspond with the number in the industry database, the system will display the customer profile and the customer will able to generate an invoice and move to payment requirement before it moves to delivery units. Figure 6 shows the activity diagram for creating invoice in the goods distribution unit. The customer utilizes his assigned registration number which will be verified for accessing the system. This validation will either deny the customer access or make him/her able to place an order. Each order has an automated invoice that is generated and sent to the GD manager for approval. Such approval is what is used for carrying out payment and the delivery is made.

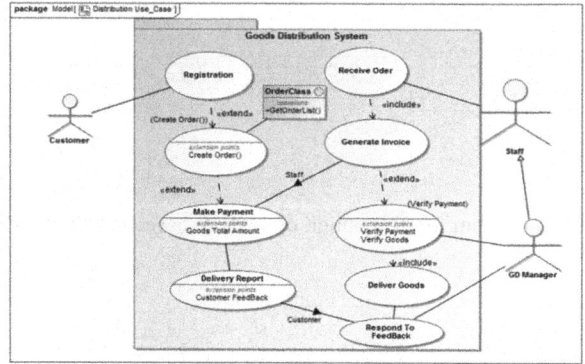

Fig. 3. Use case diagram for goods distribution unit

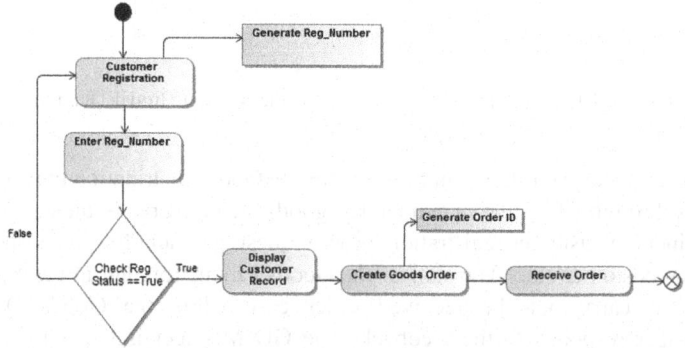

Fig. 4. Activity diagram for the customers registration

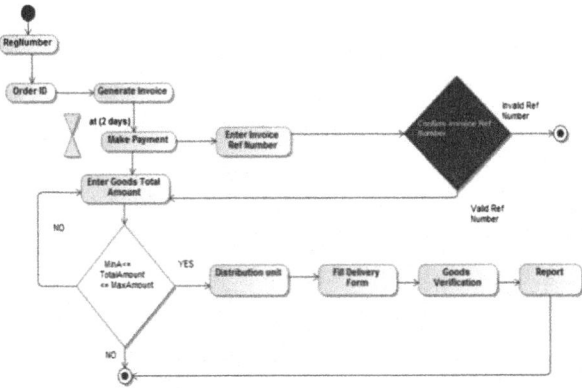

Fig. 5. Activity diagram for the orders of goods requirement.

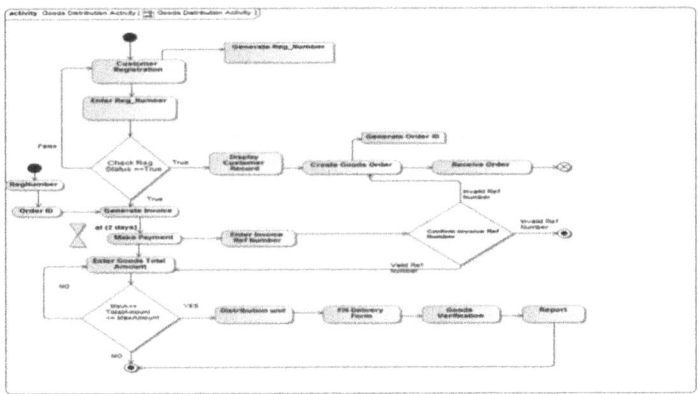

Fig. 6. Activity diagram for creating invoice in distribution unit

The eventual class diagram drawn for the Food and Beverage domain registration, good distribution and goods order systems are shown in Figs. 7, 8 and 9. Each classes shown indicates their function and data types in the figures. This help ascertain the requirements for the individual classes that will aid the workability of the systems.

Figure 10 shows the sequence diagram which reveals the step by step procedure of how the actions will be performed by different actors of the Goods distribution system. The diagram shows the sequence and how it will be carried out from the beginning to the end of the business goal.

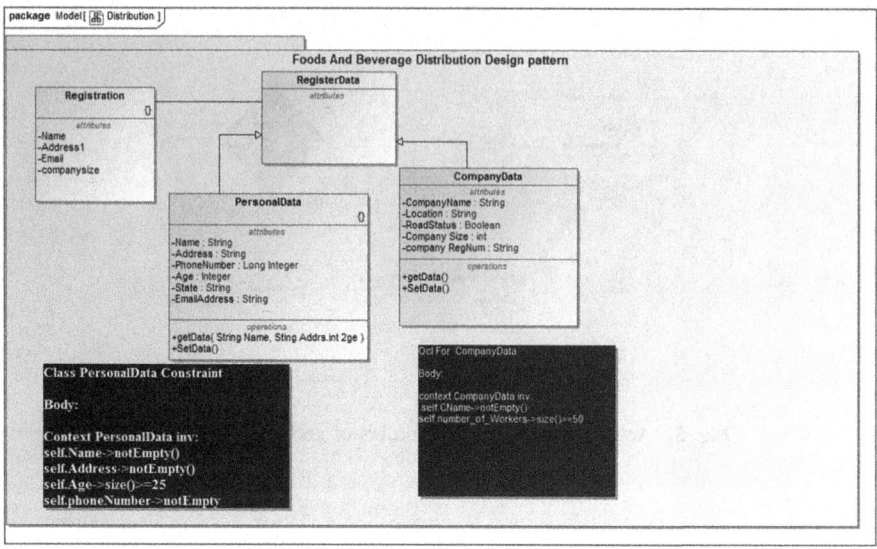

Fig. 7. Class diagram for the registration of the foods & beverages domain

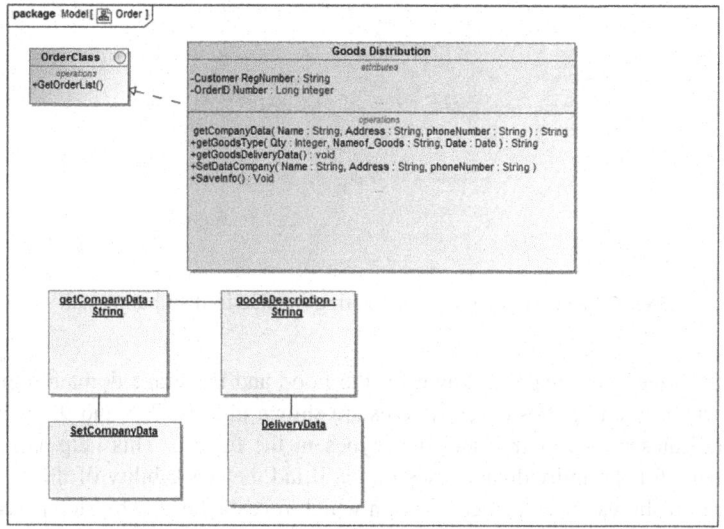

Fig. 8. Class diagram for goods distribution system

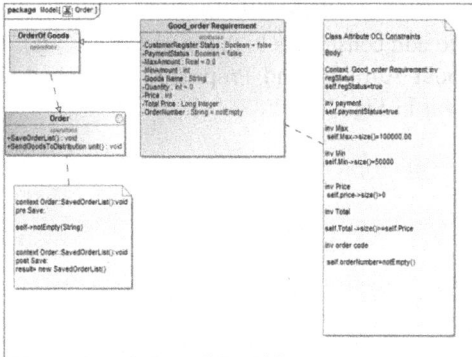

Fig. 9. Class diagram for orders of goods system

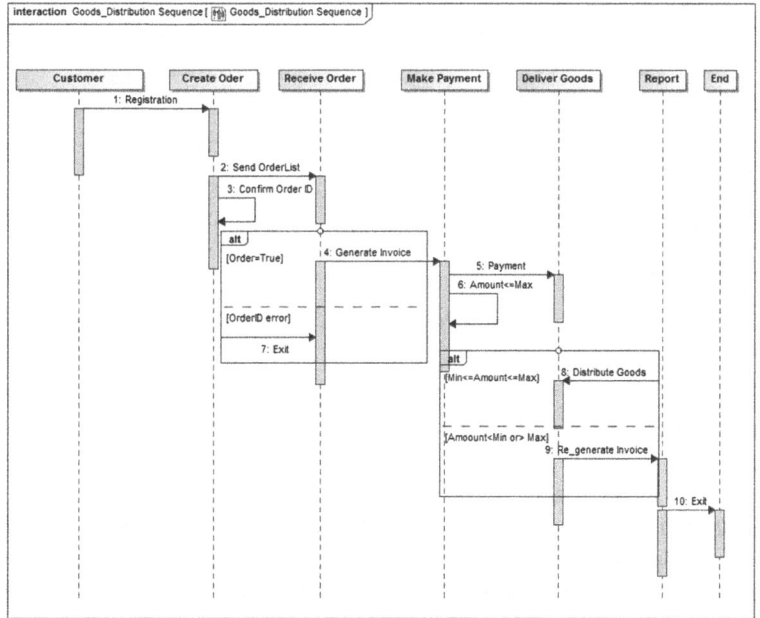

Fig. 10. Sequence diagram for registration in the foods & beverages domain

4   Model Validation

Every constraint that needs to be included in the class diagram model was added together with their contexts. The constraints with the contexts were expressed with context link to the proper diagram. The constraints identification of Post – and Pre – conditions as well as the derive and initialize constraints were not easy as their contexts are not classes but variables and functions. Papyrus software was used in validation process of Design class diagrams. This tool has the functionality of using OCL (Object Constraint Language) to add constraints to the model (elements). Also, the OCL codes used are written for both Attribute and Properties or Method. The eclipse papyrus implementation is shown in Fig. 11.

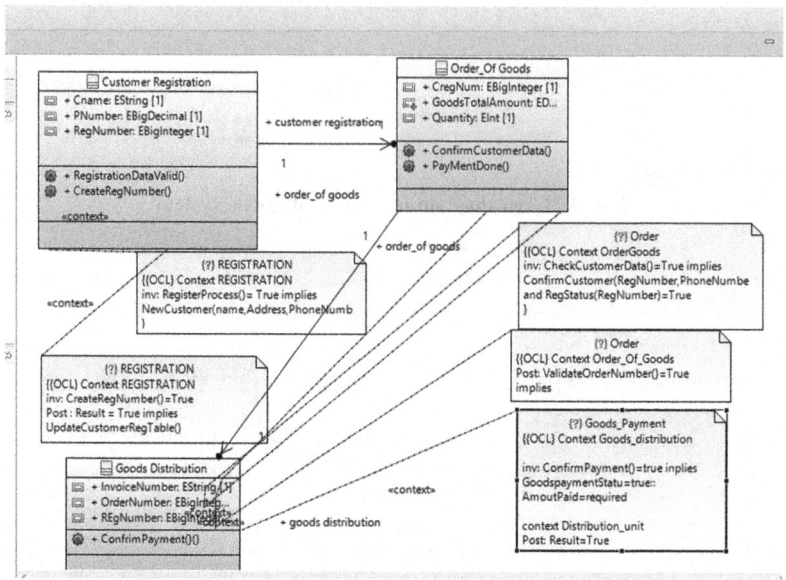

Fig. 11. The operational constraint-based class diagram of the foods & beverages distribution system

5   Result and Discussion

The problem of incorporating compliance requirements into software development of a business domain is due to the complexity of the requirements implementation. This work was implemented with OCL verifiable architecture. The flow, processes and activities were represented in UML design using Papyrus modeling tool. The purpose of modeling is to create a platform that makes implementation easy. The correctness of this model was verified through model validation using Papyrus and STAR-UML. The Compliance Requirements were implemented using Java Language in Netbean 8.0. The outputs of Prototype Application implementing all compliances were presented. Three case studies were used in this work: the e-distribution of food and beverages, e-banking and e-health. However, for the purpose of result discussion, e-distribution of food and beverages was used. When the application is launched, the home page interface pops up as seen in Fig. 12. The customer has to register in order to have customer registration number, which is a unique key to the customer. The constraint here is when the customer did not follow the procedure to register; the customer would not have access to the system.

Fig. 12. E-distribution system home page

For a new customer, there is a button to access the new registration platform.

After successful registration, the customer is granted a unique key generated by the system to access system. This is displayed in Fig. 13.

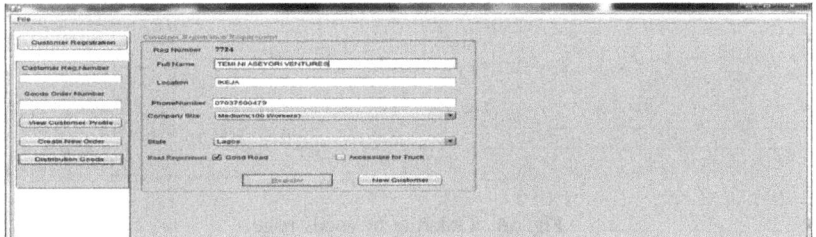

Fig. 13. Customer registration requirements page

As displayed in Fig. 14, when a customer click the view customer profile button, it will pop up the customer profile automatically showing that the customer profile is added to the industry database. If invalid registration number is supplied, application displays "Incorrect Customer Registration Number" indicating no database record (Fig. 15). This is system access constraint. With the unique key, access is granted to order of goods, and the system generates order number used to generate the invoice number as shown in Fig. 16. Figures 17 and 18 show the Goods distribution report page and the database respectively.

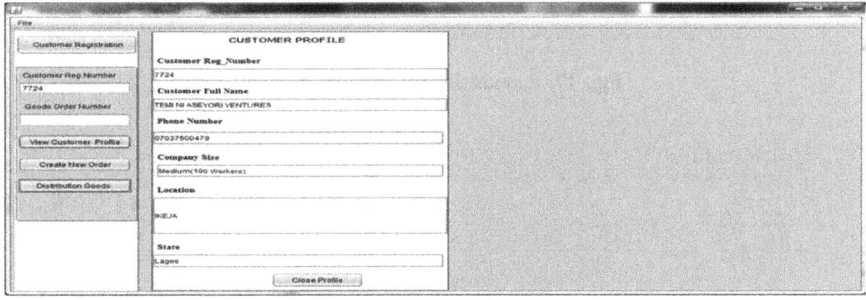

Fig. 14. Customer profile page

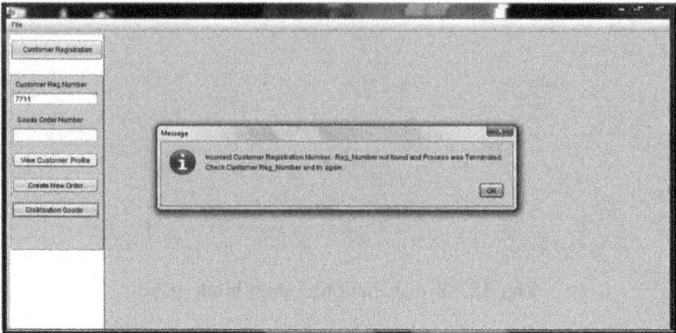

Fig. 15. Incorrect customer registration page

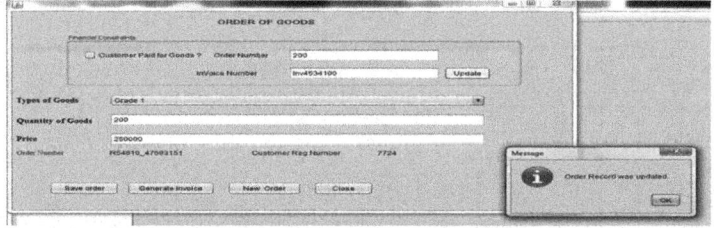

Fig. 16. Ordering of goods page

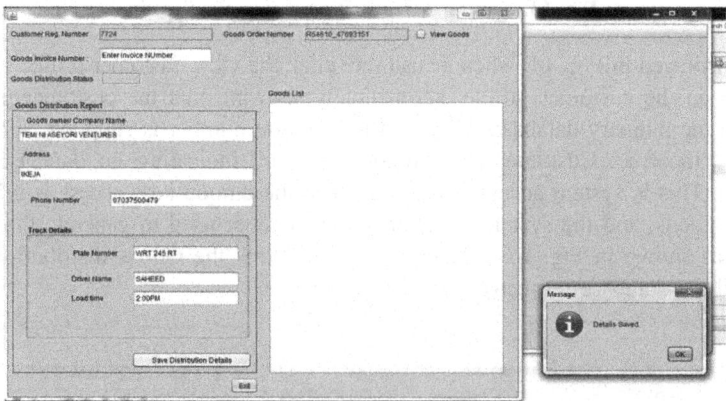

Fig. 17. Goods distribution report page

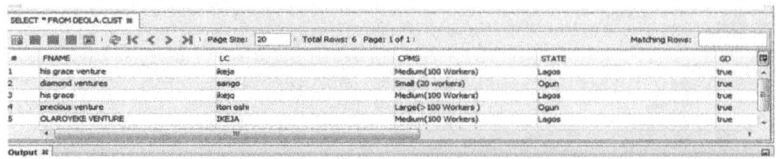

Fig. 18. Industry database page

6 Conclusion

The validation of models of industrial systems and the profile itself based on OCL constraints has been proven useful in several ways. It has been shown that the profile complies with UML as it is required. With different Industry having the records of their clients in different location, it has become essential to have a medium through which these databases can be accessed within different branches of these industries. An industry should also have a medium of accessing the information of its clients in other industries. In this research work, the e-distribution case study has been considered in the incorporation of compliance into software designs of systems before development. Validating these models has aided the discovering of some breaches in the activities of existing systems. The validation of the model using Papyrus further aided the proofs of this. The designing of models of the system profiles with UML (which is a standard modeling language) bridges the communication between end users and system developers. The OCL based validation of the model was achieved by adding some OCL constraint. With the successful validation, developers conversant with UML can utilize the models as the starting point for system development by performing an automated code generation with any tool from the model. In future, these validated models can be implemented into software systems that will be used in evaluating the compliance flaws that exist when systems are first modeled and validated before implementation and when they are not.

References

1. Elgammal, A., Turetken, O., van den Heuvel, W., Papazoglou, M.: Formalizing and applying compliance patterns for business process compliance. Softw. Syst. Model. **15**(1), 119–146 (2016)
2. Sadiq, S., Governatori, G., Namiri, K.: Modeling control objectives for business process compliance. In: Alonso, G., Dadam, P., Rosemann, M. (eds.) BPM 2007. LNCS, vol. 4714, pp. 149–164. Springer, Heidelberg (2007). https://doi.org/10.1007/978-3-540-75183-0_12
3. Abdullah, N.S., Indulska, M., Sadiq, S.: A study of compliance management in information system research. In: 17th European Conference on Information Systems (ECIS 2009 Proceedings), Verona, Italy, vol. 9 (2009)
4. Deloitte: Compliance Risk Assessments: The Third Ingredient in a World-Class Ethics and Compliance Program. Deloitte Development LLC, USA (2015)
5. Georgakopoulous, D., Hornick, M., Sheth, A.: An overview of workflow management: from process modelling to workflow automation infrastructure. Distrib. Parallel Databases **3**(2), 119–153 (1995)
6. Gupta, J., Gosain, A., Nagpal, S.: Empirical validation of object oriented data warehouse design quality metrics. In: Wyld, D.C., Wozniak, M., Chaki, N., Meghanathan, N., Nagamalai, D. (eds.) ACITY 2011. CCIS, vol. 198, pp. 320–329. Springer, Heidelberg (2011). https://doi.org/10.1007/978-3-642-22555-0_33
7. Lisboa-Filho, J., Sampaio, G.B., Nalon, F.R., Borges, K.A.D.V.: A UML profile for conceptual modeling in GIS domain. In: Proceedings of the International Workshop on Domain Engineering at CAiSE 2010, Hammamet, Tunisia, pp. 18–31 (2010)

8. Kim, H.K., Hyun, Y.: Design for U- health care hybrid control systems. Int. J. Softw. Eng. Appl. **8**(2), 375–384 (2014)
9. Sunguk, L.: UML for database systems and computer application. Int. J. Database Theor. Appl. **5**(1), 157–164 (2012)
10. Kaur, A., Arora, R.: Application of UML in real-time embedded systems. Int. J. Softw. Eng. Appl. (IJSEA) **3**(2), 59–70 (2012)
11. Alhumaidan, F.: A Critical Analysis and treatment of important UML diagrams enhancing Modelling point. Intell. Inf. Manag. **4**, 231–237 (2012)
12. Jakimi, A., El Koutbi, M.: An object-oriented approach to UML scenarios engineering and code generation. Int. J. Comput. Theor. Eng. **1**(1), 1783–8201 (2009)
13. Pham, T., Le Thanh, N.: Checking the compliance of business process in business process life cycle. In: 10th International Web Rule Symposium (RuleML 2016), CEUR 1620, New York, United States (2016)
14. Gottingen: Computer Science and Information System Reports. Technical reports, University of Jyväskylä, Finland (2010)
15. Nemuraite, L., Ceponiene, L., Vedrickas, G.: Representation of business rules in UML&OCL models for developing information systems. In: Stirna, J., Persson, A. (eds.) The Practice of Enterprise Modeling PoEM 2008. LNBIP, vol. 15, pp. 182–196. Springer, Heidelberg (2008). https://doi.org/10.1007/978-3-540-89218-2_14
16. Bubel, R., Hahnle, R.: Integration of informal and formal development of object-oriented safety-critical software: a case study with the key system. Int. J. Tools Softw. Transf. **7**(3), 197–211 (2005)
17. Milley, J., Peters, D.K.: Software Specification and Testing Using UML and OCL. Faculty of Engineering and Applied Science MUN St. John's, Newfoundland (2005)
18. Rumpe, B.: Agile modeling with the UML. In: Wirsing, M., Knapp, A., Balsamo, S. (eds.) RISSEF 2002. LNCS, vol. 2941, pp. 297–309. Springer, Heidelberg (2004). https://doi.org/10.1007/978-3-540-24626-8_21
19. Eriksson, H., Penker, M.: Business Modeling with UML, 1st edn. Wiley, New York (2000)
20. Petre, M.: UML in practice. In: Proceedings of the 2013 International Conference on Software Engineering, ICSE 2013, pp. 722–731. ACM Digital Library, San Francisco (2013)
21. Dennis, A., Wixom, B.A., Roth, R.M.: System Analysis and Design, 5th edn. Wiley, New York (2012)
22. Chang, C.H., Lu, C.W., Hsiung, P.A.: Pattern-based framework for modularized software development and evolution robustness. Inf. Softw. Technol. **53**(4), 307–316 (2011)
23. Sohr, K., Ahn, G.-J., Gogolla, M., Migge, L.: Specification and validation of authorisation constraints using UML and OCL. In: di Vimercati, SdC, Syverson, P., Gollmann, D. (eds.) ESORICS 2005. LNCS, vol. 3679, pp. 64–79. Springer, Heidelberg (2005). https://doi.org/10.1007/11555827_5
24. Monye, F.N.: Law of Consumer Protection, 1st edn. Spectrum Books, Ibadan (2003)
25. Pollit, R.G.: Standards Organisation of Nigeria (SON). SON J. **1**(5), 14 (1990)

Software R&D Process Framework for Process Tailoring with EPF Cases

SeungYong Choi[1], JeongAh Kim[1], and SunTae Kim[2(✉)]

[1] Department of Computer Education, Catholic Kwandong University,
24, Beomil-ro 579beon-gil, Gangneung-si, Gangwon-do, South Korea
{boromi,Clara}@cku.ac.kr
[2] Department of Software Engineering, Chonbuk National University,
567, Baekje-daero, Deokjin-gu, Jeonju-si, Jeollabuk-do, South Korea
stkim@jbnu.ac.kr

Abstract. Process tailoring is to make, alter, or adapt a process description for a particular end. Process tailoring is not a simple work because of the following difficulties. First, it should generate a project-specific software process each time that is executed, second, it can be considered as a reuse activity of the standard software process, third, it needs various experiences and involves an intimate knowledge of several aspects of software engineering. To resolve these difficulties, we proposed a software research and development (R&D) process framework that can make, alter, or adapt efficiently software process that will be applied to certain software projects by reusing software process assets constructed. We expect that R&D project tailors can efficiently establish software processes to apply reusable legacy software process assets to specific projects through the proposed process framework for process tailoring. If they make, alter, or adapt their own software processes founded on the proposed process framework, they can have an effect on reducing their efforts to reapplying software processes.

Keywords: EPF · Process framework · Process reuse · Process tailoring
SPEM

1 Introduction

Standard software process provides the following benefits [1].

- reducing problems related with training, reviews and tool support
- enhancing easiness in measurement of the process and quality
- Enhancing communication among team members
- Controlling of software development and ensuring consistent outcomes
- Helping train new project personnel
- Enhancing the performance, predictability and reliability of work processes

Unfortunately, there is no unique software process since appropriateness depends on various organizations, project and product characteristics, and what is even worse, all these characteristics evolve continuously [2].

© Springer International Publishing AG, part of Springer Nature 2018
O. Gervasi et al. (Eds.): ICCSA 2018, LNCS 10963, pp. 527–538, 2018.
https://doi.org/10.1007/978-3-319-95171-3_41

Process tailoring is making, altering, or adapting a process description for a particular end [3]. For example, a project tailors its defined process from the organization's set of standard processes to meet the objectives, constraints, and environment of the project. That is, tailoring is the act of adapting a standard software process to meet the needs of a specific project [4].

So, process tailoring should generate a project-specific software process each time that is executed and also can be considered as a reuse activity of the standard software process [1, 5, 6, 26, 30]. Moreover, process tailoring needs various experiences and involves an intimate knowledge of several aspects of software engineering [7]. Therefore, process tailoring is not a simple work.

Hence, we suggest a software R&D process framework that can make, alter, or adapt efficiently software process that will be applied to certain software projects by reusing software process assets constructed.

We expect that R&D project tailors can efficiently establish software processes to apply reusable legacy software process assets to specific projects through the proposed process framework for process tailoring. If they make, alter, or adapt their own software processes founded on the proposed process framework, they can have an effect on reducing their efforts to reapplying software processes.

The remainder of this paper is structured as follows: we review related researches about SPEM and EPF earlier in this paper. Then, we present software R&D process framework for process tailoring as the topic of this paper. And finally, we mention the conclusion and the future direction at the end of this paper.

2   Related Works

2.1   SPEM

Software Process Engineering Meta-model (SPEM) [8] was created by Object Management Group (OMG) is a meta-model to define software processes and their components with Unified Modeling Language (UML).

SPEM aims at providing organizations with means to define a conceptual framework offering the necessary concepts for modeling, interchanging, documenting, managing and presenting their development methods and processes [8, 9, 28].

The core idea of SPEM is that a development process is a collaboration of multiple process elements to achieve a specific project goal [10]. SPEM is founded on three basic process elements that encapsulate the main features of a software process such as activities, process roles, and work products.

SPEM that can be readily applied to concrete system and software development processes is widely used in practice [11]. For example, the architecture of the well-known Rational Unified Process (RUP) process framework is based on the SPEM, and its extension is supported by a set of tools, including IBM Rational Method Composer [11].

SPEM can be examined in relation to project management and software life cycle processes definition [11, 22–25, 29]. Also, SPEM supports plug-in mechanisms for method content as well as processes represented as work breakdown structures [12] and supports the definition of contributions to and replacements in a work breakdown structure without directly modifying it, but by building a plug-in to it [12, 18, 19].

SPEM has the following goals of being a standard for software process [13, 14].

- Definition: Providing unambiguous semantics
- Presentation: Providing clear notational guidance
- Representation: Providing a concrete modular, configurable, and reusable meta-schema
- Interchange: Define standard format for process content interchange
- Planning: SPEM processes must fit to be used as planning template
- Enactment: Fit for direct enactment and execution metrics.

2.2 EPF

Eclipse Process Framework (EPF) Composer [15, 16, 27] is a process modeling tool platform and extensible conceptual framework based on SPEM for authoring, maintaining, and customizing software development processes [10, 17, 20, 31, 32].

EPF aims at producing a customizable software process engineering framework, which supports different process methods, project types, and development styles [14]. EPF Composer also provides three sample process frameworks, i.e. OpenUP/Basic, Extreme Programming, and Scrum [21]. Users can choose and customize existing process frameworks or create new ones [10]. These frameworks can be transformed into Electronic Process Guides (EPGs) [10]. This provides convenient access and assists navigation of the process model for process performers [10].

EPF Composer based on SPEM supports to easily define process, role, template, and guideline, and so on. EPF method composer library contains method plugins and method configurations [14].

Method content and processes are organized as method plugins [14]. EPF composer clearly distinguishes method content and processes which provides standard set of method and process definitions [14].

EPF Composer has the following goals for benefits [14].

- To provide an extensible framework and exemplary tools for software process engineering. This contains method and process authoring, library management, configuring and publishing a process
- To provide exemplary and extensible process content for a range of software development and management processes supporting iterative, agile, and incremental development, and applicable to a broad set of development platforms and applications

3 Software R&D Process Framework

Research and Development Process Framework (RDPF) based on the formal meta-model is the authoring, tailoring, and managing tool about various processes to perform R&D projects.

It is important to define the framework based on the meta-model and the processes based on the framework. These environments for establishing R&D processes can improve consistency, traceability, and reusability between activities and work products. Furthermore, those can improve consistency, traceability, and reusability between development processes and management processes.

RDPF is defined as the following principles for maximizing effectiveness, productivity, and usability of the proposed framework.

3.1   Design Principles of RDPF

(1) Meta model-driven

RDPF (Fig. 1) is based on SPEM 2.0. RDPF is defined by the meta-model of it. And the meta-model of it is defined as the sub-class of SPEM 2.0. RDPF based on SPEM 2.0 also accepts all the earmarks of Model Driven Architecture (MDA).

Because RDPF has compatibility with UML, RDPF has higher degrees of object-oriented expressiveness and can ensure completeness and integrity of MDA model.

RDPF based on the formal meta-model can significantly improve interoperability, traceability, consistency, and reusability of the process model in comparison with the informal framework.

The concerns of RDPF are classified by viewpoints of stakeholders related to the process. Stakeholders related to the process broadly classify the roles into three types: a method content manager managing methodologies as assets, a process quality manager establishing processes of projects, and a project manager applying established processes to projects.

These criteria, RDPF defines three different points of view such as method contents, processes, and roles.

(2) Method class-centric

SPEM 2.0 is the process meta-model of OMG. It demands to define the core units such as activities, work products, and roles.

EPF which is the process authoring tool based on SPEM 2.0 provides the functions defining activities, work products, and roles independently and assembling those unconstrainedly.

SPEM 2.0 defines three independently authoring units about methodologies like method contents, process patterns, processes. And it defines activities, work products, and roles by each authoring unit.

Actually, process units such as activities, work products, and roles have a very close association.

3.2   RDPF Meta-Model

The meta-model of RDPF (Fig. 2) consists of method content and process.

Method content is comprised of method class that is aggregation of work products and activities. and method component that is aggregation of method classes.

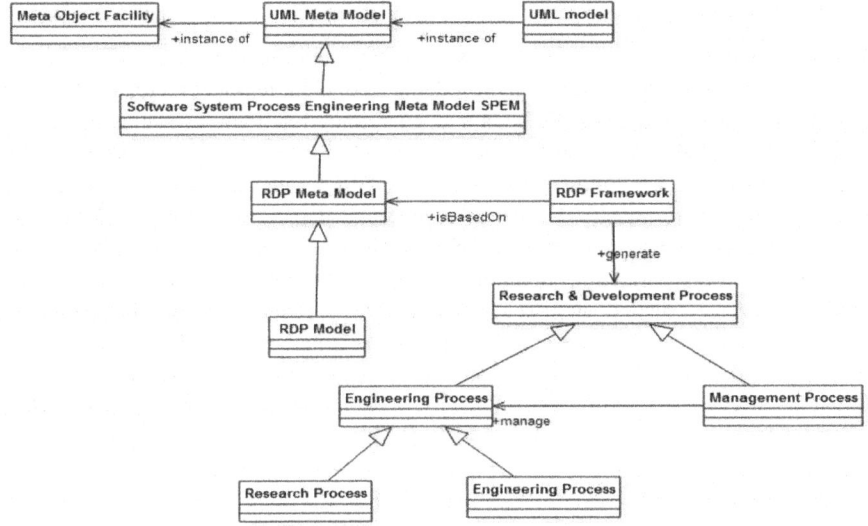

Fig. 1. A proposed framework: RDPF

Method class is defined as reusable class units centering around work products. Method component is generally defined as model units that are the structure of method classes. Model is commonly independent activity units looking at things from a different perspective. Process is managerial units that are composed of the ordered activities in achieving milestones.

The types of process are process component and delivery process. Process component is assembled with method components by the ordered activities. Delivery process is created by configuring process components on the order of activities.

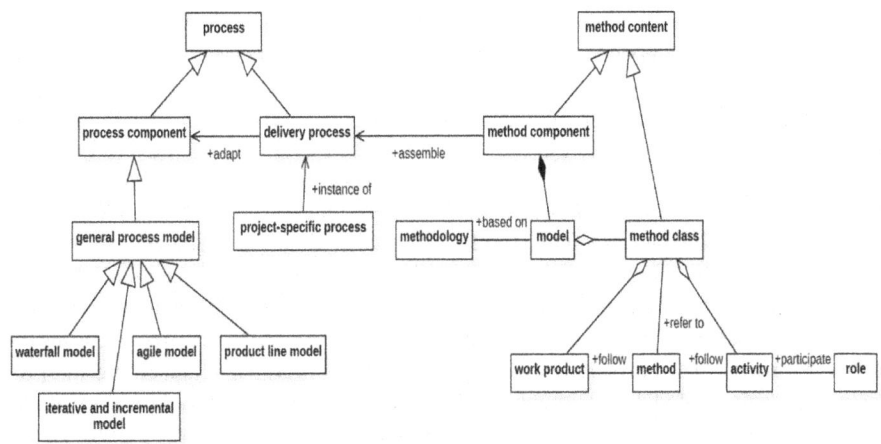

Fig. 2. A meta-model of RDPF

(1) **Method Class**

Method class is a set of independent work products and allied activities (Fig. 3).

In general, process defines work products and their templates created for each activity. And process defines methods and guidelines for doing activities or making work products. Method class defines steps to do activities or make work products with templates. Software development methodology is to define methods, procedures, criteria, and so on and is mostly defined by a particular paradigm. For instance, there are various software development methodologies such as object-oriented methodology founded on object paradigm, function-oriented methodology founded on function paradigm, service-oriented architecture methodology founded on service paradigm, agile methodology emphasizing agility, feature-oriented methodology centering on feature, and the like. Because software development methodologies based on the particular paradigms have different perspectives, even if the same software is developed in the R&D project, the ways on how to identify, express, and structure the target things can vary according to each software development methodology.

Each software development methodology defines the methods which are applied to the activities for developing the software and are expressed to the model created during software development. For example, in case of object-oriented methodology, a method about use case modeling is defined for identifying and specifying system requirements and a use case diagram is also offered for representing those.

In case of feature-oriented methodology, a method about feature modeling is defined for identifying commonalities and variabilities of various software's belonging to a domain and for developing the target software around analysis results of variabilities. A feature diagram is also offered to represent those.

So, methodologies guide how to apply their own perspectives to software development activities. Methods applicable to activities may vary according to perspectives founded on methodologies, but there are applicable methods regardless of perspectives by methodologies such as literature review, prioritizing requirements, domain expert interview, review, walkthrough, inspection, etc.

For this reason, we distinguish between method classes dependent on the paradigm and method classes independent of the paradigm. And method classes dependent on the paradigm are distinguished by paradigms. It is essential to create work products from software development methodologies because models have to be represented during the software development.

Modeling language should be usually used to represent models. UML exists as the typical modeling language but is not everything to define all software models. There are the various modeling languages such as Systems Modeling Language (SysUML) for representing the systems engineering models, feature modeling language for representing the feature models, Entity–Relationship (ER) modeling language for representing the databases, Architecture Description Language (ADL) for representing the architectures, Business Process Modeling Notation (BPMN) for representing the processes, and so on. Modeling language alone cannot represent all models. For example, in case of object-oriented methodology, BPMN or flow chart should be used to represent complex processes or the inside of the module. And ER model should be also used to represent the data region. Therefore, modeling languages are in no way dependent on software development methodologies.

Proposed process framework supports to create modeling packages independent of software development methodologies and to define methods based on each modeling language.

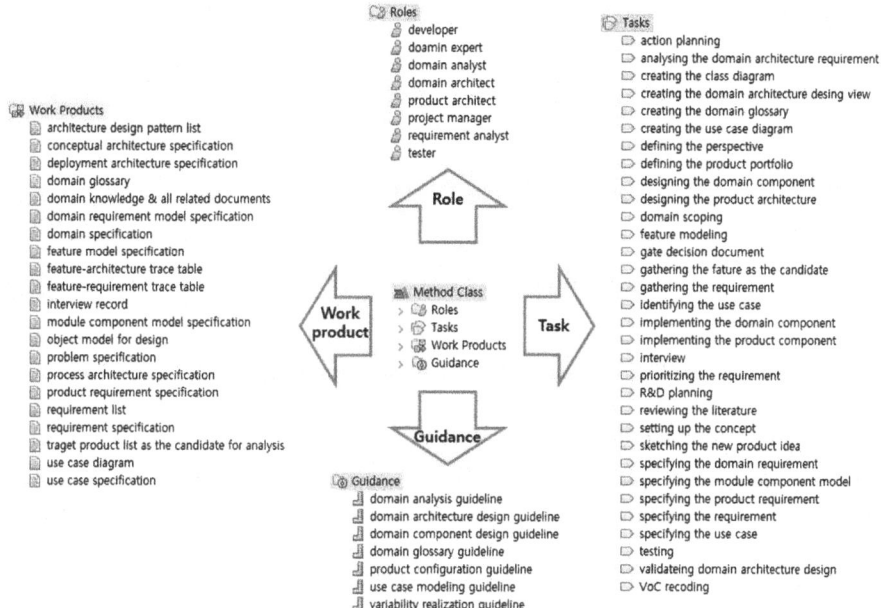

Fig. 3. A case of method class definition

(2) **Method Component**

Method component is the independent unit forming processes depending on paradigms of software development and the basic unit comprising R&D processes.

There are various models as method components such as research model, requirement model, analysis model, design model, development model, validation model, transition model, and so on. Method component also means the container of method classes for each model.

In other words, method component is to define the set of method classes that are grouped as the logical unit for establishing the model by viewpoints of software development methodologies during software development.

As method component means the model defined by each software development methodology and to combine method classes that compose each model, these method components can provide model types established in advance and methods for establishing the model to workers related R&D projects (Fig. 4).

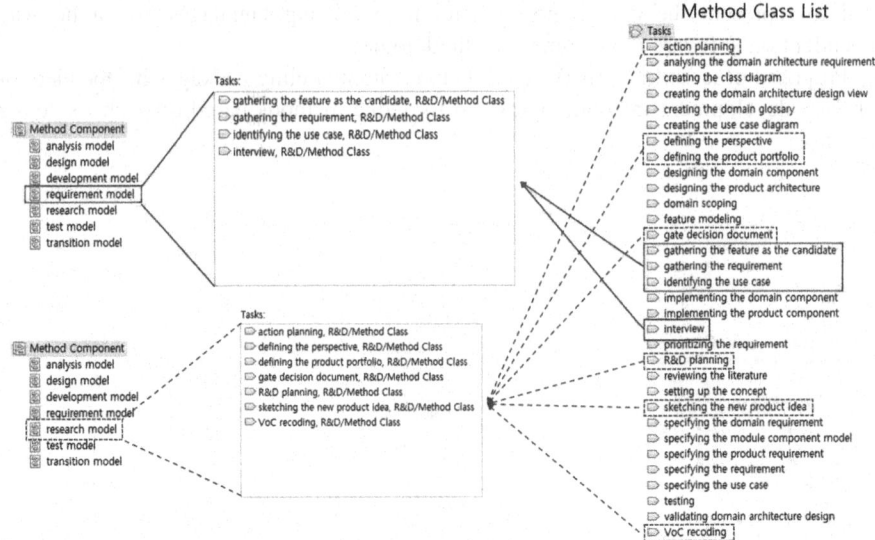

Fig. 4. A case of method component definition

(3) Process Component

Process component is the unit that consists of actual delivery processes reflecting the time concept and is comprised of composite components assembling already defined method components.

Process component is used in the same sense like process pattern or capability pattern on SPEM. Capability pattern of SPEM is the simple package type, however, process component of RDPF meta-model has the encapsulated and standardized interface.

Namely, process component is the process unit reusable in common for defining delivery process to each actual project.

The type of process component can be the process component of UP style (e.g. inception component, elaboration component, construction component, transition

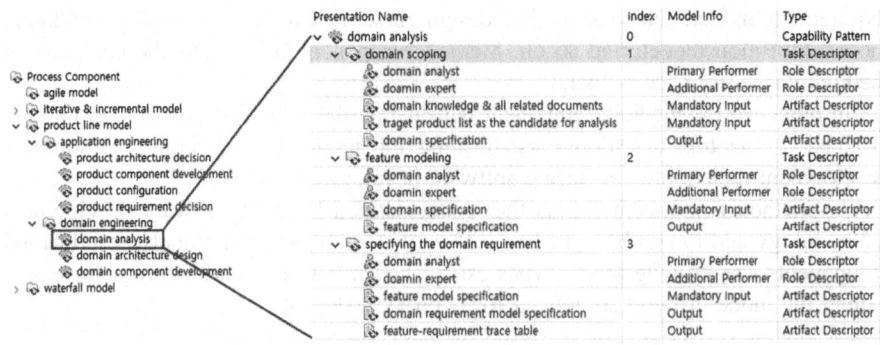

Fig. 5. A case of process component definition

component, etc.) and can also be process components of various types such as Agile or Service-Oriented Architecture (SOA) style (Fig. 5).

(4) **Delivery Process**

Delivery process means to be reflected on actual projects and is composed of several process components. Each process component has one or more method components. Process component is to assemble defined method components by the standard performed universally. But, all things (e.g. the target system, the workforce, the particular environment, and so on.) considered, all standard processes and methodologies cannot be applied to process components.

R&D workers, in view of the R&D situation, may need to assemble the objectoriented design process and the feature-oriented development process for conducting R&D projects. Therefore, delivery process can redefine method components in process components and method classes in method components. And it can also assemble other process components, other method components, and other method classes.

There are two different ways to define delivery processes. First, delivery process is defined by reusing already defined process components. Delivery process is defined by supplementing or extending process components with assembling already defined them. In this case, the first way can considerably facilitate the process definition because most of already defined process components is reused. Second, delivery process is defined by redefining new process components in it. Delivery process is defined by recomposing method components in process components because new process components are defined. Thus, the second way requires a more effort than the first way but it is flexible to define project-specific processes.

In order to do so, EPF can define process components in the delivery process and method components in each process component by the drag-and-drop function (Figs. 6 and 7).

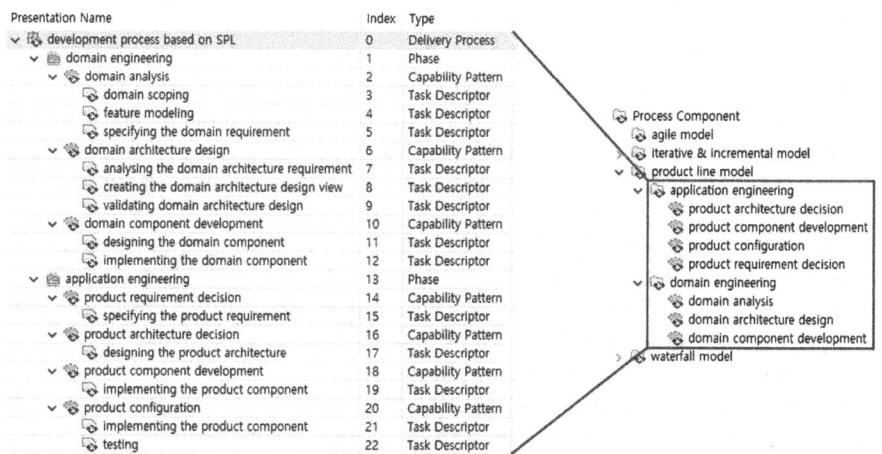

Fig. 6. A case of delivery process definition

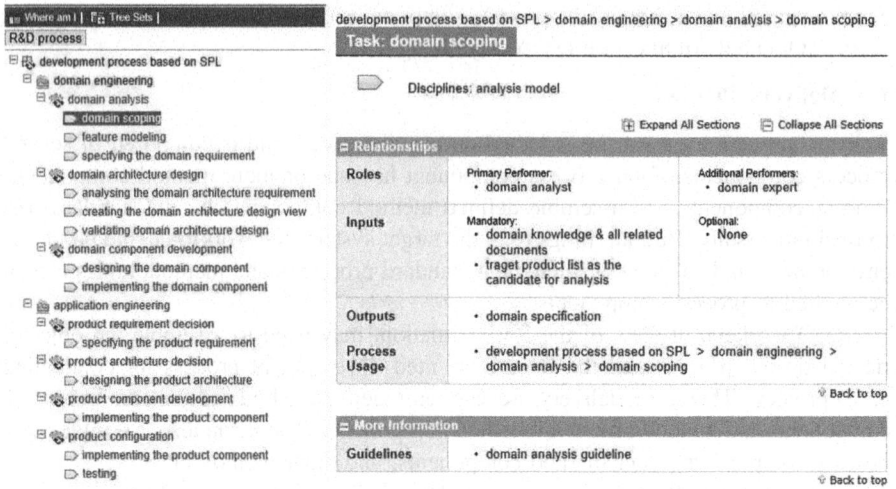

Fig. 7. A case of web publishing about delivery process

4   Conclusions

Process tailoring is to make, alter, or adapt a process description for a particular end. Process tailoring is not a simple work because it:

- should generate a project-specific software process each time that is executed
- can be considered as a reuse activity of the standard software process
- needs various experiences and involves an intimate knowledge of several aspects of software engineering

To resolve these difficulties, we proposed a software R&D process framework that can make, alter, or adapt efficiently software process that will be applied to certain software projects by reusing software process assets constructed.

Proposed RDPF based on SPEM 2.0 is the authoring, tailoring, and managing tool about various processes to perform R&D projects. It can significantly improve interoperability, traceability, consistency, and reusability of the process model for the informal framework. Also, it can support to create modeling packages independent of software development methodologies and to define methods based on each modeling language.

We expect that R&D project tailors can efficiently establish software processes to apply reusable legacy software process assets to specific projects through the proposed process framework for process tailoring. If they make, alter, or adapt their own software processes founded on the proposed process framework, they can have an effect on reducing their efforts to reapplying software processes.

In the future, we will need to apply a proposed process framework to many software R&D domains and improve it through more case studies.

Acknowledgements. This research was supported by Next-Generation Information Computing Development Program through the National Research Foundation of Korea (NRF) funded by the Ministry of Science, ICT & Future Planning (NRF- 2014M3C4A7030503). SunTae Kim is the corresponding author.

References

1. Pereira, E.B., Bastos, R.M., Oliveira, T.C.: A systematic approach to process tailoring. In: Systems Engineering and Modeling, ICSEM 2007, pp. 71–78. IEEE (2007)
2. Hurtado Alegría, J.A., Bastarrica, M.C., Quispe, A., Ochoa, S.F.: An MDE approach to software process tailoring. In: Proceedings of the 2011 International Conference on Software and Systems Process, pp. 43–52. ACM (2011)
3. CMMI Product Team: CMMI for Development, Version 1.2. Carnegie Mellon University, Software Engineering Institute, August 2006
4. Ginsberg, M.P., Quinn, L.H.: Process tailoring and the software capability maturity model. Technical Report, Software Engineering Institute (SEI), November 1995
5. Yoon, I., Min, S., Bae, D.: Tailoring and verifying software process. In: Software Engineering Conference, APSEC 2001, Eighth Asia-Pacific, pp. 202–209. IEEE (2001)
6. Kellner, M.I.: Connecting reusable software process elements and components. In: Proceedings of the 10th International Software Process Workshop, Process Support of Software Product Lines, pp. 8–11. IEEE (1996)
7. Barreto, A., Murta, L.G.P., Rocha, A.R.C.: Software process definition: a reuse-based approach. J. Univ. Comput. Sci. **17**(13), 1765–1799 (2011)
8. OMG: Software & Systems Process Engineering Meta-Model Specification, version 2.0 (2008)
9. Bendraou, R., Combemale, B., Crégut, X., Gervais, M.P.: Definition of an Executable SPEM 2.0. In: Software Engineering Conference, APSEC 2007, 14th Asia-Pacific, pp. 390–397. IEEE (2007)
10. Chiam, Y.K., Staples, M., Zhu, L.: Representation of quality attribute techniques using SPEM and EPF composer. In: 16th EuroSPI Conference (2009)
11. Nikulsins, V., Nikiforova, O.: Tool integration to support SPEM model transformations in eclipse. Sci. J. Riga Tech. Univ. Comput. Sci. **41**(1), 60–67 (2010)
12. Henderson-Sellers, B., Gonzalez-Perez, C.: A comparison of four process metamodels and the creation of a new generic standard. Inf. Softw. Technol. **47**(1), 49–65 (2005)
13. Haumer, P.: Second Revised SPEM 2.0 Submission. OMG Meeting, St. Louis (2006)
14. Terävä, H.: Software process modeling with eclipse process framework and SPEM 2.0. Master's Thesis, University of Turku, Finland (2007)
15. Tuft, B.: Eclipse Process Framework (EPF) Composer - Installation, Introduction, Tutorial and Manual (2010)
16. http://www.eclipse.org/epf/
17. Haumer, P.: Eclipse Process Framework Composer: Part 1 and Part 2. Technical report, IBM Rational Software (2006)
18. Combemale, B., Crégut, X., Caplain, A., Coulette, B.: Towards a rigorous use of SPEM. In: Proceedings of Eighth International Conference on Enterprise Information Systems INSTICC (2006)
19. Rougemaille, S., Migeon, F., Millan, T., Gleizes, M.P.: Methodology fragments definition in SPEM for designing adaptive methodology: a first step. In: International Workshop on Agent-Oriented Software Engineering, pp. 74–85 (2008)

20. McGregor, J.: Mix and match. J. Object Technol. **7**(6), 7–16 (2008)
21. Fujita, H., Zualkernan, I.A.: An ontology-driven approach for generating assessments for the scrum software process. In: Proceedings of the seventh SoMeT_08, pp. 190–205. IOS Press, The Netherlands (2008)
22. Martínez-Ruiz, T., García, F., Piattini, M.: Towards a SPEM v2. 0 extension to define process lines variability mechanisms. In: Lee, R. (eds.) Software Engineering Research, Management and Applications, pp. 115–130. Springer, Heidelberg (2008). https://doi.org/10.1007/978-3-540-70561-1_9
23. García-Magariño, I., Gómez-Rodríguez, A., González-Moreno, J.C.: Definition of process models for agent-based development. In: Luck, M., Gomez-Sanz, J.J. (eds.) AOSE 2008. LNCS, vol. 5386, pp. 60–73. Springer, Heidelberg (2009). https://doi.org/10.1007/978-3-642-01338-6_5
24. Alegría, J.A.H., Lagos, A., Bergel, A., Bastarrica, M.C.: Software process model blueprints. In: Münch, J., Yang, Y., Schäfer, W. (eds.) ICSP 2010. LNCS, vol. 6195, pp. 273–284. Springer, Heidelberg (2010). https://doi.org/10.1007/978-3-642-14347-2_24
25. Koudri, A., Champeau, J.: MODAL: a SPEM extension to improve co-design process models. In: Münch, J., Yang, Y., Schäfer, W. (eds.) ICSP 2010. LNCS, vol. 6195, pp. 248–259. Springer, Heidelberg (2010). https://doi.org/10.1007/978-3-642-14347-2_22
26. Costache, D., Kalus, G., Kuhrmann, M.: Design and validation of feature-based process model tailoring: a sample implementation of PDE. In: Proceedings of the 19th ACM SIGSOFT Symposium and the 13th European Conference on Foundations of Software Engineering, pp. 464–467. ACM (2011)
27. Garcia, F., Vizcaino, A., Ebert, C.: Process management tools. IEEE Softw. **28**(2), 15–18 (2011)
28. Aoussat, F., Oussalah, M., Nacer, M.A.: SPEM extension with software process architectural concepts. In: IEEE 35th Annual Computer Software and Applications Conference, pp. 215–223. IEEE (2011)
29. Elvesæter, B., Benguria, G., Ilieva, S.: A comparison of the Essence 1.0 and SPEM 2.0 specifications for software engineering methods. In: Proceedings of the Third Workshop on Process-Based Approaches for Model-Driven Engineering. ACM (2013)
30. Gallina, B., Kashiyarandi, S., Martin, H., Bramberger, R.: Modeling a safety-and automotive-oriented process line to enable reuse and flexible process derivation. In: Computer Software and Applications Conference Workshops (COMPSACW), pp. 504–509. IEEE (2014)
31. Choi, S.Y., Choi, J.Y., Kim, J.A., Choi, J.Y., Cho, Y.H., Hong, J.E.: Process tailoring practice with EPF. In: Proceedings of the 10th Asia Pacific International Conference on Information Science and Technology, APIC-IST 2015, pp. 115–120 (2015)
32. Choi, S.Y., Choi, J.Y., Kim, J.A., Choi, J.Y., Cho, Y.H., Hong, J.E.: Software R&D process tailoring practice with EPF. Int. J. Appl. Eng. Res. **10**(5), 3979–3982 (2015)

Performance Evaluation of Visual Descriptors for Image Indexing in Content Based Image Retrieval Systems

Oluwole A. Adegbola[1], David O. Aborisade[1], Segun I. Popoola[2(✉)], and Aderemi A. Atayero[2]

[1] Department of Electronic and Electrical Engineering,
Ladoke Akintola University of Technology, Ogbomoso, Nigeria
{oaadegbola, doaborisade}@lautech.edu.ng
[2] Department of Electrical and Information Engineering,
Covenant University, Ota, Nigeria
{segun.popoola, atayero}@covenantuniversity.edu.ng

Abstract. In practice, appropriate computer vision and image processing techniques are usually employed to obtain image visual features. Central to functional Content Based Image Retrieval (CBIR) system is effective indexing and fast searching of images based on the visual features. Effective indexing is also essential to make CBIR system scalable for large image databases and incorporation of advanced technique such as machine learning based relevance feedback (RF). However, it is extremely difficult to know the particular feature model(s) to be used to uniquely identify certain groups of images, while including many feature models can incur dimensionality problem. In this paper, Colour Moment (CM), Gabor Wavelet (GW), and Wavelet Moment (WM) are used to encode the low-level information at global and sub-global image levels. A query by feature example retrieval (QVER) was implemented to test the retrieval performance of each feature descriptor by computing average mean precision value for L1 and L2 distance measure. Taking average of the recalls, the average mean precision values of 0.6501, 0.6330 and 0.6380 were obtained for 54-dimensional CM (CM54), 48-dimensional GW (GW48) and 40-dimensional WM (WM40) respectively. The results reveal that colour descriptor computed using only the first two statistical moments at sub-global image level gave better retrieval performance than those computed at global image level, while the converse is true for texture descriptors. Hence, CM54, GW48, and WM40 are recommended for CM, GW, and WM feature models respectively.

Keywords: Visual descriptors · Feature model · Image indexing
Content Based Image Retrieval (CBIR) · Relevance feedback (RF)

1 Introduction

The pixel values of image are the simplest form of visual feature derivable from the image [1, 2]. It is viewed as a direct approach to image indexing and retrieval, where query image pixel values are compared with database images pixel values using some

© Springer International Publishing AG, part of Springer Nature 2018
O. Gervasi et al. (Eds.): ICCSA 2018, LNCS 10963, pp. 539–549, 2018.
https://doi.org/10.1007/978-3-319-95171-3_42

distance measure. Whereas the use of this type of feature has been reported to yield some level of success in application like character recognition, it is however not efficient in broad domain of Content Based Image Retrieval System (CBIR) system. There are two obvious reasons for this: first, pixel values are highly sensitive to changes in image properties like resolution, image dimension and transformation, such as, rotation). The second is that it is not suitable for use in vector space computation of image similarity measure, owing to the dimension of the resulting feature vector. For instance, if an (n × m) pixel image in RGB colour space is to be represented in feature vector space using its pixel values, the dimension of such feature vector will be (3 × n × m). Obviously, storage requirement will be an issue and also computation of image similarity measure will be highly complex. Thus, actual pixel values are rarely used as feature in CBIR system.

In practice, appropriate computer vision and image processing techniques are usually employed to obtain image visual features. Such visual features overcome those previously identified shortcomings. In generic system, it is the norm to use combination of several different visual features to represent the image. This is with a view to capturing the unique properties of selected image. As stated earlier, these features include colour, texture, shape and spatial information, out of which colour and texture are the two most commonly used. The shape features are not as commonly used, since image segmentation is a necessity for meaningful shape properties to be captured.

Colour attributes are considered the most used low-level features for image indexing and search in large database and according to Feng and Chua [3], colour is the most extensively used visual content for image retrieval. Colour features have been used in several CBIR systems [4–10]. This extensive use of colour is justified by several factors. First, its three-dimensional values make its discrimination capability superior to the single dimensional grey values of images thereby facilitating the identification and extraction of object from scene. Second, it is easier for humans to discern changes in shades and intensities of colour image than to note the difference in the intensity of grey scale image [11]. Other merits of colour, as basis for image analysis, over texture and shape include: cheaper computing cost and simpler process for extracting colour information from image.

Moreover, it is common practice to combine colour feature with other features like texture and/or shape in order to capture the unique common characteristics of a group of selected images. There exist many CBIR systems with such features combination approach for image retrieval [12–18]. Finally, before an image can be described/characterized by colour features there are three key issues for consideration, these are: colour space, colour quantization and colour descriptors.

A colour space is a notation by which colour is specified according to certain specification, usually in the form of turples [19]. Therefore, each pixel of the image can be represented as a point in 3-dimensional colour space, where each dimension is viewed as a basic channel of the colour model like, the colour channels of an image in RGB format will be red, green and blue. There is no agreement on which is the best, except that one desirable characteristic of an appropriate colour space for image retrieval is its uniformity [8]. Concept of uniformity implies that two colour pairs that are equal in similarity distance in a colour space are perceived as equal by viewers.

Each of those colour spaces is designed/formulated for different applications and purposes.

Texture is another significant low-level property of majority of images. Texture, unlike colour is not well defined. It can be viewed as the representation of visual content over a region of pixel depicting repetition of pattern or patterns over such region in an image. Though its definition is vague, it plays a very important role in human visual perception and recognition. It provides important information in image classification as it describes the content of many real-world images such as, fruit skin, clouds, trees, bricks and fabrics. Hence texture is important feature in defining high-level semantics for image retrieval purpose [20]. In addition, texture analysis techniques have been used in other areas such as, classification and segmentation [21]. Basically, texture representation approaches can be classified into two categories namely, structural and statistical [22, 23].

Structural approaches describe texture by identifying structural primitives and their placement rules. The placement rule may include various shapes such as rectangles, circles, spheres etc. hence they tend to be most effective when applied to textures that are very regular. Examples of structural approach include morphological operator and adjacency graph. The difficulty associated with the identification of the primitives defined by the approach is one major weakness in this approach, more detail on structural approach for texture analysis can be found in [23, 24].

The second main approach characterizes texture by statistical distribution of the image intensity. Methods used to extract useful texture information include Fourier power spectra, Tamura features, Wold decomposition and multi-resolution filtering techniques such as Gabor filtering and wavelet transform [25–28]. Useful statistics such as mean, variance and standard deviation, of the magnitude of the transformed coefficients are used to represent texture feature. Among the various texture features, Gabor feature and wavelets are widely used for image retrieval and have been reported to well match the result of human vision study [20, 29, 30]. Statistical methods have been shown to have high capability in describing very good candidate feature for indexing and retrieval in generic CBIR system.

Central to functional CBIR system is effective indexing and fast searching of images based on the visual features. Effective indexing is also essential to make CBIR system scalable for large image databases. Unlike the traditional database system that can be effectively indexed using a simple one dimensional data structure, meaningful CBIR system cannot be developed with only one type of visual features. As such, a combination of different visual features at different levels is needed to identify and classify images in different contexts. This usually results in high dimensionality of image feature vectors that are not well suited to traditional indexing structures. The implication of this is that indexing structure for CBIR system also has to be multidimensional.

In a generic system, it is extremely difficult to know the particular feature model(s) to be used to uniquely identify certain groups of images. Therefore, a combination of several image feature models is usually employed with the assumption that at least one will have the ability to capture the unique identity of the targeted images. In this paper, the performance of different colour and texture feature descriptors are evaluated on selected local image databases using average mean precision value. Colour Moment (CM), Gabor Wavelet (GW), and Wavelet Moment (WM) are used to encode the low-level information. The materials and method are explained in Sect. 2. The results of this study are discussed in Sect. 3. The conclusion of this research is summarized in Sect. 4.

2   Materials and Methods

In this work, generic domain image database consisting of local/indigenous concepts was created in addition to standard databases acquired online. These image databases covered various image categories and themes; these were employed for experimental purposes. The details on the image databases are presented in Table 1.

Table 1. Selected ground truth image databases

Name of database	Number of classes	Number of images/class	Properties
DB10 (Corel)	10	100	Strong within class low-level visual diversity, clearly defined high-level semantics of each class. Most appropriate for RF evaluation
DB100 (Columbia colour database)	100	72	Sufficient visual variability within each class, unique class identity not subject to interpretation. Contains sufficient number of image for RF
DB20 (Various sources)	20	100	Reasonable level of overlapping high-level semantics and high variability in terms of source and image size

2.1   Image Preprocessing

It is not uncommon for such image databases to have variations in terms of image format and size. Therefore, in order to index the image database for the developed CBIR system, image preprocessing such as image resizing, image partitioning and colour space transformation are done. The images are resized to (a × a) pixels, the choice of this dimension will make it possible to partition each image into (b × b) equal tiles, with choice of a and b dependent on image database. The essence of this is to facilitate feature extraction and comparison at a finer resolution. In addition, images are transformed to HSV colour space to facilitate feature extraction of non-device-dependent colour features.

2.2   Feature Descriptors

Once all the necessary preprocessing steps are carried out, the next thing is to transform the image database into feature database by extracting appropriate low-level features. The low-level features used are colour and texture features. Two colour descriptors (Colour moments and HSV colour histogram) and two texture descriptors (Gabor filters and wavelet moments) are used to encode the low-level information. Shape features are not being considered because to extract useful shape attributes, image segmentation is in most cases required. Secondly, the proposed CBIR system is expected to perform retrieval at image level and not at object level.

2.2.1   Colour Feature Descriptors

Two colour feature descriptors were used to represent the images at global level and partitioned levels. The partitioning is done with a view to discovering whether retrieval performance can be enhanced by taking into account the spatial information of colour properties. At the global level, for each colour channel, three statistical moments namely the mean, standard deviation and skewness are computed, using Eqs. (1)-(3) for mean (μ_i), standard deviation (σ_i) and skewness (S_i) respectively. N is the total number of pixels and f_{ij} is the pixel value respectively. This resulted into a 9-dimensional feature vector; it is denoted by CM9. To extract colour moments at the partitioned level, the images were first resized to ($a \times a$) pixels and then partitioned into (3×3) equal tiles. For each partition, two options were considered: first, two statistical moments are computed resulting into an ($6 \times 3 \times 3$) -dimensional feature vector; second, three statistical moments are computed resulting into an ($9 \times 3 \times 3$) -dimensional feature vector.

$$\mu_i = \frac{1}{N}\sum_{j=1}^{N} f_{ij} \tag{1}$$

$$\sigma_i = \left(\frac{1}{N}\sum_{j=1}^{N} \left(f_{ij} - \mu_i\right)^2\right)^{\frac{1}{2}} \tag{2}$$

$$S_i = \left(\frac{1}{N}\sum_{j=1}^{N} \left(f_{ij} - \mu_i\right)^3\right)^{\frac{1}{3}} \tag{3}$$

The second colour attribute computed is the HSV colour histogram. First a colour quantization is performed to reduce the number of colours. This may lower the quality of information retained in the image, but will also allow histograms to be computed and used in practical situation namely CBIR. Then the colour histogram, which represents the estimation of the statistical distribution of colours in the image, was computed using the model of Eq. (4). This resulted into a feature vector of dimension $\mathbb{R}^d$, where d is dependent on the number of bins used for quantizing each of the colour channels. Let I be an image of size m $\times$ n pixels where each pixel (i, j) belongs to the colour space $C : \mathbf{c}(i,j) \in C$; where $\mathbf{c}(i, j)$ is a three-dimensional vector. The colour histogram simply gives an approximation of the statistical distribution of colours in the image I:

$$h(c) = \frac{1}{mn} \sum_{i=0}^{m-1} \sum_{i=0}^{n-1} \delta(I(i,j) - c) \qquad (4)$$

where $c \in C$, $I(i, j)$ is the colour of pixel (i, j) in image I and $\delta(.)$ is the Dirac unitary impulse function.

2.2.2   Texture Feature Descriptors

For an image $I(x, y)$, with $(p \times q)$ pixels, its Gabor wavelet is defined by Eq. 5.

$$W_{mn}(x,y) = \sum_{x_1} \sum_{y_1} I(x_1, y_1) \Psi^*_{mn}(x - x_1, y - y_1) \qquad (5)$$

where Ψ^*_{mn} is the complex conjugate of the generating function; m and n are the orientations and scales. To extract texture information, a set of Gabor filter banks was applied to cover the entire frequency spectrum of the image. This resulted into creation of multichannel representation of the image, where each original pixel is described by a vector of the filter's response values at the pixel's location. For this work, useful frequency information is obtained from images by applying a set of Gabor filters ranging across four scales and six orientations. Each filter output, that is, image channel, is encoded by its mean and its standard deviation as represented by Eq. 6.

$$\mu_{mn} = \frac{1}{pq} \sum_x \sum_y |W_{mn}|, \sigma_{mn} = \frac{1}{pq} \left[\sum_x \sum_y (|W_{mn}| - \mu_{mn})^2 \right]^{\frac{1}{2}} \qquad (6)$$

to yield a 48-dimensional real-valued feature vector to represent the image as given by Eq. 7.

$$f = [\mu_{00}, \sigma_{00}, \ldots, \mu_{mn}, \sigma_{mn}] \qquad (7)$$

3   Results and Discussion

Figure 1 shows the comparison of CM6 (6-dimensional CM), CM9 (9-dimensional CM), CM54 (54-dimensional CM) and CM81 (81-dimensional CM) descriptors on the databases using the Euclidean distance (L2) metric. The mean precision performance is the combined precisions of the databases. Taking average of the recalls, the average mean precision for CM6, CM9, CM54 and CM81 are 0.6414, 0.6400, 0.6501 and 0.6480 respectively. This result reveals that the 54-dimensional colour moment (CM54) gives the best performance, having the highest average mean precision value. The comparison of the colour moments using the Manhattan distance (L1) metric is presented in Fig. 2. The average mean precision for CM6, CM9, CM54 and CM81 are 0.6320, 0.6314, 0.6424 and 0.6406 respectively. These results show that the CM54 descriptor gives the highest average mean precision value. Since the results obtained with the Euclidean distance (L2) metric agree with the results obtained with the Manhattan distance (L1) metric, the CM54 is selected for the colour moment feature model.

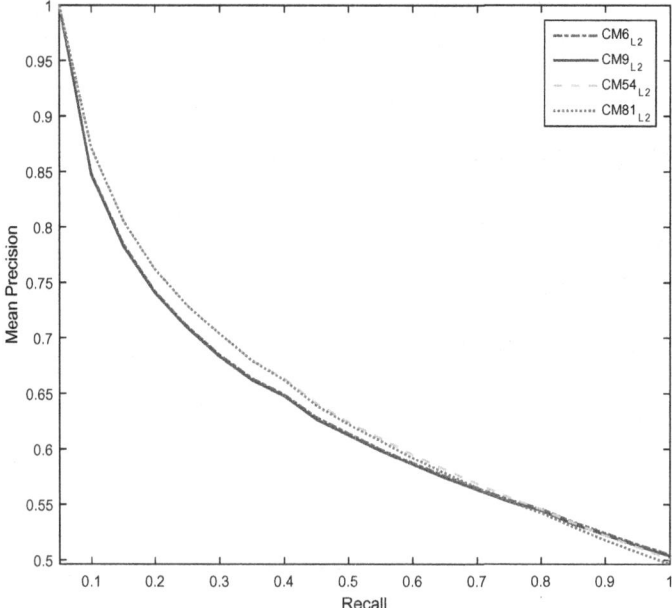

Fig. 1. Comparison of CM on the databases with L2 metric.

The comparison of the GW48 (48-dimensional Gabor wavelet), GW432 (432-dimensional Gabor wavelet), WM40 (40-dimensional Wavelet Moment) and WM160 (160-dimensional Wavelet Moment) using the Euclidean distance (L2) metric is presented in Fig. 3. The average mean precision for GW48 and GW432 are 0.6330 and 0.5887 respectively; while the average mean precision for WM40 and WM160 are 0.6313 and 0.6148 respectively. This reveals that the GW48 gives higher precision than the GW432. Also, the WM40 gives higher precision than the WM160. Figure 4 shows the comparison of the GW48, GW432, WM40 and WM160 using the Manhattan distance (L1) metric. The GW48 gives average mean precision value 0.5970 while GW432 gives 0.5953. The average mean precision value for WM40 and WM160 are 0.6380 and 0.6253 respectively. The results reveal that for both the Manhattan distance (L1) and Euclidean distance (L2) metrics, the GW48 gives better precision than GW432 while the WM40 gives better precision than WM160. Hence, the GW48 is selected for the Gabor wavelet feature model and WM40 is selected for the wavelet moment feature model.

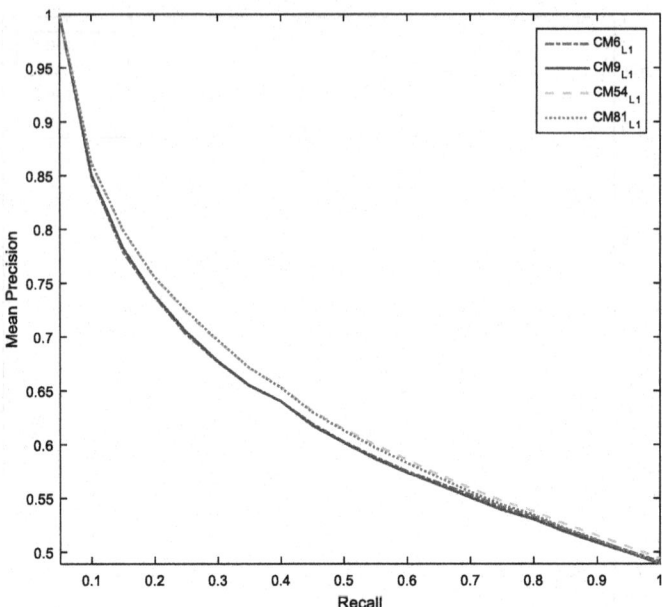

Fig. 2. Comparison of CM on the databases with L1 metric

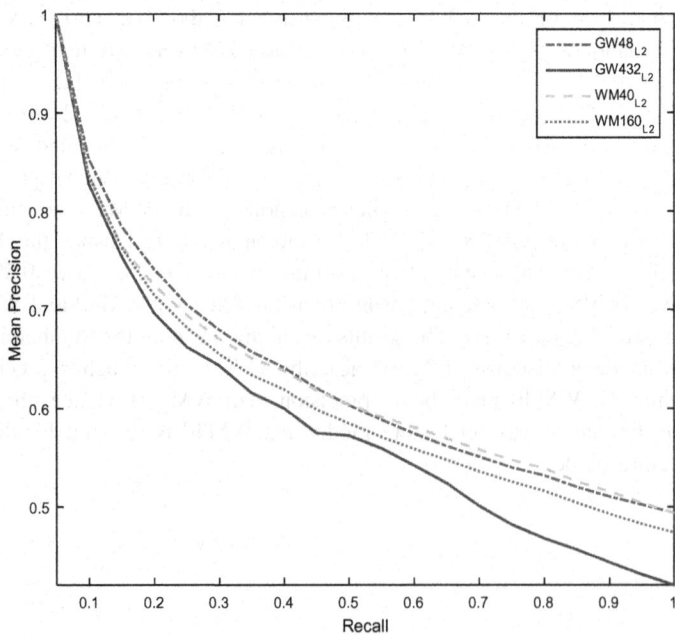

Fig. 3. Comparison of GW and WM on the databases with L2 metric

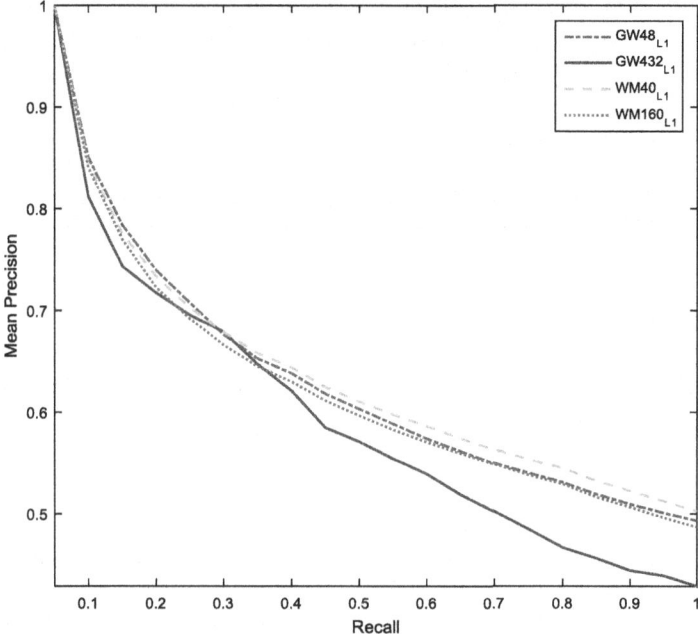

Fig. 4. Comparison of GW and WM on the databases with L1 metric

4   Conclusion

In practice, appropriate computer vision and image processing techniques are usually employed to obtain image visual features. Such visual features overcome those previously identified shortcomings. In generic system, it is the norm to use combination of several different visual features to represent the image. This is with a view to capturing the unique properties of selected image. As stated earlier, these features include colour, texture, shape and spatial information, out of which colour and texture are the two most commonly used. The shape features are not as commonly used, since image segmentation is a necessity for meaningful shape properties to be captured.

In this paper, the performance of different colour and texture feature descriptors were evaluated on selected local image databases using average mean precision value. Colour Moment (CM), Gabor Wavelet (GW), and Wavelet Moment (WM) were used to encode the low-level information. Taking average of the recalls, the average mean precision for 6-dimensional CM (CM6), 9-dimensional CM (CM9), 54-dimensional CM (CM54), and 81-dimensional CM (CM81) descriptors using the Euclidean distance (L2)) are 0.6414, 0.6400, 0.6501 and 0.6480 respectively. Using, Manhattan distance (L1), the average mean precision for CM6, CM9, CM54 and CM81 are 0.6320, 0.6314, 0.6424 and 0.6406 respectively. These results show that the CM54 descriptor has the better retrieval performance. On the other hand, findings show that, for both L1 and L2 metrics, the 48-dimensional GW (GW48) gave better precision than 432-dimensional GW (GW432) while the 40-dimensional WM (WM40) gave better precision than 160-

dimensional WM (WM160). The findings establish that: the first two statistical moments are sufficient to encode colour information; colour descriptor yields better retrieval results at sub-global image level while texture information is better captured at global image level. Hence, CM54, GW48, and WM40 are recommended for CM, GW, and WM feature models respectively.

Acknowledgment. The authors wish to appreciate the Center for Research, Innovation, and Discovery (CU-CRID) of Covenant University, Ota, Nigeria for partial funding of this research.

References

1. Lowe, D.G.: Distinctive image features from scale-invariant keypoints. Int. J. Comput. Vis. **60**(2), 91–110 (2004)
2. Viola, P., Jones, M.: Rapid object detection using a boosted cascade of simple features. In: Proceedings of the 2001 IEEE Computer Society Conference on Computer Vision and Pattern Recognition CVPR 2001. IEEE (2001)
3. Feng, H., Chua, T.-S.: A bootstrapping approach to annotating large image collection. In: Proceedings of the 5th ACM SIGMM International Workshop on Multimedia Information Retrieval. ACM (2003)
4. Hughes, J.F., Foley, J.D.: Computer Graphics: Principles and Practice. Pearson Education, New York (2014)
5. Huang, J., Kumar, S.R., Mitra, M.: Combining supervised learning with color correlograms for content-based image retrieval. In: Proceedings of the Fifth ACM International Conference on Multimedia. ACM (1997)
6. Huang, J., et al.: Spatial color indexing and applications. Int. J. Comput. Vis. **35**(3), 245–268 (1999)
7. Jain, A.K.: Fundamentals of Digital Image Processing. Prentice-Hall Inc., Upper Saddle River (1989)
8. Mathias, E., Conci, A.: Comparing the influence of color spaces and metrics in content-based image retrieval. In: Proceedings of SIBGRAPI 1998 International Symposium on Computer Graphics, Image Processing, and Vision. IEEE (1998)
9. Stricker, M.A., Orengo, M.: Similarity of color images. In: International Society for Optics and Photonics Storage and Retrieval for Image and Video Databases III (1995)
10. Swain, M.J., Ballard, D.H.: Color indexing. Int. J. Comput. Vis. **7**(1), 11–32 (1991)
11. Rui, Y., Huang, T.S., Chang, S.-F.: Image retrieval: current techniques, promising directions, and open issues. J. Vis. Commun. Image Representation **10**(1), 39–62 (1999)
12. Huang, R., Dong, S., Du, M.: A semantic retrieval approach by color and spatial location of image regions. In: International Congress on Image and Signal Processing CISP 2008. IEEE (2008)
13. Marukatat, S.: Image annotation using label propagation algorithm. In: Proceedings of 5th International Conference on Electrical Engineering/Electronics, Computer, Telecommunications and Information Technology ECTI-CON 2008. IEEE (2008)
14. Akbas, E., Vural, F.T.Y.: Automatic image annotation by ensemble of visual descriptors. In: IEEE Conference on Computer Vision and Pattern Recognition CVPR 2007. IEEE (2007)
15. Qi, X., Han, Y.: Incorporating multiple SVMs for automatic image annotation. Pattern Recogn. **40**(2), 728–741 (2007)

16. Shao, W., Naghdy, G., Phung, S.L.: Automatic annotation of digital images using colour structure and edge direction. In: IEEE International Conference on Signal Processing and Communications ICSPC 2007. IEEE (2007)
17. Li, J., Wang, J.Z., Wiederhold, G.: IRM: integrated region matching for image retrieval. In: Proceedings of the Eighth ACM International Conference on Multimedia. ACM (2000)
18. Tsai, C.-F., McGarry, K., Tait, J.: CLAIRE: a modular support vector image indexing and classification system. ACM Trans. Inf. Syst. (TOIS) 24(3), 353–379 (2006)
19. Meskaldji, K., Boucherkha, S., Chikhi, S.: Color quantization and its impact on color histogram based image retrieval accuracy. In: First International Conference on Networked Digital Technologies. NDT 2009. IEEE (2009)
20. Liu, Y., et al.: A survey of content-based image retrieval with high-level semantics. Pattern Recogn. 40(1), 262–282 (2007)
21. Jain, R., Kasturi, R., Schunck, B.G.: Machine Vision, vol. 5. McGraw-Hill, New York (1995)
22. Haralick, R.M., Shanmugam, K.: Textural features for image classification. IEEE Trans. Syst. Man Cybern. 6, 610–621 (1973)
23. Haralick, R.M.: Statistical and structural approaches to texture. Proc. IEEE 67(5), 786–804 (1979)
24. Levine, M.D.: Vision in Man and Machine. McGraw-Hill College, New York (1985)
25. Tamura, H., Mori, S., Yamawaki, T.: Textural features corresponding to visual perception. IEEE Trans. Syst. Man Cybern. 8(6), 460–473 (1978)
26. Francos, J.M.: 7 Orthogonal decompositions of 2D random fields and their applications for 2D spectral estimation. Handb. Stat. 10, 207–227 (1993)
27. Liu, F., Picard, R.W.: Periodicity, directionality, and randomness: wold features for image modeling and retrieval. IEEE Trans. Pattern Anal. Mach. Intell. 18(7), 722–733 (1996)
28. Daugman, J.G.: Complete discrete 2-D Gabor transforms by neural networks for image analysis and compression. IEEE Trans. Acoust. Speech Sig. Process. 36(7), 1169–1179 (1988)
29. Ma, W.-Y., Manjunath, B.: Edge flow: a framework of boundary detection and image segmentation. In: Proceedings of 1997 IEEE Computer Society Conference on Computer Vision and Pattern Recognition. IEEE (1997)
30. Wang, J.Z., Li, J., Wiederhold, G.: SIMPLIcity: semantics-sensitive integrated matching for picture libraries. IEEE Trans. Pattern Anal. Mach. Intell. 23(9), 947–963 (2001)

Model Checking of TTCAN
Protocol Using UPPAAL

Liu Shuxin and Noriaki Yoshiura[✉]

Department of Information and Computer Sciences, Saitama University,
255, Shimo-ookubo, Sakura-ku, Saitama, Japan
yoshiura@fmx.ics.saitama-u.ac.jp

Abstract. Recent years, vehicles are becoming more and more intelligent and automatic. Some experts estimate that more than 80% of all current innovations within vehicles are based on distributed electronic systems. The critical parts of such systems are the services provided by the underlying distributed control networks. TTCAN is the extension of the standard Controller Area Network (CAN), which is the most widely adopted in-vehicle network. As the complexity of TTCAN protocol, formal verification is the best choice to verify the specification correctness of TTCAN protocol. The previous researches are only able to verify the models of TTCAN protocol with no more than three nodes. If there are four nodes in the model, it meets two problems: state space explosion and magnanimous verification time. This paper proposes a novel method and the model of TTCAN protocol with 4 nodes can be verified. TTCAN is the extension of the standard Controller Area Network (CAN), which is the most widely adopted in-vehicle network.

1 Introduction

Today the electrical and software contents of vehicles can account for up to 23 percentages of the vehicle manufacturing cost [11]. Vehicle control systems vary widely in functionality from seat heating to automatic driving. The safety of vehicle control systems is critical for automatic industry.

The Controller Area Network (CAN) [2,3] has become the most successful vehicle network in the world. In traditional CAN networks, all the data transmissions are event-triggered. The communication peak loads occur when the transmissions of messages are requested at the same time. Fortunately, the non-destructive arbitration mechanism of CAN network guarantees the sequential transmissions of all the messages following their identifier priorities. However, one potential defect of the classic CAN network is the message starvation problem. In other words, CAN network cannot guarantee the transmission delay of the messages with relatively lower priorities.

The Time-Triggered Controller Area Network (TTCAN) [5,8] which is the extension of the standard CAN protocol shows a new solution to this problem. Currently the TTCAN [9,10] protocol has already been prototyped both in software by NEC and in hardware by Bosch and Hitachi. The communications of

© Springer International Publishing AG, part of Springer Nature 2018
O. Gervasi et al. (Eds.): ICCSA 2018, LNCS 10963, pp. 550–564, 2018.
https://doi.org/10.1007/978-3-319-95171-3_43

TTCAN are based on the periodic transmission of a reference message from a time master. Periodic transmissions also introduce a system wide global network time with high precision. This enables TTCAN to provide a high network throughput and help to ensure the real-time capability that is required by most embedded systems.

Formal verification [6], unlike testing or simulation, is a mathematical proof of correctness with respect to a given specified formal system and a given set of requirement specifications. In this paper, the TTCAN protocol is abstracted as several time automata and the requirement specifications are expressed in the form of TCTL [15] formulas. UPPAAL [1,12] is a toolbox for verification of real-time systems jointly developed by Uppsala University and Aalborg University. It has been applied successfully in case studies ranging from communication protocols to multimedia applications.

TTCAN protocol is huge and complicated and model checking of it meets two problems: state space explosion and massive verification time. In the previous researches, there are no more than three nodes in the model of TTCAN protocol [14].

This thesis proposes a novel method for the verification of TTCAN protocol. This method enables to reduce the required state space and verification time. By this method, the model of TTCAN protocol is able to be smaller and contains more than three nodes. First, we divide the whole TTCAN protocol into two no-connection phases. One phase is to determine the next time master among potential time masters. The other is to transmit messages and handle the errors. Then we assume that the first phase is always true and focused on verifying the second phase. After that, we analyse the verification results and determine that TTCAM protocol is safe and correct.

2   TTCAN

The CAN [7] specifications ISO 11898-1 (high speed) and ISO-11519-2 (low speed) define the physical layer and data link layer for the CAN communications protocol. As these are the only two layers defined in the standard, it is possible to use a separate higher layer protocol to assign a message schedule implementation based on either an event driven or time triggered model. The new session layer specification ISO 11898-4 (draft), for Time Triggered Controller Area Network (TTCAN) [4] will provide the first internationally accepted ISO Time-Triggered specification for any automotive protocol.

2.1   Basic Cycle and System Matrix

A prerequisite for synchronous scheduling in a distributed network application is the concept of a global time base to which all scheduling actions are referred. In TTCAN each node participating in the time-triggered schedule holds a replica of global time in the form of a counter. The time-triggered schedule is composed of a fixed sequence of time slots, or time windows, rather like in a Time Division

Multiple Access (TDMA) protocol. The sequence of TDMA slots in which each electronic module (network node) sends its message frames forms a basic cycle. Each message frame is called a time window. All of the basic cycles have the same size in the temporal domain.

When a basic cycle is finished, the next basic cycle is started. The system matrix is made up of all the basic cycles and the number of the basic cycles determines the length of the system matrix. After a system matrix is completed, a repeat of the system matrix is started by the same transmission pattern. Figure 1 illustrates a system matrix consisting of four basic cycles. In this figure, each line is a basic 3 cycle, consisting of five time windows. The Time Master is used to transmit the value of the clock in a time message, called Reference Message. M(1,1) means that Node 1 sends a message with priority 1 during this time window. Free and Arbitrate means free messages and arbitrate messages.

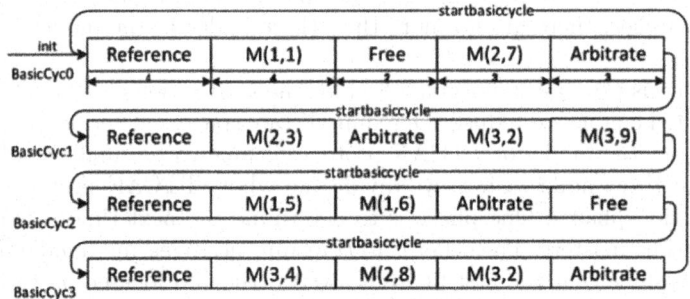

Fig. 1. System matrix

2.2 Time Windows

In TTCAN, four kinds of time windows are designed including reference window, exclusive time window, arbitration time window and free time window.

Reference window is used to transmit reference messages. The reference message is used to synchronize all the nodes. Each basic cycle in TTCAN is started with a reference window. During the reference window, transmitting or receiving other messages are not allowed on the bus except the reference message.

Exclusive time windows are used to transmit periodic messages. In exclusive time windows, specific messages are transmitted. No other message can be scheduled to access the bus during the exclusive time windows.

Arbitration time windows are used to transmit a periodic messages. This type of time windows is assigned to more than one messages. Several nodes may have a scheduled message to be transmitted during this type of time windows.

Every message has its own priority. The message with the highest priority will be allowed to be transmitted during the arbitration time window.

Free time windows are reserved for future extension of the network. Transmitting or receiving messages are not allowed during this type of time windows.

2.3   Error Handling Mechanism

In TTCAN, each node has a message status counter (MSC). The message status counters associates with every message exchanged in the exclusive time windows. The message status counter register is a counter used to track errors which occur by the messages in exclusive time windows. The MSC has a bounded range of zero to seven.

The MSC is incremented or decremented according to the error condition or normal condition. For example, if a message fails in being transmitted, the MSC of its node is incremented by one. If the message is transmitted successfully, the MSC is decremented by one. If an MSC reaches a value of seven, then an error handling procedure is initiated and the system will be stopped.

3   Model Checking and UPPAAL

In software and hardware design of complex systems, more time and effort are spent on verification than on construction. Techniques are sought to reduce and ease the verification efforts while increasing their coverage. Model checking is a verification technique that explores all possible system states in a brute-force manner. Similar to a computer chess program that checks all possible moves, a model checker, the software that performs the model checking, examines all possible system scenarios in a systematic manner. In this way, it can be shown that whether a given system model satisfies a certain property or not.

Totally there are three phases of the model checking process. First, the modeling phase: model the system under consideration using the model description language of the model checker at hand and formalize the property to be checked using the property specification language. Second, the running phase: run the model checker to check the validity of the property in the system model. Third, the analysis phase: check if the property is satisfied. If violated, analyze and generate a counterexample bisimulation. Figure 2 illustrates all the phases of model checking process.

3.1   Model and Property

The prerequisite inputs to model checking are a model of the system under consideration and a formal characterization of the property to be checked. Models of systems describe the behavior of systems in an distinct and precise way. They are mostly expressed using finite state automata, consisting of a finite set of states and a finite set of transitions. States contain the information about the current values of variables and the previously executed statements. Transitions describe how the system execute from one state to another. In this research, timed automata are used. Timed automata are finite state machines extended with clock variables. Timed automata is specially utilized for the model checking of real-time systems. The definition of timed automaton is defined as follows:

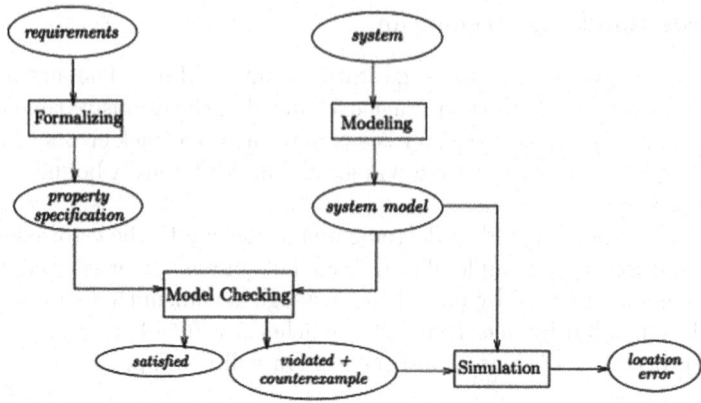

Fig. 2. Schematic view of the model checking approach

A timed automaton is a tuple $A = (Q, \Sigma, C, E, q_0)$

- Q is a finite set. The elements of Q are called the states of A.
- Σ is a finite set called the alphabet or actions of A.
- C is a finite set called the clocks of A.
- $E \subseteq Q \times \Sigma \times B(C) \times P(C) \times Q$ is a set of edges, called transitions of A where $B(C)$ is the set of boolean clock constraints involving clocks from C and $P(C)$ is the powerset of C.
- q_0 is an element of Q, called the initial state.

To make a rigorous system verification possible, properties should also be described in a precise manner. This is typically done using a property specification language, e.g. linear temporal logic (LTL), Computational Tree Logic and so on. This research focuses on a simplified version of Timed Computational Tree Logic (TCTL).

The syntax of the logic Timed Computation Tree Logic is defined as follows:
$$\phi ::= a|g|\phi_1 \wedge \phi_2|\neg\phi|E(\phi_1 U^J \phi_2)|A(\phi_1 U^J \phi_2)$$

- a is an atomic action
- g is a clock constraint
- E means "for some paths";
- A means "for all paths";
- J is an interval whose bounds are natural numbers;

Compared with LTL, TCTL adds two important concepts: First, the branching time are considered in TCTL. A and E are called path quantifiers. They enable to express that in a given state a property should be hold for all paths starting from this state or for some paths starting from this state. Second, clock variables and clock constraints can be used in TCTL formulas. This enables to verify the correctness of clocks and their values directly.

3.2 Model Checker UPPAAL

The model checker UPPAAL is based on the theory of timed automata and its modeling language offers additional features such as bounded integer variables and urgency locations. The query language of UPPAAL, used to specify properties to be checked, is a subset of TCTL (Timed Computational Tree Logic).

The simulator component of the tool suite facilitates examination of the system behaviour in a graphical context. The target system is loaded from the graphical editor into the simulator and one can examine possible execution traces of a system during the early designing and modeling stage. The user gives the option to direct the course of the execution trace when a number of alternative paths exist. The simulator is also able to perform a random execution trace. The execution path is retained in the simulator memory after a simulation and may be saved to a file. Previously saved execution traces may also be loaded and reviewed. The simulator also allows viewing of diagnostic traces generated by the verifier. This feature enables the user to examine the execution trace resulting from the verification of a system requirements specification.

4 Method and Architecture

4.1 Problem

TTCAN is a complicated and massive time-triggered protocol. The model checking of TTCAN requires an enormous amount of verification time and costs a great deal of state space. The verification time and state space increase exponentially with the increase of the nodes in the model. In most of the previous researches about the model checking of TTCAN protocol, the models with three nodes are verified successfully. If there are more than three nodes, the model checker will meet two problems: state space explosion and verification time.

4.2 Method

In TTCAN protocol, some nodes are the potential time masters. These nodes are not only used to send and receive messages, but also compete to be the time master. When the system starts to execute, the potential time master with the highest priority will be the new time master. The time master broadcasts the reference message within the reference time window. All the nodes are synchronized by the reference message.

Due to the relationship between the potential time master arbitration and the message transmission, TTCAN protocol is divided into two phases in this research. The first phase is selecting the new time master among the potential time masters. The second phase is the message transmitting phase. In this paper, the first phase is assumed to be always true. This paper focuses on the second phase, the safety of the message transmission in TTCAN protocol. By this method, the model of TTCAN protocol can be verified in practical state space and verification time.

4.3   Architecture

In this research, the architecture of TTCAN protocol is configured to be a master controllers mode (one master and several controllers). As the first phase of TTCAN is assumed to be true, only one node is appeared as the time master connected to the bus and broadcasts the reference messages. There are four nodes in the TTCAN network architecture, called Node0, Node1, Node2 and Node3.

Exclusive and Arbitration messages can be transmitted among the nodes via the bus. In the four nodes, there are sixteen messages with the identities define from one to sixteen, shown in Table 1. For example, Node0 has two exclusive messages whose identities are four and nine, and three arbitration messages whose identities are eleven, fifteen and sixteen. In this research, the identity is also the priority of the message. The lower identity the message is, the higher priority it has.

Table 1. The architecture of TTCAN protocol

Node number	Exclusive message	Arbitration
Node0	4,9	11,15,16
Node1	1,5,6	10,12
Node2	3,7,8	14
Node3	2	13

5   Model

5.1   Overview of Model

The model of TTCAN [13] network consists of five main processes. They are SystemMatrix, ArbitrationMachine, Nodes, Bus Arbitrating and TimeMaster. The Nodes process transmits and receives exclusive or arbitration messages according to the schedule of the system matrix. The Bus Arbitrating process and the ArbitrationMachine process are used to receive the arbitration messages and determine which node can transmit message within the arbitration time window. The TimeMaster process is the model of time master in TTCAN protocol. Therefore, the model is a parallel composition of SystemMatrix, ArbitrationMachine, Nodes, Bus Arbitrating and TimeMaster.

5.2   SystemMatrix

The SystemMatrix process is shown in Fig. 3, which defines the global static schedule for all nodes. In this research, the SystemMatrix process contains four basic cycle: Basiccycle0, Basiccycle1, Basiccycle2 and Basiccycle3. Each basic cycle has sixteen network time units (NTU) assigned to five time windows with four, four, two, three and three time units. According to the list of basic cycles in the SystemMatrix process, Basiccycle0 is scheduled firstly. Afterwards, Basiccycle1, Basiccycle2 andBasiccycle3 are executed before returning to the beginning of the system matrix again.

The regular structure of SystemMatrix is a 2-dimensional matrix, where a row represents a basic cycle, and a column of time windows contains the same number of time units. Clock t indicates the number of network time units. The variable w trigger is used to count the number of processes which are executed within the current window. The function signal (1,1,exclu) means that the message with identity one will be transmitted by Node1 in the exclusive time window. This function is used to broadcast the schedule information to all the nodes. Four kinds of time windows are represented in the SystemMatrix process.

There are also three channels in the SystemMatrix process. They are ref, info and arbi signal channels. The ref channel transmits a signal to the TimeMaster process, then the TimeMaster process synchronizes all the nodes by broadcasting a signal via its syn channel. The info channel appears within the exclusive time windows and arbitration time windows. The info channel is used to inform all the nodes that the message transmission is beginning. The signal along the arbi signal channel is transmitted to the ArbitrationMachine process.

5.3 Nodes

The Nodes process describes behaviors of all the nodes, shown in Fig. 4. All the nodes perform as the same behaviors. So the parameterized process Nodes(x) is built. The main role of the Nodes process is to transmit, receive messages and handle the error conditions. After the nodes are synchronized by receiving the signals via syn channel of the TimeMaster process and info channel of the

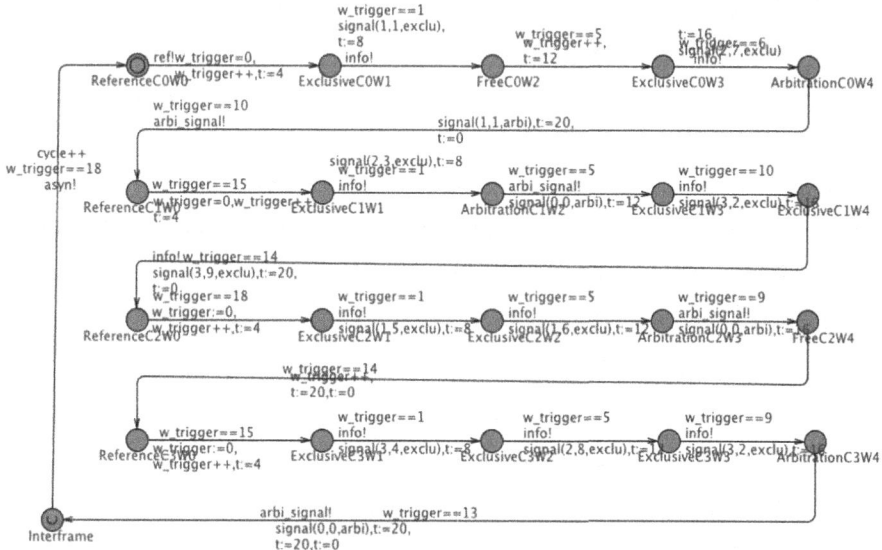

Fig. 3. SystemMatrix process

SystemMatrix process, the nodes get a message identity, a node identity and a message type. The message identity is the identity of the exclusive message which is transmitted in the current exclusive time window. The node identity is the transmitting node in the current time window. And there are two types of messages in TTCAN protocol. They are exclu which means exclusive messages and arbi which means arbitration windows. Each node needs to compare the information with its own after it receives. In total, there are three conditions after comparing.

1. Arbitration:
   The message type is Arbi. Each node chooses one of its arbitration messages and sends it to the Bus Arbitrating process. If there is no arbitration message which needs to be transmitted, the node send a message with identity seventeen, which means no message in this research. Finally, the process returns to the synchronising location and waits for the next time window.
2. Exclusive and discard:
   The message type is exclu, but the node identity does not equal to the current node identity. This means that the current window is an exclusive time window and the current node is not allowed to transmitted This node discard this signal and go back to the synchronising location.
3. Exclusive and access:
   The message type is exclu and the node identity equals to the current node. This means that the current node get the permission to transmit an exclusive message within the current time window. The node has 50% possibility for sending the exclusive message successfully, and 50% possibility for making an error. If the exclusive message is transmitted successfully, the process goes

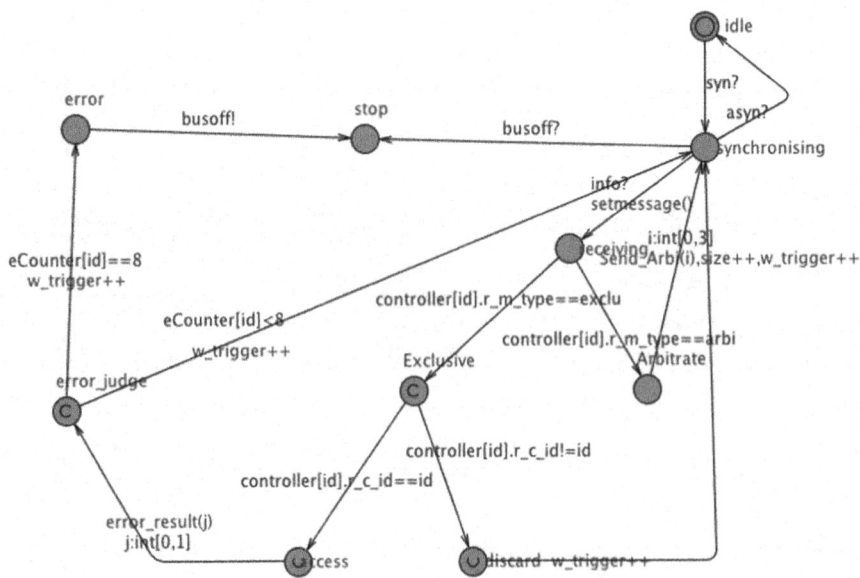

Fig. 4. The parameterized process Nodes

back to the synchronising location. If not, the error handling mechanism will be executed.

Error handling mechanism is also realized in the Nodes process. Each node has its own error counter, ranged from zero to seven. The initial value of the error counter is zero. When an exclusive message is transmitted successfully, the corresponding error counter is decremented by one. If the message fails in being transmitted, the corresponding error counter is incremented by one. If the value of any error counter reaches the value eight, the corresponding node goes to the stop location and broadcasts an error signal through the busoff channel. Then the other nodes receive the error signal and go to the stop location. So that the system stops. Figure 5 is the flow chart of error handling mechanism.

5.4   Arbitration Machine

The role of the ArbitrationMachine process is to receive the arbitration starting signal and synchronize all the nodes. There are three channels used in this process. They are arbi signal, ar and info channels.

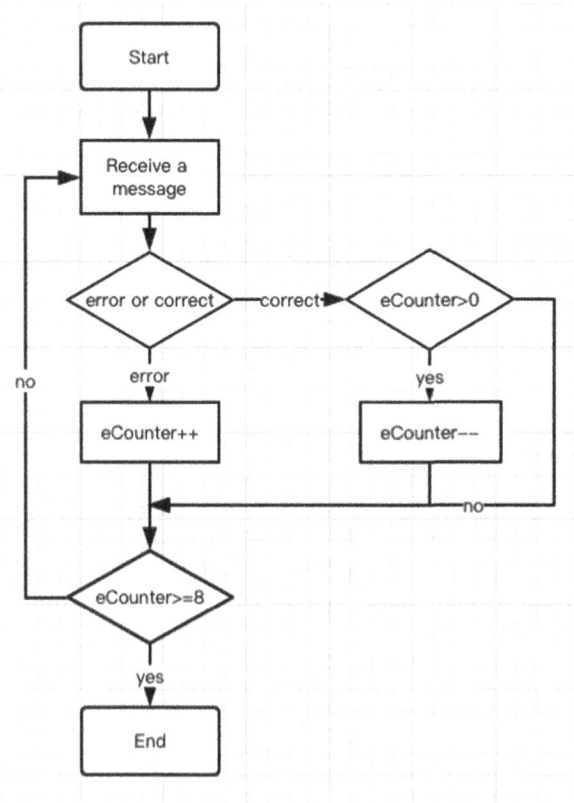

Fig. 5. The flow chart of error handling mechanism

The arbi signal channel receives the signal from the SystemMatrix process. After receiving the signal, the ArbitrationMachine process broadcasts the arbitration starting signal to the Nodes processes and the Bus Arbitrating process. The signal transmitted via the are channel initializes the Bus Arbitrating process. Figure 6 is the ArbitrationMachine process.

5.5 Bus Arbitrating

The Bus Arbitrating process handles the arbitration messages and determines the node identity and the message identity for the current arbitration time window. The determination of the node identity and the message identity is realized by the function compare(); Variable winner pr means the message with the highest priority among all of the arbitration messages within the current arbitration time window; Variable winner id indicates the node identity holding the winner pr message. Variable winner id ranges from 0 to 4. When variable winner pr equals 17, variable winner id will equal to 4. It means that there is no message to be transmitted within the current arbitration time window. Figure 7 is the Bus Arbitrating process.

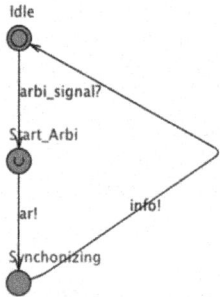

Fig. 6. ArbitrationMachine process

5.6 TimeMaster

The TimeMaster process is used to synchronize all the nodes. There are two channels in the TimeMaster process. They are ref and syn channels. The TimeMaster process receives the signal from the SystemMatrix process via ref channel, then synchronize all the nodes by sending a signal via the syn channel. Figure 8 is the TimeMaster process.

6   Verification

6.1   Properties

1. Deadlock:
   First of all, the model should be deadlock free. There are two situations of deadlock. First is normal deadlock, in which two or more than two processes occupy the same resources at the same time and want others to release the resources. The second is that the system stops because of some errors. In the tool UPPAAL, there is a primitive to describe the first situation.
   A[ ] not deadlock
   The second situation is given here. When the number of errors in one node adds up to the maximize number 8, the system reaches a stopping state and terminates. This is referred as an exception as below:
   A[ ] (eCounter[0] < 8 and eCounter[1] < 8 and eCounter[2] < 8 and eCounter[3] < 8) imply not deadlock
2. Priority safety:
   In an arbitration time window, the safety of message priority determines the correctness of the arbitration mechanism. This specification can be illustrated as follows: In the arbitration time windows, if the Bus Arbitrating process receives more than one message, the highest priority message must always be transmitted.

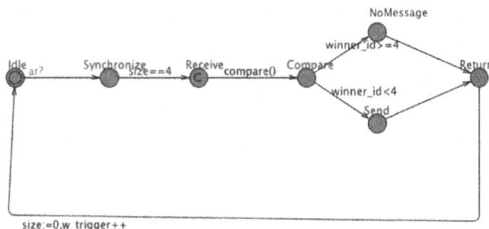

Fig. 7. Bus arbitrating process

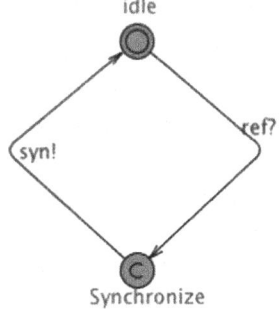

Fig. 8. TimeMaster process

- A[ ] BusArbi.Compare and Arbitration[0].messageid==16 and (Arbitration[1].messageid==10 or Arbitration[1].messageid==12 or Arbitration[2].messageid==14 or A rbitration[3].messageid==13) imply not winner id==0
- A[ ] BusArbi.Compare and Arbitration[0].messageid==15 and (Arbitration[1].messageid==10 or Arbitration[1].messageid==12 or Arbitration[2].messageid==14 or Arbitration[3].messageid==13) imply not winner id==0
- A[ ] BusArbi.Compare and Arbitration[2].messageid==14 and (Arbitration[1].messageid==10 or Arbitration[1].messageid==12 or Arbitration[3].messageid==13 or A rbitration[0].messageid==11) imply not winner id==2
- A[ ] BusArbi.Compare and Arbitration[3].messageid==13 and (Arbitration[1].messageid==10 or Arbitration[1].messageid==12 or Arbitration[0].messageid==11) im ply winner id==0 or winner id==1
- A[ ] BusArbi.Compare and Arbitration[1].messageid==12 and Arbitration[0].message id==11 imply winner id==0
- A[ ] BusArbi.Compare and Arbitration[1].messageid==12 and Arbitration[0].message id==11 imply winner id==0
- A[ ] BusArbi.Compare and Arbitration[1].messageid==10 and Arbitration[0].message id==11 imply winner id==1

3. Exclusive window:
In TTCAN protocol, the exclusive messages guarantee the latency of those lower priority messages. Exclusive time window is used to transmit the specified message at the specified time interval.
System.ExclusiveC0W1 and Con1.Exclusive → Con1.access
System.ExclusiveC0W3 and Con2.Exclusive → Con2.access
System.ExclusiveC1W1 and Con2.Exclusive → Con2.access
System.ExclusiveC1W3 and Con3.Exclusive → Con3.access
System.ExclusiveC1W4 and Con3.Exclusive → Con3.access
System.ExclusiveC2W1 and Con1.Exclusive → Con1.access
System.ExclusiveC2W2 and Con1.Exclusive → Con1.access
System.ExclusiveC3W1 and Con2.Exclusive → Con2.access
System.ExclusiveC3W2 and Con2.Exclusive → Con2.access
System.ExclusiveC3W3 and Con3.Exclusive → Con3.access

4. Free window:
Free windows are reserved for the further network extension. So no messages can be transmitted within the free windows.
A[ ] System.FreeC2W4 imply e m==0 A[ ] System.FreeC0W2 imply e m==1

6.2   Experiment Environment

The individual verification computations consume varying amounts of computational time and memory depending on the system configuration and requirement specification. The system is verified on an i86 based platform, employing

Table 2. Verification results

Propety name	Number of properties	Required memory	Verification time	Correctness
Deadlock free	1	1291 MB	123.695s	Unsatisfied
Deadlock free and exception	1	4575 MB	559.031 s	Satisfied
Priority safety	7	44684 MB	1841.981 s	Satisfied
Exclusive window	10	51779 MB	3340.545 s	Satisfied
Free window	2	12701 MB	510.144 s	Satisfied

an Intel Core i5 2.9 GHz processor, with a 24 GB 1600 MHz DDR3 memory, running macOS Sierra version 10.12.5. The UPPAAL verification engine is version 4.1.20-beta3(1), July 2014.

6.3   Verification Result

Table 2 shows that, except the deadlock free property, all the properties are satisfied. Though deadlock free property is not satisfied, the exception of it is satisfied. These properties proves the correctness of TTCAN protocol. In the previous researches, similar properties are verified. However, there are at most three nodes in the previous works. If more than three nodes, the verification time and state space are too large to be verified. In this research, the model of TTCAN is divided into two phases and the second phase is verified. Therefore, in the case of more than three nodes, the safety of message transmission in TTCAN protocol can be verified.

Through the table below, it indicates that this research does not only increase the number of nodes, but also reduces the verification time and required memory.

7   Conclusion

In this research, I have modeled and verified message transmission and error handling of TTCAN protocol using the model checker UPPAAL. All the properties have been described in terms of timed CTL formulas and UPPAAL has been used to verify whether the model caters the specifications. Finally, I am able to conclude that the TTCAN protocol satisfies the specifications.

As the model of TTCAN protocol is divided into two phases and this research focuses on message transmitting and error handling, the first phase, in which the system determines the new time master among potential time masters, has not been verified. In the future work, the first phase will be verified. After that, I will combine the verification results of both two phases, so that the whole TTCAN protocol will be verified.

References

1. Holzmann, G.J.: The Spin Model Checker-Primer and Reference Manual. Published by Addison Wesley (2004)
2. Pan, C., Guo, J., Zhu, L., Shi, J., Zhu, H., Zhou, X.: Modeling and verification of CAN bus with application layer using UPPAAL. In: Electronic Notes in Theoretical Computer Science, vol. 309, no. C, pp. 31–49 (2014)
3. Corrigan, S.: Controller Area Network Physical Layer Requirements. Published by Texas Instruments (2008)
4. Saha, I., Roy, S.: A finite state analysis of time-triggered CAN (TTCAN) protocol using Spin. In: Proceeding of International Conference on Computing: Theory and Applications, pp. 77–81 (2007)
5. Rodriguez-Navas, G., Proenza, J., Hansson, H.: Using UPPAAL to model and verify a clock synchronization protocol for the controller area network. In: Proceedings of 2005 IEEE Conference on Emerging Technologies and Factory Automation, pp. 495–502 (2005)
6. Kauer, M., Soudbakhsh, D., Dip, G., Samarjit, C., Anuradha, A.M.: Fault-tolerant control synthesis and verification of distributed embedded systems. In: Proceeding in Design, Automation & Test in Europe Conference & Exhibition, no. 56, pp. 1–6 (2014)
7. Johansson, K.H., Torngren, T., Nielsen, L.: Vehicle applications of controller area network. In: Handbook of Networked and Embedded Control Systems, pp. 741–765 (2005)
8. International Organization for Standardization: Road vehicles-Controller area network (CAN)-Part 4: Time-triggered communication (2015)
9. Keating, D., McInnes, A., Hayes, M.: Model checking a TTCAN implementation. In: Proceedings of the 2011 Fourth IEEE International Conference on Software Testing, Verification and Validation, pp. 387–396 (2011)
10. Wu, X., Ling, H., Dong, Y.: On modeling and verifying of application protocols of TTCAN in flight-control system with UPPAAL. In: Proceedings of International Conference on Embedded Software and Systems, pp. 572–577 (2009)
11. Szilagyi, C., Koopman, P.: Low cost multicast authentication via validity voting in time-triggered embedded control networks. In: Proceeding of the 5th Workshop on Embedded Systems Security, pp. 1–10 (2010)
12. Behrmann, G., David, A., Larsen, K.G.: A Tutorial on UPPAAL 4.0. Department of Computer Science. Aalborg University (2006)
13. Leen, G.: Development and Formal Verification of TTCAN (Time-Triggered Controller Area Network). Lambert Academic Publishing (2010)
14. Ran, Q., Wu, X., Li, X., Shi, J., Guo, J., Zhu, H.: Modeling and verifying the TTCAN protocol using timed CSP. In: Proceedings of Theoretical Aspects of Software Engineering Conference, pp. 90–97 (2014)
15. Byg, J., Jacobsen, M., Jacobsen, L.: TCTL-preserving translations from timed-arc petri nets to networks of timed automata. Theor. Comput. Sci. **537**, 3–28 (2014)

Processing of Design and Manufacturing Workflows in a Large Enterprise

Alexander Afanasyev$^{(\boxtimes)}$, Maria Ukhanova$^{(\boxtimes)}$, Irina Ionova$^{(\boxtimes)}$,
and Nikolay Voit$^{(\boxtimes)}$ (iD)

Ulyanovsk State Technical University, Ulyanovsk, Russia
{a.afanasev,n.voit}@ulstu.ru, mari-u@inbox.ru,
epira@mail.ru

Abstract. The paper deals with the problem of design and manufacturing workflows in a large enterprise. As an example of a workflow, we presented the author's model of coordination of design documentation (DD) based on the Petri net. The model was analyzed for possible errors in system designing.

Keywords: Workflow · Process · Manufacturing

1 Introduction

In the modern world, any large enterprise requires the design and manufacturing production planning to be faster for launching a product to market as soon as possible, for improving product's quality, and reducing production costs. Today, it is impossible to fulfill these requirements without end-to-end design technology, which is based on computer-aided design of technical documentation, project management systems, electronic document management, and a single information space. In order to solve these problems, many software products are developed. These are CAD\CAE, CAM\CAPP, PDM\PLM, and ERP systems. The diagram of the relationship between these systems is shown in Fig. 1.

Modern CAD systems include several interconnected components. First of all, these are Computer Aided Designed (CAD) used for designing documents and Computer Aided Engineering (CAE) used for engineering calculations. In Russia, typical CAD/CAE systems are Kompas-3D, T-Flex CAD, T-FLEX Analysis, Solidworks, Altium Designer, Autodesk Simulation, Unigraphics NX CAE, etc. Several other tools for the design of technological documentation, which include the means of automated development of technical processes CAPP (Computer Aided Production Planning) and means of automated production - CAM (Computer Aided Mechanical). Typical representatives of CAPP systems for the Russian market are Vertical [29], T-FLEX Technology [30], ADEM TDM [31], Sprut TP [32], etc., and CAM systems - Unigraphics NX [33], CAM350 [34], etc. PDM-systems (Product Data Management) act as a single information space in which the developed technical documentation and electronic structure of a product are stored. PDM technology allows managing the product structure and projects and provide multi-user access to documents in real-time. PLM-systems (Product Lifecycle Management) present a technology of managing the

© Springer International Publishing AG, part of Springer Nature 2018
O. Gervasi et al. (Eds.): ICCSA 2018, LNCS 10963, pp. 565–576, 2018.
https://doi.org/10.1007/978-3-319-95171-3_44

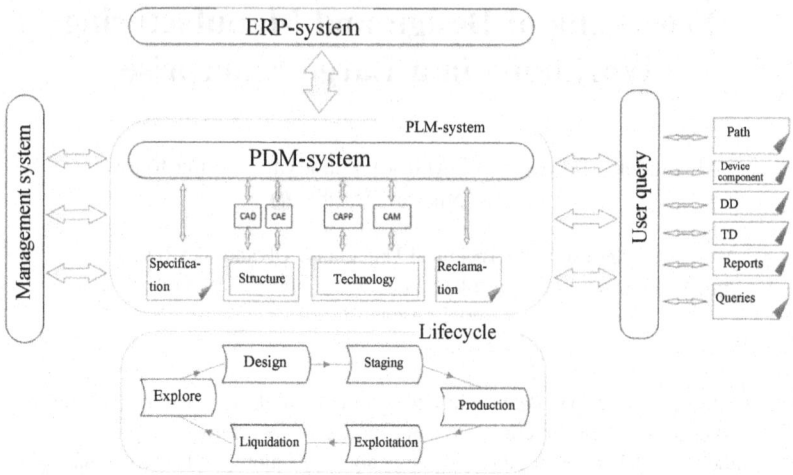

Fig. 1. The diagram of relations between CAD, CAM, PDM and ERP systems.

entire lifecycle of a product. It is a software solution that controls engineering data and information of a product, and also manages all product-related processes throughout the lifecycle of a product, from its conception, through design and manufacturing, to the end of a product. Today, many such systems have been developed by Russia and other countries: Loodsman-PLM, T-Flex-PLM, Siemens-PLM, Lotsia PLM, etc. Such PLM-systems are very effective for end-to-end design and allow a design development of a 3D model of a product to integrate into manufacturing production planning, which leads to time-reduction in design and manufacturing production planning (DMPP). ERP-systems (Enterprise Resource Planning System) are systems of planning and production management. Such information systems are used to control and plan the resources. They are used by enterprises for procurement and accounting of raw materials, production management of a product, task planning for workshops. Alpha, Lotsia ERP, 1C ERP, SAP can be used as examples of ERP-systems.

Faster coordination process of design and manufacturing documentation is based on the creation of workflows. The introduction of workflow technology in an enterprise allows one to formalize the structure and sequence of documentation passing procedures. Business effects statistics from the introduction of workflow technology are presented in Table 1 [1–14]. However, product lifecycle management systems do not always meet the needs of many large enterprises. The workflow in PLM-systems is often too closely related to the flow of information and with low agility to make alternative decisions in real-time. These factors always lead to excessively long and costly cycles of workflow system implementation, processes' reengineering and systems' reconfiguration. The processes of reengineering are not only slow and expensive, but also often impossible.

Moreover, most workflow systems allow modeling workflows, but they lack effective methods for verifying the diagrammatical models of workflows and associated semantic components as texts and program modules. These problems will be discussed below.

Table 1. Statistics of business effects from the introduction of end-to-end workflow technology [28].

Business effects	% improvement
Reduction of quantity errors in technical documentation	by 70%
Time-reduction in design and manufacturing production planning (DMPP)	by 20–60%
Cost-reduction in preparing and issuing technical documentation	by 40%
Time-reduction in searching information	by 40%
Time-reduction for documentation coordination	1,5–7
Faster time-to-market	by 25–75%
Reduction in reject rate	by 40%

The purpose of this paper is to develop a model for coordinating design documentation in the form of a workflow and analysis of this model. The design tools of ASCON and RC ASCON-Volga are used as a basis for representation, development and maintenance.

2 Features of Design and Manufacturing Workflows in a Large Enterprise

Each enterprise has its own characteristics in products' production [15–26]. For large enterprises is typical:

- a large number of nomenclature positions for manufacturing;
- short terms for production planning;
- design documentation of in-house and external developments;
- a long cycle of design documentation coordination and changes;
- production according to 2D drawings;
- a large organizational structure of the enterprise;
- complex interaction between units.

Large industrial enterprises producing mainly special purpose equipment use 2D models mainly. In this case, designers draw a 3D model just to understand the design. Based on the documentation in 2D, production engineers develop their own 3D models in order to describe the technology or develop a control program for CNC machines. It makes the development time longer.

It should be noted that it is necessary to detect errors at the design stage as early as possible. As you know, the later an error is found, the more expensive it is to correct it. The most expensive errors are those introduced at the production stage. But also, at the development of the product manufacturing technology stage, errors in engineering lead to an imminent delay in the design-engineering preproduction, since the designer will have not only to develop a product change, but also to coordinate it, and this takes considerable time.

Therefore, the trend of end-to-end manufacturing solutions based on 3D models and workflow management systems is gaining momentum. Figure 2 shows a 3D model of the gear's motion (from designing to technology) [14].

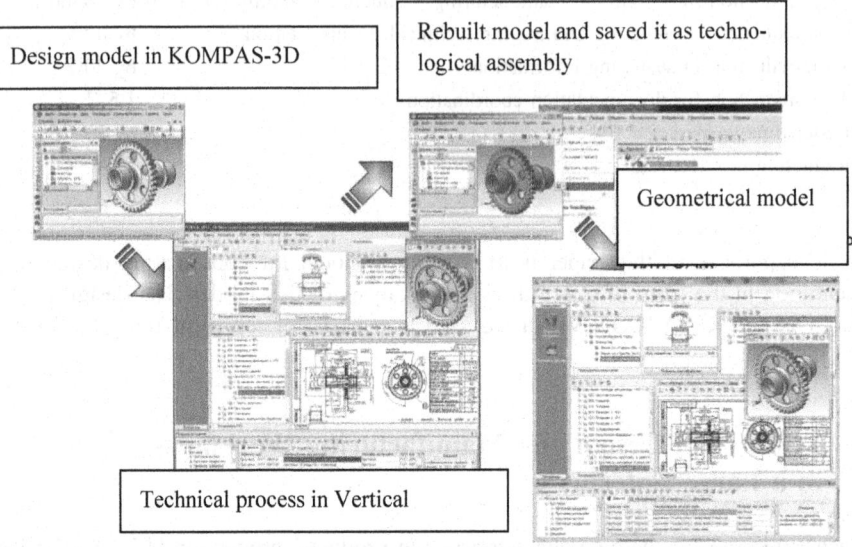

Fig. 2. A diagram of a 3D model of the gear's motion (from designing to technology).

3   Design Stages in Design and Manufacturing Workflows

We propose the following design stages in design and manufacturing workflows:

- a formal description of main business processes of design and manufacturing preproduction;
- workflow model building based on a formal description of business processes;
- an analysis of developed model properties of a design and manufacturing workflow;
- a data processing error analysis.

Below, the design stages in design and manufacturing pre-production will be described more detailed.

4   Structural-Functional Diagram of Design and Manufacturing Workflows

The effective interaction of all enterprise's units and structures makes this enterprise more effective. Data flows displaying the essence of the production process move along the chain.

In order to describe design and manufacturing workflows of any enterprise, we should identify the main processes of design and manufacturing pre-production. Figure 3 represents a developed processes diagram of design and manufacturing pre-production, which is one of the examples of normative design workflows.

In this diagram, we identify two major workflows, which deal with the design and manufacturing pre-production processes. These processes solve different problems, and the successful mastering of a new product is their goal. Let us consider them more detailed.

The design processes of pre-production workflows include the solution of the following problems:

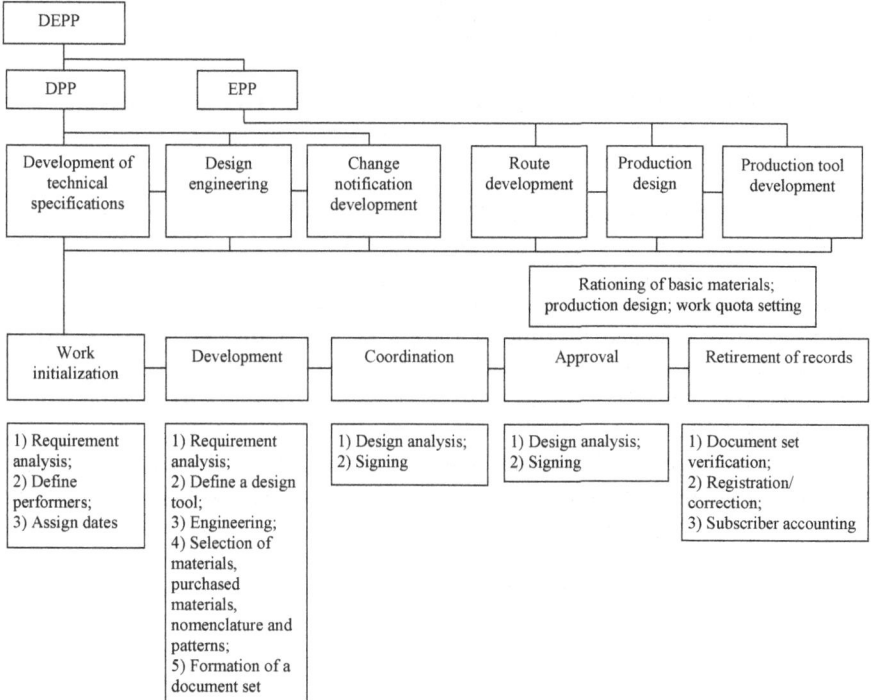

Fig. 3. Diagram of processes of design and manufacturing production planning

1. Identify the requirements for a new product.
2. Analyze a new product nomenclature.
3. Schedule the works on mastering or developing a new product.
4. Analyze customer claims.
5. Identify the requirements for a malfunction repair.
6. Develop and coordinate technical specifications for work.
7. Develop and coordinate design documentation (DD).
8. Develop and coordinate DD correction.

The manufacturing pre-production succeeds after the design pre-production. Manufacturing pre-production workflows have to solve the following problems.

1. Analyze the possibility of manufacturing a new product.
2. Analyze the equipment for manufacturing a new product.
3. Make a decision of the equipment procurement.
4. Schedule the work for developing a new product manufacturing technology.
5. Develop a route for making a nomenclature of product components.
6. Develop a manufacturing process with control programs.
7. Determine the labor-intensive manufacture of a product.
8. Set norms of direct materials of a product nomenclature.
9. Development of industrial equipment.

It is easy to understand that the workflows are interrelated.

5 Modeling a Standard Workflow of Design Documentation Coordination

Let us consider one of design pre-production tasks in order to create a model of design and manufacturing workflows: a standard process model for detailed design documentation coordination.

In order to build a model, we designed a business process for the DD development and coordination, defined the rules for the CD set's formation, chose tasks, and identified their performers. A special software called Workflow Designer of Project Management System (PMS) by RC Ascon-Volga was used as a tool for designing a workflow model.

We built a sequence of tasks; developed scripts in order to change the documents' states in the coordination process and filling the matching attributes in Loodsman:

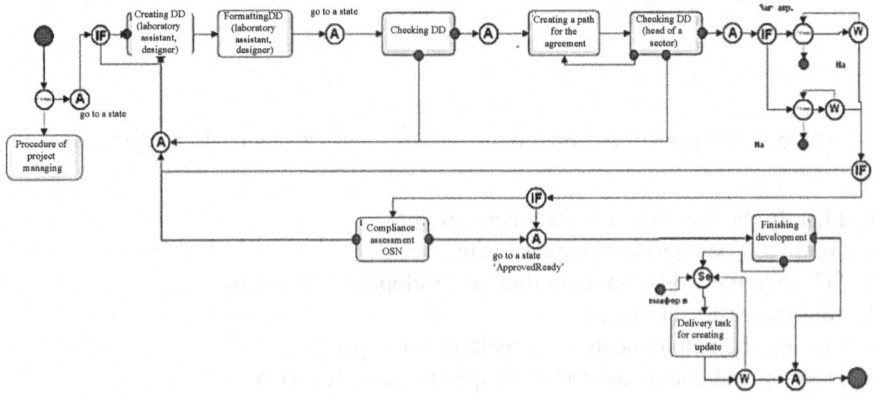

Fig. 4. Model of design coordination of DD in the specialized language of the ASCON-Volga company.

PLM. Figure 4 represents the workflow model for the DD development and coordination in the specialized language of PMS.

We use Petri nets in order to simulate a process of design coordination, and evaluate properties as safety, liveness and deadlocks. Petri nets were used to analyze the developed model for DD coordination (Fig. 4). The model was developed in Visual Object Net++. The design documentation coordination model based on Petri nets is shown in Fig. 5.

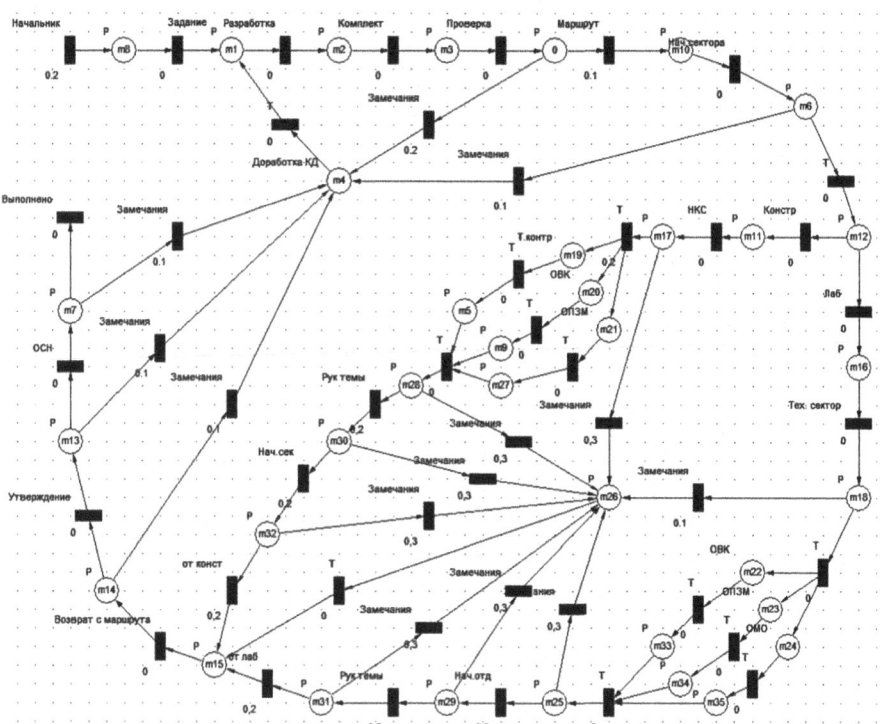

Fig. 5. Model of DD development and coordination.

6 Analysis of Workflow Model Properties of DD Coordination

The developed model of design documentation coordination was tested in the specialized software Visual Object Net++. The model was tested for the following properties:

- reachability – it establishes that the final state of the system will be achieved in any sequence of transitions from *i* position. This property also means that when the end position of this network is reached, there are no chips in the intermediate positions;
- safety – it establishes that there are no deadlocks, loops, dead ends in the processes;

- liveness – it establishes that the system does not contain unnecessary positions that will never be fulfilled. Lack of liveliness means either redundancy of a business process in the projected system, or indicates the possibility of loops, dead ends, locks.

The analysis of the workflow model of the design documentation coordination, presented in Fig. 5, showed that some properties of the network depend on the qualification of a designer. So:

- The model does not have a very good reachability property, since it may accumulate chips in m_1 position. The number of chips that can accumulate in the specified position depends primarily on the qualification of a designer who develops the design documentation. The lower the qualification of a designer, the more times the documentation will be returned for revision, which means that the more chips will accumulate in m_1 position;
- The model has a good liveliness property, because there is no redundancy in the business process. This property also depends on the qualification of a designer. The higher the qualification of a designer of design documentation, the smaller the "liveliness" of the workflow, since many operations associated with the completion of the design documentation will not be performed;
- The model has a good security feature, since there are no hang-ups, loops, dead ends and locks.

As a result of the analysis, a paradox of the liveliness property was discovered. It is traditionally believed that the higher the indicator of the liveliness property, the better the system model was developed. However, in reality, the higher the qualification of a designer, the less errors he makes, and the documentation is less often sent for revision. Therefore, it is better for a design and manufacturing production planning. As a result, the model blocks responsible for sending the design documentation for revision are used less often. And this leads to a deterioration in the quality of liveliness.

It should be noted that any process of coordinating documentation, both design and manufacturing, contains blocks of code that allow you to operate objects, their states and their attributes in the process of coordination. For example, changing the state of an object in the coordination process, for managing its lifecycle, or filling in an authorization signature at the coordination stages.

As you know, any program code can contain errors. And the more lines of program code, the more errors a programmer can tolerate. Errors are divided into two types: syntax errors or semantic errors. Syntactic errors can be easily identified, any compilers of code or specially written unit tests do this. Most of these errors are detected at the time of writing the code. And if syntax errors are found and fixed quite easily and quickly, it is very difficult to identify semantic errors, since they often occur at the stage of the application execution.

Semantic errors are divided into two groups.

1. Logical errors

Errors of this type can be identified by constructing a logic model of the program code. The analysis of the model will reveal deadlock situations, the feasibility of the program.

This question is considered in detail in many sources, therefore methods of revealing such errors in this paper will not be described.

2. Errors of data integrity

Most errors of this type can be avoided if the architect of the information system intelligently projects data integrity constraints at the database level: determines whether the value of the attribute can be empty, sets foreign keys, imposes a unique constraint, and establishes the validity of the entered value. In some cases, this is not possible.

To identify errors of this type requires the development of a special software application that verifies the possibility of filling the attribute with valid values. As a method for determining such errors, it is proposed to use the Checklist, which lists all the necessary attributes of the coordination process. For example, when coordinating the design documentation, the list of attributes of the document is filled. For the correct operation of the program, you need to develop a Checklist, which lists the invalid errors.

Checklist of errors in the coordination of design documentation:

- check the presence of the specified attributes for all possible types of design documentation.
- check the mandatory attributes.
- check the documentation files.

7 Conclusion and Future Works

Features of design and manufacturing production planning in a large enterprise are analyzed. A structural and functional scheme of typical design workflows processes has been developed. A list of tasks to be solved in the process of design and manufacturing production planning has been determined. We developed workflow models for the development and coordination of the design documentation based on the specialized language Ascon-Volga RC and Petri nets, and also analyzed the workflow model of the design documentation coordination, which has the properties of liveliness, safety, and reachability. As a result of the research work, the analysis of the types of errors that occurred in verifying the diagrammatical workflow was made. The future directions of our work will deal with the development of methods for eliminating the errors of diagrammatical workflows, using the classification of permissible structural error types.

Acknowledgments. This research is supported by the grant of the Ministry of Education and Science of the Russian Federation, the project No. 2.1615.2017/4.6. The reported study was funded by RFBR and Government of Ulyanovsk Region according to the research project No. 16-47-732152.

References

1. Afanas'ev, A.N., Voit, N.N., Bochkov, S.I., Uhanova, M.E., Ionova, I.S.: Razrabotka i issledovanie virtual'nyh rabochih mest v srede OPENSIM. Vestnik Ul'yanovskogo gosudarstvennogo tehnicheskogo universiteta **4**(76), 43–47 (2016). (in Russia). https://elibrary.ru/item.asp?id=27645868. Accessed 15 Mar 2018
2. Afanas'ev, A.N., Voit, N.N., Uhanova, M.E., Ionova, I.S., Epifanov, V.V.: Analiz konstruktorsko-tehnologicheskih potokov rabot v usloviyah krupnogo radiotehnicheskogo predpriyatiya. Radiotehnika **6**, 49–58 (2017). (in Russia). http://www.radiotec.ru/article/19581#. Accessed 15 Mar 2017
3. Karpov, Y.G.: Model Shecking. Verifikaciya parallel'nyh i raspredelennyh programmnyh sistem. BHV-Peterburg (2010). (in Russia)
4. Goncharuk, Y.O.: Problemy sozdaniya i vnedreniya modeli biznes-processov predpriyatiya v forme WorkflowSystem. Resursoeffektivnym tehnologiyam-energiyu i entuziazm molodyh: sbornik nauchnyh trudov VI Vserossiiskoi konferencii, pp. 263–272 (2015). (in Russia)
5. Awad, A., Puhlmann, F.: Structural detection of deadlocks in business process models. In: Abramowicz, W., Fensel, D. (eds.) BIS 2008. LNBIP, vol. 7, pp. 239–250. Springer, Heidelberg (2008). https://doi.org/10.1007/978-3-540-79396-0_21
6. Aguilar, J.C.P., et al.: Model checking of BPMN models for reconfigurable workflows. arXiv preprint (2016). arXiv:1607.00478
7. Janssen, W., Mateescu, R., Mauw, S., Fennema, P., van der Stappen, P.: Model checking for managers. In: Dams, D., Gerth, R., Leue, S., Massink, M. (eds.) SPIN 1999. LNCS, vol. 1680, pp. 92–107. Springer, Heidelberg (1999). https://doi.org/10.1007/3-540-48234-2_7
8. Kheldoun, A., Barkaoui, K., Ioualalen, M.: Specification and verification of complex business processes - a high-level petri net-based approach. In: Motahari-Nezhad, H.R., Recker, J., Weidlich, M. (eds.) BPM 2015. LNCS, vol. 9253, pp. 55–71. Springer, Cham (2015). https://doi.org/10.1007/978-3-319-23063-4_4
9. Afanasyev, A.N., Voit, N.N., Ukhanova, M.E., Ionova, I.S.: Treatment design-engineering workflows in large enterprises
10. Trohalinyu, I.: Locman: PLM 2017: Bylo i stalo. Obzor novyh vozmozhnostei v upravlenii dannymi ob izdeliyah mashinostroeniya. SAPR i grafika (2017). (in Russia)
11. Kochan, I.: T-FLEXPLM na mezhdunarodnom rynke. SAPR i grafika (2017). (in Russia)
12. Egorov, P.: Proekt "Razvitie SAPR" na baze Kompleksa ASKON. SAPR i grafika (2017). (in Russia)
13. Vedmid', P., Vlasov, V.: PLM sistemy menedzhmenta kachestva. SAPR i grafika (2017). (in Russia)
14. Skvoznaya 3D-tehnologiya ASKON dlya predpriyatii mashinostroeniya (in Russia). http://ct3d.ru. Accessed 15 Mar 2017
15. Afanas'ev, A.N., Voit, N.N.: Razrabotka i issledovanie sredstv izvlecheniya iz SAPR KOMPAS-3D i predstavleniya v veb-sistemah konstruktorskogo opisaniya, 3D-modelei promyshlennyh detalei i sborok. V sbornike: Sistemy proektirovaniya, tehnologicheskoi podgotovki proizvodstva i upravleniya etapami zhiznennogo cikla promyshlennogo produkta (SAD/CAM/PDM - 2015) Trudy mezhdunarodnoi konferencii, pp. 208–212 (2015). (in Russia)
16. Afanas'ev, A.N., Voit, N.N.: Komponentnaya avtomatizirovannaya obuchayushaya sistema SAPR na osnove gibridnoi neironnoi seti. Avtomatizaciya. Sovremennye tehnologii **3**, 14–18 (2009)

17. Afanas'ev, A.N., Voit, N.N.: Razrabotka komponentno-servisnoi platformy obucheniya: diagrammy ispol'zovaniya i deyatel'nosti programmnogo komponenta scenariya na UML-yazyke. Vestnik Ul'yanovskogo gosudarstvennogo tehnicheskogo universiteta **1**(57), 66–68 (2012). (in Russia)
18. Afanas'ev, A.N., Voit, N.N.: Realizaciya konstruktora scenariya obuchayushih kursov. Vestnik Ul'yanovskogo gosudarstvennogo tehnicheskogo universiteta **1**(53), 54–59 (2011)
19. Afanas'ev, A.N., Voit, N.N.: Razrabotka metodov nechetkoi parametricheskoi adaptivnoi diagnostiki obuchaemogo inzhenera. Avtomatizaciya processov upravleniya **3**, 51–56 (2009). (in Russia)
20. Afanas'ev, A.H., Igonin, A.G., Afanas'eva, T.V., Voit, N.N.: Ispol'zovanie neirosemanticheskih setei dlya avtomatizirovannogo proektirovaniya vychislitel'noi tehniki. Avtomatizaciya. Sovremennye tehnologii **1**, 21–24 (2008). (in Russia)
21. Afanasyev, A.N., Voit, N.N., Kirillov, S.Y.: Development of RYT-grammar for analysis and control dynamic workflows. In: 2017 International Conference on Computing Networking and Informatics (ICCNI), pp. 1–4 (2017). https://doi.org/10.1109/iccni.2017.8123797, http://ieeexplore.ieee.org/stamp/stamp.jsp?tp=&arnumber=8123797&isnumber=8123766. Accessed 15 Mar 2017
22. Voit, N.N.: Development of timed RT-grammars for analysis of business process at manufacturing and in cyber-physical systems. In: 2017 International Conference on Computing Networking and Informatics (ICCNI), pp. 1–5 (2017). https://doi.org/10.1109/iccni.2017.8123798, http://ieeexplore.ieee.org/stamp/stamp.jsp?tp=&arnumber=8123798&isnumber=812376. Accessed 15 Mar 2017
23. Afanasyev, A.N., Voit, N.N., Gainullin, R.F.: Diagrammatic models processing in designing the complex automated systems. In: 10th IEEE International Conference on Application of Information and Communication Technologies (AICT) 2016, pp. 441–445 (2016)
24. Afanasyev, A., Voit, N.: Intelligent agent system to analysis manufacturing process models. In: First International Scientific Conference « Intelligent Information Technologies for Industry » (IITI 2016), Advances in Intelligent Systems and Computing, Russia, vol. 451, pp. 395–403 (2016)
25. Afanasyev, A.N., Voit, N.N., Voevodin, E.Y., Gainullin, R.F.: Control of UML diagrams in designing automated systems software. In: 9th IEEE International Conference on Application of Information and Communication Technologies, AICT-2015, pp. 285–288 (2015)
26. Afanasyev, A., Voit, N.: Multi-agent system to analyse manufacturing process models. In: International Conference on Fuzzy Logic and Intelligent Technologies in Nuclear Science - FLINS2016, France, pp. 444–449 (2016)
27. Afanasyev, A., Voit, N., Gaynullin, R.: The analysis of diagrammatic models of workflows in design of the complex automated systems. In: Abraham, A., Kovalev, S., Tarassov, V., Snášel, V. (eds.) Proceedings of the First International Scientific Conference "Intelligent Information Technologies for Industry" (IITI'16). AISC, vol. 450, pp. 227–236. Springer, Cham (2016). https://doi.org/10.1007/978-3-319-33609-1_20
28. Statistics of business effects from the introduction of end-to-end workflow technology. https://sd7.ascon.ru/Public/Промышленный%20форум%202018/02_Роль%20САПР%20в%20производстве%20готовой%20продукции_Иванов_E.pdf. Accessed 12 May 2018
29. Vertical. https://ascon.ru/products/420/review/. Accessed 12 May 2018
30. T-FLEX Technology. http://tflex.com. Accessed 12 May 2018
31. ADEM TDM. http://www.dietz-cadcam.de/index.php?id=32&L=2. Accessed 12 May 2018

32. Sprut TP. https://www.sprut.ru/products-and-solutions/products/sprut-tp/. Accessed 12 May 2018
33. Unigraphics NX. https://www.plm.automation.siemens.com/global/en/products/nx/nx-for-design.html. Accessed 12 May 2018
34. CAM350. https://www.innofour.com/412/eda/pcb-systems-design/dfm-npi/cam350. Accessed 12 May 2018

Graph Database Indexing Layer
for Logic-Based Tree Pattern Matching Over
Intensional XML Document Databases

Abdullah Alrefae$^{(\boxtimes)}$, Jinli Cao, and Eric Pardede

Department of Computer Science and Information Technology,
La Trobe University, Melbourne, VIC 3086, Australia
afalrefae@students.latrobe.edu.au,
{j.cao,E.Pardede}@latrobe.edu.au

Abstract. Most XML query evaluation approaches are based on the technique of tree pattern query matching (TPQ) to find similar occurrences of the query's path and conditions. Mainly, two types of constraints are matched to evaluate a given query, including hierarchical structure constraints and value-based constraints. However, TPQ technique falls short when it comes to matching the logic-based constraints and non-hierarchical relationships between nodes and entities in the XML document and database. In this paper, we overcome this shortage by providing an abstract graph database layer that provides a logic-based graph relational model to inspect and resolve the logics of the query to choose most relevant nodes in the XML document. Only the subtrees of the relevant nodes will be traversed in the document and the other subtrees will be skipped. We propose the application of graph database as an indexing layer that defines conceptual linking between database entities, beside logic-based assertions and constraints to evaluate XML queries over this layer to find most related entities and traverse only their related nodes in the XML document. In addition, we propose a mapping criteria and algorithm between XQuery and Cypher, which is a query language for Neo4j graph database.

Keywords: Intensional XML · Tree pattern query (TPQ) · Graph database
Logic-based constraints · Neo4j

1 Introduction

Most of the XML query evaluation approaches are based on the technique of tree pattern query matching (TPQ) to find similar occurrences of the query's path and conditions. Typically, there are two types of constraints to be matched while traversing an XML document. First, match the hierarchical structure in the path expression, such as //A[/B]//C, which defines all nodes C under node A with at least one node B as child. In this example, the structural relationship between A and B is a parent-child (P-C) relation, while the structural relationship between A and C is ancestor-descendant (A-D) relation. Second, match the simple value condition, such as //A[/B]//C[X = y], which defines the node C with the aforementioned structure, and satisfies the predicate of having an element X with value y [1].

© Springer International Publishing AG, part of Springer Nature 2018
O. Gervasi et al. (Eds.): ICCSA 2018, LNCS 10963, pp. 577–588, 2018.
https://doi.org/10.1007/978-3-319-95171-3_45

A number of proposed techniques to improve the efficiency of traversing XML documents exploit the indexing of regional encoding scheme (described in Sect. 2.2, below) to optimize the evaluation of tree pattern matching process [2]. These techniques can be categorized based on their fundamental aims and methodology into two types. First, optimization by minimizing the size of the tree pattern into a small Twig pattern by using stack indexing algorithms, such as TwigStack [3] and Holistic Twig Joins [4]. Second, optimization by conducting a Global query pattern tree (G-QPT) based on collecting possible ordered pattern trees for a given query into a single rooted general query [5]. In general, most of these techniques proposed different approaches to improve the process of matching the hierarchical structure linking between nodes, and evaluating queries based on node-names and static values defined in the predicates [6].

However, in real-time systems that store their operational data in XML format, the predicate values can be stored as URI collections that need to be materialized on demand to overwrite its content, i.e. after receiving a related query, to find the most recent values [7]. This URI collections (a.k.a. intensional nodes) may need to extract data from decentralized data sources that is prompted by the infrastructure of service-oriented systems and cloud computing [8].

Problem Definition: The implementation of traditional TPQ matching process will be impractical for documents with such URI collections. The difficulty is due to the absence of simple values in predicate nodes, the variation of the external sources to be invoked, and in some cases the enormous number of value nodes to be materialized in large document.

Assume the following example, in Fig. 1, we show a sample tree of an XML document for hospitals in Melbourne, Australia. This document is part of a proposed Intensional XML-enabled Web-based Real-time decision support system [9]. Let's say we want to check the current availability of Emergency Departments (ED), to help in workload distribution or reduce congestion in emergency departments and avoid overcrowded hospitals. The following XPath expression will be part of the query.

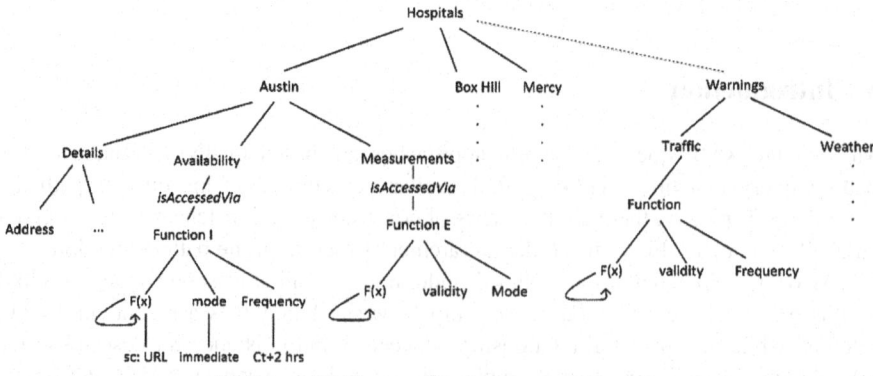

N.B. "isAccessedVia" is not part of the document nodes, it is a semantic annotation

Fig. 1. Tree representation of an XML document with intensional data parts

doc("hospitals.axml")/hospitals/hospital[availability="available"]/measurement   (1)

It is impractical to use most of the existing indexing approaches, that rely on key values, to index documents with intensional parts. The values for these parts, such as availability, are changeable or unavailable.

In addition, with data sizes incrementally increase and with more demand for real-time query answering, these intensional parts start to appear everywhere in the document. Therefore, the process of materializing all the intensional parts in the document, to prepare the document for the traditional TPQ matching traversing, will include many unnecessary materialization processes for unrelated nodes. Practically, we need to minimize the number of intensional nodes that will be materialized.

Proposed Solution: We propose the addition of logic-based relationships between database entities. The definition of assertions and constraints to build the logic-based relationships can vary from one database to another based on content type.

For instance, in our predefined hospitals database, assume the following XQuery, that is derived from the predefined XPath expression in (1), asking for the available hospitals:

```
let service Find-alternative($x) be
for $ed in doc("hospitals.axml")//Hospitals,
    $sub in $ed(name=$x)/suburb
where contains ($ed/support, $sub) and
      $ed/Availability=available and
      $ed/Measurements/LWBS<3 and
      $ed/Measurements/LOS<2
return <f>{$ed/name}</f>
```

In processing such query, we need to consider two main constraints: (1) Location-dependent constraint, i.e. alternative emergency department (ED) need to be in the nearby hospital; and (2) Time-dependent constraint, i.e. real-time measurements in the alternative emergency department need to be currently below predefined risk levels.

Traditionally, such queries are processed with the common TPQ techniques, which depend on the traversing of the document's tree, based on tag-names and values defined in the query. However, such hierarchical traversal will not consider the time and location constraints. The process of extracting the constraints' values from the query, based on predefined rules and assertions, will be described in the following sections.

In addition, we propose an abstract graph database layer that provides a relation-based indexing model to inspect and resolve the assertions and logics of the query and come up with most relevant nodes (subtrees) in the XML database to process the TPQ matching over them.

The remaining parts of this paper will be as follow. Preliminary techniques and concepts in relation to our proposal will be defined in the next section. The third section will represent our proposed approach of graph database layer, and other related evaluation techniques that include conceptual data linking and logic-based assertions and constraints. Finally, section four concludes our paper. It will summarize the proposed solution of this paper and discuss the research issues for future directions.

2   Preliminaries

XML document database consists of multiple hierarchically structured, unranked, node-labeled trees to form a forest, where each tree represents a document. To facilitate the discussions of proposed solutions, the related concepts and techniques are presented in this section.

2.1   Intensional XML Document (Active XML)

The form of XML documents with URI collections, that define service calls to the sources of these parts of the document, has been defined as part of the so-called Active XML (AXML for short) [10, 11]. AXML is a markup language framework that is based on AXML documents and AXML services. AXML document is an extension of XML document, with embedded calls (AXML subtree) to interrogate web services, beside other parts of the data that are defined explicitly in the documents as in normal XML documents. AXML is a useful solution for integration of data and services over peer-to-peer environment because the embedded service calls in AXML documents will give the flexibility to authorize distributed systems cooperation and find other sources of data at run time (see Fig. 2).

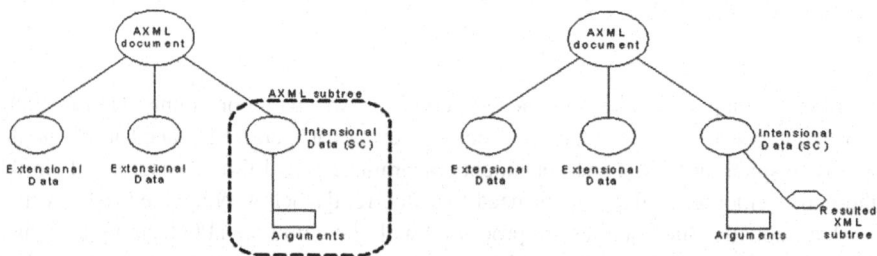

Fig. 2. AXML document before materialization (left) and after materialization (right)

The AXML framework has the following characteristics [12] that differentiate it from normal XML system and make it powerful project for data integration:

- The possibility to manage calls activation and the lifespan of the resulted data: by appending some parameters to determine *when* the service call should be activated and for *how long* the results must be considered valid.
- Support the services with intensional data: by providing AXML services that accept data with intensional input/output data.

– Allow continues services: by supporting the use and creation of Web services that may return a stream of answers, when such action is required.

These advantages of AXML framework promoted the adoption of its documents as metadata format in our proposed web-based real-time decision support system [13]. However, the nature of AXML document that stores service calls instead of static values invalidates the implementation of TPQ matching technique to traverse such documents, which we address in this paper.

2.2   Tree Pattern Matching Techniques

Most of recent proposed techniques to improve the efficiency of TPQ matching over XML databases share the following techniques to build their proposed approaches and define their rules.

Document Encoding and Position Representation of Occurrences of Elements and String Values in XML Database [3]. It is a join-based matching technique that depends on numerical annotation of elements in the XML tree. The numbering methodologies vary in position details provided for each element. In general, they show the regional encoding as a 3-tuple (DocId, LeftPos:RightPos, LevelNum). These encodings represent the flowing [14]:

DocID: Document's identifier
LeftPos: Counting number of the start word of the element, from the beginning of the document
RightPos: Counting number of the end word of the document, from the beginning of the document
LevelNum: Nesting depth of the element in the document

Recording these position details of elements facilitates the process of defining structural relationships between tree nodes [15]. For instance, for a node pair (a, d), node d is a descendent of node a, if and only if, $a.LeftPos < d.LeftPos < d.RightPos < a.RightPos$. This numbering scheme can also be a foundation for other techniques, such as inverted list and index structure, as shown below.

Inverted Lists Model. After annotating elements in XML document with their regional encoding, we can build an inverted list based on document's tags, with one sequence for each document tag, to reflect the regional encoding details for each element [16].

Index Structure. It is a part of the inverted list that defines the regional encoding for value nodes to satisfy a particular predicate [16].

The implementation of these techniques varies from one approach to another to according to indexing structure and matching format. Some approaches proposed to index XML document into join stacks or sequences. They map the XML document into stacks or B^+ tree element lists, respectively, to narrow the query matching on related stacks or subsequences [15]. However, these structural summaries only represent the encoding positions of elements as in B^+-tree, and the connection of entities based on their hierarchical structure as in stack-assisted matching. They do not consider the logical connections between entities, which we propose in this paper.

2.3 NoSQL Graph Database

NoSQL database can generally be categorized into four types, as explained in Table 1, below [17].

Table 1. NoSQL databases types.

NoSQL Database	Storing methodology	Example
Key-value stores	Store every node as a key with its value	Riak, Voldemort
Column Family\ BigTable Clones	Store data in columns to query large datasets	HBase, Hypertable
Document databases	Store every record with its data and complex data structure as a document with an associated key	CouchDB, MongoDB
Graph databases	Store information as a connected network of data	Allegro Graph, Neo4j

Because of its powerful, agile, and flexible data model, NoSQL provides solutions to most of the relational databases' issues [17]. NoSQL data model capabilities include, the manipulation of large data sets with different structures, faster schema iteration, frequent code pushes, and better treatment of geographically distributed resources.

Graph database, in particular, provides a powerful solution to overcome data complexity issues (see Fig. 3).

To improve the efficiency of QTP matching over intensional XML database, we propose a graph database layer as covering index for element nodes. It defines structured conceptual linking between nodes based on their logic-based relationships, as will be demonstrated below.

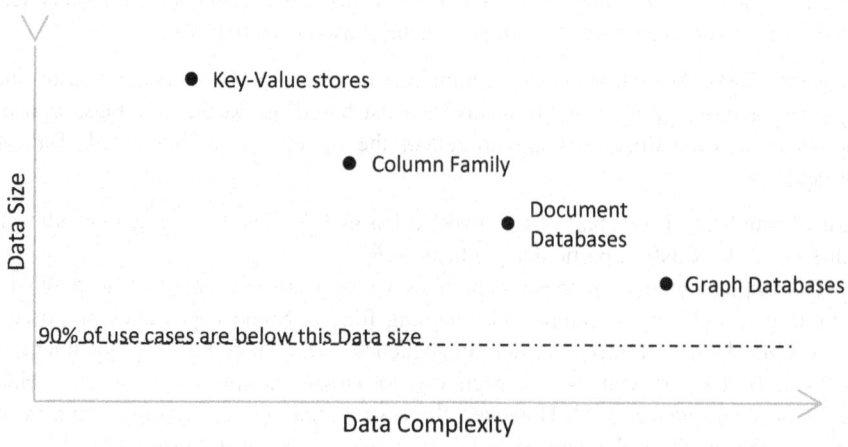

Fig. 3. NoSQL data models, in regards to data complexity and data size [18].

3   Graph Database Abstract Layer

In this section, we propose the application of logic-based definitions and connections in a form of a graph data model on top the XML data model (tree model). By using the model, we apply queries on the graph data model and filter out the most related tags in XML documents. Then we apply the query only on these matching XML tree nodes.

The application of logic-based graph database as a covering index layer empowers the system with a number of advantages, including the following.

- Schema matching is unnecessary, as graph database is schema free or schema optional. This advantage gives the system the required agility to change. Include, add or remove properties to nodes on the fly, without requirement to update other nodes to include the new properties.
- The ability to query high complex data, better than traditional TPQ or any other NoSQL query techniques.
- Provide a real relational database, as it connects any relational nodes from any level or type, in the form of triples (subject, object, predicate).
- The data mode is very intuitive, and the query processing speed is fast.

The graph database model maintains good performance with complex data sets, like social networks. Nevertheless, it can also be a promising solution for other applications, such as fraud detection, and our application of real time recommendations.

3.1   Linked Data Model

The graph database model represents data in triples (subject, object, and predicate) where each of the subject and object can represent a different entity or resource, while the predicate represents the relationship between them. This mechanism of linking data located in different resources builds a linked data model that can help in decision making process by manipulating the relationships between the different resources.

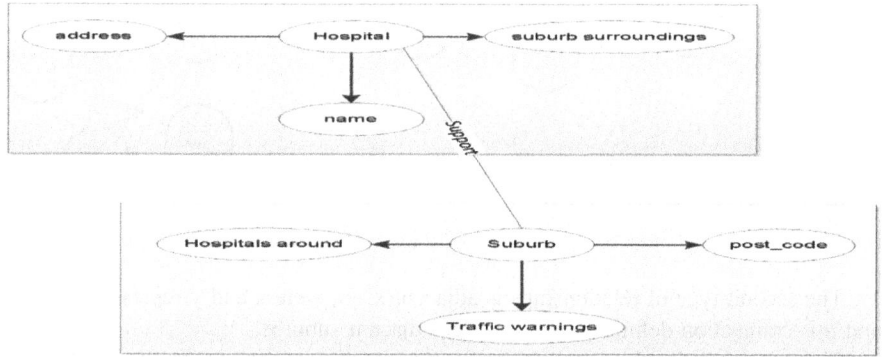

Fig. 4. Conceptual linking in a linked data model

In Fig. 4, we show a conceptual linking example between two different tags, where the hospital, suburb and support respectively represent the subject, object, and relationship type in triple.

3.2   Logical Assertions and Constraints Definition

To build a linked data model between different tags in a database, we need to define assertions and constraints that define the logic-based relationships between tags.

For our emergency department's example, we can define the following functions and axioms to organize the relationships between database elements: (1) Domain: Hospitals (Emergency departments); (2) Unary predicates: Hospital(x), Suburb(x); (3) Relationships: nearby(x, y), adjacent(x, y), support(x, y); and (4) Functions: alternate(x), can_replace(x, y).

In our example, the domain of interest is hospital emergency departments in Melbourne (Victoria, Australia). Our master data include, Hospitals and Suburbs, therefore we define these entities as unary predicates (Hospital(x) and Suburb(x)). Types of connections that have been used to build the graph database for our system include, nearby(x, y) where x and y are hospitals and this relationship represents a connection between geographically nearby hospitals, as shown in Fig. 5.

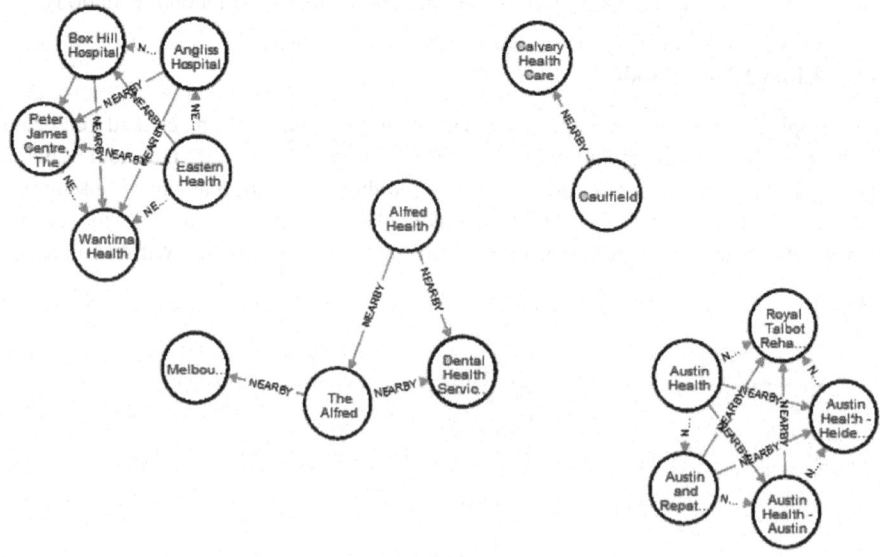

Fig. 5. Nearby relationships between hospitals

The second type of relationships is adjacent(x, y), were x and y represent suburbs, and this connection defines geographically adjacent suburbs.

The other relationship type is support(x, y), were x represents hospital and y represents suburb that is supported by the hospital x, because x is the closest hospital(s) to the suburb y, as shown in Fig. 6.

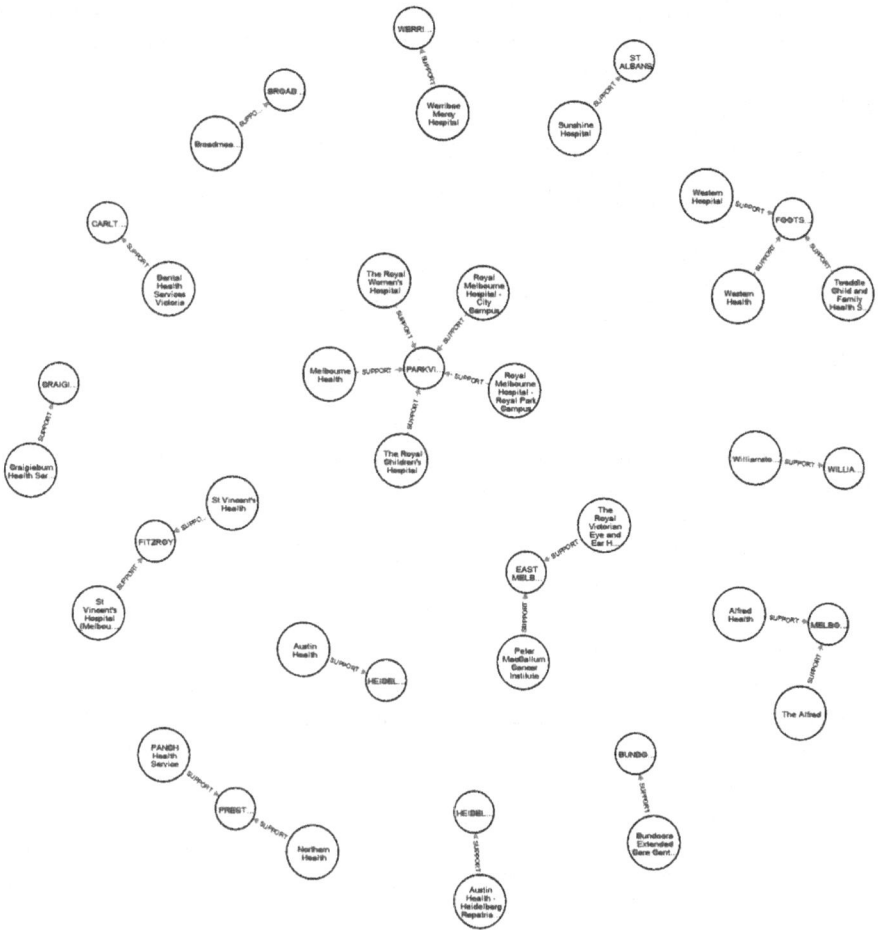

Fig. 6. Support relationships between hospitals and suburbs

After the graph database is built, based on the aforementioned predicates and relationships, we can define a number of axioms to find real-time recommendations and answer logic-based queries. Axioms can include:

$$\text{Axioms} : \forall x, y \, alternate(x) = y \leftrightarrow hospital(y) \wedge nearby(x, y) \tag{2}$$

$$\text{OR} \, \forall x, y \, can\_replace(x, y) \leftrightarrow x \neq y \wedge \exists p \, support(x, p) \wedge support(y, p) \tag{3}$$

Axiom (2) defines an alternative for hospital x, if hospital x is unavailable for any reason (e.g. overcrowded) and need to find best possible recommendations for alternatives, and axiom (3) has almost a similar purpose, but with the use of different relationships.

To answer queries and recommendation requests based on these functions and axioms, we need to extract the required details from the original XQuery as follows:

```
let service Find-alternative (Austin) be
// variable $x from general query has been declare
for $ed in doc("hospitals.axml")//Hospitals,
    $sub in $ed(name=$x)/suburb
where contains ($ed/support, $sub) and
      $ed/Availability=available and
      $ed/Measurements/LWBS<3 and
      $ed/Measurements/LOS<2
return <f>{$ed/name}/f>
```

$$(4)$$

Variables and predicates can be extracted to build an equivalent graph database query. Below, we present an equivalent Cypher query that is used to query a graph database called Neo4j:

```
Match (x:Ed {name:"Austin"})-[:SUPPORT]->(s:Suburb)<-[:SUPPORT]-(h:ED)
RETURN DISTINCT h.name;
```

$$(5)$$

As we can see in the two equivalent queries, the variable declaration in the XQuery (Austin, in a circle) has been extracted and used in the Cypher query as a start node. The node tag in the XQuery (Ed, in a solid square) has been used in the Cypher query as a label name. In addition, the property name (support, in dashed rectangle) has been extracted and used in the Cypher query as a predicate, i.e. relationship type.

In general, Table 2 shows the mapping criteria between XQuery for XML databases and Cypher for Neo4j graph databases.

The Cypher query (5) is equivalent to the XPath expressions in the XQuery (4). It is a replacement of the traversal process. The resulted nodes will then be the only subtrees to be checked for other predicates in the XQuery.

Table 2. XQuery and Cypher mapping criteria

XQuery	Cypher
x: variable name	Start node
Node tag or label	Label name
Property node	Relationship (predicate)

For the automation of the mapping, we defined an algorithm to transform XQuery to Cypher, as follows.

Mapping Algorithm

---

1. for (variable (X)   //variable_name
       of type(T)   //node_tag
       and constraint (C)   //property Condition
       with value(V)   //property value
2.   do (match ((X)
       of lable(T)
       with relation(C)
       to (V)
       and (Y)
       of label(T)
       With relation(C)
       to (V))
3.   Return Y))
4. Output: List of [Y]

In the evaluation of the predefined Cypher query (5) on the graph database, it has returned three nodes (Mercy Public Hospital, St. Vincent's Health, and Western Health) in 122 ms.

Consequently, only these three nodes will be traversed in the XML database and the predefined conditions in the XQuery (4) will be applied on these nodes to match the most relevant node after materializing the corresponding intensional web services.

4   Conclusion

This paper presented logic-based graph database indexing for XML database. It overcomes the issue of processing TPQ matching on large XML databases with intensional nodes that required to be materialized before processing the query.

We have defined the conceptual linking methodology that is based on the triples data model (subject, object, predicate) to build the graph database. In addition, we defined the logical assertions and constraints to organize the connections between the database's entities.

The contributions of the paper also include the proposal of the mapping techniques and the general algorithm to extract the logical assertions and constraints from the XQuery and build the relevant graph database's query. The example of Melbourne metropolitan's hospitals has been presented to evaluate our proposed technique.

Acknowledgments. This research paper is part of my research candidature, which is financially sponsored by the Ministry of Higher Education in Saudi Arabia.

References

1. Lu, J., Ling, T.W., Bao, Z., Wang, C.: Extended XML tree pattern matching: theories and algorithms. IEEE Trans. Knowl. Data Eng. **23**(3), 402–416 (2011)
2. Hachicha, M., Darmont, J.: A survey of XML tree patterns. IEEE Trans. Knowl. Data Eng. **25**(1), 29–46 (2013)
3. Bruno, N., Koudas, N., Srivastava, D.: Holistic twig joins: optimal XML pattern matching. In: Proceedings of the 2002 ACM SIGMOD International Conference on Management of Data, Madison, Wisconsin, pp. 310–321 (2002)
4. Jiang, H., Wang, W., Lu, H., Yu, J.X.: Holistic twig joins on indexed XML documents. In: Proceedings of the 29th International Conference on Very Large Data Bases, vol. 29, Berlin, Germany, pp. 273–284
5. Chen, Y.: Discovering ordered tree patterns from XML queries. In: Dai, H., Srikant, R., Zhang, C. (eds.) PAKDD 2004. LNCS (LNAI), vol. 3056, pp. 559–563. Springer, Heidelberg (2004). https://doi.org/10.1007/978-3-540-24775-3_66
6. Zhang, N., Kacholia, V., Ozsu, M.T.: A succinct physical storage scheme for efficient evaluation of path queries in XML. In: Proceedings of the 20th International Conference on Data Engineering, Boston, MA, USA, pp. 54–65
7. Milo, T., Abiteboul, S., Amann, B., Benjelloun, O., Ngoc, F.: Exchanging intensional XML data. ACM Trans. Database Syst. **30**(1), 1–40 (2005)
8. Demirkan, H., Delen, D.: Leveraging the capabilities of service-oriented decision support systems: putting analytics and big data in cloud. Decis. Support Syst. **55**(1), 412–421 (2013)
9. Alrefae, A., Cao, J.: Intensional XML-enabled web-based real-time decision support system. In: 2017 International Conference on Computing Networking and Informatics (ICCNI), 29–31 October 2017, pp. 1–10 (2017)
10. Abiteboul, S., Benjelloun, O., Milo, T.: The active XML project: an overview. VLDB J. **17**, 1019–1040 (2007)
11. Phan, V.B., Pardede, E.: Active XML (AXML) research: survey on the representation, system architecture, data exchange mechanism and query evaluation. J. Netw. Comput. Appl. **37**(1), 348–364 (2014)
12. Milo, T.: Peer-to-peer data integration with active XML. In: Grumbach, S., Sui, L., Vianu, V. (eds.) ASIAN 2005. LNCS, vol. 3818, pp. 11–18. Springer, Heidelberg (2005). https://doi.org/10.1007/11596370_2
13. Alrefae, A., Cao, J.: Web-based real-time decision support system active XML-based metadata. In: 2014 Global Summit on Computer & Information Technology (GSCIT), 14–16 June 2014, pp. 1–4 (2014)
14. Lu, J.: XML Tree Pattern Processing. In: An Introduction to XML Query Processing and Keyword Search, pp. 90–156 (2013). 4.2 XML structural join
15. Moro, M.M., Vagena, Z., Tsotras, V.J.: Tree-pattern queries on a lightweight XML processor. In: Proceedings of the 31st International Conference on Very Large Data Bases, Trondheim, Norway, pp. 205–216
16. Wu, X., Theodoratos, D., Hui Wang, W., Sellis, T.: Optimizing XML queries: bitmapped materialized views vs. indexes. Inf. Syst. **38**(6), 863–884 (2013)
17. NoSQL Database Explained. MongoDB, Inc. https://www.mongodb.com/nosql-explained
18. Webber, J., Robinson, I.: How graph databases relate to other NoSQL data models

Development of Interactive Tools
for Intelligent Engineering Education System

Alexander Afanasyev$^{(\boxtimes)}$ and Nikolay Voit$^{(\boxtimes)}$ (iD)

Ulyanovsk State Technical University, Ulyanovsk, Russia
{a.afanasev, n.voit}@ulstu.ru

Abstract. Increasing the students' motivation for learning is related to the effective management of the student's development process, which requires the skills of conducting an active dialogue, organizing communication methods, jointly searching for solutions by an educator. The main methodological innovations of this direction are connected with the use of interactive learning methods, which help an educator and student to interact.

Keywords: Learning management system · Moodle · Interactive learning tools

1 Introduction

Increasing the students' motivation for learning is related to the effective management of the student's development process, which requires the skills of conducting an active dialogue, organizing communication methods, jointly searching for solutions by an educator.

The main methodological innovations of this direction are connected with the use of interactive learning methods, which help an educator and student to interact.

The goal of this research work is to improve the quality of education which is based on the active use of e-Learning and distance technologies through the interactive learning tools development in Moodle LMS.

2 Problem

The goal of this research work is to improve the quality of education which is based on the active use of e-Learning and distance technologies through the interactive learning tools development in Moodle LMS.

In order to achieve this goal, we had to solve the following tasks.

1. The "Student's identification" project was developed in order to allow Moodle to identify an Internet user during the final testing of a discipline. The essence of the project is that the browser working with Moodle takes pictures of a user and enters them into the statistics of the discipline's e-learning system, and an educator gets this statistic.
2. The "Rating of educational material's sections in the network course" service was developed. The rating is formed on the basis of student's reviews and comments,

O. Gervasi et al. (Eds.): ICCSA 2018, LNCS 10963, pp. 589–598, 2018.
https://doi.org/10.1007/978-3-319-95171-3_46

which allows educators to identify sections with a decreasing rating and sections with an increasing rating. Comments and evaluations of course elements are reflected in a summary table with fields called "course element", "average score", and "number of evaluations".

3. New types of interactive question tests were developed: (a) drag and drop onto image questions; (b) drag and drop markers questions. This type of a test question allows a student to mark certain areas on the image using special markers; (c) drag and drop into text questions; (d) the "Setsplitting" questions allow an educator to create questions, in which a student can split elements in groups; (e) matching questions, (f) short answer questions.

4. The "Practical test work" project was developed. It offers students to develop a test task for the learned material. There are three question types: a short answer from the keyboard; a multiple choice question; a matching question.

5. The "Automated point-rating system (PRS)" project was developed, which contributes to: (a) improving the quality of the learning process by inuring the skills and abilities of systematic, rhythmic, independent work during the whole period of study; (b) increasing the students' motivation for mastering educational programs by means of a higher differentiation of the evaluation of their current work, as well as raising the level of the educational process organization in the university; (c) the implementation of a quality management system that allows educators to quickly optimize the organization of students' independent work on the basis of an analysis of the students' performance indicators, and to timely eliminate shortcomings in mastering and consolidating the learning materials; (d) obtaining an objective and more accurate assessment of the knowledge and level of students' professional training in the learning process.

3   Models of E-Learning in a Modern Technical University

The most promising direction of the educational process organization is the distance educational technologies development in all forms of the university's education. In this case, the general principles of constructing the traditional educational process remain. As the distance educational technologies are introduced, the requirements for the quality of educational materials and the provision of training sessions and examinations with educational eContent are sharply increased.

The search and implementation of new opportunities are related to the following models implemented in our university: (a) training with Web-based technologies (Web-based learning takes up to 30% time in this model); (b) blended training (traditional learning and e-Learning mutually complement each other; the educator's workload is reduced; the need for classrooms in the university is reduced; the efficiency of the educator's work is increased); (c) online learning (almost the whole educational process (90–100%) is over Internet. It is characterized by high interactivity of educational content). Bachelor's degree programs are realized using Web-based technologies and blended training; master's degree programs use blended and online training; online learning is mainly realized in part-time education programs and additional education.

3.1 Development of Expert System

To use in Virtual world, we create an expert system. In order to analyze trainee's actions, an ES was developed. It is a separate service that receives a record of trainee's actions, analyzes it and makes the necessary recommendations [6–16].

The analysis of data is based on the production model of knowledge with a direct inference. This model allows us to present knowledge as the following type of sentences: "IF condition, THEN action1, OTHERWISE action2". The expert systems of the production type include a rule's (knowledge's) base, working memory and a rule's interpreter (solver) that implements a certain technique of logical inference. The direct inference realizes the strategy "from facts to conclusions".

Rules for a virtual workplace of a radio fitter are given as:

1. IF "$!REG.RW$", THEN "You inserted the operation panel into the wrong connector of the special voltage pad".
2. IF "$(SCREW.POT_1 || SCREW.POT_2)$ && $(!REG.RW_R)$", THEN "You did not connect the optical cable before adjustment".
3. IF "$(SCREW.POT_1 || SCREW.POT_2)$ && $(!LB.LBO)$", THEN "You did not connect the load panel up before adjustment".
4. IF "$(SCREW.POT_1 || SCREW.POT_2)$ && $(!DIV)$", THEN "You did not set the divider before adjustment".
5. IF "$(SCREW.POT_1 || SCREW.POT_2)$ && $(!V.VO)$", THEN "You did not switch on the voltmeter before adjustment".
6. IF "$(SCREW.POT_1 || SCREW.POT_2)$ && $(!V.VS)$", THEN "You did not connect the voltmeter up before adjustment".
7. IF "$(SCREW.POT_1 || SCREW.POT_2.)$ && $(!LB.LBO)$", THEN "You did not switch on the operation panel before adjustment".

A virtual industrial environment was designed and developed on basis of the OpenSim and Unity-3D platforms.

The ES structure is shown in Fig. 1. The ES has a "Rule's editor" web interface for making, editing, deleting and checking rules.

A report of trainers' actions is generated during the work with the simulator. It consists of the current state of the simulator, the object with which a student interacted, and the type of interaction. The REST JSON-based report is sent to the ES server. The received data are analyzed via "Rule's base" module's rule, then a message with a list of recommendations is formed.

Below it is described an example of the ES operation. Let us assume that a student inserted the operation panel into the wrong connector when adjusting the radio electronic equipment. The JSON state object passed by the expert system is given as:

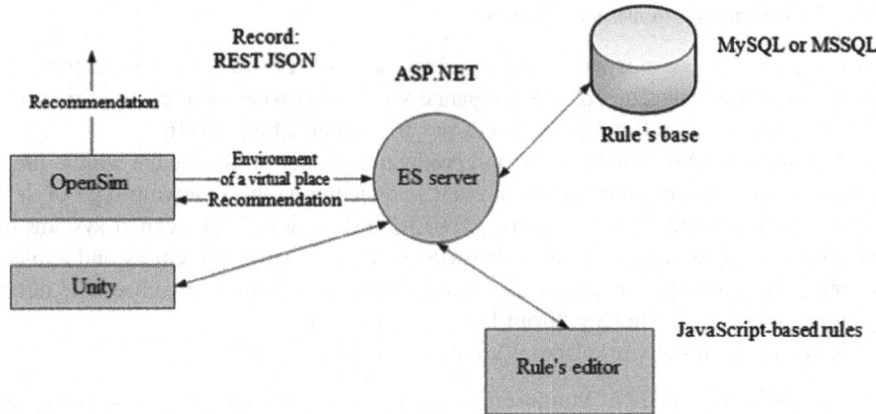

Fig. 1. The structure of the expert system.

```
{
"object":"50",
"action":"click",
"context":"adjuster",
"state":
{
"OperationPanelFork":
        {"rightParent":false},
    "VoltmeterFork":
        {"rightParent":true},
    "CableToLoadUnit":
        {"greenWire":false},
    "CableIntoCheckUnit":
        {"redWire":false},
    "kVC":
        {"blueWire":false},
    "kVZ":
        {"yellowWire":false},
    "PlaceForTheDivider":
        {"Divider":false}
        . . .
    }
}
```

After processing the request and searching for the erroneously inserted parameter, the following message will be sent: "You inserted the operation panel into the wrong connector of the special voltage pad".

4   Interactivity Is an Objective Need for an Online Course

Today it becomes obvious that it is necessary to manage the student's development process, which means a priority in the educator's work for a dialogue, methods of communication, a joint search for solutions, various creative activities. The main methodological innovations are connected with the use of interactive teaching methods facilitating the interaction between educators and students. The essence of interactive learning is the students' involvement in the cognitive process, during which students have the opportunity to understand and reflect on what they know and think. In the process of joint activity, students make their special individual contribution, at the same time there is an exchange of knowledge, ideas, and activity methods. It allows students to obtain new knowledge and develop cognitive activity. Indeed, interactive forms of conducting classes arouse interest among students, encourage the active participation of everyone in the learning process, contribute to the effective mastering of educational materials, form opinions and attitudes of a student; form life skills, and modify their behavior. Modern pedagogy highlights interactive teaching forms such as creative tasks, work in small groups, educational games, use of public resources, social projects; studying and consolidating new material; testing; discussion of issues; solving problems; trainings. The basis of interactive approaches is interactive exercises and tasks that are performed by students. The main difference between interactive exercises and tasks is that they are aimed not only at consolidating the earlier learned educational material, but also on learning a new one. Training based on interactive educational technologies involves the new experience formation of the theoretical comprehension through application.

In [1], interactive learning methods (ILMs) allow students to intensify the understanding, mastering and creative application of knowledge in performing practical tasks. ILMs increase motivation and involvement of participants in solving the discussed problems. ILMs form the ability to justify one's positions, develop the ability to listen to a different point of view. ILMs allow one to get new experience of activity; the use of ILMs makes it possible to control the mastering of knowledge and the ability to apply the acquired knowledge, abilities and skills in different situations more flexible and humane.

5   Creative Developments for Moodle

We have identified the need for user identification based on the analysis of opportunities for testing knowledge in the Moodle environment. The known methods for identifying the Internet user (browser identification; the use of biometric indicators; image matching) have become the basis for our university's project "Moodle-Browser Client". The project identifies the Internet user during the final testing of a discipline. The essence of the project is that the browser while working with the system takes photos of a user/student, the photo is entered into the statistics report of the passed discipline in an e-learning system (ELS). The statistics report is given to an educator.

The project requires the educator's participation in the identification process, but we have identified the benefits of implementing the project: the conditions for recognizing learning outcomes and constructing an individual learning path are realized. The project was tested by part-time and full-time students (more than 160 students).

The use of Moodle's resources for the organization of training in separate academic disciplines in the UlSTU with the use of distance educational technologies implies the evaluation of the service for the organization of automatic subscription to courses, the creation of conditions for studying a particular course and obtaining statistics with grades for performed tests (assignments) and workshops. The service is designed for university's full-time and part-time students wishing to study a separate academic discipline using distance educational technologies. It is also recommended to university's students wishing to make up academic deficiencies upon graduation from academic leave; when coming back to the university for continuing education; when changing the profile of training, specialty, the form of education within the university; when enrolling for a second higher education (including parallel education); when transferring from other universities.

In order to improve the learning materials contained in the individual (separate) materials of the network course, the "Rating of the educational material's sections in the network course" service was developed. The rating is formed on the basis of student's reviews and comments, which allows educators to identify sections with a decreasing rating (in the future these sections should be edited) and sections with an increasing rating (these sections can vary based on comments). Comments and evaluations of the course elements are reflected in the summary table with the fields called course's element, average score, and the number of evaluations.

The new types of interactive tests that we use in Moodle are: (a) drag and drop onto image questions (this type of question allows educators to create test questions in which a student drags words, images or both of them from a list and drop them into predefined gaps on a base image); (b) drag and drop markers questions (markers are dragged onto an area on a background image, this type of question allows a student to mark certain areas on an image using special markers, which can be either one or several); (c) drag and drop into text questions (this type of question allows a student to create fields in the text that indicate a missed word or phrase, and at the same time create replies, in the form of blocks with words or phrases that can fill in blanks with drag and drop); (d) type of question "Setsplitting" allows an educator to create questions in which a student can split elements in several groups (from 2 to 5); (e) matching questions (matching questions have a content area and a list of names or statements which must be correctly matched against another list of names or statements); (f) short answer question. In a short answer question, the student types in a word or phrase in response to a question (that may include an image). Answers may or may not be case sensitive. The answer could be a word or a phrase, but it must match one of your acceptable answers exactly. It's a good idea to keep the required answer as short as possible to avoid missing a correct answer that's phrased differently.

The creative ideas of Knowledge Relative Assessment System by Bekker's method served as the basis for testing "Practical test work" (a new toolkit). It asks students to develop a test for the learned material by themselves. There are three templates: a short answer from the keyboard; a multiple-choice question; a compliance test. The developed test is sent for the educator's assessment. If the evaluation is positive, the test is automatically added to the general question bank concerned with a specific topic of a discipline.

6 The Automated Point-Rating System

The introduced automated point-rating system (PRS) contributes to: (a) improving the quality of the learning process through the implementation of skills and abilities of systematic, rhythmic, independent work during the whole period of learning; (b) increasing the students' motivation for mastering educational programs by means of a higher differentiation of the evaluation of their current educational work, as well as raising the level of the educational process organization in the university; (c) implementing a quality management system of education that allows students to quickly optimize the organization of students' independent work on the basis of analyzing the students' progress indicators, and to timely eliminate shortcomings in mastering and consolidating the discipline's material; (d) obtaining an objective and more accurate evaluation of knowledge and level of students' professional training in the learning process.

The assessment of students' progress within the PRS is based on points of theme tests, boundary tests and posttests. The discipline's final grade is determined by the sum of the points received by a student for theme tests, boundary tests, posttests, and an exam or a final test.

7 Integration of Moodle with Interactive Services

Increased research interest is the integration with virtual worlds, representing a 3D virtual environment, where users acquire avatar's appearances and properties (their graphical representation). For example, the virtual platform vAcademia [2] represents services for conducting and attending training courses, meetings, presentations, trainings. The use of Web 2.0 technologies in combination with the capabilities of the virtual world, which allows educators to create interactive educational content. Users can communicate and interact with each other in the virtual world through chat and also voice with the help of a microphone or video conferencing. Within the research, the IDDO ULSTU staff developed a prototype of a virtual classroom based on the tools [4] such as educational whiteboards with a set of tools and educator and student's workplaces. The classroom allows a student's monitor screen to be displayed with the output of a running application or video from a student's webcam.

Integration with the ePortfolio [3] and with our university's developments allows students to realize his/her portfolio of achievements where a student can accumulate individual, educational, creative and personal achievements. The ePortfolio of achievements is an approval of the educational progress and professional growth.

The use of website's services opens new interactive features [5], due to which educators, tutors, and others can develop interactive applications quickly, and post them on the website with a link to the developed application. The service also allows authors to create interactive crosswords, tests with text input (the application allows authors/educators to create tasks in which a student has to give a verbal answer to the question); closed tests; tasks with audio/video content (the application allows educators/authors to organize the work of students with video files, insert tasks into the videos, instructions, focus on certain details); tasks like "find on a map" (using the application you can develop tasks in which students have to determine the location of various objects on a map), etc.

8   Virtual Intelligent Training Worlds

One of the effective forms of engineering training is the development and use of virtual and additional reality. The use of virtual worlds for acquisition of certain skills and competences increases an effectiveness of training through the maximum approximation to real conditions, from both the point of the objective environment's view and possible actions.

We have developed the virtual workplaces for radio assemblers, adjusters and fitters; the mathematical models of these workplaces are offered, including a composition and description of the permitted actions. The software for the said virtual workplaces has been developed on basis of the UNITY platform. Intellectualization of virtual worlds is connected with the developed expert system (ES) for trainee's actions assessment. This ES knowledge base is founded on the production rules. The direct logical inference is used to issue the recommendations to a trainee.

These virtual workplaces have been embedded into the corporate training environment of a company which is one of the Ulyanovsk State Technical University's (UlSTU's) partners, and are used to upgrade its employees' skills.

These virtual workplaces are also widely used by the UlSTU for students' training in both bachelor's degree program and secondary vocational training program in "Radio-engineering systems and complexes". Students and postgraduates of the Information Systems and Technologies Faculty of the UlSTU are involved to the development of the virtual workplaces' software and 3D models.

The conducted pedagogical experiment demonstrates that the use of intelligent virtual workplaces has sufficiently favored to improve a quality and effectiveness of training in fitting, assembly and adjustment of the radio electronic equipment, as well as to reduce the total period of training by 20–30% and to increase the trainees' motivation.

9   Structure of Virtual Industrial World

The virtual world is understood as a simulated environment, "populated" by users communicating with each other through "avatars" – graphic characters. In the industrial virtual world, the organization's production processes are modeled.

Virtual industrial worlds can be represented as a set of special technologies that simulate the tools of real workplaces, the nomenclature of components and accompanying documents and intended for use in both enterprises and universities.

For the expert system's (ES's) operation, it is necessary to develop workplace's models, simulators of which are used in a virtual industrial environment, and analyze the actions that will be an object of a research in the ES.

The logical-algebraic models of workplaces presented in a virtual industrial environment and using the ES as a module of the action's evaluation are developed and described below.

10 Conclusion and Future Works

The search for new opportunities and their expansion helps to improve the educator-student interaction by immersing oneself in the problem field of tasks, consistency in the choice of means and methods for the learning tasks performance. The further researches will be focused on including novelty in the learning process, based on the peculiarities of the dynamics of life and activity's development, the specificity of various learning technologies and the individual's needs, and also the need to implement professional standards requirements. It is necessary to emphasize that there is a need to develop mechanisms and procedures for automated assessment of competences (including Moodle's tools) in the run-up to the federal state educational standard of the fourth generation. The use of virtual industrial worlds facilitates increasing the effectiveness of training and reducing the cost of expendables. Virtual workplaces are designed taking into account the scalability of the virtual system and the requirements for technological processes. The conducted pedagogical experiment demonstrates that the use of intelligent virtual workplaces has sufficiently favored to improve a quality and effectiveness of training in fitting, assembly and adjustment of the radio electronic equipment, as well as to reduce the total period of training by 20-30% and to increase the trainees' motivation.

Acknowledgments. This research is supported by the grant of the Ministry of Education and Science of the Russian Federation, the project No. 2.1615.2017/4.6. The reported study was funded by RFBR and Government of Ulyanovsk Region according to the research project No. 16-47-732152.

References

1. Panina, T.: Modern Methods for Activating Education: The Textbook. Academy, Moscow (2009)
2. Panyukova, S., Gostin, A., Kuliyeva, G.: Development of a Student's Web-Portfolio: Methodical Recommendations: The Textbook. Ryazan State Radio Engineering University, Ryazan (2013)
3. Virtual Academia. http://www.vacademia.com/. Accessed 15 Mar 2018
4. SDK Peasantry. http://www.krestianstvo.org/books/doc/sdk2tutorial/ru/index.html. Accessed 15 Mar 2018
5. LearningApps.org. http://learningapps.org/about.php. Accessed 15 Mar 2018

6. Afanasyev, A., Voit, N., Voevodin, E., Egorova, T., Novikova, O.: Methods and tools for the development, implementation and use of the intelligent distance learning environment. In: 8th International Technology, Education and Development Conference, INTED-2014, pp. 3120–3124 (2014)

7. Afanasyev, A., Voit, N., Egorova, T., Novikova, O.: Intelligent learning environments. In: 9th International Technology, Education and Development Conference, INTED-2015, pp. 4493–4502 (2015)

8. Afanasyev, A.N., Voit, N.N.: Intelligent learning environments for corporations. In: 9th IEEE International Conference on Application of Information and Communication Technologies, AICT – 2015, pp. 107–112 (2015). https://doi.org/10.1109/icaict.2015.7338527

9. Afanasyev, A., Voit, N., Kanev, D., Afanaseva, T.: Organization, development and implementation of intelligent learning environments. In: 10th International Technology, Education and Development Conference, INTED-2016, pp. 2232–2242 (2016). https://doi.org/10.21125/inted.2016.1470

10. Afanasyev, A.N., Voit, N.N., Kanev, D.S.: Development of intelligent learning system based on the ontological approach. In: 10th IEEE International Conference on Application of Information and Communication Technologies (AICT), pp. 690–694 (2016). https://doi.org/10.1109/icaict.2016.7991794

11. Afanasyev, A., Voit, N., Kanev, D.: Intelligent and virtual training environment. In: Proceedings of International conference on Fuzzy Logic and Intelligent Technologies in Nuclear Science - FLINS2016, pp. 246–251 (2016). https://doi.org/10.1142/9789813146976_0041

12. Afanasyev, A., Voit, N., Kanev, D., Afanasyeva, T.: Development and use of a virtual laboratory of measuring devices. In: 20th International Conference on Interactive Collaborative Learning, ICL 2017, pp. 890–897 (2017). http://www.icl-conference.org/icl2017/proceedings.php

13. Afanasyev, A., Voit, N., Ionova, I., Ukhanova, M., Yepifanov, V.: Development of the intelligent system of engineering education for corporate use in the university and enterprises. In: Auer, M.E., Guralnick, D., Simonics, I. (eds.) ICL 2017. AISC, vol. 715, pp. 716–727. Springer, Cham (2018). https://doi.org/10.1007/978-3-319-73210-7_84

14. Afanasyev, A.N., Voit, N.N., Kanev, D.S.: Development of expert systems for evaluating user's actions in training systems and virtual laboratories. In: 2017 IEEE 11th International Conference on Application of Information and Communication Technologies (AICT), pp. 297–300 (2017)

15. Voit, N.N., Afanasyev, A.N., Gulshin, V.A., Bochkov, S.I.: Design of the industrial virtual worlds based on the Opensim platform. In: 2017 IEEE 11th International Conference on Application of Information and Communication Technologies (AICT), pp. 301–304 (2017)

16. Afanasyev, A., Afanasyeva, T., Voit, N., Ionova, I., Ukhanova, M.: University - Enterprise Intelligent Corporate Training System. Edulearn 17, 5355–5365. https://doi.org/10.21125/edulearn.2017.2209, https://library.iated.org/view/AFANASYEV2017UNI. Accessed 15 Mar 2018

Performance Evaluation of MQTT Broker Servers

Biswajeeban Mishra[✉] ⓘ

Department of Software Engineering, Dugonicster 13, Szeged 6720, Hungary
mishra@inf.u-szeged.hu

Abstract. Internet of Things (IoT) is a rapidly growing research field, which has enormous potential to enrich our lives for a smarter and better world. Significant improvements in telemetry technology make it possible to quickly connect things (i.e. different smart devices) situated at different geographical locations. Telemetry technology helps to monitor and measure the devices from remote locations, making them even more useful and productive at a low cost of management. MQTT (MQ Telemetry Transport) is a lightweight messaging protocol that meets today's smarter communication needs. The protocol is used for machine-to-machine communication and plays a pivotal role in IoT. In case the network bandwidth is low, or a network has high latency, and for devices having limited processing capabilities and memory, MQTT is able to distribute telemetry information using a publish/subscribe communication pattern. It enables IoT devices to send or publish information on a topic head to a server (i.e. MQTT broker), then it sends the information out to those clients that have previously subscribed to that topic. This paper puts several publicly available brokers and locally deployed brokers into experiment and compares their performance by subscription throughput i.e., in how much time a broker pushes a data packet to the client (the subscriber) or how much time a data packet takes to reach the client (the subscriber) from the broker. MQTT brokers based on the latest MQTT v3.1.1 version were evaluated. The paper also includes mqtt-stresser and mqtt-bench stress test results of both locally and publicly deployed brokers.

Keywords: Internet of Things · MQTT · MQTT brokers · Cloud computing

1 Introduction

With the rise of the Internet of Things (IoT), billions of embedded smart devices and sensors are interconnected, and they exchange data using the existing Internet infrastructure. They enormously impact and improve our life. In today's fast-growing world, many IoT application areas exist, starting from manufacturing, automobile, agriculture, energy management, environmental monitoring to smart cities and defense sector. For example, a patient's real-time health data, such as blood pressure, heart-bit rate, etc. can be monitored by a doctor from a far distant location. The supplying company can trace leakage in oil and gas pipelines from a central control room, and supply can immediately be stopped to avoid accidents [1]. Trespassing events across the borders of a

© Springer International Publishing AG, part of Springer Nature 2018
O. Gervasi et al. (Eds.): ICCSA 2018, LNCS 10963, pp. 599–609, 2018.
https://doi.org/10.1007/978-3-319-95171-3_47

nation can be detected and notified to the appropriate authorities for necessary action. All these IoT networks use several radio technologies such as RFID (radio-frequency identification), WLAN (wireless local area network), WPAN (wireless personal area network) or WMAN (wireless metropolitan area networks)[1] to create a Machine-to-Machine (M2M) network [2]. No matter which radio technology is used to operate an M2M network, the end device or machine must make their data available to the Internet [2, 3]. Many M2M data transfer protocols are available for IoT systems, amongst them, MQTT, CoAP, AMQP, and HTTP are the widely accepted ones [4–7]. Considering message size vs. message overhead, power consumption vs. resource requirement, reliability/QoS vs. interoperability, bandwidth vs. latency, security vs. provisioning, or M2M/IoT usage vs. standardization, MQTT stands tall among all [2]. In this paper we have investigated the performance of several MQTT brokers, and compared their properties concerning subscription throughput. The research question was- *In standard domestic deployment use case, is there any difference in performance of different MQTT broker distributions at standard TCP/IP level? And how the same brokers' performance varies when they are put under stress test?* In the following section we discuss a bit more about MQTT protocol. In Sect. 3, details of the test scenario for public and locally deployed brokers are given. Evaluation results are discussed in Sect. 4. Finally, the paper is concluded in Sect. 5.

2 More About MQTT

In this section we briefly discuss the basic components of MQTT. First subsection talks about MQTT protocol and MQTT Packet format. Second gives information about MQTT Quality of Service levels and the MQTT control packets associated with various QoS levels.

2.1 MQTT Packet Format

MQTT works over IANA registered TCP port numbers 8883 and 1883. The port number 8883 is used for using MQTT over SSL/TSL, and 1883 is used for non-TLS communications [11]. In MQTT, MQTT brokers play a major role. A client otherwise called as a publisher usually sends its messages to a broker (MQTT Server) on different topic-tags and consumers otherwise known as receivers subscribe to these topics to receive the messages. An MQTT Broker can handle up to 45 thousand concurrent connected MQTT clients [13] and is responsible for authenticating (publishers and subscribers) receiving, filtering, sorting and sending messages to clients. A plaintext MQTT message has a fixed-length header of 2 Bytes: an optional message-length header, and a message payload header. The first eight bits of MQTT TCP Packet Format is used as fixed MQTT header, where the first four bits represent the Message Type, the fifth bit is used for the duplicate (DUP) flag, the sixth and seventh bits are

---

[1] The IEEE 802.16 Working Group on Broadband Wireless Access Standards, http://www.ieee802. org/16/.

used for the QoS (Quality of Service) level and the eighth bit is used for "retain" message service. The second 8 bits are reserved for the variable length header, and the optional header which can be used for TLS payloads [11, 12] See Fig. 1.

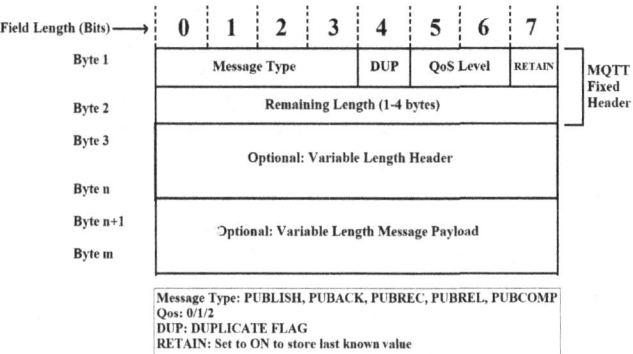

Fig. 1. TCP MQTT Packet Format

2.2 Quality of Service

MQTT provides three 'Quality of service' levels for delivering messages to an MQTT Broker and to any client (ranging from 0 to 2). In QoS 0, a message will not be acknowledged by the receiver or stored and delivered by the sender, only the payload is sent or received. This is often called "fire and forget." It is the minimal level and guarantees the best delivery effort. Only PUBLISH MQTT Control Packet is used to publish messages. In QoS 1 acknowledgment is assured. Data loss may occur. At least once delivery is guaranteed. Here PUBACK (Publish Acknowledgement) control packet is used. The client keeps a copy of the message until it receives PUBACK- Control Packet from the server for Publication Acknowledgement. If PUBACK does not get received within a stipulated time, the client resends the PUBLISH packet, and the duplicate (DUP) flag is set to 1. The (DUP) flag is used only for internal purposes by the programmers, and the broker continues to send PUBACK control packet regardless of the status of the DUP flag. In QoS 2, data delivery is assured. Exactly once delivery is guaranteed. QoS uses PUBLISH- Publish messages, PUBREC - Publish Received, PUBREL - Publish Release, and PUBCOMP - Publish Complete MQTT control packets. When the broker receives a QoS 2 PUBLISH packet, it processes the request and acknowledges the publishing client with a PUBREC message. After the client receives the PUBREC, it discards previously stored PUBLISH packet as PUBREC packet confirms the client that broker has successfully received the message and responds the server with a PUBREL packet. As the PUBREL packet reaches the server, it discards all the stored information about the publishing partner and sends a PUB-COMP packet to it to mark the completion of the process. The server stores an identifying reference to the publishing partner until it sends PUBCOMP message. This process eliminates the possibility of duplicate delivery of messages [10–12].

3 Test Scenario

3.1 For Publicly Available Brokers

In this section we introduce the test scenario for evaluation of publicly available MQTT brokers [4], the considered ones are mentioned in Table 1. In our experiment See 0, live environment event data were sent from a Raspberry PI3 Board to the cloud using the MQTT Protocol. So, on Raspberry PI Board side, an MQTT client, called "publisher" was created using a Node-Red programming language See Fig. 2. to read environment event values from onboard temperature, humidity, and pressure sensors, and publish them on a given topic-tag to an MQTT message broker server at a rate of approximately one message per second. On the receiving end, another MQTT client, called "subscriber" was created to subscribe to the publishing topic, and receive data See Fig. 3. Eclipse Foundation recommended MQTT data capture tool 'MQTT Spy' [16] was used to capture, save and analyze the received data. The goal was to evaluate overall topic-specific message load and broker payload of each broker. The evaluation parameters are depicted in Table 2.

Table 1. Publicly hosted MQTT Brokers

Type	Mosquitto	HiveMQ	Bevywise
Address	test.mosquitto.org	broker.mqttdashboard.com	mqttserver.com
Port	1883	1883	1883 (TCP)
Sign-up needs	No	No	Yes

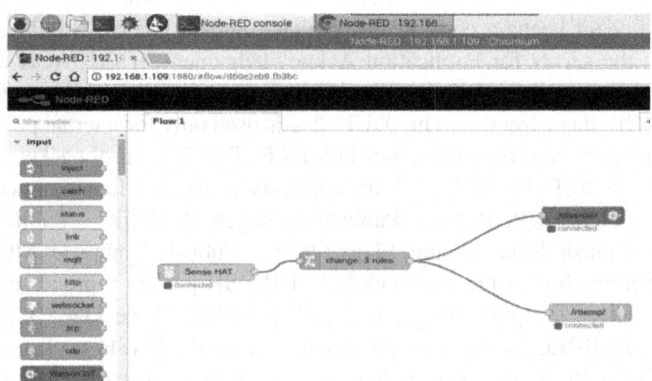

Fig. 2. NodeRed program flow to send RPi sensor data to public Brokers

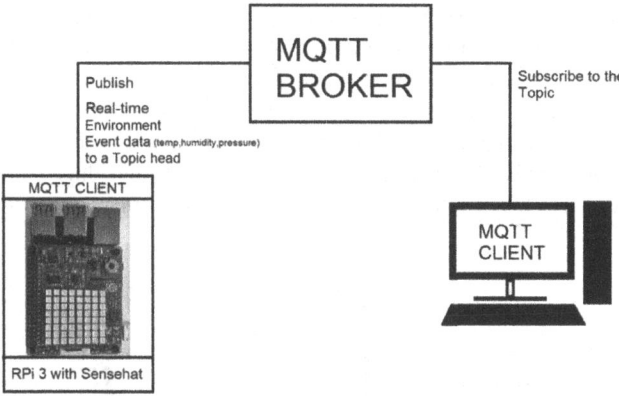

Fig. 3. Public broker experiment scenario

Table 2. Published message properties and publishing conditions for public Brokers

QoS	0/1/2
Payload	14 Bytes
Keep Alive Time (in seconds)	60
Clean Session	True
Total Number of message published	1000

3.2 For Locally Deployed Brokers

The following MQTT brokers are deployed in a local computing environment with default server configurations: ActiveMQ v5.15.2[2], Bevywise MQTT Route[3], HiveMQ 3.3[4], Mosquitto-1.4.14[5], and RabbitMQ v3.7.2[6]. Concerning the local test environment, all servers (broker and client instances) were deployed in a hardware and software setup shown in Table 3.

Table 3. Local hardware and software configurations

Hardware		Software	
Processor	Intel® Core™i5-5200U CPU@ 2.20 GHz × 4	OS	Ubuntu 16.04.3
		OS TYPE	64-bit
RAM	8 GB	KERNEL VERSION	4.10.0-42-generic
Disk	SATA 3.0, 6.0 Gb/s 5400 rpm	JAVA VERSION	Java version "9.0.1"

---

[2] http://activemq.apache.org.

[3] https://www.bevywise.com/mqtt-broker/.

[4] https://www.hivemq.com.

[5] https://mosquitto.org.

[6] https://www.rabbitmq.com.

In the locally deployed MQTT brokers' test scenario, See Fig. 4, the goal was to evaluate overall message rate and broker payload in a given context (QoS 0/1/2, 1 topics, 1 client); the parameters are same as shown in Table 2, only the payload were raised to 31 Bytes. A JavaScript program was created to simulate the sensors in a house. The script simulated and published temperature and humidity sensor values of a room on a unique topic, 1000 times (1 message/second) and thus a total number of 1000 messages were taken into account to calculate performance statistics of a given broker server.

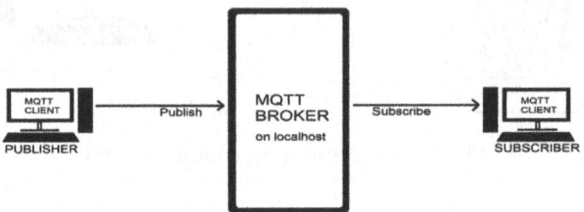

Fig. 4. Locally deployed broker servers' experiment scenario

Publishing JavaScript

```
function publish()
{
  var Thread = Java.type("java.lang.Thread");

  for (i = 0; i< 1000; i++)
  {
    mqttspy.publish("home/bedroom1",
        "{ " +
        "temp: " + (19 + Math.floor((Math.random() * 10) +
1) / 10) + ", " +
        "humidity: " + (59 + Math.floor((Math.random() *
10) + 1) / 10) + ", " +
        "}", 1, false);
    try
    {
      Thread.sleep(1000);
    }
    catch(err)
    {
      return false;
    }
  }
  return true;
}
publish();
```

Keep Alive Time. Keep Alive Time is usually measured in seconds. To call the connect function of an MQTT client, it has to be provided with four parameters as shown below:

```
connect(host, port=1883, keepalive=60, bind_address="")
```

The purpose of keep alive parameter is to ensure that the underlying connection between client and broker is still open to communicate. It is the client's responsibility to confirm that the interval between Control Packets being sent should not exceed the Keep-Alive value. If there is no data flow over an open Connection during specified keep alive period, then the client will send a PINGREQ packet and wait to receive a PINGRESP from the broker. This exchange of message affirms that the connection is open and working. The Keep-Alive is expressed as a 16-bit word and measured in seconds [11].

4   Evaluation Results

4.1   Public Brokers (Public Test Case Scenario Results)

In our public test case scenario, we found that at standard Transport Layer level over TCP/IP, there is a very small difference in performance between different publicly deployed MQTT Broker, but at QoS 0 and QoS 2 level the message load rate See Fig. 5 of Mosquitto Broker was significantly higher than other public brokers.

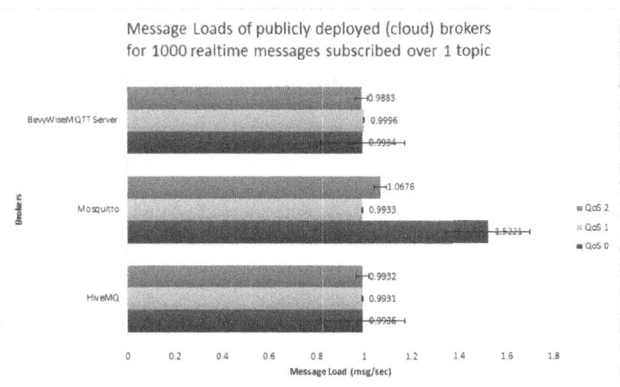

Fig. 5. Message load rate of public brokers

If we sort the brokers according to the server to client message delivery time, at QoS 0 Mosquitto consumed least time to deliver the messages to the client, then came HiveMQ and then MQTT Server. At QoS 1 level MQTT Server performed the best, Mosquitto came second, and HiveMQ reserved the third position. At QoS 2 level Mosquitto again topped the list, HiveMQ was on the second position, MQTT Server secured the third place. See Fig. 6.

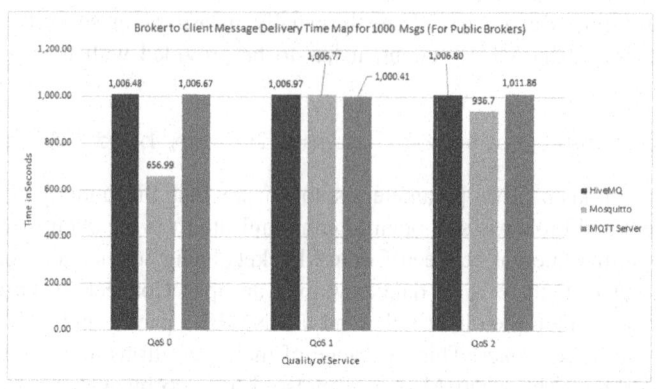

Fig. 6. Broker to client message delivery time map (Public Brokers)

4.2 Locally Deployed Brokers

Local Test Case Scenario Results. In our local test case scenario, we found very little difference in performance between the locally deployed brokers overstandard TCP/IP. We also found that RabbitMQ does not support QoS2 subscriptions. RabbitMQ automatically downgrades QoS 2 [11], publishes and subscribes to QoS 1See Fig. 7. If we sort the brokers in an ascending order according to the server to client message delivery time, at QoS 0, HiveMQ delivered the messages first and then RabbitMQ, Mosquitto, MQTT Route, and Active MQ followed accordingly. At QoS 1 HiveMQ topped the list and Mosquitto, RabbitMQ, MQTT Route and Active MQ occupied the second, third, fourth and fifth position respectively. At QoS 2 HiveMQ again secured the first position, then came Mosquitto, MQTT Route, and ActiveMQ one after another. See Figs. 8, 9 and 10.

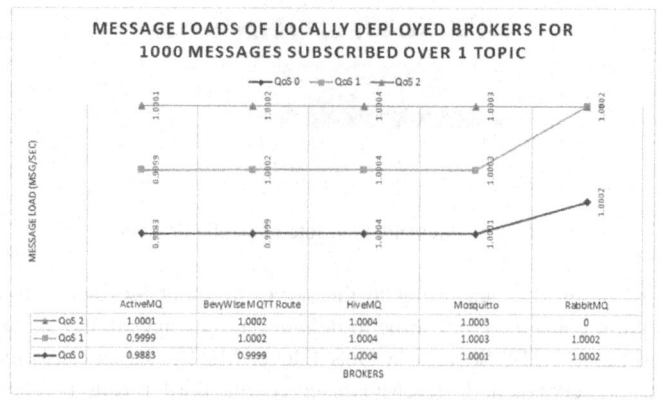

Fig. 7. Message load rate, locally deployed brokers.

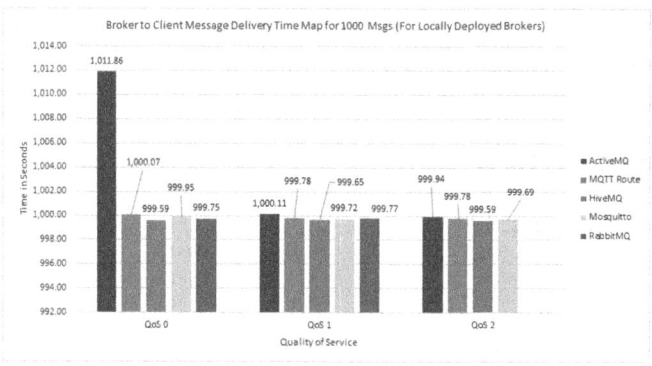

Fig. 8. Broker to client message delivery time map (Local Brokers)

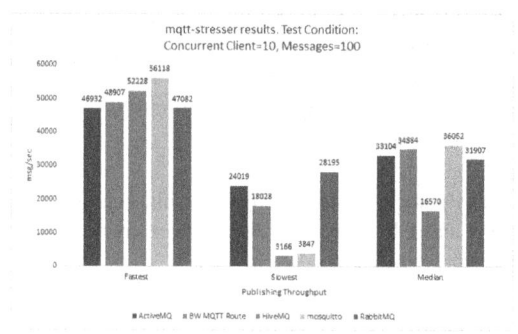

Fig. 9. Broker to client message delivery time map (Public Brokers)

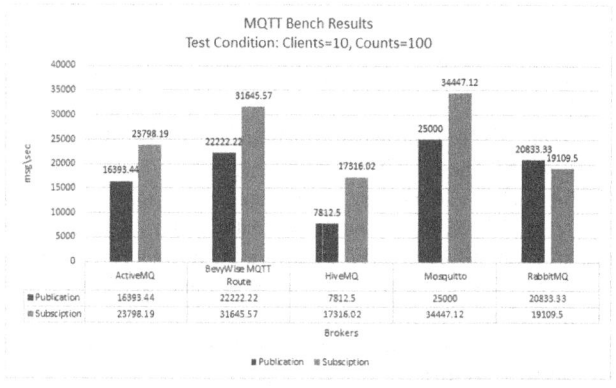

Fig. 10. Broker to client message delivery time map (Public Brokers)

Benchmark Results:

Benchmark tool: mqtt-stresser [17]
Concurrent Clients: 10
Number of Messages: 100
Benchmark tool: mqtt-bench [18]
Concurrent Clients: 10
Number of Messages: 100

5   Conclusion

The Internet of Things paradigm is a rapidly growing research field, which has a great potential to ease our lives and to create a better world. There are many M2 M data transfer protocols available for IoT systems, including MQTT, CoAP, AMQP, and HTTP. In this paper we investigated the performance of MQTT brokers and compared their properties by subscription throughput under a specific publishing condition. Our results showed very small difference in the performance of MQTT brokers in standard domestic deployment use case. On the other hand, we found stress testing results of MQTT brokers very inspiring, and we plan to continue this research line in the future with increased number of load conditions.

Acknowledgements. The author would like to show his gratitude to his colleagues: Attila Kertesz, Tamás Pflanzner and Tibor Gyimothy for their constructive comments and suggestions that made this research work possible.

References

1. Lampkin, V., et al.: Building Smarter Planet Solutions with MQTT and IBM WebSphere MQ, Telemetry. IBM Redbooks publication, 268 p. (2012)
2. Naik, N.:Choice of effective messaging protocols for IoT systems: MQTT, CoAP, AMQP and HTTP. In: IEEE International Systems Engineering Symposium, Vienna, pp. 1–7 (2017)
3. Karagiannis, V., Chatzimisios, P., Vazquez-Gallego, F., Alonso- Zarate, J.: A survey on application layer protocols for the Internet of Things. Trans. IoT Cloud Comput. 3(1), 11–17 (2015)
4. Bellavista, P., Zanni, A.: Towards better scalability for IoT-cloud interactions via combined exploitation of MQTT and CoAP. In: IEEE 2nd International Forum on Research and Technologies for Society and Industry Leveraging a better tomorrow (RTSI) (2016)
5. Gazis, V., Gortz, M., Huber, M., Leonardi, A., Mathioudakis, K., Wiesmaier, A., Zeiger, F., Vasilomanolakis, E.: A survey of technologies for the Internet of Things. In: Proceedings of 2015 IEEE International Wireless Communications and Mobile Computing Conference, pp. 1090–1095 (2015)
6. Foster, A.: Messaging technologies for the industrial internet and the Internet of Things whitepaper PrismTech. (2015)
7. Kovatsch, M., Lanter, M., Shelby, Z.: Californium: scalable cloud services for the Internet of Things with CoAP. In: IEEE International Conference on Internet of Things, pp. 1–6 (2014)

8. Stephen, N.: Power Profiling: HTTPS Long Polling vs. MQTT with SSL, on Android (2015). http://stephendnicholas.com/archives/1217. Accessed 04 Apr 2018
9. Lee, S., Kim, H., Hong, D.K., Ju, H.: Correlation analysis of MQTT loss and delay according to Qos level. In: The International Conference on Information Networking (ICOIN), pp. 714–717, January 2013
10. Pahomqtt c client library: Quality of service. http://www.eclipse.org/paho/files/mqttdoc/MQTTClient/html/qos.html. Accessed 19 June 2017
11. MQTT Version 3.1.1, 28 October 2018. http://docs.oasis-open.org/mqtt/mqtt/v3.1.1/os/mqtt-v3.1.1-os.html. Accessed 04 Apr 2018
12. Fehrenbach, P.: Messaging Queues in the IoT Under Pressure-Stress Testing the Mosquitto MQTT Broker, FakultätInformatik Hochschule Furtwangen University, 10 May 2017. https://blog.it-securityguard.com/wp-content/uploads/2017/10/IOT_Mosquitto_Pfehrenbach.pdf Accessed 04 Apr 2018
13. Nistsp 800-132, recommendation for password-based key derivation part1: Storage applications. http://nvlpubs.nist.gov/nistpubs/Legacy/SP/nistspecialpublication800-132.pdf. Accessed 04 Mar 2018
14. Public Brokers. https://github.com/mqtt/mqtt.github.io/wiki/public_brokers. Accessed 04 Apr 2018
15. Github- mqtt-spy. https://github.com/eclipse/paho.mqtt-spy. Accessed 15 Mar 2018
16. RabbitMQ Documentation. https://www.rabbitmq.com/documentation.html. Accessed 04 Apr 2018
17. Github- mqttstresser. https://github.com/inovex/mqtt-stresser. Accessed 15 Mar 2018
18. MQTT Bench mqtt-bench. https://github.com/takanorig/mqtt-bench. Accessed 15 Mar 2018

Water Treatment Monitoring System at San Jose de Chaltura, Imbabura - Ecuador

Marcelo León[1]([⊠]), Maritza Ruíz[2], Lídice Haz[3], Robert Montalvan[1],
Viviana Pinos Medrano[3], and Silvia Medina Anchundia[3]

[1] Universidad Estatal Península de Santa Elena, La Libertad, Ecuador
marceloleonll@hotmail.com,
robertmontalvan@hotmail.com
[2] Universidad de las Fuerzas Armadas, Sangolquí, Ecuador
marilolita3@hotmail.com
[3] Universidad de Guayaquil, Guayaquil, Ecuador
victoria.haz@hotmail.com,
{viviana.pinosm, silvia.medinaa}@ug.edu.ec

Abstract. Water reuse is a necessary process because water is excessively used and increasingly it is becoming scarcer. Water after being used by industry and domestic use and once treated, it can be applied to recharge aquifers, discharge into receiving bodies without contaminating them or being reused mainly in green areas and/or agriculture. Its reuse could be possible after a treatment, which aims to eliminate as many pollutants as may be otherwise harmful. This research describes the cur-rent situation of a wastewater treatment plant in at San José de Chaltura parish of canton Antonio Ante located in the province of Imbabura in Ecuador; and a process that was formulated to the treatment and decontamination of water through a system of pervasive monitoring. Experimentation was carried out by treating the wastewater by triplicate for 15 days, using biological reactors and combinations of aquatic plants. In general, results show the best aquatic species to raise quality of treated wastewater in agricultural use as irrigation water was duckweed since it managed to decrease its initial value for total coliforms and fecal coliforms.

Keywords: Water treatment · Water pollution · Pervasive information systems
Territorial planning

1 Introduction

1.1 A Subsection Sample

Water is constantly circulating around the planet as liquid, solid or gaseous states; this is why water is considered an important resource on both origin and continuation of life on Earth. Water conservation directly implies providing a positive contribution to the hydrological cycle but it is negatively affecting its quality due to anthropogenic influence. There is "wastewater" that must be treated to avoid serious contamination problems. This natural resource, considered vital for being an essential element in the development of life but its worldwide distribution is unequal, for that reason some

© Springer International Publishing AG, part of Springer Nature 2018
O. Gervasi et al. (Eds.): ICCSA 2018, LNCS 10963, pp. 610–624, 2018.
https://doi.org/10.1007/978-3-319-95171-3_48

governments invest a large part of their budget in conservation and treatment to enhance water supply. In Ecuador, water distribution is irregular [1]. Therefore, the introduction of radical technological changes that favors minimization of waste, improving the availability and quality of water, is perceived positively in the short term. In this way, environmental management carried out by the autonomous municipal governments favors territorial planning by providing more personalized and faster services.

Business intelligence applied to public services administration facilitates the ability to obtain, store and analyze data immediately, facilitating decision making, and providing an environment of proactive and reactive interaction among business stakeholders [2]. In this sense, institutions seek multiple alternatives to increase knowledge through the modeling of the information generated in the business intelligence processes. Design and implementation of ubiquitous information systems adapted to specific execution environments facilitates the generation of dynamically generated data and the development of pervasive business intelligence (PBI) [3, 4]. The emer-gence of PBI is a natural evolution of business intelligence applications in organizations, with applications from the strategic level to the operational level.

Thus, to minimize the impact of liquid waste on the quality of surface water, an integrative approach must be followed that takes advantage of all opportunities: from administrative and operational management in the industry to natural processes, based on reliable quantitative information and the use of current technological tools. [5].

This study focuses on solving contamination problems from biological wastewater at San José de Chaltura water treatment plant. It preliminary evaluation of water source through fecal coliforms analysis reported an average value of 6.74×105 CFU/100 mL, value that exceeded safe limits according to Ministerial Agreement No. 097-A published at the Official Registry 387 on November 4, 2015, whose permissible limit for fecal coliforms in waters destined for agricultural use is: 1000 NMP/100 mL.

A current diagnosis of the treatment plant was made in order to make a proposition that will decrease the value of fecal coliforms. The experiment consisted of a study for 15 days performed 3 times utilizing biological reactors $(50 \times 30 \times 30)$ cm^3 and combinations of aquatic plants water hyacinth (Eich-hornia crassipes), water duck-weed (Lemma minor), cyperus (Cyperus helferi) and water ferns (Azolla carolina). The values of BOD5, COD, fecal coliforms, total coliforms in the laboratory were reviewed in addition to the use of environmental sensors, values of relative humidity (RH), atmospheric pressure, conductivity and temperature were reported.

2 Current Situation of Water Treatment Plant at Parroquia San José de Chaltura

Imbabura has 6 counties: Antonio Ante, Cotacachi, Ibarra, Otavalo, Pimampiro and San Miguel de Urcuqui, which are mainly urban and rural parishes. The parishes have greenhouses, poultry farms, animal breeding, among others. In these activities, irrigation water from the different channels and ditches are used, the supply of crop products covers other counties, pasishes and provinces at the national level [2015].

The study was carried out in Chaltura rural parish, which belongs to Antonio Ante County from province of Imbabura. Its geographical location is shown in Fig. 1.

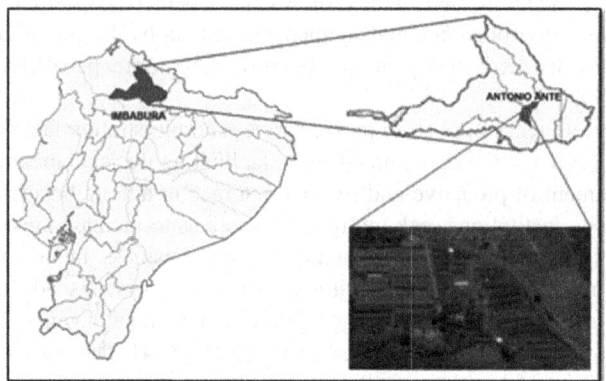

Fig. 1. Geographical location of water treatment plant at Chaltura

According to the Ecuadorian Water Regulatory Agency (SENAGUA) the greater amount of treated wastewater is used for irrigation in activities such as agriculture and livestock [6]. San Francisco de Natabuela and San José de Chaltura have biolog-ical wastewater treatment facilities in which aquatic plants are being used. Current pro-duction flow is 10.3 L per second.

The wastewater treatment plant at San José de Chaltura has several processes, initial-ly pre-treatment in which there is a grid filter, unsander and a flow distributor. In the primary treatment, there are two sedimentary tanks. A secondary treatment, in which there are 38 tanks that treat the wastewater with floating aquatic plants (Lechuguinas or water hyacinth) distributed in 4 platforms that are found connected in series [7].

The industrial development of Antonio Ante County began in 1975 with small fabric factories that are found in the area along with vegetables and fruit crops that account 16% of produce in Ecuador. The water resource began to be deficient by year 1980 due to an increase in population and by the year 2000 government began to take action with management of the water resource. The main water polluters were textiles and wastewater from their parishes [6].

The water after having been used in domestic consumption, factories, livestock activities among others, originate a waste water which appears dirty and contaminated; it contains fats, detergents, organic matter, industry and livestock waste, herbicides and pesticides, among others. This wastewater before being returned to the nature or to the nearest river must be treated to avoid contamination [8].

Quality of waste water is deficient in canton Antonio Ante which it has a treatment plant in San José de Chaltura and does not guarantee treated water is optimal for crops irrigation of the area. By 2019 an increase in the flow for irrigation will be projected that will cover an approximate area of 7,926 ha, affecting 43,518 people that live in the area with an average temperature of 15.7 °C, Average annual precipitation of 714 mm and humidity of 65–85% [6].

The wastewater treatment plant of San José Chaltura was built to treat a flow of 10.53 L/s in the year 2028 but is currently with an average input flow of 10.3 L/s, this flow supplies for the irrigation of the agricultural crops and the cattle ranch of the parishes of Chaltura and Natabuela that are commercialized between the parishes, within the province and even at national level [6].

Physical, chemical and biological parameters analysis of water source, a much higher value was reported on fecal coliforms results of 6.74 $\times$ 105 CFU/100 mL compared to a regulatory standard of 1000 MPN/100 mL in waters used on agriculture. The excess of this value or the presence of these bacteria causes several negative effects to the environment and public health of those who inhabit the area or people who consume its produce. This is why is necessary to carry out a treatment that guaran-tees the quality of the water source according to current regulations [7].

3 Methodology

A pilot scale analysis was performed for the secondary treatment. Ponds were replaced by reactors with dimensions (0.50 $\times$ 0.30 $\times$ 0.30) cm^3 in length, width and depth respectively. The experiment was performed with aquatic plants: water duckweed (Lemma minor), water hyacinth (Eichhornia crassipes), water fern (Azolla caroliniana) and cyperus (Cyperus helferi).

The aquatic plants were combined to study in triplicate the growth and effectiveness in the reactors for 15 days (days: 0, 7, 12, 15) of experimentation. Computer applied techniques for information analysis helped determine the results of fecal coliforms, total coliforms, biochemical oxygen demand (BOD5), chemical oxygen demand (COD) and establish the best combination to reduce the value of coliforms.

3.1 Biochemistry Oxygen Demand Analysis (DBO$_5$)

BOD5 is a measure of the amount of oxygen required by microorganisms within a period of five days at 20 °C to stabilize biodegradable organic matter under aerobic conditions. This measure was taken in triplicate according to the method described in the Ecuadorian Technical Standard INEN 1202: 2013, which is based on the study Standard Methods for Water and Wastewater Examination. 5210. Biochemical Oxygen Demand, 22nd edition [9].

In the process, one liter of saturated distilled water solution was inoculated at a temperature of approximately 20 °C $\pm$ 1 °C mixed with 1 cm^3 of phosphate buffer, magnesium sulfate, calcium chloride and ferric chloride with the most satisfactory inoculum for the water analyzed. The sample must be free of chlorine for which it was left to stand (1 to 2 h), and to eliminate the presence of residual chlorine, it is kept at a temperature of 20 °C $\pm$ 3 °C and pH between 6 and 8 (it is used H2SO4 and NaOH as appropriate), then inoculated dilutions were prepared (INEN 1202:2013, 2013).

Dilutions and control were incubated for 5 days at 20 °C in bottles with a hydraulic seal then dissolved oxygen was determined in the incubated samples and in the control, applying modification to nitrite, following Winkler's method, considering the confidence dilutions with residual dissolved oxygen minimum of 1–2 mg/L minimum. If the control was inoculated, it was corrected, trying to reduce the inoculum oxygen by 40% to 70% (INEN 1202:2013, 2013).

3.2 Oxygen Chemical Demand Analysis (DQO)

The COD was determined according to Ecuadorian Technical Standard INEN 1203: 2013. The sample was refluxed with excess $K_2Cr_2O_7$ (potassium dichromate) in H_2SO_4 (sulfuric acid), then the remaining potassium dichromate was titrated to determinate the reduced amount using ferrous sulfate, ammonium using ferroin as indicator and it is considered that the amount of oxidizable organic matter is proportional to the dichromate consumed.

For the analysis, 50 cm^3 of sample was placed in an Erlenmeyer flask of reflux of 500 cm^3 with pieces of pumice stone or glass beads, 1 g of $HgSO_4$ and slowly and with stirring add 5 cm^3 of the sulfuric acid reagent, then cooled for avoid losses of volatile substances in the sample while adding 25 cm^3 of 0.25 N $K_2Cr_2O_7$. Then connect the flask to the condenser, heat the mixture and reflux for 2 h, dilute the mixture approximately twice with water distilled to titrate with ferrous sulfate and ammonium solution using 2 to 3 drops of ferroin indicator until a change of color from greenish blue to reddish brown [9].

3.3 Total Coliforms Analysis

This analysis was performed in triplicate by the most probable determination with multiple tubes according to NTE INEN 1205: 32013, 10–1 solutions were prepared (450 mL of peptonada water with 50 mL of sample), 10–2 (90 mL of peptonade water with 10 mL of sample), 10–3 (10 mL of the previous solution with 90 mL of peptonade water). Approximately 10 cm^3 of lauryl triptose broth was placed in a test tube and then a 2 cm^3 tube inverted with 1 cm^3 of the previous solutions was placed separately. Then test tubes were covered at 35 °C for 24 h and finally confirmed if there was gas production [9].

3.4 Fecal Coliform Analysis

The result of total coliforms was confirmed, if this is positive, the confirmatory Escherichia coli test was analyzed three times following methodology detailed in NTE INEN 1205: 2013 according to the most probable determination of bacteria with multiple tubes, for this it was transferred the fluid from 2 to 3 positive tubes obtained during the previous test and incubated at 44.5 ± 0.1 °C for 24 to 48 h, considering as positive the tubes that show turbidity and gas production. Two tubes were then inoculated with Eschericha coli broth at an approximate temperature of 35 °C for 24 h before adding the Kovac reactive and then irradiating with a UV light source, observing fluorescence and peformed the reading [9].

4   Results and Discussion

In the Chaltura wastewater treatment plant there are 3 different processes: pretreatment, primary treatment and secondary treatment that meet specific objectives to achieve decontamination. Treated wastewater serves for a future reuse is given by consumption for agricultural uses (45–70)%, for industrial uses (15–20)% and municipal services (8–15)%, for this process all the water treated is used for agricultural uses [10].

4.1   Pretreatment

This process allows water conditioning by eliminating coarse solids, sands, plastic, bottles and other materials that arrive with the current to the plant and to guarantee efficiency of subsequent treatment. Water source enters treatment plant for solids removal to the grid box, to then it pass to the desander and finally to the flow distributor, as shown in Figs. 2, 3 and 4 respectively [11].

Fig. 2. Grid box. From Mantilla (2017)

Fig. 3. Desander. From Mantilla (2017)

Fig. 4. Flow regulator box. From Mantilla (2017)

4.2   Primary Treatment

Primary treatment has the purpose of eliminating the solids in suspension of the residual water that is being treated and that will go on to the secondary treatment [12]. In the process there are two circular sedimentation tanks that remove sedimentable solids, they are built in reinforced concrete whose dimensions are about 2.80 m high and 11.20 m in diameter, are connected to each other with a valve and have an opening that allows to inspect the wastewater decontamination process.

4.3   Secondary Treatment

Secondary treatment of wastewater that will be reused in agriculture is carried out by means of aquatic plants. Water lentil (Lemma minor) and water hyacinth (Eichhornia crassipes), distributed in 5 platforms (Atuntaqui, Chaltura, Imbaya, Natabuela and San Roque) that have in their totality 38 ponds built in reinforced concrete, the same ones that are connected in series and have a total volume of approximately 5000 cubic meters. In Fig. 5 the distribution of the ponds is observed.

Aquatic plants are mainly responsible for the oxidation of organic matter to reduce levels of BOD5, in addition to absorbing pollutant elements of wastewater, are collected from the ponds manually every fifteen days to be processed and used as organic fertilizer. In the final disposal of treated water to be used in agriculture, there is a box with grids that prevents the passage of waste from aquatic marshes used in the process.

Determination of Species and of Water Plants Combination Utilized in Secondary Water Treatment

In order to determine effectiveness of treatments in ten reactors, fecal coliforms, total coliforms, Biochemical Oxygen Demand (BOD5), Chemical Oxygen Demand (COD) for 15 days were analyzed in triplicate (0, 7, 12, 15) of experimentation.

Then, in order to determine species and combinations of aquatic plants, a secondary treatment was performed on a pilot scale using glass reactors with dimensions (0.50 × 0.30 × 0.30) cm^3 in length, width and depth respectively.

For this analysis, the behavior of aquatic plants of the ten reactors for the 4 established parameters was studied. Table 1 shows the treatments prepared with the corresponding composition for further development of this research.

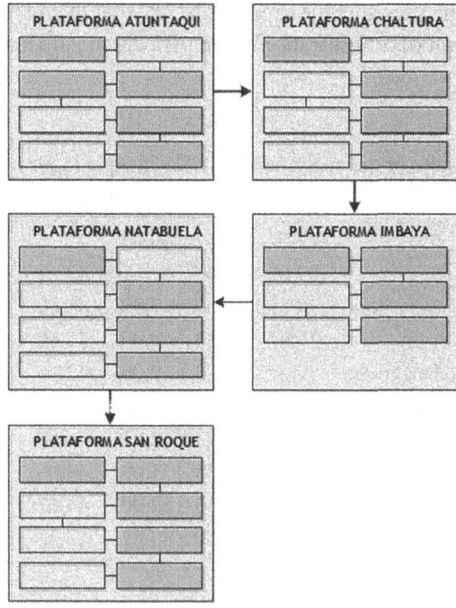

Fig. 5. Water treatment plant platform distribution and ponds

Table 1. Treatments used to determine the composition of aquatic plants that allows defining the reactor with maximum removals of fecal coliforms.

Treatment	Composition
T1	Azolla caroliniana (Helecho de agua)
T2	Cyperus helferi (Cyperus)
T3	Eichhornia crassipes (Jacinto de agua)
T4	Lemma minor (Lenteja de agua)
T5	Azolla caroliniana y Eichhornia crassipes
T6	Azolla caroliniana y Lemma minor
T7	Cyperus helferi y Eichhornia crassipes
T8	Cyperus helferi y Eichhornia crassipes
T9	Cyperus helferi y Lemma minor
T10	Eichhornia crassipes y Lemma minor

DBO5 Analysis

The Oxygen Biochemical Demand (BOD5), with values lower than 110 mg/L is considered weak pollution according to the degree of contamination of established urban wastewater [13]. In the preliminary evaluation, lab results performed by treatment plant report a value of approximately 80 mg/L that are within the norm value for this variable.

In Table 2, it can be seen that the greatest decrease of this parameter is with T3 with an approximate removal of 50% for the Oxygen Biochemical Demand that is within the norm.

Table 2. Results of the analyzes for BOD5 in aquatic plant combinations

	Day 0	Day 7	Day 12	Day 15	Removal
Azolla	79,67	58,67	49,00	41,33	48,12%
Cyperus	79,67	64,67	50,67	43,67	45,19%
Hyacinth	79,67	54,67	45,00	40,00	49,79%
Duckweed	79,67	61,33	49,00	42,00	47,28%
Cyperus & Duckweed	79,67	61,33	49,00	42,00	47,28%
Azolla & Cyperus	79,67	61,67	49,33	42,67	46,45%
Cyperus & Hyacinth	79,67	66,33	52,67	44,00	44,77%
Azolla & Duckweed	79,67	65,33	51,00	44,00	44,77%
Hyacinth & Duckweed	79,67	68,33	53,00	44,67	43,94%
Hyacinth & Azolla	79,67	62,00	49,67	43,33	45,61%

DQO Analysis

In Fig. 6(a), medians chart with intervals of 95.0% confidence is observed, making a comparison of several samples according to the days of analysis of the Chemical Oxygen Demand, having a removal between 47%–38% with the use of the four aquatic plants selected for this research. In Fig. 6(b) there is a decrease in the parameter as a function of the time of analysis, so that each moment requires less oxygen for the oxidation of organic matter in the wastewater.

In COD experimentation it showed a dispersion of similar results in the four days of taking results as shown in Fig. 6(c). In the analysis of the data, a decrease in the COD quantification was observed as a function of the study time obtaining an approximate removal of 50% as confirmed in Table 3.

Table 3. Results of the analyzes for COD in aquatic plant combinations

	Day 0	Day 7	Day 12	Day 15	Removal
Azolla	132,09	105,19	91,03	76,05	42,43%
Cyperus	132,09	111,31	96,71	80,37	39,15%
Hyacinth	132,09	96,00	83,48	71,15	46,14%
Duckweed	132,09	105,75	91,13	76,96	41,74%
Cyperus & Duckweed	132,09	115,56	101,10	82,12	37,83%
Azolla & Cyperus	132,09	114,31	98,99	81,34	38,42%
Cyperus & Hyacinth	132,09	112,01	98,15	80,75	38,87%
Azolla & Duckweed	132,09	108,70	95,61	80,31	39,20%
Hyacinth & Duckweed	132,09	108,47	92,38	78,32	40,71%
Hyacinth & Azolla	132,09	108,45	91,54	77,28	41,50%

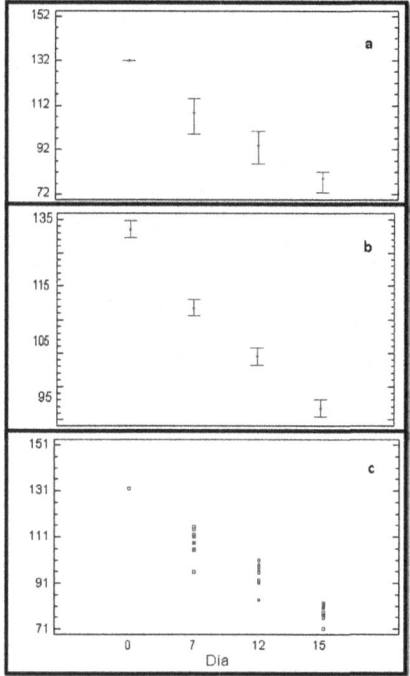

Fig. 6. Median plot (a), analysis by the means method and 95% of Tukey HSD (b), scatter plot (c) for the COD in the ten combinations of aquatic plants with respect to the days of analysis (0, 7, 12, 15) to environmental conditions of water treatment plant at Chaltura.

Total Coliform Analysis

Total presence of coliforms is difficult to control, humans throw daily in their droppings between 109 and 1011 coliforms that contaminate water that is in contact making it unfit for human consumption, so it is important to control this parameter in all treatments [14].

Table 4 shows the results for the 10 treatments in the total coliform analysis and in Fig. 7(c) and 7(a) shows the dispersion of results and distribution of the means respectively, of which it can be concluded that on day 7 the values are still few dispersed while on day 12 and day 15 this variable is more accentuated by the variability of the results, a trend that is corroborated in the analysis of means with intervals of 95.0% confidence for the 4 days of experimentation.

In Fig. 7(b) the statistical analysis of the data is shown in the study of the total coliforms of the wastewater of Treatment Plant at Chaltura showing that all are outside the norm, which establishes a maximum value of 1000 NMP/100 mL to allocate the treated water for agricultural use, in addition to the existence of an atypical data for day 12 and a dispersion that increases as it passes the days of analysis.

Table 4. Results of the analyzes for total coliforms in the combinations of aquatic plants

	Day 0	Day 7	Day 12	Day 15	Removal
T1	2,20E+06	2,07E+06	2,02E+06	2,10E+06	9,18E+04
T2	9,66E+05	1,10E+06	1,02E+06	1,03E+06	6,76E+04
T3	2,22E+05	2,02E+05	2,13E+05	2,12E+05	1,02E+04
T4	1,91E+05	1,95E+05	1,88E+05	1,91E+05	3,27E+03
T5	8,36E+04	8,30E+04	8,76E+04	8,47E+04	2,55E+03
T6	9,62E+01	9,60E+01	9,57E+01	9,59E+01	2,73E–01
T7	2,20E+06	2,07E+06	2,02E+06	2,10E+06	9,18E+04
T8	9,66E+05	1,10E+06	1,02E+06	1,03E+06	6,76E+04
T9	2,22E+05	2,02E+05	2,13E+05	2,12E+05	1,02E+04
T10	1,91E+05	1,95E+05	1,88E+05	1,91E+05	3,27E+03

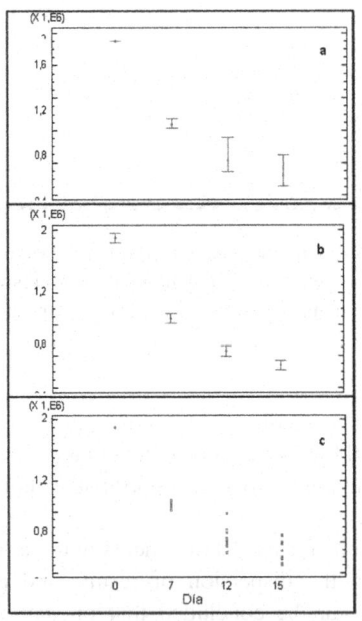

Fig. 7. Median plot (a), analysis by means of means and 95% of Tukey HSD (b), scatter plot (c) for total coliforms in the ten combinations of aquatic plants with respect to the days of analysis (0, 7, 12, 15) to environmental conditions of the water treatment plant

Fecal Coliforms
Wastewater has microorganisms that usually come from human excreta and cause gastrointestinal infections. The isolation of fecal coliforms is complex, which is why it is the cause of some diseases and makes the water unsafe to be ingested by living beings [14, 15].

Table 5 shows the results of the analysis for fecal coliforms and in Fig. 8(c) and (b) the dispersion of the data and the range with their means are shown, considering as variables the days (0, 7, 12, 15) of investigation, with the means method and 95% of Tukey HSD having the P-value of the F-test less than 0.05, so it can be assured that there is a statistically significant difference.

Table 5. Results of analyzes for fecal coliforms in aquatic plant combinations

	Day 0	Day 7	Day 12	Day 15	Removal
T1	5,54E+05	3,10E+05	1,64E+05	3,41E+04	93,85%
T2	5,54E+05	4,51E+05	2,86E+05	1,41E+05	74,58%
T3	5,54E+05	2,61E+05	1,61E+05	2,46E+04	95,56%
T4	5,54E+05	2,51E+05	1,04E+05	1,40E+04	97,47%
T5	5,54E+05	4,17E+05	2,81E+05	1,01E+05	81,81%
T6	5,54E+05	3,42E+05	1,98E+05	5,09E+04	90,82%
T7	5,54E+05	3,28E+05	1,77E+05	3,95E+04	92,87%
T8	5,54E+05	3,94E+05	2,78E+05	8,54E+04	84,59%
T9	5,54E+05	3,92E+05	2,78E+05	7,31E+04	86,81%
T10	5,54E+05	3,30E+05	1,87E+05	4,24E+04	92,35%

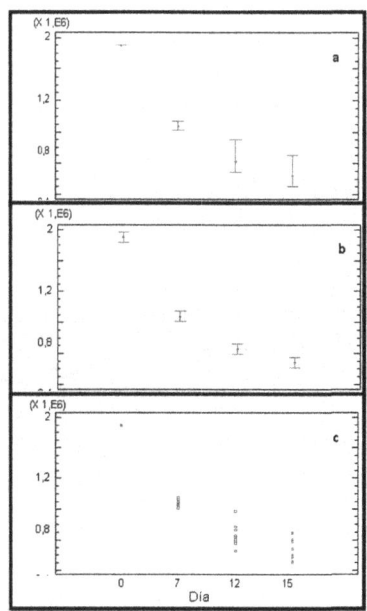

Fig. 8. Median plot (a), analysis by means of means and 95% of Tukey HSD (b), scatter plot (c) for fecal coliforms in the ten combinations of aquatic plants with respect to the days of analysis (0, 7, 12, 15) to environmental conditions of the water treatment plant

4.4   System to Improve the Wastewater Treatment Plant
at San Jose de Chaltura

The best combination of aquatic plants that was established in this study, was organized into four reactors connected in series simulating the real situation in the plant platforms with their ponds, scheme shown in Fig. 9, also kept The average retention time of 6.39 days calculated in the system.

Fig. 9. Outline of the reactors in the analysis with Lentil de agua

The diagnosis was based on the combination of aquatic plants in glass reactors for the simulation system of the real platforms of the wastewater treatment plant. The effectiveness in the system was analyzed in triplicate for 15 days (0, 5, 10, 13, 15) for BOD5, COD and microbiological study of fecal coliforms, total coliforms. In addition, environmental sensors were used as shown in Fig. 10, to record daily in triplicate during the fifteen days of the start of the study the relative humidity (RH), barometric pressure, ambient temperature (Ta), temperature of the reactor (Tr), conductivity, dissolved oxygen (DO), hydrogen potential (pH).

Fig. 10. Outline of the reactors with Lentil de agua, in the analysis with environmental sensors

In relation with the collection and analysis of data, the implementation of the pervasive system would provide the data in real time in each of its processes as shown in Fig. 11. This makes it easier for senior management to make decisions about the parameters required to treat water and optimize its use. In this study, it was determined

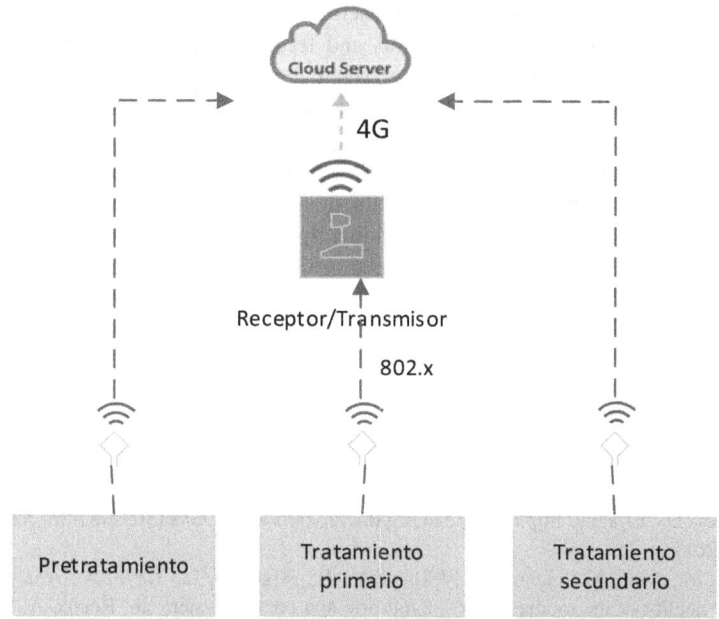

Fig. 11. Scheme of operation of the system for wastewater treatment

that the best combination for the treatment of wastewater is the aquatic plant, duckweed. A tertiary chlorination treatment is proposed that guarantees an approximate value of 850 NMP/100 mL for total coliforms and 108 NMP/100 mL for fecal coliforms to decontaminate wastewater from the water treatment plant at Chaltura, quantification that is below the norm value, fulfilling thus with the TULAS and the Ministerial Agreement 097-A in force for the parish.

5   Conclusions

The implementation of a pervasive business system (PBI) facilitates decision-making at all levels of the organization through timely analysis, alerts and feedback tools. These systems generate the information in real time according to the environment for which they are designed. The system must provide the data in real time, facilitating the decision making to the top management, in relation to the state of the water during the treatment process.

In this context, comparisons are presented for the DBO5 parameter, obtaining values of 40.0 mg/L when treated with water hyacinth, while the COD decreases to 71.15 mg/L when using the same macrophyte, with removals of approximately 50% for both cases. The total and fecal coliforms despite having the greatest decrease with water duckweed did not reach those regulated by TULAS or Ministerial Agreement No. 097-A, reporting approximate data of 1.04E+05 and 1.40E+04 respectively with percentage removals close to 98%. The presented data showed the reduction of the four parameters (BOD5, COD, total coliforms and fecal coliforms), reporting higher efficiency with water hyacinth and water duckweed, a situation that corroborates the use of these two aquatic plants for the treatment current in the wáter treatment plant at San José de Chaltura.

For further studies, the formation of halogenated compounds that can be generated by the chlorination of the contaminated effluent should be considered, in addition to its consequences for the environment and indirectly for human health by ingesting food that has been hydrated with this irrigation water. The study of aquatic species that are used to fertilize surrounded lands the sector it requires a new analysis to ensure that its composition does not cause negative environmental impacts that may be harmful in the future.

References

1. Montes, D.: El agua. http://www.fao.org/docrep/006/W1309S/w1309s06.htm. Accessed 08 Aug 2017
2. León, M., Ruiz, M., Guarda, T., Montalvan, R., Arguello, L., Tapia, A.: Analysis of the water quality of the monjas river: monitoring and control system. In: Rocha, Á., Adeli, H., Reis, L., Costanzo, S. (eds.) World Conference on Information Systems and Technologies, pp. 363–374. Springer, Cham (2018). https://doi.org/10.1007/978-3-319-77700-9_36
3. Ortiz, S.: Taking business intelligence to the masses. Computer **43**, 12–15 (2010)
4. Portela, F., Santos, M.F., Machado, J., Abelha, A., Silva, Á., Rua, F.: Pervasive and intelligent decision support in intensive medicine – the complete picture. In: Bursa, M., Khuri, S., Renda, M.E. (eds.) ITBAM 2014. LNCS, vol. 8649, pp. 87–102. Springer, Cham (2014). https://doi.org/10.1007/978-3-319-10265-8_9
5. Buitron, R.: ¿Quiénes, en verdad, tienen que dejar de desperdiciar agua en Ecuador? Gkillcity **230**, 171–172 (2015)
6. Cevallos, J.: Plan de Desarrollo y Ordenamiento Territorial-PDOT. GAD, Ibarra (2011)
7. Mantilla, P.: Evaluación preliminar de la planta de tratamiento de aguas residuales de las parroquias de Chaltura y Natabuela del cantón Antonio Ante, de la provincia de Imbabura. Pontificia Universidad Católica del Ecuador, Ibarra (2017)
8. Giuseppina, D.: La contaminación de aguas en Ecuador. Tallpa, Quito (2007)
9. NTE INEN 1203:2013. Demanda Química de Oxígeno, 1era ed. Quito, Ecuador (2013)
10. Elias, X.: Reciclaje de Residuos insdustriales, 2da edn. Diaz Santos, Madrid (2012)
11. Ramalho, R.: Tratamiento de aguas residuales. Reverte S. A, Barcelona (2003)
12. Moreno, L.: La depuracion de aguas residuales urbanas de pequeñas poblaciones mediante infiltracion directa en el terreno, 2da edn. Henares, Madrid (2008)
13. Osorio, F., Torres, J., Sánchez, M.: Tratamiento de aguas para la eliminación de mcroorganismos y agentes contaminantes, 2da edn. Díaz Santos, Madrid (2010)
14. Rigola, M.: Tratamiento de aguas industriale: Aguas de proceso y residuales 1, era edn. Impreandes, Barcelona (2015)
15. López, C., Buitron, G., García, H., Cervantes, F.: Tratamiento biológico de aguas residuales - Principios, modelación y diseño. IWA Press, London (2014)

Non-linear Behavior of the Distribution of Deformities in the Periodontal Ligament by Varying the Size of the Root: Finite Element Analysis

Luis Fernando Vargas Tamayo[1(✉)],
Leonardo Emiro Contreras Bravo[1(✉)],
and Ricardo Augusto Ríos Linares[2(✉)]

[1] Universidad Distrital Francisco José de Caldas, Bogotá, Colombia
{lufvargast,lecontrerasb}@udistrital.edu.co
[2] Universidad Libre, Bogotá, Colombia
ricardoa.riosl@unilibrebog.edu.co

Abstract. The objective of this study was to simulate through finite elements the deformation of the periodontal ligament of an upper right central incisor under the action of a 1 N load applied in two specific positions: The center of the clinical crown (CCC) and the center of the anatomical crown (CAC). For the periodontal ligament, a non-linear behavior was used to better recreate the deformities within the area, assuming it as a material with a hyperelastic behavior. Additionally, two crown-to-root ratios were used (1:1 and 1:1.5) to analyze the effect over the induced charge in the tooth root and its impact on the deformities of the periodontal ligament. In the cases where the load was applied in the CAC, fewer deformations were obtained than for the cases in which the load was applied in the CCC. In the scenarios with 1:1.5 ratios, the deformities were fewer than for the scenarios with 1:1 crown-to-root ratios.

Keywords: Crown-to-root ratio · Normal periodontal · Non-linear analysis
Periodontal ligament

1 Introduction

Orthodontics is a branch of odontology in charge of correcting the position of dental pieces through the application of loads via brackets, wires or elastic materials [1] in terms of the requirements and morphology of the patient.

In these types of treatments, shifting movements affect the teeth, the periodontal ligament and the bone that supports them [2], as well as the distribution of the efforts in these same elements which directly depend on the bracket's position. It is ultimately the bracket who applies the load on the tooth's crown. Two locations of the bracket were simulated: one in the center of the anatomic crown (CAC) and another one in the center of the clinical crown (CCC), so that the effect of the difference of the distances between the selected positions would be evidenced in the behavior of the periodontal ligament.

© Springer International Publishing AG, part of Springer Nature 2018
O. Gervasi et al. (Eds.): ICCSA 2018, LNCS 10963, pp. 625–634, 2018.
https://doi.org/10.1007/978-3-319-95171-3_49

The periodontal ligament is a tissue constituted by collagen fibers which has a hard-to-replicate orthotropic behavior recurring in some cases to mathematical models [3], and in other cases to experimental data obtained from mechanical trials in dental structures from corpses [4, 5] so it can be included in the simulations through finite elements by applying non-linear models. Several studies have been carried out regarding the behavior of this tissue, starting with linear [6–8], bilinear [9] and non-linear [10, 11] behaviors and non-linear analyses based on experimental data [4, 12–14] achieving results which are close to reality. Other studies have been made under different types of loads produced by internal media (tongue, contact between teeth) [15–17], or orthodontic loads [18, 19] due to the recreation of different setups.

Furthermore, the simulation through finite elements has become a widely used tool [9] to solve complex problems in several areas not only in Engineering but in fields such as odontology. Hence, orthodontic treatments can be recreated (movements, efforts and shifts) and even the behavior of the mechanical interactions between the bone and the implant and between the transepithelium – prosthesis, among others. In this study, the distribution of the efforts in the periodontal ligament was analyzed as well as its non-linear behavior for the four cases numbered as follows:

- Upper central incisor with 1:1 crown-to-root ratio, normal periodontal and bracket i CAC (Set 1)
- Upper central incisor with 1:1 crown-to-root ration, normal periodontal and bracket in CCC (Set 2)
- Upper central incisor with 1:1.5 crown-to-root ration, normal periodontal and bracket in CAC (Set 2)
- Upper central incisor with 1:1.5 crown-to-root ration, normal periodontal and bracket in CCC (Set 2)

For all the analyses, the applied load was equal to 1 N positioned in the bracket slot, perpendicularly to it in the direction of the tooth crown.

2   Materials and Methods

2.1   Geometric Reconstruction

Based on the patient's tomography, a reconstruction of the alveolar bone and the original incisor was made and then the tooth was modified to obtain an incisor with 1:1.5 crown-to-root ratio (Fig. 1a). The modeling of the ligament was achieved by building a surface in the common area between the tooth root and the alveolar bone which was given a thickness of 0.25 mm (Fig. 1b).

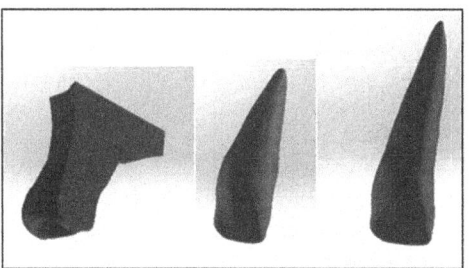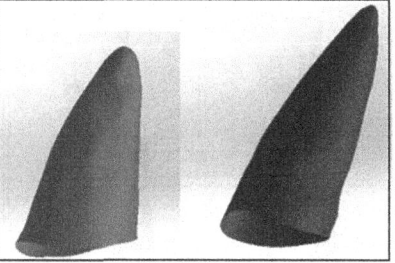

Fig. 1. (a) Examples of reconstructed geometries (from left to right): Alveolar bone, 1:1 tooth ratio and 1:1.5 tooth ratio. (b) Geometries of the periodontal ligaments for teeth with crown-to-root ratios: 1:1 on the left and 1:1.5 on the right.

Then, the bracket was drawn with the 2017 academic version of the SolidWorks software using pictures of it as a base for the definition of the contours of the most relevant details of the geometry (Fig. 2).

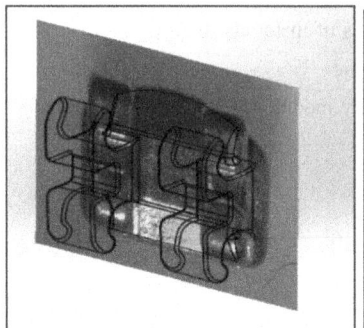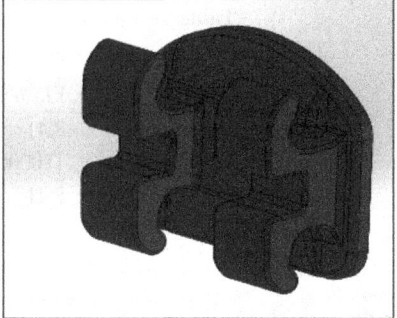

Fig. 2. Modeling process of the bracket: Base picture (left), Final geometry (Right).

Positioning the tooth and the bracket in separate files, the adhesive material's geometry is then obtained. The assembly of the different structures that were previously generated to obtain the complete sets for each simulation was carried out in SolidWorks 2017 with the two locations of the bracket (CCC and CAC) (Fig. 3a). To assure the correct position of the bracket in the anatomical and clinical crowns, their length of arc was measured to find their average distance and then locate the center of the bracket (Fig. 3b).

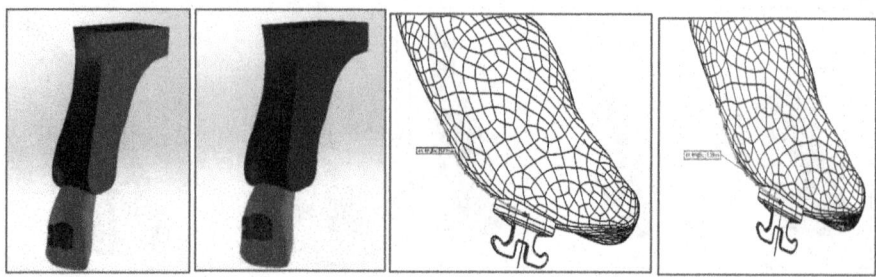

Fig. 3. (a) CCC (left) and CAC (right) model for the tooth with 1:1 ratio. (b) Arc length Anatomical: 5.89 mm (left) and Clinical: 6.39 mm (right)

2.2 Properties of the Materials

After importing the different models to the ANSYS WORKBENCH 18, it is proceeded to assign the materials to each structure drawn with the materials in the following Table 1.

Table 1. Linear properties of materials [6, 20]

Structure	Material	Properties	
		Elasticity module (MPa)	Poisson ratio
Enamel		8.41	0.33
Bracket	Titanium *	110000	0.3
Adhesive		8.41	0.33
Alveolar Bone		3.45×10^5	0.3

For the periodontal ligament, a non-linear behavior was defined according to the properties from the following Table 2.

Table 2. Non-linear properties of the periodontal ligament [12]

Effort (Mpa)	Unitary deformation (m/m)
0	0
0.0251	0.0008
0.0473	0.0021
0.0755	0.0051
0.1009	0.102
0.1266	0.197
0.1526	0.0374
0.1789	0.0706
0.1883	0.0882
0.2051	0.1309

These data were entered into the ANSYS assuming them as the result of a biaxial test of a hyperelastic material, so that its behavior could be recreated during the analysis. Figure 4 shows the curve that the ANSYS software developed from the previous data.

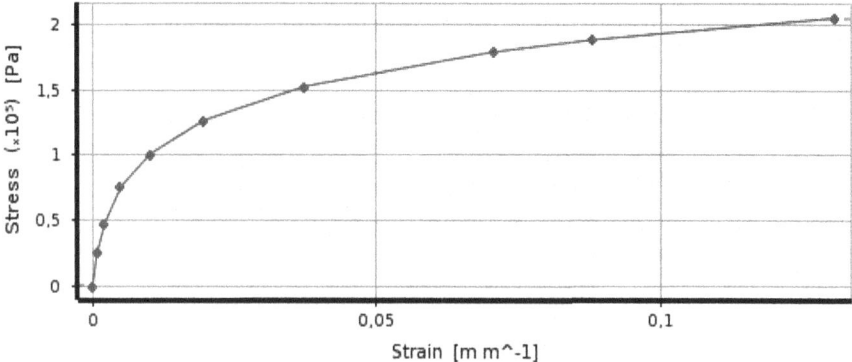

Fig. 4. Strain – Stress curve for Periodontal Ligament material properties

In this case, Ansys WorkBench assumes that the behavior of the material assigned to the Periodontal Ligament can be modeled as a set of linear sections with different slopes and not as a continuous curve, as a result of subjecting the material to a stretch in two coplanar directions, test which is used in biological tissues.

2.3 Definition of the Frontier Conditions

In all the study models, two restrictions were defined: one in the upper section and another one in the rear section of the bone (Fig. 5).

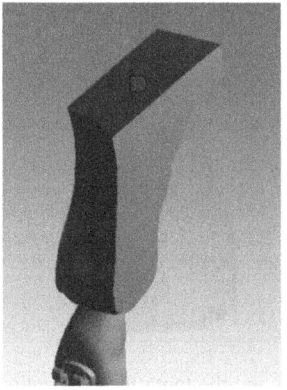 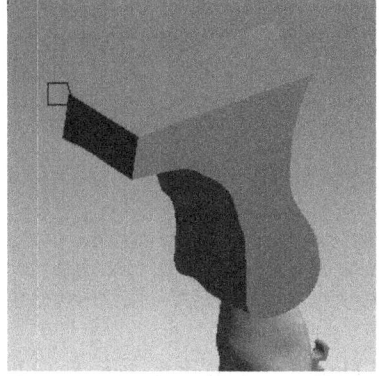

Fig. 5. Definition of the support models: Upper (left) and rear (right) sections of the bone.

The application of the load in the simulations was made by assuming a force of contact between the wire and the bracket slot with a value of 1 N applied perpendicularly to the slot. In Fig. 6, the ANSYS WorkBench program decomposes the force with respect to the global coordinate system since the set is inclined with the system due to the inclination of both the tooth and the bracket related to the assembly. It is noteworthy to mention that vectorial decomposition does not affect the simulation since the last load acting on the system is the resulting one with a magnitude of 1 N (Fig. 6).

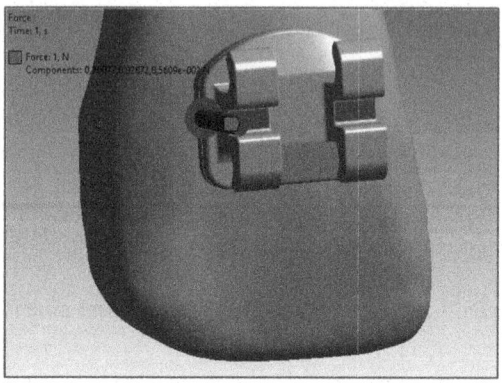

Fig. 6. Load applied to the models.

2.4   Finite Elements Analysis

For the finite elements analysis, it was proceeded to mesh each set, aiming at high refinement in the contact areas in order to reduce the numerical errors that can be induced by an inaccurate element size in such areas (Fig. 7).

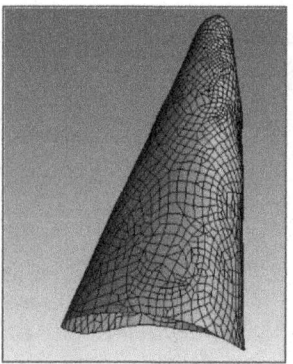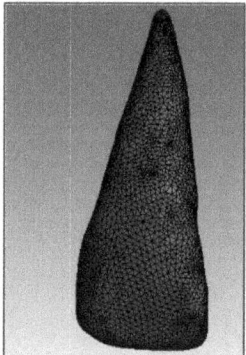

Fig. 7. Meshing of the periodontal ligament and the tooth for a 1:1 ratio

The data obtained from the meshing operation for all four simulated models was the following.

Table 3. Mesh density of the models

Model	Crown-to-root ratio	Position of the bracket	Number of elements	Number of nodes
1	1:1	CCA	460131	657219
2		CCC	460122	657126
3	1:1.5	CCA	456046	656733
4		CCC	455937	656496

As seen in Table 3, there are variations between the number of nodes and elements belonging to the mesh of the anatomical and clinical models for the same crown-to-root ratio due to the modification of the adhesive material's geometry. This can be explained by the fact that the change on the bracket's position changes the curvature of the tooth's surface hence affecting the adhesive material's thickness.

To include the behavior of the ligament in ANSYS WorkBench, the non-linear option was activated as well as the allowance of large deformities and 10 sub steps were defined for each analysis. Additionally, the contact areas between the constitutive elements of the models were defined as bonded in order to avoid any type of separation between the common surfaces during the problem solving task.

3 Results and Discussion

After the ANSYS WorkBench software solved each model in an approximate time of 12 h, the following results were obtained.

3.1 Models with 1:1 Crown-to-Root Ratio

When the bracket is placed in the center of the anatomical crown (CAC), the deformities for that model are fewer (7.92748×10^{-3} mm) than the ones obtained when the bracket is placed in the center of the clinical crown (8.10752×10^{-3} mm) as evidenced in Fig. 8. The difference in the results lies in the positioning of the bracket in the center of the anatomical crown as its distance to the resistance center is smaller than when it is placed in the CAC. Hence, the momentum linked to the applied force is reduced as well as the reaction of the root.

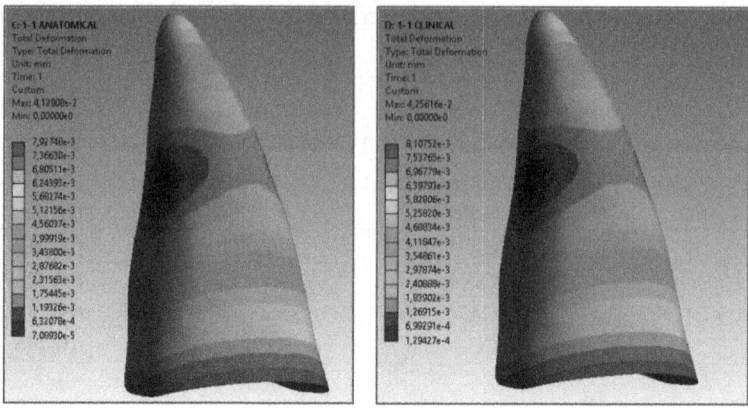

Fig. 8. Distribution of ligament deformities for CAC and CCC cases

3.2   Models with 1:1.5 Crown-to-Root Ratio

As for the 1:1 ratio model, the bracket placed in the center of the anatomical crown (CAC) has fewer deformities in the periodontal ligament (5.6605×10^{-6} mm) than the ones obtained when the bracket is located in the center of the clinical crown (5.7757×10^{-6} mm) as seen in Fig. 9. The effect of the bracket's position on the crown is once again confirmed in the results obtained. Furthermore, the deformities were smaller in the 1:1.5 ratio than in the previous scenario since a longer root canal reduces the force induced on it. Hence, the deformities in the ligament are reduced.

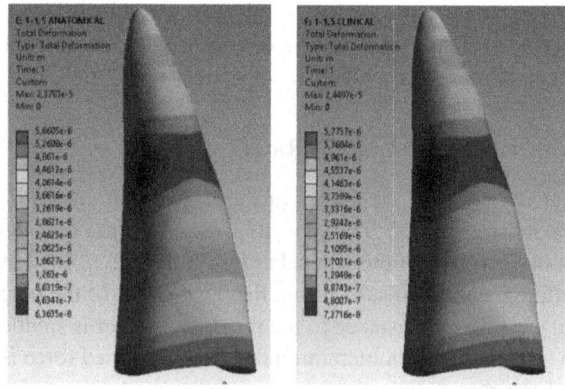

Fig. 9. Distribution of ligament deformities for CAC and CCC cases

After comparing the behavior of the deformities of the periodontal ligament (Fig. 10) for all four cases, it is clear that the values obtained for the location of the bracket in the center of the anatomical crown are smaller than in the CCC case. Additionally, a larger crown-to-root ratio reduces deformities.

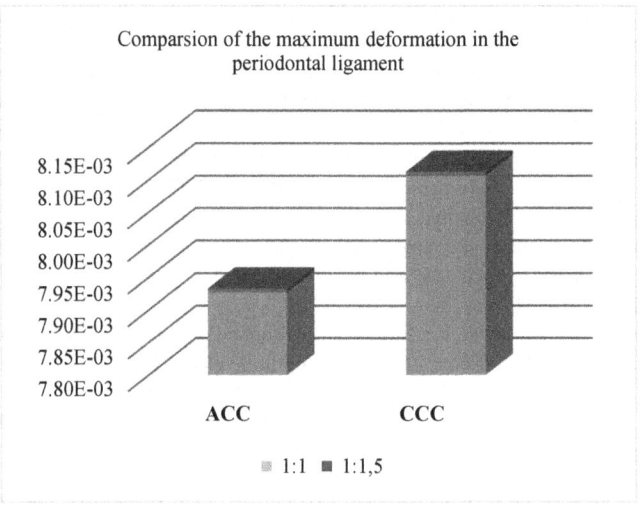

Fig. 10. Comparison between the periodontal ligament deformities in the analyzed cases

4   Conclusions

Deformities in the periodontal ligament with non-linear behavior were assessed in both load cases (CCC and CAC) with a 1 N force and crown-to-root ratios (1:1 and 1:1.5) for a total of four scenarios simulated with finite element analysis in the upper right central incisor.

In general, the crown-to-root ratio was deformities in the periodontal ligament were smaller when the bracket was placed in the center of the anatomical crown (for ratio $1:1 \rightarrow 7.92748 \times 10^{-3}$ mm and for ratio $1:1.5 \rightarrow 5.6605 \times 10^{-6}$ mm). This was caused by a smaller distance between the point of the force's application and the center of resistance which is normally found between the first third and half of the root canal.

Finally, comparing the deformities in the periodontal ligament of the model with 1:1 and 1:1.5 ratios revealed that the deformities were smaller in the latter by a 103 factor due to the increase of the root's length and the shifting of the center of resistance.

References

1. Andersen, K.L.: Determination of stress levels and profiles in the periodontal ligament by means of an improved three-dimensional finite element model for various types of orthodontic and natural force systems. J. Biomed. Eng. **13**(4), 293–303 (1991)
2. Cai, Y.: Finite element method analysis of the periodontal ligament in mandibular canine movement with transparent tooth correction treatment. BMC Oral Health **15**, 106 (2015)
3. Zhurov, A.: A constitutive model for the periodontal ligament as a compressible transversely isotropic visco-hyperelastic tissue. Comput. Methods Biomech. Biomed. Eng. **10**, 223–225 (2007)

4. Toms, S.R.: Nonlinear stress-strain behavior of periodontal ligament under orthodontic loading. Am. J. Orthod. Dentofac. Orthop. **122**(2), 174–179 (2002)
5. Zhao, Z.: The adaptive response of periodontal ligament to orthodontic force loading - a combined biomechanical and biological study. Clin. Biomech. (Bristol, Avon) **Suppl 1**, S59–S66 (2008)
6. Hemanth, M.: Stress induced in the periodontal ligament under orthodontic loading (part I): a finite element method study using linear analysis. J. Int. Oral Health **7**, 129–133 (2015)
7. Hemanth, M., et al.: An analysis of the stress induced in the periodontal ligament during extrusion and rotation movements: a finite element method linear study part I. J. Contemp. Dent. Pract. **16**(9), 740–743 (2015). https://doi.org/10.5005/jp-journals-10024-1750
8. Fongsamootr, T., Suttakul, P.: Effect of periodontal ligament on stress distribution and displacement of tooth and bone structure using finite element simulation. Eng. J. **19**(2), 99–108 (2015)
9. Cossetin, E., Nóbrega, S.H.S.d., Carvalho, M.G.F.d.: Study of tension in the periodontal ligament using the finite elements method. Dent. Press J. Orthod. **17**, 47–49 (2012)
10. Tuna, M., Sunbuloglu, E., Bozdag, E.: Finite element simulation of the behavior of the periodontal ligament: a validated nonlinear contact model. J. Biomech. **47**(12), 2883–2890 (2014)
11. Qian, L., et al.: Deformation analysis of the periodontium considering the viscoelasticity of the periodontal ligament. Dent. Mater. **25**(10), 1285–1292 (2009)
12. Hemanth, M., et al.: Stress induced in periodontal ligament under orthodontic loading (part II): a comparison of linear versus non-linear fem study. J. Int. Oral Health JIOH **9**, 114–118 (2015)
13. Hemanth, M., et al.: An analysis of the stress induced in the periodontal ligament during extrusion and rotation movements- part ii: a comparison of linear vs nonlinear FEM study. J. Contemp. Dent. Pract. **16**, 819–823 (2015)
14. Van Schepdael, A., Geris, L., Vander Sloten, J.: Analytical determination of stress patterns in the periodontal ligament during orthodontic tooth movement. Med. Eng. Phys. **35**(3), 403–410 (2013)
15. Lombardo, L., et al.: Three-dimensional finite-element analysis of a central lower incisor under labial and lingual loads. Prog. Orthod. **13**(2), 154–163 (2012)
16. Poiate, I.A.V.P., et al.: Three-dimensional stress distribution in the human periodontal ligament in masticatory, parafunctional, and trauma loads: finite element analysis. J. Periodontol. **80**(11), 1859–1867 (2009)
17. Weijun, Y., et al.: Stress distribution in the mandibular central incisor and periodontal ligament while opening the bite: a finite element analysis. Biomed. Res. **23**, 343–348 (2012)
18. McGuinness, N.J.P., et al.: A stress analysis of the periodontal ligament under various orthodontic loadings. Eur. J. Orthod. **13**, 231–242 (2013)
19. Wilson, A.N., et al.: The finite element analysis of stress in the periodontal ligament when subject to vertical orthodontic forces. Br. J. Orthod. **21**, 161–167 (1994)
20. Elsaka, S.E., Hammad, S.M., Ibrahim, N.F.: Evaluation of stresses developed in different bracket-cement-enamel systems using finite element analysis with in vitro bond strength tests. Prog. Orthod. **15**(1), 33 (2014)

Formal Modeling of the Key Determinants of Hepatitis C Virus (HCV) Induced Adaptive Immune Response Network: An Integrative Approach to Map the Cellular and Cytokine-Mediated Host Immune Regulations

Ayesha Obaid[1], Anam Naz[1], Shifa Tariq Ashraf[1],
Faryal Mehwish Awan[1], Aqsa Ikram[1], Muhammad Tariq Saeed[2],
Abida Raza[3], Jamil Ahmad[2], and Amjad Ali[1(✉)]

[1] Atta-ur-Rahman School of Applied Biosciences (ASAB),
National University of Sciences and Technology (NUST),
Islamabad 44,000, Pakistan
`amjaduni@gmail.com, amjad.ali@asab.nust.edu.pk`
[2] Research Center for Modeling and Simulation (RCMS),
National University of Sciences and Technology (NUST), Islamabad, Pakistan
[3] National Institute of Lasers and Optronics (NILOP), Islamabad, Pakistan

Abstract. HCV is a major causative agent of liver infection and is the leading cause of Hepatocellular carcinoma (HCC). To understand the complexity in interactions within the HCV induced immune signaling networks, a logic-based diagram is generated based on multiple reported interactions. A simple conceptual framework is presented to explore the key determinants of the immune system and their functions during HCV infection. Furthermore, an abstracted sub-network is modeled qualitatively which consists of both the key cellular and cytokine components of the HCV induced immune system. In the presence of NS5A protein of HCV, the behaviors and the interplay amongst the natural killer (NK) and T regulatory (Tregs) cells along with cytokines such as IFN-γ, IL-10, IL-12 are predicted. The overall modelling approach followed in this study comprises of prior knowledge-based logical interaction network, network abstraction, parameter estimation, regulatory network construction and analysis through state graph, enabling the prediction of paths leading to both, disease state and a homeostatic path/cycle predicted based on maximum betweenness centrality. To study the continuous dynamics of the network, Petri net (PN) model was generated. The analysis implicates the critical role of IFN-γ producing NK cells in recovery while, the role of IL-10 and IL-12 in pathogenesis. The predictive ability of the model implicates that IL-12 has a dual role under varying circumstances and leads to varying disease outcomes. This model attempts to reduce the noisy biological data and captures a holistic view of the key determinants of the HCV induced immune response.

Keywords: HCV · System biology · Biological regulatory network of HCV
HCV petri net · IL-10 · IL-12

© Springer International Publishing AG, part of Springer Nature 2018
O. Gervasi et al. (Eds.): ICCSA 2018, LNCS 10963, pp. 635–649, 2018.
https://doi.org/10.1007/978-3-319-95171-3_50

1 Introduction

Hepatitis C Virus (HCV) is the major cause of hepatitis C disease leading to 0.35 million deaths every year [1]. The existing treatment by PEGylated interferon-alpha and ribavirin (PegIFN-α/RBV) deliver inadequate efficacy in clearance of viremia and are poorly tolerated by patients. Direct acting antivirals (DAAs) have proved effective in certain cases however drug resistance and therapeutic failure still pose a challenge to biologists [2]. A well-defined antiviral and immunomodulatory therapy is need of the hour to restore HCV-specific immune response in order to clear the virus effectively from the host. The complex interconnected signaling and regulatory pathways are difficult to analyze as a single system via conventional mathematical approaches such as ordinary differential equations (ODEs) [3]. ODEs require details of the kinetics of each reaction which are difficult to obtain. Thus, the analysis of abstracted biological regulatory sub-networks within the complex pathway and formerly studying them via Biological Regulatory Network (BRN) modeling and analysis approaches pose a better alternative. A well-known mathematical formalism of René Thomas [4] was applied to formulate the HCV induced immune response BRN, which uses graph theory to explore the evolution of states/genes within the modeled system. Qualitative modeling such as BRN analysis is suitable enough for performing model checking based reasoning to estimate and then apply unknown parameters of the entities in the BRN [3]. The HCV induced immune signaling pathway is activated through the HCV particle entering the hepatocytes and releasing its RNA [5]. Figure 1 represents the illustration of the pathways involved in immune clearance of the infection. The linear genomic RNA molecule of HCV contains a single open reading frame (ORF), which encodes for a precursor polyprotein of ∼3 k amino acid residues [6]. The virus replicates by cleaving the polyprotein of HCV in three structural proteins (core, E1, E2), also seven non-structural proteins (p7, NS2, NS3, NS4A, NS4B, NS5A, NS5B) [7]. HCV structural proteins constitute critical constituents of HCV virions, while HCV non-structural proteins are involved in the RNA replication and virion morphogenesis [6]. Amongst non-structural proteins, NS5A (56–58 kDa) is a phosphorylated, zinc-metalloprotein which has a significant role during virus replication and cellular pathways regulation [8]. In response to viral infection, host immune response is activated (Fig. 1). Dendritic Cells (DCs) and NK cells residing in the liver are triggered for the release of pro-inflammatory cytokines including but not limited to IFN-γ and IL-12 which play a critical role in eliminating the virus either directly or by indirect activation of supporter immune function. Thus, NK cells start an early host defense against viral pathogens [9]. They are a major source of interferon gamma (IFN-γ) which inhibits viral replication without destroying liver cells. As a result, CD4+ and CD8+ T-cells are activated which act by destroying cells catalytically and non-catalytically [9] by the secretion of antiviral cytokines IFN-γ and TNF-α [5, 10]. Diverse kinds of Tregs cells are known to be involved in HCV immunology [11]. Tregs are involved in the inhibition of HCV-specific T-cells during acute infection, which contributes in T-cell failure and leads to chronic infection, also it protects from related tissue injury during HCV chronic infection [9]. On the other hand, several mechanisms in relation to HCV-specific defects in immunity have been proposed in previous studies [5]. HCV proteins directly or indirectly inhibit host cellular responses via various signaling pathways. Amongst them, failure to sustain rigorous and effective immune response include (i) lack of CD4+ T-cell help, (ii) constant antigen triggering, (iii) Tregs action (iv) reduced potential of cytotoxic T-cells, (v) reduced secretion of Th1-type cytokines (v) a reduced proliferative capacity in response to ex vivo antigenic stimulation [10].

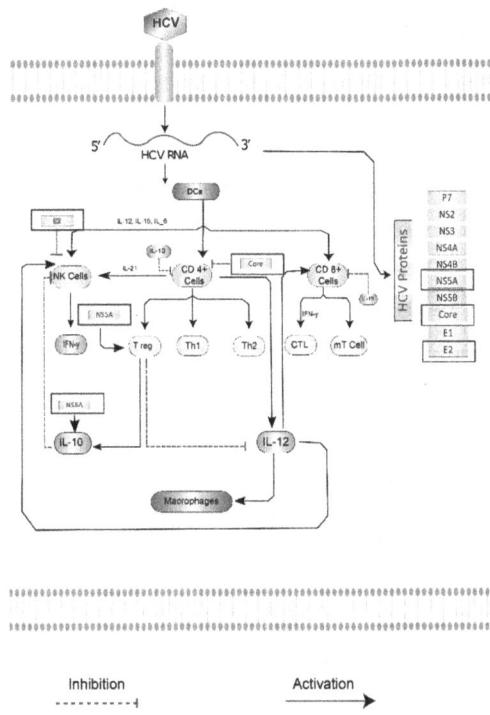

Fig. 1. Prior knowledge-based logical interaction network of Hepatitis C Virus (HCV) induced immune response.

The study was focused on the main antagonist cytokine players involved in the cellular immune response i.e. IL-10 and IL-12. These cytokines are responsible to mediate the signaling and functional activity of Tregs and NK cells. IL-10 has been implicated as a cytokine responsible for the failure of immune response to clear infection [12]. HCV, in turn also augments IL-10, and inhibits NK cells and IL-12 which results in the activation of Tregs [13–17]. IL-10 is considered to be an anti-inflammatory as well as an immunomodulatory cytokine [15]. Once infection occurs, IL-10 inhibits NK cells, Th1 cells, macrophages and the activity of pro-inflammatory cytokines (including IL-12 and TNF-α) [12]. As a result, IL-10 can hinder pathogen clearance as well as limit the damage caused by immunopathology. A critical balance between both pro-inflammatory and anti-inflammatory response determines the outcome of infection. Also, it is worth mentioning that, it is not necessary that maximum pathogen control or clearance will ensure disease recovery because a higher inflammatory response may lead to greater tissue damage.

It is known that the side effects and complications during infection are the consequence of superfluous immune activation leading to tissue injury. IL-12, on the other hand, is known to be a pro-inflammatory cytokine which activates CD4+ and CD8+ T cells, promoting infection clearance. It also stimulates the cytotoxic function of NK cells and T-cells by stimulating the release of IFN-γ [11, 14, 18]. IL-12 restricts the function of Tregs thus inducing viral clearance [11]. To characterize the behaviors of NK cells and Tregs under the influence of IL-10 and IL-12 during the presence of HCV infection, a BRN was constructed and analyzed.

2 Methods

The methodology followed for the construction of BRN and analysis has been represented in Fig. 2.

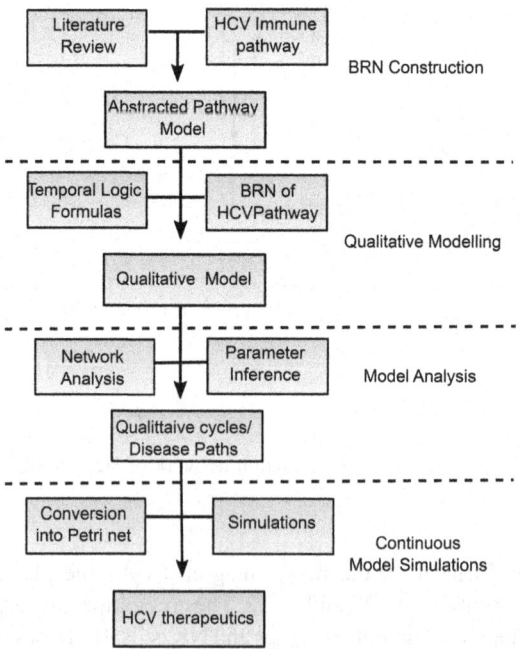

Fig. 2. Workflow of the methodology adopted in the current study.

2.1 Abstraction of the Prior Knowledge Based Interaction Network

To characterize the cytokines mediated HCV clearance and the role of NK cells in the viral clearance, the prior knowledge based logical diagram (Fig. 1) is reduced to form a BRN. However, constructing a BRN for a large set of entities, with an increased number of nodes, renders a very large state graph and suffers from state space explosion. Also, one of the limitations of BRN formalism is that once the number of entities increases roughly from seven, it becomes challenging to assign parameters and hence the interpretation of state graph [19]. Thus, the complex signaling network from literature (Fig. 1) was abstracted since, if an entity (enzymes, cytokines, etc.) activates/deactivates a downstream process via several intermediate entities, the network can be reduced by omitting intermediate entities to show the final effect of the activation or inhibition on that particular entity being studied. This method allows us to model the complex biological networks using BRN analysis tools while preserving the core functions of signaling network. This kind of abstraction has been explained in detail by Naldi *et al.* and Saadatpour *et al.* [20, 21].

2.2   Qualitative Framework for Modeling the Hepatitis C Virus (HCV) Induced Immune Regulations and Construction of Network

To simplify the analysis of biological behaviors and construction of the BRN models, the Rene' Thomas formalism is best alternative as it does not require quantitative data such as the exact concentrations and kinetic reaction rates, [8]. Qualitative model assembly involves only the qualitative thresholds and associated logical parameters [3, 4, 20]. The qualitative thresholds are adjusted per the literature findings and the logical parameters are computed by computational tree logic (CTL) using SMBioNet tool [22]. The generated parameters are then used to interpret the BRN into a qualitative model. In CTL, experimental observations from the literature are programmed in the form of formulas by means of a set of quantifiers that describe conditions to discover various states or paths initiating from a starting state. The detailed semantics of the kinetic logic formalism [8] and the formal definitions have already been discussed in the studies of Ahmad *et al.* and Saeed *et al.* [3, 23]. The detailed semantics of the quantifiers can be found in Ahmad *et al.* [3].

2.3   Hepatitis C Virus (HCV) Induced BRN Construction and Analysis

The BRN of the abstracted biological pathway is constructed using GINsim and GENOTECH tools [24, 25]. BRN consists of nodes, representatives of the biological entities, while the directed arcs amongst them show the interactions amongst them. There are two types of interactions/connections. Activating connection is represented by a solid line and +1 integer, while the negative connection is represented by −1 integer. Each of the entity in the modeled BRN is allocated a set of logical parameters (generated via SMBioNet) which generates a state graph (the qualitative model) depicting the likely steady state and cyclic behaviors of the BRN. The state graph is generated via GENOTECH and GINsim tools [24, 25] to identify various paths leading to the diseased/deadlock state or the homeostatic state. The imperative paths involved in disease progression and the recovery are identified by the analysis of the network and related state graph.

2.4   Petri Net Model of the Hepatitis C Virus (HCV)-Induced Regulatory Network

The biological pathways are continuous in nature, thus, to study the network dynamics, generated BRN is converted to a PN. It allows the study various biological behaviors in a continuous manner. GINsim [25] lets the export of BRN into a PN format to be studied via SNOOPY tool [26]. A PN is a directed bipartite graph in which places (represented by circles) and transitions (represented by squares) represent entities of a pathway and the processes in between them respectively. Furthermore, the places and transition are connected via directed arcs to allow the flow of tokens in the modeled pathway. The transition firings can influence the number of tokens assigned to the target place through the source, referred to as the *token-count*. This kind of modeling enables the flow of signals via directed protein interactions in a cellular pathway. The "simulation run" property of PN allows the study of continuous dynamics of the proteins/genes involved in the signaling pathway. The detailed methodology is discussed in Obaid et al. [27].

3   Results and Discussion

3.1   Abstraction of the Prior Knowledge Based Interaction Network and then Analysis of the Abstracted Model

The reduced BRN is shown in Fig. 3, while it is abridged to allow for easy interpretation and study of the state graph, however, the essence of the interactions and their functions are preserved in the reduced pathway network.

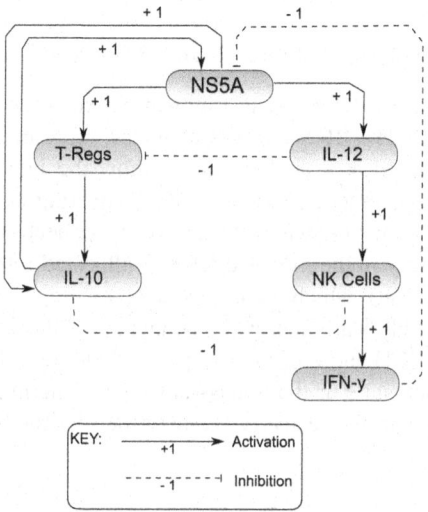

Fig. 3. Biological Regulatory Network (BRN) depicting HCV mediated immune regulation: There are six nodes representing T-regulatory cells (Tregs), IL-10, NS5A (HCV non-structural protein 5 A), IL-12, IFN-γ, NK cells. The integers −1 and +1 are used with the directed arcs to show activation (+1 with a straight line) and inhibition (−1with dashed line) mediated by the viral and host cellular components.

The reduced network was then employed to model the BRN. There are six nodes representing T-regulatory cells (Tregs), IL-10, NS5A (HCV non-structural protein 5 A), IL-12, IFN-γ, NK cells. The integers -1 and $+1$ are used with the directed arcs to show activation ($+1$ with a straight line) and inhibition (-1 with dashed line) mediated by the viral and host cellular components. NS5A is a multifunctional protein which is a part of HCV replication complex. It also exerts its effect on host cellular pathways via protein-protein interactions and effects host immune response. That is why it is a highly important protein for HCV replication and poses a very important therapeutic target.

3.2 Hepatitis C Virus (HCV) Regulatory Network Constructed with Estimated Parameters Based on Biological Observation

The parameters for the construction of a regulatory network are estimated such that they can ensure the interactions amongst the BRN entities according to the experimental observations. It maintains the interdependencies of contributing entities on each other (activation or deactivation). To estimate all the plausible combination of parameters

Table 1. Related **biological observations and the corresponding CTL Formula:** The experimental observations are converted into temporal logic formulas. The CTL formula is constructed using state quantifiers (X, F, G), path quantifiers (E, A) and implication ($\rightarrow$). The first part of implication shows a sufficient condition or a cause of the second part on the right side (effect). The formula further contains temporal operator F and G representing the Future and Global (all the time). Moreover, CTL operator A represents all the possible behaviors (dynamics or trajectories). Now the CTL formula represents that in the future of all behaviors, a state always exists where NS5A, Tregs, and IL10 are expressed (at qualitative level 1) and NK cells and IFN-γ are not expressed (at qualitative level 0). Furthermore, this state is caused by the qualitative state (NS5A=0&Treg=0&IFNy=1&NKCells=1&IL10=0)

	Biological Observations	References	CTL formula
1	NS5A inhibits NK cells function via inducing imbalance in inflammatory cytokines	[13, 28]	(NS5A=0&Treg=0&IFNy=1&NKCells=1&IL10=0)$\rightarrow$ AF(AG(NS5A=1&Treg=1&IL10=1&NKCells=0&IFNy=0))
2	NK cells produce IFN-γ which in turn inhibits HCV production	[29]	
3	Tregs modulates the immune system by decreasing it intensity thus indirectly augmenting HCV production	[30, 31]	
4	HCV augments the activation of IL-10	[32]	
5	IL-10 inhibits IL-12	[14]	

which satisfies the CTL formula based on the biological observations, SMBioNet [22] is used (explained in the Methods section). Table 1 represents the encoded CTL formula and the related biological observations from the literature.

The encoded CTL depicts these observations during inhibition of HCV infection i.e. NS5A = 0, during which the host poses an effective inflammatory response. The expression of Tregs is also downregulated (Treg = 0) during effective clearance of infection by increasing the inflammatory response. IFNγ = 1, depicting the ample expression of IFNγ by NK cells and IL-10 = 0. This CTL was used by SMBioNet and based on which it generated six sets of parameters, each set representing a specific model. Each of the generated parameters set was then further subjected to analysis in the GENOTECH tool [24] so that a state graph can be generated. Each of the state graphs was intensely studied for cycles, diseased state, and recovery/homeostatic conditions. Out of six, one model was selected whose state graph correctly represented and conformed to the biological observations from literature. The selected parameters are presented in Table 2. The BRN generated using the selected set of parameters in GENOTECH as well as GINsim tool was used [25] to check for any ambiguity, and a state graph was generated for further analysis.

Table 2. Selection of logical parameters generated via SMBioNet

Parameter	Resources	Range of values	Selected parameters
K_{Treg}	{}	0	0
K_{Treg}	{NS5A}	0, 1	1
K_{Treg}	{IL-12, NS5A}	0, 1	1
K_{IL10}	{}	0	0
K_{IL10}	{NS5A}	0, 1	1
K_{IL10}	{Treg}	0, 1	1
K_{IL10}	{NS5A, Treg}	0, 1	1
K_{NS5A}	{}	0	0
K_{NS5A}	{IFNy}	1	1
K_{IL12}	{}	0	0
K_{IL12}	{NS5A}	1	1
K_{IFNy}	{}	0	0
K_{IFNy}	{NK Cells}	1	1
$K_{NK\ Cells}$	{}	0	0
$K_{NK\ Cells}$	{IL-12}	0, 1	1
$K_{NK\ Cells}$	{IL-10}	0, 1	0
$K_{NK\ Cells}$	{IL-12, IL-10}	0, 1	0

3.3 Analysis of the State Graph for Identification of Pathophysiological Paths, Cycles, and Homeostasis

The state graph signifies all probable transitions from one state to another, and each state displays the relative expression of each entity at a specific point in time. The sequence of entities in any given state is "Tregs, IL-10, NS5A, IL10, IFN-γ, NK cells".

"1" represents the upregulation of an entity and "0" represents the downregulation of an entity in the same sequence stated above. As all states in a state graph progress asynchronously, thus, in every successor state, level of only one entity can change its level at a time. The state graph was analyzed for those states showing important biological behaviors, in terms of either disease progression or recovery. The state "001010" marks the initiation of HCV infection. Thus "Tregs = 0, IL-10 = 0, NS5A = 1, IL-12 = 0, IFN-γ = 1, NK cells = 0" constitutes an initial state of the disease progression in the system. It depicts that as soon as HCV infects the cells it immediately starts the production of its proteins (NS5A) via efficient translation of its viral genome at the endoplasmic reticulum [7]. Further analysis revealed that the system can lead to either a diseased state "111100" (represented by red color in the graph) or a reset state "000000". The disease or stable state is an irreversible state and called a deadlock. In the state graph, it is presented by "Tregs = 1, IL-10 = 1, NS5A = 1, IL-12 = 1, IFN-γ = 0, NK cells = 0". The chronic activation of Tregs, IL-10, NS5A (HCV), and IL-12 and downregulation/deactivation of NK cells and IFN-γ will lead to chronic infection from which reversal is only possible through intervention by various kinds of treatments to block the intermediate paths prior to reaching this state [7, 14, 30, 32]. On the other hand, such state is also identified in the graph "000000" also known as reset or recovery state exhibited by "Tregs = 0, IL-10 = 0, NS5A = 0, IL-12 = 0, IFN-γ = 0, NK cells = 0" which is characterized by low titers of HCV proteins in the system and is part of homeostasis cycle. The state graph with the presence of two types of behaviors (Homeostasis/deadlock) in the same state graph shows that the host immune system can either work efficiently to stabilize the biological system or move towards such a pathogenic state from which no further state is possible. The analysis of the state graph revealed the most probable and biologically plausible paths which lead towards a stable state (111100) and shown in red (Fig. 4). The shortest but biologically correct diseased path from the initial state "001001" comes out to be, "001001, 001000, 001010, 101010, 101000, 111000, 1111000". While several other downstream bifurcation paths also arise and shown in Fig. 4 which leads to a stable state. It is worth noting that majority of the states in the disease pathway are having an activated NS5A and deactivated NK cells in high proportions. This demonstrates that either the system remains in the cycle by overcoming the infection or moves towards diseased state when the host immune system is overwhelmed by viral proteins. One very interesting observation pertains to the expression of IL-12 and its role in the pathogenesis. The upregulation of IL-12 in a diseased state is an interesting prediction of the model. Classically, IL-12 is known to be an activator of CD4+ and CD8+ T cells, NK cells, and macrophages and negative regulator of Tregs [33]. It has been shown that IL-12 leads the system towards clearance of infection by promoting the differentiation of naïve T-cells [33, 34]. However, the prediction of upregulated IL-12 in pathogenesis by our model implicates that IL-12 is differentially regulated in chronic infection. It conforms to the earlier observation by Pockros et al. 2003 and other groups have shown in a small pilot study that despite the pro-cytolytic function of IL-12, IL-12 monotherapy is not useful against chronic HCV [18, 35]. It follows the same pattern in our model as well depicting strong induction in the disease state. It warrants for further studies to decipher the exact mechanism by which IL-12 may lead the system towards the pathogenic state. A study by

Orange et al. 1994 on LCMV reported that IL-12 can affect the infection both ways. Either it works towards eliminating the viral infection or detrimental to the host depending primarily on the induced environment ant and intracellular stimuli it receives. The exact mechanism and the circumstances involved also needs to be studied further to study whether it can be a therapeutic target for HCV.

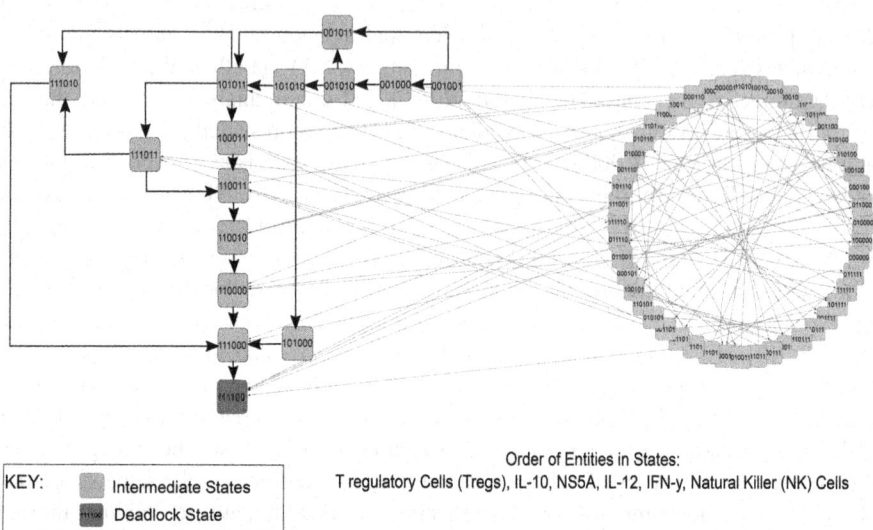

Order of Entities in States:
T regulatory Cells (Tregs), IL-10, NS5A, IL-12, IFN-y, Natural Killer (NK) Cells

KEY: Intermediate States
        Deadlock State

Fig. 4. The disease paths leading to a pathogenic deadlock state singled out from the state space: The main diseased paths including the shortest route to a stable state from the initial state has been isolated and represented in pink color leading to a stable state in red color. The alternate trajectories have also been highlighted which shows that there are multiple routes to a diseased state. (Color figure online)

3.4 Prediction of Cycles Based on Maximum Betweenness Centrality Leading to Homeostasis

The host immune systems' main players such as IFN-γ and NK cells move the system towards maintaining immune homeostasis. We are interested in that cycle which follows a well-ordered, efficient pattern/path and keeps the system in homeostatic condition. Since the model shows cycles of varying lengths, therefore, it is important to identify the most plausible biological cycle(s). Hence, we employed "betweenness centrality" computed by Cytoscape tool [36] that is able to sort all of the states in the graph on the basis of their maximum betweenness centralities. Betweenness centrality has wide application in the graph theory based analysis as it highlights those nodes which are central to the state graph/diagram. It calculates those nodes that lie in the shortest paths maximum number of times. The most probable cycle has been singled out in Fig. 5.

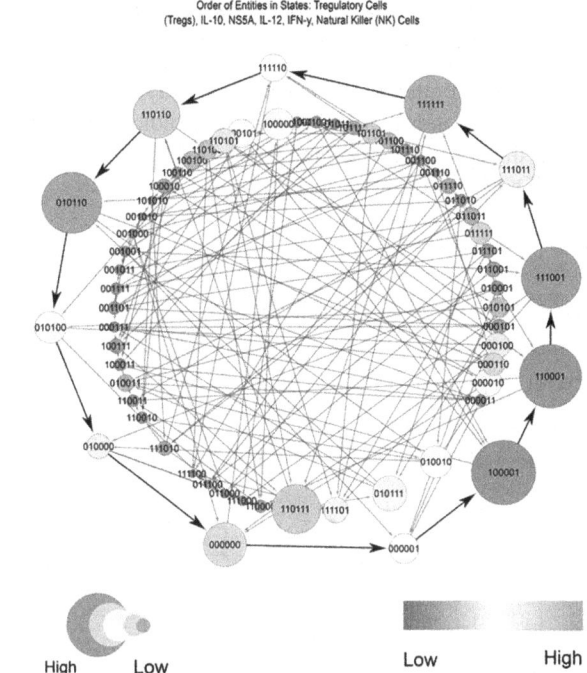

Fig. 5. State graph of Hepatitis C Virus (HCV) mediated immune response based on betweenness centrality: The size and color of the nodes have been scaled according to betweenness centrality using Cytoscape tool [36]. The most probable recovery cycle has been singled out for analysis.

The cycle "000000, 000001, 100001, 110001, 111001, 111011, 111111, 111110, 110110, 010110, 010100, 010000, 000000" shows the sequence of events occurring in the cyclic path. The host immune system works competently to protect it from going into a pathogenic state, as a result, the system remains in a cyclic behavior. As this cycle has maximum betweenness centrality it represents that all other paths must pass through this cycle serving as a bridge for all other nodes in the state space. The intrahepatic activation of NK cells via immune-related cytokines occurs through dendritic cells [37]. NK cells lie at the junction of innate and adaptive immunity and exert its function by releasing IFN-γ in the hepatocytes. IFN-γ act as a main mediator of the host adaptive immunity by activating CD4+ and CD8+ cellular responses [38]. IFN-γ also acts to nullify the effects of IL-10 [17]. The IL-10 cytokine is an immune modulatory cytokine, which dampens the inflammatory responses to protect host tissue, as a result, helping HCV infection and virus proliferation [15]. IL-12 helps to tip the balance of immune response towards clearance of infection by inhibiting the effects of Tregs [11, 14]. Tregs also act as immunomodulators thus it is necessary to attenuate their function to overcome the infection (HCV). Enhanced IFN-γ activation is the indicator of robust immune response along with the downregulation of IL-10.

3.5 Petri Net (PN) Model for Continuous Dynamic Analysis of the Hepatitis C Virus (HCV) Induced Immune Regulation

The BRN in GINsim was exported to PN format for the dynamic analysis of properties and holistic behavior of proteins of the model. As biological systems behavior is continuous in nature, the generated discrete PN was further exported into a continuous PN format using SNOOPY tool shown in Fig. 6.

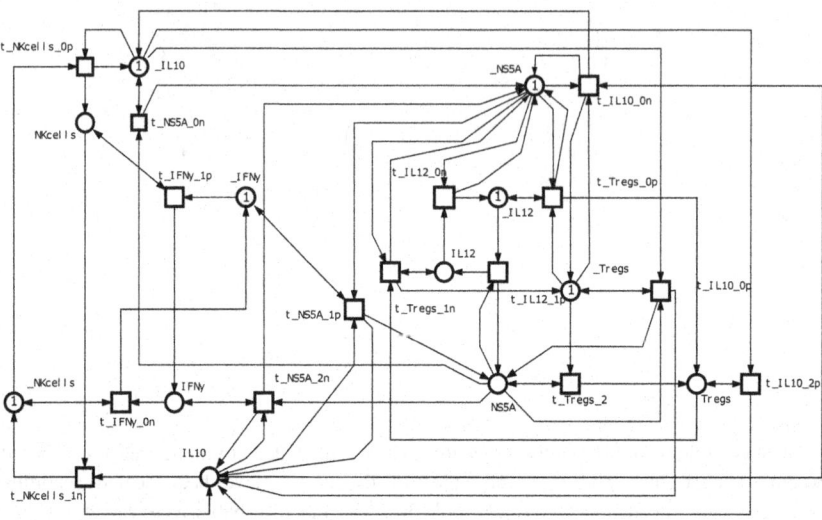

Fig. 6. Illustration of the continuous Petri net (PN): A place is depicted by a circle representing cellular enzymes, receptor complexes, and various proteins. A continuous transition is shown as a box, representative of all cellular processes. A directed arc connects a place with a transition and vice versa. Weights of the arcs are equal to 1 unless mentioned otherwise. "_" represents deactivated state of an entity. "P" presents positive regulation, "n" represents negative regulation. The number of transitions represents the number and type of regulation in the BRN provided.

The converted PN consists of two types of places for each entity of the network. One prime place (representing activated state) and another complementary state (representing deactivated state). Similarly, their associated transitions have been labeled "p" and "n" to differentiate among activating signal and deactivating signal. The biological proteins have different activation status during an infection. Therefore, it is necessary to include the deactivated places for the proteins to cater for the intracellular inhibiting signals being received. Also, the transitions created by GINsim represent each SMBioNet generated parameter exclusively which helps in the analysis of the dynamics of the modeled BRN. It has been discussed previously that the network connectivity is a single most determinant factor for signal propagation in the signaling pathway [39, 40]. The specific kinetic parameters for each reaction is difficult to obtain thus we rely on the structure of PN only. The reason behind such assumption is that the biological signaling pathways have evolved to such an extent that the connectivity of the network has a stabilizing effect on the proteins and other related interactions of the system. The generated PN is simulated with Mass action kinetics (1) for all the transitions and the markings in the places represent the presence of tokens. The simulation property of the PN was used to study the evolution of proteins and their relative changes with time. The simulation results are shown in Fig. 7A truthfully represents the stable state "111100" of the state graph in which the levels of NK cells and IFN-γ are downregulated as compared to Tregs, IL-10, NS5A, and IL-12. On the other hand, Fig. 7B shows the recovery of the NK cells and IFN-γ leading to downregulation of HCV NS5A and associated factors. It emphasizes the role of NK cells in clearance of infection.

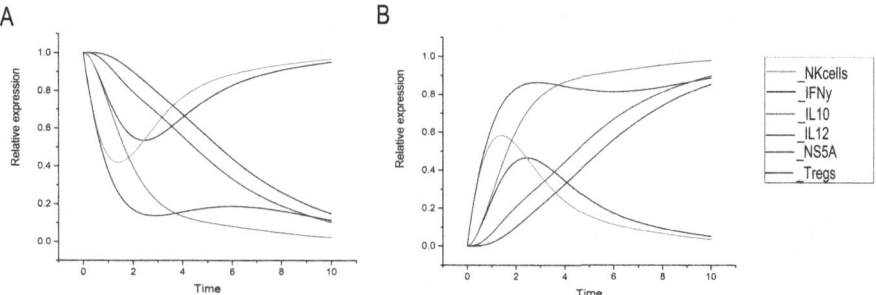

Fig. 7. Petri net (PN) analysis through simulation runs: x-axis shows time units while the y-axis represents relative activity change of the entities. A shows the diseased state where NK cells (Pink line) and IFN-γ (black line) are downregulated. B represents the recovery state where HCV NS5A (green line) is downregulated by the activation of NK cells (pink line) and IFN-γ (black line). (Color figure online)

4   Conclusion

Various computational and mathematical approaches are in practice, helping in finding new potential targets for therapeutic intervention which are expensive to explore otherwise. BRN construction represents an efficient alternative to model biological networks as compared to conventional mathematical approaches such as models based on ODEs. The developed BRN model of immune regulation and the role of HCV NS5A in antagonizing the effects of host immune control has been studied exclusively. Focus has been put on the IL-10 and IL-12 cytokines mediated regulation from the initial state to terminal state. It can be concluded that the global immunomodulatory effects of IL-10 help in the viral control of host machinery. The effects of IL-10 are more profound as compared to IL-12, which results in a pathogenic state. Also, it is observed that the IL-12 overexpression benefits the pathogenic state more as compared to its anti-viral effects. The host immune system does work to recover the system but it is overwhelmed by the efficient HCV immune evasion process. Any diversion from the diseased paths either via host immune recovery or therapeutic intervention to stabilize the levels of IFN-γ producing NK cells will lead the system towards recovery.

Acknowledgement. This research is supported by Higher Education Commission (HEC) of Pakistan, NRPU grant no. 4362.

References

1. Lechmann, M., et al.: Hepatitis C virus–like particles induce virus specific humoral and cellular immune responses in mice. Hepatology **34**(2), 417–423 (2001)
2. Cento, V., Chevaliez, S., Perno, C.F.: Resistance to direct-acting antiviral agents: clinical utility and significance. Curr. Opin. HIV AIDS **10**(5), 381–389 (2015)
3. Ahmad, J., et al.: Formal modeling and analysis of the mal-associated biological regulatory network: insight into cerebral malaria. PLoS ONE **7**(3), e33532 (2012)
4. Bernot, G., et al.: Application of formal methods to biological regulatory networks: extending Thomas' asynchronous logical approach with temporal logic. J. Theor. Biol. **229** (3), 339–347 (2004)
5. Rehermann, B.: Hepatitis C virus versus innate and adaptive immune responses: a tale of coevolution and coexistence. J. Clin. Investig. **119**(7), 1745–1754 (2009)
6. Moradpour, D., Penin, F., Rice, C.M.: Replication of hepatitis C virus. Nat. Rev. Microbiol. **5**(6), 453 (2007)
7. Bartenschlager, R., Lohmann, V., Penin, F.: The molecular and structural basis of advanced antiviral therapy for hepatitis C virus infection. Nat. Rev. Microbiol. **11**(7), 482 (2013)
8. Samaga, R., Klamt, S.: Modeling approaches for qualitative and semi-quantitative analysis of cellular signaling networks. Cell Commun. Signal. **11**(1), 43 (2013)
9. Rosen, H.R.: Emerging concepts in immunity to hepatitis C virus infection. J. Clin. Investig. **123**(10), 4121 (2013)
10. Thimme, R., Binder, M., Bartenschlager, R.: Failure of innate and adaptive immune responses in controlling hepatitis C virus infection. FEMS Microbiol. Rev. **36**(3), 663–683 (2012)
11. Zhao, J., Zhao, J., Perlman, S.: Differential effects of IL-12 on Tregs and non-Treg T cells: roles of IFN-γ, IL-2 and IL-2R. PLoS ONE **7**(9), e46241 (2012)
12. Moore, K.W., et al.: Interleukin-10 and the interleukin-10 receptor. Annu. Rev. Immunol. **19** (1), 683–765 (2001)
13. Sene, D., et al.: Hepatitis C virus (HCV) evades NKG2D-dependent NK cell responses through NS5A-mediated imbalance of inflammatory cytokines. PLoS Pathog. **6**(11), e1001184 (2010)
14. Aste-Amezaga, M., et al.: Molecular mechanisms of the induction of IL-12 and its inhibition by IL-10. J. Immunol. **160**(12), 5936–5944 (1998)
15. Blackburn, S.D., Wherry, E.J.: IL-10, T cell exhaustion and viral persistence. Trends Microbiol. **15**(4), 143–146 (2007)
16. Fiorentino, D.F., et al.: IL-10 inhibits cytokine production by activated macrophages. J. Immunol. **147**(11), 3815–3822 (1991)
17. Hu, X., et al.: IFN-γ suppresses IL-10 production and synergizes with TLR2 by regulating GSK3 and CREB/AP-1 proteins. Immunity **24**(5), 563–574 (2006)
18. Barth, H., et al.: Analysis of the effect of IL-12 therapy on immunoregulatory T-cell subsets in patients with chronic hepatitis C infection. Hepatogastroenterology **50**(49), 201–206 (2003)
19. Richard, A., et al.: Boolean models of biosurfactants production in Pseudomonas fluorescens. PLoS ONE **7**(1), e24651 (2012)

20. Naldi, A., Remy, E., Thieffry, D., Chaouiya, C.: A reduction of logical regulatory graphs preserving essential dynamical properties. In: Degano, P., Gorrieri, R. (eds.) CMSB 2009. LNCS, vol. 5688, pp. 266–280. Springer, Heidelberg (2009). https://doi.org/10.1007/978-3-642-03845-7_18

21. Saadatpour, A., Albert, R., Reluga, T.C.: A reduction method for Boolean network models proven to conserve attractors. SIAM J. Appl. Dyn. Syst. **12**(4), 1997–2011 (2013)

22. Khalis, Z., et al.: The SMBioNet method for discovering models of gene regulatory networks. Genes Genomes Genomics **3**(1), 15–22 (2009)

23. Saeed, M.T., et al.: Formal modeling and analysis of the hexosamine biosynthetic pathway: role of O-linked N-acetylglucosamine transferase in oncogenesis and cancer progression. PeerJ **4**, e2348 (2016)

24. Ahmad, J., et al.: Hybrid modelling and dynamical analysis of gene regulatory networks with delays. ComPlexUs **3**(4), 231–251 (2006)

25. Gonzalez, A.G., et al.: GINsim: a software suite for the qualitative modelling, simulation and analysis of regulatory networks. Biosystems **84**(2), 91–100 (2006)

26. Heiner, M., Herajy, M., Liu, F., Rohr, C., Schwarick, M.: Snoopy – a unifying petri net tool. In: Haddad, S., Pomello, L. (eds.) PETRI NETS 2012. LNCS, vol. 7347, pp. 398–407. Springer, Heidelberg (2012). https://doi.org/10.1007/978-3-642-31131-4_22

27. Obaid, A., et al.: Modeling and analysis of innate immune responses induced by the host cells against hepatitis C virus infection. Integr. Biol. **7**(5), 544–559 (2015)

28. Tseng, C.-T.K., Klimpel, G.R.: Binding of the hepatitis C virus envelope protein E2 to CD81 inhibits natural killer cell functions. J. Exp. Med. **195**(1), 43–50 (2002)

29. Frese, M., et al.: Interferon-γ inhibits replication of subgenomic and genomic hepatitis C virus RNAs. Hepatology **35**(3), 694–703 (2002)

30. Belkaid, Y., Rouse, B.T.: Natural regulatory T cells in infectious disease. Nat. Immunol. **6**(4), 353–360 (2005)

31. Sturm, N., et al.: Characterization and role of intra-hepatic regulatory T cells in chronic hepatitis C pathogenesis. J. Hepatol. **53**(1), 25–35 (2010)

32. Brady, M.T., et al.: Hepatitis C virus non-structural protein 4 suppresses Th1 responses by stimulating IL-10 production from monocytes. Eur. J. Immunol. **33**(12), 3448–3457 (2003)

33. Wang, K.S., Frank, D.A., Ritz, J.: Interleukin-2 enhances the response of natural killer cells to interleukin-12 through up-regulation of the interleukin-12 receptor and STAT4. Blood **95**(10), 3183–3190 (2000)

34. Eckels, D.D., et al.: Immunobiology of hepatitis C virus (HCV) infection: the role of CD4 T cells in HCV infection. Immunol. Rev. **174**(1), 90–97 (2000)

35. Pockros, P.J., et al.: A multicenter study of recombinant human interleukin 12 for the treatment of chronic hepatitis C virus infection in patients nonresponsive to previous therapy. Hepatology **37**(6), 1368–1374 (2003)

36. Shannon, P., et al.: Cytoscape: a software environment for integrated models of biomolecular interaction networks. Genome Res. **13**(11), 2498–2504 (2003)

37. Cook, K.D., Waggoner, S.N., Whitmire, J.K.: NK cells and their ability to modulate T cells during virus infections. Crit. Rev. Immunol. **34**(5), 359–388 (2014)

38. Lanford, R.E., et al.: Antiviral effect and virus-host interactions in response to alpha interferon, gamma interferon, poly (i)-poly (c), tumor necrosis factor alpha, and ribavirin in hepatitis C virus subgenomic replicons. J. Virol. **77**(2), 1092–1104 (2003)

39. Ruths, D., et al.: The signaling petri net-based simulator: a non-parametric strategy for characterizing the dynamics of cell-specific signaling networks. PLoS Comput. Biol. **4**, 0005 (2008)

40. Polak, M.E., et al.: Petri net computational modelling of langerhans cell interferon regulatory factor network predicts their role in T cell activation. Sci. Rep. **7**(1), 668 (2017)

Location Aware Personalized News Recommender System Based on Twitter Popularity

Sunita Tiwari[✉], Manjeet Singh Pangtey, and Sushil Kumar

G B Pant Government Engineering College, Delhi, India
sunita.tiwari@gbpec.edu.in

Abstract. The mobile and handheld devices have become an indispensable part of life in this era of technological advancement. Further, the ubiquity of location acquisition technologies like global positioning system (GPS) has opened the new avenues for location aware applications for mobile devices. Reading online news is becoming increasingly popular way to gather information from news sources around the globe. Users can search and read the news of their preference wherever they want. The news preferences of individuals are influenced by several factors including the geographical contexts and the recent trends on social media. In this work we propose an approach to recommend the personalized news to the users based on their individual preferences. The model for user preferences are learned implicitly for individual users. Also, the popularity of trending articles floating around the twitter are exploited to provide news interesting recommendations to the user. We believe that the interest of the user, popularity of article and other attributes of news are implicitly fuzzy in nature and therefore we propose to exploit this for generating the recommendation score for articles to be recommended. The prototype is developed for testing and evaluation of proposed approach and the results of the evaluation are motivating.

Keywords: Fuzzy clustering · User profiling · Social network
Recommender systems · Information filtering

1 Introduction

With the wide spread popularity of World Wide Web (WWW), a huge amount of information is being produced at very fast pace every day. People are able to get access to content across the globe in real time. However, due to the increasing volume and ubiquity of access the human being face difficulty in processing this voluminous amount of information and this scenario has motivated the development of recommender system applications. A recommender system is a software application which aims to the ease the problem of information by providing the product and/or service recommendations to the users which might interest them [2, 3, 20, 23].

News recommendation is relatively newer and interesting application area for recommender systems. The online news are available to the user and the notifications for new news articles are being provided with the help of RSS feeds in real time.

© Springer International Publishing AG, part of Springer Nature 2018
O. Gervasi et al. (Eds.): ICCSA 2018, LNCS 10963, pp. 650–658, 2018.
https://doi.org/10.1007/978-3-319-95171-3_51

In contrast to other existing recommendation domains like movies, videos, merchandise etc. the news recommender systems are characterized by lack of explicit user ratings and requirement of real time recommendation generation. As soon as the news articles are published, the news recommender system should be able to generate the recommendations of these article to the user whom are potential readers for these articles. Also, these recommender system should be able to infer the user's interest in a news article implicitly without them being explicitly specifying the same.

The news recommender system should take into consideration the long term user preference motivated by user's professional and educational background etc. along with short term trends influenced by the current affairs, current location and context etc. It is also observed that the users read the news on the go using their handheld devices. Several news aggregator Apps such as Yahoo News, News360 m Apple News etc. provides news to the user but most of these apps do very little or no personalization of content. They mostly use the static user profile information available with them or the recent trending news in social networks to provide news notifications to the users.

The aim of the proposed work is to provide fresh and personalized news content to the users that are relevant to their interest in a particular location with minimal explicit user interactions. Most of the recommender systems face the problem of cold start i.e. how to recommend the item to the user for which no or very little information is available [2, 3]. Traditional recommender systems use the selected topics from user profile. We aim to exploit the power of twitter to address this problem.

The rest of the paper is organized as follows. Section 2 discusses the related work and the proposed work is introduced in Sect. 3. The discussion of the proposed approach is given in Sect. 4. Finally Sect. 5 concludes the paper.

2   Related Work

Recommender System is a well-researched area [2–5, 9, 18–20]. A lot of research work can be found in literature related to news recommender system is available in literature. Some of the relevant literature are presented in this section.

Danial Billsus et al. in year 2000, proposed an intelligent hybrid user model for news classification called Daily Learner [6]. The first agent in this work focused on personalization of news contents and the second one focuses on the ubiquity of information. The system was evaluated on a user base of 300 users. Liang et al. in year 2002 [14] proposed an approach to analyze the behaviors of user from their browsing patterns and tested this approach for news recommender system. A time based strategy for analyzing the profile of a user is proposed. This approach outperforms the headlines based approach. In year 2010, Liu et al. [15], also proposed a news recommender system based on the click behavior pattern of user. They analyzed the google news to establish that the user news interest changes over time and personalized the news content using collaborative filtering concept. NewsRec is the SVM driven recommender system proposed by Bomhardt et al. in year 2004 [7]. In year 2005, R Baeza-Yates presented the ranking model based on time segments for news recommendation.

In year 2007, Lee et al. [12] proposed MONERS, a mobile web news recommendation system which includes news article attributes and user preferences with reference to the categories and news articles. Cantador et al. in year 2008 and IJntema et al. [8, 10] in year 2010 proposed ontology based new recommendation approach. Li et al. in year 2010 [13] presented personalized recommendation of news articles as a contextual bandit problem.

Twitter has been used by several researchers to develop new recommendation system. Some of the important contribution in this light are as follows. In [16] Phelan et al. proposed a real time topical news recommendation using twitter in year 2009. This work exploits the real time micro blogging activates of a user as basis for promoting the news stories. In 2011, Phelan et al. [17], proposed a service called Buzzer that adapts to the conversations that are taking place on Twitter ranking the RSS subscriptions. In a work by Abel et al. in year 2011 [1], the authors presented a framework for modeling users on twitter to enrich tweets and identifies topics and entities used in the tweets. Jonnalagedda et al. in [11] presented personalized news recommender system which rank the new article.

In contrast to existing contributions we present the approach in which implicit user interest is inferred from the topics in tweet and use fuzzy clustering to identify the user preferences. The location based trending news feed are take into consideration for recommending and personalizing the news contents.

3   Proposed System Design

The proposed system design is shown in Fig. 1. The main components of the proposed system are discussed in this section.

3.1   Mobile Client

The mobile client is a registered user who is the target user for the news recommendation based on his/her personal preferences, recent trends on twitter and the current geographical location of the user. Using the GPS (Global Positioning System) technology the current location of the user is obtained by the recommender system module. The mobile client will receive the recommendations. This service is a push based service i.e. user does not request the recommendation but it is provided by the recommendations engine automatically.

3.2   User Profile DB

The profiles of all the registered users are stored in a user profile DB (database). These profiles are learned and enriched over time by implicitly learning their news preferences. The user preferences are learnt by observing the user's news reading patterns and learnt from the twitter behavior of the user. Details of profile learning is presented in Sect. 3.3 in detail.

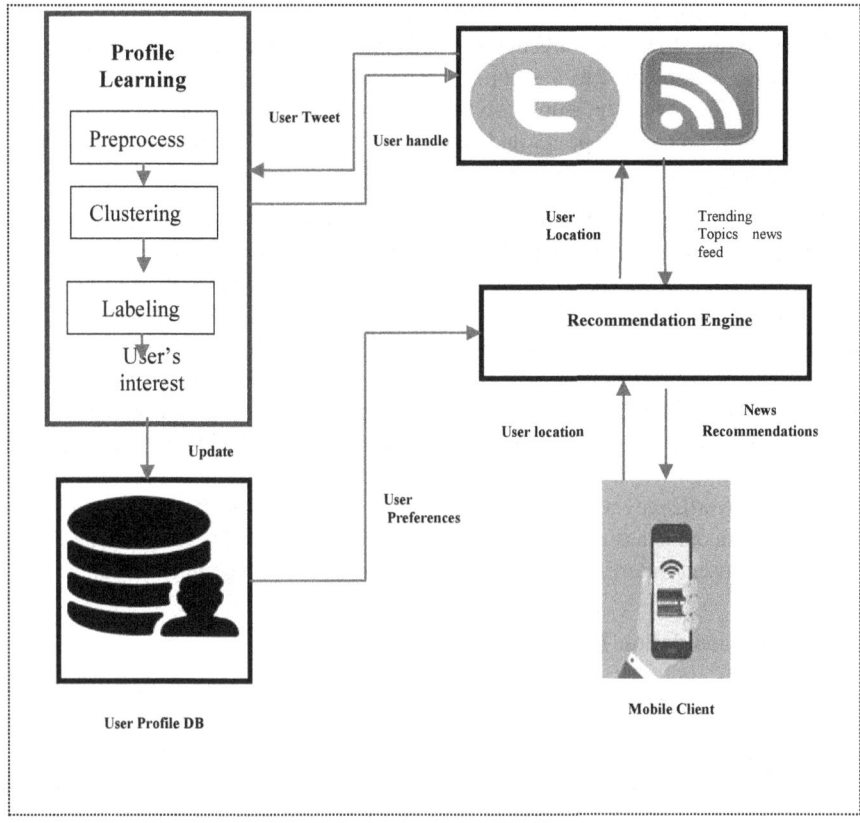

Fig. 1. System design

3.3 User Profile Learning

In this section we discuss the method to construct the profile of a user by analyzing the twitter message posted by him/her. It is difficult to learn the information directly from the tweets due to the limited size of tweets. However, by identifying the topic of discussion in tweets we can infer some important information. We exploit this feature of tweets to create the profile of a user.

Twitter profile of a user is a rich source of information about that user. It contain information about user's name, twitter handle, user's location, textual description about user, interests of user, verified mark, profile creation date etc. Using the API users/show we can retrieve such information. We can collect the user tweets by using statuses/user timeline from the REST API. APIs in twitter data are classified in two REST API and Streaming API. The REST API is useful in pulling the information about an individual user. We have used the twitter REST API to interact with our system. Streaming API provide a continuous information updates without interaction with user. Using this API call we retrieve the tweets from the user we need to identify the topic user is discussing in his/her tweet. First we preprocess the tweets by performing following-

1. Lowercase- convert the words in lowercase.
2. Tokenize- the string are converted in words based on the whitespaces. Now the data in a tweet is converted to a group of words.
3. Stopword Removal- the stopwords are removed from this group of words.
4. Stemming- remove the prefix and suffix from the word to reduce it to its stem.
5. Vectorization – convert the sequence of words to a vector.

The group of words collected from all the tweets are clustered using fuzzy k means clustering as few words may belong to more than one topic. For example start can be used for sports person and also for an actor. Once the clusters are obtained they are assigned a label. The number of clusters are identified based on the predefined categories of news such as sports, movies, politics etc. we had identified ten such categories and cluster the words in one of the ten categories. For clustering cosine similarity measure is used which is obtained using word2vec model. The word2vec model generates word embedding, based on which a cosine similarity score between -1 and 1 is obtained, where 1 meaning that the two words are same, 0 meaning no relation and -1 meaning opposite relation. This model (word2vec) was first trained on Google News dataset. We have used the naïve Bayes model to assign label to each cluster. Once the label is assigned the top five categories of users' interest are identified and used for news recommendation.

3.4   Recommendation Engine

The tweet data contains two metadata namely tweet location and account location. The tweet location is one which is shared at the time of tweet. Home location is the location which is given by the user in his/her public profile. Figure 2 shows the home location and tweet location. There are various methods by which we may filter the tweets by

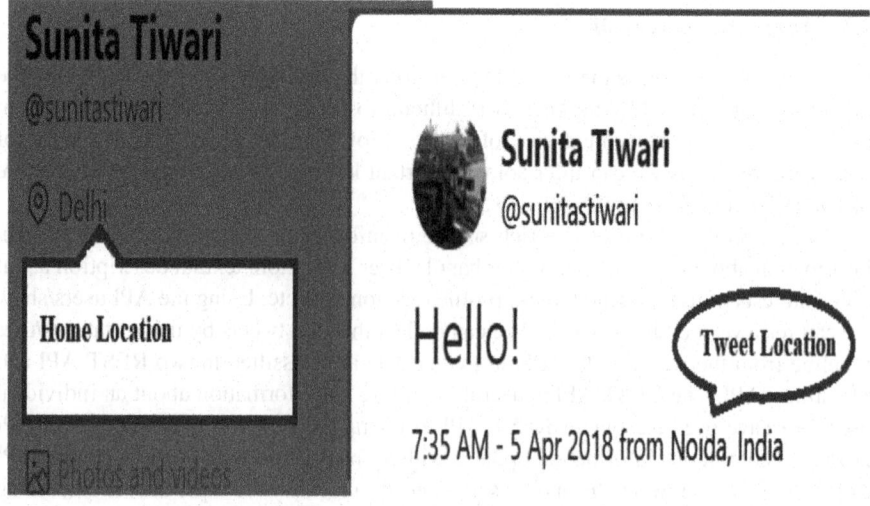

Fig. 2. Location information on twitter

tweet location. Recommendation engine retrieves the data related to user's current location.

Twitter developer make available an API for retrieving the trending topics near a location using a query of form https://api.twitter.com/1.1/trends/place.json. The result of this query is a group of trending objects which includes the name of the trending topic. We have created the RSS feed for the trending topics for the individual location. These trending topics are further ranked based on the personal interest of the user inferred by profile learning module as discussed in Sect. 3.3. The global trends are also considered for the topics in which user have high interest. The news items finally recommended to the user matches the interest of the user and recent topics trending locally.

3.5 Results

The proposed system is implemented and tested on a data sample of size 32. The accuracy of proposed recommender system turned out to be 89.2%. we have also calculated the precision and it is about 91.3%. The accuracy of proposed system

4 Discussion

For evaluating the recommendation the application is tested for 23 users for a period of time. The users are recommended with news articles and they are asked to rate their experience for using the recommendation application once every day on a scale of 1 to 10. The average rating of the user is considered after a particular period. The average

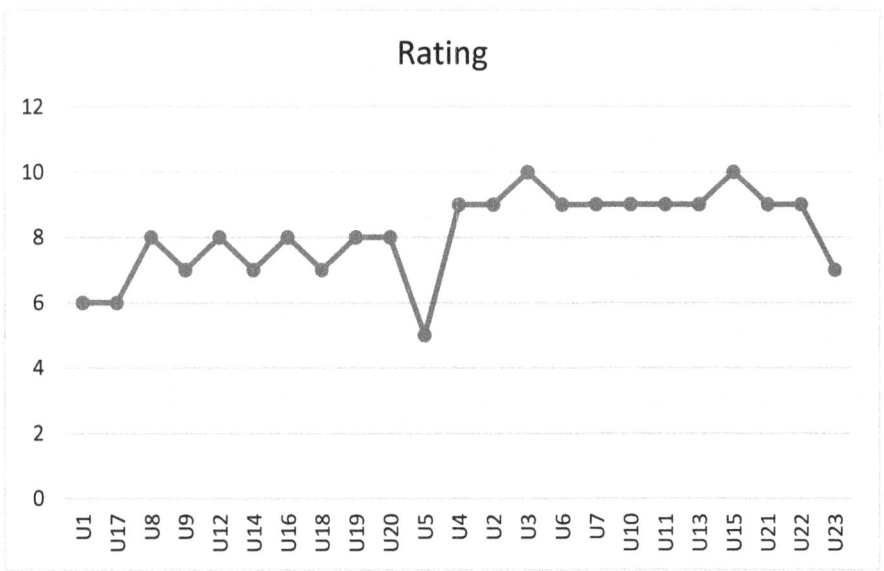

Fig. 3. Average user ratings

rating of all users is 8.17 and the Fig. 3 shows the satisfaction level of users' satisfaction.

Further, to validate the satisfaction level we have conducted explicit survey of their opinion about the relevance of news article recommended to them. The Fig. 4 shows that around 87% users have good experience with the recommendation and they have rated the application with good and very good reviews.

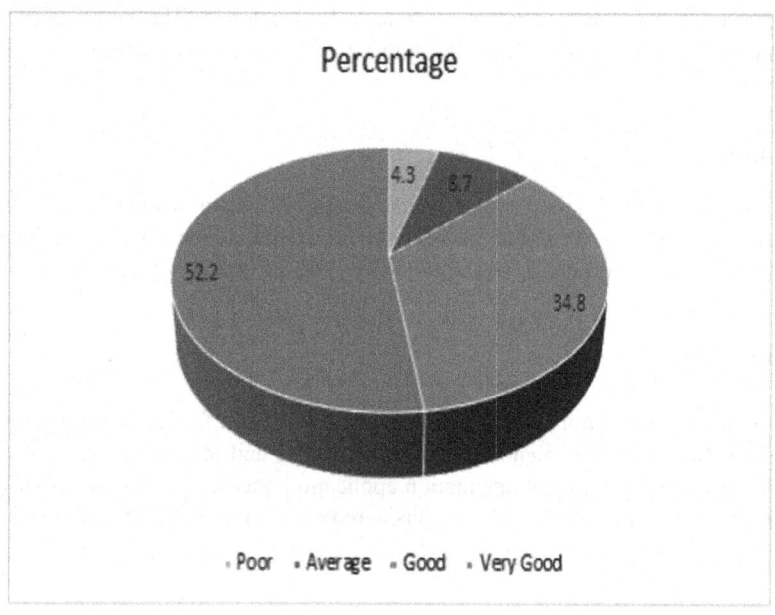

Fig. 4. User feedback

5 Conclusion and Future Directions

The personalization of news recommendation is a way to ease the problem of information overload and makes the job of getting the news content from different sources easy for user. This paper present the personalized news recommender system for mobile users to provide the location aware news content. The recommendation also take care of local and global trends on tweeter for taking care of diversification factor of news content. This work also infer the interest area of user implicitly from the tweeting patterns of the user without much intervention of user. In future we aim to include the facebook feeds to enrich the user experience. Also, evaluation on more number of user is the next agenda.

References

1. Abel, F., Gao, Q., Houben, G.-J., Tao, K.: Analyzing user modeling on twitter for personalized news recommendations. In: Konstan, Joseph A., et al. (eds.) UMAP 2011. LNCS, vol. 6787, pp. 1–12. Springer, Heidelberg (2011). https://doi.org/10.1007/978-3-642-22362-4_1
2. Adomavicius, G., Mobasher, B., Ricci, F., Tuzhilin, A.: Context-aware recommender systems. AI Mag. **32**(3), 67–80 (2011)
3. Adomavicius, G., Tuzhilin, A.: Toward the next generation of recommender systems: a survey of the state-of-the-art and possible extensions. IEEE Trans. Know. Data Eng. (IEEE) **17**(6), 734–749 (2005)
4. Berjani, B., Strufe, T.: A recommendation system for spots in location-based online social networks. In: Proceedings of the 4th Workshop on Social Network Systems, Salzburg, Austria. ACM (2011)
5. Burke, R.: Hybrid recommender systems: survey and experiments. User Model. User-Adap. Inter. **12**(4), 331–370 (2002)
6. Billsus, D., Pazzani, Michael J.: A hybrid user model for news story classification. In: Kay, J. (ed.) UM99 User Modeling. CICMS, vol. 407, pp. 99–108. Springer, Vienna (1999). https://doi.org/10.1007/978-3-7091-2490-1_10
7. Bomhardt, C.: NewsRec, a SVM-driven personal recommendation system for news websites. In: Proceedings of the 2004 IEEE/WIC/ACM International Conference on Web Intelligence, pp. 545–548. IEEE Computer Society, September 2004
8. Cantador, I., Bellogín, A., Castells, P.: Ontology-based personalised and context-aware recommendations of news items. In: IEEE/WIC/ACM International Conference on Web Intelligence and Intelligent Agent Technology, WI-IAT 2008, vol. 1, pp. 562–565. IEEE, December 2008
9. Gemmell, J., Shepitsen, A., Mobasher, B., Burke, R.: Personalization in folksonomies based on tag clustering. In: Intelligent Techniques for Web Personalization & Recommender Systems, vol. 12 (2008)
10. IJntema, W., Goossen, F., Frasincar, F., Hogenboom, F.: Ontology-based news recommendation. In: Proceedings of the 2010 EDBT/ICDT Workshops, p. 16. ACM, March 2010
11. Jonnalagedda, N., Gauch, S.: Personalized news recommendation using twitter. In: 2013 IEEE/WIC/ACM International Joint Conferences on Web Intelligence (WI) and Intelligent Agent Technologies (IAT), vol. 3, pp. 21–25. IEEE, November 2013
12. Lee, H.J., Park, S.J.: MONERS: a news recommender for the mobile web. Expert Syst. Appl. **32**(1), 143–150 (2007)
13. Li, L., Chu, W., Langford, J., Schapire, R.E.: A contextual-bandit approach to personalized news article recommendation. In: Proceedings of the 19th International Conference on World Wide Web, pp. 661–670. ACM, April 2010
14. Liang, T.P., Lai, H.J.: Discovering user interests from web browsing behavior: an application to internet news services. In: Proceedings of the 35th Annual Hawaii International Conference on System Sciences, HICSS, pp. 2718–2727. IEEE, January 2002
15. Liu, J., Dolan, P., Pedersen, E.R.: Personalized news recommendation based on click behavior. In: Proceedings of the 15th International Conference on Intelligent User Interfaces, pp. 31–40. ACM, February 2010
16. Phelan, O., McCarthy, K., Smyth, B.: Using twitter to recommend real-time topical news. In: Proceedings of the Third ACM Conference on Recommender Systems, pp. 385–388. ACM, October 2009

17. Phelan, O., McCarthy, K., Bennett, M., Smyth, B.: Terms of a feather: content-based news recommendation and discovery using Twitter. In: Clough, P., et al. (eds.) ECIR 2011. LNCS, vol. 6611, pp. 448–459. Springer, Heidelberg (2011). https://doi.org/10.1007/978-3-642-20161-5_44

18. Tiwari, S., Kaushik, S.: Modeling personalized recommendations of unvisited tourist places using genetic algorithms. In: Chu, W., Kikuchi, S., Bhalla, S. (eds.) DNIS 2015. LNCS, vol. 8999, pp. 264–276. Springer, Cham (2015). https://doi.org/10.1007/978-3-319-16313-0_20

19. Tiwari, S., Kaushik, S.: Evolving recommendations from past travel sequences using soft computing techniques. Int. J. Comput. Sci. Eng. **14**(3), 242–254 (2017)

20. Tiwari, S., Kaushik, S., Jagwani, P.: Location based recommender systems: architecture, trends and research areas (2012)

21. Tiwari, S., Kaushik, S.: Mining popular places in a geo-spatial region based on GPS data using semantic information. In: Madaan, A., Kikuchi, S., Bhalla, S. (eds.) DNIS 2013. LNCS, vol. 7813, pp. 262–276. Springer, Heidelberg (2013). https://doi.org/10.1007/978-3-642-37134-9_20

22. Tiwari, S., Kaushik, S.: Information enrichment for tourist spot recommender system using location aware crowdsourcing. In: 2014 IEEE 15th International Conference on Mobile Data Management (MDM), vol. 2, pp. 11–14. IEEE, July 2014

23. Tiwari, S., Kaushik, S.: A non functional properties based web service recommender system. In: 2010 International Conference on Computational Intelligence and Software Engineering (CiSE), pp. 1–4. IEEE, December 2010

An Improved Generalized Regression Neural Network for Type II Diabetes Classification

Moeketsi Ndaba[1][✉], Anban W. Pillay[1,2], and Absalom E. Ezugwu[1]

[1] School of Mathematics, Statistics and Computer Science,
University of Kwazulu-Natal, Westville Campus,
Private Bag X54001, Durban 4000, South Africa
ndaba.max@gmail.com, {pillay4,ezugwuA}@ukzn.ac.za
[2] Centre for Artificial Intelligence Research (CAIR), Durban, South Africa

Abstract. This paper proposes an improved Generalized Regression Neural Network (KGRNN) for the diagnosis of type II diabetes. Diabetes, a widespread chronic disease, is a metabolic disorder that develops when the body does not make enough insulin or is unable to use insulin effectively. Type II diabetes is the most common type and accounts for an estimated 90% of cases. The novel KGRNN technique reported in this study uses an enhanced K-Means clustering technique (CVE-K-Means) to produce cluster centers (centroids) that are used to train the network. The technique was applied to the Pima Indian diabetes dataset, a widely used benchmark dataset for Diabetes diagnosis. The technique outperforms the best known GRNN techniques for Type II diabetes diagnosis in terms of classification accuracy and computational time and obtained a classification accuracy of 86% with 83% sensitivity and 87% specificity. The Area Under the Receiver Operating Characteristic Curve (ROC) of 87% was obtained.

Keywords: Diabetes classification · Artificial Neural Networks
Generalized Neural Network

1 Introduction

Diabetes is one of the most challenging and widespread chronic diseases in the world [22] with an estimated 425 million diagnosed cases worldwide [8]. This number is expected to rise to 629 million by 2045 [8]. There are three types of diabetes: Type I (insulin-dependent diabetes), Type II (non-insulin-dependent diabetes) and gestational diabetes which affects pregnant women. Type II diabetes is the most prevalent form of the disease afflicting an estimated 90% of diabetics. The disease is especially devastating in low and middle income countries where two thirds of people living with diabetes have inadequate control and management of the disease due to limited continuous access to anti diabetic

© Springer International Publishing AG, part of Springer Nature 2018
O. Gervasi et al. (Eds.): ICCSA 2018, LNCS 10963, pp. 659–671, 2018.
https://doi.org/10.1007/978-3-319-95171-3_52

treatments such as insulin and limited access to quality professional health assistance [8]. In 2014 alone, approximately 4.9 million deaths have been attributed to diabetes related illnesses [8]. Late diagnosis of the disease makes it especially dangerous. 80% of complications related to type II diabetes can be prevented or delayed by early diagnosis or early identification of people at risk [4]. This demonstrates that the traditional methods for diagnosing and managing the disease are not sufficient to contain its spread.

The accelerating adoption of information systems technologies in the medical and health care sector has contributed to the increasing availability of data pertaining to diabetes; including symptoms, risk factors and socioeconomic data. These large datasets provide an opportunity for the application of data-driven approaches such as various Machine Learning (ML) techniques, to aid health professionals in making more accurate and timely diagnoses. Machine Learning (ML) techniques have been shown to be effective in quick and cost effective diagnosis. This is especially important in developing countries where the disease burden is high but health systems are generally poorly resourced.

The diagnosis of diabetes may be considered a classification problem and thus various machine learning techniques such as Artificial Neural Networks (ANNs), Logistic Regression (LR), and K-Nearest Neighbours (KNN) may be employed. These techniques are known to perform well in classification problems. ANNs are biologically inspired computer programs which simulate the way the human brain processes information [2]. ANNs have an information processing structure that is composed of a large number of interconnected processing units called neurons. ANNs use an activation function and a training algorithm such as the Back-Propagation algorithm to learn from the data. A Multi-Layer Perceptron (MLP) is a widely used ANN to solve diagnosis problems.

The KNN algorithm is a lazy-learning algorithm which classifies test instances based on their similarity with training instances in a feature space. KNN is regarded as a lazy learning technique because it stores training instances during learning and only uses them during classification. LR is a statistical regression technique that is used to model a relationship between one dependent variable and one or more independent variables. The dependent variable of the LR takes a categorical value to represent a binary outcome. This makes the algorithm more suitable to solve classification problems such as diabetes diagnosis.

In this paper, an improved Generalized Regression Neural Network (GRNN) is proposed to diagnose type II diabetes. The algorithm was improved by hybridizing it with an efficient K-Means clustering algorithm. The efficacy of the improved GRNN network was tested on the Pima Indian dataset including three additional datasets that were produced by preprocessing the Pima Indian dataset. The performance of the algorithm in these datasets was compared with other studies in literature.

This rest of the paper is organized as follows: Sect. 2 presents related work, Sect. 3 details the methodology and Sect. 4 gives the experimental results and discussion. Lastly, the conclusion and pointers to future work are given in Sect. 5.

2 Related Work

Artificial Neural Networks (ANNs) have been successfully used to replace conventional pattern recognition methods in disease diagnosis systems. Mehmet et al. [5] conducted a diabetes classification study using six different types of ANNs: Probabilistic Neural Network (PNN), Learning Vector Quantization (LVQ), Feed- Forward Networks (FFN), Cascade-Forward Networks (CFN), Distributed Time Delay Networks (DTDN) and Time Delay Networks (TDN)). They [5] also applied the artificial immune system and a Gini algorithm derived from decision tree algorithms for classification. Their studies used the Pima Indian diabetes dataset to train and test the algorithms. The best classification accuracy of 76% was achieved by the DTDN, followed by LVQ with a classification accuracy of 73%. The Gini algorithm produced the lowest classification accuracy of 66%. The remaining algorithms produced a classification accuracy between 68% and 72%.

Adeyemo and Akinwonmi [1], proposed the use of Generalized Regression Neural Network (GRNN) and the Probabilistic Neural Network to classify diabetes using patient data obtained from the Family Medicine Clinic of the Wesley Guild Unit at the University Teaching Hospital of Nigeria. Both networks used *tanh* as the activation function. Their GRNN achieved a classification accuracy of 84% while the PNN achieved an accuracy of 76%. Pradhan and Kumar Sahu [14] implemented a Multi Layer Back-propagation (MLBP) ANN with a single hidden layer with five neurons and a Genetic Algorithm (GA) for feature selection. They applied 10-fold cross validation for training and testing the network and achieved a classification accuracy of 72.2% with a Mean Square Error of 1.683.

Asha et al. [10] suggested that instead of gradient-based learning techniques for MLPBP networks, one may apply the commonly used optimization algorithms such as Genetic Algorithms, Particle Swarm Optimization (PSO), and Ant Colony Optimization (ACO) to determine the best network weights. They used a GA to initialize and optimize the connection weights of the MLBP network. The GA provided was used to determine various parameters such as the number of hidden layers, features to select, and efficient network learning rate. The GA also allowed the network to efficiently initialize the connection weights. Their study also identified features to be selected by applying a mixture of Decision Tree (DT) and GA-CFS (Correlation Feature Selection) algorithms. These algorithms (DT and GA-CFS) were used as input to the hybrid model of the MLPBP network and GA to classify diabetes. A classification accuracy of 84% was achieved by this hybrid of GA and MLPBP network.

Vijayan et al. [21] proposed the use of KNN, a K-Means clustering algorithm and an Amalgam KNN on Pima Indian dataset. The Amalgam algorithm was a hybrid of the KNN and K-Means clustering algorithm. Their KNN and K-Means clustering algorithm achieved classification accuracies of 73% and 77% respectively. The Amalgam KNN algorithm achieved an accuracy of 80%. The Amalgam KNN algorithm produced improved results by using K-Means clustering to identify and remove instances that were erroneously classified by the KNN.

KNN and K-Means clustering algorithms produced average results because the selected values of k and the dataset was not preprocessed to reduce noise.

Nai-Aruna and Moungmaia [13] used a hybrid of LR with ensemble methods. They selected Boosting and Bagging ensemble methods. Ensemble methods are designed to improve the stability and the accuracy of ML algorithms. Nai-Aruna and Moungmaia [13] applied the hybdridized LR algorithm on patient data from the Sawanpracharak Regional Hospital in Thailand. The hybrid of LR and Boosting achieved the classification accuracy of 82.308% while the hybrid of LR and Bagging achieved an accuracy of 82.318%. An accuracy of 82.308% was obtained with the standard LR algorithm. These results show that ensemble methods were not effective in significantly improving the classification accuracy of the LR model.

3   Methodology

3.1   Datasets and Data Preprocessing

The population for the dataset is the Pima Indian population in Phoenix, Arizona, USA but restricted to Pima Indian Females older than 20 years [17]. This population has been under study since 1965 by the National Institute of Diabetes and Digestive and Kidney Diseases due to the high incidence rate of diabetes. The Pima Indian females participated in standardized diabetes examinations and Type II diabetes was diagnosed using the WHO Type II diabetes diagnosis criteria [16]. A patient was considered diabetic when their two hour post-load plasma glucose was at least 200 mg/dl (11.1 mmol/l) at any survey examination [21]. The Pima Indian dataset has 768 observations with nine attributes. Five hundred of these patients were diabetic and each patient had only one record. The attributes in the dataset are given below and basic statistical properties of the dataset are given in Table 1.

1. Number of times pregnant (PREG)
2. Plasma Glucose Concentration at 2 h in an Oral Glucose Tolerance Test (GLUC)
3. Diastolic Blood Pressure in mm Hg (PRESS)
4. Triceps Skin Fold Thickness (mm) (SKIN)
5. 2-Hour Serum Insulin Uh/ml) (INSU)
6. Body Mass Index (Weight in kg/(Height in cm)) (BMI)
7. Diabetes Pedigree Function (PDF)
8. Age in years (AGE)
9. Diabetes Class Variable (0 for no diabetes or 1 for diabetes presence)

Raw data is susceptible to missing values, noise, and inconsistency [12]. These factors affect the quality of the dataset and consequently the performance of ML techniques [12]. To improve the quality of the dataset and ultimately the results of ML techniques, raw data is preprocessed. Data preprocessing deals with the preparation and transformation of the initial dataset before applying

Table 1. Statistical properties of the dataset

Feature	Minimum	Maximum	Mean	Variance	Standard deviation
Number of times pregnant	0.00	17.00	3.85	11.34	3.37
Plasma glucose concentration	0.00	199.00	120.89	1020.92	31.95
Diastolic blood pressure (mm Hg)	0.00	122.00	69.11	374.16	19.34
Triceps skin fold thickness (mm)	0.00	99.00	20.54	254.14	15.94
2-h serum insulin (Uh/ml)	0.00	846.00	79.80	13263.89	115.17
Body mass index (Weight in kg/(Height in in.))	0.00	67.10	31.99	62.08	7.88
Diabetes pedigree function	0.08	2.42	0.47	0.11	0.33
Age (years)	21.00	81.00	33.22	138.12	11.75

ML techniques. Data preprocessing techniques are divided into the following categories: Dataset Cleaning, Dataset Transformation, Dataset Reduction and Dataset Integration.

The Pima Indian dataset has approximately 10% of instances with attributes that have missing values. The Min-Max Normalization technique was employed to re-scale the values in the dataset to be in the same range [0,1] and various pre-processing techniques were applied to the original dataset to produce three additional datasets:

1. A dataset with all instances with missing values removed.
2. A dataset with missing attribute values replaced by the mean value of that attribute (except attributes: number of times pregnant and class variable).
3. A dataset with insignificant features that were excluded using a learner-based feature selection technique (Random Forest algorithm).

In this study, the original un-preprocessed dataset is referred to as A-[Unprocessed]. The dataset formed as a result of applying preprocessing method 1 is called B-[Excl Missing]. The dataset formed as a result of applying method 2 is called C-[Replaced by Mean]. Dataset D-[Extracted Features] is the dataset formed after applying feature extraction using the Random Forest algorithm.

Table 2 provides an overview of basic properties of these derived datasets including the original dataset.

Table 2. Properties of diabetes dataset A, B, C and D.

Measure	A-[Unprocessed]	B-[Excl Missing]	C-[Replaced by Mean]	D-[Extracted Features]
Number of instances	768	359	768	359
Number of positive instances	268	128	268	128
Number of negative instances	500	231	500	231
Number of instances with missing values	409	0	0	0

3.2   Improved Generalized Regression Neural Network

A Generalized Regression Neural Network (GRNN) is a special case of the Radial Basis Function Network that is based on kernel regression networks. A GRNN does not require an iterative training procedure as is the case for back propagation networks. It is known that the feedforward back-propagation network suffers from sensitivity to randomly assigned initial weights. A GRNN does not suffer from this problem because it uses the target value as a weight connection between pattern and summation layer neurons instead of using randomized weights. A GRNN provides an estimate of continuous variables by converging into either a linear or nonlinear regression surface. This type of artificial neural network (ANN) has a simple yet powerful structure of four layers: a input layer, a pattern layer, a summation layer, and an output layer. A GRNN estimates the output by using a weighted average of the outputs of the training dataset. An output weight is computed by using a distance measure between the training data and test data. If the distance between the training data and test data is small, then more weight is allocated to the output, otherwise less weight is allocated to the output. The activation function of the GRNN is given as follows:

$$
y_i = \frac{\sum_{i=1}^{n} g_i.w_{ij}}{\sum_{i=1}^{n} g_i}
$$

where: w_{ij} is the target output corresponding to input training vector x_i, $g_i = e^{-\frac{D_i^2}{2.\sigma^2}}$ is the output of a hidden layer neuron i. Here, $D_i^2 = (x - v_i)^T(x - v_i)$ is the squared distance between the input vector x and the training vector v. v_i is the training vector i at neuron i. σ is a constant controlling the size of the receptive region.

In a GRNN the distance D_i between the training sample and the test instance x is used to measure how well each training sample can represent the position of x. Figure 1 shows the structure of the proposed KGRNN network. This network has four layers. The first layer has nine neurons representing the nine attributes in the dataset (including the class label T). The hidden layer has 49 neurons representing 49 RBF activation functions with 49 centroids. The summation layer has two neurons that compute the weighted and unweighted sum of outputs from the hidden layer. Finally, the output neuron computes the final classification value.

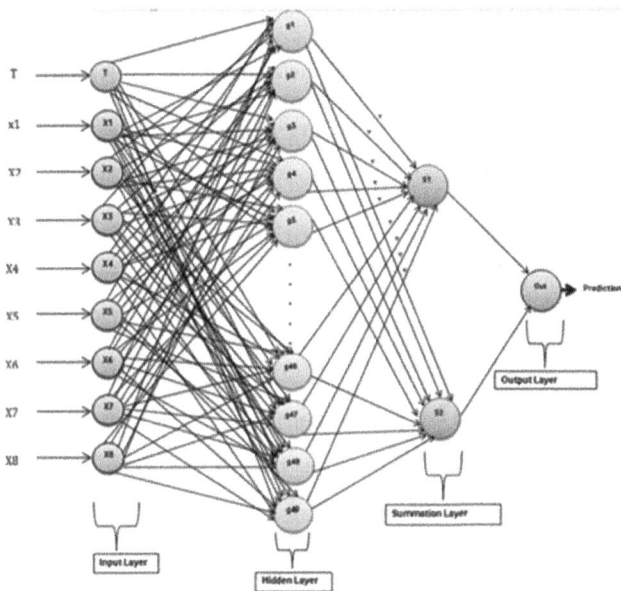

Fig. 1. KGRNN architecture

The proposed GRNN (KGRNN) uses an enhanced K-Means clustering technique to produce cluster centers (centroids) which are used as the training set for the network instead of all instances in the training set. The enhanced K-Means clustering technique (CVE-K-Means) finds quality clusters by searching for an optimal value of k within a pre-defined range of values. In order to obtain quality clusters, the CVE-K-Means algorithm also selects initial cluster centers by computing the distance between each training instance and the origin. The distance is then used to initially assign training instances to appropriate clusters based on their proximity to the origin. The pseudocode for KGRNN is given in Algorithm 1.

Algorithm 1. Pseudocode for KGRNN Algorithm

Data: A set D of n instances where $D = d_1, d_2, d_3, ..., d_i, .., d_n$ is a set of test
        examples. A set C of k-centroids (with $k < n$) produced by
        CVE-K-Means Algorithm using training set.
Result: A classification accuracy of the network given all instances from D as
        input
begin

    Make each centroid C_i in the dataset C be the centre point for each neuron
    N_i in the hidden layer of GRNN network   */* number of neurons in the
    hidden layer is = number of centroids */*
    numClassified ← 0   */* Counter of correctly classified test instances */*
    for *each instance d_i in D* **do**

        input layer of the network receives d_i attributes as input
        input layer passes inputs to all neurons in the hidden layer
        Hidden layer receives the input from input layer
        for *each neuron in the hidden layer* **do**

            D_i ← distance(input,C_i)
            Gaussian activation function $g_i = e^{-\frac{D_i^2}{2.\sigma^2}}$
            Transfer the result of the activation function as input to neurons in
            the summation layer

        Summation Layer
        numerator ← $\sum_{i=1}^{n}(weight_i * GaussianOutput_i)$

        denominator ← $\sum_{i=1}^{n}(GaussianOutput_i)$

        Output Layer
        Output ← numerator/denominator
        if *result is less than 0.5* **then**
          └ classification = 0
        else
          └ classification = 1
        if *classification matches class label of d_i* **then**
          └ increment numClassified

    /* Finish classifying given test instances   */
    Overall accuracy = numClassified / size of D
    Return classification accuracy of KGRNN

---

4   Results and Discussion

The KGRNN was implemented in the Java programming language on a machine
with an Intel i5 vPro processor running at 2.30 GHz, with 8 GB RAM and using
the JDK 1.8 software. Feature extraction using the Random Forest algorithm was
implemented in the Weka Machine Learning tool [9]. Five standard performance
measures were used in this study to evaluate the KGRNN. These performance
measures are: Classification accuracy, Sensitivity, Specificity, Positive Predictive

Value (PPV), and Negative Predictive Value (NPV). The proposed KGRNN network was configured with 49 neurons in the pattern layer and 0.19 was used as the smoothing factor σ. the forty-nine centroids that were produced by CVE-K-Means algorithm were used as a training set.

With this configuration, the network achieved the highest classification accuracy of 86% with 83% Sensitivity and 87% Specificity using the dataset D-[Extracted Features]. The second highest classification accuracy of 85% was achieved on dataset B-[Excl Missing] using $\sigma = 0.08$ and 49 centroids as training instances. The network performed poorly on two datasets A-[Unprocessed] and C-[Replaced by Mean]. It achieved the highest classification accuracy of 66% on dataset A-[Unprocessed] using 49 centroids and $\sigma = 0.09$. On dataset C-[Replaced by Mean] it achieved the highest classification accuracy of 71% using 49 centroids as training set and $\sigma = 0.05$.

Figure 2 gives the performance results for KGRNN technique using 49 training centroids and different values of σ. The influence of different values of the smoothing factor across the four datasets was also investigated. The results of this investigation are given in Fig. 3.

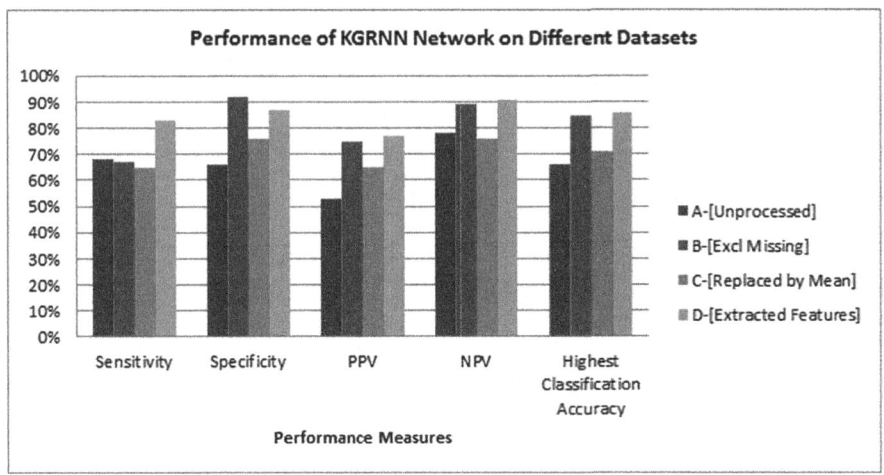

Fig. 2. Performance measures for KGRNN network.

The impact of using centroids as the training set for the KGRNN on its execution time was evaluated by recording the time the network took to train and classify diabetes as the number of centroids used increased. The performance results in Fig. 4 show that as the number of centroids increased from 5 to 140, the time it took the network to train and classify test cases also steadily increased. The results also show that it takes the network even longer to train and perform classification when data is not preprocessed.

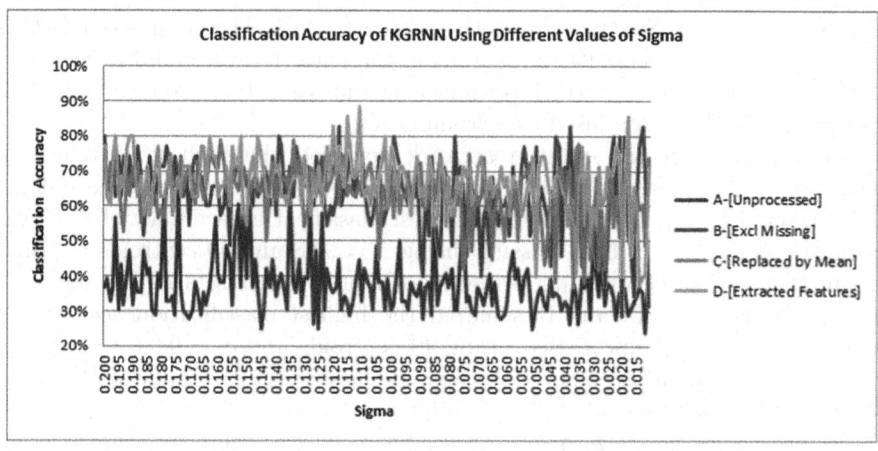

Fig. 3. KGRNN accuracy using different values of sigma and datasets.

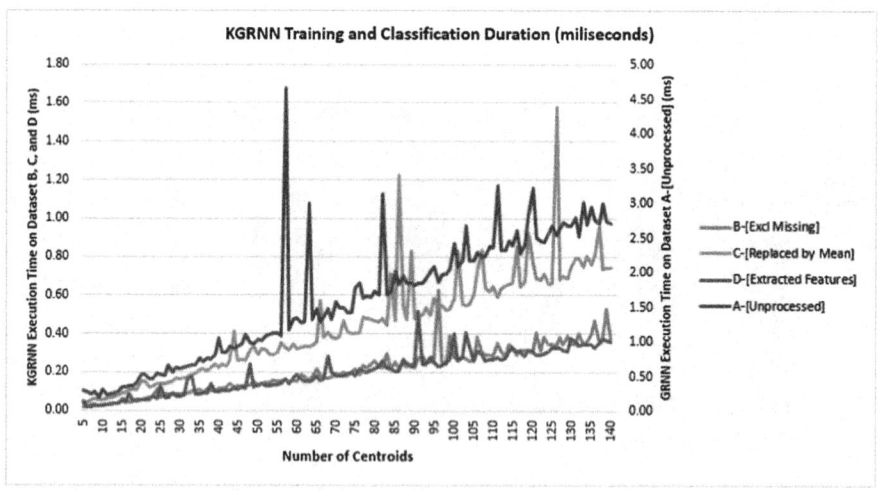

Fig. 4. KGRNN execution time for different number of centroids.

The ROC curve with AUC of 87% for KGRNN is given in Fig. 5. The ROC curve was plotted by training and testing the network using dataset D-[Extracted Features], 49 centroids as the training set and $\sigma = 1.9$. The KGRNN technique outperformed by 1% the standard GRNN technique proposed by Alby and Shivakumar [3]. The GRNN proposed by [3] obtained the highest diabetes classification accuracy known in literature for a GRNN. Table 3 compares the performance of KGRNN to other artificial neural networks in the literature.

The performance results show that the selection of relevant features using feature extraction techniques positively contributed towards the network's improved results by enhancing the quality of the dataset. The network struggled to obtain

Table 3. Accuracy comparison of KGRNN network with other ANNs

Year	Reference	Algorithm	Highest accuracy	σ
2017	This study	KGRNN	86%	0.19
2017	[3]	GRNN	85%	Not Reported
2017	[15]	RBM ANN	85%	-
2011	[1]	GRNN	84%	Not Reported
2016	[20]	CNN	83%	-
2016	[18]	PNN	81%	-
2003	[11]	GRNN	80%	2.5
2016	[7]	GA-MLPNN	79%	-
2017	[6]	RBFN	70%	-
2014	[19]	VGRNN	57%	Not reported

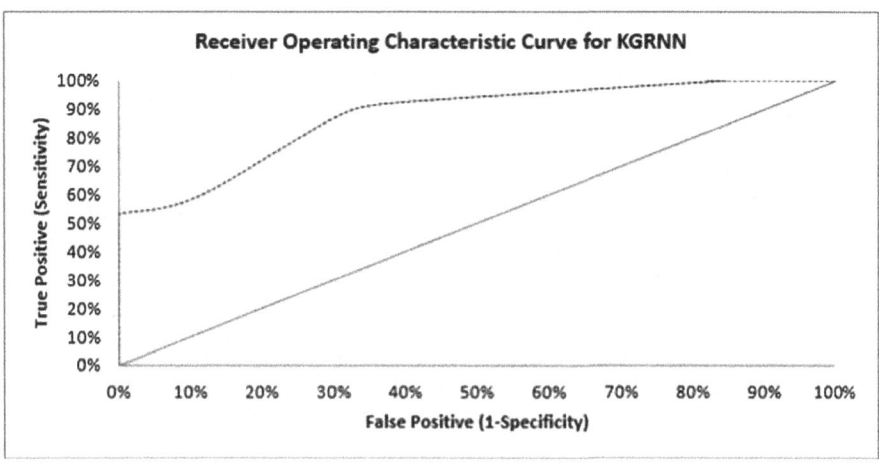

Fig. 5. ROC curve for KGRNN network

good results on dataset A-[Unprocessed] and dataset C-[Replaced by Mean]. This suggests that the network is sensitive to noise and varying attribute scales in the data. The utilization of cluster centers as the training set for the KGRNN network ensured that the network obtained improved results in less computation time compared to utilizing the entire training set. The computation time of the standard GRNN significantly increases as the number of training instances increases. This inefficiency of GRNN is effectively addressed by KGRNN.

5   Conclusion and Future Work

In this study, the diabetes diagnosis problem was addressed using an improved Generalized Regression Neural Network. The network employed the Gaussian function as its activation function during training. To improve the computational time of the network, an improved K-Means clustering technique was employed to produce quality cluster centers that were used by the network as a training set. KGRNN was able to accurately identify 83% of diabetic individuals and 87% of non-diabetic individuals during testing. Data preprocessing proved to be another significant contributor in the good performance of KGRNN. The experimental results showed that type II diabetes can be efficiently and quickly diagnosed using KGRNN.

Future work could include employing different data preprocessing techniques and different algorithm parameters. To determine the efficacy of the proposed algorithm, it would be beneficial to apply it to other benchmark problems in the future.

References

1. Adeyemo, A., Akinwonmi, A.: On the diagnosis of diabetes mellitus using artificial neural network models **4** (2011)
2. Agatonovic-Kustrin, B.: Basic concepts of artificial neural network (ANN) modeling and its application in pharmaceutical research. J. Pharm. Biomed. Anal. **22**(5) (2000)
3. Alby, S., Shivakumar, B.: A prediction model for type 2 diabetes using adaptive neuro-fuzzy interface. J. Biomed. Res., S69–S74 (2018). Special Issue
4. Barakat, N.H., Bradley, A.P., Barakat, M.N.H.: Intelligible support vector machines for diagnosis of diabetes mellitus. Trans. Info. Tech. Biomed. **14**(4), 1114–1120 (2010). https://doi.org/10.1109/TITB.2009.2039485
5. Bozkurt, M., Yurtay, N., Yilmaz, Z., Sertkaya, C.: Comparison of difierent methods for determining diabetes **22**, 1044–1055 (2014)
6. Cheruku, R., Edla, D.R., Kuppili, V.: Diabetes classification using radial basis function network by combining cluster validity index and bat optimization with novel fitness function. Int. J. Comput. Intell. Syst. **10**, 247–265 (2017)
7. Choubey, D.K.: GA-MLP NN: a hybrid intelligent system for diabetes disease diagnosis. Int. J. Intell. Syst. Appl. **1**, 49–59 (2016)
8. Indian Dental Association 6th Edition Committee: Follow-up to the political declaration of the high-level meeting of the General Assembly on the prevention and control of non-communicable diseases, 6th edn. IDF (2013)
9. Frank, E., Hall, M.A., Witten, I.H.: The WEKA Workbench. Online Appendix for Data Mining: Practical Machine Learning Tools and Techniques, 4th edn. Morgan Kaufmann (2016)
10. Karegowda, A.G., Manjunath, A., Jayaram, M.: Application of genetic algorithm optimized neural network connection weights for medical diagnosis of pima Indians diabetes. Int. J. Soft Comput. (IJSC) **2** (2011)
11. Kayaer, K., Yildirim, T.: Medical diagnosis on pima Indian diabetes using general regression neural networks. In: Proceedings of the International Conference on Artificial Neural Networks and Neural Information Processing (2003)
12. Kotsiantis, S.B., Kanellopoulos, D., Pintelas, P.E.: Data preprocessing for supervised leaning. Int. J. Comput. Sci. **1**(2) (2006)
13. Nai-Aruna, N., Moungmaia, R.: Comparison of classifiers for the risk of diabetes prediction. In: 7th International Conference on Advances in Information Technology, vol. 69, pp. 132–142 (2015)

14. Pradhan, M., Sahu, R.K.: Predict the onset of diabetes disease using artificial neural network (ANN). Int. J. Comput. Sci. Emerg. Technol. **2** (2011)

15. Ramesh, S., Balaji, H.: Optimal predictive analytics of pima diabetics using deep learning. Int. J. Database Theor. Appl. **10**, 47–62 (2017)

16. Shanker, M., Hu, M., Hung, M.: Estimating probabilities of diabetes mellitus, using neural networks. SAR QSAR Environ. Res. **11**(2), 133–147 (2000)

17. Smith, J., Everhart, J., Dickson, W., Knowler, W., Johannes, R.: Using the ADAP learning algorithm to forecast the onset of diabetes mellitus. In: Symposium on Computer Applications and Medical Care, pp. 261–265. IEEE Computer Society Press (1988)

18. Soltani, Z.: A new artificial neural networks approach for diagnosing diabetes disease type II. Int. J. Adv. Comput. Sci. Appl. **7** (2016)

19. Sujatha, V.: An intelligent expert based system neural network for the diagnosis of type2 diabetes patient. Int. J. Innovative Res. Adv. Eng. **1**(2) (2014)

20. Tharani, S., Yamini, C.: Classification using convolutional neural network for heart and diabetics datasets. Int. J. Adv. Res. Comput. Commun. Eng. **5**(12) (2016)

21. Vijayan, V., Ravikumar, A., VeluC., M., Kashwan, K.R., Karegowda, A.G., Cios, K.J., Moore, G.W.: Study of data mining algorithms for prediction and diagnosis of diabetes mellitus (2014)

22. WHO: Global health risks global health risks who mortality and burden of disease attributable to selected major risks. World Health Organization (2009)

Global Software Development: Key Performance Measures of Team in a SCRUM Based Agile Environment

Chamundeswari Arumugam[1(✉)], Srinivasan Vaidayanthan[2], and Harini Karuppuchamy[3]

[1] Department of Computer Science and Engineering,
SSN College of Engineering, Kalavakkam, Tamil Nadu, India
chamundeswaria@ssn.edu.in
[2] VIT Business School, VIT University, Chennai, India
[3] Department of Psychology, Shasun Jain College for Women,
Chennai, Tamil Nadu, India
harinikc.0805@gmail.com

Abstract. This paper is intended to study the key performance indicators of team members working in an Agile project environment in a Global Software Development setup. Practitioners from nine different projects were chosen to respond to the survey measuring the escaped defects, team member's velocity, deliverables and effort based performance indicators. These indicators are vital to any Agile project in a Global Software Development setup. The observed performance indicators were compared against the Gold Standard industry benchmarks to enable academicians and practitioners to take necessary course corrections to stay in the best case scenarios.

Keywords: Agile · Scrum · Global software development · Metrics function
Performance index

1 Introduction

Nowadays the software development has shifted completely to global software development [1, 2], and crowd source development [14]. The concentration of this paper is centric to global software development. Global software development is widely rooted in software organization to improve the productivity. There are many challenges for the organization and people who are involved in global software development. But people reinforce themselves in spite of the risk they undergo. People are ready to accept the challenges irrespective of the risk they undergo due to the benefits they acquire. On the other hand, the organizations are also facing challenges in global software development. The proper knowledge and skilled people should be hired to produce the end result. But organization comes forward to accept these challenges due to the cost cutting strategies.

Global software development strategy undergoes four stages in the development process as stated by Pressman [12]. Forming, storming, norming, and performing are

© Springer International Publishing AG, part of Springer Nature 2018
O. Gervasi et al. (Eds.): ICCSA 2018, LNCS 10963, pp. 672–682, 2018.
https://doi.org/10.1007/978-3-319-95171-3_53

the four global software development stages, the software practitioners undergo to produce the end result. Forming stages lets the team members in a project to commit on a task, while storming exposes the team members to let out their task plan to his peer members. Norming stage lets the team members to share their knowledge to his peer members, while performing determines each team members' achievement in the task, they committed. Team members should develop strong team spirit in all the four stages for the success of the project.

Agile environment is an innovative, evolvable, proactive approach that allows software development team members to learn new skills and grow by teaching others. Also, visible progress charts offer concrete ways to see progress of every member of the team. Though the agile environments produce promising best results, however the factors that influence team members in Global Software Development (GSD) are of concern. The main objective of this paper is to measure the performance of the software practitioners who are working on GSD in agile scrum environment.

The organization of the papers proceeds as follows. Section 2 discusses the related literature survey about this work. Section 3 briefly outlines the agile scrum methodology used this paper. Proposed work and the metrics related to measure the team member performance is defined and discussed in Sect. 4. Results and discussion is discussed in Sect. 5. Section 6 provides the conclusion and future enhancement of this work.

2 Literature Survey

Ashay et al. [1] highlighted factors that influence the team members' efficiency, effectiveness and productivity in global projects. Task, cultural, and distribution related factors were taken up in this work to understand the influence of virtual teams. Daniel et al. [3] unfolds the developer unhappiness based on response received from 181 questionnaires from participants. Based on quantitative and qualitative survey, recommends, working conditions of software developers need to be improved. Emily et al. [5] investigated the team performance using the team factors. 20 software development teams participated in this investigation to measure extended teamwork model factors. Communication, co-ordination of expertise, cohesion, trust, cooperation, value diversity and project performance factors was taken up to verify the project success in this investigation.

Fabian et al. [6] made an attempt to understand, how the experience of software developers can improve the software performance. Factors like communication, team spirit and team identity plays a vital role in software development process. Itanaua et al. [8] identified psychological factors that interfere directly with a work team that follows agile method. Concluded in their investigation, that trust that has more impact on the team members when compared to other factors like feelings, and maturity. Paul et al. [11] uncovered 53 attributes of great software engineers, beyond technical expertise, and their outcomes for measurement or assessment in their project or teams. Rafael et al. [13] provides guidelines to managers to set up virtual team to develop quality product.

Ronnie et al. [17] investigated job rotation is an important organization practice and has more positive impacts than negative. However, suggested the managers should be aware of them and deploy tactics to balance them. Lucas et al. [9] laid a fact that group maturity in agile team has more contribution to both industry and academia to understand team agility. Georgieos et al. [7] suggests that adopting agile on large, distributed projects improves employee satisfaction. Has a positive impact on customer satisfaction as well. Manal et al. [10] proposed estimation model at early stage on distributed projects. Serhat et al. [18] studied direct and indirect measure affecting multinational team performance and their interrelations. Identified eleven factors that affects the team performance. Also the relationship between these eleven factors was projected.

Ricardo et al. [16] proposed a model for distributed projects using stochastic automata networks (SAN) formalism to estimate, the coordination for specific project configurations. The literature survey reveals that many types of performance measures to study the team performance was proposed. In this paper, the business perspective of agile scrum framework is analyzed to study the team member performance index using the metrics.

3 Overview

Agile methodology is one of a life cycle process model that can be applied for developing GSD projects. The projects which follow agile process, have sprints or iterations for 2 weeks to 2 months. After iteration a product will be delivered. It enables the customer to provide feedback after iteration. Also enables the changes to be incorporated after iteration, feedback. But it can have one or more iteration to deliver the final product. Thus, the software is developed incrementally and delivered in iterations. The style of management followed in Agile depends on the team members. Unknown risks are more and need to be focused by team members. Agile methodology [15] has many methods to adapt for software development. Scrum, Extreme programming are two different types of methods. In this paper, scrum method which is widely used for performance measurement [17] is explored.

Scrum is one of the process method in Agile methodology. Scrum concentrates on team based development environment. In a GSD project, scrum development team members comprise of product owner, scrum master, and team members. Product owner may be clients or someone from the organization who will validate product delivery as per the plan. Scrum master sets up team, sprint meeting and takes care on removing the project obstacles that impacts productivity. The scrum master facilities and encourages the team members in decision making and problem solving capabilities. Task assignment, responsibility is empowered by team members. Team members, who belong to cross-functional group, decide how to break the tasks, and how to allocate tasks to individuals, throughout the sprint or iteration. Thus the team member is responsible for the task and product delivery at the end each iteration. The hierarchy diagram representation followed in this paper is shown in Fig. 1.

Scrum development team members can work on onsite and offshore environment in GSD projects. The scrum master, and product owner can be distributed on onsite or

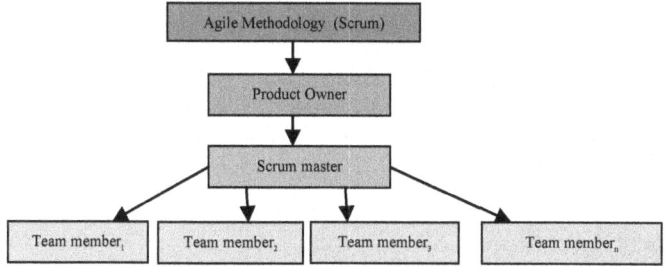

Fig. 1. Hierarchy diagram

offshore environment. Similarly, team members can be either onsite or offshore. It varies from one project to another, depending on the client. The various scenarios, scrum development team, may be located depends on the nature of project and it is shown in Table 1. In this context, the performance factors to measure team members are introduced, examined and measured here for scenario 2 and 3.

Table 1. Scrum development team

Scenario	Onsite	Offshore
1	Product owner	–
	Scrum master	
	Team members	
2	Product owner	
		Scrum master
		Team members
3	Product owner	
	Scrum master	
		Team members

The authorized product owner has an entire documentation for the project, called as product backlog. The product backlog contains the features that need to be addressed in the software. It also contains the associated activities for each feature. This document can be refined, reviewed, and revised. The scrum master has an entire documentation for the project, called as sprint backlog. The sprint backlog contains the user stories and plans to execute the user stories in form of units. The user stories are further split into tasks. Many user stories consist of one sprint. Scrum master negotiate with product owner, the number of units to be delivered in each sprint. A team member commits on a task in each sprint and delivers the product. The context diagram related to this is represented in Fig. 2.

In a positive scenario, a team member in scrum, commit on a task and completes without defects, without affecting the business. There are many negative scenarios as well. For example, a team member may complete the committed task and deliver in time. But the delivered code may prone to defect during integration. Also, there may be

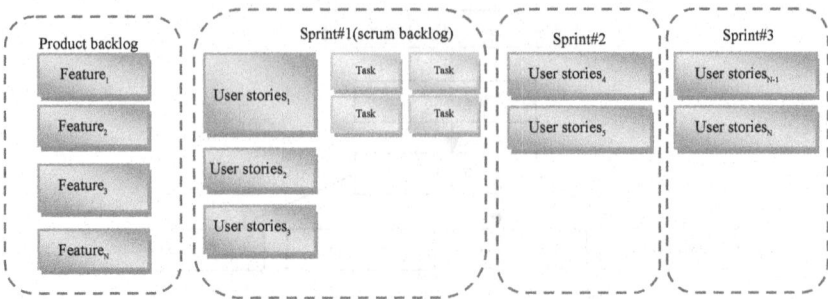

Fig. 2. Context diagram of scrum backlog

a scenario, where a team member may not have the knowledge skill to complete the task. Thus, this paper analyses the individual team members in scrum, and measure their performance towards successful product delivery.

4   Metrics Defined

In GSD projects, individual team member performance can determine the success of an organization. Continually measuring individual team member performance can be a tough task but it's the best effective way to build productive team. To build productive team, measurement is a stepping stone. Four research questions have been taken up here for performance measurement of individual team member. The Key Performance Indicator (KPI), four research questions and measurement goal is discussed in Table 2. A metric is a measurement function [4], and to develop a set of metrics, a list of quality factor need to be created.

Table 2. Defining Measurement Goal

KPI	Research question	Defining measurement goal	Indirect/Direct measurement
Escaped defects	Do defects escaped in each sprint?	To measure the individual team members escaped defects produced in the delivered product in each sprint.	Direct
Team member velocity	Are the tasks completed in user stories as per commitments?	How well the team member is bonded to his committed task?	Direct
Deliverables	Is the product in each sprint delivered within specified deadline?	To measure the work dedication of a team member	Direct
Effort	Are the efforts spent towards bug fixing equal to development efforts?	Extra effort spent by a member to complete his task.	Indirect

Research Question#1. Do defects escape in each sprint?

Escaped defect is an important metrics, to measure the defects that are existing in the delivered product. The defects need to tracked and corrected by a team member who has developed. This direct metrics affects the business of an organization. The best case is finding in the sprint#1 and worst case is finding in the sprint#N. The metric function F_1, associated with research question is given is Eq. 1.

$$\text{Escaped defects}_{\text{sprint}\#i} = \frac{\text{No. of Escaped defects of a team member in a sprint}}{\text{Total no. of escaped defects in a sprint}} \qquad (1)$$

Research question #2. Are the tasks completed in user stories as per commitments?

A sprint consists of many user stories. A user stories comprises of many tasks, to which a team member is committed. One sprint, execute period is short with a span of two or three weeks, depending on a project. The number of tasks, a team member can commit within this period of one sprint may range from one to many depending on the team members. Suppose, if a team member is not performing well, then the tasks are distributed among the other members. So, there is a chance of increase in the task that he is committed. This is a direct metric, and it is linked with the project budget of the organization. The metric function F_2, associated with research question #2 is given in Eq. 2.

$$\text{Team member velocity}_{\text{sprint}\#i} = \frac{\text{No. of task completed in a sprint}}{\text{Total no. of committed tasks in a sprint}} \qquad (2)$$

Research question #3. Is the product in each sprint delivered within specified deadline?

Deliverable is an important metrics, to measure the time spent on the product to deliver a product within the planned cycle time. The number of hours needs to be tracked and managed by a team member to complete the committed task. This is a direct measure. It affects the productivity and hence the business of the organization. The metric function F_3, associated with research question #3 is given is Eq. 3.

$$\text{Deliverables}_{\text{sprint}\#i} = \frac{\text{Total hrs spent to complete task in a sprint}}{\text{Total planned cycle duration in a sprint(hrs)}} \qquad (3)$$

Research question #4. Are the efforts spent towards bug fixing equal to development efforts?

Extra effort spent by a member to complete his task is an important metrics to measure the total effort spent to deliver a defect free product. The number of hours worked to fix the bugs will be greater than the time spent to develop the product. This is indirect measure and it affects the business of the organization. The metrics function F_4, associated with research question #4, is given in Eq. 4.

$$\text{Effort}_{\text{sprint}\#i} = \frac{\text{No. of extra hours worked to fix bugs}}{\text{Total hrs spent to complete task in a sprint} + \text{No. of extra hrs worked to fix}} \tag{4}$$

Standard 1061 [19] lays out several validation criteria for developing a metrics. Correlation, consistency, tracking, predictability, discrimination factor, and reliability are the criteria, need to be looked in. All metrics defined in Eqs. 1 to 4 follows the validation criteria. The defined metrics are correlated by the defined terms. Consistency is ensured, as it follows a monotonic function. Metric function changes from sprint$_1$ to sprint$_2$, the output also varies. Given a value of output, Y, it is possible to predict the metric function, F. A wide range of best, average and worst values are associated with each metric function, F. Thus, all metric function can demonstrate a reliable value of the application of the metric.

5 Methodology

Following the context given in this paper, this research uses survey method for its assessment and addressing of the research questions. Judgmental or purposive sampling is used to select companies that practiced the SCRUM based Agile development. Survey questionnaire was distributed to ten companies executing their SCRUM projects. Barring the rejection by one, responses were received from nine companies. Four defined metrics in Sect. 4 were assessed by framing seven questions to extract the response from practitioners. Software practitioners who are executing the agile scrum projects and practices in their organization were encouraged to fill their responses. The form was filled by software practitioners representing nine different agile projects. The set of seven questions used in the survey are listed in Table 3.

Table 3. Defining measurement goal

No.	Question
1	How many defects you anticipate in your committed task in a sprint or iteration?
2	How many defects will be anticipated by all team members in a sprint?
3	How many task you will commit in a sprint?
4	How many task you will complete in a sprint?
5	How many hours you spent to complete task in a sprint?
6	What is the planned cycle duration in a sprint?
7	How many extra hours you work to fix bugs you created in a sprint?

The working experience of practitioners ranged from five to ten years. Male and female practitioners who belonged to age group from 21 to 47 filled up the form. A set of sample data collected is represented in Table 4.

Table 4. Sample Metrics Data.

Team member	F_1	F_2	F_3	F_4	Average
SP-1	0.3	0.5	1.00	0.22	0.51
SP-2	0.1	1.00	0.10	0.11	0.33
SP-3	0.20	1.00	0.80	0.17	0.54
SP-4	0.33	1.00	0.63	0.29	0.56
SP-5	0.20	1.67	0.63	0.20	0.67
SP-6	1.00	0.80	1.00	0.11	0.73
SP-7	0.20	1.00	0.30	0.00	0.38
SP-8	0.33	1.00	1.00	0.09	0.61
SP-9	0.50	1.00	0.67	0.91	0.77
Average	0.35	1.00	0.68	0.23	

6   Results and Discussion

Industry benchmark, best case, average case, and worst case of the four metric functions are represented in Table 5.

Table 5. Industry benchmark for four metrics functions.

Metric function	Industry benchmark	Best case	Average case	Worst case
F_1	0.1	0.1 – 0.2	0.2 – 0.3	>0.3
F_2	1.0	1.0–0.9	0.9 – 0.8	<0.8
F_3	1.0	1.0–0.9	0.9 – 0.8	<0.8
F_4	0.1	0.1 – 0.2	0.2 – 0.3	<0.3

The graph is plotted to analyse the various metric function of a team member. Figure 3 represent the metric function for different software practitioners. From the metric function, it is clear that escaped defects is very less and as well it is connected with effort. The less the defects the less effort to clear the bugs. Well co-related. Normally the complete: commit ratio seems to be equal, and in certain scenario it may extend beyond 1. This clearly signifies that the practitioners are sharing task. Many experienced practitioners are able to complete the committed task within the plan cycle duration. Metric F_2 and F_3 is co-related.

Figure 4 represents the different software practitioners performance index. The performance index of SP-1, to SP-9 are 0.51, 0.33, 0.54, 0.56, 0.67, 0.73, 0.38, 0.61. and 0.77 Considering all the nine data, it is clear, that SP-9 performance index is highest and SP-2 and SP-7 is lowest and need some attention. Thus the performance index can be measured by using the four metrics. As expected, the individual performance indices for the nine different projects fall in the best, average and worst case benchmarks as observed in the industry, given in Table 5 above. The indices that are falling in the average to worst case require some course corrections to move them to the best case standards as deemed fit for the performance indices measured.

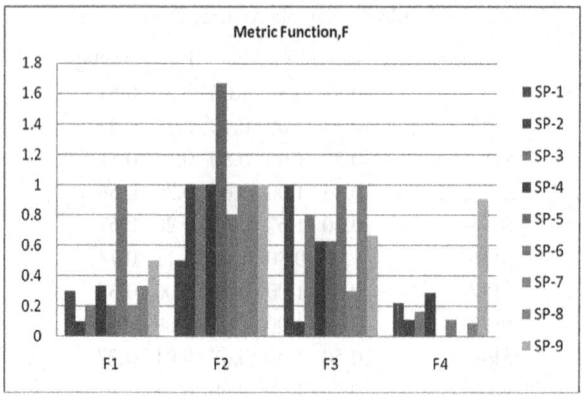

Fig. 3. Metric function for different software practitioners

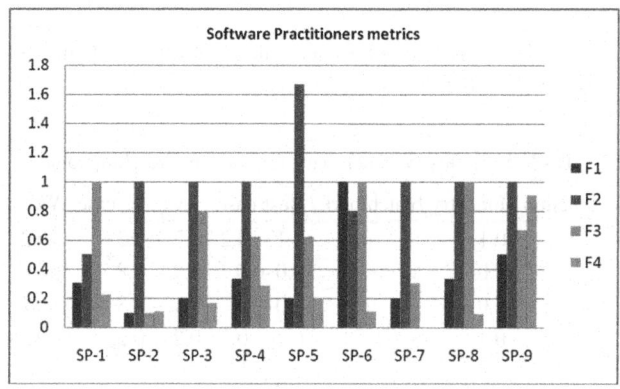

Fig. 4. Different software practitioners' performance index

7 Conclusion

With Agile projects getting into center stage, it's very critical to have right set of metrics to measure team performance and act upon right signals. In this context, this paper has taken a deep dive into various set of metrics to measure team performance in a SCRUM based Agile projects. These early warning signals can provide right view for PMs to manage the project and trigger right course correction at right time. As a further scope for research the same set of metrics can be measured in a Scaled Agile or XP based Agile projects and validate the findings. The procedure can be repeated for the Only Offshore based projects as well.

References

1. Ashay, S., Johanna, B.: Factors affecting team performance in globally distributed setting. In: Proceedings of the 52nd ACM Conference on Computers and People Research, pp. 25–33 (2014)
2. Chamundeswari, A., Sriraghav, K., Baskaran, K.: Global software development: a design framework to measure the risk of the global practitioners. In: ACM International Conference on Computer and Communication Technology (2017)
3. Daniel, G., Fabian, F., Xiaofeng, W., Pekka, A.: Consequences of unhappiness while developing software. In: Proceedings of the 2nd International Workshop on Emotion Awareness in Software Engineering, pp. 42–47 (2017)
4. Cem, K., Walter, P.B.: Software engineering metrics: what do they measure and how do we know? In: Proceedings of the 10th International Software Metrics Symposium, Metrics (2004)
5. Emily, W., Ariadi, N., Joost, V., Aske, P.: Towards high performance software teamwork. In: Proceedings of the 17th International Conference on Evaluation and Assessment in Software Engineering, pp. 212–215 (2013)
6. Fabian, F., Marko, I., Petri, K., Jürgen, M., Virpi, R., Pekka, A.: How do software developers experience team performance in lean and agile environments? In: Proceedings of the 18th International Conference on Evaluation and Assessment in Software Engineering, p. 7 (2014)
7. Georgios, P.: Moving from traditional to agile software development methodologies also on large, distributed projects. In: International Conference on Strategic Innovative Marketing, IC-SIM 2014, Spain, Procedia - Social and Behavioral Sciences, vol. 175, pp. 455–463 (2015)
8. Itanauã, F.B., Marcela, P.O., Priscila, B.S.R., Tancicleide, C.S.G., Fabio, Q.B.D.S.: Towards understanding the relationships between interdependence and trust in software development: a qualitative research. In: 10th International Workshop on Cooperative and Human Aspects of Software Engineering, pp. 66–69 (2017)
9. Lucas, G., Richard, T., Robert, F.: Group development and group maturity when building agile teams: a qualitative and quantitative investigation at eight large companies. J. Syst. Softw. **124**, 104–119 (2017)
10. Manal, E.B.: Analogy-based software development effort estimation in global software development. In: IEEE 10th International Conference on Global Software Engineering Workshops, pp. 51–54 (2015)
11. Paul, L., Andrew, J.K., Jiamin, Z.: What makes a great software engineer? In: 37th International Conference on Software Engineering, pp. 700–710 (2015)
12. Pressman, R.: Software Engineering: A Practitioner's Approach. McGraw-Hill (2005)
13. Rafael, P., Marcelo, P., Sabrina, M.: Virtual team configurations that promote better product quality. In: Proceedings of the 10th ACM/IEEE International Symposium on Empirical Software Engineering and Measurement (2016)
14. Razieh, L.S., Ye, Y., Guenther, R., David, M.: Leveraging Crowdsourcing for team elasticity: an empirical evaluation at TopCoder. In: IEEE/ACM 39th International Conference on Software Engineering: Software Engineering in Practice Track, pp. 103–112 (2017)
15. Ricardo, B., Darja, Š., Lars-Ola, D.: Experiences from measuring learning and performance in large-scale distributed software development. In: Proceedings of the 10th ACM/IEEE International Symposium on Empirical Software Engineering and Measurement, vol. 17 (2016)

16. Ricardo, M.C., Paulo, F., Lucelene, L., Afonso, S., Alan, R.S., Thais, W.: Stochastic performance analysis of global software development teams. ACM Trans. Softw. Eng. Methodol. **25**(3), 26:1–26:32 (2016)

17. Ronnie, E.S.S., Fabio, Q.B.D.S., Cleyton, V.C.D.M., Cleviton, V.F.M.: Building a theory of job rotation in software engineering from an instrumental case study. In: Proceedings of the 38th International Conference on Software Engineering, pp. 971–981 (2016)

18. Serhat, S., Ramazan, K., Bulent S.: Factors affecting multinational team performance. In: 12th International Strategic Management Conference, ISMC, Procedia - Social and Behavioral Sciences, vol. 25, no. 3, pp. 60–69 (2016)

19. IEEE, IEEE Std. 1061-1998: Standard for a Software Quality Metrics Methodology, revision. IEEE Standards Department, Piscataway, NJ (1998)

Cloud Applications Management – Issues and Developments

I. Odun-Ayo[1(✉)], B. Odede[1], and R. Ahuja[2]

[1] Department of Computer and Information Sciences,
Covenant University, Ota, Nigeria
isaac.odun-ayo@covenantuniversity.edu.ng,
blessingodede@gmail.com
[2] University of Delhi, New Delhi, India
ravinahujadce@gmail.com

Abstract. Cloud computing is a platform that dictates the mode of operations within most data centers. Cloud computing relieves its consumer's from investment in IT infrastructure. Cloud consumers are provided with on-demand services at affordable cost. Cloud service providers offer custom made applications that can be used by a variety of users to handle routine tasks. Cloud service providers also offer their users programming interfaces that enables developers design and deploy applications efficiently. In addition, it is very important for cloud service providers to regulate resources based on the workload on the applications and provide computational resources and storage. Despite cloud computing benefits, it is difficult for cloud users to port applications from one platform to another, this difficulty is inevitable because of the cost and complexity of porting such applications. In addition, it is essential for the cloud service providers to adjust resources based on workloads or failures on the system. This paper discusses key concepts of cloud applications management, issues and development and also reviews recent related literature on cloud application management. This paper examines present trends in the area of cloud application management and provides a guide for future research. In this paper, the main objective is to answer the following questions: what is the current development and trend in cloud application management? Papers published in journals, conferences and white papers were analyzed. The result in this review shows that there is insufficient discussion in the area of trust management and security as it relates to cloud applications management. This would be beneficial to prospective cloud users, researchers and cloud service providers alike.

Keywords: Cloud computing · Management · Applications · Workloads

This work was supported in part by the Covenant University Centre for Research Innovation and Discovery (CUCRID).

O. Gervasi et al. (Eds.): ICCSA 2018, LNCS 10963, pp. 683–694, 2018.
https://doi.org/10.1007/978-3-319-95171-3_54

1 Introduction

"CLOUD computing is a model for enabling universal, on-demand and convenient network access to a shared pool of configurable computing resources (e.g., networks, servers, storage, applications, and services) that can be rapidly provisioned and released with minimal management effort or service provider interaction" [1]. Cloud computing and its enabling technologies is dynamically changing the face of the IT world. Cloud computing is offering beneficial services to big and small enterprises alike. Organizations are gradually out-sourcing and migrating their applications to the cloud. Cloud computing provides scalable, elastic, on-demand compute and storage services via the Internet to cloud users. Cloud computing offers three important services such as Platform-as-a-Service (PaaS), Infrastructure-as-a-Service (IaaS) and Software-as-a-Service (SaaS) [1]. SaaS enables cloud service providers deploy custom made applications to the cloud. Applications such as Microsoft Office 365 are essential for routine activities for cloud consumers. Cloud users does not need to worry about license or having to install an application. PaaS enables the creation and deployment of applications to the cloud by cloud consumers based on infrastructure provided by cloud service providers (CSP) [2]. Programming platform with suitable application programming interfaces is provided to the user. IaaS entails the provision of compute resource, network bandwidth and storage by major CSPs to users at a cost. The CSPs operate large cloud date centers sometimes spanning different geographical location around the world. Cloud computing offers four important deployment models such as community, hybrid, public and private clouds. Community clouds deals with organizations with shared common interest and it could be managed by a third party based on an agreed policy. Hybrid clouds is a combination of either community, public or private clouds [2]. Hybrid clouds take advantage of the benefits of the various cloud models by deploying less critical information to public clouds, while core information are retained on the private cloud. Private clouds are fully owned by individual organizations using in-house staff only for access. The private cloud can be on-premise or off-premise and could be managed by a third party. Private clouds provide secure cloud services. Public clouds are managed and owned by major CSPs. They have huge infrastructure to provide various kinds of services on a pay-as-you-go basis to customers. Public clouds are considered less secure.

A major operation that takes place on the cloud is the utilization of different kind of applications through the various service and deployment models. Cloud applications have become popular tools for businesses everywhere [2]. Cloud applications are cloud hosted-tools that help businesses collaborate, communicate, and share information within their domain. Some businesses even use cloud applications to manage relationship with their customers. Cloud applications are incredibly convenient as they host an organization's data in the cloud, and such data can be accessed anywhere and at any time using devices that can connect to the Internet.

Application management is making applications perform optimally at all times by ensuring that they are secure and well-maintained. Within an enterprise where the environment is always changing, desperate use of cloud application can lead to clutter and accidental loss of information. Sometimes clutters such as application of user profile and other information may cause the enterprise to lose track of licenses under management. In case of cloud storage applications, a user may accidentally delete an important folder or document leading to critical loss. People may leave an organization or change their rules. Users who leave may still have access to the enterprise's SaaS profiles and data which could leak either personal identifiable information (PII) confidential data.

Cloud applications management allows an enterprise to handle these problems and other issues. Usually cloud application have their own management platforms in the form of "settings" or "Admin" options. Every application has its own set of monitoring tools, and administrators can usually see snapshots of recent activities and manually customize notification alerts. Third party applications that manage cloud applications are also available to the administrator. Third party applications make up for what traditional applications cannot monitor or manage. Such third party applications provide a single view of all the cloud applications of that organization. It is also possible to manage multiple cloud applications at once.

The aim of this paper is to discuss cloud applications management issues and development. This paper examines cloud services management process. Thereafter, activities in the industry is highlighted. The rest of the paper is as follow. Section 2 is an overview of related literature contributed by other researchers. Section 3 discusses cloud applications management activities. Section 4 examines current trends in the cloud services industry. Section 5 concludes and suggests future research area.

2   Related Work

SeaClouds in [3] examines the problem of deploying applications across multiple cloud services. The major objective of the seacloud framework is the utilization of these complex solutions (applications). An overview of mobile cloud computing applications, framework, approaches and architecture in [4] discusses very important aspects of mobile cloud computing. It also extensively discusses the diverse applications of mobile cloud computing. Challenges of QoE Management for Cloud Applications in [5] examines multimedia cloud application. The multimedia cloud applications are discussed using the quality of experience scheme. Development and Management of Cloud Solutions in [6] discusses the management flow of the automation utilized by cloud providers for application access. An abstract method is proposed for efficient management of application interfaces. Managing NFC Payment Applications through Cloud Computing in [7] explores the use of near field communication for data transmission. A framework is proposed for using the cloud to manage near field communication. Cloud services for managing smart grid Information in the Cloud: Opportunities, Model, and applications in [8] examines the smart grid technology. The main focus is how cloud computing can be used to enhance smart grid in terms of information management.

Managing Wearable Sensor Data through Cloud Computing in [9] presents issues in health care technologies. Storage and interoperability among others can be resolved using the cloud as suggested in the work. The main focus is a wearable gadgets that can be used to manage information using cloud services. iOverbook used for managing cloud-based real-time solutions in a resource-overbooked data center in [10] focuses on overbooking of user applications in relation to the resources of cloud service providers. An iOverbook framework is proposed to handle overbooking of resources and also ensure that real-time applications are not affected. Applying MDE to counter the Issues of Managing Multiple Cloud Solutions in [11] examines the issues of vendor lock-in and interoperability in the field of cloud applications. To ease the complexity of managing cloud solutions a framework is proposed. An effective framework for managing energy consumption in cloud services infrastructure in [12] focuses on the issues of power consumption in data centers. To manage this effectively a model was proposed which is considered better than other similar algorithms, enhancing the activities of dynamic cloud users. Designing and operating time critical solutions in cloud infrastructure the state-of-the-art and the switch framework in [13] is concerned with time critical applications. The application framework, co-programming and control infrastructure was created to enhance programmability and controllability of applications. Self-managing Cloud Native Solution, Design, implementation, and experience in [14] focuses on the disparity between deployed applications and their management. A native model was designed to enable self-managing applications on the cloud.

3 Cloud Applications Management

3.1 Application Management Strategy

There are benefits such as cost saving, scalability and accessibility when utilizing the cloud to host an application instead of hosting it on premises. However, there are several issues like moving from a network that can be controlled to another that the enterprise has no control over. With cloud applications, bandwidth needs, traffic utilization and impact of other applications affect the performance on the cloud, compared to using such applications on–premises [15]. Despite the enormous benefit of the cloud, there are issue that will affect performance of applications [15].

Loss of Visibility
Utilizing applications on– premises enables the enterprise to have applications run on servers in the data center with users within its vicinity. It is easy to know immediately if an application is up or down, and if there are power issues. In addition, the network part from user to application is simple with only a limited number of hardware involved. However, on the cloud the enterprise does not know where the application resides and where the user resides. Wherever there is a problem there is little understanding of the source within the underlying infrastructure supporting the application delivery, making it difficult to even participate in the troubleshooting or the optimization process [15].

Loss of Control
An enterprise will always lose some control wherever an application is outsourced to the cloud, but it's difficult to determine how much control will be lost. When an application has a problem, the enterprise lacks the ability to change the path of the application over the WAN, make QoS policy changes or address security concerns

[15]. Due to the fact that the enterprise lacks visibility, it is difficult to decide on the course of action to take.

Inability to Influence Service Level Agreement

Every cloud provider has a SLA, but when guarantees are not met, the effect on the provider is minimal and there is often no compensation for the loss of business to the consumer. It is having visibility and control over the network that translates into other enterprise's ability to optimize application performance. There are measures that can be taken to mitigate the issues of loss of control visibility and maintaining SLA. Such measures are discussed below: [15]

a. *The Cloud Path.* The cloud application is on one end while the cloud user is at another end. If the application is on a public cloud, and accessed by a user remotely, it is difficult to determine the path. To manage an application efficiently, the enterprise must have the ability to determine the path of the application, as well as the path of a problem when it occurs.

b. *Bandwidth Reservation.* Setting up local bandwidth reservation is easy on-premises. The enterprise has no control on the path or the hardware involved in that path. It is therefore important to measure and control the bandwidth utilized to avoid congestion.

c. *Quality of Service.* In terms of the QoS and SLA, an enterprise must place a network priority on a given cloud application for optimum management. This is to ensure that QoS guarantees are met.

d. *Latency.* The latency is a factor of the QoS, bandwidth and the path of the applications. Latency affects the user's trust in the application. Latency is a critical issues because not all devices or system permit unacceptable latency. So, it is important to gain control over these issue for optimum management.

There are certain strategies to ensure that an application utilization is optimized.

a. *Hosting On Private Clouds.* Private cloud has dedicated infrastructure or connectivity to an organization. The private cloud provides an organization with a secondary data center for hosting an application and for disaster recovery. Hence, it becomes easy to have control and optimize the use of applications.

b. *Control Cloud Access.* There are public clouds that provide some measure of control. When using a public cloud to host an application, an enterprise can centralize the connectivity to the application by retuning all application traffic through the organizations network, thereby increasing the security and providing some ability to monitor and control traffic. There are third party cloud management application tools that can be utilized. In addition, the enterprise Admin can monitor the page load times, transaction times, and server times up. It is possible to guess what the user experience is like through this process.

3.2 Autonomic Computing

To effectively manage cloud deployed applications, it is necessary that reactions to frequent occurring events are built into the applications [16]. Autonomic computing can be used to develop a cloud application software which knows how it reacts to changes in it [3]. Autonomic computing was first used in 2001 to describe computing systems that are self-managing [20]. To achieve this, IBM proposed a framework for autonomic computing control which is called control MAPE – K [16]. The sensors obtain data about the managed element [16]. The information can be the response time to cloud services, CPU and memory utilization. The effectors changes are carried out to effectively manage the element. The changes could be removing or adding virtual machines (VMs) to cloud application (replication) or changing configuration parameters in a virtual machine [16]. The information obtained by the sensor enables the autonomic manager to monitor the managed element and execute changes through the effectors. The autonomic manager is a component used for monitoring the system, analysis of the metrics, plan corrective action and execute them [16].

3.3 Application Security

Cloud applications hosted on the Internet are subjected to web security issues. Cloud application need security different from traditional security because of multi–tenancy, virtualization and colocation of sensor resources. The following threats were identified in [17].

a. Injections like SQL, OS, and LDAP.
b. Problems of session management and broken authentication.
c. Problem of insecurity and direct object reference.
d. Issues of forward and invalidated redirection.
e. Problem with security misconfiguration.
f. Issues of request forgery.
g. Issues of unknown vulnerable components.
h. Issues of missing method level access control.
i. Issues of important information exposure.
j. Issues of managing Cross Side Scripting.

Cloud services and solutions on PaaS and SaaS layers requires effective security measures to have secure design and execution framework model [18]. Cloud security alliance recommends that the security to any cloud solution must be provided without any assumption about any external environment [10]. The following are recommendations for securing applications [10]

a. Security and privacy requirements must be defined in accordance to the necessities of cloud implementation and deployment.
b. The attack and vulnerability vectors specific to cloud services infrastructure must be implemented and included in the security requirement.
c. A secure system development life cycle and system architecture process should be maintained and deployed.
d. Routine security checks and penetration testing for web-based applications should be carried out.
e. Annual testing should be carried out periodically to ensure secure management of web-based applications.

4   Analysis and Discussion

In this section cloud applications management issues including security as reviewed in related literature are presented. Table 1 presents a summary of related literature that examined current cloud applications management issues, security risk and solution trends.

4.1   Virtualization

The security vulnerabilities associated with software applications is applied to all virtual instances, however VMs security is very complex [19]. If a particular virtual machine is infected it automatically infects other virtual machines because it's not necessary to bypass other components which include the network infrastructure. The infected virtual machines are then executed against the hypervisor software attacks [21]. The problem is that it may have a negative impact on any organization that uses cloud service applications as sensitive information can be accessed by unauthorized users during such attacks. Unauthorized access of information occurs because of the shared resources used by virtual machines [22]. A PaaS framework, should focus on isolating the application programming interface invocation including the currently executing service. In SaaS framework, isolation should focus on the transactions executed on the same instance [23]. From the core literature examined, only 20% of the papers focused on this issue.

4.2   Integrity and Data Privacy

Data integrity and privacy ensures that data are isolated privately and prevented from attackers, including preventing unauthorized modification of sensitive information. The major setback of using this mechanism is the problem of limited control cloud consumers or users have over the cloud servers and the data that is deployed or residing in storage [24]. Information residing in any IaaS framework can be secured by using cryptography techniques to encrypt information in order to eliminate the problem of sensitive information being accessed by unauthorized users [23]. The legitimate information owners do not have the capabilities necessary to manage their cryptography keys. Enabling the CSPs manage cryptography keys could solve this issue but the management of complex or large length of cryptography keys is a complex task and the CSPs require a very complex security mechanism of achieving this. Information residing in any cloud infrastructure may be corrupted by both administrative or management exceptions as well as attacks [25]. Most CSPs charge consumers certain amount of fee for deploying and downloading information. This means that downloading large information that enables integrity and authentication of information is not a visible approach for solving the problem. Some approach for solving this problem has been proposed which include allocating a third party agent that is appointed by the CSP to periodically monitor the integrity of information [24]. The integrity of applications becomes a serious issue because the CSPs provide the software the consumers or users utilizes [26]. Again, from the major papers reviewed on this topic, only 33% of them sufficiently discussed the issue of data privacy and integrity.

Table 1. Cloud application management issues

Authors	Virtualization	Data privacy	Deduplication	DDOS	Loss of control and availability	Trust management	Security models
Chen, D., & Zhao, H. (2012).		x					
Sabahi, F. (2011).			x				
Trivedi, K., & Pasley, K. (2012).			x				
Behl, A., & Behl, K. (2012).	x	x					
Bouayad, A., Blilat, A., El Houda Mejhed, N., & El Ghazi, M. (2012).	x						
Khalil, I. M., Khreishah, A., Bouktif, S., & Ahmad, A. (2013).					x		
Xiao, Z., & Xiao, Y. (2013).	x	x			x		
Tari, Z. (2014).		x			x		
Grobauer, B., Walloschek, T., & Stocker, E. (2011).							
Varadharajan, V., & Tupakula, U. (2014).					x		
Liu, M., Dou, W., Yu, S., & Zhang, Z. (2015).				x			
Subashini, S., & Kavitha, V. (2011).							x
Zissis, D., & Lekkas, D. (2012).		x			x		
Rahman, M., & Cheung, W. M. (2014) a.					x		
Rahman, M., & Cheung, W. M. (2014) b.				x			

4.3 Deduplication

Deduplication is a method where only a single copy of each file is stored in the server, regardless of the number of clients requesting storage of the same information.

Implementing this mechanism enables efficient utilization of network bandwidth as well as cloud servers. However, redundancy and duplication of information may result in access to vital and sensitive information. For example, a cloud server leveraging this platform might receive a request for information to be stored, however this information already exist on the cloud server. The cloud server then informs the client requesting the information that the information is inexistence in the storage, and as such cannot be transferred [29].

4.4   Denial of Service

Denial of Service attack or Distributed Denial of Service (DDoS) is a major security vulnerability in cloud computing. Denial of Service or DDoS generally functions by the attacker transferring large amounts of information packets to an organization's network. The objective of any DDoS attack is to deny legitimate users access to the server by overloading the server's capacity and bandwidth [27]. This is achievable when the host server is unable to execute any information causing many virtual machines to disrupt their services, effectively making them inaccessible TO the users [27]. The solution to Denial of Service attacks is the deployment of firewall [28]. However, the deployment of firewall in a cloud computing infrastructure comes with a lot problem. A framework such as a centralized firewall to secure a cloud infrastructure environment against a number of vulnerabilities can be implemented. However, centralized firewalls has a lot of disadvantages. Since cloud service infrastructure executes many different services, while the package arrival rate allowed will be different for each service. In order to use a centralized firewall, the ruleset will increase, and individual users cannot specify separate rules for their cloud infrastructure [28]. Issuing a decentralized firewall platform would eliminate this problem. Deploying this platform is very effective and reduces cost [28]. Despite the effect of DDoS attacks on any organizations infrastructure, only 13% of the papers examined, discussed this topic.

4.5   Loss of Control and Availability

In this case, vulnerability is associated with the fact that cloud service consumers or users does not have privilege to the hardware infrastructure being used. This problem has severe implications for the cloud service users. The most important approach is to evaluate if deploying vital information violates existing contract or terms of use with legitimate owners of the information [30]. If storing important information on cloud services is viewed as violating the privacy of information because of loss of control and availability, organization should not proceed with their plans to deploy information to the cloud. Apart from this, choosing a trustworthy cloud service provider is very important. Organizations looking forward to migrate to cloud infrastructure must make a careful and important evaluation of the CSPs security measures and privacy measures [25].

Ensuring information is secured properly against vulnerabilities with the use of backups is essential. Obtaining routine backup on a local system of every user information stored in the cloud is a very secure method. However, this approach defeats some of the purpose of cloud computing and it is not economical. Identifying who is responsible if a backup failed or if a backup is tampered with is equally important [31].

The issue of loss of control and availability is of major concern to users at all level on the cloud, but the focus on this topic was done by only 33% of the papers used in the analysis.

4.6 Trust Management

Trust Management is implemented to counter the issues of applications with centralized security especially where heterogeneity of policy languages is involved. As suggested in [32], trust management methods are divided into several categories such as prediction, policy, recommendation and reputation. Recommendation method takes advantage of the knowledge of the users about the various parties involved. Reputation method is used to provide feedbacks by cloud infrastructure, because users of cloud service infrastructure can downgrade the reputation of a particular cloud service provider. Policy method uses a set of instructions which enables each process to assume a specific responsibility to grant authorization. Prediction method is used when there is no prior information concerning the communication of cloud services. Among the very important papers selected for this analysis, none of them discussed trust management with respect to cloud applications management.

4.7 Security Models

In [33], a security framework for cloud computing consisting of governance, compliance and risk management is discussed. Cloud computing security requirements is significantly different from the manual frameworks due to its robust and dynamic nature. It is important to note that this framework can be used for each type of cloud infrastructure such as community, public, private and hybrid. Among the papers selected for this analysis, only 6% discussed issues relating to security in terms of cloud applications management.

5 Conclusion

Cloud computing offers the ability to deploy and utilize applications on the cloud. CSPs also provide custom applications for users to utilize anytime, anywhere from the Internet. Managing applications on the cloud is essential both for the CSP and the cloud users. There are several issues associated with managing cloud applications including security considerations. There are measures that should be taken by enterprises to ensure that applications are properly managed. In addition, there are cloud application management tools to enhance easy management of applications. Increasing number of applications in business requires increase in the number tools needed to manage applications on the cloud. Some core topics related to cloud applications management were examined. Clearly, there is need for more work in the area of trust management and security in managing applications on the cloud.

Acknowledgment. We acknowledge the support and sponsorship provided by Covenant University through the Centre for Research, Innovation and Discovery (CUCRID).

References

1. Mell, P., Grance, T.: The NIST Definition of Cloud Computing. NIST Special Publication 800-145 (2011)
2. BetterCloud: Cloud Application Management (2015). https://www.bettercloud.com/glossary-cloud-application-management/
3. Brogi, A., Ibrahim, A., Soldani, J., Carrasco, J., Cubo, J., Pimentel, E., D'Andria, F.: SeaClouds: a European project on seamless management of multi-cloud applications. SIGSOFT Softw. Eng. Notes 39(1), 1–4 (2014). 39-1-2014-0163-5948. https://doi.org/10.1145/2557833.2557844
4. Dinh, H.T., Lee, C., Niyato, D., Wang, P.: A survey of mobile cloud computing: architecture, applications, and approaches. Wirel. Commun. Mob. Comput. 13(18), 1587–1611 (2011)
5. Hoßfeld, T.: Challenges of QoE management for cloud applications. IEEE Commun. Mag. 50(4), 20–27 (2012)
6. Fehling, C., Leymann, F., Rütschlin, J., Schumm, D.: Pattern-based development and management of cloud applications. Future Internet 4, 110–141 (2012). https://doi.org/10.3390/fi4010110
7. Pourghomi, P., Ghinea, G.: Managing NFC payment applications through cloud computing. In: The 7th International Conference for Internet Technology and Secured Transactions (ICITST-2012) (2012)
8. Fang, X., Misra, S., Xue, G., Yang, D.: Managing smart grid information in the cloud: opportunities, model, and applications. IEEE Netw. 26(4), 32–38 (2015). https://doi.org/10.1109/mnet.2012.6246750
9. Doukas, C., Maglogiannis, I.: Managing wearable sensor data through cloud computing. In: 2011 Third IEEE International Conference on Coud Computing Technology and Science (2011). https://doi.org/10.1109/cloudcom.2011.65
10. Caglar, F., Gokhale, A.: iOverbook: Managing Cloud-based Soft Real-time Applications in a Resource Overbooked Data Center. https://pdfs.semanticscholar.org/f42c/56380367fa638f389eeb3eae67ab8a6c075e.pdf
11. Ferry, N., Song, H., Rossini, A., Chauvel, F., Solberg, A.: CloudMF: Applying MDE to Tame the Complexity of Managing Multi-Cloud Applications (2013). http://cloudml.org/wp-content/uploads/nordicloud13_pres.pdf
12. Abd, S.K., Al-Haddad, S.A.R., Hashim, F., Abdullah, A.B.H.J., Yussof, S.: An effective approach for managing power consumption in cloud computing infrastructure. J. Comput. Sci. 21, 349–360 (2016). http://dx.doi.org/10.1016/j.jocs.2016.11.007
13. Zhaoa, Z., Martin, P., Wang, J., Taal, A., Jones, A., Taylor, I., Stankovski, V., Vega, I.G., Suciu, G., Ulisses, A., de Laat, C.: Developing and operating time critical applications in clouds: the state of the art and the SWITCH approach. Proc. Comput. Sci. 68(2015), 17–28 (2015). https://doi.org/10.1016/j.procs.2015.09.220
14. Toffetti, G., Brunner, S., Blöchlinger, M., Spillner, J., Bohnert, T.M.: Self-managing cloud-native applications: design, implementation, and experience. Future Gener. Comput. Syst. (2016). https://doi.org/10.1016/j.future.2016.09.002
15. Fortinet: Securing Cloud Applications (2017). www.fortinet.com
16. Huebscher, M.C., Mccann, J.A.: A survey of autonomic computing—degrees, models and applications (2009). Accessed 24 May 2017
17. Ali, M., Khan, S.U., Vasilakos, A.V.: Security in cloud computing: opportunities and challenges. Inf. Sci. 305(2015), 357–383 (2015)

18. Velte, A.T., Velte, T.J., Elsenpeter, R.C., Elsenpeter, R.C.: Cloud Computing: A Practical Approach, pp. 250–251. The McGraw-Hill, New York (2010). ISBN 978-0-07-162695-8

19. Cloud Management Tools: Cloud Native Application Management, 1 October 2017. https://cloud.google.com/products/management/

20. App Dynamics: Cloud Application Management (2017). https://www.appdynamics.com/solutions/cloud-application-management/

21. Mishra, A., Mathur, R., Jain, S., Singh Rathore, J.: Cloud computing security. Int. J. Recent Innov. Trends Comput. Commun. (IJRITCC), pp. 36–39 (2013). http://www.ijritcc.org/download/IJRITCC_1309.pdf

22. Tari, Z.: Security and privacy in cloud computing. IEEE Cloud Comput. 1(1), 54–57 (2014). https://doi.org/10.1109/MCC.2014.20

23. Behl, A., Behl, K.: An analysis of cloud computing security issues. In: 2012 World Congress on Information and Communication Technologies (WICT), pp. 109–114 (2012). http://doi.org/10.1109/WICT.2012.6409059

24. Chen, D., Zhao, H.: Data security and privacy protection issues in cloud computing. In: 2012 International Conference on Computer Science and Electronics Engineering (ICCSEE), vol. 1, pp. 647–651 (2012). http://doi.org/10.1109/ICCSEE.2012.193

25. Xiao, Z., Xiao, Y.: Security and privacy in cloud computing. IEEE Commun. Surv. Tutorials 15(2), 843–859 (2013). https://doi.org/10.1109/SURV.2012.060912.00182

26. Zissis, D., Lekkas, D.: Addressing cloud computing security issues. Future Gener. Comput. Syst. 28(3), 583–592 (2012). https://doi.org/10.1016/j.future.2010.12.006

27. Rahman, M., Cheung, W.M.: Analysis of cloud computing vulnerabilities. Int. J. Innov. Sci. Res. 2(2), 308–312 (2014a). http://www.issr-journals.org/links/papers.php?journal=ijisr&application=pdf&article=IJISR-14-120-07

28. Liu, M., Dou, W., Yu, S., Zhang, Z.: A decentralized cloud firewall framework with resources provisioning cost optimization. IEEE Trans. Parallel Distrib. Syst. 26(3), 621–631 (2015). https://doi.org/10.1109/TPDS.2014.2314672

29. Li, J., Li, J., Xie, D., Cai, Z.: Secure auditing and deduplicating data in cloud. IEEE Trans. Comput. PP(99), 1 (2015). http://doi.org/10.1109/TC.2015.2389960

30. Al-Anzi, F.S., Salman, A.A., Jacob, N.K., Soni, J.: Towards robust, scalable and secure network storage in Cloud Computing. In: 2014 Fourth International Conference on Digital Information and Communication Technology and it's Applications (DICTAP), pp. 51–55 (2014). http://doi.org/10.1109/DICTAP.2014.6821656

31. Khalil, I.M., Khreishah, A., Bouktif, S., Ahmad, A.: Security concerns in cloud computing. In: 2013 Tenth International Conference on Information Technology: New Generations (ITNG), pp. 411–416 (2013). http://doi.org/10.1109/ITNG.2013.127

32. Noor, T.H., Sheng, Q.Z., Zeadally, S., Yu, J.: Trust management of services in cloud environments: obstacles and solutions. ACM Comput. Surv. 46(1), 12:1–12:30 (2013). http://doi.org/10.1145/2522968.2522980

33. Al-Anzi, F.S., Yadav, S.K., Soni, J.: Cloud computing: security model comprising governance, risk management and compliance. In: 2014 International Conference on Data Mining and Intelligent Computing (ICDMIC), pp. 1–6 (2014). http://doi.org/10.1109/ICDMIC.2014.6954232

IoT-Enabled Alcohol Detection System for Road Transportation Safety in Smart City

Stanley Uzairue[1], Joshua Ighalo[2], Victor O. Matthews[1],
Frances Nwukor[3], and Segun I. Popoola[1(✉)]

[1] Department of Electrical and Information Engineering,
Covenant University, Ota, Nigeria
{stanley.uzairue,
segun.popoola}@covenantuniversity.edu.ng
[2] Department of Electrical and Electronics Engineering,
Federal University, Oye-Ekiti, Nigeria
[3] Department of Electrical and Electronics Engineering,
Petroleum Training Institute, Effurun, Warri, Nigeria

Abstract. In this paper, an alcohol detection system was developed for road transportation safety in smart city using Internet of Things (IoT) technology. Two Blood Alcohol Content (BAC) thresholds are set and monitored with the use of a microcontroller. When the first threshold is reached, the developed system transmits the BAC level of the driver and the position coordinates of the vehicle to the central monitoring unit. At the reach of the second BAC threshold, the IoT-enabled alcohol detection system shuts down the vehicle's engine, triggers an alarm and puts on the warning light indicator. A prototype of this scenario is designed and implemented such that a Direct Current (DC) motor acted as the vehicle's engine while a push button served as its ignition system. The efficiency of this system is tested to ensure proper functionality. The deployment of this system will help in reducing the incidence of drunk driving-related road accidents in smart cities.

Keywords: Internet of Things · Road transportation safety · Accident control
Smart city

1 Introduction

Drunk driving is a very dangerous behavior because excessive consumption of alcohol causes distortion in thought pattern of drivers. The investigation conducted by the World Health Organization in 2008 shows that about 50%–60% of traffic accidents are related to drunk driving [1]. In present times, the cases of traffic accident caused by drunk driving has increased rapidly. It has, therefore, become evident that drunk driving does great harm to public security.

Different technologies and techniques have been adopted to reduce the incidence of road accidents due to drunk driving by motorists. The alcohol detector in [2] is made up of the alcohol sensor, Alternating Current (AC) power supply, LM 358 Operational Amplifier (Op-Amp), and Liquid Crystal Display (LCD) circuitry. This device displays

© Springer International Publishing AG, part of Springer Nature 2018
O. Gervasi et al. (Eds.): ICCSA 2018, LNCS 10963, pp. 695–704, 2018.
https://doi.org/10.1007/978-3-319-95171-3_55

the results of the alcohol sensor as it senses the alcohol molecules in air present around it, and displays a warning text when it crosses the fixed threshold set by the LM358 Op Amp. The drawback of this system was that it required whosoever to be tested to be close to the AC power outlet due to the system running on AC power. Also, the LM358 op amp which was acting as a comparator in the circuit and came with a preset value 5 for the threshold upon crossed, had no response such as an alarm to warn that the threshold has been crossed. This system was required two participants i.e. one person to carry out the testing and note when the threshold is crossed and the other as the person being tested. This system was nowhere close to proving a means of inhibiting a driver if he/she were drunk not to mention real time implementation [2].

James and John [3] proposed an alcohol detection system that alerts the driver through his/her cell phone. The major components of this system was the GSM module and the LM358 module. This system was a huge advancement from breath analyzers as it was based on GSM technology using the GSM module and dumped the use of an alarm circuit but still employed the LM358 Op-Amp. The system alerted via text messages using a GSM module and had a unique ringtone for such text messages set on the cell phone. Its major demerit was the lack of an LCD unit and an alarm circuit which could be useful in cases where the driver is not in possession of his/her phone. Another drawback is the presence of the LM358 Op-Amp as a comparator instead of using a microcontroller to allow for flexibility in changing the blood alcohol concentration (BAC) threshold due to probability in changes of body chemistry of the driver. The issue of cellphone batteries running down also comes up implying that the system would be inactive in the state that a cellphone battery is dead. Also, with most drivers in the habit of keeping their cellphones in the vibration or silent mode while driving, this inhibited the alerting property of the work [3].

Another alcohol detection system was developed in [4] based on PIC16F877A microcontroller. The presence of the microcontroller allowed for ease of manipulation of the threshold depending on body chemistry. The presence of the microcontroller gave room for addition of other features in the future. The only major drawback was the system's inability for a direct real time implementation due to it being powered by an AC power supply, as the alcohol sensor wouldn't have the opportunity to have at least 3 h full run in time it would get if on DC supply (vehicle battery) to give the sensor the degree of accuracy it requires for its operation [4].

Figure 1 shows the graphical representation of the fatalities and fatality rate for the past decades. We can see the decreasing order of the chart and as such we can deduce that in few decades to come and with the recommendation and implementation of our proposed embedded alcohol trigger device enclosed in cars that there might be no accident caused by drunk driving.

The aim of this paper is to reduce road accidents related to drunk driving to the barest minimum by using Internet of Things (IoT) technology. With the help of this system, drivers under the influence of alcohol can be detected, monitored, and tracked by relevant law enforcement agency in the smart city. The Internet of Things (IoT) is the most recent communication display in which the objects of regular day to day existence will be outfitted with microcontrollers, transceivers for digital communication, and appropriate convention stacks that will make them ready to speak with each other and with the clients, turning into a fundamental piece of the Internet.

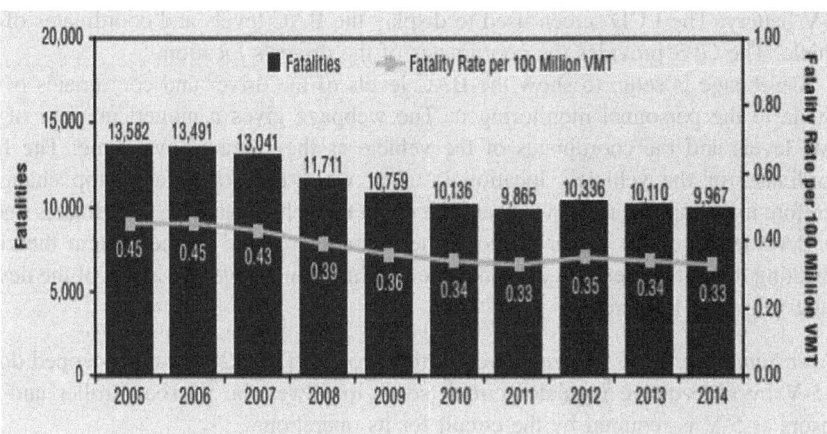

Fig. 1. Fatalities and fatality rate per 100 million VMT in alcohol-impaired-driving crashes, 2005–2014 [5]

This system is a very innovative system which will help to keep the roads free from drunk driving related accidents by not only shutting down the vehicle engine upon sensing the drunken state of the driver but would also help road traffic officials to be able to track down the vehicle inhabiting the drunk driver before the vehicle is shut down and allow for quick evacuation of the vehicle and the driver by the authorities so as to prevent traffic on such road.

The system is divided into sections; the interlock section and the monitoring section. The interlock section is made up the MQ-3 Sensor (alcohol sensor) which senses the alcohol molecules in the air breathe by the driver, an ATMEGA 328P microcontroller, a buzzer, an LCD screen, LED, Wireless Fidelity (Wi-Fi) modem, DC motor, Global Positioning System (GPS) and a push button as the ignition key. The monitoring system is a webpage built to view the BAC concentration levels of the driver as well as the coordinates of the vehicle. The system is powered by a 12-V DC source. The system has two thresholds, first (pre-drunk threshold) for communicating the BAC level and coordinates of the vehicle to the monitoring system and the second (drunk threshold) for shutting down the engine of the vehicle.

2   Materials and Methods

The IoT drunk driving monitoring system is a groundbreaking system with huge application I the field of smart cities and smart transportation. The system monitors the unsafe BAC levels and coordinates of the driver while in a drunk state through a web page. To make this possible, the hardware section of the system positioned in the vehicle makes use of the MQ3 sensor (Alcohol sensor) which senses the alcohol molecules in the air around the driver to determine if the driver is drunk or sober. The system makes use of the Arduino ATmega 328PU microcontroller, LCD screen, GPS, buzzer, DC motor, and WI-FI modem for sending data. The hardware is powered by a

12-V battery. The LCD screen used to display the BAC levels and coordinates of the vehicle. The GPS provides the coordinates of the driver's location.

A webpage is setup to show the BAC levels of the driver and coordinates of the vehicle to the personnel monitoring it. The webpage gives a numerical view of the BAC levels and the coordinates of the vehicle as they change over time. The final coordinates of the vehicle's location is taken when the coordinates stop changing therefore implying that the device has shut down the vehicle at those coordinates due to the BAC levels of the driver crossing the second threshold of the system therefore indicating that the driver is in a drunk state. At this drunk stage, the alarm of the device in the vehicle is triggered.

Power Supply: A 12-V was employed in this project. This 12-V is then stepped down to 5-V by the voltage regulator circuit so as to power the microcontroller and the sensors as 5-V is required by the circuit for its operation.

Alcohol Sensor: The simple gas sensor - MQ3 is appropriate for recognizing liquor, this sensor can be utilized as a part of a breathalyzer. It has a high affectability to liquor and little affectability to Benzene. The affectability can be balanced by the potentiometer. Tin oxide (SnO2) is Sensitive material of MQ-3 gas sensor is, which has a lower conductivity in clean air. At the point when the objective liquor gas exists, the sensor's conductivity is higher alongside the gas concentration rising, utilizing a straightforward resistive circuit changes over difference in conductivity to the relating yield flag of gas focus.

Arduino Uno: Arduino is a microcontroller board in view of the ATmega328P. It has 14 digital in-put/yield pins (of which 6 can be utilized as PWM yields), 6 simple sources of info, a 16 MHz quartz precious stone, a USB association, a power jack, an ICSP header and a reset catch. It contains everything expected to help the microcontroller. Arduino Software (IDE) were the reference variants of Arduino, now advanced to more up to date discharges. The Uno board is the first in a progression of USB Arduino sheets, and the reference show for the Arduino stage; for a broad rundown of present, past or obsolete sheets see the Arduino record of sheets.

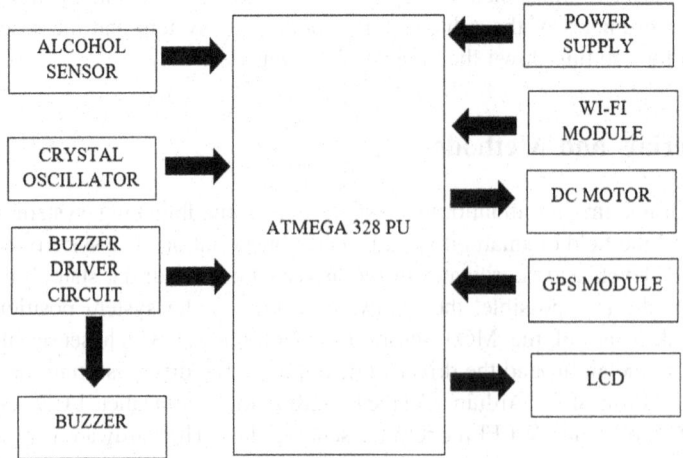

Fig. 2. Block diagram of the system

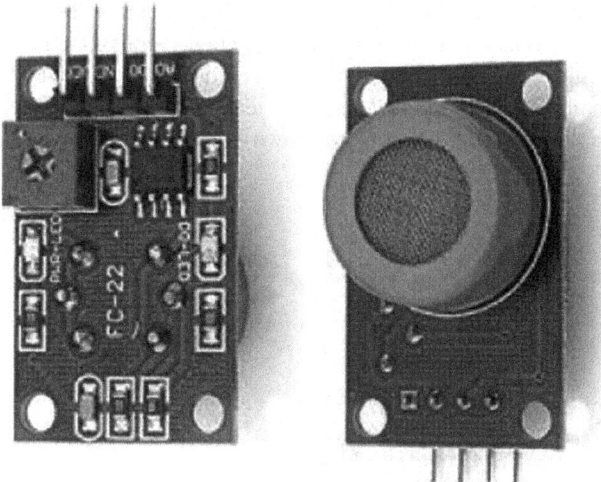

Fig. 3. MQ3 gas sensor

Wi-Fi Module: The ESP8266 Wi-Fi Module is an independent SOC with incorporated TCP/IP convention stack that can give any micro-controller access to your Wi-Fi arrange. The ESP8266 is able to do either facilitating an application or offloading all Wi-Fi organizing capacities from another application processor. Each ESP8266 module comes pre-modified with an AT summon set firmware. The ESP8266 module is a to a great degree financially savvy board with an enormous, and consistently developing, group.

Fig. 4. Arduino Uno

GPS Module: The Neo-6M GPS Module is an independent GPS receivers including the elite u-box 6 positioning motor. They have a minimized design, power and memory alternatives. The GPS is a space based satellite route framework that gives area and time data in every single climate condition, anyplace on or close to the Earth where there is an unhampered observable pathway to at least four GPS satellites. The framework gives basic capacities to military, common and business clients around the globe. It is kept up by the United States government and is unreservedly open to anybody with a GPS recipient. The components of the developed system are shown in Figs. 2, 3, 4, 5 and 6. The flowchart and the circuit diagram are shown in Figs. 7 and 8 respectively.

Fig. 5. Wi-Fi Module

Fig. 6. GPS Module

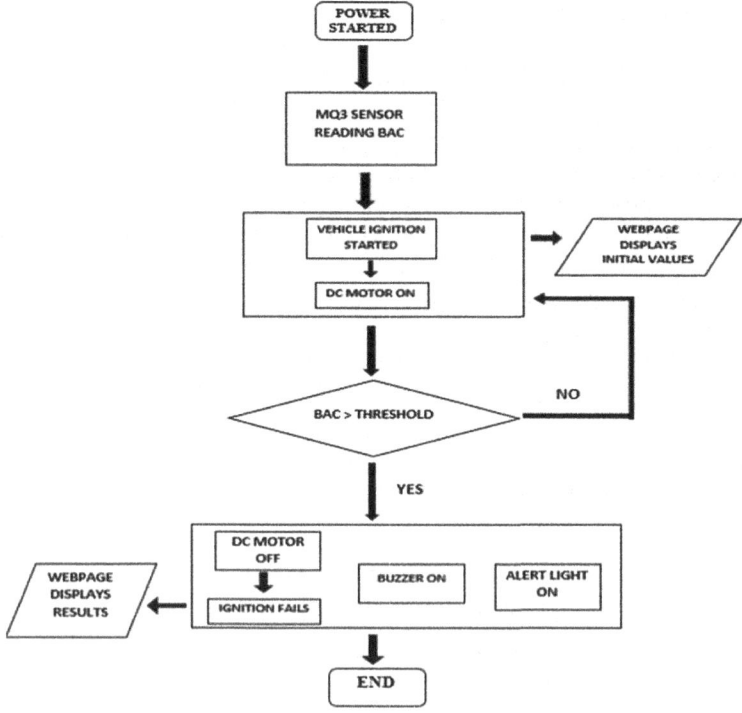

Fig. 7. Flow chart of system

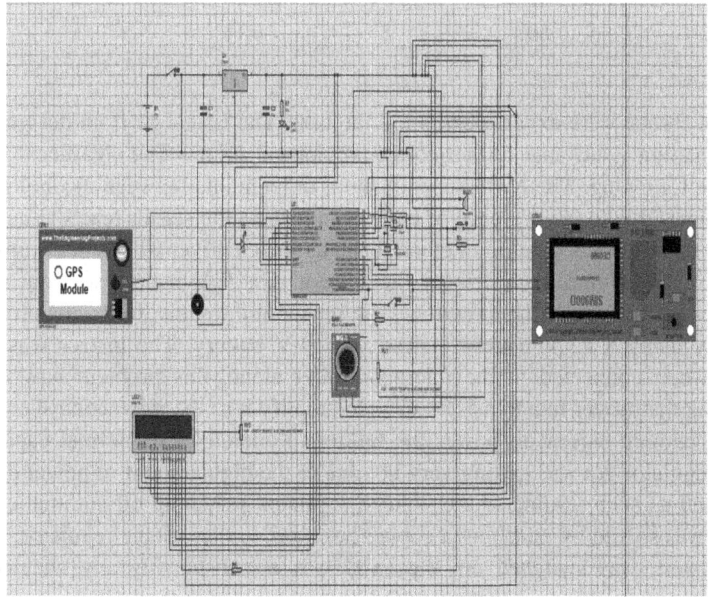

Fig. 8. Circuit diagram of the system

3   Results and Discussion

The developed system involved the use of ATMEGA 328P with Wi-Fi module. The embedded device is connected to the internet by the ADC and Wi-Fi Module. The alcohol sensor and GPS is connected to Arduino UNO board for monitoring. The ADC converts the corresponding sensor and coordinate reading to its digital value and from that value the corresponding environmental parameter will be evaluated. The sensed data (BAC levels & coordinates) is automatically sent to the web server, when a proper connection is established with server device. Table 1 shows the results taken from placing a specific volume of alcohol at specific distances from the MQ3 sensor as highlighted in Table 1. The analog value of the blood alcohol concentration at each distance is also gotten. The set threshold for the project was 244 (analog value) i.e. 0.5 g/l (BAC value). Figure 9 shows the graph of the blood alcohol concentration against the distance between the sensor and the volume of alcohol. It is deduced from the graph that as the distance increases the BAC & analog value decreases *i.e.* Distance between the sensor and the volume of alcohol is inversely proportional to blood alcohol concentration and the analog value.

Table 1. BAC (g/l) vs Distance (cm)

Distance (cm)	Analog value	BAC (g/l)
0	320	0.66
10	260	0.53
20	155	0.32
30	126	0.26
40	94	0.19
50	87	0.18

A few issues were experienced amid the task. The issues go from design issues to implementation issues and furthermore development issues. The significant issues are as per the following. The MQ3 sensor cannot differentiate between alcohol molecules and perfumes due to the presence of ethanol in both as the sensor reacts to any form of matter with high concentration of ethanol and as such a driver who is not drunk and has used a lot of perfume could trigger the system. The 9 V battery was not supplying enough current to power the circuit and the sensor at the same time. This problem was solved by using a 12 V battery instead of a 9-V battery. The buzzer was not loud enough when connected to the microcontroller alone, this problem was solved by connecting the buzzer to a transistor so as to amplify it as the microcontroller port does not have enough current to power the buzzer to operate at its normal capacity. The voltage regulator got was getting very hot due to the high amount of power dissipating as heat and as such leading to the voltage regulator switching off automatically. This problem was solved by attaching a copper heat sink to the voltage regulator. When the whole system was switched on, the LCD was not displaying any characters, this problem was solved by connecting a 10 K potentiometer to the LCD as it was used to tune the contrast of the LCD. Other problems include soldering and measurement errors but these problems were solved by proper troubleshooting with serious care in the construction of the project.

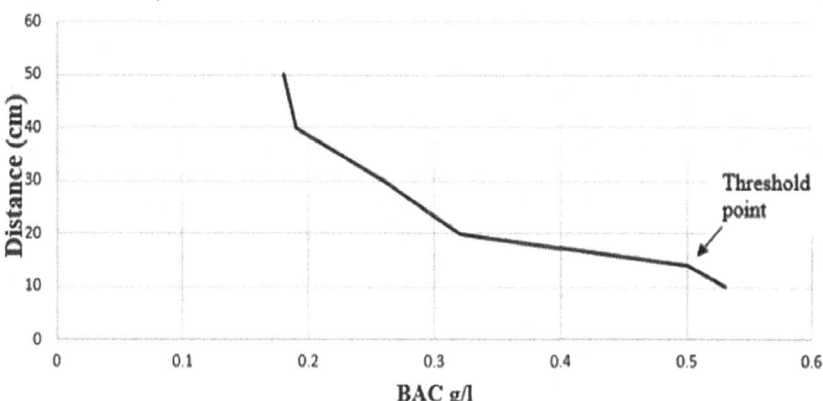

Fig. 9. Graph of blood alcohol concentration versus distance between sensor and alcohol

4 Conclusion

In this paper, an alcohol detection system was developed for road transportation safety in smart city using Internet of Things (IoT) technology. This system not only curbs drunk driving by automatically shutting down the vehicle that contains the drunk driver but also allows for traffic authorities to easily locate the shutdown vehicles using the coordinates of the vehicle sent to web server. The technologies which are used in the proposed system are good enough to ensure the perfect shut down and pick up of the drunk driven vehicle.

There are no projects that cannot be improved. Enhancements have to be carried out so as to improve the efficiency of this system. One of the improvements that could be made on this system in the future is that it should be made smaller. The smaller the system, the more convenient the alcohol system is, the more likely drivers will accept it. There should be proper positioning of the alcohol sensor so as to allow convenient reading of the driver's alcohol consumption quantity with or without the aid of the driver.

Some options for where the sensor can be placed include: (1) an element that can help differentiate the ethanol quantity in alcohol and perfumes should be introduced into the sensor so as to prevent the issue of the system being triggered due to use of large amount of perfume by the driver; (2) a cable can be put near the driver's seat and then connected with the ignition of the car. This means the alcohol detection system can be another key to the car. The driver should blow to the system before he/she start the car. If the value of the alcohol concentration is above the system's threshold value, the system will stop the car starting. So a drunk driver would not be able to start the car which will prevent the behavior of drunk driving. It is not only safe to the driver, but can ensure the passengers would not be hit because of the driver's drunk driving.

Acknowledgment. The authors wish to appreciate the Center for Research, Innovation, and Discovery (CU-CRID) of Covenant University, Ota, Nigeria, for partly funding this research.

References

1. Killoran, A., et al.: Review of effectiveness of laws limiting blood alcohol concentration levels to reduce alcohol-related road injuries and deaths. Final report. Centre for Public Health Excellence (NICE), London (2010)
2. Lee, J.D., et al.: Assessing the feasibility of vehicle-based sensors to detect alcohol impairment. National Highway Traffic Safety Administration, Washington, DC (2010)
3. James, N., John, T.P.: Alcohol detection system. IJRCCT 3(1), 059–064 (2014)
4. Phani, S.A., et al.: Liquor detection through automatic motor locking system: in built (LDAMLS). Int. J. Comput. Eng. Res. (IJCER) 4(7), 2250–3005 (2014)
5. Federal Highway Administration. Highway Statistics 2014 - Policy (2014). https://www.fhwa.dot.gov/policyinformation/statistics/2014/

Workshop Challenges, Trends and Innovations in VGI (VGI 2018)

Volunteered Geographic Information, Open Data, and Citizen Participation: A Review for Post-seismic Events Reconstruction in Mexico

Rodrigo Tapia-McClung$^{(\boxtimes)}$ (iD)

Centro de Investigación en Ciencias de Información Geoespacial,
Contoy 137, Col. Lomas de Padierna, Tlalpan, 14240 CDMX, Mexico
rtapia@centrogeo.edu.mx

Abstract. This work in progress presents the initial idea to support the creation of an online platform that includes and is updated with citizen and volunteer-generated data together with verified data from official sources. Its goal is to help society and government deal with situations when facing an emergency such as the one that occurred in Mexico City on September 19, 2017, after a 7.1-degree earthquake hit the city, causing death, injuries, and damage throughout the city's infrastructure. This proposal draws inspiration from previous experiences in crowdmapping exercises and from the fact that volunteer citizens acted as first respondents on the ground, collected and published *in-situ* data to social networks and online repositories, verified these crowdsourced data, and put together online portals to broadcast this information to other citizens to make the best decisions as fast as possible in order to direct rescue efforts, people, resources, food, etc., but unfortunately most of these citizen efforts quickly faded away and are no longer operational. Hopefully, in the long run, a more robust platform that brings together different volunteer citizen efforts and governmental points of view will prove useful and effective for disaster emergency management in the city and the country.

Keywords: Volunteer geographic information · Citizen sensors
Social and natural problems · Earthquake

1 Introduction

Volunteered Geographic Information (VGI) and citizen sensing have gained popularity in different settings along with other ways of participating, whether as non-experts creating and sharing geospatial data, generating geospatial data after natural disasters, citizens solving specific problems and sharing knowledge and ideas or citizens collaborating with scientists in a more general type of participation [1]. Of particular interest is the fact that citizens have become increasingly more interested in embracing these types of participation as

© Springer International Publishing AG, part of Springer Nature 2018
O. Gervasi et al. (Eds.): ICCSA 2018, LNCS 10963, pp. 707–721, 2018.
https://doi.org/10.1007/978-3-319-95171-3_56

means to observe what happens around them and, whenever possible, analyze collectively-gathered data and, based on it, make decisions that will help improve their everyday life. Furthermore, the Open Government Data (OGD) philosophy and policies have become important in pushing governments and "public bodies that produce and commission huge quantities of data and information [...] to make their data sets available" so that "public institutions become more transparent and accountable to citizens" [2].

In particular, Mexican Government has been gradually shifting towards the use of open standards and publishing open data. This, however, is only the beginning as there are usually many dependencies that presume to publish open data, but unfortunately lack to fully adhere to the eight principles of open government data. It is not uncommon to find data sets that do not comply with one or more of these eight principles and it is still important to "distinguish between government transparency and open data" [3].

On the day of the 32nd anniversary of one of the more devastating earthquakes in the history of Mexico, an 8.1-magnitude quake off the coast of the state of Michoacán, the country was struck by yet another devastating 7.1-magnitude earthquake on September 19, 2017 [4]. There were several differences in both events worth noticing. Firstly, the time of occurrence was around 7 am in 1985 and 1 pm in 2017. Secondly, the epicenter of the 1985 event was located more than 350 km away from the capital, Mexico City, and about 28 km beneath the surface while in 2017 it was located about 120 km away from the city at a depth of 48 km. Thirdly, the 1985 one was followed by two significant aftershocks (a 7.5-magnitude the day after and a 7.0-magnitude about seven months later) while for the 2017 one there is no agreement on this (the United States Geological Survey reports no aftershocks [5], but the National Seismological Service reported 38. The author's search on the service's web page returned 16 events associated with the epicenter's state [6]). Fourthly, in 1985 there were official figures of 9,500 deaths, 3,000 people injured, although unofficial figures estimate around 40,000 deaths [7], 137 damaged schools while in 2017 those figures were less than 400 deaths, around 4,500 people injured and 250 houses destroyed. Additionally, in 1985 the government rejected international aid and the president addressed the nation 36 h after the earthquake. In 2017, international aid was welcome and the president addressed the country via social networks and televised messages within minutes.

In both cases, it was the citizenry who played the role of the first respondent. Armed forces arrived only later, once rescue operations were underway. Above all, one significant difference 32 years apart was the way some citizens responded and pushed the government to react in accordance. In September 1985, many civilians were at the forefront of the aftermath, but back then the society was not-so-well organized. Nonetheless, they spearheaded both search and rescue operations and were eventually replaced by the armed forces. In 2017, however, several individuals and organizations got together to put forward different online platforms to help report were help and rescue were needed, and to redirect supplies and people to where they were needed the most. Due to different citizens ideas and efforts, there were several platforms available for users to report and it is likely there was repeated information among them.

Even though these crowdmapping exercises led to different data sets available that were used to help direct efforts during the aftermath of the earthquake they, unfortunately, faded away once the government took part in the so-called reconstruction process. Several funds from different origins were put forward and said to be made available for citizens in need of economic aid to rebuild their home or to pay rent in the meantime. At the time of writing, six months after the event, it is not entirely clear how many different funds are available, how much money is available on each, and how can citizens access them.

The initial agglutination of 30 organizations (later expanded to 77) from very different origins and interests was amassed in one single social movement, a civic platform called #Epicentro, whose main goal was to "set the basis on which reconstruction was to take place, with a social perspective for it to be resilient, participatory, inclusive, equitable, sustainable, and effective" [8]. Three lines of action gear #Epicentro: the follow-up on the origins and use of financial resources destined for the reconstruction process; social, human rights, gender, childhood, and youth perspectives throughout the reconstruction; and responsibilities and damage repair [8]. Again, six months later, it seems as if not much has happened in terms of financial resources, reconstruction and damage repair.

It is in this sense that this paper frames the proposal of a platform that profits from crowdmapping and citizen sensing exercises and existing VGI to build a comprehensive database that can build from citizen experience, testimony, and advice, but one that can also be complemented with official data to leverage the quality of citizen-collected data. The idea is to enhance existing efforts to include information about various different sources of funding, citizens' resources, experiences, stories, best practices, and advice to navigate the bureaucratic conundrums one would have to sort in order to gain access to the governmental or another type of financial support for reconstruction. As will be explained later on, many efforts were put forward immediately after the disaster, but they did not endure. It is the intention of this work in progress, therefore, to eventually be able to provide affected citizens with some sort of support that can accompany and help them throughout the different stages of the recovery process after an emergency.

The rest of this paper is organized as follows. Section 2 presents work related to crisis mapping, especially some of the platforms that were launched in the aftermath of the 2017 earthquake in Mexico City. Section 3 presents the work in progress and sketches the main ideas towards building this VGI platform. Section 4 presents an initial discussion and future work to be carried out.

2 Related Work on Mapping Crisis Events

In the event of an emergency situation such as an earthquake in an urban setting, the first thing to happen is rescue operations. First responders, usually citizens, take spontaneous charge of the situation and a civil chain of command is set that can last anywhere from hours to a few days. Afterward, this operations and command are relieved by the armed forces or some governmental entity. The next step involves the government and society resisting the aftermath of the event. Eventually, the reconstruction process begins once there is an initial accord on the different governmental bodies and financial institutions on how to proceed and set priorities on how to carry on. In the meantime, those affected by the event have to partially recover and adapt to their current situation. These two stages can and usually take months or years to complete. Figure 1 presents a schematic diagram of the response cycle for an emergency. Cutter gives more insights into the use of Geographic Information Science in emergency management in [9]. In 1999, Morrow had already put forward the idea of mapping vulnerable groups to have an effective emergency management in the event of a hurricane [10].

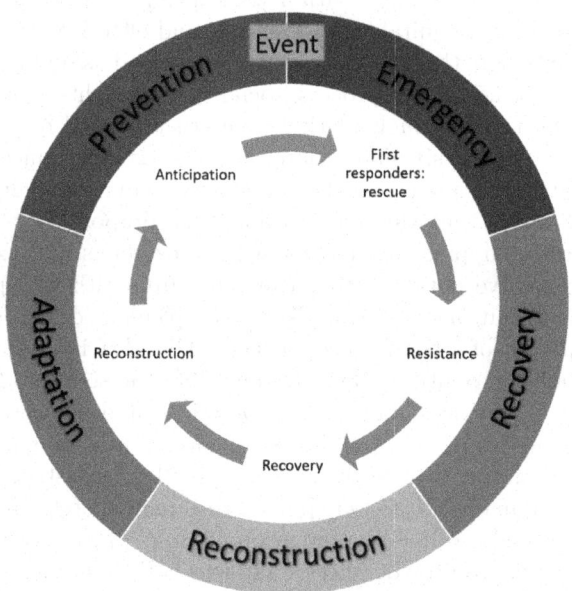

Fig. 1. Diagram of a disaster cycle. Source: author's elaboration. (Color figure online)

Several groups have developed methodologies to contribute to post-emergency events. For example, The Information Technology for Humanitarian Assistance, Cooperation and Action (ITHACA) association has experience in "providing an operational emergency mapping service since 2007" [11]. The International Working Group on Satellite Emergency Mapping (IWG-SEM) published the Emergency Mapping Guidelines, where Emergency Mapping is defined as "the creation of maps, geo-information products and spatial analyses dedicated to providing situational awareness emergency management and immediate crisis information for response by means of extraction of reference (pre-event) and crisis (post-event) geographic information/data from satellite or aerial imagery" [12] and draws from years of experience of involvement in relevant projects where both Geomatics and Remote Sensing play a crucial role. Member organizations of the IWG-SEM do not directly participate in rescue or relief operations, but their goal is to quickly and efficiently provide geospatial information within hours or days to support relief activities after an emergency. Following these guidelines, delineation maps and grading maps can be created to help assess the extent of the event together with its damage grade and spatial distribution, respectively. There is usually still the need, however, to ground-truth what can be derived from remotely sensed procedures.

One of the first accounts of an online platform to help during relief efforts relates to the 7.0 magnitude earthquake that struck Haiti in 2010. It led to several efforts to aid humanitarian help and relief by using information technologies (IT). Zook et al. report on the development and use of CrisisCamp Haiti, OpenStreetMap, Ushahidi, and GeoCommons [13]. One of the key points of these developments was putting forward the need of first-respondents to know where things *were*. After such an impactful event, many landmarks were no longer existent and visual references useful for directions were lacking. International help could use maps but, unfortunately, these lacked adequate coverage. As a result, "the power of crowdsourced online mapping and the potential for new avenues of interaction between physically distant places" was made evident [13]. The use of OpenStreetMap (OSM) became essential in reconstructing the basic cartography of many parts of the country. CrisisCamp put together the use of social networks to "make the recovery effort in Haiti easier through the application of technologies" [13]. Additionally, other tools developed for a more efficient communication between individuals and groups allowed people in need to ask for specific help and people willing to provide assistance, to offer it. Ushahidi allowed users on the island to report incidents via SMS messages, which would later be processed by volunteers to translate them form Creole, put them on a map and make those reports available to agencies. The GeoCommons project allowed "ensuring that information was discoverable, interoperable, and could be repurposed across the wide variety of stakeholders involved in relief efforts" [13]. It provided online and offline functionality to bring together many datasets from both volunteers and official sources. Putting aside issues of quality, ground-truthing, intellectual property, and regulation, crowdsourced data "were ultimately crucial for first responders, aid workers, and even U.S. military humanitarian efforts on the ground" [13]. This is relevant to note, as first responders usually are civil society members, not government officials or others who might act based on specific rescue protocols. As such, civilians usually don't have access to data useful in locating collapsed buildings, supply routes or other sources of information that could help them prioritize rescue operations.

Specific to the Mexico City earthquake, on September 20, one day after the earthquake, the Advanced Rapid Imaging and Analysis (ARIA) team at NASA's Jet Propulsion Laboratory (JPL) made available a detailed map obtained from processing synthetic aperture radar (SAR) images from the Copernicus Sentinel-1A and Sentinel-1B satellites, operated by the European Space Agency (ESA).

Using a yellow-to-red color scale, the map depicts "areas with increasingly more significant ground and building surface change" and point out that "this damage proxy map should be used as guidance to identify damaged areas" [14].

The International Disasters Charter emitted Activation CC636 for the earthquake on September 20, 2017 [15]. It contains several damage assessment maps for different parts of the country, most of which indicate that there was no field validation and that damaged structures detected from satellite imagery comprise a preliminary analysis. It is clear that in order to better help relief efforts on the ground, some sort of rapid *in situ* evaluation is required. The previous examples of assessment procedures are characterized by being remotely acquired with no validation in the field. It is in this sense that the use of VGI becomes another powerful data collection technique right after an emergency. Goodchild and Glennon express their concern about the quality of VGI, but support its use in such settings since "during emergencies time is the essence, and the risks associated with volunteered information are often outweighed by the benefits of its use" [16].

From the governmental part, Mexico City is supposed to have a *risk map*, but the outcry of many sectors is for the government to make it publicly available if it even exists. This is important as it can become much more difficult to properly tend the emergency without official sources of identified risks. Again, this points to the relevance volunteers play in the immediateness of the emergency event. It is interesting to note, however, that after the 2017 earthquake, several data sources and studies started to become publicly available and were used for exploratory and explanatory analyses, but not for anticipation or prevention [17–19].

Citizen groups became first responders and spearheaded rescue operations on the ground and also made broadcasts via social networks about the situation in real-time. This involvement was also made evident in the development of several platforms aimed at collecting and publishing data for others to help and participate in the decision-making process. It was a very interesting exercise of self-organization at different levels. Some of these platforms are described next.

2.1 Citizen Platforms for the Mexico City Earthquake

The availability of mapping platforms and APIs (such as Google Maps, Carto, Mapbox, Mapillary, WikiMapia) allowed citizens to quickly envision their use to crowdmap data relevant to the earthquake such as damaged or collapsed buildings, the location of people trapped inside them, shelters, and collection centers. Again, it was the citizenry who spearheaded this, not the government itself. These citizen groups or individuals made an effort to publicize as much as possible their own platform with their own approach, so a larger effort was diluted. It might have been possible that by joining forces a larger audience could have been reached and a more robust platform been built. Nonetheless, these efforts were rewarded with considerable recognition from the society. Especially when it is taken into account that the government took a little longer to respond by publishing a survey to collect data and by using volunteer data.

Some of the citizen groups who participated in these efforts are well-established social activists that have a history of being involved in many different societal needs. For instance, the Humanitarian OpenStreetMap Team (HOT OSM) helped collect and made available data useful in getting an idea of the impact and extent of the earthquake [20, 21]. The collaborative map from [18] unfortunately is reported as being frozen on September 21 at noon. It now redirects to a map published by the Google Crisis Response team which contains the locations of collapsed buildings, collection centers, and shelters and was later updated to include satellite imagery from different sources and time frames [22]. However, its last data entry is from October 8, 2017. Cívica Digital invited coders and programmers to help develop an app to help find the most pressing needs by area in order to link them with collection centers, send help, and notify. The idea was to allow people to find places to look for help and use this information to help coordinate efforts more efficiently. This seemed to be a very interesting and promising idea but, unfortunately, the project only has a mockup and its latest commit was five days after the earthquake [23].

A particularly interesting citizen movement was #Verificado19S [24] which took the task of verifying if the information available on the news and social media was actually true. At first, they concentrated their efforts on building a collaborative database to pinpoint the locations where buildings had been damaged or collapsed. Afterward, additional layers of data were incorporated into their platform and it allowed for citizens to enter new reports (the movement would organize a team on the field to verify these new real-time reports). In response, the federal government, on its online open data portal, launched a survey for citizens to report damages, shelters, and collection centers. This data collection exercise was then visualized as a Carto map [25] with other layers available, making it possible to distinguish between *citizen* and *official* reports. The data set is available for download on the government's open data portal and only contains data collected during September 2017 [26].

Another movement, Manos a la Obra [27], consisting of people from the MIT's Department of Urban Studies and Planning and Harvard's Graduate School of Design, designed a platform to ask for, or offer help. By means of an online survey, people were asked what they needed (separated into 12 different categories) or what they could offer to help and where it was needed. They collected about 1,800 data points. Data collection only lasted for about one month after the earthquake.

One month after the earthquake, on October 20, 20 society organizations that had previously and independently responded to the earthquake emergency joined together to create the #CIUDADanía19s movement as an effort to "strengthen and organize in the medium and long-term the spirit of collaboration, empathy, and solidarity born from the debris, social networks, data, and maps" [28].

The *Laboratory for the City* is "Mexico City's new experimental office for civic innovation and urban creativity". It is a "space for rethinking, reimagining, and reinventing the way citizens and government can work together towards a more open, more livable and more imaginative city" [29]. They quickly realized it was a once-in-a-lifetime opportunity to open up and support many of the citizen efforts that were taking place. They launched the #Iniciativas19 platform, a place to bring together many citizen initiatives that had different goals in different topics, but in one way or another can be framed in the Laboratory's post-earthquake program. It lists around 40 initiatives, some of which may have received financial support to continue with their development. It includes some of the aforementioned efforts but unfortunately does not seem to make a more robust initiative by bringing together the strengths of those which are similar or trying to improve on some possible weaknesses.

Mexico City's Reconstruction, Recovery, and Transformation Commission was put in place on October 26, 2017 [30]. On January 12, 2018, the Reconstruction Plan [31] was published. As a response to citizens and organizations that had put forward their own platforms for data collections and sharing, the local government launched *Plataforma CDMX* which aims at locating "each individual building and person affected by the earthquake in order to guarantee that programs and help are received in order, certainty, and transparency" [32]. This platform contains an online map showing 6 classes: collapsed buildings, demolitions, high risk, medium risk, low risk, and first evacuations, together with an overall statistical view of the situation. Additionally, a *Post-seismic evaluation* site is available that shows a color-coded map with dots indicating buildings that have been checked for damage and have been classified as fine, with a warning or critical conditions (green, yellow or red). It also includes basic statistics for the number of post-seismic building evaluation reports in each municipality and lists available resources from Mexico City's Disaster Fund, stating that 3 million pesos out of the 1,616 millions assigned have been allocated. An additional *Evaluation viewer* module is available but is not open to the public.

On February 15, 2018, five months after the earthquake had occurred, the chairman appointed by Mexico City's mayor resigned from the reconstruction commission, along with other members, based on claims that the local Congress was pushing its own agenda. As was mentioned before, initial efforts to crowdmap data to help direct efforts during the aftermath of the earthquake, unfortunately, faded away quickly. It is important to note that even the official survey was closed, implying that there was no more data to be collected or updated.

3   Towards Building an Emergency Reconstruction Platform: Work in Progress

The aforementioned group #Verificado19S was supported by volunteer citizens in receiving reports on collapsed buildings, gas leaks, structural damage, shelter availability, collection centers and actually verifying them, spearheading the initial relief and rescuing efforts. It is thus clear that the citizenry is capable enough to organize itself in times of need to manage emergencies. Collaborative crisis mapping is one means towards achieving this self-organization.

Based on this, the driving idea behind this work in progress is inspired by the use of a digital platform for collective mapping reported in [33] and further developed that aims at supporting a dialogue between society and government around a given issue of mutual interest, in this case, the post-earthquake reconstruction.

The idea of this platform is for it to be capable of informing citizens of current governmental actions and capabilities to be tended, relief programs being implemented, the number of financial resources available, etc. Most importantly, the government itself would be able to locate where these actions are taking place in real time. From the referred platform, it is already possible to validate volunteered information by citizen peers. Users can up or down vote contributions. Contributors can post pictures that provide evidence of their report. These contributions, being located on a map, allow for a quick state of affairs if it is needed to show citizens or government officials how and where things are happening.

Many of the technological aspects of the proposed platform have already been used in other instances. What is likely to be more important and difficult to implement, is the political will for this to move forward. As can be seen from the previous section, it is not easy to convince the government to push forward in terms of open data and access to it.

In this sense, the current state of affairs in the world, the number of online transactions taking place every minute, the amount of terabytes being transfer every second by citizens gives us a different perspective on this matter: if people are already transferring huge amounts of data, why not use it towards a greater good? Why not rally them towards a situational awareness and preparedness the whole community can benefit from?

From the previous section it is noticeable that many of these first responders were acting from their good will and their stamina quickly, and naturally, faded. How, then, could citizens become enabled for a more continuous support and knowledge of their city in the event of a disaster? Would it be possible to achieve a quicker and better response if these spontaneous efforts were somehow better directed?

In this setting, citizens are avid to receive relevant information to improve both social and natural resilience in the city. They are also willing to contribute to the generation of a far greater risk prevention culture that would enable society to better face disasters.

Recalling Fig. 1, the disaster cycle usually lasts several months or even years. Therefore, this proposed platform would not only be intended for its use as a quick response immediately after the emergency. Rather, it would be a comprehensive hierarchical system that would integrate data from several different sources, both official and not, and would provide both citizens and government officials with relevant information for each type of user. It is clear that in both cases, these users would benefit from this platform in the decision-making process prior to and in the midst of an emergency.

Risk atlases are usually intended for the professional user or the scientist caring about processes at the landscape level. Citizens need something else. Something they can make their own. They need to see what could happen at the street level. In their home; in their office or school; on their commute. Providing information with regards to matters that citizens care for in their everyday life would set the basis for an extended prevention culture and would pave the road for a far-reaching vulnerability reading in each neighborhood.

Unfortunately, political issues plague many of these situations. It is unfathomable that politicians find ways to embezzle funds destined to help citizens. In many cases, they end up resigning and the reconstruction process gets stuck. This, far from providing some kind of certainty and assurance to a citizen in need, only makes it more complicated and difficult to endure. Therefore, it is imperative that regulations for accessing funding for these processes are well established from the beginning and do not depend on a group of people being part of a commission or the local congress.

The purpose of this system would be twofold: one, to help prepare citizens and governments before an emergency occurs and two, during the reconstruction process, to help establish a dialog between the two parts allowing governments to inform citizens and letting these get information about available programs and funding, how to gain access to them, eligibility criteria and conditions, together with the ability to monitor the assignment of resources and the execution of actions towards the reconstruction. At the same time, citizens would contribute their ground-truth volunteer data that would greatly enhance the platform repository which, in turn, would be used to better inform both citizens and government.

As mentioned before, this work in progress looks into profiting from bringing together other efforts that have looked into some of the same issues presented here and have proposed individual solutions. As such, its goal is not to build a new platform from scratch but rather bring together the best modules of the different available ones so they serve a greater purpose. It is an approach that expects and invites all those developers and people involved in the creation and maintenance of other solutions to join forces in order to create a more robust one for the society. Initial steps consider identifying and collecting different modules that would comprise the core of the platform, together with those that would be activated and used whenever there is an emergency or disaster and the cycle from Fig. 1 is underway along with their associated data sources. Once this process is completed, the meticulous task of merging their different available capabilities and scopes will take place. The modules should include location reporting of damaged buildings and their conditions, ways to verify various sources of volunteer data (including damage inventories), put them on a map and update them as often as possible, incorporate maps and layers from different authoritative sources (official risk maps, cadaster, infrastructure, emergency and evacuation routes, and other relevant government data) and agencies and teams (local research groups, NASA/JPL, HOT (OSM), USGS, NOAA), and a way to link citizens' needs and help offers (including the locations and conditions of collection centers and shelters).

Additionally, different geographical data sets that have been identified to be incorporated into the proposed platform include what has already been published by different groups, individuals, and volunteers in different repositories and data outlets in terms of the September 2017 earthquake itself (Carto maps, Google layers, open government data portals), together with maps published by different organizations and university groups, official building locations and conditions, risk maps published by the government and cadastral data. Other non-geographical datasets include funding and reconstruction programs along with their eligibility criteria and conditions, government spending and financial records related to different actions about the reconstruction process.

It would be desirable to have as many sources as possible to be available as RESTful services or accessible via APIs for them to be easily incorporated into the platform. They should also maintain a history of how, they if at all, have been changed or updated throughout time. It will be important to detect which of these are being updated more continuously than the rest in order to pay close attention to their required resources to guarantee their availability and guarantee that the system can be kept up-to-date on a daily basis and, in times of need, updated in real-time.

As mentioned before, a lot of information became available after the emergency, but there is still the need to organize it in a far more accessible way. As it currently stands, one needs to navigate too many sites in order to find adequate information. Even though it has significantly improved after the initial emergency, it is still a cumbersome process. Figure 2 shows a schematic diagram of different inputs and outputs the proposed platform could use and benefit from.

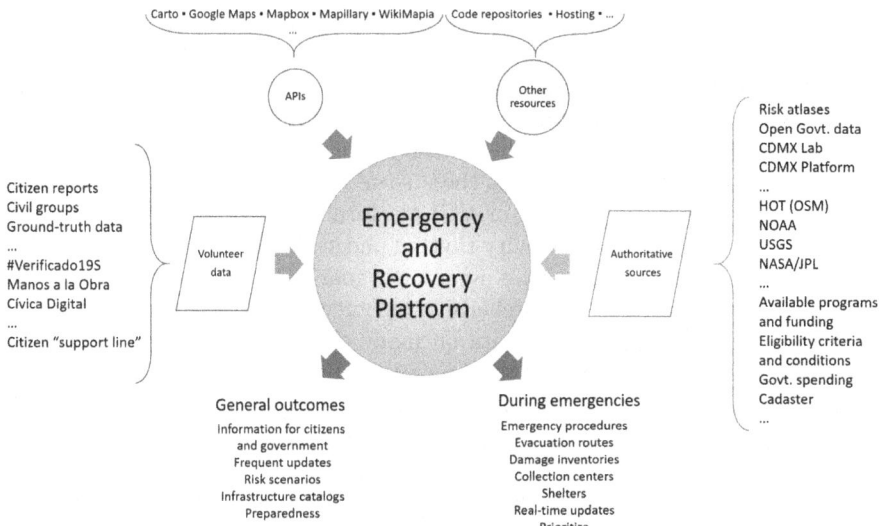

Fig. 2. Diagram of example inputs and outputs for the proposed emergency and recovery platform. Source: author's elaboration.

This approach would strive for the use of open source technologies aligned with the inclusion of interoperable formats to guarantee the coexistence of varied sources of information, be user-centered designed, provide users with valuable and important up-to-date information to be used in rescue and relief operations, and include crowdsourced data during the first stages of a crisis event that would tend to fade out as official and verified data becomes available. This condition ties together with the need for the government to actually adopt the principles of open data as it is not unusual to find "open data sets" that are actually far from being open. It is expected that additional modules might be needed and many more sources will be identified during the collection process.

As mentioned before, this rests upon the political will of many that would need to see the greater good beyond their own for this sort of proposal to reach its best. Different government and civil institutions and organizations would have to agree to share information in open standards, and a culture of transparency would need to prevail.

4   Initial Discussion and Future Work

Societies are shaken when catastrophic events occur. Mexico City was indeed shaken in September 2017, and it is struggling to recover. Slowly but surely, its residents will overcome the grief and difficulties being faced after the earthquake. Despite political arguments and differences, once again citizens have proved they can come together in a time of need and crisis for society's greater good.

During the first moments of an emergency, as already stated by others, it is important to leverage the advantages volunteer data can provide over the lack of official sources. This was again confirmed in the days after September 19, 2017, where civil society was out on the streets collecting data to help make better decisions in the initial stages of the recovery process.

It is unfortunate, however, that these societal efforts that aim at collecting data and creating crowdmapping or VGI platforms quickly fade away as society pushes to recover its normal activity rhythm and strive to regain normality. This work in progress proposes to have a common goal between society and government and push towards a comprehensive emergency and disaster management platform that not only amasses data on many different topics and regions but also makes it fairly accessible to the general public.

The idea behind this work in progress of a proposed platform or system could provide a way for society and government to initiate a dialog towards a more complete emergency and disaster management culture in the city and the country. It seems many of the volunteers who put forward ideas, code, platforms, and data somehow shared the same purpose and only in very few cases forces were joined. Many other efforts seem to have been duplicated. In this sense, it would be a much better option to bring together representatives of different groups and sectors to discuss ideas and move forward with their implementation.

However, a digital platform would not necessarily resolve these communication and emergency management issues. Some portions of the city were out of electricity for several days, so an online platform would be rendered useless for these locations. This effort should also contemplate the matter of re-educating the population in terms of what needs or can be done in the event of an emergency. For instance, as mentioned before, citizens would need to have a sound idea of what can happen at their street level, at home, work, school or during a commute.

An idea of bringing some of the resources mentioned here, and many more, to a single place, is to facilitate the required information for those in need and help them avoid the myriad of repositories and websites that inform of similar things. Instead, it would be suitable to have different sections that contain information with respect to different topics.

It will be interesting to see how local and federal government officials take this chance to harness the power of citizens and volunteers, especially their ubiquity and ability to collect data that can become useful. With this in mind, it would be possible to think about transitioning to a better-prepared society, one in which citizens are actively participating in taking care of themselves. Here is a chance for government officials to prove their worth and look up to a better and brighter future that looks into taking citizens into account on what they are seeing and experiencing on a regular basis.

A great deal of lobbying will have to take place to bring the attention of certain sectors of the government that still are not convinced of the usefulness of citizen sensors and science and of what volunteers can bring to an ever-changing process of adaptation in a city that sits on fragile grounds, one that has an will continue to be struck by earthquakes but has overcome these natural disasters.

These are prosperous and certainly very interesting times for citizen science and volunteer geography in Mexico City. Hopefully, authorities will share this progressive vision and will accompany scientists, citizens scientists, and volunteers in this journey that has high hopes of being beneficial for everyone in the city.

Future steps for this work in progress involve finishing collecting all the existing modules that are considered to be relevant at this stage and move towards a proper integration of their capabilities. For the time being, the idea of newer functionality is not considered, as it is deemed more important to have all the initial pieces of this large puzzle put together first, but will be considered later on. Another step is to detect all the current data sources (volunteered or not, verified or not) and classify them by type of source, how they can be accessed, how often they might be updated and what their relevance might be for the platform. An important step will be to present an initial pitch of the platform to the relevant authorities and interested citizen groups in order to get feedback from each side (as potential and expected users) and detect points in common and points in conflict and improve the conceptual computational design of the platform from that initial assessment.

References

1. Kar, B., Sieber, R., Haklay, M., Ghose, R.: Public participation GIS and participatory GIS in the era of GeoWeb. Cartogr. J. **53**, 296–299 (2016)
2. Organisation for Economic Co-operation and Development (OECD): Open Government Data. http://www.oecd.org/gov/digital-government/open-government-data.html
3. Open Government Working Group: The Annotated 8 Principles of Open Government Data. http://opengovdata.org/
4. National Geophysical Data Center/World Data Service (NGDC/WDS): Significant Earthquake Database. National Geophysical Data Center, NOAA. https://doi.org/10.7289/V5TD9V7K.
5. U.S. Geological Survey (USGS): M 7.1 - 1km E of Ayutla, Mexico. https://earthquake.usgs.gov/earthquakes/eventpage/us2000ar20#executive
6. Servicio Sismológico Nacional: Catálogo de sismos. http://www2.ssn.unam.mx:8080/catalogo/
7. Servicio Sismológico Nacional: El sismo del 85 en cifras. https://web.archive.org/web/20080610175800/http://www.ssn.unam.mx/website/jsp/Carteles/sismo85.jsp
8. #Epicentro: Plataforma cívica para reconstrucción social con integridad. https://www.tm.org.mx/epicentrocom/
9. Cutter, S.L.: GI science, disasters, and emergency management. Trans. GIS. **7**, 439–446 (2003)
10. Morrow, B.H.: Identifying and mapping community vulnerability. Disasters **23**, 1–18 (1999)
11. Information Technology for Humanitarian Assistance, Cooperation and Action (ITHACA): Emergency Mapping. http://www.ithacaweb.org/projects/rapid-mapping/
12. International Working Group on Satellite-based Emergency Mapping (IWG-SEM): Emergency Mapping Guidelines. http://www.un-spider.org/sites/default/files/IWG_SEM_EmergencyMappingGuidelines_v1_Final.pdf
13. Zook, M., Graham, M., Shelton, T., Gorman, S.: Volunteered geographic information and crowdsourcing disaster relief: a case study of the Haitian earthquake. World Med. Heal. Pol. **2**, 6–32 (2010)
14. NASA - Jet Propulsion Laboratory (JPL): Space Images—Satellite Radar Detects Damage from Sept. 19, 2017 Raboso, Mexico, Quake. https://www.jpl.nasa.gov/spaceimages/details.php?id=pia21963
15. International Disasters Charter: Earthquake in Mexico. https://disasterscharter.org/web/guest/activations/-/article/earthquake-in-mexico-activation-553-
16. Goodchild, M.F., Glennon, J.A.: Crowdsourcing geographic information for disaster response: a research frontier. Int. J. Digit. Earth. **3**, 231–241 (2010)
17. Instituto Nacional de Geografía y Estadística (INEGI): Mapa Digital de México. http://gaia.inegi.org.mx/desastres
18. Colegio de Ingenieros Civiles de México: Sismos México. https://www.sismosmexico.org/mapas
19. Atlas Nacional de Riesgos: Sistema de información geográfica sobre riesgos. http://www.atlasnacionalderiesgos.gob.mx/archivo/visor-capas.html
20. Humanitarian OpenStreetMap Team (HOT OSM): Mexico Earthquake. https://tasks.hotosm.org/?sort_by=priority&direction=asc&search=mexican+earthquake

21. OpenStreetMap Wiki: 2017 Mexico Earthquakes. https://wiki.openstreetmap.org/wiki/2017_Mexico_Earthquakes
22. Google Crisis Response: Sismo en México. http://google.org/crisismap/google.com/puebla-mexico-earthquake-es
23. Cívica Digital: Quake Relief MX. https://github.com/civica-digital/quake-relief-cdmx
24. Verificado 19S. Plataforma digital para verificar información. http://www.verificado19s.org/
25. Presidencia de la República: Carto map for Sismo 19S. https://cedn.carto.com/builder/1fc22592-67af-452a-b8c9-21428b4f3519/embed
26. Datos Abiertos de México: Reportes ciudadanos de afectaciones por el sismo 19-S. https://datos.gob.mx/busca/dataset/reportes-ciudadanos-de-afectaciones-por-el-sismo-19-s
27. Manos a la Obra: https://manos-a-la-obra.github.io/mapa_ayuda/
28. Ciudadanía 19S. http://ciudadania19s.org.mx/2017/10/16/que-es-ciudadania19s/
29. Agencia de Gestión Urbana (AGU): Laboratorio Para la Ciudad (LabCDMX). http://labcd.mx/el-laboratorio/
30. CDMX-Comunicación Social: Instalación de la Comisión para la Reconstrucción, Recuperación y Transformación de la Ciudad de México en una CDMX cada vez más Resiliente. http://www.comunicacion.cdmx.gob.mx/noticias/nota/instalacion-de-la-comision-para-la-reconstruccion-recuperacion-y-transformacion-de-la-ciudad-de-mexico-en-una-cdmx-cada-vez-mas-resiliente
31. Plan para la reconstrucción de la CDMX. Directrices Generales. http://www.reconstruccion.cdmx.gob.mx/storage/app/uploads/public/5a5/951/9f3/5a59519f3f047556008364.pdf
32. Plataforma CDMX. https://www.plataforma.cdmx.gob.mx/
33. Tapia-McClung, R.: Collective mapping to support citizen-government interactions using a digital platform. GI_Forum **2**, 147–156 (2016)

Workshop Virtual Reality and Applications (VRA 2018)

Object Detection with Deep Learning
for a Virtual Reality Based Training Simulator

M. Fikret Ercan[1(✉)] (iD), Qiankun Liu[1] (iD), Yasushi Amari[2] (iD),
and Takashi Miyazaki[2] (iD)

[1] Singapore Polytechnic, 500 Dover Road, Singapore 139651, Singapore
M_Fikret_ERCAN@sp.edu.sg
[2] National Institute of Technology, Nagano College, 716 Tokuma, Nagano,
Nagano Prefecture 381-8550, Japan

Abstract. Virtual Reality (VR) provides immersive user experience which
makes them a cost effective solution to employ for various training purposes.
However, a major shortcoming of VR systems is their limitation when it comes
to interacting with the environment. Typically, when users wear a head mounted
display their vision will be limited to virtual world and their external vision will
be blocked. They will not be able to see useful objects in their environment such
as controllers, buttons or even their hands. In this paper, we describe design of a
training system for aerospace industry where real and virtual images blended,
creating an augmented virtuality. The real world images are obtained from a
camera mounted on the head-mounted-display. Some of the predefined objects,
such as game controllers and user's hands, are detected via deep learning
algorithms and blended into the virtual reality images providing a more comfortable and immersive user experience. Furthermore, camera and object
detection algorithms are employed to interact with VR headset making it more
convenient tool for training simulators.

Keywords: Computer vision · Game design · Object detection
Virtual reality · Deep learning

1 Introduction

Simulators are widely used for personnel training who are operating machines or
systems at critical and/or dangerous environments. This way, operators gain a risk free
and in depth training experience before embarking on the actual machines or systems
[1, 2]. There are various driving simulators though their high cost, limited field of view
(due to use of monitors), and lack of portability is a major drawback [3–5].

In this study, we consider using VR glasses in driving simulator application which
offer an immersive experience to users. Game based learning using virtual environments becoming popular in training as the VR hardware is now low-cost and stable. It
provides a hands-on experience in a safe and risk free environment. Due to these
advantages, VR training systems found applications in diverse fields such as machine
operation and driving [6], medicine [7], mining [8] and so on. The VR training simulator presented here is developed for aircraft towing, in collaboration with our partners

© Springer International Publishing AG, part of Springer Nature 2018
O. Gervasi et al. (Eds.): ICCSA 2018, LNCS 10963, pp. 725–739, 2018.
https://doi.org/10.1007/978-3-319-95171-3_57

in aerospace industry. Operator mistakes in aircraft pushback operations may result in substantial losses due to damages made to structures or aircraft. Therefore, it is beneficial to develop operator skills before practicing with the actual tow truck. This way training can be carried out anytime instead of waiting for down-time or available aircrafts. Currently, training is handled by skilled personnel. There are existing simulators for this specific application (see for instance [9]), however they are expensive and not portable.

Training simulator discussed here provides an easy to use authoring tool for virtual environment that allow domain experts to build training scenarios. The system works with low cost VR glasses which provide a broader view to the trainees instead of limited view of the traditional simulators. A major drawback of using VR headsets in driving simulators is the completely blocked vision of the user from the actual world. In order to access driving wheel, buttons and any other game controller user needs to remove the VR headset which hinders the interactivity of the simulator and the immersive experience it can provide. We address this problem by employing a camera unit and computer vision techniques to blend selected objects from real world with the virtual reality image, providing a mixed reality experience. This allows users to perform training tasks within the virtual environment while interacting with the physical game controllers conveniently. This solution can be classified as an Augmented Virtual (AR) system referring to Milgram's taxonomy [10].

In our experiments, we use HTC VIVE which comes with front mounted cameras on VR glasses for the live stream of the actual scene. There are various other techniques presented recently which enables interaction with real environment while wearing VR headsets. Leap motion's hand gesture detection is one such example [11]. However, this system requires its custom designed hardware. There are also studies based on depth cameras such as Kinect though setting and calibrating hardware makes it difficult to use by non-experts [12]. Our primary concern in the design of the training simulator was to maintain low-cost and simplicity so that it can be used by non-experts in game design or programming. In order to achieve this objective, our solution is based on built-in camera and computer vision algorithms to detect identified objects to blend them into virtual image. Object detection in digital images is vastly studied in computer vision literature and many algorithms were developed for this purpose. For instance, Viola-Jones algorithm (for detecting faces in images) [13], Histograms of Oriented Gradients (for detecting humans) [14], Scale-Invariant Feature Transform (SIFT) [15], Speeded Up Robust Feature (SURF) [16] are some of the well-known algorithms. However, recently the performance of Deep learning and Convolutional Neural Network (CNN) based algorithms surpassed even human recognition rate which made deep learning a preferred method to use in our system.

In the following section, we will present an overview of the training simulator developed. Section 3 presents the performance of deep learning algorithm in object detection and blending with virtual images. Section 4 presents the performance of deep learning algorithm in classifying multiple objects. In order to provide a comfortable means of interaction with the training simulator, we also integrated hand gesture detection to communicate with the system and its performance is presented in Sect. 5.

2   System Architecture

The training simulator is made of three major components as shown with a block diagram in Fig. 1. These are trainer interface, trainee interface and analytics engine. An expert with no VR/AR programming proficiency can produce interactive scenarios and deploy them using trainer interface. The trainers can drag and drop game assets to create the virtual environment that fits their training purpose. Game assets include all the 2D and 3D art to create a scenario. Plenty of digital assets such as buildings, planes, tow trucks and other possible object are developed considering our application. On the other hand, game object controller module enable setting rules (such as awarding points or penalties) to control the behavior of these game assets. Trainer is then able to upload the scenario to the cloud as an xml file. Many training scenarios can be developed and shared without programming skills or the knowledge of game development. This makes the system flexible and expandable. Figure 2 shows an example training scenario created by the trainer. The system is built using development tool Unity and OpenCV.

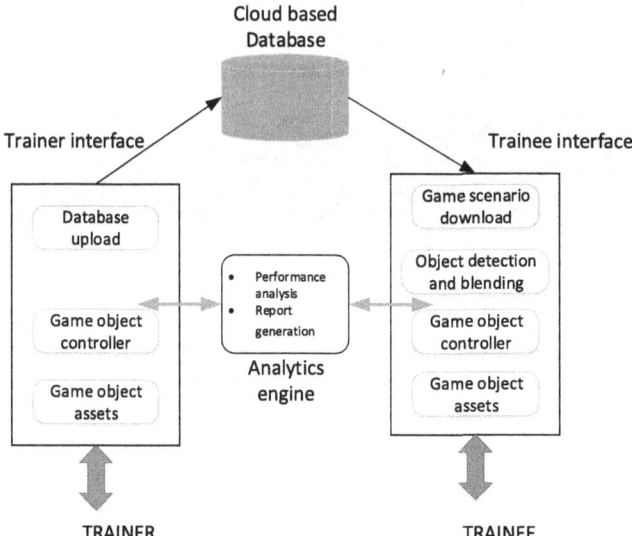

Fig. 1. The block diagram of training simulator. The trainer creates scenarios where the leaner experiences the scenario. The analytics engine provides the information about the performance trainees.

Analytics engine module is created to record and evaluate the user's performance. There are four game rules applied in the system.

Rule 1: *Staying close to the taxi line:* The purpose of this rule is to keep the plane aligned with the designated taxi line. The driver will be informed if the plane is not in the right position during the pushing process.

Rule 2: *Speed*: According to the Ground Operations Safety Manual, the pushing speed cannot exceed 5 km/h.

Rule 3: *Tow bar angle*: The driver should avoid pushing the plane in a wide angle, as it may damage both the plane and truck tires in practice. Currently, the angle is set to be within the absolute value of 75°.

Rule 4: *Collision*: This rule is to check whether the plane collide with objects such as buildings, passenger bridge and other structural elements.

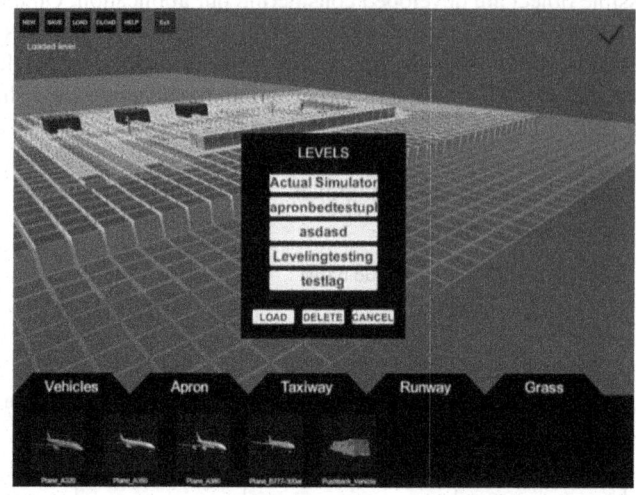

Fig. 2. A training scenario created by the user and saved in the cloud.

In the beginning, a trainee is given a score of 100. The player needs to start the tow truck engine by pressing the simulator button. Once the engine started, system starts to count time as well. A message on the task panel reminds the player to connect the tow bar which was parking at the start point. Once the push back truck is connected, trainee can start pushing the plane to the end of parking slot following the yellow taxi line. This is one of the simplest task at the beginner level. More complex scenarios are created by the trainers using trainer interface. During the training, if any of the rules violated, one point is deducted from the initial score. If trainee repeats the same mistakes, more points are deducted. After the airplane is pushed to a designated parking slot, this training simulation is passed. However, if the points are below zero or the time taken to complete the mission is more than 3 min, this level is considered as failure. At the end of the session performance of the user is reported as shown in Fig. 3. Simultaneously, performance data of trainees are recorded and stored into the database which can be viewed by the trainer and the trainee. A trainer is provided with full access to all the trainees' performance records. A video link demonstrating the operation of the training simulator can be found in [23].

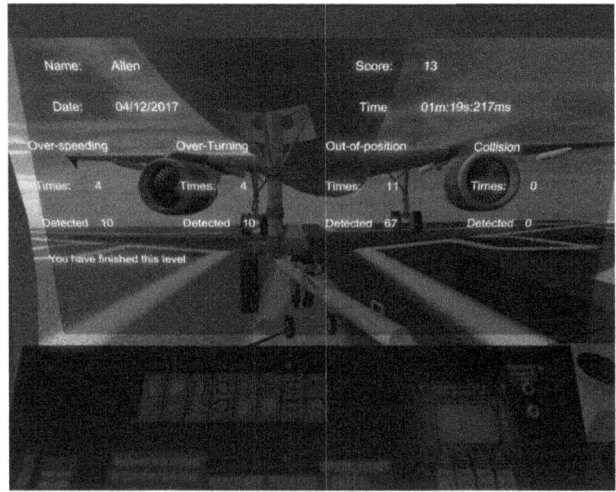

Fig. 3. Game end panel showing the result for the session.

Trainee interface enables a trainee to interact with in-game objects and physical devices such as game controllers. To begin, user selects a training scenario from the list of scenarios in the database and use their head mounted display to immerse into the task. Trainees use physical game controllers to control in-game vehicle. However, head mounted display only shows the virtual environment and blocks users view of the real world surrounding him. In the following sections, we will present our approach to tackle this problem which is the main focus of this paper.

3   Blending Virtual and Real Image

In our setup, HTC VIVE VR glasses, which comes with front mounted cameras, are used. A number of selected objects are detected from the live image feed provided by camera and the renderer blends them with the virtual image. This way user can interact with these objects without the need of taking off their VR glasses. Some of the pres-elected objects considered in our experiments are the driving wheel and human hands. There is vast research and algorithms available in the literature for detecting objects in images. We have experimented with various methods including a Haar-cascade clas-sifier [13] as well as key-point descriptors such as SURF [16] and BRIEF [17]. In our earlier trials, the best performance obtained was with Haar classifier followed with SURF algorithm. However, detection rate was not satisfactory. In particular, when there is a change in illumination, detection rate dropped dramatically. In our applica-tion, a robust object detection is needed to blend real and virtual images smoothly. Considering the effectiveness of deep learning algorithms in object detection, we implemented two deep learning algorithms for object detection and measured the performance of those methods.

3.1 Deep Learning Algorithms for Object Detection

We implemented YOLOv2 and MobileNet-SSD to recognize steering wheel and human hands since both available as open source and demonstrated good performance results.

YOLOv2

YOLOv2 is one of the recent algorithm which use deep learning for object detection [18]. The outline of the detection method is as follows. The input images are divided into grids. Each grid has some bounding boxes of constant aspect ratio called anchor. In YOLOv2, the center coordinates (x, y) and the scale of width and height (w, h) of each anchor are predicted. In addition, each anchor box has a confidence parameter indicating the probability that an object exists, and also predicts the conditional probability of what it is, if an object exists. Predictions of similar anchor boxes are performed on all grids, and only those boxes whose confidence is equal to or larger than a certain value are used as the output of the network. YOLOv2 performs object detection with these methods. In the application of neural networks for object detection, preliminary learning is generally based on VGG16 as feature extractor, however YOLOv2 uses a unique classification model called Darknet-19 which has 19 convolutional layers and 5 maxpooling layers 1 Global Average pooling layer. In the Convolutional Neural Network (CNN), it is common to put fully connected layer in the final layer and apply softmax function. Darknet-19 adopts a method of constructing all the layers with a convolution layer, and the feature map is propagated to the final layer while maintaining the accurate position information. This method is called Fully Convolutional Networks (FCN) and is often used for semantic segmentation. In addition, YOLOv2 uses all the range of an image during learning hence it can learn the surrounding context at the same time. This way erroneous detection of the background can be suppressed.

MobileNet-SSD

Another object detection algorithm based on deep learning is Single Shot MultiBox Detector (SSD) [19]. This method also produce bounding boxes of fixed size with probability scores for the presence of the object. The first part of the SSD network is called the base network and it is based on the standard VGG16 architecture which is frequently used in image classification. The SSD reduces the output size by hierarchically adding a feature map at the end of the base network so that it can handle various scales. In addition, high accuracy and detection rate are achieved by creating a discriminator for each aspect ratio. MobileNet-SSD architecture, built upon SSD described above, strive to achieve a fast and efficient detector considering mobile and embedded platforms [20]. MobileNet-SSD uses MobileNet as base network of SSD. The MobileNet model employs depthwise separable convolutions. The approach used in depthwise separable convolution is to split convolution into two stages where a 3×3 depthwise convolution is performed first followed by a 1×1 pointwise convolution. The MobileNet-SSD drastically reduced the network model and computation size and reported competitive performance when compared to larger networks [20].

3.2 Experimental Results

The data sets for deep learning is generated from two minute video recordings of eight users from the video camera of the headset while they are using the game controllers. These users are selected from various age groups and skin tones which are the typical of user profile in our environment. Subsequently, one image frame per second is extracted from the video recording, resulting in a total of 960 images. The created images are used as a dataset for hand detection. Furthermore, a video of the steering wheel is recorded for two minutes and data set for driving wheel is created the same way. Next, 120 wheel images are added to the dataset for hand detection hence creating a training set for steering wheel detector. YOLOv2 and MobileNet-SSD learn the two created datasets producing a steering wheel and human hands detector. YOLOv2 is implemented using Darknet and MobileNet-SSD is implemented using Caffe frameworks.

After the learning phase, the performance of the two networks are tested with the six new users. These users were also selected based on their age and skin tone to create a test set. Two minutes videos of the six new users while they were using the game controllers are recorded. As before, a test image set is obtained by extracting 720 images from video recordings and the learned models of YOLOv2 and MobileNet-SSD are evaluated using this data set.

A common performance measurement method in object detection is Intersect over Union (IoU) which evaluates how well the predicted bounding box overlap with the ground truth. However, in our application the correct detection of object presence and its position is more imperative. Therefore, we defined the algorithm performance based on detection rate. The objects that are recognized correctly are counted as correct detection, the objects recognized incorrectly are counted as wrong detection and the objects that cannot be detected are counted as not detected. Accuracy is defined as:

$$Accuracy = \frac{Correct\ detection}{Correct\ detection + Wrong\ detection + Not\ detected} \times 100\ [\%]$$

Table 1 shows the result of detecting steering wheel using YOLOv2 and using MobileNet-SSD. From Table 1, we can conclude that YOLOv2 and MobileNet-SSD can detect the steering wheel almost perfectly. Table 2 shows the performance of detecting human hands using YOLOv2 and using MobileNet-SSD. Results show that YOLOv2 can detect human hands almost perfectly. MobileNet-SSD has higher number of cases where hands in the image was not detected. However, accuracy of MobileNet-SSD is 96.6%, which is also a satisfactory performance for our application.

4 Multiple Classifications Using MobileNet-SSD

In the previous section, we presented steering wheel and human hand detectors using YOLOv2 and MobileNet-SSD where both networks outperformed the conventional computer vision techniques significantly. For instance, the best performance obtained for driving wheel detector using Haar classifier was 36% and with SURF algorithm was

Table 1. The performance result for detecting steering wheel.

	YOLOv2			MobileNet-SSD		
	Correct	Wrong	Undetected	Correct	Wrong	Undetected
Experiment 1	120	0	0	119	0	1
Experiment 2	120	0	0	120	0	0
Experiment 3	120	0	0	119	0	1
Experiment 4	120	0	0	120	0	0
Experiment 5	120	0	0	120	0	0
Experiment 6	120	0	0	120	0	0
Average	120	0	0	119.6	0	0.33
Accuracy	100%			99.7%		

Table 2. The performance of detecting human hand.

Person	YOLOv2			MobileNet-SSD		
	Correct	Wrong	Undetected	Correct	Wrong	Undetected
White skin (Young)	226	1	2	219	2	9
White skin (Old)	232	0	0	227	0	5
Yellow skin (Young)	232	0	4	220	0	16
Yellow skin (Old)	238	0	0	233	0	5
Dark skin (Young)	228	1	3	220	0	11
Dark skin (Old)	240	0	0	240	0	0
Average	232.67	0.33	1.5	226.5	0.33	7.67
Accuracy	99.2%			96.6%		

Table 3. The performance of detecting multiple objects (input image size 300 × 300 pixels).

User	MobileNet-SSD-300					
	Steering wheel detection			Hand detection		
	Correct	Wrong	Undetected	Correct	Wrong	Undetected
White skin (Young)	119	1	1	219	1	9
White skin (Old)	119	0	1	230	1	2
Yellow skin (Young)	118	1	2	226	2	10
Yellow skin (Old)	120	0	0	236	7	2
Dark skin (Young)	119	1	1	220	24	11
Dark skin (Old)	120	2	0	239	3	1
Only driving wheel	120	0	0	-	-	-
Average	119.29	0.71	0.71	228.33	6.33	5.83
Accuracy	98.82%			94.94%		

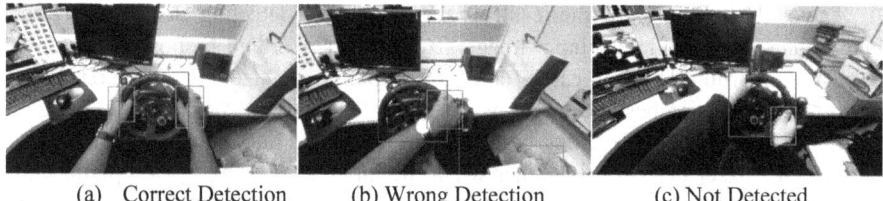

(a)   Correct Detection   (b) Wrong Detection   (c) Not Detected

Fig. 4. Examples of correct, wrong and no detections of steering wheel and human hands with MobileNet-SSD-300.

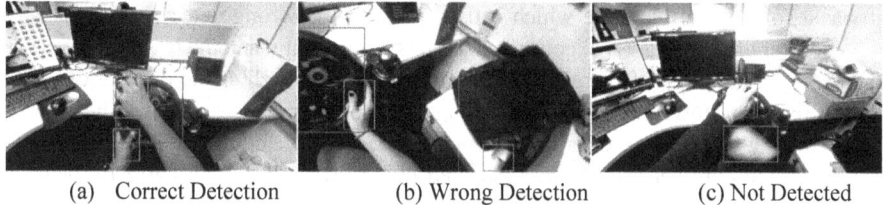

(a)   Correct Detection   (b) Wrong Detection   (c) Not Detected

Fig. 5. Examples of correct, wrong and no detections of steering wheel and human hands with MobileNet-SSD-412.

(a)Correct Detection   (b) Wrong Detection   (c) Not Detected

Fig. 6. Examples of correct, wrong and no detections of steering wheel and human hands with MobileNet-SSD-512.

12%. Our experimental results show that between the two networks, YOLOv2 slightly outperformed the MobileNet-SSD. However, when incorporated into Unity development environment [21] which is used in the development of training simulator, heavy computation time of YOLOV2 diminished the real-time processing performance by reducing it to five frames per second. Therefore, MobileNet-SSD was chosen to implement object detection in our system. Using MobileNet-SSD, we implemented a detector that can detect multiple objects such as steering wheel and human hands simultaneously. MobileNet-SSD resizes the input image and performs learning and detection. Therefore, we resize the input image to three sizes of 300×300, 412×412, 512×512 pixels and let MobileNet-SSD learn it. Two minutes videos of four users are recorded and a total of 480 images are extracted. These data added to dataset for steering wheel which is used in the previous experiment. The evaluation method is the same as before.

Tables 3, 4 and 5 show the result of simultaneously detecting steering wheel and human hands with different input image size. Figures 4, 5 and 6 shows examples of correct, and wrong detection cases for various input image sizes. From the results, we observe that the highest accuracy is obtained when the size of input image is 300 × 300 pixels when detecting both steering wheel and human hands. However, the number of correct detection is higher when the input size is larger. Comparing input image sizes 412 × 412 and 512 × 512 pixels, we observed that 412 × 412 pixels has a larger number of correct detection and a small number of wrong or not detected cases. Concluding, MobileNet-SSD-412 outperformed MobileNet-SSD-512 in these experiments. In many of the wrong detection case, a false object in the scene produced a competitive confidence rate, due to its color or texture, as learned objects. In this case, it was a soft toy in the scene which caused most of the wrong detections.

A closer observation on experimental results reveal that when the input image size is increased, the number of correct detection is increased as well as the number of wrong detection cases. However, most of the wrong detection seems to be the case where two or more steering wheels or three or more human hands are detected in one image. In most of the cases, the confidence of falsely detected object was lower than correctly detected objects in the image. Considering our application where there is only one steering wheel and a pair of human hands wrong detections can be reduced with a simple work around. Therefore, when two or more steering wheels are detected, the steering wheel with the highest confidence is selected, and when more than two human hands are detected, top two detections with highest confidence score are chosen. This method further improved the accuracy providing a smooth blending of real and virtual images as shown in Fig. 7. A video showing the operation of the system can be seen in [22].

Table 4. The performance of detecting multiple objects (input image size 412 × 412 pixels).

User	MobileNet-SSD-412					
	Steering wheel detection			Hand detection		
	Correct	Wrong	Not	Correct	Wrong	Not
White skin (Young)	119	4	1	220	2	8
White skin (Old)	120	1	0	230	5	2
Yellow skin (Young)	119	1	1	234	3	2
Yellow skin (Old)	120	1	0	236	7	2
Dark skin (Young)	120	5	0	223	36	8
Dark skin (Old)	120	0	0	240	0	0
Only driving wheel	120	0	0	-	-	-
Average	119.71	1.71	0.29	230.50	8.83	3.67
Accuracy	98.36%			94.86%		

Table 5. The performance of detecting multiple objects (input image size 512 × 512 pixels).

User	MobileNet-SSD-512					
	Steering wheel detection			Hand detection		
	Correct	Wrong	Not	Correct	Wrong	Not
White skin (Young)	118	2	2	220	1	4
White skin (Old)	118	7	2	228	1	4
Yellow skin (Young)	120	3	0	234	10	2
Yellow skin (Old)	119	0	1	237	14	1
Dark skin (Young)	120	5	0	218	48	13
Dark skin (Old)	120	3	0	240	1	0
Only driving wheel	120	1	0	-	-	-
Average	119.29	3.00	0.71	229.50	12.50	4.00
Accuracy	96.98%			93.29%		

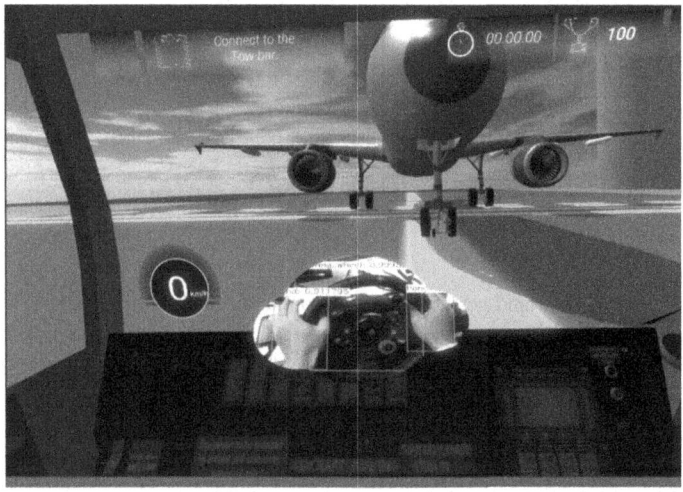

Fig. 7. User's perspective while controlling the tow truck. The driving wheel and driver's hands are detected and blended into the virtual environment.

5   Hand Gesture Detection

In our efforts to improve usability of the system, especially problem of interacting with environment while wearing VR headset, we decided to use hand gestures to communicate with the system. This way user can switch vision between real world and virtual world without the need for removing VR headset. This way user can chose to see what the camera unit mounted on the VR set is capturing or the virtual world shown by the training simulator. In order to achieve this objective, we have developed a deep learning model for detecting two hand gestures to communicate with the system.

The hand gesture shown in Fig. 8(a) is defined as start sign, and the hand gesture shown in Fig. 8(b) is defined as stop sign. These two hand gestures do not occur naturally when using the game controllers therefore they are chosen to avoid signaling the system involuntarily.

There are many algorithms for hand gesture recognition. However, in our application, the background may often be cluttered with objects, game controllers etc. Therefore, we consider each hand gesture as a separate object and develop models to detect hand gesture using MobileNet-SSD. Data from six users are collected while wearing VR headset. Two minutes videos are recorded for the two hand gestures illustrated in Fig. 8. After that image frames, with three images per second ratio, are extracted from the recorded videos resulting in a training set of 4,320 images. The size of input image is 300 × 300 pixels. In order to prevent any false detection, object with the highest confidence result is selected.

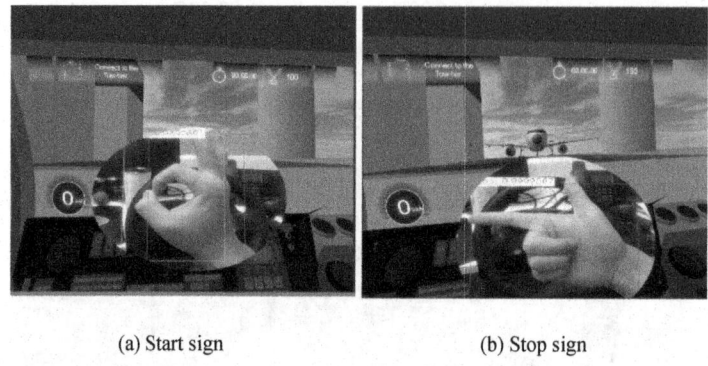

(a) Start sign   (b) Stop sign

Fig. 8. Hand gestures used for communicating with VR set.

Network is tested with data set obtained from three new users which contained 1,080 images. Performance results, given in Table 6, show highly accurate detection of these two hand gestures. The hand gesture detection is incorporated to training simulator as one of the features of the trainee interface. Once the trainee shows 'start' or 'stop' hand gestures and system detects it for a duration of 2 seconds, it will switch between virtual and real images. Two second rule is used to avoid detecting coincidental cases. When the system detects 'start' sign it stops virtual images and switches to live camera feed, similarly 'stop' sign stops live feed from camera and turns on the virtual images.

Table 6. Performance result of detecting hand gestures using test images.

	Start sign detection			Stop sign detection		
	Correct	Wrong	Undetected	Correct	Wrong	Undetected
User 1	360	0	0	360	0	0
User 2	357	1	3	358	0	2
User 3	356	0	4	360	0	0
Average	357.7	0.3	2.0	359.3	0.0	0.7
Accuracy	99.35%			99.81%		

Table 7. Real-time hand gestures detection results.

Users	Start gestures	Stop gestures
Kento	0.40	0.70
Jerome	1.00	0.50
Yanbo	0.90	1.00
Shijie	0.70	1.00
Nicholas	0.50	0.80
Warren	1.00	0.70
James	1.00	1.00
Average	79%	81%

In order to experiment final system, seven users were asked to show 'start' and 'stop' hand gestures for ten times. When a user shows the gesture but the system does not respond, it is considered as failure. Table 7 shows that the success rate is around 80%. For two users Kento and Nicholas, the success rate is rather low since our training data set did not have any samples closer to their skin tones. This can be solved by including more variety of training samples. A video link illustrating the use of gesture recognition can be found in [22].

6 Experiments with Training Simulator

The next question was to test if a trainee can improve driving skills and learn driving a tow-truck. For the experiments, ten players were asked to do ten trials on the same training scenario tackling the same complexity level. For every failed trial, trainee

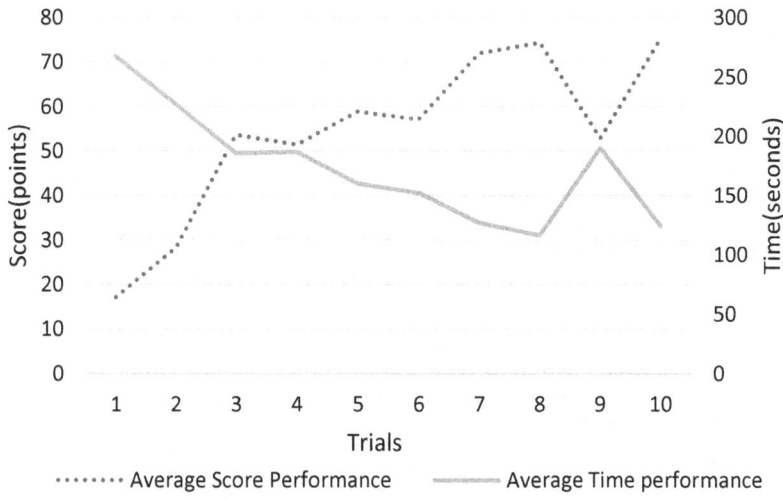

Fig. 9. Average score and time performance of users in ten trials.

receives 0 point and completion time is recorded as 300 s. The average trainee performance for each trial sessions are shown in Fig. 9. As expected, the results show that with more training a driver commits to lesser mistakes based on the game rules. Meanwhile, the time taken to complete the level also declines steadily. Going through trainee profiles, we observed that experienced drivers perform much better than regular drivers. However, after practicing several times and get to know how the pushback truck works, a novice driver's performance also improves significantly.

7   Conclusion

This paper described design of virtual reality based training system developed for aerospace industry. The system provides flexibility and portability making training available and cost effective for other industry applications. The shortcoming of VR headsets when interacting with physical game controllers is tackled by incorporating augmented virtuality using a camera and object detection algorithms. Experiments with two well-known deep learning algorithms, YOLOv2 and MobileNet-SSD, demonstrated superior detection rates which made the trainee interface of the system more user friendly. MobileNet-SSD is chosen since it is not computationally demanding. Our results show that designed system can provide an immersive experience to the user. In our future work, we aim to incorporate a better rendering when blending real and virtual images to make simulation even more immersive experience.

8   Acknowledgment

This study is sponsored by Singapore Ministry of Education under the grant number MOE2015-TIF-2-T-039.

References

1. Kading, W.: The advanced Daimler-Benz driving simulator. SAE 9530012 (1995)
2. Soma, H., Hiramatsu, K.: Driving simulator experiment on drivers' behaviour and effectiveness of danger warning against emergency braking of leading vehicle. In: Proceedings of 16th ESV, Canada (1998)
3. University of Valencia Forklift Simulator. http://www.uv.es/uvweb/university-research-institute-robotics-information-communication-technologies/en/research-groups/lsym/projects/forklift-truck-simulator-forklift-1285895484292/ProjecteInves.html?id=1285898571581. Accessed 20 Nov 2017
4. Smart Mover Ultimate Car Simulator. http://thefutureofthings.com/5741-smart-mover-ultimate-car-simulator/. Accessed 15 Sept 2017
5. University of Queensland Driving Simulator. http://www.carrsq.qut.edu.au/simulator/. Accessed 25 June 2017
6. Virtual Driver. https://www.driverinteractive.com/. Accessed 12 Feb 2018

7. Chen, L., Dayz, T.W., Tangx, W., John, N.W.: Recent developments and future challenges in medical mixed reality. In: Proceedings of 16th IEEE International Symposium on Mixed and Augmented Reality (2017)
8. Wyk, E.V., Villiers, R.: Virtual reality training applications for the mining industry. In: Proceedings of the 6th International Conference on Computer Graphics, Virtual Reality, Visualization and Interaction in Africa, Pretoria, South Africa, pp. 53–63 (2009)
9. L3 Aircraft Pushback. http://www.l-3training.com/applications/aviation/aircraft-pushback-training-simulator. Accessed 25 July 2017
10. Milgram, P., Kishino, F.: A Taxonomy of mixed reality visual displays. IEICE Trans. Inf. Syst. **E77-D**(12), 1321–1329 (1994)
11. Leap Motion. https://www.leapmotion.com/. Accessed 01 Sept 2017
12. Wang, C., Liu, Z., Chan, S.C.: Superpixel-based hand gesture recognition with kinect depth camera. IEEE Trans. Multimed. **17**(1), 29–39 (2015)
13. Viola, P.A., Jones, M.J.: Robust real-time face detection. Int. J. Comput. Vis. **57**(2), 137–154 (2004)
14. Dalal, N., Triggs, B.: Histograms of oriented gradients for human detection. In: Proceedings of IEEE Computer Society Conference on Computer Vision and Pattern Recognition (CVPR 2005), San Diego, USA, pp. 886–893 (2005)
15. Lowe, D.G.: Distinctive image features from scale-invariant key points. Int. J. Comput. Vis. **60**(2), 91–110 (2004)
16. Bay, H., Ess, A., Tuytelaars, T., Van Gool, L.J.: SURF: Speeded Up Robust Features. Comput. Vis. Image Underst. **110**(3), 346–359 (2008)
17. Calonder, M., Lepetit, V., Özuysal, M., Trzcinski, T., Strecha, C., Fua, P.: BRIEF: computing a local binary descriptor very fast. IEEE Trans. Pattern Anal. Mach. Intell. **34**(7), 1281–1298 (2012)
18. Redmon, J., Farhadi, A.: YOLO9000: Better, Faster, Stronger. arXiv preprint arXiv:1612.08242 (2016). https://arxiv.org/pdf/1612.08242.pdf. Accessed 20 Nov 2017
19. Liu, W., Anguelov, D., Erhan, D., Szegedy, C., Reed, S., Fu, C.Y., Berg, A.C.: SSD: Single Shot Multibox Detector. arXiv preprint arXiv:1512:02325 (2015). https://arxiv.org/pdf/1512.02325.pdf. Accessed 20 Nov 2017
20. Howard, A.G., Zhu, M., Chen, B., Kalenichenko, D., Wang, W., Weyand, T., Andreetto, M., Adam, H.: MobileNets: efficient convolutional neural networks for mobile vision applications. arXiv preprint arXiv:1704.04861, https://arxiv.org/pdf/1704.04861.pdf. Accessed 20 Nov 2017
21. Unity. https://unity3d.com/. Accessed 02 Dec 2017
22. Object Detection Video Demo. https://youtu.be/GoR8qaWhzSM. Accessed 8 Mar 2018
23. Project Video Demo. https://youtu.be/GnKbR5Z2bnI. Accessed 8 Mar 2018

Evaluating an Accelerometer-Based System for Spine Shape Monitoring

Katharina Stollenwerk[1]([✉]), Johannes Müllers[3], Jonas Müller[3], André Hinkenjann[2], and Björn Krüger[3]

[1] Institute of Visual Computing,
Bonn-Rhein-Sieg University of Applied Sciences,
Sankt Augustin, Germany
katharina.stollenwerk@h-brs.de
[2] Institute of Visual Computing, Hochschule Bonn-Rhein Sieg,
Sankt Augustin, Germany
[3] Gokhale Method Institute, Stanford, CA, USA

Abstract. In western societies a huge percentage of the population suffers from some kind of back pain at least once in their life. There are several approaches addressing back pain by postural modifications. Postural training and activity can be tracked by various wearable devices most of which are based on accelerometers. We present research on the accuracy of accelerometer-based posture measurements. To this end, we took simultaneous recordings using an optical motion capture system and a system consisting of five accelerometers in three different settings: On a test robot, in a template, and on actual human backs. We compare the accelerometer-based spine curve reconstruction against the motion capture data. Results show that tilt values from the accelerometers are captured highly accurate, and the spine curve reconstruction works well.

1 Introduction

Lower back pain is one of the largest diseases in the United States. In fact, 31 million Americans experience lower back pain at any given time [1]. Thus, lower back pain is the single leading cause of disability worldwide, according to the Global Burden of Disease 2010. Back pain is one of the most common reasons for missed work. In fact, back pain is the second most common reason for visits to the doctor's office, outnumbered only by upper-respiratory infections. One-half of all working Americans admit to having back pain symptoms each year [2]. Experts estimate that as much as 80% of the population will experience a back problem at some time in their lives [3], and that back pain is the largest single factor in the economical costs of $560–$635 billion per year attributed to pain in the United States [4].

There is a wide variety of interventions. Starting from invasive methods, like spinal fusion surgery, and laminectomy (decompression) surgery, over medications like cortisone injection, oral corticosteroids, or acetaminophen, to education on posture, such as yoga, physical therapy, or postural modifications.

O. Gervasi et al. (Eds.): ICCSA 2018, LNCS 10963, pp. 740–756, 2018.
https://doi.org/10.1007/978-3-319-95171-3_58

According to the crowd-sourcing platform *HealthOutcome*[1], postural modifications are the highest rated interventions [5]. Capturing and analysing motion data through training has become a standard procedure: Gait labs using motion capture setups, force plates, and other sensor technology are common. However, lab situations are not the best environment to capture and analyse a patient's natural behaviour. Thus, with emerging sensor technology, wearable devices were included into training, bringing data capturing out of the lab. So far, studies report varying results on the effectiveness of wearable devices for postural training and monitoring: The authors of [6] found that using the *UpRight*[2] device leads to positive increases in awareness of posture, emotional well-being, and decreases in pain symptoms. While the authors of a study based on the *Lumo Lift*[3] device, conclude [7]: "This study indicates that Lumo Lift is not suitable of giving posture feedback during lifting in daily life". The above mentioned studies directly focus on the impact on the user, without analysing the accuracy of the sensor systems they use. Fathi and Curran [8] use three inertial sensors, distributed over the lumbar and thoracic spine, to capture body poses. They focus on classification of various postures without assessing the quality of the captured data. Thus, we focus on the accuracy of capturing posture in this work. Only if postural features are monitored accurately, devices will be able to provide valuable data that can be enhanced to give useful feedback to the user.

The remainder of this paper is organised as follows: Sect. 2 gives an overview of the work related to motion capturing with various sensor systems. The used sensor technology is described in Sect. 3. Section 4 explains how tilt angles and positional data are computed from the used accelerometers. Our recording setup and the dataset that our experiments are based on are described in Sect. 5. An evaluation and the underlying measures are presented in Sect. 6. We discuss limitations in Sect. 7 and conclude the paper in Sect. 8.

2   Related Work

Recording and analysing human motions is well established in a wide variety of domains, such as computer animation, sport sciences [9], biology [10], and rehabilitation [11]. Optical motion capturing using passive markers and a large array of cameras has become the gold standard of capturing motions due to its high temporal and spatial resolution and accuracy [12]. This recording technique allowed the development of many enhanced applications analysing human [13,14] and animal [15,16] motions. Large databases of motion data are freely available [17,18] and a variety of techniques to handle the increasing amounts of available data have been developed [19–22]. To overcome the disadvantages of complex hardware settings (number of cameras, 42 and more markers need to be attached for full body capturing), the computer vision community is developing many approaches to compute 3D reconstructions of human poses without

---

[1] www.healthoutcome.org.
[2] www.uprightpose.com.
[3] www.lumobodytech.com.

markers from single images of video sequences [23, 24]. One orthogonal approach records motions based on the data from body-mounted cameras [25, 26].

The development of other sensor technologies allows for capturing without cameras, and thus without the restrictions of a capturing volume. Therefore, wireless EMG sensors and accelerometers have become popular and are used for motion analysis [27–29].

Based on readings from accelerometers only, various techniques have been developed to reconstruct [30–33] and classify [8, 13, 34] human poses and motions. While the above mentioned methods are able to roughly reconstruct full body motions on the basis of data from five three-axis sensors, in this work we focus on an accurate reconstruction of only a part of the human body, namely the curvature of the spine at the lower back.

3   Hardware

In this section we introduce the hardware employed in our recordings. We first give a brief overview of the motion capture system. Subsequently we provide more detailed information on the accelerometer-based system.

3.1   Motion Capture System

For the recordings, we used a ten-camera OptiTrack[4] Flex 3 system. The cameras operate at a resolution of 640×480 pixels. Throughout the recordings the frame rate was set to 100 Hz. Passive, spherical, retro-reflective markers with a diameter of 7/16 in ($\approx$11 mm) were used. As output from the motion capture system we received 3D marker trajectories, which needed further cleaning and labeling. See Sect. 5.2 for details on these processes.

3.2   Wearable

The wearable device used in the scope of this work is the $PostureSensei^{TM}$ (see Fig. 1) developed by Gokhale Method Enterprises[5]. While most posture wearables include one device, this system consists of five individual sensor units that are attached to the lower back of the user. With this approach it is possible to capture more detailed data on a larger part of the spine. Compared to readings from a single location on the body, several curvatures can be measured at once. Although a five-sensor configuration has been used, the system is in principle scalable to more or fewer sensors.

The five sensor units are technically identical and contain a three-axis accelerometer, a Bluetooth LE (low energy) module and a lithium battery. All sensors connect to one host (may be an iOS device or a computer) and stay in an energy-saving state until the measurement is started. Sampling rates of 10 Hz,

---

[4] http://optitrack.com/.
[5] http://posturesensei.com.

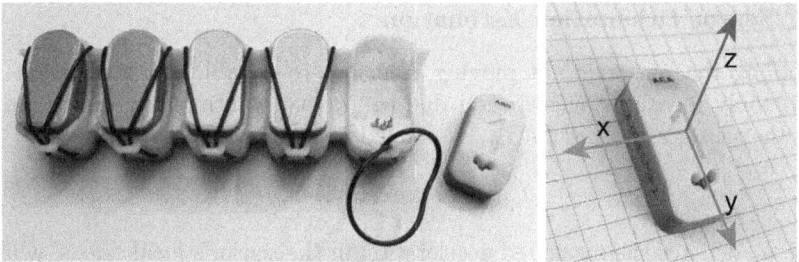

Fig. 1. Photos of the *PostureSensei*^{TM} sensor system. Four of five sensors are sitting in the charger. A single sensor has the dimensions 33 mm × 16 mm × 10 mm and is attached to a person's back with double sided tape. The right images shows a sensor's local coordinate system.

25 Hz, and 50 Hz can be configured from the host, suitable for slow motion measurements like sitting, as well as faster movements such as brisk walking [30]. At 50 Hz sampling rate, a battery runtime of eight hours allows a full work day of experimenting, while 10 Hz allow posture tracking for more than 24 h.

With a programmable full-scale-range of ±2 g (up to ±16 g)[6] and 10 bit resolution, a sensitivity of ±4 mg/LSB is achieved.

Keeping in mind that the wearables are used to reconstruct static postures due to their orientation in space, and not the actual acceleration during the movement, we shortly discuss the resulting angular resolution. To this end, it is assumed that all postures are evaluated at rest and dominated by the earth's gravitational force. Hence the resulting force on all axes equals

$$\sqrt{a_x^2 + a_y^2 + a_z^2} = 1\mathrm{g}. \tag{1}$$

In this situation, an angular resolution of roughly 0.2° is achieved. This has proven to be sufficient for all conducted measurements.

Although being very versatile for motion tracking, one has to keep in mind that with a three-axis accelerometer, rotational movements around the sensor axis pointing to the earth's centre of gravity can not be tracked.

4   Pose Reconstruction

In this section we give an overview of how we reconstruct a curve as representation for the spine shape from the accelerometers' data. First, we estimate the orientation of each sensor. The orientations from all sensors are fed into a simple model that is the basis of the spinal curve we display.

---

[6] g ≈ 9.81 m/s^2 is earth's standard acceleration due to gravity.

4.1   Sensor Orientation Estimation

Assuming the sensor is not moving, which is reasonable for static poses, the sensor only measures acceleration due to gravity pointing downwards. In this case the sensor's *forward tilt* t_{acc} is defined as follows:

$$t_{\mathrm{acc}} = \mathrm{arctan2}\,(a_z, -a_y) \tag{2}$$

Here, a_z denotes the measured acceleration in the sensor's local z-axis, while a_y is the acceleration in the sensor's local y-axis, as defined in Fig. 1.

4.2   Spine Curve Computation

The spine curve is computed based on the sensor orientations. We restrict this curve to 2D to give an easy-to-understand feedback on the user's current posture.

Attaching the sensors to a person's back with the help of an applicator, the distance between each neighbouring pair of sensors is equal. Thus, we assume equal distance in our model, too. The actual spine curve consists of two components: The first component is a line representing the forward tilt of the first (lowest) sensor. The second component consists of a series of arc segments between pairs of neighbouring sensors. The number of arc segments totals four.

The arc segments between two sensors' positions P_n and P_{n+1} is computed as follows: The tilt at the beginning and the end of the arc segments is defined by the sensor's forward tilts $t_{\mathrm{acc},n}$ and $t_{\mathrm{acc},n+1}$. The included angle δ_n is the difference between these two tilts: $\delta_n = t_{\mathrm{acc},n} - t_{\mathrm{acc},n+1}$. The distance d between the points is fixed and constant between all points in our model. From these values, the arc is already completely defined. The radius r of the underlying circle is defined as:

$$r_n = \frac{d}{|\delta_n|} \tag{3}$$

The center C_n of the circle underlying the nth arc can be computed by:

$$C_n = P_n - r_n \cdot \begin{pmatrix} \cos(t_{\mathrm{acc},n}) \\ -\sin(t_{\mathrm{acc},n}) \end{pmatrix} \tag{4}$$

The end point P_{n+1} of the arc is computed by:

$$P_{n+1} = C_n + r_n \cdot \begin{pmatrix} \cos(t_{\mathrm{acc},n+1}) \\ -\sin(t_{\mathrm{acc},n+1}) \end{pmatrix} \tag{5}$$

In case the angle is less than the inherent sensor accuracy $\Delta\delta_n \approx 0.3°$ a line is drawn instead of an arc segment, $\Delta\delta_n = \sqrt{(\Delta t_{\mathrm{acc},n})^2 + (\Delta t_{\mathrm{acc},n+1})^2}$. *PostureSensei*^{TM} comes with an app for data visualisation. Some examples of the reconstructed spine curves can be found in Fig. 2.

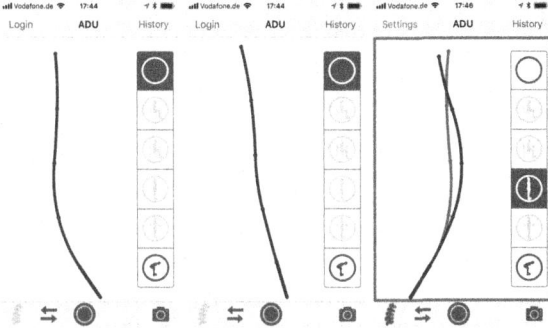

Fig. 2. Screenshots from $PostureSensei^{TM}$ app of some reconstructed spine curvatures, showing various shapes. A comparison of two curves is shown in the right image.

5   Recording Setup and Datasets

We recorded three different scenarios (robot data, template data, human posture data) with the $PostureSensei^{TM}$ sensors (at 50 Hz) and the OptiTrack system (at 100 Hz). In order to spatially track the sensors, reflective markers were attached to the sensors. These were either single spherical reflective markers or groups of four markers attached to a rigid body. The exact type and location of the markers depended on the scenario. In combination, the recorded data consists of the 3D positions of each marker or rigid body and the accelerometer data of each sensor as well as the orientation of the rigid bodies in space (4D quaternion), where applicable. The recorded datasets along with the marker setups are described in more detail in the sections below and are illustrated in Fig. 3.

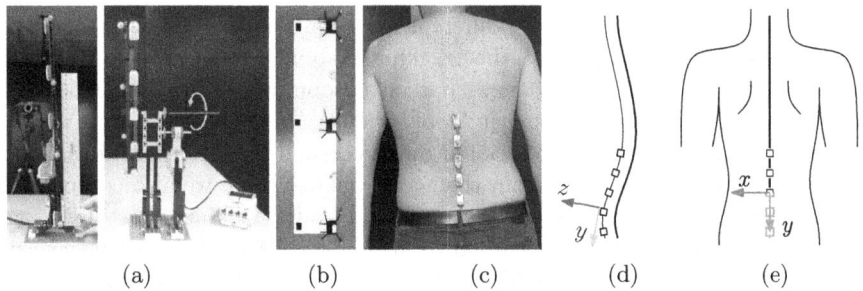

Fig. 3. Photos of the recording setups: (a) Sensors and markers mounted on the robot. (b) Sensors, markers, and rigid body assets on the synthetic template. (c) Sensors on the lumbar spine of a person. (d) and (e) Side and back view of sensor positioning on the lumbar spine (thick line) including directions of the sensor coordinate system.

5.1 Datasets

Robot. To test if the motion sensors correctly capture their orientation, we devised some tests and mounted them vertically onto a rotatable robot arm (see Fig. 3a). We used a Lego Mindstorms robot from the EV3 series. In order to track the robot arm's orienion in space, four markers were attached approximately equidistantly (13.5 cm apart from each other) to the robot arm.

We recorded two different scenarios: R380P10 and R360P10. **R380P10** consists of a 380° clockwise rotation of the motor attached to the robot arm followed by a ten-second pause. These steps are repeated 24 times. In **R360P10** the motor rotates by 360° clockwise and pauses ten seconds three consecutive times. The rotation is executed at an average of $60°\mathrm{s}^{-1}$. The 'average' arises from the motor driving the arm accelerating at the beginning of each rotation and decelerating to a stop at the end of each rotation.

Template. Here, the sensors were placed onto a 2.5 mm strong flexible PVC foam board (template, see Fig. 3b). With the sensors on the template, the template was bent stronger than usually possible for the human back.

In this scenario, rigid bodies with four spherical reflective markers each, so-called rigid body assets, were attached to three of the sensors. A single reflective spherical marker was glued to both of the remaining sensors.

Human Posture. Finally, we recorded trials with the sensors attached to a person's back as shown in Fig. 3c. We only considered static standing poses. In order to spatially track the sensors, a single reflective spherical marker was attached to the centre of every sensor.

5.2 Data Preprocessing

The recorded optical motion capture data was cleaned and temporally aligned with the accelerometer data before further processing. *Data cleaning* here refers to the semi-automatic removal of inconsistent marker data and to the consistent combination of marker data from different markers. The latter is necessary when tracking individual markers. If the tracking system loses a marker, e.g. from occlusion, it will treat it like a new marker as soon as it is no longer occluded (it does not 'know' that it just met an old friend).

In order to compare the positional data recorded with the tracking system and the tilt data t_{acc} derived from the accelerometer data, we also compute tilt angles from the tracking data. In case of rigid body tracking, the tilt t_{opt} can be directly inferred from the recorded rotation data. In the robot arm scenarios we treat the robot arm as a rigid body represented by the markers attached to it (see limitations in Sect. 7). The tilt t_{opt} of the arm is computed with respect to the tracking system's up-vector $\boldsymbol{u}$ as the angle between $\boldsymbol{u}$ and the robot arm. The robot arm is represented by an (oriented) line $\boldsymbol{m}$. With $\langle \boldsymbol{v}, \boldsymbol{w} \rangle$ denoting the dot product,

$$t_{\mathrm{opt}} = \arccos\left(\langle \boldsymbol{u}, \frac{\boldsymbol{m}}{||\boldsymbol{m}||}\rangle\right). \tag{6}$$

Other processing steps before actually comparing data from the different sources are *filtering* and *downsampling* of the OptiTrack data by a factor of two, effectively reducing the sampling rate to match the 50 Hz of the *PostureSensei*^{TM} data. For *filtering* we use a 220 ms- to 340 ms-windowed median filter (spanning 11 to 17 samples at 50 Hz) followed by a moving average filter of the same width. This removes noise from both signals. If not otherwise stated we work with the filtered data sampled at (or downsampled to) 50 Hz.

6 Results

We recorded datasets covering a variety of poses and motions that call for different evaluation strategies depending on the respective data. These strategies will be explained in more detail in Sect. 6.1. Results and their discussion can be found in Sect. 6.2.

6.1 Evaluation Strategy

Dataset Robot, R380P10. For the R380P10 dataset, we will evaluate how well the tilt computed for both systems (t_{acc} for accelerometer data and t_{opt} for tracking data) compares to one another. The data recorded in this setup, especially in the raw accelerometer data and hence the derived tilt data (see first row of Fig. 4), exhibit strong fluctuations every time the robot stops. We therefore, and because the arm oscillates for some seconds after stopping, extract the first five of the last six seconds of each step detected by both systems and compute the mean and standard deviation for each step as well as the overall mean step size (see Table 1). We furthermore compute the difference $t_{\text{opt}} - t_{\text{acc}}$ for each segment and sensor.

Dataset Robot, R360P10. This dataset was recorded in order to measure the consistency of t_{acc} and t_{opt} while moving. To this end, we divide the recorded data into parts with positive, zero, and negative gradient and analyse the non-constant segments.

In order to separate the tilt data into segments of equally signed gradients, we compute the gradient ∇f of the (filtered) tilt data f and apply a moving average with a fixed window width (of 340 ms) to ∇f. Using a threshold $T = 0.5°$, the tilt data is divided into segments of positive ($\nabla f > T$), negative ($\nabla f < -T$), and zero ($|\nabla f| \leq T$) gradient. Due to clockwise rotation, R360P10 only exhibits segments with zero and negative gradient (see second row of Fig. 4).

We compute the Pearson correlation coefficient for each found segment with negative gradient (Fig. 6 left). The Pearson correlation coefficient measures how much two signals are linearly related (e.g. by a constant offset):

$$r_{x,y} = \frac{\sum_{i=1}^{n}(x_i - \mu_x)(y_i - \mu_y)}{\sqrt{\sum_{i=1}^{n}(x_i - \mu_x)^2}\sqrt{\sum_{i=1}^{n}(y_i - \mu_y)^2}} \tag{7}$$

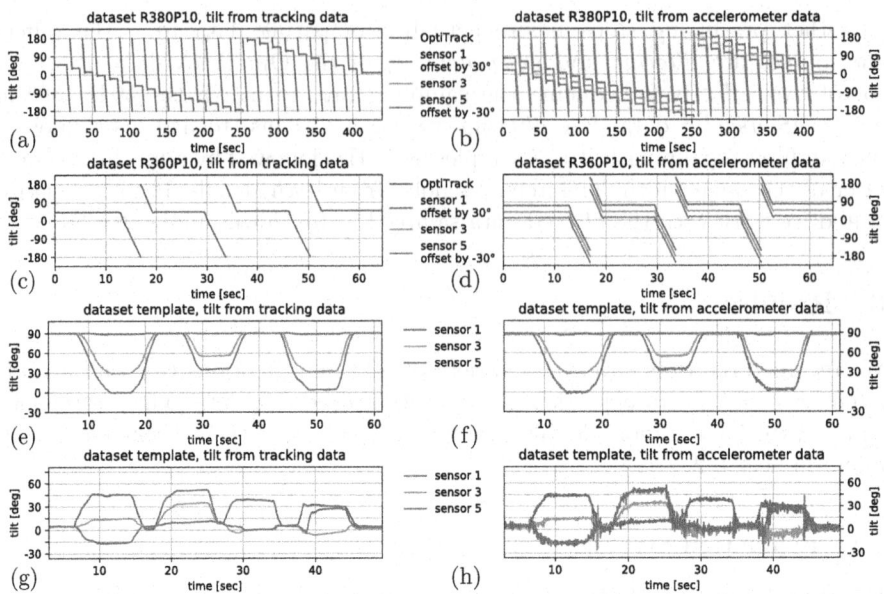

Fig. 4. Computed raw tilt values for four recordings of three scenarios. Data from the OptiTrack system are shown in the left column, data from the *PostureSensei*^{TM} are shown in the right column.

where μ_x and μ_y are the mean of x and y and $r_{x,y} \in [-1, 1]$. $r_{x,y} = \pm 1$ represents a complete positive/negative linear correlation. A value of 0 signifies that x and y are not linearly correlated.

In order to gain insight of the magnitude of a potential offset between t_{opt} and t_{acc} we compute their difference $t_{opt} - t_{acc}$.

Dataset Template. In the evaluation of the template dataset, we proceed in analogy to the evaluation of R360P10, but analyse each recording as a whole (see third row of Fig. 4 for raw tilt values). I.e. we compute the Pearson correlation coefficient and the median, mean, and standard deviation, as well as the absolute value of the tilt difference described above. The data is not split into gradient-segments. Evaluations were carried out on a per-sensor basis.

Dataset Human Posture. For the human posture dataset, we computed a 2D spine curve from the accelerometer data as described in Sect. 4.2 for all frames. All frames are leveraged to 3D. As a consequence, each sensor is represented by a single 3D position. The recorded tracking dataset represents each sensor as a single 3D position by setup design. In order to measure distances in the two datasets we interpret each of them as ordered point clouds in space, P_{opt} and P_{acc}, both ordered by sensor and frame number. Each of the two point clouds can be linearly transformed to best correspond to the other point cloud. We use a Procrustes algorithm [35] to find the best fit of the two datasets. The best-fit criterion is the minimum sum of squared distances of one point cloud P_{opt} to a scaled, translated, and rotated version P'_{acc} of the other point cloud P_{acc}. We use P_{opt} as the reference dataset because P_{acc} contains unit-less data and P_{opt} is measured in metric units of length.

The quality evaluation of the computed 2D curve data compared to the 3D positions from the tracking data is performed on the aligned raw datasets P_{opt} and P'_{acc}. To this end we first draw n random samples and extract a window of ± 100 ms width around identical frames within both datasets (10 frames each at 50 Hz). For a dataset of length l, $n = l/5$ random samples suffice to consider each single frame on average twice. We then compute the point-wise Euclidean distance of each corresponding pair of points in the two datasets within the extracted window as well as their mean and standard deviation. These state how well the best match of the two point clouds was. The distances and derived quantities are measured in millimetres (see Table 4).

6.2   Results and Discussion

Dataset Robot, R380P10. Table 1 summarises the average tilt computed from the acceleration sensors and from the tracking data in between each revolution of the robot arm, which are in very good agreement to each other (constant mean value and low standard deviations). The angles computed from neither the OptiTrack data nor the $PostureSensei^{TM}$ data match the step angle of $-380°$ programmed into the robot. As the overall mean offset between programmed rotation and measured rotation lies around $3.4°$, an average deviation of $1.61°$ per $-180°$ programmed rotation, the robot system can't be used as a third system to compare to (see limitations in Sect. 7).

We computed how much the tilt angles from OptiTrack and $PostureSensei^{TM}$ differ by computing the difference $t_{opt} - t_{acc}$ as shown in Fig. 5. Angle differences mostly lie within $[-1°, +1.6°]$. Only $PostureSensei^{TM}$ sensor 1 deviates slightly more from the OptiTrack data (by up to $-3°$) during seconds 100 to 180. Reasons for this behaviour may include, that the robot arm is not a rigid body (see limitations in Sect. 7). Nevertheless, the overall difference between the two systems $t_{opt} - t_{acc} = 0.4° \pm 0.8°$ is statistically equal to zero.

Table 1. Dataset R380P10. Means (μ) and standard deviations (σ) in degree for each detected step in the recorded robot data. The programmed rotation of the motor is denoted by a_α. For better readability we list only every fifth step.

sensor ID	data	μ a_0	σ	μ a_{-100}	σ	μ a_{-200}	σ	μ a_{-300}	σ	μ a_{-400}	σ
	t_{opt}	0.9	0.00	-82.6	0.01	-155.5	0.01	-240.9	0.00	-329.8	0.02
1	t_{acc}	-0.0	0.08	-82.4	0.07	-153.5	0.07	-242.4	0.07	-329.8	0.03
2	t_{acc}	0.0	0.12	-82.4	0.05	-155.5	0.07	-241.6	0.05	-330.7	0.06
3	t_{acc}	0.1	0.11	-82.9	0.07	-156.7	0.06	-241.1	0.07	-331.6	0.07
4	t_{acc}	0.9	0.03	-82.9	0.03	-157.3	0.06	-240.9	0.04	-330.6	0.06
5	t_{acc}	1.1	0.08	-82.3	0.08	-156.0	0.07	-240.8	0.03	-329.8	0.06

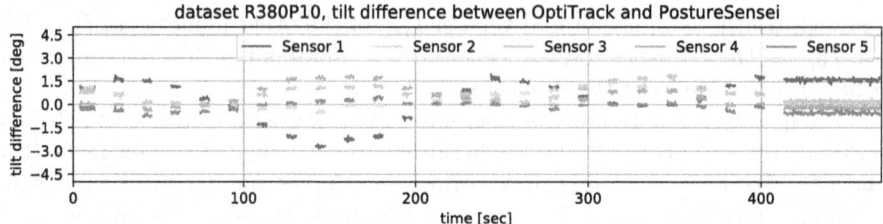

Fig. 5. Difference of t_{opt} and t_{acc} for each sensor of the $PostureSensei^{TM}$ system restricted to segments with zero gradient.

Dataset Robot, R360P10. In the second part of the robot dataset, R360P10, we compared non-constant segments of the data using the Pearson correlation coefficient. Results are depicted in Fig. 6 (left). The data decomposes into three non-constant segments. These are the segments in Fig. 4c when deleting the constant segments. The correlation coefficient is extremely high for all segments and all sensors (minimum of 0.999995).

In addition to median and mean of the absolute difference of the accelerometer-based tilt data and the tracking-based tilt data, the boxplot on the right in Fig. 6 depicts the distribution of the data. This reveals that even if the two tilt data series are highly correlated, their difference can still exhibit absolute fluctuations of up to almost 2.5°. It also shows that the difference is centred around $-1.25°$ with respect to both, median and mean. Furthermore, the difference of over half of the data is below 1.25°. More than 75 % of the differences are below 1.4°. Overall, the high similarity in shape – location of mean and median (all almost centred) as well as size of the boxplots – suggests that the differences are similarly distributed. This in turn implies a high level of consistency between the data recorded with OptiTrack and the $PostureSensei^{TM}$ sensors.

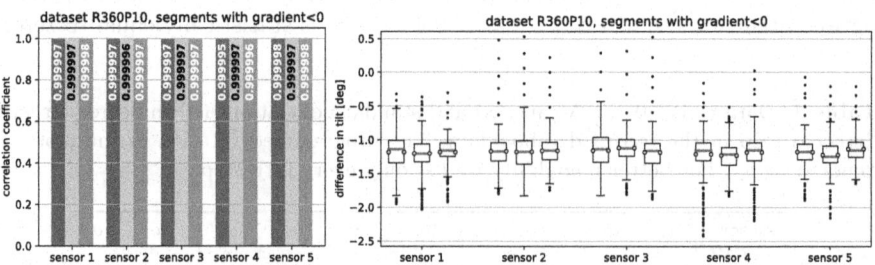

Fig. 6. Left: Pearson correlation coefficient of data segments with negative gradient of R360P10-dataset. Right: Boxplot of the difference of tilt $t_{\text{opt}} - t_{\text{acc}}$ of all such segments. Mean values are indicated by the small circles on the sides of each box, the median is drawn as blue lines. Bars and boxes are grouped by sensor and sorted by time of occurrence in the data. We used a standard boxplot as provided by matplotlib (https://matplotlib.org/api/_as_gen/matplotlib.pyplot.boxplot.html). (Color figure online)

Dataset Template. The template dataset was compared trial-wise as a whole using the Pearson correlation coefficient as well as median, mean, and standard deviation of the absolute difference of the tilt computed from tracking data and from accelerometer data. For this dataset, we evaluated filtered and unfiltered data. Table 2 lists the result of the correlation coefficient. Again, the correlation coefficient is very high for all trials and for most sensors. In the first four takes, the lower part of the template, containing sensor 1, was fixated to a flat surface, and the template was gradually bent by lifting its upper side until it reached an angle of approximately 90°. Therefore sensor 1 moves only minimally (see Fig. 4e and f), which explains the correlation coefficient of ≈ 0.5 as the data is dominated by noise. For the rest of the takes and sensors the correlation coefficient of both data types recorded indicates that there is a very strong (positive) linear relationship between the two tilt data series (filtered data minimum of 0.998, raw data minimum 0.957).

Table 2. Dataset template, all takes. Values of Pearson correlation coefficient grouped by used data type. Left side: filtered data, right side: unfiltered, raw data.

take	sensor 1	3	5	take	sensor 1	3	5	take	sensor 1	3	5	take	sensor 1	3	5
t_1f	0.592	1.000	1.000	t_5f	1.000	0.998	0.999	t_1r	0.475	1.000	1.000	t_5r	0.991	0.957	0.992
t_2f	0.587	1.000	1.000	t_6f	1.000	0.999	0.999	t_2r	0.485	0.999	1.000	t_6r	0.995	0.988	0.993
t_3f	0.587	1.000	1.000	t_7f	0.999	0.998	0.999	t_3r	0.542	1.000	1.000	t_7r	0.991	0.975	0.984
t_4f	0.537	1.000	1.000	t_8f	1.000	0.999	0.999	t_4r	0.364	0.999	1.000	t_8r	0.996	0.979	0.987

The computation of several statistical measures, such as median, mean, and standard deviation of the difference of the two tilt data series aimed at putting that linear relation better into context (see Table 3). From the table we can see that there is only slight variation in the average absolute difference of the two data series. Deviations range from $m = 0.1°$, $\mu = 0.1°$, and $\sigma = 0.1°$ (filtered data, take 6 sensor 1) to $m = 2.0°$, $mu = 1.7°$, and $\sigma = 0.6°$ (filtered data, take 4 sensor 5). These values are equally low for raw data.

Table 3. Dataset template, all takes. Median (m), means (μ), and standard deviations (σ) (all in degree) of absolute difference of tilt from tracking data and tilt from accelerometer data ($|t_{opt} - t_{acc}|$). Left side: filtered data, right side: unfiltered, raw data.

take	sensor 1 m	μ	σ	sensor 3 m	μ	σ	sensor 5 m	μ	σ	take	sensor 1 m	μ	σ	sensor 3 m	μ	σ	sensor 5 m	μ	σ
t_1f	1.3	1.1	0.7	1.3	1.4	0.3	1.6	1.7	0.4	t_1r	1.5	1.3	0.8	1.3	1.3	0.2	1.3	1.5	0.5
t_2f	1.2	1.0	0.6	1.2	1.3	0.3	1.5	1.6	0.5	t_2r	1.3	1.1	0.7	1.3	1.4	0.3	1.6	1.6	0.5
t_3f	1.3	1.2	0.8	1.5	1.4	0.4	1.9	1.7	0.5	t_3r	1.2	1.2	0.8	1.4	1.3	0.5	1.6	1.6	0.6
t_4f	1.2	1.2	0.8	1.4	1.5	0.6	2.0	1.7	0.6	t_4r	1.1	1.1	0.8	1.4	1.3	0.6	2.1	1.7	0.7
t_5f	0.6	0.8	0.8	0.9	1.1	0.7	1.4	1.4	0.8	t_5r	1.1	1.0	0.8	0.7	0.7	0.4	2.3	1.8	0.8
t_6f	0.1	0.1	0.1	0.3	0.4	0.4	0.2	0.7	0.9	t_6r	0.7	0.6	0.4	1.4	1.6	0.9	0.5	0.9	0.8
t_7f	0.5	0.5	0.4	1.0	0.8	0.4	0.9	1.1	0.8	t_7r	0.1	0.1	0.1	0.7	0.8	0.6	1.0	1.1	1.0
t_8f	0.5	0.7	0.7	0.9	1.0	0.6	1.3	1.3	0.8	t_8r	0.3	1.3	1.9	0.9	1.4	1.3	1.5	1.6	1.0

Because the overall mean of the absolute difference between the two data series is a relatively abstract description of the underlying, absolute per-sample difference, we also plotted a pair of data series together with their absolute difference in Fig. 7. For better readability we only included data from a single sensor. The depicted absolute difference exhibits a throughout slightly higher value when the tilt data exceeds 90° (e.g. seconds 1 to 10 and around second 25). This observed reoccurring difference could be attributed to minor tracking inconsistencies in the motion capturing in this range: When a registered rigid body asset is rotated close to 90° in direction of the tracking system's up-vector, the rotation computed by the tracking system tends to jitter around 90°. Peaks also occur shortly before and after constant segments. A likely cause for these is the fact that the data is not perfectly temporally aligned. Hence directional changes in the trajectory lead to higher errors in the two signals' difference.

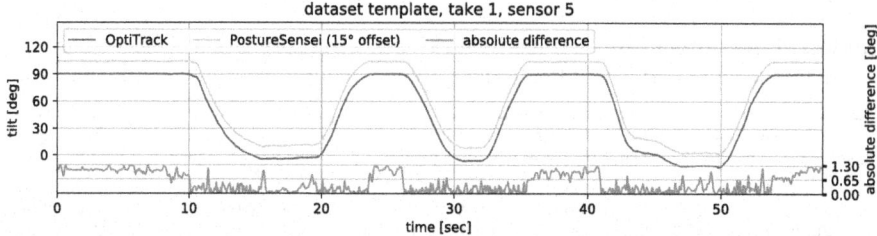

Fig. 7. Tilt from tracking data (t_{opt}, blue), from accelerometer data (t_{acc}, orange, offset by $+15°$) and their absolute difference ($|t_{opt} - t_{acc}|$, green). For better readability we plotted only one sensor. (Color figure online)

Dataset Human Posture. For the last dataset, we evaluate how well the computed 2D spine curve matches the 3D tracking data by measuring mean distances and standard deviations of the two resulting point clouds several times over different equally wide windows. Table 4 shows the resulting values. The spread of values for mean distances from 1 mm up to 8 mm with an average of $\mu = (3.4\,\text{mm} \pm 1.6\,\text{mm})$ are caused by the simplicity of the 2D spine curve model which does not incorporate factors such as skin deformation. We would like to point out that these values are obtained by comparing a set of 2D points embedded into 3D space with the native 3D coordinates of the motion capture system. The relatively small dispersion σ of usually less than 0.6 mm shows the consistency of the accelerometer data and that an even better spine curve representation can be reached by an improved model. Overall, these results show that the spine curve reconstruction is reproducible and usually highly similar to the OptiTrack recordings. This is also illustrated in Fig. 8 where visually the different reconstructions show very similar shapes.

Table 4. Dataset human posture, raw data. Mean and standard deviation (μ, σ) of the Euclidean distance between two aligned spine curves per 2D/3D sensor/marker position. $s_{i,j}$ abbreviates sensor/marker j in segment i. Values are measured in mm.

	$s_{1,1}$	$s_{1,2}$	$s_{1,3}$	$s_{1,4}$	$s_{1,5}$	$s_{2,1}$	$s_{2,2}$	$s_{2,3}$	$s_{2,4}$	$s_{2,5}$	$s_{3,1}$	$s_{3,2}$	$s_{3,3}$	$s_{3,4}$	$s_{3,5}$	$s_{4,1}$	$s_{4,2}$	$s_{4,3}$	$s_{4,4}$	$s_{4,5}$
μ	1.9	1.7	2.4	1.4	2.1	2.8	2.8	2.5	6.8	6.1	2.9	2.7	1.8	1.6	2.3	4.4	3.8	4.3	1.0	3.1
σ	0.3	0.2	0.3	0.3	0.5	0.3	0.1	0.7	0.8	1.1	0.5	0.5	0.6	0.6	0.8	0.3	0.3	0.4	0.4	0.5

	$s_{5,1}$	$s_{5,2}$	$s_{5,3}$	$s_{5,3}$	$s_{5,5}$	$s_{6,1}$	$s_{6,2}$	$s_{6,3}$	$s_{6,4}$	$s_{6,5}$	$s_{7,1}$	$s_{7,2}$	$s_{7,3}$	$s_{7,4}$	$s_{7,5}$	$s_{8,1}$	$s_{8,2}$	$s_{8,3}$	$s_{8,4}$	$s_{8,5}$
μ	3.4	3.4	1.8	1.8	2.6	4.9	3.8	3.8	1.2	3.5	4.7	4.6	2.8	2.8	3.3	7.6	6.9	5.6	2.7	5.4
σ	0.6	0.5	0.6	0.7	0.9	0.5	0.5	0.4	0.4	0.4	0.3	0.3	0.3	0.3	0.5	0.3	0.3	0.4	0.8	0.5

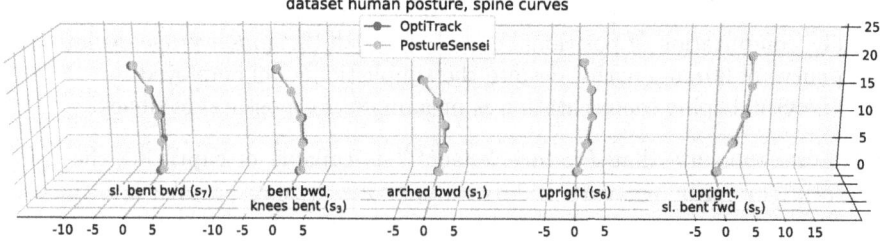

Fig. 8. Aligned computed spine curves of various segments (orange lines) and 3D positions of the sensors from OptiTrack (blue lines). (Color figure online)

7 Limitations

Limitations of the Robot Arm: As discussed in Sect. 6.2 the robot arm rotation deviates substantially from the values programmed to the motor. The arm is connected to the motor by a rubber band to minimise transferred vibrations of the activated motor to the arm. The rubber band might slip when the motor is activated, and amplify swinging after stopping the rotation. Thus, we have to rely on the motion capture data. Additionally, the assumption of a rigid body is not entirely realistic as we observe a slight bending ($<2°$) of the robot arm due to gravity.

Limitations of the Sensor System: The $PostureSensei^{TM}$ system only measures accelerations. Thus, the estimation of the tilt angles only works well if relatively static poses are considered. Otherwise, accelerations in any other direction than gravity will influence the tilt computation and thus have an impact on the displayed spine curves. However, for slow motions, like we measured on the robot and on the template, tilt estimation worked well. More advanced sensors, including magnetic field sensors or gyroscopes could be used to capture reliable posture readings from dynamic motions.

Limitations of the Pose Reconstruction: Although the presented model for pose reconstruction is simple, it yields very good results for the human posture data. An extended model could expand to 3D reconstruction and integrate the flexibility in the human skin to even better approximate the actual shape and further reduce the reconstruction error along the spine curve.

8   Conclusion and Future Work

In this paper, we reported on a series of experiments to evaluate if an accelerometer-based wearable system can be used to accurately record the lumbar spine. As baseline for the experiments we recorded data from both systems simultaneously. Our main findings are:

1. Sensor tilt values can be captured with a very high precision ($0.4° \pm 0.8°$ for a single sensor), compared against motion capture data.
2. The computation of positional data works well (3.4 mm average deviation on a curve of 30 cm length), despite the simplistic model employed.
3. The visual spine representation is meaningful for postural feedback.

Thus, we conclude that $PostureSensei^{TM}$ is capable of capturing the spinal curvature for static poses accurately and provides valuable feedback to the user.

We are planning to do user studies on the effectiveness of wearable devices in posture training in the future. Another interesting strand of research will be to explore how far the accuracy of pose reconstruction can be improved by a more advanced spine reconstruction model as well as adding more sensor modalities, such as magnetic field or gyroscopes to the wearable sensor units.

Acknowledgement. We thank Philipp Löschner and David Scherfgen for supporting us with the motion capture recordings.

References

1. Robertson, J.T.: The rape of the spine. Surg. Neurol. **39**(1), 5–12 (1993)
2. Vällfors, B.: Acute, subacute and chronic low back pain: clinical symptoms, absenteeism and working environment. Scand. J. Rehabil. Med. Suppl. **11**, 198 (1985)
3. Rubin, D.I.: Epidemiology and risk factors for spine pain. Neurol. Clin. **25**(2), 353–371 (2007). Neck and Back Pain
4. Gaskin, D.J., Richard, P.: The economic costs of pain in the united states. J. Pain **13**(8), 715–724 (2012)
5. Peleg, M., Leung, T.I., Desai, M., Dumontier, M.: Is crowdsourcing patient-reported outcomes the future of evidence-based medicine? A case study of back pain. In: ten Teije, A., Popow, C., Holmes, J.H., Sacchi, L. (eds.) AIME 2017. LNCS, vol. 10259, pp. 245–255. Springer, Cham (2017). https://doi.org/10.1007/978-3-319-59758-4_27
6. Colombo, S., Joy, M., Mason, L., Peper, E., Harvey, R., Booiman, A.: Posture change feedback training and its effect on health. In: 48th Annual Meeting of the Association for Applied Psychophysiology and Biofeedback, March 2017
7. Hellstrom, P.A.R., Åkerberg, A., Folke, M.: Posture sensor as feedback when lifting weights. In: 4th International Conference on Ambulatory Monitoring of Physical Activity and Movement, June 2015

8. Fathi, A., Curran, K.: Detection of spine curvature using wireless sensors. J. King Saud Univ. Sci. **29**(4), 553–560 (2017)
9. Noiumkar, S., Tirakoat, S.: Use of optical motion capture in sports science: a case study of golf swing. In: 2013 International Conference on Informatics and Creative Multimedia (ICICM), pp. 310–313. IEEE (2013)
10. MacIver, M., Sharabash, N., Nelson, M.: Prey-capture behavior in gymnotid electric fish: motion analysis and effects of water conductivity. J. Exp. Biol. **204**(3), 543–557 (2001)
11. Culhane, K.M., OConnor, M., Lyons, D., Lyons, G.M.: Accelerometers in rehabilitation medicine for older adults. Age Age. **34**(6), 556–560 (2005)
12. Merriaux, P., Dupuis, Y., Boutteau, R., Vasseur, P., Savatier, X.: A study of vicon system positioning performance. Sensors **17**(7), 1591 (2017)
13. Bernard, J., Dobermann, E., Vögele, A., Krüger, B., Kohlhammer, J., Fellner, D.: Visual-interactive semi-supervised labeling of human motion capture data. In: Visualization and Data Analysis (VDA 2017), January 2017
14. Chen, X., Koskela, M.: Skeleton-based action recognition with extreme learning machines. Neurocomputing **149**, 387–396 (2015)
15. Wilhelm, N., Vögele, A., Zsoldos, R., Licka, T., Krüger, B., Bernard, J.: Furyexplorer: visual-interactive exploration of horse motion capture data. In: Visualization and Data Analysis (VDA 2015), February 2015
16. Zsoldos, R., Krüger, B., Licka, T.: From maturity to old age: tasks of daily life require a different muscle use in horses. Comp. Exerc. Physiol. **10**(2), 75–88 (2014)
17. Müller, M., Röder, T., Clausen, M., Eberhardt, B., Krüger, B., Weber, A.: Documentation Mocap database HDM05. Technical report CG-2007-2, Universität Bonn, June 2007
18. CMU: Carnegie Mellon University Graphics Lab: Motion Capture Database (2013)
19. Riaz, Q., Krüger, B., Weber, A.: A relational database for human motion data. In: Gervasi, O., et al. (eds.) ICCSA 2015. LNCS, vol. 9159, pp. 234–249. Springer, Cham (2015). https://doi.org/10.1007/978-3-319-21413-9_17
20. Kapadia, M., Chiang, I.k., Thomas, T., Badler, N.I., Kider Jr., J.T., et al.: Efficient motion retrieval in large motion databases. In: Proceedings of the ACM SIGGRAPH Symposium on Interactive 3D Graphics and Games, pp. 19–28. ACM (2013)
21. Wang, P., Lau, R.W., Zhang, M., Wang, J., Song, H., Pan, Z.: A real-time database architecture for motion capture data. In: Proceedings of the 19th ACM International Conference on Multimedia, pp. 1337–1340. ACM (2011)
22. Awad, C., Courty, N., Gibet, S.: A database architecture for real-time motion retrieval. In: Seventh International Workshop on Content-Based Multimedia Indexing, CBMI 2009, pp. 225–230. IEEE (2009)
23. Pavlakos, G., Zhou, X., Derpanis, K.G., Daniilidis, K.: Coarse-to-fine volumetric prediction for single-image 3d human pose. In: 2017 IEEE Conference on Computer Vision and Pattern Recognition (CVPR), pp. 1263–1272. IEEE (2017)
24. Bogo, F., Kanazawa, A., Lassner, C., Gehler, P., Romero, J., Black, M.J.: Keep it SMPL: Automatic Estimation of 3D Human Pose and Shape from a Single Image. European Conference on Computer Vision, pp. 561–578, Springer, Cham (2016)
25. Rhodin, H., Richardt, C., Casas, D., Insafutdinov, E., Shafiei, M., Seidel, H.P., Schiele, B., Theobalt, C.: EgoCap: egocentric Marker-less motion capture with two Fisheye cameras. ACM Trans. Graph. (TOG) **35**(6), 162 (2016)
26. Shiratori, T., Park, H.S., Sigal, L., Sheikh, Y., Hodgins, J.K.: Motion capture from body-mounted cameras. ACM Trans. Graph. **30**(4), 31:1–31:10 (2011)

27. Vögele, A., Zsoldos, R., Krüger, B., Licka, T.: Novel methods for surface EMG analysis and exploration based on multi-modal gaussian mixture models. PLOS ONE **11**(6), e0157239 (2016)
28. Weiss, A., Herman, T., Plotnik, M., Brozgol, M., Maidan, I., Giladi, N., Gurevich, T., Hausdorff, J.M.: Can an accelerometer enhance the utility of the timed up & go test when evaluating patients with parkinson's disease? Med. Eng. Phys. **32**(2), 119–125 (2010)
29. Bourke, A., OBrien, J., Lyons, G.: Evaluation of a threshold-based tri-axial accelerometer fall detection algorithm. Gait Posture **26**(2), 194–199 (2007)
30. Riaz, Q., Guanhong, T., Krüger, B., Weber, A.: Motion reconstruction using very few accelerometers and ground contacts. Graph. Models **79**, 23–38 (2015)
31. Slyper, R., Hodgins, J.K.: Action capture with accelerometers. In: Proceedings of the 2008 ACM SIGGRAPH/Eurographics Symposium on Computer Animation, SCA 2008, pp. 193–199. Eurographics Association (2008)
32. Vlasic, D., Adelsberger, R., Vannucci, G., Barnwell, J., Gross, M., Matusik, W., Popović, J.: Practical motion capture in everyday surroundings. ACM Trans. Graph. **26**(3), 35 (2007)
33. Farella, E., Benini, L., Riccò, B., Acquaviva, A.: MOCA: a low-power, low-cost motion capture system based on integrated accelerometers. In: Advances in MultiMedia 2007, no. 1, p. 1 (2007)
34. Riaz, Q., Vögele, A., Krüger, B., Weber, A.: One small step for a man: estimation of gender, age, and height from recordings of one step by a single inertial sensor. Sensors **15**(12), 31999–32019 (2015)
35. Gower, J.C., Dijksterhuis, G.B.: Procrustes Problems. Volume 30 of Oxford Statistical Science Series. Oxford University Press, Oxford (2004)

An Approach to Developing Learning Objects with Augmented Reality Content

Marcelo de Paiva Guimarães[1,2](✉) (iD), Bruno Carvalho Alves[2] (iD),
Rafael Serapilha Durelli[3] (iD), Rita de F. R. Guimarães[2] (iD),
and Diego Colombo Dias[4] (iD)

[1] Federal University of São Paulo/Brazilian Open Universtiy (UAB),
São Paulo, SP, Brazil
marcelodepaiva@gmail.com
[2] Centro Universitário Campo Limpo Paulista,
Campo Limpo Paulista, SP, Brazil
bruno_finus@hotmail.com, rita.guimaraes@gmail.com
[3] Federal Universtiy of Lavras, Lavras, MG, Brazil
rafa.durelli@gmail.com
[4] Federal University of São João Del Rei, São João del Rei, MG, Brazil
diegocolombo.dias@gmail.com

Abstract. Augmented reality (AR) has become widely available to the general public. Diverse real-life AR applications, ranging from entertainment to learning, have been created. In this context, this paper describes a systematic approach to creating learning objects with an AR content. This approach yields seven steps to guide the developer: (i) requirements; (ii) design; (iii) implementation; (iv) evaluation; (v) packaging; (vi) distribution; and (vii) learning evaluation. To evaluate the proposed approach, a case study was carried out. We carried out the development and evaluation of learning objects with AR content in an elementary school. We also conducted a usability test with specialists and an experiment with 40 students, on the usage of a learning object with an AR content. The delivered lecture was compared with the use of learning objects with multimedia content (the traditional type). Post and pre-test evaluations were conducted to record the students' learning; these indicated that the proposed learning objects are more effective than the traditional type and can play a significant role in improving students' grades. As a result, we claim that the proposed approach efficiently guides the development of learning objects with AR content. Using the approach presented here, it was possible to conclude the following: (i) it can guide the developer to create learning objects with AR content; (ii) it can integrate learning objects into learning object repositories.

Keywords: Augmented Reality · Learning objects · Software development

1 Introduction

It is now becoming increasingly common for teachers take advantage of digital technologies in educational practices; this can be favorable to the learning process, bringing new possibilities and new challenges. Learning Objects (LO) [1] are an example of a

© Springer International Publishing AG, part of Springer Nature 2018
O. Gervasi et al. (Eds.): ICCSA 2018, LNCS 10963, pp. 757–774, 2018.
https://doi.org/10.1007/978-3-319-95171-3_59

digital technology tool that can be used in this new educational context. According to the Institute of Electrical and Electronic Engineers' Learning Technology Standards Committee[1], LO are "any entity, digital or non-digital that can be used, re-used or referenced during technology-supported learning". These objects can provide learning support for teachers through sets of didactic educational materials [2–5], of which main features are discoverability, reusability and interoperability.

Traditionally, digital LO use multimedia (loMU) content such as text, audio, images, animations and video. However, the recent advances in immersive and interactive technologies have driven several promising [7] resources which are capable of providing new ways to create LO; these have already become easily available to the general public, such as augmented reality (AR). AR enables users to interact with 3D objects embedded into the real world, while users keep their perception of the real world during an activity [6]. AR applications can be deployed on commodities platforms that users already have purchased for general purposes: desktops, tablets, smartphones, laptops with built-in cameras or specific devices. Moreover, it is also available devices such as Microsoft's HoloLens and Magic Leap's display.

The aim of this study is to improve traditional LO with the usage of AR (loAR), which can extend learners' interaction with and perception of their content, creating new possibilities such as different visual views. Rather than just adding extra data to the real world, AR can modify the way that learning takes place. However, the creation of models to facilitate their development is necessary in order to make their use feasible. We propose an approach to assisting the development of loAR which is an extension of its incremental development [19]. It covers the key stages of specification, modeling, implementation, evaluation, packing, distribution and learning efficiency, and was tested using a case study in an elementary school. Beyond its interesting content, the success of a loAR depends on factors such as usability and user acceptance. In the case study, we then carried a usability test with a group of three specialists [8] that allowed us to improve the object before use by the children. A controlled experimental lecture with 20 students was conducted with a loMU and other with 20 with a loRA. Post- and pre-testing were also conducted to record the students' learning.

The major contributions made by this paper are: an approach to developing loRA; a case study illustrating our approach; and a loRA for teaching animal classification. The remainder of this paper is organized as follows. Section 2 presents our approach, created to develop loAR with quality and practicality. Section 3 describes the experiment to evaluate the approach, which involved a case study carried out on the teaching of animal classification. Finally, Sect. 4 presents our conclusions.

---

[1] http://grouper.ieee.org/groups/ltsc/wg12/.

2   An Approach to Developing and Evaluating Learning Objects Based on Augmented Reality

Computational technologies are increasingly present in various educational contexts. These have modified current teaching methods and created new alternatives [9–12]. However, the efficient and effective use of these depends, among many factors, on a simple process of software development. AR has created diverse opportunities to improve the teaching-learning process [13–17], but it has several specific features that make their development and adoption difficult, such as environment illumination and object tracking. These features are not considered during conventional software development [18].

This approach extends the process of incremental development [19], which proposes that a detailed study of analysis and design is carried out before coding, so that when the code is produced, it matches the requirements. Moreover, incremental development promotes the creation of a new version for each solution evaluated by the user. This concept was maintained because LO are always subject to modifications according to the evaluation/needs of the teacher. Thus, it is expected that the loAR are capable of promoting the construction of other LO by changing their content or even their structure.

2.1   Requirements

The requirements specification is defined as the process by which the user's needs are identified, outlining a way to find a correct definition of the system to be elaborated [20], that is, defining what will be done rather than how it will be done. This phase requires the identification of stakeholders, the solution of ambiguities, the clear definition of requirements, and the promotion of communication among those involved. We propose to create a document with the following content: (1) the user's definition, which involves the acquisition and analysis of a user profile, such as education, age, gender and previous technological knowledge; (2) functional requirements, which define the actions that the loAR will be able to execute; and (3) non-functional requirements which consist of aspects that do not directly involve the user or software. For example, the physical position of the user related to capturing a marker image, and the characteristics of the physical environment (i.e. illumination, physical area and background).

Specific techniques can be used for the elicitation of requirements, such as interviews with users, questionnaires, and visits to the physical environment [21]. In our context, the participation of users, such as the teacher and the person in charge of the computational laboratory, is essential so that their needs can be correctly met. Only in this way is it possible to determine how the loAR will be applied. The use or otherwise of markers and user mobility are examples of specific AR demands that should be highlighted in this phase.

2.2 Design

The design phase describes how the application will be built [22]. It therefore establishes which hardware will be used for input and output, the types of markers, the development tools adopted, virtual objects (3D, images, textures and others) and supported platforms such as mobile, web and desktop. Although there are several points in common between most applications and AR applications, there are some striking differences; for example, AR applications generally do not use a database. The following design considerations:

- Physical environment design: most AR applications use a camera. Consequently, the illumination of the physical environment directly interferes with the tracking of objects in the scene. Thus, aspects such as this and others (i.e. ergonomic and locomotion) should be considered;
- Hardware design: an interactive AR application requires about 30 frames/second. In addition, the computer performance must be compatible. It is also essential to specify the camera adopted. Other aspects should also be evaluated to specify the equipment to be used, such as the user's mobility;
- Interaction considerations: this defines the interaction between users and virtual objects, and interaction with the environment. This project is a specific requirement of AR applications. For example, it is necessary to define whether the application is a marker or markerless solution. Our case study uses a marker solution; it was designed for children, and we therefore had to define an appropriate marker size to fit in a child's hand. The application can support diverse kinds of interaction, such as marker, mouse or a 3D mouse. This project also includes user feedback, which defines output resources such as sound;
- Visualization: most AR applications overlay 3D objects on the real world. This design aspect must consider the visual output resources that will be used, such as a mobile phone, where the user can be moving, or a desktop computer, where the user is stationary while the application is running;
- 3D virtual models: it is necessary to define the 3D objects necessary to build the AR application. This also includes textures and animations. This aspect must be based on the application goals of the teacher education plan, following the educational strategies associated with the potential and limitations of the tools; and
- The design of use: this defines how the AR application, in the format of a LO or otherwise, will be used by the teacher. For example, the project may aim only to present 3D objects with different perspectives, or to illustrate a process. If the application is used in the format of a LO, then the environment responsible for importing and displaying it (i.e. Moodle, Blackboard, Edmodo, Skillsoft, Desire2Learn and Schoology) must also be defined. The didactic strategy and the complementary didactic material must also be designed.

To promote LO reuse, a decoupling structure from the applications is desirable; this gives ease of adding new features and/or content. The results of this phase will be used by developers and other people, such as the teacher, modelers, designers and the laboratory manager, to perform their respective activities.

2.3   Implementation

There are several tools for the construction of AR applications (i.e. Vuforia[2] and Flaras[3]). Each has its own strengths, which allow the development of a variety of solutions, with or without markers, for various software platforms (IOS, Android and Windows Mobile) and with the support of several types of 3D models. An important point that distinguishes them is their ease of use. Some of these tools (such as Flaras) are targeted at end-users, which allows the teachers themselves to develop applications. However, tools such as these offer very limited features, for example only providing markers. On the other hand, low-level tools (i.e. ARToolkit[4]) require programming and a longer development time, but also provide flexibility; for example, it is possible to change the object detection algorithm.

loAR has as its content 3D models, sounds, and textures. There are several repositories, paid and otherwise, that provide ready-made objects. If the object is not ready-made, it is necessary to construct it using modeling tools such as Blender, 3D Studio and Maya; in the case of textures, tools such as Photoshop and Gimp can be used. This phase also requires other design considerations, among them, if applicable, the adequacy of the laboratory (computational resources and environment). Also, a user manual may be necessary, which may include pedagogical strategies for using the loAR.

2.4   Evaluation

The evaluation of an AR application aims to verify whether it satisfies the specified requirements. Since AR applications also rely on specific equipment such as cameras and markers, this phase is also required to validate these resources. As AR technology is new and supports unconventional types of interaction and visualization, quality analysis becomes important, especially concerning usability (that is, aspects of the user interface that may result in ease of use and a good fit for end users). Usability evaluation allows experts to make a judgment about the quality of use of a software application, and identify any problems [23–25]. A usability inspection is a low-cost evaluation method that is applied by experts, and can be applied when the application is ready.

Nielsen [26] has presented general usability metrics to determine items such as the visibility of the system status and error prevention in the use of the application. These heuristics are general and do not consider new concepts such as the use of markers and the addition of 3D objects. Kostaras and Xenos [27] have outlined guidelines for AR applications; they identified the strengths and weaknesses of making assessments through interviews, questionnaires, inspections, or usability testing. Zainuddin, Zaman, and Ahmad [28] have presented an evaluation of AR applications for deaf people. Martins, Kirner, and Kirner [29] have proposed a questionnaire to evaluate the usability of AR applications in the educational context. This phase should not be underestimated,

---

[2] https://www.vuforia.com/.

[3] http://ckirner.com/flaras2/.

[4] https://artoolkit.org/.

since the results help in the improvement of the application and, consequently, in the achievement of the objectives. Following the proposed approach, the process can return to the requirements phase if necessary. It is therefore expected that users will be satisfied with the AR application at the end of this phase.

2.5   Packaging

The packaging process encompasses an aspect of use which is based on the reuse of the LO. The phase is therefore optional, since reuse is not a requirement. However, the packaging and distribution of a loRA allows others to contribute to its evolution, increasing its lifespan.

Since loAR are digital resources that contribute to the teaching/learning process, they are composed of the AR application itself and several complementary files, such as presentation slides and exercises. The design phase therefore also takes into consideration the educational strategy which results in the creation of these materials. Initially, the packager receives as input the files (AR application and complementary materials); the metadata file is then generated and included, and finally, the LO is generated in a compact format according to the LO adopted (i.e. SCORM, Ariadne, IMS, IEE_LTSC or other).

2.6   Distribution

The possibility of reuse by end-users (students, teachers and tutors) motivates the distribution of the LO. However, for this to happen, in addition to allowing adaptation according to the aims of the developer, an adequate storage method is required that makes it easy to find, thus making it accessible [30–32]. BIOE, CESTA, LabVirt and RIVED are examples of LO repositories on the internet. They store the LO and offer search tools based on the metadata of the objects; these contain information about them, for example the relevant discipline. Repositories are the most appropriate databases for organizing, classifying and storing LO.

Storage of LO outside of repositories creates difficulties in locating them, since the search engines are not able to find them. This problem may trigger duplication of work, whereby someone unaware of the existence of an LO that meets their needs reconstructs the object. In addition to being stored in repositories, LO can reside in other places such as in a virtual learning environment, a web page, or even a shared folder on a local server.

2.7   Learning Evaluation

To determine whether a loAR creates gains, it is necessary to evaluate whether it has brought benefits to the teaching/learning process. There is thus a need to collect, analyze and quantify or qualify the results according to a predetermined quality format. There are three ways to assess a teaching/learning context: (1) summative assessment, which aims to measure student growth after instruction, and which occurs at the end of the teaching and learning process; (2) formative, which occurs during instruction in a didactic unit or a school term; and (3) diagnosis, which evaluates the conceptual and procedural knowledge that the learner dominate in a given discipline. This work proposes the use of diagnostic evaluation, since it allows the possibility of comparative pre- and post-testing to establish the evolution of the learner.

The diagnostic evaluation consists of a survey, projection, and retrospection of a learner's development situation, using elements to verify what and how he or she has learned. Thus, this evaluation makes it possible to verify to what extent previous knowledge existed and what are the difficulties. This is required to be done at the beginning of each cycle of use of the target loAR; thus, it is possible to know how much significant learning occurred during the process.

The diagnostic evaluation procedure applied to loAR should be performed as follows: pre- and post-tests should be used to measure the knowledge acquired by participants through the use of the object. The pre-test is a set of questions asked of the participants before using the loRA to determine their knowledge level about the content that will be taught. After using a loRA, learners should take a post-test with the same questions asked previously, or questions with the same level of difficulty. By comparing the pre-test scores with the post-test scores, it is possible to find out whether or not the use of the LO was successful. This phase is the final one in the construction cycle of loAR.

3   Using a Learning Object to Teach Animal Classification

To validate our approach, we carried out a case study in an elementary school classroom at Itajubá (Minas Gerais, Brazil). The class had 40 students, aged 9–10 years old. The test was performed with LO for all students; half of them with loAR, and the other half with loMU. Although the proposed approach is tailored to create a loAR, it is also can be used to develop a loMU. The difference is that the loAR uses 3D models, while the loMU uses 2D images and videos.

The requirement-gathering process used was an interview. We asked open questions to the teacher and to the school's lab coordinator. The questions concerned the difficulties faced by the students, interesting subjects, computational resources used, and which subjects would benefit from the insertion of 3D visualization.

3.1   Case Study: Requirements

During the interview, the teacher stated that students faced difficulties in understanding the classes of animals (in the field of biology). These difficulties were related to the visualization of the characteristics of each class, and especially when it was necessary to count the animals' legs. The teacher presented the textbook used to illustrate this subject [34]. Thus, we proposed the development of a loAR to assist learners in understanding the classes of animals.

The main points of the user's definition were: (1) the LO must be able to be used by users aged 9–10 years old, regardless of gender; and (2) the solution must be able to be used by users with lower levels of expertise or technical skills. The main functional requirements were: (1) the loAR should be able to recognize the marker and present the associated content (sound, 3D image). The loMU should present only 2D images, text and videos to the children; (2) the animals should be classified and presented in classes; and (3) the loAR should allow the children to rotate the visualized animals freely. The main non-functional requirements were: (1) the environment must be illuminated; (2) the application design must use a colorful and flashy interface; (3) the markers must fit the children's hands; (4) a web-based application would be desirable; and (5) the interaction will be based on fiducial markers and mouse.

These points played an important role during the development of the LO (loAR and loMU), as they were the basic criteria for decision making on the design alternatives and implementation.

3.2   Case Study: Design

In the design stage, a computational description was produced, describing in detail what the application would do:

- Physical environment design: recent technological advances allow AR applications to be run in commodities labs. The school lab had 20 computers, distributed with an adequate space between them, and was well illuminated;
- Hardware design: each computer in the local lab was equipped with Windows 7, internet access, headphones, webcam, and web browser;
- Interaction: a standard marker and mouse were used to provide user interactions to generate changes to the loAR state. We adjusted the marker size to fit the children's hands. When a child pointed the marker at the camera, and after the marker was recognized, the 3D animal was shown by the application. The children used the mouse to interact with the loMU;
- Visualization: this project considered aspects such as the children's attention and motivation; colorful and childlike images were used, which were pleasing and attractive to them. It was decided that the images in the background of the screen would have a theme of approachable and child-friendly images, including the classes of the animals, simple and colorful menus, and text with large lettering which was rounded and colored. Figure 1 presents an example of the web page design;

Fig. 1. Visualization

- 3D virtual models: taking the defined pedagogical strategy into consideration, we selected 3D animals, images, and sound from open repositories; and
- Design of use: the animal classification content was designed to run on learning management systems (LMS) as a LO.

3.3   Case Study: Implementation

Two websites were implemented using HTML, one to receive the loAR and another the loMU, and the pre- and post-test forms. The AR content was implemented using Flaras. Figure 2 depicts the website with the loAR.

Fig. 2. Learning object with AR content (loAR)-a 3D dog over a fiducial marker.

Figure 3 depicts the website with the loMU.

Fig. 3. Learning object with multimedia content (loMU).

This phase also required the assembly and preparation of the computer lab. Twenty computers were prepared. We carried out a performance test to check the children's interaction with the application.

3.4   Case Study: Evaluation

A questionnaire was prepared for our LO (loAR and loMU) usability inspection, which was carried out by three experts. Nielsen [24, 26] proposed a heuristics approach, which was adapted here. The following aspects were evaluated: (1) effectiveness: the user's ability to interact with the system to achieve its goal; (2) efficiency: the resources (time, labor and materials involved) required for the user to interact with the system and achieve its goal; (3) satisfaction: how far the user is satisfied with the system. This expresses how the system affects the user's emotions and feelings.

The severity degrees used were: strongly disagree (1); disagree (2); neither agree nor disagree (3); agree (4); strongly agree (5). The following tables have the ratings of the three experts, as well as their remarks when relevant. Table 1 represents the analysis regarding the effectiveness aspect. Although the LOs were working, the experts pointed some problems (i.e., buttons not working and designed properly, and animal sounds very low). These problems were fixed before the tests with the children.

Table 1. Verifying the effectiveness.

Checklist	Severity degree	Experts' comments
I know what is going on during the interaction	3;5;3	There are buttons that will not be used by the children in the menu below; -; The user does not know that they have to click on the animal to hear the explanation
If I put more than one marker on the interface, then I can specify one	2;4;2	I do not think so - we only select one marker at a time; -; The application works with one marker
It is possible to perform "redo" and "undo" easily	5;1;5	Yes. There is a button for this; The reset buttons did not work; No need to return
The purpose of the application is achieved	4;3;4	No. I could not even hear the explanation of each animal; The audio did not work; A child will feel lost while using it alone. If it is explained orally, it works. Despite the low audio, it fulfills the aim

Table 2 shows the evaluations regarding the LO efficiency. In general, the LO reached the aim. Almost all of the experts' comments were taken into account and fixed in the version used by the children. However, we did not alter some features; for example, although the scale of all the animals was altered, we did not add animation to reproduce behavior consistent with the real world.

Table 3 measures the experts' satisfaction. This can be considered as good for these tests. They provided important suggestions for improving the LO before the final test (i.e. the help was incomplete).

The results clearly showed that the LO were not ready. It was therefore necessary to fix these problems before the next phase. For example, the sizes of 3D objects were changed and the sound volume adjusted.

Table 2. Verifying the efficiency.

Checklist	Severity degree	Experts' comments
Load time of virtual objects is satisfactory	3;4;1	The child will be annoyed at having to activate the camera for each animal; The application took more than five seconds to load the amphibians; Sometimes it takes time to load
The virtual objects are well positioned in the scene (position, texture, scale)	4;4;5	The 3D objects should be apparent on the same scale; -; -
Animation behavior is consistent with the real world	5;2;3	-; Animals in the real world do not spin around; There is no animation regarding behavior
Actions/feedback are standardized	5;3;3	-; Audio is associated with each animal; The application does not warn about clicking on the animal
The application prevents errors (for example, the application warns when the user has shown a wrong marker)	3;2;4	The application does not work with another marker; Sometimes the 3D object got stuck, and the page had to be reloaded, and the user is not alerted; -
It's easy to remember how the application works	5;5;4	Yes, because there are few steps; -; The menu features are difficult to memorize
The learning curve is low	4;3;2	The actions are explained in the help, but it should show messages in each page to improve the learning curve; It is easy to learn, but requires training; Easy to learn after an explanation
An experienced user can use the application optimally (for example, by not watching the introductory videos)	4;5;3	There is no necessary optimization for experienced users; -; There is no optimization for experienced users
It's easy to position the marker for the camera to detect	5;4;3	-; Illumination interferes in marker detection; There are some tracking problems
The user is instructed on what to do during the interaction	3;1;4	The user does not know which subpage he/she is on; No; There is no link to download the marker anywhere
The application requires the fulfillment of specific requirements (camera, position, lighting and others)	5;1;4	The requirements are simple to fulfill; The application requires non-conventional resources; Some specific requirements are necessary to the application work
The tracking system is stable	5;3;4	Yes; The mammal did not work; Depends on the illumination
If the application detects more than one marker in the scene, it continues to function normally	5;4;5	Yes; There is a small delay; Yes

Table 3. Verifying satisfaction.

Checklist	Severity degree	Experts' comments
The number of virtual objects in the scene is appropriate	5;3;5	Yes. Only one animal is shown at a time, not overloading the child; More than one animal could be presented for each animal class; -
The number of interaction options is satisfactory (marker, keyboard, mouse, joystick)	5;3;3	-; There are a lot of buttons on the menu; The object has a predefined rotation movement that cannot be changed
The help offered is satisfactory (video, text, audio)	1;3;3	No. The help is a bit confusing and lacking in information. For example, there are two markers to be printed, but only one is spoken. Which one should be used?; The help is incomplete; The help does not clarify its use, nor the features of the buttons
I am satisfied with the interaction solution	5;3;5	-; The marker should be an appropriate size to fit in the children's hands, or it should stay on the table
I am satisfied with the freedom of movement during interaction	5;2;2	-; Having to hold the marker all the time is uncomfortable; You cannot scale an object to see it more closely

3.5 Case Study: Packaging

The LOs developed were packed into SCORM format using the tool created by Guimarães et al. [33]. This tool receives the application files as input and adds files according to the SCORM format. The packing process does not alter the application content; however, it adds files such as the metadata file imsmanifest.xml, which describes LO items (i.e. it contains links to every piece of content within the LO and a logical grouping of its component parts). As output, it generates a single ZIP file. The content of the whole application is self-contained within the ZIP file.

To validate the LO objects files, we used the Cloud Repository[5] which is an online learning tool focused on storing and distributing e-learning content. If a LO stored in this repository is altered, all LMSs are automatically updated. This repository also tracks how much of the LO content is being used, regardless of which LMS it is stored in.

3.6 Case Study: Distribution

This case study was carried out internally on the school network in which the project was applied; it was not imported and distributed via a repository. However, the LOs were ready to be inserted into the main existing LO repositories.

---

[5] http://scorm.com/scorm-solved/scorm-cloud-features/.

3.7   Case Study: Learning Evaluation

To evaluate the benefits of using loAR to teach and learn animal classes, we carried out a randomized experiment. More formally, we set out to answer the following research question (**RQ**): Are learning objects with AR content (loAR) a more effective approach to teach animal classes than learning objects with multimedia content (loMU)? The RQ outlines the issue addressed by this study and was used as the basis to formulate our hypotheses.

- **Hypothesis formulation:** we formalized our RQ into hypotheses so that statistical tests could be carried out.
- **Null hypothesis, H_0:** there is no significant difference in efficiency between the two LO (measured in terms of the children's scores), which can be formalized as follows:
- $H_0 = \mu_{loAR} = \mu_{loMU}$
- **Alternative hypothesis, H_1:** there is a significant difference in efficiency between the two LO, which can be formalized as follows:
- $H_1 = \mu_{loAR} \neq \mu_{loMU}$

Our experiment was broken down into four steps. These steps are listed in chronological order in Table 4.

Table 4. Learning evaluation stages.

Step	Description	Time
Pre-test	All students answered seven questions about animal classes	15 min.
Division of class	The class was divided into two groups of twenty students randomly	Free
Learning phase	Group A: this group went to the laboratory and was taught with the loMU	Group A: 30 min.
	Group B: this group went to the laboratory and was taught with the loAR	Group B: 30 min.
Post–test	All students answered seven questions about animal classes	15 min.

The pre-test stage consisted of an activity similar to a questionnaire in the book [34] used by the teacher. The activity consisted of one question with five alternatives for each animal class (Table 5). The questionnaire was scored from 1 to 7.

Immediately afterwards, the class was divided randomly into two groups of 20 each (Group A and Group B), and we started the lecture (30 min). Group A worked with the loMU and Group B with the loAR. Each student used a computer, and they were guided by a teacher to access the website with the LO and to navigate to it.

Figure 4 shows the scores of the children in Group A in the pre- and post-tests. The change between the results of the post-test and the pre-test was 20%, and the average hits jumped from 3.6 hits to 5 hits (Table 6); 75% of students had progressed between the first test and the second.

Table 5. Pre-test questionnaire.

Question	Alternatives
1. Which animal class does the dog belong to?	()mammals ()amphibians ()reptiles ()birds ()fish
2. Which of these animals belongs to the reptile class?	()eagle ()salamander, ()swordfish, ()snake ()giraffe
3. How many legs does an insect have?	()four ()six ()eight ()ten ()twelve
4. Which of these animals is an arachnid?	()ant ()scorpion ()ladybug ()mouse () starfish
5. Which animal class does the frog belong to?	()insects ()amphibians ()reptiles ()birds ()fish
6. Which of these animals belongs to the fish class?	()dolphin ()tilapia ()bat ()platypus ()whale
7. The duck is a …	()insect ()amphibian ()reptile ()bird ()fish

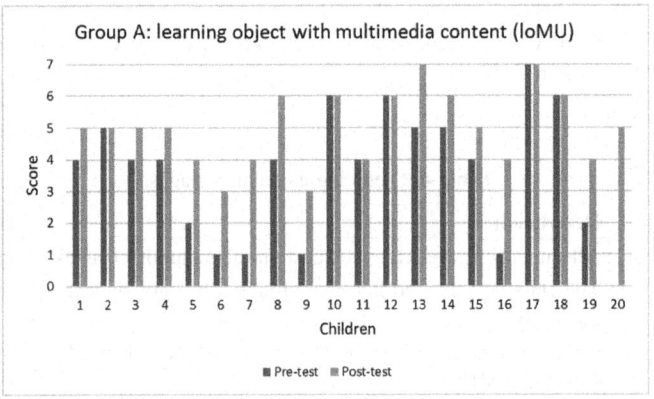

Fig. 4. Pre- and post-test scores obtained by Group A using loMU.

Table 6. Summary of the scores obtained by Group A using loMU.

	Group A: loMU	
	Pre-test	Post-test
Median	4.00	5.00
Mean	3.60	5.00
Std	2.06	1.16
Max	7	7
Min	0	3

Figure 5 shows the scores of the children in Group B in the pre- and post-tests. The change between the results of the post-test and the pre-test was 36%, and the average hits jumped from 3.2 hits to 5.7 hits (Table 7); 90% of students progressed between the first test and the second.

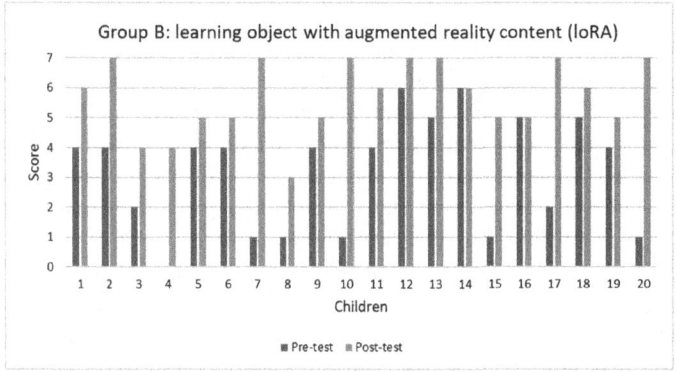

Fig. 5. Pre- and post-test scores obtained by Group B using loRA.

Table 7. Summary of the scores obtained by Group B using loRA.

	Group B: loRA	
	Pre-test	Post-test
Median	3.8	6.0
Mean	3.2	5.7
Std	1.88	1.21
Max	6	7
Min	1	3

In both cases, the standard deviation decreased after the use of the LO, indicating that its use can increase the learning process. However, in general, the children using the loMU increased their scores by 20%, while the children using loRA increased by 36%. Moreover, in the question about arachnids and insects (Question 3) the children using the loMU increased their scores by 0%, while the children using the loRA increased their scores by 45%, indicating that loAR can be of valuable assistance in subjects that require a depth view to understand the subject. In this case, it assisted the children to count the legs.

The p-value for the loMU was 0.000134602, while the p-value for loRA was 0.0000199 762496490467; the p-value for both was 1.9263E-08. (significance level 0.05), rejecting the null hypothesis. That means that the tests were significant; that is, the change in the children's scores between the pre- and post-tests was not random.

The children's teacher reported that the experiment motivated the students, especially those who did not usually pay attention during traditional classes based on the book. Although she was already aware of AR, she was surprised by the positive student involvement. The students did not have any difficulty in manipulating the marker. They become anxious to have another class with AR content.

4 Concluding Remarks

There is interest in LO that facilitate the teaching-learning process. However, an effective use of loAR that is affordable and easy to develop must be provided. This research presented a development approach tailored to create loAR with quality and practicality. As result, we expected to improve traditional LO with the usage of AR, extending learners' interaction with and perception of their content, creating new possibilities such as different visual views. Rather than just adding extra data to the real world, AR can modify the way that learning takes place

The approach presented extends the process of incremental development, a traditional software model, remodeling the concepts and adding several new steps. To test our approach, we carried out a case study which aimed to teach animal classification to children. We were able to create and validate a loAR. Moreover, our results indicate that using loAR to introduce children to animal classification can be an effective resource. During the post-test, that is, after being exposed to animal classification through a loAR, the children's scores were improved.

Although the approach presented here is an innovative work, it has limitations. These provide directions for future work in terms of extensions, experimental validations, variations and enhancements. In order to evaluate the approach differently, an experiment could be conducted in other contexts, but with some characteristics that are different from those presented in this work. For example, the development phase could be carried out using another development tool (e.g. Unity, SmartAR). The packing and distribution phases also could be validated with other tools. Finally, new experiments could also be carried out with other groups.

References

1. Wiley, D.A.: Connecting learning objects to instructional design theory: a definition, a metaphor, and a taxonomy. In: The Instructional Use of Learning Objects (2000). http://reusability.org/read/chapters/wiley.doc. Accessed 28 Feb 2018
2. McGreal, R.M.: Learning objects: a practical definition. Int. J. Instr. Technol. Distance Learn. 1, 21–32 (2004)
3. Inayat, I., Inayat, Z., Amin, R.U.: Teaching and learning object-oriented analysis and design with 3D game. In: 2016 International Conference on Frontiers of Information Technology (FIT), pp. 46–51 (2016)
4. Blanc, S., Benlloch-Dualde, J.V.: Digital learning object production in engineering courses. IEEE Revista Iberoamericana de Tecnologias del Aprendizaje 9(2), 43–48 (2014)
5. Hoff, W., Zhang, H.: Learning object and state models for AR task guidance. In: 2016 IEEE International Symposium on Mixed and Augmented Reality (ISMAR-Adjunct), pp. 272–273 (2016)

6. Azuma, R.T.: A survey of augmented reality. Presence Teleoper. Virtual Environ. **6**(4), 355–385 (1997)
7. Becker, S.A., Cummins, M., Davis, A., Hall C.G., Ananthanarayanan, V.: NMC horizon report: 2017 higher education edition (2017)
8. Nielsen, J.: Why you only need to test with 5 users (2000)
9. Cai, W.X., Li, G.S., Chen, X.H., Hong, C.Q., Zhu, S.Z., Wu, Q.H., Chen, R.: Education based new computer network simulator design and implementation. In: 2016 11th International Conference on Computer Science Education (ICCSE), pp. 933–935 (2016)
10. Paiva, V.D.F., Machado, L.D., Batista, T.V.V.: A collaborative and immersive VR simulator for education and assessment of surgical teams. In: 2015 XVII Symposium on Virtual and Augmented Reality, pp. 176–185 (2015)
11. Robinson, P.E., Carroll, J.: An online learning platform for teaching, learning, and assessment of programming. In: 2017 IEEE Global Engineering Education Conference (EDUCON), pp. 547–556 (2017)
12. Mavridis, A., Tsiatsos, T.: FGAWeb: a web platform for administrating flexible games in education. In: 2017 IEEE Global Engineering Education Conference (EDUCON), pp. 1858–1862 (2017)
13. Abbasi, F., Waseem, A., Ashraf, E.: Augmented reality based teaching in classrooms. In: 2017 International Conference on Communication, Computing and Digital Systems (C-CODE), pp. 259–264 (2017)
14. Scrivner, O., Madewell, J., Buckley, C., Perez, N.: Augmented reality digital technologies (ARDT) for foreign language teaching and learning. In: 2016 Future Technologies Conference (FTC), pp. 395–398 (2016)
15. Montenegro, R., Muñoz, L.: Improved teaching and conservation of natural sites through augmented reality. In: 2017 12th Iberian Conference on Information Systems and Technologies (CISTI), pp. 1–6 (2017)
16. Iguchi, K., Mitsuhara, H., Shishibori, M.: Evacuation instruction training system using augmented reality and a smartphone-based head mounted display. In: 2016 3rd International Conference on Information and Communication Technologies for Disaster Management (ICT-DM), pp. 1–6 (2016)
17. Nickels, S., Sminia, H., Mueller, S.C., Kools, B., Dehof, A.K., Lenhof, H.P., Hildebrandt, A.: ProteinScanAR - an augmented reality web application for high school education in biomolecular life sciences. In: 2012 16th International Conference on Information Visualisation, pp. 578–583 (2012)
18. Pressman, R.S.: Software Engineering: A Practitioner's Approach. Palgrave Macmillan, London (2005)
19. Sommerville, I.: Software Engineering, 9th edn. Addison-Wesley Publishing Company, New York (2010)
20. Wiegers, K.E., Beatty, J.: Software Requirements, 3rd edn. Microsoft Press, Redmond (2013)
21. Tiwari, S., Rathore, S.S., Gupta, A.: Selecting requirement elicitation techniques for software projects. In: 2012 CSI Sixth International Conference on Software Engineering (CONSEG), pp. 1–10. IEEE (2012)
22. Royce, W.W.: Managing the development of large software systems: concepts and techniques. In: Proceedings of the 9th International Conference on Software Engineering, pp. 328–338. IEEE Computer Society Press (1987)
23. MacKenzie, I.S.: Human-Computer Interaction: An Empirical Research Perspective, 1st edn. Morgan Kaufmann Publishers Inc., San Francisco (2013)
24. Nielsen, J., Loranger, H.: Prioritizing Web Usability. New Riders Publishing, Thousand Oaks (2006)

25. Barnum, C.M.: Usability Testing Essentials: Ready, Set...Test!, 1st edn. Morgan Kaufmann Publishers Inc., San Francisco (2010)
26. Nielsen, J.: Usability Engineering. Morgan Kaufmann Publishers Inc., San Francisco (1993)
27. Kostaras, N., Xenos, M.: Usability evaluation of augmented reality systems. Intel. Decis. Technol. **6**(2), 139–149 (2012)
28. Zainuddin, N.M.M., Zaman, H.B., Ahmad, A.: Heuristic evaluation on augmented reality courseware for the deaf. In: 2011 International Conference on User Science and Engineering (i-USEr), pp. 183–188 (2011)
29. Martins, V.F., Kirner, T.G., Kirner, C.: Subjective Usability Evaluation Criteria of Augmented Reality Applications, pp. 39–48. Springer International Publishing, Cham (2015)
30. Mahauad, J.J.M., Carvallo, J.P., Zambrano, J.S.: Educational repositories. IEEE Revista Iberoamericana de Tecnologias del Aprendizaje **11**(2), 79–86 (2016)
31. Ullrich, C., Shen, R., Borau, K.: Learning from learning objects and their repositories to create sustainable educational app environments. In: 2013 IEEE 13th International Conference on Advanced Learning Technologies, pp. 285–287 (2013)
32. Ochoa, X., Duval, E.: Quantitative analysis of learning object repositories. IEEE Trans. Learn. Technol. **2**(3), 226–238 (2009)
33. Guimarães, M.P., Alves, B., Martins, V.F., Baglie, L.S.S., Brega, J.R.F., Dias, D.R.C.: Embedding augmented reality applications into learning management systems. In: Gervasi, O., et al. (eds) ICCSA 2017. LNCS, vol. 10404, pp. 585–594. Springer, Cham (2017). https://doi.org/10.1007/978-3-319-62392-4_42
34. Santana, E., Balestri, R.: Conhecer e Crescer. 4° Ano, Escala Educacional, 3° Edition, São Paulo, 264 pages (2011)

eStreet: Virtual Reality and Wearable Devices Applied to Rehabilitation

Diego R. C. Dias[1,6]([envelope]), Iago C. Alvarenga[1], Marcelo P. Guimarães[2,3],
Luis C. Trevelin[4], Gabriela Castellano[5,6], and Alexandre F. Brandão[5,6]

[1] Federal University of São João del-Rei - UFSJ, São João del Rei, Brazil
{diegodias,iagodecastro}@ufsj.edu.br
[2] Brazilian Open University - Federal University of São Paulo, São Paulo, Brazil
marcelodepaiva@gmail.com
[3] Master Program of Faculty Campo Limpo Paulista, Faccamp,
Campo Limpo Paulista, Brazil
[4] Federal University of São Carlos - UFSCar, São Carlos, Brazil
trevelin@dc.ufscar.br
[5] State University of Campinas - UNICAMP, Campinas, Brazil
{abrandao,grabriela}@ifi.unicamp.br
[6] Brazilian Institute of Neuroscience and Neurotechnology - BRAINN,
Campinas, Brazil

Abstract. The use of virtual reality has grown in recent years due to the popularization of immersive and interactive devices, and applications in general. In areas related to medical rehabilitation, it has not been different. Several types of research have emerged in the last years integrating virtual reality as an aid to patients' rehabilitation of diverse pathologies, as for example people who suffered a stroke. The purpose of this research was to create a low-cost wearable device and provide an immersive and interactive virtual environment to perform daily life activities aiming at medical rehabilitation. In this way, virtual reality was used to support the accomplishment of activities such as functional mobility (through stationary walking) and maintenance of personal objects. The wearable device was developed using an Arduino UNO, sonars, accelerometer, and gyroscope. We also created a virtual reality environment that provides functionalities for user's movement, such as pedestrian crossing a street and moving around a virtual city. It is expected that the solution developed can assist health professionals in the rehabilitation process.

Keywords: Virtual reality · Immersive environment · Interaction
Rehabilitation

1 Introduction

Virtual reality (VR) emerged in the 1950s and has the user's immersion, interaction and engagement as some of its main features. In recent years its use

O. Gervasi et al. (Eds.): ICCSA 2018, LNCS 10963, pp. 775–789, 2018.
https://doi.org/10.1007/978-3-319-95171-3_60

has become more common on several areas, such as patient's rehabilitation solution [6,8,9,12,13,16].

Regarding immersion, the virtual environment allows the performance of several day-to-day activities, such as the Daily Life Activities (DLA) [15]. So, the higher the environment's immersion level, the more the user is expected to be engaged in the performing of some activity. In rehabilitation, the use of DLAs can provide patients who suffered a stroke with brain stimulation. Such stimulation is beneficial to the recovery of functions previously performed by the brain's lesioned areas, which are taken over by other, healthy cells [5,8,10,11].

When it comes to interaction, VR devices enable their users to move inside the virtual environment. Examples of devices include the joystick, treadmills and Kinect. However, interaction with them may not be ideal, since most of them do not allow the use of the user's natural movements, like walking. To overcome this barrier, wearable devices have arisen which are technological accessories incorporated by the user in their bodies. That type of device is expected to facilitate the performing of DLA by the user. Its main features are the monitoring of position, displacement and vital signs, or even the recognition of the presence of objects and people [3].

Aiming to make patients' rehabilitation easier, this research created a low-cost wearable device, capable of monitoring their stationary walking. To do so, Arduino and its components were used in order to perform the interaction in virtual environments. The device uses sonars that capture the distance of the user's leg to the ground, calculating its displacement and sending those data to the virtual environment via Bluetooth. Other sensors, such as a gyroscope and an accelerometer, are also used to get noise-free input data. The device's performance, as well as discussions related to calibration and walking, are presented.

In order to validate the device's usage, a virtual environment named e-Street was developed. The environment is made up of a city where the user walks virtually by means of a stationary walking. The city is equipped with traffic simulation and pedestrian crossings. The algorithms related to those activities are presented.

The main motivation and justification for this research is related to the difficulty to simulate the user's real-time movement in VR applications through low-cost wearable devices. This enables training in virtual, controlled and safe environments, which don't pose real danger to the patient when compared to an actual training environment.

This article is organized as follows. Section 2 presents the related works, highlighting innovations and difficulties to replicate the real-time movement in the virtual environments used in rehabilitation. Section 3, "Methodology", explains both the wearable device's and e-Street's development. The results and their evaluation are presented in Sect. 5. Finally, Sect. 6 reports the conclusions.

2   Related Work

The study by [13] pointed out the growth of VR and the benefits of its application in the Health area, presenting as examples the training for surgeries, the treatment of phobias and the rehabilitation of the cognitive processes. The main focus was on the potential benefits VR can provide to patients who need some form of rehabilitation. The article also mapped the rehabilitation variations, including the potential of objectively measuring the patients' behavior in reliable and safe environments, enabling the creation of standard evaluation protocols.

The study conducted by [16] brings preliminary indications that the use of VR for therapies can be provided by a context that is purposeful and encouraging of patients' rehabilitation by means of protocols. The proposed environment presents challenging and safe virtual interaction in real time. The author shows the importance of differentiating virtual environments from other media, such as videos and television, emphasizing the immersion and interaction with virtual environments, as well as the importance of devices such as gloves, treadmills and exoskeletons, which provide the user with the perceptions of tact and strength – perceptions that are useful for gaining performance in more difficult tasks. He also highlights the importance of the subject's behavior and movement features inside a virtual environment being naturally performed without losing its immersion quality.

The work done by [4] mentions that stroke patients' march improvement comes from the intensive practice of tasks, as well as from the increase in the difficulties posed. Rehabilitation time is hampered by unattractive environments. Because of that, VR has been used as a way to increase time and offer a variety of environments with controlled restrictions to maximize learning. The patients have total interaction with the environment, simulating complex physical environments, including possible dangers, with no real risk. In the study, a locomotor system was developed based on a treadmill and on the use of VR technology. The system presents challenges related to physical and temporal hurdles, as well as locomotion's cognitive characteristics. This work verified the capacity for improvement. The tests were done on five healthy elderly subjects, who had total control of their walking speed both in the treadmill and in the virtual scene. The study was then perfected, by developing several virtual environments and protocols for the treatment of the march on post-stroke patients.

The differential in the work by [14] comes from the development of shoes that interact with virtual environments with auditory and haptic feedback. The study describes a multimodal interactive space with the purpose of simulating the audiovisual elements of interactions based on walking. The users must walk in a space wearing the pair of shoes enhanced with sensors and actuators that capture their movement in order to allow the transfer of abilities. The case study used volunteers who were invited to walk directly in a straight virtual plank. The research by [14] demonstrates that walking on a straight line is a hard task in the physical word, since people tend to go in circles when there are no reference points such as the Sun or the stars.

The devices in the works of [4,16] have the objective of providing users with movement capability in the immersive environment. However, those devices are of high cost, difficult transportation and low maintainability, which cause difficulties for replicating them.

The device proposed in this article seeks to mitigate those difficulties, by being low cost, easy to transport and with high maintainability.

3   Methodology

One of the most important steps in the development of software solutions is the requirements' gathering stage, which aims to understand the target audience's desires or what they believe they desire, as well as the business rules and processes. The requirements' gathering was designed in partnership with the Brazilian Institute of Neuroscience and Neurotechnology (BRAINN) [1]. It was divided in functional and non-functional requirements, looking for "what" the system will do and "how" it will do it, standardizing directives for the building of both the wearable device and the virtual environment. These standards are extremely important, for they are related to patients' recovery.

3.1   Functional Requirements

The functional requirements describe the patient's needs the device and the virtual environment must satisfy, which are:

- Choosing movement range (MR): it allows the specialist to choose the appropriate MR for each user based on data from the sensors attached to the inferior limbs. The MR should correspond to one movement from 3 to 15 cm high, measured in relation to the ground;
- Calibrating sensors: allow the calibration of the sensors positioned on the inferior limbs in relation to the ground, with a maximum variance of one centimeter for more or for less. Once calibrated, the sensors respond to commands from the movements made;
- Autonomous Cars: lets cars interact independently around the city, complying with traffic laws; and
- Pedestrian crossings: there must be pedestrian crossings across the city, which directly interact with cars and with patients.

3.2   Non-functional Requirements

The non-functional requirements are related to issues of performance, usability, reliability, safety, availability, maintenance, and technologies involved in the development of a piece of software or a device, and they are as follows:

- Response Time: the response time between the sensors output and the VR system input should be the closest possible to the real time (avoiding delays);

- Friendly Interface: the high diversity of users regarding age, cognitive performance and previous experience with VR systems;
- Programming Language: the development of a robust, iOS- and Android-compatible system (latest releases must be considered); and
- Compatibility: multiplatform, iOS and ANDROID.

3.3 Device

The creation of the wearable device was achieved by using an Arduino UNO microcontroller, two sonars (HC-SR04), two accelerometers/gyroscopes (MPU-6050) and one Bluetooth module (HC-05). Figure 1 shows the components' connection schematics, in which the 5 V output connection of the microcontroller responsible for transmitting the power necessary for the components to work is directly connected to the 5 V inputs of the sonars and the Bluetooth module. The GND output is responsible for grounding the components, by being connected to each component's GND input. The microcontroller's outputs 10 and 8 are connected to the sonars through the TRIG input, responsible for the wave emission in the space. The outputs 11 and 9 are connected to the ECHO sonars inputs, responsible for capturing the wave in the space. The Bluetooth component uses two inputs, TXD for transmitting data and DXD for receiving TLL-type data, which are connected to Arduino UNO's TLL communication inputs, TX(1) and DX(0).

The accelerometer/gyroscope (MPU-6050) components have a different behavior from the others. They make the standard VCC and GND power connection through the 5 V and ground inputs. SCL and SDA are responsible for the communication interface and they are connected to A5 and A4 analogical inputs. And AD0 defines which address the sensor will communicate with. It is extremely important, since two components with the same communication bus are used. The AD0 input is connected to 3.3 V to define the address 0x69. When connected to GND, it defines the address 0x68.

Arduino UNO's programming aims to send back to the virtual environment, via Bluetooth, the user speed in a given moment in time. The user's leg displacement in relation to the ground and the total time it took for the user to raise it must be both captured. With that information it is possible to estimate the calculation of the speed of the movement in that moment. Due to the sensitivity of the data provided by the component, it was necessary to use a Kalman filter [7], which uses the raw data from the MPU-6050 component, to smooth the signals linearly and then to make the calculation of the user's leg angle. The measured angle can be seen in Fig. 2.

Algorithm 1 exemplifies the detailed operation of the wearable device, as well as the calculations made to get the speed. First the sensors calibration is done, seeking to normalize the user's leg distance, where the sensor was attached in relation to the ground, defining the values for zero, enabling the calculation of the user's leg displacement and disregarding its height in relation to the ground. The calibration is made according to Eq. 1, which uses an average of the

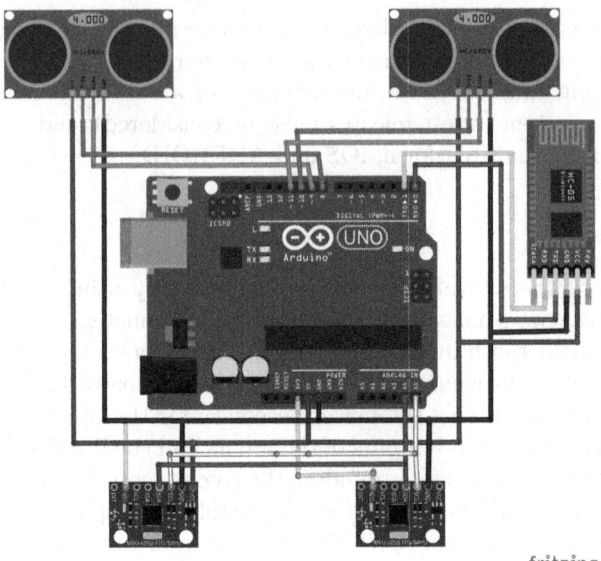

Fig. 1. Device's diagram with MPU-6050

Fig. 2. Angle obtained by the sensors on the user's leg

10 measurements for each leg in the starting (rest) position. The symbol ρ represents the value captured by the sonar.

$$\frac{\sum_1^{10} \rho_i}{10} = \rho_{cal} \tag{1}$$

The steps are done in the Arduino IDE *setup()*. The time when the user begins raising the leg is initialized in the Arduino IDE *loop()* function. This process captures the values through the sonar, looking for the highest value of

Algorithm 1. Pseudocode for the Arduino UNO with MPU6050 device programming

---

Result: Send the movement speed to the virtual environment
$calibrateComponents()$;
$initialTime \leftarrow 0$;
$newDistance \leftarrow 0$;
$distance \leftarrow 0$;
$distanceMax \leftarrow 3$;
while *True* **do**
    if $initialTime == 0$ && $distance \mathrel{!=} 0$ **then**
        | $initialTime \leftarrow getTime()$;
    end
    $newDistance \leftarrow getSonarsDistance()$;
    if $newDistance > distance$ **then**
        | $distance \leftarrow newDistance$;
    else
        $finalTime \leftarrow getTime()$;
        if $distance \geq distanceMax$ **then**
            $gyroAcc \leftarrow getGyro()$;
            $angle \leftarrow KalmanFilter(gyroAcc)$;
            $time \leftarrow finalTime - initialTime$;
            $speed \leftarrow distance * sen(angle)/time$;
            $sendSpeed()$;
            $initialTime \leftarrow 0$;
            $newDistance \leftarrow 0$;
            $distance \leftarrow 0$;
        end
    end
end

---

the leg raise. The estimated distance is calculated according to Eq. 2, which uses the leg's total displacement minus the calibration value got by Eq. 1, in which ρ is the distance captured from the sonar, ρ_{max} the largest distance captured from the sonar and ρ_{cal} is the sonar's calibrating distance.

$$\rho = \rho_{max} - \rho_{cal} \tag{2}$$

The speed v is a low estimation calculated by using the highest position ρ to which the user raised the leg over time Δt, represented in Eq. 3, being sent via Bluetooth to the virtual environment.

$$v = \frac{\rho}{\Delta t} \tag{3}$$

The distance is then calculated based on the user's knee angling. Therefore, Eq. 4 defines the new equation for distance.

$$\rho = (\rho_{max} - \rho_{cal}) \cos(\Theta) \tag{4}$$

So, the distance formula is now calculated in relation to the user's knee rotation, presented by Eq. 5, and sent via Bluetooth to the virtual environment.

$$v = \frac{\rho \cos(\Theta)}{\Delta t} \tag{5}$$

4   e-Street

For the development of the e-Street virtual environment the Unity3D game was used [2]. To do so, an example of city available on Unity's Asset Store was used and enhanced according to the requirements' gathering. A smartphone with VR glasses was used as immersive device.

4.1   Autonomous Cars

In order to simulate traffic, autonomous cars were inserted in the virtual environment, and these cars move according to an oriented graph which was created based on the city's points. Figure 3 shows several points with directed connections, indicating the cars' orientation and the direction. It also demonstrates the operation of the graph in which the cars move from point **A** to point **B** of the street. In the other street, the movement is done from point **C** to point **D**, in the opposite direction. This way the cars can move across the whole city. Another possibility is the street intersection, presented by point **E**, where the car randomly chooses the next point to go to.

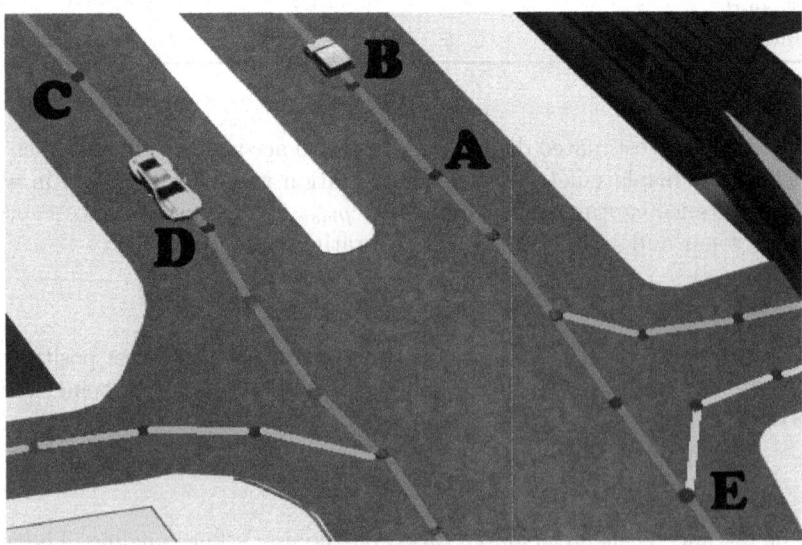

Fig. 3. Example of streets orientation

The cars have two main functionalities: (i) acceleration; and (ii) braking. Acceleration goes from the stationary state up to maximum speed set according to the type of car. In collision detection, the cars can reduce their speed when getting in touch with another vehicle. The cars have two main colliders: the one involving the car; and the front collider, which establishes contact so that the car applies the brakes. Currently the system has three types of cars with different masses:

- Sports car: Maximum speed = 20 and mass = 1,290 kg;
- Pickup: Maximum speed = 15 and mass = 1,205 kg; and
- Truck: Maximum speed = 10 and mass = 4,000 kg.

Algorithm 2 represents the cars' functionalities cycle. When the car is still and there is no obstruction, the acceleration is engaged, moving the car. When meeting any obstacle, the brake function is activated, reducing the car's speed or stopping it. The function Time.deltaTime represents the time in seconds the last frame took to complete.

Algorithm 2. Pseudocode for controlling automaton cars

Result: Autonomously control the cars in the virtual environment
controlCar();
$break \leftarrow false$;
while *True* **do**
    if $velocity \geq 0\&\&break == false$ **then**
        | $speedupCar()$;
    else
        | $breakCar()$;
    end
end

Result: Autonomously accelerate the virtual environment cars
speedupCar();
$break = false$;
if $velocity < velocityMax/2$ **then**
    | $velocity \leftarrow velocity + (Time.deltaTime/5 * velocityMax)$;
end

Result: Autonomously brake the virtual environment cars
$break = true$;
if $velocity > 0$ **then**
    | $velocity \leftarrow velocity - (Time.deltaTime * 2 * velocityMax)$;
else
    | $velocity \leftarrow 0$;
end

4.2 Pedestrian Crossings

The pedestrian crossings work according to the user's position in relation to the car. Figure 4 depicts the structure of two colliders.

The first collider, a smaller one, together with texture, is responsible for verifying the user in contact with the crossing. The second collider, larger, with no texture, is responsible for verifying the approach of cars. It only checks for the cars' existence in case the first collider is active. Therefore, if the user is not on that crossing, the environment lets the car traffic flow normally. When the user is in contact with the first sensor and the second collider detects some car approaching, a signal is sent to the car which is in contact with the second collider so that its brakes are applied. If there is no longer a user on the crossing, the car resumes accelerating and takes its course in the environment.

Fig. 4. Pedestrian crossing

A user wearing the wearable device can be seen in Fig. 5(a). The device is attached to his waist and the sensors are attached to his legs. The user visualizes the application during the use of the virtual environment in its immersive form. The image is rendered for each one of the user's eyes using a smartphone and VR glasses (Fig. 5(b)).

5   Experimental Evaluation

5.1   Device Evaluation

The wearable device developed for this research allows for a new way of interacting in the recognition of movements related to stationary walking. Figure 6

(a) User with the wearable device

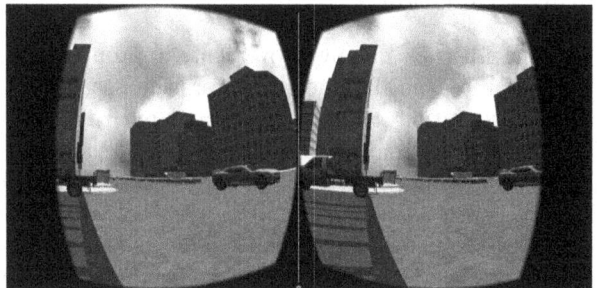

(b) How the user visualizes the immersive environment

Fig. 5. Virtual environment and its user

shows the device. A case was created and printed in a 3D printer to hold the components during the use of the device.

The objective of the evaluation was to detect possible errors emitted by the device during the execution of the application. The errors can happen due to low precision of the sonars, causing an improper movement (ghost walk) in the virtual environment. According to the requirements' gathering, the device must work with a calibration variance of 1 cm at most, and the walk with a variance from 3 to 15 cm of the leg in relation to the ground.

The evaluations were done by using the device while looking for flaws. The footstep tests involve the performing of walks through stationary walking. This way, the data gathered were mined through statistical methods for better visualization.

Fig. 6. Wearable device, including the MPU-6050

5.2   Calibration Evaluation

Theoretically, in the absence of any movement, a properly calibrated sonar should always go back to the 0 value. However, the sensing of the wave has an error, in which a variation can take place and return noisy values. It was paramount, for the study, to maximize the approach of the sonar tending to 0, with a variance of 1 cm being allowed according to the minimum requirements.

The sonars were kept static in a stand for the evaluation. Ten one-minute interactions were done to analyze the variance in movement gathering. The analysis consisted in the verification of the minimum/maximum variance values, the sonar's average and standard deviation. Table 1 presents the results obtained from the sonar regarding the left leg, right leg and the two legs combined.

Table 1. Calibration tests results (SPM - steps per minute)

Results	Left leg	Right leg	Total
Minimum	−0.6400 cm	−0.6700 cm	−0.6700 cm
Maximum	0.1200 cm	0.9600 cm	0.9600 cm
Average	−0.2701 cm	−0.0682 cm	−0.1691 cm
Standard deviation	0.2299 cm	0.2601 cm	0.2654 cm
Total of the sample	6984 spm	6984 spm	13968 spm

By analyzing Table 1, it was observed that the sonar never captured a fluctuation larger than 1 cm, for more or for less, getting an average of −0.1691 in total variance and a standard deviation of 0.2654, which are low values when compared to the required 1 cm.

5.3   Walking Evaluation

Table 2 shows the metrics used to evaluate the walking. Ten one-minute walkings were done, each one with 30 steps per minute (SPM), changing the device's precision, in order to evaluate its behavior while performing the steps capture.

Table 2. Step test table (SPM - steps per minute)

Interactions	Total time	Precision	SPM
10	1 min	2 cm	30
10	1 min	3 cm	30
10	1 min	4 cm	30

The storage of data regarding rehabilitation, such as the maximum and minimum heights and the patient's leg raise variance, are of upmost importance, since they help in the treatment validation process. Table 3 has the information with a 2-cm precision.

Table 3. Step test table with a 2-cm precision (SPM - steps per minute)

Results	Left leg	Right leg
Maximum	9.770 cm	10.510 cm
Average	6.880 cm	6.910 cm
Standard deviation	0.940 cm	1.070 cm
Total of the sample	9750 spm	9750 spm

In the 2-cm precision test, one ghost walk happened during evaluation. The left leg's maximum raise height was 9.77 cm and the right leg's one was 10.51 cm, with a variance of respectively 0.94 and 1.07 cm.

In the 3-cm precision test there was no occurrence of ghost walk during the evaluation. The maximum height reached by the right leg was 13.07 cm and the left leg's one was 14.06 with a variance of respectively 1.04 and 1.290 cm. Table 4 has the information with a 3-cm precision.

Table 4. Step test table with a 3-cm precision (SPM - steps per minute)

Results	Left leg	Right leg
Maximum	14.0600 cm	13.0700 cm
Average	7.690 cm	7.270 cm
Standard deviation	1.290 cm	1.040 cm
Total of the sample	9359 spm	9359 spm

In the 4-cm precision test there was no occurrence of ghost walk during the evaluation. The maximum height reached by the right leg was 9.26 cm and the left leg's one was 8.95 with a variance of respectively 1.03 and 1.18 cm. Table 5 has the information with a 4-cm precision.

Table 5. Step test table with a 4-cm precision (SPM - steps per minute)

Results	Left leg	Right leg
Maximum	8.9500 cm	9.2600 cm
Average	6.840 cm	7.560 cm
Standard deviation	1.180 cm	1.030 cm
Total of the sample	121411 spm	12411 spm

6   Conclusion and Future Works

The growth of VR makes possible the exploration of several areas of multidisciplinary knowledge. In this work, VR was used to tap into the possibilities of movement inside a virtual environment, in order to apply it in patients' rehabilitation, the interaction being made through the wearable device that was developed. The use of movement in VR for patients' rehabilitation is helpful due to the fact that it provides a safe and reliable environment. Virtual environments thus enable the exploration of interaction.

The wearable device developed enables the user's walking through stationary march inside the virtual application. The device building started from using sonars, which capture the user's leg displacement. The estimated speed is sent to the virtual environment via Bluetooth. The environment gets the information and handles it as a one-step displacement in the application.

The developed device is expected to enable a new way of interaction with applications aimed to rehabilitation of the inferior limbs. The device was created with the goal of meeting the need of stationary walking's movement tracking. So, as per the evaluations, it is possible to say that goal was achieved.

As a result, it was possible to envision the device in its simplest form, without accelerometer and gyroscope. Use tests with various sensitivity degrees have helped to check the low rate of ghost walk during the use of the device. Errors were detected regarding the user's legs angling though. As a possible solution for the angling issue, a new device was proposed with the addition of new components, accelerometer and gyroscope. The inclusion of those components made it necessary to use the Kalman Filter. During the search for the filter, it was observed that it could be used to enhance the entire system and not just the device user's angling measurement.

This kind of treatment still needs a long research time so it can yield actual results proving the importance of the use of VR in rehabilitation. The device developed for this research has already been applied to some patients' rehabilitation and its patent request has already been filed.

Acknowledgments. This research was partially supported by CNPq, CAPES, Fapesp, Fapemig, and Finep.

References

1. Cepid brainn. http://www.brainn.org.br/en/. Accessed 18 Feb 2018
2. Unity. https://unity3d.com. Accessed 18 Feb 2018
3. Donati, L.A.P., Prado, G.S., et al.: O computador como veste-interface: (re)configurando os espaços de atuação (2005)
4. Fung, J., Richards, C.L., Malouin, F., McFadyen, B.J., Lamontagne, A.: A treadmill and motion coupled virtual reality system for gait training post-stroke. CyberPsychol. Behav. **9**(2), 157–162 (2006)
5. Gervasi, O., Magni, R., Zampolini, M.: Nu!RehaVr: virtual reality in neuro telerehabilitation of patients with traumatic brain injury and stroke. Virtual Real. **14**(2), 131–141 (2010)
6. Jack, D., Boian, R., Merians, A.S., Tremaine, M., Burdea, G.C., Adamovich, S.V., Recce, M., Poizner, H.: Virtual reality-enhanced stroke rehabilitation. IEEE Trans. Neural Syst. Rehabil. Eng. **9**(3), 308–318 (2001)
7. Kalman, R.E.: A new approach to linear filtering and prediction problems. J. Basic Eng. **82**(1), 35–45 (1960)
8. Laver, K., George, S., Thomas, S., Deutsch, J.E., Crotty, M.: Virtual reality for stroke rehabilitation. Stroke **43**(2), e20–e21 (2012)
9. Levin, M.F., Weiss, P.L., Keshner, E.A.: Emergence of virtual reality as a tool for upper limb rehabilitation: incorporation of motor control and motor learning principles. Phys. Ther. **95**(3), 415–425 (2015)
10. McEwen, D., Taillon-Hobson, A., Bilodeau, M., Sveistrup, H., Finestone, H.: Virtual reality exercise improves mobility after stroke: an inpatient randomized controlled trial. Stroke **45**(6), 1853–1855 (2014)
11. Saposnik, G., Levin, M., Stroke Outcome Research Canada (SORCan) Working Group.: Virtual reality in stroke rehabilitation: a meta-analysis and implications for clinicians. Stroke **42**(5), 1380–1386 (2011)
12. Saposnik, G., Teasell, R., Mamdani, M., Hall, J., McIlroy, W., Cheung, D., Thorpe, K.E., Cohen, L.G., Bayley, M., et al.: Effectiveness of virtual reality using Wii gaming technology in stroke rehabilitation: a pilot randomized clinical trial and proof of principle. Stroke **41**(7), 1477–1484 (2010)
13. Schultheis, M.T., Rizzo, A.A.: The application of virtual reality technology in rehabilitation. Rehabil. Psychol. **46**(3), 296 (2001)
14. Serafin, S., Turchet, L., Nordahl, R.: Auditory feedback in a multimodal balancing task: walking on a virtual plank. In: Proceedings of Sound and Music Computing Conference (2011)
15. Silva, A.J.R., Restivo, T., Gabriel, J.: A serious game with a thermal haptic mouse. Int. J. Online Eng. (iJOE) **9**(S8), 74–76 (2013)
16. Sveistrup, H.: Motor rehabilitation using virtual reality. J. Neuroeng. Rehabil. **1**(1), 10 (2004)

An RGB-Based Gesture Framework for Virtual Reality Environments

João P. M. Ferreira[1], Diego R. C. Dias[1,4(✉)], Marcelo P. Guimarães[2,3], and Marcos A. M. Laia[1]

[1] Federal University of São João del-Rei - UFSJ, São João del Rei, Brazil
joaopmoferreira@gmail.com, diegocolombo.dias@gmail.com,
marcoslaia@gmail.com
[2] Brazilian Open University - Federal University of São Paulo, São Paulo, Brazil
marcelodepaiva@gmail.com
[3] Master Program of Faculty Campo Limpo Paulista, Faccamp,
Campo Limpo Paulista, Brazil
[4] Brazilian Institute of Neuroscience and Neurotechnology - BRAINN,
Campinas, Brazil

Abstract. Virtual reality is growing as a new interface between human and machine, new technologies improving the development of virtual reality applications, and the user's experience is extremely important for the science improvement. In order to define a new approach based on already established and easily acquired techniques of detection and tracking, an interaction framework was developed. The developed framework is able to understand basic commands through gestures performed by the user. Making use of a simple RGB camera. It is able to be used in a simple virtual reality application, allowing the user to interact with the virtual environment using natural user interface, focusing on presenting a way to interact with users without deep knowledge of computing, providing an easy-to-use interface. The results shows to be promising, and the possibilities of its uses are growing.

1 Introduction

Virtual reality (VR) is an advanced interface for computational applications where the user navigates and interacts in real-time in a 3D environment generated by computer [6].

The user interaction gestures captured from a camera to the virtual environment is done through a framework developed using the OpenCV library. OpenCV is an open source library which implements computer vision techniques [9]. In addition to being free, the present functions are optimized and can work with the most modern computer systems, such as multiprocessing GPU or multicore technologies.

Efficiency is important for real-time applications since the delays between a gesture and its response in the virtual environment can generate discomforts, such as misinterpretation of gestures. Several proprietary technologies are

O. Gervasi et al. (Eds.): ICCSA 2018, LNCS 10963, pp. 790–803, 2018.
https://doi.org/10.1007/978-3-319-95171-3_61

efficient and invisible to the user in interaction with the virtual environment. Among them, we highlight the Microsoft Kinect, which enables implementations of several tools of computer vision and interaction [5] for VR applications. However, the high cost whether of equipment acquisition or software license becomes prohibitive for a broad spectrum of commercial or non-commercial applications.

The combination of computer vision and VR techniques provides an environment where real-world objects can be captured in real-time and related to virtual objects. The area is called augmented reality (AR). AR differs from VR by the level of immersion [13]. These levels are defined by the input and output system devices. Virtual environments designed in three dimensions are mostly designed to simulate real-life situations [10]. In addition, studies in cluster computing areas and other types of arts and sciences are interesting for the scientific community advancing in general, taking into account their high interdisciplinary.

Computer vision is the area of science that studies how to make computational systems able to recognize and describe objects in a digital image [1]. The use of computer vision for capturing user movements tends to allow an interactive and intuitive means to manipulate virtual environments. This project seeks to find a natural way to manipulate objects using hands-free.

With the use of computer vision, markers can be detected or even body members can be used as a way of interaction in virtual environments. Computer vision applications can be used in several areas, such as Arts, Medicine, Engineering, among others, not being restricted only to the Computer Science area.

This paper presents a framework focused on the interaction of any VR application, using the user's body to interact with the computer, presenting the developed stage of the project, and also the results gained until this point. Indeed, the main purpose of this work is to reduce the cost of technologies which make use of RGB-D cameras, delivering results as good as the obtained using any specialized hardware. Having in mind that any portable device, as for example laptops, which have RGB cameras included in their hardware, so the technologies proposed aims to achieve a larger part of the population.

This paper is organized as follow. This section presented a brief introduction. Section 2 enumerates some papers regarding the theme. As a prove-of-concept, we proposed and developed an RGB-based framework for VR applications. In Sect. 4 we discussed results gained by the framework and compared with another approach. Finally, we performed some discussions about further work, and conclusions about the proposed framework.

2   Background

Shrivastava [11] proposed a dynamic system for hand gestures recognition using OpenCV. A hidden Markov model (HMM) technique is used in this study. The system is divided into three stages: detection and tracking, feature extraction and training, and recognition. According to the author because of the OpenCV functionalities, the recognition rate is very high and fast and can be used in real-time applications.

Gurav and Premanand [4] presented an interaction model that allows a user to control a robot using hand gestures. The gestural detection algorithms are based on several machine learning methods, such as neural networks, support vector machine, and adaptive boosting (AdaBoost). Gurav and Premanand used the AdaBoost method, which is trained with a reduced Haar-like feature set to make a robust detector. Good results were achieved about accuracy and robustness using more than four gestures.

Jia et al. [7] presented a novel hands-free control system for intelligent wheel chairs based on visual recognition of head gestures. Head gesture-based interface (HGI) was created for RoboChair users. RoboChair can be controlled according to the user's facial expression. Two techniques were combined: AdaBoost and Camshift in order to achieve good levels of accuracy, tracking, and recognition of gestures in real time. The main focus of the research is using the interface as an aid to the elderly and people with disabilities to operate RoboChair using just their head movements instead of hands.

Farhadi et al. [2] developed a computer vision based-system capable of performing interactions through arms and fingers gesturing. To reduce the effects of the environment (lighting and other noises), a depth-based camera was used. Through several tests, the authors concluded that the interaction through the fingers is superior to those generated by the arms. Also, gestures made by the arms tend to be more tiring to the users and they are less natural than the gestures made with the fingers.

Mehta et al. [8] introduce the first method for real-time 3D Human Pose Estimation with a Single RGB camera. The authors presented a comparison between the system developed and the Kinect since their system does not make use of a depth sensor they were able to introduce a solution for an outdoor application. The results presented in the paper show that low-cost technologies are being able to deliver results as good as specialized hardware.

3   The Proposed Framework

The framework developed can be resumed into 3 algorithms. The 3 main parts of the framework work together to deliver the results that will be introduced in the next section.

The 3 parts can be explicit by the flowchart (Fig. 1), which explains the methodology about the framework and show an overview regarding the project.

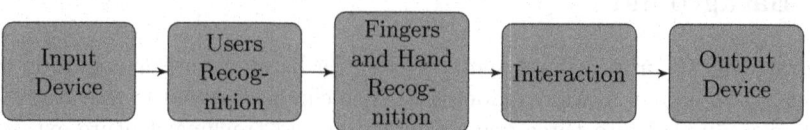

Fig. 1. Methodology adopted by the framework

The first algorithm uses digital image processing and computer vision techniques to recognize when there is or not users into the frame, and also recognize their members, defining a region of interest (ROI). That ROI can be defined using the segmentation process of an image. The segmentation process of an image defines a region and isolate interesting objects, which technique should be used is strongly dependent on the problem. So, at the end of the segmentation process, the ROI is defined [3].

At the end of the process represented by the Algorithm 1, the 3 biggest contours are the person's arms and face, and since the contours are sorted by their position, it is possible to differ the right and left arms.

OpenCV library was used to develop the Algorithm 1, having in mind that the Algorithm 1 gets the frame from an RGB-device. After that, the image is flipped to avoid the mirror effect; the grayscale image is generated, and the histogram of the frame is equalized; through OpenCV, faces are recognized from the frame. With the detected faces we can define how many people are in the scene, also a filter of skin is used to generate an image only with the user's skin. After a blur operation the image is done, and at this stage, we are able to detect the contours in the frame. With the detected contours we use sorting algorithms to sort the contours using their area and position, and with this algorithm, we are able to define the user's member.

The Algorithm 1 enables to use more than just one user in the same frame, just needing to add a statement in the switch case for more than one face detected. At next section, will be introduced some results with one and multiple users (Fig. 5).

After the recognition of the user's face and members, the framework recognizes the user's hand and fingers. This part of the project has huge importance because it is what enables the interaction. The Algorithm 2 shows how the prototype works for fingers and hands recognition in the same frame.

For recognizing hands the following Eqs. (1, 2, 3 and 4) were used. These 4 equations represent the center of mass and the normalized center of mass of a defined contour. The center of mass and the normalized center of mass are contours features.

$$m_{ji} = \sum_{x,y} (array(x,y) \cdot x^j \cdot y^i) \tag{1}$$

$$mu_{ji} = \sum_{x,y} (array(x,y) \cdot (x - \bar{x})^j \cdot (y - \bar{y})^i) \tag{2}$$

$$\bar{x} = \frac{m_{10}}{m_{00}}, \bar{y} = \frac{m_{01}}{m_{00}} \tag{3}$$

$$nu_{ji} = \frac{mu_{ji}}{m_{00}^{(i+j)/2+1}} \tag{4}$$

Algorithm 1. Recognize users

Data: RGB camera frame
Result: Contour of the user's members
1 initialization;
2 **while** *True* **do**
3 | get(frame);
4 | flip(image);
5 | cvtColor(image,gray);
6 | equalizeHist(gray);
7 | faces := detectFaces(gray);
8 | numFaces := faces.size();
9 | bin := binarize(frame,maskSkin);
10 | blured := blur(bin);
11 | contours := findContours(blured);
12 | contours := sortArea(contours);
13 | contours := sortPosition(contours);
14 | **begin**
15 | | **switch** *numFaces* **do**
16 | | | **case** *0* **do**
17 | | | | print("No person detected");
18 | | | **end**
19 | | | **case** *1* **do**
20 | | | | rightMember := contours[0];
21 | | | | userFace := contours[1];
22 | | | | leftMember := contours[2];
23 | | | **end**
24 | | | **otherwise do**
25 | | | | print("More than one person detected");
26 | | | **end**
27 | | **end**
28 | **end**
29 | **if** *Keyboard key pressed* **then**
30 | | break;
31 | **end**
32 **end**

In order to allow the fingers recognition, another arm contour feature was used. The convexity of the contour allows the prototype to recognize how many fingers are up, and through that, the user's signal can be recognized by counting the fingers.

Algorithm 2 makes use of OpenCV library to get the user's contours members. Using these, we can define the center of mass of the contour using the Eq. 3; so, using OpenCV, we can define the convexity of the contours. OpenCV makes use of the algorithm presented by [12], allowing to find the convexity defects of a contour, and with that, it is possible to define the starting and ending point of the defect. We make a comparison between the starting point and the center of

Algorithm 2. Recognize hand and fingers

Data: Contours of the recognize members
Result: Hand position and number of fingers used
1 initialization;
2 finger := 0;
3 moments := getMoments(contours);
4 handPosition := defineCenterOfMass(moments);
5 hull := convexHull(contours);
6 defects := convexityDefects(contours,hull);
7 **foreach** *defect in defects* **do**
8 | **if** *defect[3] > 20 * 256* **then**
9 | | startPoint := defect[0];
10 | | endPoint := defect[1];
11 | | **if** *startPoint.y < handPosition.y* **then**
12 | | | finger := finger + 1;
13 | | **end**
14 | **end**
15 **end**

mass, in order to be certain that the defect point is a finger. The results gained by the Algorithm 2 can be seen in Figs. 7 and 8.

Both Algorithms (1 and 2) defines the proposed framework. The combination of these algorithms enables the developer to get information, such as the position of the user's hand, and the number of user's raised fingers.

And finally, an application using the previous Algorithms 1 and 2 to simulated an virtual environment and the interaction with it. This application can be described in Algorithm 3.

The Algorithm 3 is a simply application which makes use of the proposed framework. The application uses the amount of fingers to trigger, and draw a rectangle at the user's hand until the user trigger with another amount of raised fingers. The application to simulate a virtual environment, which makes use of the proposed framework can be seen in Fig. 9.

4 Results

This section focus on the results of the developed prototype and a comparison between the Microsoft's Kinect v1 and the proposed framework. In addition, this section describes main problems and goals to the system development.

The following sections show the results obtained by some tests performed.

4.1 Users Detection

To detect users, the present framework works searching if there is a person into the scene as illustrated in Fig. 2. This was made using OpenCV library functions calls, which makes clear for the developer how the face recognition is made in fact.

Algorithm 3. Simple interaction algorithm

Data: this text
Result: Recognize users

```
 1 initialization;
 2 flag := 0;
 3 aux :=0;
 4 drawRectangleAt(Point(40,240),Point(140,340));
 5 while True do
 6 │   if center of mass is inside the rectangle AND fingers is 5 then
 7 │   │   flag := 1;
 8 │   end
 9 │   if Flag is 1 AND fingers is 0 then
10 │   │   aux ← center of mass;
11 │   │   px := Point(auxX-100,auxY-100);
12 │   │   py := Point(auxX+100,auxY+100);
13 │   │   drawRectangleAt(px,py);
14 │   end
15 │   if Flag is 1 AND fingers is 5 then
16 │   │   drawRectangleAt(px,py);
17 │   end
18 │   if Keyboard key pressed then
19 │   │   break;
20 │   end
21 end
```

Fig. 2. Face recognition with OpenCV

Once the framework detects a person's face into the scene, other parts of the user's body are detected using a skin mask into the frame. It can be noted in the Fig. 3.

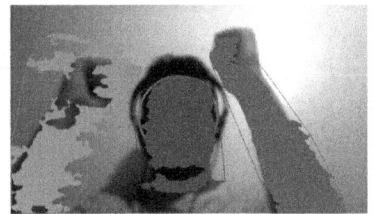

(a) Face recognition

(b) Skin recognition

Fig. 3. Members recognition example

In order to improve the results gained analyzing the previous Figs. 2 and 3, some techniques of computer vision and digital image processing were used, such as binarization and other filters in order to reduce the sensor noise. The result after the usage of this techniques is shown in Fig. 4.

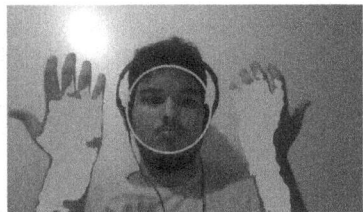

(a) Face recognition in the original input image

(b) skin recognition in the original input image

Fig. 4. Skin recognition in the input image

In order to prove the simplicity of the solution, in Fig. 5 we show the algorithm running with two users in the same scene, showing that the framework is able to recognize both users and define which arm belongs to which user (Fig. 5), which depicts that the face color ellipse is the same color used in user's members.

The next section shows the results about hand and fingers recognition developed to this framework.

4.2 Hand and Fingers Recognition

The first aim was to recognize, define and track the position of the user's hand when this stage of the project starts to work together with the framework, some interaction should be able to be simulated.

The results gained at this part of the project are shown in the Fig. 6. As seen in Algorithm 2, some contours features of the user's members were used by the framework, and the center of mass can be interpreted as user's hand.

Fig. 5. Multiple users recognition example

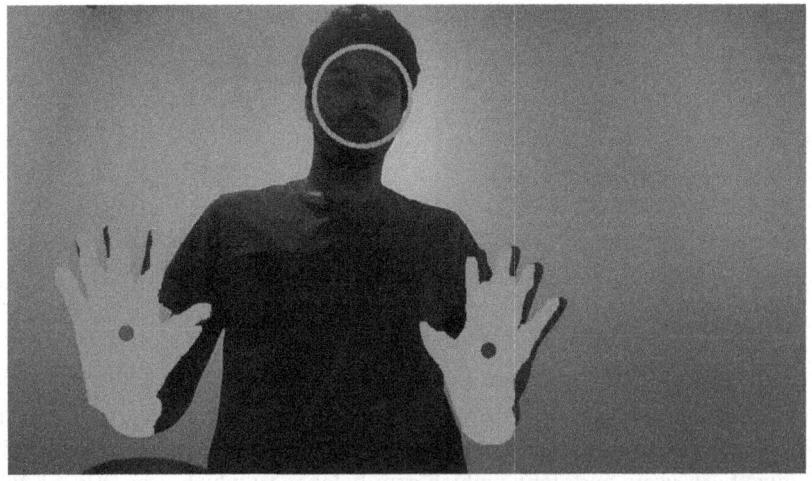

Fig. 6. Center of mass of which arm of the user

However, the prototype needs some trigger to start the interaction and stop it. To solve this problem, the fingers recognition was studied and implemented making possible to use the number of fingers recognized as a trigger to one specific function into the code.

The fingers recognition algorithm generated the results shown in the Figs. 7 and 8. Algorithm 2 shows that the convexity of the contours has a vital importance at this stage of the project.

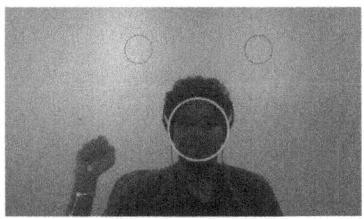

(a) Convexity contour example

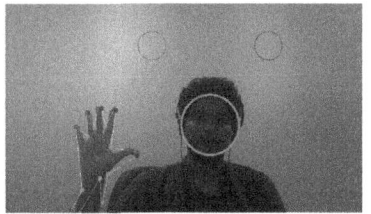

(b) Convexity contour example

Fig. 7. Convexity contour in the input image

(a) Finger recognition example

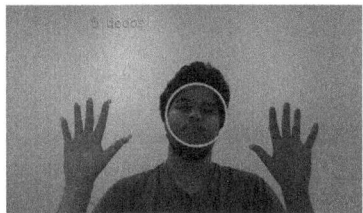

(b) Finger recognition example

Fig. 8. Finger recognition in the input image

4.3 Interaction

In this section is presented a simple application developed using the framework. A comparison between the Microsoft's Kinect v1 and the proposed framework is also introduced at the following section.

Results of the application can be seen in the Fig. 9 where a user is able to move a virtual square using his own hand to interact with the application.

As shown in Fig. 9c and e the fingers recognition makes very easy to interact with the application. In addition, the number of fingers in the frame enables the developer to trigger functions in the code and add others ways of interaction to the application.

The hand recognition makes possible to user move the square as shown in Fig. 9d, also making possible to define what object the user is interacting at that moment in an environment with more virtual objects.

4.4 Kinect vs the Proposed Framework

The Fig. 10 shows the trajectory in X-axis and Y-axis against Time. Figure 10 is the result of circles made by the user, and each line represents a hand – the red line the right hand and the blue one, the left hand –. This result was obtained using the framework and a simple RGB camera, that is a laptop webcam.

(a) Initial condition of the application

(b) Make the recognize hand match with the square's area

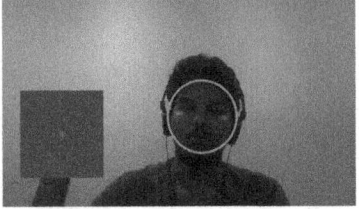

(c) Close the hand triggered the action of hold the square

(d) Moving the square together with the hand

(e) Open the hand triggered the action of leave the square at that position

(f) Moving the hand without interfering the square's position

Fig. 9. Sample of the interaction using the framework

The results presented in Fig. 11 exemplify the use of the framework against the Kinect. The graphs were generated at the same time, that means that the test was made using both systems at the same time and doing the same movements.

However, exists a distinction between the resolution of the cameras, since the Kinect uses a depth sensor to recognize and track the user's hand. In addition, the position of the sensors in the real world is different because if the sensors stay at the same position an occlusion occurs, which is not the goal of this work.

Figure 11 depicts that the results make possible to simulated a specialized hardware and property software using the developed framework. Also, VR applications which make use of specialized hardware can be re-written to run with the proposed framework.

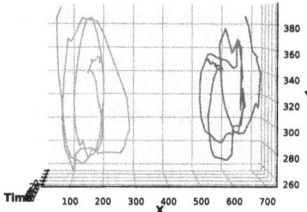

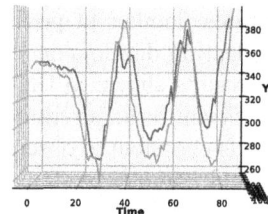

(a) Front view - graph with position of the center of mass doing circles with the hand

(b) Orthogonal view - graph with position of the center of mass doing circles with the hand

Fig. 10. Tracking of the center of the user's hand

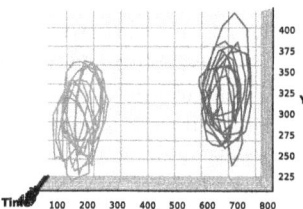

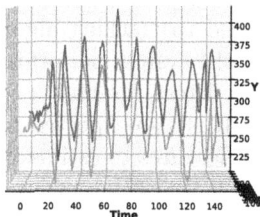

(a) Front view - graph of interaction with the proposed framework

(b) Orthogonal view - graph of interaction with the proposed framework

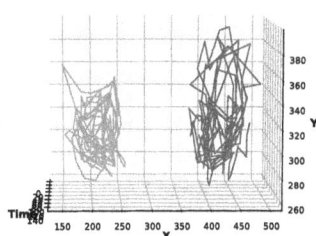

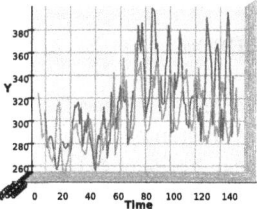

(c) Front view - graph view - of interaction with the Kinect

(d) Orthogonal view - graph of interaction with the Kinect

Fig. 11. Graphs of comparison of the Kinect with the proposed framework doing circular movements

5   Conclusions and Further Work

It is remarkable the results of the present system in comparison with property system which make uses of specialized hardware. This paper shows an uncountable number of possibilities and it might be a low-cost alternative to VR application developers.

The results shown in the previous section demonstrates that the developed framework can be an alternative to approaches of immersion in VR applications.

It is also possible to observe that low-cost technologies can be used in sophisticated and complex systems. This replacement can be done in reason of the growing power of process data, and the reduction of the cost of computational systems.

As further work, the main goal is to make the project more applicable to the society, being the framework a complete alternative to others systems, and also fully useful to developers, used as an interface which enables users to interact with the application with their own bodies.

First of all new approaches to increase the performance will be studied, taking into account that a robust framework is needed to make the system useful to developers.

Related to tracking algorithms, when such algorithms work together they increase the system performance because is no more need to do expensive operations to detect the region of interest, once ROI is already detected and being tracked. It is also expected to develop the interaction with the z-axis, using the contours features to estimate some movement at z-axis.

Finally, we intend to develop an interface as a kind of API, in order to allow the use of the system and their applications with ensuring that society gets in touch with technologies like this without any cost. At this stage will also be interesting create a dictionary of gestures.

Acknowledgments. This research was partially supported by CNPq, CAPES, Fapesp, Fapemig, and Finep.

References

1. Chehikian, A., Eklundh, J.-O., Granlund, G., Granum, E., Kittler, J., Crowley, J.L., Christensen, H.I.: Vision as Process: Basic Research on Computer Vision Systems. Springer Science & Business Media, Heidelberg (1994)
2. Farhadi-Niaki, F., Etemad, S.A., Arya, A.: Design and usability analysis of gesture-based control for common desktop tasks. In: Kurosu, M. (ed.) HCI 2013. LNCS, vol. 8007, pp. 215–224. Springer, Heidelberg (2013). https://doi.org/10.1007/978-3-642-39330-3_23
3. Gonzalez, R., Woods, R.: Digital Image Processing. Pearson Education, Limited, London (2010)
4. Gurav, R. Kadbe, P.K.: Real time finger tracking and contour detection for gesture recognition using OpenCV. In: 2015 International Conference on Industrial Instrumentation and Control (ICIC), pp. 974–977. IEEE (2015)
5. Han, J., Shao, L., Xu, D., Shotton, J.: Enhanced computer vision with microsoft kinect sensor: a review. IEEE Trans. Cybern. **43**(5), 1318–1334 (2013)
6. Hancock, D.: Virtual-reality in search of middle ground (1995)
7. Jia, P., Hu, H.H., Lu, T., Yuan, K.: Head gesture recognition for hands-free control of an intelligent wheelchair. Ind. Robot Int. J. **34**(1), 60–68 (2007)

8. Mehta, D., Sridhar, S., Sotnychenko, O., Rhodin, H., Shafiei, M., Seidel, H.-P., Xu, W., Casas, D., Theobalt, C.: VNect: real-time 3D human pose estimation with a single RGB camera. ACM Trans. Graph. (TOG) **36**(4), 44 (2017)
9. Moeslund, T.B., Granum, E.: A survey of computer vision-based human motion capture. Comput. Vis. Image Underst. **81**(3), 231–268 (2001)
10. Morie, J.F.: Inspiring the future: merging mass communication, art, entertainment and virtual environments. ACM SIGGRAPH Comput. Graph. **28**(2), 135–138 (1994)
11. Shrivastava, R.: A hidden Markov model based dynamic hand gesture recognition system using OpenCV. In: 2013 IEEE 3rd International on Advance Computing Conference (IACC), pp. 947–950. IEEE (2013)
12. Sklansky, J.: Finding the convex hull of a simple polygon. Pattern Recogn. Lett. **1**(2), 79–83 (1982)
13. Van Krevelen, D., Poelman, R.: A survey of augmented reality technologies, applications and limitations. Int. J. Virtual Real. **9**(2), 1 (2010)

Sharing Learning Objects Between Learning Platforms and Repositories

Sergio Tasso[1(✉)], Simonetta Pallottelli[1], Osvaldo Gervasi[1],
Marina Rui[2], and Antonio Laganà[3]

[1] Department of Mathematics and Computer Science, University of Perugia,
via Vanvitelli, 1, 06123 Perugia, Italy
{sergio.tasso, simonetta.pallottelli,
osvaldo.gervasi}@unipg.it
[2] Department of Chemistry and Industrial Chemistry, University of Genoa,
via Dodecaneso, 31, 16146 Genoa, Italy
marina@chimica.unige.it
[3] Department of Chemistry, Biology and Biotechnologies, University of Perugia,
via Elce di sotto 8, 06123 Perugia, Italy
lagana05@gmail.com

Abstract. The wide adoption of e-learning in several contexts requires an increasing integration of learning material from different platforms, made available to users in a secure and easy-to-use way. In the present paper the re-engineering of the Moodledata module functionalities of GLOREP federation, designed to migrate information units between several content platforms is discussed.

Keywords: Repository · Learning management systems · Content sharing
Learning object

1 Introduction

GLOREP (Grid Learning Object Repository) [1–7] is a federation of distributed repositories containing Learning Objects (LO)s from various sources. GLOREP operates since several years, serving a network of Universities and Organizations, federated in order to offer a better e-learning service and to improve the quality of courses. The present implementation of GLOREP involves the main site at the Department of Mathematics and Computer Science of Perugia University, the Department of Chemistry, Biology and Biotechnologies of the same University as well as other European universities, such as those of Genoa and Thessaloniki.

To the end of creating and sharing LO Metadata (LOM), GLOREP leverages several Moodle modules of which Moodledata [8] is the one allowing to share LOM between a Content Management System (CMS) and a Learning Management System (LMS). More precisely, Moodledata enables the user to share learning material among Moodle platforms and GLOREP repositories, which are based on Drupal CMS.

However, as discussed in Sect. 2, the previous version of Moodledata, showed some limits due both to the fact that its usage required admin permissions and because

O. Gervasi et al. (Eds.): ICCSA 2018, LNCS 10963, pp. 804–816, 2018.
https://doi.org/10.1007/978-3-319-95171-3_62

of a limited types of object managed. Furthermore, the module turned difficult and inefficient after updating the version of the basic software. This turned out to be a quite crucial aspect for the model adopted by the European Chemistry Thematic Network (ECTN) Virtual Education Community (VEC) for promoting and assessing chemical knowledge [9, 10]. As reported in ref. [11], GLOREP is a useful support to the student preparation to EChemTest® e-tests as it provides increasingly improved LOs [12–17] thanks to the cooperative effort of the VEC and ECTN members.

For these reasons, we have been working in recent times at the re-engineering of the Moodledata module as is illustrated in Sect. 3.

2   GLOREP Moddledata Architecture

The *Moodledata* module, integrated in the previous versions, allowed the administrator to search and download files on the Moodle server and possibly upload and catalog them on Drupal as LOM [18, 19]. However, both the need to move to an updated Drupal version, and the changes made to the Moodle database structure prompted a re-engineering of *Moodledata*.

The main functions of the *Moodledata* module, as sketched in Fig. 1, are:

- *Moodledata Download*: for downloading files from Moodle to Drupal;
- *Moodledata Upload* and LOM creation: to upload to Drupal the files previously downloaded by Moodle and a wide description of the LO through IEEE LOM [20].

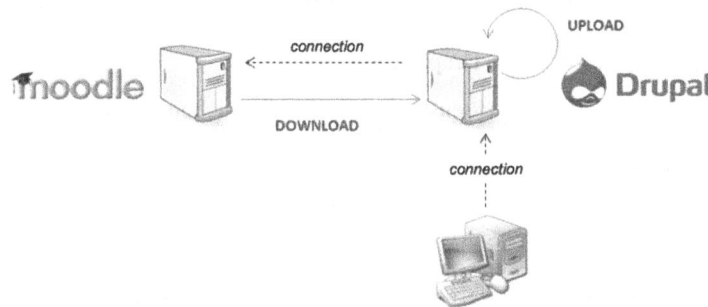

Fig. 1. The Moodledata scheme

The first part of the module, managing the download of files from Moodle, starts with the search for the materials requested by the user himself. The files that have metadata matching the criteria specified can be selected and/or deselected. While the *Download selected items* starts the actual download of the selection, a filename is assigned to the loaded files in two ways, depending on whether the file has been uploaded in Moodle individually, or as part of a collection of files loaded simultaneously into a folder.

With the download procedure, the files are copied to the *moodledata_cache* folder and the related information added to the moodledata table of the GLOREP database.

The download takes place by opening a point-to-point FTP channel, allowing a reliable transmission even for a large amount of data.

Once the download is completed, a message appears showing the number of downloaded files. A warning message appears in case the user attempts to download files already present in moodledata_cache.

The second part of the module manages the Drupal upload of the files previously downloaded by Moodle. To turn a Moodle file into a GLOREP LOM, it is necessary to create a new Linkable Object node with attached the downloaded files, then, to digit a series of data providing information associated with the Linkable Object based on the IEEE LOM standard. The *Upload selected items* starts with the uploading of the files so tagged and labeled. This creates a new Linkable Object type node to assign to all the information entered and the attached files.

The Linkable Object module uses the Field API (Application Programming Interface), present in the Drupal core, allowing to customize data fields that can be attached to Drupal entities dealing with the storing, editing, loading and viewing.

The main advantage associated with the use of the API Field is the metadata management, as Drupal fully takes care of managing the database, yet involving also the *Moodledata* module. One of the limits of the old *Moodledata* module was to restrict its use only to the administrators, but now it became imperative to extend the use of the module also to non-administrator users.

3   Implementation of GLOREP Moddledata

Generally, custom modules in Drupal consist of 3 files:

- the main module file, with extension ". module" which implements the logic to the hooks of Drupal core and contains all the information about data visualization, query and permission management;
- a file with the ". install" extension, allowing to create tables in the database and uploading data;
- a file with ". info" extension, containing the metadata concerning the module, also used to impose some criteria regarding the activation/deactivation of the module itself, moreover, describing the dependencies, the package and the minimum version of Drupal.

3.1   Preparing and Configuring the Environment

On the Drupal side two basic modules for *Moodledata*, must be installed and enabled:

- *Collabrep*: which manages the federation and the information transmission.
- *Linkable Object*: which allows to create a new type of node and checks the user permissions. Each Linkable Object can be defined, during the creation step, as a Learning Object or a Software Attachment.

When enabling the *Moodledata* module, with the .install file, we make a change to the GLOREP database by entering a new table, also called moodledata. The table, shown in Fig. 2, is crucial for the module as it takes into account the files downloaded from Moodle along with the related information.

FIELD	TYPE	NULL	KEY	EXTRA
id	int(11)	no	pri	auto_increment
user_id	int(11)	no		
course	varchar(255)	no		
name	varchar(255)	no		
author	varchar(255)	no		
description	medium text	no		
timemodified	int(11)	no		
contenthash	varchar(40)	no		

Fig. 2. The Table of Moodledata fields

Where:

- id: unique numerical identifier of the file, automatically generated
- user_id: GLOREP user identifier
- course: name of the Moodle course in which the file was created
- name: file name
- author: file author
- description: description of the content
- timemodified: date of last modification of the file, expressed through the Unix timestamp
- contenthash: encoding sha1 (hash) of the file content.

Moreover, in the file system, a new folder is added, moodledata_cache, used for temporary storage of files downloaded from Moodle while waiting for the upload. In this way, we create an intermediate phase between the two operations, download and upload, making the two steps clearer to the user and avoiding data loss. Once uploaded in Drupal, the uploaded files are deleted from the directory moodledata_cache and from moodledata table with the related information.

Here we list two methods of accessing Moodle's web services:

- Creating a new user enabled to use web services and giving access to the external application through his own credentials.
- Adding and assigning a new role to users who need to use the web service; this procedure allows the user to obtain an access token through his credentials.

We chose the second method in order to implement the module.

The first step is to create the *Moodledata* service from the *Dashboard/SiteAdministration/Plugin/Webservice/ServiceManagement/Service* screen, with the following additional functions:

- *core_files_get_files* (it returns the requested resource)
- *core_course_get_contents* (it returns the list of files belonging to the specified course)
- *core_course_get_courses* (it returns the details of the specified course)
- *core_enrol_get_users_courses* (it returns the list of courses to whom a user is registered)
- *core_user_get_users* (specifying the username, it returns a user's id)

Next, we need to create a new role, for receiving the */webservice:createtoken* and the *webservice/rest:use* pemissions. Then the role is assigned to all users who need to use the module.

The steps for activating the service are:

1. Enabling web-services.
2. Enabling Protocol REST.
3. Selecting the service *Moodledata*.
4. Adding the functions (as details specified in the previous paragraph)
5. Checking the user permissions, to ensure that the new role is correctly assigned.

3.2 Moodledata Settings and User Management

On the Drupal side, in order to access the module's functionalities, one can use the *Moodledata* menu, containing a short description of the pages to access with the first being *Settings*, used to configure the Moodle access (see Fig. 3). The involved fields are:

- Domain address of the Moodle installation.
- Username to access the Moodle account.
- Login Password.

A first check concerns the action of the *Save Moodle settings*. In this case the contents of the *Moodle address* field are checked, and then the indices of the associative array $_SESSION, useful to contain the Moodle credentials, are created. Upon

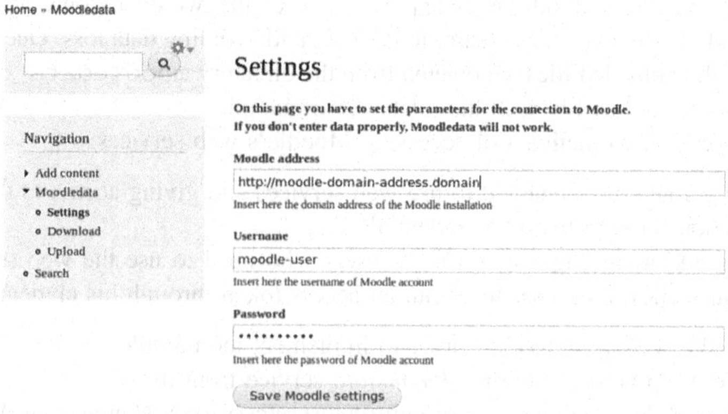

Fig. 3. Page of Moodledata settings

successful completion of the previous operations, a connection to the web-service is attempted by requesting, with a REST call, the access token for subsequent queries. Once sent the request, the information about the connection is saved and either a successful connection's or a specific error message appears.

The module is now available to any authenticated GLOREP user, without needing administrator permissions. This is made possible by dividing the information entered by each user and added to the database with a column that keeps track of who downloaded a specific resource contained in Moodle.

3.3 Moodledata Download and Storage

One of the two main functions of the module deals with downloading files from Moodle.

The screen that appears (see Fig. 4) allows searching for a file, by specifying the full name, or a part of it, through a generic string [21]. Therefore, what we are looking for, and eventually getting, is the right file contained in the Moodle folders.

We can also activate the *Advanced Search* that makes possible refining a search by combining different parameters, such as:

- *Course name*
- *File author*
- *Date of last editing* (in the format YYYY-MM-DD).

The search starts through the *Search button*. The files matching the set search criteria are shown in tabular form. The table also shows the following fields:

- *select item*: checkbox for file selection
- *course name*: the course name referred to by the file
- *filename*: file name.

By starting the *Download selected items*, the selected files will download.

A file individually loaded in Moodle will maintain the name given when loading.

If, however, the file belongs to a collection of files uploaded at the same time in a Moodle folder, it will receive a name made of `folder_name.original_file_name`. In addition to the file name, the other fields in the table are:

- `author`: file author
- `format`: file format
- `description`: a string describing the file, or any folder to which the file belongs, attributed by the Moodle user during loading.
- `last_modified`: the date of last editing (into the format YYYY-MM-DD).

The crucial update involving the re-engineering of the module consists in the replacement of the database connection with the use of Moodle web-services. cURL library in PHP has been used to implement the queries to the web-service; the cURL is very flexible and allows to establish communications with remote servers using different protocols: HTTP, HTTPS, FTP, GOPHER, TELNET, DICT, FILE, LDAP.

Thus, the cURL use made possible to carry out a series of operations on remote servers, for instance:

- Retrieving the content of a web page (scraping)
- Submitting a form
- Making authentications to protected areas
- Connecting to a web service.
- Download and storage.

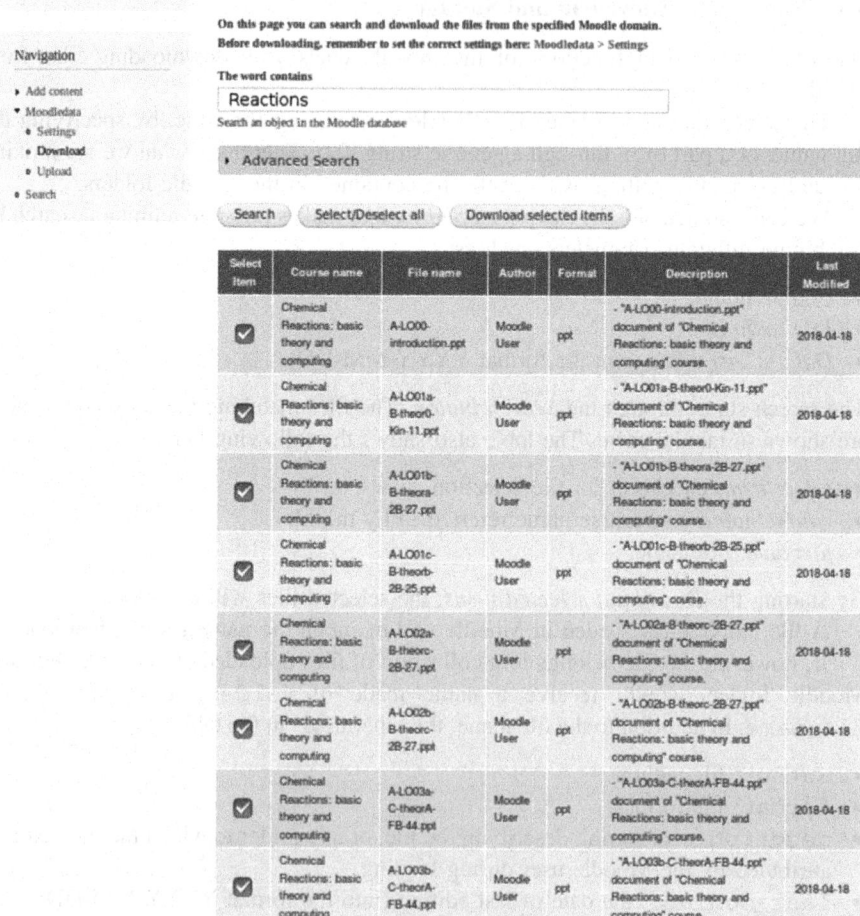

Fig. 4. Moodledata download

The *Download selected items* makes it possible, as already mentioned, to download the selected files, store them in the Moodle storage folder created at the installation, called `moodledata`, in the `filedir` subfolder. The files are stored according to the

SHA1 hash encoding of their content with the addition of the user id. This means that every file with unique content is stored just once per user, regardless of the number of times it has been loaded even with different names and it is possible to know the SHA1 hash of each file from the `contenthash` field in the Moodle database files table.

With the download function, the files are copied to the `moodledata_cache` folder and the related information added to the moodledata table of the GLOREP database. The download takes place by forwarding requests via cURL. A successful message appears showing the number of downloaded files, conversely, a warning message alerts the user when he/she tries to download files already present in `moodledata_cache`.

In the following, some basic steps of download and storage are illustrated.

Checkboxes selected on the form, at the submission time, are saved in the associative array `$selected_items`. Compared with the previous version, one needs to save also the names of the resources needed for querying the Moodle API. The *Download selected items* activates the saving, in the new associative array `$to_download`, of a progressive index and the `file_url` of the selected resources; eventually, the files are downloaded by calling the `moodledata_prepare_batch()` function. The parameters passed to this function are the associative array `$to_download` containing the file identifiers, the `file_url` of the files to be downloaded and the variable $num which indicates their number.

3.4   Moodledata Upload

The second main function of the module enables the user to upload to Drupal the files previously downloaded via *Moodledata Download*. Unlike previous versions of the module, the Upload page contains only one mandatory field: *Keywords*, since the keywords have assumed a central role in Learning-objects classing and grouping. In fact, in the evolution of GLOREP the functions of indexing and cataloguing LOMs require special attention so that the function of *Search* will have a better outcome.

Besides the *Keywords*, it is also possible to enter a title different from the pre-compiled one. All other metadata characterizing the Learning Object are now hidden to the user and passed to the Linkable Object module by default, excepting the metadata obtained from the Moodle API queries. That is:

- Course name
- File name
- Author
- Format
- Description
- Last modified
- File size

A table shows the files that can be attached to the Linkable Object. Of course, they are the files previously downloaded by Moodle, whose information is taken from the database in `moodledata`.

The *Select/Deselect All* function allows select/deselect all the files shown in Fig. 5. The function *Upload selected items* starts uploading the selected files.

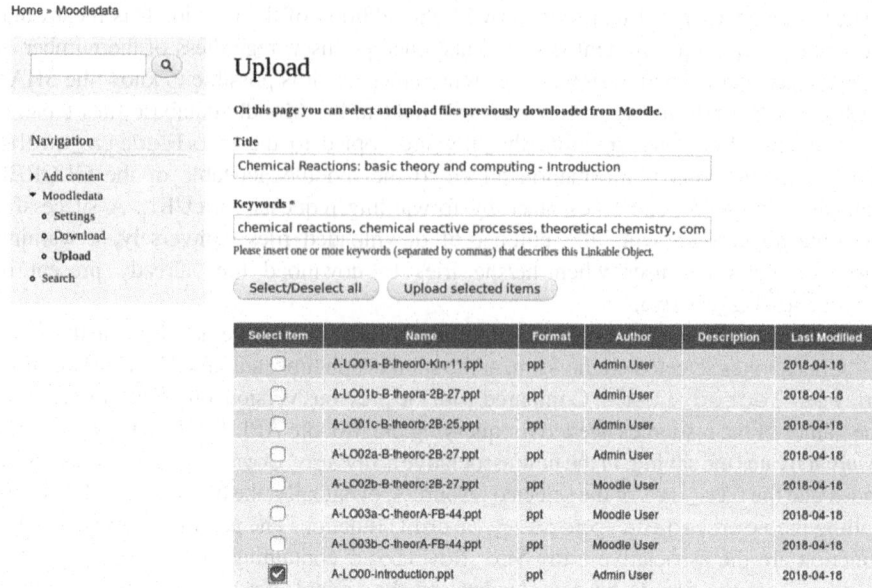

Fig. 5. Moodledata upload

This creates a new Linkable Object node to assign all the information entered and to attach the files.

These files are copied from the `moodledata_cache` folder to `sites/default/files/collabrep`, as well as the related records are removed from the `moodledata` table of the GLOREP database.

After the upload, the new Learning Object is finally available on the Drupal repositories. Note that the new Learning-Object is loaded by default in *Draft* mode to ensure the update of the metadata before making it available to a GLOREP user for download.

It should be noted the Linkable Object module does not yet support the `$file_list`; in any case it would not be able to attach more than one file at a time, indeed, the related metadata would not be properly managed, so, to add attachments, it must go to the *Edit* section of the view of the Linkable Object control.

The properties assigned to the generated node are those defined by the IEEE LOM standard.

The resulting Linkable Objects in GLOREP are show in Fig. 6.

3.5   Field and API Instance

The realization of the Linkable Object module has used one of the innovative features of Drupal 7.x: the Field API (Application Programming Interface). Present in the core of Drupal, they allow to customize data fields that can be attached to Drupal entities dealing with the storage, editing, loading and viewing.

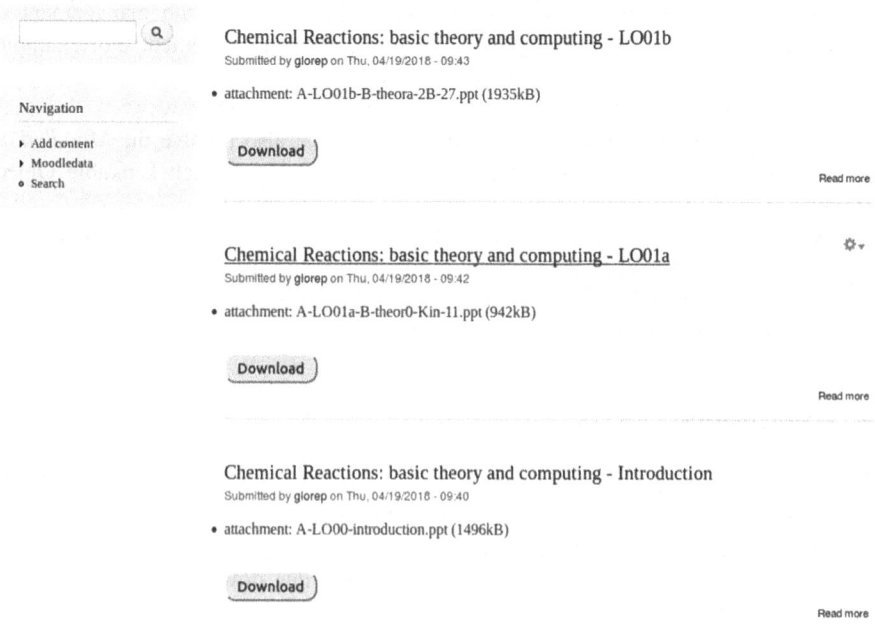

Fig. 6. Resulting linkable objects in GLOREP

For their proper functioning two primary data-structures are defined:

- *Field*: which specifies the type of data to attach to the entity;
- *Instance*: which allows to instantiate the data type.

In particular, to implement the Linkable Object module, we decided to adopt these new methods for the two fields: *body* and *files*. The *body* field contains the description of the node, the *files* field contains information about the files attached to the Linkable Object.

Drupal has also introduced a new module to attach files to Linkable Objects, the `FileField`, which is also present in the core. In order to insert an attachment to each Linkable Object it is necessary to define a new file type field.

Each `file_object` contains eight properties:

1. `fid`: file identifier
2. `uid`: user identifier
3. `filename`: file name
4. `URI`: Uniform Resource Identifier
5. `filemime`: mimetype of file
6. `filesize`: size of file in bytes
7. `status`: file status
8. `timestamp`: timestamp of the date when the file was added to the database.

The main advantage arising from the use of Field APIs is the management of metadata, as Drupal takes full responsibility for database management. For example, regarding the files, the relative fields mentioned above are stored in the table file_managed of the Drupal database in a completely automatic way.

These innovations concerning version 7.x of Drupal also involve the *Moodledata* module, thus the instantiation of the *body* and *files* fields of each Linkable Object created.

The changes are propagated by simply sending the whole object with the new metadata, this object will be then stored in the shared database, and every other server that executes the download routine, will notice that the object is a duplicate and will overwrite the existing one/s.

4   Conclusions

Updating an integrated module on Drupal now offers the possibility, to any authenticated user, to download files from Moodle which can be managed within the GLOREP federation. The result is an increase in the resources made available to the federation users. Summing up, we can upload on Drupal the files downloaded from Moodle through the creation of Linkable Object nodes, while, the problem of multiple attachments of an imported file is still open. Indeed, along this line, the future development of the module shall consist in the creation of a plug-in, useful for the administrator, to automate the procedures for activating the moodledata service on the Moodle side so as to easily manage the access required by the GLOREP users to the end of cooperatively improve the contents of the course platform [22–26].

Acknowledgements. The authors acknowledge ECTN (VEC standing committee) and the EC2E2 N 2 LLP project for stimulating debates and providing partial financial support. Thanks are due also to EGI and IGI and the related COMPCHEM VO for the use of Grid resources.

The authors are partially supported by three projects financed by Basic Research Fund, 2015, University of Perugia: *G-Lorep and EoL: interfacing between a repository of didactic-scientific material repositories and e-assessment environments* (S.Tasso), *G-Lorep and Moodle: integration between repository and LCMS (learning content management system)* (S. Pallottelli), *Computational approaches for the efficient use of General Purpose GPU Computing* (O. Gervasi).

References

1. Pallottelli, S., Tasso, S., Pannacci, N., Costantini, A., Lago, N.F.: Distributed and collaborative learning objects repositories on grid networks. In: Taniar, D., Gervasi, O., Murgante, B., Pardede, E., Apduhan, B.O. (eds.) ICCSA 2010. LNCS, vol. 6019, pp. 29–40. Springer, Heidelberg (2010). https://doi.org/10.1007/978-3-642-12189-0_3
2. Tasso, S., Pallottelli, S., Bastianini, R., Lagana, A.: Federation of distributed and collaborative repositories and its application on science learning objects. In: Murgante, B., Gervasi, O., Iglesias, A., Taniar, D., Apduhan, B.O. (eds.) ICCSA 2011. LNCS, vol. 6784, pp. 466–478. Springer, Heidelberg (2011). https://doi.org/10.1007/978-3-642-21931-3_36

3. Tasso, S., Pallottelli, S., Ferroni, M., Bastianini, R., Laganà, A.: Taxonomy management in a federation of distributed repositories: a chemistry use case. In: Murgante, B., et al. (eds.) ICCSA 2012. LNCS, vol. 7333, pp. 358–370. Springer, Heidelberg (2012). https://doi.org/10.1007/978-3-642-31125-3_28

4. Tasso, S., Pallottelli, S., Ciavi, G., Bastianini, R., Laganà, A.: An efficient taxonomy assistant for a federation of science distributed repositories: a chemistry use case. In: Murgante, B., et al. (eds.) ICCSA 2013. LNCS, vol. 7971, pp. 96–109. Springer, Heidelberg (2013). https://doi.org/10.1007/978-3-642-39637-3_8

5. Tasso, S., Pallottelli, S., Rui, M., Laganá, A.: Learning objects efficient handling in a federation of science distributed repositories. In: Murgante, B., et al. (eds.) ICCSA 2014. LNCS, vol. 8579, pp. 615–626. Springer, Cham (2014). https://doi.org/10.1007/978-3-319-09144-0_42

6. Tasso, S., Pallottelli, S., Laganà, A.: Mobile device access to collaborative distributed repositories of chemistry learning objects. In: Gervasi, O., et al. (eds.) ICCSA 2016. LNCS, vol. 9786, pp. 443–454. Springer, Cham (2016). https://doi.org/10.1007/978-3-319-42085-1_34

7. Tasso, S., Pallottelli, S., Gervasi, O., Tanase, R., Rui, M.: Synchronized content and metadata management in a federation of distributed repositories of chemical learning objects. In: Gervasi, O., et al. (eds.) ICCSA 2017. LNCS, vol. 10406, pp. 14–28. Springer, Cham (2017). https://doi.org/10.1007/978-3-319-62398-6_2

8. Pallottelli, S., Tasso, S., Rui, M., Laganà, A., Kozaris, I.: Exchange of learning objects between a learning management system and a federation of science distributed repositories. In: Gervasi, O., et al. (eds.) ICCSA 2015. LNCS, vol. 9156, pp. 371–383. Springer, Cham (2015). https://doi.org/10.1007/978-3-319-21407-8_27

9. Laganà, A., Gervasi, O., Tasso, S., Perri, D., Franciosa, F.: The ECTN virtual education community prosumer model for promoting and assessing chemical knowledge. In: Gervasi, O., et al. (eds.) ICCSA 2018. LNCS, vol. 10963, pp. 547–562. Springer, Cham (2018)

10. Gervasi, O., Tasso, S., Laganà, A.: Immersive molecular virtual reality based on X3D and web services. In: Gavrilova, M., et al. (eds.) ICCSA 2006. LNCS, vol. 3980, pp. 212–221. Springer, Heidelberg (2006). https://doi.org/10.1007/11751540_23

11. Gervasi, O., Laganà, A.: EoL: a web-based distance assessment system. In: Laganá, A., et al. (eds.) ICCSA 2004. LNCS, vol. 3044, pp. 854–862. Springer, Heidelberg (2004). https://doi.org/10.1007/978-3-540-24709-8_90

12. Laganà, A., et al.: ELCHEM: a metalaboratory to develop grid e-learning technologies and services for chemistry. In: Gervasi, O., et al. (eds.) ICCSA 2005. LNCS, vol. 3480, pp. 938–946. Springer, Heidelberg (2005). https://doi.org/10.1007/11424758_97

13. Gervasi, O., Riganelli, A., Pacifici, L., Laganà, A.: VMSLab-G: a virtual laboratory prototype for molecular science on the Grid. Future Gener. Comput. Syst. 20(5), 717–726 (2004). https://doi.org/10.1016/j.future.2003.11.015

14. Costantini, A., Tasso, S., Gervasi, O.: Visualization and web services for studying molecular properties. In: ICCSA 2009, pp. 222–228. IEEE (2009). https://doi.org/10.1109/iccsa.2009.41. ISBN 978-0-7695-3701-6

15. Vella, F., Neri, I., Gervasi, O., Tasso, S.: A simulation framework for scheduling performance evaluation on CPU-GPU heterogeneous system. In: Murgante, B., et al. (eds.) ICCSA 2012. LNCS, vol. 7336, pp. 457–469. Springer, Heidelberg (2012). https://doi.org/10.1007/978-3-642-31128-4_34

16. Mariotti, M., Gervasi, O., Vella, F., Cuzzocrea, A., Costantini, A.: Strategies and systems towards grids and clouds integration: A DBMS-based solution. Future Gener. Comput. Syst. (2017, in Press). https://doi.org/10.1016/j.future.2017.02.047

17. Costantini, A., Gervasi, O., Zollo, F., Caprini, L.: User interaction and data management for large scale grid applications. J. Grid Comput. **12**(3), 485–497 (2014). https://doi.org/10.1007/s10723-014-9300-0

18. Ahn, J., Lin, X., Khoo, M.: Dewey decimal classification based concept visualization for information retrival. In: In: CEUR Workshop Proceedings, vol. 1311, pp. 7–14 (2014)

19. McClelland, M.: Metadata standards for educational resources. Computer **36**(11), 107–109 (2003)

20. IEEE Standard for Learning Object Metadata, March 2018. http://ieeexplore.ieee.org/document/1032843

21. Laganà, A., Parker, G.A.: Chemical Reactions. Basic Theory and Computing. TCCM. Springer, Cham (2018). https://doi.org/10.1007/978-3-319-62356-6

22. Akarsh, S., Kishor, A., Niyogi, R., Milani, A., Mengoni, P.: Social cooperation in autonomous agents to avoid the tragedy of the commons. Int. J. Agric. Environ. Inf. Syst. **8**(2), 1–19 (2017). https://doi.org/10.4018/IJAEIS.2017040101

23. Franzoni, V., Li, Y., Mengoni, P., Milani, A.: Clustering facebook for biased context extraction. In: Gervasi, O., et al. (eds.) ICCSA 2017. LNCS, vol. 10404, pp. 717–729. Springer, Cham (2017). https://doi.org/10.1007/978-3-319-62392-4_52

24. Franzoni, V., Li, Y., Mengoni, P.: A path-based model for emotion abstraction on Facebook using sentiment analysis and taxonomy knowledge. In: Proceedings of the International Conference on Web Intelligence - WI 2017, pp. 947–952 (2017). https://doi.org/10.1145/3106426.3109420

25. Mengoni, P., Milani, A., Li, Y.: Clustering students interactions in eLearning systems for group elicitation. In: Gervasi, O., et al. (ed.) ICCSA 2018. LNCS (LNAI and LMBI), vol. 10963, pp. 398–413 (2018)

26. Mengoni, P., Milani, A., Li, Y.: Community graph elicitation from students' interactions in virtual learning environments. In: Gervasi, O., et al. (ed.) ICCSA 2018. LNCS (LNAI and LMBI), vol. 10963, pp. 414–425. Springer, Heidelberg (2018)

Author Index

Printed in the United States
By Bookmasters